Introduction to Stochastic Finance with Market Examples
Second Edition

Introduction to Stochastic Finance with Market Examples, Second Edition presents an introduction to pricing and hedging in discrete and continuous-time financial models, emphasizing both analytical and probabilistic methods. It demonstrates both the power and limitations of mathematical models in finance, covering the basics of stochastic calculus for finance, and details the techniques required to model the time evolution of risky assets. The book discusses a wide range of classical topics including Black–Scholes pricing, American options, derivatives, term structure modeling, and change of numéraire. It also builds up to special topics, such as exotic options, stochastic volatility, and jump processes.

New to this Edition

- New chapters on Barrier Options, Lookback Options, Asian Options, Optimal Stopping Theorem, and Stochastic Volatility
- Contains over 235 exercises and 16 problems with complete solutions available online from the instructor resources at https://bit.ly/3DCvPtm
- Added over 150 graphs and figures, for more than 250 in total, to optimize presentation
- 57 R coding examples now integrated into the book for implementation of the methods
- Substantially class-tested, so ideal for course use or self-study

With abundant exercises, problems with complete solutions, graphs and figures, and R coding examples, the book is primarily aimed at advanced undergraduate and graduate students in applied mathematics, financial engineering, and economics. It could be used as a course text or for self-study and would also be a comprehensive and accessible reference for researchers and practitioners in the field.

Nicolas Privault received a PhD degree from the University of Paris VI, France. He was with the University of Evry, France, the University of La Rochelle, France, and the University of Poitiers, France. He is currently a Professor with the School of Physical and Mathematical Sciences, Nanyang Technological University, Singapore. His research interests are in the areas of stochastic analysis and its applications.

Chapman & Hall/CRC Financial Mathematics Series

Aims and scope:

The field of financial mathematics forms an ever-expanding slice of the financial sector. This series aims to capture new developments and summarize what is known over the whole spectrum of this field. It will include a broad range of textbooks, reference works, and handbooks that are meant to appeal to both academics and practitioners. The inclusion of numerical code and concrete real-world examples is highly encouraged.

Series Editors

M.A.H. Dempster
Centre for Financial Research
Department of Pure Mathematics and Statistics
University of Cambridge, UK

Dilip B. Madan
Robert H. Smith School of Business
University of Maryland, USA

Rama Cont
Department of Mathematics
Imperial College, UK

Robert A. Jarrow
Lynch Professor of Investment Management
Johnson Graduate School of Management
Cornell University, USA

For more information about this series please visit: https://www.crcpress.com/Chapman-and-HallCRC-Financial-Mathematics-Series/book series/CHFINANCMTH

Introduction to Stochastic Finance with Market Examples

Second Edition

Nicolas Privault

Nanyang Technological University, Singapore

CRC Press
Taylor & Francis Group
Boca Raton London New York

CRC Press is an imprint of the
Taylor & Francis Group, an **informa** business

A CHAPMAN & HALL BOOK

Second edition published 2023
by CRC Press
6000 Broken Sound Parkway NW, Suite 300, Boca Raton, FL 33487-2742

and by CRC Press
4 Park Square, Milton Park, Abingdon, Oxon, OX14 4RN

© 2023 Nicolas Privault

First edition published by CRC Press 2013

CRC Press is an imprint of Taylor & Francis Group, LLC

Library of Congress Cataloging-in-Publication Data

Names: Privault, Nicolas, author.
Title: Introduction to stochastic finance with market examples / Nicolas
    Privault, Nanyang Technological University, Singapore.
Description: Second edition. | Boca Raton, FL : Chapman & Hall, CRC Press,
    2022. | Series: Chapman & Hall/CRC financial mathematics series |
    Previous edition entered under title: Stochastic finance, 2014. |
    Includes bibliographical references and index.
Identifiers: LCCN 2022022636 (print) | LCCN 2022022637 (ebook) | ISBN
    9781032288260 (hbk) | ISBN 9781032288277 (pbk) | ISBN 9781003298670
    (ebk)
Subjects: LCSH: Securities--Prices--Mathematical models. |
    Finance--Mathematical models. | Hedging (Finance)--Mathematical models.
    | Stochastic analysis.
Classification: LCC HG4636 .P85 2022 (print) | LCC HG4636 (ebook) | DDC
    332.63/2042--dc23
LC record available at https://lccn.loc.gov/2022022636
LC ebook record available at https://lccn.loc.gov/2022022637

ISBN: 978-1-032-28826-0 (hbk)
ISBN: 978-1-032-28827-7 (pbk)
ISBN: 978-1-003-29867-0 (ebk)

DOI: 10.1201/ 9781003298670

Typeset in CMR10 font
by KnowledgeWorks Global Ltd.

Publisher's note: This book has been prepared from camera-ready copy provided by the authors.

To access the Support Material: www.Routledge.com/9781032288260

Contents

Preface

This book is an introduction to a wide range of topics in financial mathematics, including Black–Scholes pricing, exotic and American options, term structure modeling and change of numéraire, stochastic volatility, and models with jumps. It presents the mathematics of pricing and hedging in discrete and continuous-time financial models, with an emphasis on the complementarity between analytical and probabilistic methods. The contents are mostly mathematical and also aim at making the reader aware of both the power and limitations of mathematical models in finance, by taking into account their conditions of applicability. The text is targeted at the advanced undergraduate and graduate levels in applied mathematics, financial engineering, and economics. It contains 235 exercises and 16 problems, as well as 19 tables and 255 figures, and includes 57 R coding examples for illustrations based on market data.

The point of view adopted is that of mainstream mathematical finance, in which the computation of fair prices is based on the absence of arbitrage hypothesis, therefore excluding riskless profit based on arbitrage opportunities and basic (buying low/selling high) trading. Similarly, this document is not concerned with any "prediction" of stock price behaviors that belong to other domains such as technical analysis, which should not be confused with the statistical modeling of asset prices.

The descriptions of the asset model, self-financing portfolios, arbitrage, and market completeness, are first given in Chapter 1 in a simple two time-step setting. These notions are then reformulated in discrete time in Chapter 2. Here, the impossibility to access future information is formulated using the notion of adapted processes, which will play a central role in the construction of stochastic calculus in continuous time.

In order to trade efficiently, it would be useful to have a formula to estimate the "fair price" of a given risky asset, helping for example to determine whether the asset is undervalued or overvalued at a given time. Although such a formula is not available, we can instead derive formulas for the pricing of options that can act as insurance contracts to protect their holders against adverse changes in the prices of risky assets. The pricing and hedging of options in discrete time, particularly in the fundamental example of the Cox–Ross–Rubinstein model, are considered in Chapter 3, with a description of the passage from discrete to continuous time that prepares the transition to the subsequent chapters.

A simplified presentation of Brownian motion, stochastic integrals, and the associated Itô formula, is given in Chapter 4, with application to stochastic asset price modeling in Chapter 5. The Black–Scholes model is presented from the angle of partial differential equation (PDE) methods in Chapter 6, with the derivation of the Black–Scholes formula by transforming the Black–Scholes PDE into the standard heat equation, which is then solved by a heat kernel argument. The martingale approach to pricing and hedging is then presented in Chapter 7, and complements the PDE approach of Chapter 6 by recovering the Black–Scholes formula via a probabilistic argument. An introduction to stochastic volatility is given in Chapter 8, followed by a presentation of volatility estimation tools including historical, local, and implied volatilities, in Chapter 9. This chapter also contains a comparison of the prices obtained by the Black–Scholes formula with actual option price market data.

Exotic options such as barrier, lookback, and Asian options are treated in Chapters 11, 12, and 13, respectively, following an introduction to the properties of the maximum of Brownian motion given in Chapter 10. Optimal stopping and exercise, with application to the pricing of American options, are considered in Chapter 15, following the presentation of background material on filtrations and stopping times in Chapter 14. The construction of forward measures by change of numéraire is given in Chapter 16 and is applied to the pricing of interest rate derivatives such as caplets, caps, and swaptions in Chapter 19, after an introduction to bond pricing and to the modeling of forward rates in Chapters 17 and 18.

Stochastic calculus with jumps is dealt with in Chapter 20 and is restricted to compound Poisson processes, which only have a finite number of jumps on any bounded interval. Those processes are used for option pricing and hedging in jump models in Chapter 21, in which we mostly focus on risk-minimizing strategies, as markets with jumps are generally incomplete. Chapter 22 contains an elementary introduction to finite difference methods for the numerical solution of PDEs and stochastic differential equations, dealing with the explicit and implicit finite difference schemes for the heat equations and the Black–Scholes PDE, as well as the Euler and Milshtein schemes for SDEs. The text is completed with an appendix containing the needed probabilistic background.

The material in this book has been used for teaching in the Masters of Science in Financial Engineering at City University of Hong Kong and at the Nanyang Technological University in Singapore. The author thanks Nicky van Foreest, Jinlong Guo, Kazuhiro Kojima, Sijian Lin, Panwar Samay, Sandu Ursu, and Ju-Yi Yen for corrections and improvements. The cover graph represents the price map of an up-and-out barrier call (or down-and-out barrier put) option price; see Chapter 11.

Nicolas Privault
2022

Introduction

Modern quantitative finance requires a strong background in fields such as stochastic calculus, optimization, partial differential equations (PDEs) and numerical methods, or even infinite dimensional analysis. In addition, the emergence of new complex financial instruments on the markets makes it necessary to rely on increasingly sophisticated mathematical tools. Not all readers of this book will eventually work in quantitative financial analysis; nevertheless, they may have to interact with quantitative analysts, and becoming familiar with the tools they employ could be an advantage. In addition, despite the availability of readymade financial calculators, it still makes sense to be able oneself to understand, design, and implement such financial algorithms. This can be particularly useful under different types of conditions, including an eventual lack of trust in financial indicators, possible unreliability of expert advice such as buy/sell recommendations, or other factors such as market manipulation. Instead of relying on predictions of stock price movements based on various tools (*e.g.* technical analysis, charting), we acknowledge that predicting the future is a difficult task, and we rely on the efficient market hypothesis. In this framework, the time evolution of the prices of risky assets will be modeled by random walks and stochastic processes.

Historical sketch

We start with a description of some of the main steps, ideas, and individuals that played an important role in the development of the field over the last century.

Robert Brown, botanist, 1828

Brown (1828) observed the movement of pollen particles as described in "A brief account of microscopical observations made in the months of June, July, and August, 1827, on the particles contained in the pollen of plants; and on the general existence of active molecules in organic and inorganic bodies." Phil. Mag. 4, 161–173, 1828.

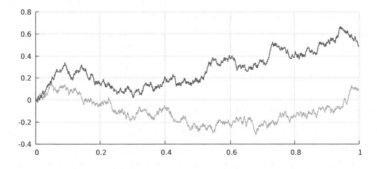

Figure 1: Two sample paths of one-dimensional Brownian motion.

Philosophical Magazine, first published in 1798, is a journal that publishes articles in the field of condensed matter describing original results, theories and concepts relating to the structure and properties of crystalline materials, ceramics, polymers, glasses, amorphous films, composites and soft matter.

Albert Einstein, physicist

Einstein received his 1921 Nobel Prize in part for investigations on the theory of Brownian motion: "... in 1905 Einstein founded a kinetic theory to account for this movement", presentation speech by S. Arrhenius, Chairman of the Nobel Committee, December 10, 1922.

Einstein (1905) "Über die von der molekularkinetischen Theorie der Wärme geforderte Bewegung von in ruhenden Flüssigkeiten suspendierten Teilchen", Annalen der Physik 17.

Louis Bachelier, mathematician, PhD 1900

Bachelier (1900) used Brownian motion for the modeling of stock prices in his PhD thesis "Théorie de la spéculation", Annales Scientifiques de l'Ecole Normale Supérieure 3 (17): 21-86, 1900.

Norbert Wiener, mathematician, founder of cybernetics

Wiener is credited, among other fundamental contributions, for the mathematical foundation of Brownian motion, published in 1923. In particular he constructed the Wiener space and Wiener measure on $\mathcal{C}_0([0,1])$ (the space of continuous functions from $[0,1]$ to $\mathbb{R}$ vanishing at 0).

Wiener (1923) "Differential space", Journal of Mathematics and Physics of the Massachusetts Institute of Technology, 2, 131-174, 1923.

Kiyoshi Itô, mathematician, C.F. Gauss Prize 2006

Itô constructed the Itô integral with respect to Brownian motion, cf. Itô, Kiyoshi, Stochastic integral. Proc. Imp. Acad. Tokyo 20, (1944), 519–524. He also constructed the stochastic calculus with respect to Brownian motion, which laid the foundation for the development of calculus for random processes, see Itô (1951) "On stochastic differential equations", in Memoirs of the American Mathematical Society.

"Renowned math wiz Itô, 93, dies." (The Japan Times, Saturday, November 15, 2008)

> Kiyoshi Itô, an internationally renowned mathematician and professor emeritus at Kyoto University died Monday of respiratory failure at a Kyoto hospital, the university said Friday. He was 93. Itô was once dubbed "the most famous Japanese in Wall Street" thanks to his contribution to the founding of financial derivatives theory. He is known for his work on stochastic differential equations and the "Itô Formula", which laid the foundation for the Black and Scholes (1973) model, a key tool for financial engineering. His theory is also widely used in fields like physics and biology.

Paul Samuelson, economist, Nobel Prize 1970

Samuelson (1965) rediscovered Bachelier's ideas and proposed geometric Brownian motion as a model for stock prices. In an interview he stated, "In the early 1950s I was able to locate by chance this unknown Bachelier (1900) book, rotting in the library of the University of Paris, and when I opened it up it was as if a whole new world was laid out before me." We refer to "Rational theory of warrant pricing" by Paul Samuelson, Industrial Management Review, p. 13–32, 1965.

In recognition of Bachelier's contribution, the Bachelier Finance Society was started in 1996 and now holds the World Bachelier Finance Congress every two years.

Robert Merton, Myron Scholes, economists

Robert Merton and Myron Scholes shared the 1997 Nobel Prize in economics: "In collaboration with Fisher Black, developed a pioneering formula for the valuation of stock options ... paved the way for economic valuations in many areas ... generated new types of financial instruments and facilitated more efficient risk management in society."[*]

Black and Scholes (1973) "The Pricing of Options and Corporate Liabilities". Journal of Political Economy 81 (3): 637–654.

The development of options pricing tools contributed greatly to the expansion of option markets and led to development several ventures such as the "Long Term Capital Management" (LTCM), founded in 1994. The fund yielded annualized returns of over 40% in its first years, but registered a loss of US$4.6 billion in less than four months in 1998, which resulted in its closure in early 2000.

Oldřich Vašíček, economist, 1977

Interest rates behave differently from stock prices, notably due to the phenomenon of mean reversion, and for this reason they are difficult to model using geometric Brownian motion. Vašíček (1977) was the first to suggest a mean-reverting model for stochastic interest rates, based on the Ornstein–Uhlenbeck process, in "An equilibrium characterization of the term structure", Journal of Financial Economics 5: 177–188.

David Heath, Robert Jarrow, Andrew Morton

These authors proposed in 1987 a general framework to model the evolution of (forward) interest rates, known as the Heath–Jarrow–Morton (HJM) model, see Heath et al. (1992) "Bond pricing and the term structure of interest rates: a new methodology for contingent claims valuation", Econometrica, (January 1992), Vol. 60, No. 1, pp 77–105.

Alan Brace, Dariusz Gatarek, Marek Musiela (BGM)

The Brace et al. (1997) model is actually based on geometric Brownian motion, and it is especially useful for the pricing of interest rate derivatives such as interest rate caps and swaptions on the LIBOR market; see "The Market Model of Interest Rate Dynamics". Mathematical Finance Vol. 7, page 127, Blackwell 1997, by Alan Brace, Dariusz Gatarek, Marek Musiela. Although LIBOR rates are being phased out, we will still use this terminology when referring to simple or linear compounded forward rates.

Financial derivatives

The following graphs exhibit a correlation between commodity (oil) prices and an oil-related asset price.

---

[*]This has to be put in relation with the modern development of *risk societies*: "societies increasingly preoccupied with the future (and also with safety), which generates the notion of risk" (Wikipedia).

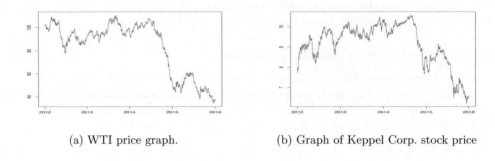

(a) WTI price graph.   (b) Graph of Keppel Corp. stock price

Figure 2: Comparison of WTI *vs* Keppel price graphs.

The study of financial derivatives aims at finding functional relationships between the price of an underlying asset (a company stock price, a commodity price, etc.) and the price of a related financial contract (an option, a financial derivative, etc.).

Option contracts

Early accounts of option contracts can also be found in *The Politics* Aristotle (BCE) by Aristotle (384-322 BCE). Referring to the philosopher Thales of Miletus (c. 624–c. 546 BCE), Aristotle writes:

> "He (Thales) knew by his skill in the stars while it was yet winter that there would be a great harvest of olives in the coming year; so, having a little money, he gave *deposits* for the use of all the olive-presses in Chios and Miletus, which he hired at a low price because no one bid against him. When the harvest-time came, and many were wanted all at once and of a sudden, he let them out at any rate which he pleased, and made a quantity of money".

In the above example, olive oil can be regarded as the underlying asset, while the oil press stands for the financial derivative. Option credit contracts appear to have been used as early as the tenth century by traders in the Mediterranean.

The derivatives market

As of year 2015, the size of the derivatives market was estimated at more than $1.2 quadrillion,* or more than 10 times the Gross World Product (GWP). See the website https://stats.bis.org/statx/toc/DER.html of the Bank for International Settlements (BIS) for up-to-date data on notional amounts outstanding and gross market value.

Next, we move to a description of (European) call and put options, which are at the basis of risk management.

European put option contracts

As previously mentioned, an important concern for the buyer of a stock at time t is whether its price S_T can decline at some future date T. The buyer of the stock may seek protection from a market crash by purchasing a contract that allows him to sell his asset

---

*One thousand trillion, or one million billion, or 10^{15}.

at time T at a guaranteed price K fixed at time t. This contract is called a put option with strike price K and exercise date T.

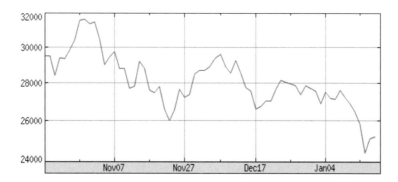

Figure 3: Graph of the Hang Seng index–holding a put option might be useful here.

Definition 1. *A (European)* put *option is a contract that gives its holder the right (but not the obligation) to* sell *a quantity of assets at a predefined price K called the strike price (or exercise price) and at a predefined date T called the maturity.*

In case the price S_T falls down below the level K, exercising the contract will give the holder of the option a gain equal to $K - S_T$ in comparison to those who did not subscribe the option contract and have to sell the asset at the market price S_T. In turn, the issuer of the option contract will register a loss also equal to $K - S_T$ (in the absence of transaction costs and other fees).

If S_T is above K, then the holder of the option contract will not exercise the option as he may choose to sell at the price S_T. In this case the profit derived from the option contract is 0.

Two possible scenarios (S_T finishing above K or below K) are illustrated in Figure 4.

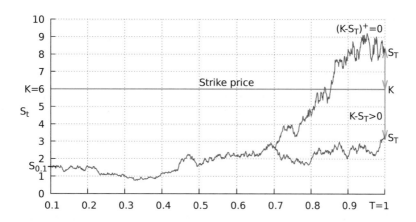

Figure 4: Two put option scenarios.

In general, the payoff of a (so-called *European*) put option contract can be written as

$$\phi(S_T) = (K - S_T)^+ := \begin{cases} K - S_T & \text{if } S_T \leqslant K, \\ 0, & \text{if } S_T \geqslant K. \end{cases}$$

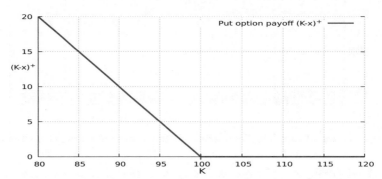

Figure 5: Payoff function of a put option with strike price $K = 100$.

Example of put option: the buy-back guarantee in currency exchange is a common example of European put option.

Cash settlement *vs* physical delivery

Physical delivery. In the case of physical delivery, the put option contract issuer will pay the strike price \$$K$ to the option contract holder in exchange for one unit of the risky asset priced S_T.

Cash settlement. In the case of a cash settlement, the put option issuer will satisfy the contract by transferring the amount $C = (K - S_T)^+$ to the option contract holder.

European call option contracts

On the other hand, if the trader aims at buying some stock or commodity, his interest will be in prices not going up, and he might want to purchase a call option, which is a contract allowing him to buy the considered asset at time T at a price not higher than a level K fixed at time t.

Definition 2. *A (European)* call *option is a contract that gives its holder the right (but not the obligation) to purchase a quantity of assets at a predefined price K called the strike price, and at a predefined date T called the maturity.*

Here, in the event that S_T goes above K, the buyer of the option contract will register a potential gain equal to $S_T - K$ in comparison to an agent who did not subscribe to the call option.

Two possible scenarios (S_T finishing above K or below K) are illustrated in Figure 6.

In general, the payoff of a (so-called European) call option contract can be written as

$$\phi(S_T) = (S_T - K)^+ := \begin{cases} S_T - K & \text{if } S_T \geqslant K, \\ 0, & \text{if } S_T \leqslant K. \end{cases}$$

Figure 6: Two call option scenarios.

According to market practice, options are often divided into a certain number n of *warrants*, the (possibly fractional) quantity n being called the *entitlement ratio*.

Example of call option: the price lock guarantee in online ticket booking is a common example of European *call* option.

Cash settlement *vs* physical delivery

Physical delivery. In the case of physical delivery, the call option contract issuer will transfer one unit of the risky asset priced S_T to the option contract holder in exchange for the strike price \$$K$. Physical delivery may include physical goods, commodities, or assets such as coffee, airline fuel, or live cattle, see Schroeder and Coffey (2018).

Cash settlement. In the case of a cash settlement, the call option issuer will fulfill the contract by transferring the amount $C = (S_T - K)^+$ to the option contract holder.

Option pricing

In order for an option contract to be fair, the buyer of the option contract should pay a fee (similar to an insurance fee) at the signature of the contract. The computation of this fee is an important issue, which is known as option *pricing*.

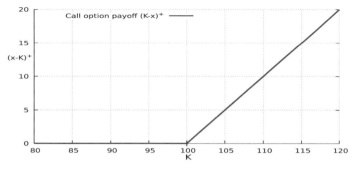

Figure 7: Payoff function of a call option with strike price $K = 100$.

Option hedging

The second important issue is that of *hedging*, *i.e.* how to manage a given portfolio in such a way that it contains the required random payoff $(K - S_T)^+$ (for a put option) or $(S_T - K)^+$ (for a call option) at the maturity date T.

Example: Fuel hedging and the four-way zero-collar option

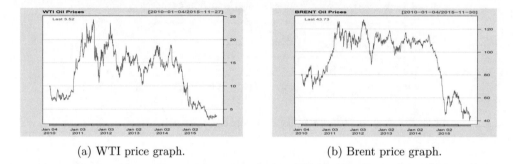

(a) WTI price graph.   (b) Brent price graph.

Figure 8: Brent and WTI price graphs.

```
1   install.packages("Quandl")
    library(Quandl);library(quantmod)
3   getSymbols("DCOILBRENTEU", src="FRED")
    chartSeries(DCOILBRENTEU,up.col="blue",theme="white",name = "BRENT Oil Prices",lwd=5)
5   BRENT = Quandl("FRED/DCOILBRENTEU",start_date="2010-01-01", end_date="2015-11-30",type="xts")
    chartSeries(BRENT,up.col="blue",theme="white",name = "BRENT Oil Prices",lwd=5)
7   getSymbols("WTI", from="2010-01-01", to="2015-11-30")
    WTI <- Ad(`WTI`)
9   chartSeries(WTI,up.col="blue",theme="white",name = "WTI Oil Prices",lwd=5)
```

The four-way call collar call option requires its holder to purchase the underlying asset (here, airline fuel) at a price specified by the blue curve in Figure 9, when the underlying asset price is represented by the red line.

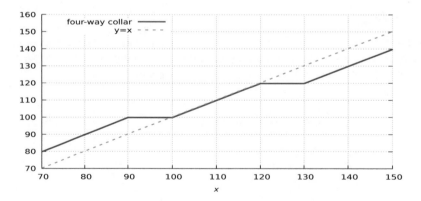

Figure 9: Price map of a four-way collar option.

The four-way call collar option contract will result into a positive or negative payoff depending on current fuel prices, as illustrated in Figure 10.

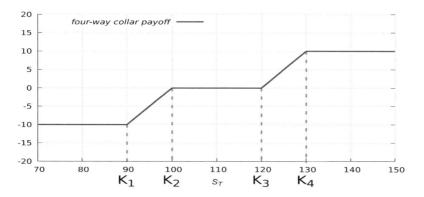

Figure 10: Payoff function of a four-way call collar option.

The four-way call collar payoff can be written as a linear combination

$$\phi(S_T) = (K_1 - S_T)^+ - (K_2 - S_T)^+ + (S_T - K_3)^+ - (S_T - K_4)^+$$

of call and put option payoffs with respective strike prices

$$K_1 = 90, \quad K_2 = 100, \quad K_3 = 120, \quad K_4 = 130.$$

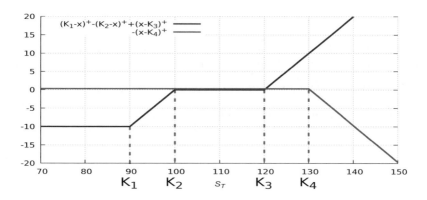

Figure 11: Four-way call collar payoff as a combination of call and put options.

Therefore, the four-way call collar option contract can be *synthesized* by:

1. purchasing a *put option* with strike price $K_1 = \$90$,

2. selling (or issuing) a *put option* with strike price $K_2 = \$100$,

3. purchasing a *call option* with strike price $K_3 = \$120$,

4. selling (or issuing) a *call option* with strike price $K_4 = \$130$.

Moreover, the call collar option contract can be made *costless* by adjusting the boundaries K_1, K_2, K_3, K_4, in which case it becomes a *zero-collar* option.

Example – The one-step 4-5-2 model

We close this introduction with a simplified example of the pricing and hedging technique in a binary model. Consider:

i) A risky underlying stock valued $S_0 = \$4$ at time $t = 0$, and taking only two possible values

$$S_1 = \begin{cases} \$5 \\ \\ \$2 \end{cases}$$

at time $t = 1$.

ii) An option contract that promises a claim payoff C whose values are defined contingent to the market data of S_1 as:

$$C := \begin{cases} \$3 & \text{if } S_1 = \$5 \\ \\ \$0 & \text{if } S_1 = \$2. \end{cases}$$

Exercise: Does C represent the payoff of a put option contract? Of a call option contract? If yes, with which strike price K?

At time $t = 0$ the option contract issuer (or writer) chooses to invest ξ units in the risky asset S, while keeping $\$\eta$ on our bank account, meaning that we invest a total amount

$$\xi S_0 + \$\eta \qquad \text{at time } t = 0.$$

Here, the amount $\$\eta$ may be positive or negative, depending on whether it corresponds to savings or to debt and is interpreted as a *liability*.

The following issues can be addressed:

a) *Hedging:* How to choose the portfolio allocation $(\xi, \$\eta)$ so that the value

$$\xi S_1 + \$\eta$$

of the portfolio matches the future payoff C at time $t = 1$?

b) *Pricing:* How to determine the amount $\xi S_0 + \$\eta$ to be invested by the option contract issuer in such a portfolio at time $t = 0$?

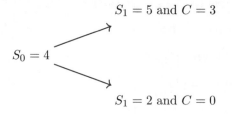

$S_1 = 5$ and $C = 3$

$S_0 = 4$

$S_1 = 2$ and $C = 0$

Hedging or *replicating* the contract means that at time $t = 1$ the portfolio value matches the future payoff C, *i.e.*

$$\xi S_1 + \$\eta = C.$$

Hedge, then price. This condition can be rewritten as

$$C = \begin{cases} \$3 = \xi \times \$5 + \$\eta & \text{if } S_1 = \$5, \\ \$0 = \xi \times \$2 + \$\eta & \text{if } S_1 = \$2, \end{cases}$$

i.e.

$$\begin{cases} 5\xi + \eta = 3, \\ 2\xi + \eta = 0, \end{cases} \quad \text{which yields} \quad \begin{cases} \xi = 1 \text{ stock}, \\ \$\eta = -\$2. \end{cases}$$

In other words, the option contract issuer purchases 1 (one) unit of the stock S at the price $S_0 = \$4$, and borrows \$2 from the bank. The price of the option contract is then given by the portfolio value

$$\xi S_0 + \$\eta = 1 \times \$4 - \$2 = \$2.$$

at time $t = 0$.

This algorithm is scalable and can be extended to recombining binary trees over multiple time steps.

Definition 3. *The* arbitrage-free price *of the option contract is defined as the initial cost* $\xi S_0 + \$\eta$ *of the portfolio hedging the claim payoff C.*

Conclusion: in order to deliver the random payoff $C = \begin{cases} \$3 & \text{if } S_1 = \$5 \\ \$0 & \text{if } S_1 = \$2. \end{cases}$ to the option contract holder at time $t = 1$, the option contract issuer (or writer) will:

1. charge $\xi S_0 + \$\eta = \$2$ (the option contract price) at time $t = 0$,

2. borrow $-\$\eta = \$2$ from the bank,

3. invest those $\$2 + \$2 = \$4$ into the purchase of $\xi = 1$ unit of stock valued at $S_0 = \$4$ at time $t = 0$,

4. wait until time $t = 1$ to find that the portfolio value has evolved into

$$C = \begin{cases} \xi \times \$5 + \$\eta = 1 \times \$5 - \$2 = \$3 & \text{if } S_1 = \$5, \\ \xi \times \$2 + \$\eta = 1 \times \$2 - \$2 = 0 & \text{if } S_1 = \$2, \end{cases}$$

so that the option contract and the equality $C = \xi S_1 + \$\eta$ can be fulfilled, allowing the option issuer to break even whatever the evolution of the risky asset price S.

In a *cash settlement*, the stock is sold at the price $S_1 = \$5$ or $S_1 = \$2$, the payoff $C = (S_1 - K)^+ = \$3$ or \$0 is issued to the option contract holder, and the loan is refunded with the remaining \$2.

In the case of *physical delivery*, $\xi = 1$ share of stock is handed in to the option holder in exchange for the strike price $K = \$2$, which is used to refund the initial \$2 loan subscribed by the issuer.

Here, the option contract price $\xi S_0 + \$\eta = \$2$ is interpreted as the cost of hedging the option. In Chapters 2 and 3, we will see that this model is scalable and extends to discrete time.

We note that the initial option contract price of $2 can be turned to $C = \$3$ (%50 profit) ... or into $C = \$0$ (total ruin).

Thinking further

1) The expected claim payoff at time $t = 1$ is

$$
\begin{aligned}
\mathbb{E}[C] &= \$3 \times \mathbb{P}(C = \$3) + \$0 \times \mathbb{P}(C = \$0) \\
&= \$3 \times \mathbb{P}(S_1 = \$5).
\end{aligned}
$$

In absence of arbitrage opportunities ("fair market"), this expected payoff $\mathbb{E}[C]$ should equal the initial amount $2 invested in the option. In that case we should have

$$
\begin{cases}
\mathbb{E}[C] = \$3 \times \mathbb{P}(S_1 = \$5) = \$2 \\[2mm]
\mathbb{P}(S_1 = \$5) + \mathbb{P}(S_1 = \$2) = 1.
\end{cases}
$$

from which we can *infer* the probabilities

$$
\begin{cases}
\mathbb{P}(S_1 = \$5) = \dfrac{2}{3} \\[4mm]
\mathbb{P}(S_1 = \$2) = \dfrac{1}{3},
\end{cases}
\tag{1}
$$

which are called *risk-neutral* probabilities. We see that under the risk-neutral probabilities, the stock S has twice more chances to go up than to go down in a "fair" market.

2) Based on the probabilities (1) we can also compute the expected value $\mathbb{E}[S_1]$ of the stock at time $t = 1$. We find

$$
\begin{aligned}
\mathbb{E}[S_1] &= \$5 \times \mathbb{P}(S_1 = \$5) + \$2 \times \mathbb{P}(S_1 = \$2) \\
&= \$5 \times \frac{2}{3} + \$2 \times \frac{1}{3} \\
&= \$4 \\
&= S_0.
\end{aligned}
$$

Here, this means that, on average, no extra profit or loss can be made from an investment on the risky stock, and the probabilities $(2/3, 1/3)$ are termed *risk-neutral* probabilities. In a more realistic model we can assume that the riskless bank account yields an interest rate equal to r, in which case the above analysis is modified by letting $\$\eta$ become $\$(1 + r)\eta$ at time $t = 1$; nevertheless, the main conclusions remain unchanged.

Market-implied probabilities

By matching the theoretical price $\mathbb{E}[C]$ to an actual market price data $\$M$ as

$$
\$M = \mathbb{E}[C] = \$3 \times \mathbb{P}(C = \$3) + \$0 \times \mathbb{P}(C = \$0) = \$3 \times \mathbb{P}(S_1 = \$5)
$$

we can infer the probabilities

$$
\begin{cases}
\mathbb{P}(S_1 = \$5) = \dfrac{\$M}{3} \\[4mm]
\mathbb{P}(S_1 = \$2) = \dfrac{3 - \$M}{3},
\end{cases}
\tag{2}
$$

which are *implied probabilities* estimated from market data, as illustrated in Figure 12. We note that the conditions

$$0 < \mathbb{P}(S_1 = \$5) < 1, \qquad 0 < \mathbb{P}(S_1 = \$2) < 1$$

are equivalent to $0 < \$M < 3$, which is consistent with financial intuition in a non-deterministic market.

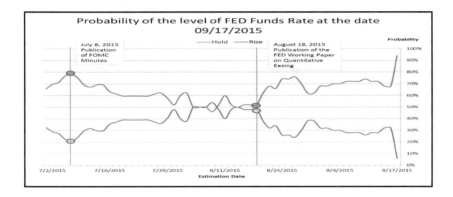

Figure 12: Implied probabilities.

Implied probabilities can be estimated using *e.g.* binary options; see for example Exercise 3.9.

The *Practitioner* expects a good model to be:

- *Robust* with respect to missing, spurious, or noisy data,

- *Fast* - prices have to be delivered daily in the morning,

- *Easy* to calibrate - parameter estimation,

- *Stable* with respect to re-calibration and the use of new data sets.

Typically, a medium-size bank manages 5,000 options and 10,000 deals daily over 1,000 possible scenarios and dozens of time steps. This can mean a hundred million computations of $\mathbb{E}[C]$ daily, or close to a billion such computations for a large bank.

The *Mathematician* tends to focus on more theoretical features, such as:

- *Elegance*,

- *Sophistication*,

- *Existence* of analytical (closed-form) solutions / error bounds,

- *Significance* to mathematical finance.

This includes:

- *Creating* new payoff functions and structured products,

- *Defining* new models for underlying asset prices,

- *Finding* new ways to compute expectations $\mathbb{E}[C]$ and hedging strategies.

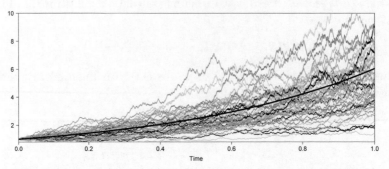

Figure 13: Fifty sample price paths used for the Monte Carlo method.

The methods involved include:

- Monte Carlo methods (60%),

- PDEs and finite differences methods (30%),

- Other analytic methods and approximation methods (10%),

+ AI and Machine Learning techniques.

Book plan

The book plan from Chapter 1 to Chapter 7 is structured in layers that repeat the main concepts (arbitrage, pricing, hedging, risk-neutral measures) in different time scale settings (one-step, discrete-time, continuous-time).

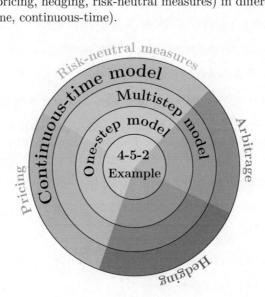

Figure 14: Book plan.

Chapter 1

Assets, Portfolios, and Arbitrage

In this chapter, the concepts of portfolio, arbitrage, market completeness, pricing, and hedging, are introduced in a simplified single-step financial model with only two time instants $t = 0$ and $t = 1$. A binary asset price model is considered as an example in Section 1.6.

1.1 Portfolio Allocation and Short Selling

We will use the following notation. An element $\bar{x}$ of $\mathbb{R}^{d+1}$ is a vector

$$\bar{x} = \left(x^{(0)}, x^{(1)}, \ldots, x^{(d)}\right)$$

made of $d + 1$ components. The scalar product $\bar{x} \cdot \bar{y}$ of two vectors $\bar{x}$, $\bar{y} \in \mathbb{R}^{d+1}$ is defined by

$$\bar{x} \cdot \bar{y} := x^{(0)}y^{(0)} + x^{(1)}y^{(1)} + \cdots + x^{(d)}y^{(d)}.$$

The vector

$$\bar{S}_0 = \left(S_0^{(0)}, S_0^{(1)}, \ldots, S_0^{(d)}\right)$$

denotes the prices at time $t = 0$ of $d + 1$ assets. Namely, $S_0^{(i)} > 0$ is the price at time $t = 0$ of asset n^o $i = 0, 1, \ldots, d$.

The asset values $S_1^{(i)} > 0$ of assets No $i = 0, 1, \ldots, d$ at time $t = 1$ are represented by the vector

$$\bar{S}_1 = \left(S_1^{(0)}, S_1^{(1)}, \ldots, S_1^{(d)}\right),$$

whose components $\left(S_1^{(1)}, \ldots, S_1^{(d)}\right)$ are random variables defined on a probability space $(\Omega, \mathcal{F}, \mathbb{P})$.

In addition we will assume that asset n° 0 is a riskless asset (of savings account type) that yields an interest rate $r > 0$, *i.e.* we have

$$S_1^{(0)} = (1 + r)S_0^{(0)}.$$

Definition 1.1. *A portfolio based on the assets $0, 1, \ldots, d$ is a vector*

$$\bar{\xi} = \left(\xi^{(0)}, \xi^{(1)}, \ldots, \xi^{(d)}\right) \in \mathbb{R}^{d+1},$$

in which $\xi^{(i)}$ represents the (possibly fractional) quantity of asset n^o i owned by an investor, $i = 0, 1, \ldots, d$.

The *price* of such a portfolio, or the cost of the corresponding investment, is given by

$$\bar{\xi} \cdot \bar{S}_0 = \sum_{i=0}^{d} \xi^{(i)} S_0^{(i)} = \xi^{(0)} S_0^{(0)} + \xi^{(1)} S_0^{(1)} + \cdots + \xi^{(d)} S_0^{(d)}$$

at time $t = 0$. At time $t = 1$, the *value* of the portfolio has evolved into

$$\bar{\xi} \cdot \bar{S}_1 = \sum_{i=0}^{d} \xi^{(i)} S_1^{(i)} = \xi^{(0)} S_1^{(0)} + \xi^{(1)} S_1^{(1)} + \cdots + \xi^{(d)} S_1^{(d)}.$$

There are various ways to construct a portfolio allocation $\left(\xi^{(i)} \right)_{i=0,1,\ldots,d}$.

i) If $\xi^{(0)} > 0$, the investor puts the amount $\xi^{(0)} S_0^{(0)} > 0$ on a savings account with interest rate r.

ii) If $\xi^{(0)} < 0$, the investor borrows the amount $-\xi^{(0)} S_0^{(0)} > 0$ with the same interest rate r.

iii) For $i = 1, 2, \ldots, d$, if $\xi^{(i)} > 0$, then the investor purchases a (possibly fractional) quantity $\xi^{(i)} > 0$ of the asset n^o i.

iv) If $\xi^{(i)} < 0$, the investor borrows a quantity $-\xi^{(i)} > 0$ of asset i and sells it to obtain the amount $-\xi^{(i)} S_0^{(i)} > 0$.

In the latter case one says that the investor *short sells* a quantity $-\xi^{(i)} > 0$ of the asset n^o i, which lowers the cost of the portfolio.

Definition 1.2. *The* short selling ratio, *or percentage of daily turnover activity related to short selling, is defined as the ratio of the number of daily short sold shares divided by daily volume.*

Profits are usually made by first buying at a low price and then selling at a high price. Short sellers apply the same rule but in the reverse time order: first sell high, and then buy low if possible, by applying the following procedure.

1. Borrow the asset n^o i.

2. At time $t = 0$, sell the asset n^o i on the market at the price $S_0^{(i)}$ and invest the amount $S_0^{(i)}$ at the interest rate $r > 0$.

3. Buy back the asset n^o i at time $t = 1$ at the price $S_1^{(i)}$, with hopefully $S_1^{(i)} < (1+r)S_0^{(i)}$.

4. Return the asset to its owner, with possibly a (small) fee $p > 0$.*

At the end of the operation the profit made on share n^o i equals

$$(1+r)S_0^{(i)} - S_1^{(i)} - p > 0,$$

which is positive provided that $S_1^{(i)} < (1+r)S_0^{(i)}$ and $p > 0$ is sufficiently small.

---

*The cost p of short selling will not be taken into account in later calculations.

1.2 Arbitrage

Arbitrage can be described as:

"the purchase of currencies, securities, or commodities in one market for immediate resale in others in order to profit from unequal prices".

In other words, an arbitrage opportunity is the possibility to make a strictly positive amount of money starting from zero, or even from a negative amount. In a sense, the existence of an arbitrage opportunity can be seen as a way to "beat" the market.

For example, *triangular arbitrage* is a way to realize arbitrage opportunities based on discrepancies in the cross-exchange rates of foreign currencies, as seen in Figure 1.1.

XE Live Exchange Rates

USD	EUR	GBP
1.00000	0.89347	0.76988
1.11923	1.00000	0.86167
1.29891	1.16054	1.00000

Figure 1.1: Examples of triangular arbitrage.

As an attempt to realize triangular arbitrage based on the data of Figure 1.1, one could:

1. Change US\$1.00 into €0.89347,

2. Change €0.89347 into £0.89347 × 0.86167 = £0.769876295,

3. Change back £0.769876295 into US\$0.769876295 × 1.2981 = US\$0.999376418,

which would actually result into a small loss. Alternatively, one could:

1. Change US\$1.00 into £0.76988,

2. Change £0.76988 into €1.16054 × 0.76988 =€0.893476535,

3. Change back €0.893476535 into US\$0.893476535 × 1.11923 = US\$1.000005742,

which would result into a small gain, assuming the absence of transaction costs.

Next, we state a mathematical formulation of the concept of arbitrage.

Definition 1.3. *A portfolio allocation $\bar{\xi} \in \mathbb{R}^{d+1}$ constitutes an arbitrage opportunity if the three following conditions are satisfied:*

i) $\bar{\xi} \cdot \bar{S}_0 \leqslant 0$ *at time $t = 0$,*   [Start from a zero-cost portfolio, or with a debt.]

ii) $\bar{\xi} \cdot \bar{S}_1 \geqslant 0$ *at time $t = 1$,*   [Finish with a nonnegative amount.]

iii) $\mathbb{P}\big(\bar{\xi} \cdot \bar{S}_1 > 0\big) > 0$ *at time $t = 1$.*   [Profit is made with nonzero probability.]

Note that there exist multiple ways to break the assumptions of Definition 1.3 in order to achieve the absence of arbitrage. For example, under the absence of arbitrage, satisfying Condition (i) means that either $\bar{\xi} \cdot \bar{S}_1$ cannot be almost surely* nonnegative (*i.e.* potential losses cannot be avoided), or $\mathbb{P}\big(\bar{\xi} \cdot \bar{S}_1 > 0\big) = 0$, (*i.e.* no strictly positive profit can be made).

---

*"Almost surely", or "*a.s.*", means "with probability one".

Realizing arbitrage

In the example below, we realize arbitrage by buying and holding an asset.

1. Borrow the amount $-\xi^{(0)}S_0^{(0)} > 0$ on the riskless asset $n^o\ 0$.

2. Use the amount $-\xi^{(0)}S_0^{(0)} > 0$ to purchase a quantity $\xi^{(i)} = -\xi^{(0)}S_0^{(0)}/S_0^{(i)}$, of the risky asset $n^o\ i \geqslant 1$ at time $t = 0$ and price $S_0^{(i)}$ so that the initial portfolio cost is

$$\xi^{(0)}S_0^{(0)} + \xi^{(i)}S_0^{(i)} = 0.$$

3. At time $t = 1$, sell the risky asset $n^o\ i$ at the price $S_1^{(i)}$, with hopefully $S_1^{(i)} > (1+r)S_0^{(i)}$.

4. Refund the amount $-(1+r)\xi^{(0)}S_0^{(0)} > 0$ with interest rate $r > 0$.

At the end of the operation the profit made is

$$
\begin{aligned}
\xi^{(i)}S_1^{(i)} - \left(-(1+r)\xi^{(0)}S_0^{(0)}\right) &= \xi^{(i)}S_1^{(i)} + (1+r)\xi^{(0)}S_0^{(0)} \\
&= -\xi^{(0)}\frac{S_0^{(0)}}{S_0^{(i)}}S_1^{(i)} + (1+r)\xi^{(0)}S_0^{(0)} \\
&= -\xi^{(0)}\frac{S_0^{(0)}}{S_0^{(i)}}\left(S_1^{(i)} - (1+r)S_0^{(i)}\right) \\
&= \xi^{(i)}\left(S_1^{(i)} - (1+r)S_0^{(i)}\right) \\
&> 0,
\end{aligned}
$$

or $S_1^{(i)} - (1+r)S_0^{(i)}$ per unit of stock invested, which is positive provided that $S_1^{(i)} > S_0^{(i)}$ and r is sufficiently small.

Arbitrage opportunities can be similarly realized using the short selling procedure described in Section 1.1.

City	Currency	US$
Tokyo	JPY 38,800	$346
Hong Kong	HK$2,956.67	$381
Seoul	KRW 378,533	$400
Taipei	NT$12,980	$404
New York	US$433	$433
Sydney	A$633.28	$483
Frankfurt	€399	$513
Paris	€399	$513
Rome	€399	$513
Brussels	€399.66	$514
London	£279.99	$527
Manila	PhP 29,500	$563
Jakarta	Rp 5,754,1676	$627

Figure 1.2: Arbitrage: Retail prices around the world for the Xbox 360 in 2006.

There are many real-life examples of situations where arbitrage opportunities can occur, such as:

– assets with different returns (finance),

– servers with different speeds (queueing, networking, computing),

– highway lanes with different speeds (driving).

In the latter two examples, the absence of arbitrage is a consequence of the fact that switching to a faster lane or server may result into congestion, thus annihilating the potential benefit of the shift.

六合彩投注換算表

MARK SIX INVESTMENT TABLE

複式 Multiple		一膽拖 One Banker with		兩膽拖 Two Bankers with		三膽拖 Three Bankers with		四膽拖 Four Bankers with		五膽拖 Five Bankers with	
所選號碼總數 No. of Selections	HK$	配腳數目 No. of Legs	HK$	配腳數目 No. of Legs	HK$	配腳數目 No. of Legs	HK$	配腳數目 No. of Legs	HK$	配腳數目 No. of Legs	HK$
7	35	6	30	5	25	4	20	3	15	2	10
8	140	7	105	6	75	5	50	4	30	3	15
9	420	8	280	7	175	6	100	5	50	4	20
10	1,050	9	630	8	350	7	175	6	75	5	25
11	2,310	10	1,260	9	630	8	280	7	105	6	30
12	4,620	11	2,310	10	1,050	9	420	8	140	7	35
13	8,580	12	3,960	11	1,650	10	600	9	180	8	40
14	15,015	13	6,435	12	2,475	11	825	10	225	9	45
15	25,025	14	10,010	13	3,575	12	1,100	11	275	10	50
49	69,919,080	48	8,561,520	47	891,825	46	75,900	45	4,950	44	220

Table 1.1: Absence of arbitrage – the Mark Six "Investment Table".

In the table of Figure 1.1, the absence of arbitrage opportunities is materialized by the fact that the price of each combination is found to be proportional to its probability, thus making the game fair and disallowing any opportunity or arbitrage that would result of betting on a more profitable combination.

In what follows, we will work under the assumption that arbitrage opportunities do not occur, and we will rely on this hypothesis for the pricing of financial instruments.

Example: share rights

Let us give a market example of pricing by the absence of arbitrage.

From March 24 to 31, 2009, HSBC issued *rights* to buy shares at the price of $28. This *right* behaves similarly to an option in the sense that it gives the right (with no obligation) to buy the stock at the discount price $K = \$28$. On March 24, the HSBC stock price closed at $41.70.

The question is: how to value the price $\$R$ of the right to buy one share? This question can be answered by looking for arbitrage opportunities. Indeed, the underlying stock can be purchased in two different ways:

1. Buy the stock directly on the market at the price of $41.70. Cost: $41.70,

   or:

2. First, purchase the right at a price R, and then the stock at a price $28. Total cost: $R+$28.

a) In case

$$\$R + \$28 < \$41.70, \tag{1.1}$$

   arbitrage would be possible for an investor who owns no stock and no rights, by

   i) Buying the right at a price R, and then
   ii) Buying the stock at a price $28, and
   iii) Reselling the stock at the market price of $41.70.

   The profit made by this investor would equal

$$\$41.70 - (\$R + \$28) > 0.$$

b) On the other hand, in case

$$\$R + \$28 > \$41.70, \tag{1.2}$$

   arbitrage would be possible for an investor who owns the rights, by:

   i) Buying the stock on the market at $41.70,
   ii) Selling the right by contract at a price R, and then
   iii) Selling the stock at $28 to that other investor.

   In this case, the profit made would equal

$$\$R + \$28 - \$41.70 > 0.$$

In the absence of arbitrage opportunities, the combination of (1.1) and (1.2) implies that R should satisfy

$$\$R + \$28 - \$41.70 = 0,$$

i.e. the arbitrage-free price of the right is given by the equation

$$\$R = \$41.70 - \$28 = \$13.70. \tag{1.3}$$

Interestingly, the *market* price of the right was $13.20 at the close of the session on March 24. The difference of $0.50 can be explained by the presence of various market factors such as transaction costs, the time value of money, or simply by the fact that asset prices are constantly fluctuating over time. It may also represent a small arbitrage opportunity, which cannot be at all excluded. Nevertheless, the absence of arbitrage argument (1.3) prices the right at $13.70, which is quite close to its market value. Thus the absence of arbitrage hypothesis appears as an accurate tool for pricing.

1.3 Risk-Neutral Probability Measures

In order to use the absence of arbitrage in the general context of pricing financial derivatives, we will need the notion of *risk-neutral probability measure*.

The next definition says that under a risk-neutral probability measure, the risky assets $n^o\ 1, 2, \ldots, d$ have same *average* rate of return as the riskless asset $n^o\ 0$.

Definition 1.4. *A probability measure* $\mathbb{P}^*$ *on* Ω *is called a* risk-neutral measure *if*

$$\mathbb{E}^*\left[S_1^{(i)}\right] = (1+r)S_0^{(i)}, \qquad i = 1, 2, \ldots, d. \tag{1.4}$$

Here, $\mathbb{E}^*$ denotes the expectation under the probability measure $\mathbb{P}^*$. Note that for $i = 0$, we have $\mathbb{E}^*\left[S_1^{(0)}\right] = S_1^{(0)} = (1+r)S_0^{(0)}$ by definition.

In other words, $\mathbb{P}^*$ is called *risk-neutral* because taking risks under $\mathbb{P}^*$ by buying a stock $S_1^{(i)}$ has a neutral effect: on average the expected yield of the risky asset equals the risk-free interest rate obtained by investing on the savings account with interest rate r, *i.e.* we have

$$\mathbb{E}^*\left[\frac{S_1^{(i)} - S_0^{(i)}}{S_0^{(i)}}\right] = r.$$

On the other hand, under a "risk premium" probability measure $\mathbb{P}^\#$, the expected return (or net discounted gain) of the risky asset $S_1^{(i)}$ would be higher than r, *i.e.* we would have

$$\mathbb{E}^\#\left[\frac{S_1^{(i)} - S_0^{(i)}}{S_0^{(i)}}\right] > r,$$

or

$$\mathbb{E}^\#\left[S_1^{(i)}\right] > (1+r)S_0^{(i)}, \qquad i = 1, 2, \ldots, d,$$

whereas under a "negative premium" measure $\mathbb{P}^\flat$, the expected return of the risky asset $S_1^{(i)}$ would be lower than r, *i.e.* we would have

$$\mathbb{E}^\flat\left[\frac{S_1^{(i)} - S_0^{(i)}}{S_0^{(i)}}\right] < r,$$

or

$$\mathbb{E}^\flat\left[S_1^{(i)}\right] < (1+r)S_0^{(i)}, \qquad i = 1, 2, \ldots, d.$$

In the sequel we will only consider probability measures $\mathbb{P}^*$ that are *equivalent* to $\mathbb{P}$, in the sense that they share the same events of zero probability.

Definition 1.5. *A probability measure* $\mathbb{P}^*$ *on* $(\Omega, \mathcal{F})$ *is said to be* equivalent *to another probability measure* $\mathbb{P}$ *when*

$$\mathbb{P}^*(A) = 0 \quad \text{if and only if} \quad \mathbb{P}(A) = 0, \quad \text{for all} \quad A \in \mathcal{F}. \tag{1.5}$$

The following Theorem 1.6 can be used to check for the existence of arbitrage opportunities and is known as the first fundamental theorem of asset pricing.

Theorem 1.6. *A market is* without *arbitrage opportunity if and only if it admits at least one* equivalent *risk-neutral probability measure* $\mathbb{P}^*$.

Proof. (i) Sufficiency. Assume that there exists a risk-neutral probability measure $\mathbb{P}^*$ equivalent to $\mathbb{P}$. Since $\mathbb{P}^*$ is risk-neutral, we have

$$\bar{\xi} \cdot \bar{S}_0 = \sum_{i=0}^d \xi^{(i)} S_0^{(i)} = \frac{1}{1+r} \sum_{i=0}^d \xi^{(i)} \mathbb{E}^* \left[S_1^{(i)} \right] = \frac{1}{1+r} \mathbb{E}^* \left[\bar{\xi} \cdot \bar{S}_1 \right]. \tag{1.6}$$

We proceed by contradiction, and suppose that the market admits an arbitrage opportunity $\bar{\xi}$ according to Definition 1.3. In this case, Definition 1.3-(ii) shows that $\bar{\xi} \cdot \bar{S}_1 \geqslant 0$, and Definition 1.3-($iii$) implies $\mathbb{P}(\bar{\xi} \cdot \bar{S}_1 > 0) > 0$, hence $\mathbb{P}^*(\bar{\xi} \cdot \bar{S}_1 > 0) > 0$ because $\mathbb{P}$ is equivalent to $\mathbb{P}^*$. We have

$$
\begin{aligned}
0 \ &< \ \mathbb{P}^*(\bar{\xi} \cdot \bar{S}_1 > 0) \\
&= \ \mathbb{P}^* \left(\bigcup_{n \geqslant 1} \{ \bar{\xi} \cdot \bar{S}_1 > 1/n \} \right) \\
&= \ \lim_{n \to \infty} \mathbb{P}^*(\bar{\xi} \cdot \bar{S}_1 > 1/n) \\
&= \ \lim_{\varepsilon \searrow 0} \mathbb{P}^*(\bar{\xi} \cdot \bar{S}_1 > \varepsilon),
\end{aligned}
$$

there exists $\varepsilon > 0$ such that $\mathbb{P}^*(\bar{\xi} \cdot \bar{S}_1 \geqslant \varepsilon) > 0$, hence

$$
\begin{aligned}
\mathbb{E}^* \left[\bar{\xi} \cdot \bar{S}_1 \right] \ &\geqslant \ \mathbb{E}^* \left[\bar{\xi} \cdot \bar{S}_1 \mathbb{1}_{\{ \bar{\xi} \cdot \bar{S}_1 \geqslant \varepsilon \}} \right] \\
&\geqslant \ \varepsilon \, \mathbb{E}^* \left[\mathbb{1}_{\{ \bar{\xi} \cdot \bar{S}_1 \geqslant \varepsilon \}} \right] \\
&= \ \varepsilon \mathbb{P}^*(\bar{\xi} \cdot \bar{S}_1 \geqslant \varepsilon) \\
&> \ 0,
\end{aligned}
$$

and by (1.6) we conclude that

$$\bar{\xi} \cdot \bar{S}_0 = \frac{1}{1+r} \mathbb{E}^* \left[\bar{\xi} \cdot \bar{S}_1 \right] > 0,$$

which contradicts Definition 1.3-(i). We conclude that the market is without arbitrage opportunities.

(ii) The proof of necessity, see Theorem 1.6 in Föllmer and Schied (2004), relies on the theorem of separation of convex sets by hyperplanes Proposition 1.7 below. It can be briefly sketched as follows in the case $d = 2$ of a portfolio including two risky assets priced $\left(S_i^{(1)}, S_i^{(2)} \right)_{i=0,1}$ with *discounted* market returns

$$R^{(1)} := \frac{S_1^{(1)} - S_0^{(1)}}{S_0^{(1)}} - r, \quad R^{(2)} := \frac{S_1^{(2)} - S_0^{(2)}}{S_0^{(2)}} - r.$$

Assume that the relation

$$\mathbb{E}_{\mathbb{Q}} \left[R^{(2)} \right] = \mathbb{E}_{\mathbb{Q}} \left[R^{(1)} \right] = 0 \tag{1.7}$$

does not hold for any $\mathbb{Q}$ in the family $\mathcal{P}$ of probability measures $\mathbb{Q}$ on Ω equivalent to $\mathbb{P}$. Applying the separation theorem Proposition 1.7 below to the convex subset

$$\mathcal{C} := \left\{ \left(\mathbb{E}_{\mathbb{Q}} \left[R^{(1)} \right], \mathbb{E}_{\mathbb{Q}} \left[R^{(2)} \right] \right) \ : \ \mathbb{Q} \in \mathcal{P} \right\} \subset \mathbb{R}^2$$

of $\mathbb{R}^2$, if (1.7) does not hold under any $\mathbb{P}^* \in \mathcal{P}$, then $(0,0) \notin \mathcal{C}$, and the convex separation Proposition 1.7 below applied to the convex sets $\mathcal{C}$ and $\{(0,0)\}$ shows the existence of $c \in \mathbb{R}$ such that

$$\mathbb{E}_\mathbb{Q}\left[R^{(1)} + cR^{(2)}\right] = \mathbb{E}_\mathbb{Q}\left[R^{(1)}\right] + c\ \mathbb{E}_\mathbb{Q}\left[R^{(2)}\right] \geqslant 0 \text{ for all } \mathbb{Q} \in \mathcal{P}, \tag{1.8}$$

and the existence of $\mathbb{P}^* \in \mathcal{P}$ such that

$$\mathbb{E}_{\mathbb{P}^*}\left[R^{(1)} + cR^{(2)}\right] = \mathbb{E}_{\mathbb{P}^*}\left[R^{(1)}\right] + c\ \mathbb{E}_{\mathbb{P}^*}\left[R^{(2)}\right] > 0, \tag{1.9}$$

up to a change of direction in both inequalities. The inequality (1.8) shows that[*]

$$R^{(1)} + cR^{(2)} \geqslant 0, \qquad \mathbb{P}^*\text{-almost surely,}$$

while (1.9) implies

$$\mathbb{P}^*\left(R^{(1)} + cR^{(2)} > 0\right) > 0. \tag{1.10}$$

Next, choosing $a \in \mathbb{R}$ such that

$$aS_0^{(0)} + S_0^{(1)} + cS_0^{(1)} = 0,$$

the portfolio allocation

$$\bar{\xi} := \left(\xi^{(0)}, \xi^{(1)}, \xi^{(2)}\right) = \left(a, 1, c\frac{S_0^{(1)}}{S_0^{(2)}}\right),$$

satisfies $\bar{\xi} \cdot \bar{S}_0 = 0$ and

$$\begin{aligned}
\bar{\xi} \cdot \bar{S}_1 &= \xi^{(0)}S_1^{(0)} + \xi^{(1)}S_1^{(1)} + \xi^{(2)}S_1^{(2)} \\
&= (1+r)aS_0^{(0)} + (1+r+R^{(1)})S_0^{(1)} + c\frac{S_0^{(1)}}{S_0^{(2)}}(1+r+R^{(2)})S_0^{(2)} \\
&= (R^{(1)} + cR^{(2)})S_0^{(1)} \\
&\geqslant 0, \qquad \mathbb{P} - a.s.,
\end{aligned}$$

hence Definition 1.3-(i)-(ii) is satisfied, and (1.10) shows that

$$\mathbb{P}^*\left(\bar{\xi} \cdot \bar{S}_1\right) = \mathbb{P}^*\left(R^{(1)} + cR^{(2)} > 0\right) > 0,$$

hence Definition 1.3-(iii) is satisfied and $\bar{\xi}$ would be an arbitrage opportunity, which contradicts our hypothesis. Therefore, there exists $\mathbb{P}^* \in \mathcal{P}$ such that (1.7) is satisfied, *i.e.*

$$\mathbb{E}_{\mathbb{P}^*}\left[S_1^{(1)}\right] = \mathbb{E}_{\mathbb{P}^*}\left[(1+r+R^{(1)})S_0^{(1)}\right] = (1+r)S_0^{(1)}$$

and

$$\mathbb{E}_{\mathbb{P}^*}\left[S_1^{(2)}\right] = \mathbb{E}_{\mathbb{P}^*}\left[(1+r+R^{(2)})S_0^{(2)}\right] = (1+r)S_0^{(2)},$$

and $\mathbb{P}^*$ is a risk-neutral probability measure. $\qquad\square$

---

[*] "Almost surely", or "*a.s.*", means "with probability one".

Next is a version of the separation theorem for convex sets, used in the above proof, which relies on the more general Theorem 1.8 below.

Proposition 1.7. *Let $\mathcal{C}$ be a convex set in $\mathbb{R}^2$ such that $(0,0) \notin \mathcal{C}$. Then, there exists $c \in \mathbb{R}$ such that, e.g.*

$$x + cy \geqslant 0,$$

for all $(x,y) \in \mathcal{C}$, and there exists $(x^*, y^*) \in \mathcal{C}$ such that

$$x^* + cy^* > 0,$$

up to a change of direction in both inequalities "$\geqslant$" and "$>$".

Proof. Theorem 1.8 below applied to $\mathcal{C}_1 := \{(0,0)\}$ and to $\mathcal{C}_2 := \mathcal{C}$ shows that for some numbers a, c we have, *e.g.*

$$0 + 0 \times c = 0 \leqslant a \leqslant x + cy$$

for all $(x,y) \in \mathcal{C}$.

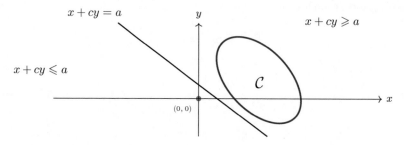

This allows us to conclude when $a > 0$. When $a = 0$, if $x + cy = 0$ for all $(x,y) \in \mathcal{C}$, then the convex set $\mathcal{C}$ is an interval part of a straight line crossing $(0,0)$, for which there exists $\tilde{c} \in \mathbb{R}$ such that $x + \tilde{c}y \geqslant 0$ for all $(x,y) \in \mathcal{C}$ and $x^* + \tilde{c}y^* > 0$ for some $(x^*, y^*) \in \mathcal{C}$, because $(0,0) \notin \mathcal{C}$.

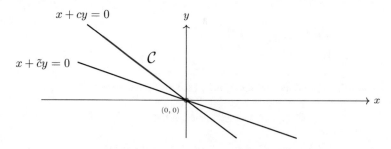

$\square$

The proof of Proposition 1.7 relies on the following result, see *e.g.* Theorem 4.14 in Hiriart-Urruty and Lemaréchal (2001).

Theorem 1.8. *Let $\mathcal{C}_1$ and $\mathcal{C}_2$ be two disjoint convex sets in $\mathbb{R}^2$. Then, there exists $a, c \in \mathbb{R}$ such that*

$$x + cy \leqslant a \qquad (x,y) \in \mathcal{C}_1,$$

and

$$a \leqslant x + cy, \qquad (x,y) \in \mathcal{C}_2,$$

up to exchange of $\mathcal{C}_1$ and $\mathcal{C}_2$.

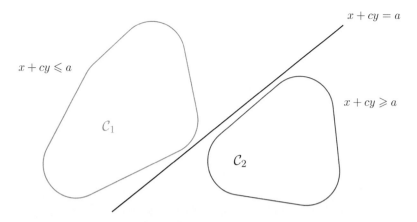

Figure 1.3: Separation of convex sets by the linear equation $x + cy = a$.

1.4 Hedging of Contingent Claims

In this section we consider the notion of contingent claim. The adjective "contingent" means:

1. Subject to chance.

2. Occurring or existing only if (certain circumstances) are the case; dependent on.

More generally, we will work according to the following broad definition, which covers contingent claims such as options, forward contracts, etc.

Definition 1.9. *A contingent claim is a financial derivative whose payoff* $C : \Omega \longrightarrow \mathbb{R}$ *is a random variable depending on the realization(s) of uncertain event(s).*

In practice, the random variable C will represent the payoff of an (option) contract at time $t = 1$.

Referring to Definition 2, the European call option with maturity $t = 1$ on the asset n^o i is a contingent claim whose payoff C is given by

$$
C = \big(S_1^{(i)} - K\big)^+ := \begin{cases} S_1^{(i)} - K & \text{if } S_1^{(i)} \geqslant K, \\ 0 & \text{if } S_1^{(i)} < K, \end{cases}
$$

where K is called the *strike price*. The claim payoff C is called "contingent" because its value may depend on various market conditions, such as $S_1^{(i)} > K$. A contingent claim is also called a financial "derivative" for the same reason.

Similarly, referring to Definition 1, the European put option with maturity $t = 1$ on the asset n^o i is a contingent claim with payoff

$$
C = \big(K - S_1^{(i)}\big)^+ := \begin{cases} K - S_1^{(i)} & \text{if } S_1^{(i)} \leqslant K, \\ 0 & \text{if } S_1^{(i)} > K, \end{cases}
$$

Definition 1.10. *A contingent claim with payoff C is said to be attainable if there exists a portfolio allocation $\bar{\xi} = \left(\xi^{(0)}, \xi^{(1)}, \ldots, \xi^{(d)}\right)$ such that*

$$C = \bar{\xi} \cdot \bar{S}_1 = \sum_{i=0}^{d} \xi^{(i)} S_1^{(i)} = \xi^{(0)} S_1^{(0)} + \xi^{(1)} S_1^{(1)} + \cdots + \xi^{(d)} S_1^{(d)},$$

with $\mathbb{P}$-probability one.

When a contingent claim with payoff C is attainable, a trader will be able to:

1. at time $t = 0$, build a portfolio allocation $\bar{\xi} = \left(\xi^{(0)}, \xi^{(1)}, \ldots, \xi^{(d)}\right) \in \mathbb{R}^{d+1}$,

2. invest the amount

$$\bar{\xi} \cdot \bar{S}_0 = \sum_{i=0}^{d} \xi^{(i)} S_0^{(i)}$$

   in this portfolio at time $t = 0$,

3. at time $t = 1$, obtain the equality

$$C = \sum_{i=0}^{d} \xi^{(i)} S_1^{(i)}$$

   and pay the claim amount C using the portfolio value

$$\bar{\xi} \cdot \bar{S}_1 = \sum_{i=0}^{d} \xi^{(i)} S_1^{(i)} = \xi^{(0)} S_1^{(0)} + \xi^{(1)} S_1^{(1)} + \cdots + \xi^{(d)} S_1^{(d)}.$$

We note that in order to attain the claim payoff C, an initial investment $\bar{\xi} \cdot \bar{S}_0$ is needed at time $t = 0$. This amount, to be paid by the buyer to the issuer of the option (the option writer), is also called the *arbitrage-free price*, or option premium, of the contingent claim and is denoted by

$$\pi_0(C) := \bar{\xi} \cdot \bar{S}_0 = \sum_{i=0}^{d} \xi^{(i)} S_0^{(i)}. \tag{1.11}$$

The action of allocating a portfolio allocation $\bar{\xi}$ such that

$$C = \bar{\xi} \cdot \bar{S}_1 = \sum_{i=0}^{d} \xi^{(i)} S_1^{(i)} \tag{1.12}$$

is called *hedging*, or *replication*, of the contingent claim with payoff C.

Definition 1.11. *In case the portfolio value $\bar{\xi} \cdot \bar{S}_1$ at time $t = 1$ exceeds the amount of the claim, i.e. when*

$$\bar{\xi} \cdot \bar{S}_1 \geqslant C,$$

we say that the portfolio allocation $\bar{\xi} = \left(\xi^{(0)}, \xi^{(1)}, \ldots, \xi^{(d)}\right)$ is super-hedging *the claim C.*

In this document, we only focus on hedging, *i.e.* on *replication* of the contingent claim with payoff C, and we will not consider super-hedging.

As a simplified illustration of the principle of hedging, one may buy an oil-related asset in order to hedge oneself against a potential price rise of gasoline. In this case, any increase in the price of gasoline that would result in a higher value of the financial derivative C would be correlated to an increase in the underlying asset value so that the equality (1.12) would be maintained.

1.5 Market Completeness

Market completeness is a strong property, stating that any contingent claim available on the market can be perfectly hedged.

Definition 1.12. *A market model is said to be* complete *if every contingent claim is attainable.*

The next result is the second fundamental theorem of asset pricing.

Theorem 1.13. *A market model without arbitrage opportunities is complete if and only if it admits only one equivalent risk-neutral probability measure* $\mathbb{P}^*$.

Proof. See the proof of Theorem 1.40 in Föllmer and Schied (2004). $\square$

Theorem 1.13 will give us a concrete way to verify market completeness by searching for a unique solution $\mathbb{P}^*$ to Equation (1.4).

1.6 Example: Binary Market

In this section we work out a simple example that allows us to apply Theorem 1.6 and Theorem 1.13. We take $d = 1$, *i.e.* the portfolio is made of

– a riskless asset with interest rate r and priced $(1 + r)S_0^{(0)}$ at time $t = 1$,

– and a risky asset priced $S_1^{(1)}$ at time $t = 1$.

We use the probability space

$$\Omega = \{\omega^-, \omega^+\},$$

which is the simplest possible nontrivial choice of probability space, made of only two possible outcomes with

$$\mathbb{P}(\{\omega^-\}) > 0 \quad \text{and} \quad \mathbb{P}(\{\omega^+\}) > 0,$$

in order for the setting to be nontrivial. In other words the behavior of the market is subject to only two possible outcomes, for example, one is expecting an important binary decision of "yes/no" type, which can lead to two distinct scenarios called ω^- and ω^+.

In this context, the asset price $S_1^{(1)}$ is given by a random variable

$$S_1^{(1)} : \Omega \longrightarrow \mathbb{R}$$

whose value depends on whether the scenario ω^-, resp. ω^+, occurs.

Precisely, we set

$$S_1^{(1)}(\omega^-) = a, \qquad \text{and} \qquad S_1^{(1)}(\omega^+) = b,$$

i.e. the value of $S_1^{(1)}$ becomes equal a under the scenario ω^-, and equal to b under the scenario ω^+, where $0 < a < b$. *

---

*The case $a = b$ leads to a trivial, constant market.

Arbitrage

The first natural question is:

　– *Arbitrage*: Does the market allow for arbitrage opportunities?

We will answer this question using Theorem 1.6, by searching for a risk-neutral probability measure $\mathbb{P}^*$ satisfying the relation

$$\mathbb{E}^*\left[S_1^{(1)}\right] = (1+r)S_0^{(1)}, \tag{1.13}$$

where $r > 0$ denotes the risk-free interest rate, cf. Definition 1.4.

In this simple framework, any measure $\mathbb{P}^*$ on $\Omega = \{\omega^-, \omega^+\}$ is characterized by the data of two numbers $\mathbb{P}^*(\{\omega^-\}) \in [0,1]$ and $\mathbb{P}^*(\{\omega^+\}) \in [0,1]$, such that

$$\mathbb{P}^*(\Omega) = \mathbb{P}^*(\{\omega^-\}) + \mathbb{P}^*(\{\omega^+\}) = 1. \tag{1.14}$$

Here, saying that $\mathbb{P}^*$ is *equivalent* to $\mathbb{P}$ simply means that

$$\mathbb{P}^*(\{\omega^-\}) > 0 \quad \text{and} \quad \mathbb{P}^*(\{\omega^+\}) > 0.$$

Although we should solve (1.13) for $\mathbb{P}^*$, at this stage it is not yet clear how $\mathbb{P}^*$ is involved in the equation. In order to make (1.13) more explicit we write the expected value as

$$\mathbb{E}^*\left[S_1^{(1)}\right] = a\mathbb{P}^*\left(S_1^{(1)} = a\right) + b\mathbb{P}^*\left(S_1^{(1)} = b\right),$$

hence Condition (1.13) for the existence of a risk-neutral probability measure $\mathbb{P}^*$ reads

$$a\mathbb{P}^*\left(S_1^{(1)} = a\right) + b\mathbb{P}^*\left(S_1^{(1)} = b\right) = (1+r)S_0^{(1)}.$$

Using the Condition (1.14) we obtain the system of two equations

$$\begin{cases} a\mathbb{P}^*(\{\omega^-\}) + b\mathbb{P}^*(\{\omega^+\}) = (1+r)S_0^{(1)} \\ \mathbb{P}^*(\{\omega^-\}) + \mathbb{P}^*(\{\omega^+\}) = 1, \end{cases} \tag{1.15}$$

with *unique* risk-neutral solution

$$\begin{cases} p^* := \mathbb{P}^*(\{\omega^+\}) = \mathbb{P}^*\left(S_1^{(1)} = b\right) = \dfrac{(1+r)S_0^{(1)} - a}{b - a} \\[3mm] q^* := \mathbb{P}^*(\{\omega^-\}) = \mathbb{P}^*\left(S_1^{(1)} = a\right) = \dfrac{b - (1+r)S_0^{(1)}}{b - a}. \end{cases} \tag{1.16}$$

In order for a solution $\mathbb{P}^*$ to exist as a probability measure, the numbers $\mathbb{P}^*(\{\omega^-\})$ and $\mathbb{P}^*(\{\omega^+\})$ must be nonnegative. In addition, for $\mathbb{P}^*$ to be equivalent to $\mathbb{P}$ they should be strictly positive from (1.5).

　We deduce that if a, b and r satisfy the condition

$$a < (1+r)S_0^{(1)} < b, \tag{1.17}$$

then there exists a risk-neutral *equivalent* probability measure $\mathbb{P}^*$ which is unique; hence by Theorems 1.6 and 1.13, the market is without arbitrage and complete.

Remark 1.14. *i) If $a = (1+r)S_0^{(1)}$, resp. $b = (1+r)S_0^{(1)}$, then $\mathbb{P}^*(\{\omega^+\}) = 0$, resp.*
$\mathbb{P}^*(\{\omega^-\}) = 0$, and $\mathbb{P}^*$ is not equivalent to $\mathbb{P}$ in the sense of Definition 1.5.

Therefore, we check from (1.16) that the condition

$$a < b \leqslant (1+r)S_0^{(1)} \qquad or \qquad (1+r)S_0^{(1)} \leqslant a < b, \qquad (1.18)$$

do not imply existence of an equivalent *risk-neutral probability measure and the absence of arbitrage opportunities in general.*

ii) If $a = b = (1+r)S_0^{(1)}$, then (1.4) admits an infinity of solutions, hence the market is without arbitrage, but it is not complete. More precisely, in this case both the riskless and risky assets yield a deterministic return rate r and the portfolio value becomes

$$\bar{\xi} \cdot \bar{S}_1 = (1+r)\bar{\xi} \cdot \bar{S}_0,$$

at time $t = 1$, hence the terminal value $\bar{\xi} \cdot \bar{S}_1$ is deterministic and this single *value can not always match the value of a contingent claim with (random) payoff C, that could be allowed to take two* distinct *values $C(\omega^-)$ and $C(\omega^+)$. Therefore, market completeness does not hold when $a = b = (1+r)S_0^{(1)}$.*

Let us give a financial interpretation of Condition (1.18).

1. If $(1+r)S_0^{(1)} \leqslant a < b$, let $\xi^{(1)} := 1$ and choose $\xi^{(0)}$ such that

$$\xi^{(0)}S_0^{(0)} + \xi^{(1)}S_0^{(1)} = 0$$

according to Definition 1.3-(i), *i.e.*

$$\xi^{(0)} = -\xi^{(1)}\frac{S_0^{(1)}}{S_0^{(0)}} < 0.$$

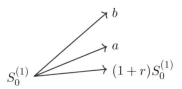

In particular, Condition (i) of Definition 1.3 is satisfied, and the investor borrows the amount $-\xi^{(0)}S_0^{(0)} > 0$ on the riskless asset and uses it to buy one unit $\xi^{(1)} = 1$ of the risky asset. At time $t = 1$ he sells the risky asset $S_1^{(1)}$ at a price at least equal to a and refunds the amount $-(1+r)\xi^{(0)}S_0^{(0)} > 0$ that he borrowed, with interest. The profit of the operation is

$$\begin{aligned}
\bar{\xi} \cdot \bar{S}_1 &= (1+r)\xi^{(0)}S_0^{(0)} + \xi^{(1)}S_1^{(1)} \\
&\geqslant (1+r)\xi^{(0)}S_0^{(0)} + \xi^{(1)}a
\end{aligned}$$

$$\begin{aligned}
&= -(1+r)\xi^{(1)}S_0^{(1)} + \xi^{(1)}a \\
&= \xi^{(1)}\big(-(1+r)S_0^{(1)} + a\big) \\
&\geqslant 0,
\end{aligned}$$

which satisfies Condition (ii) of Definition 1.3. In addition, Condition (iii) of Definition 1.3 is also satisfied because

$$\mathbb{P}(\bar{\xi}\cdot\bar{S}_1 > 0) = \mathbb{P}(S_1^{(1)} = b) = \mathbb{P}(\{\omega^+\}) > 0.$$

2. If $a < b \leqslant (1+r)S_0^{(1)}$, let $\xi^{(0)} > 0$ and choose $\xi^{(1)}$ such that

$$\xi^{(0)}S_0^{(0)} + \xi^{(1)}S_0^{(1)} = 0,$$

according to Definition 1.3-(i), *i.e.*

$$\xi^{(1)} = -\xi^{(0)}\frac{S_0^{(0)}}{S_0^{(1)}} < 0.$$

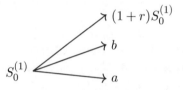

This means that the investor borrows a (possibly fractional) quantity $-\xi^{(1)} > 0$ of the risky asset, sells it for the amount $-\xi^{(1)}S_0^{(1)}$, and invests this money on the riskless account for the amount $\xi^{(0)}S_0^{(0)} > 0$. As mentioned in Section 1.1, in this case one says that the investor *shortsells* the risky asset. At time $t = 1$ she obtains $(1+r)\xi^{(0)}S_0^{(0)} > 0$ from the riskless asset, spends at most b to buy back the risky asset, and returns it to its original owner. The profit of the operation is

$$\begin{aligned}
\bar{\xi}\cdot\bar{S}_1 &= (1+r)\xi^{(0)}S_0^{(0)} + \xi^{(1)}S_1^{(1)} \\
&\geqslant (1+r)\xi^{(0)}S_0^{(0)} + \xi^{(1)}b \\
&= -(1+r)\xi^{(1)}S_0^{(1)} + \xi^{(1)}b \\
&= \xi^{(1)}\big(-(1+r)S_0^{(1)} + b\big) \\
&\geqslant 0,
\end{aligned}$$

since $\xi^{(1)} < 0$. Note that here, $a \leqslant S_1^{(1)} \leqslant b$ became

$$\xi^{(1)}b \leqslant \xi^{(1)}S_1^{(1)} \leqslant \xi^{(1)}a$$

because $\xi^{(1)} < 0$. We can check as in Part 1 above that Conditions (i)–(iii) of Definition 1.3 are satisfied.

3. Finally if $a = b \neq (1+r)S_0^{(1)}$, then (1.4) admits no solution as a probability measure $\mathbb{P}^*$ hence arbitrage opportunities exist and can be constructed by the same method as above.

Under Condition (1.17) there is an absence of arbitrage and Theorem 1.6 shows that no portfolio strategy can yield both $\bar{\xi}\cdot\bar{S}_1 \geqslant 0$ and $\mathbb{P}(\bar{\xi}\cdot\bar{S}_1 > 0) > 0$ starting from $\xi^{(0)}S_0^{(0)} + \xi^{(1)}S_0^{(1)} \leqslant 0$, however, this is less simple to show directly.

Market completeness

The second natural question is:

- *Completeness*: Is the market complete, *i.e.* are all contingent claims attainable?

In what follows we work under the condition

$$a < (1+r)S_0^{(1)} < b,$$

under which Theorems 1.6 and 1.13 show that the market is without arbitrage and complete since the risk-neutral probability measure $\mathbb{P}^*$ exists and is unique.

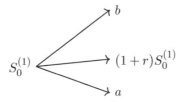

Let us recover this fact by elementary calculations. For any contingent claim with payoff C we need to show that there exists a portfolio allocation $\bar{\xi} = \left(\xi^{(0)}, \xi^{(1)}\right)$ such that $C = \bar{\xi} \cdot \bar{S}_1$, *i.e.*

$$\begin{cases} (1+r)\xi^{(0)}S_0^{(0)} + \xi^{(1)}b = C(\omega^+) \\[2mm] (1+r)\xi^{(0)}S_0^{(0)} + \xi^{(1)}a = C(\omega^-). \end{cases} \tag{1.19}$$

These equations can be solved as

$$\xi^{(0)} = \frac{bC(\omega^-) - aC(\omega^+)}{S_0^{(0)}(1+r)(b-a)} \quad \text{and} \quad \xi^{(1)} = \frac{C(\omega^+) - C(\omega^-)}{b-a}. \tag{1.20}$$

In this case, we say that the portfolio allocation $\left(\xi^{(0)}, \xi^{(1)}\right)$ *hedges* the contingent claim with payoff C. In other words, any contingent claim is attainable, and the market is indeed complete. Here, the quantity

$$\xi^{(0)}S_0^{(0)} = \frac{bC(\omega^-) - aC(\omega^+)}{(1+r)(b-a)}$$

represents the amount invested on the riskless asset. Note that if $C(\omega^+) \geqslant C(\omega^-)$, then $\xi^{(1)} \geqslant 0$ and there is not short selling.

When C has the form $C = h\left(S_1^{(1)}\right)$, we have

$$\begin{aligned} \xi^{(1)} &= \frac{C(\omega^+) - C(\omega^-)}{b-a} \\[2mm] &= \frac{h\left(S_1^{(1)}(\omega^+)\right) - h\left(S_1^{(1)}(\omega^-)\right)}{b-a} \\[2mm] &= \frac{h(b) - h(a)}{b-a}. \end{aligned}$$

Hence when $x \longmapsto h(x)$ is a non-decreasing function we have $\xi^{(1)} \geqslant 0$ and there is no short selling. This applies in particular to European call options with strike price K, for which the function $h(x) = (x - K)^+$ is non-decreasing.

In case h is a non-increasing function, which is the case in particular for European put options with payoff function $h(x) = (K - x)^+$, we will similarly find that $\xi^{(1)} \leqslant 0$, *i.e.* short selling always occurs in this case.

Arbitrage-free price

Definition 1.15. *The* arbitrage-free price $\pi_0(C)$ *of the contingent claim with payoff C is defined in (1.11) as the initial value at time $t = 0$ of the portfolio hedging C, i.e.*

$$\pi_0(C) = \bar{\xi} \cdot \bar{S}_0 = \sum_{i=0}^{d} \xi^{(i)} S_0^{(i)}, \qquad (1.21)$$

where $(\xi^{(0)}, \xi^{(1)})$ are given by (1.20).

Arbitrage-free prices can be used to ensure that financial derivatives are "marked" at their fair value (mark to market).* Note that $\pi_0(C)$ cannot be 0 since this would entail the existence of an arbitrage opportunity according to Definition 1.3.

The next proposition shows that the arbitrage-free price $\pi_0(C)$ of the claim can be computed as the expected value of its payoff C under the risk-neutral probability measure after discounting by the factor $1 + r$ in order to account for the time value of money.

Proposition 1.16. *The arbitrage-free price $\pi_0(C) = \bar{\xi} \cdot \bar{S}_0$ of the contingent claim with payoff C is given by*

$$\pi_0(C) = \frac{1}{1+r} \, \mathbb{E}^*[C]. \qquad (1.22)$$

Proof. Using the expressions (1.16) for the risk-neutral probabilities $\mathbb{P}^*(\{\omega^-\})$, $\mathbb{P}^*(\{\omega^+\})$, and (1.20) for the portfolio allocation $(\xi^{(0)}, \xi^{(1)})$, we have

$$
\begin{aligned}
\pi_0(C) &= \bar{\xi} \cdot \bar{S}_0 \\
&= \xi^{(0)} S_0^{(0)} + \xi^{(1)} S_0^{(1)} \\
&= \frac{bC(\omega^-) - aC(\omega^+)}{(1+r)(b-a)} + S_0^{(1)} \frac{C(\omega^+) - C(\omega^-)}{b-a} \\
&= \frac{1}{1+r} \left(C(\omega^-) \frac{b - S_0^{(1)}(1+r)}{b-a} + C(\omega^+) \frac{(1+r)S_0^{(1)} - a}{b-a} \right) \\
&= \frac{1}{1+r} \left(C(\omega^-) \mathbb{P}^*(S_1^{(1)} = a) + C(\omega^+) \mathbb{P}^*(S_1^{(1)} = b) \right) \\
&= \frac{1}{1+r} \, \mathbb{E}^*[C].
\end{aligned}
$$

$\square$

In the case of a European call option with strike price $K \in [a, b]$, we have $C = \left(S_1^{(1)} - K\right)^+$ and

$$
\begin{aligned}
\pi_0\left(\left(S_1^{(1)} - K\right)^+\right) &= \frac{1}{1+r} \, \mathbb{E}^* \left[\left(S_1^{(1)} - K\right)^+ \right] \\
&= \frac{1}{1+r} (b - K) \mathbb{P}^*\left(S_1^{(1)} = b\right) \\
&= \frac{1}{1+r} (b - K) \frac{(1+r)S_0^{(1)} - a}{b-a}. \\
&= \frac{b - K}{b - a} \left(S_0^{(1)} - \frac{a}{1+r} \right).
\end{aligned}
$$

---

*Not to be confused with "market-making".

In the case of a European put option, we have $C = \left(K - S_1^{(1)}\right)^+$ and

$$
\begin{aligned}
\pi_0\left(\left(K - S_1^{(1)}\right)^+\right) &= \frac{1}{1+r} \, \mathbb{E}^*\left[\left(K - S_1^{(1)}\right)^+\right] \\
&= \frac{1}{1+r}(K - a)\mathbb{P}^*\left(S_1^{(1)} = a\right) \\
&= \frac{1}{1+r}(K - a)\frac{b - (1+r)S_0^{(1)}}{b - a}. \\
&= \frac{K - a}{b - a}\left(\frac{b}{1+r} - S_0^{(1)}\right).
\end{aligned}
$$

Here, $\left(S_0^{(1)} - K\right)^+$, resp. $\left(K - S_0^{(1)}\right)^+$ is called the *intrinsic value* at time 0 of the call, resp. put option.

The simple setting described in this chapter raises several questions and remarks.

Remarks

1. The fact that $\pi_0(C)$ can be obtained by two different methods, *i.e.* an algebraic method via (1.20) and (1.21) and a probabilistic method from (1.22), is not a simple coincidence. It is actually a simple example of the deep connection that exists between probability and analysis.

    In a continuous-time setting, (1.20) will be replaced with a *partial differential equation* (PDE), and (1.22) will be computed via the *Monte Carlo* method. In practice, the quantitative analysis departments of major financial institutions can be split into a "*PDE team*" and a "*Monte Carlo* team", often trying to determine the same option prices by two different methods.

2. What if we have three possible scenarios, *i.e.* $\Omega = \{\omega^-, \omega^o, \omega^+\}$ and the random asset $S_1^{(1)}$ is allowed to take more than two values, *e.g.* $S_1^{(1)} \in \{a, b, c\}$ according to each scenario? In this case the system (1.15) would be rewritten as

$$
\begin{cases}
a\mathbb{P}^*(\{\omega^-\}) + b\mathbb{P}^*(\{\omega^o\}) + c\mathbb{P}^*(\{\omega^+\}) = (1+r)S_0^{(1)} \\
\\
\mathbb{P}^*(\{\omega^-\}) + \mathbb{P}^*(\{\omega^o\}) + \mathbb{P}^*(\{\omega^+\}) = 1,
\end{cases}
$$

    and this system of two equations with three unknowns does not admit a unique solution, hence the market can be without arbitrage, but it cannot be complete, cf. Exercise 1.5.

    Market completeness can be reached by adding a second risky asset, *i.e.* taking $d = 2$, in which case we will get three equations and three unknowns. More generally, when Ω contains $n \geqslant 2$ market scenarios, completeness of the market can be reached provided that we consider d risky assets with $d + 1 \geqslant n$. This is related to the Meta-Theorem 8.3.1 of Björk (2004a), in which the number d of traded risky underlying assets is linked to the number of random sources through arbitrage and market completeness.

Exercises

Exercise 1.1   Consider a risky asset valued $S_0 = \$3$ at time $t = 0$ and taking only two possible values $S_1 \in \{\$1, \$5\}$ at time $t = 1$, and a financial claim given at time $t = 1$ by

$$
C := \begin{cases} \$0 & \text{if } S_1 = \$5 \\ \\ \$2 & \text{if } S_1 = \$1. \end{cases}
$$

Is C the payoff of a call option or of a put option? Give the strike price of the option.

Exercise 1.2   Consider a risky asset valued $S_0 = \$4$ at time $t = 0$, and taking only two possible values $S_1 \in \{\$2, \$5\}$ at time $t = 1$. Find the portfolio allocation (ξ, η) hedging the claim payoff

$$
C = \begin{cases} \$0 & \text{if } S_1 = \$5 \\ \\ \$6 & \text{if } S_1 = \$2 \end{cases}
$$

at time $t = 1$, compute its price $V_0 = \xi S_0 + \$\eta$ at time $t = 0$, and determine the corresponding risk-neutral probability measure $\mathbb{P}^*$.

Exercise 1.3   Consider a risky asset valued $S_0 = \$4$ at time $t = 0$, and taking only two possible values $S_1 \in \{\$5, \$2\}$ at time $t = 1$, and the claim payoff

$$
C = \begin{cases} \$3 & \text{if } S_1 = \$5 \\ \\ \$0 & \text{if } S_1 = \$2. \end{cases} \qquad \text{at time } t = 1.
$$

We assume that the issuer charges $\$1$ for the option contract at time $t = 0$.

a) Compute the portfolio allocation (ξ, η) made of ξ stocks and $\$\eta$ in cash, so that:

   i) the full $\$1$ option price is invested into the portfolio at time $t = 0$,

   and

   ii) the portfolio reaches the $C = \$3$ target if $S_1 = \$5$ at time $t = 1$.

b) Compute the loss incurred by the option issuer if $S_1 = \$2$ at time $t = 1$.

Exercise 1.4

a) Consider the following market model:

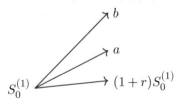

i) Does this model allow for arbitrage?

| Yes | | | No | |

ii) If this model allows for arbitrage opportunities, how can they be realized?

| By shortselling | | | By borrowing on savings | | | N.A. | |

b) Consider the following market model:

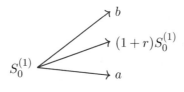

i) Does this model allow for arbitrage?

| Yes | | | No | |

ii) If this model allows for arbitrage opportunities, how can they be realized?

| By shortselling | | | By borrowing on savings | | | N.A. | |

c) Consider the following market model:

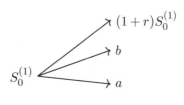

i) Does this model allow for arbitrage?

| Yes | | | No | |

ii) If this model allows for arbitrage opportunities, how can they be realized?

| By shortselling | | | By borrowing on savings | | | N.A. | |

Exercise 1.5 In a market model with two time instants $t = 0$ and $t = 1$ and risk-free interest rate r, consider

- a riskless asset valued $S_0^{(0)}$ at time $t = 0$, and value $S_1^{(0)} = (1+r)S_0^{(0)}$ at time $t = 1$.

- a risky asset with price $S_0^{(1)}$ at time $t = 0$, and three possible values at time $t = 1$, with $a < b < c$, *i.e.*:

$$S_1^{(1)} = \begin{cases} S_0^{(1)}(1+a), \\ S_0^{(1)}(1+b), \\ S_0^{(1)}(1+c). \end{cases}$$

a) Show that this market is without arbitrage but not complete.

b) In general, is it possible to hedge (or replicate) a claim with three distinct claim payoff values C_a, C_b, and C_c in this market?

Exercise 1.6 We consider a riskless asset valued $S_1^{(0)} = S_0^{(0)}$, at times $k = 0, 1$, with risk-free interest rate is $r = 0$, and a risky asset $S^{(1)}$ whose return $R_1 := (S_1^{(1)} - S_0^{(1)})/S_0^{(1)}$ can take three values $(-b, 0, b)$ at each time step, with $b > 0$ and

$$p^* := \mathbb{P}^*(R_1 = b) > 0, \quad \theta^* := \mathbb{P}^*(R_1 = 0) > 0, \quad q^* := \mathbb{P}^*(R_1 = -b) > 0,$$

a) Determine all possible risk-neutral probability measures $\mathbb{P}^*$ equivalent to $\mathbb{P}$ in the sense of Definition 1.5 in terms of the parameter $\theta^* \in (0, 1)$, from the condition $\mathbb{E}^*[R_1] = 0$.

b) We assume that the variance $\mathrm{Var}^* \left[\dfrac{S_1^{(1)} - S_0^{(1)}}{S_0^{(1)}} \right] = \sigma^2 > 0$ of the asset return is known

to be equal to σ^2. Show that this condition provides a way to select a unique risk-neutral probability measure $\mathbb{P}^*_\sigma$ under a certain condition on b and σ.

Exercise 1.7

a) Consider the following binary one-step model $(S_t)_{t=0,1,2}$ with interest rate $r = 0$ and $\mathbb{P}(S_1 = 2) = 1/3$.

$$S_0 = 1 \longrightarrow \begin{array}{c} \nearrow S_1 = 2 \\ \\ \rightarrow S_1 = 1 \end{array}$$

  i) Is the model without arbitrage?
     | Yes | | | No | |

  ii) Does there exist a risk-neutral measure $\mathbb{P}^*$ equivalent to $\mathbb{P}$ in the sense of Definition 1.5?
     | Yes | | | No | |

b) Consider the following ternary one-step model with $r = 0$, $\mathbb{P}(S_1 = 2) = 1/4$ and $\mathbb{P}(S_1 = 1) = 1/9$.

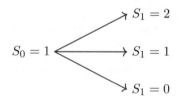

$$S_0 = 1 \begin{array}{c} \nearrow S_1 = 2 \\ \longrightarrow S_1 = 1 \\ \searrow S_1 = 0 \end{array}$$

  i) Does there exist a risk-neutral measure $\mathbb{P}^*$ equivalent to $\mathbb{P}$ in the sense of Definition 1.5?
     | Yes | | | No | |

ii) Is the model without arbitrage?

Yes | No |

iii) Is the market complete?

Yes | No |

iv) Does there exist a *unique* risk-neutral measure $\mathbb{P}^*$ equivalent to $\mathbb{P}$ in the sense of Definition 1.5?

Yes | No |

Exercise 1.8   Consider a one-step market model with two time instants $t = 0$ and $t = 1$ and two assets:

- a riskless asset π with price π_0 at time $t = 0$ and value $\pi_1 = \pi_0(1 + r)$ at time $t = 1$,

- a risky asset S with price S_0 at time $t = 0$ and random value S_1 at time $t = 1$.

We assume that S_1 can take only the values $S_0(1 + a)$ and $S_0(1 + b)$, where $-1 < a < r < b$. The *return* of the risky asset is defined as

$$R = \frac{S_1 - S_0}{S_0}.$$

a) What are the possible values of R?

b) Show that under the probability measure $\mathbb{P}^*$ defined by

$$\mathbb{P}^*(R = a) = \frac{b - r}{b - a}, \qquad \mathbb{P}^*(R = b) = \frac{r - a}{b - a},$$

   the expected return $\mathbb{E}^*[R]$ of S is equal to the return r of the riskless asset.

c) Does there exist arbitrage opportunities in this model? Explain why.

d) Is this market model complete? Explain why.

e) Consider a contingent claim with payoff C given by

$$C = \begin{cases} \xi & \text{if } R = a, \\ \eta & \text{if } R = b. \end{cases}$$

Show that the portfolio allocation (η, ξ) defined* by

$$\eta = \frac{\xi(1 + b) - \eta(1 + a)}{\pi_0(1 + r)(b - a)} \quad \text{and} \quad \xi = \frac{\eta - \xi}{S_0(b - a)},$$

hedges the contingent claim with payoff C, *i.e.* show that at time $t = 1$, we have

$$\eta \pi_1 + \xi S_1 = C.$$

Hint: Distinguish two cases $R = a$ and $R = b$.

---

*Here η is the (possibly fractional) quantity of asset π, and ξ is the quantity held of asset S.

f) Compute the arbitrage-free price $\pi_0(C)$ of the contingent claim payoff C using η, π_0, ξ, and S_0.

g) Compute $\mathbb{E}^*[C]$ in terms of a, b, r, ξ, η.

h) Show that the arbitrage-free price $\pi_0(C)$ of the contingent claim with payoff C satisfies

$$\pi_0(C) = \frac{1}{1+r} \mathbb{E}^*[C]. \tag{1.23}$$

i) What is the interpretation of Relation (1.23) above?

j) Let C denote the payoff at time $t = 1$ of a put option with strike price K=\$11 on the risky asset. Give the expression of C as a function of S_1 and K.

k) Letting $\pi_0 = S_0 = 1$, $r = 5\%$ and $a = 8$, $b = 11$, $\xi = 2$, $\eta = 0$, compute the portfolio allocation (ξ, η) hedging the contingent claim with payoff C.

l) Compute the arbitrage-free price $\pi_0(C)$ of the claim payoff C.

Exercise 1.9 A company issues share rights so that ten rights allow one to purchase three shares at the price of €6.35. Knowing that the stock is currently valued at €8, estimate the price of the right by the absence of arbitrage.

Exercise 1.10 Consider a stock valued $S_0 = \$180$ at the beginning of the year. At the end of the year, its value S_1 can be either \$152 or \$203, and the risk-free interest rate is $r = 3\%$ per year. Given a put option with strike price K on this underlying asset, find the value of K for which the price of the option at the beginning of the year is equal to the intrinsic option payoff. This value of K is called the break-even strike price. In other words, the break-even price is the value of K for which immediate exercise of the option is equivalent to holding the option until maturity.

How would a decrease in the interest rate r affect this break-even strike price?

Chapter 2

Discrete-Time Market Model

The single-step model considered in Chapter 1 is extended to a discrete-time model with $N + 1$ time instants $t = 0, 1, \ldots, N$. A basic limitation of the one-step model is that it does not allow for trading until the end of the first time period is reached, while the multistep model allows for multiple portfolio re-allocations over time. The Cox–Ross–Rubinstein (CRR) model, or binomial model, is considered as an example whose importance also lies with its computer implementability.

2.1   Discrete-Time Compounding

In this chapter, we work in a finite horizon discrete-time model indexed by $\{0, 1, \ldots, N\}$.

Investment plan

We invest an amount m each year in an investment plan that carries a constant interest rate r. At the end of the N-*th* year, the value of the amount m invested at the beginning of year $k = 1, 2, \ldots, N$ has turned into $(1 + r)^{N-k+1}m$ and the value of the plan at the end of the N-*th* year becomes

$$
\begin{aligned}
A_N : \quad &= \quad m \sum_{k=1}^{N} (1 + r)^{N-k+1} \\
&= \quad m \sum_{k=1}^{N} (1 + r)^k \\
&= \quad m(1 + r)\frac{(1 + r)^N - 1}{r},
\end{aligned}
\tag{2.1}
$$

hence the duration N of the plan satisfies

$$
N + 1 = \frac{1}{\log(1 + r)} \log\left(1 + r + \frac{rA_N}{m}\right).
$$

Loan repayment

At time $t = 0$ one borrows an amount $A_1 := A$ over a period of N years at the constant interest rate r per year.

DOI: 10.1201/9781003298670-2

Proposition 2.1. *Constant repayment. Assuming that the loan is completely repaid at the beginning of year $N + 1$, the amount m refunded every year is given by*

$$m = \frac{r(1+r)^N A}{(1+r)^N - 1} = \frac{r}{1 - (1+r)^{-N}} A. \qquad (2.2)$$

Proof. Denoting by A_k the amount owed by the borrower at the beginning of year n^o $k = 1, 2, \ldots, N$ with $A_1 = A$, the amount m refunded at the end of the first year can be decomposed as

$$m = rA_1 + (m - rA_1),$$

into rA_1 paid in interest and $m - rA_1$ in principal repayment, *i.e.* there remains

$$\begin{aligned} A_2 &= A_1 - (m - rA_1) \\ &= (1+r)A_1 - m, \end{aligned}$$

to be refunded. Similarly, the amount m refunded at the end of the second year can be decomposed as

$$m = rA_2 + (m - rA_2),$$

into rA_2 paid in interest and $m - rA_2$ in principal repayment, *i.e.* there remains

$$\begin{aligned} A_3 &= A_2 - (m - rA_2) \\ &= (1+r)A_2 - m \\ &= (1+r)((1+r)A_1 - m) - m \\ &= (1+r)^2 A_1 - m - (1+r)m \end{aligned}$$

to be refunded. After repeating the argument we find that at the beginning of year k there remains

$$\begin{aligned} A_k &= (1+r)^{k-1} A_1 - m - (1+r)m - \cdots - (1+r)^{k-2}m \\ &= (1+r)^{k-1} A_1 - m \sum_{i=0}^{k-2} (1+r)^i \\ &= (1+r)^{k-1} A_1 + m \frac{1 - (1+r)^{k-1}}{r} \end{aligned}$$

to be refunded, *i.e.*

$$A_k = \frac{m - (1+r)^{k-1}(m - rA)}{r}, \qquad k = 1, 2, \ldots, N. \qquad (2.3)$$

We also note that the repayment at the end of year k can be decomposed as

$$m = rA_k + (m - rA_k),$$

with

$$rA_k = m + (1+r)^{k-1}(rA_1 - m)$$

in interest repayment, and

$$m - rA_k = (1+r)^{k-1}(m - rA_1)$$

in principal repayment. At the beginning of year $N + 1$, the loan should be completely repaid, hence $A_{N+1} = 0$, which reads

$$(1+r)^N A + m \frac{1 - (1+r)^N}{r} = 0,$$

and yields (2.2). □

We also have

$$\frac{A}{m} = \frac{1 - (1+r)^{-N}}{r}. \tag{2.4}$$

and

$$N = \frac{1}{\log(1+r)} \log \frac{m}{m - rA} = -\frac{\log(1 - rA/m)}{\log(1+r)}.$$

Remark: One needs $m > rA$ in order for N to be finite.

The next proposition is a direct consequence of (2.2) and (2.3).

Proposition 2.2. *The k-th interest repayment can be written as*

$$rA_k = m\left(1 - \frac{1}{(1+r)^{N-k+1}}\right) = mr \sum_{l=1}^{N-k+1} (1+r)^{-l},$$

and the k-th principal repayment is

$$m - rA_k = \frac{m}{(1+r)^{N-k+1}}, \qquad k = 1, 2, \ldots, N.$$

Note that the sum of *discounted* payments at the rate r is

$$\sum_{l=1}^{N} \frac{m}{(1+r)^l} = m\frac{1 - (1+r)^{-N}}{r} = A.$$

In particular, the first interest repayment satisfies

$$rA = rA_1 = mr \sum_{l=1}^{N} \frac{1}{(1+r)^l} = m\left(1 - (1+r)^{-N}\right),$$

and the first principal repayment is

$$m - rA = \frac{m}{(1+r)^N}.$$

2.2   Arbitrage and Self-Financing Portfolios

Stochastic processes

A *stochastic process* on a probability space $(\Omega, \mathcal{F}, \mathbb{P})$ is a family $(X_t)_{t \in \mathfrak{T}}$ of random variables $X_t : \Omega \longrightarrow \mathbb{R}$ indexed by a set $\mathfrak{T}$. Examples include:

- the one-step (or two-instant) model: $\mathfrak{T} = \{0, 1\}$,

- the discrete-time model with finite horizon: $\mathfrak{T} = \{0, 1, \ldots, N\}$,

- the discrete-time model with infinite horizon: $\mathfrak{T} = \mathbb{N}$,

- the continuous-time model: $\mathfrak{T} = \mathbb{R}_+$.

For real-world examples of stochastic processes one can mention:

- the time evolution of a risky asset, *e.g.* X_t represents the price of the asset at time $t \in \mathfrak{T}$.

- the time evolution of a physical parameter - for example, X_t represents a temperature observed at time $t \in \mathfrak{T}$.

In this chapter, we focus on the finite horizon discrete-time model with $\mathfrak{T} = \{0, 1, \ldots, N\}$.

Asset price modeling

The prices at time $t = 0$ of $d + 1$ assets numbered $0, 1, \ldots, d$ are denoted by the *random vector*

$$\overline{S}_0 = \left(S_0^{(0)}, S_0^{(1)}, \ldots, S_0^{(d)} \right)$$

in $\mathbb{R}^{d+1}$. Similarly, the values at time $t = 1, 2, \ldots, N$ of assets n° $0, 1, \ldots, d$ are denoted by the *random vector*

$$\overline{S}_t = \left(S_t^{(0)}, S_t^{(1)}, \ldots, S_t^{(d)} \right)$$

on Ω, which forms a stochastic process $\left(\overline{S}_t \right)_{t=0,1,\ldots,N}$.

In what follows we assume that asset n° 0 is a riskless asset (of savings account type) yielding an interest rate r, *i.e.* we have

$$S_t^{(0)} = (1 + r)^t S_0^{(0)}, \qquad t = 0, 1, \ldots, N.$$

Portfolio strategies

Definition 2.3. *A portfolio strategy is a stochastic process* $\left(\overline{\xi}_t \right)_{t=1,2,\ldots,N} \subset \mathbb{R}^{d+1}$ *where* $\xi_t^{(k)}$ *denotes the (possibly fractional) quantity of asset n° k held in the portfolio over the time interval $(t - 1, t]$, $t = 1, 2, \ldots, N$.*

Note that the portfolio allocation

$$\overline{\xi}_t = \left(\xi_t^{(0)}, \xi_t^{(1)}, \ldots, \xi_t^{(d)} \right)$$

is decided at time $t - 1$ and remains constant over the interval $(t - 1, t]$ while the stock price changes from $S_{t-1}^{(k)}$ to $S_t^{(k)}$ over this time interval.

In other words, the quantity

$$\xi_t^{(k)} S_{t-1}^{(k)}$$

represents the amount invested in asset n^o k at the beginning of the time interval $(t-1, t]$, and

$$\xi_t^{(k)} S_t^{(k)}$$

represents the value of this investment at the end of the time interval $(t-1, t]$, $t = 1, 2, \ldots, N$.

Self-financing portfolio strategies

The opening price of the portfolio at the beginning of the time interval $(t-1, t]$ is

$$\bar{\xi}_t \cdot \bar{S}_{t-1} = \sum_{k=0}^{d} \xi_t^{(k)} S_{t-1}^{(k)},$$

when the market "opens" at time $t-1$. When the market "closes" at the end of the time interval $(t-1, t]$, it takes the closing value

$$\bar{\xi}_t \cdot \bar{S}_t = \sum_{k=0}^{d} \xi_t^{(k)} S_t^{(k)}, \tag{2.5}$$

$t = 1, 2, \ldots, N$. After the new portfolio allocation $\bar{\xi}_{t+1}$ is designed we get the new portfolio opening price

$$\bar{\xi}_{t+1} \cdot \bar{S}_t = \sum_{k=0}^{d} \xi_{t+1}^{(k)} S_t^{(k)}, \tag{2.6}$$

at the beginning of the next trading session $(t, t+1]$, $t = 0, 1, \ldots, N-1$.

Note that here, the stock price $\bar{S}_t$ is assumed to remain constant "overnight", *i.e.* from the end of $(t-1, t]$ to the beginning of $(t, t+1]$, $t = 1, 2, \ldots, N-1$.

In case (2.5) coincides with (2.6) for $t = 0, 1, \ldots, N-1$ we say that the portfolio strategy $\left(\bar{\xi}_t\right)_{t=1,2,\ldots,N}$ is *self-financing*. A non self-financing portfolio could be either bleeding money, or burning cash, for no good reason.

Definition 2.4. *A portfolio strategy* $\left(\bar{\xi}_t\right)_{t=1,2,\ldots,N}$ *is said to be* self-financing *if*

$$\bar{\xi}_t \cdot \bar{S}_t = \bar{\xi}_{t+1} \cdot \bar{S}_t, \qquad t = 1, 2, \ldots, N-1, \tag{2.7}$$

i.e.

$$\underbrace{\sum_{k=0}^{d} \xi_t^{(k)} S_t^{(k)}}_{\text{Closing value}} = \underbrace{\sum_{k=0}^{d} \xi_{t+1}^{(k)} S_t^{(k)}}_{\text{Opening price}}, \qquad t = 1, 2, \ldots, N-1.$$

The meaning of the self-financing condition (2.7) is simply that one cannot take any money in or out of the portfolio during the "overnight" transition period at time t. In other words, at the beginning of the new trading session $(t, t+1]$ one should re-invest the totality of the portfolio value obtained at the end of the interval $(t-1, t]$.

The next figure is an illustration of the self-financing condition.

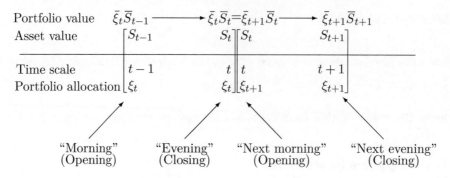

Figure 2.1: Illustration of the self-financing condition (2.7).

By (2.5) and (2.6) the self-financing condition (2.7) can be rewritten as

$$\sum_{k=0}^{d} \xi_t^{(k)} S_t^{(k)} = \sum_{k=0}^{d} \xi_{t+1}^{(k)} S_t^{(k)}, \qquad t = 0, 1, \ldots, N-1,$$

or

$$\sum_{k=0}^{d} \left(\xi_{t+1}^{(k)} - \xi_t^{(k)} \right) S_t^{(k)} = 0, \qquad t = 0, 1, \ldots, N-1.$$

Note that any portfolio strategy $\left(\bar{\xi}_t \right)_{t=1,2,\ldots,N}$ which is constant over time, *i.e.* $\bar{\xi}_t = \bar{\xi}_{t+1}$, $t = 1, 2, \ldots, N-1$, is self-financing by construction.

Here, portfolio re-allocation happens "overnight", during which time the global portfolio value remains the same due to the self-financing condition. The portfolio allocation ξ_t remains the same throughout the day, however, the portfolio value changes from morning to evening due to a change in the stock price. Also, $\bar{\xi}_0$ is not defined and its value is actually not needed in this framework.

In case $d = 1$ we are only trading $d + 1 = 2$ assets $\overline{S}_t = \left(S_t^{(0)}, S_t^{(1)} \right)$ and the portfolio allocation reads $\bar{\xi}_t = \left(\xi_t^{(0)}, \xi_t^{(1)} \right)$. In this case, the self-financing condition means that:

- In the event of an increase in the stock position $\xi_t^{(1)}$, the corresponding cost of purchase $\left(\xi_{t+1}^{(1)} - \xi_t^{(1)} \right) S_t^{(1)} > 0$ has to be *deducted from* the savings account value $\xi_t^{(0)} S_t^{(0)}$, which becomes updated as

$$\xi_{t+1}^{(0)} S_t^{(0)} = \xi_t^{(0)} S_t^{(0)} - \left(\xi_{t+1}^{(1)} - \xi_t^{(1)} \right) S_t^{(1)},$$

  recovering (2.7).

- In the event of a decrease in the stock position $\xi_t^{(1)}$, the corresponding sale profit $\left(\xi_t^{(1)} - \xi_{t+1}^{(1)} \right) S_t^{(1)} > 0$ has to be *added to* the savings account value $\xi_t^{(0)} S_t^{(0)}$, which becomes updated as

$$\xi_{t+1}^{(0)} S_t^{(0)} = \xi_t^{(0)} S_t^{(0)} + \left(\xi_t^{(1)} - \xi_{t+1}^{(1)} \right) S_t^{(1)},$$

  recovering (2.7).

Clearly, the chosen unit of time may not be the day and it can be replaced by weeks, hours, minutes, or fractions of seconds in high-frequency trading.

Portfolio value

Definition 2.5. *The portfolio opening prices at times* $t = 0, 1, \ldots, N-1$ *are defined as*

$$V_t := \bar{\xi}_{t+1} \cdot \bar{S}_t = \sum_{k=0}^{d} \xi_{t+1}^{(k)} S_t^{(k)}, \quad t = 0, 1, \ldots, N-1.$$

Under the self-financing condition (2.7), the portfolio closing values V_t at time $t = 1, 2, \ldots, N$ rewrite as

$$V_t = \bar{\xi}_t \cdot \bar{S}_t = \sum_{k=0}^{d} \xi_t^{(k)} S_t^{(k)}, \quad t = 1, 2, \ldots, N, \tag{2.8}$$

as summarized in the following table.

	V_0	V_1	V_2	$\cdots\cdots$	V_{N-1}	V_N
Opening price	$\bar{\xi}_1 \cdot \bar{S}_0$	$\bar{\xi}_2 \cdot \bar{S}_1$	$\bar{\xi}_3 \cdot \bar{S}_2$	$\cdots\cdots$	$\bar{\xi}_N \cdot \bar{S}_{N-1}$	N.A.
Closing value	N.A.	$\bar{\xi}_1 \cdot \bar{S}_1$	$\bar{\xi}_2 \cdot \bar{S}_2$	$\cdots\cdots$	$\bar{\xi}_{N-1} \cdot \bar{S}_{N-1}$	$\bar{\xi}_N \cdot \bar{S}_N$

Table 2.1: Self-financing portfolio value process.

Discounting

Summing the prices of assets considered at different times requires discounting with respect to a common date in order to compensate for possible monetary inflation. Assuming a yearly risk-free interest rate r, one dollar of year N can be added to one dollar of year $N+1$ either as $(1+r)\$1 + \$1$ if pricing occurs as of year $N+1$, or as $\$1 + (1+r)^{-1}\$1$ if pricing occurs as of year N.

My portfolio S_t grew by $b = 5\%$ this year.

Q: Did I achieve a positive return?

A:

My portfolio S_t grew by $b = 5\%$ this year.

The risk-free or inflation rate is $r = 10\%$.

Q: Did I achieve a positive return?

A:

(a) Scenario A.   (b) Scenario B.

Figure 2.2: Why apply discounting?

Definition 2.6. *Let*

$$\overline{X}_t := \left(\widetilde{S}_t^{(0)}, \widetilde{S}_t^{(1)}, \ldots, \widetilde{S}_t^{(d)} \right)$$

denote the vector of discounted asset prices, defined as:

$$\widetilde{S}_t^{(i)} = \frac{1}{(1+r)^t} S_t^{(i)}, \quad i = 0, 1, \ldots, d, \quad t = 0, 1, \ldots, N.$$

(a) *Without* inflation adjustment.   (b) *With* inflation adjustment.

Figure 2.3: Are oil prices higher in 2019 compared to 2005?

We can also write

$$\overline{X}_t := \frac{1}{(1+r)^t}\overline{S}_t, \qquad t = 0, 1, \ldots, N.$$

The *discounted* value at time 0 of the portfolio is defined by

$$\widetilde{V}_t = \frac{1}{(1+r)^t}V_t, \qquad t = 0, 1, \ldots, N.$$

For $t = 1, 2, \ldots, N$, we have

$$
\begin{aligned}
\widetilde{V}_t &= \frac{1}{(1+r)^t}\bar{\xi}_t \cdot \overline{S}_t \\
&= \frac{1}{(1+r)^t}\sum_{k=0}^{d}\xi_t^{(k)}S_t^{(k)} \\
&= \sum_{k=0}^{d}\xi_t^{(k)}\widetilde{S}_t^{(k)} \\
&= \bar{\xi}_t \cdot \overline{X}_t,
\end{aligned}
$$

while for $t = 0$ we get

$$\widetilde{V}_0 = \bar{\xi}_1 \cdot \overline{X}_0 = \bar{\xi}_1 \cdot \overline{S}_0.$$

The effect of discounting from time t to time 0 is to divide prices by $(1+r)^t$, making all prices comparable at time 0.

Arbitrage

The definition of arbitrage in discrete time follows the lines of its analog in the one-step model.

Definition 2.7. *A portfolio strategy* $\left(\bar{\xi}_t\right)_{t=1,2,\ldots,N}$ *constitutes an arbitrage opportunity if all three following conditions are satisfied:*

   i) $V_0 \leqslant 0$ *at time* $t = 0$,   [Start from a zero-cost portfolio, or with a debt.]

   ii) $V_N \geqslant 0$ *at time* $t = N$,   [Finish with a nonnegative amount.]

   iii) $\mathbb{P}(V_N > 0) > 0$ *at time* $t = N$.   [Profit is made with nonzero probability.]

2.3 Contingent Claims

Recall that from Definition 1.9, a contingent claim is given by the nonnegative random payoff C of an option contract at maturity time $t = N$. For example, in the case of the European call option of Definition 2, the payoff C is given by $C = \left(S_N^{(i)} - K\right)^+$ where K is called the strike (or exercise) price of the option, while in the case of the European put option of Definition 1 we have $C = \left(K - S_N^{(i)}\right)^+$.

The list given below is somewhat restrictive and there exists many more option types, with new ones appearing constantly on the markets.

Physical delivery *vs* cash settlement

The cash settlement realized through the payoff $C = \left(S_N^{(i)} - K\right)^+$ can be replaced by the *physical delivery* of the underlying asset in exchange for the strike price K. Physical delivery occurs only when $S_N^{(i)} > K$, in which case the underlying asset can be sold at the price $S_N^{(i)}$ by the option holder, for a payoff $S_N^{(i)} - K$. When $S_N^{(i)} > K$, no delivery occurs and the payoff is 0, which is consistent with the expression $C = \left(S_N^{(i)} - K\right)^+$. A similar procedure can be applied to other option contracts.

Vanilla options – examples

Vanilla options are options whose claim payoff depends only on the terminal value S_T of the underlying risky asset price at maturity time T.

i) *European options.*

The payoff of the European call option on the underlying asset n^o i with maturity N and strike price K is

$$C = \left(S_N^{(i)} - K\right)^+ = \begin{cases} S_N^{(i)} - K & \text{if } S_N^{(i)} \geqslant K, \\ \\ 0 & \text{if } S_N^{(i)} < K. \end{cases}$$

The *moneyness* at time $t = 0, 1, \ldots, N$ of the European call option with strike price K on the asset n^o i is the ratio

$$\mathrm{M}_t^{(i)} := \frac{S_t^{(i)} - K}{S_t^{(i)}}, \qquad t = 0, 1, \ldots, N.$$

The option is said to be "*out of the money*" (OTM) when $\mathrm{M}_t^{(i)} < 0$, "*in the money*" (ITM) when $\mathrm{M}_t^{(i)} > 0$, and "*at the money*" (ATM) when $\mathrm{M}_t^{(i)} = 0$.

The payoff of the European put option on the underlying asset n^o i with exercise date N and strike price K is

$$C = \left(K - S_N^{(i)}\right)^+ = \begin{cases} K - S_N^{(i)} & \text{if } S_N^{(i)} \leqslant K, \\ \\ 0 & \text{if } S_N^{(i)} > K. \end{cases}$$

The *moneyness* at time $t = 0, 1, \ldots, N$ of the European put option with strike price K on the asset n^o i is the ratio

$$M_t^{(i)} := \frac{K - S_t^{(i)}}{S_t^{(i)}}, \qquad t = 0, 1, \ldots, N.$$

ii) *Binary options.*

Binary (or digital) options, also called cash-or-nothing options, are options whose payoffs are of the form

$$C = \mathbb{1}_{[K,\infty)}\left(S_N^{(i)}\right) = \begin{cases} \$1 & \text{if } S_N^{(i)} \geqslant K, \\ \\ 0 & \text{if } S_N^{(i)} < K, \end{cases}$$

for binary call options, and

$$C = \mathbb{1}_{(-\infty,K]}\left(S_N^{(i)}\right) = \begin{cases} \$1 & \text{if } S_N^{(i)} \leqslant K, \\ \\ 0 & \text{if } S_N^{(i)} > K, \end{cases}$$

for binary put options.

iii) *Collar and spread options.*

Collar and spread options provide other examples of vanilla options, whose payoffs can be constructed using call and put option payoffs, see, *e.g.* Exercises 3.10 and 3.11.

Exotic options – examples

i) *Asian options.*

The payoff of an Asian call option (also called option on average) on the underlying asset n^o i with exercise date N and strike price K is

$$C = \left(\frac{1}{N+1}\sum_{t=0}^{N} S_t^{(i)} - K\right)^+.$$

The payoff of an Asian put option on the underlying asset n^o i with exercise date N and strike price K is

$$C = \left(K - \frac{1}{N+1}\sum_{t=0}^{N} S_t^{(i)}\right)^+.$$

We refer to Section 13.1 for the pricing of Asian options in continuous time. It can be shown, cf. Exercise 3.12 that Asian call option prices can be upper bounded by European call option prices.

Other examples of such options include weather derivatives (based on averaged temperatures) and volatility derivatives (based on averaged volatilities).

ii) *Barrier options.*

The payoff of a down-an-out (or knock-out) barrier call option on the underlying asset n^o i with exercise date N, strike price K and barrier level B is

$$
C = \left(S_N^{(i)} - K\right)^+ \mathbb{1}_{\left\{ \min\limits_{t=0,1,\ldots,N} S_t^{(i)} > B \right\}}
$$

$$
= \begin{cases} \left(S_N^{(i)} - K\right)^+ & \text{if } \min\limits_{t=0,1,\ldots,N} S_t^{(i)} > B, \\[2em] 0 & \text{if } \min\limits_{t=0,1,\ldots,N} S_t^{(i)} \leqslant B. \end{cases}
$$

This option is also called a Callable Bull Contract with no residual value, or turbo warrant with no rebate, in which B denotes the call price $B \geqslant K$.

The payoff of an up-and-out barrier put option on the underlying asset n^o i with exercise date N, strike price K and barrier level B is

$$
C = \left(K - S_N^{(i)}\right)^+ \mathbb{1}_{\left\{ \text{Max}\limits_{t=0,1,\ldots,N} S_t^{(i)} < B \right\}}
$$

$$
= \begin{cases} \left(K - S_N^{(i)}\right)^+ & \text{if } \text{Max}\limits_{t=0,1,\ldots,N} S_t^{(i)} < B, \\[2em] 0 & \text{if } \text{Max}\limits_{t=0,1,\ldots,N} S_t^{(i)} \geqslant B. \end{cases}
$$

This option is also called a Callable Bear Contract with no residual value, in which the call price B usually satisfies $B \leqslant K$. See Eriksson and Persson (2006) and Wong and Chan (2008) for the pricing of type R Callable Bull/Bear Contracts, or CBBCs, also called turbo warrants, which involve a rebate or residual value computed as the payoff of a down-and-in lookback option. We refer the reader to Chapters 11, 12, and 13 for the pricing and hedging of related options in continuous time.

iii) *Lookback options.*

The payoff of a floating strike lookback call option on the underlying asset n^o i with exercise date N is

$$
C = S_N^{(i)} - \min\limits_{t=0,1,\ldots,N} S_t^{(i)}.
$$

The payoff of a floating strike lookback put option on the underlying asset n^o i with exercise date N is

$$
C = \left(\text{Max}\limits_{t=0,1,\ldots,N} S_t^{(i)} \right) - S_N^{(i)}.
$$

We refer to Section 10.4 for the pricing of lookback options in continuous time.

Options in insurance and investment

Such options are involved in the statements of Exercises 2.1 and 2.2.

Vanilla *vs* exotic options

Vanilla options such as European or binary options, have a payoff $\phi(S_N^{(i)})$ that depends only on the terminal value $S_N^{(i)}$ of the underlying asset at maturity, as opposed to exotic or path-dependent options such as Asian, barrier, or lookback options, whose payoff may depend on the whole path of the underlying asset price until expiration time.

2.4 Martingales and Conditional Expectations

Before proceeding to the definition of risk-neutral probability measures in discrete time we need to introduce more mathematical tools such as conditional expectations, filtrations, and martingales.

Conditional expectations

Clearly, the expected value of any risky asset or random variable is dependent on the amount of available information. For example, the expected return on a real estate investment typically depends on the location of this investment.

In the probabilistic framework the available information is formalized as a collection $\mathcal{G}$ of events, which may be smaller than the collection $\mathcal{F}$ of all available events, *i.e.* $\mathcal{G} \subset \mathcal{F}$.[*]

The notation $\mathbb{E}[F \mid \mathcal{G}]$ represents the expected value of a random variable F given (or conditionally to) the information contained in $\mathcal{G}$, and it is read "the conditional expectation of F given $\mathcal{G}$". In a certain sense, $\mathbb{E}[F \mid \mathcal{G}]$ represents the best possible estimate of F in the mean-square sense, given the information contained in $\mathcal{G}$.

The conditional expectation satisfies the following five properties.

   i) $\mathbb{E}[FG \mid \mathcal{G}] = G\,\mathbb{E}[F \mid \mathcal{G}]$ if G depends only on the information contained in $\mathcal{G}$.

   ii) $\mathbb{E}[G \mid \mathcal{G}] = G$ when G depends only on the information contained in $\mathcal{G}$.

   iii) $\mathbb{E}[\mathbb{E}[F \mid \mathcal{H}] \mid \mathcal{G}] = \mathbb{E}[F \mid \mathcal{G}]$ if $\mathcal{G} \subset \mathcal{H}$, called the *tower property*.

   iv) $\mathbb{E}[F \mid \mathcal{G}] = \mathbb{E}[F]$ when F "does not depend" on the information contained in $\mathcal{G}$ or, more precisely stated, when the random variable F is *independent* of the σ-algebra $\mathcal{G}$.

   v) If G depends only on $\mathcal{G}$ and F is independent of $\mathcal{G}$, then

$$\mathbb{E}[h(F,G) \mid \mathcal{G}] = \mathbb{E}[h(F,x)]_{x=G}.$$

When $\mathcal{H} = \{\emptyset, \Omega\}$ is the trivial σ-algebra we have

$$\mathbb{E}[F \mid \mathcal{H}] = \mathbb{E}[F], \qquad F \in L^1(\Omega).$$

---

[*]The collection $\mathcal{G}$ is also called a σ-algebra.

Filtrations

The total amount of "information" available on the market at times $t = 0, 1, \ldots, N$ is denoted by $\mathcal{F}_t$. We assume that

$$\mathcal{F}_t \subset \mathcal{F}_{t+1}, \qquad t = 0, 1, \ldots, N-1,$$

which means that the amount of information available on the market increases over time.

Usually, $\mathcal{F}_t$ corresponds to the knowledge of the values $S_0^{(i)}, S_1^{(i)}, \ldots, S_t^{(i)}$, $i = 1, 2, \ldots, d$, of the risky assets up to time t. In mathematical notation we say that $\mathcal{F}_t$ is generated by $S_0^{(i)}, S_1^{(i)}, \ldots, S_t^{(i)}$, $i = 1, 2, \ldots, d$, and we usually write

$$\mathcal{F}_t = \sigma\big(S_0^{(i)}, S_1^{(i)}, \ldots, S_t^{(i)}, \ i = 1, 2, \ldots, d\big), \qquad t = 1, 2, \ldots, N,$$

with $\mathcal{F}_0 = \{\emptyset, \Omega\}$.

<u>Example:</u> Consider the simple random walk

$$Z_t := X_1 + X_2 + \cdots + X_t, \qquad t \geqslant 0,$$

where $(X_t)_{t \geqslant 1}$ is a sequence of independent, identically distributed $\{-1, 1\}$ valued random variables. The filtration (or information flow) $(\mathcal{F}_t)_{t \geqslant 0}$ generated by $(Z_t)_{t \geqslant 0}$ is given by $\mathcal{F}_0 = \{\emptyset, \Omega\}$, $\mathcal{F}_1 = \{\emptyset, \{X_1 = 1\}, \{X_1 = -1\}, \Omega\}$, and

$$\mathcal{F}_2 = \sigma\big(\{\emptyset, \{X_1 = 1, X_2 = 1\}, \{X_1 = 1, X_2 = -1\}, \{X_1 = -1, X_2 = 1\},$$
$$\{X_1 = -1, X_2 = -1\}, \Omega\}\big).$$

The notation $\mathcal{F}_t$ is useful to represent a quantity of information available at time t. Note that different agents or traders may work with different filtrations. For example, an insider may have access to a filtration $(\mathcal{G}_t)_{t=0,1,\ldots,N}$ which is larger than the ordinary filtration $(\mathcal{F}_t)_{t=0,1,\ldots,N}$ available to an ordinary agent, in the sense that

$$\mathcal{F}_t \subset \mathcal{G}_t, \qquad t = 0, 1, \ldots, N.$$

The notation $\mathbb{E}[F \mid \mathcal{F}_t]$ represents the expected value of a random variable F given (or conditionally to) the information contained in $\mathcal{F}_t$. Again, $\mathbb{E}[F \mid \mathcal{F}_t]$ denotes the best possible estimate of F in mean-square sense, given the information known up to time t.

We will assume that no information is available at time $t = 0$, which translates as

$$\mathbb{E}[F \mid \mathcal{F}_0] = \mathbb{E}[F]$$

for any integrable random variable F. As above, the conditional expectation with respect to $\mathcal{F}_t$ satisfies the following five properties:

i) $\mathbb{E}[FG \mid \mathcal{F}_t] = F\,\mathbb{E}[G \mid \mathcal{F}_t]$ if F depends only on the information contained in $\mathcal{F}_t$.

ii) $\mathbb{E}[F \mid \mathcal{F}_t] = F$ when F depends only on the information known at time t and contained in $\mathcal{F}_t$.

iii) $\mathbb{E}[\mathbb{E}[F \mid \mathcal{F}_{t+1}] \mid \mathcal{F}_t] = \mathbb{E}[F \mid \mathcal{F}_t]$ if $\mathcal{F}_t \subset \mathcal{F}_{t+1}$ (by the *tower property*, cf. also Relation (7.1) below).

iv) $\mathbb{E}[F \mid \mathcal{F}_t] = \mathbb{E}[F]$ when F does not depend on the information contained in $\mathcal{F}_t$.

v) If F depends only on $\mathcal{F}_t$ and G is independent of $\mathcal{F}_t$, then

$$\mathbb{E}[h(F,G) \mid \mathcal{F}_t] = \mathbb{E}[h(x,G)]_{x=F}.$$

Note that by the tower property (iii) the process $t \mapsto \mathbb{E}[F \mid \mathcal{F}_t]$ is a martingale, cf. *e.g.* Relation (7.1) for details.

Martingales

A martingale is a stochastic process whose value at time $t+1$ can be estimated using conditional expectation given its value at time t. Recall that a stochastic process $(M_t)_{t=0,1,\ldots,N}$ is said to be $(\mathcal{F}_t)_{t=0,1,\ldots,N}$-adapted if the value of M_t depends only on the information available at time t in $\mathcal{F}_t$, $t = 0,1,\ldots,N$.

Definition 2.8. *A stochastic process $(M_t)_{t=0,1,\ldots,N}$ is called a discrete-time martingale with respect to the filtration $(\mathcal{F}_t)_{t=0,1,\ldots,N}$ if $(M_t)_{t=0,1,\ldots,N}$ is $(\mathcal{F}_t)_{t=0,1,\ldots,N}$-adapted and satisfies the property*

$$\mathbb{E}[M_{t+1} \mid \mathcal{F}_t] = M_t, \qquad t = 0,1,\ldots,N-1.$$

Note that the above definition implies that $M_t \in \mathcal{F}_t$, $t = 0,1,\ldots,N$. In other words, a random process $(M_t)_{t=0,1,\ldots,N}$ is a martingale if the best possible prediction of M_{t+1} in the mean-square sense given $\mathcal{F}_t$ is simply M_t.

In discrete-time finance, the martingale property can be used to characterize risk-neutral probability measures, and for the computation of conditional expectations.

Exercise. Using the *tower property* of conditional expectation, show that Definition 2.8 can be equivalently stated by saying that

$$\mathbb{E}[M_n \mid \mathcal{F}_k] = M_k, \qquad 0 \leqslant k < n.$$

A particular property of martingales is that their expectation is constant over time.

Proposition 2.9. *Let $(Z_n)_{n \in \mathbb{N}}$ be a martingale. We have*

$$\mathbb{E}[Z_n] = \mathbb{E}[Z_0], \qquad n \geqslant 0.$$

Proof. From the tower property of conditional expectation, we have:

$$\mathbb{E}[Z_{n+1}] = \mathbb{E}[\mathbb{E}[Z_{n+1} \mid \mathcal{F}_n]] = \mathbb{E}[Z_n], \qquad n \geqslant 0,$$

hence by induction on $n \geqslant 0$, we have

$$\mathbb{E}[Z_{n+1}] = \mathbb{E}[Z_n] = \mathbb{E}[Z_{n-1}] = \cdots = \mathbb{E}[Z_1] = \mathbb{E}[Z_0], \qquad n \geqslant 0.$$

$\square$

Weather forecasting can be seen as an example of application of martingales. If M_t denotes the random temperature observed at time t, this process is a martingale when the best possible forecast of tomorrow's temperature M_{t+1} given the information known up to time t is simply today's temperature M_t, $t = 0,1,\ldots,N-1$.

Definition 2.10. *A stochastic process $(\xi_k)_{k \geqslant 1}$ is said to be predictable if ξ_k depends only on the information in $\mathcal{F}_{k-1}$, $k \geqslant 1$.*

When $\mathcal{F}_0$ simply takes the form $\mathcal{F}_0 = \{\emptyset, \Omega\}$ we find that ξ_1 is a constant when $(\xi_t)_{t=1,2,\ldots,N}$ is a predictable process. Recall that on the other hand, the process $\left(S_t^{(i)}\right)_{t=0,1,\ldots,N}$ is *adapted* as $S_t^{(i)}$ depends only on the information in $\mathcal{F}_t$, $t = 0, 1, \ldots, N$, $i = 1, 2, \ldots, d$.

The discrete-time stochastic integral (2.9) will be interpreted as the sum of discounted profits and losses $\xi_k\left(\widetilde{S}_k^{(1)} - \widetilde{S}_{k-1}^{(1)}\right)$, $k = 1, 2, \ldots, t$, in a portfolio holding a quantity ξ_k of a risky asset whose price variation is $\widetilde{S}_k^{(1)} - \widetilde{S}_{k-1}^{(1)}$ at time $k = 1, 2, \ldots, t$.

An important property of martingales is that the discrete-time stochastic integral (2.9) of a predictable process is itself a martingale, see also Proposition 7.1 for the continuous-time analog of the following proposition, which will be used in the proof of Theorem 3.5 below.

In what follows, the martingale (2.9) will be interpreted as a discounted portfolio value, in which $\widetilde{S}_k^{(1)} - \widetilde{S}_{k-1}^{(1)}$ represents the increment in the discounted asset price and ξ_k is the amount invested in that asset, $k = 1, 2 \ldots, N$.

Theorem 2.11. Martingale transform. *Given* $(X_k)_{k=0,1,\ldots,N}$ *a martingale and* $(\xi_k)_{k=1,2,\ldots,N}$ *a (bounded) predictable process, the discrete-time process* $(M_t)_{t=0,1,\ldots,N}$ *defined by*

$$M_t = \sum_{k=1}^{t} \underbrace{\xi_k(X_k - X_{k-1})}_{\text{Profit/loss}}, \qquad t = 0, 1, \ldots, N, \tag{2.9}$$

is a martingale.

Proof. Given $n > t \geq 0$, we have

$$\begin{aligned}
\mathbb{E}[M_n \mid \mathcal{F}_t] &= \mathbb{E}\left[\sum_{k=1}^{n} \xi_k(X_k - X_{k-1}) \,\Big|\, \mathcal{F}_t\right] \\
&= \sum_{k=1}^{n} \mathbb{E}\left[\xi_k(X_k - X_{k-1}) \mid \mathcal{F}_t\right] \\
&= \sum_{k=1}^{t} \mathbb{E}\left[\xi_k(X_k - X_{k-1}) \mid \mathcal{F}_t\right] + \sum_{k=t+1}^{n} \mathbb{E}\left[\xi_k(X_k - X_{k-1}) \mid \mathcal{F}_t\right] \\
&= \sum_{k=1}^{t} \xi_k(X_k - X_{k-1}) + \sum_{k=t+1}^{n} \mathbb{E}\left[\xi_k(X_k - X_{k-1}) \mid \mathcal{F}_t\right] \\
&= M_t + \sum_{k=t+1}^{n} \mathbb{E}\left[\xi_k(X_k - X_{k-1}) \mid \mathcal{F}_t\right].
\end{aligned}$$

In order to conclude to $\mathbb{E}\left[M_n \mid \mathcal{F}_t\right] = M_t$ it suffices to show that

$$\mathbb{E}\left[\xi_k(X_k - X_{k-1}) \mid \mathcal{F}_t\right] = 0, \qquad t + 1 \leq k \leq n.$$

First we note that when $0 \leq t \leq k - 1$ we have $\mathcal{F}_t \subset \mathcal{F}_{k-1}$, hence by the tower property of conditional expectations, we get

$$\mathbb{E}\left[\xi_k(X_k - X_{k-1}) \mid \mathcal{F}_t\right] = \mathbb{E}\left[\mathbb{E}\left[\xi_k(X_k - X_{k-1}) \mid \mathcal{F}_{k-1}\right] \mid \mathcal{F}_t\right].$$

Next, since the process $(\xi_k)_{k \geqslant 1}$ is predictable, ξ_k depends only on the information in $\mathcal{F}_{k-1}$, and using Property (ii) of conditional expectations we may pull out ξ_k out of the expectation since it behaves as a constant parameter given $\mathcal{F}_{k-1}$, $k = 1, 2, \ldots, n$. This yields

$$\mathbb{E}\left[\xi_k(X_k - X_{k-1}) \mid \mathcal{F}_{k-1}\right] = \xi_k \, \mathbb{E}\left[X_k - X_{k-1} \mid \mathcal{F}_{k-1}\right] = 0 \qquad (2.10)$$

since

$$
\begin{aligned}
\mathbb{E}\left[X_k - X_{k-1} \mid \mathcal{F}_{k-1}\right] &= \mathbb{E}\left[X_k \mid \mathcal{F}_{k-1}\right] - \mathbb{E}\left[X_{k-1} \mid \mathcal{F}_{k-1}\right] \\
&= \mathbb{E}\left[X_k \mid \mathcal{F}_{k-1}\right] - X_{k-1} \\
&= 0, \qquad k = 1, 2, \ldots, N,
\end{aligned}
$$

because $(X_k)_{k=0,1,\ldots,N}$ is a martingale. By (2.10), it follows that

$$
\begin{aligned}
\mathbb{E}\left[\xi_k(X_k - X_{k-1}) \mid \mathcal{F}_t\right] &= \mathbb{E}\left[\mathbb{E}\left[\xi_k(X_k - X_{k-1}) \mid \mathcal{F}_{k-1}\right] \mid \mathcal{F}_t\right] \\
&= \mathbb{E}\left[\xi_k \, \mathbb{E}\left[X_k - X_{k-1} \mid \mathcal{F}_{k-1}\right] \mid \mathcal{F}_t\right] \\
&= 0,
\end{aligned}
$$

for $k = t + 1, \ldots, n$. $\qquad\qquad\square$

2.5　Market Completeness and Risk-Neutral Measures

As in the two time step model, the concept of risk-neutral probability measure (or martingale measure) will be used to price financial claims under the absence of arbitrage hypothesis.

Definition 2.12. *A probability measure $\mathbb{P}^*$ on Ω is called a risk-neutral probability measure if under $\mathbb{P}^*$, the expected return of each risky asset equals the return r of the riskless asset, that is*

$$\mathbb{E}^*\left[S_{t+1}^{(i)} \mid \mathcal{F}_t\right] = (1+r)S_t^{(i)}, \qquad t = 0, 1, \ldots, N-1, \qquad (2.11)$$

$i = 0, 1, \ldots, d$. Here, $\mathbb{E}^*$ denotes the expectation under $\mathbb{P}^*$.

Since $S_t^{(i)} \in \mathcal{F}_t$, denoting by

$$R_{t+1}^{(i)} := \frac{S_{t+1}^{(i)} - S_t^{(i)}}{S_t^{(i)}}$$

the return of asset n^o i over the time interval $(t, t+1]$, $t = 0, 1, \ldots, N-1$, Relation (2.11) can be rewritten as

$$
\begin{aligned}
\mathbb{E}^*\left[R_{t+1}^{(i)} \mid \mathcal{F}_t\right] &= \mathbb{E}^*\left[\frac{S_{t+1}^{(i)} - S_t^{(i)}}{S_t^{(i)}} \,\middle|\, \mathcal{F}_t\right] \\
&= \mathbb{E}^*\left[\frac{S_{t+1}^{(i)}}{S_t^{(i)}} \,\middle|\, \mathcal{F}_t\right] - 1 \\
&= r, \qquad t = 0, 1, \ldots, N-1,
\end{aligned}
$$

which means that the average of the return $(S_{t+1}^{(i)} - S_t^{(i)})/S_t^{(i)}$ of asset n^o i under the risk-neutral probability measure $\mathbb{P}^*$ is equal to the risk-free interest rate r.

In other words, taking risks under $\mathbb{P}^*$ by buying the risky asset n^o i has a neutral effect, as the expected return is that of the riskless asset. The measure $\mathbb{P}^\sharp$ would yield a *positive* risk premium if we had

$$\mathbb{E}^\sharp\left[S_{t+1}^{(i)} \mid \mathcal{F}_t\right] = (1+\tilde{r})S_t^{(i)}, \qquad t = 0, 1, \ldots, N-1,$$

with $\tilde{r} > r$, and a *negative* risk premium if $\tilde{r} < r$.

In the next proposition we reformulate the definition of risk-neutral probability measure using the notion of martingale.

Proposition 2.13. *A probability measure $\mathbb{P}^*$ on Ω is a risk-neutral measure if and only if the discounted price process*

$$\widetilde{S}_t^{(i)} := \frac{S_t^{(i)}}{(1+r)^t}, \qquad t = 0, 1, \ldots, N,$$

is a martingale under $\mathbb{P}^*$, i.e.

$$\mathbb{E}^*\left[\widetilde{S}_{t+1}^{(i)} \mid \mathcal{F}_t\right] = \widetilde{S}_t^{(i)}, \qquad t = 0, 1, \ldots, N-1, \tag{2.12}$$

$i = 0, 1, \ldots, d.$

Proof. It suffices to check that by the relation $S_t^{(i)} = (1+r)^t \widetilde{S}_t^{(i)}$, Condition (2.11) can be rewritten as

$$(1+r)^{t+1}\,\mathbb{E}^*\left[\widetilde{S}_{t+1}^{(i)} \mid \mathcal{F}_t\right] = (1+r)(1+r)^t \widetilde{S}_t^{(i)},$$

$i = 1, 2, \ldots, d$, which is clearly equivalent to (2.12) after division by $(1+r)^t$, $t = 0, 1, \ldots, N-1$. $\qquad\square$

Note that, as a consequence of Propositions 2.9 and 2.13, the discounted price process $\widetilde{S}_t^{(i)} := S_t^{(i)}/(1+r)^t$, $t = 0, 1, \ldots, n$, has constant expectation under the risk-neutral probability measure $\mathbb{P}^*$, i.e.

$$\mathbb{E}^*\left[\widetilde{S}_t^{(i)}\right] = \widetilde{S}_0^{(i)}, \qquad t = 1, 2, \ldots, N,$$

for $i = 0, 1, \ldots, d.$

In the sequel we will only consider probability measures $\mathbb{P}^*$ that are *equivalent* to $\mathbb{P}$, in the sense that they share the same events of zero probability.

Definition 2.14. *A probability measure $\mathbb{P}^*$ on $(\Omega, \mathcal{F})$ is said to be* equivalent *to another probability measure $\mathbb{P}$ when*

$$\mathbb{P}^*(A) = 0 \quad \text{if and only if} \quad \mathbb{P}(A) = 0, \quad \text{for all} \quad A \in \mathcal{F}. \tag{2.13}$$

Next, we restate in discrete time the first fundamental theorem of asset pricing, which can be used to check for the existence of arbitrage opportunities.

Theorem 2.15. *A market is* without *arbitrage opportunity if and only if it admits at least one* equivalent *risk-neutral probability measure.*

Proof. See Harrison and Kreps (1979) and Theorem 5.17 of Föllmer and Schied (2004). $\qquad\square$

Next, we turn to the notion of *market completeness*, starting with the definition of attainability for a contingent claim.

Definition 2.16. *A contingent claim with payoff C is said to be attainable (at time N) if there exists a (predictable) self-financing portfolio strategy $\left(\bar{\xi}_t\right)_{t=1,2,\ldots,N}$ such that*

$$C = \bar{\xi}_N \cdot \bar{S}_N = \sum_{k=0}^{d} \xi_N^{(k)} S_N^{(k)}, \qquad \mathbb{P} - a.s. \tag{2.14}$$

In case $\left(\bar{\xi}_t\right)_{t=1,2,\ldots,N}$ is a portfolio that attains the claim payoff C at time N, *i.e.* if (2.14) is satisfied, we also say that $\left(\bar{\xi}_t\right)_{t=1,2,\ldots,N}$ *hedges* the claim payoff C. In case (2.14) is replaced by the condition

$$\bar{\xi}_N \cdot \bar{S}_N \geqslant C,$$

we talk of super-hedging.

When a self-financing portfolio $\left(\bar{\xi}_t\right)_{t=1,2,\ldots,N}$ hedges a claim payoff C, the arbitrage-free price $\pi_t(C)$ of the claim at time t is given by the value

$$\pi_t(C) = \bar{\xi}_t \cdot \bar{S}_t$$

of the portfolio at time $t = 0, 1, \ldots, N$. Recall that arbitrage-free prices can be used to ensure that financial derivatives are "marked" at their fair value (mark to market). Note that at time $t = N$, we have

$$\pi_N(C) = \bar{\xi}_N \cdot \bar{S}_N = C,$$

i.e. since exercise of the claim occurs at time N, the price $\pi_N(C)$ of the claim equals the value C of the payoff.

Definition 2.17. *A market model is said to be* complete *if every contingent claim is attainable.*

The next result can be viewed as the second fundamental theorem of asset pricing in discrete time.

Theorem 2.18. *A market model without arbitrage opportunities is complete if and only if it admits only one equivalent risk-neutral probability measure.*

Proof. See Harrison and Kreps (1979) and Theorem 5.38 of Föllmer and Schied (2004). $\qquad\square$

2.6   The Cox–Ross–Rubinstein (CRR) Market Model

We consider the discrete-time Cox–Ross–Rubinstein (Cox et al. (1979)) model, also called the *binomial model*, with $N+1$ time instants $t = 0, 1, \ldots, N$ and $d = 1$ risky asset, see Sharpe (1978). In this setting, the price $S_t^{(0)}$ of the riskless asset evolves as

$$S_t^{(0)} = S_0^{(0)}(1+r)^t, \qquad t = 0, 1, \ldots, N.$$

Let the *return* of the risky asset $S^{(1)}$ be defined as

$$R_t := \frac{S_t^{(1)} - S_{t-1}^{(1)}}{S_{t-1}^{(1)}}, \qquad t = 1, 2, \ldots, N.$$

In the CRR (or binomial) model, the return R_t is random and allowed to take only two values a and b at each time step, *i.e.*

$$R_t \in \{a, b\}, \qquad t = 1, 2, \ldots, N,$$

with $-1 < a < b$ and

$$\mathbb{P}(R_t = a) > 0, \quad \mathbb{P}(R_t = b) > 0, \qquad t = 1, 2, \ldots, N.$$

That means, the evolution of $S_{t-1}^{(1)}$ to $S_t^{(1)}$ is random and given by

$$S_t^{(1)} = \begin{cases} (1+b)S_{t-1}^{(1)} & \text{if } R_t = b \\ \\ (1+a)S_{t-1}^{(1)} & \text{if } R_t = a \end{cases} = (1+R_t)S_{t-1}^{(1)}, \qquad t = 1, \ldots, N,$$

and

$$S_t^{(1)} = S_0^{(1)} \prod_{k=1}^{t} (1 + R_k), \qquad t = 0, 1, \ldots, N.$$

Note that the price process $\left(S_t^{(1)}\right)_{t=0,1,\ldots,N}$ evolves on a binary recombining (or binomial) tree of the following type:

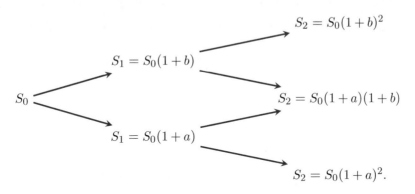

The discounted asset price is

$$\widetilde{S}_t^{(1)} = \frac{S_t^{(1)}}{(1+r)^t}, \qquad t = 0, 1, \ldots, N,$$

with

$$\widetilde{S}_t^{(1)} = \begin{cases} \dfrac{1+b}{1+r} \widetilde{S}_{t-1}^{(1)} & \text{if } R_t = b \\ \\ \dfrac{1+a}{1+r} \widetilde{S}_{t-1}^{(1)} & \text{if } R_t = a \end{cases} = \frac{1+R_t}{1+r} \widetilde{S}_{t-1}^{(1)}, \qquad t = 1, 2, \ldots, N,$$

and

$$\widetilde{S}_t^{(1)} = \frac{S_0^{(1)}}{(1+r)^t} \prod_{k=1}^t (1+R_k) = \widetilde{S}_0^{(1)} \prod_{k=1}^t \frac{1+R_k}{1+r}.$$

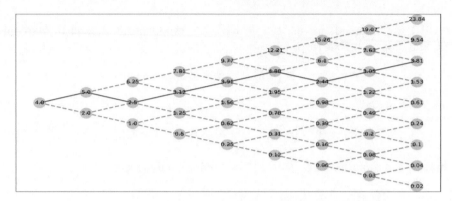

Figure 2.4: Discrete-time asset price tree in the CRR model.

In this model, the discounted value at time t of the portfolio is given by

$$\bar{\xi}_t \cdot \overline{X}_t = \xi_t^{(0)} \widetilde{S}_0^{(0)} + \xi_t^{(1)} \widetilde{S}_t^{(1)}, \qquad t = 1, 2, \dots, N.$$

The information $\mathcal{F}_t$ known in the market up to time t is given by the knowledge of $S_1^{(1)}, S_2^{(1)}, \dots, S_t^{(1)}$, which is equivalent to the knowledge of $\widetilde{S}_1^{(1)}, \widetilde{S}_2^{(1)}, \dots, \widetilde{S}_t^{(1)}$ or $R_1, R_2, \dots, R_t$, *i.e.* we write

$$\mathcal{F}_t = \sigma\big(S_1^{(1)}, S_2^{(1)}, \dots, S_t^{(1)}\big) = \sigma\big(\widetilde{S}_1^{(1)}, \widetilde{S}_2^{(1)}, \dots, \widetilde{S}_t^{(1)}\big) = \sigma(R_1, R_2, \dots, R_t),$$

$t = 0, 1, \dots, N$, where, as a convention, S_0 is a constant and $\mathcal{F}_0 = \{\emptyset, \Omega\}$ contains no information.

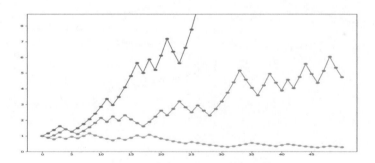

Figure 2.5: Discrete-time asset price graphs in the CRR model.

Theorem 2.19. *The CRR model is without arbitrage opportunities if and only if $a < r < b$. In this case the market is complete and the* equivalent *risk-neutral probability measure* $\mathbb{P}^*$ *is given by*

$$\mathbb{P}^*(R_{t+1} = b \mid \mathcal{F}_t) = \frac{r-a}{b-a} \quad and \quad \mathbb{P}^*(R_{t+1} = a \mid \mathcal{F}_t) = \frac{b-r}{b-a}, \tag{2.15}$$

$t = 0, 1, \ldots, N - 1$. In particular, $(R_1, R_2, \ldots, R_N)$ forms a sequence of independent and identically distributed (i.i.d.) random variables under $\mathbb{P}^*$, with

$$p^* := \mathbb{P}^*(R_t = b) = \frac{r - a}{b - a} \quad and \quad q^* := \mathbb{P}^*(R_t = a) = \frac{b - r}{b - a}, \tag{2.16}$$

$t = 1, 2, \ldots, N$.

Proof. In order to check for arbitrage opportunities we may use Theorem 2.15 and look for a risk-neutral probability measure $\mathbb{P}^*$. According to the definition of a risk-neutral measure this probability $\mathbb{P}^*$ should satisfy Condition (2.11), *i.e.*

$$\mathbb{E}^*\left[S_{t+1}^{(1)} \mid \mathcal{F}_t\right] = (1 + r)S_t^{(1)}, \qquad t = 0, 1, \ldots, N - 1.$$

Rewriting $\mathbb{E}^*\left[S_{t+1}^{(1)} \mid \mathcal{F}_t\right]$ as

$$
\begin{aligned}
\mathbb{E}^*\left[S_{t+1}^{(1)} \mid \mathcal{F}_t\right] &= \mathbb{E}^*\left[S_{t+1}^{(1)} \mid S_t^{(1)}\right] \\
&= (1 + a)S_t^{(1)}\mathbb{P}^*(R_{t+1} = a \mid \mathcal{F}_t) + (1 + b)S_t^{(1)}\mathbb{P}^*(R_{t+1} = b \mid \mathcal{F}_t),
\end{aligned}
$$

it follows that any risk-neutral probability measure $\mathbb{P}^*$ should satisfy the equations

$$
\begin{cases}
(1 + b)S_t^{(1)}\mathbb{P}^*(R_{t+1} = b \mid \mathcal{F}_t) + (1 + a)S_t^{(1)}\mathbb{P}^*(R_{t+1} = a \mid \mathcal{F}_t) = (1 + r)S_t^{(1)} \\
\mathbb{P}^*(R_{t+1} = b \mid \mathcal{F}_t) + \mathbb{P}^*(R_{t+1} = a \mid \mathcal{F}_t) = 1,
\end{cases}
$$

i.e.

$$
\begin{cases}
b\mathbb{P}^*(R_{t+1} = b \mid \mathcal{F}_t) + a\mathbb{P}^*(R_{t+1} = a \mid \mathcal{F}_t) = r \\
\mathbb{P}^*(R_{t+1} = b \mid \mathcal{F}_t) + \mathbb{P}^*(R_{t+1} = a \mid \mathcal{F}_t) = 1,
\end{cases}
$$

with solution

$$\mathbb{P}^*(R_{t+1} = b \mid \mathcal{F}_t) = \frac{r - a}{b - a} \quad and \quad \mathbb{P}^*(R_{t+1} = a \mid \mathcal{F}_t) = \frac{b - r}{b - a},$$

$t = 0, 1, \ldots, N - 1$. Since the values of $\mathbb{P}^*(R_{t+1} = b \mid \mathcal{F}_t)$ and $\mathbb{P}^*(R_{t+1} = a \mid \mathcal{F}_t)$ computed in (2.15) are non random, they are independent[*] of the information contained in $\mathcal{F}_t$ up to time t. As a consequence, under $\mathbb{P}^*$, the random variable R_{t+1} is independent of $R_1, R_2, \ldots, R_t$, hence the sequence of random variables $(R_t)_{t=0,1,\ldots,N}$ is made of *mutually independent* random variables under $\mathbb{P}^*$, and by (2.15) we have

$$\mathbb{P}^*(R_{t+1} = b) = \frac{r - a}{b - a} \quad and \quad \mathbb{P}^*(R_{t+1} = a) = \frac{b - r}{b - a}.$$

Clearly, $\mathbb{P}^*$ can be equivalent to $\mathbb{P}$ only if $r - a > 0$ and $b - r > 0$. In this case the solution $\mathbb{P}^*$ of the problem is unique by construction, hence the market is complete by Theorem 2.18. $\square$

---

[*]The relation $\mathbb{P}(A \mid B) = \mathbb{P}(A)$ is equivalent to the independence relation $\mathbb{P}(A \cap B) = \mathbb{P}(A)\mathbb{P}(B)$ of the events A and B.

As a consequence of Proposition 2.13, letting $p^* := (r-a)/(b-a)$, when $(\epsilon_1, \epsilon_2, \ldots, \epsilon_n) \in \{a, b\}^N$ we have

$$\mathbb{P}^*(R_1 = \epsilon_1, R_2 = \epsilon_2, \ldots, R_N = \epsilon_n) = (p^*)^l (1 - p^*)^{N-l},$$

where l, resp. $N - l$, denotes the number of times the term "b", resp. "a", appears in the sequence $(\epsilon_1, \epsilon_2, \ldots, \epsilon_N) \in \{a, b\}^N$.

Exercises

Exercise 2.1   Today I went to the Furong Peak mall. After exiting the Poon Way MTR station, I was met by a friendly investment consultant from NTRC Input, who recommended that I subscribe to the following investment plan. The plan requires to invest $2,550 per year over the first 10 years. No contribution is required from year 11 until year 20, and the total projected surrender value is $30,835 at maturity $N = 20$. The plan also includes a death benefit which is not considered here.

Year	Total Premiums Paid To-date ($S)	Guaranteed ($S)	Surrender Value Projected at 3.25% Non-Guaranteed ($S)	Total ($S)
1	2,550	0	0	0
2	5,100	2,460	140	2,600
3	7,650	4,240	240	4,480
4	10,200	6,040	366	6,406
5	12,750	8,500	518	9,018
10	25,499	19,440	1,735	21,175
15	25,499	22,240	3,787	26,027
20	25,499	24,000	6,835	30,835

Table 2.2: NTRC Input investment plan.

a) Compute the constant interest rate over 20 years corresponding to this investment plan.

b) Compute the projected value of the plan at the end of year 20, if the annual interest rate is $r = 3.25\%$ over 20 years.

c) Compute the projected value of the plan at the end of year 20, if the annual interest rate $r = 3.25\%$ is paid only over the first 10 years. Does this recover the total projected value $30, 835$?

Exercise 2.2 Today I went to the East mall. After exiting the Bukit Kecil MTR station, I was approached by a friendly investment consultant from Avenda Insurance, who recommended me to subscribe to the following investment plan. The plan requires me to invest $3,581 per year over the first 10 years. No contribution is required from year 11 until year 20, and the total projected surrender value is $50,862 at maturity $N = 20$. The plan also includes a death benefit which is not considered here.

Year	Total Premiums Paid To-date ($S)	Guaranteed ($S)	Surrender Value Projected at 3.25% Non-Guaranteed ($S)	Total ($S)
1	3,581	0	0	0
2	7,161	1,562	132	1,694
3	10,741	3,427	271	3,698
4	14,321	5,406	417	5,823
5	17,901	6,992	535	7,527
10	35,801	19,111	1,482	20,593
15	35,801	29,046	3,444	32,490
20	35,801	43,500	7,362	50,862

Table 2.3: Avenda Insurance investment plan.

a) Using the following graph, compute the constant interest rate over 20 years corresponding to this investment.

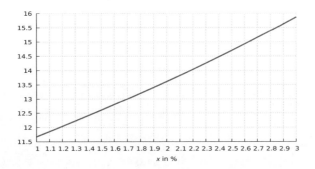

Figure 2.6: Graph of the function $x \mapsto ((1+x)^{21} - (1+x)^{11})/x$.

b) Compute the projected value of the plan at the end of year 20, if the annual interest rate is $r = 3.25\%$ over 20 years.

c) Compute the projected value of the plan at the end of year 20, if the annual interest rate $r = 3.25\%$ is paid only over the first 10 years. Does this recover the total projected value $50,862$?

Exercise 2.3   A lump sum of $100,000 is to be paid through constant yearly payments m at the end of each year over 10 years.

a) Find the value of m.

b) Assume that the amount remaining at the beginning of every year is invested at the interest rate $r = 2\%$. How does this affect the value of the constant yearly payment m?

Exercise 2.4

Today I received an SMS from Jack, and I opted for the 3K loan over 12 months.

a) Compute the *monthly* interest rate earned by Jack using the below graph of the function
$r \mapsto (1 - (1+r)^{-12})/r$.

b) Compute the *yearly* interest rate earned by Jack.

c) Should I:

    i) Block him,

    ii) Report him,

    iii) Sue him,

    iv) All of the above.

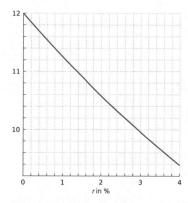

Hi Dear Customer Im Jack Here

We Power Direct understands the frustrations of bills piling up, having difficulties to make payments on time and in need of Emergency Funds. We may offer the best/right solutions for your needs.

FREE APPLY !!!
Personal/Business Loan
NO NEED UP FRONT PAYMENT !!!
Repayment On 1Year-5Year
First 88 Dear Customer Free 1 Mth

(1 Year Loan)
3K   275 x12Month
4K   370 x12Month
5K   460 x12Month

(3 Year Loan)
10K   305 x36Month
30K   920 x36Month
50K   1530 x36Month

(5 Year Loan)
20K   380 x60Month
50K   930 x60Month
100K   1850 60Month

📞 WhatsApp:
WhatsApp Number>JACK
+65 12345678
WhatsApp Link Click Here >Jack
https://1234.abcd

THIS IS A SYSTEM GENERATED MESSAGE. PLEASE REPLY HI TO ACTIVATE THE LINK ABOVE..

Exercise 2.5   Consider a two-step trinomial (or ternary) market model $(S_t)_{t=0,1,2}$ with $r = 0$ and three possible return rates $R_t \in \{-1, 0, 1\}$. Show that the probability measure $\mathbb{P}^*$ given by

$$\mathbb{P}^*(R_t = -1) := \frac{1}{4}, \quad \mathbb{P}^*(R_t = 0) := \frac{1}{2}, \quad \mathbb{P}^*(R_t = 1) := \frac{1}{4}$$

is risk-neutral.

Exercise 2.6   We consider a riskless asset valued $S_k^{(0)} = S_0^{(0)}$, $k = 0, 1, \ldots, N$, where the risk-free interest rate is $r = 0$, and a risky asset $S^{(1)}$ whose returns $R_k := \dfrac{S_k^{(1)} - S_{k-1}^{(1)}}{S_{k-1}^{(1)}}$, $k = 1, 2, \ldots, N$, form a sequence of independent identically distributed random variables taking three values $\{-b < 0 < b\}$ at each time step, with

$$p^* := \mathbb{P}^*(R_k = b) > 0, \quad \theta^* := \mathbb{P}^*(R_k = 0) > 0, \quad q^* := \mathbb{P}^*(R_k = -b) > 0,$$

$k = 1, 2, \ldots, N$. The information known to the market up to time k is denoted by $\mathcal{F}_k$.

a) Determine all possible risk-neutral probability measures $\mathbb{P}^*$ equivalent to $\mathbb{P}$ in terms of the parameter $\theta^* \in (0, 1)$.

b) Assume that the conditional variance

$$\text{Var}^* \left[\frac{S_{k+1}^{(1)} - S_k^{(1)}}{S_k^{(1)}} \,\middle|\, \mathcal{F}_k \right] = \sigma^2 > 0, \qquad k = 0, 1, \ldots, N-1, \tag{2.17}$$

of the asset return is constant and equal to σ^2. Show that this condition defines a unique risk-neutral probability measure $\mathbb{P}_\sigma^*$ under a certain condition on b and σ, and determine $\mathbb{P}_\sigma^*$ explicitly.

Exercise 2.7 We consider the discrete-time Cox–Ross–Rubinstein model with $N+1$ time instants $t = 0, 1, \ldots, N$, with a riskless asset whose price A_t evolves as $A_t = A_0(1+r)^t$, $t = 0, 1, \ldots, N$. The evolution of S_{t-1} to S_t is given by

$$S_t = \begin{cases} (1+b)S_{t-1} \\ \\ (1+a)S_{t-1} \end{cases}$$

with $-1 < a < r < b$. The *return* of the risky asset S is defined as

$$R_t := \frac{S_t - S_{t-1}}{S_{t-1}}, \qquad t = 1, 2, \ldots, N,$$

and $\mathcal{F}_t$ is generated by $R_1, R_2, \ldots, R_t$, $t = 1, 2, \ldots, N$.

a) What are the possible values of R_t?

b) Show that, under the probability measure $\mathbb{P}^*$ defined by

$$p^* = \mathbb{P}^*(R_{t+1} = b \mid \mathcal{F}_t) = \frac{r-a}{b-a}, \qquad q^* = \mathbb{P}^*(R_{t+1} = a \mid \mathcal{F}_t) = \frac{b-r}{b-a},$$

$t = 0, 1, \ldots, N-1$, the expected return $\mathbb{E}^*[R_{t+1} \mid \mathcal{F}_t]$ of S is equal to the return r of the riskless asset.

c) Show that under $\mathbb{P}^*$ the process $(S_t)_{t=0,1,\ldots,N}$ satisfies

$$\mathbb{E}^*[S_{t+k} \mid \mathcal{F}_t] = (1+r)^k S_t, \qquad t = 0, 1, \ldots, N-k, \quad k = 0, 1, \ldots, N.$$

Exercise 2.8 We consider the discrete-time Cox–Ross–Rubinstein model on $N+1$ time instants $t = 0, 1, \ldots, N$, with a riskless asset whose price A_t evolves as $A_t = A_0(1+r)^t$ with $r \geqslant 0$, and a risky asset whose price S_t is given by

$$S_t = S_0 \prod_{k=1}^{t} (1 + R_k), \qquad t = 0, 1, \ldots, N,$$

where the *asset returns* R_k are independent random variables taking two possible values a and b with $-1 < a < r < b$, and $\mathbb{P}^*$ is the probability measure defined by

$$p^* = \mathbb{P}^*(R_{t+1} = b \mid \mathcal{F}_t) = \frac{r-a}{b-a}, \qquad q^* = \mathbb{P}^*(R_{t+1} = a \mid \mathcal{F}_t) = \frac{b-r}{b-a},$$

$t = 0, 1, \ldots, N-1$, where $(\mathcal{F}_t)_{t=0,1,\ldots,N}$ is the filtration generated by $(R_t)_{t=1,2,\ldots,N}$.

a) Compute the conditional expected return $\mathbb{E}^*[R_{t+1} \mid \mathcal{F}_t]$ under $\mathbb{P}^*$, $t = 0, 1, \ldots, N-1$.

b) Show that the discounted asset price process

$$\left(\widetilde{S}_t\right)_{t=0,1,\ldots,N} := \left(\frac{S_t}{A_t}\right)_{t=0,1,\ldots,N}$$

is a (nonnegative) $(\mathcal{F}_t)$-martingale under $\mathbb{P}^*$.

Hint: Use the independence of asset returns $(R_t)_{t=1,2,\ldots,N}$ under $\mathbb{P}^*$.

c) Compute the moment $\mathbb{E}^*[(S_N)^\beta]$ for all $\beta > 0$.

Hint: Use the independence of asset returns $(R_t)_{t=1,2,\ldots,N}$ under $\mathbb{P}^*$.

d) For any $\alpha > 0$, find an upper bound for the probability

$$\mathbb{P}^*\left(S_t \geqslant \alpha A_t \text{ for some } t \in \{0, 1, \ldots, N\}\right).$$

Hint: Use the fact that when $(M_t)_{t=0,1,\ldots,N}$ is a nonnegative martingale, we have

$$\mathbb{P}^*\left(\underset{t=0,1,\ldots,N}{\text{Max}} M_t \geqslant x\right) \leqslant \frac{\mathbb{E}^*[(M_N)^\beta]}{x^\beta}, \qquad x > 0, \quad \beta \geqslant 1. \tag{2.18}$$

e) For any $x > 0$, find an upper bound for the probability

$$\mathbb{P}^*\left(\underset{t=0,1,\ldots,N}{\text{Max}} S_t \geqslant x\right).$$

Hint: Note that (2.18) remains valid for any nonnegative *sub*martingale.

Chapter 3

Pricing and Hedging in Discrete Time

We consider the pricing and hedging of financial derivatives in the N-step Cox–Ross–Rubinstein (CRR) model with $N + 1$ time instants $t = 0, 1, \ldots, N$. Vanilla options are priced and hedged using backward induction, and exotic options with arbitrary claim payoffs are dealt with using the Clark–Ocone formula in discrete time.

3.1 Pricing Contingent Claims

Let us consider an attainable contingent claim with (random) claim payoff $C \geqslant 0$ and maturity N. Recall that by the Definition 2.16 of attainability there exists a (predictable) self-financing portfolio strategy $(\xi_t)_{t=1,2,\ldots,N}$ that *hedges* the claim with payoff C, in the sense that

$$\bar{\xi}_N \bullet \bar{S}_N = \sum_{k=0}^{d} \xi_N^{(k)} S_N^{(k)} = C \tag{3.1}$$

at time N. If (3.1) holds at time N, then investing the amount

$$V_0 = \bar{\xi}_1 \bullet \bar{S}_0 = \sum_{k=0}^{d} \xi_1^{(k)} S_0^{(k)} \tag{3.2}$$

at time $t = 0$, resp.

$$V_t = \bar{\xi}_t \bullet \bar{S}_t = \sum_{k=0}^{d} \xi_t^{(k)} S_t^{(k)} \tag{3.3}$$

at times $t = 1, 2, \ldots, N$ into a self-financing hedging portfolio $(\bar{\xi}_t)_{t=1,2,\ldots,N}$ will allow one to hedge the option and to reach the perfect replication equality (3.1) at time $t = N$.

Definition 3.1. *The value (3.2)–(3.3) at time t of a (predictable) self-financing portfolio strategy $(\xi_t)_{t=1,2,\ldots,N}$ hedging an attainable claim payoff C will be called an* arbitrage-free price *of the claim payoff C at time t and denoted by $\pi_t(C)$, $t = 0, 1, \ldots, N$.*

Recall that arbitrage-free prices can be used to ensure that financial derivatives are "marked" at their fair value (mark to market).

Next we develop a second approach to the pricing of contingent claims, based on conditional expectations and martingale arguments. We will need the following lemma, in which $\widetilde{V}_t := V_t/(1+r)^t$ denotes the discounted portfolio value, $t = 0, 1, \ldots, N$.

Relation (3.4) in the following lemma has a natural interpretation by saying that when a portfolio is self-financing the value $\widetilde{V}_t$ of the (discounted) portfolio at time t is given by summing up the (discounted) trading profits and losses registered over all trading time

DOI: 10.1201/9781003298670-3

periods from time 0 to time t. Note that in (3.4), the use of the vector of discounted asset prices

$$\overline{X}_t := \left(\widetilde{S}_t^{(0)}, \widetilde{S}_t^{(1)}, \ldots, \widetilde{S}_t^{(d)} \right), \qquad t = 0, 1, \ldots, N$$

allows us to add up the discounted trading profits and losses $\bar{\xi}_t \cdot \left(\overline{X}_t - \overline{X}_{t-1} \right)$ since they are expressed in units of currency "at time 0". Indeed, in general, \$1 at time $t = 0$ cannot be added to \$1 at time $t = 1$ without proper discounting.

Lemma 3.2. *The following statements are equivalent:*

(i) *The portfolio strategy* $\left(\bar{\xi}_t \right)_{t=1,2,\ldots,N}$ *is self-financing, i.e.*

$$\bar{\xi}_t \cdot \overline{S}_t = \bar{\xi}_{t+1} \cdot \overline{S}_t, \qquad t = 1, 2, \ldots, N-1.$$

(ii) *Under discounting, we have* $\bar{\xi}_t \cdot \overline{X}_t = \bar{\xi}_{t+1} \cdot \overline{X}_t$ *for all* $t = 1, 2, \ldots, N-1$.

(iii) *The discounted portfolio value* $\widetilde{V}_t$ *can be written as the stochastic summation*

$$\widetilde{V}_t = \widetilde{V}_0 + \underbrace{\sum_{k=1}^{t} \bar{\xi}_k \cdot \left(\overline{X}_k - \overline{X}_{k-1} \right)}_{\text{Sum of profits and losses}}, \qquad t = 0, 1, \ldots, N, \qquad (3.4)$$

of discounted trading profits and losses.

Proof. First, the self-financing condition (i), *i.e.*

$$\bar{\xi}_t \cdot \overline{S}_t = \bar{\xi}_{t+1} \cdot \overline{S}_t, \qquad t = 1, 2, \ldots, N-1,$$

is clearly equivalent to (ii) by division of both sides by $(1+r)^{t-1}$.

Assuming now that (ii) holds, by (2.8) we have

$$V_0 = \bar{\xi}_1 \cdot \overline{S}_0 \quad \text{and} \quad V_t = \bar{\xi}_t \cdot \overline{S}_t = \sum_{k=0}^{d} \xi_t^{(k)} S_t^{(k)}, \qquad t = 1, 2, \ldots, N.$$

which shows that (3.4) is satisfied for $t = 1$, in addition to being satisfied for $t = 0$. Next, for $t = 2, 3, \ldots, N$ we have the telescoping identity

$$\begin{aligned}
\widetilde{V}_t &= \widetilde{V}_1 + \sum_{k=2}^{t} \left(\widetilde{V}_k - \widetilde{V}_{k-1} \right) \\
&= \widetilde{V}_1 + \sum_{k=2}^{t} \left(\bar{\xi}_k \cdot \overline{X}_k - \bar{\xi}_{k-1} \cdot \overline{X}_{k-1} \right) \\
&= \widetilde{V}_1 + \sum_{k=2}^{t} \left(\bar{\xi}_k \cdot \overline{X}_k - \bar{\xi}_k \cdot \overline{X}_{k-1} \right) \\
&= \widetilde{V}_1 + \sum_{k=2}^{t} \bar{\xi}_k \cdot \left(\overline{X}_k - \overline{X}_{k-1} \right), \qquad t = 2, 3, \ldots, N.
\end{aligned}$$

Finally, assuming that (iii) holds, we get

$$\widetilde{V}_t - \widetilde{V}_{t-1} = \bar{\xi}_t \cdot \left(\overline{X}_t - \overline{X}_{t-1} \right), \qquad t = 1, 2, \ldots, N,$$

which rewrites as

$$\bar{\xi}_t \bullet \overline{X}_t - \bar{\xi}_{t-1} \bullet \overline{X}_{t-1} = \bar{\xi}_t \bullet \left(\overline{X}_t - \overline{X}_{t-1} \right), \qquad t = 2, 3, \ldots, N,$$

or

$$\bar{\xi}_{t-1} \bullet \overline{X}_{t-1} = \bar{\xi}_t \bullet \overline{X}_{t-1}, \qquad t = 2, 3, \ldots, N,$$

which implies (ii). □

In Relation (3.4), the term $\bar{\xi}_t \bullet \left(\overline{X}_t - \overline{X}_{t-1} \right)$ represents the (discounted) trading profit and loss

$$\widetilde{V}_t - \widetilde{V}_{t-1} = \bar{\xi}_t \bullet \left(\overline{X}_t - \overline{X}_{t-1} \right),$$

of the self-financing portfolio strategy $\left(\bar{\xi}_j \right)_{j=1,2,\ldots,N}$ over the time interval $(t-1,t]$, computed by multiplication of the portfolio allocation $\bar{\xi}_t$ with the change of price $\overline{X}_t - \overline{X}_{t-1}$, $t = 1, 2, \ldots, N$.

Remark 3.3. *As a consequence of Lemma 3.2, if a contingent claim with payoff C is attainable by a (predictable) self-financing portfolio strategy $\left(\bar{\xi}_t \right)_{t=1,2,\ldots,N}$, then the discounted claim payoff*

$$\widetilde{C} := \frac{C}{(1+r)^N}$$

rewrites as the sum of discounted trading profits and losses

$$\widetilde{C} = \widetilde{V}_N = \bar{\xi}_N \bullet \overline{X}_N = \widetilde{V}_0 + \sum_{t=1}^{N} \bar{\xi}_t \bullet \left(\overline{X}_t - \overline{X}_{t-1} \right). \qquad (3.5)$$

The sum (3.4) is also referred to as a discrete-time *stochastic integral* of the portfolio strategy $\left(\bar{\xi}_t \right)_{t=1,2,\ldots,N}$ with respect to the random process $\left(\overline{X}_t \right)_{t=0,1,\ldots,N}$.

Remark 3.4. *By Proposition 2.13, the process $\left(\overline{X}_t \right)_{t=0,1,\ldots,N}$ is a martingale under the risk-neutral probability measure $\mathbb{P}^*$, hence by the martingale transform Theorem 2.11 and Lemma 3.2, $\left(\widetilde{V}_t \right)_{t=0,1,\ldots,N}$ in (3.4) is also martingale under $\mathbb{P}^*$, provided that $\left(\bar{\xi}_t \right)_{t=1,2,\ldots,N}$ is a self-financing and predictable process.*

The above remarks will be used in the proof of the next Theorem 3.5.

Theorem 3.5. *The arbitrage-free price $\pi_t(C)$ of any (integrable) attainable contingent with claim payoff C is given by*

$$\pi_t(C) = \frac{1}{(1+r)^{N-t}} \mathbb{E}^*[C \mid \mathcal{F}_t], \qquad t = 0, 1, \ldots, N, \qquad (3.6)$$

where $\mathbb{P}^*$ denotes any risk-neutral probability measure.

Proof. a) *Short proof.* Since the claim payoff C is attainable, there exists a self-financing portfolio strategy $(\xi_t)_{t=1,2,\ldots,N}$ such that $C = V_N$, i.e. $\widetilde{C} = \widetilde{V}_N$. In addition, by Theorem 2.11 Lemma 3.2 the process $(\widetilde{V}_t)_{t=0,1,\ldots,N}$ is a martingale under $\mathbb{P}^*$, hence we have

$$\widetilde{V}_t = \mathbb{E}^* \left[\widetilde{V}_N \mid \mathcal{F}_t \right] = \mathbb{E}^* \left[\widetilde{C} \mid \mathcal{F}_t \right], \qquad t = 0, 1, \ldots, N, \qquad (3.7)$$

which shows (3.8). To conclude, we note that by Definition 3.1 the arbitrage-free price $\pi_t(C)$ of the claim at time t is equal to the value V_t of the self-financing hedging C.

b) Long proof. For completeness, we include a self-contained, step-by-step derivation of (3.7) by following the argument of Theorem 2.11, as follows. By Remark 3.3 we have

$$
\mathbb{E}^* \big[\widetilde{C} \,|\, \mathcal{F}_t \big] = \mathbb{E}^* \big[\widetilde{V}_N \,|\, \mathcal{F}_t \big]
$$

$$
= \mathbb{E}^* \Bigg[\widetilde{V}_0 + \sum_{k=1}^N \bar{\xi}_k \cdot \big(\overline{X}_k - \overline{X}_{k-1} \big) \,\Big|\, \mathcal{F}_t \Bigg]
$$

$$
= \mathbb{E}^* \big[\widetilde{V}_0 \,|\, \mathcal{F}_t \big] + \sum_{k=1}^N \mathbb{E}^* \big[\bar{\xi}_k \cdot \big(\overline{X}_k - \overline{X}_{k-1} \big) \,|\, \mathcal{F}_t \big]
$$

$$
= \widetilde{V}_0 + \sum_{k=1}^t \mathbb{E}^* \big[\bar{\xi}_k \cdot \big(\overline{X}_k - \overline{X}_{k-1} \big) \,|\, \mathcal{F}_t \big] + \sum_{k=t+1}^N \mathbb{E}^* \big[\bar{\xi}_k \cdot \big(\overline{X}_k - \overline{X}_{k-1} \big) \,|\, \mathcal{F}_t \big]
$$

$$
= \widetilde{V}_0 + \sum_{k=1}^t \bar{\xi}_k \cdot \big(\overline{X}_k - \overline{X}_{k-1} \big) + \sum_{k=t+1}^N \mathbb{E}^* \big[\bar{\xi}_k \cdot \big(\overline{X}_k - \overline{X}_{k-1} \big) \,|\, \mathcal{F}_t \big]
$$

$$
= \widetilde{V}_t + \sum_{k=t+1}^N \mathbb{E}^* \big[\bar{\xi}_k \cdot \big(\overline{X}_k - \overline{X}_{k-1} \big) \,|\, \mathcal{F}_t \big],
$$

where we used Relation (3.4) of Lemma 3.2. In order to obtain (3.8) we need to show that

$$
\sum_{k=t+1}^N \mathbb{E}^* \big[\bar{\xi}_k \cdot \big(\overline{X}_k - \overline{X}_{k-1} \big) \,|\, \mathcal{F}_t \big] = 0,
$$

or

$$
\mathbb{E}^* \big[\bar{\xi}_j \cdot \big(\overline{X}_j - \overline{X}_{j-1} \big) \,|\, \mathcal{F}_t \big] = 0,
$$

for all $j = t+1, \ldots, N$. Since $0 \leqslant t \leqslant j-1$ we have $\mathcal{F}_t \subset \mathcal{F}_{j-1}$, hence by the tower property of conditional expectations we get

$$
\mathbb{E}^* \big[\bar{\xi}_j \cdot \big(\overline{X}_j - \overline{X}_{j-1} \big) \,|\, \mathcal{F}_t \big] = \mathbb{E}^* \big[\mathbb{E}^* \big[\bar{\xi}_j \cdot \big(\overline{X}_j - \overline{X}_{j-1} \big) \,|\, \mathcal{F}_{j-1} \big] \,|\, \mathcal{F}_t \big],
$$

therefore it suffices to show that

$$
\mathbb{E}^* \big[\bar{\xi}_j \cdot \big(\overline{X}_j - \overline{X}_{j-1} \big) \,|\, \mathcal{F}_{j-1} \big] = 0, \quad j = 1, 2, \ldots, N.
$$

We note that the portfolio allocation $\bar{\xi}_j$ over the time period $[j-1, j]$ is predictable, *i.e.* it is decided at time $j-1$, and it thus depends only on the information $\mathcal{F}_{j-1}$ known up to time $j-1$, hence

$$
\mathbb{E}^* \big[\bar{\xi}_j \cdot \big(\overline{X}_j - \overline{X}_{j-1} \big) \,|\, \mathcal{F}_{j-1} \big] = \bar{\xi}_j \cdot \mathbb{E}^* \big[\overline{X}_j - \overline{X}_{j-1} \,|\, \mathcal{F}_{j-1} \big].
$$

Finally we note that

$$
\begin{aligned}
\mathbb{E}^* \big[\overline{X}_j - \overline{X}_{j-1} \,|\, \mathcal{F}_{j-1} \big] &= \mathbb{E}^* \big[\overline{X}_j \,|\, \mathcal{F}_{j-1} \big] - \mathbb{E}^* \big[\overline{X}_{j-1} \,|\, \mathcal{F}_{j-1} \big] \\
&= \mathbb{E}^* \big[\overline{X}_j \,|\, \mathcal{F}_{j-1} \big] - \overline{X}_{j-1} \\
&= 0, \qquad j = 1, 2, \ldots, N,
\end{aligned}
$$

because $\big(\overline{X}_t \big)_{t=0,1,\ldots,N}$ is a martingale under the risk-neutral probability measure $\mathbb{P}^*$, and this concludes the proof of (3.7). Let

$$
\widetilde{C} = \frac{C}{(1+r)^N}
$$

denote the discounted payoff of the claim C. We will show that under any risk-neutral probability measure $\mathbb{P}^*$ the discounted value of any self-financing portfolio hedging C is given by

$$\widetilde{V}_t = \mathbb{E}^*\left[\widetilde{C}\,\middle|\,\mathcal{F}_t\right], \qquad t = 0, 1, \ldots, N, \tag{3.8}$$

which shows that

$$V_t = \frac{1}{(1+r)^{N-t}}\,\mathbb{E}^*[C \mid \mathcal{F}_t]$$

after multiplication of both sides by $(1+r)^t$. Next, we note that (3.8) follows from the martingale transform result of Theorem 2.11. $\square$

Note that (3.6) admits an interpretation in an insurance framework, in which $\pi_t(C)$ represents an insurance premium and C represents the random value of an insurance claim made by a subscriber. In this context, the premium of the insurance contract reads as the average of the values (3.6) of the random claims after discounting for the time value of money.

Remark 3.6. *By Remark 3.4 the self-financing discounted portfolio value process*

$$\left(\widetilde{V}_t\right)_{t=0,1,\ldots,N} = ((1+r)^{-t}\pi_t(C))_{t=0,1,\ldots,N}$$

hedging the claim C is a martingale under the risk-neutral probability measure $\mathbb{P}^*$. This fact can be recovered from Theorem 3.5 as in Remark 3.3, since from the tower property of conditional expectation we have

$$
\begin{aligned}
\widetilde{V}_t &= \mathbb{E}^*\left[\widetilde{C}\,\middle|\,\mathcal{F}_t\right] \\
&= \mathbb{E}^*\left[\mathbb{E}^*\left[\widetilde{C}\,\middle|\,\mathcal{F}_{t+1}\right]\,\middle|\,\mathcal{F}_t\right] \\
&= \mathbb{E}^*\left[\widetilde{V}_{t+1}\,\middle|\,\mathcal{F}_t\right], \qquad t = 0, 1, \ldots, N-1.
\end{aligned}
\tag{3.9}
$$

This will also allow us to compute V_t by backward induction on $t = 0, 1, \ldots, N-1$, starting from $V_N = C$, see (3.13) below.

In particular, for $t = 0$ we obtain the price at time 0 of the contingent claim with payoff C, i.e.

$$\pi_0(C) = \mathbb{E}^*\left[\widetilde{C}\,\middle|\,\mathcal{F}_0\right] = \mathbb{E}^*\left[\widetilde{C}\right] = \frac{1}{(1+r)^N}\,\mathbb{E}^*[C].$$

3.2   Pricing Vanilla Options in the CRR Model

In this section we consider the pricing of contingent claims in the discrete-time Cox–Ross–Rubinstein (Cox et al. (1979)) model of Section 2.6, with $d = 1$ and

$$S_t^{(0)} = S_0^{(0)}(1+r)^t, \qquad t = 0, 1, \ldots, N,$$

and

$$S_t^{(1)} = S_0^{(1)}\prod_{k=1}^{t}(1+R_k) = \left\{\begin{array}{ll} (1+b)S_{t-1}^{(1)} & \text{if } R_t = b \\[2mm] (1+a)S_{t-1}^{(1)} & \text{if } R_t = a \end{array}\right\} = (1+R_t)S_{t-1}^{(1)},$$

$t = 1, \ldots, N$. More precisely we are concerned with vanilla options whose payoffs depend on the terminal value of the underlying asset, as opposed to exotic options whose payoffs may depend on the whole path of the underlying asset price until expiration time.

Recall that the portfolio value process $(V_t)_{t=0,1,\ldots N}$ and the discounted portfolio value process $(\widetilde{V}_t)_{t=0,1,\ldots N}$ respectively satisfy

$$V_t = \bar{\xi}_t \cdot \bar{S}_t \ \text{ and } \ \widetilde{V}_t = \frac{1}{(1+r)^t} V_t = \frac{1}{(1+r)^t} \bar{\xi}_t \cdot \bar{S}_t = \bar{\xi}_t \cdot \overline{X}_t, \quad t = 0, 1, \ldots, N.$$

Here we will be concerned with the pricing of vanilla options with payoffs of the form

$$C = h\big(S_N^{(1)}\big),$$

e.g. $h(x) = (x - K)^+$ in the case of a European call option. Equivalently, the discounted claim payoff

$$\widetilde{C} = \frac{C}{(1+r)^N}$$

satisfies $\widetilde{C} = \widetilde{h}\big(S_N^{(1)}\big)$ with $\widetilde{h}(x) = h(x)/(1+r)^N$. For example in the case of the European call option with strike price K, we have

$$\widetilde{h}(x) = \frac{1}{(1+r)^N}(x - K)^+.$$

From Theorem 3.5, the discounted value of a portfolio hedging the attainable (discounted) claim payoff $\widetilde{C}$ is given by

$$\widetilde{V}_t = \mathbb{E}^* \big[\widetilde{h}\big(S_N^{(1)}\big) \,|\, \mathcal{F}_t\big], \qquad t = 0, 1, \ldots, N,$$

under the risk-neutral probability measure $\mathbb{P}^*$. As a consequence of Theorem 3.5, we have the following proposition.

Proposition 3.7. *The arbitrage-free price $\pi_t(C)$ at time $t = 0, 1, \ldots, N$ of the contingent claim with payoff $C = h\big(S_N^{(1)}\big)$ is given by*

$$\pi_t(C) = \frac{1}{(1+r)^{N-t}} \mathbb{E}^* \big[h\big(S_N^{(1)}\big) \,|\, \mathcal{F}_t\big], \qquad t = 0, 1, \ldots, N. \tag{3.10}$$

In the next proposition we implement the calculation of (3.10) in the CRR model.

Proposition 3.8. *The price $\pi_t(C)$ of the contingent claim with payoff $C = h\big(S_N^{(1)}\big)$ satisfies*

$$\pi_t(C) = v\big(t, S_t^{(1)}\big), \qquad t = 0, 1, \ldots, N,$$

where the function $v(t, x)$ is given by

$$v(t, x) = \frac{1}{(1+r)^{N-t}} \mathbb{E}^* \left[h\left(x \prod_{j=t+1}^{N} (1 + R_j)\right)\right] \tag{3.11}$$

$$= \frac{1}{(1+r)^{N-t}} \sum_{k=0}^{N-t} \binom{N-t}{k} (p^*)^k (q^*)^{N-t-k} h\big(x(1+b)^k(1+a)^{N-t-k}\big),$$

where the risk-neutral probabilities p^*, q^* are defined as

$$p^* := \frac{r - a}{b - a} \quad \text{and} \quad q^* := 1 - p^* = \frac{b - r}{b - a}. \tag{3.12}$$

Proof. From the relations

$$S_N^{(1)} = S_t^{(1)} \prod_{j=t+1}^{N} (1 + R_j),$$

and (3.10) we have, using Property (v) of the conditional expectation, see page 50, and the independence of the asset returns $\{R_1, \ldots, R_t\}$ and $\{R_{t+1}, \ldots, R_N\}$,

$$
\begin{aligned}
\pi_t(C) &= \frac{1}{(1+r)^{N-t}} \, \mathbb{E}^* \left[h(S_N^{(1)}) \mid \mathcal{F}_t \right] \\
&= \frac{1}{(1+r)^{N-t}} \, \mathbb{E}^* \left[h\left(S_t^{(1)} \prod_{j=t+1}^{N} (1 + R_j) \right) \,\Big|\, S_t^{(1)} \right] \\
&= \frac{1}{(1+r)^{N-t}} \, \mathbb{E}^* \left[h\left(x \prod_{j=t+1}^{N} (1 + R_j) \right) \right]_{x = S_t^{(1)}},
\end{aligned}
$$

where we used Property (v) of the conditional expectation, see page 50, and the independence of asset returns. Next, we note that the number of times R_j is equal to b for $j \in \{t+1, \ldots, N\}$, has a binomial distribution with parameter $(N-t, p^*)$ since the set of paths from time $t+1$ to time N containing j times "$(1+b)$" has cardinality $\binom{N-t}{j}$ and each such path has probability

$$(p^*)^j (q^*)^{N-t-j}, \qquad j = 0, \ldots, N-t.$$

In Figure 3.1 we enumerate the $120 = \binom{10}{7} = \binom{10}{3}$ possible paths corresponding to $n = 5$ and $k = 2$.

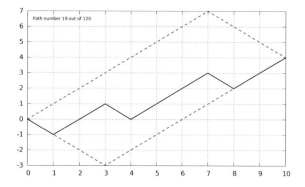

Figure 3.1: Sample of the $120 = \binom{10}{7} = \binom{10}{3}$ paths with $n = 5$ and $k = 2$.

Hence we have

$$
\begin{aligned}
\pi_t(C) &= \frac{1}{(1+r)^{N-t}} \, \mathbb{E}^* \left[h(S_N^{(1)}) \mid \mathcal{F}_t \right] \\
&= \frac{1}{(1+r)^{N-t}} \sum_{k=0}^{N-t} \binom{N-t}{k} (p^*)^k (q^*)^{N-t-k} h\big(S_t^{(1)} (1+b)^k (1+a)^{N-t-k} \big).
\end{aligned}
$$

$\square$

In the above proof we have also shown that $\pi_t(C)$ is given by the conditional expected value

$$\pi_t(C) = \frac{1}{(1+r)^{N-t}}\, \mathbb{E}^* \big[h\big(S_N^{(1)}\big) \mid \mathcal{F}_t\big] = \frac{1}{(1+r)^{N-t}}\, \mathbb{E}^* \big[h\big(S_N^{(1)}\big) \mid S_t^{(1)}\big]$$

given the value of $S_t^{(1)}$ at time $t = 0, 1, \ldots, N$, due to the Markov property of $\big(S_t^{(1)}\big)_{t=0,1,\ldots,N}$. In particular, the price of the claim with payoff C is written as the average (path integral) of the values of the contingent claim over all possible paths starting from $S_t^{(1)}$.

Market terms and data

Intrinsic value. The *intrinsic value* at time $t = 0, 1, \ldots, N$ of the option with payoff $C = h\big(S_N^{(1)}\big)$ is given by the immediate exercise payoff $h\big(S_t^{(1)}\big)$. The *extrinsic value* at time $t = 0, 1, \ldots, N$ of the option is the remaining difference $\pi_t(C) - h\big(S_t^{(1)}\big)$ between the option price $\pi_t(C)$ and the immediate exercise payoff $h\big(S_t^{(1)}\big)$. In general, the option price $\pi_t(C)$ decomposes as

$$\pi_t(C) = \underbrace{h\big(S_t^{(1)}\big)}_{\text{Intrinsic value}} + \underbrace{\pi_t(C) - h\big(S_t^{(1)}\big)}_{\text{Extrinsic value}}, \qquad t = 0, 1, \ldots, N.$$

Gearing. The *gearing* at time $t = 0, 1, \ldots, N$ of the option with payoff $C = h\big(S_N^{(1)}\big)$ is defined as the ratio

$$G_t := \frac{S_t^{(1)}}{\pi_t(C)} = \frac{S_t^{(1)}}{v\big(t, S_t^{(1)}\big)},$$

telling how many time the option price $v\big(t, S_t^{(1)}\big)$ is "contained" in the stock price $S_t^{(1)}$ at time $t = 0, 1, \ldots, N$.

Break-even price. The *break-even* price BEP_t of the underlying asset at time $t = 0, 1, \ldots, N$, see also Exercises 1.10, is the value of S for which the intrinsic option value $h\big(S_t^{(1)}\big)$ equals the option price $\pi_t(C)$. In other words, BEP_t represents the price of the underlying asset for which we would break even if the option was exercised immediately. For European call options it is given by

$$\text{BEP}_t := K + \pi_t(C) = K + v\big(t, S_t^{(1)}\big), \qquad t = 0, 1, \ldots, N.$$

whereas for European put options it is given by

$$\text{BEP}_t := K - \pi_t(C) = K - v\big(t, S_t^{(1)}\big), \qquad t = 0, 1, \ldots, N.$$

Premium. The option *premium* OP_t can be defined as the variation required from the underlying asset price in order to reach the break-even price for which the intrinsic option payoff equals the current option price, *i.e.* we have

$$\text{OP}_t := \frac{\text{BEP}_t - S_t^{(1)}}{S_t^{(1)}} = \frac{K + v\big(t, S_t^{(1)}\big) - S_t^{(1)}}{S_t^{(1)}}, \qquad t = 0, 1, \ldots, N,$$

for European call options, and

$$
\text{OP}_t := \frac{S_t^{(1)} - \text{BEP}_t}{S_t^{(1)}} = \frac{S_t^{(1)} + v\big(t, S_t^{(1)}\big) - K}{S_t^{(1)}}, \qquad t = 0, 1, \ldots, N,
$$

for European put options. The term "premium" is sometimes also used to denote the arbitrage-free price $v\big(t, S_t^{(1)}\big)$ of the option.

Pricing by backward induction in the CRR model

In the CRR model, the discounted portfolio value $\widetilde{V}_t$ can be computed by solving the *backward induction* relation (3.9), using the martingale property of the discounted portfolio value process $\big(\widetilde{V}_t\big)_{t=0,1,\ldots,N}$ under the risk-neutral probability measure $\mathbb{P}^*$.

Proposition 3.9. *The function $v(t,x)$ defined from the arbitrage-free prices of the contingent claim with payoff $C = h\big(S_N^{(1)}\big)$ at times $t = 0, 1, \ldots, N$ by*

$$
v\big(t, S_t^{(1)}\big) = V_t = \mathbb{E}^* \big[h(S_N^{(1)}) \,\big|\, \mathcal{F}_t \big]
$$

satisfies the backward recursion

$$
v(t,x) = \frac{q^*}{1+r} v\big(t+1, x(1+a)\big) + \frac{p^*}{1+r} v\big(t+1, x(1+b)\big), \qquad (3.13)
$$

with the terminal condition

$$
v(N, x) = h(x), \qquad x > 0.
$$

Proof. Namely, by the tower property of conditional expectations, letting

$$
\widetilde{v}\big(t, S_t^{(1)}\big) := \frac{1}{(1+r)^t} v\big(t, S_t^{(1)}\big), \qquad t = 0, 1, \ldots, N,
$$

we have

$$
\begin{aligned}
\widetilde{v}\big(t, S_t^{(1)}\big) &= \widetilde{V}_t \\
&= \mathbb{E}^* \big[\widetilde{h}(S_N^{(1)}) \,\big|\, \mathcal{F}_t \big] \\
&= \mathbb{E}^* \big[\mathbb{E}^* \big[\widetilde{h}(S_N^{(1)}) \,\big|\, \mathcal{F}_{t+1} \big] \,\big|\, \mathcal{F}_t \big] \\
&= \mathbb{E}^* \big[\widetilde{V}_{t+1} \,\big|\, \mathcal{F}_t \big] \\
&= \mathbb{E}^* \big[\widetilde{v}(t+1, S_{t+1}^{(1)}) \,\big|\, S_t \big] \\
&= \widetilde{v}\big(t+1, (1+a)S_t^{(1)}\big)\mathbb{P}^*(R_{t+1} = a) + \widetilde{v}\big(t+1, (1+b)S_t^{(1)}\big)\mathbb{P}^*(R_{t+1} = b) \\
&= q^*\widetilde{v}\big(t+1, (1+a)S_t^{(1)}\big) + p^*\widetilde{v}\big(t+1, (1+b)S_t^{(1)}\big),
\end{aligned}
$$

which shows that $\widetilde{v}(t,x)$ satisfies

$$
\widetilde{v}(t,x) = q^*\widetilde{v}\big(t+1, x(1+a)\big) + p^*\widetilde{v}\big(t+1, x(1+b)\big), \qquad (3.14)
$$

while the terminal condition $\widetilde{V}_N = \widetilde{h}\big(S_N^{(1)}\big)$ implies

$$
\widetilde{v}(N, x) = \widetilde{h}(x), \qquad x > 0.
$$

$\square$

The next Figure 3.2 presents a tree-based implementation of the pricing recursion (3.13).

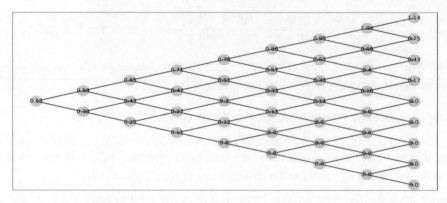

Figure 3.2: Discrete-time call option pricing tree.

Note that the discrete-time recursion (3.13) can be connected to the continuous-time Black–Scholes PDE (6.2), cf. Exercises 6.14.

3.3   Hedging Contingent Claims

The basic idea of hedging is to allocate assets in a portfolio in order to protect oneself from a given risk. For example, a risk of increasing oil prices can be hedged by buying oil-related stocks, whose value should be positively correlated with the oil price. In this way, a loss connected to increasing oil prices could be compensated by an increase in the value of the corresponding portfolio.

In the setting of this chapter, hedging an attainable contingent claim with payoff C means computing a self-financing portfolio strategy $\left(\bar{\xi}_t\right)_{t=1,2,\ldots,N}$ such that

$$\bar{\xi}_N \cdot \overline{S}_N = C, \quad i.e. \quad \bar{\xi}_N \cdot \overline{X}_N = \widetilde{C}. \tag{3.15}$$

Price, then hedge.

The portfolio allocation $\bar{\xi}_N$ can be computed by first solving (3.15) for $\bar{\xi}_N$ from the payoff values C, based on the fact that the allocation $\bar{\xi}_N$ depends only on information up to time $N-1$, by the predictability of $\left(\bar{\xi}_k\right)_{1 \leqslant k \leqslant N}$.

If the self-financing portfolio value V_t is known, for example from (3.6), *i.e.*

$$V_t = \frac{1}{(1+r)^{N-t}} \, \mathbb{E}^*[C \mid \mathcal{F}_t], \qquad t = 0, 1, \ldots, N, \tag{3.16}$$

we may similarly compute $\bar{\xi}_t$ by solving $\bar{\xi}_t \cdot \overline{S}_t = V_t$ for all $t = 1, 2, \ldots, N-1$.

Hedge, then price.

If $V_t = \pi_t(C)$ has not been computed, we can use *backward induction* to compute a self-financing portfolio strategy. Starting from the values of $\bar{\xi}_N$ obtained by solving

$$\bar{\xi}_N \cdot \overline{S}_N = C,$$

we use the self-financing condition to solve for $\bar{\xi}_{N-1}$, $\bar{\xi}_{N-2}$, ..., $\bar{\xi}_4$, down to $\bar{\xi}_3$, $\bar{\xi}_2$, and finally $\bar{\xi}_1$.

In order to implement this algorithm we can use the $N-1$ self-financing equations

$$\bar{\xi}_t \cdot \overline{X}_t = \bar{\xi}_{t+1} \cdot \overline{X}_t, \qquad t = 1, 2, \ldots, N-1, \tag{3.17}$$

allowing us in principle to compute the portfolio strategy $\left(\bar{\xi}_t\right)_{t=1,2,\ldots,N}$.

Based on the values of $\bar{\xi}_N$ we can solve

$$\bar{\xi}_{N-1} \cdot \overline{S}_{N-1} = \bar{\xi}_N \cdot \overline{S}_{N-1}$$

for $\bar{\xi}_{N-1}$, then

$$\bar{\xi}_{N-2} \cdot \overline{S}_{N-2} = \bar{\xi}_{N-1} \cdot \overline{S}_{N-2}$$

for $\bar{\xi}_{N-2}$, and successively $\bar{\xi}_2$ down to $\bar{\xi}_1$. In Section 3.3 the backward induction (3.17) will be implemented in the CRR model, see the proof of Proposition 3.10, and Exercises 3.15 and 3.4 for an application in a two-step model.

The discounted value $\widetilde{V}_t$ at time t of the portfolio claim can then be obtained from

$$\widetilde{V}_0 = \bar{\xi}_1 \cdot \overline{X}_0 \qquad \text{and} \qquad \widetilde{V}_t = \bar{\xi}_t \cdot \overline{X}_t, \qquad t = 1, 2, \ldots, N. \tag{3.18}$$

In addition we have shown in the proof of Theorem 3.5 that the price $\pi_t(C)$ of the claim payoff C at time t coincides with the value V_t of any self-financing portfolio hedging the claim payoff C, *i.e.*

$$\pi_t(C) = V_t, \qquad t = 0, 1, \ldots, N,$$

as given by (3.18). Hence the price of the claim can be computed either algebraically by solving (3.15) and (3.17) using backward induction and then using (3.18), or by a probabilistic method by a direct evaluation of the discounted expected value (3.16).

The development of hedging algorithms has increased *credit exposure* and counterparty risk when one party is unable to deliver the option payoff stated in the contract.

3.4 Hedging Vanilla Options

In this section we implement the backward induction (3.17) of Section 3.3 for the hedging of contingent claims in the discrete-time Cox–Ross–Rubinstein model. Our aim is to compute a (predictable) self-financing portfolio strategy hedging a vanilla option with payoff of the form

$$C = h\left(S_N^{(1)}\right).$$

Since the discounted price $\widetilde{S}_t^{(0)}$ of the riskless asset satisfies

$$\widetilde{S}_t^{(0)} = (1 + r)^{-t} S_t^{(0)} = S_0^{(0)},$$

we may sometimes write $S_0^{(0)}$ in place of $\widetilde{S}_t^{(0)}$. In Propositions 3.10 and 3.12 we present two different approaches to hedging and to the computation of the predictable process $\left(\xi_t^{(1)}\right)_{t=1,2,\ldots,N}$, which is also called the *Delta*.

Proposition 3.10. Price, then hedge. *The self-financing replicating portfolio strategy*

$$\left(\xi_t^{(0)}, \xi_t^{(1)}\right)_{t=1,2,\ldots,N} = \left(\xi_t^{(0)}\left(S_{t-1}^{(1)}\right), \xi_t^{(1)}\left(S_{t-1}^{(1)}\right)\right)_{t=1,2,\ldots,N}$$

hedging the contingent claim with payoff $C = h\left(S_N^{(1)}\right)$ *is given by*

$$
\begin{aligned}
\xi_t^{(1)}\left(S_{t-1}^{(1)}\right) &= \frac{v\left(t, (1+b)S_{t-1}^{(1)}\right) - v\left(t, (1+a)S_{t-1}^{(1)}\right)}{(b-a)S_{t-1}^{(1)}} \\
&= \frac{\widetilde{v}\left(t, (1+b)S_{t-1}^{(1)}\right) - \widetilde{v}\left(t, (1+a)S_{t-1}^{(1)}\right)}{(b-a)\widetilde{S}_{t-1}^{(1)}/(1+r)},
\end{aligned}
\tag{3.19}
$$

where the function $v(t,x)$ *is given by* (3.11), *and*

$$
\begin{aligned}
\xi_t^{(0)}\left(S_{t-1}^{(1)}\right) &= \frac{(1+b)v\left(t, (1+a)S_{t-1}^{(1)}\right) - (1+a)v\left(t, (1+b)S_{t-1}^{(1)}\right)}{(b-a)S_t^{(0)}} \\
&= \frac{(1+b)\widetilde{v}\left(t, (1+a)S_{t-1}^{(1)}\right) - (1+a)\widetilde{v}\left(t, (1+b)S_{t-1}^{(1)}\right)}{(b-a)S_0^{(0)}},
\end{aligned}
\tag{3.20}
$$

$t = 1, 2, \ldots, N$, *where the function* $\widetilde{v}(t,x) = (1+r)^{-t}v(t,x)$ *is given by* (3.11).

Proof. We first compute the self-financing hedging strategy $\left(\bar{\xi}_t\right)_{t=1,2,\ldots,N}$ by solving

$$\bar{\xi}_t \bullet \bar{X}_t = \widetilde{V}_t, \qquad t = 1, 2, \ldots, N,$$

from which we deduce the two equations

$$
\begin{cases}
\xi_t^{(0)}\left(S_{t-1}^{(1)}\right)S_0^{(0)} + \xi_t^{(1)}\left(S_{t-1}^{(1)}\right)\dfrac{1+a}{1+r}\widetilde{S}_{t-1}^{(1)} = \widetilde{v}\left(t, (1+a)S_{t-1}^{(1)}\right) \\[2ex]
\xi_t^{(0)}\left(S_{t-1}^{(1)}\right)S_0^{(0)} + \xi_t^{(1)}\left(S_{t-1}^{(1)}\right)\dfrac{1+b}{1+r}\widetilde{S}_{t-1}^{(1)} = \widetilde{v}\left(t, (1+b)S_{t-1}^{(1)}\right),
\end{cases}
$$

which can be solved as

$$
\begin{cases}
\xi_t^{(0)}\left(S_{t-1}^{(1)}\right) = \dfrac{(1+b)\widetilde{v}\left(t, (1+a)S_{t-1}^{(1)}\right) - (1+a)\widetilde{v}\left(t, (1+b)S_{t-1}^{(1)}\right)}{(b-a)S_0^{(0)}} \\[2ex]
\xi_t^{(1)}\left(S_{t-1}^{(1)}\right) = \dfrac{\widetilde{v}\left(t, (1+b)S_{t-1}^{(1)}\right) - \widetilde{v}\left(t, (1+a)S_{t-1}^{(1)}\right)}{(b-a)\widetilde{S}_{t-1}^{(1)}/(1+r)},
\end{cases}
$$

$t = 1, 2, \ldots, N$, which only depends on $S_{t-1}^{(1)}$, as expected, see also (1.20). This is consistent with the fact that $\xi_t^{(1)}$ represents the (possibly fractional) quantity of the risky asset to be present in the portfolio over the time period $[t-1, t]$ in order to hedge the claim payoff C at time N and is decided at time $t-1$. □

By applying (3.19) to the function $v(t, x)$ in (3.11), we find

$$\xi_t^{(1)}\big(S_{t-1}^{(1)}\big) = \frac{1}{(1+r)^{N-t}} \sum_{k=0}^{N-t} \binom{N-t}{k} (p^*)^k (q^*)^{N-t-k}$$

$$\times \frac{h\big(S_{t-1}^{(1)}(1+b)^{k+1}(1+a)^{N-t-k}\big) - h\big(S_{t-1}^{(1)}(1+b)^k(1+a)^{N-t-k+1}\big)}{(b-a)S_t^{(1)}},$$

$t = 0, 1, \ldots, N$.

The next Figure 3.3 presents a tree-based implementation of the risky hedging component (3.19).

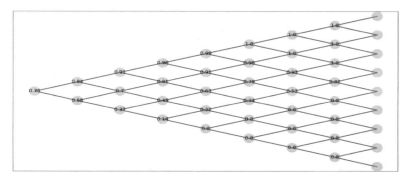

Figure 3.3: Discrete-time call option hedging strategy (risky component).

The next Figure 3.4 presents a tree-based implementation of the riskless hedging component (3.20).

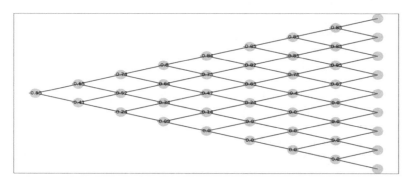

Figure 3.4: Discrete-time call option hedging strategy (riskless component).

We can also check that the portfolio strategy

$$\big(\bar{\xi}_t\big)_{t=1,2,\ldots,N} = \big(\xi_t^{(0)}, \xi_t^{(1)}\big)_{t=1,2,\ldots,N} = \big(\xi_t^{(0)}\big(S_{t-1}^{(1)}\big), \xi_t^{(1)}\big(S_{t-1}^{(1)}\big)\big)_{t=1,2,\ldots,N}$$

given by (3.19)–(3.20) is self-financing, as follows:

$$\bar{\xi}_{t+1} \cdot \overline{X}_t = \xi_{t+1}^{(0)}\big(S_t^{(1)}\big)S_0^{(0)} + \xi_{t+1}^{(1)}\big(S_t^{(1)}\big)\widetilde{S}_t^{(1)}$$

$$= S_0^{(0)} \frac{(1+b)\widetilde{v}\big(t+1, (1+a)S_t^{(1)}\big) - (1+a)\widetilde{v}\big(t+1, (1+b)S_t^{(1)}\big)}{(b-a)S_0^{(0)}}$$

$$+ \widetilde{S}_t^{(1)} \frac{\widetilde{v}(t+1, (1+b)S_t^{(1)}) - \widetilde{v}(t+1, (1+a)S_t^{(1)})}{(b-a)\widetilde{S}_t^{(1)}/(1+r)}$$

$$= \frac{(1+b)\widetilde{v}(t+1, (1+a)S_t^{(1)}) - (1+a)\widetilde{v}(t+1, (1+b)S_t^{(1)})}{b-a}$$

$$+ \frac{\widetilde{v}(t+1, (1+b)S_t^{(1)}) - \widetilde{v}(t+1, (1+a)S_t^{(1)})}{(b-a)/(1+r)}$$

$$= \frac{r-a}{b-a}\widetilde{v}(t+1, (1+b)S_t^{(1)}) + \frac{b-r}{b-a}\widetilde{v}(t+1, (1+a)S_t^{(1)})$$

$$= p^*\widetilde{v}(t+1, (1+b)S_t^{(1)}) + q^*\widetilde{v}(t+1, (1+a)S_t^{(1)})$$

$$= \widetilde{v}(t, S_t^{(1)})$$

$$= \xi_t^{(0)}(S_t^{(1)})S_0^{(0)} + \xi_t^{(1)}(S_t^{(1)})\widetilde{S}_t^{(1)}$$

$$= \bar{\xi}_t \cdot \overline{X}_t, \qquad t = 0, 1, \ldots, N-1,$$

where we used (3.14) or the martingale property of the discounted portfolio value process $\left(\widetilde{v}(t, S_t^{(1)})\right)_{t=0,1,\ldots,N}$, see Lemma 3.2.

Market terms and data

Delta. The *Delta* represents the quantity of underlying risky asset $S_t^{(1)}$ held in the portfolio over the time interval $[t-1, t]$. Here, it is denoted by $\xi_t^{(1)}(S_{t-1}^{(1)})$ for $t = 1, 2, \ldots, N$.

Effective gearing. The *effective gearing* at time $t = 1, 2, \ldots, N$ of the option with payoff $C = h(S_N^{(1)})$ is defined as the ratio

$$
\begin{aligned}
\mathrm{EG}_t &:= G_t \xi_t^{(1)} \\
&= \frac{S_t^{(1)}}{\pi_t(C)}\xi_t^{(1)} \\
&= \frac{S_t^{(1)}\left(v(t, (1+b)S_{t-1}^{(1)}) - v(t, (1+a)S_{t-1}^{(1)})\right)}{S_{t-1}^{(1)}v(t, S_t^{(1)})(b-a)} \\
&= \frac{\left(v(t, (1+b)S_{t-1}^{(1)}) - v(t, (1+a)S_{t-1}^{(1)})\right)/v(t, S_t^{(1)})}{S_{t-1}^{(1)}(b-a)/S_t^{(1)}}, \qquad t = 1, 2, \ldots, N.
\end{aligned}
$$

The effective gearing $\mathrm{EG}_t = \xi_t S_t^{(1)}/\pi_t(C)$ can be interpreted as the *hedge ratio, i.e.* the percentage of the portfolio which is invested on the risky asset. It also allows one to represent the percentage change in the option price in terms of the potential percentage change $S_{t-1}^{(1)}(b-a)/S_t^{(1)}$ in the underlying asset price when the asset return switches from a to b, as

$$\frac{\left(v(t, (1+b)S_{t-1}^{(1)}) - v(t, (1+a)S_{t-1}^{(1)})\right)}{v(t, S_t^{(1)})} = \mathrm{EG}_t \times \frac{S_{t-1}^{(1)}(b-a)}{S_t^{(1)}}.$$

By Proposition 3.8 we have the following remark.

Remark 3.11. *i) If the function $x \mapsto h(x)$ is non-decreasing, e.g. in the case of European call options, then the function $x \mapsto \widetilde{v}(t,x)$ is also non-decreasing for all fixed $t = 0,1,\ldots,N$, hence the portfolio strategy $(\xi_t^{(0)}, \xi_t^{(1)})_{t=1,2,\ldots,N}$ defined by (3.11) or (3.19) satisfies $\xi_t^{(1)} \geqslant 0$, $t = 1,2,\ldots,N$ and there is not short selling.*

ii) Similarly, we can show that when $x \mapsto h(x)$ is a non-increasing function, e.g. in the case of European put options, the portfolio allocation $\xi_t^{(1)} \leqslant 0$ is negative, $t = 1,2,\ldots,N$, i.e. short selling always occurs.

As a consequence of (3.20), the discounted amounts $\xi_t^{(0)} S_0^{(0)}$ and $\xi_t^{(1)} \widetilde{S}_t^{(1)}$ respectively invested on the riskless and risky assets are given by

$$S_0^{(0)} \xi_t^{(0)}(S_{t-1}^{(1)}) = \frac{(1+b)\widetilde{v}(t,(1+a)S_{t-1}^{(1)}) - (1+a)\widetilde{v}(t,(1+b)S_{t-1}^{(1)})}{b-a} \tag{3.21}$$

and

$$\widetilde{S}_t^{(1)} \xi_t^{(1)}(S_{t-1}^{(1)}) = (1+R_t)\frac{\widetilde{v}(t,(1+b)S_{t-1}^{(1)}) - \widetilde{v}(t,(1+a)S_{t-1}^{(1)})}{b-a},$$

$t = 1,2,\ldots,N$.

Regarding the quantity $\xi_t^{(0)}$ of the riskless asset in the portfolio at time t, from the relation

$$\widetilde{V}_t = \bar{\xi}_t \cdot \overline{X}_t = \xi_t^{(0)} \widetilde{S}_t^{(0)} + \xi_t^{(1)} \widetilde{S}_t^{(1)}, \qquad t = 1,2,\ldots,N,$$

we also obtain

$$
\begin{aligned}
\xi_t^{(0)} &= \frac{\widetilde{V}_t - \xi_t^{(1)} \widetilde{S}_t^{(1)}}{\widetilde{S}_t^{(0)}} \\
&= \frac{\widetilde{V}_t - \xi_t^{(1)} \widetilde{S}_t^{(1)}}{S_0^{(0)}} \\
&= \frac{\widetilde{v}(t,S_t^{(1)}) - \xi_t^{(1)} \widetilde{S}_t^{(1)}}{S_0^{(0)}}, \qquad t = 1,2,\ldots,N.
\end{aligned}
$$

In the next proposition we compute the hedging strategy by backward induction, starting from the relation

$$\xi_N^{(1)}(S_{N-1}^{(1)}) = \frac{h((1+b)S_{N-1}^{(1)}) - h((1+a)S_{N-1}^{(1)})}{(b-a)S_{N-1}^{(1)}},$$

and

$$\xi_N^{(0)}(S_{N-1}^{(1)}) = \frac{(1+b)h((1+a)S_{N-1}^{(1)}) - (1+a)h((1+b)S_{N-1}^{(1)})}{(b-a)S_0^{(0)}(1+r)^N},$$

that follow from (3.19)–(3.20) applied to the claim payoff function $h(\cdot)$.

Proposition 3.12. Hedge, then price. *The self-financing replicating portfolio strategy*

$$(\xi_t^{(0)}, \xi_t^{(1)})_{t=1,2,\ldots,N} = (\xi_t^{(0)}(S_{t-1}^{(1)}), \xi_t^{(1)}(S_{t-1}^{(1)}))_{t=1,2,\ldots,N}$$

hedging the contingent claim with payoff $C = h\big(S_N^{(1)}\big)$ is given from (3.19) at time $t = N$ by

$$\xi_N^{(1)}\big(S_{N-1}^{(1)}\big) = \frac{h\big((1+b)S_{N-1}^{(1)}\big) - h\big((1+a)S_{N-1}^{(1)}\big)}{(b-a)S_{N-1}^{(1)}}, \tag{3.22}$$

and

$$\xi_N^{(0)}\big(S_{N-1}^{(1)}\big) = \frac{(1+b)h\big((1+a)S_{N-1}^{(1)}\big) - (1+a)h\big((1+b)S_{N-1}^{(1)}\big)}{(b-a)S_N^{(0)}}, \tag{3.23}$$

and then inductively by

$$\begin{aligned}
\xi_t^{(1)}\big(S_{t-1}^{(1)}\big) &= \frac{(1+b)\xi_{t+1}^{(1)}\big((1+b)S_{t-1}^{(1)}\big) - (1+a)\xi_{t+1}^{(1)}\big((1+a)S_{t-1}^{(1)}\big)}{b-a} \\
&\quad + S_0^{(0)}\frac{\xi_{t+1}^{(0)}\big((1+b)S_{t-1}^{(1)}\big) - \xi_{t+1}^{(0)}\big((1+a)S_{t-1}^{(1)}\big)}{(b-a)\widetilde{S}_{t-1}^{(1)}/(1+r)},
\end{aligned} \tag{3.24}$$

and

$$\begin{aligned}
\xi_t^{(0)}\big(S_{t-1}^{(1)}\big) &= \frac{(1+a)(1+b)\widetilde{S}_{t-1}^{(1)}\big(\xi_{t+1}^{(1)}\big((1+a)S_{t-1}^{(1)}\big) - \xi_{t+1}^{(1)}\big((1+b)S_{t-1}^{(1)}\big)\big)}{(b-a)(1+r)S_0^{(0)}} \\
&\quad + \frac{(1+b)\xi_{t+1}^{(0)}\big((1+a)S_{t-1}^{(1)}\big) - (1+a)\xi_{t+1}^{(0)}\big((1+b)S_{t-1}^{(1)}\big)}{b-a},
\end{aligned} \tag{3.25}$$

$t = 1, 2, \ldots, N-1$.

The pricing function $\widetilde{v}(t,x) = (1+r)^{-t}v(t,x)$ is then given by

$$\widetilde{v}\big(t, S_t^{(1)}\big) = S_0^{(0)}\xi_t^{(0)}\big(S_{t-1}^{(1)}\big) + \widetilde{S}_t^{(1)}\xi_t^{(1)}\big(S_{t-1}^{(1)}\big), \quad t = 1, 2, \ldots, N.$$

Proof. Relations (3.22)–(3.23) follow from (3.19)–(3.20) stated at time $t = N$. Next, by the self-financing condition (3.17), we have

$$\bar{\xi}_t \cdot \overline{X}_t = \bar{\xi}_{t+1} \cdot \overline{X}_t, \qquad t = 0, 1, \ldots, N-1,$$

i.e.

$$\begin{cases}
S_0^{(0)}\xi_t^{(0)}\big(S_{t-1}^{(1)}\big) + \widetilde{S}_{t-1}^{(1)}\xi_t^{(1)}\big(S_{t-1}^{(1)}\big)\dfrac{1+b}{1+r} \\
\quad = \xi_{t+1}^{(0)}\big((1+b)S_{t-1}^{(1)}\big)S_0^{(0)} + \xi_{t+1}^{(1)}\big((1+b)S_{t-1}^{(1)}\big)\widetilde{S}_{t-1}^{(1)}\dfrac{1+b}{1+r} \\[2mm]
S_0^{(0)}\xi_t^{(0)}\big(S_{t-1}^{(1)}\big) + \widetilde{S}_{t-1}^{(1)}\xi_t^{(1)}\big(S_{t-1}^{(1)}\big)\dfrac{1+a}{1+r} \\
\quad = \xi_{t+1}^{(0)}\big((1+a)S_{t-1}^{(1)}\big)S_0^{(0)} + \xi_{t+1}^{(1)}\big((1+a)S_{t-1}^{(1)}\big)\widetilde{S}_{t-1}^{(1)}\dfrac{1+a}{1+r},
\end{cases}$$

which can be solved as

$$\begin{aligned}
\xi_t^{(1)}\big(S_{t-1}^{(1)}\big) &= \frac{(1+b)\xi_{t+1}^{(1)}\big((1+b)S_{t-1}^{(1)}\big) - (1+a)\xi_{t+1}^{(1)}\big((1+a)S_{t-1}^{(1)}\big)}{b-a} \\
&\quad + (1+r)S_0^{(0)}\frac{\xi_{t+1}^{(0)}\big((1+b)S_{t-1}^{(1)}\big) - \xi_{t+1}^{(0)}\big((1+a)S_{t-1}^{(1)}\big)}{(b-a)\widetilde{S}_{t-1}^{(1)}},
\end{aligned}$$

and

$$
\xi_t^{(0)}(S_{t-1}^{(1)}) = \frac{(1+a)(1+b)\widetilde{S}_{t-1}^{(1)}(\xi_{t+1}^{(1)}((1+a)S_{t-1}^{(1)}) - \xi_{t+1}^{(1)}((1+b)S_{t-1}^{(1)}))}{(b-a)(1+r)S_0^{(0)}}
$$
$$
+ \frac{(1+b)\xi_{t+1}^{(0)}((1+a)S_{t-1}^{(1)}) - (1+a)\xi_{t+1}^{(0)}((1+b)S_{t-1}^{(1)})}{b-a},
$$

$t = 1, 2, \ldots, N-1$. $\qquad\qquad\qquad\qquad\qquad\qquad\qquad\qquad\qquad\qquad$ $\square$

By (3.24)–(3.25), we can check that the corresponding discounted portfolio value process

$$
(\widetilde{V}_t)_{t=1,2,\ldots,N} = (\bar{\xi}_t \cdot \overline{X}_t)_{t=1,2,\ldots,N}
$$

is a martingale under $\mathbb{P}^*$:

$$
\begin{aligned}
\widetilde{V}_t &= \bar{\xi}_t \cdot \overline{X}_t \\
&= S_0^{(0)}\xi_t^{(0)}(S_{t-1}^{(1)}) + \widetilde{S}_t^{(1)}\xi_t^{(1)}(S_{t-1}^{(1)}) \\
&= \frac{(1+a)(1+b)\widetilde{S}_{t-1}^{(1)}(\xi_{t+1}^{(1)}((1+a)S_{t-1}^{(1)}) - \xi_{t+1}^{(1)}((1+b)S_{t-1}^{(1)}))}{(b-a)(1+r)} \\
&\quad + S_0^{(0)}\frac{(1+b)\xi_{t+1}^{(0)}((1+a)S_{t-1}^{(1)}) - (1+a)\xi_{t+1}^{(0)}((1+b)S_{t-1}^{(1)})}{(b-a)} \\
&\quad + \widetilde{S}_t^{(1)}\frac{(1+b)\xi_{t+1}^{(1)}((1+b)S_{t-1}^{(1)}) - (1+a)\xi_{t+1}^{(1)}((1+a)S_{t-1}^{(1)})}{b-a} \\
&\quad + (1+r)\widetilde{S}_t^{(1)}S_0^{(0)}\frac{\xi_{t+1}^{(0)}((1+b)S_{t-1}^{(1)}) - \xi_{t+1}^{(0)}((1+a)S_{t-1}^{(1)})}{(b-a)\widetilde{S}_{t-1}^{(1)}} \\
&= \frac{r-a}{b-a}S_0^{(0)}\xi_{t+1}^{(0)}(S_t^{(1)}) + \frac{b-r}{b-a}S_0^{(0)}\xi_{t+1}^{(0)}(S_t^{(1)}) \\
&\quad + \frac{(r-a)(1+b)}{(b-a)(1+r)}\widetilde{S}_t^{(1)}\xi_{t+1}^{(1)}(S_t^{(1)}) + \frac{(b-r)(1+a)}{(b-a)(1+r)}\widetilde{S}_t^{(1)}\xi_{t+1}^{(1)}(S_t^{(1)}) \\
&= p^*S_0^{(0)}\xi_{t+1}^{(0)}(S_t^{(1)}) + q^*S_0^{(0)}\xi_{t+1}^{(0)}(S_t^{(1)}) \\
&\quad + p^*\frac{1+b}{1+r}\widetilde{S}_t^{(1)}\xi_{t+1}^{(1)}(S_t^{(1)}) + q^*\frac{1+a}{1+r}\widetilde{S}_t^{(1)}\xi_{t+1}^{(1)}(S_t^{(1)}) \\
&= \mathbb{E}^*[S_0^{(0)}\xi_{t+1}^{(0)}(S_t^{(1)}) + \widetilde{S}_{t+1}^{(1)}\xi_{t+1}^{(1)}(S_t^{(1)}) \,|\, \mathcal{F}_t] \\
&= \mathbb{E}^*[\widetilde{V}_{t+1} \,|\, \mathcal{F}_t],
\end{aligned}
$$

$t = 1, 2, \ldots, N-1$, as in Remark 3.4.

The next Figure 3.5 presents a tree-based implementation of the riskless hedging component (3.20).

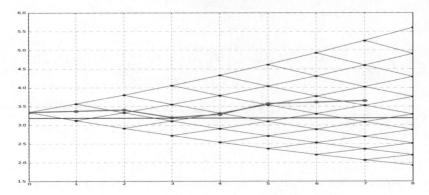

Figure 3.5: Tree of asset prices in the CRR model.

The next Figure 3.6 presents a tree-based implementation of call option prices in the CRR model.

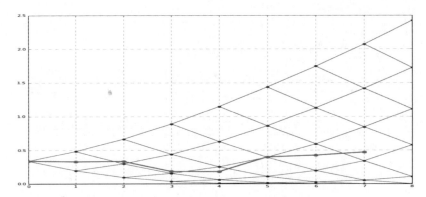

Figure 3.6: Tree of option prices in the CRR model.

The next Figure 3.7 presents a tree-based implementation of risky hedging portfolio allocation in the CRR model.

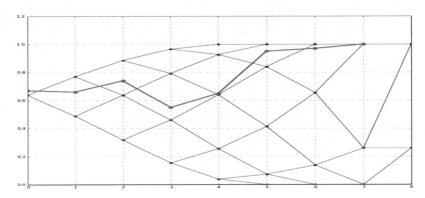

Figure 3.7: Tree of hedging portfolio allocations in the CRR model.

3.5 Hedging Exotic Options

In this section we take $p = p^*$ given by (3.12) and we consider the hedging of path-dependent options. Here we choose to use the finite difference gradient and the discrete Clark–Ocone formula of stochastic analysis, see also Föllmer and Schied (2004), Lamberton and Lapeyre (1996), Privault (2008), Chapter 1 of Privault (2009), Ruiz de Chávez (2001), or §15-1 of Williams (1991). See Di Nunno et al. (2009) and Section 8.2 of Privault (2009) for a similar approach in continuous time. Given

$$\omega = (\omega_1, \omega_2, \ldots, \omega_N) \in \Omega = \{-1, 1\}^N,$$

and $r = 1, 2, \ldots, N$, let

$$\omega_+^t := (\omega_1, \omega_2, \ldots, \omega_{t-1}, +1, \omega_{t+1}, \ldots, \omega_N)$$

and

$$\omega_-^t := (\omega_1, \omega_2, \ldots, \omega_{t-1}, -1, \omega_{t+1}, \ldots, \omega_N).$$

We also assume that the return $R_t(\omega)$ takes only two possible values

$$R_t(\omega_+^t) = b \quad \text{and} \quad R_t(\omega_-^t) = a, \qquad t = 1, 2, \ldots, N, \quad \omega \in \Omega.$$

Definition 3.13. *The operator D_t is defined on any random variable F by*

$$D_t F(\omega) = F(\omega_+^t) - F(\omega_-^t), \qquad t = 1, 2, \ldots, N. \tag{3.26}$$

We define the centered and normalized return Y_t by

$$Y_t := \frac{R_t - r}{b - a} = \begin{cases} \dfrac{b - r}{b - a} = q^*, & \omega_t = +1, \\[2mm] \dfrac{a - r}{b - a} = -p^*, & \omega_t = -1, \end{cases} \qquad t = 1, 2, \ldots, N.$$

Note that under the risk-neutral probability measure $\mathbb{P}^*$, we have

$$
\begin{aligned}
\mathbb{E}^*[Y_t] &= \mathbb{E}^*\left[\frac{R_t - r}{b - a}\right] \\
&= \frac{a - r}{b - a}\mathbb{P}^*(R_t = a) + \frac{b - r}{b - a}\mathbb{P}^*(R_t = b) \\
&= \frac{a - r}{b - a} \times \frac{b - r}{b - a} + \frac{b - r}{b - a} \times \frac{r - a}{b - a} \\
&= 0,
\end{aligned}
$$

and

$$\mathrm{Var}\,[Y_t] = p^*(q^*)^2 + q^*(p^*)^2 = p^*q^*, \qquad t = 1, 2, \ldots, N.$$

In addition, the discounted asset price increment reads

$$
\begin{aligned}
\widetilde{S}_t^{(1)} - \widetilde{S}_{t-1}^{(1)} &= \widetilde{S}_{t-1}^{(1)} \frac{1+R_t}{1+r} - \widetilde{S}_{t-1}^{(1)} \\
&= \frac{R_t - r}{1+r} \widetilde{S}_{t-1}^{(1)} \\
&= \frac{b-a}{1+r} Y_t \widetilde{S}_{t-1}^{(1)}, \qquad t = 1, 2, \ldots, N.
\end{aligned}
$$

We also have

$$
D_t Y_t = \frac{b-r}{b-a} - \left(\frac{a-r}{b-a} \right) = 1, \qquad t = 1, 2, \ldots, N,
$$

and

$$
\begin{aligned}
D_t S_N^{(1)} &= S_0^{(1)}(1+b) \prod_{\substack{k=1 \\ k \neq t}}^{N} (1+R_k) - S_0^{(1)}(1+a) \prod_{\substack{k=1 \\ k \neq t}}^{N} (1+R_k) \\
&= (b-a) S_0^{(1)} \prod_{\substack{k=1 \\ k \neq t}}^{N} (1+R_k) \\
&= S_0^{(1)} \frac{b-a}{1+R_t} \prod_{k=1}^{N} (1+R_k) \\
&= \frac{b-a}{1+R_t} S_N^{(1)}, \qquad t = 1, 2, \ldots, N.
\end{aligned}
$$

The following stochastic integral decomposition formula for the functionals of the binomial process is known as the Clark–Ocone formula in discrete time, cf. *e.g.* Privault (2009), Proposition 1.7.1.

Proposition 3.14. *For any square-integrable random variables F on Ω, we have*

$$
F = \mathbb{E}^*[F] + \sum_{k \geq 1} Y_k \, \mathbb{E}^*[D_k F \mid \mathcal{F}_{k-1}]. \tag{3.27}
$$

The Clark–Ocone formula (3.27) has the following consequence.

Corollary 3.15. *Assume that $(M_k)_{k \in \mathbb{N}}$ is a square-integrable $(\mathcal{F}_k)_{k \in \mathbb{N}}$-martingale. Then, we have*

$$
M_N = \mathbb{E}^*[M_N] + \sum_{k=1}^{N} Y_k D_k M_k, \qquad N \geq 0.
$$

Proof. We have

$$
\begin{aligned}
M_N &= \mathbb{E}^*[M_N] + \sum_{k \geq 1} Y_k \, \mathbb{E}^*[D_k M_N \mid \mathcal{F}_{k-1}] \\
&= \mathbb{E}^*[M_N] + \sum_{k \geq 1} Y_k D_k \, \mathbb{E}^*[M_N \mid \mathcal{F}_k] \\
&= \mathbb{E}^*[M_N] + \sum_{k \geq 1} Y_k D_k M_k \\
&= \mathbb{E}^*[M_N] + \sum_{k=1}^{N} Y_k D_k M_k.
\end{aligned}
$$

$\square$

In addition to the Clark–Ocone formula we also state a discrete-time analog of Itô's change of variable formula, which can be useful for option hedging. The next result extends Proposition 1.13.1 of Privault (2009) by removing the unnecessary martingale requirement on $(M_t)_{n\in\mathbb{N}}$.

Proposition 3.16. *Let $(Z_n)_{n\in\mathbb{N}}$ be an $(\mathcal{F}_n)_{n\in\mathbb{N}}$-adapted process and let $f : \mathbb{R} \times \mathbb{N} \longrightarrow \mathbb{R}$ be a given function. We have*

$$
f(Z_t, t) = f(Z_0, 0) + \sum_{k=1}^{t} D_k f(Z_k, k) Y_k
$$

$$
+ \sum_{k=1}^{t} \big(\mathbb{E}^*[f(Z_k, k) \mid \mathcal{F}_{k-1}] - f(Z_{k-1}, k-1) \big), \qquad t \geqslant 0. \qquad (3.28)
$$

Proof. First, we note that the process

$$
M_t := f(Z_t, t) - \sum_{k=1}^{t} \big(\mathbb{E}^*[f(Z_k, k) \mid \mathcal{F}_{k-1}] - f(Z_{k-1}, k-1) \big),
$$

$t = 0, 1, \ldots, N$, is a martingale under $\mathbb{P}^*$. Indeed, we have

$$
\mathbb{E}^* \left[f(Z_t, t) - \sum_{k=1}^{t} \big(\mathbb{E}^*[f(Z_k, k) \mid \mathcal{F}_{k-1}] - f(Z_{k-1}, k-1) \big) \,\Big|\, \mathcal{F}_{t-1} \right]
$$

$$
= \mathbb{E}^*[f(Z_t, t) \mid \mathcal{F}_{t-1}]
$$

$$
- \sum_{k=1}^{t} \big(\mathbb{E}^*[\mathbb{E}^*[f(Z_k, k) \mid \mathcal{F}_{k-1}] \mid \mathcal{F}_{t-1}] - \mathbb{E}^*[\mathbb{E}^*[f(Z_{k-1}, k-1) \mid \mathcal{F}_{k-1}] \mid \mathcal{F}_{t-1}] \big)
$$

$$
= \mathbb{E}^*[f(Z_t, t) \mid \mathcal{F}_{t-1}] - \sum_{k=1}^{t} \big(\mathbb{E}^*[f(Z_k, k) \mid \mathcal{F}_{k-1}] - f(Z_{k-1}, k-1) \big)
$$

$$
= f(Z_{t-1}, t-1) - \sum_{k=1}^{t-1} \big(\mathbb{E}^*[f(Z_k, k) \mid \mathcal{F}_{k-1}] - f(Z_{k-1}, k-1) \big), \qquad t \geqslant 1.
$$

Next, applying Corollary 3.15 to the martingale $(M_t)_{t=0,1,\ldots,N}$, we have

$$
f(Z_t, t) = M_t + \sum_{k=1}^{t} \big(\mathbb{E}^*[f(Z_k, k) \mid \mathcal{F}_{k-1}] - f(Z_{k-1}, k-1) \big)
$$

$$
= \mathbb{E}^*[M_t] + \sum_{k=1}^{t} Y_k D_k M_k + \sum_{k=1}^{t} \big(\mathbb{E}^*[f(Z_k, k) \mid \mathcal{F}_{k-1}] - f(Z_{k-1}, k-1) \big)
$$

$$
= f(Z_0, 0) + \sum_{k=1}^{t} Y_k D_k f(Z_k, k) + \sum_{k=1}^{t} \big(\mathbb{E}^*[f(Z_k, k) \mid \mathcal{F}_{k-1}] - f(Z_{k-1}, k-1) \big),
$$

$t \geqslant 0$, as

$$
D_k \big(\mathbb{E}^*[f(Z_k, k) \mid \mathcal{F}_{k-1}] - f(Z_{k-1}, k-1) \big) = 0, \qquad k \geqslant 1.
$$

$\square$

Note that if $(Z_t)_{t \in \mathbb{N}}$ is a discrete-time $(\mathcal{F}_t)_{t \in \mathbb{N}}$-martingale in $L^2(\Omega)$ written as

$$Z_t = Z_0 + \sum_{k=1}^{t} u_k Y_k, \qquad t \geqslant 0,$$

where $(u_t)_{t \in \mathbb{N}}$ is an $(\mathcal{F}_t)_{t \in \mathbb{N}}$-predictable process locally* in $L^2(\Omega \times \mathbb{N})$, then we have

$$D_t f(Z_t, t) = f(Z_{t-1} + q u_t, t) - f(Z_{t-1} - p u_t, t), \qquad (3.29)$$

$t = 1, 2, \ldots, N$. On the other hand, the term

$$\mathbb{E}[f(Z_t, t) - f(Z_{t-1}, t-1) \mid \mathcal{F}_{t-1}]$$

is analog to the finite variation part in the continuous-time Itô formula, and can be written as

$$p f(Z_{t-1} + q u_t, t) + q f(Z_{t-1} - p u_t, t) - f(Z_{t-1}, t-1).$$

When $(f(Z_t, t))_{t \in \mathbb{N}}$ is a martingale, Proposition 3.16 naturally recovers the decomposition

$$
\begin{aligned}
f(Z_t, t) &= f(Z_0, 0) \\
&\quad + \sum_{k=1}^{t} \big(f(Z_{k-1} + q u_k, k) - f(Z_{k-1} - p u_k, k) \big) Y_k \\
&= f(Z_0, 0) + \sum_{k=1}^{t} Y_k D_k f(Z_k, k), \qquad (3.30)
\end{aligned}
$$

that follows from Corollary 3.15 as well as from Proposition 3.14. In this case, the Clark–Ocone formula (3.27) and the change of variable formula (3.30) both coincide and we have in particular

$$D_k f(Z_k, k) = \mathbb{E}[D_k f(Z_N, N) \mid \mathcal{F}_{k-1}],$$

$k = 1, 2, \ldots, N$. For example, this recovers the martingale representation

$$
\begin{aligned}
\widetilde{S}_t^{(1)} &= S_0^{(1)} + \sum_{k=1}^{t} Y_k D_k \widetilde{S}_k^{(1)} \\
&= S_0^{(1)} + \frac{b-a}{1+r} \sum_{k=1}^{t} \widetilde{S}_{k-1}^{(1)} Y_k \\
&= S_0^{(1)} + \sum_{k=1}^{t} \widetilde{S}_{k-1}^{(1)} \frac{R_k - r}{1+r} \\
&= S_0^{(1)} + \sum_{k=1}^{t} \big(\widetilde{S}_k^{(1)} - \widetilde{S}_{k-1}^{(1)} \big),
\end{aligned}
$$

of the discounted asset price.

Our goal is to hedge an arbitrary claim payoff C on Ω, *i.e.* given an $\mathcal{F}_N$-measurable random variable C we search for a portfolio strategy $\big(\xi_t^{(0)}, \xi_t^{(1)} \big)_{t=1,2,\ldots,N}$ such that the equality

$$C = V_N = \xi_N^{(0)} S_N^{(0)} + \xi_N^{(1)} S_N^{(1)} \qquad (3.31)$$

holds, where $S_N^{(0)} = S_0^{(0)} (1+r)^N$ denotes the value of the riskless asset at time $N \geqslant 0$.

---

*i.e. $u(\cdot) \mathbb{1}_{[0,N]}(\cdot) \in L^2(\Omega \times \mathbb{N})$ for all $N > 0$.

The next proposition is the main result of this section, and provides a solution to the hedging problem under the constraint (3.31).

Proposition 3.17. Hedge, then price. *Given a contingent claim with payoff C, let $\xi_0^{(1)} = 0$,*

$$\xi_t^{(1)} = \frac{(1+r)^{-(N-t)}}{(b-a)S_{t-1}^{(1)}} \, \mathbb{E}^*[D_t C \mid \mathcal{F}_{t-1}], \qquad t = 1, 2, \ldots, N, \tag{3.32}$$

and

$$\xi_t^{(0)} = \frac{1}{S_t^{(0)}} \left((1+r)^{-(N-t)} \, \mathbb{E}^*[C \mid \mathcal{F}_t] - \xi_t^{(1)} S_t^{(1)} \right), \tag{3.33}$$

$t = 0, 1, \ldots, N$. *Then, the portfolio strategy $\left(\xi_t^{(0)}, \xi_t^{(1)}\right)_{t=1,2,\ldots,N}$ is self financing and we have*

$$V_t = \xi_t^{(0)} S_t^{(0)} + \xi_t^{(1)} S_t^{(1)} = (1+r)^{-(N-t)} \, \mathbb{E}^*[C \mid \mathcal{F}_t], \quad t = 0, 1, \ldots, N.$$

In particular we have $V_N = C$, hence $\left(\xi_t^{(0)}, \xi_t^{(1)}\right)_{t=1,2,\ldots,N}$ is a hedging strategy leading to C.

Proof. Let $\left(\xi_t^{(1)}\right)_{t=1,2,\ldots,N}$ be defined by (3.32), and consider the process $\left(\xi_t^{(0)}\right)_{t=0,1,\ldots,N}$ recursively defined by

$$\xi_0^{(0)} = (1+r)^{-N} \frac{\mathbb{E}^*[C]}{S_0^{(1)}} \quad \text{and} \quad \xi_{t+1}^{(0)} = \xi_t^{(0)} - \frac{\left(\xi_{t+1}^{(1)} - \xi_t^{(1)}\right) S_t^{(1)}}{S_t^{(0)}},$$

$t = 0, 1, \ldots, N-1$. Then, $\left(\xi_t^{(0)}, \xi_t^{(1)}\right)_{t=1,2,\ldots,N}$ satisfies the self-financing condition

$$S_t^{(0)} \left(\xi_{t+1}^{(0)} - \xi_t^{(0)}\right) + S_t^{(1)} \left(\xi_{t+1}^{(1)} - \xi_t^{(1)}\right) = 0, \qquad t = 1, 2, \ldots, N-1.$$

Let now

$$V_0 := \frac{1}{(1+r)^N} \, \mathbb{E}^*[C], \qquad V_t := \xi_t^{(0)} S_t^{(0)} + \xi_t^{(1)} S_t^{(1)}, \quad t = 1, 2, \ldots, N,$$

and

$$\widetilde{V}_t = \frac{V_t}{(1+r)^t} \qquad t = 0, 1, \ldots, N.$$

Since $\left(\xi_t^{(0)}, \xi_t^{(1)}\right)_{t=1,2,\ldots,N}$ is self-financing, by Lemma 3.2 we have

$$\widetilde{V}_t = \widetilde{V}_0 + (b-a) \sum_{k=1}^{t} \frac{1}{(1+r)^k} Y_k \xi_k^{(1)} S_{k-1}^{(1)}, \tag{3.34}$$

$t = 1, 2, \ldots, N$. On the other hand, from the Clark–Ocone formula (3.27) and the definition of $\left(\xi_t^{(1)}\right)_{t=1,2,\ldots,N}$, we have

$$\frac{1}{(1+r)^N} \, \mathbb{E}^*[C \mid \mathcal{F}_t]$$

$$= \frac{1}{(1+r)^N} \, \mathbb{E}^* \left[\mathbb{E}^*[C] + \sum_{k=0}^{N} Y_k \, \mathbb{E}^*[D_k C \mid \mathcal{F}_{k-1}] \mid \mathcal{F}_t \right]$$

$$= \frac{1}{(1+r)^N} \, \mathbb{E}^*[C] + \frac{1}{(1+r)^N} \sum_{k=0}^{t} \mathbb{E}^*[D_k C \mid \mathcal{F}_{k-1}] Y_k$$

$$= \frac{1}{(1+r)^N} \, \mathbb{E}^*[C] + (b-a) \sum_{k=0}^{t} \frac{1}{(1+r)^k} \xi_k^{(1)} S_{k-1}^{(1)} Y_k$$

$$= \tilde{V}_t$$

from (3.34). Hence

$$\tilde{V}_t = \frac{1}{(1+r)^N} \, \mathbb{E}^*[C \mid \mathcal{F}_t], \qquad t = 0, 1, \ldots, N,$$

and

$$V_t = (1+r)^{-(N-t)} \, \mathbb{E}^*[C \mid \mathcal{F}_t], \qquad t = 0, 1, \ldots, N. \tag{3.35}$$

In particular, (3.35) shows that we have $V_N = C$. To conclude the proof we note that from the relation $V_t = \xi_t^{(0)} S_t^{(0)} + \xi_t^{(1)} S_t^{(1)}$, $t = 1, 2, \ldots, N$, the process $\big(\xi_t^{(0)}\big)_{t=1,2,\ldots,N}$ coincides with $\big(\xi_t^{(0)}\big)_{t=1,2,\ldots,N}$ defined by (3.33). $\qquad\square$

Example - Vanilla options

From Proposition 3.8, the price $\pi_t(C)$ of the contingent claim with payoff $C = h\big(S_N^{(1)}\big)$ is given by

$$\pi_t(C) = v\big(t, S_t^{(1)}\big),$$

where the function $v(t, x)$ is given by

$$v\big(t, S_t^{(1)}\big) = \frac{1}{(1+r)^{N-t}} \, \mathbb{E}^*[C \mid \mathcal{F}_t]$$

$$= \frac{1}{(1+r)^{N-t}} \, \mathbb{E}^* \left[h \left(x \prod_{j=t+1}^{N} (1+R_j) \right) \right]_{x=S_t^{(1)}}.$$

Note that in this case we have $C = v\big(N, S_N^{(1)}\big)$, $\mathbb{E}[C] = v(0, M_0)$, and the discounted claim payoff $\tilde{C} = C/(1+r)^N = \tilde{v}\big(N, S_N^{(1)}\big)$ satisfies

$$\tilde{C} = \mathbb{E}\big[\tilde{C}\big] + \sum_{t=1}^{N} Y_t \, \mathbb{E}\big[D_t \tilde{v}\big(N, S_N^{(1)}\big) \mid \mathcal{F}_{t-1}\big]$$

$$= \mathbb{E}\big[\tilde{C}\big] + \sum_{t=1}^{N} Y_t D_t \tilde{v}\big(t, S_t^{(1)}\big)$$

$$= \mathbb{E}\big[\tilde{C}\big] + \sum_{t=1}^{N} \frac{1}{(1+r)^t} Y_t D_t v\big(t, S_t^{(1)}\big)$$

$$= \mathbb{E}\big[\tilde{C}\big] + \sum_{t=1}^{N} Y_t D_t \, \mathbb{E}\big[\tilde{v}\big(N, S_N^{(1)}\big) \mid \mathcal{F}_t\big]$$

$$= \mathbb{E}\big[\tilde{C}\big] + \frac{1}{(1+r)^N} \sum_{t=1}^{N} Y_t D_t \, \mathbb{E}[C \mid \mathcal{F}_t],$$

hence we have

$$\mathbb{E}\left[D_t v\big(N, S_N^{(1)}\big) \mid \mathcal{F}_{t-1}\right] = (1+r)^{N-t} D_t v\big(t, S_t^{(1)}\big), \quad t = 1, 2, \ldots, N,$$

and by Proposition 3.17 the hedging strategy for $C = h\big(S_N^{(1)}\big)$ is given by

$$
\begin{aligned}
\xi_t^{(1)} &= \frac{(1+r)^{-(N-t)}}{(b-a)S_{t-1}^{(1)}} \, \mathbb{E}\left[D_t h\big(S_N^{(1)}\big) \mid \mathcal{F}_{t-1}\right] \\
&= \frac{(1+r)^{-(N-t)}}{(b-a)S_{t-1}^{(1)}} \, \mathbb{E}\left[D_t v\big(N, S_N^{(1)}\big) \mid \mathcal{F}_{t-1}\right] \\
&= \frac{1}{(b-a)S_{t-1}^{(1)}} D_t v\big(t, S_t^{(1)}\big) \\
&= \frac{1}{(b-a)S_{t-1}^{(1)}} \Big(v\big(t, S_{t-1}^{(1)}(1+b)\big) - v\big(t, S_{t-1}^{(1)}(1+a)\big)\Big) \\
&= \frac{1}{(b-a)\widetilde{S}_{t-1}^{(1)}/(1+r)} \Big(\widetilde{v}\big(t, S_{t-1}^{(1)}(1+b)\big) - \widetilde{v}\big(t, S_{t-1}^{(1)}(1+a)\big)\Big),
\end{aligned}
$$

$t = 1, 2, \ldots, N$, which recovers Proposition 3.10 as a particular case. Note that $\xi_t^{(1)}$ is nonnegative (*i.e.* there is no short selling) when f is a non-decreasing function, because $a < b$. This is in particular true in the case of the European call option, for which we have $f(x) = (x - K)^+$.

3.6 Convergence of the CRR Model

As the pricing formulas (3.11) in the CRR model can be difficult to implement for large values on N, in this section we consider the convergence of the discrete-time model to the continuous-time Black Scholes model.

Continuous compounding – riskless asset

Consider the discretization

$$\left[0, \frac{T}{N}, \frac{2T}{N}, \ldots, \frac{(N-1)T}{N}, T\right]$$

of the time interval $[0, T]$ into N time steps.

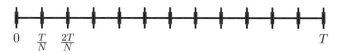

Note that

$$\lim_{N \to \infty} (1+r)^N = \infty,$$

when $r > 0$, thus we need to renormalize r so that the interest rate on each time interval becomes r_N, with $\lim_{N \to \infty} r_N = 0$. It turns out that the correct renormalization is

$$r_N := r\frac{T}{N}, \tag{3.36}$$

so that for $T \geqslant 0$,

$$
\begin{aligned}
\lim_{N \to \infty} (1 + r_N)^N &= \lim_{N \to \infty} \left(1 + r\frac{T}{N} \right)^N \\
&= \lim_{N \to \infty} \exp \left(N \log \left(1 + r\frac{T}{N} \right) \right) \\
&= e^{rT}.
\end{aligned}
\tag{3.37}
$$

Hence the price $S_t^{(0)}$ of the riskless asset is given by

$$
S_t^{(0)} = S_0^{(0)} e^{rt}, \qquad t \geqslant 0,
\tag{3.38}
$$

which solves the differential equation

$$
\frac{dS_t^{(0)}}{dt} = rS_t^{(0)}, \qquad S_0^{(0)} = 1, \quad t \geqslant 0.
\tag{3.39}
$$

We can also write

$$
dS_t^{(0)} = rS_t^{(0)} dt, \qquad \text{or} \qquad \frac{dS_t^{(0)}}{S_t^{(0)}} = rdt,
\tag{3.40}
$$

and using $dS_t^{(0)} \simeq S_{t+dt}^{(0)} - S_t^{(0)}$ we can discretize this equation by saying that the *infinitesimal return* $(S_{t+dt}^{(0)} - S_t^{(0)})/S_t^{(0)}$ of the riskless asset equals rdt on the small time interval $[t, t + dt]$, *i.e.*

$$
\frac{S_{t+dt}^{(0)} - S_t^{(0)}}{S_t^{(0)}} = rdt.
$$

In this sense, the rate r is the instantaneous interest rate per unit of time.

The same equation rewrites in *integral form* as

$$
S_T^{(0)} - S_0^{(0)} = \int_0^T dS_t^{(0)} = r \int_0^T S_t^{(0)} dt.
$$

Continuous compounding – risky asset

We recall the central limit theorem.

Theorem 3.18. *Let $(X_n)_{n \geqslant 1}$ be a sequence of independent and identically distributed random variables with finite mean $\mu = \mathbb{E}[X_1]$ and variance $\mathrm{Var}[X_1] < \infty$. We have the convergence in distribution*

$$
\lim_{n \to \infty} \frac{X_1 + \cdots + X_n - n\mu}{\sqrt{n}} = \mathcal{N}(0, \sigma^2),
$$

or equivalently

$$
\lim_{n \to \infty} \frac{X_1 + \cdots + X_n - n\mu}{\sigma\sqrt{n}} = \mathcal{N}(0, 1).
$$

The convergence in distribution of Theorem 3.18 is illustrated by the Galton board simulation of Figure 3.8, which shows the convergence of the binomial random walk to a Gaussian distribution in large time.

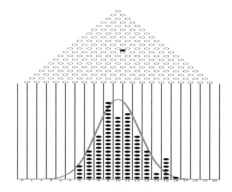

Figure 3.8: Galton board simulation.

In the CRR model we need to replace the standard Galton board by its multiplicative version, which shows that as N tends to infinity the distribution of $S_N^{(1)}$ converges to the *lognormal distribution* with probability density function of the form

$$x \longmapsto f(x) = \frac{1}{x\sigma\sqrt{2\pi T}} \exp\left(-\frac{\left(-\left(r - \sigma^2/2\right)T + \log\left(x/S_0^{(1)}\right)\right)^2}{2\sigma^2 T}\right),$$

$x > 0$, with location parameter $(r - \sigma^2/2)T + \log S_0^{(1)}$ and scale parameter $\sigma\sqrt{T}$, or log-variance $\sigma^2 T$, as illustrated in the modified Galton board of Figure 3.9 below, see also Figure 5.6 and Exercise 5.1.

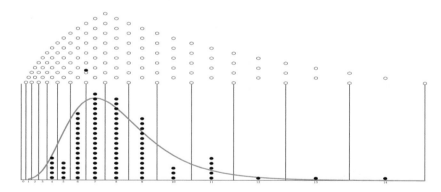

Figure 3.9: Multiplicative Galton board simulation.

Exercise: Check that f is the probability density function of $e^{\sigma X + (r - \sigma^2/2)T}$ where $X \simeq \mathcal{N}(0, T)$ is a centered Gaussian random variable with variance $T > 0$.

In addition to the renormalization (3.36) for the interest rate $r_N := rT/N$, we need to apply a similar renormalization to the coefficients a and b of the CRR model. Let $\sigma > 0$ denote a positive parameter called the volatility, which quantifies the range of random fluctuations, and let a_N, b_N be defined from

$$\frac{1 + a_N}{1 + r_N} = 1 - \sigma\sqrt{\frac{T}{N}} \quad \text{and} \quad \frac{1 + b_N}{1 + r_N} = 1 + \sigma\sqrt{\frac{T}{N}}$$

i.e.

$$a_N = (1+r_N)\left(1 - \sigma\sqrt{\frac{T}{N}}\right) - 1 \quad \text{and} \quad b_N = (1+r_N)\left(1 + \sigma\sqrt{\frac{T}{N}}\right) - 1. \qquad (3.41)$$

Consider the random return $R_k^{(N)} \in \{a_N, b_N\}$ and the price process defined as

$$S_{t,N}^{(1)} = S_0^{(1)} \prod_{k=1}^{t} (1 + R_k^{(N)}), \qquad t = 1, 2, \dots, N. \qquad (3.42)$$

Note that the risk-neutral probabilities are given by

$$
\begin{aligned}
\mathbb{P}^*\left(R_t^{(N)} = a_N\right) &= \frac{b_N - r_N}{b_N - a_N} \qquad\qquad\qquad\qquad\qquad\qquad\qquad (3.43)\\[2mm]
&= \frac{(1+r_N)(1+\sigma\sqrt{T/N}) - 1 - r_N}{(1+r_N)(1+\sigma\sqrt{T/N}) - (1+r_N)(1-\sigma\sqrt{T/N})}\\[2mm]
&= \frac{1}{2}, \quad t = 1, 2, \dots, N,
\end{aligned}
$$

and

$$
\begin{aligned}
\mathbb{P}^*\left(R_t^{(N)} = b_N\right) &= \frac{r_N - a_N}{b_N - a_N} \qquad\qquad\qquad\qquad\qquad\qquad\qquad (3.44)\\[2mm]
&= \frac{r_N - (1+r_N)(1-\sigma\sqrt{T/N}) + 1}{(1+r_N)(1+\sigma\sqrt{T/N}) - (1+r_N)(1-\sigma\sqrt{T/N})}\\[2mm]
&= \frac{1}{2}, \quad t = 1, 2, \dots, N.
\end{aligned}
$$

Continuous-time limit in distribution

We have the following convergence result.

Proposition 3.19. *Let h be a continuous and bounded function on $\mathbb{R}$. The price at time $t = 0$ of a contingent claim with payoff $C = h\big(S_{N,N}^{(1)}\big)$ converges as follows:*

$$\lim_{N\to\infty} \frac{1}{(1+rT/N)^N} \mathbb{E}^*\left[h\big(S_{N,N}^{(1)}\big)\right] = e^{-rT} \mathbb{E}\left[h\big(S_0^{(1)} e^{\sigma X + rT - \sigma^2 T/2}\big)\right] \qquad (3.45)$$

where $X \simeq \mathcal{N}(0, T)$ is a centered Gaussian random variable with variance $T > 0$.

Proof. This result is a consequence of the weak convergence in distribution of the sequence $\big(S_{N,N}^{(1)}\big)_{N\geqslant 1}$ to a lognormal distribution, see *e.g.* Theorem 5.53 page 261 of Föllmer and Schied (2004). Informally, using the Taylor expansion of the log function and (3.41), by (3.42) we have

$$
\begin{aligned}
\log S_{N,N}^{(1)} &= \log S_0^{(1)} + \sum_{k=1}^{N} \log\big(1 + R_k^{(N)}\big)\\[2mm]
&= \log S_0^{(1)} + \sum_{k=1}^{N} \log(1 + r_N) + \sum_{k=1}^{N} \log \frac{1 + R_k^{(N)}}{1 + r_N}
\end{aligned}
$$

$$
\begin{aligned}
&= \; \log S_0^{(1)} + \sum_{k=1}^{N} \log \left(1 + \frac{rT}{N}\right) + \sum_{k=1}^{N} \log \left(1 \pm \sigma \sqrt{\frac{T}{N}}\right) \\
&= \; \log S_0^{(1)} + \sum_{k=1}^{N} \frac{rT}{N} + \sum_{k=1}^{N} \left(\pm \sigma \sqrt{\frac{T}{N}} - \frac{\sigma^2 T}{2N} + o\left(\frac{T}{N}\right)\right) \\
&= \; \log S_0^{(1)} + rT - \frac{\sigma^2 T}{2} + \frac{1}{\sqrt{N}} \sum_{k=1}^{N} \pm \sqrt{\sigma^2 T} + o(1).
\end{aligned}
$$

Next, we note that by the Central Limit Theorem (CLT), the normalized sum

$$
\frac{1}{\sqrt{N}} \sum_{k=1}^{N} \pm \sqrt{\sigma^2 T}
$$

of independent Bernoulli random variables, with variance obtained from (3.43)–(3.44) as

$$
\begin{aligned}
\mathrm{Var}\left[\frac{1}{\sqrt{N}} \sum_{k=1}^{N} \pm \sqrt{\sigma^2 T}\right] &= \; 4 \frac{\sigma^2 T}{N} \sum_{k=1}^{N} (1 - \mathbb{P}^*(R_t^{(N)} = b_N)) \mathbb{P}^*(R_t^{(N)} = a_N) \\
&\simeq \; \sigma^2 T, \qquad [N \to \infty],
\end{aligned}
$$

converges in distribution to a centered $\mathcal{N}(0, \sigma^2 T)$ Gaussian random variable with variance $\sigma^2 T$. Finally, the convergence of the discount factor $(1 + rT/N)^N$ to e^{-rT} follows from (3.37). □

Note that the expectation (3.45) can be written as the Gaussian integral

$$
e^{-rT} \, \mathbb{E}\left[f\left(S_0^{(1)} e^{\sigma X + rT - \sigma^2 T/2}\right)\right] = e^{-rT} \int_{-\infty}^{\infty} f\left(S_0^{(1)} e^{\sigma \sqrt{T} x + rT - \sigma^2 T/2}\right) \frac{e^{-x^2/2}}{\sqrt{2\pi}} dx,
$$

see also Lemma 7.7 in Chapter 7, hence we have

$$
\lim_{N \to \infty} \frac{1}{(1 + rT/N)^N} \, \mathbb{E}^*\left[h\left(S_{N,N}^{(1)}\right)\right] = e^{-rT} \int_{-\infty}^{\infty} f\left(S_0^{(1)} e^{\sigma x \sqrt{T} + rT - \sigma^2 T/2}\right) \frac{e^{-x^2/2}}{\sqrt{2\pi}} dx.
$$

It is a remarkable fact that in case $h(x) = (x - K)^+$, *i.e.* when

$$
C = \left(S_T^{(1)} - K\right)^+
$$

is the payoff of the European call option with strike price K, the above integral can be computed according to the *Black–Scholes formula*, as

$$
e^{-rT} \, \mathbb{E}\left[\left(S_0^{(1)} e^{\sigma X + rT - \sigma^2 T/2} - K\right)^+\right] = S_0^{(1)} \Phi(d_+) - K e^{-rT} \Phi(d_-),
$$

where

$$
d_- = \frac{(r - \sigma^2/2)T + \log\left(S_0^{(1)}/K\right)}{\sigma \sqrt{T}}, \qquad d_+ = d_- + \sigma \sqrt{T},
$$

and

$$
\Phi(x) := \frac{1}{\sqrt{2\pi}} \int_{-\infty}^{x} e^{-y^2/2} dy, \qquad x \in \mathbb{R},
$$

is the Gaussian cumulative distribution function, see Proposition 6.3.

The Black–Scholes formula will be derived explicitly in the subsequent chapters using both PDE and probabilistic methods, cf. Propositions 6.11 and 7.6. It can be regarded as a building block for the pricing of financial derivatives, and its importance is not restricted to the pricing of options on stocks. Indeed, the complexity of the interest rate models makes it in general difficult to obtain closed-form expressions, and in many situations one has to rely on the Black–Scholes framework in order to find pricing formulas, for example in the case of interest rate derivatives as in the Black caplet formula of the BGM model, see Proposition 19.5 in Section 19.3.

Our aim later on will be to price and hedge options directly in continuous-time using stochastic calculus, instead of applying the limit procedure described in the previous section. In addition to the construction of the riskless asset price $(A_t)_{t\in\mathbb{R}_+}$ via (3.38) and (3.39) we now need to construct a mathematical model for the price of the risky asset in continuous time.

In addition to modeling the return of the riskless asset $S_t^{(0)}$ as in (3.40), the return of the risky asset $S_t^{(1)}$ over the time interval $[t, d + dt]$ will be modeled as

$$\frac{dS_t^{(1)}}{S_t^{(1)}} = \mu dt + \sigma dB_t,$$

where in comparison with (3.40), we add a "small" Gaussian random fluctuation σdB_t which accounts for market volatility. Here, the Brownian increment dB_t is multiplied by the volatility parameter $\sigma > 0$. In the next Chapter 4 we will turn to the formal definition of the stochastic process $(B_t)_{t\in\mathbb{R}_+}$ which will be used for the modeling of risky assets in continuous time.

Exercises

Exercise 3.1   (Exercise 2.5 continued). Consider a two-step trinomial market model $\left(S_t^{(1)}\right)_{t=0,1,2}$ with $r = 0$ and three possible return rates $R_t = -1, 0, 1$, and the risk-neutral probability measure $\mathbb{P}^*$ given by

$$\mathbb{P}^*(R_t = -1) := p^*, \quad \mathbb{P}^*(R_t = 0) := 1 - 2p^*, \quad \mathbb{P}^*(R_t = 1) := p^*.$$

Taking $S_0^{(1)} = 1$, price the European put option with strike price $K = 1$ and maturity $N = 2$ at times $t = 0$ and $t = 1$.

Exercise 3.2   Consider a two-step binomial market model $(S_t)_{t=0,1,2}$ with $S_0 = 1$ and stock return rates $a = 0$, $b = 1$, and a riskless account priced $A_t = (1 + r)^t$ at times $t = 0, 1, 2$, where $r = 0.5$. Price and hedge the *tunnel option* whose payoff C at time $t = 2$ is given by

$$C = \begin{cases} 3 & \text{if } S_2 = 4, \\ 1 & \text{if } S_2 = 2, \\ 3 & \text{if } S_2 = 1. \end{cases}$$

Exercise 3.3 In a two-step trinomial market model $(S_t)_{t=0,1,2}$ with interest rate $r = 0$ and three return rates $R_t = -0.5, 0, 1$, we consider a down-an-out barrier call option with exercise date $N = 2$, strike price K and barrier level B, whose payoff C is given by

$$C = (S_N - K)^+ \mathbb{1}_{\left\{ \min\limits_{t=1,2,\ldots,N} S_t > B \right\}} = \begin{cases} (S_N - K)^+ & \text{if} \quad \min\limits_{t=1,2,\ldots,N} S_t > B, \\ 0 & \text{if} \quad \min\limits_{t=1,2,\ldots,N} S_t \leqslant B. \end{cases}$$

a) Show that $\mathbb{P}^*$ given by $r^* = \mathbb{P}^*(R_t = -0.5) := 1/2$, $q^* = \mathbb{P}^*(R_t = 0) := 1/4$, $p^* = \mathbb{P}^*(R_t = 1) := 1/4$ is a risk-neutral probability measure.

b) Taking $S_0 = 1$, compute the possible values of the down-an-out barrier call option payoff C with strike price $K = 1.5$ and barrier level $B = 1$, at maturity $N = 2$.

c) Price the down-an-out barrier call option with exercise date $N = 2$, strike price $K = 1.5$ and barrier level $B = 1$, at time $t = 0$ and $t = 1$.

Hint: Use the formula

$$\pi_t(C) = \frac{1}{(1+r)^{N-t}} \mathbb{E}^*[C \mid S_t], \qquad t = 0, 1, \ldots, N,$$

where N denotes maturity time and C is the option payoff.

d) Is this market complete? Is every contingent claim attainable?

Exercise 3.4 Consider a two-step binomial random asset model $(S_k)_{k=0,1,2}$ with possible returns $a = 0$ and $b = 200\%$, and a riskless asset $A_k = A_0(1+r)^k$, $k = 0, 1, 2$ with interest rate $r = 100\%$, and $S_0 = A_0 = 1$, under the risk-neutral probabilities $p^* = (r-a)/(b-a) = 1/2$ and $q^* = (b-r)/(b-a) = 1/2$.

a) Draw a binomial tree for the possible values of $(S_k)_{k=0,1,2}$, and compute the values V_k at times $k = 0, 1, 2$ of the portfolio hedging the European *call* option on S_N with strike price $K = 8$ and maturity $N = 2$.

Hint: Consider three cases when $k = 2$, and two cases when $k = 1$.

b) Price, then hedge. Compute the self-financing hedging portfolio strategy $(\xi_k, \eta_k)_{k=1,2}$ with values

$$V_0 = \xi_1 S_0 + \eta_1 A_0, \ V_1 = \xi_1 S_1 + \eta_1 A_1 = \xi_2 S_1 + \eta_2 A_1, \ \text{and} \ V_2 = \xi_2 S_2 + \eta_2 A_2,$$

hedging the European *call* option with strike price $K = 8$ and maturity $N = 2$.

Hint: Consider two separate cases for $k = 2$ and one case for $k = 1$.

c) Hedge, then price. Compute the hedging portfolio strategy $(\xi_k, \eta_k)_{k=1,2}$ from the self-financing condition, and use it to recover the result of part (a).

Exercise 3.5 We consider a two-step binomial market model $(S_t)_{t=0,1,2}$ with $S_0 = 1$ and return rates $R_t = (S_t - S_{t-1})/S_{t-1}$, $t = 1, 2$, taking the values $a = 0$, $b = 1$, and assume that

$$p := \mathbb{P}(R_t = 1) > 0, \qquad q := \mathbb{P}(R_t = 0) > 0, \qquad t = 1, 2.$$

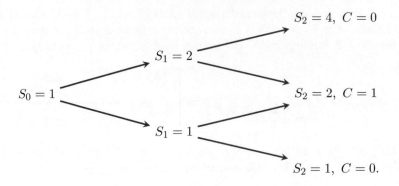

The riskless account is $A_t = \$1$ and the risk-free interest rate is $r = 0$. We consider the *tunnel option* whose payoff C at time $t = 2$ is given by

$$
C = \begin{cases}
0 & \text{if } S_2 = 4, \\
\$1 & \text{if } S_2 = 2, \\
0 & \text{if } S_2 = 1.
\end{cases}
$$

a) Build a hedging portfolio for the claim C at time $t = 1$ depending on the value of S_1.

b) Price the claim C at time $t = 1$ depending on the value of S_1.

c) Build a hedging portfolio for the claim C at time $t = 0$.

d) Price the claim C at time $t = 0$.

e) Does this model admit an equivalent risk-neutral measure in the sense of Definitions 2.12–2.14?

f) Is the model without arbitrage according to Theorem 2.15?

Exercise 3.6   Consider a discrete-time market model made of a riskless asset priced $A_k = (1 + r)^k$ and a risky asset with price S_k, $k \geqslant 0$, such that the discounted asset price process $((1 + r)^{-k} S_k)_{k \geqslant 0}$ is a martingale under a risk-neutral probability measure $\mathbb{P}^*$. Using Theorem 3.5, compute the arbitrage-free price $\pi_k(C)$ at time $k = 0, 1, \ldots, N$ of the claim C with maturity time N and affine payoff function

$$
C = h(S_N) = \alpha + \beta S_N
$$

where $\alpha, \beta \in \mathbb{R}$ are constants, in a discrete-time market with risk free rate r.

Exercise 3.7   Call-put parity.

a) Show that the relation $(x - K)^+ = x - K + (K - x)^+$ holds for any $K, x \in \mathbb{R}$.

b) From part (a), find a relation between the prices of call and put options with strike price $K > 0$ and maturity $N \geqslant 1$ in a market with risk-free rate $r > 0$.

Hints:

i) Recall that an option with payoff $\phi(S_N)$ and maturity $N \geqslant 1$ is priced at times $k = 0, 1, \ldots, N$ as $(1+r)^{-(N-k)} \, \mathbb{E}^* \left[\phi(S_N) \, | \, \mathcal{F}_k \right]$ under the risk-neutral measure $\mathbb{P}^*$.

ii) The payoff at maturity of a European call (resp. put) option with strike price K is $(S_N - K)^+$, resp. $(K - S_N)^+$.

Exercise 3.8 Consider a two-step binomial random asset model $(S_k)_{k=0,1,2}$ with possible returns $a = -50\%$ and $b = 150\%$, and a riskless asset $A_k = A_0(1+r)^k$, $k = 0, 1, 2$ with interest rate $r = 100\%$, and $S_0 = A_0 = 1$, under the risk-neutral probabilities $p^* = (r-a)/(b-a) = 3/4$ and $q^* = (b-r)/(b-a) = 1/4$.

a) Draw a binomial tree for the values of $(S_k)_{k=0,1,2}$.

b) Compute the values V_k at times $k = 0, 1, 2$ of the hedging portfolio of the European *put* option with strike price $K = 5/4$ and maturity $N = 2$ on S_N.

c) Compute the self-financing hedging portfolio strategy $(\xi_k, \eta_k)_{k=1,2}$ with values

$$V_0 = \xi_1 S_0 + \eta_1 A_0, \quad V_1 = \xi_1 S_1 + \eta_1 A_1 = \xi_2 S_1 + \eta_2 A_1, \quad \text{and } V_2 = \xi_2 S_2 + \eta_2 A_2,$$

hedging the European *put* option on S_N with strike price $K := 5/4$ and maturity $N := 2$.

Exercise 3.9 Analysis of a binary option trading website.

a) In a one-step model with risky asset prices S_0, S_1 at times $t = 0$ and $t = 1$, compute the price at time $t = 0$ of the binary call option with payoff

$$C = \mathbb{1}_{[K,\infty)}(S_1) = \begin{cases} \$1 & \text{if } S_1 \geqslant K, \\ \\ 0 & \text{if } S_1 < K, \end{cases}$$

in terms of the probability $p^* = \mathbb{P}^*(S_1 \geqslant K)$ and of the risk-free interest rate r.

b) Compute the two potential net returns obtained by purchasing one binary call option.

c) Compute the corresponding expected (net) return.

d) A website proposes to pay a return of 86% in case the binary call option matures "in the money", *i.e.* when $S_1 \geqslant K$. Compute the corresponding expected (net) return. What do you conclude?

Exercise 3.10 A *put spread collar* option requires its holder to *sell* an asset at the price $f(S)$ when its market price is at the level S, where $f(S)$ is the function plotted in Figure 3.10, with $K_1 := 80$, $K_2 := 90$, and $K_3 := 110$.

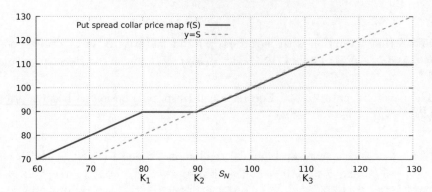

Figure 3.10: Put spread collar price map.

a) Draw the *payoff function* of the put spread collar as a function of the underlying asset price at maturity.

b) Show that this put spread collar option can be realized by purchasing and/or issuing standard European call and put options with strike prices to be specified.

   Hints: Recall that an option with payoff $\phi(S_N)$ is priced $(1+r)^{-N} \mathbb{E}^* \left[\phi(S_N) \right]$ at time 0. The payoff of the European call (resp. put) option with strike price K is $(S_N - K)^+$, resp. $(K - S_N)^+$.

Exercise 3.11 A *call spread collar* option requires its holder to *buy* an asset at the price $f(S)$ when its market price is at the level S, where $f(S)$ is the function plotted in Figure 3.10, with $K_1 := 80$, $K_2 := 100$, and $K_3 := 110$.

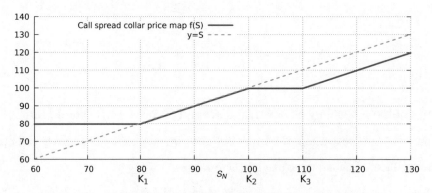

Figure 3.11: Call spread collar price map.

a) Draw the *payoff function* of the call spread collar as a function of the underlying asset price at maturity.

b) Show that this call spread collar option can be realized by purchasing and/or issuing standard European call and put options with strike prices to be specified.

   Hints: Recall that an option with payoff $\phi(S_N)$ is priced $(1+r)^{-N} \mathbb{E}^* \left[\phi(S_N) \right]$ at time 0. The payoff of the European call (resp. put) option with strike price K is $(S_N - K)^+$, resp. $(K - S_N)^+$.

Exercise 3.12 Consider an asset price $(S_n)_{n=0,1,...,N}$ which is a martingale under the risk-neutral probability measure $\mathbb{P}^*$, with respect to the filtration $(\mathcal{F}_n)_{n=0,1,...,N}$. Given the (convex) function $\phi(x) := (x - K)^+$, show that the price of an Asian option with payoff

$$\phi\left(\frac{S_1 + \cdots + S_N}{N}\right)$$

and maturity $N \geqslant 1$ is always lower than the price of the corresponding European *call* option, *i.e.* show that

$$\mathbb{E}^*\left[\phi\left(\frac{S_1 + S_2 + \cdots + S_N}{N}\right)\right] \leqslant \mathbb{E}^*[\phi(S_N)].$$

Hint: Use in the following order:

(i) the convexity inequality $\phi(x_1/N + \cdots + x_N/N) \leqslant \phi(x_1)/N + \cdots + \phi(x_N)/N$,

(ii) the martingale property $S_k = \mathbb{E}^*[S_N \mid \mathcal{F}_k]$, $k = 1, 2, \ldots, N$.

(iii) Jensen's inequality

$$\phi(\mathbb{E}^*[S_N \mid \mathcal{F}_k]) \leqslant \mathbb{E}^*[\phi(S_N) \mid \mathcal{F}_k], \qquad k = 1, 2, \ldots, N,$$

(iv) the tower property $\mathbb{E}^*[\mathbb{E}^*[\phi(S_N) \mid \mathcal{F}_k]] = \mathbb{E}^*[\phi(S_N)]$ of conditional expectations, $k = 1, 2, \ldots, N$.

Exercise 3.13 (Exercise 2.7 continued).

a) We consider a forward contract on S_N with strike price K and payoff

$$C := S_N - K.$$

Find a portfolio allocation (η_N, ξ_N) with value

$$V_N = \eta_N \pi_N + \xi_N S_N$$

at time N, such that

$$V_N = C, \tag{3.46}$$

by writing Condition (3.46) as a 2×2 system of equations.

b) Find a portfolio allocation (η_{N-1}, ξ_{N-1}) with value

$$V_{N-1} = \eta_{N-1} \pi_{N-1} + \xi_{N-1} S_{N-1}$$

at time $N - 1$, and verifying the self-financing condition

$$V_{N-1} = \eta_N \pi_{N-1} + \xi_N S_{N-1}.$$

Next, at all times $t = 1, 2, \ldots, N - 1$, find a portfolio allocation (η_t, ξ_t) with value $V_t = \eta_t \pi_t + \xi_t S_t$ verifying (3.46) and the self-financing condition

$$V_t = \eta_{t+1} \pi_t + \xi_{t+1} S_t,$$

where η_t, *resp.* ξ_t, represents the quantity of the riskless, *resp.* risky, asset in the portfolio over the time period $[t - 1, t]$, $t = 1, 2, \ldots, N - 1$.

c) Compute the arbitrage-free price $\pi_t(C) = V_t$ of the forward contract C, at time $t = 0, 1, \ldots, N$.

d) Check that the arbitrage-free price $\pi_t(C)$ satisfies the relation

$$\pi_t(C) = \frac{1}{(1+r)^{N-t}} \, \mathbb{E}^*[C \mid \mathcal{F}_t], \qquad t = 0, 1, \ldots, N.$$

Exercise 3.14 Power option. Let $(S_n)_{n \in \mathbb{N}}$ denote a binomial price process with returns -50% and $+50\%$, and let the riskless asset be valued $A_k = \$1$, $k \in \mathbb{N}$. We consider a power option with payoff $C := (S_N)^2$, and a *predictable* self-financing portfolio strategy $(\xi_k, \eta_k)_{k=1,2,\ldots,N}$ with value

$$V_k = \xi_k S_k + \eta_k A_0, \qquad k = 1, 2, \ldots, N.$$

a) Find the portfolio allocation (ξ_N, η_N) that matches the payoff $C = (S_N)^2$ at time N, i.e. that satisfies

$$V_N = (S_N)^2.$$

Hint: We have $\eta_N = -3(S_{N-1})^2/4$.

b) In the following questions we use the risk-neutral probability $p^* = 1/2$ of a $+50\%$ return.

i) Compute the portfolio value

$$V_{N-1} = \mathbb{E}^*[C \mid \mathcal{F}_{N-1}].$$

ii) Find the portfolio allocation (η_{N-1}, ξ_{N-1}) at time $N-1$ from the relation

$$V_{N-1} = \xi_{N-1} S_{N-1} + \eta_{N-1} A_0.$$

Hint: We have $\eta_{N-1} = -15(S_{N-2})^2/16$.

iii) Check that the portfolio satisfies the self-financing condition

$$V_{N-1} = \xi_{N-1} S_{N-1} + \eta_{N-1} A_0 = \xi_N S_{N-1} + \eta_N A_0.$$

Exercise 3.15 Consider the discrete-time Cox–Ross–Rubinstein model with $N+1$ time instants $t = 0, 1, \ldots, N$. The price S_t^0 of the riskless asset evolves as $S_t^0 = \pi^0(1+r)^t$, $t = 0, 1, \ldots, N$. The *return* of the risky asset, defined as

$$R_t := \frac{S_t - S_{t-1}}{S_{t-1}}, \qquad t = 1, 2, \ldots, N,$$

is random and allowed to take only two values a and b, with $-1 < a < r < b$.

The discounted asset price is given by $\widetilde{S}_t := S_t/(1+r)^t$, $t = 0, 1, \ldots, N$.

a) Show that this model admits a unique risk-neutral probability measure $\mathbb{P}^*$ and explicitly compute $\mathbb{P}^*(R_t = a)$ and $\mathbb{P}(R_t = b)$ for all $t = 1, 2, \ldots, N$, with $a = 2\%$, $b = 7\%$, $r = 5\%$.

b) Does there exist arbitrage opportunities in this model? Explain why.

c) Is this market model complete? Explain why.

d) Consider a contingent claim with payoff[*]

$$C = (S_N)^2.$$

Compute the discounted arbitrage-free price $\widetilde{V}_t$, $t = 0, 1, \ldots, N$, of a self-financing portfolio hedging the claim payoff C, *i.e.* such that

$$V_N = C = (S_N)^2, \quad \text{or} \quad \widetilde{V}_N = \widetilde{C} = \frac{(S_N)^2}{(1+r)^N}.$$

e) Compute the portfolio strategy

$$\left(\bar{\xi}_t\right)_{t=1,2,\ldots,N} = \left(\xi_t^0, \xi_t^1\right)_{t=1,2,\ldots,N}$$

associated to $\widetilde{V}_t$, *i.e.* such that

$$\widetilde{V}_t = \bar{\xi}_t \bullet \overline{X}_t = \xi_t^0 X_t^0 + \xi_t^1 X_t^1, \qquad t = 1, 2, \ldots, N.$$

f) Check that the above portfolio strategy is self-financing, *i.e.*

$$\bar{\xi}_t \bullet \overline{S}_t = \bar{\xi}_{t+1} \bullet \overline{S}_t, \qquad t = 1, 2, \ldots, N-1.$$

Exercise 3.16 We consider the discrete-time Cox–Ross–Rubinstein model with $N+1$ time instants $t = 0, 1, \ldots, N$.

The price π_t of the riskless asset evolves as $\pi_t = \pi_0(1+r)^t$, $t = 0, 1, \ldots, N$. The evolution of S_{t-1} to S_t is given by

$$S_t = \begin{cases} (1+b)S_{t-1} & \text{if } R_t = b, \\ \\ (1+a)S_{t-1} & \text{if } R_t = a, \end{cases}$$

with $-1 < a < r < b$. The *return* of the risky asset is defined as

$$R_t := \frac{S_t - S_{t-1}}{S_{t-1}}, \qquad t = 1, 2, \ldots, N.$$

Let ξ_t, *resp.* η_t, denote the (possibly fractional) quantities of the risky, *resp.* riskless, asset held over the time period $[t-1, t]$ in the portfolio with value

$$V_t = \xi_t S_t + \eta_t \pi_t, \qquad t = 0, 1, \ldots, N. \tag{3.47}$$

a) Show that

$$V_t = (1 + R_t)\xi_t S_{t-1} + (1+r)\eta_t \pi_{t-1}, \qquad t = 1, 2, \ldots, N. \tag{3.48}$$

b) Show that under the probability $\mathbb{P}^*$ defined by

$$\mathbb{P}^*(R_t = a \mid \mathcal{F}_{t-1}) = \frac{b-r}{b-a}, \qquad \mathbb{P}^*(R_t = b \mid \mathcal{F}_{t-1}) = \frac{r-a}{b-a},$$

where $\mathcal{F}_{t-1}$ represents the information generated by $\{R_1, R_2, \ldots, R_{t-1}\}$, we have

$$\mathbb{E}^*[R_t \mid \mathcal{F}_{t-1}] = r.$$

---

[*]This is the payoff of a power call option with strike price $K = 0$.

c) Under the self-financing condition

$$V_{t-1} = \xi_t S_{t-1} + \eta_t \pi_{t-1}, \qquad t = 1, 2, \ldots, N, \tag{3.49}$$

recover the martingale property

$$V_{t-1} = \frac{1}{1+r} \, \mathbb{E}^*[V_t \mid \mathcal{F}_{t-1}],$$

using the result of Question (a).

d) Let $a = 5\%$, $b = 25\%$ and $r = 15\%$. Assume that the value V_t at time t of the portfolio is \$3 if $R_t = a$ and \$8 if $R_t = b$, and compute the value V_{t-1} of the portfolio at time $t-1$.

Problem 3.17   CRR model with transaction costs (Boyle and Vorst (1992), Mel′nikov and Petrachenko (2005)). Stock broker income is generated by commissions or transaction costs representing the difference between ask prices (at which they are willing to sell an asset to their client), and bid prices (at which they are willing to buy an asset from their client).

We consider a discrete-time Cox–Ross–Rubinstein model with one risky asset priced S_t at time $t = 0, 1, \ldots, N$. The price A_t of the riskless asset evolves as

$$A_t = \rho^t, \qquad t = 0, 1, \ldots, N,$$

with $A_0 := 1$ and $\rho > 0$, and the random evolution of S_{t-1} to S_t is given by two possible returns α, β as

$$S_t = \begin{cases} \beta S_{t-1} \\ \\ \alpha S_{t-1} \end{cases}$$

$t = 1, \ldots, N$, with $0 < \alpha < \beta$.

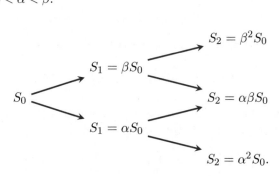

Figure 3.12: Tree of market prices with $N = 2$.

The ask and bid prices of the risky asset quoted S_t on the market are respectively given by $(1 + \lambda)S_t$, and $(1 - \lambda)S_t$ for some $\lambda \in [0, 1)$, such that

$$\begin{cases} \alpha^\uparrow := \alpha(1 + \lambda) < \beta(1 - \lambda) =: \beta_\downarrow, \\ \alpha_\downarrow := \alpha(1 - \lambda) < \beta(1 - \lambda) := \beta_\downarrow, \\ \alpha^\uparrow := \alpha(1 + \lambda) < \beta(1 + \lambda) =: \beta^\uparrow, \end{cases}$$

i.e. transaction costs are charged at the rate $\lambda \in [0, 1)$, proportionally to the traded amount.

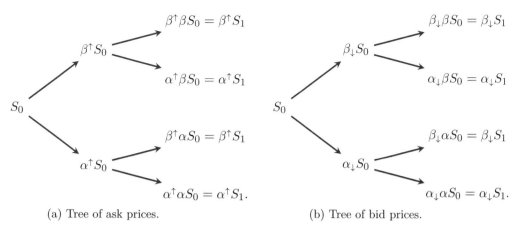

(a) Tree of ask prices. (b) Tree of bid prices.

Figure 3.13: Trees of bid and ask prices with $N = 2$.

The riskless asset is not subject to transaction costs or bid/ask prices and is priced A_t at time $t = 0, 1, \ldots, N$. We consider a predictable, self-financing replicating portfolio strategy

$$(\eta_t(S_{t-1}), \xi_t(S_{t-1}))_{t=1,2,\ldots,N}.$$

made of $\eta_t(S_{t-1})$ of the riskless asset A_t and of $\xi_t(S_{t-1})$ units of the risky asset S_t at time $t = 1, 2, \ldots, N$.

Our goal is to derive a backward recursion giving $\xi_t(S_{t-1})$, $\eta_t(S_{t-1})$ from $\xi_{t+1}(S_t)$, $\eta_{t+1}(S_t)$ for $t = N-1, N-2\ldots, 1$. The following questions are interdependent and should be treated in sequence.

a) We consider a portfolio reallocation $(\eta_t(S_{t-1}), \xi_t(S_{t-1})) \to (\eta_{t+1}(S_t), \xi_{t+1}(S_t))$ at time $t \in \{1, \ldots, N-1\}$. Write down the self-financing condition in the event of:

   i) an *increase* in the stock position from $\xi_t(S_{t-1})$ to $\xi_{t+1}(S_t)$,

   ii) a *decrease* in the stock position from $\xi_t(S_{t-1})$ to $\xi_{t+1}(S_t)$.

   The conditions are written using $\eta_t(S_{t-1})$, $\eta_{t+1}(S_t)$, $\xi_t(S_{t-1})$, $\xi_{t+1}(S_t)$, A_t, S_t and λ.

b) From Questions ai)-aii), deduce two self-financing equations in case $S_t = \alpha S_{t-1}$, and two self-financing equations in case $S_t = \beta S_{t-1}$.

c) Using the functions

$$g_\alpha(x, y) := \begin{cases} \alpha^\uparrow & \text{if } x \leqslant y, \\ \alpha_\downarrow & \text{if } x > y, \end{cases} \quad \text{and} \quad g_\beta(x, y) := \begin{cases} \beta^\uparrow & \text{if } x \leqslant y, \\ \beta_\downarrow & \text{if } x > y, \end{cases}$$

   rewrite the equations of Question (b) into a single equation in case $S_t = \alpha S_{t-1}$, and a single equation in case $S_t = \beta S_{t-1}$.

d) From the result of Question (c), derive an equation satisfied by $\xi_t(S_{t-1})$, and show that it admits a unique solution $\xi_t(S_{t-1})$.

   Hint: Show that the *piecewise affine* function

$$x \mapsto f(x, S_{t-1}) := g_\beta(x, \xi_{t+1}(\beta S_{t-1}))(x - \xi_{t+1}(\beta S_{t-1}))$$

$$-g_\alpha(x, \xi_{t+1}(\alpha S_{t-1}))(x - \xi_{t+1}(\alpha S_{t-1})) - \rho \frac{\eta_{t+1}(\beta S_{t-1}) - \eta_{t+1}(\alpha S_{t-1})}{\widetilde{S}_{t-1}}$$

   is strictly increasing in $x \in \mathbb{R}$.

e) Find the expressions of $\xi_t(S_{t-1})$ and $\eta_t(S_{t-1})$ by solving the 2×2 system of equations of Question (c).

   Hint: The expressions have to use the quantities

   $$g_\alpha(\xi_t(S_{t-1}), \xi_{t+1}(\alpha S_{t-1})), \qquad g_\beta(\xi_t(S_{t-1}), \xi_{t+1}(\beta S_{t-1})),$$

   and they should be consistent with Proposition 3.12 when $\lambda = 0$, *i.e.* when $\alpha^\uparrow = \alpha_\downarrow = 1 + a$ and $\beta^\uparrow = \beta_\downarrow = 1 + b$, with $\rho = 1 + r$.

f) Find the value of $g_\alpha(\xi_t(S_{t-1}), \xi_{t+1}(\alpha S_{t-1}))$ in the following two cases:

   i) $f(\xi_{t+1}(\alpha S_{t-1}), S_{t-1}) \geqslant 0$,

   ii) $f(\xi_{t+1}(\alpha S_{t-1}), S_{t-1}) < 0$,

   and the value of $g_\beta(\xi_t(S_{t-1}), \xi_{t+1}(\beta S_{t-1}))$ in the following two cases:

   i) $f(\xi_{t+1}(\beta S_{t-1}), S_{t-1}) \geqslant 0$,

   ii) $f(\xi_{t+1}(\beta S_{t-1}), S_{t-1}) < 0$.

g) Hedge and price the call option with strike price $K = \$2$ and $N = 2$ when $S_0 = 8$, $\rho = 1$, $\alpha = 0.5$, $\beta = 2$, and the transaction cost rate is $\lambda = 12.5\%$. Provide sufficient details of hand calculations.

   Remark: The evaluation of the terminal payoff uses the value of S_2 only and is not affected by bid/ask prices.

Figure 3.14: ₿TC/USD order book example.

In the above figure, ask prices are marked in red and bid prices are marked in green. The center column gives the quantity of the asset available at that row's bid or ask price, and the right column represents the cumulative volume of orders from the last-traded price until the current bid/ask price level. The large number in the center shows the last-traded price.

Problem 3.18 **CRR model with dividends (1).** Consider a two-step binomial model for a stock paying a dividend at the *rate* $\alpha \in (0,1)$ at times $k = 1$ and $k = 2$, and the following recombining tree represents the *ex-dividend** prices S_k at times $k = 1, 2$, starting from $S_0 = \$1$.

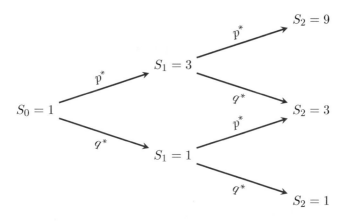

```
1   install.packages("quantmod");library(quantmod)
    getDividends("Z74.SI",from="2018-01-01",to="2018-12-31",src="yahoo")
3   getSymbols("Z74.SI",from="2018-11-16",to="2018-12-19",src="yahoo")
    dev.new(width=16,height=7)
5   myPars <- chart_pars();myPars$cex<-1.8
    myTheme <- chart_theme();myTheme$col$line.col <- "purple"
7   myTheme$rylab <- FALSE
    chart_Series(Op(`Z74.SI`),name="Opening prices (purple) - Closing prices
        (blue)",lty=4,lwd=6,pars=myPars,theme=myTheme)
9   add_TA(Cl(`Z74.SI`),lwd=3,lty=5,legend='Difference',col="blue",on = 1)
```

	Z74.SI.div
2018-07-26	0.107
2018-12-17	0.068
2018-12-18	0.068

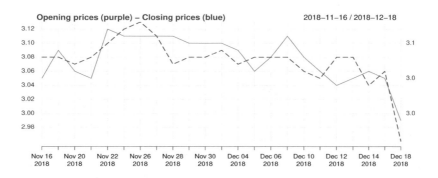

Figure 3.15: SGD0.068 dividend detached on December 18, 2018 on Z74.SI.

---

*"Ex-dividend" means after dividend payment.

The difference between the closing price on December 17 ($3.06) and the opening price on December 18 ($2.99) is $3.06 - $2.99 = $0.07. The adjusted price on December 17 ($2.992) is the closing price ($3.06) minus the dividend ($0.068).

Z74.SI	Open	High	Low	Close	Volume	Adjusted (ex-dividend)
2018-12-17	3.05	3.08	3.05	**3.06**	17441000	**2.992**
2018-12-18	**2.99**	2.99	2.96	2.96	28456400	2.960

The dividend rate α is given by $\alpha = 0.068/3.06 = 2.22\%$.

We consider a riskless asset $A_k = A_0(1+r)^k$, $k = 0, 1, 2$ with interest rate $r = 100\%$ and $A_0 = 1$, and two portfolio allocations (ξ_1, η_1) at time $k = 0$ and (ξ_2, η_2) at time $k = 1$, with the values

$$V_1 = \xi_2 S_1 + \eta_2 A_1 \tag{3.50}$$

and

$$V_0 = \xi_1 S_0 + \eta_1 A_0. \tag{3.51}$$

We make the following three assumptions:

[A] All dividends are reinvested.

[B] The portfolio strategies are self-financing.

[C] The portfolio value V_2 at time $k = 2$ hedges the European *call* option with payoff $C = (S_T - K)^+$, strike price $K = 8$, and maturity $T = 2$.

a) Using (3.50) and **[A]**, express V_2 in terms of ξ_2, η_2, S_2, A_2 and α.

b) Using (3.51) and **[A]-[B]**, express V_1 in terms of ξ_1, η_1, S_1, A_1 and α.

c) Using Assumption **[C]** and the result of Question (a), compute the portfolio allocation (ξ_2, η_2) in cases $S_1 = 1$ and $S_1 = 3$.

d) Using (3.50) and the portfolio allocation (ξ_2, η_2) obtained in Question (c), compute the portfolio value V_1 in cases $S_1 = 1$ and $S_1 = 3$.

e) From the results of Questions (b) and (d), compute the initial portfolio allocation (ξ_1, η_1).

f) Compute the initial portfolio value V_0 from the result of Question (e).

g) Knowing that the dividend rate is $\alpha = 25\%$, draw the tree of asset prices $(\bar{S}_k)_{k=1,2}$ *before* (*i.e.* without) dividend payments.

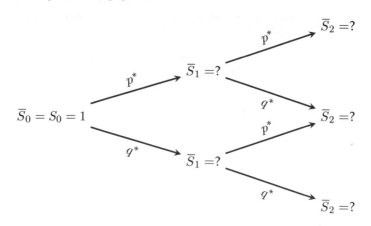

h) Compute the risk-neutral probabilities p^* and q^* under which the conditional expected return of $(\overline{S}_k)_{k=0,1,2}$ is the risk-free interest rate $r = 100\%$.

i) ✓ Check that the portfolio value V_1 found in Question (d) satisfies

$$V_1 = \frac{1}{1+r}\, \mathbb{E}^*[(S_2 - K)^+ \mid S_1].$$

j) ✓ Check that the portfolio value V_0 found in Question (f) satisfies

$$V_0 = \frac{1}{(1+r)^2}\, \mathbb{E}^*\left[(S_2 - K)^+\right] \quad \text{and} \quad V_0 = \frac{1}{1+r}\, \mathbb{E}^*[V_1].$$

Problem 3.19 CRR model with dividends (2). We consider a riskless asset priced as

$$S_k^{(0)} = S_0^{(0)}(1+r)^k, \qquad k = 0, 1, \ldots, N,$$

with $r > -1$, and a risky asset $S^{(1)}$ whose *return* is given by

$$R_k := \frac{S_k^{(1)} - S_{k-1}^{(1)}}{S_{k-1}^{(1)}}, \qquad k = 1, 2, \ldots, N,$$

with $N+1$ time instants $k = 0, 1, \ldots, N$ and $d = 1$. In the CRR model the return R_k is random and allowed to take two values a and b at each time step, *i.e.*

$$R_k \in \{a, b\}, \qquad k = 1, 2, \ldots, N,$$

with $-1 < a < 0 < b$, and the random evolution of $S_{k-1}^{(1)}$ to $S_k^{(1)}$ is given by

$$S_k^{(1)} = \left\{ \begin{array}{ll} (1+b)S_{k-1}^{(1)} & \text{if } R_k = b \\ (1+a)S_{k-1}^{(1)} & \text{if } R_k = a \end{array} \right\} = (1+R_k)S_{k-1}^{(1)}, \qquad k = 1, 2, \ldots, N, \qquad (3.52)$$

according to the tree

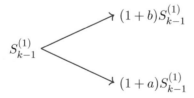

and we have

$$S_k^{(1)} = S_0^{(1)} \prod_{i=1}^{k}(1+R_i), \qquad k = 0, 1, \ldots, N.$$

The information $\mathcal{F}_k$ known to the market up to time k is given by the knowledge of $S_1^{(1)}, S_2^{(1)}, \ldots, S_k^{(1)}$, *i.e.* we write

$$\mathcal{F}_k = \sigma\left(S_1^{(1)}, S_2^{(1)}, \ldots, S_k^{(1)}\right) = \sigma(R_1, R_2, \ldots, R_k),$$

$k = 0, 1, \ldots, N$, where $S_0^{(1)}$ is a constant and $\mathcal{F}_0 = \{\emptyset, \Omega\}$ contains no information.

Under the risk-neutral probability measure $\mathbb{P}^*$ defined by

$$p^* := \mathbb{P}^*(R_k = b) = \frac{r-a}{b-a} > 0, \quad q^* := \mathbb{P}^*(R_k = a) = \frac{b-r}{b-a} > 0,$$

$k = 1, 2, \ldots, N$, the asset returns $(R_k)_{k=1,2,\ldots,N}$ form a sequence of independent identically distributed random variables.

In what follows we assume that the stock S_k pays a dividend *rate* $\alpha > 0$ at times $k = 1, 2, \ldots, N$. At the beginning of every time step $k = 1, 2, \ldots, N$, the price S_k is immediately adjusted to its *ex-dividend* level by losing $\alpha\%$ of its value. The following ten questions are interdependent and should be treated in sequence.

a) Rewrite the evolution (3.52) of $S_{k-1}^{(1)}$ to $S_k^{(1)}$ in the presence of a *daily* dividend rate $\alpha > 0$.

b) Express the dividend amount as a percentage of the ex-dividend price $S_k^{(1)}$, and show that under the risk-neutral probability measure the return of the risky asset satisfies

$$\mathbb{E}^*\left[\frac{S_{k+1}^{(1)}}{1-\alpha}\,\middle|\,\mathcal{F}_k\right] = (1+r)S_k^{(1)}, \qquad k = 0, 1, \ldots, N-1.$$

c) We consider a (predictable) portfolio strategy $(\xi_k, \eta_k)_{k=1,2,\ldots,N}$ with value process

$$V_k = \xi_{k+1} S_k^{(1)} + \eta_{k+1} S_k^{(0)}$$

at time $k = 0, 1, \ldots, N-1$. Write down the self-financing condition for the portfolio value process $(V_k)_{k=0,1,\ldots,N}$ by taking into account the reinvested dividends, and give the expression of V_N.

d) Show that under the self-financing condition, the discounted portfolio value process

$$\widetilde{V}_k := \frac{V_k}{S_k^{(0)}}, \qquad k = 0, 1, \ldots, N,$$

is a martingale under the risk-neutral probability measure $\mathbb{P}^*$.

e) Show that the price at time $k = 0, 1, \ldots, N$ of a claim with random payoff C can be written as

$$V_k = \frac{1}{(1+r)^{N-k}}\, \mathbb{E}^*[C \mid \mathcal{F}_k], \qquad k = 0, 1, \ldots, N,$$

assuming that the claim C is attained at time N by the portfolio strategy $(\xi_k, \eta_k)_{k=1,2,\ldots,N}$.

f) Compute the price at time $t = 0, 1, \ldots, N$ of a vanilla option with payoff $h(S_N^{(1)})$ using the pricing function

$$C_0(k, x, N, a, b, r)$$

$$:= \frac{1}{(1+r)^{N-k}} \sum_{l=0}^{N-k} \binom{N-k}{l} (p^*)^l (q^*)^{N-k-l} h\left(x(1+b)^l(1+a)^{N-k-l}\right)$$

of a vanilla claim with payoff $h(S_N^{(1)})$.

g) Show that the price at time $t = 0, 1, \ldots, N$ of a vanilla option with payoff function $h\big(S_N^{(1)}\big)$ can be rewritten as

$$V_k = C_\alpha\big(k, S_k^{(1)}, N, a_\alpha, b_\alpha, r_\alpha\big) := (1 - \alpha)^{N-k} C_0\big(k, S_k^{(1)}, N, a_\alpha, b_\alpha, r_\alpha\big),$$

$k = 0, 1, \ldots, N$, where the coefficients $a_\alpha, b_\alpha, r_\alpha$ will be determined explicitly.

h) Find a recurrence relation between the functions $C_\alpha\big(k, x, N, a_\alpha, b_\alpha, r_\alpha\big)$ and $C_\alpha\big(k + 1, x, N, a_\alpha, b_\alpha, r_\alpha\big)$ using the martingale property of the discounted portfolio value process $(\widetilde{V}_k)_{k=0,1,\ldots,N}$ under the risk-neutral probability measure $\mathbb{P}^*$.

i) Using the function $C_0\big(k, x, N, a_\alpha, b_\alpha, r_\alpha\big)$, compute the quantity ξ_k of risky asset $S_k^{(1)}$ allocated on the time interval $[k - 1, k)$ in a self-financing portfolio hedging the claim $C = h\big(S_N^{(1)}\big)$.

j) How are the dividends reinvested in the self-financing hedging portfolio?

Problem 3.20 We consider a *ternary tree* (or *trinomial*) model with $N + 1$ time instants $k = 0, 1, \ldots, N$ and $d = 1$ risky asset. The price $S_k^{(0)}$ of the riskless asset evolves as

$$S_k^{(0)} = S_0^{(0)}(1 + r)^k, \qquad k = 0, 1, \ldots, N,$$

with $r > -1$. Let the *return* of the risky asset $S^{(1)}$ be defined as

$$R_k := \frac{S_k^{(1)} - S_{k-1}^{(1)}}{S_{k-1}^{(1)}}, \qquad k = 1, 2, \ldots, N.$$

In this ternary tree model, the return R_k is random and allowed to take only three values a, 0 and b at each time step, *i.e.*

$$R_k \in \{a, 0, b\}, \qquad k = 1, 2, \ldots, N,$$

with $-1 < a < 0 < b$. That means, the evolution of $S_{k-1}^{(1)}$ to $S_k^{(1)}$ is random and given by

$$S_k^{(1)} = \begin{cases} (1 + b)S_{k-1}^{(1)} & \text{if } R_k = b \\ S_{k-1}^{(1)} & \text{if } R_k = 0 \\ (1 + a)S_{k-1}^{(1)} & \text{if } R_k = a \end{cases} = (1 + R_k)S_{k-1}^{(1)}, \quad k = 1, 2, \ldots, N,$$

and

$$S_k^{(1)} = S_0^{(1)} \prod_{i=1}^{k}(1 + R_i), \qquad k = 0, 1, \ldots, N.$$

The price process $\big(S_k^{(1)}\big)_{k=0,1,\ldots,N}$ evolves on a ternary tree of the form:

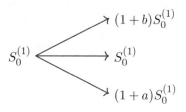

The information $\mathcal{F}_k$ known to the market up to time k is given by the knowledge of $S_1^{(1)}, S_2^{(1)}, \ldots, S_k^{(1)}$, *i.e.* we write

$$\mathcal{F}_k = \sigma\big(S_1^{(1)}, S_2^{(1)}, \ldots, S_k^{(1)}\big) = \sigma(R_1, R_2, \ldots, R_k),$$

$k = 0, 1, \ldots, N$, where, as a convention, $S_0^{(1)}$ is a constant and $\mathcal{F}_0 = \{\emptyset, \Omega\}$ contains no information. In what follows we will consider that $(R_k)_{k=1,2,\ldots,N}$ is a sequence of independent identically distributed random variables under any risk-neutral probability measure $\mathbb{P}^*$, and we denote

$$
\begin{cases}
p^* := \mathbb{P}^*(R_k = b) > 0, \\[2mm]
\theta^* := \mathbb{P}^*(R_k = 0) > 0, \\[2mm]
q^* := \mathbb{P}^*(R_k = a) > 0, \quad k = 1, 2, \ldots, N.
\end{cases}
$$

a) Determine all possible risk-neutral probability measures $\mathbb{P}^*$ equivalent to $\mathbb{P}$ in terms of the parameter $\theta^* \in (0, 1)$.

b) Give a necessary and sufficient condition for the absence of arbitrage in this ternary tree model.

    <u>Hint</u>: Use your intuition of the market to find what the condition should be, and then prove that it is necessary and sufficient. Note that we have $a < 0$ and $b > 0$, and the condition should only depend on the model parameters a, b and r.

c) When the model parameters allow for arbitrage opportunities, explain how you would exploit them if you joined the market with zero money to invest.

d) Is this ternary tree market model complete?

e) In this question we assume that the conditional variance

$$\mathrm{Var}^*\left[\frac{S_{k+1}^{(1)} - S_k^{(1)}}{S_k^{(1)}} \,\bigg|\, \mathcal{F}_k \right] = \sigma^2 > 0$$

of the asset return $(S_{k+1}^{(1)} - S_k^{(1)})/S_k^{(1)}$ given $\mathcal{F}_k$ is constant and equal to σ^2, $k = 0, 1, \ldots, N-1$. Show that this condition determines a unique value of θ^* and a unique risk-neutral probability measure $\mathbb{P}_\sigma^*$ to be written explicitly, under a certain condition on a, b, r and σ.

f) In this question and in the following we impose the condition $(1+a)(1+b) = 1$, *i.e.* we let $a := -b/(b+1)$. What does this imply on this ternary tree model and on the risk-neutral probability measure $\mathbb{P}^*$?

g) We consider a vanilla financial claim with payoff $C = h(S_N)$ and maturity N, priced as time k as

$$
\begin{aligned}
f\big(k, S_k^{(1)}\big) &= \frac{1}{(1+r)^{N-k}} \, \mathbb{E}_\theta^*\big[h(S_N) \,|\, \mathcal{F}_k\big] \\[2mm]
&= \frac{1}{(1+r)^{N-k}} \, \mathbb{E}_\theta^*\big[h(S_N) \,|\, S_k^{(1)}\big],
\end{aligned}
$$

$k = 0, 1, \ldots, N$, under the risk-neutral probability measure $\mathbb{P}^*_\theta$. Find a recurrence equation between the functions $f(k, \cdot)$ and $f(k + 1, \cdot)$, $k = 0, \ldots, N - 1$.

Hint: Use the tower property of conditional expectations.

h) Assuming that C is the payoff of the European *put* option with strike price K, give the expression of $f(N, x)$.

i) Modify the Python code below in order to make it deal with the trinomial model.

j) Taking $S_0^{(1)} = 1$, $r = 0.1$, $b = 1$, $(1 + a)(1 + b) = 1$, compute the price at time $k = 0$ of the European *put* option with strike price $K = 1$ and maturity $N = 2$ using the code of Question (i) with $\theta = 0.5$.

```
import networkx as nx
import numpy as np
import matplotlib
import matplotlib.pyplot as plt
N=2;S0=1
r = 0.1;a=-0.5;b=1; # change
# add definition of theta
p = (r-a)/(b-a) # change
q = (b-r)/(b-a) # change
def plot_tree(g):
    plt.figure(figsize=(20,10))
    pos={};lab={}
    for n in g.nodes():
        pos[n]=(n[0],n[1])
        if g.nodes[n]['value'] is not None: lab[n]=float("{0:.2f}".format(g.nodes[n]['value']))
    elarge=g.edges(data=True)
    nx.draw_networkx_labels(g,pos,lab,font_size=15)
    nx.draw_networkx_nodes(g,pos,node_color='lightblue',alpha=0.4,node_size=1000)
    nx.draw_networkx_edges(g,pos,edge_color='blue',alpha=0.7,width=3,edgelist=elarge)
    plt.ylim(-N-0.5,N+0.5)
    plt.xlim(-0.5,N+0.5)
    plt.show()
def graph_stock():
    S=nx.Graph()
    for k in range(0,N):
        for l in range(-k,k+2,2): # change range and step size
            S.add_edge((k,l),(k+1,l+1)) # add edge
            S.add_edge((k,l),(k+1,l-1))
    for n in S.nodes():
        k=n[0]
        l=n[1]
        S.nodes[n]['value']=S0*((1.0+b)**((k+l)/2))*((1.0+a)**((k-l)/2))
    return S
plot_tree(graph_stock())
```

```
def European_call_price(K):
    price = nx.Graph()
    hedge = nx.Graph()
    S = graph_stock()
    for k in range(0,N):
        for l in range(-k,k+2,2): # change range and step size
            price.add_edge((k,l),(k+1,l+1)) # add edge
            price.add_edge((k,l),(k+1,l-1))
    for l in range(-N,N+2,2): # change range and step size
        price.nodes[(N,l)]['value'] = np.maximum(S.nodes[(N,l)]['value']-K,0)

    for k in reversed(range(0,N)):
        for l in range(-k,k+2,2): # change range and step size
            price.nodes[(k,l)]['value'] =
                (price.nodes[(k+1,l+1)]['value']*p+price.nodes[(k+1,l-1)]['value']*q)/(1+r) # add theta
    return price
```

```
1  K = input("Strike K=")
   call_price = European_call_price(float(K))
3  print('Underlying asset prices:')
   plot_tree(graph_stock())
5  print('European call option prices:')
   plot_tree(call_price)
7  print('Price at time 0 of the European call option:',float("{0:.4f}".format(call_price.nodes[(0,0)]['value'])))
```

Chapter 4

Brownian Motion and Stochastic Calculus

Brownian motion is a continuous-time stochastic process having stationary and independent Gaussian distributed increments, and continuous paths. This chapter presents the constructions of Brownian motion and its associated Itô stochastic integral, which will be used for the random modeling of asset and portfolio prices in continuous time.

4.1   Brownian Motion

We start by recalling the definition of Brownian motion, which is a fundamental example of a stochastic process. The underlying probability space $(\Omega, \mathcal{F}, \mathbb{P})$ of Brownian motion can be constructed on the space $\Omega = \mathcal{C}_0(\mathbb{R}_+)$ of continuous real-valued functions on $\mathbb{R}_+$ started at 0.

Definition 4.1. *The standard Brownian motion is a stochastic process $(B_t)_{t \in \mathbb{R}_+}$ such that*

1. $B_0 = 0$,

2. The sample trajectories $t \mapsto B_t$ are continuous, with probability one.

3. For any finite sequence of times $t_0 < t_1 < \cdots < t_n$, the increments

$$B_{t_1} - B_{t_0}, B_{t_2} - B_{t_1}, \ldots, B_{t_n} - B_{t_{n-1}}$$

are mutually independent random variables.

4. For any given times $0 \leqslant s < t$, $B_t - B_s$ has the Gaussian distribution $\mathcal{N}(0, t - s)$ with mean zero and variance $t - s$.

In particular, for $t \in \mathbb{R}_+$, the random variable $B_t \simeq \mathcal{N}(0, t)$ has a Gaussian distribution with mean zero and variance $t > 0$. Existence of a stochastic process satisfying the conditions of Definition 4.1 will be covered in Section 4.2.

In Figure 4.1 we draw three sample paths of a standard Brownian motion obtained by computer simulation using (4.3). Note that there is no point in "computing" the value of B_t as it is a *random variable* for all $t > 0$. However, we can generate samples of B_t, which are distributed according to the centered Gaussian distribution with variance $t > 0$ as in Figure 4.1.

DOI: 10.1201/9781003298670-4

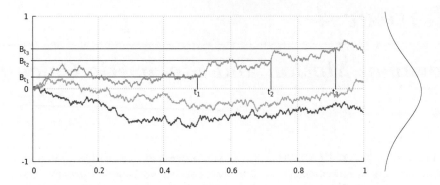

Figure 4.1: Sample paths of a one-dimensional Brownian motion.

In particular, Property *4* in Definition 4.1 implies

$$\mathbb{E}[B_t - B_s] = 0 \quad \text{and} \quad \text{Var}[B_t - B_s] = t - s, \qquad 0 \leqslant s \leqslant t,$$

and we have

$$\begin{aligned}
\text{Cov}(B_s, B_t) &= \mathbb{E}[B_s B_t] \\
&= \mathbb{E}[B_s(B_t - B_s + B_s)] \\
&= \mathbb{E}\left[B_s(B_t - B_s) + (B_s)^2\right] \\
&= \mathbb{E}[B_s(B_t - B_s)] + \mathbb{E}\left[(B_s)^2\right] \\
&= \mathbb{E}[B_s]\,\mathbb{E}[B_t - B_s] + \mathbb{E}\left[(B_s)^2\right] \\
&= \text{Var}[B_s] \\
&= s, \qquad 0 \leqslant s \leqslant t,
\end{aligned}$$

hence

$$\text{Cov}(B_s, B_t) = \mathbb{E}[B_s B_t] = \min(s, t), \qquad s, t \geqslant 0, \tag{4.1}$$

cf. also Exercise 4.2-(4.1). The following graphs present two examples of possible modeling of random data using Brownian motion.

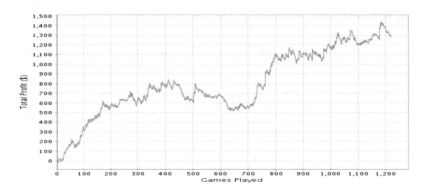

Figure 4.2: Evolution of the fortune of a poker player *vs* number of games played.

In what follows, we denote by $(\mathcal{F}_t)_{t \in \mathbb{R}_+}$ the filtration generated by the Brownian paths up to time t, defined as

$$\mathcal{F}_t := \sigma(B_s \ : \ 0 \leqslant s \leqslant t), \qquad t \geqslant 0. \tag{4.2}$$

Property 3 in Definition 4.1 shows that $B_t - B_s$ is independent of all Brownian increments taken before time s, *i.e.*

$$(B_t - B_s) \perp\!\!\!\perp (B_{t_1} - B_{t_0}, B_{t_2} - B_{t_1}, \ldots, B_{t_n} - B_{t_{n-1}}),$$

$0 \leqslant t_0 \leqslant t_1 \leqslant \cdots \leqslant t_n \leqslant s \leqslant t$, hence $B_t - B_s$ is also independent of the whole Brownian history up to time s, hence $B_t - B_s$ is in fact independent of $\mathcal{F}_s$, $s \geqslant 0$.

Definition 4.2. *A continuous-time process* $(Z_t)_{t \in \mathbb{R}_+}$ *of integrable random variables is a martingale under* $\mathbb{P}$ *and with respect to the filtration* $(\mathcal{F}_t)_{t \in \mathbb{R}_+}$ *if*

$$\mathbb{E}[Z_t \mid \mathcal{F}_s] = Z_s, \qquad 0 \leqslant s \leqslant t.$$

Note that when $(Z_t)_{t \in \mathbb{R}_+}$ is a martingale, Z_t is in particular $\mathcal{F}_t$-measurable at all times $t \geqslant 0$. As in Example 2 on page 2, we have the following result.

Proposition 4.3. *Brownian motion* $(B_t)_{t \in \mathbb{R}_+}$ *is a continuous-time* martingale.

Proof. We have

$$
\begin{aligned}
\mathbb{E}[B_t \mid \mathcal{F}_s] &= \mathbb{E}[B_t - B_s + B_s \mid \mathcal{F}_s] \\
&= \mathbb{E}[B_t - B_s \mid \mathcal{F}_s] + \mathbb{E}[B_s \mid \mathcal{F}_s] \\
&= \mathbb{E}[B_t - B_s] + B_s \\
&= B_s, \qquad 0 \leqslant s \leqslant t,
\end{aligned}
$$

because it has centered and independent increments, cf. Section 7.1. □

4.2 Three Constructions of Brownian Motion

We refer the reader to Chapter 1 of Revuz and Yor (1994) and to Theorem 10.28 in Folland (1999) for proofs of existence of Brownian motion as a stochastic process $(B_t)_{t \in \mathbb{R}_+}$ satisfying the Conditions *1-4* of Definition 4.1.

Brownian motion as a random walk

For convenience, we will informally regard Brownian motion as a random walk over infinitesimal time intervals of length Δt, whose increments

$$\Delta B_t := B_{t+\Delta t} - B_t \simeq \mathcal{N}(0, \Delta t)$$

over the time interval $[t, t + \Delta t]$ will be approximated by the Bernoulli random variable

$$\Delta B_t = \pm \sqrt{\Delta t} \tag{4.3}$$

with equal probabilities $(1/2, 1/2)$. According to this representation, the paths of Brownian motion are not differentiable, although they are continuous by Property 2, as we have

$$\frac{dB_t}{dt} \simeq \frac{\pm \sqrt{dt}}{dt} = \pm \frac{1}{\sqrt{dt}} \simeq \pm \infty. \tag{4.4}$$

Figure 4.3 presents a simulation of Brownian motion as a random walk with $\Delta t = 0.1$.

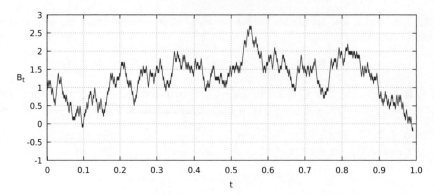

Figure 4.3: Construction of Brownian motion as a random walk with $B_0 = 1$.

Note that we have

$$\mathbb{E}[\Delta B_t] = \frac{1}{2}\sqrt{\Delta t} - \frac{1}{2}\sqrt{\Delta t} = 0,$$

and

$$\mathrm{Var}[\Delta B_t] = \mathbb{E}\left[(\Delta B_t)^2\right] = \frac{1}{2}(+\sqrt{\Delta t})^2 + \frac{1}{2}(-\sqrt{\Delta t})^2 = \frac{1}{2}\Delta t + \frac{1}{2}\Delta t = \Delta t.$$

In order to recover the Gaussian distribution property of the random variable B_T, we can split the time interval $[0, T]$ into N subintervals

$$\left(\frac{k-1}{N}T, \frac{k}{N}T\right], \qquad k = 1, 2, \ldots, N,$$

of same length $\Delta t = T/N$, with N "large".

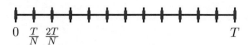

Defining the Bernoulli random variable X_k as

$$X_k := \pm\sqrt{T}$$

with equal probabilities $(1/2, 1/2)$, we have $\mathrm{Var}(X_k) = T$ and

$$\Delta B_t := \frac{X_k}{\sqrt{N}} = \pm\sqrt{\Delta t}$$

is the increment of B_t over $((k-1)\Delta t, k\Delta t]$, and we get

$$B_T \simeq \sum_{0 < t < T} \Delta B_t \simeq \frac{X_1 + X_2 + \cdots + X_N}{\sqrt{N}}.$$

Hence by the central limit theorem we recover the fact that B_T has the centered Gaussian distribution $\mathcal{N}(0, T)$ with variance T, cf. point 4 of the above Definition 4.1 of Brownian motion, and the illustration given in Figure 4.4. Indeed, the central limit theorem states that given any sequence $(X_k)_{k \geqslant 1}$ of independent identically distributed centered random variables with variance $\sigma^2 = \mathrm{Var}[X_k] = T$, the normalized sum

$$\frac{X_1 + X_2 + \cdots + X_N}{\sqrt{N}}$$

converges (in distribution) to the centered Gaussian random variable $\mathcal{N}(0, \sigma^2)$ with variance σ^2 as N goes to infinity. As a consequence, ΔB_t could in fact be replaced by any centered random variable with variance Δt in the above description.

```
1   N=1000; t <- 0:N; dt <- 1.0/N; dev.new(width=16,height=7); # Using Bernoulli samples
    nsim=100;X <- matrix((dt)^0.5*(rbinom( nsim * N, 1, 0.5)-0.5)*2, nsim, N)
3   X <- cbind(rep(0, nsim), t(apply(X, 1, cumsum))); H<-hist(X[,N],plot=FALSE);
    layout(matrix(c(1,2), nrow =1, byrow = TRUE));par(mar=c(2,2,2,0), oma = c(2, 2, 2, 2))
5   plot(t*dt, X[1, ], xlab = "", ylab = "", type = "l", ylim = c(-2, 2), col = 0,xaxs='i',las=1, cex.axis=1.6)
    for (i in 1:nsim){lines(t*dt, X[i, ], type = "l", ylim = c(-2, 2), col = i)}
7   lines(t*dt,sqrt(t*dt),lty=1,col="red",lwd=3);lines(t*dt,-sqrt(t*dt), lty=1, col="red",lwd=3)
    lines(t*dt,0*t, lty=1, col="black",lwd=2)
9   for (i in 1:nsim){points(0.999, X[i,N], pch=1, lwd = 5, col = i)}
    x <- seq(-2,2, length=100); px <- dnorm(x);par(mar = c(2,2,2,2))
11  plot(NULL , xlab="", ylab="", xlim = c(0, max(px,H$density)), ylim = c(-2,2),axes=F)
    rect(0, H$breaks[1:(length(H$breaks) - 1)], col=rainbow(20,start=0.08,end=0.6), H$density,
        H$breaks[2:length(H$breaks)]); lines(px,x, lty=1, col="black",lwd=2)
```

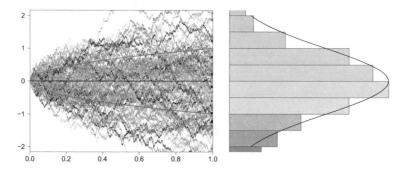

Figure 4.4: Statistics of one-dimensional Brownian paths *vs* Gaussian distribution.

Remark 4.4. *The choice of the square root in (4.3) is in fact not fortuitous. Indeed, any choice of $\pm(\Delta t)^\alpha$ with a power $\alpha > 1/2$ would lead to explosion of the process as dt tends to zero, whereas a power $\alpha \in (0, 1/2)$ would lead to a vanishing process, as can be checked from the following R code.*

Lévy's construction of Brownian motion

Figure 4.5 represents the construction of Brownian motion by successive linear interpolations, see Problem 4.20 for a proof of existence of Brownian motion based on this construction.

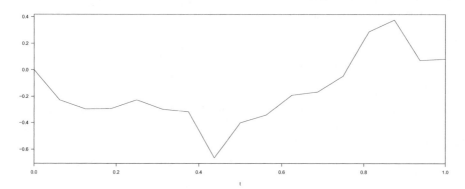

Figure 4.5: Lévy's construction of Brownian motion.

The following R code is used to generate Figure 4.5.

```
dev.new(width=16,height=7); alpha=1/2;t <- 0:1;dt <- 1; z=rnorm(1,mean=0,sd=dt^alpha)
plot(t*dt,c(0,z),xlab = "t",ylab = "",col = "blue",main = "",type = "l", xaxs="i", las = 1)
k=0;while (k<12) {readline("Press <return> to continue")
k=k+1;m <- (z+c(0,head(z,-1)))/2;y <- rnorm(length(t)-1,mean=0,sd=(dt/4)^alpha)
x <- m+y;x <- c(matrix(c(x,z), 2, byrow = T));n=2*length(t)-2;t <- 0:n
plot(t*dt/2, c(0, x), xlab = "t", ylab = "", col = "blue", main = "", type = "l", xaxs="i", las = 1);z=x;dt=dt/2}
```

Construction by series expansions

Brownian motion on $[0, T]$ can also be constructed by *Fourier synthesis* via the Paley–Wiener series expansion

$$B_t = \sum_{n \geqslant 1} X_n f_n(t) = \frac{\sqrt{2T}}{\pi} \sum_{n \geqslant 1} X_n \frac{\sin((n-1/2)\pi t/T)}{n-1/2}, \quad 0 \leqslant t \leqslant T,$$

where $(X_n)_{n \geqslant 1}$ is a sequence of independent $\mathcal{N}(0, 1)$ standard Gaussian random variables, as illustrated in Figure 4.6.

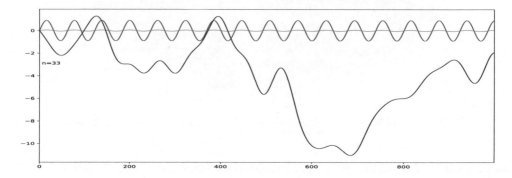

Figure 4.6: Construction of Brownian motion by series expansions.

4.3 Wiener Stochastic Integral

In this section we construct the Wiener stochastic integral of square-integrable deterministic functions of time with respect to Brownian motion.

Recall that the price S_t of risky assets was originally modeled in Bachelier (1900) as $S_t := \sigma B_t$, where σ is a volatility parameter. The stochastic integral

$$\int_0^T f(t)dS_t = \sigma \int_0^T f(t)dB_t$$

can be used to represent the value of a portfolio as a sum of profits and losses $f(t)dS_t$ where dS_t represents the stock price variation and $f(t)$ is the quantity invested in the asset S_t over the short time interval $[t, t+dt]$.

A naive definition of the stochastic integral with respect to Brownian motion would consist in letting

$$\int_0^T f(t)dB_t := \int_0^T f(t)\frac{dB_t}{dt}dt,$$

and evaluating the above integral with respect to dt. However, this definition fails because the paths of Brownian motion are not differentiable, cf. (4.4). Next we present Itô's construction of the stochastic integral with respect to Brownian motion. Stochastic integrals will be first constructed as integrals of simple step functions of the form

$$f(t) = \sum_{i=1}^{n} a_i \mathbb{1}_{(t_{i-1}, t_i]}(t), \qquad 0 \leqslant t \leqslant T, \tag{4.5}$$

i.e. the function f takes the value a_i on the interval $(t_{i-1}, t_i]$, $i = 1, 2, \ldots, n$, with $0 \leqslant t_0 < \cdots < t_n \leqslant T$, as illustrated in Figure 4.7.

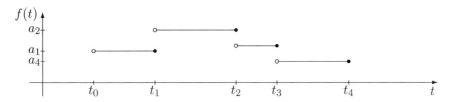

Figure 4.7: Step function $t \mapsto f(t)$.

```
ti<-c(0,2,4.5,7,9)
ai<-c(0,3,1,2,1,0)
plot(stepfun(ti,ai),xlim = c(0,10),do.points = F,main="", col = "blue")
```

Recall that the classical integral of f given in (4.5) is interpreted as the area under the curve f, and computed as

$$\int_0^T f(t)dt = \sum_{i=1}^{n} a_i(t_i - t_{i-1}).$$

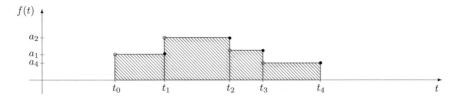

Figure 4.8: Area under the step function $t \mapsto f(t)$.

In the next Definition 4.5 we use such step functions for the construction of the stochastic integral with respect to Brownian motion. The stochastic integral (4.6) for step functions will be interpreted as the sum of profits and losses $a_i(B_{t_i} - B_{t_{i-1}})$, $i = 1, 2, \ldots, n$, in a portfolio holding a quantity a_i of a risky asset whose price variation is $B_{t_i} - B_{t_{i-1}}$ at time $i = 1, 2, \ldots, n$.

Definition 4.5. *The stochastic integral with respect to Brownian motion* $(B_t)_{t \in [0,T]}$ *of the simple step function f of the form* (4.5) *is defined by*

$$\int_0^T f(t)dB_t := \sum_{i=1}^{n} a_i(B_{t_i} - B_{t_{i-1}}). \tag{4.6}$$

In what follows, we will make a repeated use of the space $L^2([0,T])$ of *square-integrable functions*.

Definition 4.6. *Let $L^2([0,T])$ denote the space of (measurable) functions $f : [0,T] \longrightarrow \mathbb{R}$ such that*

$$\|f\|_{L^2([0,T])} := \sqrt{\int_0^T |f(t)|^2 dt} < \infty, \quad f \in L^2([0,T]). \tag{4.7}$$

In the above definition, $\|f\|_{L^2([0,T])}$ represents the *norm* of the function $f \in L^2([0,T])$.

For example, the function $f(t) := t^\alpha$, $t \in (0,T]$, belongs to $L^2([0,T])$ if and only if $\alpha > -1/2$, as we have

$$\int_0^T f^2(t)dt = \int_0^T t^{2\alpha} dt = \begin{cases} +\infty & \text{if } \alpha \leqslant -1/2, \\ \left[\dfrac{t^{1+2\alpha}}{1+2\alpha}\right]_{t=0}^{t=T} = \dfrac{T^{1+2\alpha}}{1+2\alpha} < \infty & \text{if } \alpha > -1/2, \end{cases}$$

see Figure 4.9 for an illustration.

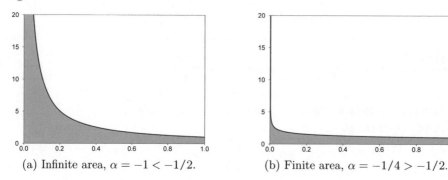

(a) Infinite area, $\alpha = -1 < -1/2$.   (b) Finite area, $\alpha = -1/4 > -1/2$.

Figure 4.9: Infinite *vs* finite area under a curve.

In the next Lemma 4.7 we determine the probability distribution of $\int_0^T f(t)dB_t$ and we show that it is independent of the particular representation (4.5) chosen for $f(t)$.

Lemma 4.7. *Let f be a simple step function f of the form (4.5). The stochastic integral $\int_0^T f(t)dB_t$ defined in (4.6) has the centered Gaussian distribution*

$$\int_0^T f(t)dB_t \simeq \mathcal{N}\left(0, \int_0^T |f(t)|^2 dt\right)$$

with mean $\mathbb{E}\left[\int_0^T f(t)dB_t\right] = 0$ and variance given by the Itô isometry

$$\mathrm{Var}\left[\int_0^T f(t)dB_t\right] = \mathbb{E}\left[\left(\int_0^T f(t)dB_t\right)^2\right] = \int_0^T |f(t)|^2 dt. \tag{4.8}$$

Proof. Recall that if $X_1, X_2, \ldots, X_n$ are independent Gaussian random variables with probability distributions $\mathcal{N}(m_1, \sigma_1^2), \ldots, \mathcal{N}(m_n, \sigma_n^2)$, then the sum $X_1 + \cdots + X_n$ is a Gaussian random variable with distribution

$$\mathcal{N}\left(m_1 + \cdots + m_n, \sigma_1^2 + \cdots + \sigma_n^2\right).$$

As a consequence, the stochastic integral

$$\int_0^T f(t)dB_t = \sum_{k=1}^n a_k(B_{t_k} - B_{t_{k-1}})$$

of the step function

$$f(t) = \sum_{k=1}^n a_k \mathbb{1}_{(t_{k-1},t_k]}(t), \qquad 0 \leqslant t \leqslant T,$$

has the centered Gaussian distribution with mean 0 and variance

$$
\begin{aligned}
\mathrm{Var}\left[\int_0^T f(t)dB_t\right] &= \mathrm{Var}\left[\sum_{k=1}^n a_k(B_{t_k} - B_{t_{k-1}})\right] \\
&= \sum_{k=1}^n \mathrm{Var}[a_k(B_{t_k} - B_{t_{k-1}})] \\
&= \sum_{k=1}^n |a_k|^2 \,\mathrm{Var}[B_{t_k} - B_{t_{k-1}}] \\
&= \sum_{k=1}^n (t_k - t_{k-1})|a_k|^2 \\
&= \sum_{k=1}^n |a_k|^2 \int_{t_{k-1}}^{t_k} dt \\
&= \sum_{k=1}^n |a_k|^2 \int_0^T \mathbb{1}_{(t_{k-1},t_k]}(t)dt \\
&= \int_0^T \sum_{k=1}^n |a_k|^2 \mathbb{1}_{(t_{k-1},t_k]}(t)dt \\
&= \int_0^T |f(t)|^2 dt,
\end{aligned}
$$

since the simple function

$$f^2(t) = \sum_{i=1}^n a_i^2 \mathbb{1}_{(t_{i-1},t_i]}(t), \qquad 0 \leqslant t \leqslant T,$$

takes the value a_i^2 on the interval $(t_{i-1}, t_i]$, $i = 1, 2, \ldots, n$, as can be checked from the following Figure 4.10.

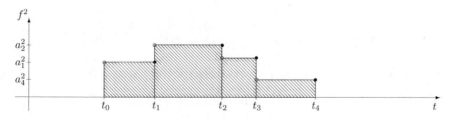

Figure 4.10: Squared step function $t \mapsto f^2(t)$.

□

The norm $\|\cdot\|_{L^2([0,T])}$ on $L^2([0,T])$ induces a *distance* between any two functions f and g in $L^2([0,T])$, defined as

$$\|f - g\|_{L^2([0,T])} := \sqrt{\int_0^T |f(t) - g(t)|^2 dt} < \infty,$$

cf. *e.g.* Chapter 3 of Rudin (1974) for details.

Definition 4.8. Convergence in $L^2([0,T])$. *We say that a sequence $(f_n)_{n\in\mathbb{N}}$ of functions in $L^2([0,T])$ converges in $L^2([0,T])$ to another function $f \in L^2([0,T])$ if*

$$\lim_{n\to\infty} \|f - f_n\|_{L^2([0,T])} = \lim_{n\to\infty} \sqrt{\int_0^T |f(t) - f_n(t)|^2 dt} = 0.$$

```
1  dev.new(width=16,height=7)
   f = function(x){exp(sin(x*1.8*pi))}
3  for (i in 3:9){n=2^i;x<-cumsum(c(0,rep(1,n)))/n;
   z<-c(NA,head(x,-1))
5  y<-c(f(x)-pmax(f(x)-f(z),0),f(1))
   t=seq(0,1,0.01);
7  plot(f,from=0,to=1,ylim=c(0.3,2.9),type="l",lwd=3,col="red",main="",xaxs="i",yaxs="i", las=1)
   lines(stepfun(x,y),do.points=F,lwd=2,col="blue",main="");
9  readline("Press <return> to continue");}
```

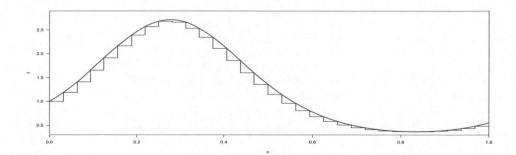

Figure 4.11: Step function approximation.

By *e.g.* Theorem 3.13 in Rudin (1974) or Proposition 2.4 page 63 of Hirsch and Lacombe (1999), we have the following result which states that the set of simple step functions f of the form (4.5) is a linear space which is dense in $L^2([0,T])$ for the norm (4.7), as stated in the next proposition.

Proposition 4.9. *For any function $f \in L^2([0,T])$ satisfying (4.7) there exists a sequence $(f_n)_{n\in\mathbb{N}}$ of simple step functions of the form (4.5), converging to f in $L^2([0,T])$ in the sense that*

$$\lim_{n\to\infty} \|f - f_n\|_{L^2([0,T])} = \lim_{n\to\infty} \sqrt{\int_0^T |f(t) - f_n(t)|^2 dt} = 0.$$

In order to extend the definition (4.6) of the stochastic integral $\int_0^T f(t)dB_t$ to any function $f \in L^2([0,T])$, *i.e.* to $f : [0,T] \longrightarrow \mathbb{R}$ measurable such that

$$\int_0^T |f(t)|^2 dt < \infty, \tag{4.9}$$

we will make use of the space $L^2(\Omega)$ of *square-integrable random variables.*

Definition 4.10. *Let $L^2(\Omega)$ denote the space of random variables $F : \Omega \longrightarrow \mathbb{R}$ such that*

$$\|F\|_{L^2(\Omega)} := \sqrt{\mathbb{E}\left[F^2\right]} < \infty.$$

The norm $\|\cdot\|_{L^2(\Omega)}$ on $L^2(\Omega)$ induces the *distance*

$$\|F - G\|_{L^2(\Omega)} := \sqrt{\mathbb{E}\left[(F - G)^2\right]} < \infty,$$

between the square-integrable random variables F and G in $L^2(\Omega)$.

Definition 4.11. *Convergence in $L^2(\Omega)$. We say that a sequence $(F_n)_{n \in \mathbb{N}}$ of random variables in $L^2(\Omega)$ converges in $L^2(\Omega)$ to another random variable $F \in L^2(\Omega)$ if*

$$\lim_{n \to \infty} \|F - F_n\|_{L^2(\Omega)} = \lim_{n \to \infty} \sqrt{\mathbb{E}\left[(F - F_n)^2\right]} = 0.$$

The next proposition allows us to extend Lemma 4.7 from simple step functions to square-integrable functions in $L^2([0, T])$.

Proposition 4.12. *The definition (4.6) of the stochastic integral $\int_0^T f(t)dB_t$ can be extended to any function $f \in L^2([0, T])$. In this case, $\int_0^T f(t)dB_t$ has the centered Gaussian distribution*

$$\int_0^T f(t)dB_t \simeq \mathcal{N}\left(0, \int_0^T |f(t)|^2 dt\right)$$

with mean $\mathbb{E}\left[\int_0^T f(t)dB_t\right] = 0$ and variance given by the Itô isometry

$$\mathrm{Var}\left[\int_0^T f(t)dB_t\right] = \mathbb{E}\left[\left(\int_0^T f(t)dB_t\right)^2\right] = \int_0^T |f(t)|^2 dt. \qquad (4.10)$$

Proof. The extension of the stochastic integral to all functions satisfying (4.9) is obtained by a denseness and Cauchy sequence argument, based on the isometry relation (4.10).

i) Given f a function satisfying (4.9), consider a sequence $(f_n)_{n \in \mathbb{N}}$ of simple functions converging to f in $L^2([0, T])$, *i.e.*

$$\lim_{n \to \infty} \|f - f_n\|_{L^2([0,T])} = \lim_{n \to \infty} \sqrt{\int_0^T |f(t) - f_n(t)|^2 dt} = 0$$

as in Proposition 4.9.

ii) By the isometry (4.10) and the triangle inequality* we have

$$\left\|\int_0^T f_k(t)dB_t - \int_0^T f_n(t)dB_t\right\|_{L^2(\Omega)}$$

$$= \sqrt{\mathbb{E}\left[\left(\int_0^T f_k(t)dB_t - \int_0^T f_n(t)dB_t\right)^2\right]}$$

---

*The triangle inequality $\|f_k - f_n\|_{L^2([0,T])} \leqslant \|f_k - f\|_{L^2([0,T])} + \|f - f_n\|_{L^2([0,T])}$ follows from the *Minkowski inequality*.

$$= \sqrt{\mathbb{E}\left[\left(\int_0^T (f_k(t) - f_n(t))dB_t\right)^2\right]}$$

$$= \|f_k - f_n\|_{L^2([0,T])}$$

$$\leqslant \|f_k - f\|_{L^2([0,T])} + \|f - f_n\|_{L^2([0,T])},$$

which tends to 0 as k and n tend to infinity, hence $\left(\int_0^T f_n(t)dB_t\right)_{n\in\mathbb{N}}$ is a Cauchy sequence in $L^2(\Omega)$ by for the $L^2(\Omega)$-norm.

iii) Since the sequence $\left(\int_0^T f_n(t)dB_t\right)_{n\in\mathbb{N}}$ is Cauchy and the space $L^2(\Omega)$ is *complete*, cf. *e.g.* Theorem 3.11 in Rudin (1974) or Chapter 4 of Dudley (2002), we conclude that $\left(\int_0^T f_n(t)dB_t\right)_{n\in\mathbb{N}}$ *converges* for the L^2-norm to a limit in $L^2(\Omega)$. In this case we let

$$\int_0^T f(t)dB_t := \lim_{n\to\infty} \int_0^T f_n(t)dB_t,$$

which also satisfies (4.10) from (4.8) From (4.10) we can check that the limit is independent of the approximating sequence $(f_n)_{n\in\mathbb{N}}$.

iv) Finally, from the convergence of Gaussian characteristic functions

$$\mathbb{E}\left[\exp\left(i\alpha \int_0^T f(t)dB_t\right)\right] = \mathbb{E}\left[\lim_{n\to\infty} \exp\left(i\alpha \int_0^T f_n(t)dB_t\right)\right]$$

$$= \lim_{n\to\infty} \mathbb{E}\left[\exp\left(i\alpha \int_0^T f_n(t)dB_t\right)\right]$$

$$= \lim_{n\to\infty} \exp\left(-\frac{\alpha^2}{2} \int_0^T |f_n(t)|^2 dt\right)$$

$$= \exp\left(-\frac{\alpha^2}{2} \int_0^T |f(t)|^2 dt\right),$$

$f \in L^2([0,T])$, $\alpha \in \mathbb{R}$, we check that $\int_0^T f(t)dB_t$ has the centered Gaussian distribution

$$\int_0^T f(t)dB_t \simeq \mathcal{N}\left(0, \int_0^T |f(t)|^2 dt\right).$$

□

The next corollary is obtained by bilinearity from the Itô isometry (4.10).

Corollary 4.13. *The stochastic integral with respect to Brownian motion $(B_t)_{t\in\mathbb{R}_+}$ satisfies the isometry*

$$\mathbb{E}\left[\int_0^T f(t)dB_t \int_0^T g(t)dB_t\right] = \int_0^T f(t)g(t)dt,$$

for all square-integrable deterministic functions $f, g \in L^2([0,T])$.

Proof. Applying the Itô isometry (4.10) to the processes $f + g$ and $f - g$ and the relation $xy = (x + y)^2/4 - (x - y)^2/4$, we have

$$\mathbb{E}\left[\int_0^T f(t)dB_t \int_0^T g(t)dB_t\right]$$

$$= \frac{1}{4}\mathbb{E}\left[\left(\int_0^T f(t)dB_t + \int_0^T g(t)dB_t\right)^2 - \left(\int_0^T f(t)dB_t - \int_0^T g(t)dB_t\right)^2\right]$$

$$= \frac{1}{4}\mathbb{E}\left[\left(\int_0^T (f(t) + g(t))dB_t\right)^2\right] - \frac{1}{4}\mathbb{E}\left[\left(\int_0^T (f(t) - g(t))dB_t\right)^2\right]$$

$$= \frac{1}{4}\int_0^T (f(t) + g(t))^2 dt - \frac{1}{4}\int_0^T (f(t) - g(t))^2 dt$$

$$= \frac{1}{4}\int_0^T \left((f(t) + g(t))^2 - (f(t) - g(t))^2\right)dt$$

$$= \int_0^T f(t)g(t)dt.$$

$\square$

For example, the Wiener stochastic integral $\int_0^T e^{-t}dB_t$ is a random variable having centered Gaussian distribution with variance

$$\mathbb{E}\left[\left(\int_0^T e^{-t}dB_t\right)^2\right] = \int_0^T e^{-2t}dt$$

$$= \left[-\frac{1}{2}e^{-2t}\right]_{t=0}^{t=T}$$

$$= \frac{1}{2}(1 - e^{-2T}),$$

as follows from the Itô isometry (4.8).

Remark 4.14. *The Wiener stochastic integral $\int_0^T f(s)dB_s$ is a Gaussian random variable which cannot be "computed" in the way standard integral are computed via the use of primitives. However, when $f \in L^2([0,T])$ is in $\mathcal{C}^1([0,T])$,[*] we have the integration by parts relation*

$$\int_0^T f(t)dB_t = f(T)B_T - \int_0^T B_t f'(t)dt. \tag{4.11}$$

When $f \in L^2(\mathbb{R}_+)$ is in $\mathcal{C}^1(\mathbb{R}_+)$ we also have following formula

$$\int_0^\infty f(t)dB_t = -\int_0^\infty B_t f'(t)dt, \tag{4.12}$$

provided that $\lim_{t\to\infty} t|f(t)|^2 = 0$ and $f \in L^2(\mathbb{R}_+)$, cf. e.g. Exercise 4.5 and Remark 2.5.9 in Privault (2009).

---

[*]This means that the function f is continuously differentiable on $[0,T]$.

4.4   Itô Stochastic Integral

In this section we extend the Wiener stochastic integral from deterministic functions in $L^2([0,T])$ to random square-integrable (random) *adapted* processes. For this, we will need the notion of *measurability*.

The extension of the stochastic integral to adapted random processes is actually necessary in order to compute a portfolio value when the portfolio process is no longer deterministic. This happens in particular when one needs to update the portfolio allocation based on random events occurring on the market.

A random variable F is said to be $\mathcal{F}_t$-*measurable* if the knowledge of F depends only on the information known up to time t. As an example, if $t =$today,

- the date of the past course exam is $\mathcal{F}_t$-measurable, because it belongs to the past.

- the date of the next Chinese new year, although it refers to a future event, is also $\mathcal{F}_t$-measurable because it is known at time t.

- the date of the next typhoon is not $\mathcal{F}_t$-measurable since it is not known at time t.

- the maturity date T of the European option is $\mathcal{F}_t$-measurable for all $t \in [0,T]$, because it has been determined at time 0.

- the exercise date τ of an American option after time t (see Section 15.1) is not $\mathcal{F}_t$-measurable because it refers to a future random event.

In the next definition, $(\mathcal{F}_t)_{t \in [0,T]}$ denotes the information flow defined in (4.2), *i.e.*

$$\mathcal{F}_t := \sigma(B_s \ : \ 0 \leqslant s \leqslant t), \qquad t \geqslant 0.$$

Definition 4.15. *A stochastic process $(X_t)_{t \in [0,T]}$ is said to be $(\mathcal{F}_t)_{t \in [0,T]}$-adapted if X_t is $\mathcal{F}_t$-measurable for all $t \in [0,T]$.*

For example,

- $(B_t)_{t \in \mathbb{R}_+}$ is an $(\mathcal{F}_t)_{t \in \mathbb{R}_+}$-*adapted* process,

- $(B_{t+1})_{t \in \mathbb{R}_+}$ is *not* an $(\mathcal{F}_t)_{t \in \mathbb{R}_+}$-adapted process,

- $(B_{t/2})_{t \in \mathbb{R}_+}$ is an $(\mathcal{F}_t)_{t \in \mathbb{R}_+}$-*adapted* process,

- $(B_{\sqrt{t}})_{t \in \mathbb{R}_+}$ is *not* an $(\mathcal{F}_t)_{t \in \mathbb{R}_+}$-adapted process,

- $(\text{Max}_{s \in [0,t]} B_s)_{t \in \mathbb{R}_+}$ is an $(\mathcal{F}_t)_{t \in \mathbb{R}_+}$-*adapted* process,

- $\left(\int_0^t B_s ds \right)_{t \in \mathbb{R}_+}$ is an $(\mathcal{F}_t)_{t \in \mathbb{R}_+}$-*adapted* process,

- $\left(\int_0^t f(s) dB_s \right)_{t \in [0,T]}$ is an $(\mathcal{F}_t)_{t \in [0,T]}$-*adapted* process when $f \in L^2([0,T])$.

In other words, a stochastic process $(X_t)_{t \in \mathbb{R}_+}$ is $(\mathcal{F}_t)_{t \in [0,T]}$-adapted if the value of X_t at time t depends only on information known up to time t. Note that the value of X_t may still depend on "known" future data, for example a fixed future date in the calendar, such as a maturity time $T > t$, as long as its value is known at time t.

The stochastic integral of adapted processes is first constructed as integrals of simple predictable processes.

Definition 4.16. *A simple predictable processes is a stochastic process* $(u_t)_{t \in \mathbb{R}_+}$ *of the form*

$$u_t := \sum_{i=1}^n F_i \mathbb{1}_{(t_{i-1}, t_i]}(t), \qquad t \geqslant 0, \tag{4.13}$$

where F_i *is an* $\mathcal{F}_{t_{i-1}}$-*measurable random variable for* $i = 1, 2, \ldots, n$, *and* $0 = t_0 < t_1 < \cdots < t_{n-1} < t_n = T$.

For example, a natural approximation of $(B_t)_{t \in \mathbb{R}_+}$ by a simple predictable process can be constructed as

$$u_t = \sum_{i=1}^n F_i \mathbb{1}_{(t_{i-1}, t_i]}(t) := \sum_{i=1}^n B_{t_{i-1}} \mathbb{1}_{(t_{i-1}, t_i]}(t), \qquad t \geqslant 0, \tag{4.14}$$

since $F_i := B_{t_{i-1}}$ is $\mathcal{F}_{t_{i-1}}$-measurable for $i = 1, 2, \ldots, n$, as in Figure 4.12.

```
1   N=10000; t <- 0:(N-1); dt <- 1.0/N;
    dB <- rnorm(N,mean=0,sd=sqrt(dt));X <- rep(0,N);X[1]=0
3   for (j in 2:N){X[j]=X[j-1]+dB[j]}
    plot(t/(N-1), X, xlab = "t", ylab = "", type = "l", ylim = c(1.05*min(X),1.05*max(X)), xaxs="i", yaxs="i", col
        = "blue", las = 1, cex.axis=1.6, cex.lab=1.8)
5   abline(h=0)
    t1=c(0.15,0.37,0.49,0.65,0.72,0.91)
7   Bt=c(0,X[t1[1]*N],X[t1[2]*N],X[t1[3]*N],X[t1[4]*N],X[t1[5]*N],X[t1[6]*N])
    lines(stepfun(t1,Bt),xlim =c(0,T),xlab="t",ylab=expression('N'[t]),pch=1, cex=0.8, col='black', lwd=3,
        main="")
```

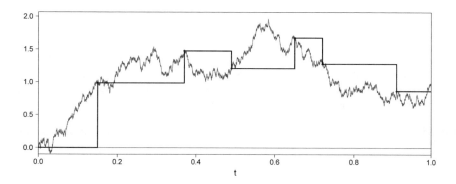

Figure 4.12: Step function approximation of Brownian motion.

The notion of simple predictable process makes full sense in the context of portfolio investment, in which F_i will represent an investment allocation decided at time t_{i-1} and to remain unchanged over the time interval $(t_{i-1}, t_i]$.

By convention, $u : \Omega \times \mathbb{R}_+ \longrightarrow \mathbb{R}$ is denoted in what follows by $u_t(\omega)$, $t \in \mathbb{R}_+$, $\omega \in \Omega$, and the random outcome ω is often dropped for convenience of notation.

Definition 4.17. *The stochastic integral with respect to Brownian motion $(B_t)_{t \in \mathbb{R}_+}$ of any simple predictable process $(u_t)_{t \in \mathbb{R}_+}$ of the form (4.13) is defined by*

$$\int_0^T u_t dB_t := \sum_{i=1}^n F_i(B_{t_i} - B_{t_{i-1}}), \tag{4.15}$$

with $0 = t_0 < t_1 < \cdots < t_{n-1} < t_n = T$.

The use of predictability in the definition (4.15) is essential from a financial point of view, as F_i will represent a portfolio allocation made at time t_{i-1} and kept constant over the trading interval $[t_{i-1}, t_i]$, while $B_{t_i} - B_{t_{i-1}}$ represents a change in the underlying asset price over $[t_{i-1}, t_i]$. See also the related discussion on self-financing portfolios in Section 5.3 and Lemma 5.14 on the use of stochastic integrals to represent the value of a portfolio.

Definition 4.18. *Let $L^2(\Omega \times [0, T])$ denote the space of stochastic processes*

$$\begin{aligned} u : \Omega \times [0, T] &\longrightarrow \mathbb{R} \\ (\omega, t) &\longmapsto u_t(\omega) \end{aligned}$$

such that

$$\|u\|_{L^2(\Omega \times [0,T])} := \sqrt{\mathbb{E}\left[\int_0^T |u_t|^2 dt\right]} < \infty, \quad u \in L^2(\Omega \times [0, T]).$$

The norm $\| \cdot \|_{L^2(\Omega \times [0,T])}$ on $L^2(\Omega \times [0, T])$ induces a *distance* between two stochastic processes u and v in $L^2(\Omega \times [0, T])$, defined as

$$\|u - v\|_{L^2(\Omega \times [0,T])} = \sqrt{\mathbb{E}\left[\int_0^T |u_t - v_t|^2 dt\right]}.$$

Definition 4.19. *Convergence in $L^2(\Omega \times [0, T])$. We say that a sequence $\left(u^{(n)}\right)_{n \in \mathbb{N}}$ of processes in $L^2(\Omega \times [0, T])$ converges in $L^2(\Omega \times [0, T])$ to another process $u \in L^2(\Omega \times [0, T])$ if*

$$\lim_{n \to \infty} \left\|u - u^{(n)}\right\|_{L^2(\Omega \times [0,T])} = \lim_{n \to \infty} \sqrt{\mathbb{E}\left[\int_0^T |u_t - u_t^{(n)}|^2 dt\right]} = 0.$$

By Lemma 1.1 of Ikeda and Watanabe (1989), pages 22 and 46, or Proposition 2.5.3 in Privault (2009), the set of simple predictable processes forms a linear space which is dense in the subspace $L^2_{ad}(\Omega \times \mathbb{R}_+)$ made of square-integrable adapted processes in $L^2(\Omega \times \mathbb{R}_+)$, as stated in the next proposition.

Proposition 4.20. *Given $u \in L^2_{ad}(\Omega \times \mathbb{R}_+)$ a square-integrable adapted process there exists a sequence $(u^{(n)})_{n \in \mathbb{N}}$ of simple predictable processes converging to u in $L^2(\Omega \times \mathbb{R}_+)$, i.e.*

$$\lim_{n \to \infty} \left\|u - u^{(n)}\right\|_{L^2(\Omega \times [0,T])} = \lim_{n \to \infty} \sqrt{\mathbb{E}\left[\int_0^T |u_t - u_t^{(n)}|^2 dt\right]} = 0.$$

The next Proposition 4.21 extends the construction of the stochastic integral from simple predictable processes to square-integrable $(\mathcal{F}_t)_{t \in [0,T]}$-adapted processes $(u_t)_{t \in \mathbb{R}_+}$ for which the value of u_t at time t can only depend on information contained in the Brownian path up to time t.

This restriction means that the Itô integrand u_t cannot depend on future information, for example a portfolio strategy that would allow the trader to "buy at the lowest" and "sell at the highest" is excluded as it would require knowledge of future market data. Note that the difference between Relation (4.16) below and Relation (4.10) is the presence of an expectation on the right-hand side.

Proposition 4.21. *The stochastic integral with respect to Brownian motion* $(B_t)_{t \in \mathbb{R}_+}$ *extends to all adapted processes* $(u_t)_{t \in \mathbb{R}_+}$ *such that*

$$\|u\|^2_{L^2(\Omega \times [0,T])} := \mathbb{E}\left[\int_0^T |u_t|^2 dt\right] < \infty,$$

with the Itô isometry

$$\left\|\int_0^T u_t dB_t\right\|^2_{L^2(\Omega)} := \mathbb{E}\left[\left(\int_0^T u_t dB_t\right)^2\right] = \mathbb{E}\left[\int_0^T |u_t|^2 dt\right]. \tag{4.16}$$

In addition, the Itô integral of an adapted process $(u_t)_{t \in \mathbb{R}_+}$ *is always a centered random variable:*

$$\mathbb{E}\left[\int_0^T u_t dB_t\right] = 0. \tag{4.17}$$

Proof. We start by showing that the Itô isometry (4.16) holds for the simple predictable process u of the form (4.13). We have

$$\mathbb{E}\left[\left(\int_0^T u_t dB_t\right)^2\right] = \mathbb{E}\left[\left(\sum_{i=1}^n F_i(B_{t_i} - B_{t_{i-1}})\right)^2\right]$$

$$= \mathbb{E}\left[\left(\sum_{i=1}^n F_i(B_{t_i} - B_{t_{i-1}})\right)\left(\sum_{j=1}^n F_j(B_{t_j} - B_{t_{j-1}})\right)\right]$$

$$= \mathbb{E}\left[\sum_{i,j=1}^n F_i F_j(B_{t_i} - B_{t_{i-1}})(B_{t_j} - B_{t_{j-1}})\right]$$

$$= \mathbb{E}\left[\sum_{i=1}^n |F_i|^2(B_{t_i} - B_{t_{i-1}})^2\right]$$

$$+ 2\,\mathbb{E}\left[\sum_{1 \leqslant i < j \leqslant n} F_i F_j(B_{t_i} - B_{t_{i-1}})(B_{t_j} - B_{t_{j-1}})\right]$$

$$= \sum_{i=1}^n \mathbb{E}\left[|F_i|^2(B_{t_i} - B_{t_{i-1}})^2\right]$$

$$+ 2 \sum_{1 \leqslant i < j \leqslant n} \mathbb{E}\left[F_i F_j(B_{t_i} - B_{t_{i-1}})(B_{t_j} - B_{t_{j-1}})\right]$$

$$= \sum_{i=1}^n \mathbb{E}[\mathbb{E}[|F_i|^2(B_{t_i} - B_{t_{i-1}})^2|\mathcal{F}_{t_{i-1}}]]$$

$$+2 \sum_{1 \leqslant i < j \leqslant n} \mathbb{E}[\mathbb{E}[F_i F_j (B_{t_i} - B_{t_{i-1}})(B_{t_j} - B_{t_{j-1}})|\mathcal{F}_{t_{j-1}}]]$$

$$= \sum_{i=1}^{n} \mathbb{E}[|F_i|^2 \, \mathbb{E}[(B_{t_i} - B_{t_{i-1}})^2|\mathcal{F}_{t_{i-1}}]]$$

$$+2 \sum_{1 \leqslant i < j \leqslant n} \mathbb{E}\Big[F_i F_j (B_{t_i} - B_{t_{i-1}}) \underbrace{\mathbb{E}[B_{t_j} - B_{t_{j-1}} \mid \mathcal{F}_{t_{j-1}}]}_{=0}\Big]$$

$$= \sum_{i=1}^{n} \mathbb{E}\left[|F_i|^2 \, \mathbb{E}\left[(B_{t_i} - B_{t_{i-1}})^2\right]\right]$$

$$+2 \sum_{1 \leqslant i < j \leqslant n} \mathbb{E}[F_i F_j (B_{t_i} - B_{t_{i-1}}) \underbrace{\mathbb{E}[B_{t_j} - B_{t_{j-1}}]}_{=0}]$$

$$= \sum_{i=1}^{n} \mathbb{E}[|F_i|^2 (t_i - t_{i-1})]$$

$$= \mathbb{E}\left[\sum_{i=1}^{n} |F_i|^2 (t_i - t_{i-1})\right]$$

$$= \mathbb{E}\left[\int_0^T |u_t|^2 dt\right],$$

where we applied the tower property of conditional expectations and the facts that $B_{t_i} - B_{t_{i-1}}$ is independent of $\mathcal{F}_{t_{i-1}}$, with

$$\mathbb{E}[B_{t_i} - B_{t_{i-1}}] = 0, \quad \mathbb{E}\left[(B_{t_i} - B_{t_{i-1}})^2\right] = t_i - t_{i-1}, \quad i = 1, 2, \ldots, n.$$

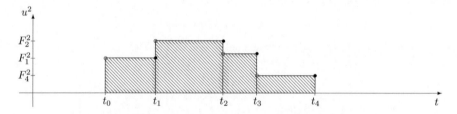

Figure 4.13: Squared simple predictable process $t \mapsto u_t^2$.

The extension of the stochastic integral to square-integrable adapted processes $(u_t)_{t \in \mathbb{R}_+}$ is obtained by a denseness and Cauchy sequence argument using the isometry (4.16), in the same way as in the proof of Proposition 4.12.

i) By Proposition 4.20 given $u \in L^2(\Omega \times [0,T])$ a square-integrable adapted process there exists a sequence $(u^{(n)})_{n \in \mathbb{N}}$ of simple predictable processes such that

$$\lim_{n \to \infty} \|u - u^{(n)}\|_{L^2(\Omega \times [0,T])} = \lim_{n \to \infty} \sqrt{\mathbb{E}\left[\int_0^T |u_t - u_t^{(n)}|^2 dt\right]} = 0.$$

ii) Since the sequence $(u^{(n)})_{n \in \mathbb{N}}$ converges it is a Cauchy sequence in $L^2(\Omega \times \mathbb{R}_+)$, hence by the Itô isometry (4.16), the sequence $\left(\int_0^T u_t^{(n)} dB_t\right)_{n \in \mathbb{N}}$ is a Cauchy sequence in $L^2(\Omega)$, therefore it admits a limit in the complete space $L^2(\Omega)$. In this case we let

$$\int_0^T u_t dB_t := \lim_{n \to \infty} \int_0^T u_t^{(n)} dB_t$$

and the limit is unique from (4.16) and satisfies (4.16).

iii) The fact that the random variable $\int_0^T u_t dB_t$ is *centered* can be proved first on simple predictable process u of the form (4.13) as

$$
\begin{aligned}
\mathbb{E}\left[\int_0^T u_t dB_t\right] &= \mathbb{E}\left[\sum_{i=1}^n F_i(B_{t_i} - B_{t_{i-1}})\right] \\
&= \sum_{i=1}^n \mathbb{E}[\mathbb{E}[F_i(B_{t_i} - B_{t_{i-1}}) \mid \mathcal{F}_{t_{i-1}}]] \\
&= \sum_{i=1}^n \mathbb{E}[F_i\, \mathbb{E}[B_{t_i} - B_{t_{i-1}} \mid \mathcal{F}_{t_{i-1}}]] \\
&= \sum_{i=1}^n \mathbb{E}[F_i\, \mathbb{E}[B_{t_i} - B_{t_{i-1}}]] \\
&= 0,
\end{aligned}
$$

and this identity extends as above from simple predictable processes to adapted processes $(u_t)_{t\in\mathbb{R}_+}$ in $L^2(\Omega \times \mathbb{R}_+)$.

$\square$

As an application of the Itô isometry (4.16), we note in particular the identity

$$
\mathbb{E}\left[\left(\int_0^T B_t dB_t\right)^2\right] = \mathbb{E}\left[\int_0^T |B_t|^2 dt\right] = \int_0^T \mathbb{E}\left[|B_t|^2\right] dt = \int_0^T t\, dt = \frac{T^2}{2},
$$

with

$$
\int_0^T B_t dB_t \overset{L^2(\Omega)}{=} \lim_{n\to\infty} \sum_{i=1}^n B_{t_{i-1}}(B_{t_i} - B_{t_{i-1}})
$$

from (4.14).

The next corollary is obtained by bilinearity from the Itô isometry (4.16) by the same argument as in Corollary 4.13.

Corollary 4.22. *The stochastic integral with respect to Brownian motion $(B_t)_{t\in\mathbb{R}_+}$ satisfies the isometry*

$$
\mathbb{E}\left[\int_0^T u_t dB_t \int_0^T v_t dB_t\right] = \mathbb{E}\left[\int_0^T u_t v_t dt\right],
$$

for all square-integrable adapted processes $(u_t)_{t\in\mathbb{R}_+}$, $(v_t)_{t\in\mathbb{R}_+}$.

Proof. Applying the Itô isometry (4.16) to the processes $u + v$ and $u - v$, we have

$$
\begin{aligned}
&\mathbb{E}\left[\int_0^T u_t dB_t \int_0^T v_t dB_t\right] \\
&= \frac{1}{4}\left(\mathbb{E}\left[\left(\int_0^T u_t dB_t + \int_0^T v_t dB_t\right)^2 - \left(\int_0^T u_t dB_t - \int_0^T v_t dB_t\right)^2\right]\right) \\
&= \frac{1}{4}\left(\mathbb{E}\left[\left(\int_0^T (u_t + v_t) dB_t\right)^2\right] - \mathbb{E}\left[\left(\int_0^T (u_t - v_t) dB_t\right)^2\right]\right) \\
&= \frac{1}{4}\left(\mathbb{E}\left[\int_0^T (u_t + v_t)^2 dt\right] - \mathbb{E}\left[\int_0^T (u_t - v_t)^2 dt\right]\right)
\end{aligned}
$$

$$= \frac{1}{4} \, \mathbb{E} \left[\int_0^T \left((u_t + v_t)^2 - (u_t - v_t)^2 \right) dt \right]$$

$$= \mathbb{E} \left[\int_0^T u_t v_t dt \right].$$

$\square$

In addition, when the integrand $(u_t)_{t \in \mathbb{R}_+}$ is not a deterministic function of time, the random variable $\int_0^T u_t dB_t$ no longer has a Gaussian distribution, except in some exceptional cases.

Definite stochastic integral

The definite stochastic integral of an adapted process $u \in L^2_{ad}(\Omega \times \mathbb{R}_+)$ over an interval $[a, b] \subset [0, T]$ is defined as

$$\int_a^b u_t dB_t := \int_0^T \mathbb{1}_{[a,b]}(t) u_t dB_t,$$

with in particular

$$\int_a^b dB_t = \int_0^T \mathbb{1}_{[a,b]}(t) dB_t = B_b - B_a, \quad 0 \leqslant a \leqslant b,$$

We also have the Chasles relation

$$\int_a^c u_t dB_t = \int_a^b u_t dB_t + \int_b^c u_t dB_t, \quad 0 \leqslant a \leqslant b \leqslant c,$$

and the stochastic integral has the following linearity property:

$$\int_0^T (u_t + v_t) dB_t = \int_0^T u_t dB_t + \int_0^T v_t dB_t, \quad u, v \in L^2(\mathbb{R}_+).$$

4.5   Stochastic Calculus

Stochastic modeling of asset returns

In the sequel we will construct the return at time $t \in \mathbb{R}_+$ of the risky asset $(S_t)_{t \in \mathbb{R}_+}$ as

$$\frac{dS_t}{S_t} = \mu dt + \sigma dB_t, \quad \text{or} \quad dS_t = \mu S_t dt + \sigma S_t dB_t. \tag{4.18}$$

with $\mu \in \mathbb{R}$ and $\sigma > 0$. Using the relation

$$X_T = X_0 + \int_0^T dX_t, \quad T > 0,$$

which holds for any process $(X_t)_{t \in \mathbb{R}_+}$, Equation (4.18) can be rewritten in integral form as

$$S_T = S_0 + \int_0^T dS_t = S_0 + \mu \int_0^T S_t dt + \sigma \int_0^T S_t dB_t, \tag{4.19}$$

hence the need to define an integral with respect to dB_t, in addition to the usual integral with respect to dt. Note that in view of the definition (4.15), this is a continuous-time extension of the notion portfolio value based on a predictable portfolio strategy.

In Proposition 4.21 we have defined the stochastic integral of square-integrable processes with respect to Brownian motion, thus we have made sense of the equation (4.19), where $(S_t)_{t \in \mathbb{R}_+}$ is an $(\mathcal{F}_t)_{t \in [0,T]}$-adapted process, which can be rewritten in differential notation as in (4.18).

This model will be used to represent the random price S_t of a risky asset at time t. Here the return dS_t/S_t of the asset is made of two components: a constant return μdt and a random return σdB_t parametrized by the coefficient σ, called the volatility.

Our goal is now to solve Equation (4.18), and for this we will need to introduce Itô's calculus in Section 4.5 after a review of classical deterministic calculus.

Deterministic calculus

The *fundamental theorem of calculus* states that for any continuously differentiable (deterministic) function f we have the integral relation

$$f(x) = f(0) + \int_0^x f'(y)dy.$$

In differential notation this relation is written as the first-order expansion

$$df(x) = f'(x)dx, \qquad (4.20)$$

where dx is "infinitesimally small". Higher-order expansions can be obtained from *Taylor's formula*, which, letting

$$\Delta f(x) := f(x + \Delta x) - f(x),$$

states that

$$\Delta f(x) = f'(x)\Delta x + \frac{1}{2}f''(x)(\Delta x)^2 + \frac{1}{3!}f'''(x)(\Delta x)^3 + \frac{1}{4!}f^{(4)}(x)(\Delta x)^4 + \cdots.$$

Note that Relation (4.20), *i.e.* $df(x) = f'(x)dx$, can be obtained by neglecting all terms of order higher than one in Taylor's formula, since $(\Delta x)^n << \Delta x$, $n \geqslant 2$, as Δx becomes "infinitesimally small".

Stochastic calculus

Let us now apply Taylor's formula to Brownian motion, taking

$$\Delta B_t = B_{t+\Delta t} - B_t \simeq \pm\sqrt{\Delta t},$$

and letting

$$\Delta f(B_t) := f(B_{t+\Delta t}) - f(B_t),$$

we have

$$\Delta f(B_t)$$
$$= f'(B_t)\Delta B_t + \frac{1}{2}f''(B_t)(\Delta B_t)^2 + \frac{1}{3!}f'''(B_t)(\Delta B_t)^3 + \frac{1}{4!}f^{(4)}(B_t)(\Delta B_t)^4 + \cdots.$$

From the construction of Brownian motion by its small increments $\Delta B_t = \pm\sqrt{\Delta t}$, it turns out that the terms in $(\Delta t)^2$ and $\Delta t \Delta B_t \simeq \pm(\Delta t)^{3/2}$ can be neglected in Taylor's formula at the first-order of approximation in Δt. However, the term of order two

$$(\Delta B_t)^2 = (\pm\sqrt{\Delta t})^2 = \Delta t$$

can no longer be neglected in front of Δt itself.

Basic Itô formula

For $f \in \mathcal{C}^2(\mathbb{R})$,[*] Taylor's formula written at the second order for Brownian motion reads

$$df(B_t) = f'(B_t)dB_t + \frac{1}{2}f''(B_t)dt, \qquad (4.21)$$

for "infinitesimally small" dt. Note that writing this formula as

$$\frac{df(B_t)}{dt} = f'(B_t)\frac{dB_t}{dt} + \frac{1}{2}f''(B_t)$$

does not make sense because the pathwise derivative

$$\frac{dB_t}{dt} \simeq \pm\frac{\sqrt{dt}}{dt} \simeq \pm\frac{1}{\sqrt{dt}} \simeq \pm\infty$$

of B_t with respect to t does not exist. Integrating (4.21) on both sides and using the relation

$$f(B_t) - f(B_0) = \int_0^t df(B_s)$$

together with (4.21), we get the integral form of Itô's formula for Brownian motion, *i.e.*

$$f(B_t) = f(B_0) + \int_0^t f'(B_s)dB_s + \frac{1}{2}\int_0^t f''(B_s)ds.$$

Itô processes

We now turn to the general expression of Itô's formula, which is stated for Itô processes.

Definition 4.23. *An Itô process is a stochastic process* $(X_t)_{t \in \mathbb{R}_+}$ *that can be written as*

$$X_t = X_0 + \int_0^t v_s ds + \int_0^t u_s dB_s, \qquad t \geqslant 0, \qquad (4.22)$$

or in differential notation

$$dX_t = v_t dt + u_t dB_t,$$

where $(u_t)_{t \in \mathbb{R}_+}$ *and* $(v_t)_{t \in \mathbb{R}_+}$ *are square-integrable adapted processes.*

Given $(t, x) \mapsto f(t, x)$ a smooth function of two variables on $\mathbb{R}_+ \times \mathbb{R}$, from now on we let $\dfrac{\partial f}{\partial t}$ denote partial differentiation with respect to the *first* (time) variable in $f(t, x)$, while $\dfrac{\partial f}{\partial x}$ denotes partial differentiation with respect to the *second* (price) variable in $f(t, x)$.

Theorem 4.24. *(Itô formula for Itô processes). For any Itô process* $(X_t)_{t \in \mathbb{R}_+}$ *of the form* (4.22) *and any* $f \in \mathcal{C}_b^{1,2}(\mathbb{R}_+ \times \mathbb{R})$,[†] *we have*

---

[*]This means that f is twice continuously differentiable on $[0, T]$.

[†]This means that f is continuously differentiable on $t \in [0, T]$ and twice differentiable in $c \in \mathbb{R}$, with bounded derivatives.

$$
\begin{aligned}
f(t, X_t) \\
= \quad & f(0, X_0) + \int_0^t \frac{\partial f}{\partial s}(s, X_s)ds + \int_0^t v_s \frac{\partial f}{\partial x}(s, X_s)ds + \int_0^t u_s \frac{\partial f}{\partial x}(s, X_s)dB_s \\
& + \frac{1}{2}\int_0^t |u_s|^2 \frac{\partial^2 f}{\partial x^2}(s, X_s)ds.
\end{aligned} \tag{4.23}
$$

Proof. The proof of the Itô formula can be outlined as follows in the case where $(X_t)_{t\in\mathbb{R}_+} = (B_t)_{t\in\mathbb{R}_+}$ is a standard Brownian motion and $f(x)$ does not depend on time t. We refer to Theorem II-32, page 79 of Protter (2004) for the general case.

Let $\{0 = t_0^n \leqslant t_1^n \leqslant \cdots \leqslant t_n^n = t\}$, $n \geqslant 1$, be a refining sequence of partitions of $[0, t]$ tending to the identity. We have the telescoping identity

$$
f(B_t) - f(B_0) = \sum_{k=1}^n \left(f(B_{t_i^n}) - f(B_{t_{i-1}^n}) \right),
$$

and from Taylor's formula

$$
f(y) - f(x) = (y - x)\frac{\partial f}{\partial x}(x) + \frac{1}{2}(y - x)^2 \frac{\partial^2 f}{\partial x^2}(x) + R(x, y),
$$

where the remainder $R(x, y)$ satisfies $R(x, y) \leqslant o(|y - x|^2)$, we get

$$
\begin{aligned}
f(B_t) - f(B_0) = \quad & \sum_{k=1}^n (B_{t_i^n} - B_{t_{i-1}^n})\frac{\partial f}{\partial x}(B_{t_{i-1}^n}) + \frac{1}{2}\sum_{k=1}^n |B_{t_i^n} - B_{t_{i-1}^n}|^2 \frac{\partial^2 f}{\partial x^2}(B_{t_{i-1}^n}) \\
& + \sum_{k=1}^n R(B_{t_i^n}, B_{t_{i-1}^n}).
\end{aligned}
$$

It remains to show that as n tends to infinity the above converges to

$$
f(B_t) - f(B_0) = \int_0^t \frac{\partial f}{\partial x}(B_s)dB_s + \frac{1}{2}\int_0^t \frac{\partial^2 f}{\partial x^2}(B_s)ds.
$$

$\square$

From the relation

$$
\int_0^t df(s, X_s) = f(t, X_t) - f(0, X_0),
$$

we can rewrite (4.23) as

$$
\begin{aligned}
\int_0^t df(s, X_s) = \quad & \int_0^t v_s \frac{\partial f}{\partial x}(s, X_s)ds + \int_0^t u_s \frac{\partial f}{\partial x}(s, X_s)dB_s \\
& + \int_0^t \frac{\partial f}{\partial s}(s, X_s)ds + \frac{1}{2}\int_0^t |u_s|^2 \frac{\partial^2 f}{\partial x^2}(s, X_s)ds,
\end{aligned}
$$

which allows us to rewrite (4.23) in differential notation, as

$$
\begin{aligned}
df(t, X_t) \\
= \quad & \frac{\partial f}{\partial t}(t, X_t)dt + v_t \frac{\partial f}{\partial x}(t, X_t)dt + u_t \frac{\partial f}{\partial x}(t, X_t)dB_t + \frac{1}{2}|u_t|^2 \frac{\partial^2 f}{\partial x^2}(t, X_t)dt.
\end{aligned} \tag{4.24}
$$

In case the function $x \mapsto f(x)$ does not depend on the time variable t we get

$$df(X_t) = u_t \frac{\partial f}{\partial x}(X_t)dB_t + v_t \frac{\partial f}{\partial x}(X_t)dt + \frac{1}{2}|u_t|^2 \frac{\partial^2 f}{\partial x^2}(X_t)dt.$$

Taking $u_t = 1$, $v_t = 0$ and $X_0 = 0$ in (4.22) yields $X_t = B_t$, in which case the Itô formula (4.23)–(4.24) reads

$$f(t, B_t) = f(0, B_0) + \int_0^t \frac{\partial f}{\partial s}(s, B_s)ds + \int_0^t \frac{\partial f}{\partial x}(s, B_s)dB_s + \frac{1}{2}\int_0^t \frac{\partial^2 f}{\partial x^2}(s, B_s)ds,$$

i.e. in differential notation:

$$df(t, B_t) = \frac{\partial f}{\partial t}(t, B_t)dt + \frac{\partial f}{\partial x}(t, B_t)dB_t + \frac{1}{2}\frac{\partial^2 f}{\partial x^2}(t, B_t)dt. \qquad (4.25)$$

Bivariate Itô formula

Next, consider two Itô processes $(X_t)_{t \in \mathbb{R}_+}$ and $(Y_t)_{t \in \mathbb{R}_+}$ written in *integral form* as

$$X_t = X_0 + \int_0^t v_s ds + \int_0^t u_s dB_s, \qquad t \geqslant 0,$$

and

$$Y_t = Y_0 + \int_0^t b_s ds + \int_0^t a_s dB_s, \qquad t \geqslant 0,$$

or in *differential notation* as

$$dX_t = v_t dt + u_t dB_t, \quad \text{and} \quad dY_t = b_t dt + a_t dB_t, \qquad t \geqslant 0.$$

The Itô formula can also be written for functions $f \in \mathcal{C}^{1,2,2}(\mathbb{R}_+ \times \mathbb{R}^2)$ of two state variables as

$$df(t, X_t, Y_t) = \frac{\partial f}{\partial t}(t, X_t, Y_t)dt + \frac{\partial f}{\partial x}(t, X_t, Y_t)dX_t + \frac{1}{2}|u_t|^2 \frac{\partial^2 f}{\partial x^2}(t, X_t, Y_t)dt$$

$$+ \frac{\partial f}{\partial y}(t, X_t, Y_t)dY_t + \frac{1}{2}|a_t|^2 \frac{\partial^2 f}{\partial y^2}(t, X_t, Y_t)dt + u_t a_t \frac{\partial^2 f}{\partial x \partial y}(t, X_t, Y_t)dt. \qquad (4.26)$$

Itô multiplication table

Applying the bivariate Itô formula (4.26) to be function $f(x, y) = xy$ shows that

$$d(X_t Y_t) = X_t dY_t + Y_t dX_t + a_t u_t dt = X_t dY_t + Y_t dX_t + dX_t \cdot dY_t \qquad (4.27)$$

where the product $dX_t \cdot dY_t$ is computed according to the *Itô rule*

$$dt \cdot dt = 0, \qquad dt \cdot dB_t = 0, \qquad dB_t \cdot dB_t = dt, \qquad (4.28)$$

which can be encoded in the following Itô multiplication table:

$\cdot$	dt	dB_t
dt	0	0
dB_t	0	dt

Table 4.1: Itô multiplication table.

It follows from the Itô Table 4.1 that

$$
\begin{aligned}
dX_t \cdot dY_t &= (v_t dt + u_t dB_t) \cdot (b_t dt + a_t dB_t) \\
&= b_t v_t (dt)^2 + b_t u_t dt dB_t + a_t v_t dt dB_t + a_t u_t (dB_t)^2 \\
&= a_t u_t dt.
\end{aligned}
$$

Hence we also have

$$
\begin{aligned}
(dX_t)^2 &= (v_t dt + u_t dB_t)^2 \\
&= (v_t)^2 (dt)^2 + (u_t)^2 (dB_t)^2 + 2u_t v_t (dt \cdot dB_t) \\
&= (u_t)^2 dt,
\end{aligned}
$$

according to the Itô Table 4.1. Consequently, (4.24) can be rewritten as

$$
df(t, X_t) = \frac{\partial f}{\partial t}(t, X_t)dt + \frac{\partial f}{\partial x}(t, X_t)dX_t + \frac{1}{2}\frac{\partial^2 f}{\partial x^2}(t, X_t)dX_t \cdot dX_t, \tag{4.29}
$$

and the Itô formula for functions $f \in \mathcal{C}^{1,2,2}(\mathbb{R}_+ \times \mathbb{R}^2)$ of two state variables can be rewritten as

$$
\begin{aligned}
df(t, X_t, Y_t) &= \frac{\partial f}{\partial t}(t, X_t, Y_t)dt + \frac{\partial f}{\partial x}(t, X_t, Y_t)dX_t + \frac{1}{2}\frac{\partial^2 f}{\partial x^2}(t, X_t, Y_t)(dX_t)^2 \\
&+ \frac{\partial f}{\partial y}(t, X_t, Y_t)dY_t + \frac{1}{2}\frac{\partial^2 f}{\partial y^2}(t, X_t, Y_t)(dY_t)^2 + \frac{\partial^2 f}{\partial x \partial y}(t, X_t, Y_t)(dX_t \cdot dY_t).
\end{aligned}
$$

Examples

Applying Itô's formula (4.25) to B_t^2 with

$$
B_t^2 = f(t, B_t) \quad \text{and} \quad f(t, x) = x^2,
$$

and

$$
\frac{\partial f}{\partial t}(t, x) = 0, \qquad \frac{\partial f}{\partial x}(t, x) = 2x, \qquad \frac{1}{2}\frac{\partial^2 f}{\partial x^2}(t, x) = 1,
$$

we find

$$
\begin{aligned}
d(B_t^2) &= df(B_t) \\
&= \frac{\partial f}{\partial t}(t, B_t)dt + \frac{\partial f}{\partial x}(t, B_t)dB_t + \frac{1}{2}\frac{\partial^2 f}{\partial x^2}(t, B_t)dt \\
&= 2B_t dB_t + dt.
\end{aligned}
$$

Note that from the Itô Table 4.1 we could also write directly

$$d(B_t^2) = B_t dB_t + B_t dB_t + (dB_t)^2 = 2B_t dB_t + dt.$$

Next, by integration in $t \in [0, T]$ we find

$$B_T^2 = B_0 + 2\int_0^T B_s dB_s + \int_0^T dt = 2\int_0^T B_s dB_s + T, \qquad (4.30)$$

hence the relation

$$\int_0^T B_s dB_s = \frac{1}{2}\left(B_T^2 - T\right), \qquad (4.31)$$

see Exercise 4.13 for the probability distribution of $\int_0^T B_s dB_s$.

Similarly, we have

i) $d(B_t^3) = 3(B_t)^2 dB_t + 3B_t dt.$

Letting $f(x) := x^3$ with $f'(x) = 3x^2$ and $f''(x) = 6x$, we have

$$d(B_t^3) = df(B_t) = f'(B_t)dB_t + \frac{1}{2}f''(B_t)dt = 3(B_t)^2 dB_t + 3B_t dt.$$

ii) $d(\sin B_t) = \cos(B_t)dB_t - \frac{1}{2}\sin(B_t)dt.$

Letting $f(x) := \sin(x)$ with $f'(x) = \cos(x)$, $f''(x) = -\sin(x)$, we have

$$\begin{aligned} d\sin(B_t) &= df(B_t) \\ &= f'(B_t)dB_t + \frac{1}{2}f''(B_t)dt \\ &= \cos(B_t)dB_t - \frac{1}{2}\sin(B_t)dt. \end{aligned}$$

iii) $d\mathrm{e}^{B_t} = \mathrm{e}^{B_t}dB_t + \frac{1}{2}\mathrm{e}^{B_t}dt.$

Letting $f(x) := \mathrm{e}^x$ with $f'(x) = \mathrm{e}^x$, $f''(x) = \mathrm{e}^x$, we have

$$\begin{aligned} d\mathrm{e}^{B_t} &= df(B_t) \\ &= f'(B_t)dB_t + \frac{1}{2}f''(B_t)dt \\ &= \mathrm{e}^{tB_t}dB_t + \frac{1}{2}\mathrm{e}^{tB_t}dt. \end{aligned}$$

iv) $d\log B_t = \frac{1}{B_t}dB_t - \frac{1}{2(B_t)^2}dt.$

Letting $f(x) := \log x$ with $f'(x) = 1/x$ and $f''(x) = -1/x^2$, we have

$$d \log B_t = df(B_t) = f'(B_t)dB_t + \frac{1}{2}f''(B_t)dt = \frac{dB_t}{B_t} - \frac{dt}{2(B_t)^2}.$$

v) $d\,\mathrm{e}^{tB_t} = B_t\,\mathrm{e}^{tB_t}\,dt + \dfrac{t^2}{2}\,\mathrm{e}^{tB_t}\,dt + t\,\mathrm{e}^{tB_t}\,dB_t.$

Letting $f(t,x) := \mathrm{e}^{xt}$ with

$$\frac{\partial f}{\partial t}(t,x) = x\,\mathrm{e}^{xt}, \quad \frac{\partial f}{\partial x}(t,x) = t\,\mathrm{e}^{xt}, \quad \frac{\partial^2 f}{\partial x^2}(t,x) = t^2\,\mathrm{e}^{xt},$$

we have

$$\begin{aligned}
d\,\mathrm{e}^{tB_t} &= df(t,B_t) \\
&= \frac{\partial f}{\partial t}(t,B_t)dt + \frac{\partial f}{\partial x}(t,B_t)dB_t + \frac{1}{2}\frac{\partial^2 f}{\partial x^2}(t,B_t)dt \\
&= B_t\,\mathrm{e}^{tB_t}\,dt + t\,\mathrm{e}^{tB_t}\,dB_t + \frac{t^2}{2}\,\mathrm{e}^{tB_t}\,dt.
\end{aligned}$$

vi) $d\cos(2t + B_t) = -2\sin(2t + B_t)dt - \sin(2t + B_t)dB_t + \dfrac{1}{2}\cos(2t + B_t)dt.$

Letting $f(t,x) := \cos(2t + x)$ with

$$\frac{\partial f}{\partial t}(t,x) = -2\sin(2t + x), \quad \frac{\partial f}{\partial x}(t,x) = -\sin(2t + x), \quad \frac{\partial^2 f}{\partial x^2}(t,x) = \cos(2t + x),$$

we have

$$\begin{aligned}
d\cos(2t + B_t) &= df(t,B_t) \\
&= \frac{\partial f}{\partial t}(t,B_t)dt + \frac{\partial f}{\partial x}(t,B_t)dB_t + \frac{1}{2}\frac{\partial^2 f}{\partial x^2}(t,B_t)dt \\
&= -2\sin(2t + B_t)dt - \sin(2t + B_t)dB_t + \frac{1}{2}\cos(2t + B_t)dt.
\end{aligned}$$

Stochastic differential equations

In addition to geometric Brownian motion there exists a large family of stochastic differential equations that can be studied, although most of the time they cannot be explicitly solved. Let now

$$\sigma : \mathbb{R}_+ \times \mathbb{R}^n \longrightarrow \mathbb{R}^d \otimes \mathbb{R}^n$$

where $\mathbb{R}^d \otimes \mathbb{R}^n$ denotes the space of $d \times n$ matrices, and

$$b : \mathbb{R}_+ \times \mathbb{R}^n \longrightarrow \mathbb{R}$$

satisfy the global Lipschitz condition

$$\|\sigma(t,x) - \sigma(t,y)\|^2 + \|b(t,x) - b(t,y)\|^2 \leqslant K^2\|x - y\|^2,$$

$t \in \mathbb{R}_+$, $x, y \in \mathbb{R}^n$. Then there exists a unique "strong" solution to the stochastic differential equation

$$X_t = X_0 + \int_0^t b(s, X_s)ds + \int_0^t \sigma(s, X_s)dB_s, \quad t \geqslant 0, \tag{4.32}$$

i.e. in differential notation

$$dX_t = b(t, X_t)dt + \sigma(t, X_t)dB_t, \quad t \geqslant 0,$$

where $(B_t)_{t \in \mathbb{R}_+}$ is a d-dimensional Brownian motion, see *e.g.* Protter (2004), Theorem V-7. In addition, the solution process $(X_t)_{t \in \mathbb{R}_+}$ of (4.32) has the *Markov property*, see § V-6 of Protter (2004).

The term $\sigma(s, X_s)$ in (4.32) will be interpreted later on in Chapters 8–9 as a *local volatility* component.

Stochastic differential equations can be used to model the behavior of a variety of quantities, such as

- stock prices,

- interest rates,

- exchange rates,

- weather factors,

- electricity/energy demand,

- commodity (*e.g.* oil) prices, etc.

Next, we consider several examples of stochastic differential equations that can be solved explicitly using Itô's calculus, in addition to geometric Brownian motion. See *e.g.* § II-4.4 of Kloeden and Platen (1999) for more examples of explicitly solvable stochastic differential equations.

Examples of stochastic differential equations

1. Consider the mean-reverting stochastic differential equation

$$dX_t = -\alpha X_t dt + \sigma dB_t, \quad X_0 = x_0, \tag{4.33}$$

with $\alpha > 0$ and $\sigma > 0$.

```
N=10000; t <- 0:(N-1); dt <- 1.0/N;alpha=5; sigma=0.4;
dB <- rnorm(N,mean=0,sd=sqrt(dt));X <- rep(0,N);X[1]=0.5
for (j in 2:N){X[j]=X[j-1]-alpha*X[j-1]*dt+sigma*dB[j]}
plot(t*dt, X, xlab = "t", ylab = "", type = "l", ylim = c(-0.5,1), col = "blue")
abline(h=0)
```

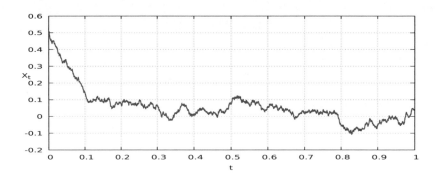

Figure 4.14: Simulated path of (4.33) with $\alpha = 10$, $\sigma = 0.2$ and $X_0 = 0.5$.

We look for a solution of the form

$$X_t = a(t)Y_t = a(t)\left(x_0 + \int_0^t b(s)dB_s\right)$$

where $a(\cdot)$ and $b(\cdot)$ are deterministic functions of time. After applying Theorem 4.24 to the Itô process $x_0 + \int_0^t b(s)dB_s$ of the form (4.22) with $u_t = b(t)$ and $v(t) = 0$, and to the function $f(t, x) = a(t)x$, we find

$$
\begin{aligned}
dX_t &= d(a(t)Y_t)\\
&= Y_t a'(t)dt + a(t)dY_t\\
&= Y_t a'(t)dt + a(t)b(t)dB_t.
\end{aligned}
\tag{4.34}
$$

By identification of (4.33) with (4.34), we get

$$
\begin{cases}
a'(t) = -\alpha a(t)\\
\\
a(t)b(t) = \sigma,
\end{cases}
$$

hence $a(t) = a(0)\,e^{-\alpha t} = e^{-\alpha t}$ and $b(t) = \sigma/a(t) = \sigma\,e^{\alpha t}$, which shows that

$$X_t = x_0\,e^{-\alpha t} + \sigma \int_0^t e^{-(t-s)\alpha}dB_s, \qquad t \geqslant 0, \tag{4.35}$$

Using integration by parts, we can also write

$$X_t = x_0\,e^{-\alpha t} + \sigma B_t - \sigma\alpha \int_0^t e^{-(t-s)\alpha}B_s ds, \qquad t \geqslant 0, \tag{4.36}$$

Remark: the solution of the equation (4.33) *cannot* be written as a function $f(t, B_t)$ of t and B_t as in the proof of Proposition 5.15.

2. Consider the stochastic differential equation

$$dX_t = tX_t dt + e^{t^2/2}dB_t, \qquad X_0 = x_0. \tag{4.37}$$

```
N=10000; T<-2.0; t <- 0:(N-1); dt <- T/N;
dB <- rnorm(N,mean=0,sd= sqrt(dt));X <- rep(0,N);X[1]=0.5
for (j in 2:N){X[j]=X[j-1]+j*X[j-1]*dt*dt+exp(j*dt*j*dt/2)*dB[j]}
plot(t*dt, X, xlab = "t", ylab = "", type = "l", ylim = c(-0.5,10), col = "blue")
abline(h=0)
```

Looking for a solution of the form $X_t = a(t)\left(X_0 + \int_0^t b(s)dB_s\right)$, where $a(\cdot)$ and $b(\cdot)$ are deterministic functions of time, we get $a'(t)/a(t) = t$ and $a(t)b(t) = e^{t^2/2}$, hence $a(t) = e^{t^2/2}$ and $b(t) = 1$, which yields $X_t = e^{t^2/2}(X_0 + B_t)$, $t \geqslant 0$.

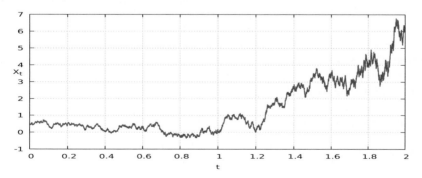

Figure 4.15: Simulated path of (4.37).

3. Consider the stochastic differential equation

$$dY_t = (-2\alpha Y_t + \sigma^2)dt + 2\sigma\sqrt{Y_t}dB_t, \qquad (4.38)$$

where $\alpha \in \mathbb{R}$ and $\sigma > 0$.

```
1   N=10000; t <- 0:(N-1); dt <- 1.0/N;mu=-5;sigma=1;
    dB <- rnorm(N,mean=0,sd=sqrt(dt));Y <- rep(0,N);Y[1]=0.5
3   for (j in 2:N){ Y[j]=max(0,Y[j-1]+(2*mu*Y[j-1]+sigma*sigma)*dt+2*sigma*sqrt(Y[j-1])*dB[j])}
    plot(t*dt, Y, xlab = "t", ylab = "", type = "l", ylim = c(-0.1,1), col = "blue")
5   abline(h=0)
```

Letting $X_t := \sqrt{Y_t}$, we find that $dX_t = -\alpha X_t dt + \sigma dB_t$, hence by (4.35) we obtain

$$Y_t = (X_t)^2 = \left(e^{-\alpha t}\sqrt{Y_0} + \sigma \int_0^t e^{-(t-s)\alpha}dB_s \right)^2.$$

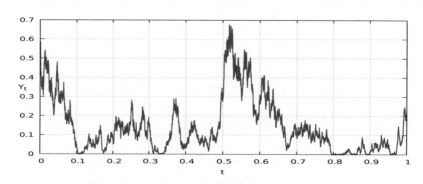

Figure 4.16: Simulated path of (4.38) with $\alpha = -5$ and $\sigma = 1$.

Exercises

Exercise 4.1 Compute $\mathbb{E}[B_t B_s]$ in terms of $s, t \geqslant 0$.

Exercise 4.2 Let $(B_t)_{t\in\mathbb{R}_+}$ denote a standard Brownian motion. Let $c > 0$. Among the following processes, tell which is a standard Brownian motion and which is not. Justify your answer.

a) $(X_t)_{t\in\mathbb{R}_+} := \left(B_{c+t} - B_c \right)_{t\in\mathbb{R}_+}$,

b) $(X_t)_{t\in\mathbb{R}_+} := \left(B_{ct^2} \right)_{t\in\mathbb{R}_+}$,

c) $(X_t)_{t\in\mathbb{R}_+} := \left(cB_{t/c^2} \right)_{t\in\mathbb{R}_+}$,

d) $(X_t)_{t\in\mathbb{R}_+} := \left(B_t + B_{t/2} \right)_{t\in\mathbb{R}_+}$.

Exercise 4.3 Let $(B_t)_{t \in \mathbb{R}_+}$ denote a standard Brownian motion. Compute the stochastic integrals

$$\int_0^T 2 dB_t \quad \text{and} \quad \int_0^T \left(2 \times \mathbb{1}_{[0,T/2]}(t) + \mathbb{1}_{(T/2,T]}(t)\right) dB_t$$

and determine their probability distributions (including mean and variance).

Exercise 4.4 Determine the probability distribution (including mean and variance) of the stochastic integral $\int_0^{2\pi} \sin(t) \, dB_t$.

Exercise 4.5 Let $T > 0$. Show that for $f : [0, T] \mapsto \mathbb{R}$ a differentiable function such that $f(T) = 0$, we have

$$\int_0^T f(t) dB_t = -\int_0^T f'(t) B_t dt.$$

Hint: Apply Itô's calculus to $t \mapsto f(t) B_t$.

Exercise 4.6 Let $(B_t)_{t \in \mathbb{R}_+}$ denote a standard Brownian motion.

a) Find the probability distribution of the stochastic integral $\int_0^1 t^2 dB_t$.

b) Find the probability distribution of the stochastic integral $\int_0^1 t^{-1/2} dB_t$.

Exercise 4.7 Given $(B_t)_{t \in \mathbb{R}_+}$ a standard Brownian motion and $n \geqslant 1$, let the random variable X_n be defined as

$$X_n := \int_0^{2\pi} \sin(nt) dB_t, \qquad n \geqslant 1.$$

a) Give the probability distribution of X_n for all $n \geqslant 1$.

b) Show that $(X_n)_{n \geqslant 1}$ is a sequence of identically distributed and pairwise independent random variables.

Hint: We have $\sin a \sin b = \dfrac{1}{2} \big(\cos(a - b) - \cos(a + b) \big)$, $a, b \in \mathbb{R}$.

Exercise 4.8 Apply the Itô formula to the process $X_t := \sin^2(B_t)$, $t \geqslant 0$.

Exercise 4.9 Let $(B_t)_{t \in \mathbb{R}_+}$ denote a standard Brownian motion.

a) Using the Itô isometry and the known relations

$$B_T = \int_0^T dB_t \quad \text{and} \quad B_T^2 = T + 2 \int_0^T B_t dB_t,$$

compute the third and fourth moments $\mathbb{E}[B_T^3]$ and $\mathbb{E}[B_T^4]$.

b) Give the third and fourth moments of the centered normal distribution with variance σ^2.

Exercise 4.10 Let $(B_t)_{t\in\mathbb{R}_+}$ denote a standard Brownian motion. Given $T > 0$, find the stochastic integral decomposition of $(B_T)^3$ as

$$(B_T)^3 = C + \int_0^T \zeta_{t,T} dB_t \qquad (4.39)$$

where $C \in \mathbb{R}$ is a constant and $(\zeta_{t,T})_{t\in[0,T]}$ is an adapted process to be determined.

Exercise 4.11 Let $f \in L^2([0,T])$, and consider a standard Brownian motion $(B_t)_{t\in[0,T]}$.

a) Compute the conditional expectation

$$\mathbb{E}\left[e^{\int_0^T f(s)dB_s} \middle| \mathcal{F}_t\right], \qquad 0 \leqslant t \leqslant T,$$

where $(\mathcal{F}_t)_{t\in[0,T]}$ denotes the filtration generated by $(B_t)_{t\in[0,T]}$.

b) Using the result of Question (a), show that the process

$$t \longmapsto \exp\left(\int_0^t f(s)dB_s - \frac{1}{2}\int_0^t f^2(s)ds\right), \qquad 0 \leqslant t \leqslant T,$$

is an $(\mathcal{F}_t)_{t\in[0,T]}$-martingale, where $(\mathcal{F}_t)_{t\in[0,T]}$ denotes the filtration generated by $(B_t)_{t\in[0,T]}$.

c) By applying the result of Question (b) to the function $f(t) := \sigma\mathbb{1}_{[0,T]}(t)$, show that the geometric Brownian motion process $\left(e^{\sigma B_t - \sigma t^2/2}\right)_{t\in[0,T]}$ is an $(\mathcal{F}_t)_{t\in[0,T]}$-martingale for any $\sigma \in \mathbb{R}$.

Exercise 4.12 Consider two assets whose prices $S_t^{(1)}$, $S_t^{(2)}$ follow the Bachelier dynamics

$$dS_t^{(1)} = \mu S_t^{(1)} dt + \sigma_1 dW_t^{(1)}, \quad dS_t^{(2)} = \mu S_t^{(2)} dt + \sigma_2 dW_t^{(2)}, \quad t \in [0,T],$$

where $\left(W_t^{(1)}\right)_{t\in[0,T]}$, $\left(W_t^{(2)}\right)_{t\in[0,T]}$ are two Brownian motions with correlation $\rho \in [-1,1]$, *i.e.* we have $dW_t^{(1)} \cdot dW_t^{(2)} = \rho dt$. Show that the spread $S_t := S_t^{(2)} - S_t^{(1)}$ also satisfies an equation of the form

$$dS_t = \mu S_t dt + \sigma dW_t,$$

where $\mu \in \mathbb{R}$, $(W_t)_{t\in\mathbb{R}_+}$ is a standard Brownian motion, and $\sigma > 0$ should be given in terms of σ_1, σ_2 and ρ.

Hint: By the Lévy characterization theorem, Brownian motion $(W_t)_{t\in\mathbb{R}_+}$ is the only continuous martingale such that $dW_t \cdot dW_t = dt$.

Exercise 4.13

a) Compute the moment generating function

$$\mathbb{E}\left[\exp\left(\beta \int_0^T B_t dB_t\right)\right]$$

for all $\beta < 1/T$.

Hint: Expand $(B_T)^2$ using the Itô formula as in (4.30).

b) Find the probability distribution of the stochastic integral $\beta \int_0^T B_t dB_t$.

Exercise 4.14

a) Solve the stochastic differential equation

$$dX_t = -bX_t dt + \sigma e^{-bt} dB_t, \qquad t \geqslant 0, \tag{4.40}$$

where $(B_t)_{t \in \mathbb{R}_+}$ is a standard Brownian motion and $\sigma, b \in \mathbb{R}$.

b) Solve the stochastic differential equation

$$dX_t = -bX_t dt + \sigma e^{-at} dB_t, \qquad t \geqslant 0, \tag{4.41}$$

where $(B_t)_{t \in \mathbb{R}_+}$ is a standard Brownian motion and $a, b, \sigma > 0$ are positive constants.

Exercise 4.15   Given $T > 0$, let $(X_t)_{t \in [0,T)}$ denote the solution of the stochastic differential equation

$$dX_t = \sigma dB_t - \frac{X_t}{T-t} dt, \qquad t \in [0, T), \tag{4.42}$$

under the initial condition $X_0 = 0$ and $\sigma > 0$.

a) Show that

$$X_t = (T - t) \int_0^t \frac{\sigma}{T-s} dB_s, \qquad 0 \leqslant t < T.$$

Hint: Start by computing $d(X_t/(T-t))$ using the Itô formula.

b) Show that $\mathbb{E}[X_t] = 0$ for all $t \in [0, T)$.

c) Show that $\mathrm{Var}[X_t] = \sigma^2 t(T-t)/T$ for all $t \in [0, T)$.

d) Show that $\lim_{t \to T} X_t = 0$ in $L^2(\Omega)$. The process $(X_t)_{t \in [0,T]}$ is called a *Brownian bridge*.

Exercise 4.16   Exponential Vašíček (1977) model (1). Consider a Vasicek process $(r_t)_{t \in \mathbb{R}_+}$ solving of the stochastic differential equation

$$dr_t = (a - br_t)dt + \sigma dB_t, \qquad t \geqslant 0,$$

where $(B_t)_{t \in \mathbb{R}_+}$ is a standard Brownian motion and $\sigma, a, b > 0$ are positive constants. Show that the exponential $X_t := e^{r_t}$ satisfies a stochastic differential equation of the form

$$dX_t = X_t(\widetilde{a} - \widetilde{b}f(X_t))dt + \sigma g(X_t)dB_t,$$

where the coefficients $\widetilde{a}$ and $\widetilde{b}$ and the functions $f(x)$ and $g(x)$ are to be determined.

Exercise 4.17   Exponential Vasicek model (2). Consider a short-term rate interest rate process $(r_t)_{t \in \mathbb{R}_+}$ in the exponential Vasicek model:

$$dr_t = (\eta - a \log r_t)r_t dt + \sigma r_t dB_t, \tag{4.43}$$

where η, a, σ are positive parameters and $(B_t)_{t \in \mathbb{R}_+}$ is a standard Brownian motion.

a) Find the solution $(Z_t)_{t \in \mathbb{R}_+}$ of the stochastic differential equation

$$dZ_t = -aZ_t dt + \sigma dB_t$$

as a function of the initial condition Z_0, where a and σ are positive parameters.

b) Find the solution $(Y_t)_{t \in \mathbb{R}_+}$ of the stochastic differential equation

$$dY_t = (\theta - aY_t)dt + \sigma dB_t \tag{4.44}$$

as a function of the initial condition Y_0. *Hint:* Let $Z_t := Y_t - \theta/a$.

c) Let $X_t = e^{Y_t}$, $t \in \mathbb{R}_+$. Determine the stochastic differential equation satisfied by $(X_t)_{t \in \mathbb{R}_+}$.

d) Find the solution $(r_t)_{t \in \mathbb{R}_+}$ of (4.43) in terms of the initial condition r_0.

e) Compute the conditional mean* $\mathbb{E}[r_t | \mathcal{F}_u]$.

f) Compute the conditional variance

$$\mathrm{Var}[r_t | \mathcal{F}_u] := \mathbb{E}[r_t^2 | \mathcal{F}_u] - (\mathbb{E}[r_t | \mathcal{F}_u])^2$$

of r_t, $0 \leqslant u \leqslant t$, where $(\mathcal{F}_u)_{u \in \mathbb{R}_+}$ denotes the filtration generated by the Brownian motion $(B_t)_{t \in \mathbb{R}_+}$.

g) Compute the asymptotic mean and variance $\lim_{t \to \infty} \mathbb{E}[r_t]$ and $\lim_{t \to \infty} \mathrm{Var}[r_t]$.

Exercise 4.18 Cox–Ingersoll–Ross (CIR) model. Consider the equation

$$dr_t = (\alpha - \beta r_t)dt + \sigma\sqrt{r_t}dB_t \tag{4.45}$$

modeling the variations of a short-term interest rate process r_t, where α, β, σ and r_0 are positive parameters and $(B_t)_{t \in \mathbb{R}_+}$ is a standard Brownian motion.

a) Write down the equation (4.45) in integral form.

b) Let $u(t) = \mathbb{E}[r_t]$. Show, using the integral form of (4.45), that $u(t)$ satisfies the differential equation

$$u'(t) = \alpha - \beta u(t),$$

and compute $\mathbb{E}[r_t]$ for all $t \geqslant 0$.

c) By an application of Itô's formula to r_t^2, show that

$$dr_t^2 = r_t(2\alpha + \sigma^2 - 2\beta r_t)dt + 2\sigma r_t^{3/2}dB_t. \tag{4.46}$$

d) Using the integral form of (4.46), find a differential equation satisfied by $v(t) := \mathbb{E}[r_t^2]$ and compute $\mathbb{E}[r_t^2]$ for all $t \geqslant 0$.

e) Show that

$$\mathrm{Var}[r_t] = r_0 \frac{\sigma^2}{\beta}\left(e^{-\beta t} - e^{-2\beta t}\right) + \frac{\alpha\sigma^2}{2\beta^2}\left(1 - e^{-\beta t}\right)^2, \quad t \geqslant 0.$$

---

*One may use the Gaussian moment generating function $\mathbb{E}[e^X] = e^{\alpha^2/2}$ for $X \simeq \mathcal{N}(0, \alpha^2)$.

Problem 4.19 Itô-Tanaka formula. Let $(B_t)_{t \in \mathbb{R}_+}$ be a standard Brownian motion started at $B_0 \in \mathbb{R}$.

a) Does the Itô formula apply to the European call option payoff function $f(x) := (x - K)^+$? Why?

b) For every $\varepsilon > 0$, consider the approximation $f_\varepsilon(x)$ of $f(x) := (x - K)^+$ defined by

$$
f_\varepsilon(x) := \begin{cases}
x - K & \text{if } x > K + \varepsilon, \\[2mm]
\dfrac{1}{4\varepsilon}(x - K + \varepsilon)^2 & \text{if } K - \varepsilon < x < K + \varepsilon, \\[2mm]
0 & \text{if } x < K - \varepsilon.
\end{cases}
$$

Plot the graph of the function $x \mapsto f_\varepsilon(x)$ for $\varepsilon = 1$ and $K = 10$.

c) Using the Itô formula, show that

$$
\begin{aligned}
f_\varepsilon(B_T) \;=\;& f_\varepsilon(B_0) + \int_0^T f_\varepsilon'(B_t)dB_t \\
&+ \frac{1}{4\varepsilon}\ell\left(\{t \in [0,T] \; : \; K - \varepsilon < B_t < K + \varepsilon\}\right),
\end{aligned} \tag{4.47}
$$

where ℓ denotes the measure of time length (Lebesgue measure) in $\mathbb{R}$.

d) Show that $\lim_{\varepsilon \to 0} \| \mathbb{1}_{[K,\infty)}(\cdot) - f_\varepsilon'(\cdot)\|_{L^2(\mathbb{R}_+)} = 0$.

e) Show, using the Itô isometry,[*] that the limit

$$
\mathcal{L}^K_{[0,T]} := \lim_{\varepsilon \to 0} \frac{1}{2\varepsilon}\ell(\{t \in [0,T] \; : \; K - \varepsilon < B_t < K + \varepsilon\})
$$

exists in $L^2(\Omega)$, and prove the Itô-Tanaka formula

$$
(B_T - K)^+ = (B_0 - K)^+ + \int_0^T \mathbb{1}_{[K,\infty)}(B_t)dB_t + \frac{1}{2}\mathcal{L}^K_{[0,T]}. \tag{4.48}
$$

The quantity $\mathcal{L}^K_{[0,T]}$ is called the *local time* spent by Brownian motion at the level K.

Problem 4.20 Lévy's construction of Brownian motion. The goal of this problem is to prove the existence of standard Brownian motion $(B_t)_{t \in [0,1]}$ as a stochastic process satisfying the four properties of Definition 4.1, *i.e.*:

1. $B_0 = 0$ almost surely,

2. The sample trajectories $t \mapsto B_t$ are continuous, with probability 1.

3. For any finite sequence of times $t_0 < t_1 < \cdots < t_n$, the increments

$$
B_{t_1} - B_{t_0}, B_{t_2} - B_{t_1}, \ldots, B_{t_n} - B_{t_{n-1}}
$$

are independent.

---

[*]Hint: Show that $\displaystyle\lim_{\varepsilon \to 0} \mathbb{E}\left[\int_0^T \left(\mathbb{1}_{[K,\infty)}(B_t) - f_\varepsilon'(B_t)\right)^2 dt\right] = 0$.

4. For any given times $0 \leqslant s < t$, $B_t - B_s$ has the Gaussian distribution $\mathcal{N}(0, t - s)$ with mean zero and variance $t - s$.

The construction will proceed by the linear interpolation scheme illustrated in Figure 4.5. We work on the space $\mathcal{C}_0([0, 1])$ of continuous functions on $[0, 1]$ started at 0, with the norm

$$\|f\|_\infty := \operatorname*{Max}_{t \in [0,1]} |f(t)|$$

and the distance

$$\|f - g\|_\infty := \operatorname*{Max}_{t \in [0,1]} |f(t) - g(t)|.$$

The following ten questions are interdependent.

a) Show that for any Gaussian random variable $X \simeq \mathcal{N}(0, \sigma^2)$, we have

$$\mathbb{P}(|X| \geqslant \varepsilon) \leqslant \frac{\sigma}{\varepsilon \sqrt{\pi/2}} e^{-\varepsilon^2 / (2\sigma^2)}, \qquad \varepsilon > 0.$$

Hint: Start from the inequality $\mathbb{E}[(X - \varepsilon)^+] \geqslant 0$ and compute the left-hand side.

b) Let X and Y be two independent centered Gaussian random variables with variances α^2 and β^2. Show that the conditional distribution

$$\mathbb{P}(X \in dx \mid X + Y = z)$$

of X given $X + Y = z$ is Gaussian with mean $\alpha^2 z / (\alpha^2 + \beta^2)$ and variance $\alpha^2 \beta^2 / (\alpha^2 + \beta^2)$.

Hint: Use the definition

$$\mathbb{P}(X \in dx \mid X + Y = z) := \frac{\mathbb{P}(X \in dx \text{ and } X + Y \in dz)}{\mathbb{P}(X + Y \in dz)}$$

and the formulas

$$d\mathbb{P}(X \leqslant x) := \frac{1}{\sqrt{2\pi\alpha^2}} e^{-x^2 / (2\alpha^2)} dx, \quad d\mathbb{P}(Y \leqslant x) := \frac{1}{\sqrt{2\pi\beta^2}} e^{-x^2 / (2\beta^2)} dx,$$

where dx (resp. dy) represents a "small" interval $[x, x + dx]$ (resp. $[y, y + dy]$).

c) Let $(B_t)_{t \in \mathbb{R}_+}$ denote a standard Brownian motion and let $0 < u < v$. Give the distribution of $B_{(u+v)/2}$ given that $B_u = x$ and $B_v = y$.

Hint: Note that given that $B_u = x$, the random variable B_v can be written as

$$B_v = (B_v - B_{(u+v)/2}) + (B_{(u+v)/2} - B_u) + x, \tag{4.49}$$

and apply the result of Question (b) after identifying X and Y in the above decomposition (4.49).

d) Consider the random sequences

$$
\begin{cases}
Z^{(0)} = \left(0, Z_1^{(0)}\right) \\[4pt]
Z^{(1)} = \left(0, Z_{1/2}^{(1)}, Z_1^{(0)}\right) \\[4pt]
Z^{(2)} = \left(0, Z_{1/4}^{(2)}, Z_{1/2}^{(1)}, Z_{3/4}^{(2)}, Z_1^{(0)}\right) \\[4pt]
Z^{(3)} = \left(0, Z_{1/8}^{(3)}, Z_{1/4}^{(2)}, Z_{3/8}^{(3)}, Z_{1/2}^{(1)}, Z_{5/8}^{(3)}, Z_{3/4}^{(2)}, Z_{7/8}^{(3)}, Z_1^{(0)}\right) \\[4pt]
\quad\vdots \qquad \vdots \\[4pt]
Z^{(n)} = \left(0, Z_{1/2^n}^{(n)}, Z_{2/2^n}^{(n)}, Z_{3/2^n}^{(n)}, Z_{4/2^n}^{(n)}, \ldots, Z_1^{(n)}\right) \\[4pt]
Z^{(n+1)} = \left(0, Z_{1/2^{n+1}}^{(n+1)}, Z_{1/2^n}^{(n)}, Z_{3/2^{n+1}}^{(n+1)}, Z_{2/2^n}^{(n+1)}, Z_{5/2^{n+1}}^{(n+1)}, Z_{3/2^n}^{(n+1)}, \ldots, Z_1^{(n+1)}\right)
\end{cases}
$$

with $Z_0^{(n)} = 0$, $n \geqslant 0$, defined recursively as

i) $Z_1^{(0)} \simeq \mathcal{N}(0,1)$,

ii) $Z_{1/2}^{(1)} \simeq \dfrac{Z_0^{(0)} + Z_1^{(0)}}{2} + \mathcal{N}(0, 1/4)$,

iii) $Z_{1/4}^{(2)} \simeq \dfrac{Z_0^{(1)} + Z_{1/2}^{(1)}}{2} + \mathcal{N}(0, 1/8)$, $\quad Z_{3/4}^{(2)} \simeq \dfrac{Z_{1/2}^{(1)} + Z_1^{(0)}}{2} + \mathcal{N}(0, 1/8)$,

and more generally

$$
Z_{(2k+1)/2^{n+1}}^{(n+1)} = \frac{Z_{k/2^n}^{(n)} + Z_{(k+1)/2^n}^{(n)}}{2} + \mathcal{N}(0, 1/2^{n+2}), \qquad k = 0, 1, \ldots, 2^n - 1,
$$

where $\mathcal{N}(0, 1/2^{n+2})$ is an independent centered Gaussian sample with variance $1/2^{n+2}$, and $Z_{k/2^n}^{(n+1)} := Z_{k/2^n}^{(n)}$, $k = 0, 1, \ldots, 2^n$.

In what follows we denote by $\left(Z_t^{(n)}\right)_{t \in [0,1]}$ the continuous-time random path obtained by linear interpolation of the sequence points in $\left(Z_{k/2^n}^{(n)}\right)_{k=0,1,\ldots,2^n}$.

Draw a sample of the first four linear interpolations $\left(Z_t^{(0)}\right)_{t \in [0,1]}$, $\left(Z_t^{(1)}\right)_{t \in [0,1]}$, $\left(Z_t^{(2)}\right)_{t \in [0,1]}$, $\left(Z_t^{(3)}\right)_{t \in [0,1]}$, and label the values of $Z_{k/2^n}^{(n)}$ on the graphs for $k = 0, 1, \ldots, 2^n$ and $n = 0, 1, 2, 3$.

e) Using an induction argument, explain why for all $n \geqslant 0$ the sequence

$$
Z^{(n)} = \left(0, Z_{1/2^n}^{(n)}, Z_{2/2^n}^{(n)}, Z_{3/2^n}^{(n)}, Z_{4/2^n}^{(n)}, \ldots, Z_1^{(n)}\right)
$$

has same distribution as the sequence

$$
B^{(n)} := \left(B_0, B_{1/2^n}, B_{2/2^n}, B_{3/2^n}, B_{4/2^n}, \ldots, B_1\right).
$$

Hint: Compare the constructions of Questions (c) and (d) and note that under the above linear interpolation, we have

$$Z^{(n)}_{(2k+1)/2^{n+1}} = \frac{Z^{(n)}_{k/2^n} + Z^{(n)}_{(k+1)/2^n}}{2}, \qquad k = 0, 1, \ldots, 2^n - 1.$$

f) Show that for any $\varepsilon_n > 0$ we have

$$\mathbb{P}(\|Z^{(n+1)} - Z^{(n)}\|_\infty \geqslant \varepsilon_n) \leqslant 2^n \mathbb{P}(|Z^{(n+1)}_{1/2^{n+1}} - Z^{(n)}_{1/2^{n+1}}| \geqslant \varepsilon_n).$$

Hint: Use the inequality

$$\mathbb{P}\left(\bigcup_{k=0}^{2^n-1} A_k\right) \leqslant \sum_{k=0}^{2^n-1} \mathbb{P}(A_k)$$

for a suitable choice of events $(A_k)_{k=0,1,\ldots,2^n-1}$.

g) Use the results of Questions (a) and (f) to show that for any $\varepsilon_n > 0$ we have

$$\mathbb{P}\left(\|Z^{(n+1)} - Z^{(n)}\|_\infty \geqslant \varepsilon_n\right) \leqslant \frac{2^{n/2}}{\varepsilon_n \sqrt{2\pi}} \, e^{-\varepsilon_n^2 2^{n+1}}.$$

h) Taking $\varepsilon_n = 2^{-n/4}$, show that

$$\mathbb{P}\left(\sum_{n \geqslant 0} \|Z^{(n+1)} - Z^{(n)}\|_\infty < \infty\right) = 1.$$

Hint: Show first that

$$\sum_{n \geqslant 0} \mathbb{P}\left(\|Z^{(n+1)} - Z^{(n)}\|_\infty \geqslant 2^{-n/4}\right) < \infty,$$

and apply the *Borel–Cantelli lemma*.

i) Show that with probability one, the sequence $\left\{(Z^{(n)}_t)_{t \in [0,1]}, \ n \geqslant 1\right\}$ converges uniformly on $[0, 1]$ to a continuous (random) function $(Z_t)_{t \in [0,1]}$.

Hint: Use the fact that $\mathcal{C}_0([0,1])$ is a *complete space* for the $\|\cdot\|_\infty$ norm.

j) Argue that the limit $(Z_t)_{t \in [0,1]}$ is a standard Brownian motion on $[0, 1]$ by checking the four relevant properties.

Problem 4.21   Consider $(B_t)_{t \in \mathbb{R}_+}$ a standard Brownian motion, and for any $n \geqslant 1$ and $T > 0$, define the discretized quadratic variation

$$Q^{(n)}_T := \sum_{k=1}^{n} (B_{kT/n} - B_{(k-1)T/n})^2, \qquad n \geqslant 1.$$

a) Compute $\mathbb{E}\left[Q^{(n)}_T\right]$, $n \geqslant 1$.

b) Compute $\mathrm{Var}[Q^{(n)}_T]$, $n \geqslant 1$.

c) Show that

$$\lim_{n \to \infty} Q_T^{(n)} = T,$$

where the limit is taken in $L^2(\Omega)$, that is, show that

$$\lim_{n \to \infty} \|Q_T^{(n)} - T\|_{L^2(\Omega)} = 0,$$

where

$$\|Q_T^{(n)} - T\|_{L^2(\Omega)} := \sqrt{\mathbb{E}\left[(Q_T^{(n)} - T)^2\right]}, \qquad n \geqslant 1.$$

d) By the result of Question (c), show that the limit

$$\int_0^T B_t dB_t := \lim_{n \to \infty} \sum_{k=1}^n (B_{kT/n} - B_{(k-1)T/n}) B_{(k-1)T/n}$$

exists in $L^2(\Omega)$, and compute it.

Hint: Use the identity

$$(x - y)y = \frac{1}{2}(x^2 - y^2 - (x - y)^2), \qquad x, y \in \mathbb{R}.$$

e) Consider the modified quadratic variation defined by

$$\widetilde{Q}_T^{(n)} := \sum_{k=1}^n (B_{(k-1/2)T/n} - B_{(k-1)T/n})^2, \qquad n \geqslant 1.$$

Compute the limit $\lim_{n \to \infty} \widetilde{Q}_T^{(n)}$ in $L^2(\Omega)$ by repeating the steps of Questions (a)–(c).

f) By the result of Question (e), show that the limit

$$\int_0^T B_t \circ dB_t := \lim_{n \to \infty} \sum_{k=1}^n (B_{kT/n} - B_{(k-1)T/n}) B_{(k-1/2)T/n}$$

exists in $L^2(\Omega)$, and compute it.

Hint: Use the identities

$$(x - y)y = \frac{1}{2}(x^2 - y^2 - (x - y)^2),$$

and

$$(x - y)x = \frac{1}{2}(x^2 - y^2 + (x - y)^2), \qquad x, y \in \mathbb{R}.$$

g) More generally, by repeating the steps of Questions (e) and (f), show that for any $\alpha \in [0, 1]$ the limit

$$\int_0^T B_t \circ d^\alpha B_t := \lim_{n \to \infty} \sum_{k=1}^n (B_{kT/n} - B_{(k-1)T/n}) B_{(k-\alpha)T/n}$$

exists in $L^2(\Omega)$, and compute it.

h) Comparison with deterministic calculus. Compute the limit

$$\lim_{n\to\infty} \sum_{k=1}^{n} (k-\alpha)\frac{T}{n}\left(k\frac{T}{n} - (k-1)\frac{T}{n}\right)$$

for all values of α in $[0,1]$.

Exercise 4.22   Let $(B_t)_{t\in\mathbb{R}_+}$ be a standard Brownian motion generating the information flow $(\mathcal{F}_t)_{t\in\mathbb{R}_+}$.

a) Let $0 \leqslant t \leqslant T$. What is the probability distribution of $B_T - B_t$?

b) Show that

$$\mathbb{E}[(B_T)^+ \mid \mathcal{F}_t] = \sqrt{\frac{T-t}{2\pi}}\, \mathrm{e}^{-B_t^2/(2(T-t))} + B_t\Phi\left(\frac{B_t}{\sqrt{T-t}}\right),$$

$0 \leqslant t \leqslant T$, where Φ denotes the standard Gaussian cumulative distribution function.
Hint: Use the time splitting decomposition $B_T = B_T - B_t + B_t$.

c) Let $\sigma > 0$, $\nu \in \mathbb{R}$, and $X_t := \sigma B_t + \nu t$, $t \geqslant 0$. Compute e^{X_t} by applying the Itô formula

$$f(X_t) = f(X_0) + \int_0^t u_s \frac{\partial f}{\partial x}(X_s)dB_s + \int_0^t v_s \frac{\partial f}{\partial x}(X_s)ds + \frac{1}{2}\int_0^t u_s^2 \frac{\partial^2 f}{\partial x^2}(X_s)ds$$

to $f(x) = \mathrm{e}^x$, where X_t is written as $X_t = X_0 + \int_0^t u_s dB_s + \int_0^t v_s ds$, $t \geqslant 0$.

d) Let $S_t = \mathrm{e}^{X_t}$, $t \geqslant 0$, and $r > 0$. For which value of ν does $(S_t)_{t\in\mathbb{R}_+}$ satisfy the stochastic differential equation

$$dS_t = rS_t dt + \sigma S_t dB_t \quad ?$$

Exercise 4.23   Show that for any $\beta \in \mathbb{R}$ we have

$$\mathbb{E}[(\beta - B_T)^+ \mid \mathcal{F}_t] = \sqrt{\frac{T-t}{2\pi}}\, \mathrm{e}^{-(\beta-B_t)^2/(2(T-t))} + (\beta - B_t)\Phi\left(\frac{\beta - B_t}{\sqrt{T-t}}\right),$$

$0 \leqslant t \leqslant T$.

Hint: Use the time splitting decomposition $B_T = B_T - B_t + B_t$.

Chapter 5

Continuous-Time Market Model

The continuous-time market model allows for the incorporation of portfolio re-allocation algorithms in a stochastic dynamic programming setting. This chapter starts with a review of the concepts of assets, self-financing portfolios, risk-neutral probability measures, and arbitrage in continuous time. We also state and solve the equation satisfied by geometric Brownian motion, which will be used for the modeling of continuous asset price processes.

5.1 Asset Price Modeling

The prices at time $t \geqslant 0$ of $d+1$ assets numbered n^o $0, 1, \ldots, d$ is denoted by the *random* vector

$$\overline{S}_t = \left(S_t^{(0)}, S_t^{(1)}, \ldots, S_t^{(d)}\right)$$

which forms a stochastic process $(\overline{S}_t)_{t \in \mathbb{R}_+}$. As in discrete time, the asset n° 0 is a riskless asset (of savings account type) yielding an interest rate r, *i.e.* we have

$$S_t^{(0)} = S_0^{(0)} \, e^{rt}, \qquad t \geqslant 0.$$

Definition 5.1. Discounting. *Let*

$$\overline{X}_t := \left(\widetilde{S}_t^{(0)}, \widetilde{S}_t^{(1)}, \ldots, \widetilde{S}_t^{(d)}\right), \qquad t \in \mathbb{R},$$

denote the vector of discounted asset prices, defined as:

$$\widetilde{S}_t^{(k)} = e^{-rt} S_t^{(k)}, \qquad t \geqslant 0, \quad k = 0, 1, \ldots, d.$$

We can also write

$$\overline{X}_t := e^{-rt} \overline{S}_t, \qquad t \geqslant 0.$$

The concept of discounting is illustrated in the following figures.

My portfolio S_t grew by $b = 5\%$ this year.

Q: Did I achieve a positive return?

A:

My portfolio S_t grew by $b = 5\%$ this year.

The risk-free or inflation rate is $r = 10\%$.

Q: Did I achieve a positive return?

A:

(a) Scenario A.

(b) Scenario B.

DOI: 10.1201/9781003298670-5

(a) *Without* inflation adjustment.   (b) *With* inflation adjustment.

Figure 5.1: Why apply discounting?

Definition 5.2. *A portfolio strategy is a stochastic process* $(\bar{\xi}_t)_{t \in \mathbb{R}_+} \subset \mathbb{R}^{d+1}$, *where* $\xi_t^{(k)}$ *denotes the (possibly fractional) quantity of asset n° k held at time $t \geqslant 0$.*

The *value* at time $t \geqslant 0$ of the portfolio strategy $(\bar{\xi}_t)_{t \in \mathbb{R}_+} \subset \mathbb{R}^{d+1}$ is defined by

$$V_t := \bar{\xi}_t \bullet \overline{S}_t = \sum_{k=0}^{d} \xi_t^{(k)} S_t^{(k)}, \qquad t \geqslant 0.$$

The *discounted* value of the portfolio is defined by

$$
\begin{aligned}
\widetilde{V}_t &:= e^{-rt} V_t \\
&= e^{-rt} \bar{\xi}_t \bullet \overline{S}_t \\
&= e^{-rt} \sum_{k=0}^{d} \xi_t^{(k)} S_t^{(k)} \\
&= \sum_{k=0}^{d} \xi_t^{(k)} \widetilde{S}_t^{(k)} \\
&= \bar{\xi}_t \bullet \overline{X}_t, \qquad t \geqslant 0.
\end{aligned}
$$

The effect of discounting from time t to time 0 is to divide prices by e^{rt}, making all prices comparable at time 0.

5.2   Arbitrage and Risk-Neutral Measures

In continuous-time, the definition of arbitrage follows the lines of its analogs in the one-step and discrete-time models. In what follows we will only consider *admissible* portfolio strategies whose total value V_t remains nonnegative for all times $t \in [0, T]$.

Definition 5.3. *A portfolio strategy* $(\xi_t^{(k)})_{t \in [0,T], k=0,1,\ldots,d}$ *with value*

$$V_t = \bar{\xi}_t \bullet \overline{S}_t = \sum_{k=0}^{d} \xi_t^{(k)} S_t^{(k)}, \qquad t \in [0, T],$$

constitutes an arbitrage opportunity if all three *following conditions are satisfied:*

i) $V_0 \leqslant 0$ *at time* $t = 0$,   [Start from a zero-cost portfolio, or with a debt.]

ii) $V_T \geqslant 0$ *at time* $t = T$,   [Finish with a nonnegative amount.]

iii) $\mathbb{P}(V_T > 0) > 0$ *at time* $t = T$.   [Profit is made with nonzero probability.]

Roughly speaking, (ii) means that the investor wants no loss, (iii) means that he wishes to sometimes make a strictly positive gain, and (i) means that he starts with zero capital or even with a debt.

Next, we turn to the definition of risk-neutral probability measures (or martingale measures) in continuous time, which states that under a risk-neutral probability measure $\mathbb{P}^*$, the return of the risky asset over the time interval $[u, t]$ equals the return of the riskless asset given by

$$S_t^{(0)} = e^{(t-u)r} S_u^{(0)}, \qquad 0 \leqslant u \leqslant t.$$

Recall that the filtration $(\mathcal{F}_t)_{t \in \mathbb{R}_+}$ is generated by Brownian motion $(B_t)_{t \in \mathbb{R}_+}$, *i.e.*

$$\mathcal{F}_t = \sigma(B_u \ : \ 0 \leqslant u \leqslant t), \qquad t \geqslant 0.$$

Definition 5.4. *A probability measure* $\mathbb{P}^*$ *on* Ω *is called a risk-neutral measure if it satisfies*

$$\mathbb{E}^* \left[S_t^{(k)} \mid \mathcal{F}_u \right] = e^{(t-u)r} S_u^{(k)}, \qquad 0 \leqslant u \leqslant t, \quad k = 1, 2, \ldots, d. \tag{5.1}$$

where $\mathbb{E}^*$ *denotes the expectation under* $\mathbb{P}^*$.

As in the discrete-time case, $\mathbb{P}^\sharp$ would be called a risk premium measure if it satisfied

$$\mathbb{E}^\sharp \left[S_t^{(k)} \mid \mathcal{F}_u \right] > e^{(t-u)r} S_u, \qquad 0 \leqslant u \leqslant t, \quad k = 1, 2, \ldots, d,$$

meaning that by taking risks in buying $S_t^{(i)}$, one could make an expected return higher than that of the riskless asset

$$S_t^{(0)} = e^{(t-u)r} S_u^{(0)}, \qquad 0 \leqslant u \leqslant t.$$

Similarly, a negative risk premium measure $\mathbb{P}^\flat$ satisfies

$$\mathbb{E}^\flat \left[S_t^{(k)} \mid \mathcal{F}_u \right] < e^{(t-u)r} S_u^{(k)}, \qquad 0 \leqslant u \leqslant t, \quad k = 1, 2, \ldots, d.$$

From the relation

$$S_t^{(0)} = e^{(t-u)r} S_u^{(0)}, \qquad 0 \leqslant u \leqslant t,$$

we interpret (5.1) by saying that the expected return of the risky asset $S_t^{(k)}$ under $\mathbb{P}^*$ equals the return of the riskless asset $S_t^{(0)}$, $k = 1, 2, \ldots, d$. Recall that the discounted (in \$ at time 0) price $\widetilde{S}_t^{(k)}$ of the risky asset n^o k is defined by

$$\widetilde{S}_t^{(k)} := e^{-rt} S_t^{(k)} = \frac{S_t^{(k)}}{S_t^{(0)} / S_0^{(0)}}, \qquad t \geqslant 0, \quad k = 0, 1, \ldots, d,$$

i.e. $S_t^{(0)} / S_0^{(0)}$ plays the role of a *numéraire* in the sense of Chapter 16.

As in the discrete-time case, see Proposition 2.13, the martingale property in continuous time, see Definition 4.2, can be used to characterize risk-neutral probability measures, for the derivation of pricing partial differential equations (PDEs), and for the computation of conditional expectations.

Proposition 5.5. *The probability measure $\mathbb{P}^*$ is risk-neutral if and only if the discounted risky asset price process $(\widetilde{S}_t^{(k)})_{t\in\mathbb{R}_+}$ is a martingale under $\mathbb{P}^*$, $k = 1, 2, \ldots, d$.*

Proof. If $\mathbb{P}^*$ is a risk-neutral probability measure, we have

$$
\begin{aligned}
\mathbb{E}^*\left[\widetilde{S}_t^{(k)} \mid \mathcal{F}_u\right] &= \mathbb{E}^*\left[\mathrm{e}^{-rt}S_t^{(k)} \mid \mathcal{F}_u\right] \\
&= \mathrm{e}^{-rt}\,\mathbb{E}^*\left[S_t^{(k)} \mid \mathcal{F}_u\right] \\
&= \mathrm{e}^{-rt}\mathrm{e}^{(t-u)r}S_u^{(k)} \\
&= \mathrm{e}^{-ru}S_u^{(k)} \\
&= \widetilde{S}_u^{(k)}, \qquad 0 \leqslant u \leqslant t,
\end{aligned}
$$

hence $(\widetilde{S}_t^{(k)})_{t\in\mathbb{R}_+}$ is a martingale under $\mathbb{P}^*$, $k = 1, 2, \ldots, d$. Conversely, if $(\widetilde{S}_t^{(k)})_{t\in\mathbb{R}_+}$ is a martingale under $\mathbb{P}^*$, then

$$
\begin{aligned}
\mathbb{E}^*\left[S_t^{(k)} \mid \mathcal{F}_u\right] &= \mathbb{E}^*\left[\mathrm{e}^{rt}\widetilde{S}_t^{(k)} \mid \mathcal{F}_u\right] \\
&= \mathrm{e}^{rt}\,\mathbb{E}^*\left[\widetilde{S}_t^{(k)} \mid \mathcal{F}_u\right] \\
&= \mathrm{e}^{rt}\widetilde{S}_u^{(k)} \\
&= \mathrm{e}^{(t-u)r}S_u^{(k)}, \qquad 0 \leqslant u \leqslant t, \quad k = 1, 2, \ldots, d,
\end{aligned}
$$

hence the probability measure $\mathbb{P}^*$ is risk-neutral according to Definition 5.4. $\qquad\square$

In what follows we will only consider probability measures $\mathbb{P}^*$ that are *equivalent* to $\mathbb{P}$, in the sense that they share the same events of zero probability.

Definition 5.6. *A probability measure $\mathbb{P}^*$ on $(\Omega, \mathcal{F})$ is said to be* equivalent *to another probability measure $\mathbb{P}$ when*

$$
\mathbb{P}^*(A) = 0 \quad \textit{if and only if} \quad \mathbb{P}(A) = 0, \quad \textit{for all} \quad A \in \mathcal{F}. \tag{5.2}
$$

Next, we note that the first fundamental theorem of asset pricing also holds in continuous time, and can be used to check for the existence of arbitrage opportunities.

Theorem 5.7. *A market is* without *arbitrage opportunity if and only if it admits at least one* equivalent *risk-neutral probability measure $\mathbb{P}^*$.*

Proof. See Harrison and Pliska (1981) and Chapter VII-4a of Shiryaev (1999). $\qquad\square$

5.3 Self-Financing Portfolio Strategies

Let $\xi_t^{(i)}$ denote the (possibly fractional) quantity invested at time t over the time interval $[t, t+dt)$, in the asset $S_t^{(k)}$, $k = 0, 1, \ldots, d$, and let

$$
\bar{\xi}_t = \left(\xi_t^{(k)}\right)_{k=0,1,\ldots,d}, \qquad \bar{S}_t = \left(S_t^{(k)}\right)_{k=0,1,\ldots,d}, \quad t \geqslant 0,
$$

denote the associated portfolio value and asset price processes. The portfolio value V_t at time $t \geqslant 0$ is given by

$$
V_t = \bar{\xi}_t \cdot \bar{S}_t = \sum_{k=0}^{d} \xi_t^{(k)}S_t^{(k)}, \qquad t \geqslant 0. \tag{5.3}
$$

Our description of portfolio strategies proceeds in four equivalent formulations (5.4), (5.6) (5.7) and (5.8), which correspond to different interpretations of the self-financing condition.

Self-financing portfolio update

The portfolio strategy $(\bar{\xi}_t)_{t \in \mathbb{R}_+}$ is self-financing if the portfolio value remains constant after updating the portfolio from $\bar{\xi}_t$ to $\bar{\xi}_{t+dt}$, *i.e.*

$$\bar{\xi}_t \cdot \overline{S}_{t+dt} = \sum_{k=0}^{d} \xi_t^{(k)} S_{t+dt}^{(k)} = \sum_{k=0}^{d} \xi_{t+dt}^{(k)} S_{t+dt}^{(k)} = \bar{\xi}_{t+dt} \cdot \overline{S}_{t+dt}, \qquad (5.4)$$

which is the continuous-time analog of the self-financing condition already encountered in the discrete setting of Chapter 2, see Definition 2.4. A major difference with the discrete-time case of Definition 2.4, however, is that the continuous-time differentials dS_t and $d\xi_t$ do not make pathwise sense as continuous-time stochastic integrals are defined by L^2 limits, cf. Proposition 4.21, or by convergence in probability.

Portfolio value	$\bar{\xi}_t \cdot \overline{S}_t$	$\longrightarrow$	$\bar{\xi}_t \cdot \overline{S}_{t+dt} = \bar{\xi}_{t+dt} \cdot \overline{S}_{t+dt}$	$\longrightarrow$	$\bar{\xi}_{t+dt} \cdot \overline{S}_{t+2dt}$
Asset value	S_t		S_{t+dt} $\;$ S_{t+dt}		S_{t+2dt}
Time scale	t		$t+dt$ $\;$ $t+dt$		$t+2dt$
Portfolio allocation	ξ_t		ξ_t $\;$ ξ_{t+dt}		ξ_{t+dt}

Figure 5.2: Illustration of the self-financing condition (5.4).

Equivalently, Condition (5.4) can be rewritten as

$$\sum_{k=0}^{d} S_{t+dt}^{(k)} (\xi_{t+dt}^{(k)} - \xi_t^{(k)}) = 0, \qquad (5.5)$$

or, letting

$$d\xi_t^{(k)} := \xi_{t+dt}^{(k)} - \xi_t^{(k)}, \qquad k = 0, 1, \ldots, d,$$

denote the respective variations in portfolio allocations, as

$$\sum_{k=0}^{d} S_{t+dt}^{(k)} d\xi_t^{(k)} = 0. \qquad (5.6)$$

Condition (5.5) can be rewritten as

$$\sum_{k=0}^{d} S_t^{(k)} (\xi_{t+dt}^{(k)} - \xi_t^{(k)}) + \sum_{k=0}^{d} (S_{t+dt}^{(k)} - S_t^{(k)}) (\xi_{t+dt}^{(k)} - \xi_t^{(k)}) = 0,$$

which shows that (5.4) and (5.6) are equivalent to

$$\overline{S}_t \cdot d\bar{\xi}_t + d\overline{S}_t \cdot d\bar{\xi}_t = \sum_{k=0}^{d} S_t^{(k)} d\xi_t^{(k)} + \sum_{k=0}^{d} dS_t^{(k)} \cdot d\xi_t^{(k)} = 0 \qquad (5.7)$$

in differential notation.

Self-financing portfolio differential

In practice, the self-financing portfolio property will be characterized by the following proposition, which states that the value of a self-financing portfolio can be written as the sum of its trading Profits and Losses (P/L).

Proposition 5.8. *A portfolio strategy* $(\xi_t^{(k)})_{t \in [0,T], k=0,1,...,d}$ *with value*

$$V_t = \bar{\xi}_t \cdot \bar{S}_t = \sum_{k=0}^{d} \xi_t^{(k)} S_t^{(k)}, \qquad t \geqslant 0,$$

is self-financing according to (5.4) *if and only if the relation*

$$dV_t = \sum_{k=0}^{d} \underbrace{\xi_t^{(k)} dS_t^{(k)}}_{\text{P/L for asset n}^o\ k} \tag{5.8}$$

holds.

Proof. By Itô's calculus we have

$$dV_t = \sum_{k=0}^{d} \xi_t^{(k)} dS_t^{(k)} + \sum_{k=0}^{d} S_t^{(k)} d\xi_t^{(k)} + \sum_{k=0}^{d} dS_t^{(k)} \cdot d\xi_t^{(k)},$$

which shows that (5.7) is equivalent to (5.8).   □

Market Completeness

We refer to Definition 1.9 for the definition of contingent claim.

Definition 5.9. *A contingent claim with payoff* C *is said to be attainable if there exists a (self-financing) portfolio strategy* $(\xi_t^{(k)})_{t \in [0,T], k=0,1,...,d}$ *such that at the maturity time* T *the equality*

$$V_T = \bar{\xi}_T \cdot \bar{S}_T = \sum_{k=0}^{d} \xi_T^{(k)} S_T^{(k)} = C$$

holds (almost surely) between random variables.

When a claim with payoff C is attainable, its price at time t will be given by the value V_t of a self-financing portfolio hedging C.

Definition 5.10. *A market model is said to be* complete *if every contingent claim is attainable.*

The next result is the continuous-time statement of the second fundamental theorem of asset pricing.

Theorem 5.11. *A market model without arbitrage opportunities is complete if and only if it admits only one* equivalent *risk-neutral probability measure* $\mathbb{P}^*$.

Proof. See Harrison and Pliska (1981) and Chapter VII-4a of Shiryaev (1999).   □

5.4 Two-Asset Portfolio Model

In the Black and Scholes (1973) model, one can show the existence of a unique risk-neutral probability measure, hence the model is without arbitrage and complete. From now on we work with $d = 1$, *i.e.* with a market based on a riskless asset with price $(A_t)_{t \in \mathbb{R}_+}$ and a risky asset with price $(S_t)_{t \in \mathbb{R}_+}$.

Self-financing portfolio strategies

Let ξ_t and η_t denote the (possibly fractional) quantities respectively invested at time t over the time interval $[t, t+dt)$, into the risky asset S_t and riskless asset A_t, and let

$$\bar{\xi}_t = (\eta_t, \xi_t), \qquad \bar{S}_t = (A_t, S_t), \qquad t \geqslant 0,$$

denote the associated portfolio value and asset price processes. The portfolio value V_t at time t is given by

$$V_t = \bar{\xi}_t \cdot \bar{S}_t = \eta_t A_t + \xi_t S_t, \qquad t \geqslant 0.$$

Our description of portfolio strategies proceeds in four equivalent formulations presented below in Equations (5.9), (5.10), (5.12) and (5.13), which correspond to different interpretations of the self-financing condition.

Self-financing portfolio update

The portfolio strategy $(\eta_t, \xi_t)_{t \in \mathbb{R}_+}$ is self-financing if the portfolio value remains constant after updating the portfolio from (η_t, ξ_t) to $(\eta_{t+dt}, \xi_{t+dt})$, *i.e.*

$$\bar{\xi}_t \cdot \bar{S}_{t+dt} = \eta_t A_{t+dt} + \xi_t S_{t+dt} = \eta_{t+dt} A_{t+dt} + \xi_{t+dt} S_{t+dt} = \bar{\xi}_{t+dt} \cdot \bar{S}_{t+dt}. \tag{5.9}$$

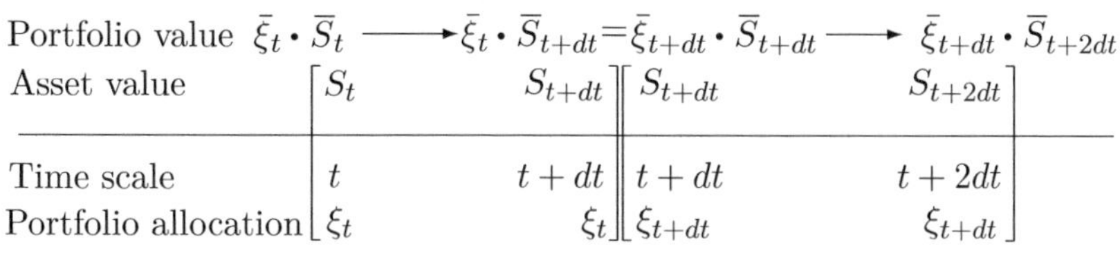

$$\begin{array}{llll}
\text{Portfolio value } \bar{\xi}_t \cdot \bar{S}_t \longrightarrow & \bar{\xi}_t \cdot \bar{S}_{t+dt} = \bar{\xi}_{t+dt} \cdot \bar{S}_{t+dt} \longrightarrow & & \bar{\xi}_{t+dt} \cdot \bar{S}_{t+2dt} \\
\text{Asset value} \quad \begin{bmatrix} S_t & S_{t+dt} \end{bmatrix} & \begin{bmatrix} S_{t+dt} & & S_{t+2dt} \end{bmatrix} \\
\hline
\text{Time scale} \quad \begin{bmatrix} t & t+dt \end{bmatrix} & \begin{bmatrix} t+dt & & t+2dt \end{bmatrix} \\
\text{Portfolio allocation} \begin{bmatrix} \xi_t & \xi_t \end{bmatrix} & \begin{bmatrix} \xi_{t+dt} & & \xi_{t+dt} \end{bmatrix}
\end{array}$$

Figure 5.3: Illustration of the self-financing condition (5.9).

Equivalently, Condition (5.9) can be rewritten as

$$A_{t+dt} d\eta_t + S_{t+dt} d\xi_t = 0, \tag{5.10}$$

where

$$d\eta_t := \eta_{t+dt} - \eta_t \quad \text{and} \quad d\xi_t := \xi_{t+dt} - \xi_t$$

denote the respective changes in portfolio allocations, hence we have

$$A_{t+dt}(\eta_t - \eta_{t+dt}) = S_{t+dt}(\xi_{t+dt} - \xi_t). \tag{5.11}$$

In other words, when one sells a (possibly fractional) quantity $\eta_t - \eta_{t+dt} > 0$ of the riskless asset valued A_{t+dt} at the end of the time interval $[t, t+dt]$ for the total amount

$A_{t+dt}(\eta_t - \eta_{t+dt})$, one should entirely spend this income to buy the corresponding quantity $\xi_{t+dt} - \xi_t > 0$ of the risky asset for the same amount $S_{t+dt}(\xi_{t+dt} - \xi_t) > 0$.

Similarly, if one sells a quantity $-d\xi_t > 0$ of the risky asset S_{t+dt} between the time intervals $[t, t + dt]$ and $[t + dt, t + 2dt]$ for a total amount $-S_{t+dt}d\xi_t$, one should entirely use this income to buy a quantity $d\eta_t > 0$ of the riskless asset for an amount $A_{t+dt}d\eta_t > 0$, *i.e.*

$$A_{t+dt}d\eta_t = -S_{t+dt}d\xi_t.$$

Condition (5.11) can also be rewritten as

$$S_t(\xi_{t+dt} - \xi_t) + A_t(\eta_{t+dt} - \eta_t) + (S_{t+dt} - S_t)(\xi_{t+dt} - \xi_t)$$
$$+ (A_{t+dt} - A_t) \cdot (\eta_{t+dt} - \eta_t) = 0,$$

which shows that (5.9) and (5.10) are equivalent to

$$S_t d\xi_t + A_t d\eta_t + dS_t \cdot d\xi_t + dA_t \cdot d\eta_t = 0 \tag{5.12}$$

in differential notation, with

$$dA_t \cdot d\eta_t \simeq (A_{t+dt} - A_t) \cdot (\eta_{t+dt} - \eta_t) = rA_t(dt \cdot d\eta_t) = 0$$

in the sense of Itô's calculus, by the Itô multiplication Table 4.1. This yields the following proposition, which is also consequence of Proposition 5.8.

Proposition 5.12. *A portfolio allocation* $(\xi_t, \eta_t)_{t \in \mathbb{R}_+}$ *with value*

$$V_t = \eta_t A_t + \xi_t S_t, \qquad t \geqslant 0,$$

is self-financing according to (5.9) if and only if the relation

$$dV_t = \underbrace{\eta_t dA_t}_{\text{Risk-free P/L}} + \underbrace{\xi_t dS_t}_{\text{Risky P/L}} \tag{5.13}$$

holds.

Proof. By Itô's calculus we have

$$dV_t = [\eta_t dA_t + \xi_t dS_t] + [S_t d\xi_t + A_t d\eta_t + dS_t \cdot d\xi_t + dA_t \cdot d\eta_t],$$

which shows that (5.12) is equivalent to (5.13). Equivalently, we can also check the equality

$$\begin{aligned} dV_t &= V_{t+dt} - V_t \\ &= \eta_{t+dt}A_{t+dt} + \xi_{t+dt}S_{t+dt} - (\eta_t A_t + \xi_t S_t) \\ &= \eta_t(A_{t+dt} - A_t) + \xi_t(S_{t+dt} - S_t) + S_t(\xi_{t+dt} - \xi_t) + A_t(\eta_{t+dt} - \eta_t) \\ &\quad + (S_{t+dt} - S_t)(\xi_{t+dt} - \xi_t) + (A_{t+dt} - A_t)(\eta_{t+dt} - \eta_t). \end{aligned}$$

$\square$

Let

$$\widetilde{V}_t := e^{-rt}V_t \qquad \text{and} \qquad \widetilde{S}_t := e^{-rt}S_t, \qquad t \geqslant 0,$$

respectively denote the discounted portfolio value and discounted risky asset price at time $t \geqslant 0$.

Geometric Brownian motion

Recall that the riskless asset price process $(A_t)_{t\in\mathbb{R}_+}$ admits the following equivalent constructions:

$$\frac{A_{t+dt} - A_t}{A_t} = rdt, \qquad \frac{dA_t}{A_t} = rdt, \qquad A_t' = rA_t, \quad t \geqslant 0,$$

with the solution

$$A_t = A_0\,\mathrm{e}^{rt}, \qquad t \geqslant 0, \tag{5.14}$$

where $r > 0$ is the risk-free interest rate.* The risky asset price process $(S_t)_{t\in\mathbb{R}_+}$ will be modeled using a geometric Brownian motion defined from the equation

$$\frac{S_{t+dt} - S_t}{S_t} = \frac{dS_t}{S_t} = \mu dt + \sigma dB_t, \qquad t \geqslant 0, \tag{5.15}$$

see Section 5.5, which can be solved numerically according to the following R code.

```
N=2000; t <- 0:N; dt <- 1.0/N;mu=0.5; sigma=0.2; nsim <- 10; X <- matrix(0, nsim, N+1)
dB <- matrix(rnorm(nsim*N,mean=0,sd=sqrt(dt)), nsim, N+1)
for (i in 1:nsim){X[i,1]=1.0;
for (j in 1:N+1){X[i,j]=X[i,j-1]+mu*X[i,j-1]*dt+sigma*X[i,j-1]*dB[i,j]}}
plot(t*dt, rep(0, N+1), xlab = "Time", ylab = "Geometric Brownian motion", lwd=2, ylim =
    c(min(X),max(X)), type = "l", col = 0,las=1, cex.axis=1.5,cex.lab=1.5, xaxs='i', yaxs='i')
for (i in 1:nsim){lines(t*dt, X[i, ], lwd=2, type = "l", col = i)}
```

Note that by Proposition 5.15 below, we also have

$$S_t = S_0 \exp\left(\sigma B_t + \left(\mu - \frac{1}{2}\sigma^2\right)t\right), \qquad t \geqslant 0,$$

which can be simulated by the following R code.

```
N=2000; t <- 0:N; dt <- 1.0/N; mu=0.5;sigma=0.2; nsim <- 10; par(oma=c(0,1,0,0))
X <- matrix(rnorm(nsim*N,mean=0,sd=sqrt(dt)), nsim, N)
X <- cbind(rep(0, nsim), t(apply(X, 1, cumsum)))
for (i in 1:nsim){X[i,] <- exp(mu*t*dt+sigma*X[i,]-sigma*sigma*t*dt/2)}
plot(t*dt, rep(0, N+1), xlab = "Time", ylab = "Geometric Brownian motion", lwd=2, ylim =
    c(min(X),max(X)), type = "l", col = 0,las=1,cex.axis=1.5,cex.lab=1.6, xaxs='i', yaxs='i')
for (i in 1:nsim){lines(t*dt, X[i, ], lwd=2, type = "l", col = i)}
```

The next Figure 5.4 presents sample paths of geometric Brownian motion.

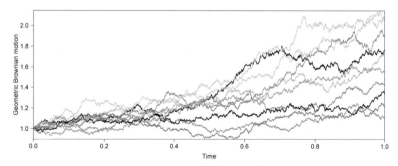

Figure 5.4: Ten sample paths of geometric Brownian motion $(S_t)_{t\in\mathbb{R}_+}$.

---

*"Anyone who believes exponential growth can go on forever in a finite world is either a madman or an economist", K. E. Boulding (1973), page 248.

Lemma 5.13. Discounting lemma. *Consider an asset price process* $(S_t)_{t\in\mathbb{R}_+}$ *be as in* (5.15), *i.e.*

$$dS_t = \mu S_t dt + \sigma S_t dB_t, \quad t \geqslant 0.$$

Then, the discounted asset price process $\big(\widetilde{S}_t\big)_{t\in\mathbb{R}_+} = \big(e^{-rt}S_t\big)_{t\in\mathbb{R}_+}$ *satisfies the equation*

$$d\widetilde{S}_t = (\mu - r)\widetilde{S}_t dt + \sigma\widetilde{S}_t dB_t.$$

Proof. By (4.27) and the Itô multiplication table 4.1, we have

$$
\begin{aligned}
d\widetilde{S}_t &= d(e^{-rt}S_t) \\
&= S_t d(e^{-rt}) + e^{-rt}dS_t + (d\,e^{-rt}) \cdot dS_t \\
&= -r e^{-rt}S_t dt + e^{-rt}dS_t + (-r e^{-rt}S_t dt) \cdot dS_t \\
&= -r e^{-rt}S_t dt + \mu e^{-rt}S_t dt + \sigma e^{-rt}S_t dB_t \\
&= (\mu - r)\widetilde{S}_t dt + \sigma\widetilde{S}_t dB_t.
\end{aligned}
$$

$\square$

In the next Lemma 5.14, which is the continuous-time analog of Lemma 3.2, we show that when a portfolio is self-financing, its discounted value is a gain process given by the sum over time of discounted trading profits and losses (number of risky assets ξ_t times discounted price variation $d\widetilde{S}_t$).

Note that in Equation (5.16) below, no profit or loss arises from trading the discounted riskless asset $\widetilde{A}_t := e^{-rt}A_t = A_0$, because its price remains constant over time.

Lemma 5.14. *Let* $(\eta_t, \xi_t)_{t\in\mathbb{R}_+}$ *be a portfolio strategy with value*

$$V_t = \eta_t A_t + \xi_t S_t, \qquad t \geqslant 0.$$

The following statements are equivalent:

(i) *the portfolio strategy* $(\eta_t, \xi_t)_{t\in\mathbb{R}_+}$ *is self-financing,*

(ii) *the discounted portfolio value* $\widetilde{V}_t$ *can be written as the stochastic integral sum*

$$\widetilde{V}_t = \widetilde{V}_0 + \int_0^t \underbrace{\xi_u d\widetilde{S}_u}_{\text{Discounted P/L}}, \qquad t \geqslant 0, \tag{5.16}$$

of discounted profits and losses.

Proof. Assuming that (i) holds, the self-financing condition and (5.14)–(5.15) show that

$$
\begin{aligned}
dV_t &= \eta_t dA_t + \xi_t dS_t \\
&= r\eta_t A_t dt + \mu\xi_t S_t dt + \sigma\xi_t S_t dB_t \\
&= rV_t dt + (\mu - r)\xi_t S_t dt + \sigma\xi_t S_t dB_t, \qquad t \geqslant 0,
\end{aligned}
$$

where we used $V_t = \eta_t A_t + \xi_t S_t$, hence

$$e^{-rt}dV_t = r e^{-rt}V_t dt + (\mu - r)e^{-rt}\xi_t S_t dt + \sigma e^{-rt}\xi_t S_t dB_t, \quad t \geqslant 0,$$

and

$$
\begin{aligned}
d\widetilde{V}_t &= d\left(\mathrm{e}^{-rt}V_t\right) \\
&= -r\,\mathrm{e}^{-rt}V_t dt + \mathrm{e}^{-rt}dV_t \\
&= (\mu - r)\xi_t\,\mathrm{e}^{-rt}S_t dt + \sigma\xi_t\,\mathrm{e}^{-rt}S_t dB_t \\
&= (\mu - r)\xi_t\widetilde{S}_t dt + \sigma\xi_t\widetilde{S}_t dB_t \\
&= \xi_t d\widetilde{S}_t, \qquad t \geqslant 0,
\end{aligned}
$$

i.e. (5.16) holds by integrating on both sides as

$$
\widetilde{V}_t - \widetilde{V}_0 = \int_0^t d\widetilde{V}_u = \int_0^t \xi_u d\widetilde{S}_u, \qquad t \geqslant 0.
$$

(ii) Conversely, if (5.16) is satisfied we have

$$
\begin{aligned}
dV_t &= d(\mathrm{e}^{rt}\widetilde{V}_t) \\
&= r\,\mathrm{e}^{rt}\widetilde{V}_t dt + \mathrm{e}^{rt}d\widetilde{V}_t \\
&= r\,\mathrm{e}^{rt}\widetilde{V}_t dt + \mathrm{e}^{rt}\xi_t d\widetilde{S}_t \\
&= rV_t dt + \mathrm{e}^{rt}\xi_t d\widetilde{S}_t \\
&= rV_t dt + \mathrm{e}^{rt}\xi_t\widetilde{S}_t((\mu - r)dt + \sigma dB_t) \\
&= rV_t dt + \xi_t S_t((\mu - r)dt + \sigma dB_t) \\
&= r\eta_t A_t dt + \mu\xi_t S_t dt + \sigma\xi_t S_t dB_t \\
&= \eta_t dA_t + \xi_t dS_t,
\end{aligned}
$$

hence the portfolio is self-financing according to Definition 5.8. $\qquad\square$

As a consequence of Relation (5.16), the problem of hedging a claim payoff C with maturity T also reduces to that of finding the process $(\xi_t)_{t\in[0,T]}$ appearing in the decomposition of the discounted claim payoff $\widetilde{C} = \mathrm{e}^{-rT}C$ as a stochastic integral:

$$
\widetilde{C} = \widetilde{V}_T = \widetilde{V}_0 + \int_0^T \xi_t d\widetilde{S}_t,
$$

see Section 7.5 on hedging by the martingale method.

Example. *Power options in the Bachelier model.*

In the Bachelier (1900) model with interest rate $r = 0$, the underlying asset price can be modeled by Brownian motion $(B_t)_{t\in\mathbb{R}_+}$, and may therefore become negative.[*] The claim payoff $C = (B_T)^2$ of a power option with at maturity $T > 0$ admits the stochastic integral decomposition

$$
(B_T)^2 = T + 2\int_0^T B_t dB_t
$$

which shows that the claim can be hedged using $\xi_t = 2B_t$ units of the underlying asset at time $t \in [0, T]$, see Exercise 6.1.

---

[*]Negative oil prices have been observed in May 2020 when the prices of oil futures contracts fell below zero.

Similarly, in the case of power claim payoff $C = (B_T)^3$ we have

$$(B_T)^3 = 3\int_0^T \left(T - t + (B_t)^2\right)dB_t,$$

cf. Exercise 4.10.

Note that according to (5.16), the (non-discounted) self-financing portfolio value V_t can be written as

$$V_t = e^{rt}V_0 + (\mu - r)\int_0^t e^{(t-u)r}\xi_u S_u du + \sigma\int_0^t e^{(t-u)r}\xi_u S_u dB_u, \quad t \geqslant 0. \tag{5.17}$$

5.5 Geometric Brownian Motion

In this section we solve the stochastic differential equation

$$dS_t = \mu S_t dt + \sigma S_t dB_t$$

which is used to model the S_t the risky asset price at time t, where $\mu \in \mathbb{R}$ and $\sigma > 0$. This equation is rewritten in *integral form* as

$$S_t = S_0 + \mu\int_0^t S_s ds + \sigma\int_0^t S_s dB_s, \quad t \geqslant 0. \tag{5.18}$$

```
N=1000; t <- 0:N; dt <- 1.0/N; sigma=0.2; mu=0.5
dB <- rnorm(N,mean=0,sd=sqrt(dt));
plot(t*dt, exp(mu*t*dt), xlab = "time", ylab = "Geometric Brownian motion", type = "l", ylim = c(0.75, 2),
    col = 1,lwd=3)
lines(t*dt, exp(sigma*c(0,cumsum(dB))+mu*t*dt-sigma*sigma*t*dt/2),xlab = "time",type = "l",ylim = c(0,
    4), col = 4)
```

The next Figure 5.5 presents an illustration of the geometric Brownian process of Proposition 5.15.

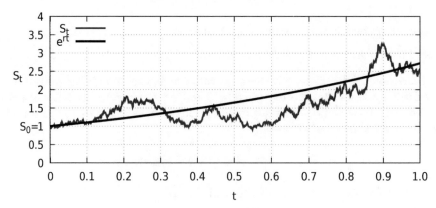

Figure 5.5: Geometric Brownian motion started at $S_0 = 1$, with $\mu = r = 1$ and $\sigma^2 = 0.5$.

Proposition 5.15. *The solution of the stochastic differential equation*

$$dS_t = \mu S_t dt + \sigma S_t dB_t \tag{5.19}$$

is given by

$$S_t = S_0 \exp\left(\sigma B_t + \left(\mu - \frac{1}{2}\sigma^2\right)t\right), \qquad t \geqslant 0. \tag{5.20}$$

Proof. *a*) Using log-returns. We apply Itô's formula to the Itô process $(S_t)_{t\in\mathbb{R}_+}$ with $v_t = \mu S_t$ and $u_t = \sigma S_t$, by taking

$$f(S_t) = \log S_t, \qquad \text{with} \qquad f(x) := \log x.$$

This yields the log-return dynamics

$$
\begin{aligned}
d\log S_t &= f'(S_t)dS_t + \frac{1}{2}f''(S_t)dS_t \cdot dS_t \\
&= \mu S_t f'(S_t)dt + \sigma S_t f'(S_t)dB_t + \frac{\sigma^2}{2}S_t^2 f''(S_t)dt \\
&= \mu dt + \sigma dB_t - \frac{\sigma^2}{2}dt,
\end{aligned}
$$

hence

$$
\begin{aligned}
\log S_t - \log S_0 &= \int_0^t d\log S_s \\
&= \left(\mu - \frac{\sigma^2}{2}\right)\int_0^t ds + \sigma \int_0^t dB_s \\
&= \left(\mu - \frac{\sigma^2}{2}\right)t + \sigma B_t,
\end{aligned}
$$

and

$$S_t = S_0 \exp\left(\left(\mu - \frac{\sigma^2}{2}\right)t + \sigma B_t\right), \qquad t \geqslant 0.$$

b) Let us provide an alternative proof by searching for a solution of the form

$$S_t = f(t, B_t)$$

where $f(t, x)$ is a function to be determined. By Itô's formula (4.25) we have

$$dS_t = df(t, B_t) = \frac{\partial f}{\partial t}(t, B_t)dt + \frac{\partial f}{\partial x}(t, B_t)dB_t + \frac{1}{2}\frac{\partial^2 f}{\partial x^2}(t, B_t)dt.$$

Comparing this expression to (5.19) and identifying the terms in dB_t we get

$$
\begin{cases}
\dfrac{\partial f}{\partial x}(t, B_t) = \sigma S_t, \\[3mm]
\dfrac{\partial f}{\partial t}(t, B_t) + \dfrac{1}{2}\dfrac{\partial^2 f}{\partial x^2}(t, B_t) = \mu S_t.
\end{cases}
$$

Using the relation $S_t = f(t, B_t)$, these two equations rewrite as

$$
\begin{cases}
\dfrac{\partial f}{\partial x}(t, B_t) = \sigma f(t, B_t), \\[3mm]
\dfrac{\partial f}{\partial t}(t, B_t) + \dfrac{1}{2}\dfrac{\partial^2 f}{\partial x^2}(t, B_t) = \mu f(t, B_t).
\end{cases}
$$

Since B_t is a Gaussian random variable taking all possible values in $\mathbb{R}$, the equations should hold for all $x \in \mathbb{R}$, as follows:

$$
\begin{cases}
\dfrac{\partial f}{\partial x}(t, x) = \sigma f(t, x), & (5.21a) \\[2em]
\dfrac{\partial f}{\partial t}(t, x) + \dfrac{1}{2}\dfrac{\partial^2 f}{\partial x^2}(t, x) = \mu f(t, x). & (5.21b)
\end{cases}
$$

To find the solution $f(t, x) = f(t, 0)\, e^{\sigma x}$ of (5.21a) we let $g(t, x) = \log f(t, x)$ and rewrite (5.21a) as

$$
\frac{\partial g}{\partial x}(t, x) = \frac{\partial}{\partial x}\log f(t, x) = \frac{1}{f(t, x)}\frac{\partial f}{\partial x}(t, x) = \sigma,
$$

i.e.

$$
\frac{\partial g}{\partial x}(t, x) = \sigma,
$$

which is solved as

$$
g(t, x) = g(t, 0) + \sigma x,
$$

hence

$$
f(t, x) = e^{g(t,0)}\, e^{\sigma x} = f(t, 0)\, e^{\sigma x}.
$$

Plugging back this expression into the second equation (5.21b) yields

$$
e^{\sigma x}\frac{\partial f}{\partial t}(t, 0) + \frac{1}{2}\sigma^2\, e^{\sigma x} f(t, 0) = \mu f(t, 0)\, e^{\sigma x},
$$

i.e.

$$
\frac{\partial f}{\partial t}(t, 0) = \left(\mu - \frac{\sigma^2}{2}\right) f(t, 0).
$$

In other words, we have $\dfrac{\partial g}{\partial t}(t, 0) = \mu - \sigma^2/2$, which yields

$$
g(t, 0) = g(0, 0) + \left(\mu - \frac{\sigma^2}{2}\right) t,
$$

i.e.

$$
\begin{aligned}
f(t, x) &= e^{g(t,x)} = e^{g(t,0) + \sigma x} \\
&= e^{g(0,0) + \sigma x + (\mu - \sigma^2/2)t} \\
&= f(0, 0)\, e^{\sigma x + (\mu - \sigma^2/2)t}, \qquad t \geqslant 0.
\end{aligned}
$$

We conclude that

$$
S_t = f(t, B_t) = f(0, 0)\, e^{\sigma B_t + (\mu - \sigma^2/2)t},
$$

and the solution to (5.19) is given by

$$
S_t = S_0\, e^{\sigma B_t + (\mu - \sigma^2/2)t}, \qquad t \geqslant 0.
$$

$\square$

Conversely, taking $S_t = f(t, B_t)$ with $f(t, x) = S_0 \, e^{\mu t + \sigma x - \sigma^2 t/2}$, we may apply Itô's formula to check that

$$
\begin{aligned}
dS_t &= df(t, B_t) \\
&= \frac{\partial f}{\partial t}(t, B_t)dt + \frac{\partial f}{\partial x}(t, B_t)dB_t + \frac{1}{2}\frac{\partial^2 f}{\partial x^2}(t, B_t)dt \\
&= \left(\mu - \frac{\sigma^2}{2}\right) S_0 \, e^{\mu t + \sigma B_t - \sigma^2 t/2}dt + \sigma S_0 \, e^{\mu t + \sigma B_t - \sigma^2 t/2}dB_t \\
&\quad + \frac{1}{2}\sigma^2 S_0 \, e^{\mu t + \sigma B_t - \sigma^2 t/2}dt \\
&= \mu S_0 \, e^{\mu t + \sigma B_t - \sigma^2 t/2}dt + \sigma S_0 \, e^{\mu t + \sigma B_t - \sigma^2 t/2}dB_t \\
&= \mu S_t dt + \sigma S_t dB_t.
\end{aligned}
\tag{5.22}
$$

Exercises

Exercise 5.1 Show that at any time $T > 0$, the random variable $S_T := S_0 \, e^{\sigma B_T + (\mu - \sigma^2/2)T}$ has the *lognormal distribution* with probability density function

$$
x \longmapsto f(x) = \frac{1}{x\sigma\sqrt{2\pi T}} \, e^{-(-(\mu - \sigma^2/2)T + \log(x/S_0))^2/(2\sigma^2 T)}, \quad x > 0,
$$

with log-variance σ^2 and log-mean $(\mu - \sigma^2/2)T + \log S_0$, see Figures 3.9 and 5.6.

```
N=1000; t <- 0:N; dt <- 1.0/N; nsim <- 100 # using Bernoulli samples
sigma=0.2;r=0.5;a=(1+r*dt)*(1-sigma*sqrt(dt))-1;b=(1+r*dt)*(1+sigma*sqrt(dt))-1
X <- matrix(a+(b-a)*rbinom( nsim * N, 1, 0.5), nsim, N)
X<-cbind(rep(0,nsim),t(apply((1+X),1,cumprod))); X[,1]=1;H<-hist(X[,N],plot=FALSE);
    dev.new(width=16,height=7);
layout(matrix(c(1,2), nrow =1, byrow = TRUE)); par(mar=c(2,2,2,0), oma = c(2, 2, 2, 2))
plot(t*dt,X[1,],xlab="time",ylab="",type="l",ylim=c(0.8,3), col = 0,xaxs='i',las=1, cex.axis=1.6)
for (i in 1:nsim){lines(t*dt, X[i, ], xlab = "time", type = "l", col = i)}
lines((1+r*dt)^t, type="l", lty=1, col="black",lwd=3,xlab="",ylab="", main="")
for (i in 1:nsim){points(0.999, X[i,N], pch=1, lwd = 5, col = i)}; x <- seq(0.01,3, length=100);
px <- exp(-(-(r-sigma^2/2)+log(x))^2/2/sigma^2)/x/sigma/sqrt(2*pi); par(mar = c(2,2,2,2))
plot(NULL , xlab="", ylab="", xlim = c(0, max(px,H$density)),ylim=c(0.8,3),axes=F, las=1)
rect(0, H$breaks[1:(length(H$breaks) - 1)], col=rainbow(20,start=0.08,end=0.6), H$density,
    H$breaks[2:length(H$breaks)])
lines(px,x, type="l", lty=1, col="black",lwd=3,xlab="",ylab="", main="")
```

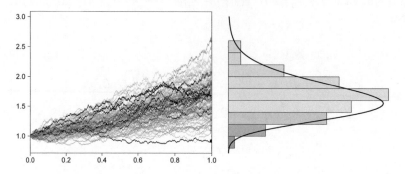

Figure 5.6: Statistics of geometric Brownian paths *vs* lognormal distribution.

Exercise 5.2

a) Consider the stochastic differential equation

$$dS_t = rS_tdt + \sigma S_tdB_t, \qquad t \geqslant 0, \tag{5.23}$$

where $r, \sigma \in \mathbb{R}$ are constants and $(B_t)_{t\in\mathbb{R}_+}$ is a standard Brownian motion. Compute $d\log S_t$ using the Itô formula.

b) Solve the ordinary differential equation $df(t) = cf(t)dt$ and the stochastic differential equation (5.23).

c) Compute the lognormal mean and variance

$$\mathbb{E}[S_t] = S_0\,\mathrm{e}^{rt} \quad \text{and} \quad \mathrm{Var}[S_t] = S_0^2\,\mathrm{e}^{2rt}\big(\mathrm{e}^{\sigma^2 t} - 1\big), \quad t \geqslant 0,$$

using the Gaussian moment generating function (MGF) formula.

d) Recover the lognormal mean and variance of Question (c) by deriving differential equations for the functions $u(t) := \mathbb{E}[S_t]$ and $v(t) := \mathbb{E}\big[S_t^2\big]$, $t \geqslant 0$, using stochastic calculus.

Exercise 5.3   Assume that $(B_t)_{t\in\mathbb{R}_+}$ and $(W_t)_{t\in\mathbb{R}_+}$ are standard Brownian motions, correlated according to the Itô rule $dW_t \cdot dB_t = \rho dt$ for $\rho \in [-1, 1]$, and consider the solution $(Y_t)_{t\in\mathbb{R}_+}$ of the stochastic differential equation $dY_t = \mu Y_t dt + \eta Y_t dW_t$, $t \geqslant 0$, where $\mu, \eta \in \mathbb{R}$ are constants. Compute $df(S_t, Y_t)$, for f a $\mathcal{C}^2$ function on $\mathbb{R}^2$ using the bivariate Itô formula (4.26).

Exercise 5.4   Consider the asset price process $(S_t)_{t\in\mathbb{R}_+}$ given by the stochastic differential equation

$$dS_t = rS_tdt + \sigma S_tdB_t.$$

Find the stochastic integral decomposition of the random variable S_T, *i.e.* find the *constant* $C(S_0, r, T)$ and the process $(\zeta_{t,T})_{t\in[0,T]}$ such that

$$S_T = C(S_0, r, T) + \int_0^T \zeta_{t,T}dB_t. \tag{5.24}$$

Hint: Use the fact that the discounted price process $(X_t)_{t\in[0,T]} := (\mathrm{e}^{-rt}S_t)_{t\in[0,T]}$ satisfies the relation $dX_t = \sigma X_t dB_t$.

Exercise 5.5   Consider $(B_t)_{t\in\mathbb{R}_+}$ a standard Brownian motion generating the filtration $(\mathcal{F}_t)_{t\in\mathbb{R}_+}$ and the process $(S_t)_{t\in\mathbb{R}_+}$ defined by

$$S_t = S_0 \exp\left(\int_0^t \sigma_s dB_s + \int_0^t u_s ds\right), \qquad t \geqslant 0,$$

where $(\sigma_t)_{t\in\mathbb{R}_+}$ and $(u_t)_{t\in\mathbb{R}_+}$ are $(\mathcal{F}_t)_{t\in[0,T]}$-adapted processes.

a) Compute dS_t using Itô calculus.

b) Show that S_t satisfies a stochastic differential equation to be determined.

Exercise 5.6   Consider $(B_t)_{t\in\mathbb{R}_+}$ a standard Brownian motion generating the filtration $(\mathcal{F}_t)_{t\in\mathbb{R}_+}$, and let $\sigma > 0$.

a) Compute the mean and variance of the random variable S_t defined as

$$S_t := 1 + \sigma \int_0^t e^{\sigma B_s - \sigma^2 s/2} dB_s, \qquad t \geqslant 0. \tag{5.25}$$

b) Express $d\log(S_t)$ using (5.25) and the Itô formula.

c) Show that $S_t = e^{\sigma B_t - \sigma^2 t/2}$ for $t \geqslant 0$.

Exercise 5.7   We consider a leveraged fund with factor $\beta : 1$ on an index $(S_t)_{t\in\mathbb{R}_+}$ modeled as the geometric Brownian motion

$$dS_t = rS_t dt + \sigma S_t dB_t, \qquad t \geqslant 0,$$

under the risk-neutral probability measure $\mathbb{P}^*$. Examples of leveraged funds include *ProShares Ultra S&P500* and *ProShares UltraShort S&P500*.

a) Find the portfolio allocation (ξ_t, η_t) of the leveraged fund value

$$F_t = \xi_t S_t + \eta_t A_t, \qquad t \geqslant 0,$$

where $A_t := A_0\, e^{rt}$ represents the risk-free money market account price.

Hint: Leveraging with a factor $\beta : 1$ means that the risky component of the portfolio should represent β times the invested amount βF_t at any time $t \geqslant 0$.

b) Find the stochastic differential equation satisfied by $(F_t)_{t\in\mathbb{R}_+}$ under the self-financing condition $dF_t = \xi_t dS_t + \eta_t dA_t$.

c) Find the relation between the fund value F_t and the index S_t by solving the stochastic differential equation obtained for F_t in Question (b). For simplicity we take $F_0 := S_0^\beta$.

Exercise 5.8   Consider two assets whose prices $S_t^{(1)}$, $S_t^{(2)}$ at time $t \in [0,T]$ follow the geometric Brownian dynamics

$$dS_t^{(1)} = \mu S_t^{(1)} dt + \sigma_1 S_t^{(1)} dW_t^{(1)} \quad \text{and} \quad dS_t^{(2)} = \mu S_t^{(2)} dt + \sigma_2 S_t^{(2)} dW_t^{(2)},$$

$t \in [0,T]$, where $\left(W_t^{(1)}\right)_{t\in[0,T]}$, $\left(W_t^{(2)}\right)_{t\in[0,T]}$ are two Brownian motions with correlation $\rho \in [-1,1]$, *i.e.* we have $\mathbb{E}\left[W_t^{(1)} W_t^{(2)}\right] = \rho t$.

a) Compute $\mathbb{E}\left[S_t^{(i)}\right]$, $t \in [0,T]$, $i = 1,2$.

b) Compute Var $\left[S_t^{(i)}\right]$, $t \in [0,T]$, $i = 1,2$.

c) Compute Var $\left[S_t^{(2)} - S_t^{(1)}\right]$, $t \in [0,T]$.

Exercise 5.9 Solve the stochastic differential equation

$$dX_t = h(t)X_t dt + \sigma X_t dB_t,$$

where $\sigma > 0$ and $h(t)$ is a deterministic, integrable function of $t \geqslant 0$.

Hint: Look for a solution of the form $X_t = f(t) e^{\sigma B_t - \sigma^2 t/2}$, where $f(t)$ is a function to be determined, $t \geqslant 0$.

Exercise 5.10 Let $(B_t)_{t \in \mathbb{R}_+}$ denote a standard Brownian motion generating the filtration $(\mathcal{F}_t)_{t \in \mathbb{R}_+}$.

a) Letting $X_t := \sigma B_t + \nu t$, $\sigma > 0$, $\nu \in \mathbb{R}$, compute $S_t := e^{X_t}$ by the Itô formula

$$f(X_t) = f(X_0) + \int_0^t u_s \frac{\partial f}{\partial x}(X_s)dB_s + \int_0^t v_s \frac{\partial f}{\partial x}(X_s)ds + \frac{1}{2}\int_0^t u_s^2 \frac{\partial^2 f}{\partial x^2}(X_s)ds, \quad (5.26)$$

applied to $f(x) = e^x$, by writing X_t as $X_t = X_0 + \int_0^t u_s dB_s + \int_0^t v_s ds$.

b) Let $r > 0$. For which value of ν does $(S_t)_{t \in \mathbb{R}_+}$ satisfy the stochastic differential equation

$$dS_t = rS_t dt + \sigma S_t dB_t \quad ?$$

c) Given $\sigma > 0$, let $X_t := (B_T - B_t)\sigma$, and compute $\mathrm{Var}[X_t]$, $0 \leqslant t \leqslant T$.

d) Let the process $(S_t)_{t \in \mathbb{R}_+}$ be defined by $S_t = S_0 e^{\sigma B_t + \nu t}$, $t \geqslant 0$. Show that the conditional probability that $S_T > K$ given $S_t = x$ can be computed as

$$\mathbb{P}(S_T > K \mid S_t = x) = \Phi\left(\frac{\log(x/K) + (T-t)\nu}{\sigma\sqrt{T-t}}\right), \quad 0 \leqslant t < T.$$

Hint: Use the time splitting decomposition

$$S_T = S_t \frac{S_T}{S_t} = S_t e^{(B_T - B_t)\sigma + (T-t)\nu}, \quad 0 \leqslant t \leqslant T.$$

Problem 5.11 Stop-loss/start-gain strategy (Lipton (2001) § 8.3.3., Exercise 4.19 continued). Let $(B_t)_{t \in \mathbb{R}_+}$ be a standard Brownian motion started at $B_0 \in \mathbb{R}$.

a) We consider a simplified foreign exchange model, in which the AUD is a risky asset and the AUD/SGD exchange rate at time t is modeled by B_t, *i.e.* AU\$1 equals SG\$$B_t$ at time t. A foreign exchange (FX) European call option gives to its holder the right (but not the obligation) to receive AU\$1 in exchange for $K = $ SG\$1 at maturity T. Give the option payoff at maturity, quoted in SGD.

In what follows, for simplicity we assume no time value of money ($r = 0$), *i.e.* the (riskless) SGD account is priced $A_t = A_0 = 1$, $0 \leqslant t \leqslant T$.

b) Consider the following hedging strategy for the European call option of Question (a):

   i) If $B_0 > 1$, charge the premium $B_0 - 1$ at time 0, and borrow SG\$1 to purchase AU\$1.

   ii) If $B_0 < 1$, issue the option for free.

   iii) From time 0 to time T, purchase* AU\$1 every time B_t crosses $K = 1$ from below, and sell† AU\$1 each time B_t crosses $K = 1$ from above.

Show that this strategy effectively hedges the foreign exchange European call option at maturity T.

Hint: Note that it suffices to consider four scenarios based on $B_0 < 1$ *vs* $B_0 < 1$ and $B_T > 1$ *vs* $B_T < 1$.

c) Determine the quantities η_t of SGD cash and ξ_t of (risky) AUDs to be held in the portfolio and express the portfolio value

$$V_t = \eta_t + \xi_t B_t$$

at all times $t \in [0, T]$.

d) Compute the integral summation

$$\int_0^t \eta_s dA_s + \int_0^t \xi_s dB_s$$

of portfolio profits and losses at any time $t \in [0, T]$.

Hint: Apply the Itô-Tanaka formula (4.48), see Question (e) in Exercise 4.19.

e) Is the portfolio strategy $(\eta_t, \xi_t)_{t \in [0,T]}$ self-financing? How to interpret the answer in practice?

---

*We need to borrow SG\$1 if this is the first AUD purchase.
†We use the SG\$1 product of the sale to refund the loan.

Chapter 6

Black–Scholes Pricing and Hedging

The Black and Scholes (1973) PDE is a Partial Differential Equation that is used for the pricing of vanilla options under the absence of arbitrage and self-financing portfolio assumptions. In this chapter, we derive the Black–Scholes PDE and present its solution by the heat kernel method, with application to the pricing and hedging of European call and put options.

6.1 The Black–Scholes PDE

In this chapter, we work in a market based on a riskless asset with price $(A_t)_{t\in\mathbb{R}_+}$ given by

$$\frac{A_{t+dt} - A_t}{A_t} = rdt, \qquad \frac{dA_t}{A_t} = rdt, \qquad \frac{dA_t}{dt} = rA_t, \quad t \geqslant 0,$$

with

$$A_t = A_0 \, e^{rt}, \qquad t \geqslant 0,$$

and a risky asset with price $(S_t)_{t\in\mathbb{R}_+}$ modeled using a geometric Brownian motion defined from the equation

$$\frac{dS_t}{S_t} = \mu dt + \sigma dB_t, \quad t \geqslant 0, \tag{6.1}$$

which admits the solution

$$S_t = S_0 \exp\left(\sigma B_t + \mu t - \frac{1}{2}\sigma^2 t\right), \qquad t \geqslant 0,$$

see Proposition 5.15.

```
1  library(quantmod)
   getSymbols("0005.HK",from="2016-02-15",to="2017-05-11",src="yahoo")
3  Marketprices<-Ad(`0005.HK`); myPars <- chart_pars();myPars$cex<-1.2
   myTheme <- chart_theme();myTheme$col$line.col <- "blue"
5  chart_Series(Marketprices,pars=myPars, theme = myTheme)
```

The *adjusted close price* Ad() is the closing price after adjustments for applicable splits and dividend distributions.

The next Figure 6.1 presents a graph of underlying asset price market data, which is compared to the geometric Brownian motion simulations of Figures 5.4 and 5.5.

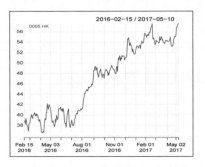 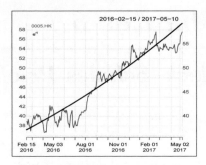

Figure 6.1: Graph of underlying market prices.

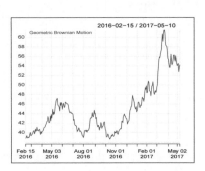 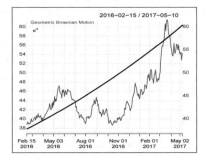

Figure 6.2: Graph of simulated geometric Brownian motion.

The R package Sim.DiffProc can be used to estimate the coefficients of a geometric Brownian motion fitting observed market data.

```
library("Sim.DiffProc")
fx <- expression( theta[1]*x ); gx <- expression( theta[2]*x )
fitsde(data = as.ts(Marketprices), drift = fx, diffusion = gx, start = list(theta1=1, theta2=1),pmle="euler")
```

In the sequel, we start by deriving the Black and Scholes (1973) Partial Differential Equation (PDE) for the value of a self-financing portfolio. Note that the drift parameter μ in (6.1) is absent in the PDE (6.2), and it does not appear as well in the Black and Scholes (1973) formula (6.11).

Proposition 6.1. *Let $(\eta_t, \xi_t)_{t \in \mathbb{R}_+}$ be a portfolio strategy such that*

(i) the portfolio strategy $(\eta_t, \xi_t)_{t \in \mathbb{R}_+}$ is self-financing,

(ii) the portfolio value $V_t := \eta_t A_t + \xi_t S_t$, takes the form

$$V_t = g(t, S_t), \qquad t \geqslant 0,$$

for some function $g \in \mathcal{C}^{1,2}(\mathbb{R}_+ \times \mathbb{R}_+)$ of t and S_t.

Then, the function $g(t, x)$ satisfies the Black and Scholes (1973) PDE

$$rg(t,x) = \frac{\partial g}{\partial t}(t,x) + rx\frac{\partial g}{\partial x}(t,x) + \frac{1}{2}\sigma^2 x^2 \frac{\partial^2 g}{\partial x^2}(t,x), \quad x > 0, \qquad (6.2)$$

and $\xi_t = \xi_t(S_t)$ is given by the partial derivative

$$\xi_t = \xi_t(S_t) = \frac{\partial g}{\partial x}(t, S_t), \qquad t \geqslant 0. \qquad (6.3)$$

Proof. (i) First, we note that the self-financing condition (5.8) in Proposition 5.8 implies

$$
\begin{aligned}
dV_t &= \eta_t dA_t + \xi_t dS_t \\
&= r\eta_t A_t dt + \mu\xi_t S_t dt + \sigma\xi_t S_t dB_t \\
&= rV_t dt + (\mu - r)\xi_t S_t dt + \sigma\xi_t S_t dB_t \\
&= rg(t, S_t)dt + (\mu - r)\xi_t S_t dt + \sigma\xi_t S_t dB_t,
\end{aligned}
\tag{6.4}
$$

$t \geqslant 0$. We now rewrite (5.18) under the form of an Itô process

$$
S_t = S_0 + \int_0^t v_s ds + \int_0^t u_s dB_s, \qquad t \geqslant 0,
$$

as in (4.22), by taking

$$
u_t = \sigma S_t, \quad \text{and} \quad v_t = \mu S_t, \qquad t \geqslant 0.
$$

(ii) By (4.24), the application of Itô's formula Theorem 4.24 to $V_t = g(t, S_t)$ leads to

$$
\begin{aligned}
dV_t &= dg(t, S_t) \\
&= \frac{\partial g}{\partial t}(t, S_t)dt + \frac{\partial g}{\partial x}(t, S_t)dS_t + \frac{1}{2}(dS_t)^2\frac{\partial^2 g}{\partial x^2}(t, S_t) \\
&= \frac{\partial g}{\partial t}(t, S_t)dt + v_t\frac{\partial g}{\partial x}(t, S_t)dt + u_t\frac{\partial g}{\partial x}(t, S_t)dB_t + \frac{1}{2}|u_t|^2\frac{\partial^2 g}{\partial x^2}(t, S_t)dt \\
&= \frac{\partial g}{\partial t}(t, S_t)dt + \mu S_t\frac{\partial g}{\partial x}(t, S_t)dt + \frac{1}{2}\sigma^2 S_t^2\frac{\partial^2 g}{\partial x^2}(t, S_t)dt + \sigma S_t\frac{\partial g}{\partial x}(t, S_t)dB_t.
\end{aligned}
\tag{6.5}
$$

By respective identification of components in dB_t and dt in (6.4) and (6.5), we get

$$
\begin{cases}
rg(t, S_t)dt + (\mu - r)\xi_t S_t dt = \dfrac{\partial g}{\partial t}(t, S_t)dt + \mu S_t\dfrac{\partial g}{\partial x}(t, S_t)dt + \dfrac{1}{2}\sigma^2 S_t^2\dfrac{\partial^2 g}{\partial x^2}(t, S_t)dt, \\[2ex]
\xi_t S_t\sigma dB_t = S_t\sigma\dfrac{\partial g}{\partial x}(t, S_t)dB_t,
\end{cases}
$$

hence

$$
\begin{cases}
rg(t, S_t) = \dfrac{\partial g}{\partial t}(t, S_t) + rS_t\dfrac{\partial g}{\partial x}(t, S_t) + \dfrac{1}{2}\sigma^2 S_t^2\dfrac{\partial^2 g}{\partial x^2}(t, S_t), \\[2ex]
\xi_t = \dfrac{\partial g}{\partial x}(t, S_t), \qquad 0 \leqslant t \leqslant T,
\end{cases}
\tag{6.6}
$$

which yields (6.2) after substituting S_t with $x > 0$. $\qquad\square$

The derivative giving ξ_t in (6.3) is called the *Delta* of the option price, see Proposition 6.4 below. The amount invested on the riskless asset is

$$
\eta_t A_t = V_t - \xi_t S_t = g(t, S_t) - S_t\frac{\partial g}{\partial x}(t, S_t),
$$

and η_t is given by

$$
\begin{aligned}
\eta_t &= \frac{V_t - \xi_t S_t}{A_t} \\
&= \frac{1}{A_t}\left(g(t, S_t) - S_t\frac{\partial g}{\partial x}(t, S_t)\right) \\
&= \frac{1}{A_0\, e^{rt}}\left(g(t, S_t) - S_t\frac{\partial g}{\partial x}(t, S_t)\right).
\end{aligned}
$$

In the next Proposition 6.2 we add a terminal condition $g(T, x) = f(x)$ to the Black–Scholes PDE (6.2) in order to price a claim payoff C of the form $C = h(S_T)$. As in the discrete-time case, the arbitrage-free price $\pi_t(C)$ at time $t \in [0, T]$ of the claim payoff C is defined to be the value V_t of the self-financing portfolio hedging C.

Proposition 6.2. *Under the assumptions of Proposition 6.1, the arbitrage-free price $\pi_t(C)$ at time $t \in [0, T]$ of the (vanilla) option with claim payoff $C = h(S_T)$ is given by $\pi_t(C) = g(t, S_t)$ and the hedging allocation ξ_t is given by the partial derivative (6.3), where the function $g(t, x)$ is solution of the following Black–Scholes PDE:*

$$
\begin{cases}
rg(t, x) = \dfrac{\partial g}{\partial t}(t, x) + rx\dfrac{\partial g}{\partial x}(t, x) + \dfrac{1}{2}\sigma^2 x^2 \dfrac{\partial^2 g}{\partial x^2}(t, x), \\[2mm]
g(T, x) = h(x), \quad x > 0.
\end{cases}
\tag{6.7}
$$

Proof. Proposition 6.1 shows that the solution $g(t, x)$ of (6.2), $g \in \mathcal{C}^{1,2}(\mathbb{R}_+ \times \mathbb{R}_+)$, represents the value $V_t = \eta_t A_t + \xi_t S_t = g(t, S_t)$, $t \in \mathbb{R}_+$, of a self-financing portfolio strategy $(\eta_t, \xi_t)_{t \in \mathbb{R}_+}$. By Definition 3.1, $\pi_t(C) := V_t = g(t, S_t)$ is the arbitrage-free price at time $t \in [0, T]$ of the vanilla option with claim payoff $C = h(S_T)$. $\qquad\square$

The absence of the drift parameter μ from the PDE (6.7) can be understood in the next forward contract example, in which the claim payoff can be hedged by leveraging on the value S_t of the underlying asset, independently of the trend parameter μ.

Example – Forward contracts

The holder of a long forward contract is committed to purchasing an asset at the price K at maturity time T, while the contract issuer has the obligation to hand in the asset priced S_T in exchange for the amount K at maturity time T.

Clearly, the contract has the claim payoff $C = S_T - K$, and it can be hedged by simply holding $\xi_t = 1$ asset in the portfolio at all times $t \in [0, T]$. Denoting by V_t the option price at time $t \in [0, T]$, the amount $S_t - V_t$ has to be borrowed at time t in order to purchase the asset. As the amount K received at maturity T should be used to refund the loan at time T, we should have $(S_t - V_t)\,\mathrm{e}^{(T-t)r} = K$, hence

$$
V_t = S_t - K\,\mathrm{e}^{-(T-t)r}, \quad 0 \leqslant t \leqslant T.
\tag{6.8}
$$

We note that the riskless allocation $\eta_t = -K\,\mathrm{e}^{-rT}$ is also constant over time $t \in [0, T]$ due to self-financing.

More precisely, the forward contract can be realized by the option issuer via the following steps:

a) At time t, *receive* the option premium $V_t := S_t - \mathrm{e}^{-(T-t)r}K$ from the option buyer.

b) *Borrow* $\mathrm{e}^{-(T-t)r}K$ from the bank, to be refunded at maturity.

c) *Buy* the risky asset using the amount $S_t - \mathrm{e}^{-(T-t)r}K + \mathrm{e}^{-(T-t)r}K = S_t$.

d) *Hold* the risky asset until maturity (do nothing, constant portfolio strategy).

e) At maturity T, *hand in* the asset to the option holder, who will pay the amount K in return.

f) Use the amount $K = e^{(T-t)r} e^{-(T-t)r} K$ to *refund* the lender of $e^{-(T-t)r} K$ borrowed at time t.

On the other hand, the payoff C of the long forward contract can be written as $C = S_T - K = h(S_T)$ where h is the (affine) payoff function $h(x) = x - K$, and the Black–Scholes PDE (6.7) admits the easy solution

$$g(t,x) = x - K e^{-(T-t)r}, \qquad x > 0, \quad 0 \leqslant t \leqslant T, \tag{6.9}$$

showing that the price at time $t \in [0, T]$ of the long forward contract is

$$g(t, S_t) = S_t - K e^{-(T-t)r}, \qquad 0 \leqslant t \leqslant T.$$

In addition, the Delta of the option price is given by

$$\xi_t = \frac{\partial g}{\partial x}(t, S_t) = 1, \qquad 0 \leqslant t \leqslant T,$$

which recovers the static, "hedge and forget" strategy, cf. Exercise 6.7.

Forward contracts can be used for physical delivery, *e.g.* for live cattle. In the case of European options, the basic "hedge and forget" constant strategy

$$\xi_t = 1, \quad \eta_t = \eta_0, \quad 0 \leqslant t \leqslant T,$$

will hedge the option only if

$$S_T + \eta_0 A_T \geqslant (S_T - K)^+,$$

i.e. if $-\eta_0 A_T \leqslant K \leqslant S_T$.

Future contracts

For a future contract expiring at time T, we take $K = S_0 e^{rT}$ and the contract is usually quoted at time t in terms of the forward price

$$e^{(T-t)r}\left(S_t - K e^{-(T-t)r}\right) = e^{(T-t)r} S_t - K = e^{(T-t)r} S_t - S_0 e^{rT},$$

discounted at time T, or simply using $e^{(T-t)r} S_t$. Future contracts are *non-deliverable* forward contracts which are "marked to market" at each time step via a cash flow exchange between the two parties, ensuring that the absolute difference $|e^{(T-t)r} S_t - K|$ is being credited to the buyer's account if $e^{(T-t)r} S_t > K$, or to the seller's account if $e^{(T-t)r} S_t < K$.

6.2 European Call Options

Recall that in the case of the European call option with strike price K the payoff function is given by $h(x) = (x - K)^+$ and the Black–Scholes PDE (6.7) reads

$$\begin{cases} r g_c(t,x) = \dfrac{\partial g_c}{\partial t}(t,x) + rx \dfrac{\partial g_c}{\partial x}(t,x) + \dfrac{1}{2}\sigma^2 x^2 \dfrac{\partial^2 g_c}{\partial x^2}(t,x) \\[2mm] g_c(T,x) = (x-K)^+. \end{cases} \tag{6.10}$$

The next proposition will be proved in Sections 6.5–6.6, see Proposition 6.11.

Proposition 6.3. *The solution of the PDE* (6.10) *is given by the* Black–Scholes *formula for call options*

$$g_c(t,x) = \mathrm{Bl}(x, K, \sigma, r, T-t) = x\Phi\big(d_+(T-t)\big) - K\,\mathrm{e}^{-(T-t)r}\Phi\big(d_-(T-t)\big), \quad (6.11)$$

with

$$d_+(T-t) := \frac{\log(x/K) + (r + \sigma^2/2)(T-t)}{|\sigma|\sqrt{T-t}} \tag{6.12}$$

and

$$d_-(T-t) := \frac{\log(x/K) + (r - \sigma^2/2)(T-t)}{|\sigma|\sqrt{T-t}}, \tag{6.13}$$

$0 \leqslant t < T$.

We note the relation

$$d_+(T-t) = d_-(T-t) + |\sigma|\sqrt{T-t}, \qquad 0 \leqslant t < T. \tag{6.14}$$

Here, "log" denotes the *natural logarithm* "ln", and

$$\Phi(x) := \mathbb{P}(X \leqslant x) = \frac{1}{\sqrt{2\pi}} \int_{-\infty}^{x} \mathrm{e}^{-y^2/2} dy, \qquad x \in \mathbb{R},$$

denotes the standard Gaussian Cumulative Distribution Function (CDF) of a standard normal random variable $X \simeq \mathcal{N}(0,1)$, with the relation

$$\Phi(-x) = 1 - \Phi(x), \qquad x \in \mathbb{R}. \tag{6.15}$$

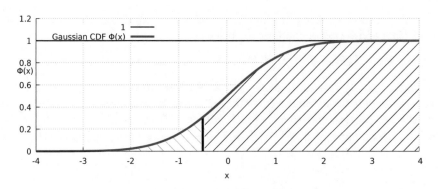

Figure 6.3: Graph of the Gaussian Cumulative Distribution Function (CDF).

In other words, the European call option with strike price K and maturity T is priced at time $t \in [0, T]$ as

$$\begin{aligned} g_c(t, S_t) &= \mathrm{Bl}(S_t, K, \sigma, r, T-t) \\ &= S_t\Phi\big(d_+(T-t)\big) - K\,\mathrm{e}^{-(T-t)r}\Phi\big(d_-(T-t)\big), \quad 0 \leqslant t \leqslant T. \end{aligned}$$

The following R script is an implementation of the Black–Scholes formula for European call options in R.

```
1   BSCall <- function(S, K, r, T, sigma)
    {d1 <- (log(S/K)+(r+sigma^2/2)*T)/(sigma*sqrt(T));d2 <- d1 - sigma * sqrt(T)
3   BSCall = S*pnorm(d1) - K*exp(-r*T)*pnorm(d2)
    BSCall}
```

In comparison with the discrete-time Cox–Ross–Rubinstein (CRR) model of Section 2.6, the interest in the formula (6.11) is to provide an analytical solution that can be evaluated in a single step, which is computationally much more efficient.

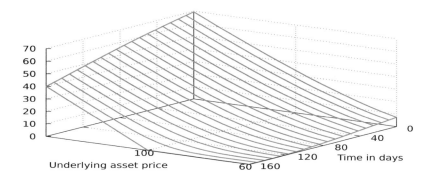

Figure 6.4: Solution of the Black–Scholes PDE (call option).

The next proposition is proved by a direct differentiation of the Black–Scholes function, and will be recovered later using a probabilistic argument in Proposition 7.13 below.

Proposition 6.4. *The Black–Scholes Delta of the European call option is given by*

$$\xi_t = \xi_t(S_t) = \frac{\partial g_c}{\partial x}(t, S_t) = \Phi\big(d_+(T - t)\big) \in [0, 1], \tag{6.16}$$

where $d_+(T - t)$ is given by (6.12).

Proof. From Relation (6.14), we note that the standard normal probability density function

$$\varphi(x) = \Phi'(x) = \frac{1}{\sqrt{2\pi}}\, \mathrm{e}^{-x^2/2}, \qquad x \in \mathbb{R},$$

satisfies

$$
\begin{aligned}
\varphi\big(d_+(T - t)\big) &= \varphi\left(\frac{\log(x/K) + (r + \sigma^2/2)(T - t)}{|\sigma|\sqrt{T - t}}\right) \\
&= \frac{1}{\sqrt{2\pi}}\exp\left(-\frac{1}{2}\left(\frac{\log(x/K) + (r + \sigma^2/2)(T - t)}{|\sigma|\sqrt{T - t}}\right)^2\right) \\
&= \frac{1}{\sqrt{2\pi}}\exp\left(-\frac{1}{2}\left(\frac{\log(x/K) + (r - \sigma^2/2)(T - t)}{|\sigma|\sqrt{T - t}} + |\sigma|\sqrt{T - t}\right)^2\right) \\
&= \frac{1}{\sqrt{2\pi}}\exp\left(-\frac{1}{2}(d_-(T - t))^2 - (T - t)r - \log\frac{x}{K}\right) \\
&= \frac{K}{x\sqrt{2\pi}}\,\mathrm{e}^{-(T-t)r}\exp\left(-\frac{1}{2}(d_-(T - t))^2\right) \\
&= \frac{K}{x}\,\mathrm{e}^{-(T-t)r}\varphi(d_-(T - t)),
\end{aligned}
$$

hence by (6.11) we have

$$\frac{\partial g_c}{\partial x}(t,x) = \frac{\partial}{\partial x}\left(x\Phi\left(\frac{\log(x/K) + (r + \sigma^2/2)(T-t)}{|\sigma|\sqrt{T-t}}\right)\right) \tag{6.17}$$

$$-Ke^{-(T-t)r}\frac{\partial}{\partial x}\left(\Phi\left(\frac{\log(x/K) + (r - \sigma^2/2)(T-t)}{|\sigma|\sqrt{T-t}}\right)\right)$$

$$= \Phi\left(\frac{\log(x/K) + (r + \sigma^2/2)(T-t)}{|\sigma|\sqrt{T-t}}\right)$$

$$+x\frac{\partial}{\partial x}\Phi\left(\frac{\log(x/K) + (r + \sigma^2/2)(T-t)}{|\sigma|\sqrt{T-t}}\right)$$

$$-Ke^{-(T-t)r}\frac{\partial}{\partial x}\Phi\left(\frac{\log(x/K) + (r - \sigma^2/2)(T-t)}{|\sigma|\sqrt{T-t}}\right)$$

$$= \Phi\left(\frac{\log(x/K) + (r + \sigma^2/2)(T-t)}{|\sigma|\sqrt{T-t}}\right)$$

$$+\frac{1}{|\sigma|\sqrt{T-t}}\varphi\left(\frac{\log(x/K) + (r + \sigma^2/2)(T-t)}{|\sigma|\sqrt{T-t}}\right)$$

$$-\frac{Ke^{-(T-t)r}}{x|\sigma|\sqrt{T-t}}\varphi\left(\frac{\log(x/K) + (r - \sigma^2/2)(T-t)}{|\sigma|\sqrt{T-t}}\right)$$

$$= \Phi(d_+(T-t)) + \frac{1}{|\sigma|\sqrt{T-t}}\varphi(d_+(T-t)) - \frac{Ke^{-(T-t)r}}{x|\sigma|\sqrt{T-t}}\varphi(d_-(T-t))$$

$$= \Phi(d_+(T-t)).$$

$\square$

As a consequence of Proposition 6.4, the Black–Scholes call price splits into a risky component $S_t\Phi(d_+(T-t))$ and a riskless component $-Ke^{-(T-t)r}\Phi(d_-(T-t))$, as follows:

$$g_c(t,S_t) = \underbrace{S_t\Phi(d_+(T-t))}_{\text{Risky investment (held)}} - \underbrace{Ke^{-(T-t)r}\Phi(d_-(T-t))}_{\text{Risk free investment (borrowed)}}, \quad 0 \leqslant t \leqslant T. \tag{6.18}$$

See Exercise 6.4 for a computation of the boundary values of $g_c(t,x)$, $t \in [0,T)$, $x > 0$. The following R script is an implementation of the Black–Scholes Delta for European call options.

```
DeltaCall <- function(S, K, r, T, sigma)
{d1 <- (log(S/K)+(r+sigma^2/2)*T)/(sigma*sqrt(T))
DeltaCall = pnorm(d1);DeltaCall}
```

In Figure 6.5 we plot the Delta of the European call option as a function of the underlying asset price and of the time remaining until maturity.

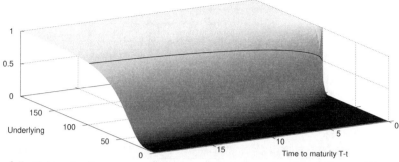

Figure 6.5: Delta of a European call option with strike price $K = 100$, $r = 3\%$, $\sigma = 10\%$.

The *Gamma* of the European call option is defined as the first derivative or sensitivity of Delta with respect to the underlying asset price. It also represents the second derivative of the option price with respect to the underlying asset price. This gives

$$
\begin{aligned}
\gamma_t &= \frac{1}{S_t |\sigma| \sqrt{T-t}} \Phi'\big(d_+(T-t)\big) \\
&= \frac{1}{S_t |\sigma| \sqrt{2(T-t)\pi}} \exp\left(-\frac{1}{2} \left(\frac{\log(S_t/K) + (r + \sigma^2/2)(T-t)}{|\sigma| \sqrt{T-t}} \right)^2 \right) \\
&\geqslant 0.
\end{aligned}
$$

In particular, a positive value of γ_t implies that the Delta $\xi_t = \xi_t(S_t)$ should increase when the underlying asset price S_t increases. In other words, the position ξ_t in the underlying asset should be increased by additional purchases if the underlying asset price S_t increases.

In Figure 6.6 we plot the (truncated) value of the Gamma of a European call option as a function of the underlying asset price and of time to maturity.

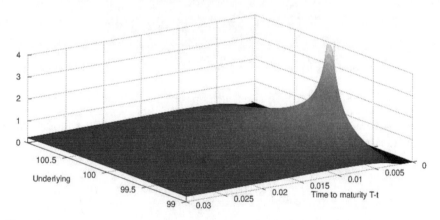

Figure 6.6: Gamma of European call and put options with strike price $K = 100$.

As Gamma is always nonnegative, the Black–Scholes hedging strategy is to keep buying the risky underlying asset when its price increases, and to sell it when its price decreases, as can be checked from Figure 6.6.

Numerical example - Hedging a call option

In Figure 6.7 we consider the historical stock price of HSBC Holdings (0005.HK) over one year:

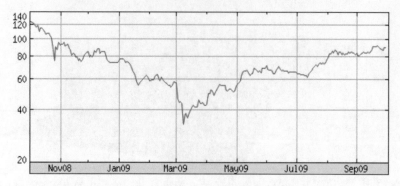

Figure 6.7: Graph of the stock price of HSBC Holdings.

Consider the call option issued by Societe Generale on December 31, 2008 with strike price K=\$63.704, maturity T = October 5, 2009, and an entitlement ratio of 100, meaning that one option contract is divided into 100 *warrants*, cf. page 7. The next graph gives the time evolution of the Black–Scholes portfolio value

$$t \longmapsto g_c(t, S_t)$$

driven by the market price $t \longmapsto S_t$ of the risky underlying asset as given in Figure 6.7, in which the number of days is counted from the origin and not from maturity.

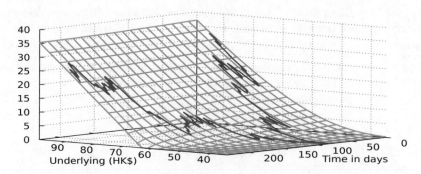

Figure 6.8: Path of the Black–Scholes price for a call option on HSBC.

As a consequence of (6.18), in the Black–Scholes call option hedging model, the amount invested in the risky asset is

$$
\begin{aligned}
S_t \xi_t &= S_t \Phi\big(d_+(T-t)\big) \\
&= S_t \Phi\left(\frac{\log(S_t/K) + (r + \sigma^2/2)(T-t)}{|\sigma|\sqrt{T-t}} \right) \\
&\geqslant 0,
\end{aligned}
$$

which is always nonnegative, *i.e.* there is no short selling, and the amount invested on the riskless asset is

$$
\begin{aligned}
\eta_t A_t &= -K e^{-(T-t)r} \Phi\big(d_-(T-t)\big) \\
&= -K e^{-(T-t)r} \Phi\left(\frac{\log(S_t/K) + (r - \sigma^2/2)(T-t)}{|\sigma|\sqrt{T-t}} \right) \\
&\leqslant 0,
\end{aligned}
$$

which is always nonpositive, *i.e.* we are constantly borrowing money on the riskless asset, as noted in Figure 6.9.

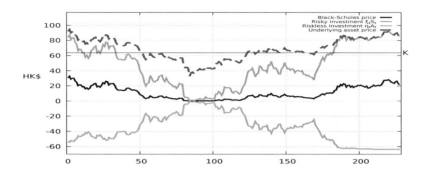

Figure 6.9: Time evolution of a hedging portfolio for a call option on HSBC.

A comparison of Figure 6.9 with market data can be found in Figures 9.9a and 9.9b below.

Cash settlement. In the case of a cash settlement, the option issuer will satisfy the option contract by selling $\xi_T = 1$ stock at the price $S_T = \$83$, refund the $K = \$63$ risk-free investment, and hand in the remaining amount $C = (S_T - K)^+ = 83 - 63 = \$20$ to the option holder.

Physical delivery. In the case of physical delivery of the underlying asset, the option issuer will deliver $\xi_T = 1$ stock to the option holder in exchange for $K = \$63$, which will be used together with the portfolio value to refund the risk-free loan.

6.3 European Put Options

Similarly, in the case of the European put option with strike price K the payoff function is given by $h(x) = (K - x)^+$ and the Black–Scholes PDE (6.7) reads

$$
\begin{cases}
rg_{\mathrm{p}}(t, x) = \dfrac{\partial g_{\mathrm{p}}}{\partial t}(t, x) + rx\dfrac{\partial g_{\mathrm{p}}}{\partial x}(t, x) + \dfrac{1}{2}\sigma^2 x^2 \dfrac{\partial^2 g_{\mathrm{p}}}{\partial x^2}(t, x), \\[2ex]
g_{\mathrm{p}}(T, x) = (K - x)^+,
\end{cases}
\tag{6.19}
$$

The next proposition can be proved from the call-put parity of Propositions 6.6 and 6.11, see Sections 6.5–6.6.

Proposition 6.5. *The solution of the PDE* (6.19) *is given by the* Black–Scholes *formula for put options*

$$g_{\mathrm{p}}(t,x) = K\,\mathrm{e}^{-(T-t)r}\Phi\big(-d_-(T-t)\big) - x\Phi\big(-d_+(T-t)\big), \qquad (6.20)$$

with

$$d_+(T-t) = \frac{\log(x/K) + (r + \sigma^2/2)(T-t)}{|\sigma|\sqrt{T-t}} \qquad (6.21)$$

and

$$d_-(T-t) = \frac{\log(x/K) + (r - \sigma^2/2)(T-t)}{|\sigma|\sqrt{T-t}}, \qquad (6.22)$$

$0 \leqslant t < T,$

In other words, the European put option with strike price K and maturity T is priced at time $t \in [0,T]$ as

$$g_{\mathrm{p}}(t,S_t) = K\,\mathrm{e}^{-(T-t)r}\Phi\big(-d_-(T-t)\big) - S_t\Phi\big(-d_+(T-t)\big), \qquad 0 \leqslant t \leqslant T.$$

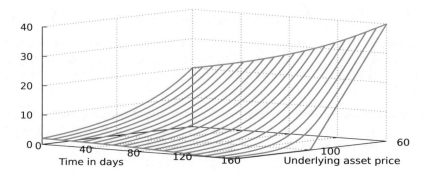

Figure 6.10: Solution of the Black–Scholes PDE (put option).

The following R script is an implementation of the Black–Scholes formula for European put options in R.

```
1  BSPut <- function(S, K, r, T, sigma)
   {d1 = (log(S/K)+(r+sigma^2/2)*T)/(sigma*sqrt(T));d2 = d1 - sigma * sqrt(T);
3  BSPut = K*exp(-r*T) * pnorm(-d2) - S*pnorm(-d1);BSPut}
```

Call-put parity

Proposition 6.6. *Call-put parity. We have the relation*

$$S_t - K\,\mathrm{e}^{-(T-t)r} = g_{\mathrm{c}}(t,S_t) - g_{\mathrm{p}}(t,S_t), \qquad 0 \leqslant t \leqslant T, \qquad (6.23)$$

between the Black–Scholes prices of call and put options, in terms of the forward contract price $S_t - K\,\mathrm{e}^{-(T-t)r}$.

Proof. The call-put parity (6.23) is a consequence of the relation

$$x - K = (x - K)^+ - (K - x)^+$$

satisfied by the terminal call and put payoff functions in the linear Black–Scholes PDE (6.7), which is solved as

$$x - K\,\mathrm{e}^{-(T-t)r} = g_{\mathrm{c}}(t,x) - g_{\mathrm{p}}(t,x)$$

for $t \in [0, T]$, since $x - K e^{-(T-t)r}$ is the pricing function of the long forward contract with payoff $S_T - K$, see (6.8). It can also be verified directly from (6.11) and (6.20) as

$$
\begin{aligned}
g_c(t, x) - g_p(t, x) &= x\Phi(d_+(T - t)) - K e^{-(T-t)r}\Phi(d_-(T - t)) \\
&\quad - \left(K e^{-(T-t)r}\Phi(-d_-(T - t)) - x\Phi(-d_+(T - t))\right) \\
&= x\Phi(d_+(T - t)) - K e^{-(T-t)r}\Phi(d_-(T - t)) \\
&\quad - K e^{-(T-t)r}(1 - \Phi(d_-(T - t))) + x(1 - \Phi(d_+(T - t))) \\
&= x - K e^{-(T-t)r}.
\end{aligned}
$$

$\square$

The *Delta* of the Black–Scholes put option can be obtained by differentiation of the call-put parity relation (6.23) and Proposition 6.4.

Proposition 6.7. *The* Delta *of the Black–Scholes put option is given by*

$$
\xi_t = -(1 - \Phi(d_+(T - t))) = -\Phi(-d_+(T - t)) \in [-1, 0], \quad 0 \leqslant t \leqslant T.
$$

Proof. By the call-put parity relation (6.23) and Proposition 6.4, we have

$$
\begin{aligned}
\frac{\partial g_p}{\partial x}(t, S_t) &= \frac{\partial g_c}{\partial x}(t, S_t) - 1 \\
&= \Phi(d_+(T - t)) - 1 \\
&= -\Phi(-d_+(T - t)), \quad 0 \leqslant t \leqslant T,
\end{aligned}
$$

where we applied (6.15). $\square$

As a consequence of Proposition 6.7, the Black–Scholes put price splits into a risky component $-S_t\Phi(-d_+(T - t))$ and a riskless component $K e^{-(T-t)r}\Phi(-d_-(T - t))$, as follows:

$$
g_p(t, S_t) = \underbrace{K e^{-(T-t)r}\Phi(-d_-(T - t))}_{\text{Risk−free investment (savings)}} - \underbrace{S_t\Phi(-d_+(T - t))}_{\text{Risky investment (short)}}, \quad 0 \leqslant t \leqslant T. \tag{6.24}
$$

```
DeltaPut <- function(S, K, r, T, sigma)
{d1 <- (log(S/K)+(r+sigma^2/2)*T)/(sigma*sqrt(T)); DeltaPut = -pnorm(-d1);DeltaPut}
```

In Figure 6.11 we plot the Delta of the European put option as a function of the underlying asset price and of the time remaining until maturity.

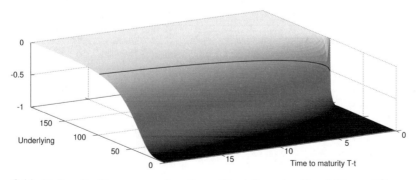

Figure 6.11: Delta of a European put option with strike price $K = 100$, $r = 3\%$, $\sigma = 10\%$.

Numerical example - Hedging a put option

For one more example, we consider a put option issued by BNP Paribas on November 4, 2008 with strike price K=$77.667, maturity T = October 5, 2009, and entitlement ratio 92.593, cf. page 7. In the next Figure 6.12, the number of days is counted from the origin, not from maturity.

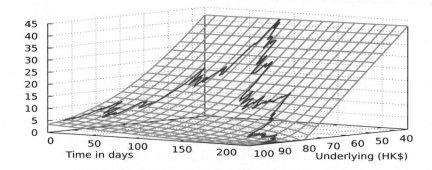

Figure 6.12: Path of the Black–Scholes price for a put option on HSBC.

As a consequence of (6.24), the amount invested on the risky asset for the hedging of a put option is

$$-S_t\Phi\big(-d_+(T-t)\big) = -S_t\Phi\left(-\frac{\log(S_t/K) + (r+\sigma^2/2)(T-t)}{|\sigma|\sqrt{T-t}}\right)$$
$$\leqslant 0,$$

i.e. there is always short selling, and the amount invested on the riskless asset priced $A_t = \mathrm{e}^{rt}$, $t \in [0,T]$, is

$$\eta_t A_t = K\mathrm{e}^{-(T-t)r}\Phi\big(-d_-(T-t)\big)$$
$$= K\mathrm{e}^{-(T-t)r}\Phi\left(-\frac{\log(S_t/K) + (r-\sigma^2/2)(T-t)}{|\sigma|\sqrt{T-t}}\right)$$
$$\geqslant 0,$$

which is always nonnegative, *i.e.* we are constantly saving money on the riskless asset, as noted in Figure 6.13.

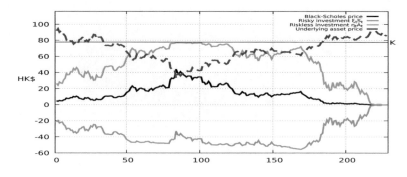

Figure 6.13: Time evolution of the hedging portfolio for a put option on HSBC.

In the above example the put option finished out of the money (OTM) so that no cash settlement or physical delivery occurs. A comparison of Figure 6.9 with market data can be found in Figures 9.10a and 9.10b below.

6.4 Market Terms and Data

The following Table 6.1 provides a summary of formulas for the computation of Black–Scholes sensitivities, also called *Greeks*.*

		Call option	Put option
Option price	$g(t, S_t)$	$S_t\Phi(d_+(T-t)) - K\,e^{-(T-t)r}\Phi(d_-(T-t))$	$K\,e^{-(T-t)r}\Phi(-d_-(T-t)) - S_t\Phi(-d_+(T-t))$
Delta (Δ)	$\dfrac{\partial g}{\partial x}(t, S_t)$	$\Phi(d_+(T-t)) \geqslant 0$	$-\Phi(-d_+(T-t)) \leqslant 0$
Gamma (Γ)	$\dfrac{\partial^2 g}{\partial x^2}(t, S_t)$	$\dfrac{\Phi'(d_+(T-t))}{S_t|\sigma|\sqrt{T-t}} \geqslant 0$	
Vega	$\dfrac{\partial g}{\partial \sigma}(t, S_t)$	$S_t\sqrt{T-t}\,\Phi'(d_+(T-t)) \geqslant 0$	
Theta (Θ)	$\dfrac{\partial g}{\partial t}(t, S_t)$	$-\dfrac{S_t|\sigma|\Phi'(d_+(T-t))}{2\sqrt{T-t}} - rK\,e^{-(T-t)r}\Phi(d_-(T-t)) \leqslant 0$	$-\dfrac{S_t|\sigma|\Phi'(d_+(T-t))}{2\sqrt{T-t}} + rK\,e^{-(T-t)r}\Phi(d_-(T-t))$
Rho (ρ)	$\dfrac{\partial g}{\partial r}(t, S_t)$	$(T-t)K\,e^{-(T-t)r}\Phi(d_-(T-t))$	$-(T-t)K\,e^{-(T-t)r}\Phi(-d_-(T-t))$

Table 6.1: Black–Scholes Greeks.

From Table 6.1 we can conclude that call option prices are increasing functions of the underlying asset price S_t, of the interest rate r, and of the volatility parameter σ. Similarly, put option prices are decreasing functions of the underlying asset price S_t, of the interest rate r, and increasing functions of the volatility parameter σ, see also Exercise 6.13.

Parameter	Variation of call option prices	Variation of put option prices
Underlying S_t	Increasing ↗	Decreasing ↘
Volatility σ	Increasing ↗	Increasing ↗
Time t	Decreasing ↘ if $r \geqslant 0$	Depends on the underlying price level if $r > 0$
	Depends on the underlying price level if $r < 0$	Decreasing ↘ if $r \leqslant 0$
Interest rate r	Increasing ↗	Increasing ↘

Table 6.2: Variations of Black–Scholes prices.

---

*"Every class feels like attending a Greek lesson" (AY2018-2019 student feedback).

The change of sign in the sensitivity Theta (Θ) with respect to time t can be verified in the following Figure 6.14 when $r > 0$.

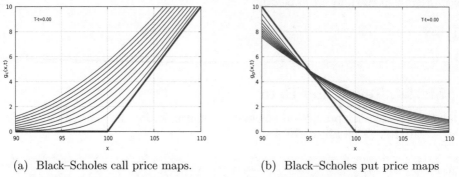

(a) Black–Scholes call price maps.   (b) Black–Scholes put price maps

Figure 6.14: Time-dependent solutions of the Black–Scholes PDE with $r = +3\% > 0$.

The next two figures show the variations of call and put option prices as functions of time when $r < 0$.

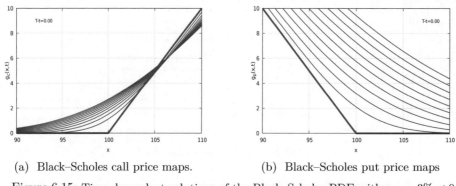

(a) Black–Scholes call price maps.   (b) Black–Scholes put price maps

Figure 6.15: Time-dependent solutions of the Black–Scholes PDE with $r = -3\% < 0$.

The next two figures show the variations of call and put option prices as functions of time when $r = 0$.

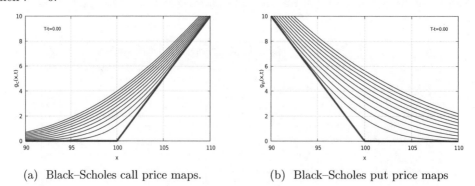

(a) Black–Scholes call price maps.   (b) Black–Scholes put price maps

Figure 6.16: Time-dependent solutions of the Black–Scholes PDE with $r = 0$.

<u>**Intrinsic value.**</u> The *intrinsic value* at time $t \in [0, T]$ of the option with claim payoff $C = h\big(S_T^{(1)}\big)$ is given by the immediate exercise payoff $h\big(S_t^{(1)}\big)$. The *extrinsic value* at time $t \in [0, T]$ of the option is the remaining difference $\pi_t(C) - h\big(S_t^{(1)}\big)$ between the

option price $\pi_t(C)$ and the immediate exercise payoff $h(S_t^{(1)})$. In general, the option price $\pi_t(C)$ decomposes as

$$\pi_t(C) = \underbrace{h(S_t^{(1)})}_{\text{Intrinsic value}} + \underbrace{\pi_t(C) - h(S_t^{(1)})}_{\text{Extrinsic value}}, \qquad 0 \leqslant t \leqslant T].$$

<u>Gearing.</u> The *gearing* at time $t \in [0,T]$ of the option with claim payoff $C = h(S_T)$ is defined as the ratio

$$G_t := \frac{S_t}{\pi_t(C)} = \frac{S_t}{g(t, S_t)}, \qquad 0 \leqslant t \leqslant T.$$

<u>Effective gearing.</u> The *effective gearing* at time $t \in [0,T]$ of the option with claim payoff $C = h(S_T)$ is defined as the ratio

$$
\begin{aligned}
\text{EG}_t \;\; :=&\;\; G_t \xi_t \\
=&\;\; \frac{\xi_t S_t}{\pi_t(C)} \\
=&\;\; \frac{S_t}{\pi_t(C)} \frac{\partial g}{\partial x}(t, S_t) \\
=&\;\; \frac{S_t}{g(t, S_t)} \frac{\partial g}{\partial x}(t, S_t) \\
=&\;\; S_t \frac{\partial}{\partial x} \log g(t, S_t), \qquad 0 \leqslant t \leqslant T.
\end{aligned}
$$

The effective gearing

$$\text{EG}_t = \frac{\xi_t S_t}{\pi_t(C)}$$

can be interpreted as the *hedge ratio*, *i.e.* the percentage of the portfolio which is invested on the risky asset. When written as

$$\frac{\Delta g(t, S_t)}{g(t, S_t)} = \text{EG}_t \times \frac{\Delta S_t}{S_t},$$

the effective gearing gives the relative variation, or percentage change, $\Delta g(t, S_t)/g(t, S_t)$ of the option price $g(t, S_t)$ from the relative variation $\Delta S_t/S_t$ in the underlying asset price.

The ratio $\text{EG}_t = S_t \partial \log g(t, S_t)/\partial x$ can also be interpreted as an *elasticity coefficient*.

<u>Break-even price.</u> The *break-even* price BEP_t of the underlying asset is the value of S for which the intrinsic option value $h(S)$ equals the option price $\pi_t(C)$ at time $t \in [0,T]$. For European call options it is given by

$$\text{BEP}_t := K + \pi_t(C) = K + g(t, S_t), \qquad t = 0, 1, \dots, N.$$

whereas for European put options it is given by

$$\text{BEP}_t := K - \pi_t(C) = K - g(t, S_t), \qquad 0 \leqslant t \leqslant T.$$

Premium. The option *premium* OP_t can be defined as the variation required from the underlying asset price in order to reach the break-even price, *i.e.* we have

$$\mathrm{OP}_t := \frac{\mathrm{BEP}_t - S_t}{S_t} = \frac{K + g(t, S_t) - S_t}{S_t}, \qquad 0 \leqslant t \leqslant T,$$

for European call options, and

$$\mathrm{OP}_t := \frac{S_t - \mathrm{BEP}_t}{S_t} = \frac{S_t + g(t, S_t) - K}{S_t}, \qquad 0 \leqslant t \leqslant T,$$

for European put options. The term "premium" is sometimes also used to denote the arbitrage-free price $g(t, S_t)$ of the option.

6.5 The Heat Equation

In the next proposition we notice that the solution $f(t, x)$ of the Black–Scholes PDE (6.7) can be transformed into a solution $g(t, y)$ of the simpler *heat equation* by a change of variable and a time inversion $t \longmapsto T - t$ on the interval $[0, T]$ so that the terminal condition at time T in the Black–Scholes equation (6.25) becomes an initial condition at time $t = 0$ in the heat equation (6.28).

Proposition 6.8. *Assume that $f(t, x)$ solves the Black–Scholes call pricing PDE*

$$\begin{cases} rf(t, x) = \dfrac{\partial f}{\partial t}(t, x) + rx \dfrac{\partial f}{\partial x}(t, x) + \dfrac{1}{2}\sigma^2 x^2 \dfrac{\partial^2 f}{\partial x^2}(t, x), \\[2mm] f(T, x) = (x - K)^+, \end{cases} \tag{6.25}$$

with terminal condition $h(x) = (x - K)^+$, $x > 0$. Then, the function $g(t, y)$ defined by

$$g(t, y) = \mathrm{e}^{rt} f\left(T - t, \; \mathrm{e}^{|\sigma|y + (\sigma^2/2 - r)t}\right) \tag{6.26}$$

solves the heat equation (6.28) with initial condition

$$\psi(y) := h\left(\mathrm{e}^{|\sigma|y}\right), \qquad y \in \mathbb{R}, \tag{6.27}$$

i.e. we have

$$\begin{cases} \dfrac{\partial g}{\partial t}(t, y) = \dfrac{1}{2}\dfrac{\partial^2 g}{\partial y^2}(t, y) \\[2mm] g(0, y) = h\left(\mathrm{e}^{|\sigma|y}\right). \end{cases} \tag{6.28}$$

Proposition 6.8 will be proved in Section 6.6. It will allow us to solve the Black–Scholes PDE (6.25) based on the solution of the heat equation (6.28) with initial condition $\psi(y) = h\left(\mathrm{e}^{|\sigma|y}\right)$, $y \in \mathbb{R}$, by inversion of Relation (6.26) with $s = T - t$, $x = \mathrm{e}^{|\sigma|y + (\sigma^2/2 - r)t}$, *i.e.*

$$f(s, x) = \mathrm{e}^{-(T-s)r} g\left(T - s, \; \frac{-(\sigma^2/2 - r)(T - s) + \log x}{|\sigma|}\right).$$

Next, we focus on the *heat equation*

$$\frac{\partial \varphi}{\partial t}(t,y) = \frac{1}{2}\frac{\partial^2 \varphi}{\partial y^2}(t,y) \tag{6.29}$$

which is used to model the diffusion of heat over time through solids. Here, the data of $g(x,t)$ represents the temperature measured at time t and point x. We refer the reader to Widder (1975) for a complete treatment of this topic.

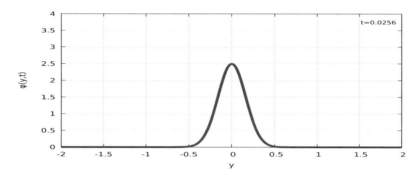

Figure 6.17: Heat equation solution.

Proposition 6.9. *The fundamental solution of the heat equation* (6.29) *is given by the Gaussian probability density function*

$$\varphi(t,y) := \frac{1}{\sqrt{2\pi t}}\,e^{-y^2/(2t)}, \qquad y \in \mathbb{R},$$

with variance $t > 0$.

Proof. The proof is done by a direct calculation, as follows:

$$
\begin{aligned}
\frac{\partial \varphi}{\partial t}(t,y) &= \frac{\partial}{\partial t}\left(\frac{e^{-y^2/(2t)}}{\sqrt{2\pi t}}\right) \\
&= -\frac{e^{-y^2/(2t)}}{2t^{3/2}\sqrt{2\pi}} + \frac{y^2}{2t^2}\frac{e^{-y^2/(2t)}}{\sqrt{2\pi t}} \\
&= \left(-\frac{1}{2t} + \frac{y^2}{2t^2}\right)\varphi(t,y),
\end{aligned}
$$

and

$$
\begin{aligned}
\frac{1}{2}\frac{\partial^2 \varphi}{\partial y^2}(t,y) &= -\frac{1}{2}\frac{\partial}{\partial y}\left(\frac{y}{t}\frac{e^{-y^2/(2t)}}{\sqrt{2\pi t}}\right) \\
&= -\frac{e^{-y^2/(2t)}}{2t\sqrt{2\pi t}} + \frac{y^2}{2t^2}\frac{e^{-y^2/(2t)}}{\sqrt{2\pi t}} \\
&= \left(-\frac{1}{2t} + \frac{y^2}{2t^2}\right)\varphi(t,y), \qquad t > 0,\ y \in \mathbb{R}.
\end{aligned}
$$

$\square$

In Section 6.6 the heat equation (6.29) will be shown to be equivalent to the Black–Scholes PDE after a change of variables. In particular this will lead to the explicit solution of the Black–Scholes PDE.

Proposition 6.10. *The heat equation*

$$
\begin{cases}
\dfrac{\partial g}{\partial t}(t, y) = \dfrac{1}{2} \dfrac{\partial^2 g}{\partial y^2}(t, y) \\[3mm]
g(0, y) = \psi(y)
\end{cases}
\tag{6.30}
$$

with bounded and continuous initial condition

$$
g(0, y) = \psi(y)
$$

has the solution

$$
g(t, y) = \int_{-\infty}^{\infty} \psi(z)\, e^{-(y-z)^2/(2t)} \frac{dz}{\sqrt{2\pi t}}, \qquad y \in \mathbb{R}, \quad t > 0.
\tag{6.31}
$$

Proof. We have

$$
\begin{aligned}
\frac{\partial g}{\partial t}(t, y) &= \frac{\partial}{\partial t} \int_{-\infty}^{\infty} \psi(z)\, e^{-(y-z)^2/(2t)} \frac{dz}{\sqrt{2\pi t}} \\[2mm]
&= \int_{-\infty}^{\infty} \psi(z) \frac{\partial}{\partial t} \left(\frac{e^{-(y-z)^2/(2t)}}{\sqrt{2\pi t}} \right) dz \\[2mm]
&= \frac{1}{2} \int_{-\infty}^{\infty} \psi(z) \left(\frac{(y-z)^2}{t^2} - \frac{1}{t} \right) e^{-(y-z)^2/(2t)} \frac{dz}{\sqrt{2\pi t}} \\[2mm]
&= \frac{1}{2} \int_{-\infty}^{\infty} \psi(z) \frac{\partial^2}{\partial y^2} e^{-(y-z)^2/(2t)} \frac{dz}{\sqrt{2\pi t}} \\[2mm]
&= \frac{1}{2} \frac{\partial^2}{\partial y^2} \int_{-\infty}^{\infty} \psi(z)\, e^{-(y-z)^2/(2t)} \frac{dz}{\sqrt{2\pi t}} \\[2mm]
&= \frac{1}{2} \frac{\partial^2 g}{\partial y^2}(t, y).
\end{aligned}
$$

On the other hand, it can be checked that at time $t = 0$ we have

$$
\begin{aligned}
\lim_{t \to 0} \int_{-\infty}^{\infty} \psi(z)\, e^{-(y-z)^2/(2t)} \frac{dz}{\sqrt{2\pi t}} &= \lim_{t \to 0} \int_{-\infty}^{\infty} \psi(y+z)\, e^{-z^2/(2t)} \frac{dz}{\sqrt{2\pi t}} \\[2mm]
&= \psi(y), \qquad y \in \mathbb{R},
\end{aligned}
$$

see also (6.32) below. $\qquad\square$

The next Figure 6.18 shows the evolution of $g(t, x)$ with initial condition based on the European call payoff function $h(x) = (x - K)^+$, i.e.

$$
g(0, y) = \psi(y) = h\big(e^{|\sigma|y}\big) = \big(e^{|\sigma|y} - K\big)^+, \qquad y \in \mathbb{R}.
$$

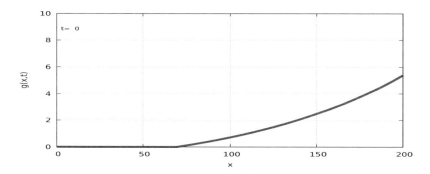

Figure 6.18: Heat equation solution.

Let us provide a second proof of Proposition 6.10, this time using Brownian motion and stochastic calculus.

Proof of Proposition 6.10. First, we note that under the change of variable $x = z - y$ we have

$$
\begin{aligned}
g(t,y) &= \int_{-\infty}^{\infty} \psi(z)\, e^{-(y-z)^2/(2t)}\, \frac{dz}{\sqrt{2\pi t}} \\
&= \int_{-\infty}^{\infty} \psi(y+x)\, e^{-x^2/(2t)}\, \frac{dx}{\sqrt{2\pi t}} \\
&= \mathbb{E}[\psi(y+B_t)] \\
&= \mathbb{E}[\psi(y-B_t)],
\end{aligned}
$$

where $(B_t)_{t\in\mathbb{R}_+}$ is a standard Brownian motion and $B_t \simeq \mathcal{N}(0,t)$, $t \geqslant 0$, with the initial condition

$$
g(0,y) = \mathbb{E}[\psi(y+B_0)] = \mathbb{E}[\psi(y)] = \psi(y). \tag{6.32}
$$

Applying Itô's formula to $\psi(y - B_t)$ and using the fact that the expectation of the stochastic integral with respect to Brownian motion is zero, see Relation (4.17) in Proposition 4.21, we find

$$
\begin{aligned}
g(t,y) &= \mathbb{E}[\psi(y-B_t)] \\
&= \mathbb{E}\left[\psi(y) - \int_0^t \psi'(y-B_s)dB_s + \frac{1}{2}\int_0^t \psi''(y-B_s)ds\right] \\
&= \psi(y) - \mathbb{E}\left[\int_0^t \psi'(y-B_s)dB_s\right] + \frac{1}{2}\mathbb{E}\left[\int_0^t \psi''(y-B_s)ds\right] \\
&= \psi(y) + \frac{1}{2}\int_0^t \mathbb{E}\left[\frac{\partial^2 \psi}{\partial y^2}(y-B_s)\right]ds \\
&= \psi(y) + \frac{1}{2}\int_0^t \frac{\partial^2}{\partial y^2}\mathbb{E}[\psi(y-B_s)]ds \\
&= \psi(y) + \frac{1}{2}\int_0^t \frac{\partial^2 g}{\partial y^2}(s,y)ds.
\end{aligned}
$$

Hence we have

$$
\begin{aligned}
\frac{\partial g}{\partial t}(t, y) &= \frac{\partial}{\partial t} \mathbb{E}[\psi(y - B_t)] \\
&= \frac{1}{2} \frac{\partial^2}{\partial y^2} \mathbb{E}[\psi(y - B_t)] \\
&= \frac{1}{2} \frac{\partial^2 g}{\partial y^2}(t, y).
\end{aligned}
$$

Regarding the initial condition, we check that

$$
g(0, y) = \mathbb{E}[\psi(y - B_0)] = \mathbb{E}[\psi(y)] = \psi(y).
$$

□

The expression $g(t, y) = \mathbb{E}[\psi(y - B_t)]$ provides a probabilistic interpretation of the heat diffusion phenomenon based on Brownian motion. Namely, when $\psi_\varepsilon(y) := \mathbb{1}_{[-\varepsilon, \varepsilon]}(y)$, we find that

$$
\begin{aligned}
g_\varepsilon(t, y) &= \mathbb{E}[\psi_\varepsilon(y - B_t)] \\
&= \mathbb{E}[\mathbb{1}_{[-\varepsilon, \varepsilon]}(y - B_t)] \\
&= \mathbb{P}(y - B_t \in [-\varepsilon, \varepsilon]) \\
&= \mathbb{P}(y - \varepsilon \leqslant B_t \leqslant y + \varepsilon)
\end{aligned}
$$

represents the probability of finding B_t within a neighborhood $[y - \varepsilon, y + \varepsilon]$ of the point $y \in \mathbb{R}$.

6.6   Solution of the Black–Scholes PDE

In this section we solve the Black–Scholes PDE by the kernel method of Section 6.5 and a change of variables. This solution method uses the change of variables (6.26) of Proposition 6.8 and a time inversion from which the terminal condition at time T in the Black–Scholes equation becomes an initial condition at time $t = 0$ in the heat equation.

Next, we provide the proof Proposition 6.8.

Proof of Proposition 6.8. Letting $s = T - t$ and $x = e^{|\sigma|y + (\sigma^2/2 - r)t}$ and using Relation (6.26), *i.e.*

$$
g(t, y) = e^{rt} f\left(T - t, e^{|\sigma|y + (\sigma^2/2 - r)t}\right),
$$

we have

$$
\begin{aligned}
\frac{\partial g}{\partial t}(t, y) &= r e^{rt} f\left(T - t, e^{|\sigma|y + (\sigma^2/2 - r)t}\right) - e^{rt} \frac{\partial f}{\partial s}\left(T - t, e^{|\sigma|y + (\sigma^2/2 - r)t}\right) \\
&\quad + \left(\frac{\sigma^2}{2} - r\right) e^{rt} e^{|\sigma|y + (\sigma^2/2 - r)t} \frac{\partial f}{\partial x}\left(T - t, e^{|\sigma|y + (\sigma^2/2 - r)t}\right) \\
&= r e^{rt} f(T - t, x) - e^{rt} \frac{\partial f}{\partial s}(T - t, x) + \left(\frac{\sigma^2}{2} - r\right) e^{rt} x \frac{\partial f}{\partial x}(T - t, x) \\
&= \frac{1}{2} e^{rt} x^2 \sigma^2 \frac{\partial^2 f}{\partial x^2}(T - t, x) + \frac{\sigma^2}{2} e^{rt} x \frac{\partial f}{\partial x}(T - t, x), \quad (6.33)
\end{aligned}
$$

where on the last step we used the Black–Scholes PDE. On the other hand we have

$$\frac{\partial g}{\partial y}(t,y) = |\sigma|\, e^{rt}\, e^{|\sigma|y+(\sigma^2/2-r)t}\frac{\partial f}{\partial x}\big(T-t,\, e^{|\sigma|y+(\sigma^2/2-r)t}\big)$$

and

$$\begin{aligned}
\frac{1}{2}\frac{\partial g^2}{\partial y^2}(t,y) &= \frac{\sigma^2}{2}\, e^{rt}\, e^{|\sigma|y+(\sigma^2/2-r)t}\frac{\partial f}{\partial x}\big(T-t,\, e^{|\sigma|y+(\sigma^2/2-r)t}\big)\\
&\quad + \frac{\sigma^2}{2}\, e^{rt}\, e^{2|\sigma|y+2(\sigma^2/2-r)t}\frac{\partial^2 f}{\partial x^2}\big(T-t,\, e^{|\sigma|y+(\sigma^2/2-r)t}\big)\\
&= \frac{\sigma^2}{2}\, e^{rt}x\frac{\partial f}{\partial x}(T-t,x) + \frac{\sigma^2}{2}\, e^{rt}x^2\frac{\partial^2 f}{\partial x^2}(T-t,x).
\end{aligned} \tag{6.34}$$

We conclude by comparing (6.33) with (6.34), which shows that $g(t,x)$ solves the heat equation (6.30) with initial condition

$$g(0,y) = f\big(T, e^{|\sigma|y}\big) = h\big(e^{|\sigma|y}\big).$$

□

In the next proposition we provide a proof of Proposition 6.3 by deriving the Black–Scholes formula (6.11) from the solution of the PDE (6.25). The Black–Scholes formula will also be recovered by a probabilistic argument via the computation of an expected value in Proposition 7.6.

Proposition 6.11. *When $h(x) = (x - K)^+$, the solution of the Black–Scholes PDE (6.25) is given by*

$$f(t,x) = x\Phi\big(d_+(T-t)\big) - K\, e^{-(T-t)r}\Phi\big(d_-(T-t)\big), \qquad x > 0,$$

where

$$\Phi(x) = \frac{1}{\sqrt{2\pi}}\int_{-\infty}^{x} e^{-y^2/2}dy, \qquad x \in \mathbb{R},$$

and

$$\begin{cases}
d_+(T-t) := \dfrac{\log(x/K) + (r + \sigma^2/2)(T-t)}{|\sigma|\sqrt{T-t}},\\[4mm]
d_-(T-t) := \dfrac{\log(x/K) + (r - \sigma^2/2)(T-t)}{|\sigma|\sqrt{T-t}},
\end{cases}$$

$x > 0$, $t \in [0,T)$.

Proof. By inversion of Relation (6.26) with $s = T - t$ and $x = e^{|\sigma|y+(\sigma^2/2-r)t}$, we get

$$f(s,x) = e^{-(T-s)r}g\left(T-s, \frac{-(\sigma^2/2-r)(T-s) + \log x}{|\sigma|}\right)$$

and

$$h(x) = \psi\left(\frac{\log x}{|\sigma|}\right), \qquad x > 0, \quad \text{or} \quad \psi(y) = h\big(e^{|\sigma|y}\big), \qquad y \in \mathbb{R}.$$

Hence, using the solution (6.31) and Relation (6.27), we get

$$f(t,x) = e^{-(T-t)r} g\left(T-t, \frac{-(\sigma^2/2-r)(T-t)+\log x}{|\sigma|}\right)$$

$$= e^{-(T-t)r}\int_{-\infty}^{\infty} \psi\left(\frac{-(\sigma^2/2-r)(T-t)+\log x}{|\sigma|}+z\right) e^{-z^2/(2(T-t))}\frac{dz}{\sqrt{2(T-t)\pi}}$$

$$= e^{-(T-t)r}\int_{-\infty}^{\infty} h\left(x\, e^{|\sigma|z-(\sigma^2/2-r)(T-t)}\right) e^{-z^2/(2(T-t))}\frac{dz}{\sqrt{2(T-t)\pi}}$$

$$= e^{-(T-t)r}\int_{-\infty}^{\infty} \left(x\, e^{|\sigma|z-(\sigma^2/2-r)(T-t)} - K\right)^{+} e^{-z^2/(2(T-t))}\frac{dz}{\sqrt{2(T-t)\pi}}$$

$$= e^{-(T-t)r}$$
$$\times \int_{\frac{(-r+\sigma^2/2)(T-t)+\log(K/x)}{|\sigma|}}^{\infty} \left(x\, e^{|\sigma|z-(\sigma^2/2-r)(T-t)} - K\right) e^{-z^2/(2(T-t))}\frac{dz}{\sqrt{2(T-t)\pi}}$$

$$= x\, e^{-(T-t)r}\int_{-d_-(T-t)\sqrt{T-t}}^{\infty} e^{|\sigma|z-(\sigma^2/2-r)(T-t)}\, e^{-z^2/(2(T-t))}\frac{dz}{\sqrt{2(T-t)\pi}}$$
$$-K\, e^{-(T-t)r}\int_{-d_-(T-t)\sqrt{T-t}}^{\infty} e^{-z^2/(2(T-t))}\frac{dz}{\sqrt{2(T-t)\pi}}$$

$$= x\int_{-d_-(T-t)\sqrt{T-t}}^{\infty} e^{|\sigma|z-(T-t)\sigma^2/2-z^2/(2(T-t))}\frac{dz}{\sqrt{2(T-t)\pi}}$$
$$-K\, e^{-(T-t)r}\int_{-d_-(T-t)\sqrt{T-t}}^{\infty} e^{-z^2/(2(T-t))}\frac{dz}{\sqrt{2(T-t)\pi}}$$

$$= x\int_{-d_-(T-t)\sqrt{T-t}}^{\infty} e^{-(z-(T-t)|\sigma|)^2/(2(T-t))}\frac{dz}{\sqrt{2(T-t)\pi}}$$
$$-K\, e^{-(T-t)r}\int_{-d_-(T-t)\sqrt{T-t}}^{\infty} e^{-z^2/(2(T-t))}\frac{dz}{\sqrt{2(T-t)\pi}}$$

$$= x\int_{-d_-(T-t)\sqrt{T-t}-(T-t)|\sigma|}^{\infty} e^{-z^2/(2(T-t))}\frac{dz}{\sqrt{2(T-t)\pi}}$$
$$-K\, e^{-(T-t)r}\int_{-d_-(T-t)\sqrt{T-t}}^{\infty} e^{-z^2/(2(T-t))}\frac{dz}{\sqrt{2(T-t)\pi}}$$

$$= x\int_{-d_-(T-t)-|\sigma|\sqrt{T-t}}^{\infty} e^{-z^2/2}\frac{dz}{\sqrt{2\pi}} - K\, e^{-(T-t)r}\int_{-d_-(T-t)}^{\infty} e^{-z^2/2}\frac{dz}{\sqrt{2\pi}}$$

$$= x\left(1-\Phi\left(-d_+(T-t)\right)\right) - K\, e^{-(T-t)r}\left(1-\Phi\left(-d_-(T-t)\right)\right)$$

$$= x\Phi\left(d_+(T-t)\right) - K\, e^{-(T-t)r}\Phi\left(d_-(T-t)\right),$$

where we used the relation (6.15), *i.e.*

$$1-\Phi(a) = \Phi(-a), \qquad a \in \mathbb{R}.$$

$\square$

Exercises

Exercise 6.1 Bachelier (1900) model. Consider a market made of a riskless asset valued $A_t = A_0$ with zero interest rate, $t \geqslant 0$, and a risky asset whose price S_t is modeled by a standard Brownian motion as $S_t = B_t$, $t \geqslant 0$.

a) Show that the price $g(t, B_t)$ of the option with claim payoff $C = (B_T)^2$ satisfies the heat equation

$$-\frac{\partial g}{\partial t}(t, y) = \frac{1}{2}\frac{\partial^2 g}{\partial y^2}(t, y)$$

with terminal condition $g(T, x) = x^2$.

b) Find the function $g(t, x)$ by solving the PDE of Question (a).

   Hint: Try a solution of the form $g(t, x) = x^2 + f(t)$.

c) Find the risky asset allocation ξ_t hedging the claim payoff $C = (B_T)^2$, and the amount $\eta_t A_t = \eta_t A_0$ invested in the riskless asset.

See Exercises 6.11 and 7.16-7.17 for extensions to nonzero interest rates.

Exercise 6.2 Consider a risky asset price $(S_t)_{t \in \mathbb{R}}$ modeled in the Cox et al. (1985) (CIR) model as

$$dS_t = \beta(\alpha - S_t)dt + \sigma\sqrt{S_t}dB_t, \qquad \alpha, \beta, \sigma > 0, \tag{6.35}$$

and let $(\eta_t, \xi_t)_{t \in \mathbb{R}_+}$ be a portfolio strategy whose value $V_t := \eta_t A_t + \xi_t S_t$, takes the form $V_t = g(t, S_t)$, $t \geqslant 0$. Figure 6.19 presents a random simulation of the solution to (6.35) with $\alpha = 0.025$, $\beta = 1$, and $\sigma = 1.3$.

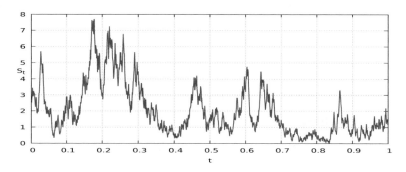

Figure 6.19: Graph of the CIR short rate $t \mapsto r_t$ with $\alpha = 2.5\%$, $\beta = 1$, and $\sigma = 1.3$.

```
N=10000; t <- 0:(N-1); dt <- 1.0/N;a=0.025; b=2; sigma=0.05;
dB <- rnorm(N,mean=0,sd=sqrt(dt));R <- rep(0,N);R[1]=0.01
for (j in 2:N){R[j]=max(0,R[j-1]+(a-b*R[j-1])*dt+sigma*sqrt(R[j-1])*dB[j])}
plot(t, R, xlab = "t", ylab = "", type = "l", ylim = c(0,0.02), col = "blue")
abline(h=0,col="black",lwd=2)
```

Based on the self-financing condition written as

$$
\begin{aligned}
dV_t &= rV_tdt - r\xi_tS_tdt + \xi_tdS_t \\
&= rV_tdt - r\xi_tS_tdt + \beta(\alpha - S_t)\xi_tdt + \sigma\xi_t\sqrt{S_t}dB_t, \quad t \geqslant 0, \quad (6.36)
\end{aligned}
$$

derive the PDE satisfied by the function $g(t, x)$ using the Itô formula.

Exercise 6.3 Black–Scholes PDE with dividends. Consider a riskless asset with price $A_t = A_0 e^{rt}$, $t \geqslant 0$, and an underlying asset price process $(S_t)_{t\in\mathbb{R}_+}$ modeled as

$$
dS_t = (\mu - \delta)S_tdt + \sigma S_tdB_t,
$$

where $(B_t)_{t\in\mathbb{R}_+}$ is a standard Brownian motion and $\delta > 0$ is a continuous-time dividend rate. By absence of arbitrage, the payment of a dividend entails a drop in the stock price by the same amount occurring generally on the *ex-dividend date*, on which the purchase of the security no longer entitles the investor to the dividend amount. The list of investors entitled to dividend payment is consolidated on the *date of record*, and payment is made on the *payable date*.

```
1  getSymbols("0005.HK",from="2010-01-01",to=Sys.Date(),src="yahoo")
   getDividends("0005.HK",from="2010-01-01",to=Sys.Date(),src="yahoo")
```

a) Assuming that the portfolio with value $V_t = \xi_tS_t + \eta_tA_t$ at time t is self-financing and that dividends are continuously reinvested, write down the portfolio variation dV_t.

b) Assuming that the portfolio value V_t takes the form $V_t = g(t, S_t)$ at time t, derive the Black–Scholes PDE for the function $g(t, x)$ with its terminal condition.

c) Compute the price at time $t \in [0, T]$ of the European call option with strike price K by solving the corresponding Black–Scholes PDE.

d) Compute the Delta of the option.

Exercise 6.4

a) Check that the Black–Scholes formula (6.11) for European call options

$$
g_c(t, x) = x\Phi\big(d_+(T - t)\big) - Ke^{-(T-t)r}\Phi\big(d_-(T - t)\big),
$$

satisfies the following boundary conditions:

i) at $x = 0$, $g_c(t, 0) = 0$,

ii) at maturity $t = T$,

$$
g_c(T, x) = (x - K)^+ = \begin{cases} x - K, & x > K \\[2mm] 0, & x \leqslant K, \end{cases}
$$

and

$$
\lim_{t \nearrow T} \Phi(d_+(T - t)) = \begin{cases} 1, & x > K \\[2mm] \dfrac{1}{2}, & x = K \\[2mm] 0, & x < K, \end{cases}
$$

iii) as time to maturity tends to infinity,

$$\lim_{T \to \infty} \mathrm{Bl}(x, K, \sigma, r, T - t) = x, \qquad t \geqslant 0.$$

b) Check that the Black–Scholes formula (6.20) for European put options

$$g_\mathrm{p}(t, x) = K\,e^{-(T-t)r}\Phi\big(-d_-(T-t)\big) - x\Phi\big(-d_+(T-t)\big)$$

satisfies the following boundary conditions:

  i) at $x = 0$, $g_\mathrm{p}(t, 0) = K\,e^{-(T-t)r}$,

  ii) as x tends to infinity, $g_\mathrm{p}(t, \infty) = 0$ for all $t \in [0, T)$,

  iii) at maturity $t = T$,

$$g_\mathrm{p}(T, x) \;\;=\;\; (K - x)^+ = \begin{cases} 0, & x > K \\[2mm] K - x, & x \leqslant K, \end{cases}$$

and

$$-\lim_{t \nearrow T} \Phi(-d_+(T - t)) \;\;=\;\; \begin{cases} 0, & x > K \\[2mm] -\dfrac{1}{2}, & x = K \\[2mm] -1, & x < K, \end{cases}$$

  iv) as time to maturity tends to infinity,

$$\lim_{T \to \infty} \mathrm{Bl}_\mathrm{p}(S_t, K, \sigma, r, T - t) = 0, \qquad t \geqslant 0.$$

Exercise 6.5 Power option (Exercise 3.14 continued). Power options can be used for the pricing of realized variance and volatility swaps, see § 8.2. Let $(S_t)_{t \in \mathbb{R}_+}$ denote a geometric Brownian motion solution of

$$dS_t = \mu S_t dt + \sigma S_t dB_t,$$

where $(B_t)_{t \in \mathbb{R}_+}$ is a standard Brownian motion, with $\mu \in \mathbb{R}$ and $\sigma > 0$.

a) Let $r \geqslant 0$. Solve the Black–Scholes PDE

$$rg(x, t) = \frac{\partial g}{\partial t}(x, t) + rx\frac{\partial g}{\partial x}(x, t) + \frac{\sigma^2}{2}x^2\frac{\partial^2 g}{\partial x^2}(x, t) \tag{6.37}$$

with terminal condition $g(x, T) = x^2$, $x > 0$, $t \in [0, T]$.

Hint: Try a solution of the form $g(x, t) = x^2 f(t)$, and find $f(t)$.

b) Find the respective quantities ξ_t and η_t of the risky asset S_t and riskless asset $A_t = A_0\,e^{rt}$ in the portfolio with value

$$V_t = g(S_t, t) = \xi_t S_t + \eta_t A_t, \qquad 0 \leqslant t \leqslant T,$$

hedging the contract with claim payoff $C = (S_T)^2$ at maturity.

Exercise 6.6   On December 18, 2007, a call warrant has been issued by Fortis Bank on the stock price S of the MTR Corporation with maturity $T = 23/12/2008$, strike price $K = $ HK\$ 36.08 and <u>entitlement ratio=10</u>. Recall that in the Black–Scholes model, the price at time t of the European claim on the underlying asset priced S_t with strike price K, maturity T, interest rate r and volatility $\sigma > 0$ is given by the Black–Scholes formula as

$$f(t, S_t) = S_t \Phi\big(d_+(T-t)\big) - K e^{-(T-t)r} \Phi\big(d_-(T-t)\big),$$

where

$$
\begin{cases}
d_-(T-t) = \dfrac{(r - \sigma^2/2)(T-t) + \log(S_t/K)}{|\sigma|\sqrt{T-t}}, \\[4mm]
d_+(T-t) = d_-(T-t) + |\sigma|\sqrt{T-t} = \dfrac{(r + \sigma^2/2)(T-t) + \log(S_t/K)}{|\sigma|\sqrt{T-t}}.
\end{cases}
$$

Recall that by Proposition 6.4 we have

$$\frac{\partial f}{\partial x}(t, S_t) = \Phi\big(d_+(T-t)\big), \qquad 0 \leqslant t \leqslant T.$$

a) Using the values of the Gaussian cumulative distribution function, compute the Black–Scholes price of the corresponding call option at time $t =$ November 7, 2008 with $S_t =$ HK\$ 17.200, assuming a volatility $\sigma = 90\% = 0.90$ and an *annual* risk-free interest rate $r = 4.377\% = 0.04377$,

b) Still using the Gaussian cumulative distribution function, compute the quantity of the risky asset required in your portfolio at time $t =$ November 7, 2008 in order to hedge one such option at maturity $T = 23/12/2008$.

c) Figure 1 represents the Black–Scholes price of the call option as a function of $\sigma \in [0.5, 1.5] = [50\%, 150\%]$.

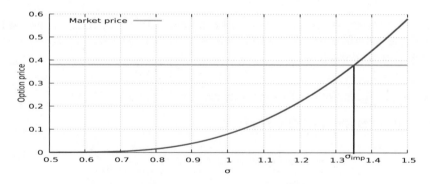

Figure 6.20: Option price as a function of the volatility $\sigma > 0$.

```
BSCall <- function(S, K, r, T, sigma)
{d1 <- (log(S/K)+(r+sigma^2/2)*T)/(sigma*sqrt(T));d2 <- d1 - sigma * sqrt(T)
BSCall = S*pnorm(d1) - K*exp(-r*T)*pnorm(d2);BSCall}
sigma <- seq(0.5,1.5, length=100);
plot(sigma,BSCall(17.2,36.08,0.04377,46/365,sigma) , type="l",lty=1, xlab="Sigma", ylab="Black--Scholes
    Call Price", ylim = c(0,0.6),col="blue",lwd=3);grid()
abline(h=0.23,col="red",lwd=3)
```

Knowing that the closing price of the warrant on November 7, 2008 was HK\$ 0.023, which value can you infer for the implied volatility σ at this date?

Exercise 6.7 Forward contracts. Recall that the price $\pi_t(C)$ of a claim payoff $C = h(S_T)$ of maturity T can be written as $\pi_t(C) = g(t, S_t)$, where the function $g(t, x)$ satisfies the *Black–Scholes PDE*

$$
\begin{cases}
rg(t, x) = \dfrac{\partial g}{\partial t}(t, x) + rx\dfrac{\partial g}{\partial x}(t, x) + \dfrac{1}{2}\sigma^2 x^2 \dfrac{\partial^2 g}{\partial x^2}(t, x), \\[2mm]
g(T, x) = h(x), \hspace{4cm} (1)
\end{cases}
$$

with terminal condition $g(T, x) = h(x)$, $x > 0$.

a) Assume that C is a forward contract with payoff

$$
C = S_T - K,
$$

at time T. Find the function $h(x)$ in (1).

b) Find the solution $g(t, x)$ of the above PDE and compute the price $\pi_t(C)$ at time $t \in [0, T]$.
   Hint: search for a solution of the form $g(t, x) = x - \alpha(t)$ where $\alpha(t)$ is a function of t to be determined.

c) Compute the quantities

$$
\xi_t = \frac{\partial g}{\partial x}(t, S_t)
$$

and η_t of risky and riskless assets in a self-financing portfolio hedging C, assuming $A_0 = \$1$.

d) Repeat the above questions with the terminal condition $g(T, x) = x$.

Exercise 6.8

a) Solve the Black–Scholes PDE

$$
rg(t, x) = \frac{\partial g}{\partial t}(t, x) + rx\frac{\partial g}{\partial x}(t, x) + \frac{\sigma^2}{2}x^2\frac{\partial^2 g}{\partial x^2}(t, x) \hspace{2cm} (6.38)
$$

with terminal condition $g(T, x) = 1$, $x > 0$.

Hint: Try a solution of the form $g(t, x) = f(t)$ and find $f(t)$.

b) Find the respective quantities ξ_t and η_t of the risky asset S_t and riskless asset $A_t = A_0 e^{rt}$ in the portfolio with value

$$
V_t = g(t, S_t) = \xi_t S_t + \eta_t A_t
$$

hedging the contract with claim payoff $C = \$1$ at maturity.

Exercise 6.9 Log contracts can be used for the pricing and hedging of realized variance swaps, see § 8.2 and Exercise 8.6.

a) Solve the PDE

$$0 = \frac{\partial g}{\partial t}(x,t) + rx\frac{\partial g}{\partial x}(x,t) + \frac{\sigma^2}{2}x^2\frac{\partial^2 g}{\partial x^2}(x,t) \qquad (6.39)$$

with the terminal condition $g(x,T) := \log x$, $x > 0$.

Hint: Try a solution of the form $g(x,t) = f(t) + \log x$, and find $f(t)$.

b) Solve the Black–Scholes PDE

$$rh(x,t) = \frac{\partial h}{\partial t}(x,t) + rx\frac{\partial h}{\partial x}(x,t) + \frac{\sigma^2}{2}x^2\frac{\partial^2 h}{\partial x^2}(x,t) \qquad (6.40)$$

with the terminal condition $h(x,T) := \log x$, $x > 0$.

Hint: Try a solution of the form $h(x,t) = u(t)g(x,t)$, and find $u(t)$.

c) Find the respective quantities ξ_t and η_t of the risky asset S_t and riskless asset $A_t = A_0 e^{rt}$ in the portfolio with value

$$V_t = g(S_t,t) = \xi_t S_t + \eta_t A_t$$

hedging a log contract with claim payoff $C = \log S_T$ at maturity.

Exercise 6.10 Binary options. Consider a price process $(S_t)_{t\in\mathbb{R}_+}$ given by

$$\frac{dS_t}{S_t} = rdt + \sigma dB_t, \qquad S_0 = 1,$$

under the risk-neutral probability measure $\mathbb{P}^*$. The binary (or digital) *call* option is a contract with maturity T, strike price K, and payoff

$$C_d := \mathbb{1}_{[K,\infty)}(S_T) = \begin{cases} \$1 & \text{if } S_T \geqslant K, \\[2mm] 0 & \text{if } S_T < K. \end{cases}$$

a) Derive the Black–Scholes PDE satisfied by the pricing function $C_d(t, S_t)$ of the binary call option, together with its terminal condition.

b) Show that the solution $C_d(t,x)$ of the Black–Scholes PDE of Question (a) is given by

$$\begin{aligned} C_d(t,x) &= e^{-(T-t)r}\Phi\left(\frac{(r-\sigma^2/2)(T-t)+\log(x/K)}{|\sigma|\sqrt{T-t}}\right) \\ &= e^{-(T-t)r}\Phi(d_-(T-t)), \end{aligned}$$

where

$$d_-(T-t) := \frac{(r-\sigma^2/2)(T-t)+\log(S_t/K)}{|\sigma|\sqrt{T-t}}, \qquad 0 \leqslant t < T.$$

Exercise 6.11

a) Bachelier (1900) model. Solve the stochastic differential equation

$$dS_t = \alpha S_t dt + \sigma dB_t \qquad (6.41)$$

in terms of $\alpha, \sigma \in \mathbb{R}$, and the initial condition S_0.

b) Write down the Bachelier PDE satisfied by the function $C(t, x)$, where $C(t, S_t)$ is the price at time $t \in [0, T]$ of the contingent claim with claim payoff $C = \phi(S_T) = \exp(S_T)$, and identify the process Delta $(\xi_t)_{t \in [0,T]}$ that hedges this claim.

c) Solve the Black–Scholes PDE of Question (b) with the terminal condition $\phi(x) = e^x$, $x \in \mathbb{R}$.

Hint: Search for a solution of the form

$$C(t, x) = \exp\left(-(T - t)r + xh(t) + \frac{\sigma^2}{4r}(h^2(t) - 1)\right), \tag{6.42}$$

where $h(t)$ is a function to be determined, with $h(T) = 1$.

d) Compute the portfolio strategy $(\xi_t, \eta_t)_{t \in [0,T]}$ that hedges the contingent claim with claim payoff $C = \exp(S_T)$.

Exercise 6.12

a) Show that for every fixed value of S, the function

$$d \longmapsto h(S, d) := S\Phi\left(d + |\sigma|\sqrt{T}\right) - Ke^{-rT}\Phi(d),$$

reaches its maximum at $d_*(S) := \dfrac{\log(S/K) + (r - \sigma^2/2)T}{|\sigma|\sqrt{T}}.$

Hint: The maximum is reached when the partial derivative $\dfrac{\partial h}{\partial d}$ vanishes.

b) By the differentiation rule

$$\frac{d}{dS}h(S, d_*(S)) = \frac{\partial h}{\partial S}(S, d_*(S)) + d'_*(S)\frac{\partial h}{\partial d}(S, d_*(S)),$$

recover the value of the Black–Scholes Delta.

Exercise 6.13

a) Compute the Black–Scholes call and put *Vega* by differentiation of the Black–Scholes function

$$g_c(t, x) = \text{Bl}(x, K, \sigma, r, T - t) = x\Phi\left(d_+(T - t)\right) - Ke^{-(T-t)r}\Phi\left(d_-(T - t)\right),$$

with respect to the volatility parameter $\sigma > 0$, knowing that

$$
\begin{aligned}
-\frac{1}{2}\left(d_-(T - t)\right)^2 &= -\frac{1}{2}\left(\frac{\log(x/K) + (r - \sigma^2/2)(T - t)}{|\sigma|\sqrt{T - t}}\right)^2 \\
&= -\frac{1}{2}\left(d_+(T - t)\right)^2 + (T - t)r + \log\frac{x}{K}. \tag{6.43}
\end{aligned}
$$

How do the Black–Scholes call and put prices behave when subjected an increase in the volatility parameter σ?

b) Compute the Black–Scholes Rho by differentiation of the Black–Scholes function $g_c(t, x)$. How do the Black–Scholes call and put prices behave when subjected an increase in the interest rate parameter r?

Exercise 6.14 Consider the backward induction relation (3.14), *i.e.*

$$\tilde{v}(t, x) = (1 - p_N^*)\tilde{v}(t + 1, x(1 + a_N)) + p_N^*\tilde{v}(t + 1, x(1 + b_N)),$$

using the renormalizations $r_N := rT/N$ and

$$a_N := (1 + r_N)(1 - |\sigma|\sqrt{T/N}) - 1, \quad b_N := (1 + r_N)(1 + |\sigma|\sqrt{T/N}) - 1,$$

of Section 3.6, $N \geqslant 1$, with

$$p_N^* = \frac{r_N - a_N}{b_N - a_N} \quad \text{and} \quad p_N^* = \frac{b_N - r_N}{b_N - a_N}.$$

a) Show that the Black–Scholes PDE (6.2) of Proposition 6.1 can be recovered from the induction relation (3.14) when the number N of time steps tends to infinity.

b) Show that the expression of the Delta $\xi_t = \dfrac{\partial g_c}{\partial x}(t, S_t)$ can be similarly recovered from the finite difference relation (3.19), *i.e.*

$$\xi_t^{(1)}(S_{t-1}) = \frac{v(t, (1 + b_N)S_{t-1}) - v(t, (1 + a_N)S_{t-1})}{S_{t-1}(b_N - a_N)}$$

as N tends to infinity.

Problem 6.15 (Leung and Sircar (2015)) *ProShares Ultra S&P500* and *ProShares UltraShort S&P500* are leveraged investment funds that seek daily investment results, before fees and expenses, that correspond to β times (βx) the daily performance of the S&P500[®], with respectively $\beta = 2$ for *ProShares Ultra* and $\beta = -2$ for *ProShares UltraShort*. Here, *leveraging* with a factor $\beta : 1$ aims at multiplying the potential return of an investment by a factor β. The following ten questions are interdependent and should be treated in sequence.

a) Consider a risky asset priced $S_0 := \$4$ at time $t = 0$ and taking two possible values $S_1 = \$5$ and $S_1 = \$2$ at time $t = 1$. Compute the two possible returns (in %) achieved when investing \$4 in one share of the asset S, and the expected return under the risk-neutral probability measure, assuming that the risk-free interest rate is zero.

b) Leveraging. Still based on an initial \$4 investment, we decide to leverage by a factor $\beta = 3$ by borrowing another $(\beta - 1) \times \$4 = 2 \times \$4$ at rate zero to purchase a total of $\beta = 3$ shares of the asset S. Compute the two returns (in %) possibly achieved in this case, and the expected return under the risk-neutral probability measure, assuming that the risk-free interest rate is zero.

c) Denoting by F_t the ProShares value at time t, how much should the fund invest in the underlying asset priced S_t, and how much \$ should it borrow or save on the risk-free market at any time t in order to leverage with a factor $\beta : 1$?

d) Find the portfolio allocation (ξ_t, η_t) for the fund value

$$F_t = \xi_t S_t + \eta_t A_t, \qquad t \geqslant 0,$$

according to Question (c), where $A_t := A_0\, e^{rt}$ is the riskless money market account.

e) We choose to model the S&P500 index S_t as the geometric Brownian motion

$$dS_t = rS_t dt + \sigma S_t dB_t, \qquad t \geqslant 0,$$

under the risk-neutral probability measure $\mathbb{P}^*$. Find the stochastic differential equation satisfied by $(F_t)_{t\in\mathbb{R}_+}$ under the self-financing condition $dF_t = \xi_t dS_t + \eta_t dA_t$.

f) Is the discounted fund value $(e^{-rt}F_t)_{t\in\mathbb{R}_+}$ a martingale under the risk-neutral probability measure $\mathbb{P}^*$?

g) Find the relation between the fund value F_t and the index S_t by solving the stochastic differential equation obtained for F_t in Question (e). For simplicity we normalize $F_0 := S_0^\beta$.

h) Write the price at time $t = 0$ of the call option with claim payoff $C = (F_T - K)^+$ on the ProShares index using the Black–Scholes formula.

i) Show that when $\beta > 0$, the Delta at time $t \in [0, T)$ of the call option with claim payoff $C = (F_T - K)^+$ on *ProShares Ultra* is equal to the Delta of the call option with claim payoff $C = (S_T - K_\beta(t))^+$ on the S&P500, for a certain strike price $K_\beta(t)$ to be determined explicitly.

j) When $\beta < 0$, find the relation between the Delta at time $t \in [0, T)$ of the call option with claim payoff $C = (F_T - K)^+$ on *ProShares UltraShort* and the Delta of the *put* option with claim payoff $C = (K_\beta(t) - S_T)^+$ on the S&P500.

Chapter 7

Martingale Approach to Pricing and Hedging

In the *martingale approach* to the pricing and hedging of financial derivatives, option prices are expressed as the expected values of discounted option payoffs. This approach relies on the construction of risk-neutral probability measures by the Girsanov theorem, and the associated hedging portfolios are obtained via stochastic integral representations.

7.1 Martingale Property of the Itô Integral

Recall (Definition 4.2) that an integrable process $(X_t)_{t \in \mathbb{R}_+}$ is said to be a *martingale* with respect to the filtration $(\mathcal{F}_t)_{t \in \mathbb{R}_+}$ if

$$\mathbb{E}[X_t \mid \mathcal{F}_s] = X_s, \qquad 0 \leqslant s \leqslant t.$$

In what follows,

$$L^2(\Omega) := \{F : \Omega \to \mathbb{R} \ : \ \mathbb{E}[|F|^2] < \infty\}$$

denotes the space of square-integrable random variables.

Examples of martingales (i)

1. Given $F \in L^2(\Omega)$ a square-integrable random variable and $(\mathcal{F}_t)_{t \in \mathbb{R}_+}$ a filtration, the process $(X_t)_{t \in \mathbb{R}_+}$ defined by

$$X_t := \mathbb{E}[F \mid \mathcal{F}_t], \qquad t \geqslant 0,$$

is an $(\mathcal{F}_t)_{t \in \mathbb{R}_+}$-martingale under $\mathbb{P}$. Indeed, since $\mathcal{F}_s \subset \mathcal{F}_t$, $0 \leqslant s \leqslant t$, it follows from the tower property of conditional expectations that

$$\mathbb{E}[X_t \mid \mathcal{F}_s] = \mathbb{E}[\mathbb{E}[F \mid \mathcal{F}_t] \mid \mathcal{F}_s] = \mathbb{E}[F \mid \mathcal{F}_s] = X_s, \quad 0 \leqslant s \leqslant t. \qquad (7.1)$$

2. Any integrable stochastic process $(X_t)_{t \in \mathbb{R}_+}$ whose increments $(X_{t_1} - X_{t_0}, \ldots, X_{t_n} - X_{t_{n-1}})$ are mutually independent and centered under $\mathbb{P}$ (*i.e.* $\mathbb{E}[X_t] = 0$, $t \in \mathbb{R}_+$) is a martingale with respect to the filtration $(\mathcal{F}_t)_{t \in \mathbb{R}_+}$ generated by $(X_t)_{t \in \mathbb{R}_+}$, as we have

$$
\begin{aligned}
\mathbb{E}[X_t \mid \mathcal{F}_s] &= \mathbb{E}[X_t - X_s + X_s \mid \mathcal{F}_s] \\
&= \mathbb{E}[X_t - X_s \mid \mathcal{F}_s] + \mathbb{E}[X_s \mid \mathcal{F}_s] \\
&= \mathbb{E}[X_t - X_s] + X_s \\
&= X_s, \qquad 0 \leqslant s \leqslant t. \qquad (7.2)
\end{aligned}
$$

DOI: 10.1201/9781003298670-7

In particular, the standard Brownian motion $(B_t)_{t\in\mathbb{R}_+}$ is a martingale because it has centered and independent increments. This fact is also consequence of Proposition 7.1 below as B_t can be written as

$$B_t = \int_0^t dB_s, \qquad t \geqslant 0.$$

3. The driftless geometric Brownian motion

$$X_t := X_0 e^{\sigma B_t - \sigma^2 t/2} \tag{7.3}$$

is a martingale. Indeed, using the Gaussian moment generating function identity, we have

$$
\begin{aligned}
\mathbb{E}[X_t \mid \mathcal{F}_s] &= \mathbb{E}\left[X_0 e^{\sigma B_t - \sigma^2 t/2} \mid \mathcal{F}_s\right] \\
&= X_0 e^{-\sigma^2 t/2} \mathbb{E}\left[e^{\sigma B_t} \mid \mathcal{F}_s\right] \\
&= X_0 e^{-\sigma^2 t/2} \mathbb{E}\left[e^{(B_t - B_s)\sigma + \sigma B_s} \mid \mathcal{F}_s\right] \\
&= X_0 e^{-\sigma^2 t/2 + \sigma B_s} \mathbb{E}\left[e^{(B_t - B_s)\sigma} \mid \mathcal{F}_s\right] \\
&= X_0 e^{-\sigma^2 t/2 + \sigma B_s} \mathbb{E}\left[e^{(B_t - B_s)\sigma}\right] \\
&= X_0 e^{-\sigma^2 t/2 + \sigma B_s} \exp\left(\mathbb{E}[(B_t - B_s)\sigma] + \frac{1}{2}\operatorname{Var}[(B_t - B_s)\sigma]\right) \\
&= X_0 e^{-\sigma^2 t/2 + \sigma B_s} e^{(t-s)\sigma^2/2} \\
&= X_0 e^{\sigma B_s - \sigma^2 s/2} \\
&= X_s, \qquad 0 \leqslant s \leqslant t.
\end{aligned}
$$

The following result shows that the Itô integral yields a martingale with respect to the Brownian filtration $(\mathcal{F}_t)_{t\in\mathbb{R}_+}$. It is the continuous-time analog of the discrete-time Theorem 2.11.

Proposition 7.1. *The stochastic integral process* $\left(\int_0^t u_s dB_s\right)_{t\in\mathbb{R}_+}$ *of a square-integrable adapted process* $u \in L^2_{\mathrm{ad}}(\Omega \times \mathbb{R}_+)$ *is a martingale, i.e.:*

$$\mathbb{E}\left[\int_0^t u_\tau dB_\tau \;\Big|\; \mathcal{F}_s\right] = \int_0^s u_\tau dB_\tau, \qquad 0 \leqslant s \leqslant t. \tag{7.4}$$

In particular, $\int_0^t u_s dB_s$ is $\mathcal{F}_t$-measurable, $t \geqslant 0$, and since $\mathcal{F}_0 = \{\emptyset, \Omega\}$, Relation (7.4) applied with $t = 0$ recovers the fact that the Itô integral is a centered random variable:

$$\mathbb{E}\left[\int_0^t u_s dB_s\right] = \mathbb{E}\left[\int_0^t u_s dB_s \;\Big|\; \mathcal{F}_0\right] = \int_0^0 u_s dB_s = 0, \qquad t \geqslant 0.$$

Proof. The statement is first proved in case $(u_t)_{t\in\mathbb{R}_+}$ is a simple predictable process, and then extended to the general case, cf. *e.g.* Proposition 2.5.7 in Privault (2009). For example, for u a predictable step process of the form

$$u_s := F\mathbb{1}_{[a,b]}(s) = \begin{cases} F & \text{if } s \in [a,b], \\ 0 & \text{if } s \notin [a,b], \end{cases}$$

with F an $\mathcal{F}_a$-measurable random variable and $t \in [a, b]$, by Definition 4.17 we have

$$
\begin{aligned}
\mathbb{E}\left[\int_0^\infty u_s dB_s \mid \mathcal{F}_t\right] &= \mathbb{E}\left[\int_0^\infty F\mathbb{1}_{[a,b]}(s)dB_s \mid \mathcal{F}_t\right] \\
&= \mathbb{E}[(B_b - B_a)F \mid \mathcal{F}_t] \\
&= F\,\mathbb{E}[B_b - B_a \mid \mathcal{F}_t] \\
&= F(B_t - B_a) \\
&= \int_a^t u_s dB_s \\
&= \int_0^t u_s dB_s, \qquad a \leqslant t \leqslant b.
\end{aligned}
$$

On the other hand, when $t \in [0, a]$ we have

$$
\int_0^t u_s dB_s = 0,
$$

and we check that

$$
\begin{aligned}
\mathbb{E}\left[\int_0^\infty u_s dB_s \mid \mathcal{F}_t\right] &= \mathbb{E}\left[\int_0^\infty F\mathbb{1}_{[a,b]}(s)dB_s \mid \mathcal{F}_t\right] \\
&= \mathbb{E}[F(B_b - B_a) \mid \mathcal{F}_t] \\
&= \mathbb{E}[\mathbb{E}[F(B_b - B_a) \mid \mathcal{F}_a] \mid \mathcal{F}_t] \\
&= \mathbb{E}[F\,\mathbb{E}[B_b - B_a \mid \mathcal{F}_a] \mid \mathcal{F}_t] \\
&= 0, \qquad 0 \leqslant t \leqslant a,
\end{aligned}
$$

where we used the tower property of conditional expectations and the fact that Brownian motion $(B_t)_{t \in \mathbb{R}_+}$ is a martingale:

$$
\mathbb{E}[B_b - B_a \mid \mathcal{F}_a] = \mathbb{E}[B_b \mid \mathcal{F}_a] - B_a = B_a - B_a = 0.
$$

The extension from simple processes to square-integrable processes in $L^2_{\mathrm{ad}}(\Omega \times \mathbb{R}_+)$ can be proved as in Proposition 4.21. Indeed, given $(u^{(n)})_{n \in \mathbb{N}}$ be a sequence of simple predictable processes converging to u in $L^2(\Omega \times [0, T])$ cf. Lemma 1.1 of Ikeda and Watanabe (1989), pages 22 and 46, by Fatou's Lemma, Jensen's inequality and the Itô isometry (4.16), we have:

$$
\begin{aligned}
&\mathbb{E}\left[\left(\int_0^t u_s dB_s - \mathbb{E}\left[\int_0^\infty u_s dB_s \mid \mathcal{F}_t\right]\right)^2\right] \\
&= \mathbb{E}\left[\lim_{n\to\infty}\left(\int_0^t u_s^{(n)} dB_s - \mathbb{E}\left[\int_0^\infty u_s dB_s \mid \mathcal{F}_t\right]\right)^2\right] \\
&\leqslant \liminf_{n\to\infty} \mathbb{E}\left[\left(\int_0^t u_s^{(n)} dB_s - \mathbb{E}\left[\int_0^\infty u_s dB_s \mid \mathcal{F}_t\right]\right)^2\right] \\
&= \liminf_{n\to\infty} \mathbb{E}\left[\left(\mathbb{E}\left[\int_0^\infty u_s^{(n)} dB_s - \int_0^\infty u_s dB_s \mid \mathcal{F}_t\right]\right)^2\right] \\
&\leqslant \liminf_{n\to\infty} \mathbb{E}\left[\mathbb{E}\left[\left(\int_0^\infty u_s^{(n)} dB_s - \int_0^\infty u_s dB_s\right)^2 \mid \mathcal{F}_t\right]\right] \\
&= \liminf_{n\to\infty} \mathbb{E}\left[\left(\int_0^\infty (u_s^{(n)} - u_s)dB_s\right)^2\right] \\
&= \liminf_{n\to\infty} \mathbb{E}\left[\int_0^\infty |u_s^{(n)} - u_s|^2 ds\right]
\end{aligned}
$$

$$= \liminf_{n \to \infty} \|u^{(n)} - u\|^2_{L^2(\Omega \times [0,T])}$$
$$= 0,$$

where we used the Itô isometry (4.16). We conclude that

$$\mathbb{E}\left[\int_0^\infty u_s dB_s \,\Big|\, \mathcal{F}_t\right] = \int_0^t u_s dB_s, \qquad t \geqslant 0,$$

for $u \in L^2_{\mathrm{ad}}(\Omega \times \mathbb{R}_+)$ a square-integrable adapted process, which leads to (7.4) after applying this identity to the process $(\mathbb{1}_{[0,t]} u_s)_{s \in \mathbb{R}_+}$, *i.e.*

$$\mathbb{E}\left[\int_0^t u_\tau dB_\tau \,\Big|\, \mathcal{F}_s\right] = \mathbb{E}\left[\int_0^\infty \mathbb{1}_{[0,t]}(\tau) u_\tau dB_\tau \,\Big|\, \mathcal{F}_s\right]$$
$$= \int_0^s \mathbb{1}_{[0,t]}(\tau) u_\tau dB_\tau$$
$$= \int_0^s u_\tau dB_\tau, \qquad 0 \leqslant s \leqslant t.$$

$\square$

Examples of martingales (*ii*)

1. The martingale property of the driftless geometric Brownian motion (7.3) can also be recovered from Proposition 7.1, since by Proposition 5.15, $(X_t)_{t \in \mathbb{R}_+}$ satisfies the stochastic differential equation

$$dX_t = \sigma X_t dB_t,$$

which shows that X_t can be written using the Brownian stochastic integral

$$X_t = X_0 + \sigma \int_0^t X_u dB_u, \qquad t \geqslant 0.$$

2. Consider an asset price process $(S_t)_{t \in \mathbb{R}_+}$ given by the stochastic differential equation

$$dS_t = \mu S_t dt + \sigma S_t dB_t, \qquad t \geqslant 0, \tag{7.5}$$

with $\mu \in \mathbb{R}$ and $\sigma > 0$. By the *Discounting Lemma 5.13*, the discounted asset price process $\widetilde{S}_t := \mathrm{e}^{-rt} S_t$, $t \geqslant 0$, satisfies the stochastic differential equation

$$d\widetilde{S}_t = (\mu - r)\widetilde{S}_t dt + \sigma \widetilde{S}_t dB_t,$$

and the discounted asset price

$$\widetilde{S}_t = \mathrm{e}^{-rt} S_t = S_0 \, \mathrm{e}^{(\mu-r)t + \sigma B_t - \sigma^2 t/2}, \qquad t \geqslant 0,$$

is a martingale under $\mathbb{P}$ when $\mu = r$. The case $\mu \neq r$ will be treated in Section 7.3 using risk-neutral probability measures, see Definition 5.4, and the Girsanov Theorem 7.3, see (7.16) below.

3. The discounted value

$$\widetilde{V}_t = \mathrm{e}^{-rt} V_t, \qquad t \geqslant 0,$$

of a self-financing portfolio is given by

$$\widetilde{V}_t = \widetilde{V}_0 + \int_0^t \xi_u d\widetilde{S}_u, \qquad t \geqslant 0,$$

cf. Lemma 5.14 is a martingale when $\mu = r$ by Proposition 7.1 because

$$\widetilde{V}_t = \widetilde{V}_0 + \sigma \int_0^t \xi_u \widetilde{S}_u dB_u, \qquad t \geqslant 0,,$$

since we have

$$d\widetilde{S}_t = \widetilde{S}_t((\mu - r)dt + \sigma dB_t) = \sigma \widetilde{S}_t dB_t$$

by the *Discounting Lemma 5.13*. Since the Black–Scholes theory is in fact valid for any value of the parameter μ we will look forward to including the case $\mu \neq r$ in the sequel.

7.2 Risk-Neutral Probability Measures

Recall that by definition, a risk-neutral measure is a probability measure $\mathbb{P}^*$ under which the discounted asset price process

$$\left(\widetilde{S}_t\right)_{t \in \mathbb{R}_+} := \left(e^{-rt} S_t\right)_{t \in \mathbb{R}_+}$$

is a *martingale*, see Definition 5.4 and Proposition 5.5.

Consider an asset price process $(S_t)_{t \in \mathbb{R}_+}$ given by the stochastic differential equation (7.5). Note that when $\mu = r$, the discounted asset price process $\left(\widetilde{S}_t\right)_{t \in \mathbb{R}_+} = \left(S_0 e^{\sigma B_t - \sigma^2 t/2}\right)_{t \in \mathbb{R}_+}$ is a martingale under $\mathbb{P}^* = \mathbb{P}$, which is a risk-neutral probability measure.

In this section we address the construction of a risk-neutral probability measure $\mathbb{P}^*$ in the general case $\mu \neq r$ using the Girsanov Theorem 7.3 below. For this, we note that by the *Discounting Lemma 5.13*, the relation

$$d\widetilde{S}_t = (\mu - r)\widetilde{S}_t dt + \sigma \widetilde{S}_t dB_t$$

where $\mu - r$ is the risk premium, can be rewritten as

$$d\widetilde{S}_t = \sigma \widetilde{S}_t d\widehat{B}_t, \tag{7.6}$$

where $\left(\widehat{B}_t\right)_{t \in \mathbb{R}_+}$ is a drifted Brownian motion given by

$$\widehat{B}_t := \frac{\mu - r}{\sigma} t + B_t, \qquad t \geqslant 0,$$

where the drift coefficient $\nu := (\mu - r)/\sigma$ is the "Market Price of Risk" (MPoR). The MPoR represents the difference between the return μ expected when investing in the risky asset S_t, and the risk-free interest rate r, measured in units of volatility σ.

From (7.6) and Propositions 5.5 and 7.1 we note that the risk-neutral probability measure can be constructed as a probability measure $\mathbb{P}^*$ under which $(\widehat{B}_t)_{t \in \mathbb{R}_+}$ is a standard Brownian motion.

Let us come back to the informal approximation of Brownian motion via its infinitesimal increments:

$$\Delta B_t = \pm \sqrt{\Delta t},$$

with

$$\mathbb{P}\big(\Delta B_t = +\sqrt{\Delta t}\,\big) = \mathbb{P}\big(\Delta B_t = -\sqrt{\Delta t}\,\big) = \frac{1}{2},$$

and

$$\mathbb{E}[\Delta B_t] = \frac{1}{2}\sqrt{\Delta t} - \frac{1}{2}\sqrt{\Delta t} = 0.$$

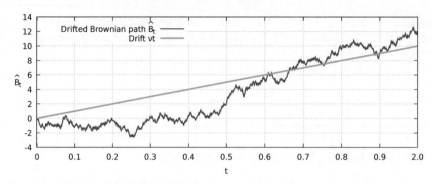

Figure 7.1: Drifted Brownian path $\big(\widehat{B}_t\big)_{t\in\mathbb{R}_+}$.

Clearly, given $\nu \in \mathbb{R}$, the drifted process

$$\widehat{B}_t := \nu t + B_t, \qquad t \geqslant 0,$$

is no longer a standard Brownian motion because it is not centered:

$$\mathbb{E}\big[\widehat{B}_t\big] = \mathbb{E}[\nu t + B_t] = \nu t + \mathbb{E}[B_t] = \nu t \neq 0,$$

cf. Figure 7.1. This identity can be formulated in terms of infinitesimal increments as

$$\mathbb{E}[\nu \Delta t + \Delta B_t] = \frac{1}{2}(\nu \Delta t + \sqrt{\Delta t}\,) + \frac{1}{2}(\nu \Delta t - \sqrt{\Delta t}\,) = \nu \Delta t \neq 0.$$

In order to make $\nu t + B_t$ a centered process (*i.e.* a standard Brownian motion, since $\nu t + B_t$ conserves all the other properties *(i)*–*(iii)* in the definition of Brownian motion, one may change the probabilities of ups and downs, which have been fixed so far equal to $1/2$.

That is, the problem is now to find two numbers $p^*, q^* \in [0,1]$ such that

$$\begin{cases} p^*(\nu \Delta t + \sqrt{\Delta t}\,) + q^*(\nu \Delta t - \sqrt{\Delta t}\,) = 0 \\[2mm] p^* + q^* = 1. \end{cases}$$

The solution to this problem is given by

$$p^* := \frac{1}{2}(1 - \nu\sqrt{\Delta t}\,) \quad \text{and} \quad q^* := \frac{1}{2}(1 + \nu\sqrt{\Delta t}\,). \tag{7.7}$$

Definition 7.2. *We say that a probability measure* $\mathbb{Q}$ *is absolutely continuous with respect to another probability measure* $\mathbb{P}$ *if there exists a nonnegative random variable* $F : \Omega \longrightarrow \mathbb{R}$ *such that* $\mathbb{E}[F] = 1$, *and*

$$\frac{d\mathbb{Q}}{d\mathbb{P}} = F, \qquad i.e. \qquad d\mathbb{Q} = F d\mathbb{P}. \tag{7.8}$$

In this case, F *is called the Radon–Nikodym density of* $\mathbb{Q}$ *with respect to* $\mathbb{P}$.

Relation (7.8) is equivalent to the relation

$$
\begin{aligned}
\mathbb{E}_{\mathbb{Q}}[G] &= \int_{\Omega} G(\omega) \mathrm{d}\mathbb{Q}(\omega) \\
&= \int_{\Omega} G(\omega) \frac{\mathrm{d}\mathbb{Q}}{\mathrm{d}\mathbb{P}}(\omega) \mathrm{d}\mathbb{P}(\omega) \\
&= \int_{\Omega} G(\omega) F(\omega) \mathrm{d}\mathbb{P}(\omega) \\
&= \mathbb{E}\left[FG\right],
\end{aligned}
$$

for any random variable G integrable under $\mathbb{Q}$.

Coming back to Brownian motion considered as a discrete random walk with independent increments $\pm\sqrt{\Delta t}$, we try to construct a new probability measure denoted $\mathbb{P}^*$, under which the drifted process $\widehat{B}_t := \nu t + B_t$ will be a standard Brownian motion. This probability measure will be defined through its Radon–Nikodym density

$$
\begin{aligned}
\frac{\mathrm{d}\mathbb{P}^*}{\mathrm{d}\mathbb{P}} &:= \frac{\mathbb{P}^*(\Delta B_{t_1} = \epsilon_1\sqrt{\Delta t}, \ldots, \Delta B_{t_N} = \epsilon_N\sqrt{\Delta t})}{\mathbb{P}(\Delta B_{t_1} = \epsilon_1\sqrt{\Delta t}, \ldots, \Delta B_{t_N} = \epsilon_N\sqrt{\Delta t})} \\
&= \frac{\mathbb{P}^*(\Delta B_{t_1} = \epsilon_1\sqrt{\Delta t}) \cdots \mathbb{P}^*(\Delta B_{t_N} = \epsilon_N\sqrt{\Delta t})}{\mathbb{P}(\Delta B_{t_1} = \epsilon_1\sqrt{\Delta t}) \cdots \mathbb{P}(\Delta B_{t_N} = \epsilon_N\sqrt{\Delta t})} \\
&= \frac{1}{(1/2)^N} \mathbb{P}^*(\Delta B_{t_1} = \epsilon_1\sqrt{\Delta t}) \cdots \mathbb{P}^*(\Delta B_{t_N} = \epsilon_N\sqrt{\Delta t}),
\end{aligned}
\tag{7.9}
$$

$\epsilon_1, \epsilon_2, \ldots, \epsilon_N \in \{-1, 1\}$, with respect to the historical probability measure $\mathbb{P}$, obtained by taking the product of the above probabilities divided by the reference probability $1/2^N$ corresponding to the symmetric random walk.

Interpreting $N = T/\Delta t$ as an (infinitely large) number of discrete time steps and under the identification $[0, T] \simeq \{0 = t_0, t_1, \ldots, t_N = T\}$, this Radon–Nikodym density (7.9) can be rewritten as

$$
\frac{\mathrm{d}\mathbb{P}^*}{\mathrm{d}\mathbb{P}} \simeq \frac{1}{(1/2)^N} \prod_{0 < t < T} \left(\frac{1}{2} \mp \frac{1}{2}\nu\sqrt{\Delta t} \right)
\tag{7.10}
$$

where 2^N becomes a normalization factor. Using the expansion

$$
\begin{aligned}
\log\left(1 \pm \nu\sqrt{\Delta t}\right) &= \pm\nu\sqrt{\Delta t} - \frac{1}{2}(\pm\nu\sqrt{\Delta t})^2 + o(\Delta t) \\
&= \pm\nu\sqrt{\Delta t} - \frac{\nu^2}{2}\Delta t + o(\Delta t),
\end{aligned}
$$

for small values of Δt, this Radon–Nikodym density can be informally shown to converge as follows as N tends to infinity, *i.e.* as the time step $\Delta t = T/N$ tends to zero:

$$
\begin{aligned}
\frac{\mathrm{d}\mathbb{P}^*}{\mathrm{d}\mathbb{P}} &= 2^N \prod_{0 < t < T} \left(\frac{1}{2} \mp \frac{1}{2}\nu\sqrt{\Delta t} \right) \\
&= \prod_{0 < t < T} \left(1 \mp \nu\sqrt{\Delta t} \right) \\
&= \exp\left(\log \prod_{0 < t < T} \left(1 \mp \nu\sqrt{\Delta t} \right) \right) \\
&= \exp\left(\sum_{0 < t < T} \log\left(1 \mp \nu\sqrt{\Delta t} \right) \right)
\end{aligned}
$$

$$\simeq \exp\left(\nu \sum_{0<t<T} \mp\sqrt{\Delta t} - \frac{1}{2}\sum_{0<t<T}(\mp\nu\sqrt{\Delta t})^2\right)$$

$$= \exp\left(-\nu\sum_{0<t<T}\pm\sqrt{\Delta t} - \frac{\nu^2}{2}\sum_{0<t<T}\Delta t\right)$$

$$= \exp\left(-\nu\sum_{0<t<T}\Delta B_t - \frac{\nu^2}{2}\sum_{0<t<T}\Delta t\right)$$

$$= \exp\left(-\nu B_T - \frac{\nu^2}{2}T\right),$$

based on the identifications

$$B_T \simeq \sum_{0<t<T}\pm\sqrt{\Delta t} \quad\text{and}\quad T \simeq \sum_{0<t<T}\Delta t.$$

Informally, the drifted process $\left(\widehat{B}_t\right)_{t\in[0,T]} = (\nu t + B_t)_{t\in[0,T]}$ is a standard Brownian motion under the probability measure $\mathbb{P}^*$ defined by its Radon–Nikodym density

$$\frac{d\mathbb{P}^*}{d\mathbb{P}} = \exp\left(-\nu B_T - \frac{\nu^2}{2}T\right).$$

The following R code is rescaling probabilities as in (7.7) based on the value of the drift μ.

```
nsim <- 100; N=2000; t <- 0:N; dt <- 1.0/N; nu=3; p=0.5*(1-nu*(dt)^0.5);
dB <- matrix((dt)^0.5*(rbinom( nsim * N, 1, p)-0.5)*2, nsim, N)
X <- cbind(rep(0, nsim), t(apply(dB, 1, cumsum)))
plot(t, X[1, ], xlab = "Time", ylab = "", type = "l", ylim = c(-2*N*dt,2*N*dt), col =
    0,cex.axis=1.4,cex.lab=1.4,xaxs="i", mgp = c(1, 2, 0), las=1)
for (i in 1:nsim){lines(t,t*nu*dt+X[i,],type="l",col=i+1,lwd=2)}
```

The discretized illustration in Figure 7.2 displays the drifted Brownian motion $\widehat{B}_t := \nu t + B_t$ under the shifted probability measure $\mathbb{P}^*$ in (7.10) using the above R code with $N = 100$. The code makes big transitions less frequent than small transitions, resulting into a standard, centered Brownian motion under $\mathbb{P}^*$.

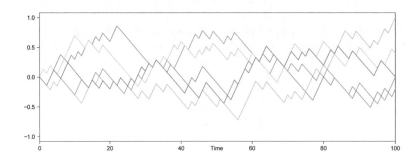

Figure 7.2: Drifted Brownian motion paths under a shifted Girsanov measure.

7.3 Change of Measure and the Girsanov Theorem

In this section we restate the Girsanov Theorem in a more rigorous way, using changes of probability measures. The Girsanov Theorem can actually be extended to shifts by adapted processes $(\psi_t)_{t \in [0,T]}$ as follows, cf. *e.g.* Theorem III-42, page 141 of Protter (2004). An extension of the Girsanov Theorem to jump processes will be covered in Section 20.5. Recall also that here, $\Omega := \mathcal{C}_0([0,T])$ is the Wiener space and $\omega \in \Omega$ is a continuous function on $[0,T]$ starting at 0 in $t = 0$. The Girsanov Theorem 7.3 will be used in Section 7.4 for the construction of a unique risk-neutral probability measure $\mathbb{P}^*$, showing absence of arbitrage and completeness in the Black–Scholes market, see Theorems 5.7 and 5.11.

Theorem 7.3. *Let* $(\psi_t)_{t \in [0,T]}$ *be an adapted process satisfying the Novikov integrability condition*

$$\mathbb{E}\left[\exp\left(\frac{1}{2}\int_0^T |\psi_t|^2 dt\right)\right] < \infty, \tag{7.11}$$

and let $\mathbb{Q}$ *denote the probability measure defined by the Radon–Nikodym density*

$$\frac{d\mathbb{Q}}{d\mathbb{P}} = \exp\left(-\int_0^T \psi_s dB_s - \frac{1}{2}\int_0^T |\psi_s|^2 ds\right).$$

Then

$$\widehat{B}_t := B_t + \int_0^t \psi_s ds, \qquad 0 \leqslant t \leqslant T,$$

is a standard Brownian motion under $\mathbb{Q}$.

In the case of the simple shift

$$\widehat{B}_t := B_t + \nu t, \qquad 0 \leqslant t \leqslant T,$$

by a drift νt with constant $\nu \in \mathbb{R}$, the process $(\widehat{B}_t)_{t \in \mathbb{R}_+}$ is a standard (centered) Brownian motion under the probability measure $\mathbb{Q}$ defined by

$$d\mathbb{Q}(\omega) = \exp\left(-\nu B_T - \frac{\nu^2}{2}T\right)d\mathbb{P}(\omega).$$

For example, the fact that $\widehat{B}_T$ has a centered Gaussian distribution under $\mathbb{Q}$ can be recovered as follows:

$$
\begin{aligned}
\mathbb{E}_{\mathbb{Q}}\left[f(\widehat{B}_T)\right] &= \mathbb{E}_{\mathbb{Q}}[f(\nu T + B_T)] \\
&= \int_\Omega f(\nu T + B_T)d\mathbb{Q} \\
&= \int_\Omega f(\nu T + B_T)\exp\left(-\nu B_T - \frac{1}{2}\nu^2 T\right)d\mathbb{P} \\
&= \int_{-\infty}^\infty f(\nu T + x)\exp\left(-\nu x - \frac{1}{2}\nu^2 T\right)e^{-x^2/(2T)}\frac{dx}{\sqrt{2\pi T}} \\
&= \int_{-\infty}^\infty f(\nu T + x)e^{-(\nu T + x)^2/(2T)}\frac{dx}{\sqrt{2\pi T}} \\
&= \int_{-\infty}^\infty f(y)e^{-y^2/(2T)}\frac{dy}{\sqrt{2\pi T}} \\
&= \mathbb{E}_{\mathbb{P}}[f(B_T)],
\end{aligned}
$$

i.e.

$$\mathbb{E}_{\mathbb{Q}}[f(\nu T + B_T)] \quad = \quad \int_\Omega f(\nu T + B_T) \mathrm{d}\mathbb{Q} \tag{7.12}$$

$$= \quad \int_\Omega f(B_T) \mathrm{d}\mathbb{P}$$

$$= \quad \mathbb{E}_{\mathbb{P}}[f(B_T)],$$

showing that, under $\mathbb{Q}$, $\nu T + B_T$ has the centered $\mathcal{N}(0, T)$ Gaussian distribution with variance T. For example, taking $f(x) = x$, Relation (7.12) recovers the fact that $\widehat{B}_T$ is a centered random variable under $\mathbb{Q}$, *i.e.*

$$\mathbb{E}_{\mathbb{Q}}\left[\widehat{B}_T\right] = \mathbb{E}_{\mathbb{Q}}[\nu T + B_T)] = \mathbb{E}_{\mathbb{P}}[B_T] = 0.$$

The Girsanov Theorem 7.3 also allows us to extend (7.12) as

$$\mathbb{E}_{\mathbb{P}}[F(\cdot)] \quad = \quad \mathbb{E}\left[F\left(B_\cdot + \int_0^\cdot \psi_s ds\right) \exp\left(-\int_0^T \psi_s dB_s - \frac{1}{2}\int_0^T |\psi_s|^2 ds\right)\right]$$

$$= \quad \mathbb{E}_{\mathbb{Q}}\left[F\left(B_\cdot + \int_0^\cdot \psi_s ds\right)\right], \tag{7.13}$$

for all random variables $F \in L^1(\Omega)$, see also Exercise 7.25.

When applied to the (constant) market price of risk (or Sharpe ratio)

$$\psi_t := \frac{\mu - r}{\sigma},$$

the Girsanov Theorem 7.3 shows that the process

$$\widehat{B}_t := \frac{\mu - r}{\sigma} t + B_t, \qquad 0 \leqslant t \leqslant T, \tag{7.14}$$

is a standard Brownian motion under the probability measure $\mathbb{P}^*$ defined by

$$\frac{\mathrm{d}\mathbb{P}^*}{\mathrm{d}\mathbb{P}} = \exp\left(-\frac{\mu - r}{\sigma} B_T - \frac{(\mu - r)^2}{2\sigma^2} T\right). \tag{7.15}$$

Hence by Proposition 7.1 the discounted price process $(\widetilde{S}_t)_{t \in \mathbb{R}_+}$ solution of

$$d\widetilde{S}_t = (\mu - r)\widetilde{S}_t dt + \sigma \widetilde{S}_t dB_t = \sigma \widetilde{S}_t d\widehat{B}_t, \qquad t \geqslant 0, \tag{7.16}$$

is a martingale under $\mathbb{P}^*$, therefore $\mathbb{P}^*$ is a risk-neutral probability measure. We also check that $\mathbb{P}^* = \mathbb{P}$ when $\mu = r$.

In the sequel, we consider probability measures $\mathbb{Q}$ that are *equivalent* to $\mathbb{P}$ in the sense that they share the same events of zero probability, see Definition 1.5. Precisely, recall that a probability measure $\mathbb{Q}$ on $(\Omega, \mathcal{F})$ is said to be *equivalent* to another probability measure $\mathbb{P}$ when

$$\mathbb{Q}(A) = 0 \quad \text{if and only if} \quad \mathbb{P}(A) = 0, \quad \text{for all} \quad A \in \mathcal{F}.$$

Note that when $\mathbb{Q}$ is defined by (7.8), it is *equivalent* to $\mathbb{P}$ if and only if $F > 0$ with $\mathbb{P}$-probability one.

7.4 Pricing by the Martingale Method

In this section we give the expression of the Black–Scholes price using expectations of discounted payoffs.

Recall that according to the first fundamental theorem of asset pricing Theorem 5.7, a continuous market is without arbitrage opportunities if and only if there exists (at least) an equivalent risk-neutral probability measure $\mathbb{P}^*$ under which the discounted price process

$$\widetilde{S}_t := \mathrm{e}^{-rt} S_t, \qquad t \geqslant 0,$$

is a martingale under $\mathbb{P}^*$. In addition, when the risk-neutral probability measure is unique, the market is said to be *complete*.

The equation

$$\frac{dS_t}{S_t} = \mu dt + \sigma dB_t, \qquad t \geqslant 0,$$

satisfied by the price process $(S_t)_{t \in \mathbb{R}_+}$ can be rewritten using (7.14) as

$$\frac{dS_t}{S_t} = rdt + \sigma d\widehat{B}_t, \qquad t \geqslant 0, \tag{7.17}$$

with the solution

$$S_t = S_0 \, \mathrm{e}^{\mu t + \sigma B_t - \sigma^2 t/2} = S_0 \, \mathrm{e}^{rt + \sigma \widehat{B}_t - \sigma^2 t/2}, \qquad t \geqslant 0. \tag{7.18}$$

By the discounting Lemma 5.13, we have

$$
\begin{aligned}
d\widetilde{S}_t &= (\mu - r)\widetilde{S}_t dt + \sigma \widetilde{S}_t dB_t \\
&= \sigma \widetilde{S}_t \left(\frac{\mu - r}{\sigma} dt + dB_t \right) \\
&= \sigma \widetilde{S}_t d\widehat{B}_t, \qquad t \geqslant 0,
\end{aligned}
\tag{7.19}
$$

hence the discounted price process

$$
\begin{aligned}
\widetilde{S}_t &:= \mathrm{e}^{-rt} S_t \\
&= S_0 \, \mathrm{e}^{(\mu - r)t + \sigma B_t - \sigma^2 t/2} \\
&= S_0 \, \mathrm{e}^{\sigma \widehat{B}_t - \sigma^2 t/2}, \qquad t \geqslant 0,
\end{aligned}
$$

is a martingale under the probability measure $\mathbb{P}^*$ defined by (7.15). We note that $\mathbb{P}^*$ is a risk-neutral probability measure equivalent to $\mathbb{P}$, also called martingale measure, whose existence and uniqueness ensure the absence of arbitrage and completeness according to Theorems 5.7 and 5.11.

Therefore, by Lemma 5.14 the discounted value $\widetilde{V}_t$ of a self-financing portfolio can be written as

$$
\begin{aligned}
\widetilde{V}_t &= \widetilde{V}_0 + \int_0^t \xi_u d\widetilde{S}_u \\
&= \widetilde{V}_0 + \sigma \int_0^t \xi_u \widetilde{S}_u d\widehat{B}_u, \qquad t \geqslant 0,
\end{aligned}
$$

and by Proposition 7.1 it becomes a martingale under $\mathbb{P}^*$.

As in Chapter 3, the value V_t at time t of a self-financing portfolio strategy $(\xi_t)_{t\in[0,T]}$ hedging an attainable claim payoff C will be called an *arbitrage-free price* of the claim payoff C at time t and denoted by $\pi_t(C)$, $t \in [0,T]$. Arbitrage-free prices can be used to ensure that financial derivatives are "marked" at their fair value ("mark to market").

Theorem 7.4. *Let $(\xi_t, \eta_t)_{t\in[0,T]}$ be a portfolio strategy with value*

$$V_t = \eta_t A_t + \xi_t S_t, \qquad 0 \leqslant t \leqslant T,$$

and let C be a contingent claim payoff, such that

(i) $(\xi_t, \eta_t)_{t\in[0,T]}$ is a self-financing portfolio, and

(ii) $(\xi_t, \eta_t)_{t\in[0,T]}$ hedges the claim payoff C, i.e. we have $V_T = C$.

Then, the arbitrage-free price of the claim payoff C is given by the portfolio value

$$\pi_t(C) = V_t = e^{-(T-t)r} \, \mathbb{E}^*[C \mid \mathcal{F}_t], \qquad 0 \leqslant t \leqslant T, \tag{7.20}$$

where $\mathbb{E}^*$ denotes expectation under the risk-neutral probability measure $\mathbb{P}^*$.

Proof. Since the portfolio strategy $(\xi_t, \eta_t)_{t\in\mathbb{R}_+}$ is self-financing, by Lemma 5.14 and (7.19) the discounted portfolio value $\widetilde{V}_t = e^{-rt}V_t$ satisfies

$$\widetilde{V}_t = V_0 + \int_0^t \xi_u d\widetilde{S}_u = \widetilde{V}_0 + \sigma \int_0^t \xi_u \widetilde{S}_u d\widehat{B}_u, \qquad t \geqslant 0,$$

which is a martingale under $\mathbb{P}^*$ from Proposition 7.1, hence

$$
\begin{aligned}
\widetilde{V}_t &= \mathbb{E}^*\left[\widetilde{V}_T \mid \mathcal{F}_t\right] \\
&= \mathbb{E}^*[e^{-rT}V_T \mid \mathcal{F}_t] \\
&= \mathbb{E}^*[e^{-rT}C \mid \mathcal{F}_t] \\
&= e^{-rT} \, \mathbb{E}^*[C \mid \mathcal{F}_t],
\end{aligned}
$$

which implies

$$V_t = e^{rt}\widetilde{V}_t = e^{-(T-t)r} \, \mathbb{E}^*[C \mid \mathcal{F}_t], \qquad 0 \leqslant t \leqslant T.$$

$\square$

Black–Scholes PDE for vanilla options by the martingale method

The martingale method can be used to recover the Black–Scholes PDE of Proposition 6.1. As the process $(S_t)_{t\in\mathbb{R}_+}$ has the Markov property, see Section 4.5, § V-6 of Protter (2004) and Definition 7.14 below, the value

$$
\begin{aligned}
V_t &= e^{-(T-t)r} \, \mathbb{E}^*[\phi(S_T) \mid \mathcal{F}_t] \\
&= e^{-(T-t)r} \, \mathbb{E}^*[\phi(S_T) \mid S_t], \qquad 0 \leqslant t \leqslant T,
\end{aligned}
$$

of the portfolio at time $t \in [0,T]$ can be written from (7.20) as a function

$$V_t = g(t, S_t) = e^{-(T-t)r} \, \mathbb{E}^*[\phi(S_T) \mid S_t] \tag{7.21}$$

of t and S_t, $0 \leqslant t \leqslant T$.

Proposition 7.5. *Assume that ϕ is a Lipschitz payoff function, and that $(S_t)_{t \in \mathbb{R}_+}$ is the geometric Brownian motion*

$$(S_t)_{t \in \mathbb{R}_+} = \left(S_0 \, e^{\sigma \widehat{B}_t + (r - \sigma^2/2)t} \right)_{t \in \mathbb{R}_+}$$

where $(\widehat{B}_t)_{t \in \mathbb{R}_+}$ is a standard Brownian motion under $\mathbb{P}^*$. Then, the function $g(t, x)$ defined in (7.21) is in $\mathcal{C}^{1,2}([0, T] \times \mathbb{R}_+)$ and solves the Black–Scholes PDE

$$\begin{cases} rg(t, x) = \dfrac{\partial g}{\partial t}(t, x) + rx \dfrac{\partial g}{\partial x}(t, x) + \dfrac{1}{2}x^2 \sigma^2 \dfrac{\partial^2 g}{\partial x^2}(t, x) \\[2mm] g(T, x) = \phi(x), \quad x > 0. \end{cases}$$

Proof. It can be checked by integrations by parts that the function $g(t, x)$ defined by

$$g(t, S_t) = e^{-(T-t)r} \, \mathbb{E}^*[\phi(S_T) \mid S_t] = e^{-(T-t)r} \, \mathbb{E}^*[\phi(xS_T/S_t)]_{|x=S_t},$$

$0 \leqslant t \leqslant T$, is in $\mathcal{C}^{1,2}([0, T] \times \mathbb{R}_+)$ when ϕ is a Lipschitz function, from the properties of the lognormal distribution of S_T. We note that by (4.24), the application of Itô's formula Theorem 4.24 to $V_t = g(t, S_t)$ and (7.17) with $u_t = \sigma S_t$ and $v_t = rS_t$ leads to

$$d\left(e^{-rt} g(t, S_t) \right) = -r \, e^{-rt} g(t, S_t) dt + e^{-rt} dg(t, S_t)$$

$$= -r \, e^{-rt} g(t, S_t) dt + e^{-rt} \frac{\partial g}{\partial t}(t, S_t) dt$$

$$+ e^{-rt} \frac{\partial g}{\partial x}(t, S_t) dS_t + \frac{1}{2} e^{-rt} (dS_t)^2 \frac{\partial^2 g}{\partial x^2}(t, S_t)$$

$$= -r \, e^{-rt} g(t, S_t) dt + e^{-rt} \frac{\partial g}{\partial t}(t, S_t) dt$$

$$+ v_t \, e^{-rt} \frac{\partial g}{\partial x}(t, S_t) dt + u_t \, e^{-rt} \frac{\partial g}{\partial x}(t, S_t) d\widehat{B}_t + \frac{1}{2} e^{-rt} |u_t|^2 \frac{\partial^2 g}{\partial x^2}(t, S_t) dt$$

$$= -r \, e^{-rt} g(t, S_t) dt + e^{-rt} \frac{\partial g}{\partial t}(t, S_t) dt$$

$$+ rS_t \, e^{-rt} \frac{\partial g}{\partial x}(t, S_t) dt + \frac{1}{2} e^{-rt} \sigma^2 S_t^2 \frac{\partial^2 g}{\partial x^2}(t, S_t) dt + \sigma \, e^{-rt} S_t \frac{\partial g}{\partial x}(t, S_t) d\widehat{B}_t. \quad (7.22)$$

By Lemma 5.14 and Proposition 7.1, the discounted price $\widetilde{V}_t = e^{-rt} g(t, S_t)$ of a self-financing hedging portfolio is a martingale under the risk-neutral probability measure $\mathbb{P}^*$, therefore from *e.g.* Corollary II-6-1, page 72 of Protter (2004), all terms in dt should vanish in the above expression of $d\left(e^{-rt} g(t, S_t) \right)$, showing that

$$-rg(t, S_t) + \frac{\partial g}{\partial t}(t, S_t) + rS_t \frac{\partial g}{\partial x}(t, S_t) + \frac{1}{2}\sigma^2 S_t^2 \frac{\partial^2 g}{\partial x^2}(t, S_t) = 0,$$

and leads to the Black–Scholes PDE

$$rg(t, x) = \frac{\partial g}{\partial t}(t, x) + rx \frac{\partial g}{\partial x}(t, x) + \frac{1}{2}\sigma^2 x^2 \frac{\partial^2 g}{\partial x^2}(t, x), \qquad x > 0.$$

$\square$

From (7.22) in the proof of Proposition 7.5, we also obtain the stochastic integral expression

$$\begin{aligned} e^{-rT} \phi(S_T) &= e^{-rT} g(T, S_T) \\ &= g(0, S_0) + \int_0^T d\left(e^{-rt} g(t, S_t) \right) \\ &= g(0, S_0) + \sigma \int_0^T e^{-rt} S_t \frac{\partial g}{\partial x}(t, S_t) d\widehat{B}_t, \end{aligned}$$

see also Proposition 5.14, and Proposition 7.11 below.

Forward contracts

The long forward contract with payoff $C = S_T - K$ is priced as

$$
\begin{aligned}
V_t &= e^{-(T-t)r} \, \mathbb{E}^*[S_T - K \mid \mathcal{F}_t] \\
&= e^{-(T-t)r} \, \mathbb{E}^*[S_T \mid \mathcal{F}_t] - K e^{-(T-t)r} \\
&= S_t - K e^{-(T-t)r}, \quad 0 \leqslant t \leqslant T,
\end{aligned}
$$

which recovers the Black–Scholes PDE solution (6.9), *i.e.*

$$
g(t, x) = x - K e^{-(T-t)r}, \qquad x > 0, \quad 0 \leqslant t \leqslant T.
$$

European call options

In the case of European call options with payoff function $\phi(x) = (x - K)^+$ we recover the Black–Scholes formula (6.11), cf. Proposition 6.11, by a probabilistic argument.

Proposition 7.6. *The price at time $t \in [0, T]$ of the European call option with strike price K and maturity T is given by*

$$
\begin{aligned}
g(t, S_t) &= e^{-(T-t)r} \, \mathbb{E}^*\big[(S_T - K)^+ \mid \mathcal{F}_t\big] \qquad\qquad (7.23) \\
&= S_t \Phi\big(d_+(T - t)\big) - K e^{-(T-t)r} \Phi\big(d_-(T - t)\big), \quad 0 \leqslant t \leqslant T,
\end{aligned}
$$

with

$$
\begin{cases}
d_+(T - t) := \dfrac{\log(S_t / K) + (r + \sigma^2/2)(T - t)}{\sigma\sqrt{T - t}}, \\[3mm]
d_-(T - t) := \dfrac{\log(S_t / K) + (r - \sigma^2/2)(T - t)}{\sigma\sqrt{T - t}}, \quad 0 \leqslant t < T,
\end{cases}
$$

where "log" denotes the natural logarithm *"ln" and Φ is the standard Gaussian Cumulative Distribution Function.*

Proof. The proof of Proposition 7.6 is a consequence of (7.20) and Lemma 7.7 below. Using the relation

$$
\begin{aligned}
S_T &= S_0 \, e^{rT + \sigma \widehat{B}_T - \sigma^2 T/2} \\
&= S_t \, e^{(T-t)r + (\widehat{B}_T - \widehat{B}_t)\sigma - (T-t)\sigma^2/2}, \qquad 0 \leqslant t \leqslant T,
\end{aligned}
$$

that follows from (7.18), by Theorem 7.4 the value at time $t \in [0, T]$ of the portfolio hedging C is given by

$$
\begin{aligned}
V_t &= e^{-(T-t)r} \, \mathbb{E}^*[C \mid \mathcal{F}_t] \\
&= e^{-(T-t)r} \, \mathbb{E}^*\big[(S_T - K)^+ \mid \mathcal{F}_t\big] \\
&= e^{-(T-t)r} \, \mathbb{E}^*\big[(S_t \, e^{(T-t)r + (\widehat{B}_T - \widehat{B}_t)\sigma - (T-t)\sigma^2/2} - K)^+ \mid \mathcal{F}_t\big] \\
&= e^{-(T-t)r} \, \mathbb{E}^*\big[(x \, e^{(T-t)r + (\widehat{B}_T - \widehat{B}_t)\sigma - (T-t)\sigma^2/2} - K)^+\big]_{|x=S_t} \\
&= e^{-(T-t)r} \, \mathbb{E}^*\big[(e^{m(x) + X} - K)^+\big]_{|x=S_t}, \qquad 0 \leqslant t \leqslant T,
\end{aligned}
$$

where

$$m(x) := (T-t)r - \frac{\sigma^2}{2}(T-t) + \log x$$

and

$$X := (\widehat{B}_T - \widehat{B}_t)\sigma \simeq \mathcal{N}(0, (T-t)\sigma^2)$$

is a centered Gaussian random variable with variance

$$\operatorname{Var}[X] = \operatorname{Var}\left[(\widehat{B}_T - \widehat{B}_t)\sigma\right] = \sigma^2 \operatorname{Var}\left[\widehat{B}_T - \widehat{B}_t\right] = (T-t)\sigma^2$$

under $\mathbb{P}^*$. Hence by Lemma 7.7 below we have

$$
\begin{aligned}
g(t, S_t) &= V_t \\
&= e^{-(T-t)r}\, \mathbb{E}^*\left[\left(e^{m(x)+X} - K\right)^+\right]_{|x=S_t} \\
&= e^{-(T-t)r}\, e^{m(S_t)+\sigma^2(T-t)/2}\Phi\left(v + \frac{m(S_t) - \log K}{v}\right) \\
&\quad - K\, e^{-(T-t)r}\Phi\left(\frac{m(S_t) - \log K}{v}\right) \\
&= S_t \Phi\left(v + \frac{m(S_t) - \log K}{v}\right) - K\, e^{-(T-t)r}\Phi\left(\frac{m(S_t) - \log K}{v}\right) \\
&= S_t \Phi\big(d_+(T-t)\big) - K\, e^{-(T-t)r}\Phi\big(d_-(T-t)\big),
\end{aligned}
$$

$0 \leqslant t \leqslant T$. $\square$

Relation (7.23) can also be written as

$$
\begin{aligned}
e^{-(T-t)r}\, \mathbb{E}^*\left[(S_T - K)^+ \mid \mathcal{F}_t\right] &= e^{-(T-t)r}\, \mathbb{E}^*\left[(S_T - K)^+ \mid S_t\right] \qquad (7.24) \\
&= S_t \Phi\left(\frac{\log(S_t/K) + (r + \sigma^2/2)(T-t)}{\sigma\sqrt{T-t}}\right) \\
&\quad - K\, e^{-(T-t)r}\Phi\left(\frac{\log(S_t/K) + (r - \sigma^2/2)(T-t)}{\sigma\sqrt{T-t}}\right), \qquad 0 \leqslant t \leqslant T.
\end{aligned}
$$

Lemma 7.7. *Let $X \simeq \mathcal{N}(0, v^2)$ be a centered Gaussian random variable with variance $v^2 > 0$. We have*

$$\mathbb{E}\left[(e^{m+X} - K)^+\right] = e^{m+v^2/2}\Phi(v + (m - \log K)/v) - K\Phi((m - \log K)/v).$$

Proof. We have

$$
\begin{aligned}
\mathbb{E}\left[(e^{m+X} - K)^+\right] &= \frac{1}{\sqrt{2\pi v^2}}\int_{-\infty}^{\infty}(e^{m+x} - K)^+ e^{-x^2/(2v^2)}dx \\
&= \frac{1}{\sqrt{2\pi v^2}}\int_{-m+\log K}^{\infty}(e^{m+x} - K)\, e^{-x^2/(2v^2)}dx \\
&= \frac{e^m}{\sqrt{2\pi v^2}}\int_{-m+\log K}^{\infty} e^{x-x^2/(2v^2)}dx - \frac{K}{\sqrt{2\pi v^2}}\int_{-m+\log K}^{\infty} e^{-x^2/(2v^2)}dx \\
&= \frac{e^{m+v^2/2}}{\sqrt{2\pi v^2}}\int_{-m+\log K}^{\infty} e^{-(v^2-x)^2/(2v^2)}dx - \frac{K}{\sqrt{2\pi}}\int_{(-m+\log K)/v}^{\infty} e^{-y^2/2}dy \\
&= \frac{e^{m+v^2/2}}{\sqrt{2\pi v^2}}\int_{-v^2-m+\log K}^{\infty} e^{-y^2/(2v^2)}dy - K\Phi((m - \log K)/v) \\
&= e^{m+v^2/2}\Phi(v + (m - \log K)/v) - K\Phi((m - \log K)/v),
\end{aligned}
$$

where we used Relation (6.15). $\square$

Call-put parity

Let

$$P(t, S_t) := e^{-(T-t)r} \, \mathbb{E}^* \left[(K - S_T)^+ \mid \mathcal{F}_t \right], \qquad 0 \leqslant t \leqslant T,$$

denote the price of the put option with strike price K and maturity T.

Proposition 7.8. *Call-put parity. We have the relation*

$$C(t, S_t) - P(t, S_t) = S_t - e^{-(T-t)r} K \tag{7.25}$$

between the Black–Scholes prices of call and put options, in terms of the forward contract price $S_t - K e^{-(T-t)r}$.

Proof. From Theorem 7.4, we have

$$
\begin{aligned}
&C(t, S_t) - P(t, S_t) \\
&= e^{-(T-t)r} \, \mathbb{E}^*[(S_T - K)^+ \mid \mathcal{F}_t] - e^{-(T-t)r} \, \mathbb{E}^*[(K - S_T)^+ \mid \mathcal{F}_t] \\
&= e^{-(T-t)r} \, \mathbb{E}^*[(S_T - K)^+ - (K - S_T)^+ \mid \mathcal{F}_t] \\
&= e^{-(T-t)r} \, \mathbb{E}^*[S_T - K \mid \mathcal{F}_t] \\
&= e^{-(T-t)r} \, \mathbb{E}^*[S_T \mid \mathcal{F}_t] - K e^{-(T-t)r} \\
&= S_t - e^{-(T-t)r} K, \qquad 0 \leqslant t \leqslant T,
\end{aligned}
$$

as we have $\mathbb{E}^*[S_T \mid \mathcal{F}_t] = e^{(T-t)r} S_t$, $t \in [0, T]$, under the risk-neutral probability measure $\mathbb{P}^*$. $\qquad\square$

European put options

Using the *call-put parity* Relation (7.25) we can recover the European put option price (6.11) from the European call option price (6.11)–(7.23).

Proposition 7.9. *The price at time $t \in [0, T]$ of the European put option with strike price K and maturity T is given by*

$$
\begin{aligned}
P(t, S_t) &= e^{-(T-t)r} \, \mathbb{E}^*[(K - S_T)^+ \mid \mathcal{F}_t] \\
&= K e^{-(T-t)r} \Phi\left(-d_-(T - t) \right) - S_t \Phi\left(-d_+(T - t) \right), \quad 0 \leqslant t \leqslant T,
\end{aligned}
$$

with

$$
\begin{cases}
d_+(T - t) := \dfrac{\log(S_t/K) + (r + \sigma^2/2)(T - t)}{\sigma\sqrt{T - t}}, \\[2ex]
d_-(T - t) := \dfrac{\log(S_t/K) + (r - \sigma^2/2)(T - t)}{\sigma\sqrt{T - t}}, \quad 0 \leqslant t < T,
\end{cases}
$$

where "log" denotes the natural logarithm *"ln" and Φ is the standard Gaussian Cumulative Distribution Function.*

Proof. By the *call-put parity* (7.25), we have

$$
\begin{aligned}
P(t, S_t) &= C(t, S_t) - S_t + e^{-(T-t)r} K \\
&= S_t \Phi\left(d_+(T - t) \right) + e^{-(T-t)r} K - S_t - e^{-(T-t)r} K \Phi\left(d_-(T - t) \right)
\end{aligned}
$$

$$
\begin{aligned}
&= -S_t\big(1 - \Phi\big(d_+(T-t)\big)\big) + e^{-(T-t)r}K\big(1 - \Phi\big(d_-(T-t)\big)\big) \\
&= -S_t\Phi\big(-d_+(T-t)\big) + e^{-(T-t)r}K\Phi\big(-d_-(T-t)\big).
\end{aligned}
$$

$\square$

7.5 Hedging by the Martingale Method

Hedging exotic options

In the next Proposition 7.10 we compute a self-financing hedging strategy leading to an arbitrary square-integrable random claim payoff $C \in L^2(\Omega)$ of an exotic option admitting a stochastic integral decomposition of the form

$$
C = \mathbb{E}^*[C] + \int_0^T \zeta_t d\widehat{B}_t, \tag{7.26}
$$

where $(\zeta_t)_{t\in[0,t]}$ is a square-integrable adapted process, see for example page 163. Consequently, the mathematical problem of finding the stochastic integral decomposition (7.26) of a given random variable has important applications in finance. The process $(\zeta_t)_{t\in[0,T]}$ can be computed using the Malliavin gradient on the Wiener space, see, *e.g.* Di Nunno et al. (2009) or § 8.2 of Privault (2009).

Simple examples of stochastic integral decompositions include the relations

$$
(B_T)^2 = T + 2\int_0^T B_t dB_t,
$$

cf. Exercises 6.1 and 7.1, and

$$
(B_T)^3 = 3\int_0^T \big(T - t + B_t^2\big)dB_t,
$$

see Exercise 4.10. In the sequel, recall that the risky asset follows the equation

$$
\frac{dS_t}{S_t} = \mu dt + \sigma dB_t, \qquad t \geqslant 0, \qquad S_0 > 0,
$$

and by (7.16), the discounted asset price $\widetilde{S}_t := e^{-rt}S_t$

$$
d\widetilde{S}_t = \sigma\widetilde{S}_t d\widehat{B}_t, \qquad t \geqslant 0, \qquad \widetilde{S}_0 = S_0 > 0, \tag{7.27}
$$

where $(\widehat{B}_t)_{t\in\mathbb{R}_+}$ is a standard Brownian motion under the risk-neutral probability measure $\mathbb{P}^*$. The following proposition applies to arbitrary square-integrable payoff functions, in particular it covers exotic and path-dependent options.

Proposition 7.10. *Consider a random claim payoff $C \in L^2(\Omega)$ and the process $(\zeta_t)_{t\in[0,T]}$ given by (7.26), and let*

$$
\xi_t = \frac{e^{-(T-t)r}}{\sigma S_t}\zeta_t, \tag{7.28}
$$

$$
\eta_t = \frac{e^{-(T-t)r}\,\mathbb{E}^*[C \mid \mathcal{F}_t] - \xi_t S_t}{A_t}, \qquad 0 \leqslant t \leqslant T. \tag{7.29}
$$

Then, the portfolio allocation $(\xi_t, \eta_t)_{t \in [0,T]}$ *is self-financing, and letting*

$$V_t = \eta_t A_t + \xi_t S_t, \qquad 0 \leqslant t \leqslant T, \tag{7.30}$$

we have

$$V_t = e^{-(T-t)r} \, \mathbb{E}^*[C \mid \mathcal{F}_t], \qquad 0 \leqslant t \leqslant T. \tag{7.31}$$

In particular we have

$$V_T = C, \tag{7.32}$$

i.e. the portfolio allocation $(\xi_t, \eta_t)_{t \in [0,T]}$ *yields a hedging strategy leading to the claim payoff C at maturity, after starting from the initial value*

$$V_0 = e^{-rT} \, \mathbb{E}^*[C].$$

Proof. Relation (7.31) follows from (7.29) and (7.30), and it implies

$$V_0 = e^{-rT} \, \mathbb{E}^*[C] = \eta_0 A_0 + \xi_0 S_0$$

at $t = 0$, and (7.32) at $t = T$. It remains to show that the portfolio strategy $(\xi_t, \eta_t)_{t \in [0,T]}$ is self-financing. By (7.26) and Proposition 7.1 we have

$$
\begin{aligned}
V_t &= \eta_t A_t + \xi_t S_t \\
&= e^{-(T-t)r} \, \mathbb{E}^*[C \mid \mathcal{F}_t] \\
&= e^{-(T-t)r} \, \mathbb{E}^* \left[\mathbb{E}^*[C] + \int_0^T \zeta_u d\widehat{B}_u \;\middle|\; \mathcal{F}_t \right] \\
&= e^{-(T-t)r} \left(\mathbb{E}^*[C] + \int_0^t \zeta_u d\widehat{B}_u \right) \\
&= e^{rt} V_0 + e^{-(T-t)r} \int_0^t \zeta_u d\widehat{B}_u \\
&= e^{rt} V_0 + \sigma \int_0^t \xi_u S_u e^{(t-u)r} d\widehat{B}_u \\
&= e^{rt} V_0 + \sigma e^{rt} \int_0^t \xi_u \widetilde{S}_u d\widehat{B}_u.
\end{aligned}
$$

By (7.27) this shows that the portfolio strategy $(\xi_t, \eta_t)_{t \in [0,T]}$ given by (7.28)–(7.29) and its discounted portfolio value $\widetilde{V}_t := e^{-rt} V_t$ satisfy

$$\widetilde{V}_t = V_0 + \int_0^t \xi_u d\widetilde{S}_u, \qquad 0 \leqslant t \leqslant T,$$

which implies that $(\xi_t, \eta_t)_{t \in [0,T]}$ is self-financing by Lemma 5.14. $\qquad \square$

The above proposition shows that there always exists a hedging strategy starting from

$$V_0 = \mathbb{E}^*[C] e^{-rT}.$$

In addition, since there exists a hedging strategy leading to

$$\widetilde{V}_T = e^{-rT} C,$$

then $(\widetilde{V}_t)_{t \in [0,T]}$ is necessarily a martingale, with

$$\widetilde{V}_t = \mathbb{E}^* \left[\widetilde{V}_T \mid \mathcal{F}_t \right] = e^{-rT} \, \mathbb{E}^*[C \mid \mathcal{F}_t], \qquad 0 \leqslant t \leqslant T,$$

and initial value

$$\widetilde{V}_0 = \mathbb{E}^* \left[\widetilde{V}_T \right] = e^{-rT} \, \mathbb{E}^*[C].$$

Hedging vanilla options

In practice, the hedging problem can now be reduced to the computation of the process $(\zeta_t)_{t\in[0,T]}$ appearing in (7.26). This computation, called Delta hedging, can be performed by the application of the Itô formula and the Markov property, see *e.g.* Protter (2001). The next lemma allows us to compute the process $(\zeta_t)_{t\in[0,T]}$ in case the payoff C is of the form $C = \phi(S_T)$ for some function ϕ.

Proposition 7.11. *Assume that ϕ is a Lipschitz payoff function. Then, the function $C(t,x)$ defined from the Markov property of $(S_t)_{t\in[0,T]}$ by*

$$C(t,S_t) := \mathbb{E}^*[\phi(S_T) \mid \mathcal{S}_t] = \mathbb{E}^*[\phi(S_T) \mid S_t]$$

is in $\mathcal{C}^{1,2}([0,T]\times\mathbb{R})$, and the stochastic integral decomposition

$$\phi(S_T) = \mathbb{E}^*\left[\phi(S_T)\right] + \int_0^T \zeta_t d\widehat{B}_t \tag{7.33}$$

is given by

$$\zeta_t = \sigma S_t \frac{\partial C}{\partial x}(t,S_t), \qquad 0 \leqslant t \leqslant T. \tag{7.34}$$

In addition, the self-financing hedging strategy $(\xi_t)_{t\in[0,T]}$ satisfies

$$\xi_t = e^{-(T-t)r}\frac{\partial C}{\partial x}(t,S_t), \qquad 0 \leqslant t \leqslant T. \tag{7.35}$$

Proof. It can be checked as in the proof of Proposition 7.5 the function $C(t,x)$ is in $\mathcal{C}^{1,2}([0,T]\times\mathbb{R})$. Therefore, we can apply the Itô formula to the process

$$t \mapsto C(t,S_t) = \mathbb{E}^*[\phi(S_T) \mid \mathcal{F}_t],$$

which is a martingale from the tower property of conditional expectations as in (7.42). From the fact that the finite variation term in the Itô formula vanishes when $(C(t,S_t))_{t\in[0,T]}$ is a martingale, (see *e.g.* Corollary II-6-1 page 72 of Protter (2004)), we obtain:

$$C(t,S_t) = C(0,S_0) + \sigma\int_0^t S_u \frac{\partial C}{\partial x}(u,S_u)d\widehat{B}_u, \quad 0 \leqslant t \leqslant T, \tag{7.36}$$

with $C(0,S_0) = \mathbb{E}^*[\phi(S_T)]$. Letting $t = T$, we obtain (7.34) by uniqueness of the stochastic integral decomposition (7.33) of $C = \phi(S_T)$. Finally, (7.35) follows from (7.28) and (7.34) by applying Proposition 7.10. $\square$

By (7.34) and the relation

$$S_T = S_0 e^{\sigma B_T + \mu T - \sigma^2 T/2} = S_t e^{(B_T-B_t)\sigma+(T-t)\mu-(T-t)\sigma^2/2},$$

we also have

$$\begin{aligned}
\zeta_t &= \sigma S_t \left(\frac{\partial}{\partial x}\mathbb{E}^*[\phi(S_T)\mid S_t = x]\right)_{x=S_t} \\
&= \sigma S_t \left(\frac{\partial}{\partial x}\mathbb{E}^*\left[\phi\left(x\frac{S_T}{S_t}\right)\right]\right)_{x=S_t}, \qquad 0 \leqslant t \leqslant T,
\end{aligned}$$

hence

$$\xi_t = \frac{1}{\sigma S_t}e^{-(T-t)r}\zeta_t \tag{7.37}$$

$$= \mathrm{e}^{-(T-t)r} \left(\frac{\partial}{\partial x} \, \mathbb{E}^* \left[\phi \left(x \frac{S_T}{S_t} \right) \right] \right)_{x=S_t}$$

$$= \mathrm{e}^{-(T-t)r} \, \mathbb{E}^* \left[\frac{S_T}{S_t} \phi' \left(x \frac{S_T}{S_t} \right) \right]_{x=S_t}, \qquad 0 \leqslant t \leqslant T,$$

which recovers the formula (6.3) for the Delta of a vanilla option. As a consequence we have $\xi_t \geqslant 0$ and there is no short selling when the payoff function ϕ is non-decreasing.

In the case of European options, the process ζ can be computed via the next proposition which follows from Proposition 7.11 and the relation

$$C(t,x) = \mathbb{E}^* \left[f(S_{t,T}^x) \right], \qquad 0 \leqslant t \leqslant T, \; x > 0.$$

Corollary 7.12. *Assume that $C = (S_T - K)^+$. Then, for $0 \leqslant t \leqslant T$ we have*

$$\zeta_t = \sigma S_t \, \mathbb{E}^* \left[\frac{S_T}{S_t} \mathbb{1}_{[K,\infty)} \left(x \frac{S_T}{S_t} \right) \right]_{|x=S_t}, \qquad 0 \leqslant t \leqslant T, \tag{7.38}$$

and

$$\xi_t = \mathrm{e}^{-(T-t)r} \, \mathbb{E}^* \left[\frac{S_T}{S_t} \mathbb{1}_{[K,\infty)} \left(x \frac{S_T}{S_t} \right) \right]_{|x=S_t}, \qquad 0 \leqslant t \leqslant T. \tag{7.39}$$

By evaluating the expectation (7.38) in Corollary 7.12 we can recover the formula (6.16) in Proposition 6.4 for the Delta of the European call option in the Black–Scholes model. In that sense, the next proposition provides another proof of the result of Proposition 6.4.

Proposition 7.13. *The Delta of the European call option with payoff function $f(x) = (x - K)^+$ is given by*

$$\xi_t = \Phi\big(d_+(T-t)\big) = \Phi \left(\frac{\log(S_t/K) + (r + \sigma^2/2)(T-t)}{\sigma\sqrt{T-t}} \right), \qquad 0 \leqslant t \leqslant T.$$

Proof. By Proposition 7.10 and Corollary 7.12, we have

$$\xi_t = \frac{1}{\sigma S_t} \mathrm{e}^{-(T-t)r} \zeta_t$$

$$= \mathrm{e}^{-(T-t)r} \, \mathbb{E}^* \left[\frac{S_T}{S_t} \mathbb{1}_{[K,\infty)} \left(x \frac{S_T}{S_t} \right) \right]_{|x=S_t}$$

$$= \mathrm{e}^{-(T-t)r}$$

$$\times \mathbb{E}^* \left[\mathrm{e}^{(\widehat{B}_T - \widehat{B}_t)\sigma - (T-t)\sigma^2/2 + (T-t)r} \mathbb{1}_{[K,\infty)} \left(x \, \mathrm{e}^{(\widehat{B}_T - \widehat{B}_t)\sigma - (T-t)\sigma^2/2 + (T-t)r} \right) \right]_{|x=S_t}$$

$$= \frac{1}{\sqrt{2(T-t)\pi}} \int_{(T-t)\sigma/2 - (T-t)r/\sigma + \sigma^{-1}\log(K/S_t)}^{\infty} \mathrm{e}^{\sigma y - (T-t)\sigma^2/2 - y^2/(2(T-t))} dy$$

$$= \frac{1}{\sqrt{2(T-t)\pi}} \int_{-d_-(T-t)/\sqrt{T-t}}^{\infty} \mathrm{e}^{-(y-(T-t)\sigma)^2/(2(T-t))} dy$$

$$= \frac{1}{\sqrt{2\pi}} \int_{-d_-(T-t)}^{\infty} \mathrm{e}^{-(y-(T-t)\sigma)^2/2} dy$$

$$= \frac{1}{\sqrt{2\pi}} \int_{-d_+(T-t)}^{\infty} \mathrm{e}^{-y^2/2} dy$$

$$= \frac{1}{\sqrt{2\pi}} \int_{-\infty}^{d_+(T-t)} \mathrm{e}^{-y^2/2} dy$$

$$= \Phi\big(d_+(T-t)\big).$$

$\square$

Proposition 7.13, combined with Proposition 7.6, shows that the Black–Scholes self-financing hedging strategy is to hold a (possibly fractional) quantity

$$\xi_t = \Phi\big(d_+(T-t)\big) = \Phi\left(\frac{\log(S_t/K) + (r + \sigma^2/2)(T-t)}{\sigma\sqrt{T-t}}\right) \geqslant 0 \qquad (7.40)$$

of the risky asset, and to borrow a quantity

$$-\eta_t = K\,e^{-rT}\Phi\left(\frac{\log(S_t/K) + (r - \sigma_t^2/2)(T-t)}{\sigma\sqrt{T-t}}\right) \geqslant 0 \qquad (7.41)$$

of the riskless (savings) account, see also Corollary 16.18 in Chapter 16.

As noted above, the result of Proposition 7.13 recovers (6.17) which is obtained by a direct differentiation of the Black–Scholes function as in (6.3) or (7.37).

Markovian semi-groups

For completeness, we provide the definition of Markovian semi-groups which can be used to reformulate the proofs of this section.

Definition 7.14. *The Markov semi-group* $(P_t)_{0 \leqslant t \leqslant T}$ *associated to* $(S_t)_{t \in [0,T]}$ *is the mapping* P_t *defined on functions* $f \in \mathcal{C}_b^2(\mathbb{R})$ *as*

$$P_t f(x) := \mathbb{E}^*[f(S_t) \mid S_0 = x], \qquad t \geqslant 0.$$

By the Markov property and time homogeneity of $(S_t)_{t \in [0,T]}$ we also have

$$P_t f(S_u) := \mathbb{E}^*[f(S_{t+u}) \mid \mathcal{F}_u] = \mathbb{E}^*[f(S_{t+u}) \mid S_u], \qquad t, u \geqslant 0,$$

and the semi-group $(P_t)_{0 \leqslant t \leqslant T}$ satisfies the composition property

$$P_s P_t = P_t P_s = P_{s+t} = P_{t+s}, \qquad s, t \geqslant 0,$$

as we have, using the Markov property and the tower property of conditional expectations as in (7.42),

$$\begin{aligned}
P_s P_t f(x) &= \mathbb{E}^*[P_t f(S_s) \mid S_0 = x] \\
&= \mathbb{E}^*\big[\,\mathbb{E}^*[f(S_t) \mid S_0 = y]_{y=S_s} \mid S_0 = x\big] \\
&= \mathbb{E}^*\big[\,\mathbb{E}^*[f(S_{t+s}) \mid S_s = y]_{y=S_s} \mid S_0 = x\big] \\
&= \mathbb{E}^*\big[\,\mathbb{E}^*[f(S_{t+s}) \mid \mathcal{F}_s] \mid S_0 = x\big] \\
&= \mathbb{E}^*[f(S_{t+s}) \mid S_0 = x] \\
&= P_{t+s} f(x), \qquad s, t \geqslant 0.
\end{aligned}$$

Similarly, we can show that the process $(P_{T-t}f(S_t))_{t \in [0,T]}$ is an $\mathcal{F}_t$-martingale as in Example (*i*) above, see (7.1), *i.e.*:

$$\begin{aligned}
\mathbb{E}^*[P_{T-t}f(S_t) \mid \mathcal{F}_u] &= \mathbb{E}^*\big[\,\mathbb{E}^*[f(S_T) \mid \mathcal{F}_t] \mid \mathcal{F}_u\big] \\
&= \mathbb{E}^*[f(S_T) \mid \mathcal{F}_u] \\
&= P_{T-u}f(S_u), \qquad 0 \leqslant u \leqslant t \leqslant T, \qquad (7.42)
\end{aligned}$$

and we have

$$P_{t-u}f(x) = \mathbb{E}^*[f(S_t) \mid S_u = x] = \mathbb{E}^*\left[f\left(x\frac{S_t}{S_u}\right)\right], \qquad 0 \leqslant u \leqslant t. \qquad (7.43)$$

Exercises

Exercise 7.1   (Exercise 6.1 continued). Consider a market made of a riskless asset priced $A_t = A_0$ with zero interest rate, $t \geqslant 0$, and a risky asset whose price modeled by a standard Brownian motion as $S_t = B_t$, $t \geqslant 0$. Price the vanilla option with payoff $C = (B_T)^2$, and recover the solution of the Black–Scholes PDE of Exercise 6.1.

Exercise 7.2   Given the price process $(S_t)_{t \in \mathbb{R}_+}$ defined as the geometric Brownian motion

$$S_t := S_0 \, e^{\sigma B_t + (r - \sigma^2/2)t}, \qquad t \geqslant 0,$$

price the option with payoff function $\phi(S_T)$ by writing $e^{-rT} \, \mathbb{E}^*[\phi(S_T)]$ as an integral with respect to the lognormal probability density function, see Exercise 5.1.

Exercise 7.3   (See Exercise 6.15). Consider an asset price $(S_t)_{t \in \mathbb{R}_+}$ given by the stochastic differential equation

$$dS_t = r S_t dt + \sigma S_t dB_t, \tag{7.44}$$

where $(B_t)_{t \in \mathbb{R}_+}$ is a standard Brownian motion, with $r \in \mathbb{R}$ and $\sigma > 0$.

a) Find the stochastic differential equation satisfied by the power $(S_t^p)_{t \in \mathbb{R}_+}$ of order $p \in \mathbb{R}$ of $(S_t)_{t \in \mathbb{R}_+}$.

b) Using the Girsanov Theorem 7.3 and the discounting Lemma 5.13, construct a probability measure under which the discounted process $(e^{-rt} S_t^p)_{t \in \mathbb{R}_+}$ is a martingale.

Exercise 7.4   Consider an asset price process $(S_t)_{t \in \mathbb{R}_+}$ which is a martingale under the risk-neutral probability measure $\mathbb{P}^*$ in a market with interest rate $r = 0$, and let ϕ be a convex payoff function. Show that, for any two maturities $T_1 < T_2$ and $p, q \in [0,1]$ such that $p + q = 1$ we have

$$\mathbb{E}^*[\phi(pS_{T_1} + qS_{T_2})] \leqslant \mathbb{E}^*[\phi(S_{T_2})],$$

i.e. the price of the basket option with payoff $\phi(pS_{T_1} + qS_{T_2})$ is upper bounded by the price of the option with payoff $\phi(S_{T_2})$.

Hints:

i) For ϕ a convex function we have $\phi(px + qy) \leqslant p\phi(x) + q\phi(y)$ for any $x, y \in \mathbb{R}$ and $p, q \in [0,1]$ such that $p + q = 1$.

ii) Any convex function $(\phi(S_t))_{t \in \mathbb{R}_+}$ of a martingale $(S_t)_{t \in \mathbb{R}_+}$ is a *sub*martingale.

Exercise 7.5   Consider an underlying asset price process $(S_t)_{t \in \mathbb{R}_+}$ under a risk-neutral measure $\mathbb{P}^*$ with risk-free interest rate r.

a) Does the European *call* option price $C(K) := e^{-rT} \, \mathbb{E}^*[(S_T - K)^+]$ increase or decrease with the strike price K? Justify your answer.

b) Does the European *put* option price $C(K) := e^{-rT} \, \mathbb{E}^*[(K - S_T)^+]$ increase or decrease with the strike price K? Justify your answer.

Exercise 7.6 Consider an underlying asset price process $(S_t)_{t\in\mathbb{R}_+}$ under a risk-neutral measure $\mathbb{P}^*$ with risk-free interest rate r.

a) Show that the price at time t of the European call option with strike price K and maturity T is lower bounded by the positive part $\left(S_t - K e^{-(T-t)r}\right)^+$ of the corresponding forward contract price, *i.e.* we have the *model-free* bound

$$e^{-(T-t)r}\, \mathbb{E}^*[(S_T - K)^+ \mid \mathcal{F}_t] \geqslant \left(S_t - K e^{-(T-t)r}\right)^+, \quad 0 \leqslant t \leqslant T.$$

b) Show that the price at time t of the European put option with strike price K and maturity T is lower bounded by $K e^{-(T-t)r} - S_t$, *i.e.* we have the *model-free* bound

$$e^{-(T-t)r}\, \mathbb{E}^*[(K - S_T)^+ \mid \mathcal{F}_t] \geqslant \left(K e^{-(T-t)r} - S_t\right)^+, \quad 0 \leqslant t \leqslant T.$$

Exercise 7.7 The following two graphs describe the payoff functions ϕ of *bull spread* and *bear spread* options with payoff $\phi(S_N)$ on an underlying asset priced S_N at maturity time N.

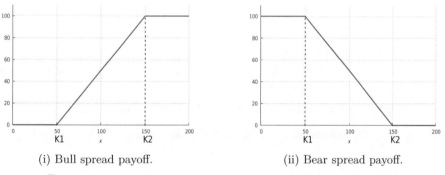

(i) Bull spread payoff. (ii) Bear spread payoff.

Figure 7.3: Payoff functions of bull spread and bear spread options.

a) Show that in each case (i) and (ii) the corresponding option can be realized by purchasing and/or short selling standard European call and put options with strike prices to be specified.

b) Price the bull spread option in cases (i) and (ii) using the Black–Scholes formula.

Hint: An option with payoff $\phi(S_T)$ is priced $e^{-rT}\, \mathbb{E}^*[\phi(S_T)]$ at time 0. The payoff of the European call (resp. put) option with strike price K is $(S_T - K)^+$, resp. $(K - S_T)^+$.

Exercise 7.8 Given two strike prices $K_1 < K_2$, we consider a long box spread option with maturity $N \geqslant 1$, realized as the combination of four legs:

- One *long* call with strike price K_1 and payoff function $(x - K_1)^+$,

- One *short* put with strike price K_1 and payoff function $-(K_1 - x)^+$,

- One *short* call with strike price K_2 and payoff function $-(x - K_2)^+$,

- One *long* put with strike price K_2 and payoff function $(K_2 - x)^+$.

The risk-free interest rate is denoted by $r \geqslant 0$.

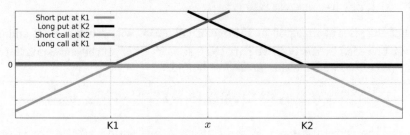

Figure 7.4: Graphs of call/put payoff functions.

a) Find the payoff of the long box spread option in terms of K_1 and K_2.

b) Price the long box spread option at times $k = 0, 1, \ldots, N$ using K_1, K_2 and the interest rate r.

c) From Table 7.1 below, find a choice of strike prices $K_1 < K_2$ that can be used to build a long box spread option on the Hang Seng Index (HSI).

d) Price the option built in part (c) in index points, and then in HK\$.

Hints.

i) The closing prices in Table 7.1 are warrant prices quoted in index points.

ii) Warrant prices are converted to option prices by multiplication by the number given in the "Entitlement Ratio" column.

iii) The conversion from index points to HK\$ is given in Table 7.2.

e) Would you buy the option priced in part (d) ? Here we can take $r = 0$ for simplicity.

DERIVATIVE WARRANT SEARCH

Link to Relevant Exchange Traded Options

Updated: 2 March 2021

| | | | | | Basic Data | | | | | | | | | | | Market Data | | | |
DW Code	Issuer	UL	Call/Put	DW Type	Listing (D-M-Y)	Maturity (D-M-Y)	Strike Currency	Strike	Entitle-ment Ratio^	Total Issue Size	O/S (%)	Delta (%)	IV. (%)	Trading Currency	Day High	Day Low	Closing Price	T/O ('000)
17334	HT	HSI	Put	Standard	12-11-2020	28-05-2021		-24600	10000	400,000,000	5.11	(0.001)	33.268	HKD	0.034	0.025	0.034	314
17535	UB	HSI	Put	Standard	13-11-2020	28-05-2021		-24600	10000	300,000,000	22.07	(0.001)	29.507	HKD	0.025	0.017	0.023	132
17589	CS	HSI	Put	Standard	13-11-2020	28-05-2021		-24900	9500	425,000,000	8.61	(0.001)	30.838	HKD	0.033	0.028	0.033	80
18242	UB	HSI	Put	Standard	19-11-2020	28-05-2021		-25000	9500	300,000,000	18.51	(0.001)	29.028	HKD	0.030	0.023	0.029	265
18606	SG	HSI	Put	Standard	23-11-2020	29-06-2021		-25088	10000	300,000,000	8.01	(0.002)	30.968	HKD	0.054	0.042	0.053	459
19399	HT	HSI	Put	Standard	02-12-2020	29-06-2021		-25200	10000	400,000,000	0.06	(0.002)	32.190	HKD	0.000	0.000	0.061	0
19485	BI	HSI	Put	Standard	03-12-2020	29-06-2021		-25200	10000	150,000,000	21.41	(0.002)	28.154	HKD	0.044	0.037	0.044	59
22857	VT	HSI	Put	Standard	27-02-2020	29-06-2021		-25000	8000	80,000,000	22.45	(0.002)	30.905	HKD	0.065	0.043	0.064	1,165
26601	BI	HSI	Call	Standard	28-12-2020	29-06-2021		-25200	11000	150,000,000	0.00	0.018	25.347	HKD	0.390	0.360	0.370	84
27489	BP	HSI	Call	Standard	18-09-2020	29-06-2021		-25000	7500	80,000,000	2.95	0.009	28.392	HKD	0.590	0.540	0.540	6
28231	HS	HSI	Call	Standard	30-09-2020	29-06-2021		-25118	7500	200,000,000	0.00	0.012	24.897	HKD	0.000	0.000	0.570	0

^ The entitlement ratio in general represents the number of derivative warrants required to be exercised into one share or one unit of the underlying asset (subject to any adjustments as may be necessary to reflect any capitalization, rights issue, distribution or the like).

Delayed data on Delta and Implied Volatility of Derivative Warrants are provided by Reuters.
Users should not use such data provided by Reuters for commercial purposes without its prior written consent.

For underlying stock price, please refer to Securities Prices of Market Data.

Table 7.1: Call and put options on the Hang Seng Index (HSI).

CONTRACT SUMMARY		
Item	**Standard Options**	**Flexible Options**
Underlying Index	Hang Seng Index	
HKATS Code	HSI	XHS
Contract Multiplier	HK$50 per index point	
Minimum Fluctuation	One index point	
Contract Months	Short-dated Options:- Spot, next three calendar months & next three calendar quarter months and Long-dated Options:- the next 3 months of June & December and the following 3 December months	Any calendar month not further out than the longest term of expiry months that are available for trading
Exercise Style	European Style	
Option Premium	Quoted in whole index points	

Table 7.2: Contract summary.

Exercise 7.9 Butterfly options. A long call butterfly option is designed to deliver a limited payoff when the future volatility of the underlying asset is expected to be low. The payoff function of a long call butterfly option is plotted in Figure 7.5, with $K_1 := 50$ and $K_2 := 150$.

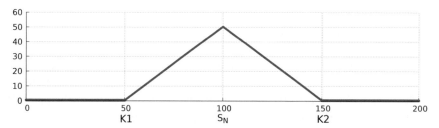

Figure 7.5: Long call butterfly payoff function.

a) Show that the long call butterfly option can be realized by purchasing and/or issuing standard European call or put options with strike prices to be specified.

b) Price the long call butterfly option using the Black–Scholes formula.

c) Does the hedging strategy of the long call butterfly option involve holding or shorting the underlying stock?

Hints: Recall that an option with payoff $\phi(S_N)$ is priced in discrete time as $(1+r)^{-N}\,\mathbb{E}^*[\phi(S_N)]$ at time 0. The payoff of the European call (resp. put) option with strike price K is $(S_N - K)^+$, resp. $(K - S_N)^+$.

Exercise 7.10 Forward contracts revisited. Consider a risky asset whose price S_t is given by $S_t = S_0\,e^{\sigma B_t + rt - \sigma^2 t/2}$, $t \geqslant 0$, where $(B_t)_{t\in\mathbb{R}_+}$ is a standard Brownian motion. Consider a forward contract with maturity T and payoff $S_T - \kappa$.

a) Compute the price C_t of this claim at any time $t \in [0,T]$.

b) Compute a hedging strategy for the option with payoff $S_T - \kappa$.

Exercise 7.11 Option pricing with dividends (Exercise 6.3 continued). Consider an underlying asset price process $(S_t)_{t \in \mathbb{R}_+}$ paying dividends at the continuous-time rate $\delta > 0$, and modeled as

$$dS_t = (\mu - \delta)S_t dt + \sigma S_t dB_t,$$

where $(B_t)_{t \in \mathbb{R}_+}$ is a standard Brownian motion.

a) Show that as in Lemma 5.14, if $(\eta_t, \xi_t)_{t \in \mathbb{R}_+}$ is a portfolio strategy with value

$$V_t = \eta_t A_t + \xi_t S_t, \qquad t \geqslant 0,$$

where the dividend yield δS_t per share is continuously reinvested in the portfolio, then the discounted portfolio value $\widetilde{V}_t$ can be written as the stochastic integral

$$\widetilde{V}_t = \widetilde{V}_0 + \int_0^t \xi_u d\widetilde{S}_u, \qquad t \geqslant 0,$$

b) Show that, as in Theorem 7.4, if $(\xi_t, \eta_t)_{t \in [0,T]}$ hedges the claim payoff C, *i.e.* if $V_T = C$, then the arbitrage-free price of the claim payoff C is given by

$$\pi_t(C) = V_t = e^{-(T-t)r} \mathbb{E}^*[C \mid \mathcal{F}_t], \qquad 0 \leqslant t \leqslant T,$$

where $\mathbb{E}^*$ denotes expectation under a risk-neutral probability measure $\mathbb{P}^*$.

c) Compute the price at time $t \in [0, T]$ of a European call option in a market with dividend rate δ by the martingale method.

d) Compute the Delta of the option.

Exercise 7.12 Forward start options (Rubinstein (1991)). A *forward start* European call option is an option whose holder receives at time T_1 (*e.g.* your birthday) the value of a standard European call option *at the money* and with maturity $T_2 > T_1$. Price this birthday present at any time $t \in [0, T_1]$, *i.e.* compute the price

$$e^{-(T_1-t)r} \mathbb{E}^* \left[e^{-(T_2-T_1)r} \mathbb{E}^* \left[(S_{T_2} - S_{T_1})^+ \mid \mathcal{F}_{T_1} \right] \mid \mathcal{F}_t \right]$$

at time $t \in [0, T_1]$, of the *forward start* European call option using the Black–Scholes formula

$$\begin{aligned} \mathrm{Bl}(x, K, \sigma, r, T - t) \; = \; & x \Phi \left(\frac{\log(x/K) + (r + \sigma^2/2)(T-t)}{|\sigma|\sqrt{T-t}} \right) \\ & - K e^{-(T-t)r} \Phi \left(\frac{\log(x/K) + (r - \sigma^2/2)(T-t)}{|\sigma|\sqrt{T-t}} \right), \end{aligned}$$

$0 \leqslant t < T$.

Exercise 7.13 Cliquet option. Let $0 = T_0 < T_1 < \cdots < T_n$ denote a sequence of financial settlement dates, and consider a risky asset priced as the geometric Brownian motion $S_t = S_0 e^{\sigma B_t + rt - \sigma^2 t/2}$, $t \geqslant 0$, where $(B_t)_{t \in \mathbb{R}_+}$ is a standard Brownian motion under the risk-neutral measure $\mathbb{P}^*$. Compute the price at time $t = 0$ of the cliquet option whose payoff consists in the sum of n payments $(S_{T_k}/S_{T_{k-1}} - K)^+$ made at times T_k, $k = 1, \ldots, n$. For this, use the Black–Scholes formula

$$\begin{aligned} e^{-rT} \mathbb{E}^*[(S_T - \kappa)^+] \; = \; & S_0 \Phi \left(\frac{\log(S_0/\kappa) + (r + \sigma^2/2)T}{|\sigma|\sqrt{T}} \right) \\ & - \kappa e^{-rT} \Phi \left(\frac{\log(S_0/\kappa) + (r - \sigma^2/2)T}{|\sigma|\sqrt{T}} \right), \qquad T > 0. \end{aligned}$$

Exercise 7.14 Log contracts. (Exercise 6.9 continued), see also Exercise 8.6. Consider the price process $(S_t)_{t \in [0,T]}$ given by

$$\frac{dS_t}{S_t} = rdt + \sigma dB_t$$

and a riskless asset valued $A_t = A_0 e^{rt}$, $t \in [0,T]$, with $r > 0$. Compute the arbitrage-free price

$$C(t, S_t) = e^{-(T-t)r} \, \mathbb{E}^*[\log S_T \mid \mathcal{F}_t],$$

at time $t \in [0,T]$, of the log contract with payoff $\log S_T$.

Exercise 7.15 Power option. (Exercise 6.5 continued). Consider the price process $(S_t)_{t \in [0,T]}$ given by

$$\frac{dS_t}{S_t} = rdt + \sigma dB_t$$

and a riskless asset valued $A_t = A_0 e^{rt}$, $t \in [0,T]$, with $r > 0$. In this problem, $(\eta_t, \xi_t)_{t \in [0,T]}$ denotes a portfolio strategy with value

$$V_t = \eta_t A_t + \xi_t S_t, \qquad 0 \leqslant t \leqslant T.$$

a) Compute the arbitrage-free price

$$C(t, S_t) = e^{-(T-t)r} \, \mathbb{E}^* \left[|S_T|^2 \mid \mathcal{F}_t \right],$$

at time $t \in [0,T]$, of the power option with payoff $C = |S_T|^2$.

b) Compute a self-financing hedging strategy $(\eta_t, \xi_t)_{t \in [0,T]}$ hedging the claim payoff $|S_T|^2$.

Exercise 7.16 Bachelier (1900) model (Exercise 6.11 continued).

a) Consider the solution $(S_t)_{t \in \mathbb{R}_+}$ of the stochastic differential equation

$$dS_t = \alpha S_t dt + \sigma dB_t.$$

For which value α_M of α is the discounted price process $\tilde{S}_t = e^{-rt} S_t$, $0 \leqslant t \leqslant T$, a martingale under $\mathbb{P}$?

b) For each value of α, build a probability measure $\mathbb{P}_\alpha$ under which the discounted price process $\tilde{S}_t = e^{-rt} S_t$, $0 \leqslant t \leqslant T$, is a martingale.

c) Compute the arbitrage-free price

$$C(t, S_t) = e^{-(T-t)r} \, \mathbb{E}_\alpha \left[e^{S_T} \mid \mathcal{F}_t \right]$$

at time $t \in [0,T]$ of the contingent claim with payoff $\exp(S_T)$, and recover the result of Exercise 6.11.

d) Explicitly compute the portfolio strategy $(\eta_t, \xi_t)_{t \in [0,T]}$ that hedges the contingent claim with payoff $\exp(S_T)$.

e) Check that this strategy is self-financing.

Exercise 7.17 Compute the arbitrage-free price

$$C(t, S_t) = e^{-(T-t)r} \mathbb{E}_{\alpha} \left[(S_T)^2 \mid \mathcal{F}_t \right]$$

at time $t \in [0, T]$ of the power option with payoff $(S_T)^2$ in the framework of the Bachelier (1900) model of Exercise 7.16.

Exercise 7.18 (Exercise 5.8 continued, see Proposition 4.1 in Carmona and Durrleman (2003)). Consider two assets whose prices $S_t^{(1)}$, $S_t^{(2)}$ at time $t \in [0, T]$ follow the geometric Brownian dynamics

$$dS_t^{(1)} = r S_t^{(1)} dt + \sigma_1 S_t^{(1)} dW_t^{(1)} \quad dS_t^{(2)} = r S_t^{(2)} dt + \sigma_2 S_t^{(2)} dW_t^{(2)} \quad t \in [0, T],$$

where $\left(W_t^{(1)} \right)_{t \in [0,T]}$, $\left(W_t^{(2)} \right)_{t \in [0,T]}$ are two standard Brownian motions with correlation $\rho \in [-1, 1]$ under a risk-neutral probability measure $\mathbb{P}^*$, with $dW_t^{(1)} \cdot dW_t^{(2)} = \rho dt$.

Estimate the price $e^{-rT} \mathbb{E}^*[(S_T - K)^+]$ of the spread option on $S_T := S_T^{(2)} - S_T^{(1)}$ with maturity $T > 0$ and strike price $K > 0$ by matching the first two moments of S_T to those of a Gaussian random variable.

Exercise 7.19 (Exercise 6.2 continued). Price the option with vanilla payoff $C = \phi(S_T)$ using the noncentral Chi square probability density function (17.10) of the Cox et al. (1985) (CIR) model.

Exercise 7.20 Let $(B_t)_{t \in \mathbb{R}_+}$ be a standard Brownian motion generating a filtration $(\mathcal{F}_t)_{t \in \mathbb{R}_+}$. Recall that for $f \in \mathcal{C}^2(\mathbb{R}_+ \times \mathbb{R})$, Itô's formula for $(B_t)_{t \in \mathbb{R}_+}$ reads

$$
\begin{aligned}
f(t, B_t) \;=\; & f(0, B_0) + \int_0^t \frac{\partial f}{\partial s}(s, B_s) ds \\
& + \int_0^t \frac{\partial f}{\partial x}(s, B_s) dB_s + \frac{1}{2} \int_0^t \frac{\partial^2 f}{\partial x^2}(s, B_s) ds.
\end{aligned}
$$

a) Let $r \in \mathbb{R}$, $\sigma > 0$, $f(x, t) = e^{rt + \sigma x - \sigma^2 t/2}$, and $S_t = f(t, B_t)$. Compute $df(t, B_t)$ by Itô's formula, and show that S_t solves the stochastic differential equation

$$dS_t = r S_t dt + \sigma S_t dB_t,$$

where $r > 0$ and $\sigma > 0$.

b) Show that

$$\mathbb{E}\left[e^{\sigma B_T} \mid \mathcal{F}_t \right] = e^{\sigma B_t + (T-t)\sigma^2/2}, \qquad 0 \leqslant t \leqslant T.$$

Hint: Use the independence of increments of $(B_t)_{t \in [0,T]}$ in the time splitting decomposition

$$B_T = (B_t - B_0) + (B_T - B_t),$$

and the Gaussian moment generating function $\mathbb{E}\left[e^{\alpha X} \right] = e^{\alpha^2 \eta^2/2}$ when $X \simeq \mathcal{N}(0, \eta^2)$.

c) Show that the process $(S_t)_{t \in \mathbb{R}_+}$ satisfies

$$\mathbb{E}[S_T \mid \mathcal{F}_t] = e^{(T-t)r} S_t, \qquad 0 \leqslant t \leqslant T.$$

d) Let $C = S_T - K$ denote the payoff of a forward contract with exercise price K and maturity T. Compute the discounted expected payoff

$$V_t := e^{-(T-t)r} \mathbb{E}[C \mid \mathcal{F}_t].$$

e) Find a self-financing portfolio strategy $(\xi_t, \eta_t)_{t\in\mathbb{R}_+}$ such that

$$V_t = \xi_t S_t + \eta_t A_t, \qquad 0 \leqslant t \leqslant T,$$

where $A_t = A_0 e^{rt}$ is the price of a riskless asset with fixed interest rate $r > 0$. Show that it recovers the result of Exercise 6.7-(c).

f) Show that the portfolio allocation $(\xi_t, \eta_t)_{t\in[0,T]}$ found in Question (e) *hedges* the payoff $C = S_T - K$ at time T, *i.e.* show that $V_T = C$.

Exercise 7.21 Binary options. Consider a price process $(S_t)_{t\in\mathbb{R}_+}$ given by

$$\frac{dS_t}{S_t} = rdt + \sigma dB_t, \qquad S_0 = 1,$$

under the risk-neutral probability measure $\mathbb{P}^*$. A binary (or digital) *call*, resp. *put*, option is a contract with maturity T, strike price K, and payoff

$$C_d := \begin{cases} \$1 & \text{if } S_T \geqslant K, \\ \\ 0 & \text{if } S_T < K, \end{cases} \qquad resp. \quad P_d := \begin{cases} \$1 & \text{if } S_T \leqslant K, \\ \\ 0 & \text{if } S_T > K. \end{cases}$$

Recall that the prices $\pi_t(C_d)$ and $\pi_t(P_d)$ at time t of the binary call and put options are given by the discounted expected payoffs

$$\pi_t(C_d) = e^{-(T-t)r} \mathbb{E}[C_d \mid \mathcal{F}_t] \quad \text{and} \quad \pi_t(P_d) = e^{-(T-t)r} \mathbb{E}[P_d \mid \mathcal{F}_t]. \tag{7.45}$$

a) Show that the payoffs C_d and P_d can be rewritten as

$$C_d = \mathbb{1}_{[K,\infty)}(S_T) \quad \text{and} \quad P_d = \mathbb{1}_{[0,K]}(S_T).$$

b) Using Relation (7.45), Question (a), and the relation

$$\mathbb{E}\left[\mathbb{1}_{[K,\infty)}(S_T) \mid S_t = x\right] = \mathbb{P}^*(S_T \geqslant K \mid S_t = x),$$

show that the price $\pi_t(C_d)$ is given by

$$\pi_t(C_d) = C_d(t, S_t),$$

where $C_d(t, x)$ is the function defined by

$$C_d(t, x) := e^{-(T-t)r}\mathbb{P}^*(S_T \geqslant K \mid S_t = x).$$

c) Using the results of Exercise 5.10-(d) and of Question (b), show that the price $\pi_t(C_d) = C_d(t, S_t)$ of the binary call option is given by the function

$$\begin{aligned} C_d(t, x) &= e^{-(T-t)r}\Phi\left(\frac{(r-\sigma^2/2)(T-t) + \log(x/K)}{\sigma\sqrt{T-t}}\right) \\ &= e^{-(T-t)r}\Phi(d_-(T-t)), \end{aligned}$$

where

$$d_-(T-t) = \frac{(r-\sigma^2/2)(T-t) + \log(S_t/K)}{\sigma\sqrt{T-t}}.$$

d) Assume that the binary option holder is entitled to receive a "return amount" $\alpha \in [0,1]$ in case the underlying asset price ends out of the money at maturity. Compute the price at time $t \in [0,T]$ of this modified contract.

e) Using Relation (7.45) and Question (a), prove the call-put parity relation

$$\pi_t(C_d) + \pi_t(P_d) = e^{-(T-t)r}, \qquad 0 \leqslant t \leqslant T. \tag{7.46}$$

If needed, you may use the fact that $\mathbb{P}^*(S_T = K) = 0$.

f) Using the results of Questions (e) and (c), show that the price $\pi_t(P_d)$ of the binary put option is given as

$$\pi_t(P_d) = e^{-(T-t)r}\Phi\big(-d_-(T-t)\big).$$

g) Using the result of Question (c), compute the Delta

$$\xi_t := \frac{\partial C_d}{\partial x}(t, S_t)$$

of the binary call option. Does the Black–Scholes hedging strategy of such a call option involve short selling? Why?

h) Using the result of Question (f), compute the Delta

$$\xi_t := \frac{\partial P_d}{\partial x}(t, S_t)$$

of the binary put option. Does the Black–Scholes hedging strategy of such a put option involve short selling? Why?

Exercise 7.22 Computation of Greeks. Consider an underlying asset whose price $(S_t)_{t \in \mathbb{R}_+}$ is given by a stochastic differential equation of the form

$$dS_t = rS_t dt + \sigma(S_t)dB_t,$$

where $\sigma(x)$ is a Lipschitz coefficient, and an option with payoff function ϕ and price

$$C(x, T) = e^{-rT}\mathbb{E}[\phi(S_T) \mid S_0 = x],$$

where $\phi(x)$ is a twice continuously differentiable ($\mathcal{C}^2$) function, with $S_0 = x$. Using the Itô formula, show that the sensitivity

$$\text{Theta}_T = \frac{\partial}{\partial T}\big(e^{-rT}\mathbb{E}[\phi(S_T) \mid S_0 = x]\big)$$

of the option price with respect to maturity T can be expressed as

$$\begin{aligned}
\text{Theta}_T &= -r\,e^{-rT}\mathbb{E}[\phi(S_T) \mid S_0 = x] + r\,e^{-rT}\mathbb{E}\big[S_t\phi'(S_T) \mid S_0 = x\big] \\
&\quad + \frac{1}{2}e^{-rT}\mathbb{E}\big[\phi''(S_T)\sigma^2(S_T) \mid S_0 = x\big].
\end{aligned}$$

Problem 7.23   Chooser options. In this problem we denote by $C(t, S_t, K, T)$, resp. $P(t, S_t, K, T)$, the price at time t of the European call, resp. put, option with strike price K and maturity T, on an underlying asset priced $S_t = S_0 e^{\sigma B_t + rt - \sigma^2 t/2}$, $t \geqslant 0$, where $(B_t)_{t \in \mathbb{R}_+}$ is a standard Brownian motion under the risk-neutral probability measure

a) Prove the call-put parity formula

$$C(t, S_t, K, T) - P(t, S_t, K, T) = S_t - K e^{-(T-t)r}, \qquad 0 \leqslant t \leqslant T. \qquad (7.47)$$

b) Consider an option contract with maturity T, which entitles its holder to receive at time T the value of the European put option with strike price K and maturity $U > T$.

Write down the price this contract at time $t \in [0, T]$ using a conditional expectation under the risk-neutral probability measure $\mathbb{P}^*$.

c) Consider now an option contract with maturity T, which entitles its holder to receive at time T either the value of a European call option or a European put option, whichever is higher. The European call and put options have same strike price K and same maturity $U > T$.

Show that at maturity T, the payoff of this contract can be written as

$$P(T, S_T, K, U) + \mathrm{Max}\left(0, S_T - K e^{-(U-T)r}\right).$$

Hint: Use the call-put parity formula (7.47).

d) Price the contract of Question (c) at any time $t \in [0, T]$ using the call and put option pricing functions $C(t, x, K, T)$ and $P(t, x, K, U)$.

e) Using the Black–Scholes formula, compute the self-financing hedging strategy $(\xi_t, \eta_t)_{t \in [0,T]}$ with portfolio value

$$V_t = \xi_t S_t + \eta_t e^{rt}, \qquad 0 \leqslant t \leqslant T,$$

for the option contract of Question (c).

f) Consider now an option contract with maturity T, which entitles its holder to receive at time T the value of either a European call or a European put option, whichever is *lower*. The two options have same strike price K and same maturity $U > T$.

Show that the payoff of this contract at maturity T can be written as

$$C(T, S_T, K, U) - \mathrm{Max}\left(0, S_T - K e^{-(U-T)r}\right).$$

g) Price the contract of Question (f) at any time $t \in [0, T]$.

h) Using the Black–Scholes formula, compute the self-financing hedging strategy $(\xi_t, \eta_t)_{t \in [0,T]}$ with portfolio value

$$V_t = \xi_t S_t + \eta_t e^{rt}, \qquad 0 \leqslant t \leqslant T,$$

for the option contract of Question (f).

i) Give the price and hedging strategy of the contract that yields the sum of the payoffs of Questions (c) and (f).

j) What happens when $U = T$? Give the payoffs of the contracts of Questions (c), (f) and (i).

Problem 7.24　(Peng (2010)). Consider a risky asset priced

$$S_t = S_0 e^{\sigma B_t + \mu t - \sigma^2 t/2}, \quad i.e. \quad dS_t = \mu S_t dt + \sigma S_t dB_t, \quad t \geqslant 0,$$

a riskless asset valued $A_t = A_0 e^{rt}$, and a self-financing portfolio allocation $(\eta_t, \xi_t)_{t \in \mathbb{R}_+}$ with value

$$V_t := \eta_t A_t + \xi_t S_t, \quad t \geqslant 0.$$

a) Using the portfolio self-financing condition $dV_t = \eta_t dA_t + \xi_t dS_t$, show that we have

$$V_T = V_t + \int_t^T (rV_s + (\mu - r)\xi_s S_s) ds + \sigma \int_t^T \xi_s S_s dB_s.$$

b) Show that under the risk-neutral probability measure $\mathbb{P}^*$ the portfolio value V_t satisfies the *Backward Stochastic Differential Equation* (BSDE)

$$V_t = V_T - \int_t^T rV_s ds - \int_t^T \pi_s d\widehat{B}_s, \tag{7.48}$$

where $\pi_t := \sigma \xi_t S_t$ is the risky amount invested on the asset S_t, multiplied by σ, and $(\widehat{B}_t)_{t \in \mathbb{R}_+}$ is a standard Brownian motion under $\mathbb{P}^*$.

Hint: the Girsanov Theorem 7.3 states that

$$\widehat{B}_t := B_t + \frac{(\mu - r)t}{\sigma}, \quad t \geqslant 0,$$

is a standard Brownian motion under $\mathbb{P}^*$.

c) Show that under the risk-neutral probability measure $\mathbb{P}^*$, the discounted portfolio value $\widetilde{V}_t := e^{-rt} V_t$ can be rewritten as

$$\widetilde{V}_T = \widetilde{V}_0 + \int_0^T e^{-rs} \pi_s d\widehat{B}_s. \tag{7.49}$$

d) Express $dv(t, S_t)$ by the Itô formula, where $v(t, x)$ is a $\mathcal{C}^2$ function of t and x.

e) Consider now a more general BSDE of the form

$$V_t = V_T - \int_t^T f(s, S_s, V_s, \pi_s) ds - \int_t^T \pi_s dB_s, \tag{7.50}$$

with terminal condition $V_T = g(S_T)$. By matching (7.50) to the Itô formula of Question (d), find the PDE satisfied by the function $v(t, x)$ defined as $V_t = v(t, S_t)$.

f) Show that when

$$f(t, x, v, z) = rv + \frac{\mu - r}{\sigma} z,$$

the PDE of Question (e) recovers the standard Black–Scholes PDE.

g) Assuming again $f(t, x, v, z) = rv + \dfrac{\mu - r}{\sigma} z$ and taking the terminal condition

$$V_T = (S_0 e^{\sigma B_T + (\mu - \sigma^2/2)T} - K)^+,$$

give the process $(\pi_t)_{t \in [0, T]}$ appearing in the stochastic integral representation (7.49) of the discounted claim payoff $e^{-rT}(S_0 e^{\sigma B_T + (\mu - \sigma^2/2)T} - K)^+$.[*]

---

[*]General Black–Scholes knowledge can be used for this question.

h) From now on we assume that short selling is penalized* at a rate $\gamma > 0$, *i.e.* $\gamma S_t |\xi_t| dt$ is subtracted from the portfolio value change dV_t whenever $\xi_t < 0$ over the time interval $[t, t + dt]$. Rewrite the self-financing condition using $(\xi_t)^- := -\min(\xi_t, 0)$.

i) Find the BSDE of the form (7.50) satisfied by $(V_t)_{t \in \mathbb{R}_+}$, and the corresponding function $f(t, x, v, z)$.

j) Under the above penalty on short selling, find the PDE satisfied by the function $u(t, x)$ when the portfolio value V_t is given as $V_t = u(t, S_t)$.

k) *Differential interest rate.* Assume that one can borrow only at a rate R which is higher[†] than the risk-free interest rate $r > 0$, *i.e.* we have

$$dV_t = R \eta_t A_t dt + \xi_t dS_t$$

when $\eta_t < 0$, and

$$dV_t = r \eta_t A_t dt + \xi_t dS_t$$

when $\eta_t > 0$. Find the PDE satisfied by the function $u(t, x)$ when the portfolio value V_t is given as $V_t = u(t, S_t)$.

l) Assume that the portfolio differential reads

$$dV_t = \eta_t dA_t + \xi_t dS_t - dU_t,$$

where $(U_t)_{t \in \mathbb{R}_+}$ is a non-decreasing process. Show that the corresponding portfolio strategy $(\xi_t)_{t \in \mathbb{R}_+}$ is superhedging the claim payoff $V_T = C$.

Exercise 7.25 Girsanov Theorem. Assume that the Novikov integrability condition (7.11) is not satisfied. How does this modify the statement (7.13) of the Girsanov Theorem 7.3?

Problem 7.26 The Capital Asset Pricing Model (CAPM) of W.F. Sharpe (1990 Nobel Prize in Economics) is based on a linear decomposition

$$\frac{dS_t}{S_t} = (r + \alpha)dt + \beta \times \left(\frac{dM_t}{M_t} - rdt \right)$$

of stock returns dS_t/S_t into:

- a risk-free interest rate[‡] r,

- an excess return α,

- a risk premium given by the difference between a benchmark market index return dM_t/M_t and the risk free rate r.

The coefficient β measures the sensitivity of the stock return dS_t/S_t with respect to the market index returns dM_t/M_t. In other words, β is the relative volatility of dS_t/S_t with respect to dM_t/M_t, and it measures the risk of $(S_t)_{t \in \mathbb{R}_+}$ in comparison to the market index $(M_t)_{t \in \mathbb{R}_+}$.

---

*SGX started to penalize naked short sales with an interim measure in September 2008.

[†]Regular savings account usually pays r=0.05% per year. Effective Interest Rates (EIR) for borrowing could be as high as R=20.61% per year.

[‡]The risk-free interest rate r is typically the yield of the *10-year Treasury bond*.

If $\beta > 1$, resp. $\beta < 1$, then the stock price S_t is more volatile (*i.e.* more risky), resp. less volatile (*i.e.* less risky), than the benchmark market index M_t. For example, if $\beta = 2$, then S_t goes up (or down) twice as much as the index M_t. Inverse Exchange-Traded Funds (IETFs) have a negative value of β. On the other hand, a fund which has a $\beta = 1$ can track the index M_t.

Vanguard 500 Index Fund (VFINX) has a $\beta = 1$ and can be considered as replicating the variations of the S&P 500 index M_t, while *Invesco S&P 500 (SPHB)* has a $\beta = 1.42$, and *Xtrackers Low Beta High Yield Bond ETF (HYDW)* has a β close to 0.36 and $\alpha = 6.36$.

In what follows, we assume that the benchmark market is represented by an index fund $(M_t)_{t\in\mathbb{R}_+}$ whose value is modeled according to

$$\frac{dM_t}{M_t} = \mu dt + \sigma_M dB_t, \tag{7.51}$$

where $(B_t)_{t\in\mathbb{R}_+}$ is a standard Brownian motion. The asset price $(S_t)_{t\in\mathbb{R}_+}$ is modeled in a stochastic version of the CAPM as

$$\frac{dS_t}{S_t} = rdt + \alpha dt + \beta\left(\frac{dM_t}{M_t} - rdt\right) + \sigma_S dW_t, \tag{7.52}$$

with an additional stock volatility term $\sigma_S dW_t$, where $(W_t)_{t\in\mathbb{R}_+}$ is a standard Brownian motion independent of $(B_t)_{t\in\mathbb{R}_+}$, with

$$\mathrm{Cov}(B_t, W_t) = 0 \quad \text{and} \quad dB_t \cdot dW_t = 0, \quad t \geqslant 0.$$

The following 10 questions are interdependent and should be treated in sequence.

a) Show that β coincides with the regression coefficient

$$\beta = \frac{\mathrm{Cov}(dS_t/S_t, dM_t/M_t)}{\mathrm{Var}[dM_t/M_t]}.$$

Hint: We have

$$\mathrm{Cov}(dW_t, dW_t) = dt, \quad \mathrm{Cov}(dB_t, dB_t) = dt, \quad \text{and} \quad \mathrm{Cov}(dW_t, dB_t) = 0.$$

b) Show that the evolution of $(S_t)_{t\in\mathbb{R}_+}$ can be written as

$$dS_t = (r + \alpha + \beta(\mu - r))S_t dt + S_t\sqrt{\beta^2\sigma_M^2 + \sigma_S^2}\,dZ_t$$

where $(Z_t)_{t\in\mathbb{R}_+}$ is a standard Brownian motion.

Hint: The standard Brownian motion $(Z_t)_{t\in\mathbb{R}_+}$ can be characterized as the only continuous (local) martingale such that $(dZ_t)^2 = dt$, see *e.g.* Theorem 7.36 page 203 of Klebaner (2005).

From now on, we assume that β is allowed to depend locally on the state of the benchmark market index M_t, as $\beta(M_t)$, $t \geqslant 0$.

c) Rewrite the equations (7.51)–(7.52) into the system

$$\begin{cases} \dfrac{dM_t}{M_t} = rdt + \sigma_M dB_t^*, \\[4mm] \dfrac{dS_t}{S_t} = rdt + \sigma_M \beta(M_t)dB_t^* + \sigma_S dW_t^*, \end{cases}$$

where $(B_t^*)_{t\in\mathbb{R}_+}$ and $(W_t^*)_{t\in\mathbb{R}_+}$ have to be determined explicitly.

d) Using the Girsanov Theorem 7.3, construct a probability measure $\mathbb{P}^*$ under which $(B_t^*)_{t\in\mathbb{R}_+}$ and $(W_t^*)_{t\in\mathbb{R}_+}$ are independent standard Brownian motions.

Hint: Only the expression of the Radon–Nikodym density $d\mathbb{P}^*/d\mathbb{P}$ is needed here.

e) Show that the market based on the assets S_t and M_t is without arbitrage opportunities.

f) Consider a portfolio strategy $(\xi_t, \zeta_t, \eta_t)_{t\in[0,T]}$ based on the three assets $(S_t, M_t, A_t)_{t\in[0,T]}$, with value

$$V_t = \xi_t S_t + \zeta_t M_t + \eta_t A_t, \qquad t \in [0,T],$$

where $(A_t)_{t\in\mathbb{R}_+}$ is a riskless asset given by $A_t = A_0\, e^{rt}$. Write down the self-financing condition for the portfolio strategy $(\xi_t, \zeta_t, \eta_t)_{t\in[0,T]}$.

g) Consider an option with payoff $C = h(S_T, M_T)$, priced as

$$f(t, S_t, M_t) = e^{-(T-t)r}\, \mathbb{E}^*[h(S_T, M_T) \mid \mathcal{F}_t], \qquad 0 \leqslant t \leqslant T.$$

Assuming that the portfolio $(V_t)_{t\in[0,T]}$ replicates the option price process $(f(t, S_t, M_t))_{t\in[0,T]}$, derive the pricing PDE satisfied by the function $f(t, x, y)$ and its terminal condition.

Hint: The following version of the Itô formula with two variables can be used for the function $f(t, x, y)$, see (4.26):

$$
\begin{aligned}
df(t, S_t, M_t) &= \frac{\partial f}{\partial t}(t, S_t, M_t)dt + \frac{\partial f}{\partial x}(t, S_t, M_t)dS_t + \frac{1}{2}(dS_t)^2\frac{\partial^2 f}{\partial x^2}(t, S_t, M_t) \\
&+ \frac{\partial f}{\partial y}(t, S_t, M_t)dM_t + \frac{1}{2}(dM_t)^2\frac{\partial^2 f}{\partial y^2}(t, S_t, M_t) + dS_t \cdot dM_t\frac{\partial^2 f}{\partial x \partial y}(t, S_t, M_t).
\end{aligned}
$$

h) Find the self-financing hedging portfolio strategy $(\xi_t, \zeta_t, \eta_t)_{t\in[0,T]}$ replicating the vanilla payoff $h(S_T, M_T)$.

i) Solve the PDE of Question (g) and compute the replicating portfolio of Question (h) when $\beta(M_t) = \beta$ is a constant and C is the European *call option* payoff on S_T with strike price K.

j) Solve the PDE of Question (g) and compute the replicating portfolio of Question (h) when $\beta(M_t) = \beta$ is a constant and C is the European *put option* payoff on S_T with strike price K.

Problem 7.27 Market bubbles occur when a financial asset becomes overvalued for various reasons, for example in the Dutch tulip bubble (1636-1637), Japan's stock market bubble (1986), dotcom bubble (2000), or US housing bubble (2009). Local martingales are used for the modeling of *market bubbles* and market crashes, see Cox and Hobson (2005), Heston et al. (2007), Jarrow et al. (2007), in which case the option call-put parity does not hold in general. In what follows we let $T > 0$ and we consider a filtration $(\mathcal{F}_t)_{t\in[0,T]}$ on $[0,T]$ with $\mathcal{F}_0 = \{\emptyset, \Omega\}$ and a probability measure $\mathbb{P}$ on $(\Omega, \mathcal{F}_T)$.

An $(\mathcal{F}_t)_{t\in[0,T]}$-adapted process $(M_t)_{t\in[0,T]}$ is called a (true) *martingale* on $[0,T]$ if

i) $\mathbb{E}[|M_t|] < \infty$ for all $t \in [0,T]$,

ii) $\mathbb{E}[M_t \mid \mathcal{F}_s] = M_s$, for all $0 \leqslant s \leqslant t$.

An $(\mathcal{F}_t)_{t\in[0,T]}$-adapted process $(M_t)_{t\in[0,T]}$ is called a *supermartingale* on $[0,T]$ if

i) $\mathbb{E}[|M_t|] < \infty$ for all $t \in [0,T]$,

ii) $\mathbb{E}[M_t \mid \mathcal{F}_s] \leqslant M_s$, for all $0 \leqslant s \leqslant t$.

An $(\mathcal{F}_t)_{t\in[0,T]}$-adapted process $(M_t)_{t\in[0,T]}$ is called a *local martingale* on $[0,T]$ if there exists a nondecreasing sequence $(\tau_n)_{n\geqslant 1}$ of $[0,T]$-valued stopping times such that

i) $\lim_{n\to\infty} \tau_n = T$ almost surely,

ii) for all $n \geqslant 1$ the stopped process $(M_{\tau_n \wedge t})_{t\in[0,T]}$ is a (true) martingale under $\mathbb{P}$.

A local martingale on $[0,T]$ which is not a true martingale is called a *strict* local martingale.

1) a) Show that any martingale $(M_t)_{t\in[0,T]}$ on $[0,T]$ is a local martingale in $[0,T]$.

   b) Show that any *non-negative* local martingale $(M_t)_{t\in[0,T]}$ is a *super*martingale.

   Hint: Use Fatou's Lemma.

   c) Show that if $(M_t)_{t\in[0,T]}$ is a non-negative and *strict* local martingale on $[0,T]$ we have $\mathbb{E}[M_T] < M_0$.

   Hint: Do the proof by contradiction using the tower property, the answer to Question (1b), and the fact that if a random variable X satisfies $X \leqslant 0$ a.s. and $\mathbb{E}[X] = 0$, then $X = 0$ a.s.

   d) Show that the call-put parity

   $$C(0, M_0) - P(0, M_0) = \mathbb{E}[M_0] - K$$

   between $C(0, M_0)$ and $P(0, M_0)$ fails when the discounted asset price process $(M_t)_{t\in[0,T]}$ is a **strict** local martingale.
   Hint: See Relation (8.4.7) in Proposition 8.9.

2) Let $(S_t)_{t\in[0,T]}$ be the solution of the stochastic differential equation

   $$dS_t = \frac{S_t}{\sqrt{T-t}}dB_t \tag{7.53}$$

   with $S_0 > 0$.

   a) Show that $(S_t)_{t\in[0,T-\varepsilon]}$ is a martingale on $[0, T-\varepsilon]$ for every $\varepsilon \in (0,T)$.

   Hint: Solve the stochastic differential equation (7.53) by the method of Proposition 6.16-*a*), and use Exercise 5.11-*b*).

   b) Find the value of S_T by a simple argument.

   c) Show that $(S_t)_{t\in[0,T]}$ is a strict local martingale on $[0,T]$.

   Hint: Consider the stopping times

   $$\tau_n := \left(\left(1 - \frac{1}{n}\right)T\right) \wedge \inf\{t \in [0,T] \;:\; |S_t| \geqslant n\}, \qquad n \geqslant 1,$$

   and use Proposition 8.1.

   d) Plot a sample graph of $(S_t)_{t\in[0,T]}$ with $T = 1$, and attach or upload it with your submission.

3) CEV model. Consider the positive strict local martingale $(S_t)_{t \in [0,T]}$ solution of $dS_t = S_t^2 dB_t$ with $S_0 > 0$, where S_t has the probability density function

$$\varphi_t(x) = \frac{S_0}{x^3 \sqrt{2\pi t}} \left(\exp\left(-\frac{(1/x - 1/S_0)^2}{2t} \right) - \exp\left(-\frac{(1/x + 1/S_0)^2}{2t} \right) \right),$$

$x > 0$, $t \in (0, T]$, see § 2.1.2 in Jacquier (2017).

a) Plot a sample graph of $(S_t)_{t \in [0,T]}$ with $T = 1$, and attach or upload it with your submission.

b) Compute $\mathbb{E}[S_T]$ and check that the condition of Question (1c) is satisfied.
   Hint: Use the change of variable $y = 1/x$ and the standard normal CDF Φ.

c) Compute the limit of $\mathbb{E}[S_T]$ as S_0 tends to infinity.

d) Compute the price $\mathbb{E}[(S_T - K)^+]$ of a European call option with strike price $K > 0$ in this model, assuming a risk-free interest rate $r = 0$.
   Hint: The final answer should be written in terms of the standard normal CDF Φ and of the normal PDF φ.

e) Show that $\mathbb{E}[(S_T - K)^+]$ is bounded uniformly in $S_0 > 0$ and $K > 0$ by a constant depending on $T > 0$.

Problem 7.28 Quantile hedging (Föllmer and Leukert (1999), §6.2 of Mel'nikov et al. (2002)). Recall that given two probability measures $\mathbb{P}$ and $\mathbb{Q}$, the *Radon–Nikodym* density $d\mathbb{P}/d\mathbb{Q}$ links the expectations of random variables F under $\mathbb{P}$ and under $\mathbb{Q}$ via the relation

$$
\begin{aligned}
\mathbb{E}_{\mathbb{Q}}[F] &= \int_\Omega F(\omega) d\mathbb{Q}(\omega) \\
&= \int_\Omega F(\omega) \frac{d\mathbb{Q}}{d\mathbb{P}}(\omega) d\mathbb{P}(\omega) \\
&= \mathbb{E}_{\mathbb{P}} \left[F \frac{d\mathbb{Q}}{d\mathbb{P}} \right].
\end{aligned}
$$

a) *Neyman–Pearson Lemma.* Given $\mathbb{P}$ and $\mathbb{Q}$ two probability measures, consider the event

$$A_\alpha := \left\{ \frac{d\mathbb{P}}{d\mathbb{Q}} > \alpha \right\}, \qquad \alpha \geq 0.$$

Show that for A any event, $\mathbb{Q}(A) \leq \mathbb{Q}(A_\alpha)$ implies $\mathbb{P}(A) \leq \mathbb{P}(A_\alpha)$.

Hint: Start by *proving* that we always have

$$\left(\frac{d\mathbb{P}}{d\mathbb{Q}} - \alpha \right) (2\mathbb{1}_{A_\alpha} - 1) \geq \left(\frac{d\mathbb{P}}{d\mathbb{Q}} - \alpha \right) (2\mathbb{1}_A - 1). \tag{7.54}$$

b) Let $C \geq 0$ denote a nonnegative claim payoff on a financial market with risk-neutral measure $\mathbb{P}^*$. Show that the Radon–Nikodym density

$$\frac{d\mathbb{Q}^*}{d\mathbb{P}^*} := \frac{C}{\mathbb{E}_{\mathbb{P}^*}[C]} \tag{7.55}$$

defines a probability measure $\mathbb{Q}^*$.

Hint: Check first that $d\mathbb{Q}^*/d\mathbb{P}^* \geq 0$, and then that $\mathbb{Q}^*(\Omega) = 1$. In the following questions we consider a nonnegative contingent claim with payoff $C \geq 0$ and maturity $T > 0$, priced $e^{-rT} \mathbb{E}_{\mathbb{P}^*}[C]$ at time 0 under the risk-neutral measure $\mathbb{P}^*$.

Budget constraint. *In what follows we will assume that no more than a certain fraction $\beta \in (0, 1]$ of the claim price $e^{-rT} \mathbb{E}_{\mathbb{P}^*}[C]$ is available to construct the initial hedging portfolio V_0 at time 0.*

Since a self-financing portfolio process $(V_t)_{t \in \mathbb{R}_+}$ started at $V_0 := \beta e^{-rT} \mathbb{E}_{\mathbb{P}^*}[C]$ may fall short of hedging the claim C when $\beta < 1$, we will attempt to maximize the probability $\mathbb{P}(V_T \geqslant C)$ of successful hedging, or, equivalently, to minimize the shortfall probability $\mathbb{P}(V_T < C)$.

For this, given A an event we consider the self-financing portfolio process $(V_t^A)_{t \in [0,T]}$ hedging the claim $C \mathbb{1}_A$, priced $V_0^A = e^{-rT} \mathbb{E}_{\mathbb{P}^*}[C \mathbb{1}_A]$ at time 0, and such that $V_T^A = C \mathbb{1}_A$ at maturity T.

c) Show that if α satisfies $\mathbb{Q}^*(A_\alpha) = \beta$, the event

$$A_\alpha = \left\{ \frac{d\mathbb{P}}{d\mathbb{Q}^*} > \alpha \right\} = \left\{ \frac{d\mathbb{P}}{d\mathbb{P}^*} > \alpha \frac{d\mathbb{Q}^*}{d\mathbb{P}^*} \right\} = \left\{ \frac{d\mathbb{P}}{d\mathbb{P}^*} > \frac{\alpha C}{\mathbb{E}_{\mathbb{P}^*}[C]} \right\}$$

maximizes $\mathbb{P}(A)$ over all possible events A, under the condition

$$e^{-rT} \mathbb{E}_{\mathbb{P}^*}\left[V_T^A\right] = e^{-rT} \mathbb{E}_{\mathbb{P}^*}[C \mathbb{1}_A] \leqslant \beta e^{-rT} \mathbb{E}_{\mathbb{P}^*}[C]. \tag{7.56}$$

Hint: Rewrite Condition (7.56) using the probability measure $\mathbb{Q}^*$, and apply the *Neyman–Pearson Lemma* of Question (a) to $\mathbb{P}$ and $\mathbb{Q}^*$.

d) Show that $\mathbb{P}(A_\alpha)$ coincides with the successful hedging probability

$$\mathbb{P}(V_T^{A_\alpha} \geqslant C) = \mathbb{P}(C \mathbb{1}_{A_\alpha} \geqslant C),$$

i.e. show that
$$\mathbb{P}(A_\alpha) = \mathbb{P}(V_T^{A_\alpha} \geqslant C) = \mathbb{P}(C \mathbb{1}_{A_\alpha} \geqslant C).$$

Hint: To prove an equality $x = y$ we can show first that $x \leqslant y$, and then that $x \geqslant y$. One inequality is obvious, and the other one follows from Question (c).

e) Check that the self-financing portfolio process $(V_t^{A_\alpha})_{t \in [0,T]}$ hedging the claim with payoff $C \mathbb{1}_{A_\alpha}$ uses only the initial budget $\beta e^{-rT} \mathbb{E}_{\mathbb{P}^*}[C]$, and that $\mathbb{P}(V_T^{A_\alpha} \geqslant C)$ maximizes the successful hedging probability.

In the next Questions (f)–(j) we assume that $C = (S_T - K)^+$ is the payoff of a European option in the Black–Scholes model

$$dS_t = rS_t dt + \sigma S_t dB_t, \tag{7.57}$$

with $\mathbb{P} = \mathbb{P}^*$, $d\mathbb{P}/d\mathbb{P}^* = 1$, and

$$S_0 := 1 \quad \text{and} \quad r = \frac{\sigma^2}{2} := \frac{1}{2}. \tag{7.58}$$

f) Solve the stochastic differential equation (7.57) with the parameters (7.58).

g) Compute the successful hedging probability

$$\mathbb{P}(V_T^{A_\alpha} \geqslant C) = \mathbb{P}(C \mathbb{1}_{A_\alpha} \geqslant C) = \mathbb{P}(A_\alpha)$$

for the claim $C =: (S_T - K)^+$ in terms of K, T, $\mathbb{E}_{\mathbb{P}^*}[C]$ and the parameter $\alpha > 0$.

h) From the result of Question (g), express the parameter α using K, T, $\mathbb{E}_{\mathbb{P}^*}[C]$, and the successful hedging probability $\mathbb{P}(V_T^{A\alpha} \geqslant C)$ for the claim $C =: (S_T - K)^+$.

i) Compute the minimal initial budget $\mathrm{e}^{-rT}\,\mathbb{E}_{\mathbb{P}^*}[C\mathbb{1}_{A_\alpha}]$ required to hedge the claim $C = (S_T - K)^+$ in terms of $\alpha > 0$, K, T and $\mathbb{E}_{\mathbb{P}^*}[C]$.

j) Taking $K := 1$, $T := 1$ and assuming a successful hedging probability of 90%, compute numerically:

   i) The European call price $\mathrm{e}^{-rT}\,\mathbb{E}_{\mathbb{P}^*}[(S_T - K)^+]$ from the Black–Scholes formula.

   ii) The value of $\alpha > 0$ obtained from Question (h).

   iii) The minimal initial budget needed to successfully hedge the European claim $C = (S_T - K)^+$ with probability 90% from Question (i).

   iv) The value of β, *i.e.* the budget reduction ratio which suffices to successfully hedge the claim $C =: (S_T - K)^+$ with 90% probability.

Problem 7.29 Log options. Log options can be used for the pricing of realized variance swaps, see § 8.2.

a) Consider a market model made of a risky asset with price $(S_t)_{t \in \mathbb{R}_+}$ as in Exercise 4.22-(d) and a riskless asset with price $A_t = \$1 \times \mathrm{e}^{rt}$ and risk-free interest rate $r = \sigma^2/2$. Show that the arbitrage-free price

$$V_t = \mathrm{e}^{-(T-t)r}\,\mathbb{E}\big[(\log S_T)^+ \mid \mathcal{F}_t\big]$$

at time $t \in [0, T]$ of a log call option with payoff $(\log S_T)^+$ is equal to

$$V_t = \sigma\,\mathrm{e}^{-(T-t)r}\sqrt{\frac{T-t}{2\pi}}\,\mathrm{e}^{-B_t^2/(2(T-t))} + \sigma\,\mathrm{e}^{-(T-t)r}B_t\Phi\left(\frac{B_t}{\sqrt{T-t}}\right).$$

b) Show that V_t can be written as

$$V_t = g(T - t, S_t),$$

where $g(\tau, x) = \mathrm{e}^{-r\tau}f(\tau, \log x)$, and

$$f(\tau, y) = \sigma\sqrt{\frac{\tau}{2\pi}}\,\mathrm{e}^{-y^2/(2\sigma^2\tau)} + y\Phi\left(\frac{y}{\sigma\sqrt{\tau}}\right).$$

c) Figure 7.6 represents the graph of $(\tau, x) \mapsto g(\tau, x)$, with $r = 0.05 = 5\%$ *per year* and $\sigma = 0.1$. Assume that the current underlying asset price is \$1 and there remains 700 days to maturity. What is the price of the option?

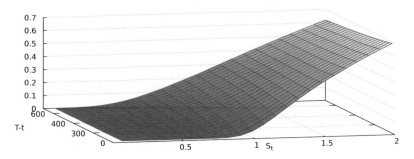

Figure 7.6: Option price as a function of underlying asset price and time to maturity.

d) Show* that the (possibly fractional) quantity $\xi_t = \dfrac{\partial g}{\partial x}(T - t, S_t)$ of S_t at time t in a portfolio hedging the payoff $(\log S_T)^+$ is equal to

$$\xi_t = e^{-(T-t)r}\frac{1}{S_t}\Phi\left(\frac{\log S_t}{\sigma\sqrt{T-t}}\right), \qquad 0 \leqslant t \leqslant T.$$

e) Figure 7.7 represents the graph of $(\tau, x) \mapsto \dfrac{\partial g}{\partial x}(\tau, x)$. Assuming that the current underlying asset price is \$1 and that there remains 700 days to maturity, how much of the risky asset should you hold in your portfolio in order to hedge one log option?

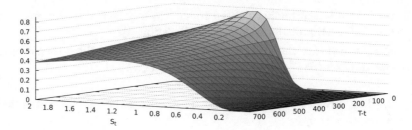

Figure 7.7: Delta as a function of underlying asset price and time to maturity.

f) Based on the framework and answers of Questions (c) and (e), should you borrow or lend the riskless asset $A_t = \$1 \times e^{rt}$, and for what amount?

g) Show that the Gamma of the portfolio, defined as $\Gamma_t = \dfrac{\partial^2 g}{\partial x^2}(T - t, S_t)$, equals

$$\Gamma_t = e^{-(T-t)r}\frac{1}{S_t^2}\left(\frac{1}{\sigma\sqrt{2(T-t)\pi}}e^{-(\log S_t)^2/(2(T-t)\sigma^2)} - \Phi\left(\frac{\log S_t}{\sigma\sqrt{T-t}}\right)\right),$$

$0 \leqslant t < T$.

h) Figure 7.8 represents the graph of Gamma. Assume that there remains 60 days to maturity and that S_t, currently at \$1, is expected to increase. Should you buy or (short) sell the underlying asset in order to hedge the option?

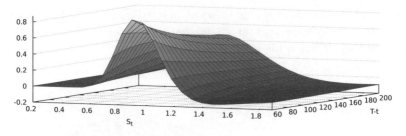

Figure 7.8: Gamma as a function of underlying asset price and time to maturity.

---

*Recall the chain rule of derivation $\dfrac{\partial}{\partial x}f(\tau, \log x) = \dfrac{1}{x}\dfrac{\partial f}{\partial y}(\tau, y)_{|y=\log x}$.

i) Let now $\sigma = 1$. Show that the function $f(\tau, y)$ of Question (b) solves the *heat equation*

$$\begin{cases} \dfrac{\partial f}{\partial \tau}(\tau, y) = \dfrac{1}{2}\dfrac{\partial^2 f}{\partial y^2}(\tau, y) \\[2mm] f(0, y) = (y)^+. \end{cases}$$

Problem 7.30 Log put options with a given strike price.

a) Consider a market model made of a risky asset with price $(S_t)_{t \in \mathbb{R}_+}$ as in Exercise 5.10, a riskless asset valued $A_t = \$1 \times e^{rt}$, risk-free interest rate $r = \sigma^2/2$ and $S_0 = 1$. Show that the arbitrage-free price

$$V_t = e^{-(T-t)r}\, \mathbb{E}^* \left[(K - \log S_T)^+ \mid \mathcal{F}_t \right]$$

at time $t \in [0, T]$ of a log call option with strike price K and payoff $(K - \log S_T)^+$ is equal to

$$V_t = \sigma e^{-(T-t)r}\sqrt{\frac{T-t}{2\pi}}\, e^{-(B_t - K/\sigma)^2/(2(T-t))} + e^{-(T-t)r}(K - \sigma B_t)\Phi\left(\frac{K/\sigma - B_t}{\sqrt{T-t}}\right).$$

b) Show that V_t can be written as

$$V_t = g(T - t, S_t),$$

where $g(\tau, x) = e^{-r\tau} f(\tau, \log x)$, and

$$f(\tau, y) = \sigma \sqrt{\frac{\tau}{2\pi}}\, e^{-(K-y)^2/(2\sigma^2 \tau)} + (K - y)\Phi\left(\frac{K - y}{\sigma\sqrt{\tau}}\right).$$

c) Figure 7.9 represents the graph of $(\tau, x) \mapsto g(\tau, x)$, with $r = 0.125$ *per year* and $\sigma = 0.5$. Assume that the current underlying asset price is \$3, that $K = 1$, and that there remains 700 days to maturity. What is the price of the option?

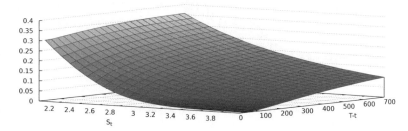

Figure 7.9: Option price as a function of underlying asset price and time to maturity.

d) Show* that the quantity $\xi_t = \dfrac{\partial g}{\partial x}(T - t, S_t)$ of S_t at time t in a portfolio hedging the payoff $(K - \log S_T)^+$ is equal to

$$\xi_t = -e^{-(T-t)r}\frac{1}{S_t}\Phi\left(\frac{K - \log S_t}{\sigma\sqrt{T-t}}\right), \qquad 0 \le t \le T.$$

---

*Recall the chain rule of derivation $\dfrac{\partial}{\partial x} f(\tau, \log x) = \dfrac{1}{x}\dfrac{\partial f}{\partial y}(\tau, y)_{|y = \log x}$.

e) Figure 7.10 represents the graph of $(\tau, x) \mapsto \frac{\partial g}{\partial x}(\tau, x)$. Assuming that the current underlying asset price is \$3 and that there remains 700 days to maturity, how much of the risky asset should you hold in your portfolio in order to hedge one log option?

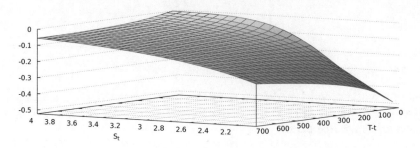

Figure 7.10: Delta as a function of underlying asset price and time to maturity.

f) Based on the framework and answers of Questions (c) and (e), should you borrow or lend the riskless asset $A_t = \$1 \times e^{rt}$, and for what amount?

g) Show that the Gamma of the portfolio, defined as $\Gamma_t = \frac{\partial^2 g}{\partial x^2}(T - t, S_t)$, equals

$$\Gamma_t = e^{-(T-t)r} \frac{1}{S_t^2} \left(\frac{1}{\sigma\sqrt{2(T - t)\pi}} e^{-(K - \log S_t)^2/(2(T-t)\sigma^2)} + \Phi\left(\frac{K - \log S_t}{\sigma\sqrt{T - t}}\right) \right),$$

$0 \leqslant t \leqslant T$.

h) Figure 7.11 represents the graph of Gamma. Assume that there remains 10 days to maturity and that S_t, currently at \$3, is expected to increase. Should you buy or (short) sell the underlying asset in order to hedge the option?

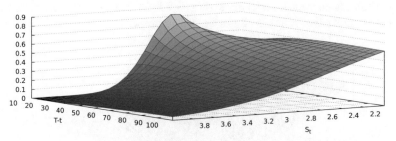

Figure 7.11: Gamma as a function of underlying asset price and time to maturity.

i) Show that the function $f(\tau, y)$ of Question (b) solves the heat equation

$$\begin{cases} \dfrac{\partial f}{\partial \tau}(\tau, y) = \dfrac{\sigma^2}{2} \dfrac{\partial^2 f}{\partial y^2}(\tau, y) \\[2mm] f(0, y) = (K - y)^+. \end{cases}$$

Chapter 8

Stochastic Volatility

Stochastic volatility refers to the modeling of volatility using time-dependent stochastic processes, in contrast to the constant volatility assumption made in the standard Black–Scholes model. In this setting, we consider the pricing of realized variance swaps and options using moment matching approximations. We also cover the pricing of vanilla options by PDE arguments in the Heston model, and by perturbation analysis approximations in more general stochastic volatility models.

8.1 Stochastic Volatility Models

Time-dependent stochastic volatility

The next Figure 8.1 refers to the EURO/SGD exchange rate, and shows some spikes that cannot be generated by Gaussian returns with constant variance.

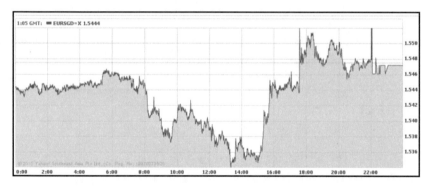

Figure 8.1: Euro / SGD exchange rate.

This type data shows that, in addition to jump models that are commonly used to take into account the slow decrease of probability tails observed in market data, other tools should be implemented in order to model a possibly random and time-varying volatility.

We consider an asset price driven by the stochastic differential equation

$$dS_t = rS_t dt + S_t \sqrt{v_t} dB_t \tag{8.1}$$

under the risk-neutral probability measure $\mathbb{P}^*$, with solution

$$S_T = S_t \exp\left((T-t)r + \int_t^T \sqrt{v_s} dB_s - \frac{1}{2} \int_t^T v_s ds \right) \tag{8.2}$$

DOI: 10.1201/9781003298670-8

where $(v_t)_{t\in\mathbb{R}_+}$ is a (possibly random) squared volatility (or variance) process adapted to the filtration $(\mathcal{F}_t)_{t\in\mathbb{R}_+}$ generated by $(B_t)_{t\in\mathbb{R}_+}$.

Time-dependent deterministic volatility

When the variance process $(v(t))_{t\in\mathbb{R}_+}$ is a deterministic function of time, the solution (8.2) of (8.1) is a lognormal random variable at time T with conditional log-variance

$$\int_t^T v(s)ds$$

given $\mathcal{F}_t$. In particular, the European call option on S_T can be priced by the Black–Scholes formula as

$$e^{-(T-t)r}\,\mathbb{E}^*[(S_T-K)^+\mid\mathcal{F}_t]=\mathrm{Bl}\big(S_t,K,r,T-t,\sqrt{\widehat{v}(t)}\big),$$

with integrated squared volatility parameter

$$\widehat{v}(t):=\frac{\int_t^T v(s)ds}{T-t},\qquad t\in[0,T).$$

Independent (stochastic) volatility

When the volatility $(v_t)_{t\in\mathbb{R}_+}$ is a random process generating a filtration $\big(\mathcal{F}_t^{(2)}\big)_{t\in\mathbb{R}_+}$, independent of the filtration $\big(\mathcal{F}_t^{(1)}\big)_{t\in\mathbb{R}_+}$ generated by the driving Brownian motion $\big(B_t^{(1)}\big)_{t\in\mathbb{R}_+}$ under $\mathbb{P}^*$, the equation (8.1) can still be solved as

$$S_T=S_t\exp\left((T-t)r+\int_t^T\sqrt{v_s}dB_s^{(1)}-\frac{1}{2}\int_t^T v_sds\right),$$

and, given $\mathcal{F}_T^{(2)}$, the asset price S_T is a lognormal random variable with random variance

$$\int_t^T v_sds.$$

In this case, taking

$$\mathcal{F}_t:=\mathcal{F}_t^{(1)}\vee\mathcal{F}_t^{(2)},\qquad 0\leqslant t\leqslant T,$$

where $\big(\mathcal{F}_t^{(1)}\big)_{t\in\mathbb{R}_+}$ is the filtration generated by $\big(B_t^{(1)}\big)_{t\in\mathbb{R}_+}$, we can still price an option with payoff $\phi(S_T)$ on the underlying asset price S_T using the tower property

$$\mathbb{E}^*[\phi(S_T)\mid\mathcal{F}_t]=\mathbb{E}^*\big[\,\mathbb{E}^*\big[\phi(S_T)\mid\mathcal{F}_t^{(1)}\vee\mathcal{F}_T^{(2)}\big]\mid\mathcal{F}_t^{(1)}\vee\mathcal{F}_t^{(2)}\big].$$

As an example, the European call option on S_T can be priced by averaging the Black–Scholes formula as follows:

$$
\begin{aligned}
&e^{-(T-t)r}\,\mathbb{E}^*[(S_T-K)^+\mid\mathcal{F}_t]\\
&\quad=\;e^{-(T-t)r}\,\mathbb{E}^*\big[\,\mathbb{E}^*\big[(S_T-K)^+\mid\mathcal{F}_t^{(1)}\vee\mathcal{F}_T^{(2)}\big]\mid\mathcal{F}_t^{(1)}\vee\mathcal{F}_t^{(2)}\big].\\
&\quad=\;e^{-(T-t)r}\,\mathbb{E}^*\left[\mathrm{Bl}\left(S_t,K,r,T-t,\sqrt{\frac{\int_t^T v_sds}{T-t}}\right)\bigg|\,\mathcal{F}_t\right]\\
&\quad=\;e^{-(T-t)r}\,\mathbb{E}^*\big[\mathrm{Bl}\big(x,K,r,T-t,\sqrt{\widehat{v}(t,T)}\big)\mid\mathcal{F}_t^{(2)}\big]_{|x=S_t},
\end{aligned}
$$

which represents an averaged version of Black–Scholes prices, with the random integrated volatility

$$\widehat{v}(t,T) := \frac{1}{T-t} \int_t^T v_s ds, \qquad 0 \leqslant t \leqslant T.$$

On the other hand, the probability distribution of the time integral $\int_t^T v_s ds$ given $\mathcal{F}_t^{(2)}$ can be computed using integral expressions, see Yor (1992) and Proposition 13.5 when $(v_t)_{t \in \mathbb{R})_+}$ is a geometric Brownian motion, and Lemma 9 in Feller (1951) or Corollary 24 in Albanese and Lawi (2005) and (17.10) when $(v_t)_{t \in \mathbb{R})_+}$ is the CIR process.

Two-factor Stochastic Volatility Models

Evidence based on financial market data, see Figure 9.14, Figure 1 of Papanicolaou and Sircar (2014) or § 2.3.1 in Fouque et al. (2011), shows that the variations in volatility tend to be negatively correlated with the variations of underlying asset prices. For this reason we need to consider an asset price process $(S_t)_{t \in \mathbb{R}_+}$ and a stochastic volatility process $(v_t)_{t \in \mathbb{R}_+}$ driven by

$$\begin{cases} dS_t = rS_t dt + \sqrt{v_t} S_t dB_t^{(1)} \\ \\ dv_t = \mu(t, v_t) dt + \beta(t, v_t) dB_t^{(2)}, \end{cases}$$

Here, $\left(B_t^{(1)}\right)_{t \in \mathbb{R}_+}$ and $\left(B_t^{(2)}\right)_{t \in \mathbb{R}_+}$ are possibly correlated Brownian motions, with

$$\mathrm{Cov}\left(B_t^{(1)}, B_t^{(2)}\right) = \rho t \quad \text{and} \quad dB_t^{(1)} \cdot dB_t^{(2)} = \rho dt,$$

where the correlation parameter ρ satisfies $-1 \leqslant \rho \leqslant 1$, and the coefficients $\mu(t,x)$ and $\beta(t,x)$ can be chosen *e.g.* from mean-reverting models (CIR) or geometric Brownian models, as follows. Note that the observed correlation coefficient ρ is usually negative, cf. *e.g.* § 2.1 in Papanicolaou and Sircar (2014) and Figures 9.14 and 9.15.

The Heston model

In the Heston (1993) model, the stochastic volatility $(v_t)_{t \in \mathbb{R}_+}$ is chosen to be a Cox et al. (1985) (CIR) process, *i.e.* we have

$$\begin{cases} dS_t = rS_t dt + S_t \sqrt{v_t} dB_t^{(1)} \\ \\ dv_t = -\lambda(v_t - m) dt + \eta \sqrt{v_t} dB_t^{(2)}, \end{cases}$$

and $\mu(t,v) = -\lambda(v - m)$, $\beta(t,v) = \eta\sqrt{v}$, where $\lambda, m, \eta > 0$.

Option pricing formulas can be derived in the Heston model using Fourier inversion and complex integrals, cf. (8.29) below.

The SABR model

In the Sigma-Alpha-Beta-Rho (σ-α-β-ρ-SABR) model Hagan et al. (2002), based on the parameters (α, β, ρ), the stochastic volatility process $(\sigma_t)_{t \in \mathbb{R}_+}$ is modeled as a geometric Brownian motion with

$$\begin{cases} dF_t = \sigma_t F_t^\beta dB_t^{(1)} \\ \\ d\sigma_t = \alpha \sigma_t dB_t^{(2)}, \end{cases}$$

where $(F_t)_{t\in\mathbb{R}_+}$ typically models a forward interest rate. Here, we have $\alpha > 0$ and $\beta \in (0,1]$, and $\left(B_t^{(1)}\right)_{t\in\mathbb{R}_+}$, $\left(B_t^{(2)}\right)_{t\in\mathbb{R}_+}$ are standard Brownian motions with the correlation

$$dB_t^{(1)} \cdot dB_t^{(2)} = \rho dt.$$

This setting is typically used for the modeling of LIBOR rates and is *not* mean-reverting, hence it is preferably used with a short time horizon. It allows in particular for short time asymptotics of Black implied volatilities that can be used for pricing by inputting them into the Black pricing formula, cf. § 3.3 in Rebonato (2009).

8.2 Realized Variance Swaps

Another look at historical volatility

When $t_k = kT/N$, $k = 0, 1, \ldots, N$, a natural estimator for the trend parameter μ can be written in terms of actual returns as

$$\widehat{\mu}_N := \frac{1}{N} \sum_{k=1}^{N} \frac{1}{t_k - t_{k-1}} \frac{S_{t_k} - S_{t_{k-1}}}{S_{t_{k-1}}},$$

or in terms of log-returns as

$$\begin{aligned}
\widehat{\mu}_N &:= \frac{1}{N} \sum_{k=1}^{N} \frac{1}{t_k - t_{k-1}} \log \frac{S_{t_k}}{S_{t_{k-1}}} \\
&= \frac{1}{T} \sum_{k=1}^{N} \left(\log(S_{t_k}) - \log(S_{t_{k-1}})\right) \\
&= \frac{1}{T} \log \frac{S_T}{S_0}.
\end{aligned}$$

Similarly, one can use the squared volatility (or realized variance) estimator

$$\begin{aligned}
\widehat{\sigma}_N^2 &:= \frac{1}{N-1} \sum_{k=0}^{N-1} \frac{1}{t_{k+1} - t_k} \left(\frac{S_{t_{k+1}} - S_{t_k}}{S_{t_k}} - (t_{k+1} - t_k)\widehat{\mu}_N\right)^2 \\
&= \frac{1}{N-1} \sum_{k=1}^{N} \frac{1}{t_k - t_{k-1}} \left(\frac{S_{t_k} - S_{t_{k-1}}}{S_{t_{k-1}}}\right)^2 - \frac{T}{N-1}(\widehat{\mu}_N)^2
\end{aligned}$$

using actual returns, or, using log-returns,*

$$\begin{aligned}
\widehat{\sigma}_N^2 &:= \frac{1}{N-1} \sum_{k=1}^{N} \frac{1}{t_k - t_{k-1}} \left(\log \frac{S_{t_k}}{S_{t_{k-1}}} - (t_k - t_{k-1})\widehat{\mu}_N\right)^2 \\
&= \frac{1}{N-1} \sum_{k=1}^{N} \frac{1}{t_k - t_{k-1}} \left(\log \frac{S_{t_k}}{S_{t_{k-1}}}\right)^2 - \frac{T}{N-1}(\widehat{\mu}_N)^2.
\end{aligned} \tag{8.3}$$

---

*We apply the identity $\sum_{k=1}^{n}\left(a_k - \sum_{l=1}^{n} a_l\right)^2 = \sum_{k=1}^{n} a_k^2 - \left(\sum_{l=1}^{n} a_l\right)^2$.

Realized variance swaps

Realized variance swaps are forward contracts that allow for the exchange of the estimated volatility (8.3) against a fixed value κ_σ. They can be priced using log-returns and expected value as

$$\mathbb{E}\left[\hat{\sigma}_N^2\right] = \frac{1}{T}\mathbb{E}\left[\sum_{k=1}^{N}\left(\log\frac{S_{t_k}}{S_{t_{k-1}}}\right)^2 - \frac{1}{N-1}\left(\log\frac{S_T}{S_0}\right)^2\right] - \kappa_\sigma^2$$

of their payoff

$$\frac{1}{T}\left(\sum_{k=1}^{N}\left(\log\frac{S_{t_k}}{S_{t_{k-1}}}\right)^2 - \frac{1}{N-1}\left(\log\frac{S_T}{S_0}\right)^2\right) - \kappa_\sigma^2,$$

where κ_σ is the volatility level. Note that the above payoff has to be multiplied by the *vega notional*, which is part of the contract, in order to convert it into currency units.

Heston model

Consider the Heston (1993) model driven by the stochastic differential equation

$$dv_t = (a - bv_t)dt + \sigma\sqrt{v_t}dW_t,$$

where $a, b, \sigma > 0$. We have

$$\mathbb{E}[v_T] = v_0 e^{-bT} + \frac{a}{b}\left(1 - e^{-bT}\right),$$

see Exercise 4.18-(b), and Exercise 8.2-(a), from which it follows that the realized variance $R_{0,T}^2 := \int_0^T v_t dt$ can be averaged as

$$
\begin{aligned}
\mathbb{E}\left[R_{0,T}^2\right] &= \mathbb{E}\left[\int_0^T v_t dt\right] \\
&= \int_0^T \mathbb{E}[v_t]dt \\
&= v_0\frac{1 - e^{-bT}}{b} + a\frac{e^{-bT} + bT - 1}{b^2}.
\end{aligned}
\tag{8.4}
$$

We can also express the variances

$$\mathrm{Var}[v_T] = v_0\frac{\sigma^2}{b}\left(e^{-bT} - e^{-2bT}\right) + \frac{a\sigma^2}{2b^2}\left(1 - e^{-bT}\right)^2,$$

cf. Exercise 4.18-(e), and

$$
\begin{aligned}
\mathrm{Var}\left[R_{0,T}^2\right] &= v_0\sigma^2\frac{1 - 2bTe^{-bT} - e^{-2bT}}{b^3} \\
&+ a\sigma^2\frac{e^{-2bT} + 2bT + 4(bT + 1)e^{-bT} - 5}{2b^4},
\end{aligned}
\tag{8.5}
$$

see *e.g.* Relation (3.3) in Prayoga and Privault (2017).

Stochastic volatility

In what follows, we assume that the risky asset price process is given by

$$\frac{dS_t}{S_t} = r dt + \sigma_t dB_t, \tag{8.6}$$

under the risk-neutral probability measure $\mathbb{P}^*$, *i.e.*

$$S_t = S_0 \exp\left(rt + \int_0^t \sigma_s dB_s - \frac{1}{2}\int_0^t \sigma_s^2 ds\right), \quad t \geqslant 0, \tag{8.7}$$

where $(\sigma_t)_{t\in\mathbb{R}_+}$ is a stochastic volatility process. In this setting, we have the following proposition.

Proposition 8.1. *Denoting by* $F_0 := e^{rT} S_0$ *the future price on* S_T, *we have the relation*

$$\mathbb{E}^*\left[\int_0^T \sigma_t^2 dt\right] = 2\,\mathbb{E}^*\left[\log \frac{F_0}{S_T}\right]. \tag{8.8}$$

Proof. From (8.7), we have

$$
\begin{aligned}
\mathbb{E}^*\left[\log \frac{S_T}{F_0}\right] &= \mathbb{E}^*\left[\log \frac{S_T}{S_0}\right] - rT \\
&= \mathbb{E}^*\left[\int_0^T \sigma_t dB_t - \frac{1}{2}\int_0^T \sigma_t^2 dt\right] \\
&= -\frac{1}{2}\,\mathbb{E}^*\left[\int_0^T \sigma_t^2 dt\right].
\end{aligned}
$$

$\square$

Independent stochastic volatility

In this subsection, we assume that the stochastic volatility process $(\sigma_t)_{t\in\mathbb{R}_+}$ in (8.6) is *independent* of the Brownian motion $(B_t)_{t\in\mathbb{R}_+}$.

Lemma 8.2. *(Carr and Lee (2008), Proposition 5.1) Assume that* $(\sigma_t)_{t\in\mathbb{R}_+}$ *is independent of* $(B_t)_{t\in\mathbb{R}_+}$. *Then, for every* $\lambda > 0$ *we have*

$$\mathbb{E}^*\left[\exp\left(\lambda \int_0^T \sigma_t^2 dt\right)\right] = e^{-rp_\lambda^{\pm}T}\,\mathbb{E}^*\left[\left(\frac{S_T}{S_0}\right)^{p_\lambda^{\pm}}\right], \tag{8.9}$$

where $p_\lambda^{\pm} := \dfrac{1}{2} \pm \sqrt{\dfrac{1}{4} + 2\lambda}$.

Proof. Letting $(\mathcal{F}_t^\sigma)_{t\in\mathbb{R}_+}$ denote the filtration generated by the process $(\sigma_t)_{t\in\mathbb{R}_+}$, we have

$$
\begin{aligned}
e^{-rp_\lambda T}\,\mathbb{E}^*\left[\left(\frac{S_T}{S_0}\right)^{p_\lambda} \Big| \mathcal{F}_T^\sigma\right] &= \mathbb{E}^*\left[\exp\left(p_\lambda \int_0^T \sigma_t dB_t - \frac{p_\lambda}{2}\int_0^T \sigma_t^2 dt\right) \Big| \mathcal{F}_T^\sigma\right] \\
&= \exp\left(-\frac{p_\lambda}{2}\int_0^T \sigma_t^2 dt\right) \mathbb{E}^*\left[\exp\left(p_\lambda \int_0^T \sigma_t dB_t\right) \Big| \mathcal{F}_T^\sigma\right] \\
&= \exp\left(-\frac{p_\lambda}{2}\int_0^T \sigma_t^2 dt\right) \exp\left(\frac{p_\lambda^2}{2}\int_0^T \sigma_t^2 dt\right)
\end{aligned}
$$

$$= \exp\left(\frac{p_\lambda}{2}(p_\lambda - 1)\int_0^T \sigma_t^2 dt\right)$$

$$= \exp\left(\lambda \int_0^T \sigma_t^2 dt\right),$$

provided that $\lambda = p_\lambda(p_\lambda - 1)/2$, and in this case we have

$$e^{-rp_\lambda T} \, \mathbb{E}^*\left[\left(\frac{S_T}{S_0}\right)^{p_\lambda}\right] = e^{-rp_\lambda T} \, \mathbb{E}^*\left[\mathbb{E}^*\left[\left(\frac{S_T}{S_0}\right)^{p_\lambda} \Big| \mathcal{F}_T^\sigma\right]\right]$$

$$= \mathbb{E}^*\left[\exp\left(\lambda \int_0^T \sigma_t^2 dt\right)\right].$$

It remains to note that the equation $\lambda = p_\lambda(p_\lambda - 1)/2$, i.e. $p_\lambda^2 - p_\lambda - 2\lambda = 0$, has for solutions

$$p_\lambda^\pm = \frac{1}{2} \pm \sqrt{\frac{1}{4} + 2\lambda},$$

with $p_\lambda^- < 0 < p_\lambda^+$ when $\lambda > 0$. □

By differentiating the moment generating function computed in Lemma 8.2 with respect to $\lambda > 0$, we can compute the first moment of the realized variance $R_{0,T}^2 = \int_0^T \sigma_t^2 dt$ in the following corollary.

Corollary 8.3. *Assume that* $(\sigma_t)_{t\in\mathbb{R}_+}$ *is independent of* $(B_t)_{t\in\mathbb{R}_+}$. *Denoting by* $F_0 := e^{rT} S_0$ *the future price on* S_T, *we have*

$$\mathbb{E}^*\left[\int_0^T \sigma_t^2 dt\right] = 2\,\mathbb{E}^*\left[\frac{S_T}{F_0} \log \frac{S_T}{F_0}\right].$$

Proof. Rewriting (8.9) as

$$\mathbb{E}^*\left[\exp\left(\lambda \int_0^T \sigma_t^2 dt\right)\right] = \mathbb{E}^*\left[\exp\left(-rp_\lambda^\pm T + p_\lambda^\pm \log \frac{S_T}{S_0}\right)\right]$$

and differentiating this relation with respect to λ, we get

$$\mathbb{E}^*\left[\int_0^T \sigma_t^2 dt \exp\left(\lambda \int_0^T \sigma_t^2 dt\right)\right] = -rp_\lambda' T\,\mathbb{E}^*\left[\exp\left(-rp_\lambda^\pm T + p_\lambda^\pm \log \frac{S_T}{S_0}\right)\right]$$

$$+ p_\lambda'\,\mathbb{E}^*\left[\exp\left(-rp_\lambda^\pm T + p_\lambda^\pm \log \frac{S_T}{S_0}\right) \log \frac{S_T}{S_0}\right]$$

$$= \mp\frac{rT}{\sqrt{2\lambda + 1/4}}\,\mathbb{E}^*\left[\exp\left(-rp_\lambda^\pm T\right)\left(\frac{S_T}{S_0}\right)^{p_\lambda^\pm}\right]$$

$$\pm \frac{1}{\sqrt{2\lambda + 1/4}}\,\mathbb{E}^*\left[\exp\left(-rp_\lambda^\pm T + p_\lambda^\pm \log \frac{S_T}{S_0}\right) \log \frac{S_T}{S_0}\right],$$

which, when $\lambda = 0$, recovers (8.8) in Lemma 8.1 as

$$\mathbb{E}^*\left[\int_0^T \sigma_t^2 dt\right] = 2rT - 2\,\mathbb{E}^*\left[\log \frac{S_T}{S_0}\right] = -2\,\mathbb{E}^*\left[\int_0^T \sigma_t dB_t - \frac{1}{2}\int_0^T \sigma_t^2 dt\right]$$

if $p_0^- = 0$, and yields

$$\mathbb{E}^*\left[\int_0^T \sigma_t^2 dt\right] = 2\,e^{-rT}\,\mathbb{E}^*\left[\frac{S_T}{S_0} \log \frac{e^{-rT} S_T}{S_0}\right]$$

for $p_0^+ = 1$. □

8.3   Realized Variance Options

In this section we consider the realized variance call option with payoff

$$\left(\int_0^T \sigma_t^2 dt - \kappa_\sigma^2 \right)^+.$$

Proposition 8.4. *In case* $\int_0^t \sigma_u^2 du \geqslant \kappa_\sigma^2$, *the price of the realized variance call option in the money is given by*

$$e^{-(T-t)r} \, \mathbb{E}^* \left[\left(\int_0^T \sigma_u^2 du - \kappa_\sigma^2 \right)^+ \Big| \mathcal{F}_t \right]$$

$$= e^{-(T-t)r} \int_0^t \sigma_u^2 du - e^{-(T-t)r} \kappa_\sigma^2 + e^{-(T-t)r} \, \mathbb{E}^* \left[\int_t^T \sigma_u^2 du \Big| \mathcal{F}_t \right].$$

Proof. In case $\int_0^t \sigma_u^2 du \geqslant \kappa_\sigma^2$, we have

$$e^{-(T-t)r} \, \mathbb{E}^* \left[\left(\int_0^T \sigma_u^2 du - \kappa_\sigma^2 \right)^+ \Big| \mathcal{F}_t \right]$$

$$= e^{-(T-t)r} \, \mathbb{E}^* \left[\left(x + \int_t^T \sigma_u^2 du - \kappa_\sigma^2 \right)^+ \Big| \mathcal{F}_t \right]_{x = \int_0^t \sigma_u^2 du}$$

$$= e^{-(T-t)r} \, \mathbb{E}^* \left[x + \int_t^T \sigma_u^2 du - \kappa_\sigma^2 \Big| \mathcal{F}_t \right]_{x = \int_0^t \sigma_u^2 du}$$

$$= e^{-(T-t)r} \int_0^t \sigma_u^2 du - e^{-(T-t)r} \kappa_\sigma^2 + e^{-(T-t)r} \, \mathbb{E}^* \left[\int_t^T \sigma_u^2 du \Big| \mathcal{F}_t \right].$$

$\square$

Lognormal approximation

When $R_{0,t}^2 := \int_0^t \sigma_u^2 du < \kappa_\sigma^2$, in order to estimate the price

$$e^{-(T-t)r} \, \mathbb{E}^* \left[\left(x + \int_t^T \sigma_u^2 du - \kappa_\sigma^2 \right)^+ \Big| \mathcal{F}_t \right]_{x = \int_0^t \sigma_u^2 du}, \tag{8.10}$$

of the realized variance call option out of the money, we can approximate $R_{t,T} := \sqrt{\int_t^T \sigma_u^2 du}$ by a lognormal random variable

$$R_{t,T} = \sqrt{\int_t^T \sigma_u^2 du} \simeq e^{\tilde{\mu}_{t,T} + \widetilde{\sigma}_{t,T} X}$$

with mean $\tilde{\mu}_{t,T}$ and variance $\eta_{t,T}^2$, where $X \simeq \mathcal{N}(0, T - t)$ is a centered Gaussian random variable with variance $T - t$.

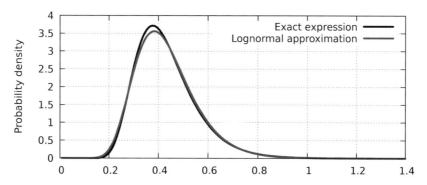

Figure 8.2: Fitting of a lognormal probability density function.

Proposition 8.5. *(Lognormal approximation by volatility swap moment matching). The probability density function $\varphi_{R_{t,T}}$ of $R_{t,T} := \sqrt{\int_t^T \sigma_u^2 du}$ can be approximated as*

$$\varphi_{R_{t,T}}(x) \approx \frac{1}{x\widetilde{\sigma}_{t,T}\sqrt{2(T-t)\pi}} \exp\left(-\frac{(\tilde{\mu}_{t,T} - \log x)^2}{2(T-t)\widetilde{\sigma}_{t,T}^2}\right), \quad x > 0, \tag{8.11}$$

where

$$\tilde{\mu}_{t,T} := \log\left(\frac{(\mathbb{E}[R_{t,T}])^2}{\sqrt{\mathbb{E}[R_{t,T}^2]}}\right) \quad and \quad \widetilde{\sigma}_{t,T}^2 := \frac{2}{T-t}\log\left(\frac{\sqrt{\mathbb{E}[R_{t,T}^2]}}{\mathbb{E}[R_{t,T}]}\right), \tag{8.12}$$

and $\mathbb{E}[R_{t,T}^2]$, $\mathbb{E}[R_{t,T}]$ can be estimated from realized variance and volatility swap prices.

Proof. The parameters $\tilde{\mu}_{t,T}$ and $\widetilde{\sigma}_{t,T}$ are estimated by matching the first and second moments $\mathbb{E}[R_{t,T}]$ and $\mathbb{E}[R_{t,T}^2]$ of $R_{t,T}$ to those of the lognormal distribution with mean $\tilde{\mu}_{t,T}$ and variance $(T-t)\widetilde{\sigma}_{t,T}^2$, which yields

$$\mathbb{E}[R_{t,T}] = e^{\tilde{\mu}_{t,T}+(T-t)\widetilde{\sigma}_{t,T}^2/2} \quad and \quad \mathbb{E}[R_{t,T}^2] = e^{2(\tilde{\mu}_{t,T}+(T-t)\widetilde{\sigma}_{t,T}^2)},$$

and (8.12). $\qquad\square$

By (8.12), the parameters $\tilde{\mu}_{t,T}$ and $\widetilde{\sigma}_{t,T}^2$ can be estimated from the realized volatility swap price

$$e^{-(T-t)r}\,\mathbb{E}^*\left[R_{t,T}\mid\mathcal{F}_t\right] = e^{-(T-t)r}\,\mathbb{E}^*\left[\sqrt{\int_t^T \sigma_u^2 du}\,\Bigg|\,\mathcal{F}_t\right],$$

and from the realized variance swap price

$$e^{-(T-t)r}\,\mathbb{E}^*\left[R_{t,T}^2\mid\mathcal{F}_t\right] = e^{-(T-t)r}\,\mathbb{E}^*\left[\int_t^T \sigma_u^2 du\,\Bigg|\,\mathcal{F}_t\right].$$

By Proposition 8.7, we can estimate the price (8.10) of the realized variance call option by approximating $R_{t,T}^2 = \int_t^T \sigma_u^2 du$ by a lognormal random variable. We refer to § 8.4 in Friz and Gatheral (2005) or to Relation (11.15) page 152 of Gatheral (2006) for the following result.

Proposition 8.6. *Under the lognormal approximation (8.11), the price*

$$\mathrm{VC}_{t,T}(\kappa_\sigma) = e^{-(T-t)r}\,\mathbb{E}\left[\left(x + R_{t,T}^2 - \kappa_\sigma^2\right)^+\right]_{x=R_{0,t}^2}$$

of the realized variance call option can be approximated as

$$\mathrm{VC}_{t,T}(\kappa_\sigma) \approx \mathrm{e}^{-(T-t)r}\, \mathbb{E}\left[R_{t,T}^2\right]\Phi(d_+) - \mathrm{e}^{-(T-t)r}\left(\kappa_\sigma^2 - R_{0,t}^2\right)\Phi(d_-), \qquad (8.13)$$

where

$$\begin{aligned}
d_+ &:= \frac{\log\left((\mathbb{E}[R_{t,T}])^2/\left(\kappa_\sigma^2 - R_{0,t}^2\right)\right)}{2\widetilde{\sigma}_{t,T}\sqrt{T-t}} + 2\widetilde{\sigma}_{t,T}\sqrt{T-t} \\[2mm]
&= \frac{-\log\left(\kappa_\sigma^2 - R_{0,t}^2\right) + 2\widetilde{\mu}_{t,T} + 4(T-t)\widetilde{\sigma}_{t,T}^2}{2\widetilde{\sigma}_{t,T}\sqrt{T-t}},
\end{aligned}$$

and

$$d_- := d_+ - 2\widetilde{\sigma}_{t,T}\sqrt{T-t} = \frac{2\widetilde{\mu}_{t,T} - \log\left(\kappa_\sigma^2 - R_{0,t}^2\right)}{2\widetilde{\sigma}_{t,T}\sqrt{T-t}},$$

and Φ denotes the standard Gaussian cumulative distribution function.

Proof. The lognormal approximation (8.13) by realized variance moment matching states that

$$\varphi_{R_{t,T}}(x) \approx \frac{1}{x\widetilde{\sigma}_{t,T}\sqrt{2(T-t)\pi}}\, \mathrm{e}^{-(-\widetilde{\mu}_{t,T}+\log x)^2/(2(T-t)\widetilde{\sigma}_{t,T}^2)}, \quad x > 0,$$

or equivalently

$$\begin{aligned}
\varphi_{R_{t,T}^2}(x) &= \frac{1}{2\sqrt{x}}\varphi_{R_{t,T}}(\sqrt{x}) \\[2mm]
&\approx \frac{1}{2x\widetilde{\sigma}_{t,T}\sqrt{2(T-t)\pi}}\, \mathrm{e}^{-(-2\widetilde{\mu}_{t,T}+\log x)^2/(2(T-t)(2\widetilde{\sigma}_{t,T})^2)}, \quad x > 0.
\end{aligned}$$

In other words, the distribution of $R_{t,T}^2$ is approximately that of $\mathrm{e}^{2\widetilde{\mu}_{t,T}+2\widetilde{\sigma}_{t,T}X}$ where $X \simeq \mathcal{N}(0, T-t)$, hence

$$\begin{aligned}
\mathrm{VC}_{t,T}(\kappa_\sigma) &= \mathrm{e}^{-(T-t)r}\, \mathbb{E}\left[\left(x + R_{t,T}^2 - \kappa_\sigma^2\right)^+\right]_{x=R_{0,t}^2} \\[2mm]
&= \mathrm{e}^{-(T-t)r} \int_{\kappa_\sigma}^\infty \left(y - \left(\kappa_\sigma^2 - R_{0,t}^2\right)\right)^+ \varphi_{R_{t,T}^2}(y)\,dy \\[2mm]
&\approx \mathrm{e}^{-(T-t)r}\, \mathbb{E}\left[\left(\mathrm{e}^{2\widetilde{\mu}_{t,T}+2\widetilde{\sigma}_{t,T}X} - \left(\kappa_\sigma^2 - x\right)\right)^+\right]_{x=R_{0,t}^2} \\[2mm]
&= \mathrm{e}^{-(T-t)r}\left(\mathrm{e}^{2\widetilde{\mu}_{t,T}+2(T-t)\widetilde{\sigma}_{t,T}^2}\Phi(d_+) - \left(\kappa_\sigma^2 - R_{0,t}^2\right)\Phi(d_-)\right) \\[2mm]
&= \mathrm{e}^{-(T-t)r}\, \mathbb{E}\left[R_{t,T}^2\right]\Phi(d_+) - \mathrm{e}^{-(T-t)r}\left(\kappa_\sigma^2 - R_{0,t}^2\right)\Phi(d_-), \qquad (8.14)
\end{aligned}$$

see Lemma 7.7. $\qquad\square$

In order to estimate the price

$$\mathrm{e}^{-(T-t)r}\, \mathbb{E}^*\left[\left(x + \int_t^T \sigma_u^2\,du - \kappa_\sigma^2\right)^+ \Big| \mathcal{F}_t\right]_{x=\int_0^t \sigma_u^2\,du},$$

of the realized variance call option when $R_{0,t} := \sqrt{\int_0^t \sigma_u^2\,du} < \kappa_\sigma$, we can also approximate $R_{t,T}^2 := \int_t^T \sigma_u^2\,du$ by a lognormal random variable

$$R_{t,T}^2 = \int_t^T \sigma_u^2\,du \simeq \mathrm{e}^{\widetilde{\mu}_{t,T}+\widetilde{\sigma}_{t,T}X}$$

with mean $\widetilde{\mu}_{t,T}$ and variance $\sigma_{t,T}^2$, where $X \simeq \mathcal{N}(0,1)$ is a standard normal random variable.

Proposition 8.7. *(Lognormal approximation by realized variance moment matching). Under the lognormal approximation, the probability density function $\varphi_{R^2_{t,T}}$ of $R^2_{t,T} := \int_t^T \sigma_u^2 du$ can be approximated as*

$$\varphi_{R^2_{t,T}}(x) \approx \frac{1}{x\widetilde{\sigma}_{t,T}\sqrt{2(T-t)\pi}} \exp\left(-\frac{(\tilde{\mu}_{t,T} - \log x)^2}{2(T-t)\widetilde{\sigma}_{t,T}^2}\right), \quad x > 0, \tag{8.15}$$

where

$$\tilde{\mu}_{t,T} := -(T-t)\frac{\widetilde{\sigma}_{t,T}^2}{2} + \log \mathbb{E}[R^2_{t,T}], \tag{8.16}$$

and

$$\widetilde{\sigma}_{t,T}^2 = \frac{1}{T-t}\log\left(1 + \frac{\mathrm{Var}[R^2_{t,T}]}{(\mathbb{E}[R^2_{t,T}])^2}\right). \tag{8.17}$$

Proof. The parameters $\tilde{\mu}_{t,T}$ and $\widetilde{\sigma}_{t,T}$ are estimated by matching the first and second moments $\mathbb{E}\left[R^2_{t,T}\right]$ and $\mathbb{E}\left[R^4_{t,T}\right]$ of $R^2_{t,T}$ to those of the lognormal distribution with mean $\tilde{\mu}_{t,T}$ and variance $(T-t)\widetilde{\sigma}_{t,T}^2$, which yields

$$\mathbb{E}\left[R^2_{t,T}\right] = e^{\tilde{\mu}_{t,T} + (T-t)\widetilde{\sigma}_{t,T}^2/2}, \qquad \mathbb{E}\left[R^4_{t,T}\right] = e^{2(\tilde{\mu}_{t,T} + (T-t)\widetilde{\sigma}_{t,T}^2)},$$

and

$$\tilde{\mu}_{t,T} = -(T-t)\frac{\widetilde{\sigma}_{t,T}^2}{2} + \log \mathbb{E}\left[R^2_{t,T}\right] \quad \text{and} \quad \widetilde{\sigma}_{t,T}^2 := \frac{1}{T-t}\log\left(\frac{\mathbb{E}\left[R^4_{t,T}\right]}{\left(\mathbb{E}\left[R^2_{t,T}\right]\right)^2}\right).$$

$\square$

By (8.16)–(8.17), the parameters $\tilde{\mu}_{t,T}$ and $\widetilde{\sigma}_{t,T}^2$ can be estimated from the realized variance swap price

$$e^{-(T-t)r}\,\mathbb{E}^*\left[R^2_{t,T} \mid \mathcal{F}_t\right] = e^{-(T-t)r}\,\mathbb{E}^*\left[\int_t^T \sigma_u^2 du \,\bigg|\, \mathcal{F}_t\right],$$

and from the realized variance power option price

$$e^{-(T-t)r}\,\mathbb{E}^*\left[R^4_{t,T} \mid \mathcal{F}_t\right] = e^{-(T-t)r}\,\mathbb{E}^*\left[\left(\int_t^T \sigma_u^2 du\right)^2 \,\bigg|\, \mathcal{F}_t\right].$$

The next proposition is obtained by the same argument as in the proof of Proposition 8.6.

Proposition 8.8. *Under the lognormal approximation* (8.15), *the price*

$$\mathrm{VC}_{t,T}(\kappa_\sigma) = e^{-(T-t)r}\,\mathbb{E}\left[(x + R^2_{t,T} - \kappa_\sigma^2)^+\right]_{x=R_{0,t}}$$

of the realized variance call option can be approximated as

$$\mathrm{VC}_{t,T}(\kappa_\sigma) \approx e^{-(T-t)r}\,\mathbb{E}\left[R^2_{t,T}\right]\Phi(d_+) - e^{-(T-t)r}\left(\kappa_\sigma^2 - R^2_{0,t}\right)\Phi(d_-), \tag{8.18}$$

where

$$
\begin{aligned}
d_+ \quad &:= \quad \frac{\log\left(\mathbb{E}\left[R^2_{t,T}\right]/\left(\kappa_\sigma^2 - R^2_{0,t}\right)\right)}{\widetilde{\sigma}_{t,T}\sqrt{T-t}} + \widetilde{\sigma}_{t,T}\frac{\sqrt{T-t}}{2} \\
&= \quad \frac{-\log\left(\kappa_\sigma^2 - R^2_{0,t}\right) + \tilde{\mu}_{t,T} + (T-t)\widetilde{\sigma}_{t,T}^2}{\widetilde{\sigma}_{t,T}\sqrt{T-t}},
\end{aligned}
$$

and

$$d_- := d_+ - \widetilde{\sigma}_{t,T}\sqrt{T-t} = \frac{\widetilde{\mu}_{t,T} - \log\left(\kappa_\sigma^2 - R_{0,t}^2\right)}{\widetilde{\sigma}_{t,T}\sqrt{T-t}},$$

and Φ *denotes the standard Gaussian cumulative distribution function.*

Note that, using the integral identity

$$\sqrt{x} = \frac{1}{2\pi}\int_0^\infty (1 - e^{-\lambda x})\frac{d\lambda}{\lambda^{3/2}},$$

see *e.g.* Relation 3.434.1 in Gradshteyn and Ryzhik (2007) and Exercise 9.7-(a), the realized volatility swap price $\mathbb{E}[R_{t,T}]$ can be expressed as

$$\mathbb{E}[R_{t,T}] = \frac{1}{2\sqrt{\pi}}\int_0^\infty \left(1 - \mathbb{E}\left[e^{-\lambda R_{t,T}^2}\right]\right)\frac{d\lambda}{\lambda^{3/2}}, \tag{8.19}$$

see § 3.1 in Friz and Gatheral (2005), where $\mathbb{E}\left[e^{-\lambda R_{t,T}^2}\right]$ can be expressed from Lemma 8.2. In particular, by *e.g.* Relation (3.25) in Brigo and Mercurio (2006), in the Cox et al. (1985) (CIR)

$$dv_t = (a - bv_t)dt + \eta\sqrt{v_t}dW_t$$

variance model with $v_t = \sigma_t^2$, we have

$$
\begin{aligned}
&\mathbb{E}\left[e^{-\lambda R_{0,T}^2}\right] \\
&= \exp\left(-\frac{2v_0\lambda(1 - e^{-\bar{b}T})}{\bar{b} + b + (\bar{b} - b)e^{-\bar{b}T}} - \frac{a}{\eta^2}(\bar{b} - b)T - \frac{2a}{\eta^2}\log\frac{\bar{b} + b + (\bar{b} - b)e^{-\bar{b}T}}{2\bar{b}}\right),
\end{aligned}
$$

where $\bar{b} := \sqrt{b^2 + 2\lambda\eta^2}$.

Gamma approximation

In case $R_{0,t}^2 = \int_0^t \sigma_u^2 du < \kappa_\sigma^2$, the realized variance call option price

$$e^{-(T-t)r}\,\mathbb{E}^*\left[\left(x + \int_t^T \sigma_u^2 du - \kappa_\sigma^2\right)^+ \middle| \mathcal{F}_t\right]_{x=\int_0^t \sigma_u^2 du}$$

can be estimated by approximating $R_{t,T}^2 = \int_t^T \sigma_u^2 du$ by a gamma random variable as in the probability density graph of Figure 8.3.

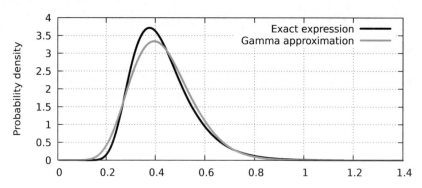

Figure 8.3: Fitting of a gamma probability density function.

Proposition 8.9. *(Gamma approximation). Under the gamma approximation the probability density function* $\varphi_{R_{t,T}^2}$ *of* $R_{t,T}^2 := \int_t^T \sigma_u^2 du$ *can be approximated as*

$$\varphi_{R_{t,T}^2}(x) \approx \frac{(x/\theta_{t,T})^{-1+\nu_{t,T}}}{\theta_{t,T}\Gamma(\nu_{t,T})}e^{-x/\theta_{t,T}}, \qquad x > 0, \tag{8.20}$$

where

$$\theta_{t,T} = \frac{\text{Var}\left[R_{t,T}^2\right]}{\mathbb{E}\left[R_{t,T}^2\right]} \quad and \quad \nu_{t,T} = \frac{\mathbb{E}\left[R_{t,T}^2\right]}{\theta_{t,T}} = \frac{\left(\mathbb{E}\left[R_{t,T}^2\right]\right)^2}{\text{Var}\left[R_{t,T}^2\right]}. \tag{8.21}$$

Proof. The parameters $\theta_{t,T}$, $\nu_{t,T}$ are estimated by matching the first and second moments of $R_{t,T}^2$ to those of the gamma distribution with scale and shape parameters $\theta_{t,T}$ and $\nu_{t,T}$, which yields

$$\mathbb{E}\left[R_{t,T}^2\right] = \nu_{t,T}\theta_{t,T} \quad and \quad \text{Var}\left[R_{t,T}^2\right] = \nu_{t,T}\theta_{t,T}^2,$$

and (8.21). □

Proposition 8.10. *Under the gamma approximation* (8.20), *the price*

$$\text{EA}(\kappa_\sigma, T) = e^{-(T-t)r}\,\mathbb{E}\left[(x + R_{t,T}^2 - \kappa_\sigma^2)^+\right]_{x=R_{0,t}^2}$$

of the realized variance call option can be approximated as

$$\text{EA}(\kappa_\sigma, T) = e^{-(T-t)r}\left(\mathbb{E}\left[R_{t,T}^2\right]Q\left(1+\nu_{t,T}, \frac{\kappa_\sigma^2}{\theta_{t,T}}\right) - \kappa_\sigma^2 Q\left(\nu_{t,T}, \frac{\kappa_\sigma^2}{\theta_{t,T}}\right)\right), \tag{8.22}$$

where

$$Q(\lambda, z) := \frac{1}{\Gamma(\lambda)}\int_z^\infty t^{\lambda-1}e^{-t}dt, \qquad z > 0,$$

is the (normalized) upper incomplete gamma function.

Proof. Using the gamma approximation

$$\varphi_{R_{t,T}^2}(x) \approx \frac{e^{-x/\theta_{t,T}}}{\Gamma(\nu_{t,T})}\frac{x^{-1+\nu_{t,T}}}{(\theta_{t,T})^{\nu_{t,T}}}, \tag{8.23}$$

where $\theta_{t,T}$ and $\nu_{t,T}$ are given by (8.21), we have

$$\begin{aligned}
\mathbb{E}\left[(R_{t,T}^2 - \kappa_\sigma^2)^+\right] &= \int_{\kappa_\sigma^2}^\infty (x-\kappa_\sigma^2)^+ \varphi_{R_{t,T}^2}(x)dx \\
&\approx \frac{1}{\Gamma(\nu_{t,T})}\int_{\kappa_\sigma^2}^\infty (x-\kappa_\sigma^2)\frac{x^{-1+\nu_{t,T}}}{(\theta_{t,T})^{\nu_{t,T}}}e^{-x/\theta_{t,T}}dx \\
&= \frac{1}{\Gamma(\nu_{t,T})}\int_{\kappa_\sigma^2}^\infty (x/\theta_{t,T})^{\nu_{t,T}}e^{-x/\theta_{t,T}}dx - \frac{\kappa_\sigma^2}{\Gamma(\nu_{t,T})}\int_{\kappa_\sigma^2}^\infty \frac{x^{-1+\nu_{t,T}}}{(\theta_{t,T})^{\nu_{t,T}}}e^{-x/\theta_{t,T}}dx \\
&= \frac{\theta_{t,T}}{\Gamma(\nu_{t,T})}\int_{\kappa_\sigma^2/\theta_{t,T}}^\infty x^{\nu_{t,T}}e^{-x}dx - \frac{\kappa_\sigma^2}{\Gamma(\nu_{t,T})}\int_{\kappa_\sigma^2/\theta_{t,T}}^\infty x^{-1+\nu_{t,T}}e^{-x}dx \\
&= \theta_{t,T}\nu_{t,T}Q\left(1+\nu_{t,T}, \frac{\kappa_\sigma^2}{\theta_{t,T}}\right) - \kappa_\sigma^2 Q\left(\nu_{t,T}, \frac{\kappa_\sigma^2}{\theta_{t,T}}\right),
\end{aligned}$$

where

$$Q(\lambda, z) := \frac{1}{\Gamma(\lambda)} \int_z^\infty t^{\lambda-1} e^{-t} dt, \qquad z > 0,$$

is the (normalized) upper incomplete gamma function, which yields

$$
\begin{aligned}
\mathrm{EA}(\kappa_\sigma, T) &= e^{-(T-t)r} \, \mathbb{E}\left[\left(x + R_{t,T}^2 - \kappa_\sigma^2 \right)^+ \right] \\
&\approx e^{-(T-t)r} \left(\nu_{t,T} \theta_{t,T} Q\left(1 + \nu_{t,T}, \frac{\kappa_\sigma^2}{\theta_{t,T}} \right) - \kappa_\sigma^2 Q\left(\nu_{t,T}, \frac{\kappa_\sigma^2}{\theta_{t,T}} \right) \right) \qquad (8.24) \\
&= e^{-(T-t)r} \left(\mathbb{E}\left[R_{t,T}^2 \right] Q\left(1 + \nu_{t,T}, \frac{\kappa_\sigma^2}{\theta_{t,T}} \right) - \kappa_\sigma^2 Q\left(\nu_{t,T}, \frac{\kappa_\sigma^2}{\theta_{t,T}} \right) \right).
\end{aligned}
$$

$\square$

Realized variance options in the Heston model

Taking $r = 0$, $t = 0$ and $R_{0,0} = 0$, and using the parameters

$$\sigma = 0.39, \quad b = 1.15, \quad a = 0.04 \times b, \quad v_0 = 0.04, \quad T = 1$$

in the Heston stochastic differential equation

$$dv_t = (a - bv_t)dt + \sigma\sqrt{v_t}dW_t,$$

in Figures 8.4-8.5 we plot the graphs of the lognormal volatility swap and realized variance moment matching approximations (8.13), (8.18), and of the gamma approximation (8.22) for realized variance call option prices with $\kappa_\sigma^2 \in [0, 0.2]$, based on the expressions (8.4)–(8.5) of $\mathbb{E}\left[R_{0,T}^2 \right]$ and $\mathrm{Var}\left[R_{0,T}^2 \right]$.

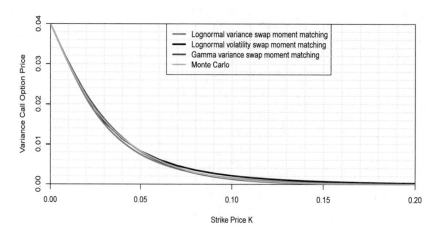

Figure 8.4: One-year variance call option prices with $b = 0.15$.

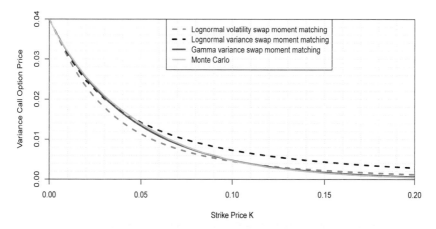

Figure 8.5: One-year variance call option prices with $b = -0.05$.

As can be checked from in Figure 8.5 with

$$\sigma = 0.39, \ b = 1.15, \ a = 0.04 \times b, \ v_0 = 0.04, \ T = 1,$$

the gamma approximation (8.22) appears to be more accurate than the lognormal approximations for large values of κ_σ^2, which can be consistent with the fact that the long run distribution of the CIR-Heston process has the gamma probability density function

$$f(x) = \frac{1}{\Gamma(2a/\sigma^2)} \left(\frac{2b}{\sigma^2} \right)^{2a/\sigma^2} x^{-1+2a/\sigma^2} e^{-2bx/\sigma^2}, \quad x > 0.$$

with shape parameter $2a/\sigma^2$ and scale parameter $\sigma^2/(2b)$, which is also the *invariant distribution* of v_t.

8.4 European Options – PDE Method

In what follows we consider an asset price process $(S_t)_{t \in \mathbb{R}_+}$ in the stochastic volatility model

$$dS_t = rS_t dt + S_t \sqrt{v_t} dB_t^{(1)}$$

under the risk-neutral probability measure $\mathbb{P}^*$, where $(v_t)_{t \in \mathbb{R}_+}$ is a squared volatility (or variance) process satisfying a stochastic differential equation of the form

$$dv_t = \mu(t, v_t)dt + \beta(t, v_t)dB_t^{(2)}.$$

Here, $\left(B_t^{(1)} \right)_{t \in \mathbb{R}_+}$ and $\left(B_t^{(2)} \right)_{t \in \mathbb{R}_+}$ are correlated standard Brownian motions started at 0 with correlation $\mathrm{Corr}\left(B_s^{(1)}, B_t^{(2)} \right) = \rho \min(s, t)$ under the risk-neutral probability measure $\mathbb{P}^*$, *i.e.* $dB_t^{(1)} \cdot dB_t^{(2)} = \rho dt$.

Proposition 8.11. *Assume that $\left(B_t^{(2)}\right)_{t\in\mathbb{R}_+}$ is also a standard Brownian motion under the risk-neutral probability measure* $\mathbb{P}^*$*. Consider a vanilla option with payoff* $h(S_T)$ *priced as*

$$V_t = f(t, v_t, S_t) = \mathrm{e}^{-(T-t)r}\,\mathbb{E}^*[h(S_T)\mid\mathcal{F}_t], \qquad 0\leqslant t\leqslant T.$$

The function $f(t, y, x)$ *satisfies the PDE*

$$
\begin{aligned}
&\frac{\partial f}{\partial t}(t, v, x) + rx\frac{\partial f}{\partial x}(t, v, x) + \frac{1}{2}vx^2\frac{\partial^2 f}{\partial x^2}(t, v, x) \\
&+ \mu(t, v)\frac{\partial f}{\partial v}(t, v, x) + \frac{1}{2}\beta^2(t, v)\frac{\partial^2 f}{\partial v^2}(t, v, x) + \rho\beta(t, v)x\sqrt{v}\frac{\partial^2 f}{\partial v\partial x}(t, v, x) \\
&= rf(t, v, x),
\end{aligned}
\tag{8.25}
$$

under the terminal condition $f(T, v, x) = h(x)$.

Proof. By Itô calculus with respect to the correlated Brownian motions $\left(B_t^{(1)}\right)_{t\in\mathbb{R}_+}$ and $\left(B_t^{(2)}\right)_{t\in\mathbb{R}_+}$, the portfolio value $f(t, v_t, S_t)$ can be differentiated as follows:

$$
\begin{aligned}
df&(t, v_t, S_t) \\
=\ & \frac{\partial f}{\partial t}(t, v_t, S_t)dt + rS_t\frac{\partial f}{\partial x}(t, v_t, S_t)dt + \sqrt{v_t}S_t\frac{\partial f}{\partial x}(t, v_t, S_t)dB_t^{(1)} \\
&+ \frac{1}{2}v_tS_t^2\frac{\partial^2 f}{\partial x^2}(t, v_t, S_t)dt + \mu(t, v_t)\frac{\partial f}{\partial v}(t, v_t, S_t)dt \\
&+ \beta(t, v_t)\frac{\partial f}{\partial v}(t, v_t, S_t)dB_t^{(2)} + \frac{1}{2}\beta^2(t, v_t)\frac{\partial^2 f}{\partial v^2}(t, v_t, S_t)dt \\
&+ \beta(t, v_t)\sqrt{v_t}S_t\frac{\partial^2 f}{\partial v\partial x}(t, v_t, S_t)dB_t^{(1)}\cdot dB_t^{(2)} \\
=\ & \frac{\partial f}{\partial t}(t, v_t, S_t)dt + rS_t\frac{\partial f}{\partial x}(t, v_t, S_t)dt + \sqrt{v_t}S_t\frac{\partial f}{\partial x}(t, v_t, S_t)dB_t^{(1)} \\
&+ \frac{1}{2}v_tS_t^2\frac{\partial^2 f}{\partial x^2}(t, v_t, S_t)dt + \mu(t, v_t)\frac{\partial f}{\partial v}(t, v_t, S_t)dt \\
&+ \beta(t, v_t)\frac{\partial f}{\partial v}(t, v_t, S_t)dB_t^{(2)} + \frac{1}{2}\beta^2(t, v_t)\frac{\partial^2 f}{\partial v^2}(t, v_t, S_t)dt \\
&+ \rho\beta(t, v_t)\sqrt{v_t}S_t\frac{\partial^2 f}{\partial v\partial x}(t, v_t, S_t)dt.
\end{aligned}
\tag{8.26}
$$

Knowing that the discounted portfolio value process $(\mathrm{e}^{-rt}f(t, v_t, S_t))_{t\in\mathbb{R}_+}$ is also a martingale under $\mathbb{P}^*$, from the relation

$$d(\mathrm{e}^{-rt}f(t, v_t, S_t)) = -r\mathrm{e}^{-rt}f(t, v_t, S_t)dt + \mathrm{e}^{-rt}df(t, v_t, S_t),$$

we obtain

$$
\begin{aligned}
&- rf(t, v_t, S_t)dt + \frac{\partial f}{\partial t}(t, v_t, S_t)dt + rS_t\frac{\partial f}{\partial x}(t, v_t, S_t)dt + \frac{1}{2}v_tS_t^2\frac{\partial^2 f}{\partial x^2}(t, v_t, S_t)dt \\
&+ \mu(t, v_t)\frac{\partial f}{\partial v}(t, v_t, S_t)dt + \frac{1}{2}\beta^2(t, v_t)\frac{\partial^2 f}{\partial v^2}(t, v_t, S_t)dt
\end{aligned}
$$

---

*When this condition is not satisfied, we need to introduce a drift that will yield a market price of volatility.

$$+ \rho\beta(t, v_t)S_t\sqrt{v_t}\frac{\partial^2 f}{\partial v \partial x}(t, v_t, S_t)dt$$
$$= 0,$$

and the pricing PDE (8.25). □

Heston model

In the Heston model with $\mu(t, v) = -\lambda(v - m)$ and $\beta(t, v) = \eta\sqrt{v}$, from (8.25) we find the Heston PDE

$$\frac{\partial f}{\partial t}(t, v, x) + rx\frac{\partial f}{\partial x}(t, v, x) + \frac{1}{2}vx^2\frac{\partial^2 f}{\partial x^2}(t, v, x) \qquad (8.27)$$
$$- \lambda(v - m)\frac{\partial f}{\partial v}(t, v, x) + \frac{1}{2}\eta^2 v\frac{\partial^2 f}{\partial v^2}(t, v, x) + \rho\eta xv\frac{\partial^2 f}{\partial v \partial x}(t, v, x) = rf(t, v, x).$$

The solution of this PDE has been expressed in Heston (1993) as a complex integral by inversion of a characteristic function.

Using the change of variable $y = \log x$ where with $g(t, v, y) = f(t, v, e^y)$, the PDE (8.27) is transformed into

$$\frac{\partial g}{\partial t}(t, v, y) + \frac{1}{2}v\frac{\partial^2 g}{\partial y^2}(t, v, y) + \left(r - \frac{v}{2}\right)\frac{\partial g}{\partial y}(t, v, x)$$
$$+ \lambda(m - v)\frac{\partial g}{\partial v}(t, v, y) + v\frac{\eta^2}{2}\frac{\partial^2 g}{\partial v^2}(t, v, y) + \rho\eta v\frac{\partial^2 g}{\partial v \partial y}(t, v, y) = rg(t, v, y).$$

The following proposition shows that the Fourier transform of $g(t, v, y)$ satisfies an affine PDE with respect to the variable v, when z is regarded as a constant parameter.

Proposition 8.12. *Assume that $\rho = 0$. The Fourier transform*

$$\widehat{g}(t, v, z) := \int_{-\infty}^{\infty} e^{-iyz}g(t, v, y)dy$$

satisfies the partial differential equation

$$\frac{\partial\widehat{g}}{\partial t}(t, v, z) + \left(irz - \frac{1}{2}vz^2\right)\widehat{g}(t, v, z) - iz\frac{1}{2}v\widehat{g}(t, v, z) \qquad (8.28)$$
$$+ (\lambda(m - v) + i\rho\eta zv)\frac{\partial\widehat{g}}{\partial v}(t, v, z) + v\frac{\eta^2}{2}\frac{\partial^2\widehat{g}}{\partial v^2}(t, v, z) = r\widehat{g}(t, v, z).$$

Proof. We apply the relations $i^2 = -1$ and

$$iz\widehat{g}(t, v, z) = \int_{-\infty}^{\infty} e^{-iyz}\frac{\partial g}{\partial y}(t, v, y)dy.$$

□

The equation (8.28) can be solved in closed form, and the final solution $g(t, v, y)$ can then be obtained by the Fourier inversion relation

$$g(t,v,y) = \frac{1}{2\pi} \int_{-\infty}^{\infty} e^{izy} \widehat{g}(t,v,z) dz, \qquad (8.29)$$

see Heston (1993), Attari (2004), Albrecher et al. (2007), and Rouah (2013) for details.

Delta hedging in the Heston model

Consider a portfolio of the form

$$V_t = \eta_t\, e^{rt} + \xi_t S_t$$

based on the riskless asset $A_t = e^{rt}$ and on the risky asset S_t. When this portfolio is self-financing we have

$$
\begin{aligned}
dV_t &= df(t, v_t, S_t) \\
&= r\eta_t\, e^{rt} dt + \xi_t dS_t \\
&= r\eta_t\, e^{rt} dt + \xi_t \big(rS_t dt + S_t \sqrt{v_t} dB_t^{(1)}\big) \\
&= rV_t dt + \xi_t S_t \sqrt{v_t} dB_t^{(1)} \\
&= rf(t, v_t, S_t) dt + \xi_t S_t \sqrt{v_t} dB_t^{(1)}.
\end{aligned}
\qquad (8.30)
$$

However, trying to match (8.26) to (8.30) yields

$$\sqrt{v_t} S_t \frac{\partial f}{\partial x}(t, v_t, S_t) dB_t^{(1)} + \beta(t, v_t)\frac{\partial f}{\partial v}(t, v_t, S_t) dB_t^{(2)} = \xi_t S_t \sqrt{v_t} dB_t^{(1)}, \qquad (8.31)$$

which admits no solution unless $\beta(t, v) = 0$, *i.e.* when volatility is deterministic. A solution to that problem is to consider instead a portfolio

$$V_t = f(t, v_t, S_t) = \eta_t\, e^{rt} + \xi_t S_t + \zeta_t P(t, v_t, S_t)$$

that includes an additional asset with price $P(t, v_t, S_t)$, which can be an option depending on the volatility v_t.

Proposition 8.13. *Assume that $\rho = 0$. The self-financing portfolio allocation $(\xi_t, \zeta_t)_{t \in [0,T]}$ in the assets $(e^{rt}, S_t, P(t, v_t, S_t))_{t \in [0,T]}$ with portfolio value*

$$V_t = f(t, v_t, S_t) = \eta_t\, e^{rt} + \xi_t S_t + \zeta_t P(t, v_t, S_t) \qquad (8.32)$$

is given by

$$\zeta_t = \frac{\dfrac{\partial f}{\partial v}(t, v_t, S_t)}{\dfrac{\partial P}{\partial v}(t, v_t, S_t)}, \qquad (8.33)$$

and

$$\xi_t = \frac{\partial f}{\partial x}(t, v_t, S_t) - \frac{\partial f}{\partial v}(t, v_t, S_t)\frac{\dfrac{\partial P}{\partial x}(t, v_t, S_t)}{\dfrac{\partial P}{\partial v}(t, v_t, S_t)}. \qquad (8.34)$$

Proof. Using (8.32), we replace (8.30) with the self-financing condition

$$
\begin{aligned}
dV_t &= df(t, v_t, S_t)\\
&= r\eta_t \, \mathrm{e}^{rt}dt + \xi_t dS_t + \zeta_t dP(t, v_t, S_t)\\
&= r\eta_t \, \mathrm{e}^{rt}dt + \xi_t(rS_t dt + S_t\sqrt{v_t}dB_t^{(1)}) + r\zeta_t S_t\frac{\partial P}{\partial x}(t, v_t, S_t)dt\\
&\quad +\zeta_t\mu(t, v_t)\frac{\partial P}{\partial v}(t, v_t, S_t)dt + \zeta_t\frac{\partial P}{\partial t}(t, v_t, S_t)dt + \frac{1}{2}\zeta_t S_t^2 v_t\frac{\partial^2 P}{\partial x^2}(t, v_t, S_t)dt\\
&\quad +\frac{1}{2}\zeta_t\beta^2(t, v_t)\frac{\partial^2 P}{\partial v^2}(t, v_t, S_t)dt + \rho\zeta_t\beta(t, v_t)S_t\sqrt{v_t}\frac{\partial^2 P}{\partial x\partial v}(t, v_t, S_t)dt\\
&\quad +\zeta_t S_t\sqrt{v_t}\frac{\partial P}{\partial x}(t, v_t, S_t)dB_t^{(1)} + \zeta_t\beta(t, v_t)\frac{\partial P}{\partial v}(t, v_t, S_t)dB_t^{(2)},\\
&= (V_t - \zeta_t P(t, v_t, S_t))rdt + \xi_t S_t\sqrt{v_t}dB_t^{(1)} + r\zeta_t S_t\frac{\partial P}{\partial x}(t, v_t, S_t)dt\\
&\quad +\zeta_t\mu(t, v_t)\frac{\partial P}{\partial v}(t, v_t, S_t)dt + \zeta_t\frac{\partial P}{\partial t}(t, v_t, S_t)dt + \frac{1}{2}\zeta_t S_t^2 v_t\frac{\partial^2 P}{\partial x^2}(t, v_t, S_t)dt\\
&\quad +\frac{1}{2}\zeta_t\beta^2(t, v_t)\frac{\partial^2 P}{\partial v^2}(t, v_t, S_t)dt + \rho\zeta_t\beta(t, v_t)S_t\sqrt{v_t}\frac{\partial^2 P}{\partial x\partial v}(t, v_t, S_t)dt\\
&\quad +\zeta_t S_t\sqrt{v_t}\frac{\partial P}{\partial x}(t, v_t, S_t)dB_t^{(1)} + \zeta_t\beta(t, v_t)\frac{\partial P}{\partial v}(t, v_t, S_t)dB_t^{(2)}\\
&= rf(t, v_t, S_t)dt + \xi_t S_t\sqrt{v_t}dB_t^{(1)} + r\zeta_t S_t\frac{\partial P}{\partial x}(t, v_t, S_t)dt\\
&\quad +\zeta_t\mu(t, v_t)\frac{\partial P}{\partial v}(t, v_t, S_t)dt + \zeta_t\frac{\partial P}{\partial t}(t, v_t, S_t)dt + \frac{1}{2}\zeta_t S_t^2 v_t\frac{\partial^2 P}{\partial x^2}(t, v_t, S_t)dt\\
&\quad +\frac{1}{2}\zeta_t\beta^2(t, v_t)\frac{\partial^2 P}{\partial v^2}(t, v_t, S_t)dt + \rho\zeta_t\beta(t, v_t)S_t\sqrt{v_t}\frac{\partial^2 P}{\partial x\partial v}(t, v_t, S_t)dt\\
&\quad +\zeta_t S_t\sqrt{v_t}\frac{\partial P}{\partial x}(t, v_t, S_t)dB_t^{(1)} + \zeta_t\beta(t, v_t)\frac{\partial P}{\partial v}(t, v_t, S_t)dB_t^{(2)},
\end{aligned}
\tag{8.35}
$$

and by matching (8.35) to (8.26), the equation (8.31) now becomes

$$
\sqrt{v_t}S_t\frac{\partial f}{\partial x}(t, v_t, S_t)dB_t^{(1)} + \beta(t, v_t)\frac{\partial f}{\partial v}(t, v_t, S_t)dB_t^{(2)}
$$
$$
= \xi_t S_t\sqrt{v_t}dB_t^{(1)} + \zeta_t S_t\sqrt{v_t}\frac{\partial P}{\partial x}(t, v_t, S_t)dB_t^{(1)} + \zeta_t\beta(t, v_t)\frac{\partial P}{\partial v}(t, v_t, S_t)dB_t^{(2)}.
$$

This leads to the equations

$$
\begin{cases}
\sqrt{v_t}S_t\dfrac{\partial f}{\partial x}(t, v_t, S_t) = \xi_t S_t\sqrt{v_t} + \zeta_t S_t\sqrt{v_t}\dfrac{\partial P}{\partial x}(t, v_t, S_t),\\[2ex]
\beta(t, v_t)\dfrac{\partial f}{\partial v}(t, v_t, S_t) = \zeta_t\beta(t, v_t)\dfrac{\partial P}{\partial v}(t, v_t, S_t),
\end{cases}
$$

which show that

$$
\zeta_t = \frac{\dfrac{\partial f}{\partial v}(t, v_t, S_t)}{\dfrac{\partial P}{\partial v}(t, v_t, S_t)},
$$

and

$$
\begin{aligned}
\xi_t \;&=\; \frac{1}{S_t\sqrt{v_t}}\left(\sqrt{v_t}S_t\frac{\partial f}{\partial x}(t,v_t,S_t)-\zeta_t S_t\sqrt{v_t}\frac{\partial P}{\partial x}(t,v_t,S_t),\right)\\[2mm]
&=\; \frac{\partial f}{\partial x}(t,v_t,S_t)-\zeta_t\frac{\partial P}{\partial x}(t,v_t,S_t)\\[2mm]
&=\; \frac{\partial f}{\partial x}(t,v_t,S_t)-\frac{\partial f}{\partial v}(t,v_t,S_t)\frac{\dfrac{\partial P}{\partial x}(t,v_t,S_t)}{\dfrac{\partial P}{\partial v}(t,v_t,S_t)}.
\end{aligned}
$$

$\square$

We note in addition that identifying the "dt" terms when equating (8.35) to (8.26) would now lead to the more complicated PDE

$$
\begin{aligned}
&(f(t,v_t,S_t)-\zeta_t P(t,v_t,S_t))r + r\zeta_t S_t\frac{\partial P}{\partial x}(t,v_t,S_t)+\zeta_t\mu(t,v_t)\frac{\partial P}{\partial v}(t,v_t,S_t)\\[2mm]
&+\zeta_t\frac{\partial P}{\partial t}(t,v_t,S_t)+\frac12\zeta_t S_t^2 v_t\frac{\partial^2 P}{\partial x^2}(t,v_t,S_t)+\frac12\zeta_t\beta^2(t,v_t)\frac{\partial^2 P}{\partial v^2}(t,v_t,S_t)\\[2mm]
&+\rho\zeta_t\beta(t,v_t)S_t\sqrt{v_t}\frac{\partial^2 P}{\partial x\partial v}(t,v_t,S_t)\\[2mm]
=\;&\frac{\partial f}{\partial t}(t,v_t,S_t)+rS_t\frac{\partial f}{\partial x}(t,v_t,S_t)+\frac12 v_t S_t^2\frac{\partial^2 f}{\partial x^2}(t,v_t,S_t)+\mu(t,v_t)\frac{\partial f}{\partial v}(t,v_t,S_t)\\[2mm]
&+\frac12\beta^2(t,v_t)\frac{\partial^2 f}{\partial v^2}(t,v_t,S_t)+\rho\beta(t,v_t)S_t\sqrt{v_t}\frac{\partial^2 f}{\partial v\partial x}(t,v_t,S_t),
\end{aligned}
$$

which can be rewritten using (8.33) as

$$
\begin{aligned}
&\frac{\partial f}{\partial v}(t,v,x)\left(-rP(t,v,x)+\frac{\partial P}{\partial t}(t,v,x)+rx\frac{\partial P}{\partial x}(t,v,x)+\mu(t,v)\frac{\partial P}{\partial v}(t,v,x)\right)\\[2mm]
&+\frac{\partial f}{\partial v}(t,v,x)\left(\frac{x^2 v}{2}\frac{\partial^2 P}{\partial x^2}(t,v,x)+\frac12\beta^2(t,v)\frac{\partial^2 P}{\partial v^2}(t,v,x)+\rho\beta(t,v)x\sqrt{v}\frac{\partial^2 P}{\partial x\partial v}(t,v,x)\right)\\[2mm]
=\;&\frac{\partial P}{\partial v}(t,v,x)\left(-rf(t,v,x)+\frac{\partial f}{\partial t}(t,v,x)+rx\frac{\partial f}{\partial x}(t,v,x)+\frac{vx^2}{2}\frac{\partial^2 f}{\partial x^2}(t,v,x)\right)\\[2mm]
&+\frac{\partial P}{\partial v}(t,v,x)\left(\mu(t,v)\frac{\partial f}{\partial v}(t,v,x)+\frac12\beta^2(t,v)\frac{\partial^2 f}{\partial v^2}(t,v,x)+\rho\beta(t,v)x\sqrt{v}\frac{\partial^2 f}{\partial v\partial x}(t,v,x)\right).
\end{aligned}
$$

Therefore, dividing both sides by $\dfrac{\partial P}{\partial v}(t,v,x)$ and letting

$$\lambda(t,v,x) \tag{8.36}$$

$$
\begin{aligned}
:=\;&\frac{1}{\frac{\partial P}{\partial v}(t,v,x)}\left(-rP(t,v,x)+rx\frac{\partial P}{\partial x}(t,v,x)+\frac{\partial P}{\partial t}(t,v,x)\right)\\[2mm]
&+\frac{1}{\frac{\partial P}{\partial v}(t,v,x)}\left(\frac{x^2 v}{2}\frac{\partial^2 P}{\partial x^2}(t,v,x)+\frac12\beta^2(t,v)\frac{\partial^2 P}{\partial v^2}(t,v,x)+\rho\beta(t,v)x\sqrt{v}\frac{\partial^2 P}{\partial x\partial v}(t,v,x)\right)
\end{aligned}
$$

$$
=\;\frac{1}{\frac{\partial f}{\partial v}(t,v,x)}\left(-rf(t,v,x)+\frac{\partial f}{\partial t}(t,v,x)+rx\frac{\partial f}{\partial x}(t,v,x)+\frac{vx^2}{2}\frac{\partial^2 f}{\partial x^2}(t,v,x)\right) \tag{8.37}
$$

$$
+\;\frac{1}{\frac{\partial f}{\partial v}(t,v,x)}\left(\frac12\beta^2(t,v)\frac{\partial^2 f}{\partial v^2}(t,v,x)+\rho\beta(t,v)x\sqrt{v}\frac{\partial^2 f}{\partial v\partial x}(t,v,x)\right) \tag{8.38}
$$

defines a function $\lambda(t, v, x)$ that depends only on the parameters (t, v, x) and not on P, without requiring $\left(B_t^{(2)}\right)_{t \in \mathbb{R}_+}$ to be a standard Brownian motion under $\mathbb{P}$. The function $\lambda(t, v, x)$ is linked to the market price of volatility risk, cf. Chapter 1 of Gatheral (2006) § 2.4.1 in Fouque et al. (2000; 2011) for details.

Combining (8.36)–(8.38) allows us to rewrite the pricing PDE as

$$\frac{\partial f}{\partial t}(t, v, x) + rx\frac{\partial f}{\partial x}(t, v, x) + \frac{vx^2}{2}\frac{\partial^2 f}{\partial x^2}(t, v, x) + \frac{1}{2}\beta^2(t, v)\frac{\partial^2 f}{\partial v^2}(t, v, x)$$

$$+\rho\beta(t, v)x\sqrt{v}\frac{\partial^2 f}{\partial v \partial x}(t, v, x) = rf(t, v, x) + \lambda(t, v, x)\frac{\partial f}{\partial v}(t, v, x),$$

and (8.25) corresponds to the choice $\lambda(t, v, x) = -\mu(t, v)$, which corresponds to a vanishing "market price of volatility risk".

8.5 Perturbation Analysis

We refer to Chapter 4 of Fouque et al. (2011) for the contents of this section. Consider the time-rescaled model

$$\begin{cases} dS_t = rS_t dt + S_t\sqrt{v_{t/\varepsilon}}dB_t^{(1)} \\ \\ dv_t = \mu(v_t)dt + \beta(v_t)dB_t^{(2)}. \end{cases} \tag{8.39}$$

We note that $v_t^{(\varepsilon)} := v_{t/\varepsilon}$ satisfies the SDE

$$\begin{aligned} dv_t^{(\varepsilon)} &= dv_{t/\varepsilon} \\ &\simeq v_{(t+dt)/\varepsilon} - v_{t/\varepsilon} \\ &= v_{t/\varepsilon+dt/\varepsilon} - v_{t/\varepsilon} \\ &= \frac{1}{\varepsilon}\mu(v_{t/\varepsilon})dt + \beta(v_{t/\varepsilon})dB_{t/\varepsilon}^{(2)}, \end{aligned}$$

with

$$\left(dB_{t/\varepsilon}^{(2)}\right)^2 \simeq \frac{dt}{\varepsilon} \simeq \frac{1}{\varepsilon}\left(dB_t^{(2)}\right)^2 \simeq \left(\frac{1}{\sqrt{\varepsilon}}dB_t^{(2)}\right)^2,$$

hence the SDE for $v_t^{(\varepsilon)}$ can be rewritten as the slow-fast system

$$dv_t^{(\varepsilon)} = \frac{1}{\varepsilon}\mu(v_t^{(\varepsilon)})dt + \frac{1}{\sqrt{\varepsilon}}\beta(v_t^{(\varepsilon)})dB_t^{(2)}.$$

In other words, $\varepsilon \to 0$ corresponds to fast mean-reversion and (8.39) can be rewritten as

$$\begin{cases} dS_t = rS_t dt + \sqrt{v_t^{(\varepsilon)}}S_t dB_t^{(1)} \\ \\ dv_t^{(\varepsilon)} = \frac{1}{\varepsilon}\mu(v_t^{(\varepsilon)})dt + \frac{1}{\sqrt{\varepsilon}}\beta(v_t^{(\varepsilon)})dB_t^{(2)}, \qquad \varepsilon > 0. \end{cases}$$

The perturbed PDE

$$\frac{\partial f_\varepsilon}{\partial t}(t,v,x) + rx\frac{\partial f_\varepsilon}{\partial x}(t,v,x) + \frac{vx^2}{2}\frac{\partial^2 f_\varepsilon}{\partial x^2}(t,v,x) + \frac{1}{\varepsilon}\mu(v)\frac{\partial f_\varepsilon}{\partial v}(t,v,x)$$
$$+ \frac{1}{2\varepsilon}\beta^2(v)\frac{\partial^2 f_\varepsilon}{\partial v^2}(t,v,x) + \frac{\rho}{\sqrt{\varepsilon}}\beta(v)x\sqrt{v}\frac{\partial^2 f_\varepsilon}{\partial v\partial x}(t,v,x) = rf_\varepsilon(t,v,x)$$

with terminal condition $f_\varepsilon(T,v,x) = (x-K)^+$ rewrites as

$$\frac{1}{\varepsilon}\mathcal{L}_0 f_\varepsilon(t,v,x) + \frac{1}{\sqrt{\varepsilon}}\mathcal{L}_1 f_\varepsilon(t,v,x) + \mathcal{L}_2 f_\varepsilon(t,v,x) = rf_\varepsilon(t,v,x), \qquad (8.40)$$

where

$$\begin{cases} \mathcal{L}_0 f_\varepsilon(t,v,x) := \frac{1}{2}\beta^2(v)\frac{\partial^2 f_\varepsilon}{\partial v^2}(t,v,x) + \mu(v)\frac{\partial f_\varepsilon}{\partial v}(t,v,x), \\[2mm] \mathcal{L}_1 f_\varepsilon(t,v,x) := \rho x\beta(v)\sqrt{v}\frac{\partial^2 f_\varepsilon}{\partial v\partial x}(t,v,x), \\[2mm] \mathcal{L}_2 f_\varepsilon(t,v,x) := \frac{\partial f_\varepsilon}{\partial t}(t,v,x) + rx\frac{\partial f_\varepsilon}{\partial x}(t,v,x) + \frac{vx^2}{2}\frac{\partial^2 f_\varepsilon}{\partial x^2}(t,v,x). \end{cases}$$

Note that

- $\mathcal{L}_0$ is the infinitesimal generator of the process $\left(v_s^1\right)_{s\in\mathbb{R}_+}$, see (8.44) below,

  and

- $\mathcal{L}_2$ is the Black–Scholes operator, *i.e.* $\mathcal{L}_2 f = rf$ is the Black–Scholes PDE.

The solution $f_\varepsilon(t,v,x)$ will be expanded as

$$f_\varepsilon(t,v,x) = f^{(0)}(t,v,x) + \sqrt{\varepsilon}f^{(1)}(t,v,x) + \varepsilon f^{(2)}(t,v,x) + \cdots \qquad (8.41)$$

with $f(T,v,x) = (x-K)^+$, $f^{(1)}(T,v,x) = 0$, and $f^{(2)}(T,v,x) = 0$. Since $\mathcal{L}_0$ contains only differentials with respect to v, we will choose $f^{(0)}(t,v,x)$ of the form

$$f^{(0)}(t,v,x) = f^{(0)}(t,x),$$

cf. § 4.2.1 of Fouque et al. (2011) for details, with

$$\mathcal{L}_0 f^{(0)}(t,x) = \mathcal{L}_1 f^{(0)}(t,x) = 0. \qquad (8.42)$$

Proposition 8.14. *(Fouque et al. (2011), § 3.2). The first-order term $f_0(t,v)$ in (8.41) satisfies the Black–Scholes PDE*

$$rf^{(0)}(t,x) = \frac{\partial f^{(0)}}{\partial t}(t,x) + rx\frac{\partial f^{(0)}}{\partial x}(t,x) + \frac{\eta^2}{2}\int_0^\infty v\phi(v)dv\frac{\partial^2 f^{(0)}}{\partial x^2}(t,x)$$

with the terminal condition $f^{(0)}(T,x) = (x-K)^+$, where $\phi(v)$ is the stationary (or invariant) probability density function of the process $\left(v_t^{(1)}\right)_{t\in\mathbb{R}_+}$.

Proof. By identifying the terms of order $1/\sqrt{\varepsilon}$ when plugging (8.41) in (8.40), we have

$$\mathcal{L}_0 f^{(1)}(t,v,x) + \mathcal{L}_1 f^{(0)}(t,x) = 0,$$

hence $\mathcal{L}_0 f^{(1)}(t,v,x) = 0$. Similarly, by identifying the terms that do not depend on ε in (8.40) and taking $f^{(1)}(t,v,x) = f^{(1)}(t,x)$, we have $\mathcal{L}_1 f^{(1)} = 0$ and

$$\mathcal{L}_0 f^{(2)}(t,v,x) + \mathcal{L}_2 f^{(0)}(t,x) = 0. \tag{8.43}$$

Using the Itô formula, we have

$$
\begin{aligned}
\mathbb{E}\left[f^{(2)}\big(t,v_s^1,x\big) \right] &= f^{(2)}\big(t,v_0^1,x\big) + \mathbb{E}\left[\int_0^s \frac{\partial f^{(2)}}{\partial x}\big(t,v_\tau^1,x\big) dB_\tau^{(2)} \right] \\
&\quad + \mathbb{E}\left[\int_0^s \left(\mu(v_\tau^1)\frac{\partial f^{(2)}}{\partial v}\big(t,v_\tau^1,x\big) + \frac{1}{2}\beta^2(v_\tau^1)\frac{\partial^2 f^{(2)}}{\partial v^2}\big(t,v_\tau^1,x\big) \right) d\tau \right] \\
&= f^{(2)}\big(t,v_0^1,x\big) + \int_0^s \mathbb{E}\left[\mathcal{L}_0 f^{(2)}\big(t,v_\tau^1,x\big) \right] d\tau.
\end{aligned}
\tag{8.44}
$$

When the process $\big(v_t^{(1)}\big)_{t\in\mathbb{R}_+}$ is started under its stationary (or invariant) probability distribution with probability density function $\phi(v)$, we have

$$\mathbb{E}\left[f^{(2)}\big(t,v_\tau^1,x\big) \right] = \int_0^\infty f^{(2)}(t,v,x)\phi(v)dv, \qquad \tau \geqslant 0,$$

hence (8.44) rewrites as

$$\int_0^\infty f^{(2)}(t,v,x)\phi(v)dv = \int_0^\infty f^{(2)}(t,v,x)\phi(v)dv + \int_0^s \int_0^\infty \mathcal{L}_0 f^{(2)}(t,v,x)\phi(v)dvd\tau.$$

By differentiation with respect to $s > 0$ this yields

$$\int_0^\infty \mathcal{L}_0 f^{(2)}(t,v,x)\phi(v)dv = 0,$$

hence by (8.43) we find

$$\int_0^\infty \mathcal{L}_2 f^{(0)}(t,x)\phi(v)dv = 0,$$

cf. § 3.2 of Fouque et al. (2011), *i.e.* we find

$$\frac{\partial f^{(0)}}{\partial t}(t,x) + rx\frac{\partial f^{(0)}}{\partial x}(t,x) + \frac{\eta^2}{2}\int_0^\infty v\phi(v)dv\frac{\partial^2 f^{(0)}}{\partial x^2}(t,x) = rf^{(0)}(t,x),$$

with the terminal condition $f^{(0)}(T,x) = (x-K)^+$. $\qquad\square$

As a consequence of Proposition 8.14, the first-order term $f^{(0)}(t,x)$ in the expansion (8.41) is the Black–Scholes function

$$f^{(0)}(t,x) = \mathrm{Bl}\left(S_t, K, r, T-t, \sqrt{\int_0^\infty v\phi(v)dv} \right),$$

with the averaged squared volatility

$$\int_0^\infty v\phi(v)dv = \mathbb{E}\left[v_\tau^1 \right], \qquad \tau \geqslant 0, \tag{8.45}$$

under the stationary distribution of the process with infinitesimal generator $\mathcal{L}_0$, *i.e.* the stationary distribution of the solution to

$$dv_t^{(1)} = \mu\big(v_t^{(1)}\big)dt + \beta\big(v_t^{(1)}\big)dB_t^{(2)}.$$

Perturbation analysis in the Heston model

We have

$$
\begin{cases}
dS_t = rS_t dt + S_t \sqrt{v_t^{(\varepsilon)}}\, dB_t^{(1)} \\[2mm]
dv_t^{(\varepsilon)} = -\dfrac{\lambda}{\varepsilon}\big(v_t^{(\varepsilon)} - m\big)dt + \eta \sqrt{\dfrac{v_t^{(\varepsilon)}}{\varepsilon}}\, dB_t^{(2)},
\end{cases}
$$

under the modified short mean-reversion time scale, and the SDE can be rewritten as

$$
dv_t^{(\varepsilon)} = -\frac{\lambda}{\varepsilon}\big(v_t^{(\varepsilon)} - m\big)dt + \eta \sqrt{\frac{v_t^{(\varepsilon)}}{\varepsilon}}\, dB_t^{(2)}.
$$

In other words, $\varepsilon \to 0$ corresponds to fast mean reversion, in which $v_t^{(\varepsilon)}$ becomes close to its mean (8.45).

Recall, cf. (17.11), that the CIR process $\big(v_t^{(1)}\big)_{t\in\mathbb{R}_+}$ has a gamma invariant (or stationary) distribution with shape parameter $2\lambda m/\eta^2$, scale parameter $\eta^2/(2\lambda)$, and probability density function ϕ given by

$$
\phi(v) = \frac{1}{\Gamma(2\lambda m/\eta^2)(\eta^2/(2\lambda))^{2\lambda m/\eta^2}} v^{-1+2\lambda m/\eta^2}\, \mathrm{e}^{-2v\lambda/\eta^2} \mathbb{1}_{[0,\infty)}(v), \quad v > 0,
$$

and mean

$$
m = \int_0^\infty v\phi(v)dv.
$$

Hence the first-order term $f^{(0)}(t,x)$ in the expansion (8.41) reads

$$
f^{(0)}(t,x) = \mathrm{Bl}\left(S_t, K, r, T-t, \sqrt{m}\right),
$$

with the averaged squared volatility

$$
m = \int_0^\infty v\phi(v)dv = \mathbb{E}\left[v_\tau^1\right], \qquad \tau \geqslant 0,
$$

under the stationary distribution of the process with infinitesimal generator $\mathcal{L}_0$, *i.e.* the stationary distribution of the solution to

$$
dv_t^{(1)} = \mu\big(v_t^{(1)}\big)dt + \beta\big(v_t^{(1)}\big)dB_t^{(2)}.
$$

In Figure 8.6, cf. Privault and She (2016), related approximations of put option prices are plotted against the value of v with correlation $\rho = -0.5$ and $\varepsilon = 0.01$ in the α-hypergeometric stochastic volatility model of Fonseca and Martini (2016), based on the series expansion of Han et al. (2013), and compared to a Monte Carlo curve requiring $300,000$ samples and $30,000$ time steps.

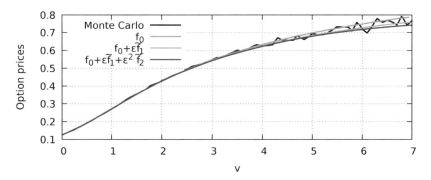

Figure 8.6: Option price approximations plotted against v with $\rho = -0.5$.

Exercises

Exercise 8.1 (Gatheral (2006), Chapter 11). Compute the expected realized variance on the time interval $[0, T]$ in the Heston model, with

$$dv_t = -\lambda(v_t - m)dt + \eta\sqrt{v_t}dB_t, \qquad 0 \leqslant t \leqslant T.$$

Exercise 8.2 Compute the variance swap rate

$$\mathrm{VS}_T := \frac{1}{T}\,\mathbb{E}\left[\lim_{n\to\infty}\sum_{k=1}^{n}\left(\frac{S_{kT/n} - S_{(k-1)T/n}}{S_{(k-1)T/n}}\right)^2\right] = \frac{1}{T}\,\mathbb{E}\left[\int_0^T \frac{1}{S_t^2}(dS_t)^2\right]$$

on the index whose level S_t is given in the following two models.

a) Heston (1993) model. Here, $(S_t)_{t\in\mathbb{R}_+}$ is given by the system of stochastic differential equations

$$\begin{cases} dS_t = (r - \alpha v_t)S_t dt + S_t\sqrt{\beta + v_t}dB_t^{(1)} \\[2mm] dv_t = -\lambda(v_t - m)dt + \gamma\sqrt{v_t}dB_t^{(2)}, \end{cases}$$

where $\left(B_t^{(1)}\right)_{t\in\mathbb{R}_+}$ and $\left(B_t^{(2)}\right)_{t\in\mathbb{R}_+}$ are standard Brownian motions with correlation $\rho \in [-1, 1]$ and $\alpha \geqslant 0$, $\beta \geqslant 0$, $\lambda > 0$, $m > 0$, $r > 0$, $\gamma > 0$.

b) SABR model with $\beta = 1$. The index level S_t is given by the system of stochastic differential equations

$$\begin{cases} dS_t = \sigma_t S_t dB_t^{(1)} \\[2mm] d\sigma_t = \alpha\sigma_t dB_t^{(2)}, \end{cases}$$

where $\alpha > 0$ and $\left(B_t^{(1)}\right)_{t\in\mathbb{R}_+}$ and $\left(B_t^{(2)}\right)_{t\in\mathbb{R}_+}$ are standard Brownian motions with correlation $\rho \in [-1, 1]$.

Exercise 8.3 Convexity adjustment (§ 2.3 of Broadie and Jain (2008)).

a) Using Taylor's formula

$$\sqrt{x} = \sqrt{x_0} + \frac{x - x_0}{2\sqrt{x_0}} - \frac{(x - x_0)^2}{8x_0^{3/2}} + o((x - x_0)^2),$$

find an approximation of $R_{0,T} = \sqrt{R_{0,T}^2}$ using $\sqrt{\mathbb{E}\left[R_{0,T}^2\right]}$ and correction terms.

b) Find an (approximate) relation between the variance swap price $\mathbb{E}^*\left[R_{0,T}^2\right]$ and the volatility swap price $\mathbb{E}^*[R_{0,T}]$ up to a correction term.

Exercise 8.4 Consider an asset price $(S_t)_{t \in \mathbb{R}_+}$ with log-return dynamics

$$d \log S_t = \mu dt + Z_{N_{t^-}} dN_t, \qquad t \geqslant 0,$$

i.e. $S_t := S_0 e^{\mu t + Y_t}$ in a pure jump Merton model, where $(N_t)_{t \in \mathbb{R}_+}$ is a Poisson process with intensity $\lambda > 0$ and $(Z_k)_{k \geqslant 0}$ is a family of independent identically distributed Gaussian $\mathcal{N}(\delta, \eta^2)$ random variables. Compute the price of the log-return variance swap

$$
\begin{aligned}
\mathbb{E}\left[\int_0^T (d \log S_t)^2 dN_t\right] &= \mathbb{E}\left[\int_0^T (\mu dt + Z_{N_{t^-}} dN_t)^2 dN_t\right] \\
&= \mathbb{E}\left[\int_0^T (Z_{N_{t^-}} dN_t)^2 dN_t\right] \\
&= \mathbb{E}\left[\int_0^T \left(\log \frac{S_t}{S_{t^-}}\right)^2 dN_t\right] \\
&= \mathbb{E}\left[\sum_{n=1}^{N_T} \left(\log \frac{S_{T_k}}{S_{T_{k-1}}}\right)^2\right]
\end{aligned}
$$

using the smoothing lemma Proposition 20.10.

Exercise 8.5 Consider an asset price $(S_t)_{t \in \mathbb{R}_+}$ given by the stochastic differential equation

$$dS_t = rS_t dt + \sigma S_t dB_t, \tag{8.46}$$

where $(B_t)_{t \in \mathbb{R}_+}$ is a standard Brownian motion, with $r \in \mathbb{R}$ and $\sigma > 0$.

a) Write down the solution $(S_t)_{t \in \mathbb{R}_+}$ of Equation (8.46) in explicit form.

b) Show by a direct calculation that Corollary 8.3 is satisfied by $(S_t)_{t \in \mathbb{R}_+}$.

Exercise 8.6 (Carr and Lee (2008)) Consider an underlying asset price $(S_t)_{t \in \mathbb{R}_+}$ given by $dS_t = rS_t dt + \sigma_t S_t dB_t$, where $(B_t)_{t \in \mathbb{R}_+}$ is a standard Brownian motion and $(\sigma_t)_{t \in \mathbb{R}_+}$ is an (adapted) stochastic volatility process. The riskless asset is priced $A_t := e^{rt}$, $t \in [0, T]$. We consider a realized variance swap with payoff $R_{0,T}^2 = \int_0^T \sigma_t^2 dt$.

a) Show that the payoff $\int_0^T \sigma_t^2 dt$ of the realized variance swap satisfies

$$\int_0^T \sigma_t^2 dt = 2 \int_0^T \frac{dS_t}{S_t} - 2 \log \frac{S_T}{S_0}. \tag{8.47}$$

b) Show that the price $V_t := \mathrm{e}^{-(T-t)r} \, \mathbb{E}^* \left[\int_0^T \sigma_t^2 dt \,\bigg|\, \mathcal{F}_t \right]$ of the variance swap at time $t \in [0, T]$ satisfies

$$V_t = L_t + 2(T - t)r \, \mathrm{e}^{-(T-t)r} + 2\,\mathrm{e}^{-(T-t)r} \int_0^t \frac{dS_u}{S_u}, \tag{8.48}$$

where

$$L_t := -2\,\mathrm{e}^{-(T-t)r} \, \mathbb{E}^* \left[\log \frac{S_T}{S_0} \,\bigg|\, \mathcal{F}_t \right]$$

is the price at time t of the log contract (see Neuberger (1994), Demeterfi et al. (1999)) with payoff $-2 \log(S_T/S_0)$, see also Exercises 6.9 and 7.14.

c) Show that the portfolio made at time $t \in [0, T]$ of:

  - one log contract priced L_t,

  - $2\,\mathrm{e}^{-(T-t)r}/S_t$ in shares priced S_t,

  - $2\,\mathrm{e}^{-rT} \left(\int_0^t \frac{dS_u}{S_u} + (T - t)r - 1 \right)$ in the riskless asset $A_t = \mathrm{e}^{rt}$,

  hedges the realized variance swap.

d) Show that the above portfolio is self-financing.

Exercise 8.7 Compute the moment $\mathbb{E}^* \left[R_{0,T}^4 \right]$ from Lemma 8.2.

Chapter 9

Volatility Estimation

Volatility estimation methods include historical, implied and local volatility, and the VIX® volatility index. This chapter presents such estimation methods, together with examples of how the Black–Scholes formula can be fitted to market data. While the market parameters r, t, S_t, T, and K used in Black–Scholes option pricing can be easily obtained from market terms and data, the estimation of volatility parameters can be a more complex task.

9.1 Historical Volatility

We consider the problem of estimating the parameters μ and σ from market data in the stock price model

$$\frac{dS_t}{S_t} = \mu dt + \sigma dB_t. \tag{9.1}$$

Historical trend estimation

By discretization of (9.1) along a family $t_0, t_1, \ldots, t_N$ of observation times as

$$\frac{S_{t_{k+1}} - S_{t_k}}{S_{t_k}} = (t_{k+1} - t_k)\mu + (B_{t_{k+1}} - B_{t_k})\sigma, \quad k = 0, 1, \ldots, N-1, \tag{9.2}$$

a natural estimator for the trend parameter μ can be constructed as

$$\widehat{\mu}_N := \frac{1}{N} \sum_{k=0}^{N-1} \frac{1}{t_{k+1} - t_k} \left(\frac{S_{t_{k+1}}^M - S_{t_k}^M}{S_{t_k}^M} \right), \tag{9.3}$$

where $(S_{t_{k+1}}^M - S_{t_k}^M)/S_{t_k}^M$, $k = 0, 1, \ldots, N-1$ denotes market returns observed at discrete times $t_0, t_1, \ldots, t_N$.

Historical log-return estimation

Alternatively, observe that, replacing[†] (9.3) by the log-returns

$$
\begin{aligned}
\log \frac{S_{t_{k+1}}}{S_{t_k}} &= \log S_{t_{k+1}} - \log S_{t_k} \\
&= \log \left(1 + \frac{S_{t_{k+1}} - S_{t_k}}{S_{t_k}} \right) \\
&\simeq \frac{S_{t_{k+1}} - S_{t_k}}{S_{t_k}},
\end{aligned}
$$

[†]This approximation does not include the correction term $(dS_t)^2/(2S_t^2)$ in the Itô formula $d\log S_t = dS_t/S_t - (dS_t)^2/(2S_t^2)$.

DOI: 10.1201/9781003298670-9

with $t_{k+1} - t_k = T/N$, $k = 0, 1, \ldots, N-1$, one can replace (9.3) with the simpler telescoping estimate

$$\frac{1}{N} \sum_{k=0}^{N-1} \frac{1}{t_{k+1} - t_k} \left(\log S_{t_{k+1}} - \log S_{t_k} \right) = \frac{1}{T} \log \frac{S_T}{S_0}.$$

Historical volatility estimation

The volatility parameter σ can be estimated by writing, from (9.2),

$$\sigma^2 \sum_{k=0}^{N-1} \frac{(B_{t_{k+1}} - B_{t_k})^2}{t_{k+1} - t_k} = \sum_{k=0}^{N-1} \frac{1}{t_{k+1} - t_k} \left(\frac{S_{t_{k+1}} - S_{t_k}}{S_{t_k}} - (t_{k+1} - t_k)\mu \right)^2,$$

which yields the (unbiased) realized variance estimator

$$\widehat{\sigma}_N^2 := \frac{1}{N-1} \sum_{k=0}^{N-1} \frac{1}{t_{k+1} - t_k} \left(\frac{S_{t_{k+1}} - S_{t_k}}{S_{t_k}} - (t_{k+1} - t_k)\widehat{\mu}_N \right)^2.$$

```
1  library(quantmod)
   getSymbols("0005.HK",from="2017-02-15",to=Sys.Date(),src="yahoo")
3  stock=Ad(`0005.HK`)
   chartSeries(stock,up.col="blue",theme="white")
```

```
   stock=Ad(`0005.HK`);logreturns=diff(log(stock));returns=(stock-lag(stock))/stock
2  times=index(returns);returns <- as.vector(returns)
   n = sum(is.na(returns))+sum(!is.na(returns))
4  plot(times,returns,pch=19,cex=0.05,col="blue", ylab="returns", xlab="n", main = '')
   segments(x0 = times, x1 = times, cex=0.05,y0 = 0, y1 = returns,col="blue")
6  abline(seq(1,n),0,FALSE);dt=1.0/365;mu=mean(returns,na.rm=TRUE)/dt
   sigma=sd(returns,na.rm=TRUE)/sqrt(dt);mu;sigma
```

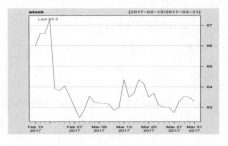

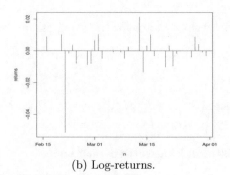

(a) Underlying asset price.   (b) Log-returns.

Figure 9.1: Graph of underlying asset price *vs* log-returns.

```
1  library(PerformanceAnalytics);
   returns <- exp(CalculateReturns(stock,method="compound")) - 1; returns[1,] <- 0
3  histvol <- rollapply(returns, width = 30, FUN=sd.annualized)
   myPars <- chart_pars();myPars$cex<-1.4
5  myTheme <- chart_theme(); myTheme$col$line.col <- "blue"
   dev.new(width=16,height=7)
7  chart_Series(stock,name="0005.HK",pars=myPars,theme=myTheme)
   add_TA(histvol,name="Historical Volatility")
```

The next Figure 9.2 presents a historical volatility graph with a 30 days rolling window.

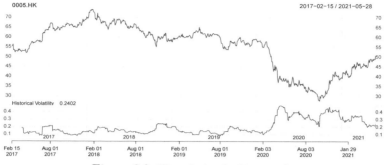

Figure 9.2: Historical volatility graph.

Parameter estimation based on historical data usually requires a lot of samples and it can only be valid on a given time interval, or as a moving average. Moreover, it can only rely on past data, which may not reflect future data.

9.2 Implied Volatility

Recall that when $h(x) = (x - K)^+$, the solution of the Black–Scholes PDE is given by

$$\text{Bl}(t, x, K, \sigma, r, T) = x\Phi\big(d_+(T - t)\big) - K\,\mathrm{e}^{-(T-t)r}\Phi\big(d_-(T - t)\big),$$

where

$$\Phi(x) = \frac{1}{\sqrt{2\pi}} \int_{-\infty}^{x} \mathrm{e}^{-y^2/2} dy, \qquad x \in \mathbb{R},$$

and

$$\begin{cases} d_+(T - t) = \dfrac{\log(x/K) + (r + \sigma^2/2)(T - t)}{\sigma\sqrt{T - t}}, \\[2mm] d_-(T - t) = \dfrac{\log(x/K) + (r - \sigma^2/2)(T - t)}{\sigma\sqrt{T - t}}. \end{cases}$$

In contrast with the historical volatility, the computation of the implied volatility can be done at a fixed time and requires much less data. Equating the Black–Scholes formula

$$\text{Bl}(t, S_t, K, \sigma, r, T) = M \tag{9.4}$$

to the observed value M of a given market price allows one to infer a value of σ when t, S_t, r, T are known, as in *e.g.* Figure 6.20.

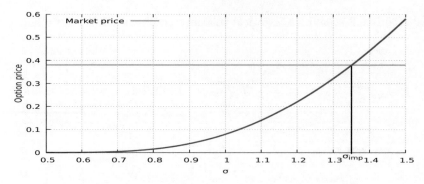

Figure 9.3: Option price as a function of the volatility σ.

This value of σ is called the implied volatility, and it is denoted here by $\sigma_{\text{imp}}(K,T)$, cf. *e.g.* Exercise 6.6. Various algorithms can be implemented to solve (9.4) numerically for $\sigma_{\text{imp}}(K,T)$, such as the bisection method and the Newton–Raphson method.

```
 1  BS <- function(S, K, T, r, sig){d1 <- (log(S/K) + (r + sig^2/2)*T) / (sig*sqrt(T))
 2  d2 <- d1 - sig*sqrt(T);return(S*pnorm(d1) - K*exp(-r*T)*pnorm(d2))}
 3  implied.vol <- function(S, K, T, r, market){
 4  sig <- 0.20;sig.up <- 10;sig.down <- 0.0001;count <- 0;err <- BS(S, K, T, r, sig) - market
 5  while(abs(err) > 0.00001 && count<1000){
 6  if(err < 0){sig.down <- sig;sig <- (sig.up + sig)/2} else{sig.up <- sig;sig <- (sig.down + sig)/2}
 7  err <- BS(S, K, T, r, sig) - market;count <- count + 1};if(count==1000){return(NA)}else{return(sig)}}
 8  market = 0.83;K = 62.8;T = 7 / 365.0;S = 63.4;r = 0.02; implied.vol(S, K, T, r, market)
 9  BS(S, K, T, r, implied.vol(S, K, T, r, market))
```

The implied volatility value can be used as an alternative way to quote the option price, based on the knowledge of the remaining parameters (such as underlying asset price, time to maturity, interest rate, and strike price). For example, market option price data provided by the Hong Kong stock exchange includes implied volatility computed by inverting the Black–Scholes formula.

```
 1  library(fOptions)
 2  market = 0.83;K = 62.8;T = 7 / 365.0;S = 63.4;r = 0.02
 3  sig=GBSVolatility(market,"c",S,K,T,r,r,1e-4,maxiter = 10000)
 4  BS(S, K, T, r, sig)
```

Option chain data in R

```
 1  getSymbols("^GSPC", src = "yahoo", from = as.Date("2018-01-01"), to = as.Date("2018-03-01"))
 2  head(GSPC)
 3  # Only the front-month expiry
 4  SPX.OPT <- getOptionChain("^SPX")
 5  AAPL.OPT <- getOptionChain("AAPL")
 6  # All expiries
 7  SPX.OPTS <- getOptionChain("^SPX", NULL)
 8  AAPL.OPTS <- getOptionChain("AAPL", NULL)
 9  # All 2021 to 2023 expiries
10  SPX.OPTS <- getOptionChain("^SPX", "2021/2023")
11  AAPL.OPTS <- getOptionChain("AAPL", "2021/2023")
```

Exporting option price data

```
write.table(AAPL.OPT$puts, file = "AAPLputs")
write.csv(AAPL.OPT$puts, file = "AAPLputs.csv")
install.packages("xlsx"); library(xlsx)
write.xlsx(AAPL.OPTS$Jun.19.2020$puts, file = "AAPL.OPTS$Jun.19.2020$puts.xlsx")
```

Volatility smiles

Given two European call options with strike prices K_1, resp. K_2, maturities T_1, resp. T_2, and prices C_1, resp. C_2, on the same stock S, this procedure should yield two estimates $\sigma_{\mathrm{imp}}(K_1, T_1)$ and $\sigma_{\mathrm{imp}}(K_2, T_2)$ of implied volatilities according to the following equations.

$$\begin{cases} \mathrm{Bl}(t, S_t, K_1, \sigma_{\mathrm{imp}}(K_1, T_1), r, T_1) = M_1, & (9.5\mathrm{a}) \\[2ex] \mathrm{Bl}(t, S_t, K_2, \sigma_{\mathrm{imp}}(K_2, T_2), r, T_2) = M_2, & (9.5\mathrm{b}) \end{cases}$$

Clearly, there is no reason a priori for the implied volatilities $\sigma_{\mathrm{imp}}(K_1, T_1)$, $\sigma_{\mathrm{imp}}(K_2, T_2)$ solutions of (9.5a)–(9.5b) to coincide across different strike prices and different maturities. However, in the standard Black–Scholes model the value of the parameter σ should be unique for a given stock S. This contradiction between a model and market data is motivating the development of more sophisticated stochastic volatility models.

Figure 9.4 presents an estimated implied volatility surface for Asian options on light sweet crude oil futures traded on the New York Mercantile Exchange (NYMEX), based on contract specifications and market data obtained from the *Chicago Mercantile Exchange* (CME).

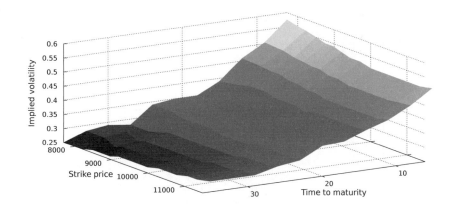

Figure 9.4: Implied volatility surface of Asian options on light sweet crude oil futures.

As observed in Figure 9.4, the volatility surface can exhibit a *smile* phenomenon, in which implied volatility is higher at a given end (or at both ends) of the range of strike price values.

```
   install.packages("jsonlite");install.packages("lubridate")
 2 library(jsonlite);library(lubridate);library(quantmod)
   # Maturity to be updated as needed
 4 maturity <- as.Date("2021-08-20", format="%Y-%m-%d")
   CHAIN <- getOptionChain("GOOG",maturity)
 6 today <- as.Date(Sys.Date(), format="%Y-%m-%d")
   getSymbols("GOOG", src = "yahoo")
 8 lastBusDay=last(row.names(as.data.frame(Ad(GOOG))))
   T <- as.numeric(difftime(maturity, lastBusDay, units = "days")/365);r = 0.02;ImpVol<-1:1;
       S=as.vector(tail(Ad(GOOG),1))
10 for (i in 1:length(CHAIN$calls$Strike)){ImpVol[i]<-implied.vol(S,CHAIN$calls$Strike[i],T,r,
       CHAIN$calls$Last[i])}
   plot(CHAIN$calls$Strike[!is.na(ImpVol)], ImpVol[!is.na(ImpVol)], xlab = "Strike price", ylab = "Implied
       volatility", lwd =3, type = "l", col = "blue")
12 fit4 <- lm(ImpVol[!is.na(ImpVol)]~poly(CHAIN$calls$Strike[!is.na(ImpVol)],4,raw=TRUE))
   lines(CHAIN$calls$Strike[!is.na(ImpVol)], predict(fit4, data.frame(x=CHAIN$calls$Strike[!is.na(ImpVol)])),
       col="red",lwd=2)
```

```
 1 currentyear<-format(Sys.Date(), "%Y")
   # Maturity to be updated as needed
 3 maturity <- as.Date("2021-12-17", format="%Y-%m-%d")
   CHAIN <- getOptionChain("^SPX",maturity)
 5 # Last trading day (may require update)
   today <- as.Date(Sys.Date(), format="%Y-%m-%d")
 7 getSymbols("^SPX", src = "yahoo")
   lastBusDay=last(row.names(as.data.frame(Ad(SPX))))
 9 T <- as.numeric(difftime(maturity, lastBusDay, units = "days")/365);r = 0.02;ImpVol<-1:1;
       S=as.vector(tail(Ad(SPX),1))
   for (i in 1:length(CHAIN$calls$Strike)){ImpVol[i]<-implied.vol(S, CHAIN$calls$Strike[i], T, r,
       CHAIN$calls$Last[i])}
11 plot(CHAIN$calls$Strike[!is.na(ImpVol)], ImpVol[!is.na(ImpVol)], xlab = "Strike price", ylab = "Implied
       volatility", lwd =3, type = "l", col = "blue")
   fit4 <- lm(ImpVol[!is.na(ImpVol)]~poly(CHAIN$calls$Strike[!is.na(ImpVol)],4,raw=TRUE))
13 lines(CHAIN$calls$Strike[!is.na(ImpVol)], predict(fit4, data.frame(x=CHAIN$calls$Strike[!is.na(ImpVol)])),
       col="red",lwd=3)
```

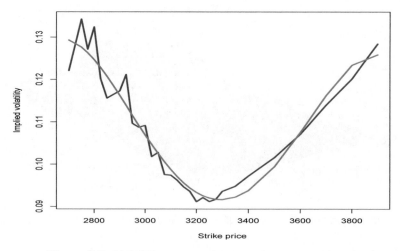

Figure 9.5: S&P500 option prices plotted against strike prices.

When reading option prices on the volatility scale, the smile phenomenon shows that the Black–Scholes formula tends to underprice extreme events for which the underlying asset price S_T is far away from the strike price K. In that sense, the Black–Scholes formula, which is modeling asset returns using Gaussian distribution tails, tends to underestimate the probability of extreme events.

Plotting the different values of the implied volatility σ as a function of K and T will yield a three-dimensional plot called the volatility surface.

Black–Scholes Formula *vs* Market Data

On July 28, 2009 a call warrant has been issued by Merrill Lynch on the stock price S of Cheung Kong Holdings (0001.HK) with strike price K=\$109.99, Maturity T = December 13, 2010, and entitlement ratio 100.

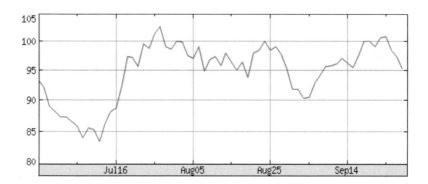

Figure 9.6: Graph of the (market) stock price of Cheung Kong Holdings.

The market price of the option (17838.HK) on September 28 was \$12.30.

The next graph in Figure 9.7a shows the evolution of the market price of the option over time. One sees that the option price is much more volatile than the underlying asset price.

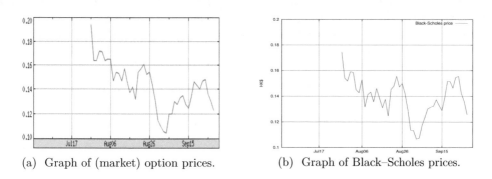

(a) Graph of (market) option prices.   (b) Graph of Black–Scholes prices.

Figure 9.7: Comparison of market option prices *vs* calibrated Black–Scholes prices.

In Figure 9.7b we have fitted the time evolution $t \mapsto g_c(t, S_t)$ of Black–Scholes prices to the data of Figure 9.7a using the market stock price data of Figure 9.6, by varying the values of the volatility σ.

Another example

Let us consider the stock price of HSBC Holdings (0005.HK) over one year:

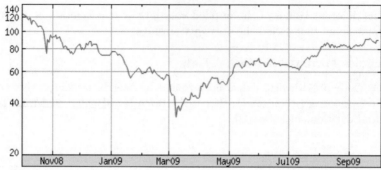

Figure 9.8: Graph of the (market) stock price of HSBC Holdings.

Next, we consider the graph of the price of the call option issued by Societe Generale on December 31, 2008 with strike price K=$63.704, maturity T = October 5, 2009, and entitlement ratio 100, cf. page 7.

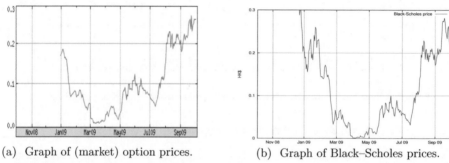

(a) Graph of (market) option prices.   (b) Graph of Black–Scholes prices.

Figure 9.9: Comparison of market option prices *vs* calibrated Black–Scholes prices.

As above, in Figure 9.9b we have fitted the path $t \longmapsto g_c(t, S_t)$ of the Black–Scholes option price to the data of Figure 9.9a using the stock price data of Figure 9.8.

In this case the option is *in the money* at maturity. We can also check that the option is worth $100 \times 0.2650 = \$26.650$ at that time, which, according to the absence of arbitrage, is quite close to the actual value $90 - \$63.703 = \$26.296$ of its payoff.

For one more example, consider the graph of the price of a put option issued by BNP Paribas on November 4, 2008 on the underlying asset HSBC, with strike price K=$77.667, maturity T = October 5, 2009, and entitlement ratio 92.593.

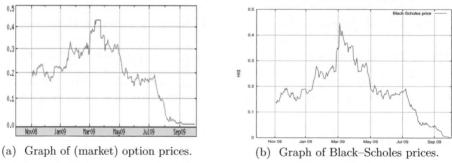

(a) Graph of (market) option prices.   (b) Graph of Black–Scholes prices.

Figure 9.10: Comparison of market option prices *vs* calibrated Black–Scholes prices.

One checks easily that at maturity, the price of the put option is worth \$0.01 (a market price cannot be lower), which almost equals the option payoff \$0, by absence of arbitrage opportunities. Figure 9.10b is a fit of the Black–Scholes put price graph

$$t \longmapsto g_{\mathrm{p}}(t, S_t)$$

to Figure 9.10a as a function of the stock price data of Figure 9.9b. Note that the Black–Scholes price at maturity is strictly equal to 0 while the corresponding market price cannot be lower than one cent.

9.3 Local Volatility

As the constant volatility assumption in the Black–Scholes model does not appear to be satisfactory due to the existence of volatility smiles, it can make more sense to consider models of the form

$$\frac{dS_t}{S_t} = rdt + \sigma_t dB_t$$

where σ_t is a random process. Such models are called stochastic volatility models.

A particular class of stochastic volatility models can be written as

$$\frac{dS_t}{S_t} = rdt + \sigma(t, S_t)dB_t \tag{9.6}$$

where $\sigma(t, x) \geqslant 0$ is a deterministic function of time t and of the underlying asset price x. Such models are called local volatility models.

As an example, consider the stochastic differential equation with local volatility

$$dY_t = rdt + \sigma Y_t^2 dB_t, \tag{9.7}$$

where $\sigma > 0$, see also Exercise 7.27.

```
dev.new(width=16,height=7)
N=10000; t <- 0:(N-1); dt <- 1.0/N;r=0.5;sigma=1.2;
Z <- rnorm(N,mean=0,sd=sqrt(dt));Y <- rep(0,N);Y[1]=1
for (j in 2:N){ Y[j]=max(0,Y[j-1]+r*Y[j-1]*dt+sigma*Y[j-1]**2*Z[j])}
plot(t*dt, Y, xlab = "t", ylab = "", type = "l", col = "blue", xaxs='i', yaxs='i', cex.lab=2, cex.axis=1.6,las=1)
abline(h=0)
```

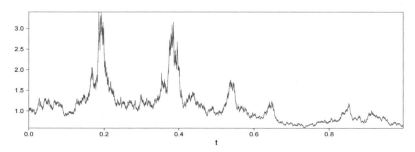

Figure 9.11: Simulated path of (9.7) with $r = 0.5$ and $\sigma = 1.2$.

In the general case, the corresponding Black–Scholes PDE for the option prices

$$g(t, x, K) := e^{-(T-t)r} \, \mathbb{E}\left[(S_T - K)^+ \mid S_t = x \right], \tag{9.8}$$

where $(S_t)_{t \in \mathbb{R}_+}$ is defined by (9.6), can be written as

$$\begin{cases} rg(t, x, K) = \dfrac{\partial g}{\partial t}(t, x, K) + rx\dfrac{\partial g}{\partial x}(t, x, K) + \dfrac{1}{2}x^2\sigma^2(t, x)\dfrac{\partial^2 g}{\partial x^2}(t, x, K), \\[2mm] g(T, x, K) = (x - K)^+, \end{cases} \tag{9.9}$$

with terminal condition $g(T, x, K) = (x - K)^+$, *i.e.* we consider European call options.

Lemma 9.1. *(Relation (1) in Breeden and Litzenberger (1978)). Consider a family* $(C^M(T, K))_{T, K > 0}$ *of market call option prices with maturities T and strike prices K given at time 0. Then, the probability density function $\varphi_T(y)$ of S_T is given by*

$$\varphi_T(K) = e^{rT}\frac{\partial^2 C^M}{\partial K^2}(T, K), \qquad K, T > 0. \tag{9.10}$$

Proof. Assume that the market option prices $C^M(T, K)$ match the Black–Scholes prices $e^{-rT}\,\mathbb{E}[(S_T - K)^+]$, $K > 0$. Letting $\varphi_T(y)$ denote the probability density function of S_T, Condition (9.13) can be written at time $t = 0$ as

$$\begin{aligned} C^M(T, K) &= e^{-rT}\,\mathbb{E}[(S_T - K)^+] \\ &= e^{-rT}\int_0^\infty (y - K)^+\varphi_T(y)dy \\ &= e^{-rT}\int_K^\infty (y - K)\varphi_T(y)dy \\ &= e^{-rT}\int_K^\infty y\varphi_T(y)dy - Ke^{-rT}\int_K^\infty \varphi_T(y)dy \\ &= e^{-rT}\int_K^\infty y\varphi_T(y)dy - Ke^{-rT}\,\mathbb{P}(S_T \geqslant K). \end{aligned} \tag{9.11}$$

By differentiation of (9.11) with respect to K, one gets

$$\begin{aligned} \frac{\partial C^M}{\partial K}(T, K) &= -e^{-rT}K\varphi_T(K) - e^{-rT}\int_K^\infty \varphi_T(y)dy + e^{-rT}K\varphi_T(K) \\ &= -e^{-rT}\int_K^\infty \varphi_T(y)dy, \end{aligned}$$

which yields (9.10) by twice differentiation of $C^M(T, K)$ with respect to K. □

In order to implement a stochastic volatility model such as (9.6), it is important to first calibrate the local volatility function $\sigma(t, x)$ to market data.

In principle, the Black–Scholes PDE (9.9) could allow one to recover the value of $\sigma(t, x)$ as a function of the option price $g(t, x, K)$, as

$$\sigma(t, x) = \sqrt{\frac{2rg(t, x, K) - 2\dfrac{\partial g}{\partial t}(t, x, K) - 2rx\dfrac{\partial g}{\partial x}(t, x, K)}{x^2\dfrac{\partial^2 g}{\partial x^2}(t, x, K)}}, \qquad x, t > 0,$$

however, this formula requires the knowledge of the option price for different values of the underlying asset price x, in addition to the knowledge of the strike price K.

The Dupire (1994) formula brings a solution to the local volatility calibration problem by providing an estimator of $\sigma(t, x)$ as a function $\sigma(t, K)$ based on the values of the strike price K.

Proposition 9.2. *(Dupire (1994), Derman and Kani (1994)) Consider a family $(C^M(T, K))_{T,K>0}$ of market call option prices at time 0 with maturity T and strike price K, and define the volatility function $\sigma(t, y)$ by*

$$
\sigma(t,y) := \sqrt{\frac{2\dfrac{\partial C^M}{\partial t}(t,y) + 2ry\dfrac{\partial C^M}{\partial y}(t,y)}{y^2 \dfrac{\partial^2 C^M}{\partial y^2}(t,y)}} = \frac{\sqrt{\dfrac{\partial C^M}{\partial t}(t,y) + ry\dfrac{\partial C^M}{\partial y}(t,y)}}{y\,\mathrm{e}^{-rT/2}\sqrt{\varphi_t(y)/2}}, \qquad (9.12)
$$

where $\varphi_t(y)$ denotes the probability density function of S_t, $t \in [0, T]$. Then, the prices generated from the Black–Scholes PDE (9.9) will be compatible with the market option prices $C^M(T, K)$ in the sense that

$$
C^M(T, K) = \mathrm{e}^{-rT}\, \mathbb{E}[(S_T - K)^+], \qquad K > 0. \tag{9.13}
$$

Proof. For any sufficiently smooth function $f \in \mathcal{C}_0^\infty(\mathbb{R})$, with $\lim_{x\to-\infty} f(x) = \lim_{x\to+\infty} f(x) = 0$, using the Itô formula we have

$$
\int_{-\infty}^{\infty} f(y)\varphi_T(y)dy = \mathbb{E}[f(S_T)]
$$

$$
= \mathbb{E}\left[f(S_0) + r\int_0^T S_t f'(S_t)dt + \int_0^T S_t f'(S_t)\sigma(t, S_t)dB_t \right.
$$
$$
\left. + \frac{1}{2}\int_0^T S_t^2 f''(S_t)\sigma^2(t, S_t)dt \right]
$$

$$
= f(S_0) + \mathbb{E}\left[r\int_0^T S_t f'(S_t)dt + \frac{1}{2}\int_0^T S_t^2 f''(S_t)\sigma^2(t, S_t)dt \right]
$$

$$
= f(S_0) + r\int_0^T \mathbb{E}[S_t f'(S_t)]dt + \frac{1}{2}\int_0^T \mathbb{E}[S_t^2 f''(S_t)\sigma^2(t, S_t)]dt
$$

$$
= f(S_0) + r\int_{-\infty}^{\infty} y f'(y) \int_0^T \varphi_t(y)dt\,dy
$$
$$
+ \frac{1}{2}\int_{-\infty}^{\infty} y^2 f''(y) \int_0^T \sigma^2(t, y)\varphi_t(y)dt\,dy,
$$

hence, after differentiating both sides of the equality with respect to T,

$$
\int_{-\infty}^{\infty} f(y)\frac{\partial \varphi_T}{\partial T}(y)dy = r\int_{-\infty}^{\infty} y f'(y)\varphi_T(y)dy + \frac{1}{2}\int_{-\infty}^{\infty} y^2 f''(y)\sigma^2(T, y)\varphi_T(y)dy.
$$

Integrating by parts in the above relation yields

$$
\int_{-\infty}^{\infty} \frac{\partial \varphi_T}{\partial T}(y)f(y)dy
$$

$$
= -r\int_{-\infty}^{\infty} f(y)\frac{\partial}{\partial y}(y\varphi_T(y))dy + \frac{1}{2}\int_{-\infty}^{\infty} f(y)\frac{\partial^2}{\partial y^2}(y^2\sigma^2(T, y)\varphi_T(y))dy,
$$

for all smooth functions $f(y)$ with compact support in $\mathbb{R}$, hence

$$\frac{\partial \varphi_T}{\partial T}(y) = -r\frac{\partial}{\partial y}(y\varphi_T(y)) + \frac{1}{2}\frac{\partial^2}{\partial y^2}(y^2\sigma^2(T,y)\varphi_T(y)), \qquad y \in \mathbb{R}.$$

From Relation (9.10) in Lemma 9.1, we have

$$\frac{\partial \varphi_T}{\partial T}(K) = r\,e^{rT}\frac{\partial^2 C^M}{\partial K^2}(T,K) + e^{rT}\frac{\partial^3 C^M}{\partial T\partial K^2}(T,K),$$

hence we get

$$-r\frac{\partial^2 C^M}{\partial y^2}(T,y) - \frac{\partial^3 C^M}{\partial T\partial y^2}(T,y)$$
$$= r\frac{\partial}{\partial y}\left(y\frac{\partial^2 C^M}{\partial y^2}(T,y)\right) - \frac{1}{2}\frac{\partial^2}{\partial y^2}\left(y^2\sigma^2(T,y)\frac{\partial^2 C^M}{\partial y^2}(T,y)\right), \qquad y \in \mathbb{R}.$$

After a first integration with respect to y under the boundary condition $\lim_{y\to+\infty} C^M(T,y) = 0$, we obtain

$$-r\frac{\partial C^M}{\partial y}(T,y) - \frac{\partial}{\partial T}\frac{\partial C^M}{\partial y}(T,y)$$
$$= ry\frac{\partial^2 C^M}{\partial y^2}(T,y) - \frac{1}{2}\frac{\partial}{\partial y}\left(y^2\sigma^2(T,y)\frac{\partial^2 C^M}{\partial y^2}(T,y)\right),$$

i.e.

$$-r\frac{\partial C^M}{\partial y}(T,y) - \frac{\partial}{\partial T}\frac{\partial C^M}{\partial y}(T,y)$$
$$= r\frac{\partial}{\partial y}\left(y\frac{\partial C^M}{\partial y}(T,y)\right) - r\frac{\partial C^M}{\partial y}(T,y) - \frac{1}{2}\frac{\partial}{\partial y}\left(y^2\sigma^2(T,y)\frac{\partial^2 C^M}{\partial y^2}(T,y)\right),$$

or

$$-\frac{\partial}{\partial y}\frac{\partial C^M}{\partial T}(T,y) = r\frac{\partial}{\partial y}\left(y\frac{\partial C^M}{\partial y}(T,y)\right) - \frac{1}{2}\frac{\partial}{\partial y}\left(y^2\sigma^2(T,y)\frac{\partial^2 C^M}{\partial y^2}(T,y)\right).$$

Integrating one more time with respect to y yields

$$-\frac{\partial C^M}{\partial T}(T,y) = ry\frac{\partial C^M}{\partial y}(T,y) - \frac{1}{2}y^2\sigma^2(T,y)\frac{\partial^2 C^M}{\partial y^2}(T,y), \qquad y \in \mathbb{R},$$

which conducts to (9.12) and is called the Dupire (1994) PDE. $\qquad \square$

Partial derivatives in time can be approximated using *forward* finite difference approximations as

$$\frac{\partial C}{\partial t}(t_i,y_j) \simeq \frac{C(t_{i+1},y_j) - C(t_i,y_j)}{\Delta t}, \tag{9.14}$$

or, using *backward* finite difference approximations, as

$$\frac{\partial C}{\partial t}(t_i,y) \simeq \frac{C(t_i,y_j) - C(t_{i-1},y_j)}{\Delta t}. \tag{9.15}$$

First-order spatial derivatives can be approximated as

$$\frac{\partial C}{\partial y}(t,y_j) \simeq \frac{C(t,y_j) - C(t_i,y_{j-1})}{\Delta y}, \quad \frac{\partial C}{\partial y}(t,y_{j+1}) \simeq \frac{C(t,y_{j+1}) - C(t_i,y_j)}{\Delta y}. \tag{9.16}$$

Reusing (9.16), second-order spatial derivatives can be similarly approximated as

$$\frac{\partial^2 C}{\partial y^2}(t, y_j) \simeq \frac{1}{\Delta y}\left(\frac{\partial C}{\partial y}(t, y_{j+1}) - \frac{\partial C}{\partial y}(t, y_j)\right) \tag{9.17}$$

$$\simeq \frac{C(t_i, y_{j+1}) + C(t_i, y_{j-1}) - 2C(t_i, y_j)}{(\Delta y)^2}.$$

Figure 9.12* presents an estimation of local volatility by the finite differences (9.14)–(9.17), based on Boeing (NYSE:BA) option price data.

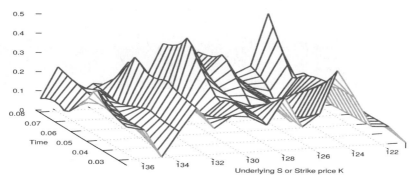

Figure 9.12: Local volatility estimated from Boeing Co. option price data.

See Achdou and Pironneau (2005) and in particular Figure 8.1 therein for numerical methods applied to local volatility estimation using spline functions instead of the discretization (9.14)–(9.17).

Based on (9.12), the local volatility $\sigma(t, y)$ can also be estimated by computing $C^M(T, y)$ from the Black–Scholes formula, from a value of the implied volatility σ.

Local volatility from put option prices

Note that by the call-put parity relation

$$C^M(T, y) = P^M(T, y) + x - y\,\mathrm{e}^{-rT}, \qquad y, T > 0,$$

where $S_0 = y$, cf. (6.23), we have

$$\begin{cases} \dfrac{\partial C^M}{\partial T}(T, y) = ry\,\mathrm{e}^{-rT} + \dfrac{\partial P^M}{\partial T}(T, y), \\[3mm] \dfrac{\partial P^M}{\partial y}(T, y) = \mathrm{e}^{-rT} + \dfrac{\partial C^M}{\partial y}(T, y), \end{cases}$$

and

$$\frac{\partial C^M}{\partial T}(T, y) + ry\frac{\partial C^M}{\partial y}(T, y) = \frac{\partial P^M}{\partial T}(T, y) + ry\frac{\partial P^M}{\partial y}(T, y).$$

Consequently, the local volatility in Proposition 9.2 can be rewritten in terms of market put option prices as

$$\sigma(t,y) := \sqrt{\frac{2\dfrac{\partial P^M}{\partial t}(t,y) + 2ry\dfrac{\partial P^M}{\partial y}(t,y)}{y^2\dfrac{\partial^2 P^M}{\partial y^2}(t,y)}} = \frac{\sqrt{\dfrac{\partial P^M}{\partial t}(t,y) + ry\dfrac{\partial P^M}{\partial y}(t,y)}}{y\mathrm{e}^{-rT/2}\sqrt{\varphi_t(y)/2}},$$

which is formally identical to (9.12) after replacing market call option prices $C^M(T,K)$ with market put option prices $P^M(T,K)$. In addition, we have the relation

$$\varphi_T(K) = \mathrm{e}^{rT}\frac{\partial^2 C^M}{\partial y^2}(T,y) = \mathrm{e}^{rT}\frac{\partial^2 P^M}{\partial y^2}(T,y) \qquad (9.18)$$

between the probability density function φ_T of S_T and the call/put option pricing functions $C^M(T,y)$, $P^M(T,y)$.

9.4   The VIX® Index

Other ways to estimate market volatility include the *CBOE Volatility Index® (VIX®)* for the S&P 500 Index (SPX). Let the asset price process $(S_t)_{t\in\mathbb{R}_+}$ satisfy

$$dS_t = rS_t dt + \sigma_t S_t dB_t,$$

i.e.

$$S_t = S_0 \exp\left(\int_0^t \sigma_s dB_s + rt - \frac{1}{2}\int_0^t \sigma_s^2 ds\right), \qquad t \geqslant 0,$$

where, as in Section 8.2, $(\sigma_t)_{t\in\mathbb{R}_+}$ denotes a stochastic volatility process.

Lemma 9.3. *Let $\phi \in \mathcal{C}^2((0,\infty))$. For all $y > 0$, we have the following version of the Taylor formula:*

$$\phi(x) = \phi(y) + (x-y)\phi'(y) + \int_0^y (z-x)^+\phi''(z)dz + \int_y^\infty (x-z)^+\phi''(z)dz,$$

$x > 0$.

Proof. We use the Taylor formula with integral remainder:

$$\phi(x) = \phi(y) + (x-y)\phi'(y) + |x-y|^2\int_0^1 (1-\tau)\phi''(\tau x + (1-\tau)y)d\tau, \quad x,y \in \mathbb{R}.$$

Letting $z = \tau x + (1-\tau)y = y + \tau(x-y)$, if $x \leqslant y$ we have

$$\begin{aligned} |x-y|^2\int_0^1 (1-\tau)\phi''(\tau x + (1-\tau)y)d\tau &= |x-y|\int_y^x \left(1 - \frac{z-y}{x-y}\right)\phi''(z)dz \\ &= \int_y^x (x-z)\phi''(z)dz \\ &= \int_y^\infty (x-z)^+\phi''(z)dz. \end{aligned}$$

If $x \geqslant y$, we have

$$
\begin{aligned}
|x-y|^2 \int_0^1 (1-\tau)\phi''(\tau x + (1-\tau)y)d\tau &= |y-x| \int_x^y \left(1 - \frac{y-z}{y-x}\right) \phi''(z)dz \\
&= \int_x^y (z-x)\phi''(z)dz \\
&= \int_0^y (z-x)^+ \phi''(z)dz.
\end{aligned}
$$

$\square$

The next Proposition 9.4, cf. Remark 5 in Friz and Gatheral (2005) and page 4 of the *CBOE white paper*, shows that the VIX$^{\circledR}$ Volatility Index defined as

$$
\text{VIX}_t := \sqrt{\frac{2\,e^{r\tau}}{\tau} \left(\int_0^{F_{t,t+\tau}} \frac{P(t,t+\tau,K)}{K^2} dK + \int_{F_{t,t+\tau}}^{\infty} \frac{C(t,t+\tau,K)}{K^2} dK \right)} \tag{9.19}
$$

at time $t > 0$ can be interpreted as an average of future volatility values, see also § 3.1.1 of Papanicolaou and Sircar (2014). Here, $\tau = 30$ days,

$$
F_{t,t+\tau} := \mathbb{E}^*[S_{t+\tau} \mid \mathcal{F}_t] = e^{r\tau} S_t
$$

represents the future price on $S_{t+\tau}$, and $P(t,t+\tau,K)$, $C(t,t+\tau,K)$ are OTM (Out-Of-the-Money) call and put option prices with respect to $F_{t,t+\tau}$, with strike price K and maturity $t+\tau$.

Proposition 9.4. *The value of the VIX$^{\circledR}$ Volatility Index at time $t \geqslant 0$ is given from the averaged realized variance swap price as*

$$
\text{VIX}_t := \sqrt{\frac{1}{\tau} \mathbb{E}^* \left[\int_t^{t+\tau} \sigma_u^2 du \,\middle|\, \mathcal{F}_t \right]}.
$$

Proof. We take $t = 0$ for simplicity. Applying Lemma 9.3 to the function

$$
\phi(x) = \frac{x}{y} - 1 - \log \frac{x}{y}
$$

with $\phi'(x) = 1/y - 1/x$ and $\phi''(x) = 1/x^2$ shows that

$$
\frac{x}{y} - 1 - \log \frac{x}{y} = \int_0^y (z-x)^+ \frac{1}{z^2} dz + \int_y^{\infty} (x-z)^+ \frac{1}{z^2} dz, \quad x,y > 0.
$$

Alternatively, we can use the following relationships which are obtained by integration by parts:

$$
\begin{aligned}
\int_0^y (z-x)^+ \frac{dz}{z^2} &= \mathbb{1}_{\{x \leqslant y\}} \int_x^y (z-x) \frac{dz}{z^2} \\
&= \mathbb{1}_{\{x \leqslant y\}} \left(\int_x^y \frac{dz}{z} - x \int_x^y \frac{dz}{z^2} \right) \\
&= \mathbb{1}_{\{x \leqslant y\}} \left(\frac{x}{y} - 1 + \log \frac{y}{x} \right),
\end{aligned}
$$

and

$$\int_y^\infty (x-z)^+ \frac{dz}{z^2} = \mathbb{1}_{\{x \geqslant y\}} \int_y^x (x-z) \frac{dz}{z^2}$$

$$= \mathbb{1}_{\{x \geqslant y\}} \left(x \int_y^x \frac{dz}{z^2} - \int_y^x \frac{dz}{z} \right)$$

$$= \mathbb{1}_{\{x \geqslant y\}} \left(\frac{x}{y} - 1 + \log \frac{y}{x} \right).$$

Hence, taking $y := F_{0,\tau} = e^{r\tau} S_0$ and $x := S_\tau$, we have

$$\frac{S_\tau}{F_{0,\tau}} - 1 + \log \frac{F_{0,\tau}}{S_\tau} = \int_0^{F_{0,\tau}} (K - S_\tau)^+ \frac{dK}{K^2} + \int_{F_{0,\tau}}^\infty (S_\tau - K)^+ \frac{dK}{K^2}. \tag{9.20}$$

Next, taking expectations under $\mathbb{P}^*$ on both sides of (9.20), we find

$$
\begin{aligned}
\text{VIX}_0^2 &= \frac{2 e^{r\tau}}{\tau} \left(\int_0^{F_{0,\tau}} \frac{P(0,\tau,K)}{K^2} dK + \int_{F_{0,\tau}}^\infty \frac{C(0,\tau,K)}{K^2} dK \right) \\
&= \frac{2}{\tau} \int_0^{F_{0,\tau}} \mathbb{E}^*[(K-S_\tau)^+] \frac{dK}{K^2} + \frac{2}{\tau} \int_{F_{0,\tau}}^\infty \mathbb{E}^*[(S_\tau - K)^+] \frac{dK}{K^2} \\
&= \frac{2}{\tau} \mathbb{E}^* \left[\int_0^{F_{0,\tau}} (K-S_\tau)^+ \frac{dK}{K^2} + \int_{F_{0,\tau}}^\infty (S_\tau - K)^+ \frac{dK}{K^2} \right] \\
&= \frac{2}{\tau} \mathbb{E}^* \left[\frac{S_\tau}{F_{0,\tau}} - 1 + \log \frac{F_{0,\tau}}{S_\tau} \right] \\
&= \frac{2}{\tau} \left(\frac{\mathbb{E}^*[S_\tau]}{F_{0,\tau}} - 1 \right) + \frac{2}{\tau} \mathbb{E}^* \left[\log \frac{F_{0,\tau}}{S_\tau} \right] \\
&= \frac{2}{\tau} \mathbb{E}^* \left[\log \frac{F_{0,\tau}}{S_\tau} \right] \\
&= \frac{1}{\tau} \mathbb{E}^* \left[\int_0^\tau \sigma_t^2 dt \right],
\end{aligned}
$$

where we applied Proposition 8.1. $\qquad\qquad\square$

The following R code allows us to estimate the VIX® index based on the discretization of (9.19) and market option prices on the S&P 500 Index (SPX). Here, the OTM put strike prices and call strike prices are listed as

$$K_1^{(p)} < \cdots < K_{n_p-1}^{(p)} < K_{n_p}^{(p)} := F_{t,t+\tau} =: K_0^{(c)} < K_1^{(c)} < \cdots < K_{n_c}^{(c)},$$

and (9.19) may for example be discretized as

$$
\begin{aligned}
\text{VIX}_t^2 &= \frac{2 e^{r\tau}}{\tau} \left(\int_0^{F_{t,t+\tau}} \frac{P(t,t+\tau,K)}{K^2} dK + \int_{F_{t,t+\tau}}^\infty \frac{C(t,t+\tau,K)}{K^2} dK \right) \\
&= \frac{2 e^{r\tau}}{\tau} \left(\sum_{i=1}^{n_p-1} \int_{K_i^{(p)}}^{K_{i+1}^{(p)}} \frac{P(t,t+\tau,K)}{K^2} dK + \sum_{i=1}^{n_c} \int_{K_{i-1}^{(c)}}^{K_i^{(c)}} \frac{C(t,t+\tau,K)}{K^2} dK \right) \\
&\simeq \frac{2 e^{r\tau}}{\tau} \left(\sum_{i=1}^{n_p-1} \int_{K_i^{(p)}}^{K_{i+1}^{(p)}} \frac{P\big(t,t+\tau,K_i^{(p)}\big)}{K^2} dK + \sum_{i=1}^{n_c} \int_{K_{i-1}^{(c)}}^{K_i^{(c)}} \frac{C\big(t,t+\tau,K_i^{(c)}\big)}{K^2} dK \right)
\end{aligned}
$$

$$= \frac{2\,e^{r\tau}}{\tau}\left(\sum_{i=1}^{n_p-1} P\!\left(t, t+\tau, K_i^{(p)}\right)\left(\frac{1}{K_i^{(p)}} - \frac{1}{K_{i+1}^{(p)}}\right)\right.$$

$$\left. + \sum_{i=1}^{n_c}\int_{K_{i-1}^{(c)}}^{K_i^{(c)}} C\!\left(t, t+\tau, K_i^{(c)}\right)\left(\frac{1}{K_{i-1}^{(c)}} - \frac{1}{K_i^{(c)}}\right)\right),$$

see page 158 of Gatheral (2006) for the implementation of the discretization of the *CBOE white paper*.

```
today <- as.Date(Sys.Date(), format="%Y-%m-%d"); getSymbols("^SPX", src = "yahoo")
lastBusDay=last(row.names(as.data.frame(Ad(SPX))))
S0 = as.vector(tail(Ad(SPX),1)); T = 30/365;r=0.02;F0 = S0*exp(r*T)
maturity <- as.Date("2021-07-07", format="%Y-%m-%d") # Choose a maturity in 30 days
SPX.OPTS <- getOptionChain("^SPX", maturity)
Call <- as.data.frame(SPX.OPTS$calls);Put <- as.data.frame(SPX.OPTS$puts)
Call_OTM <- Call[Call$Strike>F0,];Put_OTM <-Put[Put$Strike<F0,];
Call_OTM$dif = c(1/F0-1/min(Call_OTM$Strike),-diff(1/Call_OTM$Strike))
Put_OTM$dif = c(-diff(1/Put_OTM$Strike),1/max(Put_OTM$Strike)-1/F0)
VIX_imp = 100*sqrt((2*exp(r*T)/T)*(sum(Put_OTM$Last*Put_OTM$dif)
    +sum(Call_OTM$Last*Call_OTM$dif)))
getSymbols("^VIX", src = "yahoo", from = lastBusDay);VIX_market = as.vector(Ad(VIX)[1])
c("Estimated VIX"= VIX_imp, "CBOE VIX"=VIX_market)
VIX.OPTS <- getOptionChain("^VIX")
```

The following R code is fetching VIX® index data using the quantmod R package.

```
getSymbols("^GSPC",from="2000-01-01",to=Sys.Date(),src="yahoo")
getSymbols("^VIX",from="2000-01-01",to=Sys.Date(),src="yahoo")
dev.new(width=16,height=7); myPars <- chart_pars();myPars$cex<-1.4
myTheme <- chart_theme();myTheme$col$line.col <- "blue"
chart_Series(Ad(`GSPC`),name="S&P500",pars=myPars,theme=myTheme)
add_TA(Ad(`VIX`))
```

The impact of various world events can be identified on the VIX® index in Figure 9.13.

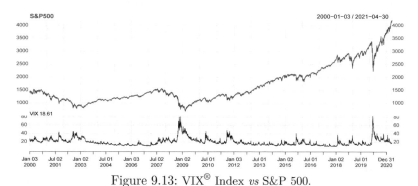

Figure 9.13: VIX® Index *vs* S&P 500.

```
getSymbols("^GSPC",from="2000-01-01",to=Sys.Date(),src="yahoo")
getSymbols("^VIX",from="2000-01-01",to=Sys.Date(),src="yahoo");SP500=Ad(`GSPC`)
SP500.rtn <- exp(CalculateReturns(SP500,method="compound")) - 1;SP500.rtn[1,] <- 0
histvol <- rollapply(SP500.rtn, width = 30, FUN=sd.annualized)
dev.new(width=16,height=7)
myPars <- chart_pars();myPars$cex<-1.4
myTheme <- chart_theme();myTheme$col$line.col <- "blue"
chart_Series(SP500,name="SP500",theme=myTheme,pars=myPars)
add_TA(histvol, name="Historical Volatility");add_TA(Ad(`VIX`), name="VIX")
```

Figure 9.14 compares the VIX® index estimate to the historical volatility of Section 9.1.

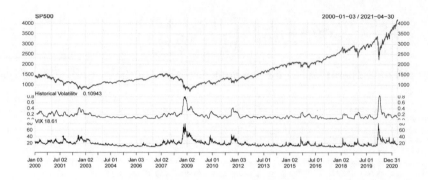

Figure 9.14: VIX® Index *vs* historical volatility for the year 2011.

We note that the variations of the stock index are negatively correlated to the variations of the VIX® index, however, the same cannot be said of the correlation to the variations of historical volatility.

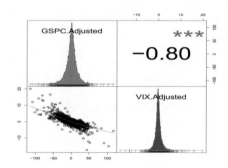

(a) Underlying returns *vs* the VIX® index.

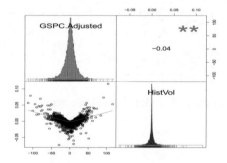

(b) Underlying returns *vs* hist. volatility.

Figure 9.15: Correlation estimates between GSPC and the VIX®.

```
1   chart.Correlation(cbind(Ad(`GSPC`)-lag(Ad(`GSPC`)),Ad(`VIX`)-lag(Ad(`VIX`))), histogram=TRUE,
        pch="+")
    colnames(histvol) <- "HistVol"
3   chart.Correlation(cbind(Ad(`GSPC`)-lag(Ad(`GSPC`)),histvol-lag(histvol)), histogram=TRUE, pch="+")
```

The next Figure 9.16 shortens the time range to year 2011 and shows the increased reactivity of the VIX® index to volatility spikes, in comparison with the moving average of historical volatility.

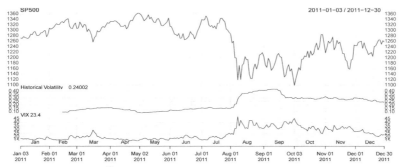

Figure 9.16: VIX® Index *vs* 30 day historical volatility for the S&P 500.

Exercises

Exercise 9.1 Consider the Black–Scholes call pricing formula

$$C(T - t, x, K) = K f\left(T - t, \frac{x}{K}\right)$$

written using the function

$$f(\tau, z) := z\Phi\left(\frac{(r + \sigma^2/2)\tau + \log z}{|\sigma|\sqrt{\tau}}\right) - e^{-r\tau}\Phi\left(\frac{(r - \sigma^2/2)\tau + \log z}{|\sigma|\sqrt{\tau}}\right).$$

a) Compute $\dfrac{\partial C}{\partial x}$ and $\dfrac{\partial C}{\partial K}$ using the function f, and find the relation between $\dfrac{\partial C}{\partial K}(T - t, x, K)$ and $\dfrac{\partial C}{\partial x}(T - t, x, K)$.

b) Compute $\dfrac{\partial^2 C}{\partial x^2}$ and $\dfrac{\partial^2 C}{\partial K^2}$ using the function f, and find the relation between $\dfrac{\partial C^2}{\partial K^2}(T - t, x, K)$ and $\dfrac{\partial C^2}{\partial x^2}(T - t, x, K)$.

c) From the Black–Scholes PDE

$$
\begin{aligned}
rC(T - t, x, K) &= \frac{\partial C}{\partial t}(T - t, x, K) + rx\frac{\partial C}{\partial x}(T - t, x, K) \\
&\quad + \frac{\sigma^2 x^2}{2}\frac{\partial^2 C}{\partial x^2}(T - t, x, K),
\end{aligned}
$$

recover the Dupire (1994) PDE for the constant volatility σ.

Exercise 9.2 The prices of call options in a certain local volatility model of the form $dS_t = S_t\sigma(t, S_t)dB_t$ with risk-free rate $r = 0$ are given by

$$C(S_0, K, T) = \sqrt{\frac{T}{2\pi}}\,e^{-(K-S_0)^2/(2T)} - (K - S_0)\Phi\left(-\frac{K - S_0}{\sqrt{T}}\right), \quad K, T > 0.$$

Recover the local volatility function $\sigma(t, x)$ of this model by applying the Dupire formula.

Exercise 9.3 Let $\sigma_{\text{imp}}(K)$ denote the implied volatility of a call option with strike price K, defined from the relation

$$M_C(K, S, r, \tau) = C(K, S, \sigma_{\text{imp}}(K), r, \tau),$$

where M_C is the market price of the call option, $C(K, S, \sigma_{\text{imp}}(K), r, \tau)$ is the Black–Scholes call pricing function, S is the underlying asset price, τ is the time remaining until maturity, and r is the risk-free interest rate.

a) Compute the partial derivative

$$\frac{\partial M_C}{\partial K}(K, S, r, \tau).$$

using the functions C and σ_{imp}.

b) Knowing that market call option prices $M_C(K, S, r, \tau)$ are *decreasing* in the strike prices K, find an upper bound for the slope $\sigma'_{\text{imp}}(K)$ of the implied volatility curve.

c) Similarly, knowing that the market *put* option prices $M_P(K, S, r, \tau)$ are *increasing* in the strike prices K, find a lower bound for the slope $\sigma'_{\text{imp}}(K)$ of the implied volatility curve.

Exercise 9.4 (Hagan et al. (2002)) Consider the European option priced as $e^{-rT}\,\mathbb{E}^*[(S_T - K)^+]$ in a local volatility model $dS_t = \sigma_{\text{loc}}(S_t)S_t dB_t$. The implied volatility $\sigma_{\text{imp}}(K, S_0)$, computed from the equation

$$\text{Bl}(S_0, K, T, \sigma_{\text{imp}}(K, S_0), r) = e^{-rT}\,\mathbb{E}^*[(S_T - K)^+],$$

is known to admit the approximation

$$\sigma_{\text{imp}}(K, S_0) \simeq \sigma_{\text{loc}}\left(\frac{K + S_0}{2}\right).$$

a) Taking a local volatility of the form $\sigma_{\text{loc}}(x) := \sigma_0 + \beta(x - S_0)^2$, estimate the implied volatility $\sigma_{\text{imp}}(K, S)$ when the underlying asset price is at the level S.

b) Express the Delta of the Black Scholes call option price given by

$$\text{Bl}(S, K, T, \sigma_{\text{imp}}(K, S), r),$$

using the standard Black–Scholes Delta and the Black–Scholes Vega.

Exercise 9.5 Show that the result of Proposition 9.4 can be recovered from Lemma 8.2 and Relation (9.18).

Exercise 9.6 (Exercise 8.7 continued). Find an expression for $\mathbb{E}^*\left[R_{0,T}^4\right]$ using call and put pricing functions.

Exercise 9.7 (Henry-Labordère (2009), § 3.5).

a) Using the gamma probability density function and integration by parts or Laplace transform inversion, prove the formula

$$\int_0^\infty \frac{e^{-\nu x} - e^{-\mu x}}{x^{\rho+1}} dx = \frac{\mu^\rho - \nu^\rho}{\rho} \Gamma(1-\rho)$$

for all $\rho \in (0,1)$ and $\mu, \nu > 0$, see Relation 3.434.1 in Gradshteyn and Ryzhik (2007).

b) By the result of Question (a), generalize the volatility swap pricing expression (8.19).

c) By Lemma 8.2 and the result of Question (b), find an expression of the volatility swap price using call and put functions.

Chapter 10

Maximum of Brownian Motion

The probability distribution of the maximum of Brownian motion on a given interval can be computed in closed form using the reflection principle. As a consequence, the expected value of the running maximum of Brownian motion can also be computed explicitly. Those properties will be applied in the next Chapters 11 and 12 to the pricing of barrier and lookback options, whose payoffs may depend on extrema of the underlying asset price process $(S_t)_{t\in[0,T]}$, as well as on its terminal value S_T.

10.1 Running Maximum of Brownian Motion

Figure 10.1 represents the running maximum process

$$X_0^t := \operatorname*{Max}_{s\in[0,t]} W_s, \qquad t \geqslant 0,$$

of Brownian motion $(W_t)_{t\in\mathbb{R}_+}$.

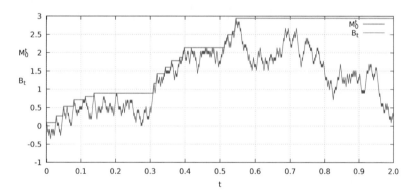

Figure 10.1: Brownian motion $(W_t)_{t\in\mathbb{R}_+}$ and its running maximum $(X_0^t)_{t\in\mathbb{R}_+}$.

Note that Brownian motion admits (almost surely) no "point of increase". More precisely, there does not exist $t > 0$ and $\varepsilon > 0$ such that

$$\operatorname*{Max}_{s\in(t-\varepsilon,t)} W_s \leqslant W_t \leqslant \operatorname*{min}_{s\in(t,t+\varepsilon)} W_s,$$

see, *e.g.* Dvoretzky et al. (1961) and Burdzy (1990). This property is illustrated in Figure 10.1, see also (10.4)–(10.5) below.

DOI: 10.1201/9781003298670-10

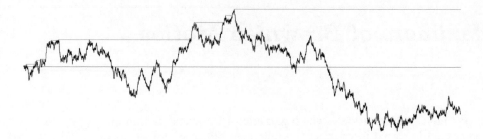

Figure 10.2: Zeroes of Brownian motion.

Related properties can be observed with the zeroes of Brownian motion which form an *uncountable* set (see *e.g.* Theorem 2.28 page 48 of Mörters and Peres (2010)) which has *zero measure* $\mathbb{P}$-almost surely, as we have

$$\mathbb{E}\left[\int_0^\infty \mathbb{1}_{\{W_t=0\}}dt\right] = \int_0^\infty \mathbb{E}\left[\mathbb{1}_{\{W_t=0\}}\right]dt = \int_0^\infty \mathbb{P}(W_t=0)dt = 0,$$

see Figure 10.2.

10.2 The Reflection Principle

Let $(W_t)_{t\in\mathbb{R}_+}$ denote the standard Brownian motion started at $W_0 = 0$. While it is well-known that $W_T \simeq \mathcal{N}(0,T)$, computing the distribution of the maximum

$$X_0^T := \operatorname*{Max}_{t\in[0,T]} W_t$$

might seem a difficult problem. However, this is not the case, due to the *reflection principle*.

Note that since $W_0 = 0$, we have

$$X_0^T = \operatorname*{Max}_{t\in[0,T]} W_t \geqslant 0,$$

almost surely, *i.e.* with probability one. Given $a > W_0 = 0$, let

$$\tau_a = \inf\{t \geqslant 0 \ : \ W_t = a\}$$

denote the first time $(W_t)_{t\in\mathbb{R}_+}$ hits the level $a > 0$. Due to the spatial symmetry of Brownian motion we note the identity

$$\mathbb{P}(W_T \geqslant a \mid \tau_a \leqslant T) = \mathbb{P}(W_T > a \mid \tau_a \leqslant T) = \mathbb{P}(W_T \leqslant a \mid \tau_a \leqslant T) = \frac{1}{2}.$$

In addition, due to the relation

$$\{X_0^T \geqslant a\} = \{\tau_a \leqslant T\}, \tag{10.1}$$

we have

$$
\begin{aligned}
\mathbb{P}(\tau_a \leqslant T) &= \mathbb{P}(\tau_a \leqslant T \text{ and } W_T > a) + \mathbb{P}(\tau_a \leqslant T \text{ and } W_T \leqslant a) \\
&= 2\mathbb{P}(\tau_a \leqslant T \text{ and } W_T \geqslant a) \\
&= 2\mathbb{P}(X_0^T \geqslant a \text{ and } W_T \geqslant a) \\
&= 2\mathbb{P}(W_T \geqslant a) \\
&= \mathbb{P}(W_T \geqslant a) + \mathbb{P}(W_T \leqslant -a) \\
&= \mathbb{P}(|W_T| \geqslant a),
\end{aligned}
$$

where we used the fact that

$$
\{W_T \geqslant a\} \subset \{X_0^T \geqslant a \text{ and } W_T \geqslant a\} \subset \{W_T \geqslant a\}.
$$

Figure 10.3 shows a graph of Brownian motion and its reflected path, with $0 < b < a < 2a - b$.

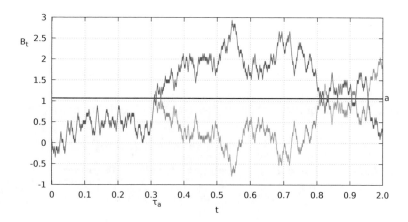

Figure 10.3: Reflected Brownian motion with $a = 1.07$.

As a consequence of the equality

$$
\mathbb{P}(\tau_a \leqslant T) = \mathbb{P}(|W_T| \geqslant a), \qquad a > 0, \tag{10.2}
$$

the maximum X_0^T of Brownian motion has *same distribution* as the absolute value $|W_T|$ of W_T. Precisely, X_0^T is a nonnegative random variable with cumulative distribution function given by

$$
\begin{aligned}
\mathbb{P}(X_0^T < a) &= \mathbb{P}(\tau_a > T) \\
&= \mathbb{P}(|W_T| < a) \\
&= \frac{1}{\sqrt{2\pi T}} \int_{-a}^{a} e^{-x^2/(2T)} dx \\
&= \frac{2}{\sqrt{2\pi T}} \int_{0}^{a} e^{-x^2/(2T)} dx, \qquad a \geqslant 0,
\end{aligned}
$$

i.e.

$$
\mathbb{P}(X_0^T \leqslant a) = \frac{2}{\sqrt{2\pi T}} \int_{0}^{a} e^{-x^2/(2T)} dx, \qquad a \geqslant 0,
$$

and probability density function

$$\varphi_{X_0^T}(a) = \frac{d\mathbb{P}(X_0^T \leqslant a)}{da} = \sqrt{\frac{2}{\pi T}}\, e^{-a^2/(2T)}\mathbb{1}_{[0,\infty)}(a), \quad a \in \mathbb{R}, \tag{10.3}$$

which vanishes over $a \in (-\infty, 0]$ because $X_0^T \geqslant 0$ almost surely.

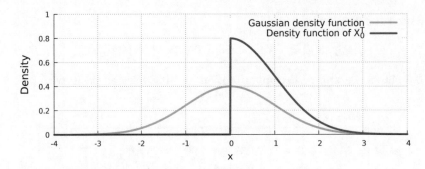

Figure 10.4: Probability density of the maximum X_0^1 of Brownian motion over [0,1].

We note that, as a consequence of the existence of the probability density function (10.3), we have

$$\mathbb{P}(W_t \leqslant 0, \ \forall t \in [0,\varepsilon]) = \mathbb{P}(X_0^\varepsilon = 0) = \int_0^0 \varphi_{X_0^\varepsilon}(a)ds = 0, \tag{10.4}$$

for all $\varepsilon > 0$. Similarly, by a symmetry argument, for all $\varepsilon > 0$ we find

$$\mathbb{P}(W_t \geqslant 0, \ \forall t \in [0,\varepsilon]) = 0 \tag{10.5}$$

Using the probability density function of X_0^T, we can price an option with payoff $\phi(X_0^T)$, as

$$\begin{aligned}
e^{-rT}\,\mathbb{E}^*\left[\phi(X_0^T)\right] &= e^{-rT}\int_{-\infty}^\infty \phi(x)d\mathbb{P}(X_0^T \leqslant x) \\
&= e^{-rT}\sqrt{\frac{2}{\pi T}}\int_0^\infty \phi(x)\,e^{-x^2/(2T)}dx.
\end{aligned}$$

Proposition 10.1. *Let $\sigma > 0$ and $(S_t)_{t\in[0,T]} := \left(S_0\,e^{\sigma W_t}\right)_{t\in[0,T]}$. The probability density function of the maximum*

$$M_0^T := \max_{t\in[0,T]} S_t$$

of $(S_t)_{t\in[0,T]}$ over the time interval $[0,T]$ is given by the truncated lognormal probability density function

$$\varphi_{M_0^T}(y) = \mathbb{1}_{[S_0,\infty)}(y)\frac{1}{\sigma y}\sqrt{\frac{2}{\pi T}}\exp\left(-\frac{1}{2\sigma^2 T}\left(\log(y/S_0)\right)^2\right), \quad y > 0,$$

see Figure 10.5.

Proof. Since $\sigma > 0$, we have

$$
\begin{aligned}
M_0^T &= \underset{t\in[0,T]}{\mathrm{Max}}\ S_t \\
&= S_0 \underset{t\in[0,T]}{\mathrm{Max}}\ \mathrm{e}^{\sigma W_t} \\
&= S_0\, \mathrm{e}^{\sigma\, \mathrm{Max}_{t\in[0,T]}\, W_t} \\
&= S_0\, \mathrm{e}^{\sigma X_0^T}.
\end{aligned}
$$

Hence $M_0^T = h\big(X_0^T\big)$ with $h(x) = S_0\, \mathrm{e}^{\sigma x}$, and

$$
h'(x) = \sigma S_0\, \mathrm{e}^{\sigma x}, \quad x \in \mathbb{R}, \quad \text{and}\ \ h^{-1}(y) = \frac{1}{\sigma}\log\left(\frac{y}{S_0}\right), \quad y > 0,
$$

hence

$$
\begin{aligned}
\varphi_{M_0^T}(y) &= \frac{1}{|h'(h^{-1}(y))|}\varphi_{X_0^T}\big(h^{-1}(y)\big) \\
&= \mathbb{1}_{[0,\infty)}\big(h^{-1}(y)\big)\frac{\sqrt{2}}{|h'(h^{-1}(y))|\sqrt{\pi T}}\, \mathrm{e}^{-(h^{-1}(y))^2/(2T)} \\
&= \mathbb{1}_{[S_0,\infty)}(y)\frac{1}{\sigma y}\sqrt{\frac{2}{\pi T}}\exp\left(-\frac{1}{2\sigma^2 T}\left(\log(y/S_0)\right)^2\right), \quad y > 0.
\end{aligned}
$$

$\square$

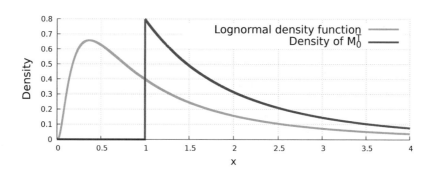

Figure 10.5: Density of the maximum $M_0^T = \mathrm{Max}_{t\in[0,T]}\, S_t$ of geometric Brownian motion with $S_0 = 1$.

When the claim payoff takes the form $C = \phi\big(M_0^T\big)$, where $S_T = S_0\, \mathrm{e}^{\sigma W_T}$, we have

$$
C = \phi\big(M_0^T\big) = \phi\big(S_0\, \mathrm{e}^{\sigma X_0^T}\big),
$$

hence

$$
\begin{aligned}
\mathrm{e}^{-rT}\,\mathbb{E}^*[C] &= \mathrm{e}^{-rT}\,\mathbb{E}^*\left[\phi\big(S_0\, \mathrm{e}^{\sigma X_0^T}\big)\right] \\
&= \mathrm{e}^{-rT}\int_{-\infty}^{\infty}\phi(S_0\, \mathrm{e}^{\sigma x})\mathrm{d}\mathbb{P}(X_0^T \leqslant x) \\
&= \sqrt{\frac{2}{\pi T}}\,\mathrm{e}^{-rT}\int_0^{\infty}\phi(S_0\, \mathrm{e}^{\sigma x})\,\mathrm{e}^{-x^2/(2T)}dx \\
&= \sqrt{\frac{2}{\pi\sigma^2 T}}\,\mathrm{e}^{-rT}\int_1^{\infty}\phi(y)\exp\left(-\frac{1}{2\sigma^2 T}\left(\log(y/S_0)\right)^2\right)\frac{dy}{y},
\end{aligned}
$$

after the change of variable $y = S_0\, \mathrm{e}^{\sigma x}$ with $dx = dy/(\sigma y)$.

The above computation is however not sufficient for practical applications as it imposes the condition $r = \sigma^2/2$. In order to do away with this condition we need to consider the maximum of *drifted* Brownian motion, and for this we have to compute the *joint* probability density function of X_0^T and W_T.

10.3   Density of the Maximum of Brownian Motion

The reflection principle also allows us to compute the *joint* probability density function of Brownian motion W_T and its maximum $X_0^T = \underset{t \in [0,T]}{\mathrm{Max}} \, W_t$. Recall that the probability density function $\varphi_{X_0^T, W_T}$ can be recovered from the joint cumulative distribution function

$$
\begin{aligned}
(x,y) \longmapsto F_{X_0^T, W_T}(x,y) \; &:= \; \mathbb{P}\big(X_0^T \leqslant x \text{ and } W_T \leqslant y\big) \\
&= \; \int_{-\infty}^{x} \int_{-\infty}^{y} \varphi_{X_0^T, W_T}(s,t) ds dt,
\end{aligned}
$$

and

$$
(x,y) \longmapsto \mathbb{P}\big(X_0^T \geqslant x \text{ and } W_T \geqslant y\big) = \int_{x}^{\infty} \int_{y}^{\infty} \varphi_{X_0^T, W_T}(s,t) ds dt,
$$

as

$$
\begin{aligned}
\varphi_{X_0^T, W_T}(x,y) \; &= \; \frac{\partial^2}{\partial x \partial y} F_{X_0^T, W_T}(x,y) && (10.6) \\
&= \; \frac{\partial^2}{\partial x \partial y} \int_{-\infty}^{x} \int_{-\infty}^{y} \varphi_{X_0^T, W_T}(s,t) ds dt && (10.7) \\
&= \; \frac{\partial^2}{\partial x \partial y} \int_{x}^{\infty} \int_{y}^{\infty} \varphi_{X_0^T, W_T}(s,t) ds dt, && x,y \in \mathbb{R}.
\end{aligned}
$$

The probability densities $\varphi_{X_0^T} : \mathbb{R} \longrightarrow \mathbb{R}_+$ and $\varphi_{W_T} : \mathbb{R} \longrightarrow \mathbb{R}_+$ of X_0^T and W_T are called the marginal densities of (X_0^T, W_T), and are given by

$$
\varphi_{X_0^T}(x) = \int_{-\infty}^{\infty} \varphi_{X_0^T, W_T}(x,y) dy, \qquad x \in \mathbb{R},
$$

and

$$
\varphi_{W_T}(y) = \int_{-\infty}^{\infty} \varphi_{X_0^T, W_T}(x,y) dx, \qquad y \in \mathbb{R}.
$$

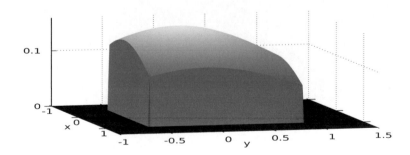

Figure 10.6: Probability $\mathbb{P}((X,Y) \in [-0.5,1] \times [-0.5,1])$ computed as a volume integral.

In order to compute the *joint* probability density function of Brownian motion W_T and its maximum $X_0^T = \underset{t \in [0,T]}{\text{Max}} W_t$ by the reflection principle, we note that for any $b \leqslant a$ we have

$$\mathbb{P}(W_T < b \mid \tau_a < T) = \mathbb{P}(W_T > a + (a - b) \mid \tau_a < T)$$

as shown in Figure 10.7, *i.e.*

$$\mathbb{P}(W_T < b \text{ and } \tau_a < T) = \mathbb{P}(W_T > 2a - b \text{ and } \tau_a < T),$$

or, by (10.1),

$$\mathbb{P}\big(X_0^T \geqslant a \text{ and } W_T < b\big) \;=\; \mathbb{P}\big(X_0^T \geqslant a \text{ and } W_T > 2a - b\big).$$

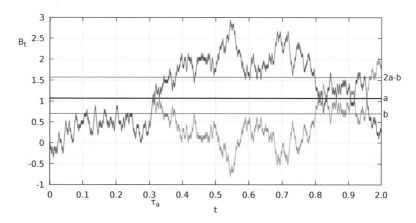

Figure 10.7: Reflected Brownian motion with $a = 1.07$.

Hence, since $2a - b \geqslant a$ we have

$$\mathbb{P}\big(X_0^T \geqslant a \text{ and } W_T < b\big) = \mathbb{P}\big(X_0^T \geqslant a \text{ and } W_T > 2a - b\big) = \mathbb{P}(W_T \geqslant 2a - b), \qquad (10.8)$$

where we used the fact that

$$\{W_T \geqslant 2a - b\} \;\subset\; \{X_0^T \geqslant 2a - b \text{ and } W_T > 2a - b\}$$
$$\subset\; \{X_0^T \geqslant a \text{ and } W_T > 2a - b\} \subset \{W_T > 2a - b\},$$

which shows that

$$\{W_T \geqslant 2a - b\} = \{X_0^T \geqslant a \text{ and } W_T > 2a - b\}.$$

Consequently, by (10.8) we find

$$\begin{aligned}
\mathbb{P}\big(X_0^T > a \text{ and } W_T \leqslant b\big) &= \mathbb{P}\big(X_0^T \geqslant a \text{ and } W_T < b\big) \\
&= \mathbb{P}(W_T \geqslant 2a - b) \\
&= \frac{1}{\sqrt{2\pi T}} \int_{2a-b}^{\infty} e^{-x^2/(2T)} dx,
\end{aligned} \qquad (10.9)$$

$0 \leqslant b \leqslant a$, which yields the joint probability density function

$$
\begin{aligned}
\varphi_{X_0^T, W_T}(a, b) &= \frac{\partial^2}{\partial a \partial b} \mathbb{P}\big(X_0^T \leqslant a \text{ and } W_T \leqslant b\big) \\
&= \frac{\partial^2}{\partial a \partial b}\big(\mathbb{P}\big(W_T \leqslant b\big) - \mathbb{P}\big(X_0^T > a \text{ and } W_T \leqslant b\big)\big) \\
&= -\frac{d\mathbb{P}\big(X_0^T > a \text{ and } W_T \leqslant b\big)}{da\,db}, \qquad a, b \in \mathbb{R}.
\end{aligned}
$$

By (10.9), we obtain the following proposition.

Proposition 10.2. *The joint probability density function* $\varphi_{X_0^T, W_T}$ *of Brownian motion* W_T *and its maximum* $X_0^T = \underset{t \in [0,T]}{\mathrm{Max}}\, W_t$ *is given by*

$$
\varphi_{X_0^T, W_T}(a, b) = \sqrt{\frac{2}{\pi}} \frac{(2a - b)}{T^{3/2}} \mathrm{e}^{-(2a-b)^2/(2T)} \mathbb{1}_{\{a \geqslant \mathrm{Max}(b,0)\}} \tag{10.10}
$$

$$
= \begin{cases} \sqrt{\dfrac{2}{\pi}} \dfrac{(2a - b)}{T^{3/2}} \mathrm{e}^{-(2a-b)^2/(2T)}, & a > \mathrm{Max}(b, 0), \\[2mm] 0, & a < \mathrm{Max}(b, 0). \end{cases}
$$

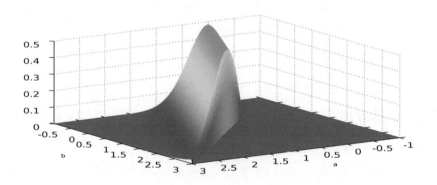

Figure 10.8: Joint probability density of W_1 and the maximum $\widehat{X}_0^1$ over $[0,1]$.

Figure 10.9 presents the corresponding *heat map* of the same graph as seen from above.

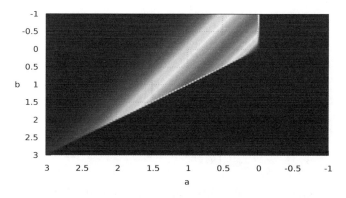

Figure 10.9: Heat map of the joint density of W_1 and its maximum $\widehat{X}_0^1$ over [0,1].

Maximum of drifted Brownian motion

Using the Girsanov Theorem, it is even possible to compute the probability density function of the maximum

$$\widehat{X}_0^T := \underset{t\in[0,T]}{\mathrm{Max}}\ \widetilde{W}_t = \underset{t\in[0,T]}{\mathrm{Max}}\ (W_t + \mu t)$$

of drifted Brownian motion $\widetilde{W}_t = W_t + \mu t$ over $t \in [0,T]$, for any $\mu \in \mathbb{R}$.

Proposition 10.3. *The joint probability density function $\varphi_{\widehat{X}_0^T, \widetilde{W}_T}$ of the drifted Brownian motion $\widetilde{W}_T := W_T + \mu T$ and its maximum $\widehat{X}_0^T = \underset{t\in[0,T]}{\mathrm{Max}}\ \widetilde{W}_t$ is given by*

$$\varphi_{\widehat{X}_0^T, \widetilde{W}_T}(a,b) = \mathbb{1}_{\{a\geqslant\mathrm{Max}(b,0)\}}\frac{1}{T}\sqrt{\frac{2}{\pi T}}(2a-b)\,e^{\mu b-(2a-b)^2/(2T)-\mu^2 T/2}$$

$$(10.11)$$

$$= \begin{cases} \dfrac{1}{T}\sqrt{\dfrac{2}{\pi T}}(2a-b)\,e^{-\mu^2 T/2+\mu b-(2a-b)^2/(2T)}, & a > \mathrm{Max}(b,0), \\[2mm] 0, & a < \mathrm{Max}(b,0). \end{cases}$$

Proof. The arguments previously applied to the standard Brownian motion $(W_t)_{t\in[0,T]}$ cannot be directly applied to $(\widetilde{W}_t)_{t\in[0,T]}$ because drifted Brownian motion is no longer symmetric in space when $\mu \neq 0$. On the other hand, the drifted process $(\widetilde{W}_t)_{t\in\mathbb{R}_+}$ is a standard Brownian motion under the probability measure $\widetilde{\mathbb{P}}$ defined from the Radon–Nikodym density

$$\frac{d\widetilde{\mathbb{P}}}{d\mathbb{P}} := e^{-\mu W_T-\mu^2 T/2}, \qquad (10.12)$$

and the joint probability density function of $(\widehat{X}_0^T, \widetilde{W}_T)$ under $\widetilde{\mathbb{P}}$ is given by (10.10). Now, using the probability density function (10.12) and the relation $\widetilde{W}_t := W_t + \mu t$, we get

$$\mathbb{P}(\widehat{X}_0^T \leqslant a \text{ and } \widetilde{W}_T \leqslant b) = \mathbb{E}\left[\mathbb{1}_{\{\widehat{X}_0^T\leqslant a \text{ and } \widetilde{W}_T\leqslant b\}}\right]$$

$$= \int_\Omega \mathbb{1}_{\{\widehat{X}_0^T\leqslant a \text{ and } \widetilde{W}_T\leqslant b\}}\,d\mathbb{P}$$

$$= \int_{\Omega} \frac{d\mathbb{P}}{d\widetilde{\mathbb{P}}} \mathbb{1}_{\{\widehat{X}_0^T \leqslant a \text{ and } \widetilde{W}_T \leqslant b\}} d\widetilde{\mathbb{P}}$$

$$= \widetilde{\mathbb{E}}\left[\frac{d\mathbb{P}}{d\widetilde{\mathbb{P}}} \mathbb{1}_{\{\widehat{X}_0^T \leqslant a \text{ and } \widetilde{W}_T \leqslant b\}}\right]$$

$$= \widetilde{\mathbb{E}}\left[e^{\mu W_T + \mu^2 T/2} \mathbb{1}_{\{\widehat{X}_0^T \leqslant a \text{ and } \widetilde{W}_T \leqslant b\}}\right]$$

$$= \widetilde{\mathbb{E}}\left[e^{\mu \widetilde{W}_T - \mu^2 T/2} \mathbb{1}_{\{\widehat{X}_0^T \leqslant a \text{ and } \widetilde{W}_T \leqslant b\}}\right]$$

$$= \sqrt{\frac{2}{\pi T}} \int_0^a \int_{-\infty}^b \mathbb{1}_{(-\infty,x]}(y) e^{\mu y - \mu^2 T/2} \frac{(2x-y)}{T} e^{-(2x-y)^2/(2T)} dydx,$$

$0 \leqslant b \leqslant a$, which yields the joint probability density function (10.11) from the differentiation

$$\varphi_{\widehat{X}_0^T, \widetilde{W}_T}(a,b) = \frac{d\mathbb{P}(\widehat{X}_0^T \leqslant a \text{ and } \widetilde{W}_T \leqslant b)}{dadb}.$$

□

The following proposition is consistent with (10.3) in case $\mu = 0$.

Proposition 10.4. *The cumulative distribution function of the maximum*

$$\widehat{X}_0^T := \operatorname*{Max}_{t\in[0,T]} \widetilde{W}_t = \operatorname*{Max}_{t\in[0,T]} (W_t + \mu t)$$

of drifted Brownian motion $\widetilde{W}_t = W_t + \mu t$ *over* $t \in [0,T]$ *is given by*

$$\mathbb{P}(\widehat{X}_0^T \leqslant a) = \Phi\left(\frac{a - \mu T}{\sqrt{T}}\right) - e^{2\mu a}\Phi\left(\frac{-a - \mu T}{\sqrt{T}}\right), \quad a \geqslant 0, \tag{10.13}$$

and the probability density function $\varphi_{\widehat{X}_0^T}$ *of* $\widehat{X}_0^T$ *satisfies*

$$\varphi_{\widehat{X}_0^T}(a) = \sqrt{\frac{2}{\pi T}} e^{-(a-\mu T)^2/(2T)} - 2\mu e^{2\mu a}\Phi\left(\frac{-a - \mu T}{\sqrt{T}}\right), \quad a \geqslant 0. \tag{10.14}$$

Proof. Letting $a \vee b := \operatorname{Max}(a,b)$, $a,b \in \mathbb{R}$, since the condition ($y \leqslant x$ and $0 \leqslant x \leqslant a$) is equivalent to the condition ($y \vee 0 \leqslant x \leqslant a$), we have

$$\mathbb{P}(\widehat{X}_0^T \leqslant a) = \sqrt{\frac{2}{\pi T}} \int_0^a \int_{-\infty}^{\infty} \mathbb{1}_{(-\infty,x]}(y) e^{\mu y - \mu^2 T/2} \frac{(2x-y)}{T} e^{-(2x-y)^2/(2T)} dydx$$

$$= \sqrt{\frac{2}{\pi T}} \int_0^a \int_{-\infty}^x e^{\mu y - \mu^2 T/2} \frac{(2x-y)}{T} e^{-(2x-y)^2/(2T)} dydx$$

$$= \sqrt{\frac{2}{\pi T}} e^{-\mu^2 T/2} \int_{-\infty}^a e^{\mu y} \int_{y\vee 0}^a \frac{(2x-y)}{T} e^{-(2x-y)^2/(2T)} dxdy.$$

Next, since

$$2(y \vee 0)^2 - y = \begin{cases} 2 \times 0 - y = -y, & y \leqslant 0, \\[2mm] 2y - y = y, & y \geqslant 0, \end{cases}$$

and using the "completion of the square" identity

$$\mu y - \frac{(2a-y)^2}{2T} - \frac{\mu^2 T}{2} = 2a\mu - \frac{1}{2T}(y - (\mu T + 2a))^2$$

and a standard changes of variables, we have

$$\mathbb{P}\big(\widehat{X}_0^T \leqslant a\big) = \sqrt{\frac{2}{\pi T}} \int_0^a \int_{-\infty}^{\infty} \mathbb{1}_{(-\infty, x]}(y)\, e^{\mu y - \mu^2 T/2} \frac{(2x-y)}{T}\, e^{-(2x-y)^2/(2T)} dy\, dx$$

$$= \frac{1}{\sqrt{2\pi T}} e^{-\mu^2 T/2} \int_{-\infty}^a \Big(e^{\mu y - (2(y \vee 0) - y)^2/(2T)} - e^{\mu y - (2a-y)^2/(2T)} \Big) dy$$

$$= \frac{1}{\sqrt{2\pi T}} \int_{-\infty}^a \Big(e^{\mu y - y^2/(2T) - \mu^2 T/2} - e^{\mu y - (2a-y)^2/(2T) - \mu^2 T/2} \Big) dy$$

$$= \frac{1}{\sqrt{2\pi T}} \int_{-\infty}^a \Big(e^{-(y - \mu T)^2/(2T)} - e^{-(y - (\mu T + 2a))^2/(2T) + 2a\mu} \Big) dy$$

$$= \frac{1}{\sqrt{2\pi T}} \int_{-\infty}^a e^{-(y - \mu T)^2/(2T)} dy - e^{2a\mu} \frac{1}{\sqrt{2\pi T}} \int_{-\infty}^a e^{-(y - (\mu T + 2a))^2/(2T)} dy$$

$$= \frac{1}{\sqrt{2\pi T}} \int_{-\infty}^{a - \mu T} e^{-y^2/(2T)} dy - e^{2a\mu} \frac{1}{\sqrt{2\pi T}} \int_{-\infty}^{-a - \mu T} e^{-y^2/(2T)} dy$$

$$= \Phi\left(\frac{a - \mu T}{\sqrt{T}}\right) - e^{2\mu a} \Phi\left(\frac{-a - \mu T}{\sqrt{T}}\right), \qquad a \geqslant 0,$$

cf. Corollary 7.2.2 and pages 297-299 of Shreve (2004) for another derivation. □

See Profeta et al. (2010) for interpretations of (10.13) and (10.15) in terms of the Black–Scholes formula.

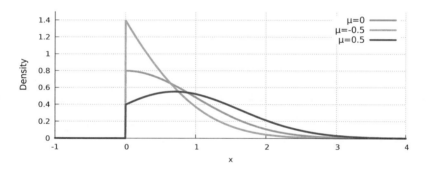

Figure 10.10: Probability density of the maximum $\widehat{X}_0^T$ of drifted Brownian motion.

We note from Figure 10.10 that small values of the maximum are more likely to occur when μ takes large negative values. As T tends to infinity, Proposition 10.4 also shows that when $\mu < 0$, the maximum of drifted Brownian motion $\big(\widetilde{W}_t\big)_{t \in \mathbb{R}_+} = (W_t + \mu t)_{t \in \mathbb{R}_+}$ over all time has an exponential distribution with parameter $2|\mu|$, *i.e.*

$$\varphi_{\widehat{X}_0^T}(a) = 2\mu\, e^{2\mu a}, \qquad a \geqslant 0.$$

Relation (10.13), resp. Relation (10.16) below, will be used for the pricing of lookback call, resp. put options in Section 10.4.

Corollary 10.5. *The cumulative distribution function of the maximum*

$$M_0^T := \underset{t \in [0,T]}{\text{Max}}\, S_t = S_0 \underset{t \in [0,T]}{\text{Max}}\, e^{\sigma W_t + (r - \sigma^2/2)t}$$

of geometric Brownian motion over $t \in [0, T]$ is given by

$$
\mathbb{P}(M_0^T \leqslant x) \;=\; \Phi\left(\frac{-(r - \sigma^2/2)T + \log(x/S_0)}{\sigma\sqrt{T}} \right) \tag{10.15}
$$
$$
- \left(\frac{S_0}{x} \right)^{1 - 2r/\sigma^2} \Phi\left(\frac{-(r - \sigma^2/2)T - \log(x/S_0)}{\sigma\sqrt{T}} \right), \quad x \geqslant S_0,
$$

and the probability density function $\varphi_{M_0^T}$ of M_0^T satisfies

$$
\varphi_{M_0^T}(x) = \frac{1}{\sigma x \sqrt{2\pi T}} \exp\left(-\frac{(-(r - \sigma^2/2)T + \log(x/S_0))^2}{2\sigma^2 T} \right)
$$
$$
+ \frac{1}{\sigma x \sqrt{2\pi T}} \left(\frac{S_0}{x} \right)^{1 - 2r/\sigma^2} \exp\left(-\frac{((r - \sigma^2/2)T + \log(x/S_0))^2}{2\sigma^2 T} \right)
$$
$$
+ \frac{1}{x} \left(1 - \frac{2r}{\sigma^2} \right) \left(\frac{S_0}{x} \right)^{1 - 2r/\sigma^2} \Phi\left(\frac{-(r - \sigma^2/2)T - \log(x/S_0)}{\sigma\sqrt{T}} \right), \quad x \geqslant S_0.
$$

Proof. Taking

$$
\widetilde{W}_t := W_t + \mu t = W_t + \frac{1}{\sigma} \left(r - \frac{\sigma^2}{2} \right) t
$$

with $\mu := r/\sigma - \sigma/2$, by (10.13) we find

$$
\mathbb{P}(M_0^T \leqslant x) = \mathbb{P}\left(e^{\sigma \widehat{X}_0^T} \leqslant \frac{x}{S_0} \right)
$$
$$
= \mathbb{P}\left(\widehat{X}_0^T \leqslant \frac{1}{\sigma} \log \frac{x}{S_0} \right)
$$
$$
= \Phi\left(\frac{-\mu T + \sigma^{-1} \log(x/S_0)}{\sqrt{T}} \right) - e^{2\mu\sigma^{-1} \log(x/S_0)} \Phi\left(\frac{-\mu T - \sigma^{-1} \log(x/S_0)}{\sqrt{T}} \right)
$$
$$
= \Phi\left(\frac{-\mu T + \sigma^{-1} \log(x/S_0)}{\sqrt{T}} \right) - \left(\frac{x}{S_0} \right)^{2\mu/\sigma} \Phi\left(\frac{-\mu T - \sigma^{-1} \log(x/S_0)}{\sqrt{T}} \right)
$$
$$
= \Phi\left(\frac{-(r - \sigma^2/2)T + \log(x/S_0)}{\sigma\sqrt{T}} \right)
$$
$$
- \left(\frac{S_0}{x} \right)^{1 - 2r/\sigma^2} \Phi\left(\frac{-(r - \sigma^2/2)T - \log(x/S_0)}{\sigma\sqrt{T}} \right).
$$

$\square$

Minimum of drifted Brownian motion

Proposition 10.6. *The joint probability density function $\varphi_{\check{X}_0^T, \widetilde{W}_T}$ of the minimum of the drifted Brownian motion $\widetilde{W}_t := W_t + \mu t$ and its value $\widetilde{W}_T$ at time T is given by*

$$\varphi_{\breve{X}{}^T_0,\widetilde{W}_T}(a,b) = \mathbb{1}_{\{a\leqslant\min(b,0)\}}\frac{1}{T}\sqrt{\frac{2}{\pi T}}(b-2a)\,\mathrm{e}^{\mu b-(2a-b)^2/(2T)-\mu^2 T/2}$$

$$= \begin{cases} \dfrac{1}{T}\sqrt{\dfrac{2}{\pi T}}(b-2a)\,\mathrm{e}^{-\mu^2 T/2+\mu b-(2a-b)^2/(2T)}, & a < \min(b,0), \\[2ex] 0, & a > \min(b,0). \end{cases}$$

Proof. We use the relations

$$\min_{t\in[0,T]}\widetilde{W}_t = -\operatorname*{Max}_{t\in[0,T]}\left(-\widetilde{W}_t\right),$$

and

$$\begin{aligned}
\breve{X}{}^T_0 &:= \min_{t\in[0,T]}\widetilde{W}_t \\
&= \min_{t\in[0,T]}(W_t+\mu t) \\
&= -\operatorname*{Max}_{t\in[0,T]}\left(-\widetilde{W}_t\right) \\
&= -\operatorname*{Max}_{t\in[0,T]}(-W_t-\mu t) \\
&\simeq -\operatorname*{Max}_{t\in[0,T]}(W_t-\mu t),
\end{aligned}$$

where the last equality "$\simeq$" follows from the identity in distribution of $(W_t)_{t\in\mathbb{R}_+}$ and $(-W_t)_{t\in\mathbb{R}_+}$, and we conclude by applying the change of variables $(a,b,\mu)\mapsto(-a,-b,-\mu)$ to (10.11). $\qquad\square$

Similarly to the above, the following proposition holds for the minimum drifted Brownian motion, and Relation (10.17) below can be obtained by changing the signs of both a and μ in Proposition 10.4.

Proposition 10.7. *The cumulative distribution function and probability density function of the minimum*

$$\breve{X}{}^T_0 := \min_{t\in[0,T]}\widetilde{W}_t = \min_{t\in[0,T]}(W_t+\mu t)$$

of the drifted Brownian motion $\widetilde{W}_t = W_t+\mu t$ over $t\in[0,T]$ are given by

$$\mathbb{P}\big(\breve{X}{}^T_0\leqslant a\big) = \Phi\left(\frac{a-\mu T}{\sqrt{T}}\right) + \mathrm{e}^{2\mu a}\Phi\left(\frac{a+\mu T}{\sqrt{T}}\right), \qquad a\leqslant 0, \qquad (10.16)$$

and

$$\varphi_{\breve{X}{}^T_0}(a) = \sqrt{\frac{2}{\pi T}}\,\mathrm{e}^{-(a-\mu T)^2/(2T)} + 2\mu\,\mathrm{e}^{2\mu a}\Phi\left(\frac{a+\mu T}{\sqrt{T}}\right), \qquad a\leqslant 0. \qquad (10.17)$$

Proof. From (10.13), the cumulative distribution function of the minimum of drifted Brownian motion can be expressed as

$$
\begin{aligned}
\mathbb{P}\big(\breve{X}_0^T \leqslant a\big) &= \mathbb{P}\left(\min_{t\in[0,T]} \widetilde{W}_t \leqslant a\right) \\
&= \mathbb{P}\left(\min_{t\in[0,T]} (W_t + \mu t) \leqslant a\right) \\
&= \mathbb{P}\left(-\max_{t\in[0,T]} (-W_t - \mu t) \leqslant a\right) \\
&= \mathbb{P}\left(-\max_{t\in[0,T]} (W_t - \mu t) \leqslant a\right) \\
&= \mathbb{P}\left(\max_{t\in[0,T]} (W_t - \mu t) \geqslant -a\right) \\
&= 1 - \mathbb{P}\left(\max_{t\in[0,T]} (W_t - \mu t) \leqslant -a\right) \\
&= 1 - \Phi\left(\frac{-a + \mu T}{\sqrt{T}}\right) + \mathrm{e}^{2\mu a}\Phi\left(\frac{a + \mu T}{\sqrt{T}}\right) \\
&= \Phi\left(\frac{a - \mu T}{\sqrt{T}}\right) + \mathrm{e}^{2\mu a}\Phi\left(\frac{a + \mu T}{\sqrt{T}}\right), \qquad a \leqslant 0,
\end{aligned}
$$

where we used the identity in distribution of $(W_t)_{t\in\mathbb{R}_+}$ and $(-W_t)_{t\in\mathbb{R}_+}$, hence the probability density function of the minimum of drifted Brownian motion is given by (10.17). $\square$

Similarly, we have

$$
\mathbb{P}\big(\breve{X}_0^T > a\big) = \Phi\left(\frac{\mu T - a}{\sqrt{T}}\right) - \mathrm{e}^{2a\mu}\Phi\left(\frac{\mu T + a}{\sqrt{T}}\right), \qquad a \leqslant 0,
$$

and, if $\mu > 0$, the minimum of the positively drifted Brownian motion $\big(\widetilde{W}_t\big)_{t\in\mathbb{R}_+} = (W_t + \mu t)_{t\in\mathbb{R}_+}$ over all time has an exponential distribution with parameter 2μ on $\mathbb{R}_-$, *i.e.*

$$
\varphi_{\breve{X}_0^T}(a) = 2\mu\,\mathrm{e}^{2\mu a}, \qquad a \leqslant 0.
$$

In addition, as in Corollary 10.5, we have the following result.

Corollary 10.8. *The cumulative distribution function of the minimum*

$$
m_0^T := \min_{t\in[0,T]} S_t = S_0 \min_{t\in[0,T]} \mathrm{e}^{\sigma W_t + (r - \sigma^2/2)t}
$$

of geometric Brownian motion over $t \in [0, T]$ is given by

$$
\mathbb{P}\big(m_0^T \leqslant x\big) = \Phi\left(\frac{-(r - \sigma^2/2)T + \log(x/S_0)}{\sigma\sqrt{T}}\right) \tag{10.18}
$$
$$
+ \left(\frac{S_0}{x}\right)^{1 - 2r/\sigma^2} \Phi\left(\frac{(r - \sigma^2/2)T + \log(x/S_0)}{\sigma\sqrt{T}}\right), \qquad 0 < x \leqslant S_0,
$$

and the probability density function $\varphi_{m_0^T}$ *of* m_0^T *satisfies*

$$\varphi_{m_0^T}(x) = \frac{1}{\sigma x \sqrt{2\pi T}} \exp\left(-\frac{(-(r-\sigma^2/2)T + \log(x/S_0))^2}{2\sigma^2 T}\right)$$

$$+ \frac{1}{\sigma x \sqrt{2\pi T}} \left(\frac{S_0}{x}\right)^{1-2r/\sigma^2} \exp\left(-\frac{((r-\sigma^2/2)T + \log(x/S_0))^2}{2\sigma^2 T}\right)$$

$$+ \frac{1}{x}\left(\frac{2r}{\sigma^2} - 1\right)\left(\frac{S_0}{x}\right)^{1-2r/\sigma^2} \Phi\left(\frac{(r-\sigma^2/2)T + \log(x/S_0)}{\sigma\sqrt{T}}\right), \quad 0 < x \leqslant S_0.$$

Proof. From (10.16) we have

$$\mathbb{P}(m_0^T \leqslant x)$$

$$= \Phi\left(\frac{-\mu T + \sigma^{-1}\log(x/S_0)}{\sqrt{T}}\right) + e^{2\mu\sigma^{-1}\log(x/S_0)}\Phi\left(\frac{\mu T + \sigma^{-1}\log(x/S_0)}{\sqrt{T}}\right)$$

$$= \Phi\left(\frac{-\mu T + \sigma^{-1}\log(x/S_0)}{\sqrt{T}}\right) + \left(\frac{x}{S_0}\right)^{2\mu/\sigma}\Phi\left(\frac{\mu T + \sigma^{-1}\log(x/S_0)}{\sqrt{T}}\right)$$

$$= \Phi\left(\frac{-(r-\sigma^2/2)T + \log(x/S_0)}{\sigma\sqrt{T}}\right)$$

$$+ \left(\frac{S_0}{x}\right)^{1-2r/\sigma^2}\Phi\left(\frac{(r-\sigma^2/2)T + \log(x/S_0)}{\sigma\sqrt{T}}\right), \quad 0 < x \leqslant S_0,$$

with $\mu := r/\sigma - \sigma/2$. The probability density function $\varphi_{m_0^T}$ is computed from

$$\varphi_{m_0^T}(x) = \frac{\partial}{\partial x}\mathbb{P}(m_0^T \leqslant x), \qquad 0 < x \leqslant S_0.$$

$\square$

10.4   Average of Geometric Brownian Extrema

Let

$$m_s^t = \min_{u\in[s,t]} S_u \quad \text{and} \quad M_s^t = \operatorname*{Max}_{u\in[s,t]} S_u,$$

$0 \leqslant s \leqslant t \leqslant T$, and let $\mathcal{M}_s^t$ be either m_s^t or M_s^t. In the lookback option case the payoff $\phi(S_T, \mathcal{M}_0^T)$ depends not only on the price of the underlying asset at maturity but it also depends on all price values of the underlying asset over the period which starts from the initial time and ends at maturity.

The payoff of such of an option is of the form $\phi(S_T, \mathcal{M}_0^T)$ with $\phi(x,y) = x - y$ in the case of lookback call options, and $\phi(x,y) = y - x$ in the case of lookback put options. We let

$$e^{-(T-t)r}\,\mathbb{E}^*\left[\phi(S_T, \mathcal{M}_0^T)|\mathcal{F}_t\right]$$

denote the price at time $t \in [0, T]$ of such an option.

Maximum selling price over $[0, T]$

In the next proposition we start by computing the average of the maximum selling price $M_0^T := \underset{t \in [0,T]}{\text{Max}} \, S_t$ of $(S_t)_{t \in [0,T]}$ over the time interval $[0, T]$. We denote

$$\delta_\pm^\tau(s) := \frac{1}{\sigma\sqrt{\tau}}\left(\log s + \left(r \pm \frac{1}{2}\sigma^2\right)\tau\right), \qquad s > 0. \tag{10.19}$$

Proposition 10.9. *The average maximum value of* $(S_t)_{t \in [0,T]}$ *over* $[0, T]$ *is given by*

$$
\begin{aligned}
\mathbb{E}^* &\left[M_0^T \mid \mathcal{F}_t \right] \tag{10.20}\\
&= M_0^t \Phi\left(-\delta_-^{T-t}\left(\frac{S_t}{M_0^t}\right)\right) + S_t \, e^{(T-t)r}\left(1 + \frac{\sigma^2}{2r}\right)\Phi\left(\delta_+^{T-t}\left(\frac{S_t}{M_0^t}\right)\right)\\
&\quad - S_t \frac{\sigma^2}{2r}\left(\frac{M_0^t}{S_t}\right)^{2r/\sigma^2}\Phi\left(-\delta_-^{T-t}\left(\frac{M_0^t}{S_t}\right)\right),
\end{aligned}
$$

where $\delta_\pm^{T-t}$ *is defined in* (10.19).

When $t = 0$ we have $S_0 = M_0^0$, and given that

$$\delta_\pm^T(1) = \frac{r \pm \sigma^2/2}{\sigma}\sqrt{T}, \tag{10.21}$$

the formula (10.20) simplifies to

$$
\begin{aligned}
\mathbb{E}^* &\left[M_0^T \right]\\
&= S_0\left(1 - \frac{\sigma^2}{2r}\right)\Phi\left(\frac{\sigma^2/2 - r}{\sigma}\sqrt{T}\right) + S_0 \, e^{rT}\left(1 + \frac{\sigma^2}{2r}\right)\Phi\left(\frac{\sigma^2/2 + r}{\sigma}\sqrt{T}\right),
\end{aligned}
$$

with

$$\mathbb{E}^*\left[M_0^T \right] = 2S_0\left(1 + \frac{\sigma^2 T}{4}\Phi\left(\sigma\frac{\sqrt{T}}{2}\right)\right) + \sigma S_0\sqrt{\frac{T}{2\pi}} \, e^{-\sigma^2 T/8}$$

when $r = 0$, cf. Exercise 12.2.

In general, when T tends to infinity we find that

$$\lim_{T \to \infty} \frac{\mathbb{E}^*\left[M_0^T \mid \mathcal{F}_t \right]}{\mathbb{E}^*[S_T \mid \mathcal{F}_t]} = \begin{cases} 1 + \dfrac{\sigma^2}{2r} & \text{if } r > 0, \\[2mm] \infty & \text{if } r = 0, \end{cases}$$

see Exercise 10.3-(d) in the case $r = \sigma^2/2$.

Proof of Proposition 10.9. We have

$$
\begin{aligned}
\mathbb{E}^*\left[M_0^T \mid \mathcal{F}_t \right] &= \mathbb{E}^*\left[\text{Max}\left(M_0^t, M_t^T\right) \mid \mathcal{F}_t \right]\\
&= \mathbb{E}^*\left[M_0^t \mathbb{1}_{\{M_0^t > M_t^T\}} \mid \mathcal{F}_t \right] + \mathbb{E}^*\left[M_t^T \mathbb{1}_{\{M_t^T > M_0^t\}} \mid \mathcal{F}_t \right]\\
&= M_0^t \, \mathbb{E}^*\left[\mathbb{1}_{\{M_0^t > M_t^T\}} \mid \mathcal{F}_t \right] + \mathbb{E}^*\left[M_t^T \mathbb{1}_{\{M_t^T > M_0^t\}} \mid \mathcal{F}_t \right]\\
&= M_0^t \mathbb{P}\left(M_0^t > M_t^T \mid \mathcal{F}_t\right) + \mathbb{E}^*\left[M_t^T \mathbb{1}_{\{M_t^T > M_0^t\}} \mid \mathcal{F}_t \right].
\end{aligned}
$$

Next, we have

$$
\mathbb{P}\big(M_0^t > M_t^T \,\big|\, \mathcal{F}_t\big) \;=\; \mathbb{P}\left(\frac{M_0^t}{S_t} > \frac{M_t^T}{S_t} \,\bigg|\, \mathcal{F}_t\right)
$$

$$
\;=\; \mathbb{P}\left(x > \frac{M_t^T}{S_t} \,\bigg|\, \mathcal{F}_t\right)_{x = M_0^t/S_t}
$$

$$
\;=\; \mathbb{P}\left(\frac{M_0^{T-t}}{S_0} < x\right)_{x = M_0^t/S_t}.
$$

On the other hand, letting $\mu := r/\sigma - \sigma/2$, from (10.13) or (10.15) in Corollary 10.5 we have

$$
\mathbb{P}\left(\frac{M_0^T}{S_0} < x\right) \;=\; \mathbb{P}\left(\operatorname*{Max}_{t \in [0,T]} e^{\sigma W_t + rt - \sigma^2 t/2} < x\right)
$$

$$
\;=\; \mathbb{P}\left(\operatorname*{Max}_{t \in [0,T]} e^{(W_t + \mu t)\sigma} < x\right)
$$

$$
\;=\; \mathbb{P}\left(\operatorname*{Max}_{t \in [0,T]} e^{\sigma \widetilde{W}_t} < x\right)
$$

$$
\;=\; \mathbb{P}\left(e^{\sigma \widehat{X}_0^T} < x\right)
$$

$$
\;=\; \mathbb{P}\left(\widehat{X}_T < \frac{1}{\sigma} \log x\right)
$$

$$
\;=\; \Phi\left(\frac{-\mu T + \sigma^{-1} \log x}{\sqrt{T}}\right) - e^{2\mu \sigma^{-1} \log x} \Phi\left(\frac{-\mu T - \sigma^{-1} \log x}{\sqrt{T}}\right)
$$

$$
\;=\; \Phi\left(-\delta_-^T\left(\frac{1}{x}\right)\right) - x^{-1+2r/\sigma^2} \Phi\left(-\delta_-^T(x)\right).
$$

Hence, we have

$$
\mathbb{P}\big(M_0^t > M_t^T \,\big|\, \mathcal{F}_t\big) \;=\; \mathbb{P}\left(\frac{M_0^{T-t}}{S_0} < x\right)_{x = M_0^t/S_t}
$$

$$
\;=\; \Phi\left(-\delta_-^{T-t}\left(\frac{S_t}{M_0^t}\right)\right) - \left(\frac{M_0^t}{S_t}\right)^{-1+2r/\sigma^2} \Phi\left(-\delta_-^{T-t}\left(\frac{M_0^t}{S_t}\right)\right).
$$

Next, we have

$$
\mathbb{E}^*\left[M_t^T \mathbb{1}_{\{M_t^T > M_0^t\}} \,\Big|\, \mathcal{F}_t\right] \;=\; S_t \, \mathbb{E}^*\left[\frac{M_t^T}{S_t} \mathbb{1}_{\{M_t^T/S_t > M_0^t/S_t\}} \,\bigg|\, \mathcal{F}_t\right]
$$

$$
\;=\; S_t \, \mathbb{E}^*\left[\mathbb{1}_{\{\operatorname{Max}_{u \in [t,T]} S_u/S_t > x\}} \operatorname*{Max}_{u \in [t,T]} \frac{S_u}{S_t} \,\bigg|\, \mathcal{F}_t\right]_{x = M_0^t/S_t}
$$

$$
\;=\; S_t \, \mathbb{E}^*\left[\mathbb{1}_{\{\operatorname{Max}_{u \in [0,T-t]} S_u/S_0 > x\}} \operatorname*{Max}_{u \in [0,T-t]} \frac{S_u}{S_0}\right]_{x = M_0^t/S_t},
$$

and by Proposition 10.4 we have

$$\mathbb{E}^* \left[\mathbb{1}_{\{\operatorname{Max}_{u \in [0,T]} S_u/S_0 > x\}} \operatorname*{Max}_{u \in [0,T]} \frac{S_u}{S_0} \right] \tag{10.22}$$

$$= \mathbb{E}^* \left[\mathbb{1}_{\{\operatorname{Max}_{u \in [0,T]} e^{\sigma \widehat{W}_u} > x\}} \operatorname*{Max}_{u \in [0,T]} e^{\sigma \widehat{W}_u} \right]$$

$$= \mathbb{E}^* \left[e^{\sigma \operatorname{Max}_{u \in [0,T]} \widehat{W}_u} \mathbb{1}_{\{\operatorname{Max}_{u \in [0,T]} \widehat{W}_u > \sigma^{-1} \log x\}} \right]$$

$$= \mathbb{E}^* \left[e^{\sigma \widehat{X}_T} \mathbb{1}_{\{\widehat{X}_T > \sigma^{-1} \log x\}} \right]$$

$$= \int_{\sigma^{-1} \log x}^{\infty} e^{\sigma z} f_{\widehat{X}_T}(z) dz$$

$$= \int_{\sigma^{-1} \log x}^{\infty} e^{\sigma z} \left(\sqrt{\frac{2}{\pi T}} e^{-(z - \mu T)^2/(2T)} - 2\mu e^{2\mu z} \Phi \left(\frac{-z - \mu T}{\sqrt{T}} \right) \right) dz$$

$$= \sqrt{\frac{2}{\pi T}} \int_{\sigma^{-1} \log x}^{\infty} e^{\sigma z - (z - \mu T)^2/(2T)} dz - 2\mu \int_{\sigma^{-1} \log x}^{\infty} e^{z(\sigma + 2\mu)} \Phi \left(\frac{-z - \mu T}{\sqrt{T}} \right) dz.$$

By a standard "completion of the square" argument, we find

$$\frac{1}{\sqrt{2\pi T}} \int_{\sigma^{-1} \log x}^{\infty} e^{\sigma z - (z - \mu T)^2/(2T)} dz$$

$$= \frac{1}{\sqrt{2\pi T}} \int_{\sigma^{-1} \log x}^{\infty} e^{-(z^2 + \mu^2 T^2 - 2(\mu + \sigma)Tz)/(2T)} dz$$

$$= \frac{1}{\sqrt{2\pi T}} e^{\sigma^2 T/2 + \mu \sigma T} \int_{\sigma^{-1} \log x}^{\infty} e^{-(z - (\mu + \sigma)T)^2/(2T)} dz$$

$$= \frac{1}{\sqrt{2\pi T}} e^{rT} \int_{-(\mu + \sigma)T + \sigma^{-1} \log x}^{\infty} e^{-z^2/(2T)} dz$$

$$= e^{rT} \Phi \left(\delta_+^T \left(\frac{1}{x} \right) \right),$$

since $\mu \sigma + \sigma^2/2 = r$. The second integral

$$\int_{\sigma^{-1} \log x}^{\infty} e^{z(\sigma + 2\mu)} \Phi \left(\frac{-z - \mu T}{\sqrt{T}} \right) dz$$

can be computed by integration by parts using the identity

$$\int_a^{\infty} v'(z) u(z) dz = u(+\infty) v(+\infty) - u(a) v(a) - \int_a^{\infty} v(z) u'(z) dz,$$

with $a := \sigma^{-1} \log x$. We let

$$u(z) = \Phi \left(\frac{-z - \mu T}{\sqrt{T}} \right) \quad \text{and} \quad v'(z) = e^{z(\sigma + 2\mu)}$$

which satisfy

$$u'(z) = -\frac{1}{\sqrt{2\pi T}} e^{-(z + \mu T)^2/(2T)} \quad \text{and} \quad v(z) = \frac{1}{\sigma + 2\mu} e^{z(\sigma + 2\mu)},$$

and using the completion of square identity

$$\frac{1}{\sqrt{2\pi T}} \int_c^b e^{\gamma y - y^2/(2T)} dy = e^{\gamma^2 T/2} \left(\Phi \left(\frac{-c + \gamma T}{\sqrt{T}} \right) - \Phi \left(\frac{-b + \gamma T}{\sqrt{T}} \right) \right) \tag{10.23}$$

for $b = +\infty$, we find

$$
\int_a^\infty e^{z(\sigma+2\mu)} \Phi\left(\frac{-z-\mu T}{\sqrt{T}}\right) dz = \int_a^\infty v'(z)u(z)dz
$$

$$
= u(+\infty)v(+\infty) - u(a)v(a) - \int_a^\infty v(z)u'(z)dz
$$

$$
= -\frac{1}{\sigma+2\mu} e^{a(\sigma+2\mu)} \Phi\left(\frac{-a-\mu T}{\sqrt{T}}\right)
$$
$$
+ \frac{1}{(\sigma+2\mu)\sqrt{2\pi T}} \int_a^\infty e^{z(\sigma+2\mu)} e^{-(z+\mu T)^2/(2T)} dz
$$

$$
= -\frac{1}{\sigma+2\mu} e^{a(\sigma+2\mu)} \Phi\left(\frac{-a-\mu T}{\sqrt{T}}\right)
$$
$$
+ \frac{1}{(\sigma+\mu)\sqrt{2\pi T}} e^{(T(\sigma+\mu)^2-\mu^2 T)/2} \int_a^\infty e^{-(z-T(\sigma+\mu))^2/(2T)} dz
$$

$$
= -\frac{1}{\sigma+2\mu} e^{a(\sigma+2\mu)} \Phi\left(\frac{-a-\mu T}{\sqrt{T}}\right)
$$
$$
+ \frac{1}{(\sigma+2\mu)\sqrt{2\pi}} e^{(T(\sigma+\mu)^2-\mu^2 T)/2} \int_{(a-T(\sigma+\mu))/\sqrt{T}}^\infty e^{-z^2/2} dz
$$

$$
= -\frac{1}{\sigma+2\mu} e^{a(\sigma+2\mu)} \Phi\left(\frac{-a-\mu T}{\sqrt{T}}\right)
$$
$$
+ \frac{1}{\sigma+2\mu} e^{(T(\sigma+\mu)^2-\mu^2 T)/2} \Phi\left(\frac{-a+T(\sigma+\mu)}{\sqrt{T}}\right)
$$

$$
= -\frac{2r}{\sigma} (x)^{2r/\sigma^2} \Phi\left(\frac{-(r/\sigma-\sigma/2)T - \sigma^{-1}\log x}{\sqrt{T}}\right)
$$
$$
+ \frac{2r}{\sigma} e^{\sigma T(\sigma+2\mu)/2} \Phi\left(\frac{T(r/\sigma+\sigma/2) - \sigma^{-1}\log x}{\sqrt{T}}\right)
$$

$$
= \frac{\sigma}{2r} e^{rT} \Phi\left(\delta_+^T\left(\frac{1}{x}\right)\right) - \frac{\sigma}{2r} x^{2r/\sigma^2} \Phi\left(-\delta_-^T(x)\right),
$$

cf. pages 317-319 of Shreve (2004) for a different derivation using double integrals. Hence we have

$$
\mathbb{E}^*\left[M_t^T \mathbb{1}_{\{M_t^T > M_0^t\}} \,\Big|\, \mathcal{F}_t\right] = S_t \mathbb{E}^*\left[\mathbb{1}_{\{\text{Max}_{u\in[0,T-t]} S_u/S_0 > x\}} \underset{u\in[0,T-t]}{\text{Max}} \frac{S_u}{S_0}\right]_{x=M_0^t/S_t}
$$

$$
= 2S_t e^{(T-t)r} \Phi\left(\delta_+^{T-t}\left(\frac{S_t}{M_0^t}\right)\right) - S_t \frac{\mu\sigma}{r} e^{(T-t)r} \Phi\left(\delta_+^{T-t}\left(\frac{S_t}{M_0^t}\right)\right)
$$
$$
+ S_t \frac{\mu\sigma}{r} \left(\frac{M_0^t}{S_t}\right)^{2r/\sigma^2} \Phi\left(-\delta_-^{T-t}\left(\frac{M_0^t}{S_t}\right)\right),
$$

and consequently this yields, since $\mu\sigma/r = 1 - \sigma^2/(2r)$,

$$
\mathbb{E}^*\left[M_0^T \,|\, \mathcal{F}_t\right] = \mathbb{E}^*\left[M_0^T \,|\, M_0^t\right]
$$
$$
= M_0^t \mathbb{P}(M_0^t > M_t^T \,|\, M_0^t) + \mathbb{E}^*\left[M_t^T \mathbb{1}_{\{M_t^T > M_0^t\}} \,|\, M_0^t\right]
$$

$$
= M_0^t \Phi\left(-\delta_-^{T-t}\left(\frac{S_t}{M_0^t}\right)\right) - S_t \left(\frac{M_0^t}{S_t}\right)^{2r/\sigma^2} \Phi\left(-\delta_-^{T-t}\left(\frac{M_0^t}{S_t}\right)\right)
$$
$$
+ 2S_t e^{(T-t)r} \Phi\left(\delta_+^{T-t}\left(\frac{S_t}{M_0^t}\right)\right)
$$

$$-S_t \left(1 - \frac{\sigma^2}{2r}\right) e^{(T-t)r} \Phi\left(\delta_+^{T-t}\left(\frac{S_t}{M_0^t}\right)\right)$$

$$+S_t \left(1 - \frac{\sigma^2}{2r}\right) \left(\frac{M_0^t}{S_t}\right)^{2r/\sigma^2} \Phi\left(-\delta_-^{T-t}\left(\frac{M_0^t}{S_t}\right)\right)$$

$$= M_0^t \Phi\left(-\delta_-^{T-t}\left(\frac{S_t}{M_0^t}\right)\right) + S_t e^{(T-t)r}\left(1 + \frac{\sigma^2}{2r}\right) \Phi\left(\delta_+^{T-t}\left(\frac{S_t}{M_0^t}\right)\right)$$

$$-S_t \frac{\sigma^2}{2r}\left(\frac{M_0^t}{S_t}\right)^{2r/\sigma^2} \Phi\left(-\delta_-^{T-t}\left(\frac{M_0^t}{S_t}\right)\right).$$

This concludes the proof of Proposition 10.9. □

See Exercise 10.5-(a) for a computation of the average minimum $\mathbb{E}^*\left[m_0^T\right] = \mathbb{E}^*\left[\min_{t\in[0,T]} S_t\right]$.

Minimum buying price over $[0, T]$

In the next proposition we compute the average of the minimum buying price $m_0^T := \min_{t\in[0,T]} S_t$ of $(S_t)_{t\in[0,T]}$ over the time interval $[0, T]$.

Proposition 10.10. *The average minimum value of $(S_t)_{t\in[0,T]}$ over $[0, T]$ is given by*

$$\mathbb{E}^*\left[m_0^T \mid \mathcal{F}_t\right] \tag{10.24}$$

$$= m_0^t \Phi\left(\delta_-^{T-t}\left(\frac{S_t}{m_0^t}\right)\right) - S_t \frac{\sigma^2}{2r}\left(\frac{m_0^t}{S_t}\right)^{2r/\sigma^2} \Phi\left(\delta_-^{T-t}\left(\frac{m_0^t}{S_t}\right)\right)$$

$$+S_t e^{(T-t)r}\left(1 + \frac{\sigma^2}{2r}\right) \Phi\left(-\delta_+^{T-t}\left(\frac{S_t}{m_0^t}\right)\right),$$

where $\delta_\pm^{T-t}$ is defined in (10.19).

We note a certain symmetry between the expressions (10.20) and (10.24).

When $t = 0$ we have $S_0 = m_0^0$, and given (10.21) the formula (10.24) simplifies to

$$\mathbb{E}^*\left[m_0^T\right] = S_0 \Phi\left(\frac{r - \sigma^2/2}{\sigma}\sqrt{T}\right) - S_0 \frac{\sigma^2}{2r}\left(\frac{m_0^t}{S_t}\right)^{2r/\sigma^2} \Phi\left(\frac{r - \sigma^2/2}{\sigma}\sqrt{T}\right)$$

$$+S_0 e^{rT}\left(1 + \frac{\sigma^2}{2r}\right) \Phi\left(-\frac{\sigma^2/2 + r}{\sigma}\sqrt{T}\right),$$

with

$$\mathbb{E}^*\left[m_0^T\right] = 2S_0\left(1 + \frac{\sigma^2 T}{4}\right) \Phi\left(-\frac{\sigma^2 T/2}{\sigma\sqrt{T}}\right) - \sigma S_0\sqrt{\frac{T}{2\pi}}\, e^{-\sigma^2 T/8}.$$

when $r = 0$, cf. Exercise 12.1.

In general, when T tends to infinity we find that

$$\lim_{T\to\infty} \frac{\mathbb{E}^* \left[m_0^T \mid \mathcal{F}_t \right]}{\mathbb{E}^* \left[S_T \mid \mathcal{F}_t \right]} = 0, \qquad r \geqslant 0,$$

see Exercise 10.3-(f) in the case $r = \sigma^2/2$.

Proof of Proposition 10.10. We have

$$
\begin{aligned}
\mathbb{E}^* \left[m_0^T \mid \mathcal{F}_t \right] &= \mathbb{E}^* \left[\min\left(m_0^t, m_t^T \right) \mid \mathcal{F}_t \right] \\
&= \mathbb{E}^* \left[m_0^t \mathbb{1}_{\{ m_0^t < m_t^T \}} \mid \mathcal{F}_t \right] + \mathbb{E}^* \left[m_t^T \mathbb{1}_{\{ m_0^t > m_t^T \}} \mid \mathcal{F}_t \right] \\
&= m_0^t \, \mathbb{E}^* \left[\mathbb{1}_{\{ m_0^t < m_t^T \}} \mid \mathcal{F}_t \right] + \mathbb{E}^* \left[m_t^T \mathbb{1}_{\{ m_0^t > m_t^T \}} \mid \mathcal{F}_t \right] \\
&= m_0^t \mathbb{P}\left(m_0^t < m_t^T \mid \mathcal{F}_t \right) + \mathbb{E}^* \left[m_t^T \mathbb{1}_{\{ m_0^t > m_t^T \}} \mid \mathcal{F}_t \right].
\end{aligned}
$$

By (10.17) we find the cumulative distribution function

$$
\mathbb{P}\left(\frac{m_0^{T-t}}{S_0} > x \right)_{x = m_0^t/S_t} = \Phi\left(\delta_-^{T-t}\left(\frac{S_t}{m_0^t} \right) \right) - \left(\frac{m_0^t}{S_t} \right)^{-1+2r/\sigma^2} \Phi\left(\delta_-^{T-t}\left(\frac{m_0^t}{S_t} \right) \right),
$$

of the minimum m_0^{T-t} of $(S_t)_{t\in\mathbb{R}_+}$ over the time interval $[0, T-t]$, hence

$$
\begin{aligned}
\mathbb{P}\left(m_0^t < m_t^T \mid \mathcal{F}_t \right) &= \mathbb{P}\left(\frac{m_0^t}{S_t} < \frac{m_t^T}{S_t} \,\Big|\, \mathcal{F}_t \right) \\
&= \mathbb{P}\left(x < \frac{m_t^T}{S_t} \,\Big|\, \mathcal{F}_t \right)_{x = m_0^t/S_t} \\
&= \mathbb{P}\left(\frac{m_0^{T-t}}{S_0} > x \right)_{x = m_0^t/S_t} \\
&= \Phi\left(\delta_-^{T-t}\left(\frac{S_t}{m_0^t} \right) \right) - \left(\frac{m_0^t}{S_t} \right)^{-1+2r/\sigma^2} \Phi\left(\delta_-^{T-t}\left(\frac{m_0^t}{S_t} \right) \right).
\end{aligned}
$$

Next, by integration with respect to the probability density function (10.16) as in (10.22) in the proof of Proposition 10.9, we find

$$
\mathbb{E}^* \left[m_t^T \mathbb{1}_{\{ m_0^t > m_t^T \}} \mid \mathcal{F}_t \right] = S_t \, \mathbb{E}^* \left[\mathbb{1}_{\{ m_0^t/S_t > m_t^T/S_t \}} \min_{u\in[t,T]} \frac{S_u}{S_t} \right]_{x = m_0^t, y = S_t}
$$

$$
= S_t \, \mathbb{E}^* \left[\mathbb{1}_{\{ \min_{u\in[t,T]} S_u/S_t < x \}} \min_{u\in[t,T]} \frac{S_u}{S_t} \right]_{x = m_0^t/S_t}
$$

$$
= S_t \, \mathbb{E}^* \left[\mathbb{1}_{\{ \min_{u\in[0,T-t]} S_u/S_0 < x \}} \min_{u\in[0,T-t]} \frac{S_u}{S_0} \right]_{x = m_0^t/S_t}
$$

$$
= 2 S_t \, \mathrm{e}^{(T-t)r} \Phi\left(-\delta_+^{T-t}\left(\frac{S_t}{m_0^t} \right) \right) - S_t \frac{\mu\sigma}{r} \mathrm{e}^{(T-t)r} \Phi\left(-\delta_+^{T-t}\left(\frac{S_t}{m_0^t} \right) \right)
$$

$$
+ S_t \frac{\mu\sigma}{r} \left(\frac{m_0^t}{S_t} \right)^{2r/\sigma^2} \Phi\left(\delta_-^{T-t}\left(\frac{m_0^t}{S_t} \right) \right).
$$

Given the relation $\mu\sigma/r = 1 - \sigma^2/(2r)$, this yields

$$
\mathbb{E}^* \left[m_0^T \mid \mathcal{F}_t \right] = m_0^t \mathbb{P} \left(\frac{m_0^{T-t}}{S_0} > x \right)_{x=m_0^t/S_t}
$$

$$
+ S_t \, \mathbb{E}^* \left[\mathbb{1}_{\{\min_{u\in[0,T-t]} S_u/S_0 < x\}} \min_{u\in[0,T-t]} \frac{S_u}{S_0} \right]_{x=m_0^t/S_t}
$$

$$
= m_0^t \Phi \left(\delta_-^{T-t} \left(\frac{S_t}{m_0^t} \right) \right) - m_0^t \left(\frac{m_0^t}{S_t} \right)^{-1+2r/\sigma^2} \Phi \left(\delta_-^{T-t} \left(\frac{m_0^t}{S_t} \right) \right)
$$

$$
+ 2 S_t \, e^{(T-t)r} \Phi \left(-\delta_+^{T-t} \left(\frac{S_t}{m_0^t} \right) \right) - S_t \, e^{(T-t)r} \frac{\mu\sigma}{r} \Phi \left(-\delta_+^{T-t} \left(\frac{S_t}{m_0^t} \right) \right)
$$

$$
+ S_t \frac{\mu\sigma}{r} \left(\frac{m_0^t}{S_t} \right)^{2r/\sigma^2} \Phi \left(\delta_-^{T-t} \left(\frac{m_0^t}{S_t} \right) \right)
$$

$$
= m_0^t \Phi \left(\delta_-^{T-t} \left(\frac{S_t}{m_0^t} \right) \right) + S_t \, e^{(T-t)r} \left(1 + \frac{\sigma^2}{2r} \right) \Phi \left(-\delta_+^{T-t} \left(\frac{S_t}{m_0^t} \right) \right)
$$

$$
- S_t \frac{\sigma^2}{2r} \left(\frac{m_0^t}{S_t} \right)^{2r/\sigma^2} \Phi \left(\delta_-^{T-t} \left(\frac{m_0^t}{S_t} \right) \right).
$$

$\square$

Exercises

Exercise 10.1   Let $(W_t)_{t\in\mathbb{R}_+}$ be standard Brownian motion, and let $a > W_0 = 0$.

a) Using the equality (10.2), find the probability density function φ_{τ_a} of the first time

$$
\tau_a := \inf\{t \geqslant 0 \ : \ W_t = a\}
$$

that $(W_t)_{t\in\mathbb{R}_+}$ hits the level $a > 0$.

b) Let $\mu \in \mathbb{R}$. By Proposition 10.4, find the probability density function $\varphi_{\tilde{\tau}_a}$ of the first time

$$
\tilde{\tau}_a := \inf\{t \geqslant 0 \ : \ \widetilde{W}_t = a\}
$$

that the drifted Brownian motion $\left(\widetilde{W}_t \right)_{t\in\mathbb{R}_+} := (W_t + \mu t)_{t\in\mathbb{R}_+}$ hits the level $a > 0$.

c) Let $\sigma > 0$ and $r \in \mathbb{R}$. By Corollary 10.5, find the probability density function φ_{τ_a} of the first time

$$
\hat{\tau}_x := \inf\{t \geqslant 0 \ : \ S_t = x\}
$$

that the geometric Brownian motion $(S_t)_{t\in\mathbb{R}_+} := \left(e^{\sigma W_t + rt - \sigma^2 t/2} \right)_{t\in\mathbb{R}_+}$ hits the level $x > 0$.

Exercise 10.2

a) Compute the mean value

$$\mathbb{E}\left[\underset{t\in[0,T]}{\text{Max}}\ \widetilde{W}_t\right] = \mathbb{E}\left[\underset{t\in[0,T]}{\text{Max}}\ (\sigma W_t + \mu t)\right]$$

of the maximum of drifted Brownian motion $\widetilde{W}_t = W_t + \mu t$ over $t \in [0,T]$, for $\sigma > 0$ and $\mu \in \mathbb{R}$. The probability density function of the maximum is given in (10.14).

b) Compute the mean value $\mathbb{E}\left[\min_{t\in[0,T]}\ \widetilde{W}_t\right] = \mathbb{E}\left[\min_{t\in[0,T]}(\sigma W_t + \mu t)\right]$ of the *minimum* of drifted Brownian motion $\widetilde{W}_t = \sigma W_t + \mu t$ over $t \in [0,T]$, for $\sigma > 0$ and $\mu \in \mathbb{R}$. The probability density function of the minimum is given in (10.17).

Exercise 10.3   Consider a risky asset whose price S_t is given by

$$dS_t = \sigma S_t dW_t + \frac{\sigma^2}{2}S_t dt, \tag{10.25}$$

where $(W_t)_{t\in\mathbb{R}_+}$ is a standard Brownian motion.

a) Solve the stochastic differential equation (10.25).

b) Compute the expected stock price value $\mathbb{E}^*[S_T]$ at time T.

c) What is the probability distribution of the maximum $\underset{t\in[0,T]}{\text{Max}}\ W_t$ over the interval $[0,T]$?

d) Compute the expected value $\mathbb{E}^*\left[M_0^T\right]$ of the maximum

$$M_0^T := \underset{t\in[0,T]}{\text{Max}}\ S_t = S_0 \underset{t\in[0,T]}{\text{Max}}\ e^{\sigma W_t} = S_0 \exp\left(\sigma \underset{t\in[0,T]}{\text{Max}}\ W_t\right).$$

of the stock price over the interval $[0,T]$.

e) What is the probability distribution of the *minimum* $\underset{t\in[0,T]}{\min}\ W_t$ over the interval $[0,T]$?

f) Compute the expected value $\mathbb{E}^*\left[m_0^T\right]$ of the *minimum*

$$m_0^T := \underset{t\in[0,T]}{\min}\ S_t = S_0 \underset{t\in[0,T]}{\min}\ e^{\sigma W_t} = S_0 \exp\left(\sigma \underset{t\in[0,T]}{\min}\ W_t\right).$$

of the stock price over the interval $[0,T]$.

Exercise 10.4   (Exercise 10.3 continued).

a) Compute the "optimal call option" prices $\mathbb{E}\left[\left(M_0^T - K\right)^+\right]$ estimated by optimally exercising at the maximum value M_0^T of $(S_t)_{t\in[0,T]}$ before maturity T.

b) Compute the "optimal put option" prices $\mathbb{E}\left[\left(K - m_0^T\right)^+\right]$ estimated by optimally exercising at the minimum value m_0^T of $(S_t)_{t\in[0,T]}$ before maturity T.

Exercise 10.5   (Exercise 10.4 continued). Consider an asset price S_t given by $S_t = S_0 e^{rt+\sigma B_t - \sigma^2 t/2}$, $t \geq 0$, where $(B_t)_{t \in \mathbb{R}_+}$ is a standard Brownian motion, with $r \geq 0$ and $\sigma > 0$.

a) Compute the average $\mathbb{E}^* \left[m_0^T \right]$ of the minimum $m_0^T := \min_{t \in [0,T]} S_t$ of $(S_t)_{t \in [0,T]}$ over $[0,T]$.

b) Compute the expected payoff $\mathbb{E} \left[\left(K - \min_{t \in [0,T]} S_t \right)^+ \right]$ for $r > 0$. Using a finite expiration American put option pricer, compare the American put option price to the above expected payoff.

c) Compute the expected payoff $\mathbb{E} \left[\left(K - \min_{t \in [0,T]} S_t \right)^+ \right]$ for $r = 0$.

Exercise 10.6   Recall that the maximum $X_0^t := \mathrm{Max}_{s \in [0,t]} W_s$ over $[0,t]$ of standard Brownian motion $(W_s)_{s \in [0,t]}$ has the probability density function

$$\varphi_{X_0^t}(x) = \sqrt{\frac{2}{\pi t}} e^{-x^2/(2t)}, \qquad x \geq 0.$$

a) Let $\tau_a = \inf\{s \geq 0 : W_s = a\}$ denote the first hitting time of $a > 0$ by $(W_s)_{s \in \mathbb{R}_+}$. Using the relation between $\{\tau_a \leq t\}$ and $\{X_0^t \geq a\}$, write down the probability $\mathbb{P}(\tau_a \leq t)$ as an integral from a to ∞.

b) Using integration by parts on $[a, \infty)$, compute the probability density function of τ_a.

Hint: the derivative of $e^{-x^2/(2t)}$ with respect to x is $-x e^{-x^2/(2t)}/t$.

c) Compute the mean value $\mathbb{E}^*[(\tau_a)^{-2}]$ of $1/\tau_a^2$.

Exercise 10.7   Using From Relation (10.11) in Proposition 10.3 and the Jacobian change of variable formula, assuming $S_0 > 0$, compute the joint probability density function of geometric Brownian motion $S_T := S_0 e^{\sigma W_T + (r - \sigma^2/2)T}$ and its maximum

$$M_0^T := \mathrm{Max}_{t \in [0,T]} S_t = S_0 \, \mathrm{Max}_{t \in [0,T]} e^{\sigma W_t + (r - \sigma^2/2)t}.$$

Chapter 11

Barrier Options

Barrier options are financial derivatives whose payoffs depend on the crossing of a certain predefined barrier level by the underlying asset price process $(S_t)_{t\in[0,T]}$. In this chapter, we consider barrier options whose payoffs depend on an extremum of $(S_t)_{t\in[0,T]}$, in addition to the terminal value S_T. Barrier options are then priced by computing the discounted expected values of their claim payoffs, or by PDE arguments.

11.1 Options on Extrema

Vanilla options with payoff $C = \phi(S_T)$ can be priced as

$$e^{-rT} \, \mathbb{E}^*[\phi(S_T)] = e^{-rT} \int_0^\infty \phi(y)\varphi_{S_T}(y)dy$$

where $\varphi_{S_T}(y)$ is the (one parameter) *probability density* function of S_T, which satisfies

$$\mathbb{P}(S_T \leqslant y) = \int_0^y \varphi_{S_T}(v)dv, \qquad y > 0.$$

Recall that typically we have

$$\phi(x) = (x - K)^+ = \begin{cases} x - K & \text{if } x \geqslant K, \\ \\ 0 & \text{if } x < K, \end{cases}$$

for the European call option with strike price K, and

$$\phi(x) = \mathbb{1}_{[K,\infty)}(x) = \begin{cases} \$1 & \text{if } x \geqslant K, \\ \\ 0 & \text{if } x < K, \end{cases}$$

for the binary call option with strike price K. On the other hand, exotic options, also called path-dependent options, are options whose payoff C may depend on the whole path

$$\{S_t \ : \ 0 \leqslant t \leqslant T\}$$

of the underlying asset price process via a "complex" operation such as averaging or computing a maximum. They are opposed to vanilla options whose payoff

$$C = \phi(S_T),$$

depend only using the terminal value S_T of the price process via a payoff function ϕ, and can be priced by the computation of path integrals, see Section 17.3.

DOI: 10.1201/9781003298670-11

For example, the payoff of an option on extrema may take the form

$$C := \phi(M_0^T, S_T),$$

where

$$M_0^T = \underset{t \in [0,T]}{\text{Max}} \, S_t$$

is the maximum of $(S_t)_{t \in \mathbb{R}_+}$ over the time interval $[0, T]$. In such situations the option price at time $t = 0$ can be expressed as

$$\mathrm{e}^{-rT} \, \mathbb{E}^* \left[\phi(M_0^T, S_T) \right] = \mathrm{e}^{-rT} \int_0^\infty \int_0^\infty \phi(x, y) \varphi_{M_0^T, S_T}(x, y) dx dy$$

where $\varphi_{M_0^T, S_T}$ is the *joint probability density* function of (M_0^T, S_T), which satisfies

$$\mathbb{P}(M_0^T \leqslant x \text{ and } S_T \leqslant y) = \int_0^x \int_0^y \varphi_{M_0^T, S_T}(u, v) du dv, \qquad x, y \geqslant 0.$$

General case

Using the joint probability density function of $\widetilde{W}_T = W_T + \mu T$ and

$$\widehat{X}_0^T = \underset{t \in [0,T]}{\text{Max}} \, \widetilde{W} = \underset{t \in [0,T]}{\text{Max}} \, (W_t + \mu t),$$

we are able to price any exotic option with payoff $\phi(\widetilde{W}_T, \widehat{X}_0^T)$, as

$$\mathrm{e}^{-(T-t)r} \, \mathbb{E}^* \left[\phi(\widehat{X}_0^T, \widetilde{W}_T) \,|\, \mathcal{F}_t \right],$$

with in particular, letting $a \vee b := \text{Max}(a, b)$,

$$\mathrm{e}^{-rT} \, \mathbb{E}^* \left[\phi(\widehat{X}_0^T, \widetilde{W}_T) \right] = \mathrm{e}^{-rT} \int_{-\infty}^\infty \int_{y \vee 0}^\infty \phi(x, y) d\mathbb{P}^* \left(\widehat{X}_0^T \leqslant x, \widetilde{W}_T \leqslant y \right).$$

In this chapter, we work in a (continuous) geometric Brownian model, in which the asset price $(S_t)_{t \in [0,T]}$ has the dynamics

$$dS_t = rS_t dt + \sigma S_t dW_t, \qquad t \geqslant 0,$$

where $\sigma > 0$ and $(W_t)_{t \in \mathbb{R}_+}$ is a standard Brownian motion under the risk-neutral probability measure $\mathbb{P}^*$. In particular, by Lemma 5.14 the value V_t of a self-financing portfolio satisfies

$$V_T \mathrm{e}^{-rT} = V_0 + \sigma \int_0^T \xi_t S_t \mathrm{e}^{-rt} dW_t, \quad t \in [0, T].$$

In order to price barrier* options by the above probabilistic method, we will use the probability density function of the maximum

$$M_0^T = \underset{t \in [0,T]}{\text{Max}} \, S_t$$

of geometric Brownian motion $(S_t)_{t \in \mathbb{R}_+}$ over a given time interval $[0, T]$ and the joint probability density function $\varphi_{M_0^T, S_T}(u, v)$ derived in Chapter 10 by the *reflection principle*.

---

*"A former MBA student in finance told me on March 26, 2004, that she did not understand why I covered barrier options until she started working in a bank" Lyuu (2021).

Proposition 11.1. *An exotic option with integrable claim payoff of the form*

$$C = \phi\big(M_0^T, S_T\big) = \phi\left(\operatorname*{Max}_{t\in[0,T]} S_t, S_T\right)$$

can be priced at time 0 as

$$\begin{aligned}
&\mathrm{e}^{-rT}\,\mathbb{E}^*[C]\\
&= \frac{\mathrm{e}^{-rT}}{T^{3/2}}\sqrt{\frac{2}{\pi}}\int_0^\infty\int_y^\infty \phi\big(S_0\,\mathrm{e}^{\sigma y}, S_0\,\mathrm{e}^{\sigma x}\big)(2x-y)\,\mathrm{e}^{-\mu^2 T/2+\mu y-(2x-y)^2/(2T)}\,dxdy\\
&\quad+\frac{\mathrm{e}^{-rT}}{T^{3/2}}\sqrt{\frac{2}{\pi}}\int_{-\infty}^0\int_0^\infty \phi\big(S_0\,\mathrm{e}^{\sigma y}, S_0\,\mathrm{e}^{\sigma x}\big)(2x-y)\,\mathrm{e}^{-\mu^2 T/2+\mu y-(2x-y)^2/(2T)}\,dxdy.
\end{aligned}$$

Proof. We have

$$S_T = S_0\,\mathrm{e}^{\sigma W_T-\sigma^2 T/2+rT} = S_0\,\mathrm{e}^{(W_T+\mu T)\sigma} = S_0\,\mathrm{e}^{\sigma\widetilde{W}_T},$$

with

$$\mu := -\frac{\sigma}{2}+\frac{r}{\sigma} \quad\text{and}\quad \widetilde{W}_T = W_T+\mu T,$$

and

$$\begin{aligned}
M_0^T &= \operatorname*{Max}_{t\in[0,T]} S_t = S_0\operatorname*{Max}_{t\in[0,T]}\mathrm{e}^{\sigma W_t-\sigma^2 t/2+rt}\\
&= S_0\operatorname*{Max}_{t\in[0,T]}\mathrm{e}^{\sigma\widetilde{W}_t} = S_0\,\mathrm{e}^{\sigma\operatorname*{Max}_{t\in[0,T]}\widetilde{W}_t}\\
&= S_0\,\mathrm{e}^{\sigma\widehat{X}_0^T},
\end{aligned}$$

we have

$$C = \phi\big(S_T, M_0^T\big) = \phi\big(S_0\,\mathrm{e}^{\sigma W_T-\sigma^2 T/2+rT}, M_0^T\big) = \phi\big(S_0\,\mathrm{e}^{\sigma\widetilde{W}_T}, S_0\,\mathrm{e}^{\sigma\widehat{X}_0^T}\big),$$

hence

$$\begin{aligned}
\mathrm{e}^{-rT}\,\mathbb{E}^*[C] &= \mathrm{e}^{-rT}\,\mathbb{E}^*\left[\phi\big(S_0\,\mathrm{e}^{\sigma\widetilde{W}_T}, S_0\,\mathrm{e}^{\sigma\widehat{X}_0^T}\big)\right]\\
&= \mathrm{e}^{-rT}\int_{-\infty}^\infty\int_{y\vee 0}^\infty \phi\big(S_0\,\mathrm{e}^{\sigma y}, S_0\,\mathrm{e}^{\sigma x}\big)d\mathbb{P}\big(\widehat{X}_0^T\leqslant x, \widetilde{W}_T\leqslant y\big)\\
&= \frac{\mathrm{e}^{-rT}}{T^{3/2}}\sqrt{\frac{2}{\pi}}\int_{-\infty}^\infty\int_{y\vee 0}^\infty \phi\big(S_0\,\mathrm{e}^{\sigma y}, S_0\,\mathrm{e}^{\sigma x}\big)(2x-y)\,\mathrm{e}^{-\mu^2 T/2+\mu y-(2x-y)^2/(2T)}\,dxdy\\
&= \frac{\mathrm{e}^{-rT}}{T^{3/2}}\sqrt{\frac{2}{\pi}}\int_0^\infty\int_y^\infty \phi\big(S_0\,\mathrm{e}^{\sigma y}, S_0\,\mathrm{e}^{\sigma x}\big)(2x-y)\,\mathrm{e}^{-\mu^2 T/2+\mu y-(2x-y)^2/(2T)}\,dxdy\\
&\quad+\frac{\mathrm{e}^{-rT}}{T^{3/2}}\sqrt{\frac{2}{\pi}}\int_{-\infty}^0\int_0^\infty \phi\big(S_0\,\mathrm{e}^{\sigma y}, S_0\,\mathrm{e}^{\sigma x}\big)(2x-y)\,\mathrm{e}^{-\mu^2 T/2+\mu y-(2x-y)^2/(2T)}\,dxdy.
\end{aligned}$$

$\square$

Pricing barrier options

The payoff of an up-and-out barrier put option on the underlying asset price S_t with exercise date T, strike price K and barrier level (or call level) B is

$$C = (K-S_T)^+\,\mathbb{1}_{\left\{\operatorname*{Max}_{0\leqslant t\leqslant T} S_t < B\right\}} = \begin{cases} (K-S_T)^+ & \text{if } \operatorname*{Max}_{0\leqslant t\leqslant T} S_t < B,\\[2ex] 0 & \text{if } \operatorname*{Max}_{0\leqslant t\leqslant T} S_t \geqslant B. \end{cases}$$

This option is also called a *Callable Bear Contract*, or a Bear CBBC with no residual value, or a turbo warrant with no rebate, in which the call level B usually satisfies $B \leqslant K$.

The payoff of a down-and-out barrier call option on the underlying asset price S_t with exercise date T, strike price K and barrier level B is

$$
C = (S_T - K)^+ \, \mathbb{1}_{\left\{ \min_{0 \leqslant t \leqslant T} S_t > B \right\}} = \begin{cases} (S_T - K)^+ & \text{if } \min_{0 \leqslant t \leqslant T} S_t > B, \\ 0 & \text{if } \min_{0 \leqslant t \leqslant T} S_t \leqslant B. \end{cases}
$$

This option is also called a *Callable Bull Contract*, or a Bull CBBC with no residual value, or a turbo warrant with no rebate, in which the call level B usually satisfies $B \geqslant K$.

Category 'R' Callable Bull/Bear Contracts, or CBBCs, also called turbo warrants, involve a rebate or residual value computed as the payoff of a down-and-in lookback option. Category 'N' Callable Bull/Bear Contracts do not involve a residual value or rebate, and they usually satisfy $B = K$. See Eriksson and Persson (2006), Wong and Chan (2008) and Exercise 11.2 for the pricing of Category 'R' CBBCs with rebate.

Option type	CBBC	Behavior	Payoff		Price	Figure
Barrier call	Bull	down-and-out (knock-out)	$(S_T - K)^+ \, \mathbb{1}_{\left\{ \min_{0 \leqslant t \leqslant T} S_t > B \right\}}$	$B \leqslant K$	(11.10)	11.4a
				$B \geqslant K$	(11.11)	11.4b
		down-and-in (knock-in)	$(S_T - K)^+ \, \mathbb{1}_{\left\{ \min_{0 \leqslant t \leqslant T} S_t < B \right\}}$	$B \leqslant K$	(11.13)	11.7a
				$B \geqslant K$	(11.14)	11.7b
		up-and-out (knock-out)	$(S_T - K)^+ \, \mathbb{1}_{\left\{ \max_{0 \leqslant t \leqslant T} S_t < B \right\}}$	$B \leqslant K$	0	N.A.
				$B \geqslant K$	(11.5)	11.1
		up-and-in (knock-in)	$(S_T - K)^+ \, \mathbb{1}_{\left\{ \max_{0 \leqslant t \leqslant T} S_t > B \right\}}$	$B \leqslant K$	BSCall	6.4
				$B \geqslant K$	(11.15)	11.8
Barrier put	Bear	down-and-out (knock-out)	$(K - S_T)^+ \, \mathbb{1}_{\left\{ \min_{0 \leqslant t \leqslant T} S_t > B \right\}}$	$B \leqslant K$	(11.12)	11.6
				$B \geqslant K$	0	N.A.
		down-and-in (knock-in)	$(K - S_T)^+ \, \mathbb{1}_{\left\{ \min_{0 \leqslant t \leqslant T} S_t < B \right\}}$	$B \leqslant K$	(11.16)	11.9
				$B \geqslant K$	BSPut	6.10
		up-and-out (knock-out)	$(K - S_T)^+ \, \mathbb{1}_{\left\{ \max_{0 \leqslant t \leqslant T} S_t < B \right\}}$	$B \leqslant K$	(11.8)	11.2a
				$B \geqslant K$	(11.9)	11.2b
		up-and-in (knock-in)	$(K - S_T)^+ \, \mathbb{1}_{\left\{ \max_{0 \leqslant t \leqslant T} S_t > B \right\}}$	$B \leqslant K$	(11.17)	11.10a
				$B \geqslant K$	(11.18)	11.10b

Table 11.1: Barrier option types.

We can distinguish between eight different variations on barrier options, according to Table 11.1.

In-out parity

We have the following parity relations between the prices of barrier options and vanilla call and put options:

$$
\begin{cases}
C_{\text{up-in}}(t) + C_{\text{up-out}}(t) = e^{-(T-t)r}\, \mathbb{E}^*[(S_T - K)^+ \mid \mathcal{F}_t], & (11.1) \\[3mm]
C_{\text{down-in}}(t) + C_{\text{down-out}}(t) = e^{-(T-t)r}\, \mathbb{E}^*[(S_T - K)^+ \mid \mathcal{F}_t], & (11.2) \\[3mm]
P_{\text{up-in}}(t) + P_{\text{up-out}}(t) = e^{-(T-t)r}\, \mathbb{E}^*[(K - S_T)^+ \mid \mathcal{F}_t], & (11.3) \\[3mm]
P_{\text{down-in}}(t) + P_{\text{down-out}}(t) = e^{-(T-t)r}\, \mathbb{E}^*[(K - S_T)^+ \mid \mathcal{F}_t], & (11.4)
\end{cases}
$$

where the price of the European call, resp. put option with strike price K are obtained from the Black–Scholes formula. Consequently, in what follows we will only compute the prices of the up-and-out barrier call and put options and of the down-and-out barrier call and put options.

Note that all knock-out barrier option prices vanish when $M_0^t > B$ or $m_0^t < B$, while the barrier up-and-out call, resp. the down-and-out barrier put option prices require $B > K$, resp. $B < K$, in order not to vanish.

11.2 Knock-Out Barrier

Up-and-out barrier call option

Let us consider an up-and-out barrier call option with maturity T, strike price K, barrier (or call level) B, and payoff

$$
C = (S_T - K)^+ \mathbb{1}_{\left\{ \underset{0 \leqslant t \leqslant T}{\text{Max}}\, S_t < B \right\}} =
\begin{cases}
S_T - K & \text{if } \underset{0 \leqslant t \leqslant T}{\text{Max}}\, S_t \leqslant B, \\[3mm]
0 & \text{if } \underset{0 \leqslant t \leqslant T}{\text{Max}}\, S_t > B,
\end{cases}
$$

with $B \geqslant K$.

Proposition 11.2. *When $K \leqslant B$, the price*

$$
e^{-(T-t)r} \mathbb{1}_{\left\{ M_0^t < B \right\}} \mathbb{E}^* \left[\left(x \frac{S_{T-t}}{S_0} - K \right)^+ \mathbb{1}_{\left\{ x \underset{0 \leqslant u \leqslant T-t}{\text{Max}} \frac{S_u}{S_0} < B \right\}} \right]_{x = S_t}
$$

of the up-and-out barrier call option with maturity T, strike price K and barrier level B is given by

$$e^{-(T-t)r} \, \mathbb{E}^* \left[(S_T - K)^+ \mathbb{1}_{\left\{ M_0^T < B \right\}} \,\middle|\, \mathcal{F}_t \right] \tag{11.5}$$

$$= S_t \mathbb{1}_{\left\{ M_0^t < B \right\}} \left\{ \Phi \left(\delta_+^{T-t} \left(\frac{S_t}{K} \right) \right) - \Phi \left(\delta_+^{T-t} \left(\frac{S_t}{B} \right) \right) \right.$$

$$- \left(\frac{B}{S_t} \right)^{1+2r/\sigma^2} \left(\Phi \left(\delta_+^{T-t} \left(\frac{B^2}{KS_t} \right) \right) - \Phi \left(\delta_+^{T-t} \left(\frac{B}{S_t} \right) \right) \right) \right\}$$

$$- e^{-(T-t)r} K \mathbb{1}_{\left\{ M_0^t < B \right\}} \left\{ \Phi \left(\delta_-^{T-t} \left(\frac{S_t}{K} \right) \right) - \Phi \left(\delta_-^{T-t} \left(\frac{S_t}{B} \right) \right) \right.$$

$$- \left(\frac{S_t}{B} \right)^{1-2r/\sigma^2} \left(\Phi \left(\delta_-^{T-t} \left(\frac{B^2}{KS_t} \right) \right) - \Phi \left(\delta_-^{T-t} \left(\frac{B}{S_t} \right) \right) \right) \right\},$$

where

$$\delta_\pm^\tau(s) = \frac{1}{\sigma\sqrt{\tau}} \left(\log s + \left(r \pm \frac{\sigma^2}{2} \right) \tau \right), \qquad s > 0. \tag{11.6}$$

The price of the up-and-out barrier call option vanishes when $B \leqslant K$.

We also have

$$e^{-(T-t)r} \, \mathbb{E}^* \left[(S_T - K)^+ \mathbb{1}_{\left\{ M_0^T < B \right\}} \,\middle|\, \mathcal{F}_t \right]$$

$$= \mathbb{1}_{\left\{ M_0^t < B \right\}} \mathrm{Bl}(S_t, K, r, T-t, \sigma) - S_t \mathbb{1}_{\left\{ M_0^t < B \right\}} \Phi \left(\delta_+^{T-t} \left(\frac{S_t}{B} \right) \right)$$

$$- B \left(\frac{B}{S_t} \right)^{2r/\sigma^2} \mathbb{1}_{\left\{ M_0^t < B \right\}} \left(\Phi \left(\delta_+^{T-t} \left(\frac{B^2}{KS_t} \right) \right) - \Phi \left(\delta_+^{T-t} \left(\frac{B}{S_t} \right) \right) \right)$$

$$+ e^{-(T-t)r} K \mathbb{1}_{\left\{ M_0^t < B \right\}} \Phi \left(\delta_-^{T-t} \left(\frac{S_t}{B} \right) \right)$$

$$+ e^{-(T-t)r} K \left(\frac{S_t}{B} \right)^{1-2r/\sigma^2} \mathbb{1}_{\left\{ M_0^t < B \right\}} \left(\Phi \left(\delta_-^{T-t} \left(\frac{B^2}{KS_t} \right) \right) - \Phi \left(\delta_-^{T-t} \left(\frac{B}{S_t} \right) \right) \right).$$

The following R code implements the up and out pricing formula (11.5).

```
dp <- function( T , r, v, s ) { ( log(s) + ( r + v*v/2.0)*T )/v/sqrt(T) }
dm <- function( T , r, v, s ) { ( log(s) + ( r - v*v/2.0)*T )/v/sqrt(T) }
ind<-function(condition) ifelse(condition,1,0)
CBBC <- function(S,K,B,T,r,sig){ S*ind(S<B)*(pnorm(dp(T,r,sig,S/K)) -pnorm(dp(T,r,sig,S/B))
    -(B/S)**(1+2*r/sig**2)*(pnorm(dp(T,r,sig,B**2/K/S)) -pnorm(dp(T,r,sig,B/S))))
    -K*exp(-r*T)*ind(S<B)*((pnorm(dm(T,r,sig,S/K)) -pnorm(dm(T,r,sig,S/B)))
    -(S/B)**(1-2*r/sig**2)*(pnorm(dm(T,r,sig,B**2/K/S)) -pnorm(dm(T,r,sig,B/S))))}
CBBC(S=90,K=100,B=120,T=1,r=0.01,sig=0.1)
library(fExoticOptions);StandardBarrierOption("cuo",90,100,120,0,1,0.01,0.01,0.1)
```

Note that taking $B = +\infty$ in the above identity (11.5) recovers the Black–Scholes formula

$$e^{-(T-t)r} \, \mathbb{E}^*[(S_T - K)^+ \mid \mathcal{F}_t] = S_t \Phi \left(\delta_+^{T-t} \left(\frac{S_t}{K} \right) \right) - e^{-(T-t)r} K \Phi \left(\delta_-^{T-t} \left(\frac{S_t}{K} \right) \right)$$

for the price of European call options.

The graph of Figure 11.1 represents the up-and-out barrier call option price given the value S_t of the underlying asset and the time $t \in [0, T]$ with $T = 220$ days.

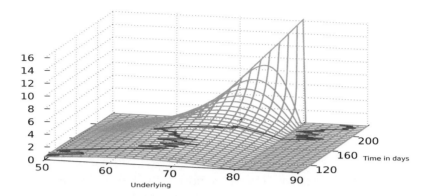

Figure 11.1: Graph of the up-and-out call option price.

Proof of Proposition 11.2. We have $C = \phi\big(S_T, M_0^T\big)$ with

$$
\phi(x, y) = (x - K)^+ \mathbb{1}_{\{y < B\}} =
\begin{cases}
(x - K)^+ & \text{if } y < B, \\[2mm]
0 & \text{if } y \geqslant B,
\end{cases}
$$

hence

$$
\begin{aligned}
& e^{-(T-t)r} \, \mathbb{E}^* \left[(S_T - K)^+ \mathbb{1}_{\left\{ M_0^T < B \right\}} \, \Big| \, \mathcal{F}_t \right] \\[2mm]
&= e^{-(T-t)r} \, \mathbb{E}^* \left[(S_T - K)^+ \mathbb{1}_{\left\{ M_0^t < B \right\}} \mathbb{1}_{\left\{ M_t^T < B \right\}} \, \Big| \, \mathcal{F}_t \right] \\[2mm]
&= e^{-(T-t)r} \mathbb{1}_{\left\{ M_0^t < B \right\}} \mathbb{E}^* \left[(S_T - K)^+ \mathbb{1}_{\left\{ \underset{t \leqslant r \leqslant T}{\mathrm{Max}} S_r < B \right\}} \, \Big| \, \mathcal{F}_t \right] \\[2mm]
&= e^{-(T-t)r} \mathbb{1}_{\left\{ M_0^t < B \right\}} \mathbb{E}^* \left[\left(x \frac{S_T}{S_t} - K \right)^+ \mathbb{1}_{\left\{ x \underset{t \leqslant r \leqslant T}{\mathrm{Max}} \frac{S_r}{S_t} > B \right\}} \right]_{x = S_t} \\[2mm]
&= e^{-(T-t)r} \mathbb{1}_{\left\{ M_0^t < B \right\}} \mathbb{E}^* \left[\left(x \frac{S_{T-t}}{S_0} - K \right)^+ \mathbb{1}_{\left\{ x \underset{0 \leqslant r \leqslant T-t}{\mathrm{Max}} \frac{S_r}{S_0} < B \right\}} \right]_{x = S_t} \\[2mm]
&= e^{-(T-t)r} \mathbb{1}_{\left\{ M_0^t < B \right\}} \mathbb{E}^* \left[\left(x \, e^{\sigma \widetilde{W}_{T-t}} - K \right)^+ \mathbb{1}_{\left\{ x \underset{0 \leqslant r \leqslant T-t}{\mathrm{Max}} e^{\sigma \widetilde{W}_r} < B \right\}} \right]_{x = S_t}.
\end{aligned}
$$

It then suffices to compute, using (10.11),

$$
\begin{aligned}
& \mathbb{E}^* \left[(S_T - K)^+ \mathbb{1}_{\left\{ M_0^T < B \right\}} \right] \\[2mm]
&= \mathbb{E}^* \left[\left(S_0 \, e^{\sigma \widetilde{W}_T} - K \right) \mathbb{1}_{\left\{ S_0 \, e^{\sigma \widetilde{W}_T} > K \right\}} \mathbb{1}_{\left\{ S_0 \, e^{\sigma \widehat{X}_0^T} < B \right\}} \right] \\[2mm]
&= \int_{-\infty}^{\infty} \int_{-\infty}^{\infty} \left(S_0 \, e^{\sigma y} - K \right) \mathbb{1}_{\{ S_0 e^{\sigma y} > K \}} \mathbb{1}_{\{ S_0 e^{\sigma x} < B \}} \, d\mathbb{P}\big(\widehat{X}_0^T \leqslant x, \widetilde{W}_T \leqslant y \big)
\end{aligned}
$$

$$= \int_{-\infty}^{\infty} \int_{-\infty}^{\infty} \left(S_0 e^{\sigma y} - K\right) \mathbb{1}_{\{\sigma y > \log(K/S_0)\}} \mathbb{1}_{\{\sigma x < \log(B/S_0)\}} \varphi_{\widehat{X}_T, \widetilde{W}_T}(x, y) dx dy$$

$$= \int_{-\infty}^{\infty} \int_{-\infty}^{\infty} \left(S_0 e^{\sigma y} - K\right) \mathbb{1}_{\{\sigma y > \log(K/S_0)\}} \mathbb{1}_{\{\sigma x < \log(B/S_0)\}} \mathbb{1}_{\{y \vee 0 < x\}} \varphi_{\widehat{X}_T, \widetilde{W}_T}(x, y) dx dy$$

$$= \frac{1}{T^{3/2}} \sqrt{\frac{2}{\pi}} \int_{\sigma^{-1} \log(K/S_0)}^{\sigma^{-1} \log(B/S_0)}$$
$$\int_{y \vee 0}^{\sigma^{-1} \log(B/S_0)} \left(S_0 e^{\sigma y} - K\right) (2x - y) e^{-\mu^2 T/2 + \mu y - (2x - y)^2/(2T)} dx dy$$

$$= \frac{e^{-\mu^2 T/2}}{T^{3/2}} \sqrt{\frac{2}{\pi}} \int_{\sigma^{-1} \log(K/S_0)}^{\sigma^{-1} \log(B/S_0)} \left(S_0 e^{\sigma y} - K\right) e^{\mu y - y^2/(2T)}$$
$$\times \int_{y \vee 0}^{\sigma^{-1} \log(B/S_0)} (2x - y) e^{2x(y - x)/T} dx dy,$$

if $B \geqslant K$ and $B \geqslant S_0$ (otherwise the option price is 0), with $\mu := r/\sigma - \sigma/2$ and $y \vee 0 = \text{Max}(y, 0)$. Letting $a = y \vee 0$ and $b = \sigma^{-1} \log(B/S_0)$, we have

$$\int_a^b (2x - y) e^{2x(y - x)/T} dx = \int_a^b (2x - y) e^{2x(y - x)/T} dx$$
$$= -\frac{T}{2} \left[e^{2x(y - x)/T} \right]_{x=a}^{x=b}$$
$$= \frac{T}{2} \left(e^{2a(y - a)/T} - e^{2b(y - b)/T} \right)$$
$$= \frac{T}{2} \left(e^{2(y \vee 0)(y - y \vee 0)/T} - e^{2b(y - b)/T} \right)$$
$$= \frac{T}{2} \left(1 - e^{2b(y - b)/T} \right),$$

hence, letting $c = \sigma^{-1} \log(K/S_0)$, we have

$$\mathbb{E}^* \left[(S_T - K)^+ \mathbb{1}_{\{M_0^T < B\}} \right]$$
$$= \frac{e^{-\mu^2 T/2}}{\sqrt{2\pi T}} \int_c^b \left(S_0 e^{\sigma y} - K\right) e^{\mu y - y^2/(2T)} \left(1 - e^{2b(y - b)/T}\right) dy$$
$$= S_0 e^{-\mu^2 T/2} \frac{1}{\sqrt{2\pi T}} \int_c^b e^{(\sigma + \mu) y - y^2/(2T)} \left(1 - e^{2b(y - b)/T}\right) dy$$
$$\quad - K e^{-\mu^2 T/2} \frac{1}{\sqrt{2\pi T}} \int_c^b e^{\mu y - y^2/(2T)} \left(1 - e^{2b(y - b)/T}\right) dy$$
$$= S_0 e^{-\mu^2 T/2} \frac{1}{\sqrt{2\pi T}} \int_c^b e^{(\sigma + \mu) y - y^2/(2T)} dy$$
$$\quad - S_0 e^{-\mu^2 T/2 - 2b^2/T} \frac{1}{\sqrt{2\pi T}} \int_c^b e^{(\sigma + \mu + 2b/T) y - y^2/(2T)} dy$$
$$\quad - K e^{-\mu^2 T/2} \frac{1}{\sqrt{2\pi T}} \int_c^b e^{\mu y - y^2/(2T)} dy$$
$$\quad + K e^{-\mu^2 T/2 - 2b^2/T} \frac{1}{\sqrt{2\pi T}} \int_c^b e^{(\mu + 2b/T) y - y^2/(2T)} dy.$$

Using Relation (10.23), we find

$$e^{-rT} \mathbb{E}^* \left[(S_T - K)^+ \mathbb{1}_{\{M_0^T < B\}} \right]$$
$$= S_0 e^{-(r + \mu^2/2) T + (\sigma + \mu)^2 T/2} \left(\Phi\left(\frac{-c + (\sigma + \mu) T}{\sqrt{T}} \right) - \Phi\left(\frac{-b + (\sigma + \mu) T}{\sqrt{T}} \right) \right)$$

$$
-S_0 \, \mathrm{e}^{-(r+\mu^2/2)T - 2b^2/T + (\sigma+\mu+2b/T)^2 T/2}
$$
$$
\times \left(\Phi\left(\frac{-c + (\sigma + \mu + 2b/T)T}{\sqrt{T}} \right) - \Phi\left(\frac{-b + (\sigma + \mu + 2b/T)T}{\sqrt{T}} \right) \right)
$$
$$
- K \, \mathrm{e}^{-rT} \left(\Phi\left(\frac{-c + \mu T}{\sqrt{T}} \right) - \Phi\left(\frac{-b + \mu T}{\sqrt{T}} \right) \right)
$$
$$
+ K \, \mathrm{e}^{-(r+\mu^2/2)T - 2b^2/T + (\mu+2b/T)^2 T/2}
$$
$$
\times \left(\Phi\left(\frac{-c + (\mu + 2b/T)T}{\sqrt{T}} \right) - \Phi\left(\frac{-b + (\mu + 2b/T)T}{\sqrt{T}} \right) \right)
$$
$$
= \; S_0 \left(\Phi\left(\delta_+^T\left(\frac{S_0}{K} \right) \right) - \Phi\left(\delta_+^T\left(\frac{S_0}{B} \right) \right) \right)
$$
$$
- S_0 \, \mathrm{e}^{-(r+\mu^2/2)T - 2b^2/T + (\sigma+\mu+2b/T)^2 T/2} \left(\Phi\left(\delta_+^T\left(\frac{B^2}{K S_0} \right) \right) - \Phi\left(\delta_+^T\left(\frac{B}{S_0} \right) \right) \right)
$$
$$
- K \, \mathrm{e}^{-rT} \left(\Phi\left(\delta_-^T\left(\frac{S_0}{K} \right) \right) - \Phi\left(\delta_-^T\left(\frac{S_0}{B} \right) \right) \right)
$$
$$
+ K \, \mathrm{e}^{-(r+\mu^2/2)T - 2b^2 T + (\mu+2b/T)^2 T/2} \left(\Phi\left(\delta_-\left(\frac{B^2}{K S_0} \right) \right) - \Phi\left(\delta_-\left(\frac{B}{S_0} \right) \right) \right),
$$

$0 \leqslant x \leqslant B$, where $\delta_\pm^T(s)$ is defined in (11.6). Given the relations

$$
-T\left(r + \frac{\mu^2}{2} \right) - 2\frac{b^2}{T} + \frac{T}{2}\left(\sigma + \mu + \frac{2b}{T} \right)^2 = 2b\left(\frac{r}{\sigma} + \frac{\sigma}{2} \right) = \left(1 + \frac{2r}{\sigma^2} \right) \log \frac{B}{S_0},
$$

and

$$
-T\left(r + \frac{\mu^2}{2} \right) - 2\frac{b^2}{T} + \frac{T}{2}\left(\mu + \frac{2b}{T} \right)^2 = -rT + 2\mu b = -rT + \left(-1 + \frac{2r}{\sigma^2} \right) \log \frac{B}{S_0},
$$

this yields

$$
\mathrm{e}^{-rT} \, \mathbb{E}^* \left[(S_T - K)^+ \mathbb{1}_{\{M_0^T < B\}} \right] \tag{11.7}
$$
$$
= \; S_0 \left(\Phi\left(\delta_+^T\left(\frac{S_0}{K} \right) \right) - \Phi\left(\delta_+^T\left(\frac{S_0}{B} \right) \right) \right)
$$
$$
- \mathrm{e}^{-rT} K \left(\Phi\left(\delta_-^T\left(\frac{S_0}{K} \right) \right) - \Phi\left(\delta_-^T\left(\frac{S_0}{B} \right) \right) \right)
$$
$$
- B \left(\frac{B}{S_0} \right)^{2r/\sigma^2} \left(\Phi\left(\delta_+^T\left(\frac{B^2}{K S_0} \right) \right) - \Phi\left(\delta_+^T\left(\frac{B}{S_0} \right) \right) \right)
$$
$$
+ \mathrm{e}^{-rT} K \left(\frac{S_0}{B} \right)^{1 - 2r/\sigma^2} \left(\Phi\left(\delta_-^T\left(\frac{B^2}{K S_0} \right) \right) - \Phi\left(\delta_-^T\left(\frac{B}{S_0} \right) \right) \right)
$$
$$
= \; S_0 \left(\Phi\left(\delta_+^T\left(\frac{S_0}{K} \right) \right) - \Phi\left(\delta_+^T\left(\frac{S_0}{B} \right) \right) \right)
$$
$$
- S_0 \left(\frac{B}{S_0} \right)^{1 + 2r/\sigma^2} \left(\Phi\left(\delta_+^T\left(\frac{B^2}{K S_0} \right) \right) - \Phi\left(\delta_+^T\left(\frac{B}{S_0} \right) \right) \right)
$$
$$
- \mathrm{e}^{-rT} K \left(\Phi\left(\delta_-^T\left(\frac{S_0}{K} \right) \right) - \Phi\left(\delta_-^T\left(\frac{S_0}{B} \right) \right) \right)
$$
$$
+ \mathrm{e}^{-rT} K \left(\frac{S_0}{B} \right)^{1 - 2r/\sigma^2} \left(\Phi\left(\delta_-^T\left(\frac{B^2}{K S_0} \right) \right) - \Phi\left(\delta_-^T\left(\frac{B}{S_0} \right) \right) \right),
$$

and this yields the result of Proposition 11.2, cf. § 7.3.3 pages 304-307 of Shreve (2004) for a different calculation. This concludes the proof of Proposition 11.2. $\qquad\square$

Up-and-out barrier put option

This option is also called a *Callable Bear Contract*, or a Bear CBBC with no residual value, or a turbo warrant with no rebate, in which B denotes the call level for the pricing of Bear CBBCs (up-and-out barrier put options) with $B \leqslant K$. The price

$$e^{-(T-t)r}\mathbb{1}_{\left\{M_0^t < B\right\}}\mathbb{E}^*\left[\left(K - x\frac{S_{T-t}}{S_0}\right)^+\mathbb{1}_{\left\{x\,\underset{0 \leqslant r \leqslant T-t}{\text{Max}}\,\frac{S_r}{S_0} < B\right\}}\right]_{x=S_t}$$

of the up-and-out barrier put option with maturity T, strike price K and barrier level B is given, if $B \leqslant K$, by

$$e^{-(T-t)r}\mathbb{E}^*\left[(K - S_T)^+\mathbb{1}_{\left\{M_0^T < B\right\}}\,\Big|\,\mathcal{F}_t\right]$$

$$= S_t\mathbb{1}_{\left\{M_0^t<B\right\}}\left(\Phi\left(\delta_+^{T-t}\left(\frac{S_t}{B}\right)\right) - 1 - \left(\frac{B}{S_t}\right)^{1+2r/\sigma^2}\left(\Phi\left(\delta_+^{T-t}\left(\frac{B}{S_t}\right)\right) - 1\right)\right)$$

$$- e^{-(T-t)r}K\mathbb{1}_{\left\{M_0^t<B\right\}}\left(\Phi\left(\delta_-^{T-t}\left(\frac{S_t}{B}\right)\right) - 1 - \left(\frac{S_t}{B}\right)^{1-2r/\sigma^2}\left(\Phi\left(\delta_-^{T-t}\left(\frac{B}{S_t}\right)\right) - 1\right)\right)$$

$$= S_t\mathbb{1}_{\left\{M_0^t<B\right\}}\left(-\Phi\left(-\delta_+^{T-t}\left(\frac{S_t}{B}\right)\right) + \left(\frac{B}{S_t}\right)^{1+2r/\sigma^2}\Phi\left(-\delta_+^{T-t}\left(\frac{B}{S_t}\right)\right)\right)$$

$$- Ke^{-(T-t)r}$$

$$\times \mathbb{1}_{\left\{M_0^t<B\right\}}\left(-\Phi\left(-\delta_-^{T-t}\left(\frac{S_t}{B}\right)\right) + \left(\frac{S_t}{B}\right)^{1-2r/\sigma^2}\Phi\left(-\delta_-^{T-t}\left(\frac{B}{S_t}\right)\right)\right).$$

$$(11.8)$$

and, if $B \geqslant K$, by

$$e^{-(T-t)r}\mathbb{E}^*\left[(K - S_T)^+\mathbb{1}_{\left\{M_0^T<B\right\}}\,\Big|\,\mathcal{F}_t\right]$$

$$= S_t\mathbb{1}_{\left\{M_0^t<B\right\}}\left(\Phi\left(\delta_+^{T-t}\left(\frac{S_t}{K}\right)\right) - 1 - \left(\frac{B}{S_t}\right)^{1+2r/\sigma^2}\left(\Phi\left(\delta_+^{T-t}\left(\frac{B^2}{KS_t}\right)\right) - 1\right)\right)$$

$$- e^{-(T-t)r}K$$

$$\times \mathbb{1}_{\left\{M_0^t<B\right\}}\left(\Phi\left(\delta_-^{T-t}\left(\frac{S_t}{K}\right)\right) - 1 - \left(\frac{S_t}{B}\right)^{1-2r/\sigma^2}\left(\Phi\left(\delta_-^{T-t}\left(\frac{B^2}{KS_t}\right)\right) - 1\right)\right)$$

$$= S_t\mathbb{1}_{\left\{M_0^t<B\right\}}\left(-\Phi\left(-\delta_+^{T-t}\left(\frac{S_t}{K}\right)\right) + \left(\frac{B}{S_t}\right)^{1+2r/\sigma^2}\Phi\left(-\delta_+^{T-t}\left(\frac{B^2}{KS_t}\right)\right)\right)$$

$$- Ke^{-(T-t)r}$$

$$\times \mathbb{1}_{\left\{M_0^t<B\right\}}\left(-\Phi\left(-\delta_-^{T-t}\left(\frac{S_t}{K}\right)\right) + \left(\frac{S_t}{B}\right)^{1-2r/\sigma^2}\Phi\left(-\delta_-^{T-t}\left(\frac{B^2}{KS_t}\right)\right)\right),$$

$$
= \mathrm{e}^{-(T-t)r}\, \mathbb{E}^{*}\left[\left(K - x\frac{S_{T-t}}{S_0}\right)^{+} \mathbb{1}_{\left\{x\,\underset{0\leqslant r\leqslant T-t}{\mathrm{Max}}\,\frac{S_r}{S_0} < B\right\}}\right]_{x=S_t}
$$

$$
= -S_t \mathbb{1}_{\left\{M_0^t < B\right\}}\Phi\left(-\delta_+^{T-t}\left(\frac{S_t}{K}\right)\right) + S_t \mathbb{1}_{\left\{M_0^t < B\right\}}\left(\frac{B}{S_t}\right)^{1+2r/\sigma^2}\Phi\left(-\delta_+^{T-t}\left(\frac{B^2}{KS_t}\right)\right)
$$

$$
+ K\mathbb{1}_{\left\{M_0^t < B\right\}}\mathrm{e}^{-(T-t)r}\Phi\left(-\delta_-^{T-t}\left(\frac{S_t}{K}\right)\right) - K\mathrm{e}^{-(T-t)r}\left(\frac{S_t}{B}\right)^{1-2r/\sigma^2}\Phi\left(-\delta_-^{T-t}\left(\frac{B^2}{KS_t}\right)\right)
$$

$$
= \mathbb{1}_{\left\{M_0^t < B\right\}}\mathrm{Bl}_{\mathrm{put}}(S_t, K, r, T-t, \sigma) + S_t\mathbb{1}_{\left\{M_0^t < B\right\}}\left(\frac{B}{S_t}\right)^{1+2r/\sigma^2}\Phi\left(-\delta_+^{T-t}\left(\frac{B^2}{KS_t}\right)\right)
$$

$$
- K\mathbb{1}_{\left\{M_0^t < B\right\}}\mathrm{e}^{-(T-t)r}\left(\frac{S_t}{B}\right)^{1-2r/\sigma^2}\Phi\left(-\delta_-^{T-t}\left(\frac{B^2}{KS_t}\right)\right). \tag{11.9}
$$

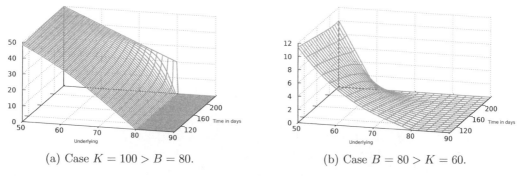

(a) Case $K = 100 > B = 80$.   (b) Case $B = 80 > K = 60$.

Figure 11.2: Graphs of the up-and-out put option prices (11.8)–(11.9).

The following Figure 11.3 shows the market pricing data of an up-and-out barrier put option on BHP Billiton Limited ASX:BHP with $B = K = \$28$ for half a share, priced at 1.79.

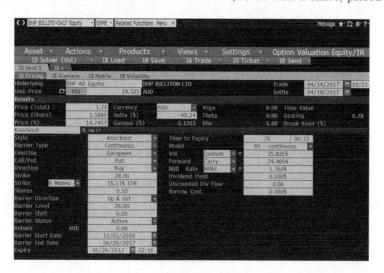

Figure 11.3: Pricing data for an up-and-out put option with $K = B = \$28$.

Down-and-out barrier call option

Let us now consider a down-and-out barrier call option on the underlying asset price S_t with exercise date T, strike price K, barrier level B, and payoff

$$
C = (S_T - K)^+ \mathbb{1}_{\left\{ \min\limits_{0 \leqslant t \leqslant T} S_t > B \right\}} =
\begin{cases}
S_T - K & \text{if } \min\limits_{0 \leqslant t \leqslant T} S_t > B, \\[2ex]
0 & \text{if } \min\limits_{0 \leqslant t \leqslant T} S_t \leqslant B,
\end{cases}
$$

with $0 \leqslant B \leqslant K$. The down-and-out barrier call option is also called a *Callable Bull Contract*, or a Bull CBBC with no residual value, or a turbo warrant with no rebate, in which B denotes the call level. When $B \leqslant K$, we have

$$
e^{-(T-t)r} \, \mathbb{E}^* \left[(S_T - K)^+ \mathbb{1}_{\left\{ \min\limits_{0 \leqslant t \leqslant T} S_t > B \right\}} \,\middle|\, \mathcal{F}_t \right] \tag{11.10}
$$

$$
= \; S_t \mathbb{1}_{\{m_0^t > B\}} \Phi\left(\delta_+^{T-t}\left(\frac{S_t}{K}\right) \right) - e^{-(T-t)r} K \mathbb{1}_{\{m_0^t > B\}} \Phi\left(\delta_-^{T-t}\left(\frac{S_t}{K}\right) \right)
$$

$$
- B \mathbb{1}_{\{m_0^t > B\}} \left(\frac{B}{S_t}\right)^{2r/\sigma^2} \Phi\left(\delta_+^{T-t}\left(\frac{B^2}{KS_t}\right) \right)
$$

$$
+ e^{-(T-t)r} K \mathbb{1}_{\{m_0^t > B\}} \left(\frac{S_t}{B}\right)^{1-2r/\sigma^2} \Phi\left(\delta_-^{T-t}\left(\frac{B^2}{KS_t}\right) \right)
$$

$$
= \; \mathbb{1}_{\{m_0^t > B\}} \mathrm{Bl}(S_t, K, r, T-t, \sigma)
$$

$$
- B \mathbb{1}_{\{m_0^t > B\}} \left(\frac{B}{S_t}\right)^{2r/\sigma^2} \Phi\left(\delta_+^{T-t}\left(\frac{B^2}{KS_t}\right) \right)
$$

$$
+ e^{-(T-t)r} K \mathbb{1}_{\{m_0^t > B\}} \left(\frac{S_t}{B}\right)^{1-2r/\sigma^2} \Phi\left(\delta_-^{T-t}\left(\frac{B^2}{KS_t}\right) \right)
$$

$$
= \; \mathbb{1}_{\{m_0^t > B\}} \mathrm{Bl}(S_t, K, r, T-t, \sigma)
$$

$$
- S_t \mathbb{1}_{\{m_0^t > B\}} \left(\frac{B}{S_t}\right)^{2r/\sigma^2} \mathrm{Bl}\left(\frac{B}{S_t}, \frac{K}{B}, r, T-t, \sigma \right),
$$

$0 \leqslant t \leqslant T$. When $B \geqslant K$, we find

$$
e^{-(T-t)r} \, \mathbb{E}^* \left[(S_T - K)^+ \mathbb{1}_{\left\{ \min\limits_{0 \leqslant t \leqslant T} S_t > B \right\}} \,\middle|\, \mathcal{F}_t \right] \tag{11.11}
$$

$$
= \; S_t \mathbb{1}_{\{m_0^t > B\}} \Phi\left(\delta_+^{T-t}\left(\frac{S_t}{B}\right) \right) - e^{-(T-t)r} K \mathbb{1}_{\{m_0^t > B\}} \Phi\left(\delta_-^{T-t}\left(\frac{S_t}{B}\right) \right)
$$

$$
- B \mathbb{1}_{\{m_0^t > B\}} \left(\frac{B}{S_t}\right)^{2r/\sigma^2} \Phi\left(\delta_+^{T-t}\left(\frac{B}{S_t}\right) \right)
$$

$$
+ e^{-(T-t)r} K \mathbb{1}_{\{m_0^t > B\}} \left(\frac{S_t}{B}\right)^{1-2r/\sigma^2} \Phi\left(\delta_-^{T-t}\left(\frac{B}{S_t}\right) \right),
$$

$S_t > B$, $0 \leqslant t \leqslant T$, see Exercise 11.1 below.

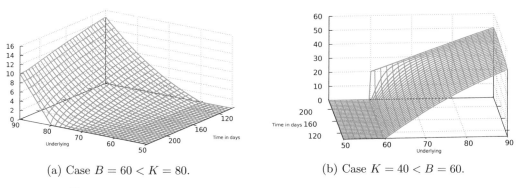

(a) Case $B = 60 < K = 80$.   (b) Case $K = 40 < B = 60$.

Figure 11.4: Graphs of the down-and-out call option price (11.10)–(11.11).

In the next Figure 11.5 we plot the down-and-out barrier call option price (11.11) as a function of volatility with $B = 349.2 > K = 346.4$, $r = 0.03$, $T = 99/365$, and $S_0 = 360$.

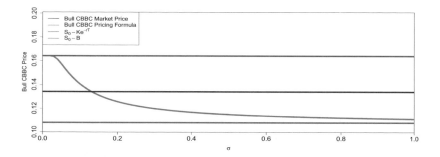

Figure 11.5: Down-and-out call option price as a function of σ.

We note that with such parameters, the down-and-out barrier call option price (11.11) is upper bounded by the forward contract price $S_0 - K\,e^{-rT}$ in the limit as σ tends to zero, and that it decreases to $S_0 - B$ in the limit as σ tends to infinity.

Down-and-out barrier put option

When $K \geqslant B$, the price

$$
e^{-(T-t)r}\mathbb{1}_{\{m_0^t > B\}}\ \mathbb{E}^*\left[\left(K - x\frac{S_{T-t}}{S_0}\right)^+ \mathbb{1}_{\left\{x\ \min\limits_{0\leqslant r\leqslant T-t} S_r/S_0 > B\right\}}\right]_{x=S_t}
$$

of the down-and-out barrier put option with maturity T, strike price K and barrier level B is given by

$$
e^{-(T-t)r}\,\mathbb{E}^*\left[(K - S_T)^+ \mathbb{1}_{\{m_0^T > B\}}\,\Big|\,\mathcal{F}_t\right]
$$

$$
= S_t\mathbb{1}_{\{m_0^t > B\}}\left\{\Phi\left(\delta_+^{T-t}\left(\frac{S_t}{K}\right)\right) - \Phi\left(\delta_+^{T-t}\left(\frac{S_t}{B}\right)\right)\right.
$$

$$
\left. - \left(\frac{B}{S_t}\right)^{1+2r/\sigma^2}\left(\Phi\left(\delta_+^{T-t}\left(\frac{B^2}{KS_t}\right)\right) - \Phi\left(\delta_+^{T-t}\left(\frac{B}{S_t}\right)\right)\right)\right\}
$$

$$-\mathrm{e}^{-(T-t)r} K \mathbb{1}_{\{m_0^t > B\}} \left\{ \Phi\left(\delta_-^{T-t}\left(\frac{S_t}{K}\right)\right) - \Phi\left(\delta_-^{T-t}\left(\frac{S_t}{B}\right)\right) \right.$$

$$\left. - \left(\frac{S_t}{B}\right)^{1-2r/\sigma^2} \left(\Phi\left(\delta_-^{T-t}\left(\frac{B^2}{KS_t}\right)\right) - \Phi\left(\delta_-^{T-t}\left(\frac{B}{S_t}\right)\right)\right) \right\}$$

$$= S_t \mathbb{1}_{\{m_0^t > B\}} \left\{ \Phi\left(-\delta_+^{T-t}\left(\frac{S_t}{B}\right)\right) - \Phi\left(-\delta_+^{T-t}\left(\frac{S_t}{K}\right)\right) \right.$$

$$\left. - \left(\frac{B}{S_t}\right)^{1+2r/\sigma^2} \left(\Phi\left(\delta_+^{T-t}\left(\frac{B^2}{KS_t}\right)\right) - \Phi\left(\delta_+^{T-t}\left(\frac{B}{S_t}\right)\right)\right) \right\}$$

$$- \mathrm{e}^{-(T-t)r} K \mathbb{1}_{\{m_0^t > B\}} \left\{ \Phi\left(-\delta_-^{T-t}\left(\frac{S_t}{B}\right)\right) - \Phi\left(-\delta_-^{T-t}\left(\frac{S_t}{K}\right)\right) \right.$$

$$\left. - \left(\frac{S_t}{B}\right)^{1-2r/\sigma^2} \left(\Phi\left(\delta_-^{T-t}\left(\frac{B^2}{KS_t}\right)\right) - \Phi\left(\delta_-^{T-t}\left(\frac{B}{S_t}\right)\right)\right) \right\}$$

$$= \mathbb{1}_{\{m_0^t > B\}} \mathrm{Bl}_{\mathrm{put}}(S_t, K, r, T-t, \sigma) + S_t \mathbb{1}_{\{m_0^t > B\}} \Phi\left(-\delta_+^{T-t}\left(\frac{S_t}{B}\right)\right) \qquad (11.12)$$

$$- B \mathbb{1}_{\{m_0^t > B\}} \left(\frac{B}{S_t}\right)^{2r/\sigma^2} \left(\Phi\left(\delta_+^{T-t}\left(\frac{B^2}{KS_t}\right)\right) - \Phi\left(\delta_+^{T-t}\left(\frac{B}{S_t}\right)\right)\right)$$

$$- \mathrm{e}^{-(T-t)r} K \mathbb{1}_{\{m_0^t > B\}} \Phi\left(-\delta_-^{T-t}\left(\frac{S_t}{B}\right)\right)$$

$$+ \mathrm{e}^{-(T-t)r} K \mathbb{1}_{\{m_0^t > B\}} \left(\frac{S_t}{B}\right)^{1-2r/\sigma^2} \left(\Phi\left(\delta_-^{T-t}\left(\frac{B^2}{KS_t}\right)\right) - \Phi\left(\delta_-^{T-t}\left(\frac{B}{S_t}\right)\right)\right),$$

while the corresponding price vanishes when $K \leqslant B$.

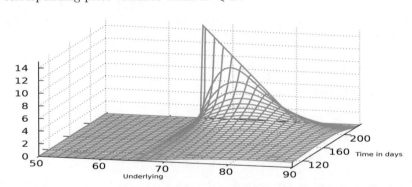

Figure 11.6: Graph of the down-and-out put option price (11.12) with $K = 80 > B = 65$.

Note that although Figures 11.2b and 11.4a, resp. 11.2a and 11.4b, appear to share some symmetry property, the functions themselves are not exactly symmetric. Regarding Figures 6.4 and 11.6, the pricing function is actually the same, but the conditions $B < K$ and $B > K$ play opposite roles.

11.3 Knock-In Barrier

Down-and-in barrier call option

When $B \leqslant K$, the price of the down-and-in barrier call option is given from the down-and-out barrier call option price (11.10) and the down-in-out call parity relation (11.2) as

$$
e^{-(T-t)r} \, \mathbb{E}^* \left[(S_T - K)^+ \mathbb{1}_{\left\{ m_0^T < B \right\}} \, \Big| \, \mathcal{F}_t \right] \tag{11.13}
$$

$$
= \mathbb{1}_{\left\{ m_0^t \leqslant B \right\}} \mathrm{Bl}(S_t, K, r, T - t, \sigma)
$$

$$
+ S_t \mathbb{1}_{\left\{ m_0^t > B \right\}} \left(\frac{B}{S_t} \right)^{1+2r/\sigma^2} \Phi\left(\delta_+^{T-t} \left(\frac{B^2}{K S_t} \right) \right)
$$

$$
- e^{-(T-t)r} K \mathbb{1}_{\left\{ m_0^t > B \right\}} \left(\frac{S_t}{B} \right)^{1-2r/\sigma^2} \Phi\left(\delta_-^{T-t} \left(\frac{B^2}{K S_t} \right) \right).
$$

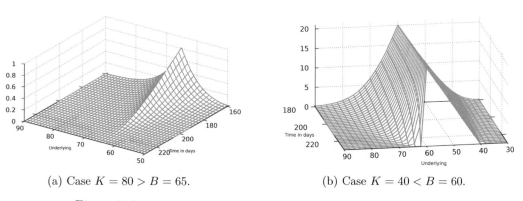

(a) Case $K = 80 > B = 65$.   (b) Case $K = 40 < B = 60$.

Figure 11.7: Graphs of the down-and-in call option price (11.13)–(11.14).

When $B \geqslant K$, the price of the down-and-in barrier call option is given from the down-and-out barrier call option price (11.11) and the down-in-out call parity relation (11.2) as

$$
e^{-(T-t)r} \, \mathbb{E}^* \left[(S_T - K)^+ \mathbb{1}_{\left\{ m_t^T < B \right\}} \, \Big| \, \mathcal{F}_t \right] \tag{11.14}
$$

$$
= \mathrm{Bl}(S_t, K, r, T - t, \sigma)
$$

$$
- S_t \mathbb{1}_{\left\{ m_0^t > B \right\}} \Phi\left(\delta_+^{T-t} \left(\frac{S_t}{B} \right) \right) + e^{-(T-t)r} K \mathbb{1}_{\left\{ m_0^t > B \right\}} \Phi\left(\delta_-^{T-t} \left(\frac{S_t}{B} \right) \right)
$$

$$
+ \mathbb{1}_{\left\{ m_0^t > B \right\}} S_t \left(\frac{B}{S_t} \right)^{1+2r/\sigma^2} \Phi\left(\delta_+^{T-t} \left(\frac{B}{S_t} \right) \right)
$$

$$
- e^{-(T-t)r} K \mathbb{1}_{\left\{ m_0^t > B \right\}} \left(\frac{S_t}{B} \right)^{1-2r/\sigma^2} \Phi\left(\delta_-^{T-t} \left(\frac{B}{S_t} \right) \right), \qquad 0 \leqslant t \leqslant T.
$$

Up-and-in barrier call option

When $B \geqslant K$, the price of the up-and-in barrier call option is given from (11.5) and the up-in-out call parity relation (11.1) as

$$
e^{-(T-t)r} \, \mathbb{E}^* \left[(S_T - K)^+ \mathbb{1}_{\{M_0^T > B\}} \,\middle|\, \mathcal{F}_t \right] \tag{11.15}
$$

$$
= \mathbb{1}_{\{M_0^t \geqslant B\}} \mathrm{Bl}(S_t, K, r, T-t, \sigma) + S_t \mathbb{1}_{\{M_0^t < B\}} \Phi\left(\delta_+^{T-t}\left(\frac{S_t}{B} \right) \right)
$$

$$
+ B \mathbb{1}_{\{M_0^t < B\}} \left(\frac{B}{S_t} \right)^{2r/\sigma^2} \left(\Phi\left(\delta_+^{T-t}\left(\frac{B^2}{KS_t} \right) \right) - \Phi\left(\delta_+^{T-t}\left(\frac{B}{S_t} \right) \right) \right)
$$

$$
- e^{-(T-t)r} K \mathbb{1}_{\{M_0^t < B\}} \Phi\left(\delta_-^{T-t}\left(\frac{S_t}{B} \right) \right)
$$

$$
- e^{-(T-t)r} K \left(\frac{S_t}{B} \right)^{1-2r/\sigma^2} \left(\Phi\left(\delta_-^{T-t}\left(\frac{B^2}{KS_t} \right) \right) - \Phi\left(\delta_-^{T-t}\left(\frac{B}{S_t} \right) \right) \right).
$$

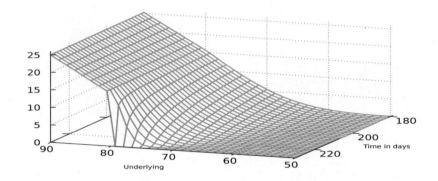

Figure 11.8: Graph of the up-and-in call option price (11.15) with $B = 80 > K = 65$.

When $B \leqslant K$, the price of the up-and-in barrier call option is given from the Black–Scholes formula and the up-in-out call parity relation (11.1) as

$$
e^{-(T-t)r} \, \mathbb{E}^* \left[(S_T - K)^+ \mathbb{1}_{\{M_0^T > B\}} \,\middle|\, \mathcal{F}_t \right] = \mathrm{Bl}(S_t, K, r, T-t, \sigma).
$$

Down-and-in barrier put option

When $B \leqslant K$, the price of the down-and-in barrier put option is given from (11.12) and the down-in-out put parity relation (11.4) as

$$
e^{-(T-t)r} \, \mathbb{E}^* \left[(K - S_T)^+ \mathbb{1}_{\{m_t^T < B\}} \,\middle|\, \mathcal{F}_t \right] \tag{11.16}
$$

$$
= \mathbb{1}_{\{m_0^t \leqslant B\}} \mathrm{Bl}_{\mathrm{put}}(S_t, K, r, T-t, \sigma) - S_t \mathbb{1}_{\{m_0^t > B\}} \Phi\left(-\delta_+^{T-t}\left(\frac{S_t}{B} \right) \right)
$$

$$
+ B \mathbb{1}_{\{m_0^t > B\}} \left(\frac{B}{S_t} \right)^{2r/\sigma^2} \left(\Phi\left(\delta_+^{T-t}\left(\frac{B^2}{KS_t} \right) \right) - \Phi\left(\delta_+^{T-t}\left(\frac{B}{S_t} \right) \right) \right)
$$

$$+ \mathrm{e}^{-(T-t)r} K \mathbb{1}_{\{m_0^t > B\}} \Phi\left(-\delta_-^{T-t}\left(\frac{S_t}{B}\right)\right)$$

$$- \mathrm{e}^{-(T-t)r} K \mathbb{1}_{\{m_0^t > B\}} \left(\frac{S_t}{B}\right)^{1-2r/\sigma^2} \left(\Phi\left(\delta_-^{T-t}\left(\frac{B^2}{KS_t}\right)\right) - \Phi\left(\delta_-^{T-t}\left(\frac{B}{S_t}\right)\right)\right),$$

$0 \leqslant t \leqslant T$.

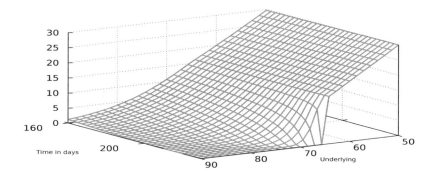

Figure 11.9: Graph of the down-and-in put option price (11.16) with $K = 80 > B = 65$.

When $B \geqslant K$, the price of the down-and-in barrier put option is given from the Black–Scholes put function and the down-in-out put parity relation (11.4) as

$$\mathrm{e}^{-(T-t)r} \mathbb{E}^*\left[(K - S_T)^+ \mathbb{1}_{\{m_t^T < B\}} \,\Big|\, \mathcal{F}_t\right] = \mathrm{Bl_{put}}(S_t, K, r, T-t, \sigma),$$

$0 \leqslant t \leqslant T$.

Up-and-in barrier put option

When $B \leqslant K$, the price of the down-and-in barrier put option is given from (11.8) and the up-in-out put parity relation (11.3) as

$$\mathrm{e}^{-(T-t)r} \mathbb{E}^*\left[(K - S_T)^+ \mathbb{1}_{\{M_0^T > B\}} \,\Big|\, \mathcal{F}_t\right] \tag{11.17}$$

$$= \mathrm{Bl_{put}}(S_t, K, r, T-t, \sigma)$$

$$- S_t \mathbb{1}_{\{M_0^t < B\}} \left(\left(\frac{B}{S_t}\right)^{1+2r/\sigma^2} \Phi\left(-\delta_+^{T-t}\left(\frac{B}{S_t}\right)\right) - \Phi\left(-\delta_+^{T-t}\left(\frac{S_t}{B}\right)\right)\right)$$

$$+ K \mathrm{e}^{-(T-t)r}$$

$$\times \mathbb{1}_{\{M_0^t < B\}} \left(\left(\frac{S_t}{B}\right)^{1-2r/\sigma^2} \Phi\left(-\delta_-^{T-t}\left(\frac{B}{S_t}\right)\right) - \Phi\left(-\delta_-^{T-t}\left(\frac{S_t}{B}\right)\right)\right).$$

$0 \leqslant t \leqslant T$.

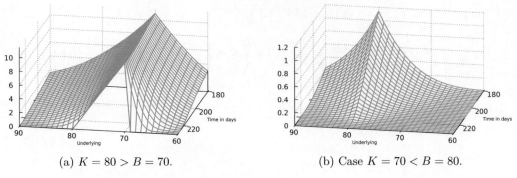

(a) $K = 80 > B = 70$.   (b) Case $K = 70 < B = 80$.

Figure 11.10: Graphs of the up-and-in put option price (11.17)–(11.18).

By (11.9) and the up-in-out put parity relation (11.3), the price of the up-and-in barrier put option is given when $B \geqslant K$ by

$$
e^{-(T-t)r} \, \mathbb{E}^* \left[(K - S_T)^+ \mathbb{1}_{\left\{ M_0^T > B \right\}} \,\Big|\, \mathcal{F}_t \right]
\tag{11.18}
$$

$$
= \; \mathbb{1}_{\left\{ M_0^t \geqslant B \right\}} \mathrm{Bl}_{\mathrm{put}}(S_t, K, r, T - t, \sigma)
$$

$$
- S_t \mathbb{1}_{\left\{ M_0^t < B \right\}} \left(\frac{B}{S_t} \right)^{1 + 2r/\sigma^2} \Phi \left(-\delta_+^{T-t} \left(\frac{B^2}{K S_t} \right) \right)
$$

$$
+ K \mathbb{1}_{\left\{ M_0^t < B \right\}} e^{-(T-t)r} \left(\frac{S_t}{B} \right)^{1 - 2r/\sigma^2} \Phi \left(-\delta_-^{T-t} \left(\frac{B^2}{K S_t} \right) \right).
$$

11.4 PDE Method

The up-and-out barrier call option price has been evaluated by probabilistic arguments in the previous sections. In this section we complement this approach with the derivation of a Partial Differential Equation (PDE) for this option price function.

The up-and-out barrier call option price can be written as

$$
e^{-(T-t)r} \, \mathbb{E}^* \left[(S_T - K)^+ \mathbb{1}_{\left\{ M_0^T < B \right\}} \,\Big|\, \mathcal{F}_t \right]
$$

$$
= \; e^{-(T-t)r} \, \mathbb{E}^* \left[(S_T - K)^+ \mathbb{1}_{\left\{ \underset{0 \leqslant r \leqslant t}{\mathrm{Max}} \, S_r < B \right\}} \mathbb{1}_{\left\{ \underset{t \leqslant r \leqslant T}{\mathrm{Max}} \, S_r < B \right\}} \,\Big|\, \mathcal{F}_t \right]
$$

$$
= \; e^{-(T-t)r} \mathbb{1}_{\left\{ \underset{0 \leqslant r \leqslant t}{\mathrm{Max}} \, S_r < B \right\}} \mathbb{E}^* \left[(S_T - K)^+ \mathbb{1}_{\left\{ \underset{t \leqslant r \leqslant T}{\mathrm{Max}} \, S_r < B \right\}} \,\Big|\, \mathcal{F}_t \right]
$$

$$
= \; \mathbb{1}_{\left\{ M_0^t < B \right\}} g(t, S_t),
$$

where the function $g(t, x)$ of t and S_t is given by

$$
g(t, x) = e^{-(T-t)r} \, \mathbb{E}^* \left[(S_T - K)^+ \mathbb{1}_{\left\{ \underset{t \leqslant r \leqslant T}{\mathrm{Max}} \, S_r < B \right\}} \,\Big|\, S_t = x \right].
\tag{11.19}
$$

Next, by the same argument as in the proof of Proposition 6.1 we derive the Black–Scholes partial differential equation (PDE) satisfied by $g(t,x)$, and written for the value of a self-financing portfolio.

Proposition 11.3. *Let $(\eta_t, \xi_t)_{t \in \mathbb{R}_+}$ be a portfolio strategy such that*

(i) $(\eta_t, \xi_t)_{t \in \mathbb{R}_+}$ is self-financing,

(ii) the portfolio value $V_t := \eta_t A_t + \xi_t S_t$, $t \geq 0$, is given as in (11.19) by

$$V_t = \mathbb{1}_{\{M_0^t < B\}} g(t, S_t), \qquad t \geq 0.$$

Then, the function $g(t,x)$ pricing the up-and-out barrier call option satisfies the Black–Scholes PDE

$$rg(t,x) = \frac{\partial g}{\partial t}(t,x) + rx\frac{\partial g}{\partial x}(t,x) + \frac{1}{2}x^2\sigma^2\frac{\partial^2 g}{\partial x^2}(t,x), \tag{11.20}$$

$t > 0$, $0 < x < B$, and ξ_t is given by

$$\xi_t = \frac{\partial g}{\partial x}(t, S_t), \qquad 0 \leq t \leq T, \tag{11.21}$$

provided that $M_0^t < B$.

Proof. By (11.19) the price at time t of the up-and-out barrier call option discounted to time 0 is given by

$$e^{-rt}\mathbb{1}_{\{M_0^t < B\}} g(t, S_t)$$

$$= e^{-rT}\mathbb{1}_{\{M_0^t < B\}}\,\mathbb{E}^*\left[(S_T - K)^+ \mathbb{1}_{\left\{\underset{t \leq r \leq T}{\text{Max}}\, S_r < B\right\}} \,\middle|\, \mathcal{F}_t\right]$$

$$= e^{-rT}\,\mathbb{E}^*\left[(S_T - K)^+ \mathbb{1}_{\{M_0^t < B\}}\mathbb{1}_{\left\{\underset{t \leq r \leq T}{\text{Max}}\, S_r < B\right\}} \,\middle|\, \mathcal{F}_t\right]$$

$$= e^{-rT}\,\mathbb{E}^*\left[(S_T - K)^+ \mathbb{1}_{\left\{\underset{0 \leq r \leq T}{\text{Max}}\, S_r < B\right\}} \,\middle|\, S_t\right],$$

which is a martingale indexed by $t \geq 0$. Next, applying the Itô formula to $t \longmapsto e^{-rt}g(t, S_t)$ "on $\{M_0^t \leq B,\ 0 \leq t \leq T\}$", we have

$$d(e^{-rt}g(t, S_t)) = -re^{-rt}g(t, S_t)dt + e^{-rt}dg(t, S_t)$$

$$= -re^{-rt}g(t, S_t)dt + e^{-rt}\frac{\partial g}{\partial t}(t, S_t)dt$$

$$+ re^{-rt}S_t\frac{\partial g}{\partial x}(t, S_t)dt + \frac{1}{2}e^{-rt}\sigma^2 S_t^2\frac{\partial^2 g}{\partial x^2}(t, S_t)dt$$

$$+ e^{-rt}\sigma S_t\frac{\partial g}{\partial x}(t, S_t)dW_t. \tag{11.22}$$

In order to derive (11.21) we note that, as in the proof of Proposition 6.1, the self-financing condition (5.8) implies

$$
\begin{aligned}
d\left(\mathrm{e}^{-rt}V_t\right) &= -r\,\mathrm{e}^{-rt}V_t dt + \mathrm{e}^{-rt}dV_t \\
&= -r\,\mathrm{e}^{-rt}V_t dt + \eta_t\,\mathrm{e}^{-rt}dA_t + \xi_t\,\mathrm{e}^{-rt}dS_t \\
&= -r(\eta_t A_t + \xi_t S_t)\,\mathrm{e}^{-rt}dt + r\eta_t A_t\,\mathrm{e}^{-rt}dt + r\xi_t S_t\,\mathrm{e}^{-rt}dt + \sigma\xi_t S_t\,\mathrm{e}^{-rt}dW_t \\
&= \sigma\xi_t S_t\,\mathrm{e}^{-rt}dW_t, \qquad t \geqslant 0,
\end{aligned}
\tag{11.23}
$$

and (11.21) follows by identification of (11.22) with (11.23) which shows that the sum of components in factor of dt have to vanish, hence

$$
-rg(t,S_t) + \frac{\partial g}{\partial t}(t,S_t) + rS_t\frac{\partial g}{\partial x}(t,S_t) + \frac{\sigma^2}{2}S_t^2\frac{\partial^2 g}{\partial x^2}(t,S_t) = 0.
$$

$\square$

In the next proposition we add a boundary condition to the Black–Scholes PDE (11.20) in order to hedge the up-and-out barrier call option with maturity T, strike price K, barrier (or call level) B, and payoff

$$
C = (S_T - K)^+ \mathbb{1}_{\left\{\underset{0\leqslant t\leqslant T}{\mathrm{Max}}\, S_t < B\right\}} = \begin{cases} S_T - K & \text{if } \underset{0\leqslant t\leqslant T}{\mathrm{Max}}\, S_t \leqslant B, \\[2mm] 0 & \text{if } \underset{0\leqslant t\leqslant T}{\mathrm{Max}}\, S_t > B, \end{cases}
$$

with $B \geqslant K$.

Proposition 11.4. *The value $V_t = \mathbb{1}_{\left\{M_0^t < B\right\}}g(t,S_t)$ of the self-financing portfolio hedging the up-and-out barrier call option satisfies the Black–Scholes PDE*

$$
\begin{cases}
rg(t,x) = \dfrac{\partial g}{\partial t}(t,x) + rx\dfrac{\partial g}{\partial x}(t,x) + \dfrac{1}{2}x^2\sigma^2\dfrac{\partial^2 g}{\partial x^2}(t,x), & \text{(11.24a)} \\[4mm]
g(t,x) = 0, \qquad x \geqslant B, \quad t \in [0,T], & \text{(11.24b)} \\[4mm]
g(T,x) = (x-K)^+\mathbb{1}_{\{x<B\}}, & \text{(11.24c)}
\end{cases}
$$

on the time-space domain $[0,T] \times [0,B]$ with terminal condition

$$
g(T,x) = (x-K)^+\mathbb{1}_{\{x<B\}}
$$

and additional boundary condition

$$
g(t,x) = 0, \qquad x \geqslant B.
\tag{11.25}
$$

Condition (11.25) holds since the price of the claim at time t is 0 whenever $S_t = B$. When $K \leqslant B$, the closed-form solution of the PDE (11.24a) under the boundary conditions (11.24b)–(11.24c) is given from (11.5) in Proposition 11.2 as

$$
g(t,x) = x \left(\Phi \left(\delta_+^{T-t} \left(\frac{x}{K} \right) \right) - \Phi \left(\delta_+^{T-t} \left(\frac{x}{B} \right) \right) \right) \tag{11.26}
$$

$$
- x \left(\frac{x}{B} \right)^{-1-2r/\sigma^2} \left(\Phi \left(\delta_+^{T-t} \left(\frac{B^2}{Kx} \right) \right) - \Phi \left(\delta_+^{T-t} \left(\frac{B}{x} \right) \right) \right)
$$

$$
- K \mathrm{e}^{-(T-t)r} \left(\Phi \left(\delta_-^{T-t} \left(\frac{x}{K} \right) \right) - \Phi \left(\delta_-^{T-t} \left(\frac{x}{B} \right) \right) \right)
$$

$$
+ K \mathrm{e}^{-(T-t)r} \left(\frac{x}{B} \right)^{1-2r/\sigma^2} \left(\Phi \left(\delta_-^{T-t} \left(\frac{B^2}{Kx} \right) \right) - \Phi \left(\delta_-^{T-t} \left(\frac{B}{x} \right) \right) \right),
$$

$$
0 < x \leqslant B, \ 0 \leqslant t \leqslant T,
$$

see Figure 6.4. We note that the expression (11.26) can be rewritten using the standard Black–Scholes formula

$$
\mathrm{Bl}(S, K, r, T, \sigma) = S \Phi \left(\delta_+^T \left(\frac{S}{K} \right) \right) - K \mathrm{e}^{-rT} \Phi \left(\delta_-^T \left(\frac{S}{K} \right) \right)
$$

for the price of the European call option, as

$$
g(t,x) = \mathrm{Bl}(x, K, r, T-t, \sigma) - x \Phi \left(\delta_+^{T-t} \left(\frac{x}{B} \right) \right) + \mathrm{e}^{-(T-t)r} K \Phi \left(\delta_-^{T-t} \left(\frac{x}{B} \right) \right)
$$

$$
- B \left(\frac{B}{x} \right)^{2r/\sigma^2} \left(\Phi \left(\delta_+^{T-t} \left(\frac{B^2}{Kx} \right) \right) - \Phi \left(\delta_+^{T-t} \left(\frac{B}{x} \right) \right) \right)
$$

$$
+ \mathrm{e}^{-(T-t)r} K \left(\frac{x}{B} \right)^{1-2r/\sigma^2} \left(\Phi \left(\delta_-^{T-t} \left(\frac{B^2}{Kx} \right) \right) - \Phi \left(\delta_-^{T-t} \left(\frac{B}{x} \right) \right) \right),
$$

$$
0 < x \leqslant B, \ 0 \leqslant t \leqslant T.
$$

Table 11.2 summarizes the boundary conditions satisfied for barrier option pricing in the Black–Scholes PDE.

Option type	CBBC	Behavior		Boundary conditions	
				Maturity T	Barrier B
Barrier call	Bull	down-and-out	$B \leqslant K$	$(x-K)^+$	0
		(knock-out)	$B \geqslant K$	$(x-K)^+\mathbb{1}_{\{x>B\}}$	0
		down-and-in	$B \leqslant K$	0	$\mathrm{Bl}(B,K,r,T-t,\sigma)$
		(knock-in)	$B \geqslant K$	$(x-K)^+\mathbb{1}_{\{x<B\}}$	$\mathrm{Bl}(B,K,r,T-t,\sigma)$
		up-and-out	$B \leqslant K$	0	0
		(knock-out)	$B \geqslant K$	$(x-K)^+\mathbb{1}_{\{x<B\}}$	0
		up-and-in	$B \leqslant K$	$(x-K)^+$	0
		(knock-in)	$B \geqslant K$	$(x-K)^+\mathbb{1}_{\{x>B\}}$	$\mathrm{Bl}(B,K,r,T-t,\sigma)$
Barrier put	Bear	down-and-out	$B \leqslant K$	$(K-x)^+\mathbb{1}_{\{x>B\}}$	0
		(knock-out)	$B \geqslant K$	0	0
		down-and-in	$B \leqslant K$	$(K-x)^+\mathbb{1}_{\{x<B\}}$	$\mathrm{Bl}_\mathrm{p}(B,K,r,T-t,\sigma)$
		(knock-in)	$B \geqslant K$	$(K-x)^+$	0
		up-and-out	$B \leqslant K$	$(K-x)^+\mathbb{1}_{\{x<B\}}$	0
		(knock-out)	$B \geqslant K$	$(K-x)^+$	0
		up-and-in	$B \leqslant K$	$(K-x)^+\mathbb{1}_{\{x>B\}}$	$\mathrm{Bl}_\mathrm{p}(B,K,r,T-t,\sigma)$
		(knock-in)	$B \geqslant K$	0	$\mathrm{Bl}_\mathrm{p}(B,K,r,T-t,\sigma)$

Table 11.2: Boundary conditions for barrier option prices.

11.5   Hedging Barrier Options

Figure 11.11 represents the value of Delta obtained from (11.21) for the up-and-out barrier call option in Exercise 11.1-(a).

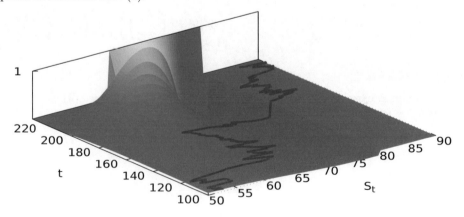

Figure 11.11: Delta of the up-and-out barrier call with $B = 80 > K = 55$.

Down-and-out barrier call option

Similarly, the price $g(t, S_t)$ at time t of the down-and-out barrier call option satisfies the Black–Scholes PDE

$$
\begin{cases}
rg(t, x) = \dfrac{\partial g}{\partial t}(t, x) + rx\dfrac{\partial g}{\partial x}(t, x) + \dfrac{1}{2}x^2\sigma^2\dfrac{\partial^2 g}{\partial x^2}(t, x), \\[2mm]
g(t, B) = 0, \quad t \in [0, T], \\[2mm]
g(T, x) = (x - K)^+ \mathbb{1}_{\{x > B\}},
\end{cases}
$$

on the time-space domain $[0, T] \times [0, B]$ with terminal condition $g(T, x) = (x - K)^+ \mathbb{1}_{\{x > B\}}$ and the additional boundary condition

$$
g(t, x) = 0, \qquad x \leqslant B,
$$

since the price of the claim at time t is 0 whenever $S_t \leqslant B$, see (11.10) and Figure 11.4a when $B \leqslant K$, and (11.11) and Figure 11.4b when $B \geqslant K$.

Exercises

Exercise 11.1 Barrier options.

a) Compute the hedging strategy of the up-and-out barrier call option on the underlying asset price S_t with exercise date T, strike price K and barrier level B, with $B \geqslant K$.

b) Compute the joint probability density function

$$
\varphi_{Y_T, W_T}(a, b) = \frac{d\mathbb{P}(Y_T \leqslant a \text{ and } W_T \leqslant b)}{da\, db}, \qquad a, b \in \mathbb{R},
$$

of standard Brownian motion W_T and its *minimum*

$$
Y_T = \min_{t \in [0, T]} W_t.
$$

c) Compute the joint probability density function

$$
\varphi_{\breve{Y}_T, \widetilde{W}_T}(a, b) = \frac{d\mathbb{P}(\breve{Y}_T \leqslant a \text{ and } \widetilde{W}_T \leqslant b)}{da\, db}, \qquad a, b \in \mathbb{R},
$$

of *drifted* Brownian motion $\widetilde{W}_T = W_T + \mu T$ and its *minimum*

$$
\breve{Y}_T = \min_{t \in [0, T]} \widetilde{W}_t = \min_{t \in [0, T]}(W_t + \mu t).
$$

d) Compute the price at time $t \in [0, T]$ of the down-and-out barrier call option on the underlying asset price S_t with exercise date T, strike price K, barrier level B, and payoff

$$
C = (S_T - K)^+ \mathbb{1}_{\left\{\min\limits_{0 \leqslant t \leqslant T} S_t > B\right\}} =
\begin{cases}
S_T - K & \text{if } \min\limits_{0 \leqslant t \leqslant T} S_t > B, \\[3mm]
0 & \text{if } \min\limits_{0 \leqslant t \leqslant T} S_t \leqslant B,
\end{cases}
$$

in cases $0 < B < K$ and $B \geqslant K$.

Exercise 11.2 Pricing Category 'R' CBBC rebates. Given $\tau > 0$, consider an asset price $(S_t)_{t \in [\tau, \infty)}$, given by

$$S_{\tau+t} = S_\tau e^{rt + \sigma W_t - \sigma^2 t/2}, \qquad t \geqslant 0,$$

where $(W_t)_{t \in \mathbb{R}_+}$ is a standard Brownian motion, with $r \geqslant 0$ and $\sigma > 0$. In what follows, $\Delta\tau$ is the *deterministic* length of the Mandatory Call Event (MCE) valuation period which commences from the time upon which a MCE occurs up to the end of the following trading session.

a) Compute the expected rebate (or residual) $\mathbb{E}\left[\left(\min_{s \in [0, \Delta\tau]} S_{\tau+s} - K \right)^+ \,\middle|\, \mathcal{F}_\tau \right]$ of a Category 'R' *CBBC Bull Contract* having expired at a given time $\tau < T$, knowing that $S_\tau = B > K > 0$, with $r > 0$.

b) Compute the expected rebate $\mathbb{E}\left[\left(\min_{s \in [0, \Delta\tau]} S_{\tau+s} - K \right)^+ \,\middle|\, \mathcal{F}_\tau \right]$ of a Category 'R' *CBBC Bull Contract* having expired at a given time $\tau < T$, knowing that $S_\tau = B > 0$, with $r = 0$.

c) Find the expression of the probability density function of the first hitting time

$$\tau_B = \inf\{t \geqslant 0 \,:\, S_t = B\}$$

of the level $B > 0$ by the process $(S_t)_{t \in \mathbb{R}_+}$.

d) Price the CBBC rebate

$$e^{-\Delta\tau} \mathbb{E}\left[e^{-\tau} \mathbb{1}_{[0,T]}(\tau) \left(\min_{t \in [\tau, \tau+\Delta\tau]} S_t - K \right)^+ \right]$$

$$= e^{-\Delta\tau} \mathbb{E}\left[e^{-r\tau} \mathbb{1}_{[0,T]}(\tau) \mathbb{E}\left[\left(\min_{t \in [\tau, \tau+\Delta\tau]} S_t - K \right)^+ \,\middle|\, \mathcal{F}_\tau \right] \right].$$

Exercise 11.3 Barrier forward contracts. Compute the price at time t of the following barrier forward contracts on the underlying asset price S_t with exercise date T, strike price K, barrier level B, and the following payoffs. In addition, compute the corresponding hedging strategies.

a) <u>Up-and-in barrier long forward contract.</u> Take

$$C = (S_T - K)\, \mathbb{1}_{\left\{ \underset{0 \leqslant t \leqslant T}{\mathrm{Max}}\, S_t > B \right\}} = \begin{cases} S_T - K & \text{if } \underset{0 \leqslant t \leqslant T}{\mathrm{Max}}\, S_t > B, \\ 0 & \text{if } \underset{0 \leqslant t \leqslant T}{\mathrm{Max}}\, S_t \leqslant B. \end{cases}$$

b) <u>Up-and-out barrier long forward contract.</u> Take

$$C = (S_T - K)\, \mathbb{1}_{\left\{ \underset{0 \leqslant t \leqslant T}{\mathrm{Max}}\, S_t < B \right\}} = \begin{cases} S_T - K & \text{if } \underset{0 \leqslant t \leqslant T}{\mathrm{Max}}\, S_t < B, \\ 0 & \text{if } \underset{0 \leqslant t \leqslant T}{\mathrm{Max}}\, S_t \geqslant B. \end{cases}$$

c) <u>Down-and-in barrier long forward contract</u>. Take

$$C = (S_T - K) \, \mathbb{1}_{\left\{ \min_{0 \leqslant t \leqslant T} S_t < B \right\}} = \begin{cases} S_T - K & \text{if } \min_{0 \leqslant t \leqslant T} S_t < B, \\ 0 & \text{if } \min_{0 \leqslant t \leqslant T} S_t \geqslant B. \end{cases}$$

d) <u>Down-and-out barrier long forward contract</u>. Take

$$C = (S_T - K) \, \mathbb{1}_{\left\{ \min_{0 \leqslant t \leqslant T} S_t > B \right\}} = \begin{cases} S_T - K & \text{if } \min_{0 \leqslant t \leqslant T} S_t > B, \\ 0 & \text{if } \min_{0 \leqslant t \leqslant T} S_t \leqslant B. \end{cases}$$

e) <u>Up-and-in barrier short forward contract</u>. Take

$$C = (K - S_T) \, \mathbb{1}_{\left\{ \underset{0 \leqslant t \leqslant T}{\text{Max}} \, S_t > B \right\}} = \begin{cases} K - S_T & \text{if } \underset{0 \leqslant t \leqslant T}{\text{Max}} \, S_t > B, \\ 0 & \text{if } \underset{0 \leqslant t \leqslant T}{\text{Max}} \, S_t \leqslant B. \end{cases}$$

f) <u>Up-and-out barrier short forward contract</u>. Take

$$C = (K - S_T) \, \mathbb{1}_{\left\{ \underset{0 \leqslant t \leqslant T}{\text{Max}} \, S_t < B \right\}} = \begin{cases} K - S_T & \text{if } \underset{0 \leqslant t \leqslant T}{\text{Max}} \, S_t < B, \\ 0 & \text{if } \underset{0 \leqslant t \leqslant T}{\text{Max}} \, S_t \geqslant B. \end{cases}$$

g) <u>Down-and-in barrier short forward contract</u>. Take

$$C = (K - S_T) \, \mathbb{1}_{\left\{ \min_{0 \leqslant t \leqslant T} S_t < B \right\}} = \begin{cases} K - S_T & \text{if } \min_{0 \leqslant t \leqslant T} S_t < B, \\ 0 & \text{if } \min_{0 \leqslant t \leqslant T} S_t \geqslant B. \end{cases}$$

h) <u>Down-and-out barrier short forward contract</u>. Take

$$C = (K - S_T) \, \mathbb{1}_{\left\{ \min_{0 \leqslant t \leqslant T} S_t > B \right\}} = \begin{cases} K - S_T & \text{if } \min_{0 \leqslant t \leqslant T} S_t > B, \\ 0 & \text{if } \min_{0 \leqslant t \leqslant T} S_t \leqslant B. \end{cases}$$

Exercise 11.4 Compute the Vega of the down-and-out and down-and-in barrier call option prices, *i.e.* compute the sensitivity of down-and-out and down-and-in barrier option prices with respect to the volatility parameter σ.

Exercise 11.5 Stability warrants. Price the up-and-out binary barrier option with payoff

$$C := \mathbb{1}_{\{S_T > K\}} \mathbb{1}_{\{M_0^T < B\}} = \mathbb{1}_{\{S_T > K \text{ and } M_0^T \leqslant B\}}$$

at time $t = 0$, with $K \leqslant B$.

Exercise 11.6 Check that the function $g(t, x)$ in (11.26) satisfies the boundary conditions

$$
\begin{cases}
g(t, B) = 0, & t \in [0, T], \\[2mm]
g(T, x) = 0, & x \leqslant K < B, \\[2mm]
g(T, x) = x - K, & K \leqslant x < B, \\[2mm]
g(T, x) = 0, & x > B.
\end{cases}
$$

Exercise 11.7 European knock-in/knock-out barrier options. Price the following vanilla options by computing their conditional discounted expected payoffs:

a) European knock-out barrier call option with payoff $(S_T - K)^+ \mathbb{1}_{\{S_T \leqslant B\}}$,

b) European knock-in barrier put option with payoff $(K - S_T)^+ \mathbb{1}_{\{S_T \leqslant B\}}$,

c) European knock-in barrier call option with payoff $(S_T - K)^+ \mathbb{1}_{\{S_T \geqslant B\}}$,

d) European knock-out barrier put option with payoff $(K - S_T)^+ \mathbb{1}_{\{S_T \geqslant B\}}$,

Chapter 12

Lookback Options

Lookback call (resp. put) options are financial derivatives that allow their holders to exercise the option by setting the strike price at the minimum (resp. maximum) of the underlying asset price process $(S_t)_{t \in [0,T]}$ over the time interval $[0, T]$. Lookback options can be priced by PDE arguments or by computing the discounted expected values of their claim payoff C, namely $C = S_T - \min_{0 \leqslant t \leqslant T} S_t$ in the case of call options, and $C = \operatorname*{Max}_{0 \leqslant t \leqslant T} S_t - S_T$ in the case of put options.

12.1 The Lookback Put Option

The standard lookback put option gives its holder the right to sell the underlying asset at its historically highest price. In this case, the floating strike price is M_0^T and the payoff is given by the terminal value

$$C = M_0^T - S_T$$

of the drawdown process $(M_0^t - S_t)_{t \in [0,T]}$. The following pricing formula for lookback put options is a direct consequence of Proposition 10.9.

Proposition 12.1. *The price at time $t \in [0, T]$ of the lookback put option with payoff $M_0^T - S_T$ is given by*

$$
\begin{aligned}
& \mathrm{e}^{-(T-t)r} \, \mathbb{E}^* \left[M_0^T - S_T \mid \mathcal{F}_t \right] \\
&= M_0^t \mathrm{e}^{-(T-t)r} \Phi \left(-\delta_-^{T-t} \left(\frac{S_t}{M_0^t} \right) \right) + S_t \left(1 + \frac{\sigma^2}{2r} \right) \Phi \left(\delta_+^{T-t} \left(\frac{S_t}{M_0^t} \right) \right) \\
&\quad - S_t \mathrm{e}^{-(T-t)r} \frac{\sigma^2}{2r} \left(\frac{M_0^t}{S_t} \right)^{2r/\sigma^2} \Phi \left(-\delta_-^{T-t} \left(\frac{M_0^t}{S_t} \right) \right) - S_t,
\end{aligned}
$$

where $\delta_\pm^T(s)$ is defined in (11.6).

Proof. We have

$$
\begin{aligned}
\mathbb{E}^* \left[M_0^T - S_T \mid \mathcal{F}_t \right] &= \mathbb{E}^* \left[M_0^T \mid \mathcal{F}_t \right] - \mathbb{E}^* [S_T \mid \mathcal{F}_t] \\
&= \mathbb{E}^* \left[M_0^T \mid \mathcal{F}_t \right] - \mathrm{e}^{(T-t)r} S_t,
\end{aligned}
$$

hence Proposition 10.9 shows that

$$
e^{-(T-t)r} \, \mathbb{E}^* \left[M_0^T - S_T \mid \mathcal{F}_t \right]
$$
$$
= e^{-(T-t)r} \, \mathbb{E}^* \left[M_0^T \mid \mathcal{F}_t \right] - e^{-(T-t)r} \, \mathbb{E}^* [S_T \mid \mathcal{F}_t]
$$
$$
= e^{-(T-t)r} \, \mathbb{E}^* \left[M_0^T \mid M_0^t \right] - S_t
$$
$$
= M_0^t e^{-(T-t)r} \Phi \left(-\delta_-^{T-t} \left(\frac{S_t}{M_0^t} \right) \right) - S_t \Phi \left(-\delta_+^{T-t} \left(\frac{S_t}{M_0^t} \right) \right)
$$
$$
+ S_t \frac{\sigma^2}{2r} \Phi \left(\delta_+^{T-t} \left(\frac{S_t}{M_0^t} \right) \right) - S_t \frac{\sigma^2}{2r} e^{-(T-t)r} \left(\frac{M_0^t}{S_t} \right)^{2r/\sigma^2} \Phi \left(-\delta_-^{T-t} \left(\frac{M_0^t}{S_t} \right) \right).
$$

$\square$

Figure 12.1 represents the lookback put option price as a function of S_t and M_0^t, for different values of the time to maturity $T - t$.

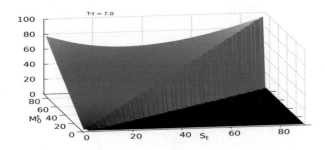

Figure 12.1: Graph of the lookback put option price (3D).

From Figures 12.1 and 12.2, we note the following.

i) When the underlying asset price S_t is close to M_0^t, an increase in the value S_t results into a higher put option price, since in this case the variation of S_t can increase the value of M_0^t.

ii) When the underlying asset price S_t is far from M_0^t, an increase in S_t is less likely to affect the value of M_0^t when time t is close to maturity T, and this results into a lower option price.

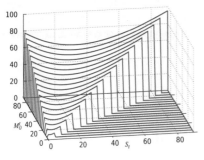

(a) Put prices as functions of S.

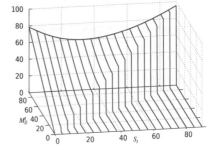

(b) Put prices as functions of M.

Figure 12.2: Graph of lookback put option prices.

Figures 12.2 and 12.3 show accordingly that, from the Delta hedging strategy for lookback put options, see Proposition 12.2 below, one should short the underlying asset when S_t is far from M_0^t, and long this asset when S_t becomes closer to M_0^t.

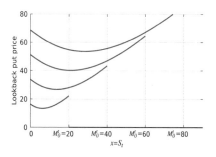

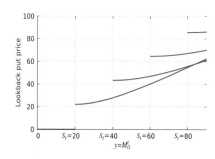

(a) Lookback put prices for fixed M_0^t.   (b) Lookback put prices for fixed S_t.

Figure 12.3: Graph of lookback put option prices (2D).

12.2 PDE Method

Since the couple (S_t, M_0^t) is a Markov process, the price of the lookback put option at time $t \in [0, T]$ can be written as a function

$$
\begin{aligned}
f\big(t, S_t, M_0^t\big) &= \mathrm{e}^{-(T-t)r}\, \mathbb{E}^* \big[\phi\big(S_T, M_0^T\big)\,\big|\, \mathcal{F}_t\big] \\
&= \mathrm{e}^{-(T-t)r}\, \mathbb{E}^* \big[\phi\big(S_T, M_0^T\big)\,\big|\, S_t,\ M_0^t\big]
\end{aligned}
\tag{12.1}
$$

of S_t and M_0^t, $0 \leqslant t \leqslant T$.

Black–Scholes PDE for lookback put option prices

In the next proposition we derive the partial differential equation (PDE) for the pricing function $f(t, x, y)$ of a self-financing portfolio hedging a lookback put option. See Exercise 12.5 for the verification of the boundary conditions (12.3a)–(12.3c).

Proposition 12.2. *The function $f(t, x, y)$ defined by*

$$
f(t, x, y) = \mathrm{e}^{-(T-t)r}\, \mathbb{E}^* \big[M_0^T - S_T \,\big|\, S_t = x,\ M_0^T = y\big], \quad t \in [0, T],\ x, y > 0,
$$

is $\mathcal{C}^2\big((0, T) \times (0, \infty)^2\big)$ and satisfies the Black–Scholes PDE

$$
rf(t, x, y) = \frac{\partial f}{\partial t}(t, x, y) + rx\frac{\partial f}{\partial x}(t, x, y) + \frac{1}{2}x^2\sigma^2\frac{\partial^2 f}{\partial x^2}(t, x, y),
\tag{12.2}
$$

$0 \leqslant t \leqslant T$, $x, y > 0$, subject to the boundary conditions

$$
\begin{cases}
f(t, 0^+, y) = e^{-(T-t)r} y, & 0 \leqslant t \leqslant T, \quad y \geqslant 0, \tag{12.3a} \\[2ex]
\dfrac{\partial f}{\partial y}(t, x, y)_{|y=x} = 0, & 0 \leqslant t \leqslant T, \quad y > 0, \tag{12.3b} \\[2ex]
f(T, x, y) = y - x, & 0 \leqslant x \leqslant y. \tag{12.3c}
\end{cases}
$$

The replicating portfolio of the lookback put option is given by

$$
\xi_t = \frac{\partial f}{\partial x}(t, S_t, M_0^t), \qquad t \in [0, T]. \tag{12.4}
$$

Proof. The existence of $f(t, x, y)$ follows from the Markov property, more precisely, from the time homogeneity of the asset price process $(S_t)_{t \in \mathbb{R}_+}$ the function $f(t, x, y)$ satisfies

$$
\begin{aligned}
f(t, x, y) &= e^{-(T-t)r} \, \mathbb{E}^* \left[\phi(S_T, M_0^T) \mid S_t = x, \ M_0^t = y \right] \\[1ex]
&= e^{-(T-t)r} \, \mathbb{E}^* \left[\phi\left(x \frac{S_T}{S_t}, \text{Max}\left(y, M_t^T \right) \right) \right] \\[1ex]
&= e^{-(T-t)r} \, \mathbb{E}^* \left[\phi\left(x \frac{S_{T-t}}{S_0}, \text{Max}\left(y, M_0^{T-t} \right) \right) \right], \quad t \in [0, T].
\end{aligned}
$$

Applying the change of variable formula to the discounted portfolio value

$$
\widetilde{f}(t, x, y) := e^{-rt} f(t, x, y) = e^{-rT} \, \mathbb{E}^* \left[\phi(S_T, M_0^T) \mid S_t = x, \ M_0^t = y \right]
$$

which is a martingale indexed by $t \in [0, T]$, we have

$$
\begin{aligned}
d\widetilde{f}(t, S_t, M_0^t) &= -r e^{-rt} f(t, S_t, M_0^t) dt + e^{-rt} df(t, S_t, M_0^t) \\[1ex]
&= -r e^{-rt} f(t, S_t, M_0^t) dt + e^{-rt} \frac{\partial f}{\partial t}(t, S_t, M_0^t) dt + r e^{-rt} S_t \frac{\partial f}{\partial x}(t, S_t, M_0^t) dt \\[1ex]
&\quad + e^{-rt} \sigma S_t \frac{\partial f}{\partial x}(t, S_t, M_0^t) dB_t + \frac{1}{2} e^{-rt} \sigma^2 S_t^2 \frac{\partial^2 f}{\partial x^2}(t, S_t, M_0^t) dt \\[1ex]
&\quad + e^{-rt} \frac{\partial f}{\partial y}(t, S_t, M_0^t) dM_0^t, \tag{12.5}
\end{aligned}
$$

according to the following extension of the Itô multiplication table 12.1.

$\cdot$	dt	dB_t	dM_0^t
dt	0	0	0
dB_t	0	dt	0
dM_0^t	0	0	0

Table 12.1: Extended Itô multiplication table.

Since $\left(\widetilde{f}(t, S_t, M_0^t) \right)_{t \in [0,T]} = \left(e^{-rT} \, \mathbb{E}^* \left[\phi(S_T, M_0^T) \mid \mathcal{F}_t \right] \right)_{t \in [0,T]}$ is a martingale under $\mathbb{P}$ and $\left(M_0^t \right)_{t \in [0,T]}$ has finite variation (it is in fact a non-decreasing process), (12.5) yields:

$$
d\widetilde{f}(t, S_t, M_0^t) = \sigma S_t \frac{\partial \widetilde{f}}{\partial x}(t, S_t, M_0^t) dB_t, \qquad t \in [0, T], \tag{12.6}
$$

and the function $f(t, x, y)$ satisfies the equation

$$\frac{\partial f}{\partial t}(t, S_t, M_0^t)dt + rS_t \frac{\partial f}{\partial x}f(t, S_t, M_0^t)dt$$

$$+ \frac{1}{2}\sigma^2 S_t^2 \frac{\partial^2 f}{\partial x^2}(t, S_t, M_0^t)dt + \frac{\partial f}{\partial y}(t, S_t, M_0^t)dM_0^t = rf(t, S_t, M_0^t)dt, \qquad (12.7)$$

which implies

$$\frac{\partial f}{\partial t}(t, S_t, M_0^t) + rS_t \frac{\partial f}{\partial x}(t, S_t, M_0^t) + \frac{1}{2}\sigma^2 S_t^2 \frac{\partial^2 f}{\partial x^2}(t, S_t, M_0^t) = rf(t, S_t, M_0^t),$$

which is (12.2), and

$$\frac{\partial f}{\partial y}(t, S_t, M_0^t)dM_0^t = 0.$$

Indeed, M_0^t increases only on a set of zero Lebesgue measure (which has no isolated points), therefore the Lebesgue measure dt and the measure dM_0^t are mutually *singular*, hence by the *Lebesgue decomposition theorem*, both components in dt and dM_0^t should vanish in (12.7) if the sum vanishes. This implies

$$\frac{\partial f}{\partial y}(t, S_t, M_0^t) = 0,$$

when $dM_0^t > 0$, hence since

$$\{S_t = M_0^t\} \quad \Longleftrightarrow \quad dM_0^t > 0$$

and

$$\{S_t < M_0^t\} \quad \Longleftrightarrow \quad dM_0^t = 0,$$

we have

$$\frac{\partial f}{\partial y}(t, S_t, S_t) = \frac{\partial f}{\partial y}(t, x, y)_{x=S_t,\ y=S_t} = 0,$$

since M_0^t hits S_t, *i.e.* $M_0^t = S_t$, only when M_0^t increases at time t, and this shows the boundary condition (12.3b).

On the other hand, (12.6) shows that

$$\phi(S_T, M_0^T) = \mathbb{E}^*[\phi(S_T, M_0^T)] + \sigma \int_0^T S_t \frac{\partial f}{\partial x}(t, x, M_0^t)_{|x=S_t}dB_t,$$

$0 \leqslant t \leqslant T$, which implies (12.4) as in the proof of Propositions 6.1 or 11.3. $\qquad\square$

In other words, the price of the lookback put option takes the form

$$f(t, S_t, M_0^t) = e^{-(T-t)r}\mathbb{E}^*[M_0^T - S_T \mid \mathcal{F}_t],$$

where the function $f(t, x, y)$ is given from Proposition 12.1 as

$$\begin{aligned}
f(t, x, y) &= ye^{-(T-t)r}\Phi\left(-\delta_-^{T-t}(x/y)\right) + x\left(1 + \frac{\sigma^2}{2r}\right)\Phi\left(\delta_+^{T-t}(x/y)\right)\\
&\quad - x\frac{\sigma^2}{2r}e^{-(T-t)r}\left(\frac{y}{x}\right)^{2r/\sigma^2}\Phi\left(-\delta_-^{T-t}(y/x)\right) - x.
\end{aligned}$$

$$(12.8)$$

Remark 12.3. *We have*
$$f(t, x, x) = xC(T - t),$$

with

$$
\begin{aligned}
C(\tau) &= e^{-r\tau}\Phi\left(-\delta_-^\tau(1)\right) + \left(1 + \frac{\sigma^2}{2r}\right)\Phi\left(\delta_+^\tau(1)\right) - \frac{\sigma^2}{2r}e^{-r\tau}\Phi\left(-\delta_-^\tau(1)\right) - 1 \\
&= e^{-r\tau}\Phi\left(-\frac{r - \sigma^2/2}{\sigma}\sqrt{\tau}\right) + \left(1 + \frac{\sigma^2}{2r}\right)\Phi\left(\frac{r + \sigma^2/2}{\sigma}\sqrt{\tau}\right) \\
&\quad - \frac{\sigma^2}{2r}e^{-r\tau}\Phi\left(-\frac{r - \sigma^2/2}{\sigma}\sqrt{\tau}\right) - 1, \qquad \tau > 0,
\end{aligned}
$$

hence

$$\frac{\partial f}{\partial x}(t, x, x) = C(T - t), \qquad t \in [0, T].$$

Scaling property of lookback put option prices

From (12.8) and the following argument we note the scaling property

$$
\begin{aligned}
f(t, x, y) &= e^{-(T-t)r}\,\mathbb{E}^*\left[M_0^T - S_T \,\middle|\, S_t = x,\ M_0^t = y\right] \\
&= e^{-(T-t)r}\,\mathbb{E}^*\left[\mathrm{Max}\left(M_0^t, M_t^T\right) - S_T \,\middle|\, S_t = x,\ M_0^t = y\right] \\
&= e^{-(T-t)r}x\,\mathbb{E}^*\left[\mathrm{Max}\left(\frac{M_0^t}{S_t}, \frac{M_t^T}{S_t}\right) - \frac{S_T}{S_t} \,\middle|\, S_t = x,\ M_0^t = y\right] \\
&= e^{-(T-t)r}x\,\mathbb{E}^*\left[\mathrm{Max}\left(\frac{y}{x}, \frac{M_t^T}{x}\right) - \frac{S_T}{x} \,\middle|\, S_t = x,\ M_0^t = y\right] \\
&= e^{-(T-t)r}x\,\mathbb{E}^*\left[\mathrm{Max}\left(M_0^t, M_t^T\right) - S_T \,\middle|\, S_t = 1,\ M_0^t = \frac{y}{x}\right] \\
&= e^{-(T-t)r}x\,\mathbb{E}^*\left[M_0^T - S_T \,\middle|\, S_t = 1,\ M_0^t = \frac{y}{x}\right] \\
&= xf(t, 1, y/x) \\
&= xg(T - t, x/y),
\end{aligned}
$$

where we let

$$g(\tau, z) :=$$

$$\frac{1}{z}e^{-r\tau}\Phi\left(-\delta_-^\tau(z)\right) + \left(1 + \frac{\sigma^2}{2r}\right)\Phi\left(\delta_+^\tau(z)\right) - \frac{\sigma^2}{2r}e^{-r\tau}\left(\frac{1}{z}\right)^{2r/\sigma^2}\Phi\left(-\delta_-^\tau\left(\frac{1}{z}\right)\right) - 1,$$

with the boundary condition

$$
\begin{cases}
\dfrac{\partial g}{\partial z}(\tau, 1) = 0, & \tau > 0, \\[2ex]
g(0, z) = \dfrac{1}{z} - 1, & z \in (0, 1].
\end{cases}
$$

$$(12.9a)$$

$$(12.9b)$$

The next Figure 12.4 shows a graph of the function $g(\tau, z)$.

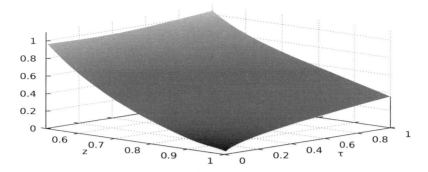

Figure 12.4: Graph of the normalized lookback put option price.

Black–Scholes approximation of lookback put option prices

Letting

$$\mathrm{Bl_p}(x, K, r, \sigma, \tau) := K\,\mathrm{e}^{-r\tau}\Phi\left(-\delta_-^\tau\left(\frac{x}{K}\right)\right) - x\Phi\left(-\delta_+^\tau\left(\frac{x}{K}\right)\right)$$

denote the standard Black–Scholes formula for the price of the European put option.

Proposition 12.4. *The lookback put option price can be rewritten as*

$$\mathrm{e}^{-(T-t)r}\,\mathbb{E}^*\left[M_0^T - S_T\,\middle|\,\mathcal{F}_t\right] = \mathrm{Bl_p}(S_t, M_0^t, r, \sigma, T - t) \tag{12.10}$$

$$+S_t\frac{\sigma^2}{2r}\left(\Phi\left(\delta_+^{T-t}\left(\frac{S_t}{M_0^t}\right)\right) - \mathrm{e}^{-(T-t)r}\left(\frac{M_0^t}{S_t}\right)^{2r/\sigma^2}\Phi\left(-\delta_-^{T-t}\left(\frac{M_0^t}{S_t}\right)\right)\right).$$

In other words, we have

$$\mathrm{e}^{-(T-t)r}\,\mathbb{E}^*\left[M_0^T - S_T\,\middle|\,\mathcal{F}_t\right] = \mathrm{Bl_p}(S_t, M_0^t, r, \sigma, T - t) + S_t h_p\left(T - t, \frac{S_t}{M_0^t}\right)$$

where the function

$$h_p(\tau, z) = \frac{\sigma^2}{2r}\Phi\left(\delta_+^\tau\left(z\right)\right) - \frac{\sigma^2}{2r}\mathrm{e}^{-r\tau}z^{-2r/\sigma^2}\Phi\left(-\delta_-^\tau\left(\frac{1}{z}\right)\right), \tag{12.11}$$

depends only on time τ and $z = S_t/M_0^t$. In other words, due to the relation

$$\begin{aligned}\mathrm{Bl_p}(x, y, r, \sigma, \tau) &= y\,\mathrm{e}^{-r\tau}\Phi\left(-\delta_-^\tau\left(\frac{x}{y}\right)\right) - x\Phi\left(-\delta_+^\tau\left(\frac{x}{y}\right)\right)\\ &= x\mathrm{Bl_p}(1, y/x, r, \sigma, \tau)\end{aligned}$$

for the standard Black–Scholes put option price formula, we observe that $f(t, x, y)$ satisfies

$$f(t, x, y) = x\mathrm{Bl_p}\left(1, \frac{y}{x}, r, \sigma, T - t\right) + xh\left(T - t, \frac{x}{y}\right),$$

i.e.

$$f(t, x, y) = xg\left(T - t, \frac{x}{y}\right),$$

with

$$g(\tau, z) = \mathrm{Bl_p}\left(1, \frac{1}{z}, r, \sigma, \tau\right) + h_p(\tau, z), \tag{12.12}$$

where the function $h_p(\tau, z)$ is a correction term given by (12.11) which is small when $z = x/y$ or τ become small.

Note that $(x, y) \longmapsto x h_p(T - t, x/y)$ also satisfies the Black–Scholes PDE (12.2), in particular $(\tau, z) \longmapsto \mathrm{Bl_p}(1, 1/z, r, \sigma, \tau)$ and $h_p(\tau, z)$ both satisfy the PDE

$$\frac{\partial h_p}{\partial \tau}(\tau, z) = z \left(r + \sigma^2 \right) \frac{\partial h_p}{\partial z}(\tau, z) + \frac{1}{2} \sigma^2 z^2 \frac{\partial^2 h_p}{\partial z^2}(\tau, z), \qquad (12.13)$$

$\tau \in [0, T]$, $z \in [0, 1]$, subject to the boundary condition

$$h_p(0, z) = 0, \qquad 0 \leqslant z \leqslant 1.$$

The next Figure 12.5b illustrates the decomposition (12.12) of the normalized look-back put option price $g(\tau, z)$ in Figure 12.4 into the Black–Scholes put price function $\mathrm{Bl_p}(1, 1/z, r, \sigma, \tau)$ and $h_p(\tau, z)$.

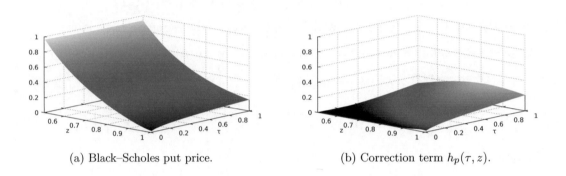

(a) Black–Scholes put price.　　　　　　　　(b) Correction term $h_p(\tau, z)$.

Figure 12.5: Normalized Black–Scholes put price and correction term in (12.12).

Note that in Figure 12.5b the condition $h_p(0, z) = 0$ is not fully respected as z tends to 1, due to numerical instabilities in the approximation of the function Φ.

12.3　The Lookback Call Option

The standard Lookback call option gives the right to buy the underlying asset at its historically lowest price. In this case, the floating strike price is m_0^T and the payoff is

$$C = S_T - m_0^T.$$

The following result gives the price of the lookback call option, cf. *e.g.* Proposition 9.5.1, page 270 of Dana and Jeanblanc (2007).

Proposition 12.5. *The price at time $t \in [0, T]$ of the lookback call option with payoff $S_T - m_0^T$ is given by*

$$e^{-(T-t)r} \, \mathbb{E}^* \left[S_T - m_0^T \mid \mathcal{F}_t \right]$$

$$= \; S_t \Phi \left(\delta_+^{T-t} \left(\frac{S_t}{m_0^t} \right) \right) - m_0^t e^{-(T-t)r} \Phi \left(\delta_-^{T-t} \left(\frac{S_t}{m_0^t} \right) \right)$$

$$+ e^{-(T-t)r} S_t \frac{\sigma^2}{2r} \left(\frac{m_0^t}{S_t} \right)^{2r/\sigma^2} \Phi \left(\delta_-^{T-t} \left(\frac{m_0^t}{S_t} \right) \right) - S_t \frac{\sigma^2}{2r} \Phi \left(-\delta_+^{T-t} \left(\frac{S_t}{m_0^t} \right) \right).$$

Proof. By Proposition 10.10 we have

$$e^{-(T-t)r} \, \mathbb{E}^* \left[S_T - m_0^T \mid \mathcal{F}_t \right] = S_t - e^{-(T-t)r} \, \mathbb{E}^* \left[m_0^T \mid \mathcal{F}_t \right]$$

$$= \; S_t \Phi \left(\delta_+^{T-t} \left(\frac{S_t}{m_0^t} \right) \right) - e^{-(T-t)r} m_0^t \Phi \left(\delta_-^{T-t} \left(\frac{S_t}{m_0^t} \right) \right)$$

$$+ e^{-(T-t)r} \frac{S_t \sigma^2}{2r} \left(\left(\frac{m_0^t}{S_t} \right)^{2r/\sigma^2} \Phi \left(\delta_-^{T-t} \left(\frac{m_0^t}{S_t} \right) \right) - e^{(T-t)r} \Phi \left(-\delta_+^{T-t} \left(\frac{S_t}{m_0^t} \right) \right) \right).$$

$\square$

Figure 12.6 represents the price of the lookback call option as a function of m_0^t and S_t for different values of the time to maturity $T - t$.

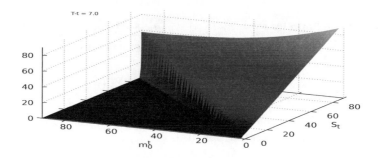

Figure 12.6: Graph of the lookback call option price.

From Figures 12.6 and 12.7, we note the following.

i) When the underlying asset price S_t is far from m_0^t, an increase in the value S_t clearly results into a higher call option price.

ii) When the underlying asset price S_t is close to m_0^t, a decrease in S_t could lead to a decrease in the value of m_0^t, however on average this appears insufficient to increase the average option payoff.

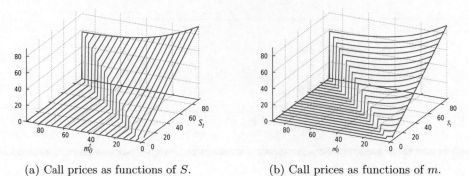

(a) Call prices as functions of S.   (b) Call prices as functions of m.

Figure 12.7: Graph of lookback call option prices.

Figures 12.7 and 12.8 show accordingly that, from the Delta hedging strategy for lookback call options, see Propositions 12.6 and 12.8, one should long the underlying asset in order to hedge a lookback call option.

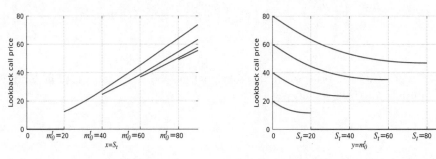

(a) Lookback call prices for fixed m_0^t.   (b) Lookback call prices for fixed S_t.

Figure 12.8: Graphs of lookback call option prices (2D).

Black–Scholes PDE for lookback call option prices

Since the couple (S_t, m_0^t) is also a Markov process, the price of the lookback call option at time $t \in [0, T]$ can be written as a function

$$
\begin{aligned}
f(t, S_t, m_0^t) &= e^{-(T-t)r} \, \mathbb{E}^* \left[\phi(S_T, m_0^T) \,|\, \mathcal{F}_t \right] \\
&= e^{-(T-t)r} \, \mathbb{E}^* \left[\phi(S_T, m_0^T) \,|\, S_t, \, m_0^t \right]
\end{aligned}
$$

of S_t and m_0^t, $0 \leqslant t \leqslant T$. By the same argument as in the proof of Proposition 12.2, we obtain the following result.

Proposition 12.6. *The function $f(t, x, y)$ defined by*

$$
f(t, x, y) = e^{-(T-t)r} \, \mathbb{E}^* \left[S_T - m_0^T \,|\, S_t = x, \, m_0^t = y \right], \quad t \in [0, T], \ x, y > 0,
$$

is $\mathcal{C}^2((0, T) \times (0, \infty)^2)$ and satisfies the Black–Scholes PDE

$$
rf(t, x, y) = \frac{\partial f}{\partial t}(t, x, y) + rx \frac{\partial f}{\partial x}(t, x, y) + \frac{1}{2} x^2 \sigma^2 \frac{\partial^2 f}{\partial x^2}(t, x, y),
$$

$0 \leqslant t \leqslant T$, $x > 0$, *subject to the boundary conditions*

$$
\begin{cases}
\lim_{y \searrow 0} f(t, x, y) = x, & 0 \leqslant t \leqslant T, \quad x > 0, & \text{(12.14a)} \\[2ex]
\dfrac{\partial f}{\partial y}(t, x, y)_{y=x} = 0, & 0 \leqslant t \leqslant T, \quad y > 0, & \text{(12.14b)} \\[2ex]
f(T, x, y) = x - y, & 0 < y \leqslant x, & \text{(12.14c)}
\end{cases}
$$

and the corresponding self-financing hedging strategy is given by

$$
\xi_t = \frac{\partial f}{\partial x}(t, S_t, m_0^t), \qquad t \in [0, T], \tag{12.15}
$$

which represents the quantity of the risky asset S_t to be held at time t in the hedging portfolio.

In other words, the price of the lookback call option takes the form

$$
f(t, S_t, m_t) = e^{-(T-t)r} \, \mathbb{E}^* \left[S_T - m_0^T \mid \mathcal{F}_t \right],
$$

where the function $f(t, x, y)$ is given by

$$
\begin{aligned}
f(t, x, y) &= x \Phi \left(\delta_+^{T-t} \left(\frac{x}{y} \right) \right) - e^{-(T-t)r} y \Phi \left(\delta_-^{T-t} \left(\frac{x}{y} \right) \right) \tag{12.16} \\
&\quad + e^{-(T-t)r} x \frac{\sigma^2}{2r} \left(\left(\frac{y}{x} \right)^{2r/\sigma^2} \Phi \left(\delta_-^{T-t} \left(\frac{y}{x} \right) \right) - e^{(T-t)r} \Phi \left(-\delta_+^{T-t} \left(\frac{x}{y} \right) \right) \right) \\
&= x - y e^{-(T-t)r} \Phi \left(\delta_-^{T-t} \left(\frac{x}{y} \right) \right) - x \left(1 + \frac{\sigma^2}{2r} \right) \Phi \left(-\delta_+^{T-t} \left(\frac{x}{y} \right) \right) \\
&\quad + x e^{-(T-t)r} \frac{\sigma^2}{2r} \left(\frac{y}{x} \right)^{2r/\sigma^2} \Phi \left(\delta_-^{T-t} \left(\frac{y}{x} \right) \right).
\end{aligned}
$$

Scaling property of lookback call option prices

We note the scaling property

$$
\begin{aligned}
f(t, x, y) &= e^{-(T-t)r} \, \mathbb{E}^* \left[S_T - m_0^T \mid S_t = x, \, m_0^t = y \right] \\
&= e^{-(T-t)r} \, \mathbb{E}^* \left[S_T - \min \left(m_0^t, m_t^T \right) \mid S_t = x, \, m_0^t = y \right] \\
&= e^{-(T-t)r} x \, \mathbb{E}^* \left[\frac{S_T}{S_t} - \min \left(\frac{m_0^t}{S_t}, \frac{m_t^T}{S_t} \right) \, \bigg| \, S_t = x, \, m_0^t = y \right] \\
&= e^{-(T-t)r} x \, \mathbb{E}^* \left[\frac{S_T}{x} - \min \left(\frac{y}{x}, \frac{m_t^T}{x} \right) \, \bigg| \, S_t = x, \, m_0^t = y \right] \\
&= e^{-(T-t)r} x \, \mathbb{E}^* \left[S_T - \min \left(m_0^t, m_t^T \right) \, \bigg| \, S_t = 1, \, m_0^t = \frac{y}{x} \right] \\
&= e^{-(T-t)r} x \, \mathbb{E}^* \left[S_T - m_0^T \, \bigg| \, S_t = 1, \, m_0^t = \frac{y}{x} \right]
\end{aligned}
$$

$$
\begin{aligned}
&= \ xf(t,1,y/x) \\
&= \ xg\left(T-t,\frac{1}{z}\right),
\end{aligned}
$$

where

$$
\begin{aligned}
g(\tau,z) &:= \\
&1 - \frac{1}{z}\,\mathrm{e}^{-r\tau}\Phi\left(\delta_{-}^{\tau}\left(z\right)\right) - \left(1+\frac{\sigma^2}{2r}\right)\Phi\left(-\delta_{+}^{\tau}\left(z\right)\right) + \frac{\sigma^2}{2r}\,\mathrm{e}^{-r\tau}z^{-2r/\sigma^2}\Phi\left(\delta_{-}^{\tau}\left(\frac{1}{z}\right)\right),
\end{aligned}
$$

with $g(\tau,1) = C(T-t)$, and

$$
f(t,x,y) = xg\left(T-t,\frac{x}{y}\right)
$$

and the boundary condition

$$
\begin{cases}
\dfrac{\partial g}{\partial z}(\tau,1) = 0, \qquad \tau > 0, & \text{(12.17a)} \\[2ex]
g(0,z) = 1 - \dfrac{1}{z}, \qquad z \geqslant 1. & \text{(12.17b)}
\end{cases}
$$

The next Figure 12.9 shows a graph of the function $g(\tau,z)$.

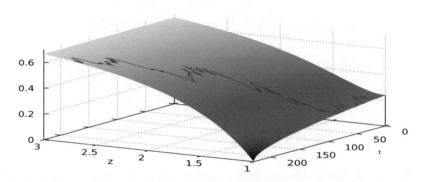

Figure 12.9: Normalized lookback call option price.

The next Figure 12.10 represents the path of the underlying asset price used in Figure 12.9.

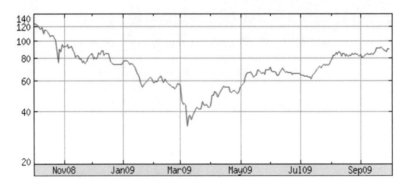

Figure 12.10: Graph of underlying asset prices.

The next Figure 12.11 represents the corresponding underlying asset price and its running minimum.

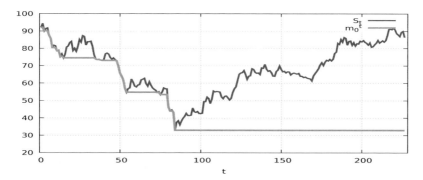

Figure 12.11: Running minimum of the underlying asset price.

Next, we represent the option price as a function of time, together with the process $\left(S_t - m_0^t\right)_{t \in \mathbb{R}_+}$.

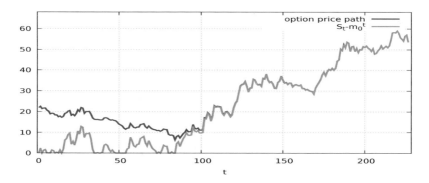

Figure 12.12: Graph of the lookback call option price.

Black–Scholes approximation of lookback call option prices

Let

$$\mathrm{Bl}_{\mathrm{c}}(S, K, r, \sigma, \tau) = S\Phi\left(\delta_+^\tau\left(\frac{S}{K}\right)\right) - K\,\mathrm{e}^{-r\tau}\Phi\left(\delta_-^\tau\left(\frac{S}{K}\right)\right)$$

denote the standard Black–Scholes formula for the price of the European call option.

Proposition 12.7. *The lookback call option price can be rewritten as*

$$\mathrm{e}^{-(T-t)r}\,\mathbb{E}^*\left[S_T - m_0^T \mid \mathcal{F}_t\right] = \mathrm{Bl}_{\mathrm{c}}(S_t, m_0^t, r, \sigma, T-t) \tag{12.18}$$

$$-S_t \frac{\sigma^2}{2r}\left(\Phi\left(-\delta_+^{T-t}\left(\frac{S_t}{m_0^t}\right)\right) - \mathrm{e}^{-(T-t)r}\left(\frac{m_0^t}{S_t}\right)^{2r/\sigma^2}\Phi\left(\delta_-^{T-t}\left(\frac{m_0^t}{S_t}\right)\right)\right).$$

In other words, we have

$$\mathrm{e}^{-(T-t)r}\,\mathbb{E}^*\left[S_T - m_0^T \mid \mathcal{F}_t\right] := \mathrm{Bl}_{\mathrm{c}}(S_t, m_0^t, r, \sigma, T-t) + S_t h_c\left(T-t, \frac{S_t}{m_0^t}\right)$$

where the correction term

$$h_c(\tau, z) = -\frac{\sigma^2}{2r}\left(\Phi\left(-\delta_+^\tau(z)\right) - e^{-r\tau}z^{-2r/\sigma^2}\Phi\left(\delta_-^\tau\left(\frac{1}{z}\right)\right)\right), \qquad (12.19)$$

is small when $z = S_t/m_0^t$ becomes large or τ becomes small. In addition, $h_p(\tau, z)$ is linked to $h_c(\tau, z)$ by the relation

$$h_c(\tau, z) = h_p(\tau, z) - \frac{\sigma^2}{2r}\left(1 - e^{-r\tau}z^{-2r/\sigma^2}\right), \qquad \tau \geqslant 0, \quad z \geqslant 0,$$

where $(z, \tau) \longmapsto e^{-r\tau}z^{-2r/\sigma^2}$ also solves the PDE (12.13). Due to the relation

$$
\begin{aligned}
\mathrm{Bl}_c(x, y, r, \sigma, \tau) &= x\Phi\left(\delta_+^\tau\left(\frac{x}{y}\right)\right) - ye^{-r\tau}\Phi\left(\delta_-^\tau\left(\frac{x}{y}\right)\right) \\
&= x\mathrm{Bl}_c\left(1, \frac{y}{x}, r, \sigma, \tau\right)
\end{aligned}
$$

for the standard Black–Scholes call price formula, recall that from Proposition 12.7, $f(t, x, y)$ can be decomposed as

$$f(t, x, y) = x\mathrm{Bl}_c\left(1, \frac{y}{x}, r, \sigma, T-t\right) + xh_c\left(T-t, \frac{x}{y}\right),$$

where $h_c(\tau, z)$ is the function given by (12.19), *i.e.*

$$f(t, x, y) = xg\left(T-t, \frac{x}{y}\right),$$

with

$$g(\tau, z) = \mathrm{Bl}_c\left(1, \frac{1}{z}, r, \sigma, \tau\right) + h_c(\tau, z), \qquad (12.20)$$

where $(x, y) \longmapsto xh_c(T-t, x/y)$ also satisfies the Black–Scholes PDE (12.2), *i.e.* $(\tau, z) \longmapsto \mathrm{Bl}_c(1, 1/z, r, \sigma, \tau)$ and $h_c(\tau, z)$ both satisfy the PDE (12.13) subject to the boundary condition

$$h_c(0, z) = 0, \qquad z \geqslant 1.$$

The next Figures 12.13a and 12.13b show the decomposition of $g(t, z)$ in (12.20) and Figures 12.9-12.10 into the sum of the Black–Scholes call price function $\mathrm{Bl}_c(1, 1/z, r, \sigma, \tau)$ and $h(t, z)$.

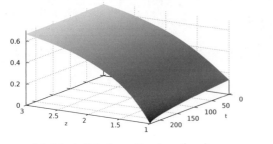

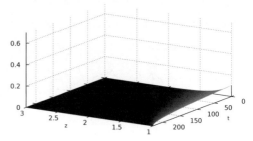

(a) Black–Scholes call price $g(\tau, z)$.   (b) Correction term $h_c(\tau, z)$.

Figure 12.13: Normalized Black–Scholes call price and correction term in (12.20).

We also note that

$$
\begin{aligned}
\mathbb{E}^* \left[M_0^T - m_0^T \mid S_0 = x \right] &= x - x\,e^{-(T-t)r} \Phi\big(\delta_-^{T-t}(1)\big) \\
&\quad - x \left(1 + \frac{\sigma^2}{2r} \right) \Phi\big(-\delta_+^{T-t}(1)\big) + x\,e^{-(T-t)r} \frac{\sigma^2}{2r} \Phi\big(\delta_-^{T-t}(1)\big) \\
&\quad + x\,e^{-(T-t)r} \Phi\big(-\delta_-^{T-t}(1)\big) + x \left(1 + \frac{\sigma^2}{2r} \right) \Phi\big(\delta_+^{T-t}(1)\big) \\
&\quad - x \frac{\sigma^2}{2r} e^{-(T-t)r} \Phi\big(-\delta_-^{T-t}(1)\big) - x \\
&= x \left(1 + \frac{\sigma^2}{2r} \right) \Big(\Phi\big(\delta_+^{T-t}(1)\big) - \Phi\big(-\delta_+^{T-t}(1)\big) \Big) \\
&\quad + x\,e^{-(T-t)r} \left(\frac{\sigma^2}{2r} - 1 \right) \Big(\Phi\big(\delta_-^{T-t}(1)\big) - \Phi\big(-\delta_-^{T-t}(1)\big) \Big).
\end{aligned}
$$

12.4 Delta Hedging for Lookback Options

In this section we compute hedging strategies for lookback call and put options by application of the Delta hedging formula (12.15). See Bermin (1998), § 2.6.1, page 29, for another approach to the following result using the Clark–Ocone formula. Here we use (12.15) instead, cf. Proposition 4.6 of El Khatib and Privault (2003).

Proposition 12.8. *The Delta hedging strategy of the lookback call option is given by*

$$
\begin{aligned}
\xi_t &= 1 - \left(1 + \frac{\sigma^2}{2r} \right) \Phi \left(-\delta_+^{T-t}\left(\frac{S_t}{m_0^t} \right) \right) \\
&\quad + e^{-(T-t)r} \left(\frac{m_0^t}{S_t} \right)^{2r/\sigma^2} \left(\frac{\sigma^2}{2r} - 1 \right) \Phi \left(\delta_-^{T-t}\left(\frac{m_0^t}{S_t} \right) \right), \qquad 0 \leqslant t \leqslant T.
\end{aligned}
\tag{12.21}
$$

Proof. By (12.15) and (12.18), we need to differentiate

$$
f(t, x, y) = \mathrm{Bl}_c(x, y, r, \sigma, T - t) + x h_c \left(T - t, \frac{x}{y} \right)
$$

with respect to the variable x, where

$$
h_c(\tau, z) = -\frac{\sigma^2}{2r} \left(\Phi\left(-\delta_+^\tau(z) \right) - e^{-r\tau} z^{-2r/\sigma^2} \Phi\left(\delta_-^\tau\left(\frac{1}{z} \right) \right) \right)
$$

is given by (12.19) First, we note that the relation

$$
\frac{\partial}{\partial x} \mathrm{Bl}_c(x, y, r, \sigma, \tau) = \Phi\left(\delta_+^\tau\left(\frac{x}{y} \right) \right)
$$

is known, cf. Propositions 6.4 and 7.13. Next, we have

$$
\frac{\partial}{\partial x} \left(x h_c\left(\tau, \frac{x}{y} \right) \right) = h_c\left(\tau, \frac{x}{y} \right) + \frac{x}{y} \frac{\partial h_c}{\partial z}\left(\tau, \frac{x}{y} \right),
$$

and

$$\frac{\partial h_c}{\partial z}(\tau, z) = -\frac{\sigma^2}{2r}\left(\frac{\partial}{\partial z}\left(\Phi\left(-\delta_+^\tau(z)\right)\right) - e^{-r\tau}z^{-2r/\sigma^2}\frac{\partial}{\partial z}\left(\Phi\left(\delta_-^\tau\left(\frac{1}{z}\right)\right)\right)\right)$$
$$- \frac{\sigma^2}{2r}\left(\frac{2r}{\sigma^2}e^{-r\tau}z^{-1-2r/\sigma^2}\Phi\left(\delta_-^\tau\left(\frac{1}{z}\right)\right)\right)$$
$$= \frac{\sigma}{2rz\sqrt{2\pi\tau}}\exp\left(-\frac{1}{2}(\delta_+^\tau(z))^2\right)$$
$$- e^{-r\tau}z^{-2r/\sigma^2}\frac{\sigma}{2rz\sqrt{2\pi\tau}}\exp\left(-\frac{1}{2}\left(\delta_-^\tau\left(\frac{1}{z}\right)\right)^2\right) - \frac{2r}{\sigma^2}e^{-r\tau}z^{-1-2r/\sigma^2}\Phi\left(\delta_-^\tau\left(\frac{1}{z}\right)\right).$$

Next, we note that

$$e^{-(\delta_-^\tau(1/z))^2/2} = \exp\left(-\frac{1}{2}(\delta_+^\tau(z))^2 - \frac{1}{2}\left(\frac{4r^2}{\sigma^2}\tau - \frac{4r}{\sigma}\delta_+^\tau(z)\sqrt{\tau}\right)\right)$$
$$= e^{-(\delta_+^\tau(z))^2/2}\exp\left(-\frac{1}{2}\left(\frac{4r^2}{\sigma^2}\tau - \frac{4r}{\sigma^2}\left(\log z + \left(r + \frac{1}{2}\sigma^2\right)\tau\right)\right)\right)$$
$$= e^{-(\delta_+^\tau(z))^2/2}\exp\left(\frac{-2r^2}{\sigma^2}\tau + \frac{2r}{\sigma^2}\log z + \frac{2r^2}{\sigma^2}\tau + r\tau\right)$$
$$= e^{r\tau}z^{2r/\sigma^2}e^{-(\delta_+^\tau(z))^2/2} \tag{12.22}$$

as in the proof of Proposition 6.4, hence

$$\frac{\partial h_c}{\partial z}\left(\tau, \frac{x}{y}\right) = -e^{-r\tau}z^{-1-2r/\sigma^2}\Phi\left(\delta_-^\tau\left(\frac{1}{z}\right)\right),$$

and

$$\frac{\partial}{\partial x}\left(xh_c\left(\tau, \frac{x}{y}\right)\right) = h_c\left(\tau, \frac{x}{y}\right) - e^{-r\tau}\left(\frac{y}{x}\right)^{2r/\sigma^2}\Phi\left(\delta_-^\tau\left(\frac{y}{x}\right)\right),$$

which concludes the proof. $\square$

We note that $\xi_t = 1 > 0$ as T tends to infinity, and that at maturity $t = T$, the hedging strategy satisfies

$$\xi_T = \begin{cases} 1 & \text{if } m_0^T < S_T, \\ 1 - \frac{1}{2}\left(1 + \frac{\sigma^2}{2r}\right) + \frac{1}{2}\left(\frac{\sigma^2}{2r} - 1\right) = 0 & \text{if } m_0^T = S_T. \end{cases}$$

In Figure 12.14 we represent the Delta of the lookback call option, as given by (12.21).

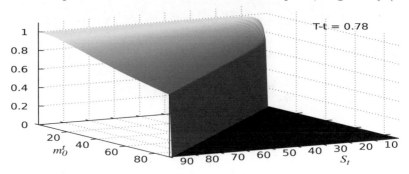

Figure 12.14: Delta of the lookback call option with $r = 2\%$ and $\sigma = 0.41$.

The above scaling procedure can be applied to the Delta of lookback call options by noting that ξ_t can be written as

$$\xi_t = \zeta\left(t, \frac{S_t}{m_0^t}\right),$$

where the function $\zeta(t, z)$ is given by

$$\zeta(t, z) = \Phi\left(\delta_+^{T-t}(z)\right) - \frac{\sigma^2}{2r}\Phi\left(-\delta_+^{T-t}(z)\right) \tag{12.23}$$
$$+ e^{-(T-t)r} z^{-2r/\sigma^2}\left(\frac{\sigma^2}{2r} - 1\right)\Phi\left(\delta_-^{T-t}\left(\frac{1}{z}\right)\right),$$

$t \in [0, T]$, $z \in [0, 1]$. The graph of the function $\zeta(t, x)$ is given in Figure 12.15.

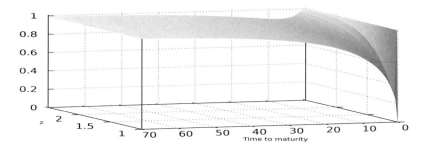

Figure 12.15: Rescaled portfolio strategy for the lookback call option.

Similar calculations using (12.4) can be carried out for other types of lookback options, such as options on extrema and partial lookback options, cf. El Khatib (2003). As a consequence of Propositions 12.5 and 12.8, we have

$$e^{-(T-t)r}\, \mathbb{E}^*\left[S_T - m_0^T \mid \mathcal{F}_t\right]$$
$$= S_t\Phi\left(\delta_+^{T-t}\left(\frac{S_t}{m_0^t}\right)\right) - m_0^t\, e^{-(T-t)r}\Phi\left(\delta_-^{T-t}\left(\frac{S_t}{m_0^t}\right)\right)$$
$$+ e^{-(T-t)r} S_t \frac{\sigma^2}{2r}\left(\frac{m_0^t}{S_t}\right)^{2r/\sigma^2}\Phi\left(\delta_-^{T-t}\left(\frac{m_0^t}{S_t}\right)\right) - S_t\frac{\sigma^2}{2r}\Phi\left(-\delta_+^{T-t}\left(\frac{S_t}{m_0^t}\right)\right)$$
$$= \xi_t S_t + m_0^t\, e^{-(T-t)r}\left(\left(\frac{S_t}{m_0^t}\right)^{1-2r/\sigma^2}\Phi\left(\delta_-^{T-t}\left(\frac{m_0^t}{S_t}\right)\right) - \Phi\left(\delta_-^{T-t}\left(\frac{S_t}{m_0^t}\right)\right)\right),$$

and the quantity of the riskless asset e^{rt} in the portfolio is given by

$$\eta_t = m_0^t\, e^{-rT}\left(\left(\frac{S_t}{m_0^t}\right)^{1-2r/\sigma^2}\Phi\left(\delta_-^{T-t}\left(\frac{m_0^t}{S_t}\right)\right) - \Phi\left(\delta_-^{T-t}\left(\frac{S_t}{m_0^t}\right)\right)\right),$$

so that the portfolio value V_t at time t satisfies

$$V_t = \xi_t S_t + \eta_t\, e^{rt}, \qquad t \geqslant 0.$$

Proposition 12.9. *The Delta hedging strategy of the lookback put option is given by*

$$\xi_t = \left(1 + \frac{\sigma^2}{2r}\right)\Phi\left(\delta_+^{T-t}\left(\frac{S_t}{M_0^t}\right)\right) \tag{12.24}$$
$$+ e^{-(T-t)r}\left(\frac{M_0^t}{S_t}\right)^{2r/\sigma^2}\left(1 - \frac{\sigma^2}{2r}\right)\Phi\left(-\delta_-^{T-t}\left(\frac{M_0^t}{S_t}\right)\right) - 1, \quad 0 \leqslant t \leqslant T.$$

Proof. By (12.15) and (12.10), we need to differentiate

$$f(t,x,y) = \mathrm{Bl_p}(x,y,r,\sigma,T-t) + x h_p\left(T-t,\frac{x}{y}\right)$$

where

$$h_p(\tau,z) = \frac{\sigma^2}{2r}\Phi\left(\delta_+^\tau(z)\right) - e^{-r\tau}\frac{\sigma^2}{2r}z^{-2r/\sigma^2}\Phi\left(-\delta_-^\tau(1/z)\right),$$

and

$$\delta_\pm^\tau(z) := \frac{1}{\sigma\sqrt{\tau}}\left(\log z + \left(r \pm \frac{1}{2}\sigma^2\right)\tau\right), \qquad z > 0.$$

We have

$$
\begin{aligned}
\frac{\partial h_p}{\partial z}(\tau,z) &= \frac{\sigma^2}{2r}\delta_+'^\tau(z)\,\varphi\left(\delta_+^\tau(z)\right) + e^{-r\tau}z^{-1-2r/\sigma^2}\Phi\left(-\delta_-^\tau\left(\frac{1}{z}\right)\right) \\
&\quad + \frac{\sigma^2}{2rz^2}\delta_-'^\tau\left(\frac{1}{z}\right)e^{-r\tau}z^{-2r/\sigma^2}\varphi\left(\delta_-^\tau\left(\frac{1}{z}\right)\right) \\
&= e^{-r\tau}z^{-1-2r/\sigma^2}\Phi\left(-\delta_-^\tau\left(\frac{1}{z}\right)\right) \\
&\quad + \frac{\sigma}{2rz\sqrt{\tau}}\left(\varphi\left(\delta_+^\tau(z)\right) - e^{-r\tau}z^{-2r/\sigma^2}\varphi\left(\delta_-^\tau\left(\frac{1}{z}\right)\right)\right).
\end{aligned}
$$

From the relation

$$
\begin{aligned}
\left(\delta_+^{T-t}(z)\right)^2 - \left(\delta_-^{T-t}\left(\frac{1}{z}\right)\right)^2 &= \left(\delta_+^{T-t}(z) + \delta_-^{T-t}\left(\frac{1}{z}\right)\right)\left(\delta_+^{T-t}(z) - \delta_-^{T-t}\left(\frac{1}{z}\right)\right) \\
&= \frac{2r}{\sigma^2}\log z + 2r(T-t),
\end{aligned}
$$

we have

$$\varphi\left(\delta_+^{T-t}(z)\right) = z^{-2r/\sigma^2}e^{-r(T-t)}\varphi\left(\delta_-^{T-t}\left(\frac{1}{z}\right)\right),$$

hence

$$\frac{\partial h_p}{\partial z}(\tau,z) = e^{-r\tau}z^{-1-2r/\sigma^2}\Phi\left(-\delta_-^\tau\left(\frac{1}{z}\right)\right).$$

Therefore, knowing that the Black–Scholes put Delta is

$$-\Phi\left(-\delta_+^{T-t}\left(\frac{x}{y}\right)\right) = -1 + \Phi\left(\delta_+^{T-t}\left(\frac{x}{y}\right)\right),$$

see *e.g.* Proposition 6.7, we have

$$
\begin{aligned}
\frac{\partial f}{\partial x}(t,x,y) &= -\Phi\left(-\delta_+^{T-t}\left(\frac{x}{y}\right)\right) + h_p\left(T-t,\frac{x}{y}\right) + \frac{x}{y}\frac{\partial h_p}{\partial z}\left(T-t,\frac{x}{y}\right) \\
&= -\Phi\left(-\delta_+^{T-t}\left(\frac{x}{y}\right)\right) + \frac{\sigma^2}{2r}\Phi\left(\delta_+^{T-t}\left(\frac{x}{y}\right)\right) \\
&\quad + e^{-(T-t)r}\left(\frac{y}{x}\right)^{2r/\sigma^2}\left(1 - \frac{\sigma^2}{2r}\right)\Phi\left(-\delta_-^{T-t}\left(\frac{y}{x}\right)\right),
\end{aligned}
$$

which yields (12.24). $\square$

Note that we have $\xi_t = \sigma^2/(2r) > 0$ as T tends to infinity. At maturity $t = T$, the hedging strategy satisfies

$$
\xi_T = \begin{cases} -1 & \text{if } M_0^T > S_T, \\[2mm] \dfrac{1}{2} + \dfrac{\sigma^2}{4r} + \dfrac{1}{2}\left(1 - \dfrac{\sigma^2}{2r}\right) - 1 = 0 & \text{if } M_0^T = S_T. \end{cases}
$$

In Figure 12.16 we represent the Delta of the lookback put option, as given by (12.24).

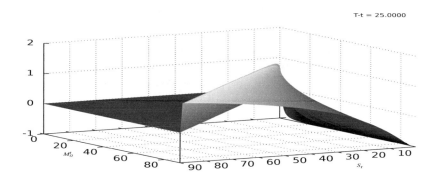

T-t = 25.0000

Figure 12.16: Delta of the lookback put option with $r = 2\%$ and $\sigma = 0.25$.

As a consequence of Propositions 12.1 and 12.9, we have

$$
\begin{aligned}
& e^{-(T-t)r}\, \mathbb{E}^*\left[M_0^T - S_T \mid \mathcal{F}_t\right] \\
&= M_0^t e^{-(T-t)r} \Phi\left(-\delta_-^{T-t}\left(\frac{S_t}{M_0^t}\right)\right) + S_t\left(1 + \frac{\sigma^2}{2r}\right)\Phi\left(\delta_+^{T-t}\left(\frac{S_t}{M_0^t}\right)\right) \\
&\quad - S_t e^{-(T-t)r}\frac{\sigma^2}{2r}\left(\frac{M_0^t}{S_t}\right)^{2r/\sigma^2}\Phi\left(-\delta_-^{T-t}\left(\frac{M_0^t}{S_t}\right)\right) - S_t \\
&= \xi_t S_t + M_0^t e^{-(T-t)r}\left(\Phi\left(-\delta_-^{T-t}\left(\frac{S_t}{M_0^t}\right)\right) - \left(\frac{S_t}{M_0^t}\right)^{1-2r/\sigma^2}\Phi\left(-\delta_-^{T-t}\left(\frac{M_0^t}{S_t}\right)\right)\right),
\end{aligned}
$$

and the quantity of the riskless asset e^{rt} in the portfolio is given by

$$
\eta_t = M_0^t e^{-rT}\left(\Phi\left(-\delta_-^{T-t}\left(\frac{S_t}{M_0^t}\right)\right) - \left(\frac{S_t}{M_0^t}\right)^{1-2r/\sigma^2}\Phi\left(-\delta_-^{T-t}\left(\frac{M_0^t}{S_t}\right)\right)\right)
$$

so that the portfolio value V_t at time t satisfies

$$
V_t = \xi_t S_t + \eta_t\, e^{rt}, \qquad t \geq 0.
$$

Exercises

Exercise 12.1

a) Give the probability density function of the maximum of drifted Brownian motion
$$\underset{t\in[0,1]}{\text{Max}}\ (B_t + \sigma t/2).$$

b) Taking $S_t := e^{\sigma B_t - \sigma^2 t/2}$, compute the expected value

$$
\mathbb{E}\left[\min_{t\in[0,1]} S_t\right] = \mathbb{E}\left[\min_{t\in[0,1]} e^{\sigma B_t - \sigma^2 t/2}\right]
$$
$$
= \mathbb{E}\left[e^{-\sigma\,\text{Max}_{t\in[0,1]}(B_t + \sigma t/2)}\right].
$$

c) Compute the "optimal exercise" price $\mathbb{E}\left[\left(K - S_0 \min_{t\in[0,1]} e^{\sigma B_t - \sigma^2 t/2}\right)^+\right]$ of a finite expiration American put option with $S_0 \leqslant K$.

Exercise 12.2   Let $(B_t)_{t\in\mathbb{R}_+}$ denote a standard Brownian motion.

a) Compute the expected value

$$
\mathbb{E}\left[\underset{t\in[0,1]}{\text{Max}}\ S_t\right] = \mathbb{E}\left[e^{\sigma\,\text{Max}_{t\in[0,1]}(B_t - \sigma t/2)}\right].
$$

b) Compute the "optimal exercise" price $\mathbb{E}\left[\left(S_0 \underset{t\in[0,1]}{\text{Max}}\ e^{\sigma B_t - \sigma^2 t/2} - K\right)^+\right]$ of a finite expiration American call option with $S_0 \geqslant K$.

Exercise 12.3   Consider a risky asset whose price S_t is given by

$$dS_t = \sigma S_t dB_t + \sigma^2 S_t dt/2,$$

where $(B_t)_{t\in\mathbb{R}_+}$ is a standard Brownian motion.

a) Compute the cumulative distribution function and the probability density function of the minimum $\min_{t\in[0,T]} B_t$ over the interval $[0,T]$?

b) Compute the price value
$$
e^{-\sigma^2 T/2}\, \mathbb{E}^*\left[S_T - \min_{t\in[0,T]} S_t\right]
$$
of a lookback call option on S_T with maturity T.

Exercise 12.4 (Dassios and Lim (2019)) The digital drawdown call option with qualifying period pays a unit amount when the drawdown period reaches one unit of time, if this happens before fixed maturity T, but only if the size of drawdown at this stopping time is larger than a prespecified K. This provides an insurance against a prolonged drawdown, if the drawdown amount is large. Specifically, the digital drawdown call option is priced as

$$\mathbb{E}^* \left[e^{-r\tau} \mathbb{1}_{\{\tau \leqslant T\}} \mathbb{1}_{\{M_0^\tau - S_\tau \geqslant K\}} \right],$$

where $M_0^t := \text{Max}_{u \in [0,t]} S_u$, $U_t := t - \text{Sup}\{0 \leqslant u \leqslant t \ : \ M_0^t = S_u\}$, and $\tau := \inf\{t \in \mathbb{R}_+ \ : \ U_t = 1\}$. Write the price of the drawdown option as a triple integral using the joint probability density function $f_{(\tau, S_\tau, M_\tau)}(t, x, y)$ of (τ, S_τ, M_τ) under the risk-neutral probability measure $\mathbb{P}^*$.

Exercise 12.5

a) Check explicitly that the boundary conditions (12.3a)–(12.3c) are satisfied.

b) Check explicitly that the boundary conditions (12.14a)–(12.14b) are satisfied.

Chapter 13

Asian Options

Asian options are special cases of average value options, whose claim payoffs are determined by the difference between the average underlying asset price over a certain time interval and a strike price K. This chapter covers several probabilistic and PDE techniques for the pricing and hedging of Asian options. Due to their dependence on averaged asset prices. Asian options are less volatile than plain vanilla options whose claim payoffs depend only on the terminal value of the underlying asset.

13.1 Bounds on Asian Option Prices

Asian options were first traded in Tokyo in 1987, and have become particularly popular in commodities trading.

Arithmetic Asian options

Given an underlying asset price process $(S_t)_{t \in [0,T]}$, the payoff of the Asian call option on $(S_t)_{t \in [0,T]}$ with exercise date T and strike price K is given by

$$C = \left(\frac{1}{T} \int_0^T S_t dt - K \right)^+.$$

Similarly, the payoff of the Asian put option on $(S_t)_{t \in [0,T]}$ with exercise date T and strike price K is

$$C = \left(K - \frac{1}{T} \int_0^T S_t dt \right)^+.$$

Due to their dependence on averaged asset prices, Asian options are less volatile than plain vanilla options whose payoffs depend only on the terminal value of the underlying asset.

As an example, Figure 13.1 presents a graph of Brownian motion and its moving average process

$$X_t := \frac{1}{t} \int_0^t B_s ds, \qquad t > 0.$$

Related exotic options include the Asian-American options, or Hawaiian options, that combine an Asian claim payoff with American style exercise, and can be priced by variational PDEs, cf. § 8.6.3.2 of Crépey (2013).

An option on average is an option whose payoff has the form

$$C = \phi(\Lambda_T, S_T),$$

DOI: 10.1201/9781003298670-13

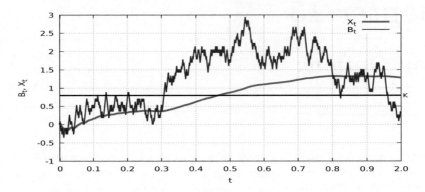

Figure 13.1: Brownian motion B_t and its moving average X_t.

where

$$\Lambda_T = S_0 \int_0^T e^{\sigma B_u + ru - \sigma^2 u/2} du = \int_0^T S_u du, \qquad T \geqslant 0.$$

- For example when $\phi(y,x) = (y/T - K)^+$ this yields the Asian call option with payoff

$$\left(\frac{1}{T} \int_0^T S_u du - K \right)^+ = \left(\frac{\Lambda_T}{T} - K \right)^+, \tag{13.1}$$

which is a path-dependent option whose price at time $t \in [0,T]$ is given by

$$e^{-(T-t)r} \mathbb{E}^* \left[\left(\frac{1}{T} \int_0^T S_u du - K \right)^+ \Bigg| \mathcal{F}_t \right]. \tag{13.2}$$

- As another example, when $\phi(y,x) := e^{-y}$ this yields the price

$$P(0,T) = \mathbb{E}^* \left[e^{- \int_0^T S_u du} \right] = \mathbb{E}^* \left[e^{-\Lambda_T} \right]$$

at time 0 of a bond with underlying short-term rate process S_t.

In the sequel, we assume that the underlying asset price process $(S_t)_{t \in \mathbb{R}_+}$ is a geometric Brownian motion satisfying the equation

$$dS_t = rS_t dt + \sigma S_t dB_t,$$

where $(B_t)_{t \in \mathbb{R}_+}$ is a standard Brownian motion under the risk-neutral probability measure $\mathbb{P}^*$.

Using the time homogeneity of the process $(S_t)_{t \in \mathbb{R}_+}$, the option with payoff $C = \phi(\Lambda_T, S_T)$ can be priced as

$$
\begin{aligned}
e^{-(T-t)r} \mathbb{E}^*[\phi(\Lambda_T, S_T) \mid \mathcal{F}_t] &= e^{-(T-t)r} \mathbb{E}^* \left[\phi \left(\Lambda_t + \int_t^T S_u du, S_T \right) \Bigg| \mathcal{F}_t \right] \\
&= e^{-(T-t)r} \mathbb{E}^* \left[\phi \left(y + x \int_t^T \frac{S_u}{S_t} du, x \frac{S_T}{S_t} \right) \right]_{y = \Lambda_t, x = S_t} \\
&= e^{-(T-t)r} \mathbb{E}^* \left[\phi \left(y + x \int_0^{T-t} \frac{S_u}{S_0} du, x \frac{S_{T-t}}{S_0} \right) \right]_{y = \Lambda_t, x = S_t}.
\end{aligned}
\tag{13.3}
$$

Using the Markov property of the process $(S_t, \Lambda_t)_{t \in \mathbb{R}_+}$, we can write down the option price as a function

$$
\begin{aligned}
f(t, S_t, \Lambda_t) &= \mathrm{e}^{-(T-t)r}\, \mathbb{E}^*[\phi(\Lambda_T, S_T) \mid \mathcal{F}_t] \\
&= \mathrm{e}^{-(T-t)r}\, \mathbb{E}^*[\phi(\Lambda_T, S_T) \mid S_t,\ \Lambda_t]
\end{aligned}
$$

of (t, S_t, Λ_t), where the function $f(t, x, y)$ is given by

$$
f(t, x, y) = \mathrm{e}^{-(T-t)r}\, \mathbb{E}^* \left[\phi \left(y + x \int_0^{T-t} \frac{S_u}{S_0} du,\, x \frac{S_{T-t}}{S_0} \right) \right].
$$

As we will see below there exists no easily tractable closed-form solution for the price of an arithmetically averaged Asian option.

Geometric Asian options

On the other hand, replacing the arithmetic average

$$
\frac{1}{T} \sum_{k=1}^n S_{t_k}(t_k - t_{k-1}) \simeq \frac{1}{T} \int_0^T S_u du
$$

with the geometric average

$$
\begin{aligned}
\prod_{k=1}^n S_{t_k}^{(t_k - t_{k-1})/T} &= \exp \left(\log \prod_{k=1}^n S_{t_k}^{(t_k - t_{k-1})/T} \right) \\
&= \exp \left(\frac{1}{T} \sum_{k=1}^n \log S_{t_k}^{t_k - t_{k-1}} \right) \\
&= \exp \left(\frac{1}{T} \sum_{k=1}^n (t_k - t_{k-1}) \log S_{t_k} \right) \\
&\simeq \exp \left(\frac{1}{T} \int_0^T \log S_u du \right)
\end{aligned}
$$

leads to closed-form solutions using the Black Scholes formula, see Exercise 13.5.

Pricing by probability density functions

We note that the prices of option on averages can be estimated numerically using the joint probability density function $\psi_{\Lambda_{T-t}, B_{T-t}}$ of (Λ_{T-t}, B_{T-t}), as follows:

$$
\begin{aligned}
f(t, x, y) &= \mathrm{e}^{-(T-t)r}\, \mathbb{E}^* \left[\phi \left(y + x \int_0^{T-t} \frac{S_u}{S_0} du,\, x \frac{S_{T-t}}{S_0} \right) \right] \\
&= \mathrm{e}^{-(T-t)r} \int_0^\infty \int_{-\infty}^\infty \phi \left(y + xz,\, x\, \mathrm{e}^{\sigma u + (T-t)r - (T-t)\sigma^2/2} \right) \psi_{\Lambda_{T-t}, B_{T-t}}(z, u) dz du,
\end{aligned}
$$

see Section 13.2 for details.

Bounds on Asian option prices

As noted in the next proposition, arithmetic Asian call option prices can be lower bounded by geometric Asian call prices, as a consequence of Jensen's inequality.

Proposition 13.1. *Let ϕ be a non-decreasing payoff function. We have the bound*

$$\mathrm{e}^{-rT}\,\mathbb{E}^*\left[\phi\left(\exp\left(\frac{1}{T}\int_0^T \log S_u du\right) - K\right)\right] \leqslant \mathrm{e}^{-rT}\,\mathbb{E}^*\left[\phi\left(\frac{1}{T}\int_0^T S_u du - K\right)\right].$$

Proof. By Jensen's inequality applied to the (concave) log function and the uniform measure with probability density function $(1/T)\mathbb{1}_{[0,T]}$ on $[0,T]$, we have

$$\exp\left(\frac{1}{T}\int_0^T \log S_t dt\right) \leqslant \exp\left(\log\left(\frac{1}{T}\int_0^T S_t dt\right)\right) = \frac{1}{T}\int_0^T S_t dt. \tag{13.4}$$

$\square$

We also note (see Lemma 1 of Kemna and Vorst (1990) and Exercise 13.7 below for the discrete-time version of that result), that the Asian call option price can be upper bounded by the corresponding European call option price using convexity arguments.

Proposition 13.2. *Assume that $r \geqslant 0$, and let ϕ be a convex and non-decreasing payoff function. We have the bound*

$$\mathrm{e}^{-rT}\,\mathbb{E}^*\left[\phi\left(\frac{1}{T}\int_0^T S_u du - K\right)\right] \leqslant \mathrm{e}^{-rT}\,\mathbb{E}^*[\phi(S_T - K)].$$

Proof. By Jensen's inequality for the uniform measure with probability density function $(1/T)\mathbb{1}_{[0,T]}$ on $[0,T]$ and for the probability measure $\mathbb{P}^*$, we have

$$\begin{aligned}
\mathrm{e}^{-rT}\,\mathbb{E}^*\left[\phi\left(\int_0^T S_u \frac{du}{T} - K\right)\right] &= \mathrm{e}^{-rT}\,\mathbb{E}^*\left[\phi\left(\int_0^T (S_u - K)\frac{du}{T}\right)\right] \\
&\leqslant \mathrm{e}^{-rT}\,\mathbb{E}^*\left[\int_0^T \phi(S_u - K)\frac{du}{T}\right] \\
&= \mathrm{e}^{-rT}\,\mathbb{E}^*\left[\int_0^T \phi\left(\mathrm{e}^{-(T-u)r}\,\mathbb{E}^*[S_T \mid \mathcal{F}_u] - K\right)\frac{du}{T}\right] \\
&= \mathrm{e}^{-rT}\,\mathbb{E}^*\left[\int_0^T \phi\left(\mathbb{E}^*[\mathrm{e}^{-(T-u)r}S_T - K \mid \mathcal{F}_u]\right)\frac{du}{T}\right] \\
&\leqslant \mathrm{e}^{-rT}\,\mathbb{E}^*\left[\int_0^T \mathbb{E}^*\left[\phi\left(\mathrm{e}^{-(T-u)r}S_T - K\right) \mid \mathcal{F}_u\right]\frac{du}{T}\right] \tag{13.5} \\
&\leqslant \mathrm{e}^{-rT}\int_0^T \mathbb{E}^*\left[\mathbb{E}^*\left[\phi(S_T - K) \mid \mathcal{F}_u\right]\right]\frac{du}{T} \tag{13.6} \\
&= \mathrm{e}^{-rT}\int_0^T \mathbb{E}^*[\phi(S_T - K)]\frac{du}{T} \\
&= \mathrm{e}^{-rT}\,\mathbb{E}^*[\phi(S_T - K)],
\end{aligned}$$

where from (13.5) to (13.6) we used the facts that $r \geqslant 0$ and ϕ is non-decreasing. $\square$

In particular, taking $\phi(x) : (x - K)^+$, Proposition 13.2 shows that Asian option prices are upper bounded by European call option prices due to the lower volatility of arithmetic averages, as

$$\mathrm{e}^{-rT}\,\mathbb{E}^*\left[\left(\frac{1}{T}\int_0^T S_u du - K\right)^+\right] \leqslant \mathrm{e}^{-rT}\,\mathbb{E}^*[(S_T - K)^+],$$

see Figure 13.2 for an illustration, as the averaging feature of Asian options reduces their underlying volatility.

```
  nSim=99999;N=1000; t <- 1:N; dt <- 1.0/N; sigma=2;r=0.5; european=0;asian=0;K=1.5
2 dev.new(width=16,height=7); par(oma=c(0,5,0,0))
  for (j in 1:nSim){S<-exp(sigma*cumsum(rnorm( N, 0,sqrt(dt)))+r*t/N-sigma**2*t/2/N);color="blue"
4 A<-sum(c(1,S))/(N+1);if (S[N]>=K) {european=european+S[N]-K}
  if (A>=K) {asian=asian+A-K};if (S[N]>A) {color="darkred"} else {color="darkgreen"}
6 plot(c(0,t/N),c(1,S), xlab = "Time", type='l', lwd = 3, ylab = "", ylim = c(0,exp(4*r)), col =
       color,main=paste("Asian Price=",format(round(asian,2)),"/", j,"=",format(round(asian/j,2)),"European
       Price=",format(round(european,2)), "/",j,"=",format(round(european/j,2))), xaxs='i',xaxt='n',yaxt='n',
       yaxs='i', yaxp = c(0,10,10), cex.lab=2, cex.main=2)
  text(0.3,6,paste("A-Payoff=",format(round(max(A-K,0),2)),", E-Payoff=", format(round(max(S[N]-K,0),2))),
       col=color,cex=2)
8 axis(1, las=1, cex.axis=2)
  axis(2, at=c(0,K,A,1,2,3,4,5,6,7,8,9,10), labels=c(0,"K","Average",1,2,3,4,5,6,7,8,9,10), las=2, cex.axis=2)
10 lines(c(0,t/N),rep(K,N+1),col = "red",lty = 1, lwd = 4);
  lines(c(0,t/N),rep(A,N+1),col = "darkgreen",lty = 2, lwd = 4); Sys.sleep(0.1)
12 if (S[N]>K || A>K) {readline(prompt = "Pause. Press <Enter> to continue...")}}}
```

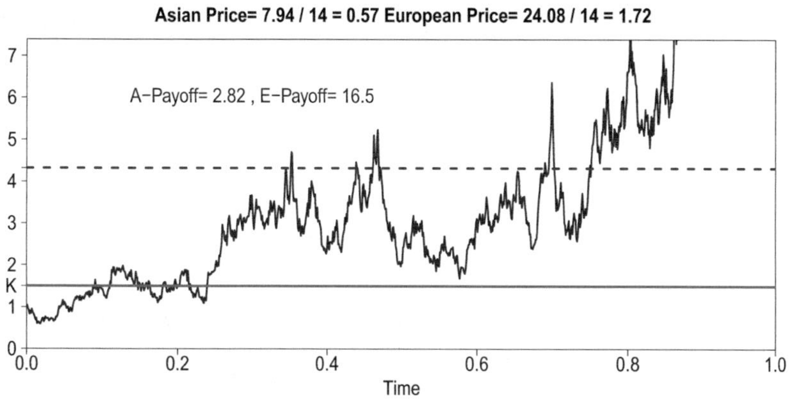

Figure 13.2: Asian option price *vs* European option price.

In the case of Asian call options we have the following result.

Proposition 13.3. *Assume that $r \geqslant 0$. We have the conditional bound*

$$
\mathrm{e}^{-(T-t)r}\,\mathbb{E}^*\left[\left(\frac{1}{T}\int_0^T S_u du - K\right)^+ \bigg| \mathcal{F}_t\right] \tag{13.7}
$$
$$
\leqslant \quad \mathrm{e}^{-(T-t)r}\,\mathbb{E}^*\left[\left(\frac{1}{T}\int_0^t S_u du + \frac{T-t}{T}S_T - K\right)^+ \bigg| \mathcal{F}_t\right]
$$

on Asian option prices, $t \in [0, T]$.

Proof. Let the function $f(t, x, y)$ be defined as

$$
f(t, S_t, \Lambda_t) = \mathbb{E}^*\left[\left(\frac{1}{T}\int_0^T S_u du - K\right)^+ \bigg| \mathcal{F}_t\right],
$$

i.e. from Proposition 13.2,

$$
f(t, x, y) \;=\; \mathbb{E}^*\left[\left(\frac{1}{T}\left(y + x\int_0^{T-t}\frac{S_u}{S_0}du\right) - K\right)^+\right]
$$
$$
\;=\; \mathbb{E}^*\left[\left(\frac{1}{T}\left(y + \frac{x}{S_0}\Lambda_{T-t}\right) - K\right)^+\right]
$$

$$= \mathbb{E}^* \left[\left(\frac{y}{T} - K + \frac{x}{TS_0} \Lambda_{T-t} \right)^+ \right]$$

$$= \frac{(T-t)x}{TS_0} \mathbb{E}^* \left[\left(\frac{yS_0}{(T-t)x} - \frac{KTS_0}{(T-t)x} + \frac{\Lambda_{T-t}}{T-t} \right)^+ \right]$$

$$\leqslant \frac{(T-t)x}{TS_0} \mathbb{E}^* \left[\left(\frac{yS_0}{(T-t)x} - \frac{KTS_0}{(T-t)x} + S_{T-t} \right)^+ \right]$$

$$= \mathbb{E}^* \left[\left(\frac{y}{T} - K + \frac{(T-t)xS_{T-t}}{TS_0} \right)^+ \right], \qquad x, y > 0,$$

which yields (13.7). $\qquad\qquad\square$

The right-hand side of the bound (13.7) can be computed from the Black–Scholes formula as

$$\mathrm{e}^{-(T-t)r} \mathbb{E}^* \left[\left(\frac{1}{T} \int_0^t S_u du + \frac{T-t}{T} S_T - K \right)^+ \middle| \mathcal{F}_t \right]$$

$$= \frac{T-t}{T} \mathrm{e}^{-(T-t)r} \mathbb{E}^* \left[\left(S_T + \frac{1}{T-t} \int_0^t S_u du - \frac{KT}{T-t} \right)^+ \middle| \mathcal{F}_t \right]$$

$$= \frac{T-t}{T} \mathrm{Bl} \left(S_t, \frac{KT}{T-t} - \frac{1}{T-t} \int_0^t S_u du, \sigma, r, T-t \right), \quad 0 \leqslant t < T.$$

See also Proposition 3.2-(ii) of Geman and Yor (1993) for lower bounds when r takes negative values. We also have the following bound which yields the behavior of Asian call option prices in large time.

Proposition 13.4. *Assume that $r \geqslant 0$. The Asian call option price satisfies the bound*

$$\mathrm{e}^{-(T-t)r} \mathbb{E}^* \left[\left(\frac{1}{T} \int_0^T S_u du - K \right)^+ \middle| \mathcal{F}_t \right] \leqslant \frac{\mathrm{e}^{-(T-t)r}}{T} \int_0^t S_u du + S_t \frac{1 - \mathrm{e}^{-(T-t)r}}{rT},$$

$t \in [0, T]$, *and tends to zero (almost surely) as time to maturity T tends to infinity:*

$$\lim_{T \to \infty} \left(\mathrm{e}^{-(T-t)r} \mathbb{E}^* \left[\left(\frac{1}{T} \int_0^T S_u du - K \right)^+ \middle| \mathcal{F}_t \right] \right) = 0, \quad t \geqslant 0.$$

Proof. Using the inequality $(x - K)^+ \leqslant x$ for $x \geqslant 0$, we have the bound

$$0 \leqslant \mathrm{e}^{-(T-t)r} \mathbb{E}^* \left[\left(\frac{1}{T} \int_0^T S_u du - K \right)^+ \middle| \mathcal{F}_t \right]$$

$$\leqslant \mathrm{e}^{-(T-t)r} \mathbb{E}^* \left[\frac{1}{T} \int_0^T S_u du \middle| \mathcal{F}_t \right]$$

$$= \mathrm{e}^{-(T-t)r} \mathbb{E}^* \left[\frac{1}{T} \int_0^t S_u du \middle| \mathcal{F}_t \right] + \mathrm{e}^{-(T-t)r} \mathbb{E}^* \left[\frac{1}{T} \int_t^T S_u du \middle| \mathcal{F}_t \right]$$

$$= \frac{\mathrm{e}^{-(T-t)r}}{T} \int_0^t \mathbb{E}^* [S_u \mid \mathcal{F}_t] du + \frac{1}{T} \mathrm{e}^{-(T-t)r} \int_t^T \mathbb{E}^* [S_u \mid \mathcal{F}_t] du$$

$$= \mathrm{e}^{-(T-t)r} \frac{1}{T} \int_0^t S_u du + \frac{1}{T} \mathrm{e}^{-(T-t)r} \int_t^T \mathrm{e}^{(u-t)r} S_t du$$

$$= \frac{1}{T} e^{-(T-t)r} \int_0^t S_u du + \frac{S_t}{T} \int_t^T e^{-(T-u)r} du$$

$$= \frac{1}{T} e^{-(T-t)r} \int_0^t S_u du + S_t \frac{1 - e^{-(T-t)r}}{rT}.$$

$\square$

Note that as T tends to infinity the Black–Scholes European call price tends to S_t, *i.e.* we have

$$\lim_{T\to\infty} \left(e^{-(T-t)r} \, \mathbb{E}^*[(S_T - K)^+ \mid \mathcal{F}_t] \right) = S_t, \quad t \geqslant 0,$$

see Exercise 6.4-aiii).

13.2 Hartman–Watson Distribution

First, we note that the numerical computation of Asian call option prices can be done using the probability density function of

$$\Lambda_T = \int_0^T S_t dt.$$

In Yor (1992), Proposition 2, the joint probability density function of

$$(\Lambda_t, B_t) = \left(\int_0^t e^{\sigma B_s - p\sigma^2 s/2} ds, \, B_t - p\sigma t/2 \right), \quad t > 0,$$

has been computed in the case $\sigma = 2$, cf. also Dufresne (2001) and Matsumoto and Yor (2005). In the next proposition, we restate this result for an arbitrary variance parameter σ after rescaling. Let $\theta(v, \tau)$ denote the function defined as

$$\theta(v, \tau) = \frac{v \, e^{\pi^2/(2\tau)}}{\sqrt{2\pi^3\tau}} \int_0^\infty e^{-\xi^2/(2\tau)} \, e^{-v\cosh\xi} \sinh(\xi) \sin\left(\pi\xi/\tau\right) d\xi, \quad v, \tau > 0. \qquad (13.8)$$

Proposition 13.5. *For all $t > 0$ we have*

$$\mathbb{P}\left(\int_0^t e^{\sigma B_s - p\sigma^2 s/2} ds \in dy, \, B_t - p\frac{\sigma t}{2} \in dz \right)$$

$$= \frac{\sigma}{2} e^{-p\sigma z/2 - p^2\sigma^2 t/8} \exp\left(-2\frac{1 + e^{\sigma z}}{\sigma^2 y} \right) \theta\left(\frac{4 e^{\sigma z/2}}{\sigma^2 y}, \frac{\sigma^2 t}{4} \right) \frac{dy}{y} dz,$$

$y > 0, \, z \in \mathbb{R}$.

The expression of this probability density function can then be used for the pricing of options on average such as (13.3), as

$$f(t, x, y) = e^{-(T-t)r} \, \mathbb{E}^*\left[\phi\left(y + x \int_0^{T-t} \frac{S_v}{S_0} dv, \, x\frac{S_{T-t}}{S_0} \right) \right]$$

$$= e^{-(T-t)r}$$

$$\times \int_0^\infty \phi\left(y + xz, \, x\, e^{\sigma u + (T-t)r - (T-t)\sigma^2/2} \right) \mathbb{P}\left(\int_0^{T-t} \frac{S_v}{S_0} dv \in dz, \, B_{T-t} \in du \right)$$

$$
= \frac{\sigma}{2} e^{-(T-t)r+(T-t)p^2\sigma^2/8} \int_0^\infty \int_{-\infty}^\infty \phi\left(y + xz, x\, e^{\sigma u + (T-t)r - (T-t)(1+p)\sigma^2/2}\right)
$$

$$
\times \exp\left(-2\frac{1 + e^{\sigma u - (T-t)p\sigma^2/2}}{\sigma^2 z} - \frac{p}{2}\sigma u\right) \theta\left(\frac{4 e^{\sigma u/2 - (T-t)p\sigma^2/4}}{\sigma^2 z}, \frac{(T-t)\sigma^2}{4}\right) du \frac{dz}{z}
$$

$$
= e^{-(T-t)r - (T-t)p^2\sigma^2/8} \int_0^\infty \int_0^\infty \phi\left(y + x/z, xv^2\, e^{(T-t)r - (T-t)\sigma^2/2}\right)
$$

$$
\times v^{-1-p} \exp\left(-2z\frac{1+v^2}{\sigma^2}\right) \theta\left(\frac{4vz}{\sigma^2}, \frac{(T-t)\sigma^2}{4}\right) dv \frac{dz}{z},
$$

which actually stands as a triple integral due to the definition (13.8) of $\theta(v, \tau)$. Note that here the order of integration between du and dz cannot be exchanged without particular precautions, at the risk of wrong computations.

By repeating the argument of (13.3) for $\phi(x, y) := (x - K)^+$, the Asian call option can be priced as

$$
e^{-(T-t)r} \mathbb{E}^*\left[\left(\frac{1}{T}\int_0^T S_u du - K\right)^+ \Big| \mathcal{F}_t\right]
$$

$$
= e^{-(T-t)r} \mathbb{E}^*\left[\left(\frac{1}{T}\left(\Lambda_t + \int_t^T S_u du\right) - K\right)^+ \Big| \mathcal{F}_t\right]
$$

$$
= e^{-(T-t)r} \mathbb{E}^*\left[\left(\frac{1}{T}\left(y + x\int_t^T \frac{S_u}{S_t} du\right) - K\right)^+ \Big| \mathcal{F}_t\right]_{x=S_t,\ y=\Lambda_t}
$$

$$
= e^{-(T-t)r} \mathbb{E}^*\left[\left(\frac{1}{T}\left(y + x\int_0^{T-t} \frac{S_u}{S_0} du\right) - K\right)^+\right]_{x=S_t,\ y=\Lambda_t}.
$$

Hence the Asian call option can be priced as

$$
f(t, S_t, \Lambda_t) = e^{-(T-t)r} \mathbb{E}^*\left[\left(\frac{1}{T}\int_0^T S_u du - K\right)^+ \Big| \mathcal{F}_t\right],
$$

where the function $f(t, x, y)$ is given by

$$
f(t, x, y) = e^{-(T-t)r} \mathbb{E}^*\left[\left(\frac{1}{T}\left(y + x\int_0^{T-t} \frac{S_u}{S_0} du\right) - K\right)^+\right]
$$

$$
= e^{-(T-t)r} \mathbb{E}^*\left[\left(\frac{1}{T}\left(y + \frac{x}{S_0}\Lambda_{T-t}\right) - K\right)^+\right], \quad x, y > 0. \tag{13.9}
$$

From Proposition 13.5, we deduce the marginal probability density function of Λ_T, also called the Hartman–Watson distribution see *e.g.* Barrieu et al. (2004).

Proposition 13.6. *The probability density function of*

$$
\Lambda_T := \int_0^T e^{\sigma B_t - p\sigma^2 t/2} dt,
$$

is given by

$$
\mathbb{P}\left(\int_0^T e^{\sigma B_t - p\sigma^2 t/2} dt \in du\right)
$$

$$
= \frac{\sigma}{2u} e^{p^2\sigma^2 T/8} \int_{-\infty}^{\infty} \exp\left(-2\frac{1 + e^{\sigma v - p\sigma^2 T/2}}{\sigma^2 u} - \frac{p}{2}\sigma v\right) \theta\left(\frac{4 e^{\sigma v/2 - p\sigma^2 T/4}}{\sigma^2 u}, \frac{\sigma^2 T}{4}\right) dv du
$$

$$
= e^{-p^2\sigma^2 T/8} \int_0^{\infty} v^{-1-p} \exp\left(-2\frac{1 + v^2}{\sigma^2 u}\right) \theta\left(\frac{4v}{\sigma^2 u}, \frac{\sigma^2 T}{4}\right) dv \frac{du}{u},
$$

$u > 0$.

From Proposition 13.6, we get

$$
\mathbb{P}(\Lambda_T / S_0 \in du) = \mathbb{P}\left(\int_0^T S_t dt \in du\right) \tag{13.10}
$$

$$
= e^{-p^2\sigma^2 T/8} \int_0^{\infty} v^{-1-p} \exp\left(-2\frac{1 + v^2}{\sigma^2 u}\right) \theta\left(\frac{4v}{\sigma^2 u}, \frac{\sigma^2 T}{4}\right) dv \frac{du}{u},
$$

where $S_t = S_0 e^{\sigma B_t - p\sigma^2 t/2}$ and $p = 1 - 2r/\sigma^2$. By (13.9), this probability density function can then be used for the pricing of Asian options, as

$$
\begin{aligned}
f(t, x, y) &= e^{-(T-t)r} \mathbb{E}^*\left[\left(\frac{1}{T}\left(y + \frac{x}{S_0}\Lambda_{T-t}\right) - K\right)^+\right] \tag{13.11} \\
&= e^{-(T-t)r} \int_0^{\infty}\left(\frac{y + xz}{T} - K\right)^+ \mathbb{P}(\Lambda_{T-t} / S_0 \in dz) \\
&= e^{-(T-t)r} \frac{\sigma}{2} e^{-(T-t)p^2\sigma^2/8} \int_0^{\infty} \int_0^{\infty}\left(\frac{y + xz}{T} - K\right)^+ \\
&\quad \times v^{-1-p} \exp\left(-2\frac{1 + v^2}{\sigma^2 z}\right) \theta\left(\frac{4v}{\sigma^2 z}, (T-t)\frac{\sigma^2}{4}\right) dv \frac{dz}{z} \\
&= \frac{1}{T} e^{-(T-t)r - (T-t)p^2\sigma^2/8} \int_{0 \vee (KT-y)/x}^{\infty} \int_0^{\infty} (xz + y - KT) \\
&\quad \times \exp\left(-2\frac{1 + v^2}{\sigma^2 z}\right) \theta\left(\frac{4v}{\sigma^2 z}, (T-t)\frac{\sigma^2}{4}\right) dv \frac{dz}{z} \\
&= \frac{4x}{\sigma^2 T} e^{-(T-t)r - (T-t)p^2\sigma^2/8} \int_0^{\infty} \int_0^{\infty}\left(\frac{1}{z} - \frac{(KT - y)\sigma^2}{4x}\right)^+ \\
&\quad \times v^{-1-p} \exp\left(-z\frac{1 + v^2}{2}\right) \theta\left(vz, (T-t)\frac{\sigma^2}{4}\right) dv \frac{dz}{z},
\end{aligned}
$$

cf. Theorem in § 5 of Carr and Schröder (2004), which is actually a triple integral due to the definition (13.8) of $\theta(v, t)$. Note that since the integrals are not absolutely convergent, here the order of integration between dv and dz cannot be exchanged without particular precautions, at the risk of wrong computations.

13.3   Laplace Transform Method

The time Laplace transform of the rescaled option price

$$C(t) := \mathbb{E}^* \left[\left(\frac{1}{t} \int_0^t S_u du - K \right)^+ \right], \qquad t > 0,$$

as

$$\int_0^\infty e^{-\lambda t} C(t) dt = \frac{\int_0^{K/2} e^{-x} x^{-2+(p+\sqrt{2\lambda+p^2})/2}(1-2Kx)^{2+(\sqrt{2\lambda+p^2}-p)/2}dx}{\lambda(\lambda-2+2p)\Gamma\left(-1+(p+\sqrt{2\lambda+p^2})/2\right)},$$

with here $\sigma := 2$, and $\Gamma(z)$ denotes the gamma function, see Relation (3.10) in Geman and Yor (1993). This expression can be used for pricing by numerical inversion of the Laplace transform using *e.g.* the Widder method, the Gaver-Stehfest method, the Durbin-Crump method, or the Papoulis method. The following Figure 13.3 represents Asian call option prices computed by the Geman and Yor (1993) method.

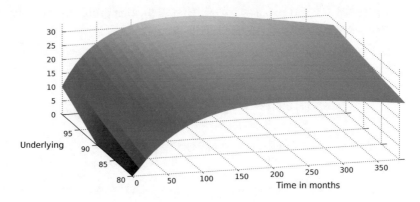

Figure 13.3: Graph of Asian call option prices with $\sigma = 1$, $r = 0.1$ and $K = 90$.

We refer to *e.g.* Carr and Schröder (2004), Dufresne (2000), and references therein for more results on Asian option pricing using the probability density function of the averaged geometric Brownian motion.

Figure 9.4 presents a graph of implied volatility surface for Asian options on light sweet crude oil futures.

13.4   Moment Matching Approximations

Lognormal approximation

Other numerical approaches to the pricing of Asian options include Levy (1992), Turn-bull and Wakeman (1992) which rely on approximations of the average price distribution based on the lognormal distribution. The lognormal distribution has the probability density function

$$g(x) = \frac{1}{\eta\sqrt{2\pi}} e^{-(\mu - \log x)^2/(2\eta^2)} \frac{dx}{x}, \qquad x > 0,$$

where $\mu \in \mathbb{R}$, $\eta > 0$, with moments

$$\mathbb{E}[X] = e^{\mu + \eta^2/2} \quad \text{and} \quad \mathbb{E}[X^2] = e^{2\mu + 2\eta^2}. \tag{13.12}$$

The approximation is implemented by matching the above first two moments to those of time integral

$$\Lambda_T := \int_0^T S_t dt$$

of geometric Brownian motion

$$S_t = S_0 e^{\sigma B_t + (r - \sigma^2/2)t}, \qquad 0 \leqslant t \leqslant T,$$

as computed in the next proposition, cf. also (7) and (8) page 480 of Levy (1992), and Exercise 13.1.

Proposition 13.7. *The first and second moments of Λ_T are given by*

$$\mathbb{E}^*[\Lambda_T] = S_0 \frac{e^{rT} - 1}{r},$$

and

$$\mathbb{E}^*\left[(\Lambda_T)^2\right] = 2S_0^2 \frac{r\, e^{(\sigma^2 + 2r)T} - (\sigma^2 + 2r) e^{rT} + (\sigma^2 + r)}{(\sigma^2 + r)(\sigma^2 + 2r)r}.$$

Proof. The computation of the first moment is straightforward. We have

$$\begin{aligned}
\mathbb{E}^*[\Lambda_T] &= \mathbb{E}^*\left[\int_0^T S_u du\right] \\
&= \int_0^T \mathbb{E}^*[S_u] du \\
&= S_0 \int_0^T e^{ru} du \\
&= S_0 \frac{e^{rT} - 1}{r}.
\end{aligned}$$

For the second moment we have, letting $p := 1 - 2r/\sigma^2$,

$$\begin{aligned}
\mathbb{E}^*\left[(\Lambda_T)^2\right] &= S_0^2 \int_0^T \int_0^T e^{-p\sigma^2 a/2 - p\sigma^2 b/2}\, \mathbb{E}^*\left[e^{\sigma B_a} e^{\sigma B_b}\right] db\, da \\
&= 2S_0^2 \int_0^T \int_0^a e^{-p\sigma^2 a/2 - p\sigma^2 b/2}\, e^{(a+b)\sigma^2/2} e^{b\sigma^2} db\, da \\
&= 2S_0^2 \int_0^T e^{-(p-1)\sigma^2 a/2} \int_0^a e^{-(p-3)\sigma^2 b/2} db\, da \\
&= \frac{4S_0^2}{(p-3)\sigma^2} \int_0^T e^{-(p-1)\sigma^2 a/2} \left(1 - e^{-(p-3)\sigma^2 a/2}\right) da \\
&= \frac{4S_0^2}{(p-3)\sigma^2} \int_0^T e^{-(p-1)\sigma^2 a/2} da - \frac{4S_0^2}{(p-3)\sigma^2} \int_0^T e^{-(p-1)\sigma^2 a/2}\, e^{-(p-3)\sigma^2 a/2} da \\
&= \frac{8S_0^2}{(p-3)(p-1)\sigma^4} \left(1 - e^{-(p-1)\sigma^2 T/2}\right) - \frac{4S_0^2}{(p-3)\sigma^2} \int_0^T e^{-(2p-4)\sigma^2 a/2} da
\end{aligned}$$

$$= \frac{8S_0^2}{(p-3)(p-1)\sigma^4}(1 - \mathrm{e}^{-(p-1)\sigma^2 T/2}) - \frac{4S_0^2}{(p-3)(p-2)\sigma^4}(1 - \mathrm{e}^{-(p-2)\sigma^2 T})$$

$$= 2S_0^2 \frac{r\,\mathrm{e}^{(\sigma^2+2r)T} - (\sigma^2+2r)\,\mathrm{e}^{rT} + (\sigma^2+r)}{(\sigma^2+r)(\sigma^2+2r)r},$$

since $r - \sigma^2/2 = -p\sigma^2/2$. $\qquad\qquad\qquad\qquad\qquad\qquad\qquad\qquad\square$

By matching the first and second moments

$$\mathbb{E}[\Lambda_T] \simeq \mathrm{e}^{\widehat{\mu}_T + \widehat{\eta}_T^2 T/2} \quad \text{and} \quad \mathbb{E}\left[\Lambda_T^2\right] \simeq \mathrm{e}^{2(\widehat{\mu}_T + \widehat{\eta}_T^2 T)}$$

of the lognormal distribution with the moments of Proposition 13.7 we estimate $\widehat{\mu}_T$ and $\widehat{\eta}_T$ as

$$\widehat{\eta}_T^2 = \frac{1}{T}\log\left(\frac{E[\Lambda_T^2]}{(\mathbb{E}^*[\Lambda_T])^2}\right) \quad \text{and} \quad \widehat{\mu}_T = \frac{1}{T}\log \mathbb{E}^*[\Lambda_T] - \frac{1}{2}\widehat{\eta}_T^2.$$

Under this approximation, the probability density function φ_{Λ_T} of $\Lambda_T = \int_0^T S_t dt$ is approximated by the lognormal probability density function

$$\varphi_{\Lambda_T}(x) \approx \frac{1}{x\sigma_{t,T}\sqrt{2(T-t)\pi}} \exp\left(-\frac{(\widehat{\mu}_T - \log x)^2}{2(T-t)\widehat{\eta}_T^2}\right), \quad x > 0.$$

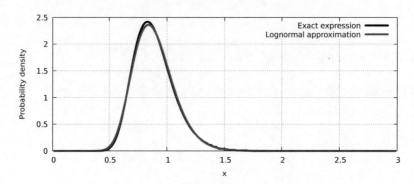

Figure 13.4: Lognormal approximation for the probability density function of Λ_T.

As a consequence of Lemma 7.7 we find the approximation

$$\mathrm{e}^{-rT}\,\mathbb{E}^*\left[\left(\frac{1}{T}\int_0^T S_t dt - K\right)^+\right] = \mathrm{e}^{-rT}\int_0^\infty \left(\frac{x}{T} - K\right)^+ \varphi_{\Lambda_T}(x)dx$$

$$\simeq \frac{\mathrm{e}^{-rT}}{\sigma_{t,T}\sqrt{2(T-t)\pi}}\int_0^\infty \left(\frac{x}{T} - K\right)^+ \exp\left(-\frac{(\widehat{\mu}_T - \log x)^2}{2(T-t)\widehat{\eta}_T^2}\right)\frac{dx}{x}$$

$$= \frac{1}{T}\mathrm{e}^{\widehat{\mu}_T + \widehat{\eta}_T^2 T/2}\Phi(d_1) - K\Phi(d_2) \qquad\qquad\qquad (13.13)$$

$$= \frac{\mathbb{E}[\Lambda_T]}{T}\Phi(d_1) - K\Phi(d_2)$$

$$= \mathrm{Bl}\left(\frac{\mathbb{E}[\Lambda_T]}{T}, K, 0, \widehat{\eta}_T, T - t\right),$$

where

$$d_1 = \frac{\log(\mathbb{E}^*[\Lambda_T]/(KT))}{\widehat{\eta}_T\sqrt{T}} + \widehat{\eta}_T\frac{\sqrt{T}}{2} = \frac{\widehat{\mu}_T T + \widehat{\eta}_T^2 T - \log(KT)}{\widehat{\eta}_T\sqrt{T}}$$

and

$$d_2 = d_1 - \widehat{\eta}_T \sqrt{T} = \frac{\log(\mathbb{E}^*[\Lambda_T]/(KT))}{\widehat{\eta}_T \sqrt{T}} - \widehat{\eta}_T \frac{\sqrt{T}}{2}.$$

The next Figure 13.5 compares the lognormal approximation to a Monte Carlo estimate of Asian call option prices with $\sigma = 0.5$, $r = 0.05$ and $K/S_t = 1.1$.

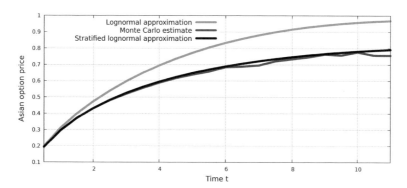

Figure 13.5: Lognormal approximation to the Asian call option price.

Figure 13.5 also includes the stratified approximation

$$e^{-rT} \mathbb{E}\left[\left(\frac{1}{T} \int_0^T S_t dt - K \right)^+ \right] \tag{13.14}$$

$$= e^{-rT} \int_0^\infty \mathbb{E}\left[\left(\frac{x}{T} - K \right)^+ \,\Big|\, S_T = y \right] \varphi_{\Lambda_T | S_T = y}(x) d\mathbb{P}(S_T \leqslant y) dx$$

$$\simeq \frac{e^{-rT}}{T} \int_0^\infty \left(e^{-p(y/x)\sigma^2(y/x)T/2 + \sigma^2(y/x)T/2} \Phi(d_+(K,y,x)) - KT\Phi(d_-(K,y,x)) \right)$$
$$\times d\mathbb{P}(S_T \leqslant y) dx,$$

cf. Privault and Yu (2016), where

$$d_\pm(K,y,x) := \frac{1}{2\sigma(y/x)\sqrt{T}} \log\left(\frac{2x(b_T(y/x) - (1+y/x)a_T(y/x))}{\sigma^2 K^2 T^2} \right) \pm \frac{\sigma(y/x)\sqrt{T}}{2}$$

and

$$\begin{cases} \sigma^2(z) := \dfrac{1}{T} \log\left(\dfrac{2}{\sigma^2 a_T(z)} \left(\dfrac{b_T(z)}{a_T(z)} - 1 - z \right) \right), \\[3mm] a_T(z) := \dfrac{1}{\sigma^2 p(z)} \left(\Phi\left(\dfrac{\log z}{\sqrt{\sigma^2 T}} + \dfrac{1}{2}\sqrt{\sigma^2 T} \right) - \Phi\left(\dfrac{\log z}{\sqrt{\sigma^2 T}} - \dfrac{1}{2}\sqrt{\sigma^2 T} \right) \right), \\[3mm] b_T(z) := \dfrac{1}{\sigma^2 q(z)} \left(\Phi\left(\dfrac{\log z}{\sqrt{\sigma^2 T}} + \sqrt{\sigma^2 T} \right) - \Phi\left(\dfrac{\log z}{\sqrt{\sigma^2 T}} - \sqrt{\sigma^2 T} \right) \right), \end{cases}$$

and

$$p(z) := \frac{1}{\sqrt{2\pi\sigma^2 T}} e^{-(\sigma^2 T/2 + \log z)^2/(2\sigma^2 T)}, \quad q(z) := \frac{1}{\sqrt{2\pi\sigma^2 T}} e^{-(\sigma^2 T + \log z)^2/(2\sigma^2 T)}.$$

Conditioning on the geometric mean price

Asian options on the arithmetic average

$$\frac{1}{T} \int_0^T S_t dt$$

have been priced by conditioning on the geometric mean underlying price

$$G := \exp\left(\frac{1}{T} \int_0^T \log S_t dt\right) \leqslant \exp\left(\log\left(\frac{1}{T} \int_0^T S_t dt\right)\right) = \frac{1}{T} \int_0^T S_t dt$$

in Curran (1994), as

$$e^{-rT} \, \mathbb{E}^*\left[\left(\frac{1}{T} \int_0^T S_u du - K\right)^+\right]$$

$$= e^{-rT} \int_0^\infty \mathbb{E}^*\left[\left(\frac{1}{T} \int_0^T S_u du - K\right)^+ \middle| G = x\right] d\mathbb{P}(G \leqslant x)$$

$$= e^{-rT} \int_0^K \mathbb{E}^*\left[\left(\frac{1}{T} \int_0^T S_u du - K\right)^+ \middle| G = x\right] d\mathbb{P}(G \leqslant x)$$

$$+ e^{-rT} \int_K^\infty \mathbb{E}^*\left[\left(\frac{1}{T} \int_0^T S_u du - K\right)^+ \middle| G = x\right] d\mathbb{P}(G \leqslant x)$$

$$= C_1 + C_2,$$

where

$$C_1 := e^{-rT} \int_0^K \mathbb{E}^*\left[\left(\frac{1}{T} \int_0^T S_u du - K\right)^+ \middle| G = x\right] d\mathbb{P}(G \leqslant x),$$

and

$$C_2 := e^{-rT} \int_K^\infty \mathbb{E}^*\left[\left(\frac{1}{T} \int_0^T S_u du - K\right)^+ \middle| G = x\right] d\mathbb{P}(G \leqslant x)$$

$$= e^{-rT} \int_K^\infty \mathbb{E}^*\left[\frac{1}{T} \int_0^T S_u du - K \middle| G = x\right] d\mathbb{P}(G \leqslant x)$$

$$= \frac{e^{-rT}}{T} \int_K^\infty \mathbb{E}^*\left[\int_0^T S_u du \middle| G = x\right] d\mathbb{P}(G \leqslant x) - K e^{-rT} \int_K^\infty d\mathbb{P}(G \leqslant x)$$

$$= \frac{e^{-rT}}{T} \mathbb{E}^*\left[\int_0^T S_u du \mathbb{1}_{\{G \geqslant K\}}\right] - K e^{-rT} \mathbb{P}(G \geqslant K).$$

The term C_1 can be estimated by a lognormal approximation given that $G = x$. As for C_2, we note that

$$G = \exp\left(\frac{1}{T} \int_0^T \log S_t dt\right)$$

$$= \exp\left(\frac{1}{T} \int_0^T \left(\mu t + \sigma B_t - \frac{\sigma^2 t}{2}\right) dt\right)$$

$$= \exp\left(\frac{T}{2}\left(\mu - \frac{\sigma^2}{2}\right) + \frac{\sigma}{T} \int_0^T B_t dt\right),$$

hence

$$\log G = \frac{T}{2}(\mu - \sigma^2/2) + \frac{\sigma}{T}\int_0^T B_t dt$$

has the Gaussian distribution $\mathcal{N}\left((\mu - \sigma^2/2)T/2, \sigma^2 T/3\right)$ with mean $(\mu - \sigma^2/2)T/2$, and variance

$$
\begin{aligned}
\mathbb{E}\left[\left(\int_0^T B_t dt\right)^2\right] &= \mathbb{E}\left[\int_0^T\int_0^T B_s B_t ds dt\right] \\
&= \int_0^T\int_0^T \mathbb{E}[B_s B_t] ds dt \\
&= 2\int_0^T\int_0^t s\, ds dt \\
&= \int_0^T t^2 dt \\
&= \frac{T^3}{3}.
\end{aligned}
$$

Hence, we have

$$
\begin{aligned}
\mathbb{P}(G \geqslant K) &= \mathbb{P}(\log G \geqslant \log K) \\
&= \mathbb{P}\left(\frac{T}{2}\left(\mu - \frac{\sigma^2}{2}\right) + \frac{\sigma}{T}\int_0^T B_t dt \geqslant \log K\right) \\
&= \mathbb{P}\left(\int_0^T B_t dt \geqslant \frac{T}{\sigma}\left(-\frac{T}{2}\left(\mu - \frac{\sigma^2}{2}\right) + \log K\right)\right) \\
&= \Phi\left(\frac{\sqrt{3}}{\sigma\sqrt{T}}\left(\frac{T}{2}\left(\mu - \frac{\sigma^2}{2}\right) - \log K\right)\right).
\end{aligned}
$$

Basket options

Basket options on the portfolio

$$A_T := \sum_{k=1}^N \alpha_k S_T^{(k)}$$

have also been priced in Milevsky (1998) by approximating A_T by a lognormal or a reciprocal gamma random variable, see also Deelstra et al. (2004) for additional conditioning on the geometric average of asset prices.

Asian basket options

Moment matching techniques combined with conditioning have been applied to Asian basket options in Deelstra et al. (2010). See also Dahl and Benth (2002) for the pricing of Asian basket options using quasi Monte Carlo simulation.

13.5   PDE Method

Two variables

The price at time t of the Asian call option with payoff (13.1) can be written as

$$f(t, S_t, \Lambda_t) = e^{-(T-t)r} \, \mathbb{E}^* \left[\left(\frac{1}{T} \int_0^T S_u du - K \right)^+ \Bigg| \mathcal{F}_t \right], \quad 0 \leqslant t \leqslant T. \qquad (13.15)$$

Next, we derive the Black–Scholes partial differential equation (PDE) for the value of a self-financing portfolio. Until the end of this chapter we model the asset price $(S_t)_{t \in [0,T]}$ as

$$dS_t = \mu S_t dt + \sigma S_t dB_t, \qquad t \geqslant 0, \qquad (13.16)$$

where $(B_t)_{t \in \mathbb{R}_+}$ is a standard Brownian motion under the historical probability measure $\mathbb{P}$.

Proposition 13.8. *Let $(\eta_t, \xi_t)_{t \in \mathbb{R}_+}$ be a self-financing portfolio strategy whose value $V_t := \eta_t A_t + \xi_t S_t$, $t \geqslant 0$, takes the form*

$$V_t = f(t, S_t, \Lambda_t), \qquad t \geqslant 0,$$

where $f \in \mathcal{C}^{1,2,1}((0,T) \times (0,\infty)^2)$ is given by (13.15). Then, the function $f(t,x,y)$ satisfies the PDE

$$rf(t,x,y) = \frac{\partial f}{\partial t}(t,x,y) + x\frac{\partial f}{\partial y}(t,x,y) + rx\frac{\partial f}{\partial x}(t,x,y) + \frac{1}{2}x^2\sigma^2\frac{\partial^2 f}{\partial x^2}(t,x,y), \quad (13.17)$$

$0 \leqslant t \leqslant T$, $x > 0$, *under the boundary conditions*

$$\begin{cases} f(t,0^+,y) = \lim_{x \searrow 0} f(t,x,y) = e^{-(T-t)r} \left(\dfrac{y}{T} - K \right)^+, & (13.18a) \\[2mm] f(t,x,0^+) = \lim_{y \searrow 0} f(t,x,y) = 0, & (13.18b) \\[2mm] f(T,x,y) = \left(\dfrac{y}{T} - K \right)^+, & (13.18c) \end{cases}$$

$0 \leqslant t \leqslant T$, $x > 0$, $y \geqslant 0$,

and ξ_t is given by

$$\xi_t = \frac{\partial f}{\partial x}(t, S_t, \Lambda_t), \qquad 0 \leqslant t \leqslant T. \qquad (13.19)$$

Proof. We note that the self-financing condition (5.8) implies

$$\begin{aligned} dV_t &= \eta_t dA_t + \xi_t dS_t \\ &= r\eta_t A_t dt + \mu \xi_t S_t dt + \sigma \xi_t S_t dB_t \\ &= rV_t dt + (\mu - r)\xi_t S_t dt + \sigma \xi_t S_t dB_t, \qquad t \geqslant 0. \end{aligned} \qquad (13.20)$$

Since $d\Lambda_t = S_t dt$, an application of Itô's formula to $f(t, x, y)$ leads to

$$
\begin{aligned}
dV_t &= f(t, S_t, \Lambda_t) = \frac{\partial f}{\partial t}(t, S_t, \Lambda_t)dt + \frac{\partial f}{\partial y}(t, S_t, \Lambda_t)d\Lambda_t \\
&\quad + \mu S_t \frac{\partial f}{\partial x}(t, S_t, \Lambda_t)dt + \frac{1}{2}S_t^2\sigma^2\frac{\partial^2 f}{\partial x^2}(t, S_t, \Lambda_t)dt + \sigma S_t\frac{\partial f}{\partial x}(t, S_t, \Lambda_t)dB_t \\
&= \frac{\partial f}{\partial t}(t, S_t, \Lambda_t)dt + S_t\frac{\partial f}{\partial y}(t, S_t, \Lambda_t)dt \\
&\quad + \mu S_t \frac{\partial f}{\partial x}(t, S_t, \Lambda_t)dt + \frac{1}{2}S_t^2\sigma^2\frac{\partial^2 f}{\partial x^2}(t, S_t, \Lambda_t)dt + \sigma S_t\frac{\partial f}{\partial x}(t, S_t, \Lambda_t)dB_t.
\end{aligned}
\tag{13.21}
$$

By respective identification of components in dB_t and dt in (13.20) and (13.21), we get

$$
\begin{cases}
r\eta_t \Lambda_t dt + \mu\xi_t S_t dt = \dfrac{\partial f}{\partial t}(t, S_t, \Lambda_t)dt + S_t\dfrac{\partial f}{\partial y}(t, S_t, \Lambda_t)dt + \mu S_t\dfrac{\partial f}{\partial x}(t, S_t, \Lambda_t)dt \\
\qquad\qquad\qquad\qquad + \dfrac{1}{2}S_t^2\sigma^2\dfrac{\partial^2 f}{\partial x^2}(t, S_t, \Lambda_t)dt, \\[2ex]
\xi_t S_t \sigma dB_t = S_t\sigma\dfrac{\partial f}{\partial x}(t, S_t, \Lambda_t)dB_t,
\end{cases}
$$

hence

$$
\begin{cases}
rV_t - r\xi_t S_t = \dfrac{\partial f}{\partial t}(t, S_t, \Lambda_t) + S_t\dfrac{\partial f}{\partial y}(t, S_t, \Lambda_t)dt + \dfrac{1}{2}S_t^2\sigma^2\dfrac{\partial^2 f}{\partial x^2}(t, S_t, \Lambda_t), \\[2ex]
\xi_t = \dfrac{\partial f}{\partial x}(t, S_t, \Lambda_t),
\end{cases}
$$

i.e.

$$
\begin{cases}
rf(t, S_t, \Lambda_t) = \dfrac{\partial f}{\partial t}(t, S_t, \Lambda_t) + S_t\dfrac{\partial f}{\partial y}(t, S_t, \Lambda_t) + rS_t\dfrac{\partial f}{\partial x}(t, S_t, \Lambda_t) \\
\qquad\qquad\qquad + \dfrac{1}{2}S_t^2\sigma^2\dfrac{\partial^2 f}{\partial x^2}(t, S_t, \Lambda_t), \\[2ex]
\xi_t = \dfrac{\partial f}{\partial x}(t, S_t, \Lambda_t).
\end{cases}
$$

$\square$

Remarks.

i) We have $\xi_T = 0$ at maturity from (13.18c) and (13.19), which is consistent with the fact that the Asian option is cash-settled at maturity and, close to maturity, its payoff $(\Lambda_T/T - K)^+$ becomes less dependent on the underlying asset price S_T.

ii) If $\Lambda_t/T \geqslant K$, by Exercise 13.8 we have

$$
\begin{aligned}
f(t, S_t, \Lambda_t) &= e^{-(T-t)r}\,\mathbb{E}^*\!\left[\left(\frac{1}{T}\int_0^T S_u du - K\right)^+ \middle| \mathcal{F}_t\right] \\
&= e^{-(T-t)r}\left(\frac{\Lambda_t}{T} - K\right) + S_t\frac{1 - e^{-(T-t)r}}{rT},
\end{aligned}
\tag{13.22}
$$

$0 \leqslant t \leqslant T$. In particular, the function

$$f(t, x, y) = e^{-(T-t)r} \left(\frac{y}{T} - K \right) + x \frac{1 - e^{-(T-t)r}}{rT},$$

$0 \leqslant t \leqslant T$, $x > 0$, $y \geqslant KT$, solves the PDE (13.17).

iii) When $\Lambda_t / T \geqslant K$, the Delta ξ_t is given by

$$\xi_t = \frac{\partial f}{\partial x}(t, S_t, \Lambda_t) = \frac{1 - e^{-(T-t)r}}{rT}, \qquad 0 \leqslant t \leqslant T. \qquad (13.23)$$

Next, we examine two methods which allow one to reduce the Asian option pricing PDE from three variables (t, x, y) to two variables (t, z). Reduction of dimensionality can be of crucial importance when applying discretization scheme whose complexity are of the form N^d where N is the number of discretization steps and d is the dimension of the problem (curse of dimensionality).

(1) One variable with time-independent coefficients

Following Lamberton and Lapeyre (1996), page 91, we define the auxiliary process

$$Z_t := \frac{1}{S_t} \left(\frac{1}{T} \int_0^t S_u du - K \right) = \frac{1}{S_t} \left(\frac{\Lambda_t}{T} - K \right), \qquad 0 \leqslant t \leqslant T.$$

With this notation, the price of the Asian call option at time t becomes

$$e^{-(T-t)r} \, \mathbb{E}^* \left[\left(\frac{1}{T} \int_0^T S_u du - K \right)^+ \Big| \mathcal{F}_t \right] = e^{-(T-t)r} \, \mathbb{E}^* \left[S_T (Z_T)^+ \big| \mathcal{F}_t \right].$$

Lemma 13.9. *The price* (13.2) *at time t of the Asian call option with payoff* (13.1) *can be written as*

$$f(t, S_t, \Lambda_t) = S_t g(t, Z_t) \qquad (13.24)$$

$$= e^{-(T-t)r} \, \mathbb{E}^* \left[\left(\frac{1}{T} \int_0^T S_u du - K \right)^+ \Big| \mathcal{F}_t \right], \qquad t \in [0, T],$$

with the relation

$$f(t, x, y) = x g \left(t, \frac{1}{x} \left(\frac{y}{T} - K \right) \right), \qquad x > 0, \ y \geqslant 0, \ 0 \leqslant t \leqslant T,$$

where

$$g(t, z) = e^{-(T-t)r} \, \mathbb{E}^* \left[\left(z + \frac{1}{T} \int_0^{T-t} \frac{S_u}{S_0} du \right)^+ \right] \qquad (13.25)$$

$$= e^{-(T-t)r} \, \mathbb{E}^* \left[\left(z + \frac{\Lambda_{T-t}}{S_0 T} \right)^+ \right],$$

with the boundary condition

$$g(T, z) = z^+, \qquad z \in \mathbb{R}.$$

Proof. For $0 \leqslant s \leqslant t \leqslant T$, we have

$$d(S_t Z_t) = \frac{1}{T} d \left(\int_0^t S_u du - K \right) = \frac{S_t}{T} dt,$$

hence

$$S_t Z_t = S_s Z_s + \int_s^t d(S_u Z_u) = S_s Z_s + \int_s^t \frac{S_u}{T} du,$$

and therefore

$$\frac{S_t Z_t}{S_s} = Z_s + \frac{1}{T} \int_s^t \frac{S_u}{S_s} du, \qquad 0 \leqslant s \leqslant t \leqslant T.$$

Since for any $t \in [0, T]$, S_t is positive and $\mathcal{F}_t$-measurable, and S_u / S_t is independent of $\mathcal{F}_t$, $u \geqslant t$, we have:

$$
\begin{aligned}
\mathrm{e}^{-(T-t)r} \, \mathbb{E}^* \left[S_T (Z_T)^+ \mid \mathcal{F}_t \right] &= \mathrm{e}^{-(T-t)r} S_t \, \mathbb{E}^* \left[\left(\frac{S_T}{S_t} Z_T \right)^+ \middle| \mathcal{F}_t \right] \\
&= \mathrm{e}^{-(T-t)r} S_t \, \mathbb{E}^* \left[\left(Z_t + \frac{1}{T} \int_t^T \frac{S_u}{S_t} du \right)^+ \middle| \mathcal{F}_t \right] \\
&= \mathrm{e}^{-(T-t)r} S_t \, \mathbb{E}^* \left[\left(z + \frac{1}{T} \int_t^T \frac{S_u}{S_t} du \right)^+ \right]_{z=Z_t} \\
&= \mathrm{e}^{-(T-t)r} S_t \, \mathbb{E}^* \left[\left(z + \frac{1}{T} \int_0^{T-t} \frac{S_u}{S_0} du \right)^+ \right]_{z=Z_t} \\
&= \mathrm{e}^{-(T-t)r} S_t \, \mathbb{E}^* \left[\left(z + \frac{\Lambda_{T-t}}{S_0 T} \right)^+ \right]_{z=Z_t} \\
&= S_t g(t, Z_t),
\end{aligned}
$$

which proves (13.25). $\qquad\qquad\qquad\qquad\qquad\qquad\qquad\qquad\qquad\qquad\qquad\qquad\qquad\qquad$ $\square$

When $\Lambda_t / T \geqslant K$ we have $Z_t \geqslant 0$, hence in this case by (13.22) and (13.24) we find

$$g(t, Z_t) = \mathrm{e}^{-(T-t)r} Z_t + \frac{1 - \mathrm{e}^{-(T-t)r}}{rT}, \qquad 0 \leqslant t \leqslant T. \tag{13.26}$$

Note that as in (13.11), $g(t, z)$ can be computed from the probability density function (13.10) of Λ_{T-t}, as

$$
\begin{aligned}
g(t, z) &= \mathbb{E}^* \left[\left(z + \frac{\Lambda_{T-t}}{S_0 T} \right)^+ \right] \\
&= \int_0^\infty \left(z + \frac{u}{T} \right)^+ d\mathbb{P} \left(\frac{\Lambda_t}{S_0} \leqslant u \right) \\
&= \mathrm{e}^{-p^2 \sigma^2 t / 8} \\
&\quad \times \int_0^\infty \left(z + \frac{u}{T} \right)^+ \int_0^\infty v^{-1-p} \exp \left(-2 \frac{1 + v^2}{\sigma^2} \right) \theta \left(\frac{4v}{\sigma^2 u}, (T-t) \frac{\sigma^2}{4} \right) dv \frac{du}{u} \\
&= \mathrm{e}^{-p^2 \sigma^2 t / 8} \\
&\quad \times \int_{(-zT) \vee 0}^\infty \left(z + \frac{u}{T} \right) \int_0^\infty v^{-1-p} \exp \left(-2 \frac{1 + v^2}{\sigma^2} \right) \theta \left(\frac{4v}{\sigma^2 u}, (T-t) \frac{\sigma^2}{4} \right) dv \frac{du}{u}
\end{aligned}
$$

$$\begin{aligned}
= \quad & z\,e^{-p^2\sigma^2 t/8} \int_{(-zT)\vee 0}^{\infty} \int_0^{\infty} v^{-1-p} \exp\left(-2\frac{1+v^2}{\sigma^2}\right) \theta\left(\frac{4v}{\sigma^2 u}, (T-t)\frac{\sigma^2}{4}\right) dv\,\frac{du}{u} \\
& + \frac{1}{T} e^{-p^2\sigma^2 t/8} \int_{(-zT)\vee 0}^{\infty} \int_0^{\infty} v^{-1-p} \exp\left(-2\frac{1+v^2}{\sigma^2}\right) \theta\left(\frac{4v}{\sigma^2 u}, (T-t)\frac{\sigma^2}{4}\right) dv\,du.
\end{aligned}$$

The next proposition gives a replicating hedging strategy for Asian options.

Proposition 13.10. *(Rogers and Shi (1995)). Let $(\eta_t, \xi_t)_{t\in\mathbb{R}_+}$ be a self-financing portfolio strategy whose value $V_t := \eta_t A_t + \xi_t S_t$, $t \in [0, T]$, is given by*

$$V_t = S_t g(t, Z_t) = S_t g\left(t, \frac{1}{S_t}\left(\frac{\Lambda_t}{T} - K\right)\right), \qquad 0 \leqslant t \leqslant T,$$

where $g \in \mathcal{C}^{1,2}((0, T) \times (0, \infty))$ is given by (13.25). Then, the function $g(t, z)$ satisfies the PDE

$$\frac{\partial g}{\partial t}(t, z) + \left(\frac{1}{T} - rz\right)\frac{\partial g}{\partial z}(t, z) + \frac{1}{2}\sigma^2 z^2 \frac{\partial^2 g}{\partial z^2}(t, z) = 0, \qquad (13.27)$$

$0 \leqslant t \leqslant T$, *under the terminal condition*

$$g(T, z) = z^+, \qquad z \in \mathbb{R}, \qquad (13.28)$$

and the corresponding replicating portfolio Delta is given by

$$\xi_t = g(t, Z_t) - Z_t \frac{\partial g}{\partial z}(t, Z_t), \qquad 0 \leqslant t \leqslant T. \qquad (13.29)$$

Proof. By (13.16) and the Itô formula applied to $1/S_t$, we have

$$\begin{aligned}
d\left(\frac{1}{S_t}\right) &= -\frac{dS_t}{(S_t)^2} + \frac{2}{2}\frac{(dS_t)^2}{(S_t)^3} \\
&= \frac{1}{S_t}\left((-\mu + \sigma^2)\,dt - \sigma dB_t\right),
\end{aligned}$$

hence

$$\begin{aligned}
dZ_t &= d\left(\frac{1}{S_t}\left(\frac{\Lambda_t}{T} - K\right)\right) \\
&= d\left(\frac{\Lambda_t}{TS_t} - \frac{K}{S_t}\right) \\
&= \frac{1}{T}d\left(\frac{\Lambda_t}{S_t}\right) - K d\left(\frac{1}{S_t}\right) \\
&= \frac{1}{T}\frac{d\Lambda_t}{S_t} + \left(\frac{\Lambda_t}{T} - K\right)d\left(\frac{1}{S_t}\right) \\
&= \frac{dt}{T} + S_t Z_t d\left(\frac{1}{S_t}\right) \\
&= \frac{dt}{T} + Z_t\left(-\mu + \sigma^2\right)dt - Z_t \sigma dB_t.
\end{aligned}$$

By the self-financing condition (5.8) we have

$$
\begin{aligned}
dV_t &= \eta_t dA_t + \xi_t dS_t \\
&= r\eta_t A_t dt + \mu \xi_t S_t dt + \sigma \xi_t S_t dB_t \\
&= rV_t dt + (\mu - r)\xi_t S_t dt + \sigma \xi_t S_t dB_t, \qquad t \geqslant 0.
\end{aligned}
\tag{13.30}
$$

Another application of Itô's formula to $f(t, S_t, Z_t) = S_t g(t, Z_t)$ leads to

$$
\begin{aligned}
d(S_t g(t, Z_t)) &= g(t, Z_t)dS_t + S_t dg(t, Z_t) + dS_t \cdot dg(t, Z_t) \\
&= g(t, Z_t)dS_t + S_t \frac{\partial g}{\partial t}(t, Z_t)dt + S_t \frac{\partial g}{\partial z}(t, Z_t)dZ_t \\
&\quad + \frac{1}{2}S_t \frac{\partial^2 g}{\partial z^2}(t, Z_t)(dZ_t)^2 + dS_t \cdot dg(t, Z_t) \\
&= \mu S_t g(t, Z_t)dt + \sigma S_t g(t, Z_t)dB_t + S_t \frac{\partial g}{\partial t}(t, Z_t)dt \\
&\quad + S_t Z_t \left(-\mu + \sigma^2\right)\frac{\partial g}{\partial z}(t, Z_t)dt + \frac{1}{T}S_t \frac{\partial g}{\partial z}(t, Z_t)dt - \sigma S_t Z_t \frac{\partial g}{\partial z}(t, Z_t)dB_t \\
&\quad + \frac{1}{2}\sigma^2 Z_t^2 S_t \frac{\partial^2 g}{\partial z^2}(t, Z_t)dt - \sigma^2 S_t Z_t \frac{\partial g}{\partial z}(t, Z_t)dt \\
&= \mu S_t g(t, Z_t)dt + S_t \frac{\partial g}{\partial t}(t, Z_t)dt + S_t Z_t \left(-\mu + \sigma^2\right)\frac{\partial g}{\partial z}(t, Z_t)dt + \frac{1}{T}S_t \frac{\partial g}{\partial z}(t, Z_t)dt \\
&\quad + \frac{1}{2}\sigma^2 Z_t^2 S_t \frac{\partial^2 g}{\partial z^2}(t, Z_t)dt - \sigma^2 S_t Z_t \frac{\partial g}{\partial z}(t, Z_t)dt \\
&\quad + \sigma S_t g(t, Z_t)dB_t - \sigma S_t Z_t \frac{\partial g}{\partial z}(t, Z_t)dB_t.
\end{aligned}
\tag{13.31}
$$

By respective identification of components in dB_t and dt in (13.30) and (13.31), we get

$$
\left\{
\begin{aligned}
r\eta_t A_t + \mu \xi_t S_t &= \mu S_t g(t, Z_t) + S_t \frac{\partial g}{\partial t}(t, Z_t) - \mu S_t Z_t \frac{\partial g}{\partial z}(t, Z_t) \\
&\quad + \frac{1}{T}S_t \frac{\partial g}{\partial z}(t, Z_t) + \frac{1}{2}\sigma^2 Z_t^2 S_t \frac{\partial^2 g}{\partial z^2}(t, Z_t), \\
\\
\xi_t S_t \sigma &= \sigma S_t g(t, Z_t) - \sigma S_t Z_t \frac{\partial g}{\partial z}(t, Z_t),
\end{aligned}
\right.
$$

hence

$$
\left\{
\begin{aligned}
rV_t - r\xi_t S_t &= S_t \frac{\partial g}{\partial t}(t, Z_t) + \frac{1}{T}S_t \frac{\partial g}{\partial z}(t, Z_t) + \frac{1}{2}\sigma^2 Z_t^2 S_t \frac{\partial^2 g}{\partial z^2}(t, Z_t), \\
\xi_t &= g(t, Z_t) - Z_t \frac{\partial g}{\partial z}(t, Z_t),
\end{aligned}
\right.
$$

i.e.

$$
\left\{
\begin{aligned}
\frac{\partial g}{\partial t}(t, z) &+ \left(\frac{1}{T} - rz\right)\frac{\partial g}{\partial z}(t, z) + \frac{1}{2}\sigma^2 z^2 \frac{\partial^2 g}{\partial z^2}(t, z) = 0, \\
\xi_t &= g(t, Z_t) - Z_t \frac{\partial g}{\partial z}(t, Z_t),
\end{aligned}
\right.
$$

under the terminal condition $g(T, z) = z^+$, $z \in \mathbb{R}$, which follows from (13.25). $\qquad \square$

When $\Lambda_t/T \geqslant K$ we have $Z_t \geqslant 0$ and (13.26) and (13.29) show that

$$
\begin{aligned}
\xi_t &= g(t, Z_t) - Z_t \frac{\partial g}{\partial z}(t, Z_t) \\
&= e^{-(T-t)r} Z_t + \frac{1 - e^{-(T-t)r}}{rT} - e^{-(T-t)r} Z_t \\
&= \frac{1 - e^{-(T-t)r}}{rT}, \qquad 0 \leqslant t \leqslant T,
\end{aligned}
$$

which recovers (13.23). Similarly, from (13.28) we recover

$$
\xi_T = g(T, Z_T) - Z_T \frac{\partial g}{\partial z}(T, Z_T) = Z_T \mathbb{1}_{\{Z_T \geqslant 0\}} - Z_T \mathbb{1}_{\{Z_T \geqslant 0\}} = 0
$$

at maturity.

We also check that

$$
\begin{aligned}
\xi_t &= e^{-(T-t)r} \sigma S_t \frac{\partial f}{\partial x} f(t, S_t, Z_t) - \sigma Z_t \frac{\partial f}{\partial z} f(t, S_t, Z_t) \\
&= e^{-(T-t)r} \left(-Z_t \frac{\partial g}{\partial z}(t, Z_t) + g(t, Z_t) \right) \\
&= e^{-(T-t)r} \left(S_t \frac{\partial g}{\partial x} \left(t, \frac{1}{x} \left(\frac{1}{T} \int_0^t S_u du - K \right) \right) \bigg|_{x = S_t} + g(t, Z_t) \right) \\
&= \frac{\partial}{\partial x} \left(x e^{-(T-t)r} g \left(t, \frac{1}{x} \left(\frac{1}{T} \int_0^t S_u du - K \right) \right) \right) \bigg|_{x = S_t}, \qquad 0 \leqslant t \leqslant T.
\end{aligned}
$$

We also find that the amount invested on the riskless asset is given by

$$
\eta_t A_t = Z_t S_t \frac{\partial g}{\partial z}(t, Z_t).
$$

Next we note that a PDE with no first-order derivative term can be obtained using time-dependent coefficients.

(2) One variable with time-dependent coefficients

Define now the auxiliary process

$$
\begin{aligned}
U_t &:= \frac{1 - e^{-(T-t)r}}{rT} + e^{-(T-t)r} \frac{1}{S_t} \left(\frac{1}{T} \int_0^t S_u du - K \right) \\
&= \frac{1}{rT} \left(1 - e^{-(T-t)r} \right) + e^{-(T-t)r} Z_t, \qquad 0 \leqslant t \leqslant T,
\end{aligned}
$$

i.e.

$$
Z_t = e^{(T-t)r} U_t + \frac{e^{(T-t)r} - 1}{rT}, \qquad 0 \leqslant t \leqslant T.
$$

We have

$$
\begin{aligned}
dU_t &= -\frac{1}{T} e^{-(T-t)r} dt + r e^{-(T-t)r} Z_t dt + e^{-(T-t)r} dZ_t \\
&= e^{-(T-t)r} \sigma^2 Z_t dt - e^{-(T-t)r} \sigma Z_t dB_t - (\mu - r) e^{-(T-t)r} Z_t dt \\
&= -e^{-(T-t)r} \sigma Z_t d\widehat{B}_t, \qquad t \geqslant 0,
\end{aligned}
$$

where

$$d\widehat{B}_t = dB_t - \sigma dt + \frac{\mu - r}{\sigma} dt = d\widetilde{B}_t - \sigma dt$$

is a standard Brownian motion under

$$d\widehat{\mathbb{P}} = e^{\sigma B_T - \sigma^2 t/2} d\mathbb{P}^* = e^{-rT} \frac{S_T}{S_0} d\mathbb{P}^*.$$

Lemma 13.11. *The Asian call option price can be written as*

$$S_t h(t, U_t) = e^{-(T-t)r} \, \mathbb{E}^* \left[\left(\frac{1}{T} \int_0^T S_u du - K \right)^+ \Bigg| \mathcal{F}_t \right],$$

where the function $h(t, y)$ is given by

$$h(t, y) = \widehat{\mathbb{E}}[(U_T)^+ \,|\, U_t = y], \qquad 0 \leqslant t \leqslant T. \tag{13.32}$$

Proof. We have

$$U_T = \frac{1}{S_T} \left(\frac{1}{T} \int_0^T S_u du - K \right) = Z_T,$$

and

$$\frac{d\widehat{\mathbb{P}}_{|\mathcal{F}_t}}{d\mathbb{P}^*_{|\mathcal{F}_t}} = e^{(B_T - B_t)\sigma - (T-t)\sigma^2/2} = \frac{e^{-rT} S_T}{e^{-rt} S_t},$$

hence the price of the Asian call option is

$$
\begin{aligned}
e^{-(T-t)r} \, \mathbb{E}^*[S_T (Z_T)^+ \,|\, \mathcal{F}_t] &= e^{-(T-t)r} \, \mathbb{E}^*[S_T (U_T)^+ \,|\, \mathcal{F}_t] \\
&= S_t \, \mathbb{E}^* \left[\frac{e^{-rT} S_T}{e^{-rt} S_t} (U_T)^+ \,\bigg|\, \mathcal{F}_t \right] \\
&= S_t \, \mathbb{E}^* \left[\frac{d\widehat{\mathbb{P}}_{|\mathcal{F}_t}}{d\mathbb{P}^*_{|\mathcal{F}_t}} (U_T)^+ \,\bigg|\, \mathcal{F}_t \right] \\
&= S_t \widehat{\mathbb{E}}[(U_T)^+ \,|\, \mathcal{F}_t].
\end{aligned}
$$

$\square$

The next proposition gives a replicating hedging strategy for Asian options. See § 7.5.3 of Shreve (2004) and references therein for a different derivation of the PDE (13.33).

Proposition 13.12. *(Večeř (2001)). Let $(\eta_t, \xi_t)_{t \in \mathbb{R}_+}$ be a self-financing portfolio strategy whose value $V_t := \eta_t A_t + \xi_t S_t$, $t \geqslant 0$, is given by*

$$V_t = S_t h(t, U_t), \qquad t \geqslant 0,$$

where $h \in \mathcal{C}^{1,2}((0, T) \times (0, \infty))$ is given by (13.32). Then, the function $h(t, z)$ satisfies the PDE

$$\frac{\partial h}{\partial t}(t, y) + \frac{\sigma^2}{2} \left(\frac{1 - e^{-(T-t)r}}{rT} - y \right)^2 \frac{\partial^2 h}{\partial y^2}(t, y) = 0, \tag{13.33}$$

under the terminal condition

$$h(T, z) = z^+,$$

and the corresponding replicating portfolio is given by

$$\xi_t = h(t, U_t) - Z_t \frac{\partial h}{\partial y}(t, U_t), \qquad 0 \leqslant t \leqslant T.$$

Proof. By the self-financing condition (13.20) we have

$$
\begin{aligned}
dV_t &= r\eta_t A_t dt + \mu \xi_t S_t dt + \sigma \xi_t S_t dB_t \\
&= rV_t dt + (\mu - r)\xi_t S_t dt + \sigma \xi_t S_t dB_t,
\end{aligned}
\tag{13.34}
$$

$t \geqslant 0$. By Itô's formula we get

$$
\begin{aligned}
d(S_t h(t, U_t)) &= h(t, U_t) dS_t + S_t dh(t, U_t) + dS_t \cdot dh(t, U_t) \\
&= \mu S_t h(t, U_t) dt + \sigma S_t h(t, U_t) dB_t \\
&\quad + S_t \left(\frac{\partial h}{\partial t}(t, U_t) dt + \frac{\partial h}{\partial y}(t, U_t) dU_t + \frac{1}{2}\frac{\partial^2 h}{\partial y^2}(t, U_t)(dU_t)^2 \right) \\
&\quad + \frac{\partial h}{\partial y}(t, U_t) dS_t \cdot dU_t \\
&= \mu S_t h(t, U_t) dt + \sigma S_t h(t, U_t) dB_t - S_t(\mu - r)\frac{\partial h}{\partial y}(t, U_t) Z_t dt \\
&\quad + S_t \left(\frac{\partial h}{\partial t}(t, U_t) dt - \sigma\frac{\partial h}{\partial y}(t, U_t) Z_t d\widetilde{B}_t + \frac{\sigma^2}{2} Z_t^2 \frac{\partial^2 h}{\partial y^2}(t, U_t) dt \right) \\
&\quad - \sigma^2 S_t \frac{\partial h}{\partial y}(t, U_t) Z_t dt \\
&= \mu S_t h(t, U_t) dt + \sigma S_t h(t, U_t) dB_t - S_t(\mu - r)\frac{\partial h}{\partial y}(t, U_t) Z_t dt \\
&\quad + S_t \left(\frac{\partial h}{\partial t}(t, U_t) dt - \sigma\frac{\partial h}{\partial y}(t, U_t) Z_t(dB_t - \sigma dt) + \frac{\sigma^2}{2} Z_t^2 \frac{\partial^2 h}{\partial y^2}(t, U_t) dt \right) \\
&\quad - \sigma^2 S_t \frac{\partial h}{\partial y}(t, U_t) Z_t dt.
\end{aligned}
\tag{13.35}
$$

By respective identification of components in dB_t and dt in (13.34) and (13.35), we get

$$
\begin{cases}
r\eta_t A_t + \mu \xi_t S_t = \mu S_t h(t, U_t) - (\mu - r)S_t Z_t \dfrac{\partial h}{\partial y}(t, U_t) dt + S_t \dfrac{\partial h}{\partial t}(t, U_t) \\
\qquad\qquad + \dfrac{\sigma^2}{2} S_t Z_t^2 \dfrac{\partial^2 h}{\partial y^2}(t, U_t), \\[2ex]
\xi_t = h(t, U_t) - Z_t \dfrac{\partial h}{\partial y}(t, U_t),
\end{cases}
$$

hence

$$
\begin{cases}
r\eta_t A_t = -rS_t(\xi_t - h(t, U_t)) + S_t \dfrac{\partial h}{\partial t}(t, U_t) + \dfrac{\sigma^2}{2} S_t Z_t^2 \dfrac{\partial^2 h}{\partial y^2}(t, U_t), \\[2ex]
\xi_t = h(t, U_t) - Z_t \dfrac{\partial h}{\partial y}(t, U_t),
\end{cases}
$$

and

$$\begin{cases} \dfrac{\partial h}{\partial t}(t,y) + \dfrac{\sigma^2}{2}\left(\dfrac{1 - e^{-(T-t)r}}{rT} - y\right)^2 \dfrac{\partial^2 h}{\partial y^2}(t,y) = 0, \\[3ex] \xi_t = h(t,U_t) + \left(\dfrac{1 - e^{-(T-t)r}}{rT} - U_t\right)\dfrac{\partial h}{\partial y}(t,U_t), \end{cases}$$

under the terminal condition

$$h(T,z) = z^+.$$

$\square$

We also find the riskless portfolio allocation

$$\eta_t A_t = e^{(T-t)r} S_t \left(U_t - \dfrac{1 - e^{-(T-t)r}}{rT}\right)\dfrac{\partial h}{\partial y}(t,U_t) = S_t Z_t \dfrac{\partial h}{\partial y}(t,U_t).$$

Exercises

Exercise 13.1 Compute the first and second moments of the time integral $\int_\tau^T S_t dt$ for $\tau \in [0,T)$, where $(S_t)_{t\in\mathbb{R}_+}$ is the geometric Brownian motion $S_t := S_0 e^{\sigma B_t + rt - \sigma^2 t/2}$, $t \geqslant 0$.

Exercise 13.2 Consider the short rate process $r_t = \sigma B_t$, where $(B_t)_{t\in\mathbb{R}_+}$ is a standard Brownian motion.

a) Find the probability distribution of the time integral $\int_0^T r_s ds$.

b) Compute the price

$$e^{-rT} \, \mathbb{E}^* \left[\left(\int_0^T r_u du - K\right)^+\right]$$

of a caplet on the forward rate $\int_0^T r_s ds$.

Exercise 13.3 Asian call option with a *negative* strike price. Consider the asset price process

$$S_t = S_0 e^{rt + \sigma B_t - \sigma^2 t/2}, \qquad t \geqslant 0,$$

where $(B_t)_{t\in\mathbb{R}_+}$ is a standard Brownian motion. Assuming that $K \leqslant 0$, compute the price

$$e^{-(T-t)r} \, \mathbb{E}^* \left[\left(\frac{1}{T}\int_0^T S_u du - K\right)^+ \middle| \mathcal{F}_t\right]$$

of the Asian option at time $t \in [0,T]$.

Exercise 13.4 Consider the Asian forward contract with payoff

$$\frac{1}{T}\int_0^T S_u du - K, \tag{13.36}$$

where $S_u = S_0 e^{\sigma B_u + ru - \sigma^2 u/2}$, $u \geqslant 0$, and $(B_u)_{u\in\mathbb{R}_+}$ is a standard Brownian motion under the risk-neutral measure $\mathbb{P}^*$.

a) Price the long forward Asian contract at any time $t \in [0, T]$.

b) Derive a call-put parity relation between the prices

$$C(t, K) := e^{-(T-t)r} \, \mathbb{E}^* \left[\left(\frac{1}{T} \int_0^T S_u du - K \right)^+ \middle| \mathcal{F}_t \right]$$

and

$$P(t, K) := e^{-(T-t)r} \, \mathbb{E}^* \left[\left(K - \frac{1}{T} \int_0^T S_u du \right)^+ \middle| \mathcal{F}_t \right]$$

of Asian call and put options.

c) Find the self-financing portfolio strategy $(\xi_t)_{t \in [0,T]}$ hedging the Asian forward contract with payoff (13.36), where ξ_t denotes the quantity invested at time $t \in [0, T]$ in the risky asset S_t.

d) Compute the numerical value of the price

$$e^{-(T-t)r} \, \mathbb{E}^* \left[\frac{1}{T} \int_0^T S_u du - K \middle| \mathcal{F}_t \right]$$

of the long forward *Asian contract* on Light Sweet Crude Oil Futures (CLZ22.NYM) using the following market data:

Issue date: 2022-01-01,

Maturity T =2022-12-31,

Strike price K =\$80,

Interest rate r =2% per year,

t =2022-04-01,

Number of business days per month: 21, per year: 252.

```
library(quantmod)
getSymbols("CLZ22.NYM",from="2022-01-01",to="2022-04-01",src="yahoo")
futures=Cl(`CLZ22.NYM`)
chartSeries(futures,up.col="blue",theme="white")
n = length(!is.na(futures))
```

Exercise 13.5   Compute the price

$$e^{-(T-t)r} \, \mathbb{E}^* \left[\left(\exp \left(\frac{1}{T} \int_0^T \log S_u du \right) - K \right)^+ \middle| \mathcal{F}_t \right], \qquad 0 \leqslant t \leqslant T.$$

at time t of the geometric Asian option with maturity T, where $S_t = S_0 e^{rt + \sigma B_t - \sigma^2 t/2}$, $t \in [0, T]$.

Hint: When $X \simeq \mathcal{N}(0, v^2)$ we have

$$\mathbb{E}^*[(e^{m+X} - K)^+] = e^{m+v^2/2} \Phi(v + (m - \log K)/v) - K \Phi((m - \log K)/v).$$

Exercise 13.6 Consider a CIR process $(r_t)_{t \in \mathbb{R}_+}$ given by

$$dr_t = -\lambda(r_t - m)dt + \sigma\sqrt{r_t}dB_t, \qquad (13.37)$$

where $(B_t)_{t \in \mathbb{R}_+}$ is a standard Brownian motion under the risk-neutral probability measure $\mathbb{P}^*$, and let

$$\Lambda_t := \frac{1}{T - \tau}\int_\tau^t r_s ds, \qquad t \in [\tau, T].$$

Compute the price at time $t \in [\tau, T]$ of the Asian option with payoff $(\Lambda_T - K)^+$, under the condition $\Lambda_t \geqslant K$.

Exercise 13.7 Consider an asset price $(S_t)_{t \in \mathbb{R}_+}$ which is a *sub*martingale under the risk-neutral probability measure $\mathbb{P}^*$, in a market with risk-free interest rate $r > 0$, and let $\phi(x) = (x - K)^+$ be the (convex) payoff function of the European call option.

Show that, for any sequence $0 < T_1 < \cdots < T_n$, the price of the option on average with payoff

$$\phi\left(\frac{S_{T_1} + \cdots + S_{T_n}}{n}\right)$$

can be upper bounded by the price of the European call option with maturity T_n, *i.e.* show that

$$\mathbb{E}^*\left[\phi\left(\frac{S_{T_1} + \cdots + S_{T_n}}{n}\right)\right] \leqslant \mathbb{E}^*[\phi(S_{T_n})].$$

Exercise 13.8 Let $(S_t)_{t \in \mathbb{R}_+}$ denote a risky asset whose price S_t is given by

$$dS_t = \mu S_t dt + \sigma S_t dB_t,$$

where $(B_t)_{t \in \mathbb{R}_+}$ is a standard Brownian motion under the risk-neutral probability measure $\mathbb{P}^*$. Compute the price at time $t \in [\tau, T]$ of the Asian option with payoff

$$\left(\frac{1}{T - \tau}\int_\tau^T S_u du - K\right)^+,$$

under the condition that

$$A_t := \frac{1}{T - \tau}\int_\tau^t S_u du \geqslant K.$$

Exercise 13.9 Pricing Asian options by PDEs. Show that the functions $g(t, z)$ and $h(t, y)$ are linked by the relation

$$g(t, z) = h\left(t, \frac{1 - e^{-(T-t)r}}{rT} + e^{-(T-t)r}z\right), \qquad 0 \leqslant t \leqslant T, \quad z > 0,$$

and that the PDE (1.35) for $h(t, y)$ can be derived from the PDE (1.33) for $g(t, z)$ and the above relation.

Exercise 13.10 (Brown et al. (2016)) Given $S_t := S_0 e^{\sigma B_t + rt - \sigma^2 t/2}$ a geometric Brownian motion and letting

$$\widetilde{Z}_t := \frac{e^{-(T-t)r}}{S_t}\left(\frac{1}{T}\int_0^t S_u du - K\right) = \frac{e^{-(T-t)r}}{S_t}\left(\frac{\Lambda_t}{T} - K\right), \qquad 0 \leqslant t \leqslant T,$$

find the PDE satisfied by the pricing function $\tilde{g}(t, z)$ such that

$$S_t \tilde{g}(t, \tilde{Z}_t) = e^{-(T-t)r} \mathbb{E}^* \left[\left(\frac{1}{T} \int_0^T S_u du - K \right)^+ \bigg| \mathcal{F}_t \right].$$

Exercise 13.11 Hedging Asian options (Yang et al. (2011)).

a) Compute the Asian option price $f(t, S_t, \Lambda_t)$ when $\Lambda_t / T \geqslant K$.

b) Compute the hedging portfolio allocation (ξ_t, η_t) when $\Lambda_t / T \geqslant K$.

c) At maturity we have $f(T, S_T, \Lambda_T) = (\Lambda_T / T - K)^+$, hence $\xi_T = 0$ and

$$\eta_T A_T = A_T \frac{e^{-rT}}{A_0} \left(\frac{\Lambda_T}{T} - K \right) \mathbb{1}_{\{\Lambda_T > KT\}} = \left(\frac{\Lambda_T}{T} - K \right)^+.$$

d) Show that the Asian option with payoff $(\Lambda_T - K)^+$ can be hedged by the self-financing portfolio

$$\xi_t = \frac{1}{S_t} \left(f(t, S_t, \Lambda_t) - e^{-(T-t)r} \left(\frac{\Lambda_t}{T} - K \right) h \left(t, \frac{1}{S_t} \left(\frac{\Lambda_t}{T} - K \right) \right) \right)$$

in the asset S_t and

$$\eta_t = \frac{e^{-rT}}{A_0} \left(\frac{\Lambda_t}{T} - K \right) h \left(t, \frac{1}{S_t} \left(\frac{\Lambda_t}{T} - K \right) \right), \qquad 0 \leqslant t \leqslant T,$$

in the riskless asset $A_t = A_0 e^{rt}$, where $h(t, z)$ is solution to a partial differential equation to be written explicitly.

Exercise 13.12 Asian options with dividends. Consider an underlying asset price process $(S_t)_{t \in \mathbb{R}_+}$ modeled as $dS_t = (\mu - \delta) S_t dt + \sigma S_t dB_t$, where $(B_t)_{t \in \mathbb{R}_+}$ is a standard Brownian motion and $\delta > 0$ is a continuous-time dividend rate.

a) Write down the self-financing condition for the portfolio value $V_t = \xi_t S_t + \eta_t A_t$ with $A_t = A_0 e^{rt}$, assuming that all dividends are reinvested.

b) Derive the Black–Scholes PDE for the function $g_\delta(t, x, y)$ such that $V_t = g_\delta(t, S_t, \Lambda_t)$ at time $t \in [0, T]$.

```
1   getDividends("Z74.SI",from="2018-01-01",to="2018-12-31",src="yahoo")
    getSymbols("Z74.SI",from="2018-11-16",to="2018-12-19",src="yahoo")
3   T <- chart_theme(); T$col$line.col <- "black"
    chart_Series(Op(`Z74.SI`),name="Opening prices (black) - Closing prices (blue)",lty=4,theme=T)
5   add_TA(Cl(`Z74.SI`),lwd=2,lty=5,legend='Difference',col="blue",on = 1)
```

	Z74.SI.div
2018-07-26	0.107
2018-12-17	0.068
2018-12-18	0.068

Figure 13.6: SGD0.068 dividend detached on December 18, 2018 on Z74.SI.

The difference between the closing price on December 17 ($3.06) and the opening price on December 18 ($2.99) is $3.06 - $2.99 = $0.07. The adjusted price on December 17 ($2.992) is the closing price ($3.06) minus the dividend ($0.068).

Z74.SI	Open	High	Low	Close	Volume	Adjusted (ex-dividend)
2018-12-17	3.05	3.08	3.05	**3.06**	17441000	**2.992**
2018-12-18	**2.99**	2.99	2.96	2.96	28456400	2.960

The dividend rate α is given by $\alpha = 0.068/3.06 = 2.22\%$.

Chapter 14

Optimal Stopping Theorem

Stopping times are random times whose value can be determined by the historical behavior of a stochastic process modeling market data. This chapter presents additional material on optimal stopping and martingales, for use in the pricing and optimal exercise of American options in Chapter 15. Applications are given to hitting probabilities for Brownian motion.

14.1 Filtrations and Information Flow

Let $(\mathcal{F}_t)_{t \in \mathbb{R}_+}$ denote the *filtration* generated by a stochastic process $(X_t)_{t \in \mathbb{R}_+}$. In other words, $\mathcal{F}_t$ denotes the collection of all events possibly generated by $\{X_s : 0 \leqslant s \leqslant t\}$ up to time t. Examples of such events include the event

$$\{X_{t_0} \leqslant a_0, \ X_{t_1} \leqslant a_1, \ \ldots, \ X_{t_n} \leqslant a_n\}$$

for $a_0, a_1, \ldots, a_n$ a given fixed sequence of real numbers and $0 \leqslant t_1 < \cdots < t_n < t$, and $\mathcal{F}_t$ is said to represent the *information* generated by $(X_s)_{s \in [0,t]}$ up to time $t \geqslant 0$.

By construction, $(\mathcal{F}_t)_{t \in \mathbb{R}_+}$ is a *non-decreasing* family of σ-algebras in the sense that we have $\mathcal{F}_s \subset \mathcal{F}_t$ (information known at time s is contained in the information known at time t) when $0 < s < t$.

One refers sometimes to $(\mathcal{F}_t)_{t \in \mathbb{R}_+}$ as the non-decreasing flow of information generated by $(X_t)_{t \in \mathbb{R}_+}$.

14.2 Submartingales and Supermartingales

Let us recall the definition of *martingale* (cf. Definition 4.2), and introduce in addition the definitions of *super*martingale and *sub*martingale.[†]

Definition 14.1. *An integrable[‡] stochastic process $(Z_t)_{t \in \mathbb{R}_+}$ is a martingale (resp. a supermartingale, resp. a submartingale) with respect to $(\mathcal{F}_t)_{t \in \mathbb{R}_+}$ if it satisfies the property*

$$Z_s = \mathbb{E}[Z_t \mid \mathcal{F}_s], \qquad 0 \leqslant s \leqslant t, \qquad \text{(martingale)}$$

[†]"This obviously inappropriate nomenclature was chosen under the malign influence of the noise level of radio's SUPERman program, a favorite supper-time program of Doob's son during the writing of Doob (1953)", cf. Doob (1984), historical notes, page 808.

[‡]This condition means that $\mathbb{E}[|Z_t|] < \infty$ for all $t \geqslant 0$.

DOI: 10.1201/9781003298670-14

resp.

$$Z_s \geqslant \mathbb{E}[Z_t \mid \mathcal{F}_s], \qquad 0 \leqslant s \leqslant t, \qquad\qquad (supermartingale)$$

resp.

$$Z_s \leqslant \mathbb{E}[Z_t \mid \mathcal{F}_s], \qquad 0 \leqslant s \leqslant t. \qquad\qquad (submartingale)$$

Clearly, a stochastic process $(Z_t)_{t \in \mathbb{R}_+}$ is a martingale if and only if it is both a *super*martingale and a *sub*martingale.

A particular property of martingales is that their expectation is constant over time $t \in \mathbb{R}_+$. In the next proposition we also check that *super*martingales have *non-increasing* expectation over time, while *sub*martingales have a *non-decreasing* expectation.

Proposition 14.2. *Let $(Z_t)_{t \in \mathbb{R}_+}$ denote an adapted integrable process.*

*a) If $(Z_t)_{t \in \mathbb{R}_+}$ is a super*martingale*, we have*

$$\mathbb{E}[Z_s] \geqslant \mathbb{E}[Z_t], \qquad 0 \leqslant s \leqslant t. \qquad\qquad (supermartingale)$$

*b) If $(Z_t)_{t \in \mathbb{R}_+}$ is a sub*martingale*, we have*

$$\mathbb{E}[Z_s] \leqslant \mathbb{E}[Z_t], \qquad 0 \leqslant s \leqslant t. \qquad\qquad (submartingale)$$

c) If $(Z_t)_{t \in \mathbb{R}_+}$ be a martingale, we have

$$\mathbb{E}[Z_s] = \mathbb{E}[Z_t], \qquad 0 \leqslant s \leqslant t. \qquad\qquad (martingale)$$

Proof. The case where $(Z_t)_{t \in \mathbb{R}_+}$ is a martingale follows from the tower property of conditional expectations, which shows that

$$\mathbb{E}[Z_t] = \mathbb{E}[\mathbb{E}[Z_t \mid \mathcal{F}_s]] = \mathbb{E}[Z_s], \qquad 0 \leqslant s \leqslant t. \qquad\qquad (14.1)$$

Regarding *super*martingales, similarly to (14.1) we have

$$\mathbb{E}[Z_t] = \mathbb{E}[\mathbb{E}[Z_t \mid \mathcal{F}_s]] \leqslant \mathbb{E}[Z_s], \qquad 0 \leqslant s \leqslant t.$$

The proof is similar in the *sub*martingale case. $\qquad\qquad\qquad\qquad\qquad \square$

Independent increments processes whose increments have negative expectation give examples of *super*martingales. For example, if $(Z_t)_{t \in \mathbb{R}_+}$ is such a stochastic process, then we have

$$
\begin{aligned}
\mathbb{E}[Z_t \mid \mathcal{F}_s] &= \mathbb{E}[Z_s \mid \mathcal{F}_s] + \mathbb{E}\left[Z_t - Z_s \mid \mathcal{F}_s\right] \\
&= \mathbb{E}[Z_s \mid \mathcal{F}_s] + \mathbb{E}[Z_t - Z_s] \\
&\leqslant \mathbb{E}[Z_s \mid \mathcal{F}_s] \\
&= Z_s, \qquad 0 \leqslant s \leqslant t.
\end{aligned}
$$

Similarly, a stochastic process with independent increments which have positive expectation will be a *sub*martingale. Brownian motion $B_t + \mu t$ with positive drift $\mu > 0$ is such an example, as in Figure 14.1 below.

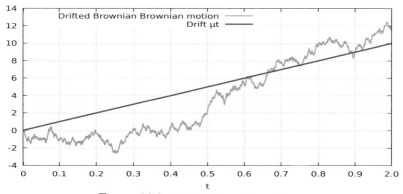

Figure 14.1: Drifted Brownian path.

The following example comes from gambling.

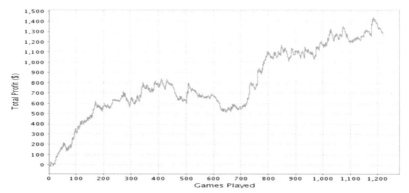

Figure 14.2: Evolution of the fortune of a poker player *vs* number of games played.

Proposition 14.3. *Jensen's inequality. Let $\varphi : \mathbb{R} \to \mathbb{R}$ be a convex function, i.e.*

$$\varphi(px + qy) \leqslant p\varphi(x) + q\varphi(y)$$

for any $p, q \in [0, 1]$ such that $p + q = 1$ and $x, y \in \mathbb{R}$. Jensen's inequality states that for X any sufficiently integrable random variable and convex function $\varphi : \mathbb{R} \to \mathbb{R}$ we have

$$\varphi(\mathbb{E}[X]) \leqslant \mathbb{E}[\varphi(X)].$$

Proof. See (3.7.1) in Hardy et al. (1988). We only consider the case where X is a discrete random variable taking values in a finite set $\{x_1, \ldots, x_n\}$, with $\mathbb{P}(X = x_i) = p_i$, $i = 1, \ldots, n$, and show by induction on $n \geqslant 1$ that

$$\phi(p_1 x_1 + p_2 x_2 + \cdots + p_n x_n) \leqslant p_1 \phi(x_1) + p_2 \phi(x_2) + \cdots + p_n \phi(x_n), \qquad (14.2)$$

$x_1, \ldots, x_n \in \mathbb{R}$, for any sequence of coefficients $p_1, p_2, \ldots, p_n \geqslant 0$ such that $p_1 + p_2 + \cdots + p_n = 1$. The inequality (14.2) clearly holds for $n = 1$, and for $n = 2$ it coincides with the convexity property of ϕ, *i.e.*

$$\phi(p_1 x_1 + p_2 x_2) \leqslant p_1 \phi(x_1) + p_2 \phi(x_2), \qquad x_1, x_2 \in \mathbb{R}.$$

Assuming that (14.2) holds for some $n \geqslant 1$ and taking $p_1, p_2, \ldots, p_{n+1} \geqslant 0$ such that $p_1 + p_2 + \cdots + p_{n+1} = 1$ and $0 < p_{n+1} < 1$ and applying (14.2) at the second-order, we have

$$
\begin{aligned}
\phi(&p_1 x_1 + p_2 x_2 + \cdots + p_{n+1} x_{n+1}) \\
&= \phi\left((1 - p_{n+1}) \frac{p_1 x_1 + p_2 x_2 + \cdots + p_n x_n}{1 - p_{n+1}} + p_{n+1} x_{n+1} \right) \\
&\leqslant (1 - p_{n+1}) \phi\left(\frac{p_1 x_1 + p_2 x_2 + \cdots + p_n x_n}{1 - p_{n+1}} \right) + p_{n+1} \phi(x_{n+1}) \\
&\leqslant (1 - p_{n+1}) \left(\frac{p_1 \phi(x_1) + p_2 \phi(x_2) + \cdots + p_n \phi(x_n)}{1 - p_{n+1}} \right) + p_{n+1} \phi(x_{n+1}) \\
&= p_1 \phi(x_1) + p_2 \phi(x_2) + \cdots + p_{n+1} \phi(x_{n+1}),
\end{aligned}
$$

and we conclude by induction. $\square$

A natural way to construct *sub*martingales is to take convex functions of martingales and to apply Jensen's inequality.

Proposition 14.4. *a) Given $(M_t)_{t \in \mathbb{R}_+}$ a martingale and $\phi : \mathbb{R} \longrightarrow \mathbb{R}$ a convex function, the process $(\phi(M_t))_{t \in \mathbb{R}_+}$ is a* sub*martingale.*

b) Given $(M_t)_{t \in \mathbb{R}_+}$ a sub*martingale and $\phi : \mathbb{R} \longrightarrow \mathbb{R}$ a non-decreasing convex function, the process $(\phi(M_t))_{t \in \mathbb{R}_+}$ is a* sub*martingale.*

Proof. By Jensen's inequality we have

$$
\phi(\mathbb{E}[M_t \mid \mathcal{F}_s]) \leqslant \mathbb{E}[\phi(M_t) \mid \mathcal{F}_s], \qquad 0 \leqslant s \leqslant t, \tag{14.3}
$$

which shows that

$$
\phi(M_s) = \phi(\mathbb{E}[M_t \mid \mathcal{F}_s]) \leqslant \mathbb{E}[\phi(M_t) \mid \mathcal{F}_s], \qquad 0 \leqslant s \leqslant t.
$$

If ϕ is convex non-decreasing and $(M_t)_{\in \mathbb{R}_+}$ is a *sub*martingale, the above rewrites as

$$
\phi(M_s) \leqslant \phi(\mathbb{E}[M_t \mid \mathcal{F}_s]) \leqslant \mathbb{E}[\phi(M_t) \mid \mathcal{F}_s], \qquad 0 \leqslant s \leqslant t,
$$

showing that $(\phi(M_t))_{t \in \mathbb{R}_+}$ is a *sub*martingale. $\square$

Similarly, $(\phi(M_t))_{t \in \mathbb{R}_+}$ will be a *super*martingale when $(M_t)_{\in \mathbb{R}_+}$ is a martingale and the function ϕ is *concave*.

As a direct application of Proposition 14.4, the process $(B_t^2)_{t \in \mathbb{R}_+}$ is a *sub*martingale as $\varphi(x) = x^2$ is a convex function. Other examples of (*super*, *sub*)-martingales include geometric Brownian motion

$$
S_t = S_0 \, e^{rt + \sigma B_t - \sigma^2 t / 2}, \qquad t \geqslant 0,
$$

which is a martingale for $r = 0$, a *super*martingale for $r \leqslant 0$, and a *sub*martingale for $r \geqslant 0$.

14.3   Optimal Stopping Theorem

Next, we turn to the definition of *stopping time*, which is based on a probability space $(\Omega, \mathcal{F}, \mathbb{P})$ and a filtration $(\mathcal{F}_t)_{t \in \mathbb{R}_+} \subset \mathcal{F}$.

Definition 14.5. *An $(\mathcal{F}_t)_{t \in \mathbb{R}_+}$-stopping time is a random variable $\tau : \Omega \longrightarrow \mathbb{R}_+ \cup \{+\infty\}$ such that*

$$\{\tau > t\} \in \mathcal{F}_t, \qquad t \geqslant 0. \tag{14.4}$$

The meaning of Relation (14.4) is that the knowledge of the event $\{\tau > t\}$ depends only on the information present in $\mathcal{F}_t$ up to time t, *i.e.* on the knowledge of $(X_s)_{0 \leqslant s \leqslant t}$.

In other words, an event occurs at a *stopping time* τ if at any time t it can be decided whether the event has already occurred ($\tau \leqslant t$) or not ($\tau > t$) based on the information $\mathcal{F}_t$ generated by $(X_s)_{s \in \mathbb{R}_+}$ up to time t.

For example, the day you bought your first car is a stopping time (one can always answer the question "did I ever buy a car"), whereas the day you will buy your *last* car may not be a stopping time (one may not be able to answer the question "will I ever buy another car").

Proposition 14.6. *Every constant time is a stopping time. In addition, if τ and θ are stopping times, then*

 i) *the minimum $\tau \wedge \theta := \min(\tau, \theta)$ of τ and θ is also a stopping time,*

 ii) *the maximum $\tau \vee \theta := \mathrm{Max}(\tau, \theta)$ of τ and θ is also a stopping time.*

Proof. Point (i) is easily checked. Regarding (ii), we have

$$\{\tau \wedge \theta > t\} = \{\tau > t \text{ and } \theta > t\} = \{\tau > t\} \cap \{\theta > t\} \in \mathcal{F}_t, \quad t \geqslant 0.$$

On the other hand, we have

$$\{\tau \vee \theta \leqslant t\} = \{\tau \leqslant t \text{ and } \theta \leqslant t\} = \{\tau > t\}^c \cap \{\theta > t\}^c \in \mathcal{F}_t, \quad t \geqslant 0,$$

which implies

$$\{\tau \vee \theta > t\} = \{\tau \vee \theta \leqslant t\}^c \in \mathcal{F}_t, \qquad t \geqslant 0.$$

$\square$

Hitting times

Hitting times provide natural examples of stopping times. The hitting time of level x by the process $(X_t)_{t \in \mathbb{R}_+}$, defined as

$$\tau_x = \inf\{t \in \mathbb{R}_+ : X_t = x\},$$

is a stopping time,* as we have (here in discrete time)

$$\begin{aligned} \{\tau_x > t\} &= \{X_s \neq x \text{ for all } s \in [0, t]\} \\ &= \{X_0 \neq x\} \cap \{X_1 \neq x\} \cap \cdots \cap \{X_t \neq x\} \in \mathcal{F}_t, \qquad t \in \mathbb{N}. \end{aligned}$$

In gambling, a hitting time can be used as an exit strategy from the game. For example, letting

$$\tau_{x,y} := \inf\{t \in \mathbb{R}_+ : X_t = x \text{ or } X_t = y\} \tag{14.5}$$

defines a hitting time (hence a stopping time) which allows a gambler to exit the game as soon as losses become equal to $x = -10$, or gains become equal to $y = +100$, whichever

---

*As a convention we let $\tau = +\infty$ in case there exists no $t \geqslant 0$ such that $X_t = x$.

comes first. Hitting times can be used to trigger for "buy limit" or "sell stop" orders in finance.

However, not every $\mathbb{R}_+$-valued random variable is a stopping time. For example the random time

$$\tau = \inf \left\{ t \in [0,T] \ : \ X_t = \sup_{s \in [0,T]} X_s \right\},$$

which represents the first time the process $(X_t)_{t \in [0,T]}$ reaches its maximum over $[0,T]$, is <u>not</u> a stopping time with respect to the filtration generated by $(X_t)_{t \in [0,T]}$. Indeed, the information known at time $t \in (0,T)$ is not sufficient to determine whether $\{\tau > t\}$.

Stopped process

Given $(Z_t)_{t \in \mathbb{R}_+}$ a stochastic process and $\tau : \Omega \longrightarrow \mathbb{R}_+ \cup \{+\infty\}$ a stopping time, the *stopped process* $(Z_{t \wedge \tau})_{t \in \mathbb{R}_+}$ is defined as

$$Z_{t \wedge \tau} := \begin{cases} Z_t & \text{if } t < \tau, \\ \\ Z_\tau & \text{if } t \geqslant \tau, \end{cases}$$

Using indicator functions, we may also write

$$Z_{t \wedge \tau} = Z_t \mathbb{1}_{\{t < \tau\}} + Z_\tau \mathbb{1}_{\{t \geqslant \tau\}}, \qquad t \geqslant 0.$$

The following Figure 14.3 is an illustration of the path of a stopped process.

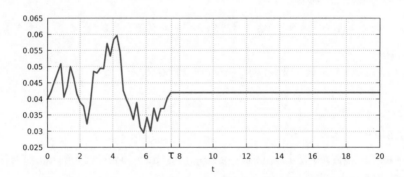

Figure 14.3: Stopped process.

Theorem 14.7 below is called the *Stopping Time* (or *Optional Sampling*, or *Optional Stopping*) Theorem, it is due to the mathematician J.L. Doob (1910-2004). It is also used in Exercise 14.6 below.

Theorem 14.7. *Assume that $(M_t)_{t \in \mathbb{R}_+}$ is a martingale with respect to $(\mathcal{F}_t)_{t \in \mathbb{R}_+}$, and that τ is an $(\mathcal{F}_t)_{t \in \mathbb{R}_+}$-stopping time. Then, the stopped process $(M_{t \wedge \tau})_{t \in \mathbb{R}_+}$ is also a martingale with respect to $(\mathcal{F}_t)_{t \in \mathbb{R}_+}$.*

Proof. We only give the proof in discrete time by applying the martingale transform argument of Theorem 2.11. Writing the telescoping sum

$$M_n = M_0 + \sum_{l=1}^{n} (M_l - M_{l-1}),$$

we have

$$M_{\tau \wedge n} = M_0 + \sum_{l=1}^{\tau \wedge n} (M_l - M_{l-1}) = M_0 + \sum_{l=1}^{n} \mathbb{1}_{\{l \leqslant \tau\}} (M_l - M_{l-1}),$$

and for $k \leqslant n$,

$$
\begin{aligned}
\mathbb{E}[M_{\tau \wedge n} \mid \mathcal{F}_k] &= \mathbb{E}\left[M_0 + \sum_{l=1}^{n} \mathbb{1}_{\{l \leqslant \tau\}} (M_l - M_{l-1}) \,\middle|\, \mathcal{F}_k\right] \\
&= M_0 + \sum_{l=1}^{n} \mathbb{E}[\mathbb{1}_{\{l \leqslant \tau\}} (M_l - M_{l-1}) \mid \mathcal{F}_k] \\
&= M_0 + \sum_{l=1}^{k} \mathbb{E}[\mathbb{1}_{\{l \leqslant \tau\}} (M_l - M_{l-1}) \mid \mathcal{F}_k] \\
&\quad + \sum_{l=k+1}^{n} \mathbb{E}[\mathbb{1}_{\{l \leqslant \tau\}} (M_l - M_{l-1}) \mid \mathcal{F}_k] \\
&= M_0 + \sum_{l=1}^{k} (M_l - M_{l-1}) \mathbb{E}[\mathbb{1}_{\{l \leqslant \tau\}} \mid \mathcal{F}_k] \\
&\quad + \sum_{l=k+1}^{n} \mathbb{E}[\mathbb{E}[(M_l - M_{l-1})\mathbb{1}_{\{l \leqslant \tau\}} \mid \mathcal{F}_{l-1}] \mid \mathcal{F}_k] \\
&= M_0 + \sum_{l=1}^{k} (M_l - M_{l-1}) \mathbb{1}_{\{l \leqslant \tau\}} \\
&\quad + \sum_{l=k+1}^{n} \mathbb{E}[\mathbb{1}_{\{l \leqslant \tau\}} \underbrace{\mathbb{E}[(M_l - M_{l-1}) \mid \mathcal{F}_{l-1}]}_{=0} \mid \mathcal{F}_k] \\
&= M_0 + \sum_{l=1}^{k} (M_l - M_{l-1}) \mathbb{1}_{\{l \leqslant \tau\}} \\
&= M_0 + \sum_{l=1}^{\tau \wedge k} (M_l - M_{l-1}) \\
&= M_{\tau \wedge k}, \qquad k = 0, 1, \ldots, n,
\end{aligned}
$$

as by the martingale property of $(M_l)_{l \in \mathbb{N}}$, we have

$$
\begin{aligned}
\mathbb{E}[(M_l - M_{l-1}) \mid \mathcal{F}_{l-1}] &= \mathbb{E}[M_l \mid \mathcal{F}_{l-1}] - \mathbb{E}[M_{l-1} \mid \mathcal{F}_{l-1}] \\
&= \mathbb{E}[M_l \mid \mathcal{F}_{l-1}] - M_{l-1} \\
&= 0, \qquad l \geqslant 1.
\end{aligned}
$$

$\square$

Remarks.

a) More generally, if $(M_t)_{t \in \mathbb{R}_+}$ is a *super* (resp. *sub*)-martingale with respect to $(\mathcal{F}_t)_{t \in \mathbb{R}_+}$, then the *stopped process* $(M_{t \wedge \tau})_{t \in \mathbb{R}_+}$ remains a *super* (resp. *sub*)-martingale with respect to $(\mathcal{F}_t)_{t \in \mathbb{R}_+}$, see *e.g.* Exercise 14.6 below for the case of *sub*martingales in discrete time.

b) Since by Theorem 14.7 the stopped process $(M_{\tau \wedge t})_{t \in \mathbb{R}_+}$ is a martingale, we find that its expected value $\mathbb{E}[M_{\tau \wedge t}]$ is constant over time $t \in \mathbb{R}_+$ by Proposition 14.2-c).

As a consequence, if $(M_t)_{t \in \mathbb{R}_+}$ is an $(\mathcal{F}_t)_{t \in \mathbb{R}_+}$-martingale and τ is a stopping time bounded by a constant $T > 0$, *i.e.* $\tau \leqslant T$ almost surely,[*] we have

$$\mathbb{E}[M_\tau] = \mathbb{E}[M_{\tau \wedge T}] = \mathbb{E}[M_{\tau \wedge 0}] = \mathbb{E}[M_0] = \mathbb{E}[M_T]. \tag{14.6}$$

c) From (14.6), if τ, ν are two stopping times *a.s. bounded* by a constant $T > 0$ and $(M_t)_{t \in \mathbb{R}_+}$ is a martingale, we have

$$\mathbb{E}[M_0] = \mathbb{E}[M_\tau] = \mathbb{E}[M_\nu] = \mathbb{E}[M_T]. \tag{14.7}$$

d) If τ, ν are two stopping times *a.s. bounded* by a constant $T > 0$ and such that $\tau \leqslant \nu$ *a.s.*, then

(i) when $(M_t)_{t \in \mathbb{R}_+}$ is a *super*martingale, we have

$$\mathbb{E}[M_0] \geqslant \mathbb{E}[M_\tau] \geqslant \mathbb{E}[M_\nu] \geqslant \mathbb{E}[M_T], \tag{14.8}$$

(ii) when $(M_t)_{t \in \mathbb{R}_+}$ is a *sub*martingale, we have

$$\mathbb{E}[M_0] \leqslant \mathbb{E}[M_\tau] \leqslant \mathbb{E}[M_\nu] \leqslant \mathbb{E}[M_T], \tag{14.9}$$

see Exercise 14.6 below for a proof in discrete time.

e) In case τ is finite with probability one (but not bounded) we may also write

$$\mathbb{E}[M_\tau] = \mathbb{E}\left[\lim_{t \to \infty} M_{\tau \wedge t} \right] = \lim_{t \to \infty} \mathbb{E}[M_{\tau \wedge t}] = \mathbb{E}[M_0], \tag{14.10}$$

provided that

$$|M_{\tau \wedge t}| \leqslant C, \qquad a.s., \quad t \geqslant 0+. \tag{14.11}$$

More generally, (14.10) holds provided that the limit and expectation signs can be exchanged, and this can be done using *e.g.* the *Dominated Convergence Theorem*. In some situations the exchange of limit and expectation signs may not be valid.[†]

In case $\mathbb{P}(\tau = +\infty) > 0$, (14.10) holds under the above conditions, provided that

$$M_\infty := \lim_{t \to \infty} M_t \tag{14.12}$$

exists with probability one.

Relations (14.8), (14.9) and (14.7) can be extended to unbounded stopping times along the same lines and conditions as (14.10), such as (14.11) applied to both τ and ν. Dealing with unbounded stopping times can be necessary in the case of hitting times.

---

[*] "$\tau \leqslant T$ almost surely" means $\mathbb{P}(\tau \leqslant T) = 1$, *i.e.* $\mathbb{P}(\tau > T) = 0$.
[†] Consider for example the sequence $M_n = n \mathbb{1}_{\{X < 1/n\}}$, $n \geqslant 1$, where $X \simeq U(0,1]$ is a uniformly distributed random variable on $(0,1]$.

f) In general, for all *a.s.* finite (bounded or unbounded) stopping times τ it remains true that

$$\mathbb{E}[M_\tau] = \mathbb{E}\left[\lim_{t\to\infty} M_{\tau\wedge t}\right] \leqslant \lim_{t\to\infty} \mathbb{E}\left[M_{\tau\wedge t}\right] \leqslant \lim_{t\to\infty} \mathbb{E}[M_0] = \mathbb{E}[M_0], \qquad (14.13)$$

provided that $(M_t)_{t\in\mathbb{R}_+}$ is a nonnegative *super*martingale, where we used Fatou's Lemma.* As in (14.10), the limit (14.12) is required to exist with probability one if $\mathbb{P}(\tau = +\infty) > 0$.

g) As a counterexample to (14.7), the random time

$$\tau := \inf\left\{t \in [0,T] \ : \ M_t = \operatorname*{Sup}_{s\in[0,T]} M_s\right\},$$

which is not a stopping time, will satisfy

$$\mathbb{E}[M_\tau] > \mathbb{E}[M_T],$$

although $\tau \leqslant T$ almost surely. Similarly,

$$\tau := \inf\left\{t \in [0,T] \ : \ M_t = \inf_{s\in[0,T]} M_s\right\},$$

is not a stopping time and satisfies

$$\mathbb{E}[M_\tau] < \mathbb{E}[M_T].$$

Martingales and stopping times as gambling strategies

When $(M_t)_{t\in[0,T]}$ is a martingale, *e.g.* a centered random walk with independent increments, the message of the Stopping Time Theorem 14.7 is that the expected gain of the exit strategy $\tau_{x,y}$ of (14.5) remains zero on average since

$$\mathbb{E}\left[M_{\tau_{x,y}}\right] = \mathbb{E}[M_0] = 0,$$

if $M_0 = 0$. Therefore, on average, this exit strategy does not increase the average gain of the player. More precisely we have

$$\begin{aligned}
0 &= M_0 = \mathbb{E}[M_{\tau_{x,y}}] = x\mathbb{P}(M_{\tau_{x,y}} = x) + y\mathbb{P}(M_{\tau_{x,y}} = y) \\
&= -10 \times \mathbb{P}(M_{\tau_{x,y}} = -10) + 100 \times \mathbb{P}(M_{\tau_{x,y}} = 100),
\end{aligned}$$

which shows that

$$\mathbb{P}(M_{\tau_{x,y}} = -10) = \frac{10}{11} \quad \text{and} \quad \mathbb{P}(M_{\tau_{x,y}} = 100) = \frac{1}{11},$$

provided that the relation $\mathbb{P}(M_{\tau_{x,y}} = x) + \mathbb{P}(M_{\tau_{x,y}} = y) = 1$ is satisfied, see below for further applications to Brownian motion.

---

* $\mathbb{E}[\lim_{n\to\infty} F_n] \leqslant \lim_{n\to\infty} \mathbb{E}[F_n]$ for any sequence $(F_n)_{n\in\mathbb{N}}$ of *nonnegative* random variables, provided that the limits exist.

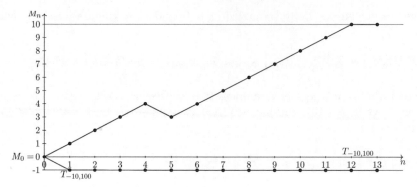

Figure 14.4: Sample paths of a gambling process $(M_n)_{n \in \mathbb{N}}$.

In the next Table 14.1 we summarize some of the results obtained in this section for bounded stopping times.

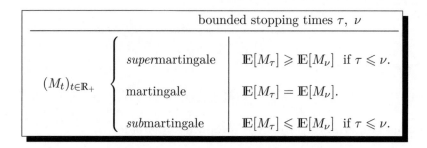

		bounded stopping times τ, ν
$(M_t)_{t \in \mathbb{R}_+}$	*super*martingale	$\mathbb{E}[M_\tau] \geqslant \mathbb{E}[M_\nu]$ if $\tau \leqslant \nu$.
	martingale	$\mathbb{E}[M_\tau] = \mathbb{E}[M_\nu]$.
	*sub*martingale	$\mathbb{E}[M_\tau] \leqslant \mathbb{E}[M_\nu]$ if $\tau \leqslant \nu$.

Table 14.1: Martingales and stopping times.

In the sequel we note that, as an application of the Stopping Time Theorem 14.7, a number of expectations can be computed in a simple and elegant way.

14.4 Drifted Brownian Motion

Brownian motion hitting a barrier

Given $a, b \in \mathbb{R}$, $a < b$, let the hitting* time $\tau_{a,b} : \Omega \longrightarrow \mathbb{R}_+$ be defined by

$$\tau_{a,b} = \inf\{t \geqslant 0 \ : \ B_t = a \text{ or } B_t = b\},$$

which is the hitting time of the boundary $\{a, b\}$ of Brownian motion $(B_t)_{t \in \mathbb{R}_+}$, $a < b \in \mathbb{R}$.

---

*Hitting times are stopping times.

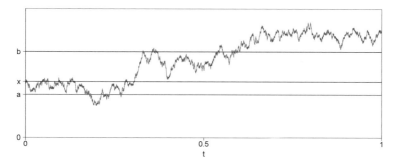

Figure 14.5: Brownian motion hitting a barrier.

Recall that Brownian motion $(B_t)_{t\in\mathbb{R}_+}$ is a martingale since it has independent increments, and those increments are centered:

$$\mathbb{E}[B_t - B_s] = 0, \qquad 0 \leqslant s \leqslant t.$$

Consequently, $(B_{\tau_{a,b}\wedge t})_{t\in\mathbb{R}_+}$ is still a martingale, and by (14.10) we have

$$\mathbb{E}[B_{\tau_{a,b}} \mid B_0 = x] = \mathbb{E}[B_0 \mid B_0 = x] = x,$$

as the exchange between limit and expectation in (14.10) can be justified since

$$|B_{t\wedge\tau_{a,b}}| \leqslant \mathrm{Max}(|a|, |b|), \qquad t \geqslant 0.$$

Hence we have

$$\begin{cases} x = \mathbb{E}[B_{\tau_{a,b}} \mid B_0 = x] = a \times \mathbb{P}(B_{\tau_{a,b}} = a \mid B_0 = x) + b \times \mathbb{P}(B_{\tau_{a,b}} = b \mid B_0 = x), \\ \mathbb{P}(X_{\tau_{a,b}} = a \mid X_0 = x) + \mathbb{P}(X_{\tau_{a,b}} = b \mid X_0 = x) = 1, \end{cases}$$

which yields

$$\mathbb{P}(B_{\tau_{a,b}} = b \mid B_0 = x) = \frac{x - a}{b - a}, \qquad a \leqslant x \leqslant b,$$

and also shows that

$$\mathbb{P}(B_{\tau_{a,b}} = a \mid B_0 = x) = \frac{b - x}{b - a}, \qquad a \leqslant x \leqslant b.$$

Note that the above result and its proof actually apply to any continuous martingale, and not only to Brownian motion.

Drifted Brownian motion hitting a barrier

Next, let us turn to the case of drifted Brownian motion

$$X_t = x + B_t + \mu t, \qquad t \geqslant 0.$$

In this case, the process $(X_t)_{t\in\mathbb{R}_+}$ is no longer a martingale and in order to use Theorem 14.7 we need to construct a martingale of a different type. Here we note that the process

$$M_t := \mathrm{e}^{\sigma B_t - \sigma^2 t/2}, \qquad t \geqslant 0,$$

is a martingale with respect to $(\mathcal{F}_t)_{t \in \mathbb{R}_+}$. Indeed, we have

$$\mathbb{E}[M_t \mid \mathcal{F}_s] = \mathbb{E}\left[e^{\sigma B_t - \sigma^2 t/2} \mid \mathcal{F}_s\right] = e^{\sigma B_s - \sigma^2 s/2}, \qquad 0 \leqslant s \leqslant t,$$

cf. *e.g.* Example 3 page 208.

By Theorem 14.7, we know that the stopped process $(M_{\tau_{a,b} \wedge t})_{t \in \mathbb{R}_+}$ is a martingale, hence its expected value is constant over time $t \in \mathbb{R}_+$ Proposition 14.2-c), and (14.10) yields

$$1 = \mathbb{E}[M_0] = \mathbb{E}[M_{\tau_{a,b}}],$$

as the exchange between limit and expectation in (14.10) can be justified since

$$|M_{t \wedge \tau_{a,b}}| \leqslant \mathrm{Max}\left(e^{\sigma|a|}, e^{\sigma|b|}\right), \qquad t \geqslant 0.$$

Next, we note that taking $\mu = -\sigma/2$, *i.e.* $\sigma = -2\mu$, we have $M_t = e^{-\sigma x} e^{\sigma X_t}$, and

$$e^{\sigma X_t} = e^{\sigma x + \sigma B_t + \sigma \mu t} = e^{\sigma x + \sigma B_t - \sigma^2 t/2} = e^{\sigma x} M_t,$$

hence

$$
\begin{aligned}
1 &= \mathbb{E}[M_{\tau_{a,b}}] \\
&= e^{-\sigma x} \mathbb{E}\left[e^{\sigma X_{\tau_{a,b}}}\right] \\
&= e^{(a-x)\sigma} \mathbb{P}(X_{\tau_{a,b}} = a \mid X_0 = x) + e^{(b-x)\sigma} \mathbb{P}(X_{\tau_{a,b}} = b \mid X_0 = x) \\
&= e^{-2(a-x)\mu} \mathbb{P}(X_{\tau_{a,b}} = a \mid X_0 = x) + e^{-2(b-x)\mu} \mathbb{P}(X_{\tau_{a,b}} = b \mid X_0 = x),
\end{aligned}
$$

under the additional condition

$$\mathbb{P}(X_{\tau_{a,b}} = a \mid X_0 = x) + \mathbb{P}(X_{\tau_{a,b}} = b \mid X_0 = x) = 1.$$

Finally, this gives

$$
\begin{cases}
\mathbb{P}(X_{\tau_{a,b}} = a \mid X_0 = x) = \dfrac{e^{\sigma x} - e^{\sigma b}}{e^{\sigma a} - e^{\sigma b}} = \dfrac{e^{-2\mu x} - e^{-2\mu b}}{e^{-2\mu a} - e^{-2\mu b}} & \text{(14.14a)} \\[4mm]
\mathbb{P}(X_{\tau_{a,b}} = b \mid X_0 = x) = \dfrac{e^{-2\mu a} - e^{-2\mu x}}{e^{-2\mu a} - e^{-2\mu b}}, & \text{(14.14b)}
\end{cases}
$$

$a \leqslant x \leqslant b$, see Figure 14.6 for an illustration with $a = 1$, $b = 2$, $x = 1.3$, $\mu = 2.0$, and $\left(e^{-2\mu a} - e^{-2\mu x}\right)/\left(e^{-2\mu a} - e^{-2\mu b}\right) = 0.7118437$.

```
1   nsim <- 1000;a=1;b=2;x=1.3;mu=2.0;N=10001; T<-2.0; t <- 0:(N-1); dt <- T/N; prob=0; time=0;
    dev.new(width=16,height=8)
3   for (i in 1:nsim){signal=0;colour="blue";Z <- rnorm(N,mean=0,sd= sqrt(dt));
    X <- c(1,N);X[1]=x;for (j in 2:N){X[j]=X[j-1]+Z[j]+mu*dt
5   if (X[j]<=a && signal==0) {signal=-1;colour="purple";time=time+j}
    if (X[j]>=b && signal==0) {signal=1;colour="blue";prob=prob+1;time=time+j}}
7   plot(t, X, xlab = "t", ylab = "", type = "l", ylim = c(-0,3), col =
        "blue",main=paste("Prob=",prob,"/",i,"=",round(prob/i, digits=5)," Time=",round(time*dt,
        digits=3),"/",i,"=",round(time*dt/i, digits=5)), xaxs="i", yaxs="i", xaxt="n",
        yaxt="n",cex.axis=1.8,cex.lab=1.8,cex.main=2)
    lines(t, x+mu*t*dt, type = "l", col = "orange",lwd=3);yticks<-c(0,a,x,b);
9   axis(side=2, at=yticks,labels = c(0,"a","x","b"), las = 2,cex.axis=1.8)
    xticks<-c(0,5000,10000)
11  axis(side=1, at=xticks,labels = c(0,"0.5","1"), las = 1,cex.axis=1.8)
    abline(h=x,lw=2); abline(h=a,col="purple",lwd=3);
13  abline(h=b,col="blue",lwd=3)# Sys.sleep(0.5)
    readline(prompt = "Pause. Press <Enter> to continue...")}
15  (exp(-2*mu*a)-exp(-2*mu*x))/(exp(-2*mu*a)-exp(-2*mu*b))
    (b*(exp(-2*mu*a)-exp(-2*mu*x))+a*(exp(-2*mu*x)-exp(-2*mu*b))
        -x*(exp(-2*mu*a)-exp(-2*mu*b)))/mu/(exp(-2*mu*a)-exp(-2*mu*b))
```

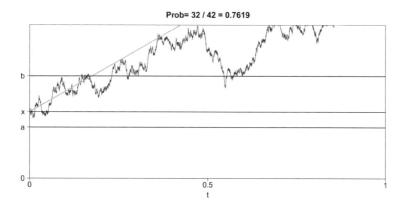

Figure 14.6: Drifted Brownian motion hitting a barrier.

Escape to infinity

Letting b tend to $+\infty$ in the above equalities shows by (14.14a)–(14.14b) that the probability $\mathbb{P}(\tau_a = +\infty)$ of escape to $+\infty$ of Brownian motion started from $x \in (a, \infty)$ is equal to

$$\mathbb{P}(\tau_a = +\infty) = \begin{cases} 1 - \mathbb{P}(X_{\tau_{a,\infty}} = a \mid X_0 = x) = 1 - e^{-2\mu(x-a)} > 0, & \mu > 0, \\ \\ 0, & \mu \leqslant 0, \end{cases}$$

i.e.

$$\mathbb{P}(\tau_a < +\infty) = \begin{cases} \mathbb{P}(X_{\tau_{a,\infty}} = a \mid X_0 = x) = e^{-2\mu(x-a)} < 1, & \mu > 0, \\ \\ 1, & \mu \leqslant 0. \end{cases} \tag{14.15}$$

Similarly, letting a tend to $-\infty$ shows that the probability $\mathbb{P}(\tau_b = +\infty)$ of escape to $-\infty$ of Brownian motion started from $x \in (-\infty, b)$ is equal to

$$\mathbb{P}(\tau_b = +\infty) = \begin{cases} 1 - \mathbb{P}(X_{\tau_{-\infty,b}} = b \mid X_0 = x) = 1 - e^{-2\mu(x-b)} > 0, & \mu < 0, \\ \\ 0, & \mu \geqslant 0, \end{cases}$$

i.e.

$$\mathbb{P}(\tau_b < +\infty) = \begin{cases} \mathbb{P}(X_{\tau_{-\infty,b}} = b \mid X_0 = x) = e^{-2\mu(x-b)} < 1, & \mu < 0, \\ \\ 1, & \mu \geqslant 0. \end{cases} \tag{14.16}$$

Mean hitting times for Brownian motion

The martingale method also allows us to compute the expectation $\mathbb{E}[B_{\tau_{a,b}}]$, after rechecking that

$$B_t^2 - t = 2 \int_0^t B_s dB_S, \qquad t \geqslant 0,$$

is also a martingale. Indeed, we have

$$
\begin{aligned}
\mathbb{E}[B_t^2 - t \mid \mathcal{F}_s] &= \mathbb{E}[(B_s + (B_t - B_s))^2 - t \mid \mathcal{F}_s] \\
&= \mathbb{E}[B_s^2 + (B_t - B_s)^2 + 2B_s(B_t - B_s) - t \mid \mathcal{F}_s] \\
&= \mathbb{E}[B_s^2 - s \mid \mathcal{F}_s] - (t-s) + \mathbb{E}[(B_t - B_s)^2 \mid \mathcal{F}_s] + 2\,\mathbb{E}[B_s(B_t - B_s) \mid \mathcal{F}_s] \\
&= B_s^2 - s - (t-s) + \mathbb{E}[(B_t - B_s)^2 \mid \mathcal{F}_s] + 2B_s\,\mathbb{E}[B_t - B_s \mid \mathcal{F}_s] \\
&= B_s^2 - s - (t-s) + \mathbb{E}[(B_t - B_s)^2] + 2B_s\,\mathbb{E}[B_t - B_s] \\
&= B_s^2 - s, \qquad 0 \leqslant s \leqslant t.
\end{aligned}
$$

Consequently the stopped process $(B_{\tau_{a,b}\wedge t}^2 - \tau_{a,b} \wedge t)_{t\in\mathbb{R}_+}$ is still a martingale by Theorem 14.7 hence the expectation $\mathbb{E}[B_{\tau_{a,b}\wedge t}^2 - \tau_{a,b} \wedge t]$ is constant over time $t \in \mathbb{R}_+$, hence by (14.10) we get[*]

$$
\begin{aligned}
x^2 &= \mathbb{E}[B_0^2 - 0 \mid B_0 = x] \\
&= \mathbb{E}[B_{\tau_{a,b}}^2 - \tau_{a,b} \mid B_0 = x] \\
&= \mathbb{E}[B_{\tau_{a,b}}^2 \mid B_0 = x] - \mathbb{E}[\tau_{a,b} \mid B_0 = x] \\
&= b^2\mathbb{P}(B_{\tau_{a,b}} = b \mid B_0 = x) + a^2\mathbb{P}(B_{\tau_{a,b}} = a \mid B_0 = x) - \mathbb{E}[\tau_{a,b} \mid B_0 = x],
\end{aligned}
$$

i.e.

$$
\begin{aligned}
\mathbb{E}[\tau_{a,b} \mid B_0 = x] &= b^2\mathbb{P}(B_{\tau_{a,b}} = b \mid B_0 = x) + a^2\mathbb{P}(B_{\tau_{a,b}} = a \mid B_0 = x) - x^2 \\
&= b^2\frac{x-a}{b-a} + a^2\frac{b-x}{b-a} - x^2 \\
&= (x-a)(b-x), \qquad a \leqslant x \leqslant b.
\end{aligned}
$$

Mean hitting time for drifted Brownian motion

Finally we show how to recover the value of the mean hitting time $\mathbb{E}[\tau_{a,b} \mid X_0 = x]$ of drifted Brownian motion $X_t = x + B_t + \mu t$. As above, the process $X_t - \mu t$ is a martingale the stopped process $(X_{\tau_{a,b}\wedge t} - \mu(\tau_{a,b} \wedge t))_{t\in\mathbb{R}_+}$ is still a martingale by Theorem 14.7. Hence the expectation $\mathbb{E}[X_{\tau_{a,b}\wedge t} - \mu(\tau_{a,b} \wedge t)]$ is constant over time $t \geqslant 0$.

Since the stopped process $\left(X_{\tau_{a,b}\wedge t} - \mu(\tau_{a,b} \wedge t)\right)_{t\in\mathbb{R}_+}$ is a martingale, we have

$$
x = \mathbb{E}[X_{\tau_{a,b}} - \mu\tau_{a,b} \mid X_0 = x],
$$

which gives

$$
\begin{aligned}
x &= \mathbb{E}[X_{\tau_{a,b}} - \mu\tau_{a,b} \mid X_0 = x] \\
&= \mathbb{E}[X_{\tau_{a,b}} \mid X_0 = x] - \mu\,\mathbb{E}[\tau_{a,b} \mid X_0 = x] \\
&= b\mathbb{P}(X_{\tau_{a,b}} = b \mid X_0 = x) + a\mathbb{P}(X_{\tau_{a,b}} = a \mid X_0 = x) - \mu\,\mathbb{E}[\tau_{a,b} \mid X_0 = x],
\end{aligned}
$$

i.e. by (14.14a),

$$
\begin{aligned}
\mu\,\mathbb{E}[\tau_{a,b} \mid X_0 = x] &= b\mathbb{P}(X_{\tau_{a,b}} = b \mid X_0 = x) + a\mathbb{P}(X_{\tau_{a,b}} = a \mid X_0 = x) - x \\
&= b\frac{\mathrm{e}^{-2\mu a} - \mathrm{e}^{-2\mu x}}{\mathrm{e}^{-2\mu a} - \mathrm{e}^{-2\mu b}} + a\frac{\mathrm{e}^{-2\mu x} - \mathrm{e}^{-2\mu b}}{\mathrm{e}^{-2\mu a} - \mathrm{e}^{-2\mu b}} - x \\
&= \frac{b\left(\mathrm{e}^{-2\mu a} - \mathrm{e}^{-2\mu x}\right) + a\left(\mathrm{e}^{-2\mu x} - \mathrm{e}^{-2\mu b}\right) - x\left(\mathrm{e}^{-2\mu a} - \mathrm{e}^{-2\mu b}\right)}{\mathrm{e}^{-2\mu a} - \mathrm{e}^{-2\mu b}},
\end{aligned}
$$

---

[*]Here we note that it can be showed that $\mathbb{E}[\tau_{a,b}] < \infty$ in order to apply (14.10).

hence

$$\mathbb{E}[\tau_{a,b} \mid X_0 = x] = \frac{b\left(e^{-2\mu a} - e^{-2\mu x}\right) + a\left(e^{-2\mu x} - e^{-2\mu b}\right) - x\left(e^{-2\mu a} - e^{-2\mu b}\right)}{\mu\left(e^{-2\mu a} - e^{-2\mu b}\right)},$$

$a \leqslant x \leqslant b$, see the code of page 412 for an illustration.

Table 14.2 presents a summary of the families of martingales used in this chapter.

Probabilities / Problem	Non drifted	Drifted
Hitting probability $\mathbb{P}(X_{\tau_{a,b}} = a, b)$	B_t	$e^{\sigma B_t - \sigma^2 t/2}$
Mean hitting time $\mathbb{E}[\tau_{a,b}]$	$B_t^2 - t$	$X_t - \mu t$

Table 14.2: List of martingales.

Exercises

Exercise 14.1 Let $(B_t)_{t \in \mathbb{R}_+}$ be a standard Brownian motion started at 0, *i.e.* $B_0 = 0$.

a) Is the process $t \longmapsto (2 - B_t)^+$ a *sub*martingale, a martingale or a *super*martingale?

b) Is the process $\left(e^{B_t}\right)_{t \in \mathbb{R}_+}$ a *sub*martingale, a martingale, or a *super*martingale?

c) Consider the random time ν defined by

$$\nu := \inf\{t \in \mathbb{R}_+ \; : \; B_t = B_{2t}\},$$

which represents the first intersection time of the curves $(B_t)_{t \in \mathbb{R}_+}$ and $(B_{2t})_{t \in \mathbb{R}_+}$.

Is ν a stopping time?

d) Consider the random time τ defined by

$$\tau := \inf\left\{t \in \mathbb{R}_+ \; : \; e^{B_t - t/2} = \alpha + \beta t\right\},$$

which represents the first time geometric Brownian motion $e^{B_t - t/2}$ crosses the straight line $t \longmapsto \alpha + \beta t$. Is τ a stopping time?

e) If τ is a stopping time, compute $\mathbb{E}[\tau]$ by the Doob Stopping Time Theorem 14.7 in each of the following two cases:

i) $\alpha > 1$ and $\beta < 0$,

ii) $\alpha < 1$ and $\beta > 0$.

Exercise 14.2 Stopping times. Let $(B_t)_{t\in\mathbb{R}_+}$ be a standard Brownian motion started at 0.

a) Consider the random time ν defined by

$$\nu := \inf\{t \in \mathbb{R}_+ \ : \ B_t = B_1\},$$

which represents the first time Brownian motion B_t hits the level B_1. Is ν a stopping time?

b) Consider the random time τ defined by

$$\tau := \inf\left\{t \in \mathbb{R}_+ \ : \ e^{B_t} = \alpha e^{-t/2}\right\},$$

which represents the first time the exponential of Brownian motion B_t crosses the path of $t \longmapsto \alpha e^{-t/2}$, where $\alpha > 1$.

Is τ a stopping time? If τ is a stopping time, compute $\mathbb{E}[e^{-\tau}]$ by applying the Stopping Time Theorem 14.7.

c) Consider the random time τ defined by

$$\tau := \inf\left\{t \in \mathbb{R}_+ \ : \ B_t^2 = 1 + \alpha t\right\},$$

which represents the first time the process $(B_t^2)_{t\in\mathbb{R}_+}$ crosses the straight line $t \longmapsto 1 + \alpha t$, with $\alpha < 1$.

Is τ a stopping time? If τ is a stopping time, compute $\mathbb{E}[\tau]$ by the Doob Stopping Time Theorem 14.7.

Exercise 14.3 Consider a standard Brownian motion $(B_t)_{t\in\mathbb{R}_+}$ started at $B_0 = 0$, and let

$$\tau_L = \inf\{t \in \mathbb{R}_+ \ : \ B_t = L\}$$

denote the first hitting time of the level $L > 0$ by $(B_t)_{t\in\mathbb{R}_+}$.

a) Compute the Laplace transform $\mathbb{E}[e^{-r\tau_L}]$ of τ_L for all $r \geqslant 0$.

Hint: Use the Stopping Time Theorem 14.7 and the fact that $\left(e^{\sqrt{2r}B_t - rt}\right)_{t\in\mathbb{R}_+}$ is a martingale when $r > 0$.

b) Find the optimal level stopping strategy depending on the value of $r > 0$ for the maximization problem

$$\underset{L>0}{\mathrm{Sup}}\ \mathbb{E}\left[e^{-r\tau_L}B_{\tau_L}\right].$$

Exercise 14.4 Consider $(B_t)_{t\in\mathbb{R}_+}$ a Brownian motion started at $B_0 = x \in [a,b]$ with $a < b$, and let

$$\tau := \inf\left\{t \in \mathbb{R}_+ \ : \ B_t = a \ \text{ or } \ B_t = b\right\}$$

denote the first exit time of the interval $[a,b]$. Show that the solution $f(x)$ of the differential equation $f''(x) = -2$ with $f(a) = f(b) = 0$ satisfies $f(x) = \mathbb{E}[\tau \mid B_0 = x]$.

Hint: Consider the process $X_t := f(B_t) - \dfrac{1}{2}\displaystyle\int_0^t f''(B_s)ds$, and apply the Doob Stopping Time Theorem 14.7.

Exercise 14.5 Consider a standard Brownian motion $(B_t)_{t \in \mathbb{R}_+}$ started at $B_0 = 0$, and let

$$\tau := \inf\{t \in \mathbb{R}_+ \ : \ B_t = \alpha + \beta t\}$$

denote the first hitting time of the straight line $t \longmapsto \alpha + \beta t$ by $(B_t)_{t \in \mathbb{R}_+}$.

a) Compute the Laplace transform $\mathbb{E}[e^{-r\tau}]$ of τ for all $r > 0$ and $\alpha \geqslant 0$.

b) Compute the Laplace transform $\mathbb{E}[e^{-r\tau}]$ of τ for all $r > 0$ and $\alpha \leqslant 0$.

Hint. Use the stopping time theorem and the fact that $\left(e^{\sigma B_t - \sigma^2 t/2}\right)_{t \in \mathbb{R}_+}$ is a martingale for all $\sigma \in \mathbb{R}$.

Exercise 14.6 (Doob–Meyer decomposition in discrete time). Let $(M_n)_{n \in \mathbb{N}}$ be a discrete-time *sub*martingale with respect to a filtration $(\mathcal{F}_n)_{n \in \mathbb{N}}$, with $\mathcal{F}_{-1} = \{\emptyset, \Omega\}$.

a) Show that there exists two processes $(N_n)_{n \in \mathbb{N}}$ and $(A_n)_{n \in \mathbb{N}}$ such that

    i) $(N_n)_{n \in \mathbb{N}}$ is a martingale with respect to $(\mathcal{F}_n)_{n \in \mathbb{N}}$,

    ii) $(A_n)_{n \in \mathbb{N}}$ is non-decreasing, *i.e.* $A_n \leqslant A_{n+1}$ *a.s.*, $n \in \mathbb{N}$,

    iii) $(A_n)_{n \in \mathbb{N}}$ is predictable in the sense that A_n is $\mathcal{F}_{n-1}$-measurable, $n \in \mathbb{N}$, and

    iv) $M_n = N_n + A_n$, $n \in \mathbb{N}$.

Hint: Let $A_0 := 0$,

$$A_{n+1} := A_n + \mathbb{E}[M_{n+1} - M_n \mid \mathcal{F}_n], \quad n \geqslant 0,$$

and define $(N_n)_{n \in \mathbb{N}}$ in such a way that it satisfies the four required properties.

b) Show that for all bounded stopping times σ and τ such that $\sigma \leqslant \tau$ *a.s.*, we have

$$\mathbb{E}[M_\sigma] \leqslant \mathbb{E}[M_\tau].$$

Hint: Use the Stopping Time Theorem 14.7 for martingales and (14.7).

Chapter 15

American Options

American options are financial derivatives that can be exercised at any time before maturity, in contrast to European options which have fixed maturities. The prices of American options are evaluated as an optimization problem, in which one has to find the optimal time to exercise in order to maximize the claim option payoff.

15.1 Perpetual American Put Options

The price of an American put option with finite expiration time $T > 0$ and strike price K can be expressed as the expected value of its discounted payoff:

$$f(t, S_t) = \sup_{\substack{t \leqslant \tau \leqslant T \\ \tau \text{ Stopping time}}} \mathbb{E}^* \left[e^{-(\tau-t)r} (K - S_\tau)^+ \,\middle|\, S_t \right],$$

under the risk-neutral probability measure $\mathbb{P}^*$, where the supremum is taken over stopping times between t and a fixed maturity T. Similarly, the price of a finite expiration American call option with strike price K is expressed as

$$f(t, S_t) = \sup_{\substack{t \leqslant \tau \leqslant T \\ \tau \text{ Stopping time}}} \mathbb{E}^* \left[e^{-(\tau-t)r} (S_\tau - K)^+ \,\middle|\, S_t \right].$$

Finite expiration American options can be found for example on the SPDR S&P 500 ETF Trust (SPY) exchange-traded fund. In this section we take $T = +\infty$, in which case we refer to these options as *perpetual* options, and the corresponding put and call options are respectively priced as

$$f(t, S_t) = \sup_{\substack{\tau \geqslant t \\ \tau \text{ Stopping time}}} \mathbb{E}^* \left[e^{-(\tau-t)r} (K - S_\tau)^+ \,\middle|\, S_t \right],$$

and

$$f(t, S_t) = \sup_{\substack{\tau \geqslant t \\ \tau \text{ Stopping time}}} \mathbb{E}^* \left[e^{-(\tau-t)r} (S_\tau - K)^+ \,\middle|\, S_t \right].$$

Two-choice optimal stopping at a fixed price level for perpetual put options

In this section we consider the pricing of perpetual put options. Given $L \in (0, K)$ a fixed price, consider the following choices for the exercise of a *put* option with strike price K:

1. If $S_t \leqslant L$, then exercise at time t.

2. Otherwise if $S_t > L$, wait until the first hitting time

$$\tau_L := \inf\{u \geqslant t \; : \; S_u \leqslant L\} \tag{15.1}$$

of the level $L > 0$, and exercise the option at time τ_L if $\tau_L < \infty$.

Note that by definition of (15.1) we have $\tau_L = t$ if $S_t \leqslant L$.

In case $S_t \leqslant L$, the payoff will be

$$(K - S_t)^+ = K - S_t$$

since $K > L \geqslant S_t$, however, in this case one would buy the option at price $K - S_t$ only to exercise it immediately for the same amount.

In case $S_t > L$, as $r > 0$ the price of the option is given by

$$
\begin{aligned}
f_L(t, S_t) &= \mathbb{E}^* \left[e^{-(\tau_L - t)r} (K - S_{\tau_L})^+ \mid S_t \right] \\
&= \mathbb{E}^* \left[e^{-(\tau_L - t)r} (K - S_{\tau_L})^+ \mathbb{1}_{\{\tau_L < \infty\}} \mid S_t \right] \\
&= \mathbb{E}^* \left[e^{-(\tau_L - t)r} (K - L)^+ \mathbb{1}_{\{\tau_L < \infty\}} \mid S_t \right] \\
&= (K - L) \mathbb{E}^* \left[e^{-(\tau_L - t)r} \mid S_t \right].
\end{aligned}
\tag{15.2}
$$

We note that the starting date t does not matter when pricing perpetual options, which have an infinite time horizon. Hence, $f_L(t, x) = f_L(x)$, $x > 0$, does not depend on $t \in \mathbb{R}_+$, and the pricing of the perpetual put option can be performed at $t = 0$. Recall that the underlying asset price is written as

$$S_t = S_0 \, e^{rt + \sigma \widehat{B}_t - \sigma^2 t / 2}, \qquad t \geqslant 0, \tag{15.3}$$

where $(\widehat{B}_t)_{t \in \mathbb{R}_+}$ is a standard Brownian motion under the risk-neutral probability measure $\mathbb{P}^*$, r is the risk-free interest rate, and $\sigma > 0$ is the volatility coefficient.

Lemma 15.1. *Assume that $r > 0$. We have*

$$\mathbb{E}^* \left[e^{-(\tau_L - t)r} \mid S_t = x \right] = \left(\frac{x}{L} \right)^{-2r/\sigma^2}, \qquad x \geqslant L. \tag{15.4}$$

Proof. We take $t = 0$ in (15.4) without loss of generality. We note that from (15.3), for all $\lambda \in \mathbb{R}$ we have

$$(S_t)^\lambda = e^{\lambda rt + \lambda \sigma \widehat{B}_t - \lambda \sigma^2 t / 2}, \qquad t \geqslant 0,$$

and the process $\left(Z_t^{(\lambda)} \right)_{t \in \mathbb{R}_+}$ defined as

$$Z_t^{(\lambda)} := (S_0)^\lambda \, e^{\lambda \sigma \widehat{B}_t - \lambda^2 \sigma^2 t / 2} = (S_t)^\lambda \, e^{-(\lambda r - \lambda(1 - \lambda)\sigma^2 / 2)t}, \qquad t \geqslant 0, \tag{15.5}$$

is a martingale under the risk-neutral probability measure $\mathbb{P}^*$. Choosing $\lambda \in \mathbb{R}$ such that

$$r = r\lambda - \lambda(1 - \lambda)\frac{\sigma^2}{2}, \tag{15.6}$$

we have

$$Z_t^{(\lambda)} = (S_t)^\lambda \, e^{-rt}, \qquad t \geqslant 0. \tag{15.7}$$

The equation (15.6) rewrites as

$$0 = \lambda^2 \frac{\sigma^2}{2} + \lambda \left(r - \frac{\sigma^2}{2} \right) - r = \frac{\sigma^2}{2} \left(\lambda + \frac{2r}{\sigma^2} \right) (\lambda - 1), \qquad (15.8)$$

with solutions

$$\lambda_+ = 1 \quad \text{and} \quad \lambda_- = -\frac{2r}{\sigma^2}.$$

Choosing the negative solution* $\lambda_- = -2r/\sigma^2 < 0$ and noting that $S_t \geqslant L$ for all $t \in [0, \tau_L]$, we obtain

$$0 \leqslant Z_t^{(\lambda_-)} = \mathrm{e}^{-rt}(S_t)^{\lambda_-} \leqslant \mathrm{e}^{-rt} L^{\lambda_-} \leqslant L^{\lambda_-}, \qquad 0 \leqslant t \leqslant \tau_L, \qquad (15.9)$$

since $r > 0$. Therefore we have $\lim_{t \to \infty} Z_t^{(\lambda_-)} = 0$, and since $\lim_{t \to \infty} Z_{\tau_L \wedge t}^{(\lambda_-)} = Z_{\tau_L}^{(\lambda_-)}$ on $\{\tau_L < \infty\}$, using (15.7), we find

$$
\begin{aligned}
L^{\lambda_-} \mathbb{E}^* \left[\mathrm{e}^{-r\tau_L} \right] &= \mathbb{E}^* \left[\mathrm{e}^{-r\tau_L} L^{\lambda_-} \mathbb{1}_{\{\tau_L < \infty\}} \right] \\
&= \mathbb{E}^* \left[\mathrm{e}^{-r\tau_L} (S_{\tau_L})^{\lambda_-} \mathbb{1}_{\{\tau_L < \infty\}} \right] \\
&= \mathbb{E}^* \left[Z_{\tau_L}^{(\lambda_-)} \mathbb{1}_{\{\tau_L < \infty\}} \right] \\
&= \mathbb{E}^* \left[\mathbb{1}_{\{\tau_L < \infty\}} \lim_{t \to \infty} Z_{\tau_L \wedge t}^{(\lambda_-)} \right] \\
&= \mathbb{E}^* \left[\lim_{t \to \infty} Z_{\tau_L \wedge t}^{(\lambda_-)} \right] &(15.10) \\
&= \lim_{t \to \infty} \mathbb{E}^* \left[Z_{\tau_L \wedge t}^{(\lambda_-)} \right] &(15.11) \\
&= \lim_{t \to \infty} \mathbb{E}^* \left[Z_0^{(\lambda_-)} \right] \\
&= (S_0)^{\lambda_-},
\end{aligned}
$$

where by (15.9) we applied the dominated convergence theorem from (15.10) to (15.11). Hence, we find

$$\mathbb{E}^* \left[\mathrm{e}^{-r\tau_L} \mid S_0 = x \right] = \left(\frac{x}{L} \right)^{-2r/\sigma^2}, \qquad x \geqslant L.$$

Note also that by (14.15) we have $\mathbb{P}(\tau_L < \infty) = 1$ if $r - \sigma^2/2 \leqslant 0$, and $\mathbb{P}(\tau_L = +\infty) > 0$ if $r - \sigma^2/2 > 0$. $\qquad \square$

Next, we apply Lemma 15.1 in order to price the perpetual American put option.

Proposition 15.2. *Assume that $r > 0$. We have*

$$
\begin{aligned}
f_L(x) &= \mathbb{E}^* \left[\mathrm{e}^{-(\tau_L - t)r} (K - S_{\tau_L})^+ \mid S_t = x \right] \\
&= \begin{cases} K - x, & 0 < x \leqslant L, \\ (K - L) \left(\dfrac{x}{L} \right)^{-2r/\sigma^2}, & x \geqslant L. \end{cases}
\end{aligned}
$$

---

* The bound (15.9) does not hold for the positive solution $\lambda_+ = 1$.

Proof. We take $t = 0$ without loss of generality.

i) The result is obvious for $S_0 = x \leqslant L$ since in this case we have $\tau_L = t = 0$ and $S_{\tau_L} = S_0 = x$ so that we only focus on the case $x > L$.

ii) Next, we consider the case $S_0 = x > L$. We have

$$
\begin{aligned}
\mathbb{E}^* \left[e^{-r\tau_L} (K - S_{\tau_L})^+ \,\middle|\, S_0 = x \right] &= \mathbb{E}^* \left[\mathbb{1}_{\{\tau_L < \infty\}} e^{-r\tau_L} (K - S_{\tau_L})^+ \,\middle|\, S_0 = x \right] \\
&= \mathbb{E}^* \left[\mathbb{1}_{\{\tau_L < \infty\}} e^{-r\tau_L} (K - L) \,\middle|\, S_0 = x \right] \\
&= (K - L)\, \mathbb{E}^* \left[e^{-r\tau_L} \,\middle|\, S_0 = x \right],
\end{aligned}
$$

and we conclude by the expression of $\mathbb{E}^* \left[e^{-r\tau_L} \,\middle|\, S_0 = x \right]$ given in Lemma 15.1. $\qquad\square$

We note that taking $L = K$ would yield a payoff always equal to 0 for the option holder, hence the value of L should be strictly lower than K. On the other hand, if $L = 0$ the value of τ_L will be infinite almost surely, hence the option price will be 0 when $r \geqslant 0$ from (15.2). Therefore there should be an optimal value L^*, which should be strictly comprised between 0 and K.

Figure 15.1 shows for $K = 100$ that there exists an optimal value $L^* = 85.71$ which maximizes the option price for all values of the underlying asset price.

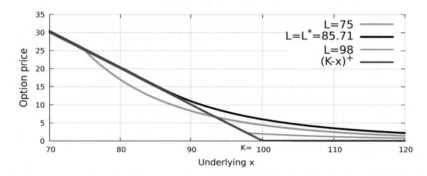

Figure 15.1: American put by exercising at τ_L for different values of L and $K = 100$.

Smooth pasting In order to compute L^* we observe that, geometrically, the slope of $f_L(x)$ at $x = L^*$ is equal to -1, *i.e.*

$$
f'_{L^*}(L^*) = -\frac{2r}{\sigma^2}(K - L^*)\frac{(L^*)^{-2r/\sigma^2 - 1}}{(L^*)^{-2r/\sigma^2}} = -1,
$$

i.e.

$$
\frac{2r}{\sigma^2}(K - L^*) = L^*,
$$

or

$$
L^* = \frac{2r}{2r + \sigma^2} K < K. \tag{15.12}
$$

We note that L^* tends to zero as σ becomes large or r becomes small, and that L^* tends to K when σ becomes small.

The same conclusion can be reached from the vanishing of the derivative of $L \mapsto f_L(x)$:

$$
\frac{\partial f_L(x)}{\partial L} = -\left(\frac{x}{L}\right)^{-2r/\sigma^2} + \frac{2r}{\sigma^2}\frac{K - L}{L}\left(\frac{x}{L}\right)^{-2r/\sigma^2} = 0,
$$

cf. page 351 of Shreve (2004). The next Figure 15.2 is a 2-dimensional animation that also shows the optimal value L^* of L.

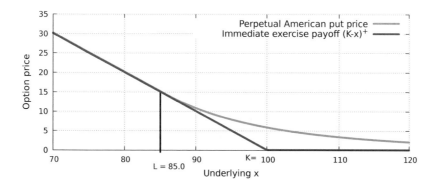

Figure 15.2: Animated graph of American put prices depending on L with $K = 100$.

The next Figure 15.3 gives another view of the put option prices according to different values of L, with the optimal value $L^* = 85.71$.

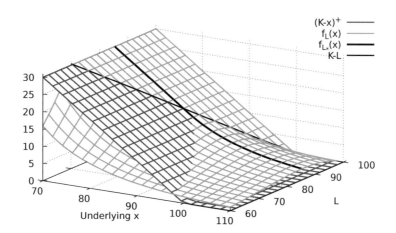

Figure 15.3: Option price as a function of L and of the underlying asset price.

In Figure 15.4, which is based on the stock price of HSBC Holdings (0005.HK) over year 2009 as in Figures 6.7-6.13, the optimal exercise strategy for an American put option with strike price K=\$77.67 would have been to exercise whenever the underlying asset price goes above $L^* = \$62$, *i.e.* at approximately 54 days, for a payoff of \$25.67. Exercising after a longer time, *e.g.* 85 days, could yield an even higher payoff of over \$65, however, this choice is not made because decisions are taken based on existing (past) information, and optimization is in expected value (or average) over all possible future paths.

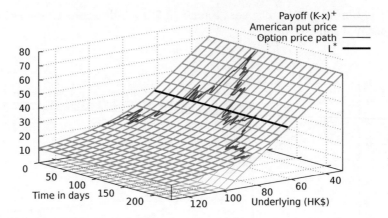

Figure 15.4: Path of the American put option price on the HSBC stock.

See Exercise 15.6 for the pricing of perpetual American put options with dividends.

15.2   PDE Method for Perpetual Put Options

Exercise. Check by hand calculations that the function f_{L^*} defined as

$$
f_{L^*}(x) :=
\begin{cases}
K - x, & 0 < x \leqslant L^* = \dfrac{2r}{2r + \sigma^2} K, \\[2ex]
\dfrac{K\sigma^2}{2r + \sigma^2} \left(\dfrac{2r + \sigma^2}{2r} \dfrac{x}{K} \right)^{-2r/\sigma^2}, & x \geqslant L^* = \dfrac{2r}{2r + \sigma^2} K,
\end{cases}
\tag{15.13}
$$

satisfies the Partial Differential Equation (PDE)

$$
\begin{aligned}
-r f_{L^*}(x) + r x f'_{L^*}(x) + \frac{1}{2}\sigma^2 x^2 f''_{L^*}(x) &= -rK \mathbb{1}_{\{x \leqslant L^*\}} \\
&= \begin{cases} -rK < 0, & 0 < x \leqslant L^* < K, \quad [\text{Exercise now}] \\ 0, & x > L^*. \quad [\text{Wait}] \end{cases}
\end{aligned}
\tag{15.14}
$$

in addition to the conditions

$$
\begin{cases}
f_{L^*}(x) = K - x, & 0 < x \leqslant L^* < K, \quad [\text{Exercise now}] \\
f_{L^*}(x) > (K - x)^+, & x > L^*, \quad [\text{Wait}]
\end{cases}
$$

see (15.13).

The above statements can be summarized in the following proposition.

Proposition 15.3. *The function* f_{L^*} *satisfies the following set of differential inequalities, or variational differential equation:*

$$
\begin{cases}
f_{L^*}(x) \geqslant (K - x)^+, & \text{(15.15a)} \\[2mm]
rx f'_{L^*}(x) + \dfrac{\sigma^2}{2} x^2 f''_{L^*}(x) \leqslant r f_{L^*}(x), & \text{(15.15b)} \\[2mm]
\left(r f_{L^*}(x) - rx f'_{L^*}(x) - \dfrac{\sigma^2}{2} x^2 f''_{L^*}(x) \right)\left(f_{L^*}(x) - (K - x)^+ \right) = 0. & \text{(15.15c)}
\end{cases}
$$

The equation (15.15c) admits an interpretation in terms of the absence of arbitrage, as shown below. By (15.14) and Itô's formula applied to

$$
dS_t = r S_t dt + \sigma S_t d\widehat{B}_t,
$$

the discounted portfolio value process

$$
\widetilde{f}_{L^*}(S_t) = \mathrm{e}^{-rt} f_{L^*}(S_t), \qquad t \geqslant 0,
$$

satisfies

$$
\begin{aligned}
& d\big(\widetilde{f}_{L^*}(S_t)\big) \\
={}& \left(-r f_{L^*}(S_t) + r S_t f'_{L^*}(S_t) + \frac{1}{2}\sigma^2 S_t^2 f''_{L^*}(S_t) \right) \mathrm{e}^{-rt} dt + \mathrm{e}^{-rt}\sigma S_t f'_{L^*}(S_t) d\widehat{B}_t \\
={}& -\mathbb{1}_{\{S_t \leqslant L^*\}} rK \mathrm{e}^{-rt} dt + \mathrm{e}^{-rt}\sigma S_t f'_{L^*}(S_t) d\widehat{B}_t \\
={}& -\mathbb{1}_{\{f_{L^*}(S_t) = (K - S_t)^+\}} rK \mathrm{e}^{-rt} dt + \mathrm{e}^{-rt}\sigma S_t f'_{L^*}(S_t) d\widehat{B}_t, & \text{(15.16)}
\end{aligned}
$$

hence we have the relation

$$
\begin{aligned}
& \widetilde{f}_{L^*}(S_T) - \widetilde{f}_{L^*}(S_t) \\
={}& -rK \int_t^T \mathbb{1}_{\{f_{L^*}(S_u) \leqslant (K - S_u)^+\}} \mathrm{e}^{-ru} du + \int_t^T \mathrm{e}^{-ru}\sigma S_u f'_{L^*}(S_u) d\widehat{B}_u,
\end{aligned}
$$

for some maturity time $T > 0$, which implies

$$
\begin{aligned}
& \mathbb{E}^*\left[\widetilde{f}_{L^*}(S_T) - \widetilde{f}_{L^*}(S_t) \mid \mathcal{F}_t \right] = \mathbb{E}^*\left[\widetilde{f}_{L^*}(S_T) \mid \mathcal{F}_t \right] - \widetilde{f}_{L^*}(S_t) \\
={}& \mathbb{E}^*\left[-rK \int_t^T \mathbb{1}_{\{f_{L^*}(S_u) \leqslant (K - S_u)^+\}} \mathrm{e}^{-ru} du + \int_t^T \mathrm{e}^{-ru}\sigma S_u f'_{L^*}(S_u) d\widehat{B}_u \,\Big|\, \mathcal{F}_t \right] \\
={}& -\mathbb{E}^*\left[rK \int_t^T \mathbb{1}_{\{f_{L^*}(S_u) \leqslant (K - S_u)^+\}} \mathrm{e}^{-ru} du \,\Big|\, \mathcal{F}_t \right],
\end{aligned}
$$

hence the following decomposition of the perpetual American put price into the sum of a European put price and an early exercise premium:

$$
\begin{aligned}
& \widetilde{f}_{L^*}(S_t) \\
={}& \mathbb{E}^*\left[\widetilde{f}_{L^*}(S_T) \mid \mathcal{F}_t \right] + rK\, \mathbb{E}^*\left[\int_t^T \mathbb{1}_{\{f_{L^*}(S_u) \leqslant (K - S_u)^+\}} \mathrm{e}^{-ru} du \,\Big|\, \mathcal{F}_t \right] \\
\geqslant{}& \underbrace{\mathrm{e}^{-rT}\, \mathbb{E}^*\left[(K - S_T)^+ \mid \mathcal{F}_t \right]}_{\text{European put price}} + \underbrace{rK\, \mathbb{E}^*\left[\int_t^T \mathbb{1}_{\{S_u \leqslant L^*\}} \mathrm{e}^{-ru} du \,\Big|\, \mathcal{F}_t \right]}_{\text{Early exercise premium}}, & \text{(15.17)}
\end{aligned}
$$

$0 \leqslant t \leqslant T$, see also Theorem 8.4.1 in § 8.4 in Elliott and Kopp (2005) on early exercise premiums. From (15.16) we also make the following observations.

a) From Equation (15.15c), $\widetilde{f}_{L^*}(S_t)$ is a martingale when

$$f_{L^*}(S_t) > (K - S_t)^+, \quad i.e. \quad S_t > L^*, \quad \text{[Wait]}$$

and in this case the expected rate of return of the hedging portfolio value $f_{L^*}(S_t)$ equals the rate r of the riskless asset, as

$$d\big(\widetilde{f}_{L^*}(S_t)\big) = \mathrm{e}^{-rt}\sigma S_t f'_{L^*}(S_t)d\widehat{B}_t,$$

or

$$d\big(f_{L^*}(S_t)\big) = d\big(\mathrm{e}^{rt}\widetilde{f}_{L^*}(S_t)\big) = rf_{L^*}(S_t)dt + \sigma S_t f'_{L^*}(S_t)d\widehat{B}_t,$$

and the investor prefers to wait.

b) On the other hand, if

$$f_{L^*}(S_t) = (K - S_t)^+, \quad i.e. \quad 0 < S_t < L^*, \quad \text{[Exercise now]}$$

the return of the hedging portfolio becomes lower than r as $d\big(\widetilde{f}_{L^*}(S_t)\big) = -rK\,\mathrm{e}^{-rt}dt + \mathrm{e}^{-rt}\sigma S_t f'_{L^*}(S_t)d\widehat{B}_t$ and

$$
\begin{aligned}
d\big(f_{L^*}(S_t)\big) &= d\big(\mathrm{e}^{rt}\widetilde{f}_{L^*}(S_t)\big)\\
&= rf_{L^*}(S_t)dt - rK\,dt + \mathrm{e}^{-rt}\sigma S_t f'_{L^*}(S_t)d\widehat{B}_t.
\end{aligned}
$$

In this case it is not worth waiting as (15.15b)–(15.15c) show that the return of the hedging portfolio is lower than that of the riskless asset, *i.e.*:

$$-rf_{L^*}(S_t) + rS_t f'_{L^*}(S_t) + \frac{1}{2}\sigma^2 S_t^2 f''_{L^*}(S_t) = -rK < 0,$$

exercise becomes immediate since the process $\widetilde{f}_{L^*}(S_t)$ becomes a (strict) *super*martingale, and (15.15c) implies $f_{L^*}(x) = (K - x)^+$.

In view of the above derivation, it should make sense to assert that $f_{L^*}(S_t)$ is the price at time t of the perpetual American put option. The next proposition confirms that this is indeed the case, and that the optimal exercise time is $\tau^* = \tau_{L^*}$.

Proposition 15.4. *The price of the perpetual American put option is given for all $t \geqslant 0$ by*

$$
\begin{aligned}
f_{L^*}(S_t) &= \operatorname*{Sup}_{\substack{\tau \geqslant t \\ \tau \text{ Stopping time}}} \mathbb{E}^*\big[\mathrm{e}^{-(\tau - t)r}(K - S_\tau)^+ \,\big|\, S_t\big]\\
&= \mathbb{E}^*\big[\mathrm{e}^{-(\tau_{L^*} - t)r}(K - S_{\tau_{L^*}})^+ \,\big|\, S_t\big]\\
&= \begin{cases} K - S_t, & 0 < S_t \leqslant L^*,\\[2mm] (K - L^*)\left(\dfrac{S_t}{L^*}\right)^{-2r/\sigma^2} = \dfrac{K\sigma^2}{2r + \sigma^2}\left(\dfrac{2r + \sigma^2}{2r}\dfrac{S_t}{K}\right)^{-2r/\sigma^2}, & S_t \geqslant L^*. \end{cases}
\end{aligned}
$$

Proof. i) Since the drift

$$-rf_{L^*}(S_t) + rS_t f'_{L^*}(S_t) + \frac{1}{2}\sigma^2 S_t^2 f''_{L^*}(S_t)$$

in Itô's formula (15.16) is nonpositive by the inequality (15.15b), the discounted portfolio value process

$$u \mapsto \mathrm{e}^{-ru} f_{L^*}(S_u), \qquad u \in [t, \infty),$$

is a *super*martingale. As a consequence, for all (*a.s.* finite) stopping times $\tau \in [t, \infty)$ we have, by (14.13),

$$\mathrm{e}^{-rt} f_{L^*}(S_t) \geqslant \mathbb{E}^* \left[\mathrm{e}^{-r\tau} f_{L^*}(S_\tau) \,\middle|\, S_t \right] \geqslant \mathbb{E}^* \left[\mathrm{e}^{-r\tau} (K - S_\tau)^+ \,\middle|\, S_t \right],$$

from (15.15a), which implies

$$\mathrm{e}^{-rt} f_{L^*}(S_t) \geqslant \sup_{\substack{\tau \geqslant t \\ \tau \text{ Stopping time}}} \mathbb{E}^* \left[\mathrm{e}^{-r\tau} (K - S_\tau)^+ \,\middle|\, S_t \right]. \tag{15.18}$$

ii) The converse inequality is obvious by Proposition 15.2, as

$$\begin{aligned} f_{L^*}(S_t) &= \mathbb{E}^* \left[\mathrm{e}^{-(\tau_{L^*} - t)r} (K - S_{\tau_{L^*}})^+ \,\middle|\, S_t \right] \\ &\leqslant \sup_{\substack{\tau \geqslant t \\ \tau \text{ Stopping time}}} \mathbb{E}^* \left[\mathrm{e}^{-(\tau - t)r} (K - S_\tau)^+ \,\middle|\, S_t \right], \end{aligned} \tag{15.19}$$

since τ_{L^*} is a stopping time larger than $t \in \mathbb{R}_+$. The inequalities (15.18) and (15.19) allow us to conclude to the equality

$$f_{L^*}(S_t) = \sup_{\substack{\tau \geqslant t \\ \tau \text{ Stopping time}}} \mathbb{E}^* \left[\mathrm{e}^{-(\tau - t)r} (K - S_\tau)^+ \,\middle|\, S_t \right].$$

$\square$

Remark. We note that the converse inequality (15.19) can also be obtained from the variational PDE (15.15a)–(15.15c) itself, without relying on Proposition 15.2. For this, taking $\tau = \tau_{L^*}$ we note that the process

$$u \mapsto \mathrm{e}^{-(u \wedge \tau_{L^*})r} f_{L^*}(S_{u \wedge \tau_{L^*}}), \qquad u \geqslant t,$$

is not only a *super*martingale, it is also a martingale until exercise at time τ_{L^*} by (15.14) since $S_{u \wedge \tau_{L^*}} \geqslant L^*$, hence we have

$$\mathrm{e}^{-rt} f_{L^*}(S_t) = \mathbb{E}^* \left[\mathrm{e}^{-(u \wedge \tau_{L^*})r} f_{L^*}(S_{u \wedge \tau_{L^*}}) \,\middle|\, S_t \right], \qquad u \geqslant t,$$

hence after letting u tend to infinity we obtain

$$\begin{aligned} \mathrm{e}^{-rt} f_{L^*}(S_t) &= \mathbb{E}^* \left[\mathrm{e}^{-r\tau_{L^*}} f_{L^*}(S_{\tau_{L^*}}) \,\middle|\, S_t \right] \\ &= \mathbb{E}^* \left[\mathrm{e}^{-r\tau_{L^*}} f_{L^*}(L^*) \,\middle|\, S_t \right] \\ &= \mathbb{E}^* \left[\mathrm{e}^{-r\tau_{L^*}} (K - S_{\tau_{L^*}})^+ \,\middle|\, S_t \right] \\ &\leqslant \sup_{\substack{\tau \geqslant t \\ \tau \text{ Stopping time}}} \mathbb{E}^* \left[\mathrm{e}^{-r\tau_{L^*}} (K - S_{\tau_{L^*}})^+ \,\middle|\, S_t \right], \end{aligned}$$

which recovers (15.19) as

$$\mathrm{e}^{-rt} f_{L^*}(S_t) \leqslant \sup_{\substack{\tau \geqslant t \\ \tau \text{ Stopping time}}} \mathbb{E}^* \left[\mathrm{e}^{-r\tau} (K - S_\tau)^+ \,\middle|\, S_t \right], \qquad t \geqslant 0.$$

15.3   Perpetual American Call Options

In this section we consider the pricing of perpetual call options.

Two-choice optimal stopping at a fixed price level for perpetual call options

Given $L > K$ a fixed price, consider the following choices for the exercise of a *call* option with strike price K:

1. If $S_t \geqslant L$, then exercise at time t.

2. Otherwise, wait until the first hitting time

$$\tau_L = \inf\{u \geqslant t \; : \; S_u = L\}$$

   and exercise the option and time τ_L.

In case $S_t \geqslant L$, the immediate exercise (or intrinsic) payoff will be

$$(S_t - K)^+ = S_t - K,$$

since $K < L \leqslant S_t$.

   In case $S_t < L$, as $r > 0$ the price of the option will be given by

$$
\begin{aligned}
f_L(S_t) &= \mathbb{E}^*\left[\,\mathrm{e}^{-(\tau_L - t)r}(S_{\tau_L} - K)^+ \,\middle|\, S_t\right] \\
&= \mathbb{E}^*\left[\,\mathrm{e}^{-(\tau_L - t)r}(S_{\tau_L} - K)^+ \mathbb{1}_{\{\tau_L < \infty\}} \,\middle|\, S_t\right] \\
&= \mathbb{E}^*\left[\,\mathrm{e}^{-(\tau_L - t)r}(L - K)^+ \,\middle|\, S_t\right] \\
&= (L - K)\,\mathbb{E}^*\left[\,\mathrm{e}^{-(\tau_L - t)r} \,\middle|\, S_t\right].
\end{aligned}
$$

Lemma 15.5. *Assume that $r > 0$. We have*

$$\mathbb{E}^*\left[\,\mathrm{e}^{-r\tau_L}\right] = \frac{S_0}{L}.$$

Proof. We only need to consider the case $S_0 = x < L$. Note that for all $\lambda \in \mathbb{R}$, the process $\left(Z_t^{(\lambda)}\right)_{t \in \mathbb{R}_+}$ defined as

$$Z_t^{(\lambda)} := (S_t)^\lambda \,\mathrm{e}^{-r\lambda t + \lambda \sigma^2 t/2 - \lambda^2 \sigma^2 t/2} = (S_0)^\lambda \,\mathrm{e}^{\lambda \sigma \widehat{B}_t - \lambda^2 \sigma^2 t/2}, \qquad t \geqslant 0,$$

defined in (15.5) is a martingale under the risk-neutral probability measure $\widetilde{\mathbb{P}}$. Hence the stopped process $\left(Z_{t \wedge \tau_L}^{(\lambda)}\right)_{t \in \mathbb{R}_+}$ is a martingale and it has constant expectation, *i.e.* we have

$$\mathbb{E}^*\left[Z_{t \wedge \tau_L}^{(\lambda)}\right] = \mathbb{E}^*\left[Z_0^{(\lambda)}\right] = (S_0)^\lambda, \qquad t \geqslant 0. \tag{15.20}$$

Choosing λ such that

$$r = r\lambda - \lambda\frac{\sigma^2}{2} + \lambda^2\frac{\sigma^2}{2},$$

i.e.

$$0 = \lambda^2 \frac{\sigma^2}{2} + \lambda \left(r - \frac{\sigma^2}{2} \right) - r = \frac{\sigma^2}{2} \left(\lambda + \frac{2r}{\sigma^2} \right) (\lambda - 1),$$

Relation (15.20) rewrites as

$$\mathbb{E}^* \left[(S_{t \wedge \tau_L})^\lambda e^{-(t \wedge \tau_L) r} \right] = (S_0)^\lambda, \qquad t \geqslant 0. \tag{15.21}$$

Choosing the positive solution* $\lambda_+ = 1$ yields the bound

$$0 \leqslant Z_t^{(\lambda_+)} = e^{-rt} S_t \leqslant S_t \leqslant L, \qquad 0 \leqslant t \leqslant \tau_L, \tag{15.22}$$

since $r > 0$ and $S_t \leqslant L$ for all $t \in [0, \tau_L]$. Hence we have $\lim_{t \to \infty} Z_t^{(\lambda_+)} = 0$, and since $\lim_{t \to \infty} Z_{\tau_L \wedge t}^{(\lambda_+)} = Z_{\tau_L}^{(\lambda_+)}$ on $\{\tau_L < \infty\}$, by (15.21)–(15.22) and the dominated convergence theorem, we get

$$
\begin{aligned}
L \, \mathbb{E}^* \left[e^{-r\tau_L} \right] &= \mathbb{E}^* \left[e^{-r\tau_L} S_{\tau_L} \mathbb{1}_{\{\tau_L < \infty\}} \right] \\
&= \mathbb{E}^* \left[\lim_{t \to \infty} e^{-(\tau_L \wedge t) r} S_{\tau_L \wedge t} \right] \\
&= \mathbb{E}^* \left[\lim_{t \to \infty} Z_{\tau_L \wedge t}^{(\lambda_+)} \right] \\
&= \lim_{t \to \infty} \mathbb{E}^* \left[Z_{\tau_L \wedge t}^{(\lambda_+)} \right] \\
&= \lim_{t \to \infty} \mathbb{E}^* \left[Z_0^{(\lambda_+)} \right] \\
&= S_0,
\end{aligned}
$$

which yields

$$\mathbb{E}^* \left[e^{-r\tau_L} \right] = \frac{S_0}{L}. \tag{15.23}$$

Note also that by (14.16) we have $\mathbb{P}(\tau_L < \infty) = 1$ if $r - \sigma^2/2 \geqslant 0$, and $\mathbb{P}(\tau_L = +\infty) > 0$ if $r - \sigma^2/2 < 0$. $\qquad \square$

Next, we apply Lemma 15.5 in order to price the perpetual American call option.

Proposition 15.6. *Assume that $r > 0$. The price of the perpetual American call option is given by $f_L(S_t)$ when $S_t < L$, where*

$$
f_L(x) = \begin{cases} x - K, & x \geqslant L \geqslant K, \\[2mm] (L - K)\dfrac{x}{L}, & 0 < x \leqslant L. \end{cases} \tag{15.24}
$$

Proof. i) The result is obvious for $S_0 = x \geqslant L$ since in this case we have $\tau_L = t = 0$ and $S_{\tau_L} = S_0 = x$ so that we only focus on the case $x < L$.
ii) Next, we consider the case $S_0 = x < L$. We have

$$
\begin{aligned}
\mathbb{E}^* \left[e^{-r\tau_L} (S_{\tau_L} - K)^+ \,\big|\, S_0 = x \right] &= \mathbb{E}^* \left[\mathbb{1}_{\{\tau_L < \infty\}} e^{-r\tau_L} (S_{\tau_L} - K)^+ \,\big|\, S_0 = x \right] \\
&= \mathbb{E}^* \left[\mathbb{1}_{\{\tau_L < \infty\}} e^{-r\tau_L} (L - K) \,\big|\, S_0 = x \right] \\
&= (L - K) \, \mathbb{E}^* \left[e^{-r\tau_L} \,\big|\, S_0 = x \right],
\end{aligned}
$$

and we conclude by the expression of $\mathbb{E}^* \left[e^{-r\tau_L} \,\big|\, S_0 = x \right]$ given in Lemma 15.1. $\qquad \square$

---

* The bound (15.22) does not hold for the negative solution $\lambda_- = -2r/\sigma^2$.

One can check from Figures 15.5 and 15.6 that the situation completely differs from the perpetual put option case, as there does not exist an optimal value L^* that would maximize the option price for all values of the underlying asset price.

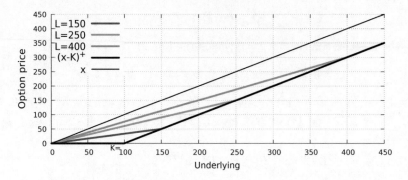

Figure 15.5: American call prices by exercising at τ_L for different values of L and $K = 100$.

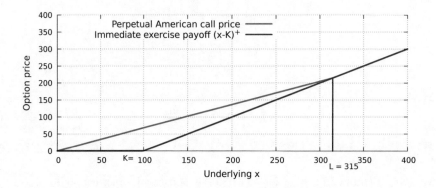

Figure 15.6: Animated graph of American option prices depending on L with $K = 100$.

The intuition behind this picture is that there is no upper limit above which one should exercise the option, and in order to price the American perpetual call option we have to let L go to infinity, *i.e.* the "optimal" exercise strategy is to wait indefinitely.

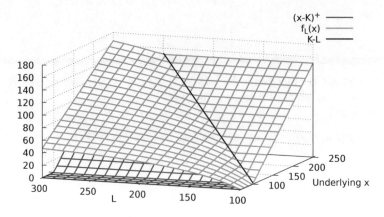

Figure 15.7: American call prices for different values of L.

We check from (15.24) that

$$\lim_{L \to \infty} f_L(x) = x - \lim_{L \to \infty} K\frac{x}{L} = x, \qquad x > 0. \tag{15.25}$$

As a consequence we have the following proposition.

Proposition 15.7. *Assume that* $r \geqslant 0$. *The price of the perpetual American call option is given by*

$$\mathop{\mathrm{Sup}}_{\substack{\tau \geqslant t \\ \tau \text{ Stopping time}}} \mathbb{E}^* \left[e^{-(\tau - t)r} (S_\tau - K)^+ \,|\, S_t \right] = S_t, \qquad t \geqslant 0. \tag{15.26}$$

Proof. For all $L > K$ we have

$$\begin{aligned} f_L(S_t) &= \mathbb{E}^* \left[e^{-(\tau_L - t)r} (S_{\tau_L} - K)^+ \,|\, S_t \right] \\ &\leqslant \mathop{\mathrm{Sup}}_{\substack{\tau \geqslant t \\ \tau \text{ Stopping time}}} \mathbb{E}^* \left[e^{-(\tau - t)r} (S_\tau - K)^+ \,|\, S_t \right], \qquad t \geqslant 0, \end{aligned}$$

hence from (15.25), taking the limit as $L \to \infty$ yields

$$S_t \leqslant \mathop{\mathrm{Sup}}_{\substack{\tau \geqslant t \\ \tau \text{ Stopping time}}} \mathbb{E}^* \left[e^{-(\tau - t)r} (S_\tau - K)^+ \,|\, S_t \right]. \tag{15.27}$$

On the other hand, since $u \mapsto e^{-(u-t)r} S_u$ is a martingale, by (14.13) we have, for all stopping times $\tau \in [t, \infty)$,

$$\mathbb{E}^* \left[e^{-(\tau - t)r} (S_\tau - K)^+ \,|\, S_t \right] \leqslant \mathbb{E}^* \left[e^{-(\tau - t)r} S_\tau \,|\, S_t \right] \leqslant S_t, \quad t \geqslant 0,$$

hence

$$\mathop{\mathrm{Sup}}_{\substack{\tau \geqslant t \\ \tau \text{ Stopping time}}} \mathbb{E}^* \left[e^{-(\tau - t)r} (S_\tau - K)^+ \,|\, S_t \right] \leqslant S_t, \qquad t \geqslant 0,$$

which shows (15.26) by (15.27). $\square$

We may also check that since $(e^{-rt} S_t)_{t \in \mathbb{R}_+}$ is a martingale, the process $t \mapsto (e^{-rt} S_t - K)^+$ is a *sub*martingale since the function $x \mapsto (x - K)^+$ is convex, hence for all bounded stopping times τ such that $t \leqslant \tau$ we have

$$(S_t - K)^+ \leqslant \mathbb{E}^* \left[(e^{-(\tau - t)r} S_\tau - K)^+ \,|\, S_t \right] \leqslant \mathbb{E}^* \left[e^{-(\tau - t)r} (S_\tau - K)^+ \,|\, S_t \right],$$

$t \geqslant 0$, showing that it is always better to wait than to exercise at time t, and the optimal exercise time is $\tau^* = +\infty$. This argument does not apply to American put options.

See Exercise 15.7 for the pricing of perpetual American call options with dividends.

15.4 Finite Expiration American Options

In this section we consider finite expiration American put and call options with strike price K. The prices of such options can be expressed as

$$f(t, S_t) = \mathop{\mathrm{Sup}}_{\substack{t \leqslant \tau \leqslant T \\ \tau \text{ Stopping time}}} \mathbb{E}^* \left[e^{-(\tau - t)r} (K - S_\tau)^+ \,|\, S_t \right],$$

and

$$f(t, S_t) = \operatorname*{Sup}_{\substack{t \leqslant \tau \leqslant T \\ \tau \text{ Stopping time}}} \mathbb{E}^* \left[e^{-(\tau - t)r} (S_\tau - K)^+ \mid S_t \right].$$

Two-choice optimal stopping at fixed times with finite expiration

We start by considering the optimal stopping problem in a simplified setting where $\tau \in \{t, T\}$ is allowed at time t to take only *two* values t (which corresponds to immediate exercise) and T (wait until maturity).

Proposition 15.8. *Assume that $r \geqslant 0$. For any stopping time $\tau \geqslant t$, the price of the European call option exercised at time τ satisfies the bound*

$$(x - K)^+ \leqslant \mathbb{E}^* [e^{-(\tau - t)r} (S_\tau - K)^+ \mid S_t = x], \qquad x, t > 0. \tag{15.28}$$

Proof. Since the function $x \mapsto x^+ = \operatorname{Max}(x, 0)$ is convex non-decreasing and the process $\left(e^{-rt} S_t - e^{-rt} K \right)_{t \in \mathbb{R}_+}$ is a *sub*martingale under $\mathbb{P}^*$ since $r \geqslant 0$, Proposition 14.4-(b) shows that that $t \mapsto \left(e^{-rt} S_t - e^{-rt} K \right)^+$ is a *sub*martingale by the Jensen inequality (14.3). Hence, by (14.13) applied to *sub*martingales, for any stopping time τ bounded by $t > 0$ we have

$$\begin{aligned}
(S_t - K)^+ &= e^{rt} (e^{-rt} S_t - e^{-rt} K)^+ \\
&\leqslant e^{rt} \mathbb{E}^* [(e^{-r\tau} S_\tau - e^{-r\tau} K)^+ \mid \mathcal{F}_t] \\
&= \mathbb{E}^* [e^{-(\tau - t)r} (S_\tau - K)^+ \mid \mathcal{F}_t],
\end{aligned}$$

which yields (15.28). □

In particular, for the deterministic time $\tau := T \geqslant t$ we get

$$(x - K)^+ \leqslant e^{-(T-t)r} \mathbb{E}^* [(S_T - K)^+ \mid S_t = x], \qquad x, t > 0.$$

as illustrated in Figure 15.8 using the Black–Scholes formula for European call options, see also Figure 6.14a. In other words, taking $x = S_t$, the payoff $(S_t - K)^+$ of immediate exercise at time t is always lower than the expected payoff $e^{-(T-t)r} \mathbb{E}^* [(S_T - K)^+ \mid S_t = x]$ given by exercise at maturity T. As a consequence, the optimal strategy for the investor is to wait until time T to exercise an American call option, rather than exercising earlier at time t. Note that the situation is completely different when $r < 0$, see Figure 6.15a.

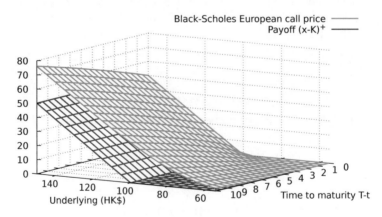

Figure 15.8: Black–Scholes call option price with $r = 3\% > 0$ *vs* $(x, t) \mapsto (x - K)^+$.

More generally, it can be shown that the price of the American call option equals the price of the corresponding European call option with maturity T, *i.e.*

$$f(t, S_t) = e^{-(T-t)r} \mathbb{E}^* \left[(S_T - K)^+ \mid S_t \right],$$

i.e. T is the optimal exercise date, see Proposition 15.10 below or §14.4 of Steele (2001) for a proof.

Put options

For put options the situation is entirely different. The Black–Scholes formula for European put options shows that the inequality

$$(K - x)^+ \leqslant e^{-(T-t)r} \, \mathbb{E}^*[(K - S_T)^+ \mid S_t = x],$$

does not always hold, as illustrated in Figure 15.9, see also Figure 6.14b.

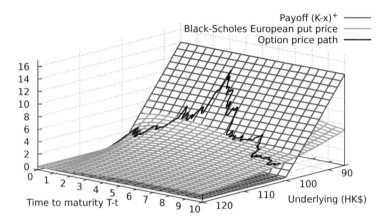

Figure 15.9: Black–Scholes put option price with $r = 3\% > 0$ *vs* $(x, t) \mapsto (K - x)^+$.

As a consequence, the optimal exercise decision for a put option depends on whether $(K - S_t)^+ \leqslant e^{-(T-t)r} \, \mathbb{E}^*[(K - S_T)^+ \mid S_t]$ (in which case one chooses to exercise at time T) or $(K - S_t)^+ > e^{-(T-t)r} \, \mathbb{E}^*[(K - S_T)^+ \mid S_t]$ (in which case one chooses to exercise at time t).

A view from above of the graph of Figure 15.9 shows the existence of an optimal frontier depending on time to maturity and on the price of the underlying asset, instead of being given by a constant level L^* as in Section 15.1, see Figure 15.10.

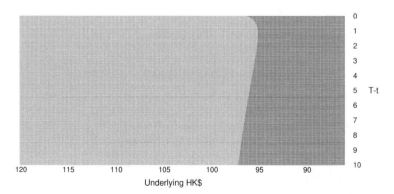

Figure 15.10: Optimal frontier for the exercise of a put option.

At a given time t, one will choose to exercise immediately if $(S_t, T - t)$ belongs to the blue area on the right, and to wait until maturity if $(S_t, T - t)$ belongs to the red area on the left.

When $r = 0$ we have $L^* = 0$, and the next remark shows that in this case it is always better to exercise the finite expiration American put option at maturity T, see also Exercise 15.9.

Proposition 15.9. *Assume that $r = 0$ and let $\phi : \mathbb{R} \longrightarrow \mathbb{R}$ be a nonnegative convex function. Then, the price of the finite expiration American option with payoff function ϕ on the underlying asset price $(S_t)_{t \in \mathbb{R}_+}$ coincides with the corresponding vanilla option price:*

$$f(t, S_t) = \underset{\substack{t \leqslant \tau \leqslant T \\ \tau \; Stopping \; time}}{Sup} \mathbb{E}^* \left[\phi(S_\tau) \, | \, S_t \right] = \mathbb{E}^* \left[\phi(S_T) \, | \, S_t \right],$$

i.e. the optimal strategy is to wait until the maturity time T to exercise the option, and $\tau^* = T$.

Proof. Since the function ϕ is convex and $(S_{t+s})_{s \in [0, T-t]}$ is a martingale under the risk-neutral measure $\mathbb{P}^*$, we know from Proposition 14.4-(a) that the process $(\phi(S_{t+s}))_{s \in [0, T-t]}$ is a *sub*martingale. Therefore, for all (bounded) stopping times τ comprised between t and T we have,

$$\mathbb{E}^*[\phi(S_\tau) \, | \, \mathcal{F}_t] \leqslant \mathbb{E}^*[\phi(S_T) \, | \, \mathcal{F}_t],$$

i.e. it is always better to wait until time T than to exercise at time $\tau \in [t, T]$, and this yields

$$\underset{\substack{t \leqslant \tau \leqslant T \\ \tau \; Stopping \; time}}{Sup} \mathbb{E}^* \left[\phi(S_\tau) \, | \, S_t \right] \leqslant \mathbb{E}^* \left[\phi(S_T) \, | \, S_t \right].$$

Since the constant T is a stopping time, it attains the above supremum. $\square$

15.5   PDE Method with Finite Expiration

Let us describe the PDE associated to American put options. After discretization $\{0 = t_0 < t_1 < \ldots < t_N = T\}$ of the time interval $[0, T]$, the optimal exercise strategy for the American put option can be described as follow at each time step:

If $f(t, S_t) > (K - S_t)^+$, wait.

If $f(t, S_t) = (K - S_t)^+$, exercise the option at time t.

Note that we cannot have $f(t, S_t) < (K - S_t)^+$.

If $f(t, S_t) > (K - S_t)^+$ the expected return of the hedging portfolio equals that of the riskless asset. This means that $f(t, S_t)$ follows the Black–Scholes PDE

$$r f(t, S_t) = \frac{\partial f}{\partial t}(t, S_t) + r S_t \frac{\partial f}{\partial x}(t, S_t) + \frac{1}{2} \sigma^2 S_t^2 \frac{\partial^2 f}{\partial x^2}(t, S_t),$$

whereas if $f(t, S_t) = (K - S_t)^+$ it is not worth waiting as the return of the hedging portfolio is lower than that of the riskless asset:

$$r f(t, S_t) \geqslant \frac{\partial f}{\partial t}(t, S_t) + r S_t \frac{\partial f}{\partial x}(t, S_t) + \frac{1}{2} \sigma^2 S_t^2 \frac{\partial^2 f}{\partial x^2}(t, S_t).$$

As a consequence, $f(t, x)$ should solve the following variational PDE, see Jaillet et al. (1990), Theorem 8.5.9 in Elliott and Kopp (2005) and Theorem 5 in Üstünel (2009):

$$
\begin{cases}
f(t, x) \geqslant f(T, x) = (K - x)^+, & (15.29a) \\[3mm]
\dfrac{\partial f}{\partial t}(t, x) + rx\dfrac{\partial f}{\partial x}(t, x) + \dfrac{\sigma^2}{2}x^2\dfrac{\partial^2 f}{\partial x^2}(t, x) \leqslant rf(t, x), & (15.29b) \\[3mm]
\left(\dfrac{\partial f}{\partial t}(t, x) + rx\dfrac{\partial f}{\partial x}(t, x) + \dfrac{\sigma^2}{2}x^2\dfrac{\partial^2 f}{\partial x^2}(t, x) - rf(t, x)\right) \\[3mm]
\qquad\qquad\qquad\qquad \times \left(f(t, x) - (K - x)^+\right) = 0, & (15.29c)
\end{cases}
$$

$x > 0$, $0 \leqslant t \leqslant T$, subject to the terminal condition $f(T, x) = (K - x)^+$. In other words, equality holds either in (15.29a) or in (15.29b) due to the presence of the term $(f(t, x) - (K - x)^+)$ in (15.29c).

The optimal exercise strategy consists in exercising the put option as soon as the equality $f(u, S_u) = (K - S_u)^+$ holds, *i.e.* at the time

$$
\tau^* = T \wedge \inf\{u \geqslant t \ : \ f(u, S_u) = (K - S_u)^+\},
$$

after which the process $\widetilde{f}_{L^*}(S_t)$ ceases to be a martingale and becomes a (strict) *super*martingale.

A simple procedure to compute numerically the price of an American put option is to use a finite difference scheme while simply enforcing the condition $f(t, x) \geqslant (K - x)^+$ at every iteration by adding the condition

$$
f(t_i, x_j) := \mathrm{Max}(f(t_i, x_j), (K - x_j)^+)
$$

right after the computation of $f(t_i, x_j)$.

The next Figure 15.11 shows a numerical resolution of the variational PDE (15.29a)-(15.29c) using the above simplified (implicit) finite difference scheme, see also Jacka (1991) for properties of the optimal boundary function. In comparison with Figure 15.4, one can check that the PDE solution becomes time-dependent in the finite expiration case.

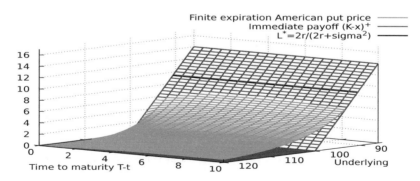

Figure 15.11: PDE estimates of finite expiration American put option prices.

In general, one will choose to exercise the put option when

$$
f(t, S_t) = (K - S_t)^+,
$$

i.e. within the blue area in Figure (15.11). We check that the optimal threshold $L^* = 90.64$ of the corresponding perpetual put option is within the exercise region, which is consistent since the perpetual optimal strategy should allow one to wait longer than in the finite expiration case.

The numerical computation of the American put option price

$$f(t, S_t) = \sup_{\substack{t \leqslant \tau \leqslant T \\ \tau \text{ Stopping time}}} \mathbb{E}^* \left[e^{-(\tau-t)r} (K - S_\tau)^+ \mid S_t \right]$$

can also be done by dynamic programming and backward optimization using the Longstaff and Schwartz (2001) (or Least Square Monte Carlo, LSM) algorithm as in Figure 15.12.

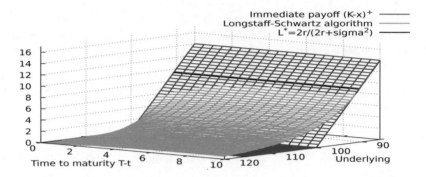

Figure 15.12: Longstaff-Schwartz estimates of finite expiration American put option prices.

In Figure 15.12 above and Figure 15.13 below the optimal threshold of the corresponding perpetual put option is again $L^* = 90.64$ and falls within the exercise region. Also, the optimal threshold is closer to L^* for large time to maturities, which shows that the perpetual option approximates the finite expiration option in that situation. In the next Figure 15.13 we compare the numerical computation of the American put option price by the finite difference and Longstaff-Schwartz methods.

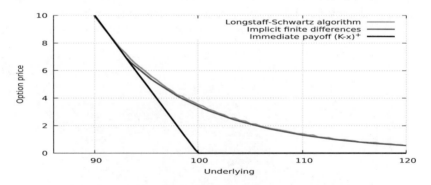

Figure 15.13: Comparison between Longstaff-Schwartz and finite differences.

It turns out that, although both results are very close, the Longstaff-Schwartz method performs better in the critical area close to exercise at it yields the expected continuously differentiable solution, and the simple numerical PDE solution tends to underestimate the optimal threshold. Also, a small error in the values of the solution translates into a large error on the value of the optimal exercise threshold.

The fOptions package in R contains a finite expiration American put option pricer based on the Barone-Adesi and Whaley (1987) approximation, see Exercise 15.4, however, the approximation is valid only for certain parameter ranges. See also Allegretto et al. (1995) for a related approximation of the early exercise premium (15.17).

The finite expiration American call option

In the next proposition we compute the price of a finite expiration American call option with an arbitrary convex payoff function ϕ.

Proposition 15.10. *Assume that $r \geqslant 0$ and let $\phi : \mathbb{R} \longrightarrow \mathbb{R}$ be a nonnegative convex function such that $\phi(0) = 0$. The price of the finite expiration American call option with payoff function ϕ on the underlying asset price $(S_t)_{t \in \mathbb{R}_+}$ is given by*

$$f(t, S_t) = \sup_{\substack{t \leqslant \tau \leqslant T \\ \tau \; Stopping \; time}} \mathbb{E}^* \left[e^{-(\tau-t)r} \phi(S_\tau) \,\middle|\, S_t \right] = e^{-(T-t)r} \mathbb{E}^* \left[\phi(S_T) \,\middle|\, S_t \right],$$

i.e. the optimal strategy is to wait until the maturity time T to exercise the option, and $\tau^* = T$.

Proof. Since the function ϕ is convex and $\phi(0) = 0$, we have

$$\phi(px) = \phi((1-p) \times 0 + px) \leqslant (1-p) \times \phi(0) + p\phi(x) = p\phi(x), \tag{15.30}$$

for all $p \in [0, 1]$ and $x \geqslant 0$. Next, taking $p := e^{-rs}$ in (15.30) we note that

$$
\begin{aligned}
e^{-rs} \mathbb{E}^* \left[\phi(S_{t+s}) \,\middle|\, \mathcal{F}_t \right] &\geqslant e^{-rs} \phi\big(\mathbb{E}^* \left[S_{t+s} \,\middle|\, \mathcal{F}_t \right] \big) \\
&\geqslant \phi\big(e^{-rs} \mathbb{E}^* \left[S_{t+s} \,\middle|\, \mathcal{F}_t \right] \big) \\
&= \phi(S_t),
\end{aligned}
$$

where we used Jensen's inequality (14.3) applied to the convex function ϕ, hence the process $s \mapsto e^{-rs} \phi(S_{t+s})$ is a *sub*martingale. Hence by the optional stopping theorem for *sub*martingales, cf (14.9), for all (bounded) stopping times τ comprised between t and T we have,

$$\mathbb{E}^* \left[e^{-(\tau-t)r} \phi(S_\tau) \,\middle|\, \mathcal{F}_t \right] \leqslant e^{-(T-t)r} \mathbb{E}^* [\phi(S_T) \,\middle|\, \mathcal{F}_t],$$

i.e. it is always better to wait until time T than to exercise at time $\tau \in [t, T]$, and this yields

$$\sup_{\substack{t \leqslant \tau \leqslant T \\ \tau \; Stopping \; time}} \mathbb{E}^* \left[e^{-(\tau-t)r} \phi(S_\tau) \,\middle|\, S_t \right] \leqslant e^{-(T-t)r} \mathbb{E}^* \left[\phi(S_T) \,\middle|\, S_t \right].$$

The converse inequality

$$e^{-(T-t)r} \mathbb{E}^* \left[\phi(S_T) \,\middle|\, S_t \right] \leqslant \sup_{\substack{t \leqslant \tau \leqslant T \\ \tau \; Stopping \; time}} \mathbb{E}^* \left[e^{-(\tau-t)r} \phi(S_\tau) \,\middle|\, S_t \right],$$

is obvious because T is a stopping time. $\qquad \square$

As a consequence of Proposition 15.10 applied to the convex function $\phi(x) = (x - K)^+$, the price of the finite expiration American call option is given by

$$
\begin{aligned}
f(t, S_t) &= \sup_{\substack{t \leqslant \tau \leqslant T \\ \tau \; Stopping \; time}} \mathbb{E}^* \left[e^{-(\tau-t)r} (S_\tau - K)^+ \,\middle|\, S_t \right] \\
&= e^{-(T-t)r} \mathbb{E}^* \left[(S_T - K)^+ \,\middle|\, S_t \right],
\end{aligned}
$$

i.e. the optimal strategy is to wait until the maturity time T to exercise the option. In the following Table 15.1 we summarize the optimal exercise strategies for the pricing of American options.

Option type	Perpetual			Finite expiration	
	Pricing	Optimal time		Pricing	Optimal time
Put option	$\begin{cases} K - S_t, & 0 < S_t \leqslant L^*, \\ (K - L^*)\left(\dfrac{S_t}{L^*}\right)^{-2r/\sigma^2}, & S_t \geqslant L^*. \end{cases}$	$\tau^* = \tau_{L^*}$		Solve the PDE (15.29a)-(15.29c) for $f(t,x)$ or use Longstaff and Schwartz (2001)	$\tau^* = T \wedge \inf\{u \geqslant t : f(u, S_u) = (K - S_u)^+\}$
Call option	S_t	$\tau^* = +\infty$		$e^{-(T-t)r}\,\mathbb{E}^*[(S_T - K)^+ \mid S_t]$	$\tau^* = T$

Table 15.1: Optimal exercise strategies.

Exercises

Exercise 15.1   Consider a two-step binomial model $(S_k)_{k=0,1,2}$ with interest rate $r = 0\%$ and risk-neutral probabilities (p^*, q^*):

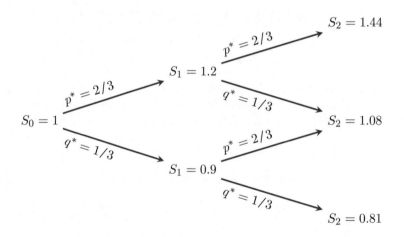

a) At time $t = 1$, would you exercise the American put option with strike price $K = 1.25$ if $S_1 = 1.2$? If $S_1 = 0.9$?

b) What would be your investment allocation at time $t = 0$?

Exercise 15.2   Let $r > 0$ and $\sigma > 0$.

a) Show that for every $C > 0$, the function $f(x) := Cx^{-2r/\sigma^2}$ solves the differential equation

$$\begin{cases} rf(x) = rxf'(x) + \dfrac{1}{2}\sigma^2 x^2 f''(x), \\[2mm] \lim_{x \to \infty} f(x) = 0. \end{cases}$$

b) Show that for every $K > 0$ there exists a unique level $L^* \in (0, K)$ and constant $C > 0$ such that $f(x)$ also solves the smooth fit conditions $f(L^*) = K - L^*$ and $f'(L^*) = -1$.

Exercise 15.3 Consider an American butterfly option with the following payoff function.

Figure 15.14: Butterfly payoff function.

Price the *perpetual* American butterfly option with $r > 0$ in the following cases.

a) $\widehat{K} \leqslant L^* \leqslant S_0$.

b) $\widehat{K} \leqslant S_0 \leqslant L^*$.

c) $0 \leqslant S_0 \leqslant \widehat{K}$.

Exercise 15.4 (Barone-Adesi and Whaley (1987)) We approximate the finite expiration American put option price with strike price K as

$$f(x,T) \simeq \begin{cases} \mathrm{BS_p}(x, T) + \alpha(x/S^*)^{-2r/\sigma^2}, & x > S^*, \qquad (15.31) \\ \\ K - x, & x \leqslant S^*, \qquad (15.32) \end{cases}$$

where $\alpha > 0$ is a parameter, $S^* > 0$ is called the *critical price*, and $\mathrm{BS_p}(x, T) = e^{-rT} K \Phi(-d_-(x, T)) - x\Phi(-d_+(x, T))$ is the Black–Scholes *put* pricing function.

a) Find the value α^* of α which achieves a smooth fit (equality of derivatives in x) between (15.31) and (15.32) at $x = S^*$.

b) Derive the equation satisfied by the critical price S^*.

Exercise 15.5 Consider the process $(X_t)_{t \in \mathbb{R}_+}$ given by $X_t := tZ$, $t \in \mathbb{R}_+$, where $Z \in \{0, 1\}$ is a Bernoulli random variable with $\mathbb{P}(Z = 1) = \mathbb{P}(Z = 0) = 1/2$. Given $\epsilon \geqslant 0$, let the random time τ_ϵ be defined as

$$\tau_\epsilon := \inf\{t > 0 \ : \ X_t > \epsilon\},$$

with $\inf \emptyset = +\infty$, and let $(\mathcal{F}_t)_{t \in \mathbb{R}_+}$ denote the filtration generated by $(X_t)_{t \in \mathbb{R}_+}$.

a) Give the possible values of τ_ϵ in $[0, \infty]$ depending on the value of Z.

b) Take $\epsilon = 0$. Is $\tau_0 := \inf\{t > 0 \ : \ X_t > 0\}$ an $(\mathcal{F}_t)_{t \in \mathbb{R}_+}$-stopping time? *Hint:* Consider the event $\{\tau_0 > 0\}$.

c) Take $\epsilon > 0$. Is $\tau_\epsilon := \inf\{t > 0 \ : \ X_t > \epsilon\}$ an $(\mathcal{F}_t)_{t \in \mathbb{R}_+}$-stopping time? *Hint:* Consider the event $\{\tau_\epsilon > t\}$ for $t \geqslant 0$.

Exercise 15.6   American put options with dividends, cf. Exercise 8.5 in Shreve (2004). Consider a dividend-paying asset priced as

$$S_t = S_0 e^{(r-\delta)t + \sigma \widehat{B}_t - \sigma^2 t/2}, \qquad t \geqslant 0,$$

where $r > 0$ is the risk-free interest rate, $\delta \geqslant 0$ is a continuous dividend rate, $(\widehat{B}_t)_{t \in \mathbb{R}_+}$ is a standard Brownian motion under the risk-neutral probability measure $\mathbb{P}^*$, and $\sigma > 0$ is the volatility coefficient. Consider the American put option with payoff

$$(\kappa - S_\tau)^+ = \begin{cases} \kappa - S_\tau & \text{if } S_\tau \leqslant \kappa, \\[2mm] 0 & \text{if } S_\tau > \kappa, \end{cases}$$

when exercised at the stopping time $\tau > 0$. Given $L \in (0, \kappa)$ a fixed level, consider the following exercise strategy for the above option:

- If $S_t \leqslant L$, then exercise at time t.

- If $S_t > L$, wait until the hitting time $\tau_L := \inf\{u \geqslant t : S_u = L\}$, and exercise the option at time τ_L.

a) Give the intrinsic option value at time $t = 0$ in case $S_0 \leqslant L$.

In what follows we work with $S_0 = x > L$.

b) Show that for all $\lambda \in \mathbb{R}$ the process $(Z_t^{(\lambda)})_{t \in \mathbb{R}_+}$ defined as

$$Z_t^{(\lambda)} := \left(\frac{S_t}{S_0}\right)^\lambda e^{-((r-\delta)\lambda - \lambda(1-\lambda)\sigma^2/2)t}$$

is a martingale under the risk-neutral probability measure $\mathbb{P}^*$.

c) Show that $(Z_t^{(\lambda)})_{t \in \mathbb{R}_+}$ can be rewritten as

$$Z_t^{(\lambda)} = \left(\frac{S_t}{S_0}\right)^\lambda e^{-rt}, \qquad t \geqslant 0,$$

for two values $\lambda_- \leqslant 0 \leqslant \lambda_+$ of λ that can be computed explicitly.

d) Choosing the negative solution λ_-, show that

$$0 \leqslant Z_t^{(\lambda_-)} \leqslant \left(\frac{L}{S_0}\right)^{\lambda_-}, \qquad 0 \leqslant t \leqslant \tau_L.$$

e) Let τ_L denote the hitting time

$$\tau_L = \inf\{u \in \mathbb{R}_+ : S_u \leqslant L\}.$$

By application of the Stopping Time Theorem 14.7 to the martingale $(Z_t)_{t \in \mathbb{R}_+}$, show that

$$\mathbb{E}^* \left[e^{-r\tau_L} \right] = \left(\frac{S_0}{L}\right)^{\lambda_-}, \tag{15.33}$$

with

$$\lambda_- := \frac{-(r - \delta - \sigma^2/2) - \sqrt{(r - \delta - \sigma^2/2)^2 + 4r\sigma^2/2}}{\sigma^2}. \tag{15.34}$$

f) Show that for all $L \in (0, K)$ we have

$$\mathbb{E}^* \left[e^{-r\tau_L} (K - S_{\tau_L})^+ \mid S_0 = x \right]$$

$$= \begin{cases} K - x, & 0 < x \leqslant L, \\[2ex] (K - L) \left(\dfrac{x}{L} \right)^{\frac{-(r-\delta-\sigma^2/2) - \sqrt{(r-\delta-\sigma^2/2)^2 + 4r\sigma^2/2}}{\sigma^2}}, & x \geqslant L. \end{cases}$$

g) Show that the value L^* of L that maximizes

$$f_L(x) := \mathbb{E}^* \left[e^{-r\tau_L} (K - S_{\tau_L})^+ \mid S_0 = x \right]$$

for every $x > 0$ is given by

$$L^* = \frac{\lambda_-}{\lambda_- - 1} K.$$

h) Show that

$$f_{L^*}(x) = \begin{cases} K - x, & 0 < x \leqslant L^* = \dfrac{\lambda_-}{\lambda_- - 1} K, \\[2ex] \left(\dfrac{1 - \lambda_-}{K} \right)^{\lambda_- - 1} \left(\dfrac{x}{-\lambda_-} \right)^{\lambda_-}, & x \geqslant L^* = \dfrac{\lambda_-}{\lambda_- - 1} K, \end{cases}$$

i) Show by hand computation that $f_{L^*}(x)$ satisfies the variational differential equation

$$\begin{cases} f_{L^*}(x) \geqslant (K - x)^+, & \text{(15.35a)} \\[2ex] (r - \delta) x f'_{L^*}(x) + \dfrac{1}{2} \sigma^2 x^2 f''_{L^*}(x) \leqslant r f_{L^*}(x), & \text{(15.35b)} \\[2ex] \left(r f_{L^*}(x) - (r - \delta) x f'_{L^*}(x) - \dfrac{1}{2} \sigma^2 x^2 f''_{L^*}(x) \right) & \text{(15.35c)} \\[1ex] \qquad \times \left(f_{L^*}(x) - (K - x)^+ \right) = 0. \end{cases}$$

j) Using Itô's formula, check that the discounted portfolio value process

$$t \mapsto e^{-rt} f_{L^*}(S_t)$$

is a *super*martingale.

k) Show that we have

$$f_{L^*}(S_0) \geqslant \sup_{\tau \text{ Stopping time}} \mathbb{E}^* \left[e^{-r\tau} (K - S_\tau)^+ \mid S_0 \right].$$

l) Show that the stopped process

$$s \mapsto e^{-(s \wedge \tau_{L^*}) r} f_{L^*}(S_{s \wedge \tau_{L^*}}), \qquad s \geqslant 0,$$

is a martingale, and that

$$f_{L^*}(S_0) \leqslant \sup_{\tau \text{ Stopping time}} \mathbb{E}^* \left[e^{-r\tau} (K - S_\tau)^+ \right].$$

m) Fix $t \in \mathbb{R}_+$ and let τ_{L^*} denote the hitting time

$$\tau_{L^*} = \inf\{u \geqslant t \ : \ S_u = L^*\}.$$

Conclude that the price of the perpetual American put option with dividend is given for all $t \in \mathbb{R}_+$ by

$$f_{L^*}(S_t) = \mathbb{E}^* \left[e^{-(\tau_{L^*}-t)r}(K - S_{\tau_{L^*}})^+ \,|\, S_t \right]$$

$$= \begin{cases} K - S_t, & 0 < S_t \leqslant \dfrac{\lambda_-}{\lambda_- - 1}K, \\[4mm] \left(\dfrac{1-\lambda_-}{K}\right)^{\lambda_- - 1}\left(\dfrac{S_t}{-\lambda_-}\right)^{\lambda_-}, & S_t \geqslant \dfrac{\lambda_-}{\lambda_- - 1}K, \end{cases}$$

where $\lambda_- < 0$ is given by (15.34), and

$$\tau_{L^*} = \inf\{u \geqslant t \ : \ S_u \leqslant L\}.$$

Exercise 15.7 American call options with dividends, see § 9.3 of Wilmott (2006). Consider a dividend-paying asset priced as $S_t = S_0 e^{(r-\delta)t+\sigma \widehat{B}_t - \sigma^2 t/2}$, $t \geqslant 0$, where $r > 0$ is the risk-free interest rate, $\delta \geqslant 0$ is a continuous dividend rate, and $\sigma > 0$.

a) Show that for all $\lambda \in \mathbb{R}$ the process $Z_t^{(\lambda)} := (S_t)^\lambda e^{-((r-\delta)\lambda - \lambda(1-\lambda)\sigma^2/2)t}$ is a martingale under $\mathbb{P}^*$.

b) Show that we have $Z_t^{(\lambda)} = (S_t)^\lambda e^{-rt}$ for two values $\lambda_- \leqslant 0$, $1 \leqslant \lambda_+$ of λ satisfying a certain equation.

c) Show that $0 \leqslant Z_t^{(\lambda_+)} \leqslant L^{\lambda_+}$ for $0 \leqslant t \leqslant \tau_L := \inf\{u \geqslant t \ : \ S_u = L\}$, and compute $\mathbb{E}^* \left[e^{-r\tau_L}(S_{\tau_L} - K)^+ \,|\, S_0 = x \right]$ when $S_0 = x < L$ and $K < L$.

Exercise 15.8 Optimal stopping for exchange options (Gerber and Shiu (1996)). We consider two risky assets S_1 and S_2 modeled by

$$S_1(t) = S_1(0) e^{\sigma_1 W_t + rt - \sigma_2^2 t/2} \quad \text{and} \quad S_2(t) = S_2(0) e^{\sigma_2 W_t + rt - \sigma_2^2 t/2}, \tag{15.36}$$

$t \geqslant 0$, with $\sigma_2 > \sigma_1 \geqslant 0$ and $r > 0$, and the perpetual optimal stopping problem

$$\operatorname*{Sup}_{\tau \ \text{Stopping time}} \mathbb{E}[e^{-r\tau}(S_1(\tau) - S_2(\tau))^+],$$

where $(W_t)_{t \in \mathbb{R}_+}$ is a standard Brownian motion under $\mathbb{P}$.

a) Find $\alpha > 1$ such that the process

$$Z_t := e^{-rt} S_1(t)^\alpha S_2(t)^{1-\alpha}, \qquad t \geqslant 0, \tag{15.37}$$

is a martingale.

b) For some fixed $L \geqslant 1$, consider the hitting time

$$\tau_L = \inf\left\{t \in \mathbb{R}_+ \ : \ S_1(t) \geqslant LS_2(t)\right\},$$

and show that

$$\mathbb{E}[e^{-r\tau_L}(S_1(\tau_L) - S_2(\tau_L))^+] = (L-1)\,\mathbb{E}[e^{-r\tau_L} S_2(\tau_L)].$$

c) By an application of the Stopping Time Theorem 14.7 to the martingale (15.37), show that we have

$$\mathbb{E}[e^{-r\tau_L}(S_1(\tau_L) - S_2(\tau_L))^+] = \frac{L-1}{L^\alpha}S_1(0)^\alpha S_2(0)^{1-\alpha}.$$

d) Show that the price of the perpetual exchange option is given by

$$\underset{\tau \text{ Stopping time}}{\text{Sup}} \mathbb{E}[e^{-r\tau}(S_1(\tau) - S_2(\tau))^+] = \frac{L^*-1}{(L^*)^\alpha}S_1(0)^\alpha S_2(0)^{1-\alpha},$$

where

$$L^* = \frac{\alpha}{\alpha - 1}.$$

e) As an application of Question (d), compute the perpetual American put option price

$$\underset{\tau \text{ Stopping time}}{\text{Sup}} \mathbb{E}[e^{-r\tau}(\kappa - S_2(\tau))^+]$$

when $r = \sigma_2^2/2$.

Exercise 15.9 Consider an underlying asset whose price is written as

$$S_t = S_0 e^{rt + \sigma B_t - \sigma^2 t/2}, \qquad t \geqslant 0,$$

where $(B_t)_{t \in \mathbb{R}_+}$ is a standard Brownian motion under the risk-neutral probability measure $\mathbb{P}^*$, $\sigma > 0$ denotes the volatility coefficient, and $r \in \mathbb{R}$ is the risk-free interest rate. For any $\lambda \in \mathbb{R}$ we consider the process $\left(Z_t^{(\lambda)}\right)_{t \in \mathbb{R}_+}$ defined by

$$
\begin{aligned}
Z_t^{(\lambda)} &:= e^{-rt}(S_t)^\lambda \\
&= (S_0)^\lambda e^{\lambda \sigma B_t - \lambda^2 \sigma^2 t/2 + (\lambda-1)(\lambda + 2r/\sigma^2)\sigma^2 t/2}, \quad t \geqslant 0. \quad (15.38)
\end{aligned}
$$

a) Assume that $r \geqslant -\sigma^2/2$. Show that, under $\mathbb{P}^*$, the process $\left(Z_t^{(\lambda)}\right)_{t \in \mathbb{R}_+}$ is a *su-permartingale* when $-2r/\sigma^2 \leqslant \lambda \leqslant 1$, and that it is a *submartingale* when $\lambda \in (-\infty, -2r/\sigma^2] \cup [1, \infty)$.

b) Assume that $r \leqslant -\sigma^2/2$. Show that, under $\mathbb{P}^*$, the process $\left(Z_t^{(\lambda)}\right)_{t \in \mathbb{R}_+}$ is a *su-permartingale* when $1 \leqslant \lambda \leqslant -2r/\sigma^2$, and that it is a *submartingale* when $\lambda \in (-\infty, 1] \cup [-2r/\sigma^2, \infty)$.

c) From this question onwards, we assume that $r < 0$. Given $L > 0$, let τ_L denote the hitting time

$$\tau_L = \inf\{u \in \mathbb{R}_+ : S_u = L\}.$$

By application of the Stopping Time Theorem 14.7 to $\left(Z_t^{(\lambda)}\right)_{t \in \mathbb{R}_+}$ to suitable values of λ, show that

$$\mathbb{E}^*\left[e^{-r\tau_L}\mathbb{1}_{\{\tau_L < \infty\}} \mid S_0 = x\right] \leqslant
\begin{cases}
\left(\dfrac{x}{L}\right)^{\text{Max}(1, -2r/\sigma^2)}, & x \geqslant L, \\[3mm]
\left(\dfrac{x}{L}\right)^{\min(1, -2r/\sigma^2)}, & 0 < x \leqslant L.
\end{cases}$$

d) Deduce an upper bound on the price

$$\mathbb{E}^* \left[e^{-r\tau_L} (K - S_{\tau_L})^+ \mid S_0 = x \right]$$

of the American put option exercised in finite time under the stopping strategy τ_L when $L \in (0, K)$ and $x \geqslant L$.

e) Show that when $r \leqslant -\sigma^2/2$, the upper bound of Question (d) increases and tends to $+\infty$ when L decreases to 0.

f) Find an upper bound on the price

$$\mathbb{E}^* \left[e^{-r\tau_L} (S_{\tau_L} - K)^+ \mathbb{1}_{\{\tau_L < \infty\}} \mid S_0 = x \right]$$

of the American call option exercised in finite time under the stopping strategy τ_L when $L \geqslant K$ and $x \leqslant L$.

g) Show that when $-\sigma^2/2 \leqslant r < 0$, the upper bound of Question (f) increases in $L \geqslant K$, and tends to S_0 as L increases to $+\infty$.

Exercise 15.10   Perpetual American binary options.

a) Compute the price

$$C_b^{\mathrm{Am}}(t, S_t) = \underset{\substack{\tau \geqslant t \\ \tau \text{ Stopping time}}}{\mathrm{Sup}} \mathbb{E}^* \left[e^{-(\tau - t)r} \mathbb{1}_{\{S_\tau \geqslant K\}} \mid S_t \right]$$

of the perpetual American binary call option.

b) Compute the price

$$P_b^{\mathrm{Am}}(t, S_t) = \underset{\substack{\tau \geqslant t \\ \tau \text{ Stopping time}}}{\mathrm{Sup}} \mathbb{E}^* \left[e^{-(\tau - t)r} \mathbb{1}_{\{S_\tau \leqslant K\}} \mid S_t \right]$$

of the perpetual American binary put option.

Exercise 15.11   Finite expiration American binary options. An American binary (or digital) call (resp. put) option with maturity $T > 0$ on an underlying asset process $(S_t)_{t \in \mathbb{R}_+} = (e^{rt + \sigma B_t - \sigma^2 t/2})_{t \in \mathbb{R}_+}$ can be exercised at any time $t \in [0, T]$, at the choice of the option holder.

The call (resp. put) option exercised at time t yields the payoff $\mathbb{1}_{[K, \infty)}(S_t)$ (resp. $\mathbb{1}_{[0,K]}(S_t)$), and the option holder wants to find an exercise strategy that will maximize his payoff.

a) Consider the following possible situations at time t:

    i) $S_t \geqslant K$,

    ii) $S_t < K$.

In each case (i) and (ii), tell whether you would choose to exercise the <u>call</u> option immediately, or to wait.

b) Consider the following possible situations at time t:

   i) $S_t > K$,

   ii) $S_t \leqslant K$.

In each case (i) and (ii), tell whether you would choose to exercise the <u>put</u> option immediately, or to wait.

c) The price $C_d^{\mathrm{Am}}(t, T, S_t)$ of an American binary call option is known to satisfy the Black–Scholes PDE

$$rC_d^{\mathrm{Am}}(t, T, x) = \frac{\partial C_d^{\mathrm{Am}}}{\partial t}(t, T, x) + rx \frac{\partial C_d^{\mathrm{Am}}}{\partial x}(t, T, x) + \frac{1}{2}\sigma^2 x^2 \frac{\partial^2 C_d^{\mathrm{Am}}}{\partial x^2}(t, T, x).$$

Based on your answers to Question (a), how would you set the boundary conditions $C_d^{\mathrm{Am}}(t, T, K)$, $0 \leqslant t < T$, and $C_d^{\mathrm{Am}}(T, T, x)$, $0 \leqslant x < K$?

d) The price $P_d^{\mathrm{Am}}(t, T, S_t)$ of an American binary put option is known to satisfy the same Black–Scholes PDE

$$rP_d^{\mathrm{Am}}(t, T, x) = \frac{\partial P_d^{\mathrm{Am}}}{\partial t}(t, T, x) + rx \frac{\partial P_d^{\mathrm{Am}}}{\partial x}(t, T, x) + \frac{1}{2}\sigma^2 x^2 \frac{\partial^2 P_d^{\mathrm{Am}}}{\partial x^2}(t, T, x). \quad (15.39)$$

Based on your answers to Question (b), how would you set the boundary conditions $P_d^{\mathrm{Am}}(t, T, K)$, $0 \leqslant t < T$, and $P_d^{\mathrm{Am}}(T, T, x)$, $x > K$?

e) Show that the optimal exercise strategy for the American binary call option with strike price K is to exercise as soon as the price of the underlying asset reaches the level K, *i.e.* at time

$$\tau_K := \inf\{u \geqslant t \ : \ S_u = K\},$$

starting from any level $S_t \leqslant K$, and that the price $C_d^{\mathrm{Am}}(t, T, S_t)$ of the American binary call option is given by

$$C_d^{\mathrm{Am}}(t, x) = \mathbb{E}\left[e^{-(\tau_K - t)r} \mathbb{1}_{\{\tau_K < T\}} \mid S_t = x\right].$$

f) Show that the price $C_d^{\mathrm{Am}}(t, T, S_t)$ of the American binary call option is equal to

$$C_d^{\mathrm{Am}}(t, T, x) = \frac{x}{K}\Phi\left(\frac{(r + \sigma^2/2)(T - t) + \log(x/K)}{\sigma\sqrt{T - t}}\right)$$
$$+ \left(\frac{x}{K}\right)^{-2r/\sigma^2}\Phi\left(\frac{-(r + \sigma^2/2)(T - t) + \log(x/K)}{\sigma\sqrt{T - t}}\right), \qquad 0 \leqslant x \leqslant K,$$

that this formula is consistent with the answer to Question (c), and that it recovers the answer to Question (a) of Exercise 15.10 as T tends to infinity.

g) Show that the optimal exercise strategy for the American binary put option with strike price K is to exercise as soon as the price of the underlying asset reaches the level K, *i.e.* at time

$$\tau_K := \inf\{u \geqslant t \ : \ S_u = K\},$$

starting from any level $S_t \geqslant K$, and that the price $P_d^{\mathrm{Am}}(t, T, S_t)$ of the American binary put option is

$$P_d^{\mathrm{Am}}(t, T, x) = \mathbb{E}[e^{-(\tau_K - t)r} \mathbb{1}_{\{\tau_K < T\}} \mid S_t = x], \qquad x \geqslant K.$$

h) Show that the price $P_d^{\mathrm{Am}}(t, T, S_t)$ of the American binary put option is equal to

$$
\begin{aligned}
P_d^{\mathrm{Am}}(t, T, x) &= \frac{x}{K} \Phi \left(\frac{-(r + \sigma^2/2)(T - t) - \log(x/K)}{\sigma\sqrt{T - t}} \right) \\
&+ \left(\frac{x}{K} \right)^{-2r/\sigma^2} \Phi \left(\frac{(r + \sigma^2/2)(T - t) - \log(x/K)}{\sigma\sqrt{T - t}} \right), \qquad x \geqslant K,
\end{aligned}
$$

that this formula is consistent with the answer to Question (d), and that it recovers the answer to Question (b) of Exercise 15.10 as T tends to infinity.

i) Does the standard call-put parity relation hold for American binary options?

Exercise 15.12 American forward contracts. Consider $(S_t)_{t \in \mathbb{R}_+}$ an asset price process given by

$$
\frac{dS_t}{S_t} = r dt + \sigma dB_t,
$$

where $r > 0$ and $(B_t)_{t \in \mathbb{R}_+}$ is a standard Brownian motion under $\mathbb{P}^*$.

a) Compute the price

$$
f(t, S_t) = \mathop{\mathrm{Sup}}_{\substack{t \leqslant \tau \leqslant T \\ \tau \text{ Stopping time}}} \mathbb{E}^* \left[e^{-(\tau - t)r} (K - S_\tau) \,\middle|\, S_t \right],
$$

and optimal exercise strategy of a finite expiration American-type short forward contract with strike price K on the underlying asset priced $(S_t)_{t \in \mathbb{R}_+}$, with payoff $K - S_\tau$ when exercised at time $\tau \in [0, T]$.

b) Compute the price

$$
f(t, S_t) = \mathop{\mathrm{Sup}}_{\substack{t \leqslant \tau \leqslant T \\ \tau \text{ Stopping time}}} \mathbb{E}^* \left[e^{-(\tau - t)r} (S_\tau - K) \,\middle|\, S_t \right],
$$

and optimal exercise strategy of a finite expiration American-type long forward contract with strike price K on the underlying asset priced $(S_t)_{t \in \mathbb{R}_+}$, with payoff $S_\tau - K$ when exercised at time $\tau \in [0, T]$.

c) How are the answers to Questions (a) and (b) modified in the case of perpetual options with $T = +\infty$?

Exercise 15.13 Consider an underlying asset price process written as

$$
S_t = S_0 e^{rt + \sigma \widehat{B}_t - \sigma^2 t/2}, \qquad t \geqslant 0,
$$

where $(\widehat{B}_t)_{t \in \mathbb{R}_+}$ is a standard Brownian motion under the risk-neutral probability measure $\mathbb{P}^*$, with $\sigma, r > 0$.

a) Show that the processes $(Y_t)_{t \in \mathbb{R}_+}$ and $(Z_t)_{t \in \mathbb{R}_+}$ defined as

$$
Y_t := e^{-rt} S_t^{-2r/\sigma^2} \quad \text{and} \quad Z_t := e^{-rt} S_t, \qquad t \geqslant 0,
$$

are both martingales under $\mathbb{P}^*$.

b) Let τ_L denote the hitting time

$$\tau_L = \inf\{u \in \mathbb{R}_+ \; : \; S_u = L\}.$$

By application of the Stopping Time Theorem 14.7 to the martingales $(Y_t)_{t \in \mathbb{R}_+}$ and $(Z_t)_{t \in \mathbb{R}_+}$, show that

$$\mathbb{E}^*\left[e^{-r\tau_L} \, | \, S_0 = x\right] \;=\; \begin{cases} \dfrac{x}{L}, & 0 < x \leqslant L, \\[2mm] \left(\dfrac{x}{L}\right)^{-2r/\sigma^2}, & x \geqslant L. \end{cases}$$

c) Compute the price $\mathbb{E}^*[e^{-r\tau_L}(K - S_{\tau_L})]$ of a short forward contract under the exercise strategy τ_L.

d) Show that for every value of $S_0 = x$ there is an optimal value L_x^* of L that maximizes $L \mapsto \mathbb{E}[e^{-r\tau_L}(K - S_{\tau_L})]$.

e) Would you use the stopping strategy

$$\tau_{L_x^*} = \inf\{u \in \mathbb{R}_+ \; : \; S_u = L_x^*\}$$

as an optimal exercise strategy for the short forward contract with payoff $K - S_\tau$?

Exercise 15.14 Let $p \geqslant 1$ and consider a power put option with payoff

$$((\kappa - S_\tau)^+)^p = \begin{cases} (\kappa - S_\tau)^p & \text{if } S_\tau \leqslant \kappa, \\ 0 & \text{if } S_\tau > \kappa, \end{cases}$$

exercised at time τ, on an underlying asset whose price S_t is written as

$$S_t = S_0 \, e^{rt + \sigma B_t - \sigma^2 t/2}, \qquad t \geqslant 0,$$

where $(B_t)_{t \in \mathbb{R}_+}$ is a standard Brownian motion under the risk-neutral probability measure $\mathbb{P}^*$, $r \geqslant 0$ is the risk-free interest rate, and $\sigma > 0$ is the volatility coefficient.

Given $L \in (0, \kappa)$ a fixed price, consider the following choices for the exercise of a *put* option with strike price κ:

i) If $S_t \leqslant L$, then exercise at time t.

ii) Otherwise, wait until the first hitting time $\tau_L := \inf\{u \geqslant t \; : \; S_u = L\}$, and exercise the option at time τ_L.

a) Under the above strategy, what is the option payoff equal to if $S_t \leqslant L$?

b) Show that in case $S_t > L$, the price of the option is equal to

$$f_L(S_t) = (\kappa - L)^p \, \mathbb{E}^*\left[e^{-(\tau_L - t)r} \, | \, S_t\right].$$

c) Compute the price $f_L(S_t)$ of the option at time t.

   Hint: Recall that by (15.4) we have $\mathbb{E}^*[e^{-(\tau_L - t)r} \, | \, S_t = x] = (x/L)^{-2r/\sigma^2}$ for $x \geqslant L$.

d) Compute the optimal value L^* that maximizes $L \mapsto f_L(x)$ for all fixed $x > 0$.

    Hint: Observe that, geometrically, the slope of $x \mapsto f_L(x)$ at $x = L^*$ is equal to $-p(\kappa - L^*)^{p-1}$.

e) How would you compute the American put option price

$$f(t, S_t) = \underset{\substack{\tau \geqslant t \\ \tau \text{ Stopping time}}}{\text{Sup}} \quad \mathbb{E}^* \left[e^{-(\tau-t)r} ((\kappa - S_\tau)^+)^p \,\middle|\, S_t \right] \quad ?$$

Exercise 15.15 Same questions as in Exercise 15.14, this time for the option with payoff $\kappa - (S_\tau)^p$ exercised at time τ, with $p > 0$.

Chapter 16

Change of Numéraire and Forward Measures

Change of numéraire is a powerful technique for the pricing of options under random discount factors by the use of forward measures. It has applications to the pricing of interest rate derivatives and other types of options, including exchange options (Margrabe formula) and foreign exchange options (Garman–Kohlhagen formula). The computation of self-financing hedging strategies by change of numéraire is treated in Section 16.5, and the change of numéraire technique will be applied to the pricing of interest rate derivatives such as bond options and swaptions in Chapter 19.

16.1 Notion of Numéraire

A *numéraire* is any strictly positive $(\mathcal{F}_t)_{t\in\mathbb{R}_+}$-adapted stochastic process $(N_t)_{t\in\mathbb{R}_+}$ that can be taken as a unit of reference when pricing an asset or a claim.

In general, the price S_t of an asset, when quoted in terms of the numéraire N_t, is given by

$$\widehat{S}_t := \frac{S_t}{N_t}, \qquad t \geqslant 0.$$

Deterministic numéraire transformations are easy to handle, as change of numéraire by a constant factor is a formal algebraic transformation that does not involve any risk. This can be the case for example when a currency is pegged to another currency,[†] for example the exchange rate of the French franc to the Euro was locked at €1 = FRF 6.55957 on December 31, 1998.

On the other hand, a random numéraire may involve new risks, and can allow for arbitrage opportunities.

Examples of numéraire processes $(N_t)_{t\in\mathbb{R}_+}$ include:

- *Money market account.*

  Given $(r_t)_{t\in\mathbb{R}_+}$ a possibly random, time-dependent and $(\mathcal{F}_t)_{t\in\mathbb{R}_+}$-adapted risk-free interest rate process, let[‡]

  $$N_t := \exp\left(\int_0^t r_s ds\right).$$

[†]Major currencies have started floating against each other since 1973, following the end of the system of fixed exchanged rates agreed upon at the Bretton Woods Conference, July 1–22, 1944.

[‡]"Anyone who believes exponential growth can go on forever in a finite world is either a madman or an economist", K.E. Boulding (1973), page 248.

DOI: 10.1201/9781003298670-16

In this case,

$$\widehat{S}_t = \frac{S_t}{N_t} = e^{-\int_0^t r_s ds} S_t, \qquad t \geqslant 0,$$

represents the discounted price of the asset at time 0.

- *Currency exchange rates*

In this case, $N_t := R_t$ denotes *e.g.* the EUR/SGD (EURSGD=X) exchange rate from a foreign currency (*e.g.* EUR) to a domestic currency (*e.g.* SGD), *i.e.* one unit of foreign currency (EUR) corresponds to R_t units of local currency (SGD). Let

$$\widehat{S}_t := \frac{S_t}{R_t}, \qquad t \geqslant 0,$$

denote the price of a local (SG) asset quoted in units of the foreign currency (EUR). For example, if $R_t = 1.63$ and $S_t = S\$1$, then

$$\widehat{S}_t = \frac{S_t}{R_t} = \frac{1}{1.63} \times \$1 \simeq €0.61,$$

and $1/R_t$ is the domestic SGD/EUR exchange rate. A question of interest is whether a local asset $\$S_t$, discounted according to a foreign risk-free rate r^f and priced in foreign currency as

$$e^{-r^f t} \frac{S_t}{R_t} = e^{-r^f t} \widehat{S}_t,$$

can be a martingale on the foreign market.

My foreign currency account S_t grew by 5% this year.	My foreign currency account S_t grew by 5% this year.
Q: Did I achieve a positive return?	The foreign exchange rate dropped by 10%.
A:	Q: Did I achieve a positive return?
	A:

(a) Scenario A.   (b) Scenario B.

Figure 16.1: Why change of numéraire?

- *Forward numéraire.*

The price $P(t,T)$ of a bond paying $P(T,T) = \$1$ at maturity T can be taken as numéraire. In this case, we have

$$N_t := P(t,T) = \mathbb{E}^* \left[e^{-\int_t^T r_s ds} \;\middle|\; \mathcal{F}_t \right], \qquad 0 \leqslant t \leqslant T.$$

Recall that

$$t \mapsto e^{-\int_0^t r_s ds} P(t,T) = \mathbb{E}^* \left[e^{-\int_0^T r_s ds} \;\middle|\; \mathcal{F}_t \right], \qquad 0 \leqslant t \leqslant T,$$

is an $\mathcal{F}_t$- martingale.

- *Annuity numéraire.*

Processes of the form

$$N_t = P(t, T_0, T_n) := \sum_{k=1}^{n} (T_k - T_{k-1}) P(t, T_k), \qquad 0 \leqslant t \leqslant T_0,$$

where $P(t, T_1), P(t, T_2), \ldots, P(t, T_n)$ are bond prices with maturities $T_1 < T_2 < \cdots < T_n$ arranged according to a *tenor structure*.

- *Combinations of the above*: for example a foreign money market account $e^{\int_0^t r_s^f ds} R_t$, expressed in local (or domestic) units of currency, where $\left(r_t^f\right)_{t \in \mathbb{R}_+}$ represents a short-term interest rate on the foreign market.

When the numéraire is a random process, the pricing of a claim whose value has been transformed under change of numéraire, *e.g.* under a change of currency, has to take into account the risks existing on the foreign market.

In particular, in order to perform a fair pricing, one has to determine a probability measure under which the transformed (or forward, or deflated) process $\widehat{S}_t = S_t / N_t$ will be a martingale, see Section 16.3 for details.

For example in case $N_t := e^{\int_0^t r_s ds}$ is the money market account, the risk-neutral probability measure $\mathbb{P}^*$ is a measure under which the discounted price process

$$\widehat{S}_t = \frac{S_t}{N_t} = e^{-\int_0^t r_s ds} S_t, \qquad t \geqslant 0,$$

is a martingale. In the next section, we will see that this property can be extended to any type of numéraire.

See Exercises 16.5 and 16.6 for other examples of numéraires.

16.2 Change of Numéraire

In this section we review the pricing of options by a change of measure associated to a numéraire N_t, cf. *e.g.* Geman et al. (1995) and references therein.

Most of the results of this chapter rely on the following assumption, which expresses the absence of arbitrage. In the foreign exchange setting where $N_t = R_t$, this condition states that the price of one unit of foreign currency is a martingale when quoted and discounted in the domestic currency.

Assumption (A). *The discounted numéraire*

$$t \mapsto M_t := e^{-\int_0^t r_s ds} N_t$$

is an $\mathcal{F}_t$-martingale under the risk-neutral probability measure $\mathbb{P}^*$.

Definition 16.1. *Given* $(N_t)_{t\in[0,T]}$ *a numéraire process, the associated* forward measure $\widehat{\mathbb{P}}$ *is defined by its Radon–Nikodym density*

$$\frac{d\widehat{\mathbb{P}}}{d\mathbb{P}^*} := \frac{M_T}{M_0} = e^{-\int_0^T r_s ds} \frac{N_T}{N_0}. \tag{16.1}$$

Recall that from Section 7.3 the above Relation (16.1) rewrites as

$$d\widehat{\mathbb{P}} = \frac{M_T}{M_0} d\mathbb{P}^* = e^{-\int_0^T r_s ds} \frac{N_T}{N_0} d\mathbb{P}^*,$$

which is equivalent to stating that

$$\begin{aligned}
\widehat{\mathbb{E}}[F] &= \int_\Omega F(\omega) d\widehat{\mathbb{P}}(\omega) \\
&= \int_\Omega F(\omega) e^{-\int_0^T r_s ds} \frac{N_T}{N_0} d\mathbb{P}^*(\omega) \\
&= \mathbb{E}^* \left[F e^{-\int_0^T r_s ds} \frac{N_T}{N_0} \right],
\end{aligned}$$

for all integrable $\mathcal{F}_T$-measurable random variables F. More generally, by (16.1) and the fact that the process

$$t \mapsto M_t := e^{-\int_0^t r_s ds} N_t$$

is an $\mathcal{F}_t$-martingale under $\mathbb{P}^*$ under Assumption (A), we find that

$$\begin{aligned}
\mathbb{E}^* \left[\frac{d\widehat{\mathbb{P}}}{d\mathbb{P}^*} \,\Big|\, \mathcal{F}_t \right] &= \mathbb{E}^* \left[\frac{N_T}{N_0} e^{-\int_0^T r_s ds} \,\Big|\, \mathcal{F}_t \right] \\
&= \mathbb{E}^* \left[\frac{M_T}{M_0} \,\Big|\, \mathcal{F}_t \right] \\
&= \frac{M_t}{M_0} \\
&= \frac{N_t}{N_0} e^{-\int_0^t r_s ds}, \qquad 0 \leqslant t \leqslant T. \tag{16.2}
\end{aligned}$$

In Proposition 16.5 we will show, as a consequence of next Lemma 16.2 below, that for any integrable random claim payoff C we have

$$\mathbb{E}^* \left[C e^{-\int_t^T r_s ds} N_T \,\big|\, \mathcal{F}_t \right] = N_t \widehat{\mathbb{E}}[C \mid \mathcal{F}_t], \qquad 0 \leqslant t \leqslant T.$$

Similarly to the above, the Radon–Nikodym density $d\widehat{\mathbb{P}}_{|\mathcal{F}_t} / d\mathbb{P}^*_{|\mathcal{F}_t}$ of $\widehat{\mathbb{P}}_{|\mathcal{F}_t}$ with respect to $\mathbb{P}^*_{|\mathcal{F}_t}$ satisfies the relation

$$\begin{aligned}
\widehat{\mathbb{E}}[F \mid \mathcal{F}_t] &= \int_\Omega F(\omega) d\widehat{\mathbb{P}}_{|\mathcal{F}_t}(\omega) \\
&= \int_\Omega F(\omega) e^{-\int_0^T r_s ds} \frac{d\widehat{\mathbb{P}}_{|\mathcal{F}_t}}{d\mathbb{P}^*_{|\mathcal{F}_t}} d\mathbb{P}^*_{|\mathcal{F}_t}(\omega) \\
&= \mathbb{E}^* \left[F \frac{d\widehat{\mathbb{P}}_{|\mathcal{F}_t}}{d\mathbb{P}^*_{|\mathcal{F}_t}} \,\Big|\, \mathcal{F}_t \right],
\end{aligned}$$

for all integrable $\mathcal{F}_T$-measurable random variables F, $0 \leqslant t \leqslant T$. Note that (16.2), which is $\mathcal{F}_t$-measurable, should not be confused with (16.3), which is $\mathcal{F}_T$-measurable.

Lemma 16.2. *We have*

$$\frac{d\widehat{\mathbb{P}}_{|\mathcal{F}_t}}{d\mathbb{P}^*_{|\mathcal{F}_t}} = \frac{M_T}{M_t} = e^{-\int_t^T r_s ds} \frac{N_T}{N_t}, \qquad 0 \leqslant t \leqslant T. \tag{16.3}$$

Proof. The proof of (16.3) relies on an abstract version of the Bayes formula. For all bounded $\mathcal{F}_t$-measurable random variable G, by (16.2), the tower property of conditional expectations we have

$$\begin{aligned}
\widehat{\mathbb{E}}[G\widehat{X}] &= \mathbb{E}^*\left[G\widehat{X} e^{-\int_0^T r_s ds} \frac{N_T}{N_0}\right] \\
&= \mathbb{E}^*\left[G \frac{N_t}{N_0} e^{-\int_0^t r_s ds} \mathbb{E}^*\left[\widehat{X} e^{-\int_t^T r_s ds} \frac{N_T}{N_t} \,\Big|\, \mathcal{F}_t\right]\right] \\
&= \mathbb{E}^*\left[G \mathbb{E}^*\left[\frac{d\widehat{\mathbb{P}}}{d\mathbb{P}^*} \,\Big|\, \mathcal{F}_t\right] \mathbb{E}^*\left[\widehat{X} e^{-\int_t^T r_s ds} \frac{N_T}{N_t} \,\Big|\, \mathcal{F}_t\right]\right] \\
&= \mathbb{E}^*\left[G \frac{d\widehat{\mathbb{P}}}{d\mathbb{P}^*} \mathbb{E}^*\left[\widehat{X} e^{-\int_t^T r_s ds} \frac{N_T}{N_t} \,\Big|\, \mathcal{F}_t\right]\right] \\
&= \widehat{\mathbb{E}}\left[G \mathbb{E}^*\left[\widehat{X} e^{-\int_t^T r_s ds} \frac{N_T}{N_t} \,\Big|\, \mathcal{F}_t\right]\right],
\end{aligned}$$

for all bounded random variables $\widehat{X}$, which shows that

$$\widehat{\mathbb{E}}[\widehat{X} \mid \mathcal{F}_t] = \mathbb{E}^*\left[\widehat{X} e^{-\int_t^T r_s ds} \frac{N_T}{N_t} \,\Big|\, \mathcal{F}_t\right],$$

i.e. (16.3) holds. $\qquad\square$

We note that in case the numéraire $N_t = e^{\int_0^t r_s ds}$ is equal to the money market account we simply have $\widehat{\mathbb{P}} = \mathbb{P}^*$.

Definition 16.3. *Given* $(X_t)_{t\in\mathbb{R}_+}$ *an asset price process, we define the process of forward (or deflated) prices*

$$\widehat{X}_t := \frac{X_t}{N_t}, \qquad 0 \leqslant t \leqslant T. \tag{16.4}$$

The process $\big(\widehat{X}_t\big)_{t\in\mathbb{R}_+}$ epresents the values at times t of X_t, expressed in units of the numéraire N_t. In the sequel, it will be useful to determine the dynamics of $\big(\widehat{X}_t\big)_{t\in\mathbb{R}_+}$ under the forward measure $\widehat{\mathbb{P}}$. The next proposition shows in particular that the process $\big(e^{\int_0^t r_s ds}/N_t\big)_{t\in\mathbb{R}_+}$ is an $\mathcal{F}_t$-martingale under $\widehat{\mathbb{P}}$.

Proposition 16.4. *Let* $(X_t)_{t\in\mathbb{R}_+}$ *denote a continuous* $(\mathcal{F}_t)_{t\in\mathbb{R}_+}$*-adapted asset price process such that*

$$t \mapsto e^{-\int_0^t r_s ds} X_t, \qquad t \geqslant 0,$$

is a martingale under $\mathbb{P}^*$*. Then, under change of numéraire,*

> *the deflated process* $\big(\widehat{X}_t\big)_{t\in[0,T]} = (X_t/N_t)_{t\in[0,T]}$ *of forward prices is an* $\mathcal{F}_t$*-martingale under* $\widehat{\mathbb{P}}$*,*

provided that $\big(\widehat{X}_t\big)_{t\in[0,T]}$ *is integrable under* $\widehat{\mathbb{P}}$*.*

Proof. We show that

$$\widehat{\mathbb{E}}\left[\frac{X_t}{N_t}\,\bigg|\,\mathcal{F}_s\right] = \frac{X_s}{N_s}, \qquad 0 \leqslant s \leqslant t, \tag{16.5}$$

using a standard characterization of conditional expectation. Namely, for all bounded $\mathcal{F}_s$-measurable random variables G we note that using (16.2) under Assumption (A) we have

$$
\begin{aligned}
\widehat{\mathbb{E}}\left[G\frac{X_t}{N_t}\right] &= \mathbb{E}^*\left[G\frac{X_t}{N_t}\frac{d\widehat{\mathbb{P}}}{d\mathbb{P}^*}\right] \\
&= \mathbb{E}^*\left[\mathbb{E}^*\left[G\frac{X_t}{N_t}\frac{d\widehat{\mathbb{P}}}{d\mathbb{P}^*}\,\bigg|\,\mathcal{F}_t\right]\right] \\
&= \mathbb{E}^*\left[G\frac{X_t}{N_t}\mathbb{E}^*\left[\frac{d\widehat{\mathbb{P}}}{d\mathbb{P}^*}\,\bigg|\,\mathcal{F}_t\right]\right] \\
&= \mathbb{E}^*\left[G\,\mathrm{e}^{-\int_0^t r_u du}\frac{X_t}{N_0}\right] \tag{16.6} \\
&= \mathbb{E}^*\left[G\,\mathrm{e}^{-\int_0^s r_u du}\frac{X_s}{N_0}\right] \tag{16.7} \\
&= \mathbb{E}^*\left[G\frac{X_s}{N_s}\mathbb{E}^*\left[\frac{d\widehat{\mathbb{P}}}{d\mathbb{P}^*}\,\bigg|\,\mathcal{F}_s\right]\right] \\
&= \mathbb{E}^*\left[\mathbb{E}^*\left[G\frac{X_s}{N_s}\frac{d\widehat{\mathbb{P}}}{d\mathbb{P}^*}\,\bigg|\,\mathcal{F}_s\right]\right] \\
&= \mathbb{E}^*\left[G\frac{X_s}{N_s}\frac{d\widehat{\mathbb{P}}}{d\mathbb{P}^*}\right] \\
&= \widehat{\mathbb{E}}\left[G\frac{X_s}{N_s}\right], \qquad 0 \leqslant s \leqslant t,
\end{aligned}
$$

where from (16.6) to (16.7)we used the fact that

$$t \mapsto \mathrm{e}^{-\int_0^t r_s ds}X_t$$

is an $\mathcal{F}_t$-martingale under $\mathbb{P}^*$. Finally, the identity

$$\widehat{\mathbb{E}}[G\widehat{X}_t] = \widehat{\mathbb{E}}\left[G\frac{X_t}{N_t}\right] = \widehat{\mathbb{E}}\left[G\frac{X_s}{N_s}\right] = \widehat{\mathbb{E}}[G\widehat{X}_s], \qquad 0 \leqslant s \leqslant t,$$

for all bounded $\mathcal{F}_s$-measurable G, implies (16.5). $\qquad\square$

Pricing using change of numéraire

The change of numéraire technique is especially useful for pricing under random interest rates, in which case an expectation of the form

$$\mathbb{E}^*\left[\mathrm{e}^{-\int_t^T r_s ds}C\,\bigg|\,\mathcal{F}_t\right]$$

becomes a *path integral*, see *e.g.* Dash (2004) for a recent account of path integral methods in quantitative finance. The next proposition is the basic result of this section, it provides a way to price an option with arbitrary payoff C under a random discount factor $\mathrm{e}^{-\int_t^T r_s ds}$ by use of the forward measure. It will be applied in Chapter 19 to the pricing of bond options and caplets, cf. Propositions 19.1, 19.3 and 19.5 below.

Proposition 16.5. *An option with integrable claim payoff $C \in L^1(\Omega, \mathbb{P}^*, \mathcal{F}_T)$ is priced at time t as*

$$\mathbb{E}^* \left[e^{-\int_t^T r_s ds} C \,\middle|\, \mathcal{F}_t \right] = N_t \widehat{\mathbb{E}} \left[\frac{C}{N_T} \,\middle|\, \mathcal{F}_t \right], \qquad 0 \leqslant t \leqslant T, \tag{16.8}$$

provided that $C/N_T \in L^1(\Omega, \widehat{\mathbb{P}}, \mathcal{F}_T)$.

Proof. By Relation (16.3) in Lemma 16.2 we have

$$
\begin{aligned}
\mathbb{E}^* \left[e^{-\int_t^T r_s ds} C \,\middle|\, \mathcal{F}_t \right] &= \mathbb{E}^* \left[\frac{d\widehat{\mathbb{P}}_{|\mathcal{F}_t}}{d\mathbb{P}^*_{|\mathcal{F}_t}} \frac{N_t}{N_T} C \,\middle|\, \mathcal{F}_t \right] \\
&= N_t \, \mathbb{E}^* \left[\frac{d\widehat{\mathbb{P}}_{|\mathcal{F}_t}}{d\mathbb{P}^*_{|\mathcal{F}_t}} \frac{C}{N_T} \,\middle|\, \mathcal{F}_t \right] \\
&= N_t \int_\Omega \frac{d\widehat{\mathbb{P}}_{|\mathcal{F}_t}}{d\mathbb{P}^*_{|\mathcal{F}_t}} \frac{C}{N_T} d\mathbb{P}^*_{|\mathcal{F}_t} \\
&= N_t \int_\Omega \frac{C}{N_T} d\widehat{\mathbb{P}}_{|\mathcal{F}_t} \\
&= N_t \widehat{\mathbb{E}} \left[\frac{C}{N_T} \,\middle|\, \mathcal{F}_t \right], \qquad 0 \leqslant t \leqslant T.
\end{aligned}
$$

Equivalently, we can write

$$
\begin{aligned}
N_t \widehat{\mathbb{E}} \left[\frac{C}{N_T} \,\middle|\, \mathcal{F}_t \right] &= N_t \mathbb{E}^* \left[\frac{C}{N_T} \frac{d\widehat{\mathbb{P}}_{|\mathcal{F}_t}}{d\mathbb{P}^*_{|\mathcal{F}_t}} \,\middle|\, \mathcal{F}_t \right] \\
&= \mathbb{E}^* \left[e^{-\int_t^T r_s ds} C \,\middle|\, \mathcal{F}_t \right], \qquad 0 \leqslant t \leqslant T.
\end{aligned}
$$

$\square$

Each application of the change of numéraire formula (16.8) will require to:

a) pick a suitable numéraire $(N_t)_{t \in \mathbb{R}_+}$ satisfying Assumption (A),

b) make sure that the ratio C/N_T takes a sufficiently simple form,

c) use the Girsanov theorem in order to determine the dynamics of asset prices under the new probability measure $\widehat{\mathbb{P}}$,

so as to compute the expectation under $\widehat{\mathbb{P}}$ on the right-hand side of (16.8).

Next, we consider further examples of numéraires and associated examples of option prices.

Examples:

a) *Money market account.*

Take $N_t := e^{\int_0^t r_s ds}$, where $(r_t)_{t \in \mathbb{R}_+}$ is a possibly random and time-dependent risk-free interest rate. In this case, Assumption (A) is clearly satisfied, we have $\widehat{\mathbb{P}} = \mathbb{P}^*$ and $d\mathbb{P}^*/d\widehat{\mathbb{P}}$, and (16.8) simply reads

$$\mathbb{E}^* \left[e^{-\int_t^T r_s ds} C \,\middle|\, \mathcal{F}_t \right] = e^{\int_0^t r_s ds} \mathbb{E}^* \left[e^{-\int_0^T r_s ds} C \,\middle|\, \mathcal{F}_t \right], \qquad 0 \leqslant t \leqslant T,$$

which yields no particular information.

b) *Forward numéraire.*

Here, $N_t := P(t,T)$ is the price $P(t,T)$ of a bond maturing at time T, $0 \leqslant t \leqslant T$, and the discounted bond price process $\left(e^{-\int_0^t r_s ds} P(t,T) \right)_{t \in [0,T]}$ is an $\mathcal{F}_t$-martingale under $\mathbb{P}^*$, *i.e.* Assumption (A) is satisfied and $N_t = P(t,T)$ can be taken as numéraire. In this case, (16.8) shows that a random claim payoff C can be priced as

$$\mathbb{E}^* \left[e^{-\int_t^T r_s ds} C \,\middle|\, \mathcal{F}_t \right] = P(t,T) \widehat{\mathbb{E}}[C \mid \mathcal{F}_t], \qquad 0 \leqslant t \leqslant T, \tag{16.9}$$

since $N_T = P(T,T) = 1$, where the forward measure $\widehat{\mathbb{P}}$ satisfies

$$\frac{d\widehat{\mathbb{P}}}{d\mathbb{P}^*} = e^{-\int_0^T r_s ds} \frac{P(T,T)}{P(0,T)} = \frac{e^{-\int_0^T r_s ds}}{P(0,T)} \tag{16.10}$$

by (16.1).

c) *Annuity numéraires.*

We take

$$N_t := \sum_{k=1}^n (T_k - T_{k-1}) P(t,T_k)$$

where $P(t,T_1), \ldots, P(t,T_n)$ are bond prices with maturities $T_1 < T_2 < \cdots < T_n$. Here, (16.8) shows that a swaption on the cash flow $P(T,T_n) - P(T,T_1) - \kappa N_T$ can be priced as

$$\mathbb{E}^* \left[e^{-\int_t^T r_s ds} (P(T,T_n) - P(T,T_1) - \kappa N_T)^+ \,\middle|\, \mathcal{F}_t \right]$$

$$= N_t \widehat{\mathbb{E}} \left[\left(\frac{P(T,T_n) - P(T,T_1)}{N_T} - \kappa \right)^+ \,\middle|\, \mathcal{F}_t \right],$$

$0 \leqslant t \leqslant T < T_1$, where $(P(T,T_n) - P(T,T_1))/N_T$ becomes a *swap rate*, cf. (18.19) in Proposition 18.11 and Section 19.5.

Girsanov theorem

We refer to *e.g.* Theorem III-35 page 132 of Protter (2004) for the following version of the Girsanov Theorem.

Theorem 16.6. *Assume that $\widehat{\mathbb{P}}$ is equivalent* to $\mathbb{P}^*$ with Radon–Nikodym density $d\widehat{\mathbb{P}}/d\mathbb{P}^*$, and let $(W_t)_{t \in [0,T]}$ be a standard Brownian motion under $\mathbb{P}^*$. Then, letting*

$$\Phi_t := \mathbb{E}^* \left[\frac{d\widehat{\mathbb{P}}}{d\mathbb{P}^*} \,\middle|\, \mathcal{F}_t \right], \qquad 0 \leqslant t \leqslant T, \tag{16.11}$$

the process $\left(\widehat{W}_t \right)_{t \in [0,T]}$ defined by

$$d\widehat{W}_t := dW_t - \frac{1}{\Phi_t} d\Phi_t \cdot dW_t, \qquad 0 \leqslant t \leqslant T, \tag{16.12}$$

is a standard Brownian motion under $\widehat{\mathbb{P}}$.

---

*This means that the Radon–Nikodym densities $d\widehat{\mathbb{P}}/d\mathbb{P}^*$ and $d\mathbb{P}^*/d\widehat{\mathbb{P}}$ exist and are strictly positive with $\mathbb{P}^*$ and $\widehat{\mathbb{P}}$-probability one, respectively.

In case the martingale $(\Phi_t)_{t \in [0,T]}$ takes the form

$$\Phi_t = \exp\left(-\int_0^t \psi_s dW_s - \frac{1}{2}\int_0^t |\psi_s|^2 ds\right), \qquad 0 \leqslant t \leqslant T,$$

i.e.

$$d\Phi_t = -\psi_t \Phi_t dW_t, \qquad 0 \leqslant t \leqslant T,$$

the Itô multiplication Table 4.1 shows that Relation (16.12) reads

$$
\begin{aligned}
d\widehat{W}_t &= dW_t - \frac{1}{\Phi_t}d\Phi_t \cdot dW_t \\
&= dW_t - \frac{1}{\Phi_t}(-\psi_t\Phi_t dW_t)\cdot dW_t \\
&= dW_t + \psi_t dt, \qquad 0 \leqslant t \leqslant T,
\end{aligned}
$$

and shows that the shifted process $\left(\widehat{W}_t\right)_{t\in[0,T]} = \left(W_t + \int_0^t \psi_s ds\right)_{t\in[0,T]}$ is a standard Brownian motion under $\widehat{\mathbb{P}}$, which is consistent with the Girsanov Theorem 7.3. The next result is another application of the Girsanov Theorem.

Proposition 16.7. *The process* $\left(\widehat{W}_t\right)_{t\in[0,T]}$ *defined by*

$$d\widehat{W}_t := dW_t - \frac{1}{N_t}dN_t \cdot dW_t, \qquad 0 \leqslant t \leqslant T, \tag{16.13}$$

is a standard Brownian motion under $\widehat{\mathbb{P}}$.

Proof. Relation (16.2) shows that Φ_t defined in (16.11) satisfies

$$
\begin{aligned}
\Phi_t &= \mathbb{E}^*\left[\frac{d\widehat{\mathbb{P}}}{d\mathbb{P}^*}\,\Big|\,\mathcal{F}_t\right] \\
&= \mathbb{E}^*\left[\frac{N_T}{N_0}e^{-\int_0^T r_s ds}\,\Big|\,\mathcal{F}_t\right] \\
&= \frac{N_t}{N_0}e^{-\int_0^t r_s ds}, \qquad 0 \leqslant t \leqslant T,
\end{aligned}
$$

hence

$$
\begin{aligned}
d\Phi_t &= d\left(\frac{N_t}{N_0}e^{-\int_0^t r_s ds}\right) \\
&= -\Phi_t r_t dt + e^{-\int_0^t r_s ds}d\left(\frac{N_t}{N_0}\right) \\
&= -\Phi_t r_t dt + \frac{\Phi_t}{N_t}dN_t,
\end{aligned}
$$

which, by (16.12), yields

$$
\begin{aligned}
d\widehat{W}_t &= dW_t - \frac{1}{\Phi_t}d\Phi_t \cdot dW_t \\
&= dW_t - \frac{1}{\Phi_t}\left(-\Phi_t r_t dt + \frac{\Phi_t}{N_t}dN_t\right)\cdot dW_t \\
&= dW_t - \frac{1}{N_t}dN_t \cdot dW_t,
\end{aligned}
$$

which is (16.13), from Relation (16.12) and the Itô multiplication Table 4.1. $\qquad\square$

The next Proposition 16.8 is consistent with the statement of Proposition 16.4, and in addition it specifies the dynamics of $(\widehat{X}_t)_{t\in\mathbb{R}_+}$ under $\widehat{\mathbb{P}}$ using the Girsanov Theorem 16.7. As a consequence, we have the next proposition, see Exercise 16.1 for another calculation based on geometric Brownian motion, and Exercise 16.10 for an extension to correlated Brownian motions.

Proposition 16.8. *Assume that* $(X_t)_{t\in\mathbb{R}_+}$ *and* $(N_t)_{t\in\mathbb{R}_+}$ *satisfy the stochastic differential equations*

$$dX_t = r_t X_t dt + \sigma_t^X X_t dW_t, \quad \text{and} \quad dN_t = r_t N_t dt + \sigma_t^N N_t dW_t, \qquad (16.14)$$

where $(\sigma_t^X)_{t\in\mathbb{R}_+}$ *and* $(\sigma_t^N)_{t\in\mathbb{R}_+}$ *are* $(\mathcal{F}_t)_{t\in\mathbb{R}_+}$*-adapted volatility processes and* $(W_t)_{t\in\mathbb{R}_+}$ *is a standard Brownian motion under* $\mathbb{P}^*$. *Then, we have*

$$d\widehat{X}_t = (\sigma_t^X - \sigma_t^N)\widehat{X}_t d\widehat{W}_t, \qquad (16.15)$$

hence $(\widehat{X}_t)_{t\in[0,T]}$ *is given by the driftless geometric Brownian motion*

$$\widehat{X}_t = \widehat{X}_0 \exp\left(\int_0^t (\sigma_s^X - \sigma_s^N)d\widehat{W}_s - \frac{1}{2}\int_0^t (\sigma_s^X - \sigma_s^N)^2 ds\right), \quad 0 \leqslant t \leqslant T.$$

Proof. First we note that by (16.13) and (16.14),

$$d\widehat{W}_t = dW_t - \frac{1}{N_t}dN_t \cdot dW_t = dW_t - \sigma_t^N dt, \qquad t \geqslant 0,$$

is a standard Brownian motion under $\widehat{\mathbb{P}}$. Next, by Itô's calculus and the Itô multiplication Table 4.1 and (16.14) we have

$$
\begin{aligned}
d\left(\frac{1}{N_t}\right) &= -\frac{1}{N_t^2}dN_t + \frac{1}{N_t^3}dN_t \cdot dN_t \\
&= -\frac{1}{N_t^2}\left(r_t N_t dt + \sigma_t^N N_t dW_t\right) + \frac{|\sigma_t^N|^2}{N_t}dt \\
&= -\frac{1}{N_t^2}\left(r_t N_t dt + \sigma_t^N N_t \left(d\widehat{W}_t + \sigma_t^N dt\right)\right) + \frac{|\sigma_t^N|^2}{N_t}dt \\
&= -\frac{1}{N_t}\left(r_t dt + \sigma_t^N d\widehat{W}_t\right), \qquad (16.16)
\end{aligned}
$$

hence

$$
\begin{aligned}
d\widehat{X}_t &= d\left(\frac{X_t}{N_t}\right) \\
&= \frac{dX_t}{N_t} + X_t d\left(\frac{1}{N_t}\right) + dX_t \cdot d\left(\frac{1}{N_t}\right) \\
&= \frac{1}{N_t}\left(r_t X_t dt + \sigma_t^X X_t dW_t\right) - \frac{X_t}{N_t}\left(r_t dt + \sigma_t^N dW_t - |\sigma_t^N|^2 dt\right) \\
&\quad - \frac{1}{N_t}\left(r_t X_t dt + \sigma_t^X X_t dW_t\right) \cdot \left(r_t dt + \sigma_t^N dW_t - |\sigma_t^N|^2 dt\right) \\
&= \frac{1}{N_t}\left(r_t X_t dt + \sigma_t^X X_t dW_t\right) - \frac{X_t}{N_t}\left(r_t dt + \sigma_t^N dW_t\right) \\
&\quad + \frac{X_t}{N_t}|\sigma_t^N|^2 dt - \frac{X_t}{N_t}\sigma_t^X \sigma_t^N dt
\end{aligned}
$$

$$
\begin{aligned}
&= \frac{X_t}{N_t}\sigma_t^X dW_t - \frac{X_t}{N_t}\sigma_t^N dW_t - \frac{X_t}{N_t}\sigma_t^X\sigma_t^N dt + X_t\frac{|\sigma_t^N|^2}{N_t}dt \\
&= \frac{X_t}{N_t}\left(\sigma_t^X dW_t - \sigma_t^N dW_t - \sigma_t^X\sigma_t^N dt + |\sigma_t^N|^2 dt\right) \\
&= \widehat{X_t}(\sigma_t^X - \sigma_t^N)dW_t - \widehat{X_t}(\sigma_t^X - \sigma_t^N)\sigma_t^N dt \\
&= \widehat{X_t}(\sigma_t^X - \sigma_t^N)d\widehat{W_t},
\end{aligned}
$$

since $d\widehat{W}_t = dW_t - \sigma_t^N dt$, $0 \leqslant t \leqslant T$. $\qquad\square$

We end this section with some comments on inverse changes of measure.

Inverse changes of measure

In the next proposition we compute the conditional inverse Radon–Nikodym density $d\mathbb{P}^*/d\widehat{\mathbb{P}}$, see also (16.2).

Proposition 16.9. *We have*

$$
\widehat{\mathbb{E}}\left[\frac{d\mathbb{P}^*}{d\widehat{\mathbb{P}}}\,\Big|\,\mathcal{F}_t\right] = \frac{N_0}{N_t}\exp\left(\int_0^t r_s ds\right), \qquad 0 \leqslant t \leqslant T, \tag{16.17}
$$

and the process

$$
t \mapsto \frac{M_0}{M_t} = \frac{N_0}{N_t}\exp\left(\int_0^t r_s ds\right), \qquad 0 \leqslant t \leqslant T,
$$

is an $\mathcal{F}_t$-martingale under $\widehat{\mathbb{P}}$.

Proof. For all bounded and $\mathcal{F}_t$-measurable random variables F we have,

$$
\begin{aligned}
\widehat{\mathbb{E}}\left[F\frac{d\mathbb{P}^*}{d\widehat{\mathbb{P}}}\right] &= \mathbb{E}^*[F] \\
&= \mathbb{E}^*\left[F\frac{N_t}{N_t}\right] \\
&= \mathbb{E}^*\left[F\frac{N_T}{N_t}\exp\left(-\int_t^T r_s ds\right)\right] \\
&= \widehat{\mathbb{E}}\left[F\frac{N_0}{N_t}\exp\left(\int_0^t r_s ds\right)\right].
\end{aligned}
$$

$\qquad\square$

By (16.16) we also have

$$
d\left(\frac{1}{N_t}\exp\left(\int_0^t r_s ds\right)\right) = -\frac{1}{N_t}\exp\left(\int_0^t r_s ds\right)\sigma_t^N d\widehat{W}_t,
$$

which recovers the second part of Proposition 16.9, *i.e.* the martingale property of

$$
t \mapsto \frac{M_0}{M_t} = \frac{1}{N_t}\exp\left(\int_0^t r_s ds\right)
$$

under $\widehat{\mathbb{P}}$.

16.3   Foreign Exchange

Currency exchange is a typical application of change of numéraire, that illustrates the absence of arbitrage principle.

Let R_t denote the foreign exchange rate, *i.e.* R_t is the (possibly fractional) quantity of local currency that correspond to one unit of foreign currency, while $1/R_t$ represents the quantity of foreign currency that correspond to a unit of local currency.

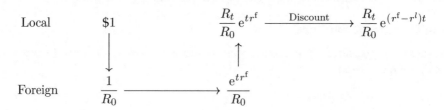

Consider an investor that intends to exploit an "overseas investment opportunity" by

a) at time 0, changing one unit of local currency into $1/R_0$ units of foreign currency,

b) investing $1/R_0$ on the foreign market at the rate r^f, which will yield the amount e^{tr^f}/R_0 at time $t > 0$,

c) changing back e^{tr^f}/R_0 into a quantity $e^{tr^f}R_t/R_0 = N_t/R_0$ of local currency.

In other words, the foreign money market account e^{tr^f} is valued $e^{tr^f}R_t$ on the local (or domestic) market, and its discounted value on the local market is

$$e^{-tr^l + tr^f}R_t, \qquad t > 0.$$

The outcome of this investment will be obtained by a martingale comparison of $e^{tr^f}R_t/R_0$ to the amount e^{tr^l} that could have been obtained by investing on the local market.

Taking

$$N_t := e^{tr^f}R_t, \qquad t \geqslant 0, \tag{16.18}$$

as *numéraire*, absence of arbitrage is expressed by Assumption (A), which states that the discounted numéraire process

$$t \mapsto e^{-r^l t}N_t = e^{-t(r^l - r^f)}R_t$$

is an $\mathcal{F}_t$-martingale under $\mathbb{P}^*$.

Next, we find a characterization of this arbitrage condition using the model parameters r, r^f, μ, by modeling the foreign exchange rates R_t according to a geometric Brownian motion (16.19).

Proposition 16.10. *Assume that the foreign exchange rate R_t satisfies a stochastic differential equation of the form*

$$dR_t = \mu R_t dt + \sigma R_t dW_t, \tag{16.19}$$

where $(W_t)_{t \in \mathbb{R}_+}$ *is a standard Brownian motion under* $\mathbb{P}^*$. *Under the absence of arbitrage Assumption (A) for the numéraire* (16.18), *we have*

$$\mu = r^l - r^f, \tag{16.20}$$

hence the exchange rate process satisfies

$$dR_t = \left(r^l - r^f\right) R_t dt + \sigma R_t dW_t. \tag{16.21}$$

under $\mathbb{P}^*$.

Proof. The equation (16.19) has solution

$$R_t = R_0 \, e^{\mu t + \sigma W_t - \sigma^2 t/2}, \qquad t \geqslant 0,$$

hence the discounted value of the foreign money market account e^{tr^f} on the local market is

$$e^{-tr^l} N_t = e^{-tr^l + tr^f} R_t = R_0 \, e^{(r^f - r^l + \mu)t + \sigma W_t - \sigma^2 t/2}, \qquad t \geqslant 0.$$

Under the absence of arbitrage Assumption (A), the process $e^{-(r^l - r^f)t} R_t = e^{-tr^l} N_t$ should be an $\mathcal{F}_t$-martingale under $\mathbb{P}^*$, and this holds provided that $r^f - r + \mu = 0$, which yields (16.20) and (16.21). $\qquad \square$

As a consequence of Proposition 16.10, under the absence of arbitrage a local investor who buys a unit of foreign currency in the hope of a higher return $r^f \gg r$ will have to face a lower (or even more negative) drift

$$\mu = r^l - r^f \ll 0$$

in his exchange rate R_t. The drift $\mu = r^l - r^f$ is also called the *cost of carrying* the foreign currency.

The local money market account $X_t := e^{tr^l}$ is valued e^{tr^l} / R_t on the foreign market, and its discounted value at time $t \geqslant 0$ on the foreign market is

$$
\begin{aligned}
\frac{e^{(r^l - r^f)t}}{R_t} &= \frac{X_t}{N_t} = \widehat{X}_t \\
&= \frac{1}{R_0} \, e^{(r^l - r^f)t - \mu t - \sigma W_t + \sigma^2 t/2} \\
&= \frac{1}{R_0} \, e^{(r^l - r^f)t - \mu t - \sigma \widehat{W}_t - \sigma^2 t/2},
\end{aligned}
\tag{16.22}
$$

where

$$
\begin{aligned}
d\widehat{W}_t &= dW_t - \frac{1}{N_t} dN_t \cdot dW_t \\
&= dW_t - \frac{1}{R_t} dR_t \cdot dW_t \\
&= dW_t - \sigma dt, \qquad t \geqslant 0,
\end{aligned}
$$

is a standard Brownian motion under $\widehat{\mathbb{P}}$ by (16.13). Under the absence of arbitrage, the process $e^{-(r^l - r^f)t} R_t$ is an $\mathcal{F}_t$-martingale under $\mathbb{P}^*$ and (16.22) is an $\mathcal{F}_t$-martingale under $\widehat{\mathbb{P}}$ by Proposition 16.4, which recovers (16.20).

```
  library(quantmod)
2 getSymbols("EURTRY=X",src = "yahoo",from = "2018-01-01",to = "2021-12-31")
  getSymbols("INTDSRTRM193N",src = "FRED")
4 Interestrate<-`INTDSRTRM193N`["2018-01-01::2021-31-12"]
  EURTRY<-Ad(`EURTRY=X`); myPars <- chart_pars();myPars$cex<-1.2
6 Cumulative<-cumprod(1+Interestrate/100/12)
  normalizedfxrate<-1+(as.numeric(last(Cumulative))-1)*(EURTRY-as.numeric(EURTRY[1]))/
        (as.numeric(last(EURTRY))-as.numeric(EURTRY[1]))
8 myTheme <- chart_theme();myTheme$col$line.col <- "blue"
  dev.new(width=16,height=8)
10 chart_Series(Cumulative,pars=myPars, theme = myTheme)
  add_TA(normalizedfxrate, col='black', lw =2, on = 1)
12 add_TA(Interestrate, col='purple', lw =2)
```

The above code plots an evolution of currency exchange rates compared with the evolution of interest rates, as shown in Figure 16.2.

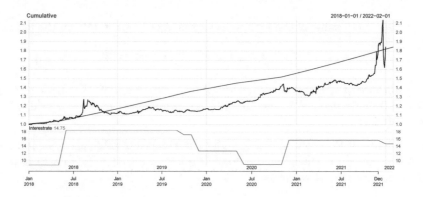

Figure 16.2: Evolution of exchange rate *vs* interest rate.

Proposition 16.11. *Under the absence of arbitrage condition* (16.20), *the inverse exchange rate* $1/R_t$ *satisfies*

$$d\left(\frac{1}{R_t}\right) = \frac{r^{\mathrm{f}} - r^l}{R_t}dt - \frac{\sigma}{R_t}d\widehat{W}_t, \qquad (16.23)$$

under $\widehat{\mathbb{P}}$, *where* $(R_t)_{t\in\mathbb{R}_+}$ *is given by* (16.21).

Proof. By (16.20), the exchange rate $1/R_t$ is written using Itô's calculus as

$$
\begin{aligned}
d\left(\frac{1}{R_t}\right) &= -\frac{1}{R_t^2}(\mu R_t dt + \sigma R_t dW_t) + \frac{1}{R_t^3}\sigma^2 R_t^2 dt \\
&= -\frac{\mu - \sigma^2}{R_t}dt - \frac{\sigma}{R_t}dW_t \\
&= -\frac{\mu}{R_t}dt - \frac{\sigma}{R_t}d\widehat{W}_t \\
&= \frac{r^{\mathrm{f}} - r^l}{R_t}dt - \frac{\sigma}{R_t}d\widehat{W}_t,
\end{aligned}
$$

where $(\widehat{W}_t)_{t\in\mathbb{R}_+}$ is a standard Brownian motion under $\widehat{\mathbb{P}}$. $\qquad\square$

Consequently, under the absence of arbitrage, a foreign investor who buys a unit of the local currency in the hope of a higher return $r \gg r^{\mathrm{f}}$ will have to face a lower (or even more negative) drift $-\mu = r^{\mathrm{f}} - r$ in his exchange rate $1/R_t$ as written in (16.23) under $\widehat{\mathbb{P}}$.

Foreign exchange options

We now price a foreign exchange call option with payoff $(R_T - \kappa)^+$ under $\mathbb{P}^*$ on the exchange rate R_T by the Black–Scholes formula as in the next proposition, also known as the Garman and Kohlhagen (1983) formula. The foreign exchange call option is designed for a local buyer of foreign currency.

Proposition 16.12. *(Garman and Kohlhagen (1983) formula for call options). Consider the exchange rate process $(R_t)_{t\in\mathbb{R}_+}$ given by (16.21). The price of the foreign exchange call option on R_T with maturity T and strike price $\kappa > 0$ is given in local currency units as*

$$
\mathrm{e}^{-(T-t)r^l}\, \mathbb{E}^* \left[(R_T - \kappa)^+ \mid \mathcal{F}_t \right] = \mathrm{e}^{-(T-t)r^f} R_t \Phi_+(t, R_t) - \kappa \mathrm{e}^{-(T-t)r^l} \Phi_-(t, R_t),
$$
$$(16.24)$$

$0 \leqslant t \leqslant T$, *where*

$$
\Phi_+(t, x) = \Phi\left(\frac{\log(x/\kappa) + (T - t)\left(r^l - r^f + \sigma^2/2\right)}{\sigma\sqrt{T - t}} \right),
$$

and

$$
\Phi_-(t, x) = \Phi\left(\frac{\log(x/\kappa) + (T - t)\left(r^l - r^f - \sigma^2/2\right)}{\sigma\sqrt{T - t}} \right).
$$

Proof. As a consequence of (16.21), we find the numéraire dynamics

$$
\begin{aligned}
dN_t &= d\left(\mathrm{e}^{tr^f} R_t \right) \\
&= r^f \mathrm{e}^{tr^f} R_t dt + \mathrm{e}^{tr^f} dR_t \\
&= r^f \mathrm{e}^{tr^f} R_t dt + \sigma \mathrm{e}^{tr^f} R_t dW_t \\
&= r^f N_t dt + \sigma N_t dW_t.
\end{aligned}
$$

Hence, a standard application of the Black–Scholes formula yields

$$
\begin{aligned}
\mathrm{e}^{-(T-t)r^l}\, \mathbb{E}^* \left[(R_T - \kappa)^+ \mid \mathcal{F}_t \right] &= \mathrm{e}^{-(T-t)r^l}\, \mathbb{E}^* \left[\left(\mathrm{e}^{-Tr^f} N_T - \kappa \right)^+ \mid \mathcal{F}_t \right] \\
&= \mathrm{e}^{-(T-t)r^l} \mathrm{e}^{-Tr^f}\, \mathbb{E}^* \left[\left(N_T - \kappa \mathrm{e}^{Tr^f} \right)^+ \mid \mathcal{F}_t \right] \\
&= \mathrm{e}^{-Tr^f} \left(N_t \Phi\left(\frac{\log(N_t \mathrm{e}^{-Tr^f}/\kappa) + (r + \sigma^2/2)(T - t)}{\sigma\sqrt{T - t}} \right) \right. \\
&\qquad \left. - \kappa \mathrm{e}^{Tr^f - (T-t)r^l} \Phi\left(\frac{\log(N_t \mathrm{e}^{-Tr^f}/\kappa) + \left(r^l - \sigma^2/2\right)(T - t)}{\sigma\sqrt{T - t}} \right) \right) \\
&= \mathrm{e}^{-Tr^f} \left(N_t \Phi\left(\frac{\log(R_t/\kappa) + (T - t)\left(r^l - r^f + \sigma^2/2\right)}{\sigma\sqrt{T - t}} \right) \right. \\
&\qquad \left. - \kappa \mathrm{e}^{Tr^f - (T-t)r^l} \Phi\left(\frac{\log(R_t/\kappa) + (T - t)\left(r^l - r^f - \sigma^2/2\right)}{\sigma\sqrt{T - t}} \right) \right) \\
&= \mathrm{e}^{-(T-t)r^f} R_t \Phi_+(t, R_t) - \kappa \mathrm{e}^{-(T-t)r^l} \Phi_-(t, R_t).
\end{aligned}
$$

A similar conclusion can be reached by directly applying (16.21). $\qquad\square$

Similarly, from (16.23) rewritten as

$$d\left(\frac{e^{tr^l}}{R_t}\right) = r^f \frac{e^{tr^l}}{R_t}dt - \sigma\frac{e^{tr^l}}{R_t}d\widehat{W}_t,$$

a foreign exchange put option with payoff $(1/\kappa - 1/R_T)^+$ can be priced under $\widehat{\mathbb{P}}$ in a Black–Scholes model by taking e^{tr^l}/R_t as underlying asset price, r^f as risk-free interest rate, and $-\sigma$ as volatility parameter. The foreign exchange put option is designed for the foreign seller of local currency, for example in a *buy back guarantee* which is a typical example of a foreign exchange put option.

Proposition 16.13. *(Garman and Kohlhagen (1983) formula for put options). Consider the exchange rate process* $(R_t)_{t\in\mathbb{R}_+}$ *given by (16.21). The price of the foreign exchange put option on* R_T *with maturity* T *and strike price* $1/\kappa > 0$ *is given in foreign currency units as*

$$e^{-(T-t)r^f}\widehat{\mathbb{E}}\left[\left(\frac{1}{\kappa} - \frac{1}{R_T}\right)^+ \Big| \mathcal{F}_t\right] \tag{16.25}$$

$$= \frac{e^{-(T-t)r^f}}{\kappa}\Phi_-\left(t, \frac{1}{R_t}\right) - \frac{e^{-(T-t)r^l}}{R_t}\Phi_+\left(t, \frac{1}{R_t}\right),$$

$0 \leqslant t \leqslant T$, *where*

$$\Phi_+(t, x) := \Phi\left(-\frac{\log(\kappa x) + (T-t)(r^f - r^l + \sigma^2/2)}{\sigma\sqrt{T-t}}\right),$$

and

$$\Phi_-(t, x) := \Phi\left(-\frac{\log(\kappa x) + (T-t)(r^f - r^l - \sigma^2/2)}{\sigma\sqrt{T-t}}\right).$$

Proof. The Black–Scholes formula (6.11) yields

$$e^{-(T-t)r^f}\widehat{\mathbb{E}}\left[\left(\frac{1}{\kappa} - \frac{1}{R_T}\right)^+ \Big| \mathcal{F}_t\right] = e^{-(T-t)r^f}e^{-Tr^l}\widehat{\mathbb{E}}\left[\left(\frac{e^{Tr^l}}{\kappa} - \frac{e^{Tr^l}}{R_T}\right)^+ \Big| \mathcal{F}_t\right]$$

$$= \frac{1}{\kappa}e^{-(T-t)r^f}\Phi_-\left(t, \frac{1}{R_t}\right) - \frac{e^{-(T-t)r^l}}{R_t}\Phi_+\left(t, \frac{1}{R_t}\right),$$

which is the symmetric of (16.24) by exchanging R_t with $1/R_t$, and r with r^f. $\square$

Call/put duality for foreign exchange options

Let $N_t = e^{tr^f}R_t$, where R_t is an exchange rate with respect to a foreign currency and r_f is the foreign market interest rate.

Proposition 16.14. *The foreign exchange call and put options on the local and foreign markets are linked by the call/put duality relation*

$$e^{-(T-t)r^l}\mathbb{E}^*\left[(R_T - \kappa)^+ \mid \mathcal{F}_t\right] = \kappa R_t e^{-(T-t)r^f}\widehat{\mathbb{E}}\left[\left(\frac{1}{\kappa} - \frac{1}{R_T}\right)^+ \Big| \mathcal{F}_t\right], \tag{16.26}$$

between a put option with strike price $1/\kappa$ and a (possibly fractional) quantity $1/(\kappa R_t)$ of call option(s) with strike price κ.

Proof. By application of change of numéraire from Proposition 16.5 and (16.8) we have

$$\widehat{\mathbb{E}}\left[\frac{1}{\mathrm{e}^{Tr^{\mathrm{f}}}R_T}\,(R_T - \kappa)^+ \,\bigg|\, \mathcal{F}_t\right] = \frac{1}{N_t}\,\mathrm{e}^{-(T-t)r^l}\,\mathbb{E}^*\left[(R_T - \kappa)^+ \,\big|\, \mathcal{F}_t\right],$$

hence

$$\begin{aligned}
\mathrm{e}^{-(T-t)r^{\mathrm{f}}}\widehat{\mathbb{E}}\left[\left(\frac{1}{\kappa} - \frac{1}{R_T}\right)^+ \,\bigg|\, \mathcal{F}_t\right] &= \mathrm{e}^{-(T-t)r^{\mathrm{f}}}\widehat{\mathbb{E}}\left[\frac{1}{\kappa R_T}\,(R_T - \kappa)^+ \,\bigg|\, \mathcal{F}_t\right]\\[2mm]
&= \frac{1}{\kappa}\mathrm{e}^{tr^{\mathrm{f}}}\widehat{\mathbb{E}}\left[\frac{1}{\mathrm{e}^{Tr^{\mathrm{f}}}R_T}\,(R_T - \kappa)^+ \,\bigg|\, \mathcal{F}_t\right]\\[2mm]
&= \frac{1}{\kappa N_t}\mathrm{e}^{tr^{\mathrm{f}}-(T-t)r^l}\,\mathbb{E}^*\left[(R_T - \kappa)^+ \,\big|\, \mathcal{F}_t\right]\\[2mm]
&= \frac{1}{\kappa R_t}\mathrm{e}^{-(T-t)r^l}\,\mathbb{E}^*\left[(R_T - \kappa)^+ \,\big|\, \mathcal{F}_t\right].
\end{aligned}$$

$\square$

In the Black–Scholes case, the duality (16.26) can be directly checked by verifying that (16.25) coincides with

$$\begin{aligned}
&\frac{1}{\kappa R_t}\mathrm{e}^{-(T-t)r^l}\,\mathbb{E}^*\left[(R_T - \kappa)^+ \,\big|\, \mathcal{F}_t\right]\\[2mm]
&= \frac{1}{\kappa R_t}\mathrm{e}^{-(T-t)r^l}\,\mathrm{e}^{-Tr^{\mathrm{f}}}\,\mathbb{E}^*\left[\left(\mathrm{e}^{Tr^{\mathrm{f}}}R_T - \kappa\mathrm{e}^{Tr^{\mathrm{f}}}\right)^+ \,\big|\, \mathcal{F}_t\right]\\[2mm]
&= \frac{1}{\kappa R_t}\mathrm{e}^{-(T-t)r^l}\,\mathrm{e}^{-Tr^{\mathrm{f}}}\,\mathbb{E}^*\left[\left(N_T - \kappa\mathrm{e}^{Tr^{\mathrm{f}}}\right)^+ \,\big|\, \mathcal{F}_t\right]\\[2mm]
&= \frac{1}{\kappa R_t}\left(\mathrm{e}^{-(T-t)r^{\mathrm{f}}}R_t\Phi_+^{\mathrm{c}}(t, R_t) - \kappa\mathrm{e}^{-(T-t)r^l}\Phi_-^{\mathrm{c}}(t, R_t)\right)\\[2mm]
&= \frac{1}{\kappa}\mathrm{e}^{-(T-t)r^{\mathrm{f}}}\Phi_+^{\mathrm{c}}(t, R_t) - \frac{\mathrm{e}^{-(T-t)r^l}}{R_t}\Phi_-^{\mathrm{c}}(t, R_t)\\[2mm]
&= \frac{1}{\kappa}\mathrm{e}^{-(T-t)r^{\mathrm{f}}}\Phi_-\left(t, \frac{1}{R_t}\right) - \frac{\mathrm{e}^{-(T-t)r^l}}{R_t}\Phi_+\left(t, \frac{1}{R_t}\right),
\end{aligned}$$

where

$$\Phi_+^{\mathrm{c}}(t, x) := \Phi\left(\frac{\log(x/\kappa) + (T-t)\left(r^l - r^{\mathrm{f}} + \sigma^2/2\right)}{\sigma\sqrt{T-t}}\right),$$

and

$$\Phi_-^{\mathrm{c}}(t, x) := \Phi\left(\frac{\log(x/\kappa) + (T-t)\left(r^l - r^{\mathrm{f}} - \sigma^2/2\right)}{\sigma\sqrt{T-t}}\right).$$

	Local market	Foreign market
Measure	$\mathbb{P}^*$	$\widehat{\mathbb{P}}$
Discount factor	$t \mapsto e^{-r^l t}$	$t \mapsto e^{-r^f t}$
Martingale	$t \mapsto e^{-tr^l} N_t = e^{-t(r^l - r^f)} R_t$	$t \mapsto \dfrac{X_t}{N_t} = \widehat{X}_t = \dfrac{e^{(r^l - r^f)t}}{R_t}$
Option	$e^{-(T-t)r^l} \mathbb{E}^*\left[(R_T - \kappa)^+ \mid \mathcal{F}_t\right]$	$e^{-(T-t)r^f} \widehat{\mathbb{E}}\left[\left(\dfrac{1}{\kappa} - \dfrac{1}{R_T}\right)^+ \mid \mathcal{F}_t\right]$
Application	Local purchase of foreign currency	Foreign selling of local currency

Table 16.1: Local *vs* foreign exchange options.

Example - Buy back guarantee

The put option priced

$$
e^{-(T-t)r^f} \widehat{\mathbb{E}}\left[\left(\frac{1}{\kappa} - \frac{1}{R_T}\right)^+ \Big| \mathcal{F}_t\right]
$$
$$
= \frac{1}{\kappa} e^{-(T-t)r^f} \Phi_-\left(t, \frac{1}{R_t}\right) - \frac{e^{-(T-t)r^l}}{R_t} \Phi_+\left(t, \frac{1}{R_t}\right)
$$

on the foreign market corresponds to a *buy back guarantee* in currency exchange. In the case of an option "at the money" with $\kappa = R_t$ and $r^l = r^f \simeq 0$, we find

$$
\widehat{\mathbb{E}}\left[\left(\frac{1}{R_t} - \frac{1}{R_T}\right)^+ \Big| \mathcal{F}_t\right] = \frac{1}{R_t} \times \left(\Phi\left(\frac{\sigma\sqrt{T-t}}{2}\right) - \Phi\left(-\frac{\sigma\sqrt{T-t}}{2}\right)\right)
$$
$$
= \frac{1}{R_t} \times \left(2\Phi\left(\frac{\sigma\sqrt{T-t}}{2}\right) - 1\right).
$$

For example, let R_t denote the USD/EUR (USDEUR=X) exchange rate from a foreign currency (USD) to a local currency (EUR), *i.e.* one unit of the foreign currency (USD) corresponds to $R_t = 1/1.23$ units of local currency (EUR). Taking $T - t = 30$ days and $\sigma = 10\%$, we find that the foreign currency put option allowing the foreign sale of one EURO back into USDs is priced at the money in USD as

$$
\widehat{\mathbb{E}}\left[\left(\frac{1}{R_t} - \frac{1}{R_T}\right)^+ \Big| \mathcal{F}_t\right] = 1.23\big(2\Phi\big(0.05 \times \sqrt{31/365}\big) - 1\big)
$$
$$
= 1.23(2 \times 0.505813 - 1)
$$
$$
= \$0.01429998
$$

per USD, or €0.011626 per exchanged unit of EURO. Based on a displayed option price of €4.5 and in order to make the contract fair, this would translate into an average amount of $4.5/0.011626 \simeq €387$ exchanged at the counter by customers subscribing to the buy back guarantee.

16.4 Pricing Exchange Options

Based on Proposition 16.4, we model the process $\widehat{X}_t$ of forward prices as a continuous martingale under $\widehat{\mathbb{P}}$, written as

$$d\widehat{X}_t = \widehat{\sigma}_t d\widehat{W}_t, \qquad t \geqslant 0, \tag{16.27}$$

where $\big(\widehat{W}_t\big)_{t\in\mathbb{R}_+}$ is a standard Brownian motion under $\widehat{\mathbb{P}}$ and $(\widehat{\sigma}_t)_{t\in\mathbb{R}_+}$ is an $(\mathcal{F}_t)_{t\in\mathbb{R}_+}$-adapted stochastic volatility process. More precisely, we assume that $\big(\widehat{X}_t\big)_{t\in\mathbb{R}_+}$ has the dynamics

$$d\widehat{X}_t = \widehat{\sigma}_t\big(\widehat{X}_t\big)d\widehat{W}_t, \tag{16.28}$$

where $x \mapsto \widehat{\sigma}_t(x)$ is a local volatility function which is Lipschitz in x, uniformly in $t \geqslant 0$. The Markov property of the diffusion process $\big(\widehat{X}_t\big)_{t\in\mathbb{R}_+}$, cf. Theorem V-6-32 of Protter (2004), shows that when $\widehat{g}$ is a deterministic payoff function, the conditional expectation $\widehat{\mathbb{E}}\big[\widehat{g}(\widehat{X}_T)\,\big|\,\mathcal{F}_t\big]$ can be written using a (measurable) function $\widehat{C}(t,x)$ of t and $\widehat{X}_t$, as

$$\widehat{\mathbb{E}}\big[\widehat{g}(\widehat{X}_T)\,\big|\,\mathcal{F}_t\big] = \widehat{C}\big(t,\widehat{X}_t\big), \qquad 0 \leqslant t \leqslant T.$$

Consequently, a vanilla option with claim payoff $C := N_T\widehat{g}(\widehat{X}_T)$ can be priced from Proposition 16.5 as

$$
\begin{aligned}
\mathbb{E}^*\left[e^{-\int_t^T r_s ds} N_T \widehat{g}(\widehat{X}_T)\,\Big|\,\mathcal{F}_t\right] &= N_t \widehat{\mathbb{E}}\big[\widehat{g}(\widehat{X}_T)\,|\,\mathcal{F}_t\big] \\
&= N_t \widehat{C}\big(t,\widehat{X}_t\big), \quad 0 \leqslant t \leqslant T.
\end{aligned}
\tag{16.29}
$$

In the next Proposition 16.15 we state the Margrabe (1978) formula for the pricing of exchange options by the zero interest rate Black–Scholes formula. It will be applied in particular in Proposition 19.3 below for the pricing of bond options. Here, $(N_t)_{t\in\mathbb{R}_+}$ denotes any numéraire process satisfying Assumption (A).

Proposition 16.15. *(Margrabe (1978) formula). Assume that $\widehat{\sigma}_t\big(\widehat{X}_t\big) = \widehat{\sigma}(t)\widehat{X}_t$, i.e. the martingale $\big(\widehat{X}_t\big)_{t\in[0,T]}$ is a (driftless) geometric Brownian motion under $\widehat{\mathbb{P}}$ with deterministic volatility $(\widehat{\sigma}(t))_{t\in[0,T]}$. Then, we have*

$$\mathbb{E}^*\left[e^{-\int_t^T r_s ds}(X_T - \kappa N_T)^+\,\Big|\,\mathcal{F}_t\right] = X_t\Phi_+^0\big(t,\widehat{X}_t\big) - \kappa N_t\Phi_-^0\big(t,\widehat{X}_t\big),$$

$$\tag{16.30}$$

$t \in [0, T]$, *where*

$$\Phi_+^0(t, x) = \Phi\left(\frac{\log(x/\kappa)}{v(t, T)} + \frac{v(t, T)}{2}\right), \quad \Phi_-^0(t, x) = \Phi\left(\frac{\log(x/\kappa)}{v(t, T)} - \frac{v(t, T)}{2}\right), \quad (16.31)$$

and $v^2(t, T) = \int_t^T \widehat{\sigma}^2(s)ds.$

Proof. Taking $g(x) := (x - \kappa)^+$ in (16.29), the call option with payoff

$$\begin{aligned}
(X_T - \kappa N_T)^+ &= N_T(\widehat{X}_T - \kappa)^+ \\
&= N_T\left(\widehat{X}_t \exp\left(\int_t^T \widehat{\sigma}(t)d\widehat{W}_t - \frac{1}{2}\int_t^T |\widehat{\sigma}(t)|^2 dt\right) - \kappa\right)^+,
\end{aligned}$$

and floating strike price κN_T is priced by (16.29) as

$$\begin{aligned}
\mathbb{E}^*\left[e^{-\int_t^T r_s ds}(X_T - \kappa N_T)^+ \,\Big|\, \mathcal{F}_t\right] &= \mathbb{E}^*\left[e^{-\int_t^T r_s ds} N_T(\widehat{X}_T - \kappa)^+ \,\Big|\, \mathcal{F}_t\right] \\
&= N_t\widehat{\mathbb{E}}\left[(\widehat{X}_T - \kappa)^+ \,\Big|\, \mathcal{F}_t\right] \\
&= N_t\widehat{C}(t, \widehat{X}_t),
\end{aligned}$$

where the function $\widehat{C}(t, \widehat{X}_t)$ is given by the Black–Scholes formula

$$\widehat{C}(t, x) = x\Phi_+^0(t, x) - \kappa\Phi_-^0(t, x),$$

with zero interest rate, since $(\widehat{X}_t)_{t \in [0,T]}$ is a driftless geometric Brownian motion which is an $\mathcal{F}_t$-martingale under $\widehat{\mathbb{P}}$, and $\widehat{X}_T$ is a lognormal random variable with variance coefficient $v^2(t, T) = \int_t^T \widehat{\sigma}^2(s)ds$. Hence we have

$$\begin{aligned}
\mathbb{E}^*\left[e^{-\int_t^T r_s ds}(X_T - \kappa N_T)^+ \,\Big|\, \mathcal{F}_t\right] &= N_t\widehat{C}(t, \widehat{X}_t) \\
&= N_t\widehat{X}_t\Phi_+^0(t, \widehat{X}_t) - \kappa N_t\Phi_-^0(t, \widehat{X}_t),
\end{aligned}$$

$t \geqslant 0$. $\qquad \square$

In particular, from Proposition 16.8 and (16.15), we can take $\widehat{\sigma}(t) = \sigma_t^X - \sigma_t^N$ when $(\sigma_t^X)_{t \in \mathbb{R}_+}$ and $(\sigma_t^N)_{t \in \mathbb{R}_+}$ are deterministic.

Examples:

a) When the short rate process $(r(t))_{t \in [0,T]}$ is a *deterministic* function of time and $N_t = e^{\int_t^T r(s)ds}$, $0 \leqslant t \leqslant T$, we have $\widehat{\mathbb{P}} = \mathbb{P}^*$ and Proposition 16.15 yields the Merton (1973) "zero interest rate" version of the Black–Scholes formula

$$\begin{aligned}
e^{-\int_t^T r(s)ds}\,\mathbb{E}^*\left[(X_T - \kappa)^+ \,\big|\, \mathcal{F}_t\right] \\
= X_t\Phi_+^0\left(t, e^{\int_t^T r(s)ds}X_t\right) - \kappa e^{-\int_t^T r(s)ds}\Phi_-^0\left(t, e^{\int_t^T r(s)ds}X_t\right),
\end{aligned}$$

where Φ_+^0 and Φ_-^0 are defined in (16.31) and $(X_t)_{t \in \mathbb{R}_+}$ satisfies the equation

$$\frac{dX_t}{X_t} = r(t)dt + \widehat{\sigma}(t)dW_t, \quad i.e. \quad \frac{d\widehat{X}_t}{\widehat{X}_t} = \widehat{\sigma}(t)dW_t, \quad 0 \leqslant t \leqslant T.$$

b) In the case of pricing under a *forward numéraire*, *i.e.* when $N_t = P(t,T)$, $t \in [0,T]$, we get

$$\mathbb{E}^* \left[e^{-\int_t^T r_s ds} (X_T - \kappa)^+ \mid \mathcal{F}_t \right] = X_t \Phi_+^0 \left(t, \widehat{X}_t \right) - \kappa P(t,T) \Phi_-^0 \left(t, \widehat{X}_t \right),$$

$0 \leqslant t \leqslant T$, since $N_T = P(T,T) = 1$. In particular, when $X_t = P(t,S)$ the above formula allows us to price a bond call option on $P(T,S)$ as

$$\mathbb{E}^* \left[e^{-\int_t^T r_s ds} (P(T,S) - \kappa)^+ \mid \mathcal{F}_t \right] = P(t,S) \Phi_+^0 \left(t, \widehat{X}_t \right) - \kappa P(t,T) \Phi_-^0 \left(t, \widehat{X}_t \right),$$

$0 \leqslant t \leqslant T$, provided that the martingale $\widehat{X}_t = P(t,S)/P(t,T)$ under $\widehat{\mathbb{P}}$ is given by a geometric Brownian motion, cf. Section 19.2.

16.5 Hedging by Change of Numéraire

In this section we reconsider and extend the Black–Scholes self-financing hedging strategies found in (7.40)–(7.41) and Proposition 7.13 of Chapter 7. For this, we use the stochastic integral representation of the forward claim payoffs and change of numéraire in order to compute self-financing portfolio strategies. Our hedging portfolios will be built on the assets (X_t, N_t), not on X_t and the money market account $B_t = e^{\int_0^t r_s ds}$, extending the classical hedging portfolios that are available in from the Black–Scholes formula, using a technique from Jamshidian (1996), cf. also Privault and Teng (2012).

Consider a claim with random payoff C, typically an interest rate derivative, cf. Chapter 19. Assume that the forward claim payoff $C/N_T \in L^2(\Omega)$ has the stochastic integral representation

$$\widehat{C} := \frac{C}{N_T} = \widehat{\mathbb{E}} \left[\frac{C}{N_T} \right] + \int_0^T \widehat{\phi}_t d\widehat{X}_t, \tag{16.32}$$

where $\left(\widehat{X}_t \right)_{t \in [0,T]}$ is given by (16.27) and $\left(\widehat{\phi}_t \right)_{t \in [0,T]}$ is a square-integrable adapted process under $\widehat{\mathbb{P}}$, from which it follows that the forward claim price

$$\widehat{V}_t := \frac{V_t}{N_t} = \frac{1}{N_t} \mathbb{E}^* \left[e^{-\int_t^T r_s ds} C \mid \mathcal{F}_t \right] = \widehat{\mathbb{E}} \left[\frac{C}{N_T} \mid \mathcal{F}_t \right], \quad 0 \leqslant t \leqslant T,$$

is an $\mathcal{F}_t$-martingale under $\widehat{\mathbb{P}}$, that can be decomposed as

$$\widehat{V}_t = \widehat{\mathbb{E}}[\widehat{C} \mid \mathcal{F}_t] = \widehat{\mathbb{E}} \left[\frac{C}{N_T} \right] + \int_0^t \widehat{\phi}_s d\widehat{X}_s, \quad 0 \leqslant t \leqslant T. \tag{16.33}$$

The next Proposition 16.16 extends the argument of Jamshidian (1996) to the general framework of pricing using change of numéraire. Note that this result differs from the standard formula that uses the money market account $B_t = e^{\int_0^t r_s ds}$ for hedging instead of N_t, cf. *e.g.* Geman et al. (1995) pages 453-454. The notion of self-financing portfolio is similar to that of Definition 5.8.

Proposition 16.16. *Letting* $\widehat{\eta}_t := \widehat{V}_t - \widehat{X}_t \widehat{\phi}_t$, *with* $\widehat{\phi}_t$ *defined in* (16.33), $0 \leqslant t \leqslant T$, *the portfolio allocation*

$$\left(\widehat{\phi}_t, \widehat{\eta}_t \right)_{t \in [0,T]}$$

with value

$$V_t = \widehat{\phi}_t X_t + \widehat{\eta}_t N_t, \qquad 0 \leqslant t \leqslant T,$$

is self-financing in the sense that

$$dV_t = \widehat{\phi}_t dX_t + \widehat{\eta}_t dN_t,$$

and it hedges the claim payoff C, i.e.

$$V_t = \widehat{\phi}_t X_t + \widehat{\eta}_t N_t = \mathbb{E}^* \left[e^{-\int_t^T r_s ds} C \,\middle|\, \mathcal{F}_t \right], \qquad 0 \leqslant t \leqslant T. \qquad (16.34)$$

Proof. In order to check that the portfolio allocation $(\widehat{\phi}_t, \widehat{\eta}_t)_{t \in [0,T]}$ hedges the claim payoff C it suffices to check that (16.34) holds since by (16.8) the price V_t at time $t \in [0,T]$ of the hedging portfolio satisfies

$$V_t = N_t \widehat{V}_t = \mathbb{E}^* \left[e^{-\int_t^T r_s ds} C \,\middle|\, \mathcal{F}_t \right], \qquad 0 \leqslant t \leqslant T.$$

Next, we show that the portfolio allocation $(\widehat{\phi}_t, \widehat{\eta}_t)_{t \in [0,T]}$ is self-financing. By *numéraire invariance*, cf. *e.g.* page 184 of Protter (2001), we have, using the relation $d\widehat{V}_t = \widehat{\phi}_t d\widehat{X}_t$ from (16.33),

$$
\begin{aligned}
dV_t &= d\big(N_t \widehat{V}_t\big) \\
&= \widehat{V}_t dN_t + N_t d\widehat{V}_t + dN_t \cdot d\widehat{V}_t \\
&= \widehat{V}_t dN_t + N_t \widehat{\phi}_t d\widehat{X}_t + \widehat{\phi}_t dN_t \cdot d\widehat{X}_t \\
&= \widehat{\phi}_t \widehat{X}_t dN_t + N_t \widehat{\phi}_t d\widehat{X}_t + \widehat{\phi}_t dN_t \cdot d\widehat{X}_t + \big(\widehat{V}_t - \widehat{\phi}_t \widehat{X}_t\big) dN_t \\
&= \widehat{\phi}_t d\big(N_t \widehat{X}_t\big) + \widehat{\eta}_t dN_t \\
&= \widehat{\phi}_t dX_t + \widehat{\eta}_t dN_t.
\end{aligned}
$$

$\square$

We now consider an application to the forward Delta hedging of European-type options with payoff $C = N_T \widehat{g}(\widehat{X}_T)$ where $\widehat{g} : \mathbb{R} \longrightarrow \mathbb{R}$ and $(\widehat{X}_t)_{t \in \mathbb{R}_+}$ has the Markov property as in (16.28), where $\widehat{\sigma} : \mathbb{R}_+ \times \mathbb{R}$ is a *deterministic* function. Assuming that the function $\widehat{C}(t, x)$ defined by

$$\widehat{V}_t := \widehat{\mathbb{E}}\big[\widehat{g}(\widehat{X}_T) \,\big|\, \mathcal{F}_t\big] = \widehat{C}(t, \widehat{X}_t)$$

is $\mathcal{C}^2$ on $\mathbb{R}_+$, we have the following corollary of Proposition 16.16, which extends the Black–Scholes Delta hedging technique to the general change of numéraire setup.

Corollary 16.17. *Letting $\widehat{\eta}_t = \widehat{C}(t, \widehat{X}_t) - \widehat{X}_t \dfrac{\partial \widehat{C}}{\partial x}(t, \widehat{X}_t), 0 \leqslant t \leqslant T$, the portfolio allocation*

$$\left(\frac{\partial \widehat{C}}{\partial x}(t, \widehat{X}_t), \widehat{\eta}_t \right)_{t \in [0,T]}$$

with value

$$V_t = \widehat{\eta}_t N_t + X_t \frac{\partial \widehat{C}}{\partial x}(t, \widehat{X}_t), \qquad t \geqslant 0,$$

is self-financing and hedges the claim payoff $C = N_T \widehat{g}(\widehat{X}_T)$.

Proof. This result follows directly from Proposition 16.16 by noting that by Itô's formula, and the martingale property of $\widehat{V}_t$ under $\widehat{\mathbb{P}}$ the stochastic integral representation (16.33) is given by

$$
\begin{aligned}
\widehat{V}_T &= \widehat{C} \\
&= \widehat{g}(\widehat{X}_T) \\
&= \widehat{C}(0, \widehat{X}_0) + \int_0^T \frac{\partial \widehat{C}}{\partial t}(t, \widehat{X}_t) dt + \int_0^T \frac{\partial \widehat{C}}{\partial x}(t, \widehat{X}_t) d\widehat{X}_t \\
&\quad + \frac{1}{2} \int_0^T \frac{\partial^2 \widehat{C}}{\partial x^2}(t, \widehat{X}_t) |\widehat{\sigma}_t|^2 dt \\
&= \widehat{C}(0, \widehat{X}_0) + \int_0^T \frac{\partial \widehat{C}}{\partial x}(t, \widehat{X}_t) d\widehat{X}_t \\
&= \widehat{\mathbb{E}}\left[\frac{C}{N_T}\right] + \int_0^T \widehat{\phi}_t d\widehat{X}_t, \qquad 0 \leqslant t \leqslant T,
\end{aligned}
$$

hence

$$
\widehat{\phi}_t = \frac{\partial \widehat{C}}{\partial x}(t, \widehat{X}_t), \qquad 0 \leqslant t \leqslant T.
$$

$\square$

In the case of an exchange option with payoff function

$$
C = (X_T - \kappa N_T)^+ = N_T(\widehat{X}_T - \kappa)^+
$$

on the geometric Brownian motion $(\widehat{X}_t)_{t \in [0,T]}$ under $\widehat{\mathbb{P}}$ with

$$
\widehat{\sigma}_t(\widehat{X}_t) = \widehat{\sigma}(t)\widehat{X}_t, \tag{16.35}
$$

where $(\widehat{\sigma}(t))_{t \in [0,T]}$ is a deterministic volatility function of time, we have the following corollary on the hedging of exchange options based on the Margrabe (1978) formula (16.30).

Corollary 16.18. *The decomposition*

$$
\mathbb{E}^*\left[e^{-\int_t^T r_s ds}(X_T - \kappa N_T)^+ \,\Big|\, \mathcal{F}_t\right] = X_t \Phi_+^0(t, \widehat{X}_t) - \kappa N_t \Phi_-^0(t, \widehat{X}_t)
$$

yields a self-financing portfolio allocation $(\Phi_+^0(t, \widehat{X}_t), -\kappa \Phi_-^0(t, \widehat{X}_t))_{t \in [0,T]}$ *in the assets* (X_t, N_t), *that hedges the claim payoff* $C = (X_T - \kappa N_T)^+$.

Proof. We apply Corollary 16.17 and the relation

$$
\frac{\partial \widehat{C}}{\partial x}(t, x) = \Phi_+^0(t, x), \qquad x \in \mathbb{R},
$$

for the function $\widehat{C}(t, x) = x\Phi_+^0(t, x) - \kappa \Phi_-^0(t, x)$, cf. Relation (6.16) in Proposition 6.4.

$\square$

Note that the Delta hedging method requires the computation of the function $\widehat{C}(t, x)$ and that of the associated finite differences, and may not apply to path-dependent claims.

Examples:

a) When the short rate process $(r(t))_{t\in[0,T]}$ is a *deterministic* function of time and $N_t = e^{\int_t^T r(s)ds}$, Corollary 16.18 yields the usual Black–Scholes hedging strategy

$$\left(\Phi_+(t,\widehat{X}_t), -\kappa e^{\int_0^T r(s)ds}\Phi_-(t,X_t)\right)_{t\in[0,T]}$$
$$= \left(\Phi_+^0\left(t, e^{\int_t^T r(s)ds}\widehat{X}_t\right), -\kappa e^{\int_0^T r(s)ds}\Phi_-^0\left(t, e^{\int_t^T r(s)ds}X_t\right)\right)_{t\in[0,T]},$$

in the assets $\left(X_t, e^{\int_0^t r(s)ds}\right)$, that hedges the claim payoff $C = (X_T - \kappa)^+$, with

$$\Phi_+(t,x) := \Phi\left(\frac{\log(x/\kappa) + \int_t^T r(s)ds + (T-t)\sigma^2/2}{\sigma\sqrt{T-t}}\right),$$

and

$$\Phi_-(t,x) := \Phi\left(\frac{\log(x/\kappa) + \int_t^T r(s)ds - (T-t)\sigma^2/2}{\sigma\sqrt{T-t}}\right).$$

b) In case $N_t = P(t,T)$ and $X_t = P(t,S)$, $0 \leqslant t \leqslant T < S$, Corollary 16.18 shows that when $\left(\widehat{X}_t\right)_{t\in[0,T]}$ is modeled as the geometric Brownian motion (16.35) under $\widehat{\mathbb{P}}$, the bond call option with payoff $(P(T,S) - \kappa)^+$ can be hedged as

$$\mathbb{E}^*\left[e^{-\int_t^T r_s ds}(P(T,S) - \kappa)^+ \mid \mathcal{F}_t\right] = P(t,S)\Phi_+\left(t,\widehat{X}_t\right) - \kappa P(t,T)\Phi_-\left(t,\widehat{X}_t\right)$$

by the self-financing portfolio allocation

$$\left(\Phi_+\left(t,\widehat{X}_t\right), -\kappa\Phi_-\left(t,\widehat{X}_t\right)\right)_{t\in[0,T]}$$

in the assets $(P(t,S), P(t,T))$, *i.e.* one needs to hold the quantity $\Phi_+\left(t,\widehat{X}_t\right)$ of the bond maturing at time S, and to short a quantity $\kappa\Phi_-\left(t,\widehat{X}_t\right)$ of the bond maturing at time T.

Exercises

Exercise 16.1   Let $(B_t)_{t\in\mathbb{R}_+}$ be a standard Brownian motion started at 0 under the risk-neutral probability measure $\mathbb{P}^*$. Consider a numéraire $(N_t)_{t\in\mathbb{R}_+}$ given by

$$N_t := N_0\, e^{\eta B_t - \eta^2 t/2}, \qquad t \geqslant 0,$$

and a risky asset $(X_t)_{t\in\mathbb{R}_+}$ given by

$$X_t := X_0\, e^{\sigma B_t - \sigma^2 t/2}, \qquad t \geqslant 0,$$

in a market with risk-free interest rate $r = 0$. Let $\widehat{\mathbb{P}}$ denote the forward measure relative to the numéraire $(N_t)_{t\in\mathbb{R}_+}$, under which the process $\widehat{X}_t := X_t/N_t$ of forward prices is known to be a <u>martingale</u>.

a) Using the Itô formula, compute

$$d\widehat{X}_t = d\left(\frac{X_t}{N_t}\right)$$

$$= \frac{X_0}{N_0} d\left(e^{(\sigma-\eta)B_t - (\sigma^2 - \eta^2)t/2}\right).$$

b) Explain why the exchange option price $\mathbb{E}^*[(X_T - \lambda N_T)^+]$ at time 0 has the Black–Scholes form

$$\mathbb{E}^*[(X_T - \lambda N_T)^+] \tag{16.36}$$

$$= X_0 \Phi\left(\frac{\log(\widehat{X}_0/\lambda)}{\widehat{\sigma}\sqrt{T}} + \frac{\widehat{\sigma}\sqrt{T}}{2}\right) - \lambda N_0 \Phi\left(\frac{\log(\widehat{X}_0/\lambda)}{\widehat{\sigma}\sqrt{T}} - \frac{\widehat{\sigma}\sqrt{T}}{2}\right).$$

Hints:

(i) Use the change of numéraire identity

$$\mathbb{E}^*[(X_T - \lambda N_T)^+] = N_0 \widehat{\mathbb{E}}[(\widehat{X}_T - \lambda)^+].$$

(ii) The forward price $\widehat{X}_t$ is a martingale under the forward measure $\widehat{\mathbb{P}}$ relative to the numéraire $(N_t)_{t \in \mathbb{R}_+}$.

c) Give the value of $\widehat{\sigma}$ in terms of σ and η.

Exercise 16.2 Let $\left(B_t^{(1)}\right)_{t \in \mathbb{R}_+}$ and $\left(B_t^{(2)}\right)_{t \in \mathbb{R}_+}$ be correlated standard Brownian motions started at 0 under the risk-neutral probability measure $\mathbb{P}^*$, with correlation $\mathrm{Corr}\left(B_s^{(1)}, B_t^{(2)}\right) = \rho \min(s, t)$, i.e. $dB_t^{(1)} \cdot dB_t^{(2)} = \rho dt$. Consider two asset prices $\left(S_t^{(1)}\right)_{t \in \mathbb{R}_+}$ and $\left(S_t^{(2)}\right)_{t \in \mathbb{R}_+}$ given by the geometric Brownian motions

$$S_t^{(1)} := S_0^{(1)} e^{rt + \sigma B_t^{(1)} - \sigma^2 t/2}, \quad \text{and} \quad S_t^{(2)} := S_0^{(2)} e^{rt + \eta B_t^{(2)} - \eta^2 t/2}, \qquad t \geqslant 0.$$

Let $\widehat{\mathbb{P}}_2$ denote the forward measure with numéraire $(N_t)_{t \in \mathbb{R}_+} := \left(S_t^{(2)}\right)_{t \in \mathbb{R}_+}$ and Radon–Nikodym density

$$\frac{d\widehat{\mathbb{P}}_2}{d\mathbb{P}^*} = e^{-rT} \frac{S_T^{(2)}}{S_0^{(2)}} = e^{\eta B_T^{(2)} - \eta^2 T/2}.$$

a) Using the Girsanov Theorem 16.7, determine the shifts $\left(\widehat{B}_t^{(1)}\right)_{t \in \mathbb{R}_+}$ and $\left(\widehat{B}_t^{(2)}\right)_{t \in \mathbb{R}_+}$ of $\left(B_t^{(1)}\right)_{t \in \mathbb{R}_+}$ and $\left(B_t^{(2)}\right)_{t \in \mathbb{R}_+}$ which are standard Brownian motions under $\widehat{\mathbb{P}}_2$.

b) Using the Itô formula, compute

$$d\widehat{S}_t^{(1)} = d\left(\frac{S_t^{(1)}}{S_t^{(2)}}\right)$$

$$= \frac{S_0^{(1)}}{S_0^{(2)}} d\left(e^{\sigma B_t^{(1)} - \eta B_t^{(2)} - (\sigma^2 - \eta^2)t/2}\right),$$

and write the answer in terms of the martingales $d\widehat{B}_t^{(1)}$ and $d\widehat{B}_t^{(2)}$.

c) Using change of numéraire, explain why the exchange option price

$$e^{-rT} \, \mathbb{E}^* \left[\left(S_T^{(1)} - \lambda S_T^{(2)} \right)^+ \right]$$

at time 0 has the Black–Scholes form

$$
e^{-rT} \, \mathbb{E}^* \left[\left(S_T^{(1)} - \lambda S_T^{(2)} \right)^+ \right] \;=\; S_0^{(1)} \Phi \left(\frac{\log \left(\widehat{S}_0^{(1)} / \lambda \right)}{\widehat{\sigma} \sqrt{T}} + \frac{\widehat{\sigma} \sqrt{T}}{2} \right)
$$
$$
- \lambda S_0^{(2)} \Phi \left(\frac{\log \left(\widehat{S}_0^{(1)} / \lambda \right)}{\widehat{\sigma} \sqrt{T}} - \frac{\widehat{\sigma} \sqrt{T}}{2} \right),
$$

where the value of $\widehat{\sigma}$ can be expressed in terms of σ and η.

Exercise 16.3 Consider two zero-coupon bond prices of the form $P(t,T) = F(t, r_t)$ and $P(t, S) = G(t, r_t)$, where $(r_t)_{t \in \mathbb{R}_+}$ is a short-term interest rate process. Taking $N_t := P(t, T)$ as a numéraire defining the forward measure $\widehat{\mathbb{P}}$, compute the dynamics of $(P(t, S))_{t \in [0, T]}$ under $\widehat{\mathbb{P}}$ using a standard Brownian motion $\left(\widehat{W}_t \right)_{t \in [0, T]}$ under $\widehat{\mathbb{P}}$.

Exercise 16.4 Forward contracts. Using a change of numéraire argument for the numéraire $N_t := P(t, T)$, $t \in [0, T]$, compute the price at time $t \in [0, T]$ of a forward (or future) contract with payoff $P(T, S) - K$ in a bond market with short-term interest rate $(r_t)_{t \in \mathbb{R}_+}$. How would you hedge this forward contract?

Exercise 16.5 (Question 2.7 page 17 of Downes et al. (2008)). Consider a price process $(S_t)_{t \in \mathbb{R}_+}$ given by $dS_t = r S_t dt + \sigma S_t dB_t$ under the risk-neutral probability measure $\mathbb{P}^*$, where $r \in \mathbb{R}$ and $\sigma > 0$, and the option with payoff

$$S_T (S_T - K)^+ = \text{Max}(S_T(S_T - K), 0)$$

at maturity T.

a) Show that the option payoff can be rewritten as

$$(S_T(S_T - K))^+ = N_T (S_T - K)^+$$

for a suitable choice of numéraire process $(N_t)_{t \in [0, T]}$.

b) Rewrite the option price $e^{-(T-t)r} \, \mathbb{E}^* \left[(S_T(S_T - K))^+ \mid \mathcal{F}_t \right]$ using a forward measure $\widehat{\mathbb{P}}$ and a change of numéraire argument.

c) Find the dynamics of $(S_t)_{t \in \mathbb{R}_+}$ under the forward measure $\widehat{\mathbb{P}}$.

d) Price the option with payoff

$$S_T (S_T - K)^+ = \text{Max}(S_T(S_T - K), 0)$$

at time $t \in [0, T]$ using the Black–Scholes formula.

Exercise 16.6 Consider the risk asset with dynamics $dS_t = rS_t dt + \sigma S_t dW_t$ with constant interest rate $r \in \mathbb{R}$ and volatility $\sigma > 0$ under the risk-neutral measure $\mathbb{P}^*$. The power call option with payoff $(S_T^n - K^n)^+$, $n \geqslant 1$, is priced at time $t \in [0, T]$ as

$$e^{-(T-t)r} \, \mathbb{E}^* \left[(S_T^n - K^n)^+ \,|\, \mathcal{F}_t \right]$$
$$= \quad e^{-(T-t)r} \, \mathbb{E}^* \left[S_T^n \mathbb{1}_{\{S_T \geqslant K\}} \,|\, \mathcal{F}_t \right] - K^n e^{-(T-t)r} \, \mathbb{E}^* \left[\mathbb{1}_{\{S_T \geqslant K\}} \,|\, \mathcal{F}_t \right]$$

under the risk-neutral measure $\mathbb{P}^*$.

a) Write down the density $\dfrac{d\widehat{\mathbb{P}}}{d\mathbb{P}^*}$ using the numéraire process

$$N_t := S_t^n \, e^{-(n-1)n\sigma^2 t/2 - (n-1)rt}, \qquad t \in [0, T].$$

b) Construct a standard Brownian motion $\widehat{W}_t$ under $\widehat{\mathbb{P}}$.

c) Compute the term $e^{-(T-t)r} \, \mathbb{E}^* \left[S_T^n \mathbb{1}_{\{S_T \geqslant K\}} \,|\, \mathcal{F}_t \right]$ using change of numéraire.

   Hint: We have

$$\mathbb{P}^*(S_T \geqslant K \,|\, \mathcal{F}_t) \quad = \quad \mathbb{E}^* \left[\mathbb{1}_{\{S_T \geqslant K\}} \,|\, \mathcal{F}_t \right]$$
$$= \quad \Phi \left(\frac{\log(S_t/K) + (r^l - \sigma^2/2)(T-t)}{\sigma\sqrt{T-t}} \right).$$

d) Price the power call option with payoff $(S_T^n - K^n)^+$ at time $t \in [0, T]$.

Exercise 16.7 Bond options. Consider two bonds with maturities T and S, with prices $P(t, T)$ and $P(t, S)$ given by

$$\frac{dP(t, T)}{P(t, T)} = r_t dt + \zeta_t^T dW_t,$$

and

$$\frac{dP(t, S)}{P(t, S)} = r_t dt + \zeta_t^S dW_t,$$

where $(\zeta^T(s))_{s \in [0, T]}$ and $(\zeta^S(s))_{s \in [0, S]}$ are deterministic volatility functions of time.

a) Show, using Itô's formula, that

$$d\left(\frac{P(t, S)}{P(t, T)} \right) = \frac{P(t, S)}{P(t, T)} (\zeta^S(t) - \zeta^T(t)) d\widehat{W}_t,$$

   where $\left(\widehat{W}_t \right)_{t \in \mathbb{R}_+}$ is a standard Brownian motion under $\widehat{\mathbb{P}}$.

b) Show that

$$P(T, S) = \frac{P(t, S)}{P(t, T)} \exp \left(\int_t^T (\zeta^S(s) - \zeta^T(s)) d\widehat{W}_s - \frac{1}{2} \int_t^T |\zeta^S(s) - \zeta^T(s)|^2 ds \right).$$

   Let $\widehat{\mathbb{P}}$ denote the forward measure associated to the numéraire

$$N_t := P(t, T), \qquad 0 \leqslant t \leqslant T.$$

c) Show that for all $S, T > 0$ the price at time t

$$\mathbb{E}^* \left[e^{-\int_t^T r_s ds} (P(T,S) - \kappa)^+ \mid \mathcal{F}_t \right]$$

of a bond call option on $P(T,S)$ with payoff $(P(T,S) - \kappa)^+$ is equal to

$$\mathbb{E}^* \left[e^{-\int_t^T r_s ds} (P(T,S) - \kappa)^+ \mid \mathcal{F}_t \right] \tag{16.37}$$
$$= P(t,S) \Phi \left(\frac{v}{2} + \frac{1}{v} \log \frac{P(t,S)}{\kappa P(t,T)} \right) - \kappa P(t,T) \Phi \left(-\frac{v}{2} + \frac{1}{v} \log \frac{P(t,S)}{\kappa P(t,T)} \right),$$

where

$$v^2 = \int_t^T |\zeta^S(s) - \zeta^T(s)|^2 ds.$$

d) Compute the self-financing hedging strategy that hedges the bond option using a portfolio based on the assets $P(t,T)$ and $P(t,S)$.

Exercise 16.8 Consider two risky assets S_1 and S_2 modeled by the geometric Brownian motions

$$S_1(t) = e^{\sigma_1 W_t + \mu t} \quad \text{and} \quad S_2(t) = e^{\sigma_2 W_t + \mu t}, \quad t \geqslant 0, \tag{16.38}$$

where $(W_t)_{t \in \mathbb{R}_+}$ is a standard Brownian motion under $\mathbb{P}$.

a) Find a condition on r, μ and σ_2 so that the discounted price process $e^{-rt} S_2(t)$ is a martingale under $\mathbb{P}$.

b) Assume that $r - \mu = \sigma_2^2/2$, and let

$$X_t = e^{(\sigma_2^2 - \sigma_1^2)t/2} S_1(t), \quad t \geqslant 0.$$

Show that the discounted process $e^{-rt} X_t$ is a martingale under $\mathbb{P}$.

c) Taking $N_t = S_2(t)$ as numéraire, show that the forward process $\widehat{X}(t) = X_t/N_t$ is a martingale under the forward measure $\widehat{\mathbb{P}}$ defined by the Radon–Nikodym density

$$\frac{d\widehat{\mathbb{P}}}{d\mathbb{P}} = e^{-rT} \frac{N_T}{N_0}.$$

Recall that

$$\widehat{W}_t := W_t - \sigma_2 t$$

is a standard Brownian motion under $\widehat{\mathbb{P}}$.

d) Using the relation

$$e^{-rT} \mathbb{E}^* [(S_1(T) - S_2(T))^+] = N_0 \widehat{\mathbb{E}} \left[\frac{(S_1(T) - S_2(T))^+}{N_T} \right],$$

compute the price

$$e^{-rT} \mathbb{E}^* [(S_1(T) - S_2(T))^+]$$

of the exchange option on the assets S_1 and S_2.

Exercise 16.9 Compute the price $e^{-(T-t)r} \mathbb{E}^* \left[\mathbb{1}_{\{R_T \geqslant \kappa\}} \mid \mathcal{F}_t \right]$ at time $t \in [0, T]$ of a cash-or-nothing "binary" foreign exchange call option with maturity T and strike price κ on the foreign exchange rate process $(R_t)_{t \in \mathbb{R}_+}$ given by

$$dR_t = (r^l - r^f)R_t dt + \sigma R_t dW_t,$$

where $(W_t)_{t \in \mathbb{R}_+}$ is a standard Brownian motion under $\mathbb{P}^*$.
Hint: We have the relation

$$\mathbb{P}^* \left(x\, e^{X + \mu} \geqslant \kappa \right) = \Phi \left(\frac{\mu - \log(\kappa/x)}{\sqrt{\mathrm{Var}[X]}} \right)$$

for $X \simeq \mathcal{N}(0, \mathrm{Var}[X])$ a centered Gaussian random variable.

Exercise 16.10 Extension of Proposition 16.8 to correlated Brownian motions. Assume that $(S_t)_{t \in \mathbb{R}_+}$ and $(N_t)_{t \in \mathbb{R}_+}$ satisfy the stochastic differential equations

$$dS_t = r_t S_t dt + \sigma_t^S S_t dW_t^S, \quad \text{and} \quad dN_t = \eta_t N_t dt + \sigma_t^N N_t dW_t^N,$$

where $(W_t^S)_{t \in \mathbb{R}_+}$ and $(W_t^N)_{t \in \mathbb{R}_+}$ have the correlation

$$dW_t^S \bullet dW_t^N = \rho dt,$$

where $\rho \in [-1, 1]$.

a) Show that $(W_t^N)_{t \in \mathbb{R}_+}$ can be written as

$$W_t^N = \rho W_t^S + \sqrt{1 - \rho^2} W_t, \qquad t \geqslant 0,$$

where $(W_t)_{t \in \mathbb{R}_+}$ is a standard Brownian motion under $\mathbb{P}^*$, independent of $(W_t^S)_{t \in \mathbb{R}_+}$.

b) Letting $X_t = S_t / N_t$, show that dX_t can be written as

$$dX_t = (r_t - \eta_t + (\sigma_t^N)^2 - \rho \sigma_t^N \sigma_t^S)X_t dt + \widehat{\sigma}_t X_t dW_t^X,$$

where $(W_t^X)_{t \in \mathbb{R}_+}$ is a standard Brownian motion under $\mathbb{P}^*$ and $\widehat{\sigma}_t$ is to be computed.

Exercise 16.11 Quanto options (Exercise 9.5 in Shreve (2004)). Consider an asset priced S_t at time t, with

$$dS_t = r S_t dt + \sigma^S S_t dW_t^S,$$

and an exchange rate $(R_t)_{t \in \mathbb{R}_+}$ given by

$$dR_t = (r - r^f)R_t dt + \sigma^R R_t dW_t^R,$$

from (16.20) in Proposition 16.10, where $(W_t^R)_{t \in \mathbb{R}_+}$ is written as

$$W_t^R = \rho W_t^S + \sqrt{1 - \rho^2} W_t, \qquad t \geqslant 0,$$

where $(W_t)_{t \in \mathbb{R}_+}$ is a standard Brownian motion under $\mathbb{P}^*$, independent of $(W_t^S)_{t \in \mathbb{R}_+}$, *i.e.* we have

$$dW_t^R \bullet dW_t^S = \rho dt,$$

where ρ is a correlation coefficient.

a) Let

$$a = r^l - r^f + \rho \sigma^R \sigma^S - (\sigma^R)^2$$

and $X_t = e^{at} S_t / R_t$, $t \geqslant 0$, and show by Exercise 16.10 that dX_t can be written as

$$dX_t = r X_t dt + \widehat{\sigma} X_t dW_t^X,$$

where $(W_t^X)_{t \in \mathbb{R}_+}$ is a standard Brownian motion under $\mathbb{P}^*$ and $\widehat{\sigma}$ is to be determined.

b) Compute the price

$$e^{-(T-t)r} \, \mathbb{E}^* \left[\left(\frac{S_T}{R_T} - \kappa \right)^+ \middle| \mathcal{F}_t \right]$$

of the quanto option at time $t \in [0, T]$.

Chapter 17

Short Rates and Bond Pricing

Short-term rates, typically daily rates, are the interest rates applied to short-term lending between financial institutions. The stochastic modeling of short-term interest rate processes is based on the mean reversion property, as in the Vasicek, CIR, CEV, and affine-type models studied in this chapter. The pricing of fixed income products, such as bonds, is considered in this framework using probabilistic and PDE arguments.

17.1 Vasicek Model

As short-term interest rates behave differently from stock prices, they require the development of specific models to account for properties such as positivity, boundedness, and return to equilibrium. The first model to capture the mean reversion property of interest rates, a property not possessed by geometric Brownian motion, is the Vašíček (1977) model, which is based on the Ornstein–Uhlenbeck process. Here, the short-term interest rate process $(r_t)_{t \in \mathbb{R}_+}$ solves the equation

$$dr_t = (a - br_t)dt + \sigma dB_t, \qquad (17.1)$$

where $a, \sigma \in \mathbb{R}$, $b > 0$, and $(B_t)_{t \in \mathbb{R}_+}$ is a standard Brownian motion, with solution

$$r_t = r_0 e^{-bt} + \frac{a}{b}(1 - e^{-bt}) + \sigma \int_0^t e^{-(t-s)b} dB_s, \quad t \geqslant 0, \qquad (17.2)$$

see Exercise 17.1. The probability distribution of r_t is Gaussian at all times t, with mean

$$\mathbb{E}[r_t] = r_0 e^{-bt} + \frac{a}{b}(1 - e^{-bt}),$$

and variance given from the Itô isometry (4.16) as

$$\begin{aligned}
\mathrm{Var}[r_t] &= \mathrm{Var}\left[\sigma \int_0^t e^{-(t-s)b} dB_s\right] \\
&= \sigma^2 \int_0^t \left(e^{-(t-s)b}\right)^2 ds \\
&= \sigma^2 \int_0^t e^{-2bs} ds \\
&= \frac{\sigma^2}{2b}(1 - e^{-2bt}), \qquad t \geqslant 0,
\end{aligned}$$

i.e.

$$r_t \simeq \mathcal{N}\left(r_0 e^{-bt} + \frac{a}{b}(1 - e^{-bt}), \frac{\sigma^2}{2b}(1 - e^{-2bt})\right), \quad t > 0.$$

DOI: 10.1201/9781003298670-17

In particular, the probability density function $f_t(x)$ of r_t at time $t > 0$ is given by

$$f_t(x) = \frac{\sqrt{b/\pi}}{\sigma\sqrt{1 - e^{-2bt}}} \exp\left(-\frac{\left(r_0 e^{-bt} + a\left(1 - e^{-bt}\right)/b - x\right)^2}{\sigma^2\left(1 - e^{-2bt}\right)/b}\right), \quad x \in \mathbb{R}.$$

In the long run,[*] *i.e.* as time t becomes large we have, assuming $b > 0$,

$$\lim_{t\to\infty} \mathbb{E}[r_t] = \frac{a}{b} \quad \text{and} \quad \lim_{t\to\infty} \text{Var}[r_t] = \frac{\sigma^2}{2b}, \tag{17.3}$$

and this distribution converges to the Gaussian $\mathcal{N}(a/b, \sigma^2/(2b))$ distribution, which is also the *invariant* (or stationary) distribution of $(r_t)_{t\in\mathbb{R}_+}$, see Exercise 17.1. In addition, the process tends to revert to its long term mean $a/b = \lim_{t\to\infty} \mathbb{E}[r_t]$ which makes the average drift vanish, *i.e.*:

$$\lim_{t\to\infty} \mathbb{E}[a - br_t] = a - b\lim_{t\to\infty} \mathbb{E}[r_t] = 0.$$

The next R code provides a numerical solution of the stochastic differential equation (17.1) using the Euler method, see Figure 17.1.

```
N=10000;t<-0:(N-1);dt<-1.0/N;nsim<-2; a=0.025;b=1;sigma=0.1;
dB <- matrix(rnorm(nsim*N,mean=0,sd=sqrt(dt)), nsim, N)
R <- matrix(0,nsim,N);R[,1]=0.03
dev.new(width=10,height=7);
for (i in 1:nsim){for (j in 2:N){R[i,j]=R[i,j-1]+(a-b*R[i,j-1])*dt+sigma*dB[i,j]}}
par(mar=c(0,1,1,1));par(oma=c(0,1,1,1));par(mgp=c(-5,1,1))
plot(t,R[1,],xlab = "Time",ylab = "",type = "l",ylim = c(R[1,1]-0.2,R[1,1]+0.2),col = 0,axes=FALSE)
axis(2, pos=0,las=1);for (i in 1:nsim){lines(t, R[i, ], xlab = "time", type = "l", col = i+0)}
abline(h=a/b,col="blue",lwd=3);abline(h=0)
```

Figure 17.1 presents a random simulation of $t \mapsto r_t$ in the Vasicek model with $r_0 = 3\%$, and shows the mean-reverting property of the process with respect to $a/b = 2.5\%$.

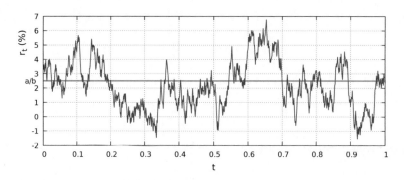

Figure 17.1: Graph of the Vasicek short rate $t \mapsto r_t$ with $a = 0.025$, $b = 1$, and $\sigma = 0.1$.

As can be checked from the simulation of Figure 17.1, the value of r_t in the Vasicek model may become negative due to its Gaussian distribution. Although real interest rates may sometimes fall below zero,[†] this can be regarded as a potential drawback of the Vasicek model.

---

[*]"But this *long run* is a misleading guide to current affairs. *In the long run* we are all dead." Keynes (1924), Ch. 3, p. 80.

[†]Eurozone interest rates turned negative in 2014.

Calibration of the Vasicek Model

The Vasicek equation (17.1), *i.e.*

$$dr_t = (a - br_t)dt + \sigma dB_t,$$

can be discretized according to a discrete-time sequence $(t_k)_{k \geqslant 0} = (t_0, t_1, t_2, \ldots)$ of time instants, as

$$r_{t_{k+1}} - r_{t_k} = (a - br_{t_k})\Delta t + \sigma Z_k, \qquad k \geqslant 0,$$

where $\Delta t := t_{k+1} - t_k$ and $(Z_k)_{k \geqslant 0}$ is a Gaussian white noise with variance Δt, *i.e.* a sequence of independent, centered and identically distributed $\mathcal{N}(0, \Delta t)$ Gaussian random variables, which yields

$$r_{t_{k+1}} = r_{t_k} + (a - br_{t_k})\Delta t + \sigma Z_k = a\Delta t + (1 - b\Delta t)r_{t_k} + \sigma Z_k, \quad k \geqslant 0.$$

Based on a set $(\tilde{r}_{t_k})_{k=0,1,\ldots,n}$ of *market data*, we consider the quadratic residual

$$\sum_{k=0}^{n-1} \left(\tilde{r}_{t_{k+1}} - a\Delta t - (1 - b\Delta t)\tilde{r}_{t_k} \right)^2 \tag{17.4}$$

which represents the (squared) quadratic distance between the observed data sequence $(\tilde{r}_{t_k})_{k=1,2,\ldots,n}$ and its predictions $\left(a\Delta t + (1 - b\Delta t)\tilde{r}_{t_k} \right)_{k=0,1,\ldots,n-1}$.

In order to minimize the residual (17.4) over a and b we use Ordinary Least Square (OLS) regression, and equate the following derivatives to zero. Namely, we have

$$\frac{\partial}{\partial a} \sum_{l=0}^{n-1} \left(\tilde{r}_{t_{l+1}} - a\Delta t - (1 - b\Delta t)\tilde{r}_{t_l} \right)^2$$

$$= -2\Delta t \left(-an\Delta t + \sum_{l=0}^{n-1} \left(\tilde{r}_{t_{l+1}} - (1 - b\Delta t)\tilde{r}_{t_l} \right) \right)$$

$$= 0,$$

hence

$$a\Delta t = \frac{1}{n} \sum_{l=0}^{n-1} \left(\tilde{r}_{t_{l+1}} - (1 - b\Delta t)\tilde{r}_{t_l} \right),$$

and

$$\frac{\partial}{\partial b} \sum_{k=0}^{n-1} \left(\tilde{r}_{t_{k+1}} - a\Delta t - (1 - b\Delta t)\tilde{r}_{t_k} \right)^2$$

$$= 2\Delta t \sum_{k=0}^{n-1} \tilde{r}_{t_k} \left(-a\Delta t + \tilde{r}_{t_{k+1}} - (1 - b\Delta t)\tilde{r}_{t_k} \right)$$

$$= 2\Delta t \sum_{k=0}^{n-1} \tilde{r}_{t_k} \left(\tilde{r}_{t_{k+1}} - (1 - b\Delta t)\tilde{r}_{t_k} - \frac{1}{n} \sum_{l=0}^{n-1} \left(\tilde{r}_{t_{l+1}} - (1 - b\Delta t)\tilde{r}_{t_l} \right) \right)$$

$$= 2\Delta t \sum_{k=0}^{n-1} \tilde{r}_{t_k} \tilde{r}_{t_{k+1}} - \frac{\Delta t}{n} \sum_{k,l=0}^{n-1} \tilde{r}_{t_k} \tilde{r}_{t_{l+1}} - \Delta t (1 - b\Delta t) \left(\sum_{k=0}^{n-1} (\tilde{r}_{t_k})^2 - \frac{1}{n} \sum_{k,l=0}^{n-1} \tilde{r}_{t_k} \tilde{r}_{t_l} \right)$$

$$= 0.$$

This leads to estimators for the parameters a and b, respectively as the empirical mean and covariance of $(\tilde{r}_{t_k})_{k=0,1,\ldots,n}$, *i.e.*

$$\begin{cases} \widehat{a}\Delta t = \dfrac{1}{n}\sum_{k=0}^{n-1}\left(\tilde{r}_{t_{k+1}} - (1-\widehat{b}\Delta t)\tilde{r}_{t_k}\right), \\[2ex] \text{and} \\[2ex] 1-\widehat{b}\Delta t = \dfrac{\displaystyle\sum_{k=0}^{n-1}\tilde{r}_{t_k}\tilde{r}_{t_{k+1}} - \dfrac{1}{n}\sum_{k,l=0}^{n-1}\tilde{r}_{t_k}\tilde{r}_{t_{l+1}}}{\displaystyle\sum_{k=0}^{n-1}(\tilde{r}_{t_k})^2 - \dfrac{1}{n}\sum_{k,l=0}^{n-1}\tilde{r}_{t_k}\tilde{r}_{t_l}} \\[4ex] \qquad\qquad = \dfrac{\displaystyle\sum_{k=0}^{n-1}\left(\tilde{r}_{t_k} - \dfrac{1}{n}\sum_{l=0}^{n-1}\tilde{r}_{t_l}\right)\left(\tilde{r}_{t_{k+1}} - \dfrac{1}{n}\sum_{l=0}^{n-1}\tilde{r}_{t_{l+1}}\right)}{\displaystyle\sum_{k=0}^{n-1}\left(\tilde{r}_{t_k} - \dfrac{1}{n}\sum_{k=0}^{n-1}\tilde{r}_{t_k}\right)^2}. \end{cases} \qquad (17.5)$$

This also yields

$$\begin{aligned} \sigma^2\Delta t &= \mathrm{Var}[\sigma Z_k] \\ &\simeq \mathbb{E}\left[\left(\tilde{r}_{t_{k+1}} - (1-b\Delta t)\tilde{r}_{t_k} - a\Delta t\right)^2\right], \qquad k \geqslant 0, \end{aligned}$$

hence σ can be estimated as

$$\widehat{\sigma}^2\Delta t = \frac{1}{n}\sum_{k=0}^{n-1}\left(\tilde{r}_{t_{k+1}} - \tilde{r}_{t_k}(1-\widehat{b}\Delta t) - \widehat{a}\Delta t\right)^2. \qquad (17.6)$$

Exercise. Show that (17.6) can be recovered by minimizing the residual

$$\eta \mapsto \sum_{k=0}^{n-1}\left(\left(\tilde{r}_{t_{k+1}} - \tilde{r}_{t_k}(1-\widehat{b}\Delta t) - \widehat{a}\Delta t\right)^2 - \eta\Delta t\right)^2$$

as a function of $\eta > 0$, see also Exercise 17.3.

Time series modeling

Defining $\widehat{r}_{t_n} := r_{t_n} - a/b$, $n \geqslant 0$, we have

$$\begin{aligned} \widehat{r}_{t_{n+1}} &= r_{t_{n+1}} - \frac{a}{b} \\ &= r_{t_n} - \frac{a}{b} + (a - br_{t_n})\Delta t + \sigma Z_n \\ &= r_{t_n} - \frac{a}{b} - b\left(r_{t_n} - \frac{a}{b}\right)\Delta t + \sigma Z_n \\ &= \widehat{r}_{t_n} - b\widehat{r}_{t_n}\Delta t + \sigma Z_n \\ &= (1-b\Delta t)\widehat{r}_{t_n} + \sigma Z_n, \qquad n \geqslant 0. \end{aligned}$$

In other words, the sequence $(\widehat{r}_{t_n})_{n\geqslant 0}$ is modeled according to an autoregressive AR(1) time series $(X_n)_{n\geqslant 0}$ with parameter $\alpha = 1 - b\Delta t$, in which the current state X_n of the system is expressed as the linear combination

$$X_n := \sigma Z_n + \alpha X_{n-1}, \qquad n \geqslant 1, \qquad (17.7)$$

where $(Z_n)_{n \geqslant 1}$ another Gaussian white noise sequence with variance Δt. This equation can be solved recursively as the causal series

$$X_n = \sigma Z_n + \alpha(\sigma Z_{n-1} + \alpha X_{n-2}) = \cdots = \sigma \sum_{k \geqslant 0} \alpha^k Z_{n-k},$$

which converges when $|\alpha| < 1$, *i.e.* $|1 - b\Delta t| < 1$, in which case the time series $(X_n)_{n \geqslant 0}$ is weakly stationary, with

$$
\begin{aligned}
\mathbb{E}[X_n] &= \sigma \sum_{k \geqslant 0} \alpha^k \, \mathbb{E}[Z_{n-k}] \\
&= \sigma \, \mathbb{E}[Z_0] \sum_{k \geqslant 0} \alpha^k \\
&= \frac{\sigma}{1 - \alpha} \, \mathbb{E}[Z_0] \\
&= 0, \qquad n \geqslant 0.
\end{aligned}
$$

The variance of X_n is given by

$$
\begin{aligned}
\mathrm{Var}[X_n] &= \sigma^2 \, \mathrm{Var}\left[\sum_{k \geqslant 0} \alpha^k Z_{n-k} \right] \\
&= \sigma^2 \Delta t \sum_{k \geqslant 0} \alpha^{2k} \\
&= \sigma^2 \Delta t \sum_{k \geqslant 0} (1 - b\Delta t)^{2k} \\
&= \frac{\sigma^2 \Delta t}{1 - (1 - b\Delta t)^2} \\
&= \frac{\sigma^2 \Delta t}{2b\Delta t - b^2 (\Delta t)^2} \\
&\simeq \frac{\sigma^2}{2b}, \qquad [\Delta t \simeq 0],
\end{aligned}
$$

which coincides with the variance (17.3) of the Vasicek process in the stationary regime.

Example - TNX yield calibration

We consider the yield of the 10 Year Treasury Note on the Chicago Board Options Exchange (CBOE), for later use in the calibration of the Vasicek model. Treasury notes usually have a maturity between one and 10 years, whereas treasury bonds have maturities beyond 10 years)

```
1  library(quantmod)
   getSymbols("^TNX",from="2012-01-01",to="2016-01-01",src="yahoo")
3  rate=Ad(`TNX`);rate<-rate[!is.na(rate)]
   dev.new(width=10,height=7);chartSeries(rate,up.col="blue",theme="white")
5  n = length(!is.na(rate))
```

The next Figure 17.2 displays the yield of the 10 Year Treasury Note.

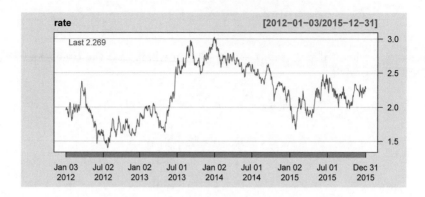

Figure 17.2: CBOE 10 Year Treasury Note (TNX) yield.

The next R code is estimating the parameters of the Vasicek model using the 10 Year Treasury Note yield data of Figure 17.2, by implementing the formulas (17.5).

```
1  ratek=as.vector(rate);ratekplus1 <- c(ratek[-1],0)
   oneminusbdt <- (sum(ratek*ratekplus1) - sum(ratek)*sum(ratekplus1)/n)/(sum(ratek*ratek) -
       sum(ratek)*sum(ratek)/n)
3  adt <- sum(ratekplus1)/n-oneminusbdt*sum(ratek)/n;
   sigmadt <- sqrt(sum((ratekplus1-oneminusbdt*ratek-adt)^2)/n)
```

Parameter estimation can also be implemented using the linear regression command

$$\mathrm{lm}(c(\mathrm{diff}(\mathrm{ratek})) \sim \mathrm{ratek}[1{:}\mathrm{length}(\mathrm{ratek}){-}1])$$

in R, which estimates the values of $a\Delta t \simeq 0.017110$ and $-b\Delta t \simeq -0.007648$ in the regression

$$r_{t_{k+1}} - r_{t_k} = (a - b r_{t_k})\Delta t + \sigma Z_k, \qquad k \geqslant 0,$$

Coefficients:

(Intercept)   ratek[1:length(ratek) - 1]

0.017110   -0.007648

```
   dev.new(width=10,height=7);
2  for (i in 1:100) {ar.sim<-arima.sim(model=list(ar=c(oneminusbdt)),n.start=100,n)
   y=adt/oneminusbdt+sigmadt*ar.sim;y=y+ratek[1]-y[1]
4  time <- as.POSIXct(time(rate), format = "%Y-%m-%d")
   yield <- xts(x = y, order.by = time);
6  chartSeries(yield,up.col="blue",theme="white",yrange=c(0,max(ratek)))
   Sys.sleep(0.5)}
```

The above R code is generating Vasicek random samples according to the AR(1) time series (17.7), see Figure 17.3.

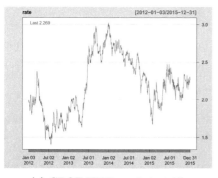

(a) CBOE TNX market yield.

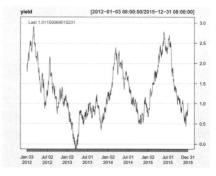

(b) Calibrated Vasicek sample path.

Figure 17.3: Calibrated Vasicek simulation *vs* market data.

The R package Sim.DiffProc can also be used to estimate the coefficients $a\Delta t$ and $b\Delta t$.

```
1  install.packages("Sim.DiffProc");library(Sim.DiffProc)
   fx <- expression( theta[1]-theta[2]*x ); gx <- expression( theta[3] )
3  fitsde(data = as.ts(ratek), drift = fx, diffusion = gx, start = list(theta1=0.1, theta2=0.1,
       theta3=0.1),pmle="euler")
```

17.2 Affine Short Rate Models

The class of short rate interest rate models admits a number of generalizations (see the references quoted in the introduction of this chapter), including the class of affine models of the form

$$dr_t = (\eta(t) + \lambda(t)r_t)dt + \sqrt{\delta(t) + \gamma(t)r_t}dB_t. \tag{17.8}$$

Such models are called *affine* because the associated bonds can be priced using an *affine* PDE of the type (17.26) below with solution of the form (17.27), as will be seen after Proposition 17.2.

The family of affine models also includes:

i) the Ho and Lee (1986) model

$$dr_t = \theta(t)dt + \sigma dB_t,$$

where $\theta(t)$ is a deterministic function of time, as an extension of the Merton model $dr_t = \theta dt + \sigma dB_t$,

ii) the Hull and White (1990) model

$$dr_t = (\theta(t) - \alpha(t)r_t)dt + \sigma(t)dB_t$$

which is a time-dependent extension of the Vasicek model (17.1), with the explicit solution

$$r_t = r_0 e^{-\int_0^t \alpha(\tau)d\tau} + \int_0^t e^{-\int_u^t \alpha(\tau)d\tau}\theta(u)du + \int_0^t \sigma(u)e^{-\int_u^t \alpha(\tau)d\tau}dB_u,$$

$t \geqslant 0$.

Cox–Ingersoll–Ross (CIR) model

The Cox et al. (1985) (CIR) model brings a solution to the positivity problem encountered with the Vasicek model, by the use the nonlinear stochastic differential equation

$$dr_t = \beta(\alpha - r_t)dt + \sigma\sqrt{r_t}dB_t, \tag{17.9}$$

with $\alpha > 0$, $\beta > 0$, $\sigma > 0$. The probability distribution of r_t at time $t > 0$ admits the noncentral Chi square probability density function given by

$$f_t(x) \tag{17.10}$$

$$= \frac{2\beta}{\sigma^2\left(1 - e^{-\beta t}\right)} \exp\left(-\frac{2\beta\left(x + r_0\,e^{-\beta t}\right)}{\sigma^2\left(1 - e^{-\beta t}\right)}\right) \left(\frac{x}{r_0\,e^{-\beta t}}\right)^{\alpha\beta/\sigma^2 - 1/2} I_{2\alpha\beta/\sigma^2 - 1}\left(\frac{4\beta\sqrt{r_0 x\,e^{-\beta t}}}{\sigma^2\left(1 - e^{-\beta t}\right)}\right),$$

$x > 0$, where

$$I_\lambda(z) := \left(\frac{z}{2}\right)^\lambda \sum_{k \geqslant 0} \frac{(z^2/4)^k}{k!\Gamma(\lambda + k + 1)}, \qquad z \in \mathbb{R},$$

is the modified Bessel function of the first kind, see Lemma 9 in Feller (1951) and Corollary 24 in Albanese and Lawi (2005). Note that $f_t(x)$ is not defined at $x = 0$ if $\alpha\beta/\sigma^2 - 1/2 < 0$, *i.e.* $\sigma^2 > 2\alpha\beta$, in which case the probability distribution of r_t admits a point mass at $x = 0$. On the other hand, r_t remains almost surely strictly positive under the Feller condition $2\alpha\beta \geqslant \sigma^2$, *cf.* the study of the associated probability density function in Lemma 4 of Feller (1951) for $\alpha, \beta \in \mathbb{R}$.

The next R code provides a numerical solution of the stochastic differential equation (17.9) using the Euler method, see Figure 17.4.

```
1  N=10000; t <- 0:(N-1); dt <- 1.0/N; nsim <- 2
   a=0.025; b=1; sigma=0.1; sd=sqrt(sigma^2/2/b)
3  X <- matrix(rnorm(nsim*N,mean=0,sd=sqrt(dt)), nsim, N)
   R <- matrix(0,nsim,N);R[,1]=0.03
5  for (i in 1:nsim){for (j in 2:N){R[i,j]=max(0,R[i,j-1]+(a-b*R[i,j-1])*dt+sigma*sqrt(R[i,j-1])*X[i,j])}}
   plot(t,R[1,],xlab="time",ylab="",type="l",ylim=c(0,R[1,1]+sd/5),col=0,axes=FALSE)
7  axis(2, pos=0)
   for (i in 1:nsim){lines(t, R[i, ], xlab = "time", type = "l", col = i+8)}
9  abline(h=a/b,col="blue",lwd=3);abline(h=0)
```

Figure 17.4 presents a random simulation of $t \mapsto r_t$ in the Cox et al. (1985) (CIR) model in the case $\sigma^2 > 2\alpha\beta$, in which the process is mean reverting with respect to $\alpha = 2.5\%$ and has a nonzero probability of hitting 0.

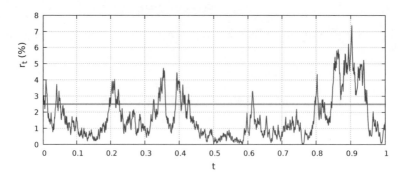

Figure 17.4: Graph of the CIR short rate $t \mapsto r_t$ with $\alpha = 2.5\%$, $\beta = 1$, and $\sigma = 1.3$.

In large time $t \to \infty$, using the asymptotics

$$I_\lambda(z) \simeq_{z \to 0} \frac{1}{\Gamma(\lambda+1)} \left(\frac{z}{2}\right)^\lambda,$$

the probability density function (17.10) becomes the gamma density function

$$f(x) = \lim_{t \to \infty} f_t(x) = \frac{1}{\Gamma(2\alpha\beta/\sigma^2)} \left(\frac{2\beta}{\sigma^2}\right)^{2\alpha\beta/\sigma^2} x^{-1+2\alpha\beta/\sigma^2} e^{-2\beta x/\sigma^2}, \quad x > 0. \qquad (17.11)$$

with shape parameter $2\alpha\beta/\sigma^2$ and scale parameter $\sigma^2/(2\beta)$, which is also the *invariant distribution* of r_t.

The family of classical mean-reverting models also includes the Courtadon (1982) model

$$dr_t = \beta(\alpha - r_t)dt + \sigma r_t dB_t,$$

where α, β, σ are nonnegative, cf. Exercise 17.5, and the exponential Vasicek model

$$dr_t = r_t(\eta - a \log r_t)dt + \sigma r_t dB_t,$$

where $a, \eta, \sigma > 0$, cf. Exercises 4.16 and 4.17.

Constant Elasticity of Variance (CEV) model

Constant Elasticity of Variance models are designed to take into account nonconstant volatilities that can vary as a power of the underlying asset price. The Marsh and Rosenfeld (1983) short-term interest rate model

$$dr_t = (\beta r_t^{\gamma-1} + \alpha r_t)dt + \sigma r_t^{\gamma/2}dB_t, \qquad (17.12)$$

where $\alpha \in \mathbb{R}$, $\beta, \sigma > 0$ are constants and $\gamma > 0$ is the variance (or diffusion) elasticity coefficient, covers most of the CEV models. Here, the elasticity coefficient is defined as ratio

$$\frac{dv^2(r)/v^2(r)}{dr/r}$$

between the relative change $dv(r)/v(r)$ in the variance $v(r)$ and the relative change dr/r in r. Denoting by $v^2(r) := \sigma^2 r^\gamma$ the variance coefficient in (17.12), constant elasticity refers to the constant ratio

$$\frac{dv^2(r)/v^2(r)}{dr/r} = 2\frac{r}{v(r)}\frac{dv(r)}{dr} = 2\frac{d\log v(r)}{d\log r} = 2\frac{d\log r^{\gamma/2}}{d\log r} = \gamma.$$

For $\gamma = 1$, (17.12) yields the Cox et al. (1985) (CIR) equation

$$dr_t = (\beta + \alpha r_t)dt + \sigma\sqrt{r_t}dB_t.$$

For $\beta = 0$ we get the standard CEV model

$$dr_t = \alpha r_t dt + \sigma r_t^{\gamma/2}dB_t,$$

and for $\gamma = 2$ and $\beta = 0$ this yields the Dothan (1978) model

$$dr_t = \alpha r_t dt + \sigma r_t dB_t,$$

which is a version of geometric Brownian motion used for short-term interest rate modeling.

17.3   Zero-Coupon and Coupon Bonds

A zero-coupon bond is a contract priced $P(t,T)$ at time $t < T$ to deliver the *face value* (or *par value*) $P(T,T) = \$1$ at time T. In addition to its value at maturity, a bond may yield a periodic *coupon* payment at regular time intervals until the maturity date.

The computation of the arbitrage-free price $P_0(t,T)$ of a zero-coupon bond based on an underlying short-term interest rate process $(r_t)_{t\in\mathbb{R}_+}$ is a basic and important issue in interest rate modeling.

Constant short rate

In case the short-term interest rate is a constant $r_t = r$, $t \geqslant 0$, a standard arbitrage argument shows that the price $P(t,T)$ of the bond is given by

$$P(t,T) = e^{-r(T-t)}, \qquad 0 \leqslant t \leqslant T.$$

Indeed, if $P(t,T) > e^{-r(T-t)}$ we could issue a bond at the price $P(t,T)$ and invest this amount at the compounded risk free rate r, which would yield $P(t,T) e^{r(T-t)} > 1$ at time T.

On the other hand, if $P(t,T) < e^{-r(T-t)}$ we could borrow $P(t,T)$ at the rate r to buy a bond priced $P(t,T)$. At maturity time T we would receive $\$1$ and refund only $P(t,T) e^{r(T-t)} < 1$.

The price $P(t,T) = e^{-r(T-t)}$ of the bond is the value of $P(t,T)$ that makes the potential profit $P(t,T) e^{r(T-t)} - 1$ vanish for both traders.

Time-dependent deterministic short rates

Similarly to the above, when the short-term interest rate process $(r(t))_{t\in\mathbb{R}_+}$ is a deterministic function of time, a similar argument shows that

$$P(t,T) = e^{-\int_t^T r(s)ds}, \qquad 0 \leqslant t \leqslant T. \tag{17.13}$$

Stochastic short rates

In case $(r_t)_{t\in\mathbb{R}_+}$ is an $(\mathcal{F}_t)_{t\in\mathbb{R}_+}$-adapted random process the formula (17.13) is no longer valid as it relies on future information, and we replace it with the averaged discounted payoff

$$P(t,T) = \mathbb{E}^*\left[e^{-\int_t^T r_s ds} \,\middle|\, \mathcal{F}_t\right], \qquad 0 \leqslant t \leqslant T, \tag{17.14}$$

under a risk-neutral probability measure $\mathbb{P}^*$. It is natural to write $P(t,T)$ as a conditional expectation under a martingale measure, as the use of conditional expectation helps to "filter out" the (random/unknown) future information past time t contained in $\int_t^T r_s ds$. The expression (17.14) makes sense as the "best possible estimate" of the future quantity $e^{-\int_t^T r_s ds}$ in mean-square sense, given the information known up to time t.

Coupon bonds

Pricing bonds with nonzero coupon is not difficult since in general the amount and periodicity of coupons are deterministic.* In the case of a succession of coupon payments

---

*However, coupon default cannot be excluded.

$c_1, c_2, \ldots, c_n$ at times $T_1, T_2, \ldots, T_n \in (t, T]$, another application of the above absence of arbitrage argument shows that the price $P_c(t, T)$ of the coupon bond with discounted (deterministic) coupon payments is given by the linear combination of zero-coupon bond prices

$$
\begin{aligned}
P_c(t, T) \quad &:= \quad \mathbb{E}^* \left[\sum_{k=1}^{n} c_k\, \mathrm{e}^{-\int_t^{T_k} r_s ds} \,\bigg|\, \mathcal{F}_t \right] + \mathbb{E}^* \left[\mathrm{e}^{-\int_t^{T} r_s ds} \,\bigg|\, \mathcal{F}_t \right] \\
&= \quad \sum_{k=1}^{n} c_k\, \mathbb{E}^* \left[\mathrm{e}^{-\int_t^{T_k} r_s ds} \,\bigg|\, \mathcal{F}_t \right] + P_0(t, T) \\
&= \quad P_0(t, T) + \sum_{k=1}^{n} c_k P_0(t, T_k), \qquad 0 \leqslant t \leqslant T_1, \qquad (17.15)
\end{aligned}
$$

which represents the present value at time t of future $\$c_1, \$c_2, \ldots, \$c_n$ receipts respectively at times $T_1, T_2, \ldots, T_n$, in addition to a terminal $\$1$ principal payment.

In the case of a constant coupon rate c paid at regular time intervals $\tau = T_{k+1} - T_k$, $k = 0, 1, \ldots, n-1$, with $T_0 = t$, $T_n = T$, and a constant deterministic short rate r, we find

$$
\begin{aligned}
P_c(T_0, T_n) \quad &= \quad \mathrm{e}^{-rn\tau} + c \sum_{k=1}^{n} \mathrm{e}^{-(T_k - T_0)r} \\
&= \quad \mathrm{e}^{-rn\tau} + c \sum_{k=1}^{n} \mathrm{e}^{-kr\tau} \\
&= \quad \mathrm{e}^{-rn\tau} + c \frac{\mathrm{e}^{-r\tau} - \mathrm{e}^{-r(n+1)\tau}}{1 - \mathrm{e}^{-r\tau}}.
\end{aligned}
$$

In terms of the discrete-time interest rate $\tilde{r} := \mathrm{e}^{r\tau} - 1$, we also have

$$
P_c(T_0, T_n) = \frac{c}{\tilde{r}} + \frac{\tilde{r} - c}{(1 + \tilde{r})^n \tilde{r}}.
$$

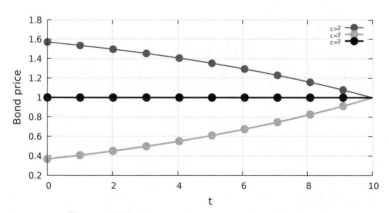

Figure 17.5: Discrete-time coupon bond pricing.

In the case of a continuous-time coupon rate $c > 0$, the above discrete-time calculation (17.15) can be reinterpreted as follows:

$$
\begin{aligned}
P_c(t,T) &= P_0(t,T) + c \int_t^T P_0(t,u)\,du \qquad (17.16)\\
&= P_0(t,T) + c \int_t^T e^{-(u-t)r}\,du\\
&= e^{-(T-t)r} + c \int_0^{T-t} e^{-ru}\,du\\
&= e^{-(T-t)r} + \frac{c}{r}\left(1 - e^{-(T-t)r}\right),\\
&= \frac{c}{r} + \frac{r-c}{r}e^{-(T-t)r}, \qquad 0 \leqslant t \leqslant T, \qquad (17.17)
\end{aligned}
$$

where the coupon bond price $P_c(t,T)$ solves the ordinary differential equation

$$
dP_c(t,T) = (r-c)\,e^{-(T-t)r}\,dt = -c\,dt + rP_c(t,T)\,dt, \qquad 0 \leqslant t \leqslant T,
$$

see also Figure 17.6 below.

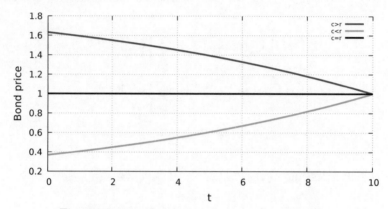

Figure 17.6: Continuous-time coupon bond pricing.

In what follows, we will mostly consider zero-coupon bonds priced as $P(t,T) = P_0(t,T)$, $0 \leqslant t \leqslant T$, in the setting of stochastic short rates.

Martingale property of discounted bond prices

The following proposition shows that Assumption (A) of Chapter 16 is satisfied, in other words, the bond price process $t \mapsto P(t,T)$ can be used as a numéraire.

Proposition 17.1. *The discounted bond price process*

$$
t \mapsto \widetilde{P}(t,T) := e^{-\int_0^t r_s\,ds} P(t,T)
$$

is a martingale under $\mathbb{P}^*$.

Proof. By (17.14) we have

$$
\begin{aligned}
\widetilde{P}(t,T) &= e^{-\int_0^t r_s\,ds} P(t,T)\\
&= e^{-\int_0^t r_s\,ds} \mathbb{E}^*\left[e^{-\int_t^T r_s\,ds} \,\middle|\, \mathcal{F}_t\right]
\end{aligned}
$$

$$= \mathbb{E}^* \left[e^{- \int_0^t r_s ds} e^{- \int_t^T r_s ds} \mid \mathcal{F}_t \right]$$

$$= \mathbb{E}^* \left[e^{- \int_0^T r_s ds} \mid \mathcal{F}_t \right], \qquad 0 \leqslant t \leqslant T,$$

and this suffices in order to conclude, since by the tower property of conditional expectations, see, *e.g.* Example 1 page 207, any process $(X_t)_{t \in \mathbb{R}_+}$ of the form $t \mapsto X_t := \mathbb{E}^*[F \mid \mathcal{F}_t]$, $F \in L^1(\Omega)$, is a martingale, see also Relation (7.1). In other words, we have

$$\mathbb{E}^* \left[\widetilde{P}(t,T) \mid \mathcal{F}_u \right] = \mathbb{E}^* \left[\mathbb{E}^* \left[e^{- \int_0^T r_s ds} \mid \mathcal{F}_t \right] \mid \mathcal{F}_u \right]$$

$$= \mathbb{E}^* \left[e^{- \int_0^T r_s ds} \mid \mathcal{F}_u \right]$$

$$= \widetilde{P}(u,T), \qquad 0 \leqslant u \leqslant t.$$

$\square$

17.4 Bond Pricing PDE

We assume from now on that the underlying short rate process solves the stochastic differential equation

$$dr_t = \mu(t, r_t) dt + \sigma(t, r_t) dB_t \tag{17.18}$$

where $(B_t)_{t \in \mathbb{R}_+}$ is a standard Brownian motion under $\mathbb{P}^*$. Note that specifying the dynamics of $(r_t)_{t \in \mathbb{R}_+}$ under the historical probability measure $\mathbb{P}$ will also lead to a notion of market price of risk (MPoR) for the modeling of short rates.

As all solutions of stochastic differential equations such as (17.18) have the *Markov property*, cf. *e.g.* Theorem V-32 of Protter (2004), the arbitrage-free price $P(t,T)$ can be rewritten as a function $F(t, r_t)$ of r_t, *i.e.*

$$P(t,T) = \mathbb{E}^* \left[e^{- \int_t^T r_s ds} \mid \mathcal{F}_t \right]$$

$$= \mathbb{E}^* \left[e^{- \int_t^T r_s ds} \mid r_t \right]$$

$$= F(t, r_t), \tag{17.19}$$

and depends on (t, r_t) only, instead of depending on the whole information available in $\mathcal{F}_t$ up to time t, meaning that the pricing problem can now be formulated as a search for the function $F(t,x)$.

Proposition 17.2. *(Bond pricing PDE). Consider a short rate $(r_t)_{t \in \mathbb{R}_+}$ modeled by a diffusion equation of the form*

$$dr_t = \mu(t, r_t) dt + \sigma(t, r_t) dB_t.$$

The bond pricing PDE for $P(t,T) = F(t, r_t)$ as in (17.19) is written as

$$x F(t,x) = \frac{\partial F}{\partial t}(t,x) + \mu(t,x) \frac{\partial F}{\partial x}(t,x) + \frac{1}{2} \sigma^2(t,x) \frac{\partial^2 F}{\partial x^2}(t,x), \tag{17.20}$$

$t \geqslant 0$, $x \in \mathbb{R}$, *subject to the terminal condition*

$$F(T,x) = 1, \qquad x \in \mathbb{R}. \tag{17.21}$$

In addition, the bond price dynamics is given by

$$dP(t,T) = r_t P(t,T)dt + \sigma(t,r_t)\frac{\partial F}{\partial x}(t,r_t)dB_t. \tag{17.22}$$

Proof. By Itô's formula, we have

$$
\begin{aligned}
d\left(e^{-\int_0^t r_s ds} P(t,T)\right) &= -r_t e^{-\int_0^t r_s ds} P(t,T)dt + e^{-\int_0^t r_s ds} dP(t,T) \\
&= -r_t e^{-\int_0^t r_s ds} F(t,r_t)dt + e^{-\int_0^t r_s ds} dF(t,r_t) \\
&= -r_t e^{-\int_0^t r_s ds} F(t,r_t)dt + e^{-\int_0^t r_s ds}\frac{\partial F}{\partial x}(t,r_t)dr_t \\
&\quad + \frac{1}{2}e^{-\int_0^t r_s ds}\frac{\partial^2 F}{\partial x^2}(t,r_t)(dr_t)^2 + e^{-\int_0^t r_s ds}\frac{\partial F}{\partial t}(t,r_t)dt \\
&= -r_t e^{-\int_0^t r_s ds} F(t,r_t)dt + e^{-\int_0^t r_s ds}\frac{\partial F}{\partial x}(t,r_t)(\mu(t,r_t)dt + \sigma(t,r_t)dB_t) \\
&\quad + e^{-\int_0^t r_s ds}\left(\frac{1}{2}\sigma^2(t,r_t)\frac{\partial^2 F}{\partial x^2}(t,r_t) + \frac{\partial F}{\partial t}(t,r_t)\right)dt \\
&= e^{-\int_0^t r_s ds}\sigma(t,r_t)\frac{\partial F}{\partial x}(t,r_t)dB_t \\
&\quad + e^{-\int_0^t r_s ds}\left(-r_t F(t,r_t) + \mu(t,r_t)\frac{\partial F}{\partial x}(t,r_t) + \frac{1}{2}\sigma^2(t,r_t)\frac{\partial^2 F}{\partial x^2}(t,r_t) + \frac{\partial F}{\partial t}(t,r_t)\right)dt.
\end{aligned}
\tag{17.23}
$$

Given that $t \mapsto e^{-\int_0^t r_s ds} P(t,T)$ is a martingale, the above expression (17.23) should only contain terms in dB_t (cf. Corollary II-6-1, page 72 of Protter (2004)), and all terms in dt should vanish inside (17.23). This leads to the identities

$$
\begin{cases}
r_t F(t,r_t) = \mu(t,r_t)\dfrac{\partial F}{\partial x}(t,r_t) + \dfrac{1}{2}\sigma^2(t,r_t)\dfrac{\partial^2 F}{\partial x^2}(t,r_t) + \dfrac{\partial F}{\partial t}(t,r_t) \\[3mm]
d\left(e^{-\int_0^t r_s ds} P(t,T)\right) = e^{-\int_0^t r_s ds}\sigma(t,r_t)\dfrac{\partial F}{\partial x}(t,r_t)dB_t,
\end{cases}
\tag{17.24a}
$$

which lead to (17.20) and (17.22). Condition (17.21) is due to the fact that $P(T,T) = \$1$. $\square$

By (17.24a), the proof of Proposition 17.2 also shows that

$$
\begin{aligned}
\frac{dP(t,T)}{P(t,T)} &= \frac{1}{P(t,T)}d\left(e^{\int_0^t r_s ds} e^{-\int_0^t r_s ds} P(t,T)\right) \\
&= \frac{1}{P(t,T)}\left(r_t P(t,T)dt + e^{\int_0^t r_s ds} d\left(e^{-\int_0^t r_s ds} P(t,T)\right)\right) \\
&= r_t dt + \frac{1}{P(t,T)} e^{\int_0^t r_s ds} d\left(e^{-\int_0^t r_s ds} P(t,T)\right) \\
&= r_t dt + \frac{1}{F(t,r_t)}\frac{\partial F}{\partial x}(t,r_t)\sigma(t,r_t)dB_t \\
&= r_t dt + \sigma(t,r_t)\frac{\partial}{\partial x}\log F(t,r_t)dB_t.
\end{aligned}
\tag{17.25}
$$

In the case of an interest rate process modeled by (17.8), we have

$$\mu(t,x) = \eta(t) + \lambda(t)x, \qquad \text{and} \qquad \sigma(t,x) = \sqrt{\delta(t) + \gamma(t)x},$$

hence (17.20) yields the *affine* PDE

$$xF(t,x) = \frac{\partial F}{\partial t}(t,x) + (\eta(t) + \lambda(t)x)\frac{\partial F}{\partial x}(t,x) + \frac{1}{2}(\delta(t) + \gamma(t)x)\frac{\partial^2 F}{\partial x^2}(t,x) \tag{17.26}$$

with time-dependent coefficients, $t \geqslant 0$, $x \in \mathbb{R}$.

Note that more generally, all affine short rate models as defined in Relation (17.8), including the Vasicek model, will yield a bond pricing formula of the form

$$P(t,T) = e^{A(T-t) + r_t C(T-t)}, \tag{17.27}$$

cf. *e.g.* § 3.2.4. in Brigo and Mercurio (2006).

Vašíček (1977) model

In the Vasicek case

$$dr_t = (a - br_t)dt + \sigma dB_t,$$

the bond price takes the form

$$F(t,r_t) = P(t,T) = e^{A(T-t) + r_t C(T-t)},$$

where $A(\cdot)$ and $C(\cdot)$ are deterministic functions of time, see (17.33)–(17.34) below, and (17.25) yields

$$\frac{dP(t,T)}{P(t,T)} = r_t dt + \sigma C(T-t)dB_t \tag{17.28}$$

$$= r_t dt - \frac{\sigma}{b}\left(1 - e^{-(T-t)b}\right)dB_t,$$

since $F(t,x) = e^{A(T-t) + xC(T-t)}$.

Probabilistic solution of the Vasicek PDE

Next, we solve the PDE (17.20), written with $\mu(t,x) = a - bx$ and $\sigma(t,x) = \sigma$ in the Vašíček (1977) model

$$dr_t = (a - br_t)dt + \sigma dB_t \tag{17.29}$$

as

$$\begin{cases} xF(t,x) = \dfrac{\partial F}{\partial t}(t,x) + (a - bx)\dfrac{\partial F}{\partial x}(t,x) + \dfrac{\sigma^2}{2}\dfrac{\partial^2 F}{\partial x^2}(t,x), \\[2mm] F(T,x) = 1. \end{cases} \tag{17.30}$$

For this, Proposition 17.3 relies on a direct computation of the conditional expectation

$$F(t,r_t) = P(t,T) = \mathbb{E}^*\left[e^{-\int_t^T r_s ds} \mid \mathcal{F}_t\right]. \tag{17.31}$$

See also Exercise 17.7 for a closed-form bond pricing formula in the Cox et al. (1985) (CIR) model.

Proposition 17.3. *The zero-coupon bond price in the Vasicek model (17.29) can be expressed as*

$$P(t,T) = e^{A(T-t)+r_t C(T-t)}, \qquad 0 \leqslant t \leqslant T, \tag{17.32}$$

where $A(x)$ and $C(x)$ are functions of time to maturity given by

$$C(x) := -\frac{1}{b}\left(1 - e^{-bx}\right), \tag{17.33}$$

and

$$
\begin{aligned}
A(x) \ &:= \ \frac{4ab - 3\sigma^2}{4b^3} + \frac{\sigma^2 - 2ab}{2b^2}x + \frac{\sigma^2 - ab}{b^3}e^{-bx} - \frac{\sigma^2}{4b^3}e^{-2bx} \\
&= \ -\left(\frac{a}{b} - \frac{\sigma^2}{2b^2}\right)(x + C(x)) - \frac{\sigma^2}{4b}C^2(x), \qquad x \geqslant 0.
\end{aligned}
\tag{17.34}
$$

Proof. Recall that in the Vasicek model (17.29), the short rate process $(r_t)_{t \in \mathbb{R}_+}$ solution of (17.29) has the expression

$$r_t = g(t) + \int_0^t h(t,s)dB_s = r_0 e^{-bt} + \frac{a}{b}\left(1 - e^{-bt}\right) + \sigma \int_0^t e^{-(t-s)b}dB_s,$$

see Exercise 17.1, where g and h are the deterministic functions

$$g(t) := r_0 e^{-bt} + \frac{a}{b}\left(1 - e^{-bt}\right), \qquad t \geqslant 0,$$

and

$$h(t,s) := \sigma e^{-(t-s)b}, \qquad 0 \leqslant s \leqslant t.$$

Using the fact that Wiener integrals are Gaussian random variables and the Gaussian moment generating function, and exchanging the order of integration between ds and du over $[t,T]$ according to the following picture,

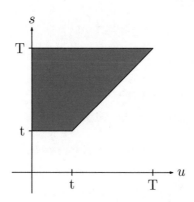

we have

$$
\begin{aligned}
P(t,T) &= \mathbb{E}^*\left[e^{-\int_t^T r_s ds} \,\Big|\, \mathcal{F}_t\right] \\
&= \mathbb{E}^*\left[e^{-\int_t^T (g(s) + \int_0^s h(s,u)dB_u)ds} \,\Big|\, \mathcal{F}_t\right] \\
&= \exp\left(-\int_t^T g(s)ds\right) \mathbb{E}^*\left[e^{-\int_t^T \int_0^s h(s,u)dB_u ds} \,\Big|\, \mathcal{F}_t\right]
\end{aligned}
$$

$$= \exp\left(-\int_t^T g(s)ds\right) \mathbb{E}^*\left[e^{-\int_0^T \int_{\text{Max}(u,t)}^T h(s,u)dsdB_u} \,\Big|\, \mathcal{F}_t\right]$$

$$= \exp\left(-\int_t^T g(s)ds - \int_0^t \int_{\text{Max}(u,t)}^T h(s,u)dsdB_u\right) \mathbb{E}^*\left[e^{-\int_t^T \int_{\text{Max}(u,t)}^T h(s,u)dsdB_u} \,\Big|\, \mathcal{F}_t\right]$$

$$= \exp\left(-\int_t^T g(s)ds - \int_0^t \int_t^T h(s,u)dsdB_u\right) \mathbb{E}^*\left[e^{-\int_t^T \int_u^T h(s,u)dsdB_u} \,\Big|\, \mathcal{F}_t\right]$$

$$= \exp\left(-\int_t^T g(s)ds - \int_0^t \int_t^T h(s,u)dsdB_u\right) \mathbb{E}^*\left[e^{-\int_t^T \int_u^T h(s,u)dsdB_u}\right]$$

$$= \exp\left(-\int_t^T g(s)ds - \int_0^t \int_t^T h(s,u)dsdB_u + \frac{1}{2}\int_t^T \left(\int_u^T h(s,u)ds\right)^2 du\right)$$

$$= \exp\left(-\int_t^T \left(r_0 e^{-bs} + \frac{a}{b}(1 - e^{-bs})\right)ds - \sigma \int_0^t \int_t^T e^{-(s-u)b}dsdB_u\right)$$

$$\times \exp\left(\frac{\sigma^2}{2}\int_t^T \left(\int_u^T e^{-(s-u)b}ds\right)^2 du\right)$$

$$= \exp\left(-\int_t^T \left(r_0 e^{-bs} + \frac{a}{b}(1 - e^{-bs})\right)ds - \frac{\sigma}{b}(1 - e^{-(T-t)b})\int_0^t e^{-(t-u)b}dB_u\right)$$

$$\times \exp\left(\frac{\sigma^2}{2}\int_t^T e^{2bu}\left(\frac{e^{-bu} - e^{-bT}}{b}\right)^2 du\right)$$

$$= \exp\left(-\frac{r_t}{b}(1 - e^{-(T-t)b}) + \frac{1}{b}(1 - e^{-(T-t)b})\left(r_0 e^{-bt} + \frac{a}{b}(1 - e^{-bt})\right)\right)$$

$$\times \exp\left(-\int_t^T \left(r_0 e^{-bs} + \frac{a}{b}(1 - e^{-bs})\right)ds + \frac{\sigma^2}{2}\int_t^T e^{2bu}\left(\frac{e^{-bu} - e^{-bT}}{b}\right)^2 du\right)$$

$$= e^{A(T-t)+r_t C(T-t)}, \tag{17.35}$$

where $A(x)$ and $C(x)$ are the functions given by (17.33) and (17.34). $\qquad\square$

Analytical solution of the Vasicek PDE

In order to solve the PDE (17.30) analytically, we may start by looking for a solution of the form

$$F(t,x) = e^{A(T-t)+xC(T-t)}, \tag{17.36}$$

where $A(\cdot)$ and $C(\cdot)$ are functions to be determined under the conditions $A(0) = 0$ and $C(0) = 0$. Substituting (17.36) into the PDE (17.20) with the Vasicek coefficients $\mu(t,x) = (a - bx)$ and $\sigma(t,x) = \sigma$ shows that

$$\begin{aligned} x e^{A(T-t)+xC(T-t)} &= -(A'(T-t) + xC'(T-t))\, e^{A(T-t)+xC(T-t)} \\ &\quad + (a - bx)C(T-t)\, e^{A(T-t)+xC(T-t)} \\ &\quad + \frac{1}{2}\sigma^2 C^2(T-t)\, e^{A(T-t)+xC(T-t)}, \end{aligned}$$

i.e.

$$x = -A'(T-t) - xC'(T-t) + (a - bx)C(T-t) + \frac{1}{2}\sigma^2 C^2(T-t).$$

By identification of terms for $x = 0$ and $x \neq 0$, this yields the system of Riccati and linear differential equations

$$\begin{cases} A'(s) = aC(s) + \dfrac{\sigma^2}{2}C^2(s) \\[2mm] C'(s) = -1 - bC(s), \end{cases}$$

which can be solved to recover the above value of $P(t,T) = F(t, r_t)$ via

$$C(s) = -\frac{1}{b}\left(1 - e^{-bs}\right)$$

and

$$\begin{aligned} A(t) &= A(0) + \int_0^t A'(s)ds \\[2mm] &= \int_0^t \left(aC(s) + \frac{\sigma^2}{2}C^2(s)\right)ds \\[2mm] &= \int_0^t \left(\frac{a}{b}\left(1 - e^{-bs}\right) + \frac{\sigma^2}{2b^2}\left(1 - e^{-bs}\right)^2\right)ds \\[2mm] &= \frac{a}{b}\int_0^t \left(1 - e^{-bs}\right)ds + \frac{\sigma^2}{2b^2}\int_0^t \left(1 - e^{-bs}\right)^2 ds \\[2mm] &= \frac{4ab - 3\sigma^2}{4b^3} + \frac{\sigma^2 - 2ab}{2b^2}t + \frac{\sigma^2 - ab}{b^3}e^{-bt} - \frac{\sigma^2}{4b^3}e^{-2bt}, \qquad t \geqslant 0. \end{aligned}$$

The next Figure 17.7 shows both a Monte Carlo and an analytical estimation of Vasicek bond prices.

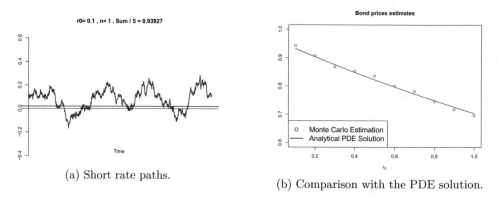

(a) Short rate paths.

(b) Comparison with the PDE solution.

Figure 17.7: Comparison of Monte Carlo and analytical PDE solutions.

Vasicek bond price simulations

In this section we consider again the Vasicek model, in which the short rate $(r_t)_{t \in \mathbb{R}_+}$ is solution to (17.1). Figure 17.8 presents a random simulation of the zero-coupon bond price (17.32) in the Vasicek model with $\sigma = 10\%$, $r_0 = 2.96\%$, $b = 0.5$, and $a = 0.025$. The graph of the corresponding deterministic zero-coupon bond price with $r = r_0 = 2.96\%$ is also shown in Figure 17.8.

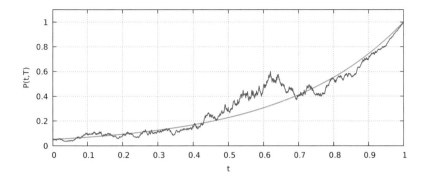

Figure 17.8: Graphs of $t \mapsto F(t, r_t) = P(t, T)$ *vs* $t \mapsto e^{-r_0(T-t)}$.

Figure 17.9 presents a random simulation of the coupon bond price (17.16) in the Vasicek model with $\sigma = 2\%$, $r_0 = 3.5\%$, $b = 0.5$, $a = 0.025$, and coupon rate $c = 5\%$. The graph of the corresponding deterministic coupon bond price (17.17) with $r = r_0 = 3.5\%$ is also shown in Figure 17.9.

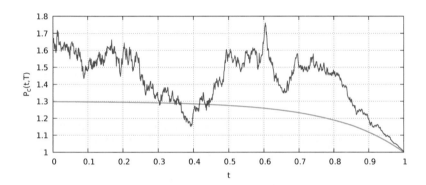

Figure 17.9: Graph of $t \mapsto P_c(t, T)$ for a bond with a 5% coupon rate.

Zero-coupon bond price and yield data

The following zero-coupon public bond price data was downloaded from *EMMA* at the Municipal Securities Rulemaking Board.

ORANGE CNTY CALIF PENSION OBLIG CAP APPREC-TAXABLE-REF-SER A (CA)
CUSIP: 68428LBB9
Dated Date: 06/12/1996 (June 12, 1996)
Maturity Date: 09/01/2016 (September 1, 2016)
Interest Rate: 0.0%
Principal Amount at Issuance: $26,056,000
Initial Offering Price: 19.465

```
1  library(quantmod);getwd()
   bondprice <- read.table("bond_data_R.txt",col.names =
       c("Date","HighPrice","LowPrice","HighYield","LowYield","Count","Amount"))
3  head(bondprice)
   time <- as.POSIXct(bondprice$Date, format = "%Y-%m-%d")
5  price <- xts(x = bondprice$HighPrice, order.by = time)
   yield <- xts(x = bondprice$HighYield, order.by = time)
7  dev.new(width=10,height=7);
   chartSeries(price,up.col="blue",theme="white")
9  chartSeries(yield,up.col="blue",theme="white")
```

	Date	HighPrice	LowPrice	HighYield	LowYield	Count	Amount
1	2016-01-13	99.082	98.982	1.666	1.501	2	20000
2	2015-12-29	99.183	99.183	1.250	1.250	1	10000
3	2015-12-21	97.952	97.952	3.014	3.014	1	10000
4	2015-12-17	99.141	98.550	2.123	1.251	5	610000
5	2015-12-07	98.770	98.770	1.714	1.714	2	10000
6	2015-12-04	98.363	98.118	2.628	2.280	2	10000

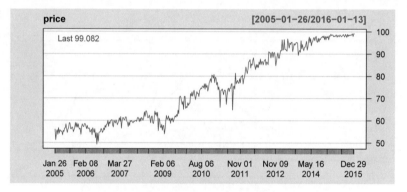

Figure 17.10: Orange Cnty Calif bond prices.

The next Figure 17.11 plots the *bond yield* $y(t,T)$ defined as

$$y(t,T) = -\frac{\log P(t,T)}{T-t}, \quad \text{or} \quad P(t,T) = e^{-(T-t)y(t,T)}, \qquad 0 \leqslant t \leqslant T.$$

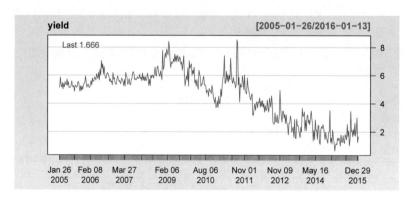

Figure 17.11: Orange Cnty Calif bond yields.

Bond pricing in the Dothan model

In the Dothan (1978) model, the short-term interest rate process $(r_t)_{t \in \mathbb{R}_+}$ is modeled according to a geometric Brownian motion

$$dr_t = \mu r_t dt + \sigma r_t dB_t, \qquad (17.37)$$

where the volatility $\sigma > 0$ and the drift $\mu \in \mathbb{R}$ are constant parameters and $(B_t)_{t \in \mathbb{R}_+}$ is a standard Brownian motion. In this model the short-term interest rate r_t remains always positive, while the proportional volatility term σr_t accounts for the sensitivity of the volatility of interest rate changes to the level of the rate r_t.

On the other hand, the Dothan model is the only lognormal short rate model that allows for an analytical formula for the zero-coupon bond price

$$P(t,T) = \mathbb{E}^* \left[e^{-\int_t^T r_s ds} \,\middle|\, \mathcal{F}_t \right], \qquad 0 \leqslant t \leqslant T.$$

For convenience of notation we let $p = 1 - 2\mu/\sigma^2$ and rewrite (17.37) as

$$dr_t = (1-p)\frac{\sigma^2}{2} r_t dt + \sigma r_t dB_t,$$

with solution

$$r_t = r_0 e^{\sigma B_t - p\sigma^2 t/2}, \qquad t \geqslant 0. \qquad (17.38)$$

By the Markov property of $(r_t)_{t \in \mathbb{R}_+}$, the bond price $P(t,T)$ is a function $F(t, r_t)$ of r_t and time $t \in [0,T]$:

$$P(t,T) = F(t, r_t) = \mathbb{E}^* \left[e^{-\int_t^T r_s ds} \,\middle|\, r_t \right], \qquad 0 \leqslant t \leqslant T. \qquad (17.39)$$

By computation of the conditional expectation (17.39) using (13.10) we easily obtain the following result, cf. Proposition 1.2 of Pintoux and Privault (2011), where the function $\theta(v,t)$ is defined in (13.8).

Proposition 17.4. *The zero-coupon bond price $P(t,T) = F(t, r_t)$ is given for all $p \in \mathbb{R}$ by*

$$F(t,x) \qquad (17.40)$$

$$= e^{-\sigma^2 p^2 (T-t)/8} \int_0^\infty \int_0^\infty e^{-ux} \exp\left(-2\frac{(1+z^2)}{\sigma^2 u}\right) \theta\left(\frac{4z}{\sigma^2 u}, \frac{(T-t)\sigma^2}{4}\right) \frac{du}{u} \frac{dz}{z^{p+1}},$$

$x > 0$.

Proof. By Proposition 13.5, cf. Proposition 2 in Yor (1992), the probability distribution of the time integral $\int_0^{T-t} e^{\sigma B_s - p\sigma^2 s/2} ds$ is given by

$$\mathbb{P}\left(\int_0^{T-t} e^{\sigma B_s - p\sigma^2 s/2} ds \in dy \right)$$

$$= \int_{-\infty}^\infty \mathbb{P}\left(\int_0^t e^{\sigma B_s - p\sigma^2 s/2} ds \in dy, \ B_t - p\sigma t/2 \in dz \right)$$

$$= \frac{\sigma}{2} \int_{-\infty}^\infty e^{-p\sigma z/2 - p^2 \sigma^2 t/8} \exp\left(-2\frac{1 + e^{\sigma z}}{\sigma^2 y}\right) \theta\left(\frac{4 e^{\sigma z/2}}{\sigma^2 y}, \frac{\sigma^2 t}{4}\right) \frac{dy}{y} dz$$

$$= e^{-(T-t)p^2 \sigma^2/8} \int_0^\infty \exp\left(-2\frac{1 + z^2}{\sigma^2 y}\right) \theta\left(\frac{4z}{\sigma^2 y}, \frac{(T-t)\sigma^2}{4}\right) \frac{dz}{z^{p+1}} \frac{dy}{y}, \qquad y > 0,$$

where the exchange of integrals is justified by the Fubini theorem and the nonnegativity of integrands. Hence, by (13.10) and (17.38) we find

$$
\begin{aligned}
F(t, r_t) &= P(t, T) \\
&= \mathbb{E}^* \left[\exp\left(-\int_t^T r_s ds \right) \Big| \mathcal{F}_t \right] \\
&= \mathbb{E}^* \left[\exp\left(-r_t \int_t^T e^{\sigma(B_s - B_t) - \sigma^2 p(s-t)/2} ds \right) \Big| \mathcal{F}_t \right] \\
&= \mathbb{E}^* \left[\exp\left(-x \int_t^T e^{\sigma(B_s - B_t) - \sigma^2 p(s-t)/2} ds \right) \right]_{x = r_t} \\
&= \mathbb{E}^* \left[\exp\left(-x \int_0^{T-t} e^{\sigma B_s - \sigma^2 ps/2} ds \right) \right]_{x = r_t} \\
&= \int_0^\infty e^{-r_t y}\, \mathbb{P}\left(\int_0^{T-t} e^{\sigma B_s - p\sigma^2 s/2} ds \in dy \right) \\
&= e^{-(T-t)p^2 \sigma^2/8} \int_0^\infty e^{-r_t y} \int_0^\infty \exp\left(-2 \frac{1+z^2}{\sigma^2 y} \right) \theta\left(\frac{4z}{\sigma^2 y}, \frac{(T-t)\sigma^2}{4} \right) \frac{dz}{z^{p+1}} \frac{dy}{y}.
\end{aligned}
$$

$\square$

The zero-coupon bond price $P(t, T) = F(t, r_t)$ in the Dothan model can also be written for all $p \in \mathbb{R}$ as

$$
\begin{aligned}
F(t, x) &= \frac{(2x)^{p/2}}{2\pi^2 \sigma^p} \int_0^\infty u\, e^{-(p^2 + u^2)\sigma^2 t/8} \sinh(\pi u) \left| \Gamma\left(-\frac{p}{2} + i\frac{u}{2} \right) \right|^2 K_{iu}\left(\frac{\sqrt{8x}}{\sigma} \right) du \\
&\quad + \frac{(2x)^{p/2}}{\sigma^p} \sum_{k \geqslant 0} \frac{2(p - 2k)^+}{k!(p-k)!} e^{\sigma^2 k(k-p)t/2} K_{p-2k}\left(\frac{\sqrt{8x}}{\sigma} \right), \quad x > 0,\ t > 0,
\end{aligned}
$$

cf. Corollary 2.2 of Pintoux and Privault (2010), see also Privault and Uy (2013) for numerical computations. Zero-coupon bond prices in the Dothan model can also be computed by the conditional expression

$$
\mathbb{E}\left[\exp\left(-\int_0^T r_t dt \right) \right] = \int_0^\infty \mathbb{E}\left[\exp\left(-\int_0^T r_t dt \right) \Big| r_T = z \right] d\mathbb{P}(r_T \leqslant z), \tag{17.41}
$$

where r_T has the lognormal distribution

$$
d\mathbb{P}(r_T \leqslant z) = d\mathbb{P}(r_0 e^{\sigma B_T - p\sigma^2 T/2} \leqslant z) = \frac{1}{z\sqrt{2\pi\sigma^2 T}} e^{-(p\sigma^2 T/2 + \log(z/r_0))^2/(2\sigma^2 T)}.
$$

In Proposition 17.5 we note that the conditional Laplace transform

$$
\mathbb{E}\left[\exp\left(-\int_0^T r_t dt \right) \Big| r_T = z \right]
$$

cf. (17.45) above, can be computed by a closed-form integral expression based on the modified Bessel function of the second kind

$$
K_\zeta(z) := \frac{z^\zeta}{2^{\zeta+1}} \int_0^\infty \exp\left(-u - \frac{z^2}{4u} \right) \frac{du}{u^{\zeta+1}}, \quad \zeta \in \mathbb{R},\ z \in \mathbb{C}, \tag{17.42}
$$

cf. *e.g.* Watson (1995) page 183, provided that the real part $\mathcal{R}(z^2)$ of $z^2 \in \mathbb{C}$ is positive.

Proposition 17.5. *(Privault and Yu (2016), Proposition 4.1). Taking $r_0 = 1$, for all $\lambda, z > 0$ we have*

$$\mathbb{E}\left[\exp\left(-\lambda \int_0^T r_s ds\right) \mid r_T = z\right] = \frac{4\,e^{-\sigma^2 T/8}}{\pi^{3/2}\sigma^2 p(z)}\sqrt{\frac{\lambda}{T}} \tag{17.43}$$

$$\times \int_0^\infty e^{2(\pi^2-\xi^2)/(\sigma^2 T)} \sin\left(\frac{4\pi\xi}{\sigma^2 T}\right) \sinh(\xi)\frac{K_1\big(\sqrt{8\lambda}\sqrt{1 + 2\sqrt{z}\cosh\xi + z}/\sigma\big)}{\sqrt{1 + 2\sqrt{z}\cosh\xi + z}}\,d\xi.$$

Note however that the numerical evaluation of (17.43) can fail for small values of $T > 0$, and for this reason the integral can be estimated by a gamma approximation as in (17.44) below. Under the gamma approximation we can approximate the conditional bond price on the Dothan short rate r_t as

$$\mathbb{E}\left[\exp\left(-\lambda \int_0^T r_t dt\right) \mid r_T = z\right] \simeq (1 + \lambda\theta(z))^{-\nu(z)},$$

where the parameters $\nu(z)$ and $\theta(z)$ are determined by conditional moment fitting to a gamma distribution, as

$$\theta(z) := \frac{\text{Var}[\Lambda_T \mid S_T = z]}{\mathbb{E}[\Lambda_T \mid S_T = z]}, \quad \nu(z) := \frac{(\mathbb{E}[\Lambda_T \mid S_T = z])^2}{\text{Var}[\Lambda_T \mid S_T = z]} = \frac{\mathbb{E}[\Lambda_T \mid S_T = z]}{\theta},$$

cf. Privault and Yu (2016), which yields

$$\mathbb{E}\left[\exp\left(-\lambda \int_0^T r_s ds\right)\right] \simeq \int_0^\infty (1 + \lambda\theta(z))^{-\nu(z)} \, d\mathbb{P}(r_T \leqslant z). \tag{17.44}$$

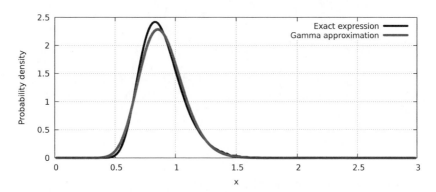

Figure 17.12: Fitting of a gamma probability density function.

The quantity $\theta(z)$ is also known in physics as the *Fano factor* or *dispersion index* that measures the dispersion of the probability distribution of Λ_T given that $S_T = z$. Figures 17.13 shows that the stratified gamma approximation (17.44) matches the Monte Carlo estimate, while the use of the integral expressions (17.41) and (17.43) leads to numerical instabilities.

Related computations for yield options in the Cox et al. (1985) (CIR) model can also be found in Prayoga and Privault (2017).

Path integrals in option pricing

Let $\hbar$ denote the Planck constant, and let $S(x(\cdot))$ denote the action functional given as

$$S(x(\cdot)) = \int_0^t L(x(s), \dot{x}(s), s) ds = \int_0^t \left(\frac{1}{2}m(\dot{x}(s))^2 - V(x(s))\right) ds,$$

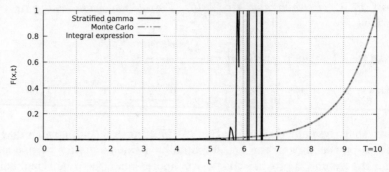

Figure 17.13: Approximation of Dothan bond prices $t \mapsto F(t, x)$ with $\sigma = 0.3$ and $T = 10$.

where $L(x(s), \dot{x}(s), s)$ is the Lagrangian

$$L(x(s), \dot{x}(s), s) := \frac{1}{2} m (\dot{x}(s))^2 - V(x(s)).$$

In physics, the Feynman path integral

$$\psi(y, t) := \int_{x(0)=x, \ x(t)=y} \mathcal{D}x(\cdot) \exp\left(\frac{i}{\hbar} S(x(\cdot))\right)$$

solves the Schrödinger equation

$$i\hbar \frac{\partial \psi}{\partial t}(x, t) = -\frac{\hbar^2}{2m} \frac{\partial^2 \psi}{\partial x^2}(x, t) + V(x(t))\psi(x, t).$$

After the Wick rotation $t \mapsto -it$, the function

$$\phi(y, t) := \int_{x(0)=x, \ x(t)=y} \mathcal{D}x(\cdot) \exp\left(-\frac{1}{\hbar} S(x(\cdot))\right)$$

solves the heat equation

$$\hbar \frac{\partial \phi}{\partial t}(x, t) = -\frac{\hbar^2}{2m} \frac{\partial^2 \phi}{\partial x^2}(x, t) + V(x(t))\phi(x, t).$$

By reformulating the action functional $S(x(\cdot))$ as

$$
\begin{aligned}
S(x(\cdot)) &= \int_0^t \left(\frac{1}{2} m (\dot{x}(s))^2 + V(x(s))\right) ds \\
&\simeq \sum_{i=1}^N \left(\frac{(x(t_i) - x(t_{i-1}))^2}{2(t_i - t_{i-1})^2} + V(x(t_{i-1}))\right) \Delta t_i,
\end{aligned}
$$

we can rewrite the Euclidean path integral as

$$
\begin{aligned}
\phi(y, t) &= \int_{x(0)=x, \ x(t)=y} \mathcal{D}x(\cdot) \exp\left(-\frac{1}{\hbar} S(x(\cdot))\right) \\
&= \int_{x(0)=x, \ x(t)=y} \mathcal{D}x(\cdot) \exp\left(-\frac{1}{2\hbar} \sum_{i=1}^N \frac{(x(t_i) - x(t_{i-1}))^2}{2\Delta t_i} - \frac{1}{\hbar} \sum_{i=1}^N V(x(t_{i-1}))\right) \\
&= \mathbb{E}^*\left[\exp\left(-\frac{1}{\hbar} \int_0^t V(B_s) ds\right) \Big| B_0 = x, B_t = y\right].
\end{aligned}
$$

This type of path integral computation

$$\phi(y,t) = \mathbb{E}^* \left[\exp\left(-\int_0^t V(B_s)ds \right) \,\Big|\, B_0 = x, B_t = y \right]. \tag{17.45}$$

is particularly useful for bond pricing, as (17.45) can be interpreted as the price of a bond with short-term interest rate process $(r_t)_{t\in\mathbb{R}_+} := (V(B_t))_{t\in\mathbb{R}_+}$ conditionally to the value of the endpoint $B_t = y$, cf. (17.43) below. It can also be useful for exotic option pricing, cf. Chapter 13, and for risk management, see *e.g.* Kakushadze (2015). The path integral (17.45) can be estimated either by closed-form expressions using Partial Differential Equations (PDEs) or probability densities, by approximations such as (conditional) Moment matching, or by Monte Carlo estimation, from the paths of a Brownian bridge as shown in Figure 17.14.

Figure 17.14: Brownian bridge.

Exercises

Exercise 17.1   We consider the stochastic differential equation

$$dr_t = (a - br_t)dt + \sigma dB_t, \tag{17.46}$$

where $a, \sigma \in \mathbb{R}$, $b > 0$.

a) Show that the solution of (17.46) is

$$r_t = r_0 e^{-bt} + \frac{a}{b}\left(1 - e^{-bt}\right) + \sigma \int_0^t e^{-(t-s)b}dB_s, \quad t \geqslant 0. \tag{17.47}$$

b) Show that the Gaussian $\mathcal{N}(a/b, \sigma^2/(2b))$ distribution is the *invariant* (or stationary) distribution of $(r_t)_{t\in\mathbb{R}_+}$.

Exercise 17.2   (Brody et al. (2018)) In the mean-reverting Vasicek model (17.47) with $b > 0$, compute:

i) The asymptotic bond yield, or exponential long rate of interest

$$r_\infty := -\lim_{T\to\infty} \frac{\log P(t,T)}{T-t}.$$

ii) The long-bond return

$$L_t := \lim_{T \to \infty} \frac{P(t,T)}{P(0,T)}.$$

Hint: Start from $\log(P(t,T)/P(0,T))$.

Exercise 17.3   Consider the Chan–Karolyi–Longstaff–Sanders (CKLS) interest rate model (Chan et al. (1992)) parametrized as

$$dr_t = (a - br_t)dt + \sigma r_t^\gamma dB_t,$$

and time-discretized as

$$
\begin{aligned}
r_{t_{k+1}} &= r_{t_k} + (a - br_{t_k})\Delta t + \sigma r_{t_k}^\gamma Z_k \\
&= a\Delta t + (1 - b\Delta t)r_{t_k} + \sigma r_{t_k}^\gamma Z_k, \quad k \geqslant 0,
\end{aligned}
$$

where $\Delta t := t_{k+1} - t_k$ and $(Z_k)_{k \geqslant 0}$ is an *i.i.d.* sequence of $\mathcal{N}(0, \Delta t)$ random variables. Assuming that $a, b, \gamma > 0$ are known, find an unbiased estimator $\widehat{\sigma}^2$ for the variance coefficient σ^2, based on a market data set $(\tilde{r}_{t_k})_{k=0,1,\dots,n}$.

Exercise 17.4   Let $(B_t)_{t \in \mathbb{R}_+}$ denote a standard Brownian motion started at 0 under the risk-neutral probability measure $\mathbb{P}^*$. We consider a short-term interest rate process $(r_t)_{t \in \mathbb{R}_+}$ in a Ho–Lee model with constant deterministic volatility, defined by

$$dr_t = adt + \sigma dB_t, \tag{17.48}$$

where $a \in \mathbb{R}$ and $\sigma > 0$. Let $P(t,T)$ denote the arbitrage-free price of a zero-coupon bond in this model:

$$P(t,T) = \mathbb{E}^*\left[\exp\left(-\int_t^T r_s ds\right) \,\Big|\, \mathcal{F}_t\right], \quad 0 \leqslant t \leqslant T. \tag{17.49}$$

a) State the bond pricing PDE satisfied by the function $F(t,x)$ defined *via*

$$F(t,x) := \mathbb{E}^*\left[\exp\left(-\int_t^T r_s ds\right) \,\Big|\, r_t = x\right], \quad 0 \leqslant t \leqslant T.$$

b) Compute the arbitrage-free price $F(t, r_t) = P(t,T)$ from its expression (17.49) as a conditional expectation.

   Hint: One may use the *integration by parts* relation

$$
\begin{aligned}
\int_t^T B_s ds &= TB_T - tB_t - \int_t^T s dB_s \\
&= (T - t)B_t + T(B_T - B_t) - \int_t^T s dB_s \\
&= (T - t)B_t + \int_t^T (T - s)dB_s,
\end{aligned}
$$

   and the Gaussian moment generating function $\mathbb{E}[e^{\lambda X}] = e^{\lambda^2 \eta^2 / 2}$ for $X \simeq \mathcal{N}(0, \eta^2)$.

c) Check that the function $F(t,x)$ computed in Question (b) does satisfy the PDE derived in Question (a).

Exercise 17.5 Consider the Courtadon (1982) model

$$dr_t = \beta(\alpha - r_t)dt + \sigma r_t dB_t, \tag{17.50}$$

where α, β, σ are nonnegative, which is a particular case of the Chan–Karolyi–Longstaff–Sanders (CKLS) model (Chan et al. (1992)) with $\gamma = 1$. Show that the solution of (17.50) is given by

$$r_t = \alpha\beta \int_0^t \frac{S_t}{S_u}du + r_0 S_t, \qquad t \geqslant 0, \tag{17.51}$$

where $(S_t)_{t\in\mathbb{R}_+}$ is the geometric Brownian motion solution of $dS_t = -\beta S_t dt + \sigma S_t dB_t$ with $S_0 = 1$.

Exercise 17.6 Consider the Marsh and Rosenfeld (1983) short-term interest rate model

$$dr_t = \left(\beta r_t^{\gamma-1} + \alpha r_t\right)dt + \sigma r_t^{\gamma/2}dB_t$$

where $\alpha \in \mathbb{R}$ and $\beta, \sigma, \gamma > 0$.

a) Letting $R_t := r_t^{2-\gamma}$, $t \geqslant 0$, find the stochastic differential equation satisfied by $(R_t)_{t\in\mathbb{R}_+}$.

b) Given that the discounted bond price process is a martingale, derive the bond pricing PDE satisfied by the function $F(t, x)$ such that

$$F(t, r_t) = P(t, T) = \mathbb{E}^* \left[e^{-\int_t^T r_s ds} \,\Big|\, \mathcal{F}_t \right] = \mathbb{E}^* \left[e^{-\int_t^T r_s ds} \,\Big|\, r_t \right].$$

Exercise 17.7 Consider the Cox et al. (1985) (CIR) process $(r_t)_{t\in\mathbb{R}_+}$ solution of

$$dr_t = -ar_t dt + \sigma\sqrt{r_t}dB_t,$$

where $a, \sigma > 0$ are constants $(B_t)_{t\in\mathbb{R}_+}$ is a standard Brownian motion started at 0.

a) Write down the bond pricing PDE for the function $F(t, x)$ given by

$$F(t, x) := \mathbb{E}^* \left[\exp\left(-\int_t^T r_s ds \right) \,\Big|\, r_t = x \right], \qquad 0 \leqslant t \leqslant T.$$

Hint: Use Itô calculus and the fact that the discounted bond price is a martingale.

b) Show that the PDE found in Question (a) admits a solution of the form $F(t, x) = e^{A(T-t)+xC(T-t)}$ where the functions $A(s)$ and $C(s)$ satisfy ordinary differential equations to be also written down together with the values of $A(0)$ and $C(0)$.

Exercise 17.8 Convertible bonds. Consider an underlying asset price process $(S_t)_{t\in\mathbb{R}_+}$ given by

$$dS_t = rS_t dt + \sigma S_t dB_t^{(1)},$$

and a short-term interest rate process $(r_t)_{t\in\mathbb{R}_+}$ given by

$$dr_t = \gamma(t, r_t)dt + \eta(t, r_t)dB_t^{(2)},$$

where $\left(B_t^{(1)}\right)_{t\in\mathbb{R}_+}$ and $\left(B_t^{(2)}\right)_{t\in\mathbb{R}_+}$ are two correlated Brownian motions under the risk-neutral probability measure $\mathbb{P}^*$, with $dB_t^{(1)} \cdot dB_t^{(2)} = \rho dt$. A convertible bond is made of a corporate bond priced $P(t,T)$ at time $t \in [0,T]$, that can be exchanged into a quantity $\alpha > 0$ of the underlying company's stock priced S_τ at a future time τ, whichever has a higher value, where α is a *conversion rate*.

a) Find the payoff of the convertible bond at time τ.

b) Rewrite the convertible bond payoff at time τ as the linear combination of $P(\tau,T)$ and a call option payoff on S_τ, whose strike price is to be determined.

c) Write down the convertible bond price at time $t \in [0,\tau]$ as a function $C(t, S_t, r_t)$ of the underlying asset price and interest rate, using a discounted conditional expectation, and show that the discounted corporate bond price

$$e^{-\int_0^t r_s ds} C(t, S_t, r_t), \qquad t \in [0,\tau],$$

is a martingale.

d) Write down $d\left(e^{-\int_0^t r_s ds} C(t, S_t, r_t)\right)$ using the Itô formula and derive the pricing PDE satisfied by the function $C(t,x,y)$ together with its terminal condition.

e) Taking the bond price $P(t,T)$ as a numéraire, price the convertible bond as a European option with strike price $K = 1$ on an underlying asset priced $Z_t := S_t/P(t,T)$, $t \in [0,\tau]$ under the forward measure $\widehat{\mathbb{P}}$ with maturity T.

f) Assuming the bond price dynamics

$$dP(t,T) = r_t P(t,T)dt + \sigma_B(t)P(t,T)dB_t,$$

determine the dynamics of the process $(Z_t)_{t\in\mathbb{R}_+}$ under the forward measure $\widehat{\mathbb{P}}$.

g) Assuming that $(Z_t)_{t\in\mathbb{R}_+}$ can be modeled as a geometric Brownian motion, price the convertible bond using the Black–Scholes formula.

Exercise 17.9 Bond duration. Compute the duration

$$D_c(0,n) := -\frac{1+r}{P_c(0,n)} \frac{\partial}{\partial r} P_c(0,n)$$

of a discrete-time coupon bond priced as

$$\begin{aligned} P_c(0,n) &= \frac{1}{(1+r)^n} + c\sum_{k=1}^{n} \frac{1}{(1+r)^k} \\ &= \frac{c}{r} + \left(1 - \frac{c}{r}\right)\frac{1}{(1+r)^n}, \end{aligned}$$

where $r > 0$, and $c \geqslant 0$ denotes the coupon rate. What happens when n becomes large?

Exercise 17.10   Let $(r_t)_{t \in \mathbb{R}_+}$ denote a short-term interest rate process. For any $T > 0$, let $P(t,T)$ denote the price at time $t \in [0,T]$ of a zero-coupon bond defined by the stochastic differential equation

$$\frac{dP(t,T)}{P(t,T)} = r_t dt + \sigma_t^T dB_t, \qquad 0 \leqslant t \leqslant T, \tag{17.52}$$

under the terminal condition $P(T,T) = 1$, where $(\sigma_t^T)_{t \in [0,T]}$ is an adapted process. We define the forward measure $\widehat{\mathbb{P}}$ by

$$\mathbb{E}^* \left[\frac{d\widehat{\mathbb{P}}}{d\mathbb{P}^*} \,\middle|\, \mathcal{F}_t \right] = \frac{P(t,T)}{P(0,T)} e^{-\int_0^t r_s ds}, \qquad 0 \leqslant t \leqslant T.$$

Recall that

$$B_t^T := B_t - \int_0^t \sigma_s^T ds, \qquad 0 \leqslant t \leqslant T,$$

is a standard Brownian motion under $\widehat{\mathbb{P}}$.

a) Solve the stochastic differential equation (17.52).

b) Derive the stochastic differential equation satisfied by the discounted bond price process

$$t \mapsto e^{-\int_0^t r_s ds} P(t,T), \qquad 0 \leqslant t \leqslant T,$$

and show that it is a martingale.

c) Show that

$$\mathbb{E}^* \left[e^{-\int_0^T r_s ds} \,\middle|\, \mathcal{F}_t \right] = e^{-\int_0^t r_s ds} P(t,T), \qquad 0 \leqslant t \leqslant T.$$

d) Show that

$$P(t,T) = \mathbb{E}^* \left[e^{-\int_t^T r_s ds} \,\middle|\, \mathcal{F}_t \right], \qquad 0 \leqslant t \leqslant T.$$

e) Compute $P(t,S)/P(t,T)$, $0 \leqslant t \leqslant T$, show that it is a martingale under the forward measure $\widehat{\mathbb{P}}$ with maturity T, and that

$$P(T,S) = \frac{P(t,S)}{P(t,T)} \exp \left(\int_t^T (\sigma_s^S - \sigma_s^T) dB_s^T - \frac{1}{2} \int_t^T (\sigma_s^S - \sigma_s^T)^2 ds \right).$$

f) Assuming that $(\sigma_t^T)_{t \in [0,T]}$ and $(\sigma_t^S)_{t \in [0,S]}$ are deterministic functions of time, compute the price

$$\mathbb{E}^* \left[e^{-\int_t^T r_s ds} (P(T,S) - \kappa)^+ \,\middle|\, \mathcal{F}_t \right] = P(t,T) \widehat{\mathbb{E}} \left[(P(T,S) - \kappa)^+ \,\middle|\, \mathcal{F}_t \right]$$

of a bond option with strike price κ.

Recall that if X is a Gaussian random variable with mean $m(t)$ and variance $v^2(t)$ given $\mathcal{F}_t$, we have

$$\mathbb{E} \left[(e^X - K)^+ \,\middle|\, \mathcal{F}_t \right]$$
$$= e^{m(t) + v^2(t)/2} \Phi \left(\frac{v(t)}{2} + \frac{1}{v(t)} (m(t) + v^2(t)/2 - \log K) \right)$$
$$- K \Phi \left(-\frac{v(t)}{2} + \frac{1}{v(t)} (m(t) + v^2(t)/2 - \log K) \right)$$

where $\Phi(x)$, $x \in \mathbb{R}$, denotes the Gaussian cumulative distribution function.

Exercise 17.11   (Exercise 4.18 continued). Write down the bond pricing PDE for the function

$$F(t,x) = \mathbb{E}^* \left[e^{-\int_t^T r_s ds} \,\middle|\, r_t = x \right]$$

and show that in case $\alpha = 0$ the corresponding bond price $P(t,T)$ equals

$$P(t,T) = e^{-r_t B(T-t)}, \qquad 0 \leqslant t \leqslant T,$$

where

$$B(x) := \frac{2(e^{\gamma x} - 1)}{2\gamma + (\beta + \gamma)(e^{\gamma x} - 1)}, \qquad x \in \mathbb{R},$$

with $\gamma = \sqrt{\beta^2 + 2\sigma^2}$.

Exercise 17.12   Consider a zero-coupon bond with prices $P(1,2) = 91.74\%$ and $P(0,2) = 83.40\%$ at times $t = 0$ and $t = 1$.

a) Compute the corresponding yields $y_{0,1}$, $y_{0,2}$ and $y_{1,2}$ at times $t = 0$ and $t = 1$.

b) Assume that $\$0.1$ coupons are paid at times $t = 1$ and $t = 2$. Price the corresponding coupon bond at times $t = 0$ and $t = 1$ using the yields y_0 and y_1.

Exercise 17.13   Consider the Vasicek process $(r_t)_{t \in \mathbb{R}_+}$ solution of the equation

$$dr_t = (a - br_t)dt + \sigma dB_t. \tag{17.53}$$

a) Consider the discretization

$$r_{t_{k+1}} := r_{t_k} + (a - br_{t_k})\Delta t \pm \sigma\sqrt{\Delta t}, \qquad k = 0, 1, 2, \dots$$

of the equation (17.53) with $p(r_{t_0}) = p(r_{t_1}) = 1/2$ and

$$\mathbb{E}[\Delta r_{t_1}] = (a - br_{t_0})\Delta t + \sigma p(r_{t_0})\sqrt{\Delta t} - \sigma q(r_{t_0})\sqrt{\Delta t} = (a - br_{t_0})\Delta t$$

and

$$\mathbb{E}[\Delta r_{t_2}] = (a - br_{t_1})\Delta t + \sigma p(r_{t_0})\sqrt{\Delta t} - \sigma q(r_{t_0})\sqrt{\Delta t} = (a - br_{t_1})\Delta t.$$

Does this discretization lead to a (recombining) binomial tree?

b) Using the Girsanov Theorem, find a probability measure $\mathbb{Q}$ under which the process $(r_t/\sigma)_{t \in [0,T]}$ with

$$\frac{dr_t}{\sigma} = \frac{a - br_t}{\sigma}dt + dB_t$$

is a standard Brownian motion.

Hint: By the Girsanov Theorem, the process $X_t = X_0 + \int_0^t u_s ds + B_t$ is a martingale under the probability measure $\mathbb{Q}$ with Radon–Nikodym density

$$\frac{d\mathbb{Q}}{d\mathbb{P}} = \exp\left(-\int_0^T u_t dB_t - \frac{1}{2}\int_0^T (u_t)^2 dt \right)$$

with respect to $\mathbb{P}$.

c) Prove the Radon–Nikodym derivative approximation

$$2^{T/\Delta t} \prod_{0<t<T} \left(\frac{1}{2} \pm \frac{a - br_t}{2\sigma} \sqrt{\Delta t} \right)$$

$$\simeq \exp\left(\frac{1}{\sigma^2} \int_0^T (a - br_t) dr_t - \frac{1}{2\sigma^2} \int_0^T (a - br_t)^2 dt \right). \qquad (17.54)$$

d) Using (17.54), show that the Vasicek process can be discretized along the *binomial* tree

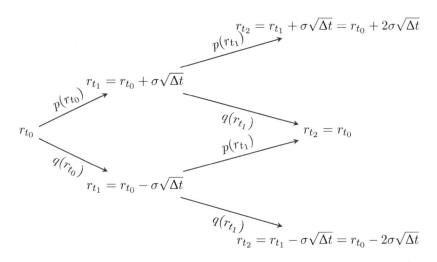

with

$$\mathbb{E}[\Delta r_{t_1} \mid r_{t_0}] = (a - br_{t_0})\Delta t \quad \text{and} \quad \mathbb{E}[\Delta r_{t_2} \mid r_{t_1}] = (a - br_{t_1})\Delta t,$$

where $\Delta r_{t_1} := r_{t_1} - r_{t_0}$, $\Delta r_{t_2} := r_{t_2} - r_{t_1}$, and the probabilities $p(r_{t_0})$, $q(r_{t_0})$, $p(r_{t_1})$, $q(r_{t_1})$ will be computed explicitly.

The use of binomial (or recombining) trees can make the implementation of the Monte Carlo method easier as their size grows linearly instead of exponentially.

Exercise 17.14   Black–Derman–Toy model (Black et al. (1990)).   Consider a one-step interest rate model, in which the short-term interest rate r_0 on $[0,1]$ can turn into two possible values $r_1^u = r_0 e^{\mu \Delta t + \sigma\sqrt{\Delta t}}$ and $r_1^d = r_0 e^{\mu \Delta t - \sigma\sqrt{\Delta t}}$ on the time interval $[1,2]$ with equal probabilities $1/2$ at time $\Delta t = 1$ year and volatility $\sigma = 22\%$ per year, and a zero-coupon bonds with prices $P(0,1)$ and $P(0,2)$ at time $t = 0$.

a) Write down the value of $P(1,2)$ using r_1^u and r_1^d.

b) Write down the value of $P(0,2)$ using r_1^u, r_1^d and r_0.

c) Estimate the value of r_0 from the market price $P(0,1) = 91.74$.

d) Estimate the values of r_1^u and r_1^d from the market price $P(0,2) = 83.40$.

Exercise 17.15 Consider a yield curve $(f(t,t,T))_{0 \leqslant t \leqslant T}$ and a bond paying coupons $c_1, c_2, \ldots, c_n$ at times $T_1, T_2, \ldots, T_n$ until maturity T_n, and priced as

$$P(t, T_n) = \sum_{k=1}^{n} c_k \, e^{-(T_k - t)f(t,t,T_k)}, \qquad 0 \leqslant t \leqslant T_1,$$

where c_n is inclusive of the last coupon payment and the nominal \$1 value of the bond. Let $\widetilde{f}(t, t, T_n)$ denote the *compounded yield to maturity* defined by equating

$$P(t, T_n) = \sum_{k=1}^{n} c_k \, e^{-(T_k - t)\widetilde{f}(t,t,T_n)}, \qquad 0 \leqslant t \leqslant T_1, \tag{17.55}$$

i.e. $\widetilde{f}(t, t, T_n)$ solves the equation

$$F\big(t, \widetilde{f}(t, t, T_n)\big) = P(t, T_n), \qquad 0 \leqslant t \leqslant T_1,$$

with

$$F(t, x) := \sum_{k=1}^{n} c_k \, e^{-(T_k - t)x}, \qquad 0 \leqslant t \leqslant T_1.$$

The *bond duration* $D(t, T_n)$ is the relative sensitivity of $P(t, T_n)$ with respect to $\widetilde{f}(t, t, T_n)$, defined as

$$D(t, T_n) := -\frac{1}{P(t, T_n)} \frac{\partial F}{\partial x}\big(t, \widetilde{f}(t, t, T_n)\big), \qquad 0 \leqslant t \leqslant T_1.$$

The *bond convexity* $C(t, T_n)$ is defined as

$$C(t, T_n) := \frac{1}{P(t, T_n)} \frac{\partial^2 F}{\partial x^2}\big(t, \widetilde{f}(t, t, T_n)\big), \qquad 0 \leqslant t \leqslant T_1.$$

a) Compute the bond duration in case $n = 1$.

b) Show that the *bond duration* $D(t, T_n)$ can be interpreted as an average of times to maturity weighted by the respective discounted bond payoffs.

c) Show that the *bond convexity* $C(t, T_n)$ satisfies

$$C(t, T_n) = (D(t, T_n))^2 + (S(t, T_n))^2,$$

where

$$(S(t, T_n))^2 := \sum_{k=1}^{n} w_k (T_k - t - D(t, T_n))^2$$

measures the dispersion of the duration of the bond payoffs around the portfolio duration $D(t, T_n)$.

d) Consider now the zero-coupon yield defined as

$$P(t, t + \alpha(T_n - t)) = \exp\big(-\alpha(T_n - t)f_\alpha(t, t, T_n)\big),$$

where $\alpha \in (0, 1)$, *i.e.*

$$f_\alpha(t, t, T_n) := -\frac{1}{\alpha(T_n - t)} \log P(t, t + \alpha(T_n - t)), \qquad 0 \leqslant t \leqslant T_n.$$

Compute the bond duration associated to the yield $f_\alpha(t, t, T_n)$ in affine bond pricing models of the form

$$P(t, T) = e^{A(T-t) + r_t B(T-t)}, \qquad 0 \leqslant t \leqslant T.$$

e) (Wu (2000)) Compute the bond duration associated to the yield $f_\alpha(t, t, T_n)$ in the Vasicek model, in which

$$B(T - t) := \frac{1 - e^{-(T-t)b}}{b}, \qquad 0 \leqslant t \leqslant T.$$

Chapter 18

Forward Rates

Forward rates are interest rates used in Forward Rate Agreements (FRA) for financial transactions, such as loans, that can take place at a future date. This chapter deals with the modeling of forward rates and swap rates in the Heath–Jarrow–Morton (HJM) and Brace-Gatarek-Musiela (BGM) models. It also includes a presentation of the Nelson and Siegel (1987) and Svensson (1994) curve parametrizations for yield curve fitting, and an introduction to two-factor interest rate models.

18.1 Construction of Forward Rates

A forward interest rate contract (or Forward Rate Agreement, FRA) gives to its holder the possibility to lock an interest rate denoted by $f(t, T, S)$ at present time t for a loan to be delivered over a future period of time $[T, S]$, with $t \leqslant T \leqslant S$.

The rate $f(t, T, S)$ is called a forward interest rate. When $T = t$, the *spot* forward rate $f(t, t, T)$ coincides with the *yield*, see Relation (18.3) below.

Figure 18.1 presents a typical yield curve on the LIBOR (London Interbank Offered Rate) market with $t =$07 May 2003.

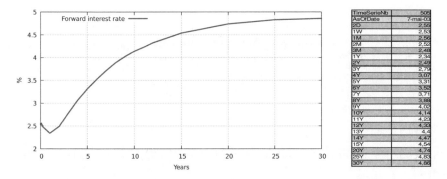

TimeSerieNb	505
AsOfDate	7-mai-03
2D	2,55
1W	2,53
1M	2,56
2M	2,52
3M	2,48
1Y	2,34
2Y	2,49
3Y	2,79
4Y	3,07
5Y	3,31
6Y	3,52
7Y	3,71
8Y	3,88
9Y	4,02
10Y	4,14
11Y	4,23
12Y	4,33
13Y	4,4
14Y	4,47
15Y	4,54
20Y	4,74
25Y	4,83
30Y	4,86

Figure 18.1: Graph of the spot forward rate $S \mapsto f(t, t, S)$.

Maturity transformation, i.e. the ability to transform short-term borrowing (debt with short maturities, such as deposits) into long term lending (credits with very long maturities, such as loans), is among the roles of banks. Profitability is then dependent on the difference between long rates and short rates.

DOI: 10.1201/9781003298670-18

Another example of market data is given in the next Figure 18.2, in which the red and blue curves refer respectively to July 21 and 22, 2011.

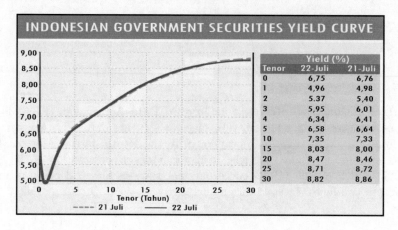

Figure 18.2: Market example of yield curves, cf. (18.3).

Long maturities usually correspond to higher rates as they carry an increased risk. The dip observed with short maturities can correspond to a lower motivation to lend/invest in the short-term.

Forward rates from bond prices

Let us determine the arbitrage or "fair" value of the forward interest rate $f(t,T,S)$ by implementing the Forward Rate Agreement using the instruments available in the market, which are bonds priced at $P(t,T)$ for various maturity dates $T > t$.

The loan can be realized using the available instruments (here, bonds) on the market, by proceeding in two steps:

1) At time t, borrow the amount $P(t,S)$ by issuing (or short selling) one bond with maturity S, which means refunding \$1 at time S.

2) Since the money is only needed at time T, the rational investor will invest the amount $P(t,S)$ over the period $[t,T]$ by buying a (possibly fractional) quantity $P(t,S)/P(t,T)$ of a bond with maturity T priced $P(t,T)$ at time t. This will yield the amount

$$\$1 \times \frac{P(t,S)}{P(t,T)}$$

at time $T > 0$.

As a consequence, the investor will actually receive $P(t,S)/P(t,T)$ at time T, to refund \$1 at time S.

The corresponding forward rate $f(t,T,S)$ is then given by the relation

$$\frac{P(t,S)}{P(t,T)} \exp\left((S-T)f(t,T,S)\right) = \$1, \qquad 0 \leqslant t \leqslant T \leqslant S, \tag{18.1}$$

where we used exponential compounding, which leads to the following definition (18.2).

Definition 18.1. *The forward rate $f(t, T, S)$ at time t for a loan on $[T, S]$ is given by*

$$f(t, T, S) = \frac{\log P(t, T) - \log P(t, S)}{S - T}. \tag{18.2}$$

The *spot* forward rate $f(t, t, S)$ coincides with the *yield* $y(t, S)$, with

$$f(t, t, S) = y(t, S) = -\frac{\log P(t, S)}{T - t}, \quad \text{or} \quad P(t, S) = e^{-(S-t)f(t,t,S)}, \tag{18.3}$$

$0 \leqslant t \leqslant S$.

Proposition 18.2. *The instantaneous forward rate $f(t, T) = f(t, T, T)$ is defined by taking the limit of $f(t, T, S)$ as $S \searrow T$, and satisfies*

$$f(t, T) := \lim_{S \searrow T} f(t, T, S) = -\frac{1}{P(t, T)} \frac{\partial P}{\partial T}(t, T). \tag{18.4}$$

Proof. We have

$$
\begin{aligned}
f(t, T) : &= \lim_{S \searrow T} f(t, T, S) \\
&= -\lim_{S \searrow T} \frac{\log P(t, S) - \log P(t, T)}{S - T} \\
&= -\lim_{\varepsilon \searrow 0} \frac{\log P(t, T + \varepsilon) - \log P(t, T)}{\varepsilon} \\
&= -\frac{\partial}{\partial T} \log P(t, T) \\
&= -\frac{1}{P(t, T)} \frac{\partial P}{\partial T}(t, T).
\end{aligned}
$$

$\square$

The above equation (18.4) can be viewed as a differential equation to be solved for $\log P(t, T)$ under the initial condition $P(T, T) = 1$, which yields the following proposition.

Proposition 18.3. *The bond price $P(t, T)$ can be recovered from the instantaneous forward rate $f(t, s)$ as*

$$P(t, T) = \exp\left(-\int_t^T f(t, s) ds\right), \quad 0 \leqslant t \leqslant T. \tag{18.5}$$

Proof. We check that

$$
\begin{aligned}
\log P(t, T) &= \log P(t, T) - \log P(t, t) \\
&= \int_t^T \frac{\partial}{\partial s} \log P(t, s) ds \\
&= -\int_t^T f(t, s) ds.
\end{aligned}
$$

$\square$

Proposition 18.3 also shows that

$$
\begin{aligned}
f(t,t,t) &= f(t,t) \\
&= \frac{\partial}{\partial T} \int_t^T f(t,s)ds_{|T=t} \\
&= -\frac{\partial}{\partial T} \log P(t,T)_{|T=t} \\
&= -\frac{1}{P(t,T)_{|T=t}} \frac{\partial P}{\partial T}(t,T)_{|T=t} \\
&= -\frac{1}{P(T,T)} \frac{\partial}{\partial T} \mathbb{E}^* \left[e^{-\int_t^T r_s ds} \;\middle|\; \mathcal{F}_t \right]_{|T=t} \\
&= \mathbb{E}^* \left[r_T e^{-\int_t^T r_s ds} \;\middle|\; \mathcal{F}_t \right]_{|T=t} \\
&= \mathbb{E}^*[r_t \mid \mathcal{F}_t] \\
&= r_t, \quad\quad (18.6)
\end{aligned}
$$

i.e. the short rate r_t can be recovered from the instantaneous forward rate as

$$
r_t = f(t,t) = \lim_{T \searrow t} f(t,T).
$$

As a consequence of (18.1) and (18.5) the forward rate $f(t,T,S)$ can be recovered from (18.2) and the instantaneous forward rate $f(t,s)$, as:

$$
\begin{aligned}
f(t,T,S) &= \frac{\log P(t,T) - \log P(t,S)}{S-T} \\
&= -\frac{1}{S-T} \left(\int_t^T f(t,s)ds - \int_t^S f(t,s)ds \right) \\
&= \frac{1}{S-T} \int_T^S f(t,s)ds, \quad 0 \leqslant t \leqslant T < S. \quad\quad (18.7)
\end{aligned}
$$

Similarly, as a consequence of (18.3) and (18.5) we have the next proposition.

Proposition 18.4. *The* spot *forward rate or* yield *$f(t,t,T)$ can be written in terms of bond prices as*

$$
f(t,t,T) = -\frac{\log P(t,T)}{T-t} = \frac{1}{T-t} \int_t^T f(t,s)ds, \quad 0 \leqslant t < T. \quad\quad (18.8)
$$

Differentiation with respect to T of the above relation shows that the yield $f(t,t,T)$ and the instantaneous forward rate $f(t,s)$ are linked by the relation

$$
\frac{\partial f}{\partial T}(t,t,T) = -\frac{1}{(T-t)^2} \int_t^T f(t,s)ds + \frac{1}{T-t} f(t,T), \quad 0 \leqslant t < T,
$$

from which it follows that

$$
\begin{aligned}
f(t,T) &= \frac{1}{T-t} \int_t^T f(t,s)ds + (T-t) \frac{\partial f}{\partial T}(t,t,T) \\
&= f(t,t,T) + (T-t) \frac{\partial f}{\partial T}(t,t,T), \quad 0 \leqslant t < T.
\end{aligned}
$$

Forward Vašíček (1977) rates

In this section we consider the Vasicek model, in which the short rate process is the solution (17.2) of (17.1) as illustrated in Figure 17.1.

In the Vasicek model, the forward rate is given by

$$
\begin{aligned}
f(t,T,S) &= -\frac{\log P(t,S) - \log P(t,T)}{S-T} \\
&= -\frac{r_t(C(S-t) - C(T-t)) + A(S-t) - A(T-t))}{S-T} \\
&= -\frac{\sigma^2 - 2ab}{2b^2} \\
&\quad -\frac{1}{S-T}\left(\left(\frac{r_t}{b} + \frac{\sigma^2 - ab}{b^3}\right)\left(e^{-(S-t)b} - e^{-(T-t)b}\right) - \frac{\sigma^2}{4b^3}\left(e^{-2(S-t)b} - e^{-2(T-t)b}\right)\right),
\end{aligned}
$$

and the spot forward rate, or yield, satisfies

$$
\begin{aligned}
f(t,t,T) &= -\frac{\log P(t,T)}{T-t} = -\frac{r_t C(T-t) + A(T-t)}{T-t} \\
&= -\frac{\sigma^2 - 2ab}{2b^2} + \frac{1}{T-t}\left(\left(\frac{r_t}{b} + \frac{\sigma^2 - ab}{b^3}\right)\left(1 - e^{-(T-t)b}\right) - \frac{\sigma^2}{4b^3}\left(1 - e^{-2(T-t)b}\right)\right),
\end{aligned}
$$

with the mean

$$
\begin{aligned}
&\mathbb{E}[f(t,t,T)] \\
&= -\frac{\sigma^2 - 2ab}{2b^2} + \frac{1}{T-t}\left(\left(\frac{\mathbb{E}[r_t]}{b} + \frac{\sigma^2 - ab}{b^3}\right)\left(1 - e^{-(T-t)b}\right) - \frac{\sigma^2}{4b^3}\left(1 - e^{-2(T-t)b}\right)\right) \\
&= -\frac{\sigma^2 - 2ab}{2b^2} + \frac{1}{T-t}\left(\frac{r_0}{b}e^{-bt} + \frac{a}{b^2}\left(1 - e^{-bt}\right) + \frac{\sigma^2 - ab}{b^3}\right)\left(1 - e^{-(T-t)b}\right) \\
&\quad -\frac{\sigma^2}{4b^3(T-t)}\left(1 - e^{-2(T-t)b}\right).
\end{aligned}
$$

In this model, the forward rate $t \mapsto f(t,t,T)$ can be represented as in the following Figure 18.3, with $a = 0.06$, $b = 0.1$, $\sigma = 0.1$, $r_0 = \%1$ and $T = 50$.

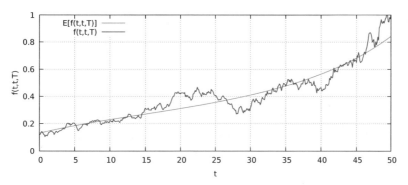

Figure 18.3: Forward rate process $t \mapsto f(t,t,T)$.

We note that the Vasicek forward rate curve $t \mapsto f(t, t, T)$ appears flat for small values of t, *i.e.* longer rates are more stable, while shorter rates show higher volatility or risk. Similar features can be observed in Figure 18.4 for the instantaneous short rate given by

$$
\begin{aligned}
f(t, T) : \ &= \ -\frac{\partial}{\partial T} \log P(t, T) \qquad\qquad\qquad (18.9) \\
&= \ r_t \mathrm{e}^{-(T-t)b} + \frac{a}{b}\left(1 - \mathrm{e}^{-(T-t)b}\right) - \frac{\sigma^2}{2b^2}\left(1 - \mathrm{e}^{-(T-t)b}\right)^2,
\end{aligned}
$$

from which the relation $\lim_{T \searrow t} f(t, T) = r_t$ can be easily recovered. We can also evaluate the mean

$$
\begin{aligned}
\mathbb{E}[f(t, T)] \ &= \ \mathbb{E}[r_t]\mathrm{e}^{-(T-t)b} + \frac{a}{b}\left(1 - \mathrm{e}^{-(T-t)b}\right) - \frac{\sigma^2}{2b^2}\left(1 - \mathrm{e}^{-(T-t)b}\right)^2 \\
&= \ r_0 \mathrm{e}^{-bT} + \frac{a}{b}\left(1 - \mathrm{e}^{-bT}\right) - \frac{\sigma^2}{2b^2}\left(1 - \mathrm{e}^{-(T-t)b}\right)^2.
\end{aligned}
$$

The instantaneous forward rate $t \mapsto f(t, T)$ can be represented as in the following Figure 18.4, with $a = 0.06$, $b = 0.1$, $\sigma = 0.1$ and $r_0 = \%1$.

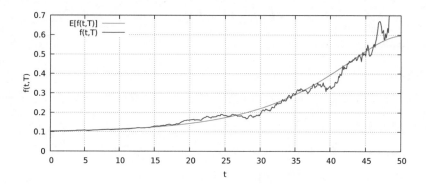

Figure 18.4: Instantaneous forward rate process $t \mapsto f(t, T)$.

Yield curve data

We refer to Chapter III-12 of Charpentier (2014) on the R package "YieldCurve" Guirreri (2015) for the following R code and further details on yield curve and interest rate modeling using R.

```
install.packages("YieldCurve");require(YieldCurve);data(FedYieldCurve)
first(FedYieldCurve,'3 month');last(FedYieldCurve,'3 month')
mat.Fed=c(0.25,0.5,1,2,3,5,7,10);n=50
plot(mat.Fed, FedYieldCurve[n,], type="o",xlab="Maturities structure in years", ylab="Interest rates values",
    col = "blue", lwd=3)
title(main=paste("Federal Reserve yield curve observed at",time(FedYieldCurve[n]), sep=" ")));grid()
```

European Central Bank (ECB) data can be similarly obtained by the next R code.

```
1  data(ECBYieldCurve);first(ECBYieldCurve,'3 month');last(ECBYieldCurve,'3 month')
   mat.ECB<-c(3/12,0.5,1,2,3,4,5,6,7,8,9,10,11,12,13,14,15,16,17,18,19,20,21,22,23, 24,25,26,27,28, 29,30)
3  dev.new(width=16,height=7)
   for (n in 200:400) {
5  plot(mat.ECB, ECBYieldCurve[n,], type="o",xlab="Maturity structure in years", ylab="Interest rates
         values",ylim=c(3.1,5.1),col="blue",lwd=2,cex.axis=1.5,cex.lab=1.5)
   title(main=paste("European Central Bank yield curve observed at",time(ECBYieldCurve[n], sep=" ")))
7  grid();Sys.sleep(0.5)}
```

The next Figure 18.5 represents the output of the above script.

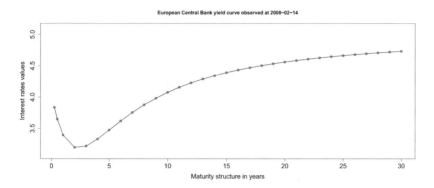

Figure 18.5: European Central Bank yield curves.

Yield curve inversion

Increasing yield curves are typical of economic expansion phases. Decreasing yield curves can occur when central banks attempt to limit inflation by tightening interest rates, such as in the case of an economic recession. In this case, uncertainty triggers increased investment in long bonds whose rates tend to drop as a consequence, while reluctance to lend in the short term can lead to higher short rates.

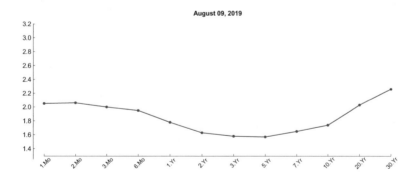

Figure 18.6: August 2019 Federal Reserve yield curve inversion.

The above Figure 18.6 illustrates a Federal Reserve (FED) yield curve inversions occurring in February and August 2019.

LIBOR (London Interbank Offered) Rates

Recall that the forward rate $f(t, T, S)$, $0 \leqslant t \leqslant T \leqslant S$, is defined using exponential compounding, from the relation

$$f(t, T, S) = -\frac{\log P(t, S) - \log P(t, T)}{S - T}. \tag{18.10}$$

In order to compute swaption prices one prefers to use forward rates as defined on the London InterBank Offered Rates (LIBOR) market instead of the standard forward rates given by (18.10). Other types of LIBOR rates include EURIBOR (European Interbank Offered Rates), HIBOR (Hong Kong Interbank Offered Rates), SHIBOR (Shanghai Interbank Offered Rates), SIBOR (Singapore Interbank Offered Rates), TIBOR (Tokyo Interbank Offered Rates), etc. Most LIBOR rates have been replaced by alternatives such as the Secured Overnight Financing Rate (SOFR) starting with the end of year 2021, see below, page 521.

The forward LIBOR rate $L(t, T, S)$ for a loan on $[T, S]$ is defined using linear compounding, *i.e.* by replacing (18.10) with the relation

$$1 + (S - T)L(t, T, S) = \frac{P(t, T)}{P(t, S)}, \qquad t \geqslant T,$$

which yields the following definition.

Definition 18.5. *The forward LIBOR rate $L(t, T, S)$ at time t for a loan on $[T, S]$ is given by*

$$L(t, T, S) = \frac{1}{S - T}\left(\frac{P(t, T)}{P(t, S)} - 1\right), \qquad 0 \leqslant t \leqslant T < S. \tag{18.11}$$

Note that (18.11) above yields the same formula for the (LIBOR) instantaneous forward rate

$$
\begin{aligned}
L(t, T) : &= \lim_{S \searrow T} L(t, T, S) \\
&= \lim_{S \searrow T} \frac{P(t, T) - P(t, S)}{(S - T)P(t, S)} \\
&= \lim_{\varepsilon \searrow 0} \frac{P(t, T) - P(t, T + \varepsilon)}{\varepsilon P(t, T + \varepsilon)} \\
&= \frac{1}{P(t, T)} \lim_{\varepsilon \searrow 0} \frac{P(t, T) - P(t, T + \varepsilon)}{\varepsilon} \\
&= -\frac{1}{P(t, T)} \frac{\partial P}{\partial T}(t, T) \\
&= -\frac{\partial}{\partial T} \log P(t, T) \\
&= f(t, T),
\end{aligned}
$$

as in (18.4). In addition, Relation (18.11) shows that the LIBOR rate can be viewed as a forward price $\widehat{X}_t = X_t / N_t$ with numéraire $N_t = (S - T)P(t, S)$ and $X_t = P(t, T) - P(t, S)$, according to Relation (16.4) of Chapter 16. As a consequence, from Proposition 16.4, the LIBOR rate $(L(t,T,S))_{t \in [T,S]}$ is a martingale under the forward measure $\widehat{\mathbb{P}}$ defined by

$$\frac{d\widehat{\mathbb{P}}}{d\mathbb{P}^*} = \frac{1}{P(0,S)} e^{-\int_0^S r_t dt}.$$

SOFR (Secured Overnight Financing) Rates

The repurchase agreement ("repo") market is a market where government treasury securities can be borrowed on the short term. The SOFR rate is a measure of the cost of borrowing which is estimated using overnight activity on the repo market. In that sense, the SOFR, which is transaction-based, differs from LIBOR which is relied on a survey of a panel of banks and subject to manipulation. On the other hand, an important difference is that LIBOR rates are *forward-looking* using a term structure, whereas SOFR rates are *backward-looking*.

The next definition uses the integral convention $\int_a^b = -\int_b^a$, $a < b$.

Definition 18.6. *The* backward-looking *bond price is defined for $t \geqslant T$ as*

$$P(t,T) = \mathbb{E}\left[e^{-\int_t^T r_u du} \,\Big|\, \mathcal{F}_t\right] = \mathbb{E}\left[e^{\int_T^t r_u du} \,\Big|\, \mathcal{F}_t\right] = e^{\int_T^t r_u du}, \quad t \geqslant T.$$

The forward SOFR rate $R(t,T,S)$ for a loan on $[T,S]$ is defined using linear compounding with the relation

$$1 + (S-T)R(t,T,S) = \frac{P(t,T)}{P(t,S)}, \qquad 0 \leqslant T \leqslant t,$$

which yields the following definition.

Definition 18.7. *The forward SOFR rate $R(t,T,S)$ at time t for a loan on $[T,S]$ is given by*

$$R(t,T,S) = \frac{1}{S-T}\left(\frac{P(t,T)}{P(t,S)} - 1\right), \qquad 0 \leqslant T \leqslant t \leqslant S. \qquad (18.12)$$

In particular, the spot Effective Federal Funds Rate (EFFR) is given for $t = S$ as

$$R(S,T,S) = \frac{1}{S-T}\left(e^{\int_T^S r_u du} - 1\right).$$

The following proposition, see Rutkowski and Bickersteth (2021), uses the forward S-measure $\mathbb{P}_S$ defined by its Randon-Nikodym

$$\frac{d\mathbb{P}_S}{d\mathbb{P}^*} := e^{-\int_0^S r_s ds} P(0,S),$$

with the numéraire process $N_t := P(t,S)$, $t \in [0,S]$, see Definition 16.1.

Proposition 18.8. *The (simply compounded) SOFR forward rate $(R(t,T,S))_{t \in [T,S]}$ is a martingale under the forward S-measure $\mathbb{P}_S$, i.e. we have*

$$R(t,T,S) = \mathbb{E}_S[R(S,T,S) \mid \mathcal{F}_t] = \mathbb{E}_S\left[\frac{1}{S-T}\left(e^{\int_T^S r_u du} - 1\right) \,\Big|\, \mathcal{F}_t\right],$$

$T \leqslant t \leqslant S$.

Proof. We have

$$
\begin{aligned}
R(t,T,S) &= \frac{1}{S-T}\left(\frac{P(t,T)}{P(t,S)}-1\right) \\
&= \frac{1}{S-T}\left(\frac{\mathrm{e}^{\int_T^t r_u du}}{P(t,S)}-1\right) \\
&= \frac{1}{S-T}\left(\frac{1}{P(t,S)}\,\mathbb{E}[P(t,T)\mid\mathcal{F}_t]-1\right) \\
&= \frac{1}{S-T}\left(\frac{1}{P(t,S)}\,\mathbb{E}\left[\mathrm{e}^{\int_T^t r_u du}\,\Big|\,\mathcal{F}_t\right]-1\right) \\
&= \frac{1}{S-T}\left(\frac{1}{P(t,S)}\,\mathbb{E}\left[\mathrm{e}^{-\int_t^S r_u du}\mathrm{e}^{\int_T^S r_u du}\,\Big|\,\mathcal{F}_t\right]-1\right) \\
&= \frac{1}{S-T}\left(\mathbb{E}_S\left[\mathrm{e}^{\int_T^S r_u du}\,\Big|\,\mathcal{F}_t\right]-1\right) \\
&= \frac{1}{S-T}\left(\mathbb{E}_S[P(S,T)\mid\mathcal{F}_t]-1\right) \\
&= \mathbb{E}_S[R(S,T,S)\mid\mathcal{F}_t], \qquad T\leqslant t\leqslant S.
\end{aligned}
$$

$\square$

18.2 LIBOR/SOFR Swap Rates

The first interest rate swap occurred in 1981 between the World Bank, which was interested in borrowing German Marks and Swiss Francs, and IBM, which already had large amounts of those currencies but needed to borrow U.S. dollars.

The vanilla interest rate swap makes it possible to exchange a sequence of variable LIBOR rates $L(t,T_k,T_{k+1})$, $k=1,2,\ldots,n-1$, against a fixed rate κ over a succession of time intervals $[T_i,T_{i+1}),\ldots,[T_{j-1},T_j]$ defining a *tenor structure*, see Section 19.1 for details.

Making the agreement fair results into an exchange of cashflows

$$
\underbrace{(T_{k+1}-T_k)L(t,T_k,T_{k+1})}_{\text{floating leg}}-\underbrace{(T_{k+1}-T_k)\kappa}_{\text{fixed leg}},
$$

at the dates $T_{i+1},\ldots T_j$ between the two parties, therefore generating a cumulative discounted cash flow

$$
\sum_{k=i}^{j-1}\mathrm{e}^{-\int_t^{T_{k+1}} r_s ds}(T_{k+1}-T_k)\big(L(t,T_k,T_{k+1})-\kappa\big),
$$

at time $t=T_0$, in which we used simple (or linear) interest rate compounding. This corresponds to a *payer swap*, in which the swap holder receives the *floating leg* and pays the *fixed leg* κ, whereas the holder of a *seller swap* receives the *fixed leg* κ and pays the *floating leg*.

The above cash flow is used to make the contract fair, and it can be priced *at time t* as

$$\mathbb{E}^* \left[\sum_{k=i}^{j-1} (T_{k+1} - T_k) \, \mathrm{e}^{-\int_t^{T_{k+1}} r_s ds} \big(L(t, T_k, T_{k+1}) - \kappa \big) \, \Big| \, \mathcal{F}_t \right]$$

$$= \sum_{k=i}^{j-1} (T_{k+1} - T_k)(L(t, T_k, T_{k+1}) - \kappa) \, \mathbb{E}^* \left[\mathrm{e}^{-\int_t^{T_{k+1}} r_s ds} \, \Big| \, \mathcal{F}_t \right]$$

$$= \sum_{k=i}^{j-1} (T_{k+1} - T_k) P(t, T_{k+1}) \big(L(t, T_k, T_{k+1}) - \kappa \big). \tag{18.13}$$

The swap rate $S(t, T_i, T_j)$ is by definition the value of the rate κ that makes the contract fair by making the above cash flow $\mathcal{C}(t)$ vanish.

Definition 18.9. *The LIBOR swap rate $S(t, T_i, T_j)$ is the value of the break-even rate κ that makes the contract fair by making the cash flow (18.13) vanish, i.e.*

$$\sum_{k=i}^{j-1} (T_{k+1} - T_k) P(t, T_{k+1}) \big(L(t, T_k, T_{k+1}) - \kappa \big) = 0. \tag{18.14}$$

The next Proposition 18.10 makes use of the annuity numéraire

$$P(t, T_i, T_j) \; := \; \mathbb{E}^* \left[\sum_{k=i}^{j-1} (T_{k+1} - T_k) \, \mathrm{e}^{-\int_t^{T_{k+1}} r_s ds} \, \Big| \, \mathcal{F}_t \right] \tag{18.15}$$

$$= \sum_{k=i}^{j-1} (T_{k+1} - T_k) \, \mathbb{E}^* \left[\mathrm{e}^{-\int_t^{T_{k+1}} r_s ds} \, \Big| \, \mathcal{F}_t \right]$$

$$= \sum_{k=i}^{j-1} (T_{k+1} - T_k) P(t, T_{k+1}), \qquad 0 \leqslant t \leqslant T_2,$$

which represents the present value at time t of future \$1 receipts at times $T_i, \ldots, T_j$, weighted by the lengths $T_{k+1} - T_k$ of the time intervals $(T_k, T_{k+1}]$, $k = i, \ldots, j-1$.

The time intervals $(T_{k+1} - T_k)_{k=i,\ldots,j-1}$ in the definition (18.15) of the annuity numéraire can be replaced by coupon payments $(c_{k+1})_{k=i,\ldots,j-1}$ occurring at times $(T_{k+1})_{k=i,\ldots,j-1}$, in which case the annuity numéraire becomes

$$P(t, T_i, T_j) \; := \; \mathbb{E}^* \left[\sum_{k=i}^{j-1} c_{k+1} \, \mathrm{e}^{-\int_t^{T_{k+1}} r_s ds} \, \Big| \, \mathcal{F}_t \right]$$

$$= \sum_{k=i}^{j-1} c_{k+1} \, \mathbb{E}^* \left[\mathrm{e}^{-\int_t^{T_{k+1}} r_s ds} \, \Big| \, \mathcal{F}_t \right]$$

$$= \sum_{k=i}^{j-1} c_{k+1} P(t, T_{k+1}), \qquad 0 \leqslant t \leqslant T_i, \tag{18.16}$$

which represents the value at time t of the future coupon payments discounted according to the bond prices $(P(t, T_{k+1}))_{k=i,\ldots,j-1}$. This expression can also be used to define *amortizing swaps*, in which the value of the notional decreases over time, or *accreting swaps* in which the value of the notional increases over time.

LIBOR Swap rates

The LIBOR *swap rate* $S(t, T_i, T_j)$ is defined by solving Relation (18.14) for the forward rate $S(t, T_k, T_{k+1})$, *i.e.*

$$\sum_{k=i}^{j-1}(T_{k+1} - T_k)P(t, T_{k+1})\big(L(t, T_k, T_{k+1}) - S(t, T_i, T_j)\big) = 0. \tag{18.17}$$

Proposition 18.10. *The LIBOR swap rate $S(t, T_i, T_j)$ is given by*

$$S(t, T_i, T_j) = \frac{1}{P(t, T_i, T_j)} \sum_{k=i}^{j-1}(T_{k+1} - T_k)P(t, T_{k+1})L(t, T_k, T_{k+1}), \tag{18.18}$$

$0 \leqslant t \leqslant T_i$.

Proof. By definition, $S(t, T_i, T_j)$ is the (fixed) break-even rate over $[T_i, T_j]$ that will be agreed in exchange for the family of forward rates $L(t, T_k, T_{k+1})$, $k = i, \ldots, j-1$, and it solves (18.17), *i.e.* we have

$$\sum_{k=i}^{j-1}(T_{k+1} - T_k)P(t, T_{k+1})L(t, T_k, T_{k+1}) - P(t, T_i, T_j)S(t, T_i, T_j)$$

$$= \sum_{k=i}^{j-1}(T_{k+1} - T_k)P(t, T_{k+1})L(t, T_k, T_{k+1})$$

$$\quad -S(t, T_i, T_j)\sum_{k=i}^{j-1}(T_{k+1} - T_k)P(t, T_{k+1})$$

$$= \sum_{k=i}^{j-1}(T_{k+1} - T_k)P(t, T_{k+1})L(t, T_k, T_{k+1}) - S(t, T_i, T_j)P(t, T_i, T_j)$$

$$= 0,$$

which shows (18.18) by solving the above equation for $S(t, T_i, T_j)$.   □

The LIBOR swap rate $S(t, T_i, T_j)$ is defined by the same relation as (18.14), with the forward rate $L(t, T_k, T_{k+1})$ replaced with the LIBOR rate $L(t, T_k, T_{k+1})$. In this case, using the Definition 18.11 of LIBOR rates we obtain the next corollary.

Corollary 18.11. *The LIBOR swap rate $S(t, T_i, T_j)$ is given by*

$$S(t, T_i, T_j) = \frac{P(t, T_i) - P(t, T_j)}{P(t, T_i, T_j)}, \qquad 0 \leqslant t \leqslant T_i. \tag{18.19}$$

Proof. By (18.18), (18.11) and a telescoping summation argument we have

$$
\begin{aligned}
S(t, T_i, T_j) &= \frac{1}{P(t, T_i, T_j)} \sum_{k=i}^{j-1} (T_{k+1} - T_k) P(t, T_{k+1}) L(t, T_k, T_{k+1}) \\
&= \frac{1}{P(t, T_i, T_j)} \sum_{k=i}^{j-1} P(t, T_{k+1}) \left(\frac{P(t, T_k)}{P(t, T_{k+1})} - 1 \right) \\
&= \frac{1}{P(t, T_i, T_j)} \sum_{k=i}^{j-1} (P(t, T_k) - P(t, T_{k+1})) \\
&= \frac{P(t, T_i) - P(t, T_i)}{P(t, T_i, T_j)}.
\end{aligned}
\tag{18.20}
$$

$\square$

By (18.19), the bond prices $P(t, T_i)$ can be recovered from the values of the forward swap rates $S(t, T_i, T_j)$.

Clearly, a simple expression for the swap rate such as that of Corollary 18.11 cannot be obtained using the standard (*i.e.* non-LIBOR) rates defined in (18.10). Similarly, it will not be available for amortizing or accreting swaps because the telescoping summation argument does not apply to the expression (18.16) of the annuity numéraire.

When $n = 2$, the LIBOR swap rate $S(t, T_1, T_2)$ coincides with the LIBOR rate $L(t, T_1, T_2)$, as from (18.16) we have

$$
\begin{aligned}
S(t, T_1, T_2) &= \frac{P(t, T_1) - P(t, T_2)}{P(t, T_1, T_2)} \\
&= \frac{P(t, T_1) - P(t, T_2)}{(T_2 - T_1) P(t, T_2)} \\
&= L(t, T_1, T_2).
\end{aligned}
\tag{18.21}
$$

Similarly to the case of LIBOR rates, Relation (18.19) shows that the LIBOR swap rate can be viewed as a forward price with (annuity) numéraire $N_t = P(t, T_i, T_j)$ and $X_t = P(t, T_i) - P(t, T_j)$. Consequently the LIBOR swap rate $(S(t, T_i, T_j)_{t \in [T, S]}$ is a martingale under the forward measure $\widehat{\mathbb{P}}$ defined from (16.1) by

$$
\frac{d\widehat{\mathbb{P}}}{d\mathbb{P}^*} = \frac{P(T_i, T_i, T_j)}{P(0, T_i, T_j)} e^{-\int_0^{T_i} r_t dt}.
$$

SOFR Swap rates

The expressions

$$
S(t, T_i, T_j) = \frac{1}{P(t, T_i, T_j)} \sum_{k=i}^{j-1} (T_{k+1} - T_k) P(t, T_{k+1}) R(t, T_k, T_{k+1})
\tag{18.22}
$$

and

$$S(t, T_i, T_j) = \frac{P(t, T_i) - P(t, T_j)}{P(t, T_i, T_j)}, \qquad T_i \leqslant t \leqslant T_j, \tag{18.23}$$

defining the SOFR swap rate $S(t, T_i, T_j)$ are identical to the ones defining the LIBOR swap rate in (18.18) and (18.19) by taking $t \geqslant T_i$ in the case of the SOFR swap rate.

18.3 The HJM Model

In this section we turn to the modeling of instantaneous forward rate curves. From the beginning of this chapter we have started with the modeling of the short rate $(r_t)_{t \in \mathbb{R}_+}$, followed by its consequences on the pricing of bonds $P(t, T)$ and on the expressions of the forward rates $f(t, T, S)$ and $L(t, T, S)$.

In this section we choose a different starting point and consider the problem of directly modeling the instantaneous forward rate $f(t, T)$. The graph given in Figure 18.7 presents a possible random evolution of a forward interest rate curve using the Musiela convention, *i.e.* we will write

$$g(x) = f(t, t + x) = f(t, T), \tag{18.24}$$

under the substitution $x = T - t$, $x \geqslant 0$, and represent a sample of the instantaneous forward curve $x \mapsto f(t, t + x)$ for each $t \geqslant 0$.

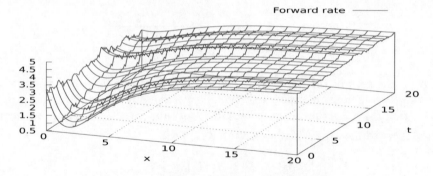

Figure 18.7: Stochastic process of forward curves.

Definition 18.12. *In the Heath–Jarrow–Morton (HJM) model, the instantaneous forward rate $f(t, T)$ is modeled under $\mathbb{P}^*$ by a stochastic differential equation of the form*

$$d_t f(t, T) = \alpha(t, T)dt + \sigma(t, T)dB_t, \qquad 0 \leqslant t \leqslant T, \tag{18.25}$$

where $t \mapsto \alpha(t, T)$ and $t \mapsto \sigma(t, T)$, $0 \leqslant t \leqslant T$, are allowed to be random, $(\mathcal{F}_t)_{t \in [0,T]}$-adapted, processes.

In the above equation, the date T is fixed and the differential d_t is with respect to the time variable t.

Under basic Markovianity assumptions, a HJM model with deterministic coefficients $\alpha(t, T)$ and $\sigma(t, T)$ will yield a short rate process $(r_t)_{t \in \mathbb{R}_+}$ of the form

$$dr_t = (a(t) - b(t)r_t)dt + \sigma(t)dB_t,$$

see § 7.4 in Privault (2021), which is the Hull and White (1990) model, with the explicit solution

$$r_t = r_s e^{-\int_s^t b(\tau)d\tau} + \int_s^t e^{-\int_u^t b(\tau)d\tau} a(u)du + \int_s^t \sigma(u) e^{-\int_u^t b(\tau)d\tau} dB_u,$$

$0 \leqslant s \leqslant t.$

The HJM condition

How to "encode" absence of arbitrage in the defining HJM Equation (18.25) is an important question. Recall that under the absence of arbitrage, the bond price $P(t, T)$ has been constructed as

$$P(t, T) = \mathbb{E}^* \left[\exp \left(- \int_t^T r_s ds \right) \mid \mathcal{F}_t \right] = \exp \left(- \int_t^T f(t, s)ds \right), \qquad (18.26)$$

cf. Proposition 18.3, hence the discounted bond price process is given by

$$t \mapsto \exp \left(- \int_0^t r_s ds \right) P(t, T) = \exp \left(- \int_0^t r_s ds - \int_t^T f(t, s)ds \right) \qquad (18.27)$$

is a martingale under $\mathbb{P}^*$ by Proposition 17.1 and Relation (18.5) in Proposition 18.3. This shows that $\mathbb{P}^*$ is a risk-neutral probability measure, and by the first fundamental theorem of asset pricing Theorem 5.7 we conclude that the market is without arbitrage opportunities.

Proposition 18.13. *(HJM Condition Heath et al. (1992)). Under the condition*

$$\alpha(t, T) = \sigma(t, T) \int_t^T \sigma(t, s)ds, \qquad 0 \leqslant t \leqslant T, \qquad (18.28)$$

which is known as the HJM absence of arbitrage condition, *the discounted bond price process (18.27) is a martingale, and the probability measure $\mathbb{P}^*$ is risk-neutral.*

Proof. Using the process $(X_t)_{t \in [0,T]}$ defined as

$$X_t := \int_t^T f(t, s)ds = -\log P(t, T), \qquad 0 \leqslant t \leqslant T,$$

such that $P(t, T) = e^{-X_t}$, we rewrite the spot forward rate, or yield

$$f(t, t, T) = \frac{1}{T - t} \int_t^T f(t, s)ds,$$

see (18.8), as

$$f(t, t, T) = \frac{1}{T - t} \int_t^T f(t, s)ds = \frac{X_t}{T - t}, \qquad 0 \leqslant t \leqslant T,$$

where the dynamics of $t \mapsto f(t, s)$ is given by (18.25). We also use the extended *Leibniz integral rule*

$$d_t \int_t^T f(t, s)ds = -f(t, t)dt + \int_t^T d_t f(t, s)ds = -r_t dt + \int_t^T d_t f(t, s)ds,$$

see (18.6). This identity can be checked in the particular case where $f(t,s) = g(t)h(s)$ is a smooth function that satisfies the separation of variables property, as

$$
\begin{aligned}
d_t \left(\int_t^T g(t)h(s)ds \right) &= d_t \left(g(t) \int_t^T h(s)ds \right) \\
&= \int_t^T h(s)ds\, dg(t) + g(t)d_t \int_t^T h(s)ds \\
&= g'(t) \left(\int_t^T h(s)ds \right) dt - g(t)h(t)dt.
\end{aligned}
$$

We have

$$
\begin{aligned}
d_t X_t &= d_t \int_t^T f(t,s)ds \\
&= -f(t,t)dt + \int_t^T d_t f(t,s)ds \\
&= -f(t,t)dt + \int_t^T \alpha(t,s)ds\,dt + \int_t^T \sigma(t,s)ds\,dB_t \\
&= -r_t dt + \left(\int_t^T \alpha(t,s)ds \right) dt + \left(\int_t^T \sigma(t,s)ds \right) dB_t,
\end{aligned}
$$

hence

$$
|d_t X_t|^2 = \left(\int_t^T \sigma(t,s)ds \right)^2 dt.
$$

By Itô's calculus, we find

$$
\begin{aligned}
d_t P(t,T) &= d_t e^{-X_t} \\
&= -e^{-X_t} d_t X_t + \frac{1}{2} e^{-X_t} (d_t X_t)^2 \\
&= -e^{-X_t} d_t X_t + \frac{1}{2} e^{-X_t} \left(\int_t^T \sigma(t,s)ds \right)^2 dt \\
&= -e^{-X_t} \left(-r_t dt + \int_t^T \alpha(t,s)ds\,dt + \int_t^T \sigma(t,s)ds\,dB_t \right) \\
&\quad + \frac{1}{2} e^{-X_t} \left(\int_t^T \sigma(t,s)ds \right)^2 dt,
\end{aligned}
$$

and the discounted bond price satisfies

$$
\begin{aligned}
&d_t \left(\exp\left(-\int_0^t r_s ds \right) P(t,T) \right) \\
&= -r_t \exp\left(-\int_0^t r_s ds - X_t \right) dt + \exp\left(-\int_0^t r_s ds \right) d_t P(t,T) \\
&= -r_t \exp\left(-\int_0^t r_s ds - X_t \right) dt - \exp\left(-\int_0^t r_s ds - X_t \right) d_t X_t \\
&\quad + \frac{1}{2} \exp\left(-\int_0^t r_s ds - X_t \right) \left(\int_t^T \sigma(t,s)ds \right)^2 dt \\
&= -r_t \exp\left(-\int_0^t r_s ds - X_t \right) dt \\
&\quad - \exp\left(-\int_0^t r_s ds - X_t \right) \left(-r_t dt + \int_t^T \alpha(t,s)ds\,dt + \int_t^T \sigma(t,s)ds\,dB_t \right)
\end{aligned}
$$

$$+\frac{1}{2}\exp\left(-\int_0^t r_s ds - X_t\right)\left(\int_t^T \sigma(t,s)ds\right)^2 dt$$

$$= -\exp\left(-\int_0^t r_s ds - X_t\right)\int_t^T \sigma(t,s)ds dB_t$$

$$-\exp\left(-\int_0^t r_s ds - X_t\right)\left(\int_t^T \alpha(t,s)ds - \frac{1}{2}\left(\int_t^T \sigma(t,s)ds\right)^2\right)dt.$$

Thus, the discounted bond price process

$$t \mapsto \exp\left(-\int_0^t r_s ds\right)P(t,T)$$

will be a martingale provided that

$$\int_t^T \alpha(t,s)ds - \frac{1}{2}\left(\int_t^T \sigma(t,s)ds\right)^2 = 0, \qquad 0 \leqslant t \leqslant T. \tag{18.29}$$

Differentiating the above relation with respect to T yields

$$\alpha(t,T) = \sigma(t,T)\int_t^T \sigma(t,s)ds,$$

which is in fact equivalent to (18.29). □

Forward Vasicek rates in the HJM model

The HJM coefficients in the Vasicek model are in fact deterministic, for example, taking $a = 0$, by (18.9) we have

$$d_t f(t,T) = \sigma^2 e^{-(T-t)b}\int_t^T e^{(t-s)b}ds dt + \sigma e^{-(T-t)b}dB_t,$$

i.e.

$$\alpha(t,T) = \sigma^2 e^{-(T-t)b}\int_t^T e^{(t-s)b}ds = \sigma^2 e^{-(T-t)b}\frac{1 - e^{-(T-t)b}}{b},$$

and $\sigma(t,T) = \sigma e^{-(T-t)b}$, and the HJM condition reads

$$\alpha(t,T) = \sigma^2 e^{-(T-t)b}\int_t^T e^{(t-s)b}ds = \sigma(t,T)\int_t^T \sigma(t,s)ds. \tag{18.30}$$

Random simulations of the Vasicek instantaneous forward rates are provided in Figures 18.8 and 18.9 using the Musiela convention (18.24).

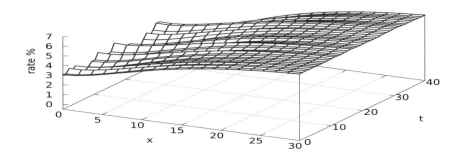

Figure 18.8: Forward instantaneous curve $(t,x) \mapsto f(t,t+x)$ in the Vasicek model.

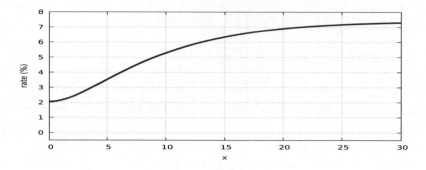

Figure 18.9: Forward instantaneous curve $x \mapsto f(0,x)$ in the Vasicek model.

HJM-SOFR Model

In the HJM-SOFR model, the instantaneous forward rate $f(t,T)$ is extended to $t > T$ by taking

$$d_t f(t,T) = \mathbb{1}_{\{t \leqslant T\}} \alpha(t,T)dt + \mathbb{1}_{\{t \leqslant T\}} \sigma(t,T)dB_t, \qquad t \geqslant T,$$

i.e.

$$f(t,T) = f(T,T) = r_T, \qquad t \geqslant T,$$

see Lyashenko and Mercurio (2020).

18.4   Yield Curve Modeling

In the Nelson and Siegel (1987) parametrization the instantaneous forward rate curves are parametrized by 4 coefficients z_1, z_2, z_3, z_4, as

$$g(x) = z_1 + (z_2 + z_3 x)\,e^{-xz_4}, \qquad x \geqslant 0.$$

An example of a graph obtained by the Nelson–Siegel parametrization is given in Figure 18.10, for $z_1 = 1$, $z_2 = -10$, $z_3 = 100$, $z_4 = 10$.

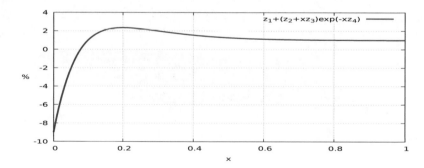

Figure 18.10: Graph of $x \mapsto g(x)$ in the Nelson–Siegel model.

The Svensson (1994) parametrization has the advantage to reproduce two humps instead of one, the location and height of which can be chosen *via* 6 parameters z_1, z_2, z_3, z_4, z_5, z_6 as

$$g(x) = z_1 + (z_2 + z_3 x)\,\mathrm{e}^{-xz_4} + z_5 x\,\mathrm{e}^{-xz_6}, \qquad x \geqslant 0.$$

A typical graph of a Svensson parametrization is given in Figure 18.11, for $z_1 = 6.6$, $z_2 = -5$, $z_3 = -100$, $z_4 = 10$, $z_5 = -1/2$, $z_6 = 1$.

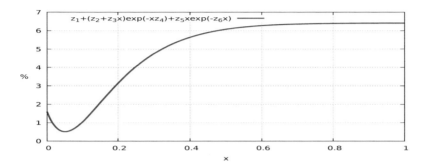

Figure 18.11: Graph of $x \mapsto g(x)$ in the Svensson model.

Figure 18.12 presents a fit of the market data of Figure 18.1 using a Svensson curve.

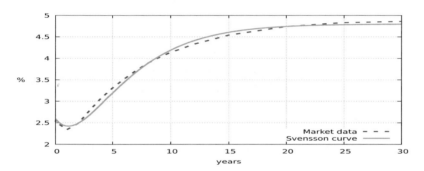

Figure 18.12: Fitting of a Svensson curve to market data.

Vasicek parametrization

In the Vasicek model, the instantaneous forward rate process is given from (18.9) and (18.24) as

$$f(t, T) = \frac{a}{b} - \frac{\sigma^2}{2b^2} + \left(r_t - \frac{a}{b} + \frac{\sigma^2}{b^2}\right)\mathrm{e}^{-bx} - \frac{\sigma^2}{2b^2}\mathrm{e}^{-2bx}, \tag{18.31}$$

in the Musiela notation ($x = T - t$), and we have

$$\frac{\partial f}{\partial T}(t, T) = \left(a - br_t - \frac{\sigma^2}{b}(1 - \mathrm{e}^{-(T-t)b})\right)\mathrm{e}^{-(T-t)b}.$$

We check that the derivative $\partial f/\partial T$ vanishes when $a - br_t + a - \sigma^2(1 - \mathrm{e}^{-bx})/b = 0$, *i.e.*

$$\mathrm{e}^{-bx} = 1 + \frac{b}{\sigma^2}(br_t - a),$$

which admits at most one solution, provided that $a > br_t$. As a consequence, the possible forward curves in the Vasicek model are limited to one change of "regime" per curve, as illustrated in Figure 18.13 for various values of r_t, and in Figure 18.14.

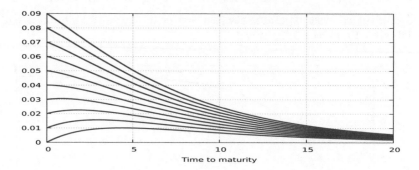

Figure 18.13: Graphs of forward rates with $b = 0.16$, $a/b = 0.04$, $r_0 = 2\%$, $\sigma = 4.5\%$.

The next Figure 18.14 is also using the parameters $b = 0.16$, $a/b = 0.04$, $r_0 = 2\%$, and $\sigma = 4.5\%$.

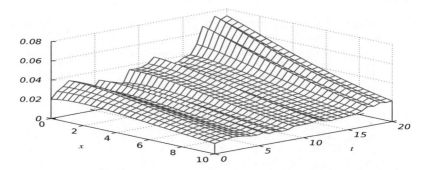

Figure 18.14: Forward instantaneous curve $(t, x) \mapsto f(t, t+x)$ in the Vasicek model.

One may think of constructing an instantaneous forward rate process taking values in the Svensson space, however, this type of modeling is not consistent with the absence of arbitrage, and it can be proved that the HJM curves cannot live in the Nelson–Siegel or Svensson spaces, see §3.5 of Björk (2004b). In other words, it can be shown that the forward yield curves produced by the Vasicek model are included neither in the Nelson–Siegel space, nor in the Svensson space. In addition, the Vasicek yield curves do not appear to correctly model the market forward curves cf. also Figure 18.1 above.

Another way to deal with the curve fitting problem is to use deterministic shifts for the fitting of one forward curve, such as the initial curve at $t = 0$, cf. *e.g.* § 6.3 in Privault (2021).

Fitting the Nelson–Siegel and Svensson models to yield curve data

Recall that in the Nelson–Siegel parametrization the instantaneous forward rate curves are parametrized by four coefficients z_1, z_2, z_3, z_4, as

$$f(t, t+x) = z_1 + (z_2 + z_3 x)\, e^{-x z_4}, \qquad x \geqslant 0. \tag{18.32}$$

Taking $x = T - t$, the yield $f(t, t, T)$ is given as

$$
\begin{aligned}
f(t, t, T) &= \frac{1}{T - t} \int_t^T f(t, s) ds \\
&= \frac{1}{x} \int_0^x f(t, t + y) dy \\
&= z_1 + \frac{z_2}{x} \int_0^x e^{-y z_4} dy + \frac{z_3}{x} \int_0^x y \, e^{-y z_4} dy \\
&= z_1 + z_2 \frac{1 - e^{-x z_4}}{x z_4} + z_3 \frac{1 - e^{-x z_4} + x \, e^{-x z_4}}{x z_4}.
\end{aligned}
$$

The yield $f(t, t, T)$ can be reparametrized as

$$
f(t, t + x) = z_1 + (z_2 + z_3 x) \, e^{-x z_4} = \beta_0 + \beta_1 \, e^{-x/\lambda} + \frac{\beta_2}{\lambda} x \, e^{-x/\lambda}, \qquad x \geqslant 0,
$$

cf. Charpentier (2014), with $\beta_0 = z_1$, $\beta_1 = z_2$, $\beta_2 = z_3 / z_4$, $\lambda = 1 / z_4$.

```
require(YieldCurve);data(ECBYieldCurve)
mat.ECB<-c(3/12,0.5,1,2,3,4,5,6,7,8,9,10,11,12,13,14,15,16,17,18,19,20,21,22,23, 24,25,26,27,28,29,30)
first(ECBYieldCurve, '1 month');Nelson.Siegel(first(ECBYieldCurve, '1 month'), mat.ECB)
```

```
for (n in seq(from=70, to=290, by=10)) {
ECB.NS <- Nelson.Siegel(ECBYieldCurve[n,], mat.ECB)
ECB.S <- Svensson(ECBYieldCurve[n,], mat.ECB)
ECB.NS.yield.curve <- NSrates(ECB.NS, mat.ECB)
ECB.S.yield.curve <- Srates(ECB.S, mat.ECB,"Spot")
plot(mat.ECB, as.numeric(ECBYieldCurve[n,]), type="o", lty=1, col=1,ylab="Interest rates", xlab="Maturity
    in years", ylim=c(3.2,4.8))
lines(mat.ECB, as.numeric(ECB.NS.yield.curve), type="l", lty=3,col=2,lwd=2)
lines(mat.ECB, as.numeric(ECB.S.yield.curve), type="l", lty=2,col=6,lwd=2)
title(main=paste("ECB yield curve observed at",time(ECBYieldCurve[n], sep=" "),"vs fitted yield curve"))
legend('bottomright', legend=c("ECB data","Nelson--Siegel","Svensson"),col=c(1,2,6), lty=1, bg='gray90')
grid();Sys.sleep(2.5)}
```

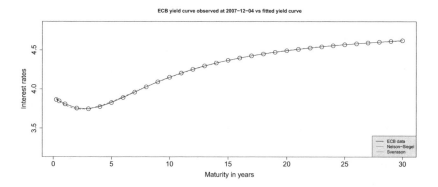

Figure 18.15: ECB data *vs* fitted yield curve.

18.5   Two-Factor Model

The correlation problem is another issue of concern when using the affine models considered so far, see (17.8) and (17.27). Let us compare three bond price simulations with maturity $T_1 = 10$, $T_2 = 20$, and $T_3 = 30$ based on the same Brownian path, as given in Figure 18.16. Clearly, the bond prices

$$F(r_t, T_i) = P(t, T_i) = e^{A(t,T_i)r_t C(t,T_i)}, \qquad 0 \leqslant t \leqslant T_i, \quad i = 1, 2,$$

with maturities T_1 and T_2 are linked by the relation

$$P(t, T_2) = P(t, T_1) \exp\left(A(t, T_2) - A(t, T_1) + r_t(C(t, T_2) - C(t, T_1))\right), \tag{18.33}$$

meaning that bond prices with different maturities could be deduced from each other, which is unrealistic.

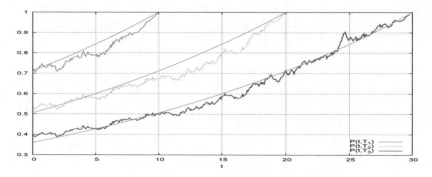

Figure 18.16: Graph of $t \mapsto P(t, T_1), P(t, T_2), P(t, T_3)$.

In affine short rate models, by (18.33), $\log P(t, T_1)$ and $\log P(t, T_2)$ are linked by the affine relationship

$$\log P(t, T_2) = \log P(t, T_1) + A(t, T_2) - A(t, T_1) + r_t(C(t, T_2) - C(t, T_1))$$
$$= \log P(t, T_1) + A(t, T_2) - A(t, T_1) + (C(t, T_2) - C(t, T_1))\frac{\log P(t, T_1) - A(t, T_1)}{C(t, T_1)}$$
$$= \left(1 + \frac{C(t, T_2) - C(t, T_1)}{A(t, T_1)}\right)\log P(t, T_1) + A(t, T_2) - A(t, T_1)\frac{C(t, T_2)}{C(t, T_1)}$$

with constant coefficients, which yields the perfect correlation or anticorrelation

$$\mathrm{Cor}(\log P(t, T_1), \log P(t, T_2)) = \pm 1,$$

depending on the sign of the coefficient $1 + (C(t, T_2) - C(t, T_1))/A(t, T_1)$, cf. § 6.4 in Privault (2021),

A solution to the correlation problem is to consider a two-factor model based on two control processes $(X_t)_{t\in\mathbb{R}_+}$, $(Y_t)_{t\in\mathbb{R}_+}$ which are solution of

$$\begin{cases} dX_t = \mu_1(t, X_t)dt + \sigma_1(t, X_t)dB_t^{(1)}, \\ \\ dY_t = \mu_2(t, Y_t)dt + \sigma_2(t, Y_t)dB_t^{(2)}, \end{cases} \tag{18.34}$$

where $\left(B_t^{(1)}\right)_{t\in\mathbb{R}_+}$, $\left(B_t^{(2)}\right)_{t\in\mathbb{R}_+}$ are correlated Brownian motion, with

$$\text{Cov}\left(B_s^{(1)}, B_t^{(2)}\right) = \rho\min(s,t), \qquad s,t \geqslant 0, \tag{18.35}$$

and

$$dB_t^{(1)} \cdot dB_t^{(2)} = \rho dt, \tag{18.36}$$

for some correlation parameter $\rho \in [-1,1]$. In practice, $\left(B^{(1)}\right)_{t\in\mathbb{R}_+}$ and $\left(B^{(2)}\right)_{t\in\mathbb{R}_+}$ can be constructed from two independent Brownian motions $\left(W^{(1)}\right)_{t\in\mathbb{R}_+}$ and $\left(W^{(2)}\right)_{t\in\mathbb{R}_+}$, by letting

$$\begin{cases} B_t^{(1)} = W_t^{(1)}, \\ B_t^{(2)} = \rho W_t^{(1)} + \sqrt{1-\rho^2}W_t^{(2)}, & t \geqslant 0, \end{cases}$$

and Relations (18.35) and (18.36) are easily satisfied from this construction.

In two-factor models one chooses to build the short-term interest rate r_t *via*

$$r_t := X_t + Y_t, \qquad t \geqslant 0.$$

By the previous standard arbitrage arguments we define the price of a bond with maturity T as

$$\begin{aligned} P(t,T) : &= \mathbb{E}^*\left[\exp\left(-\int_t^T r_s ds\right)\Big|\,\mathcal{F}_t\right] \\ &= \mathbb{E}^*\left[\exp\left(-\int_t^T r_s ds\right)\Big|\,X_t,\,Y_t\right] \\ &= \mathbb{E}^*\left[\exp\left(-\int_t^T (X_s+Y_s)ds\right)\Big|\,X_t,\,Y_t\right] \\ &= F(t,X_t,Y_t), \end{aligned} \tag{18.37}$$

since the couple $(X_t,Y_t)_{t\in\mathbb{R}_+}$ is Markovian. Applying the Itô formula with two variables to

$$t \mapsto F(t,X_t,Y_t) = P(t,T) = \mathbb{E}^*\left[\exp\left(-\int_t^T r_s ds\right)\Big|\,\mathcal{F}_t\right],$$

and using the fact that the discounted process

$$t \mapsto e^{-\int_0^t r_s ds}P(t,T) = \mathbb{E}^*\left[\exp\left(-\int_0^T r_s ds\right)\Big|\,\mathcal{F}_t\right]$$

is an $\mathcal{F}_t$-martingale under $\mathbb{P}^*$, we can derive the PDE

$$-(x+y)F(t,x,y) + \mu_1(t,x)\frac{\partial F}{\partial x}(t,x,y) + \mu_2(t,y)\frac{\partial F}{\partial y}(t,x,y)$$

$$+\frac{1}{2}\sigma_1^2(t,x)\frac{\partial^2 F}{\partial x^2}(t,x,y) + \frac{1}{2}\sigma_2^2(t,y)\frac{\partial^2 F}{\partial y^2}(t,x,y)$$

$$+\rho\sigma_1(t,x)\sigma_2(t,y)\frac{\partial^2 F}{\partial x \partial y}(t,x,y) + \frac{\partial F}{\partial t}(t,x,y) = 0, \tag{18.38}$$

on $\mathbb{R}^2$ for the bond price $P(t,T)$. In the Vasicek model

$$
\begin{cases}
dX_t = -aX_t dt + \sigma dB_t^{(1)}, \\
dY_t = -bY_t dt + \eta dB_t^{(2)},
\end{cases}
$$

this yields the solution $F(t,x,y)$ of (18.38) as

$$
P(t,T) = F(t, X_t, Y_t) = F_1(t, X_t) F_2(t, Y_t) \exp\left(\rho U(t,T)\right), \tag{18.39}
$$

where $F_1(t, X_t)$ and $F_2(t, Y_t)$ are the bond prices associated to X_t and Y_t in the Vasicek model, and

$$
U(t,T) := \frac{\sigma\eta}{ab}\left(T - t + \frac{e^{-(T-t)a} - 1}{a} + \frac{e^{-(T-t)b} - 1}{b} - \frac{e^{-(a+b)(T-t)} - 1}{a+b}\right)
$$

is a correlation term which vanishes when $\left(B_t^{(1)}\right)_{t\in\mathbb{R}_+}$ and $\left(B_t^{(2)}\right)_{t\in\mathbb{R}_+}$ are independent, *i.e.* when $\rho = 0$, cf. Ch. 4, Appendix A in Brigo and Mercurio (2006), § 6.5 of Privault (2021).

Partial differentiation of $\log P(t,T)$ with respect to T leads to the instantaneous forward rate

$$
f(t,T) = f_1(t,T) + f_2(t,T) - \rho\frac{\sigma\eta}{ab}\left(1 - e^{-(T-t)a}\right)\left(1 - e^{-(T-t)b}\right), \tag{18.40}
$$

where $f_1(t,T)$, $f_2(t,T)$ are the instantaneous forward rates corresponding to X_t and Y_t respectively, cf. § 6.5 of Privault (2021).

An example of a forward rate curve obtained in this way is given in Figure 18.17.

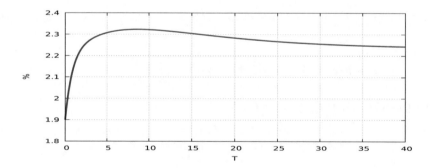

Figure 18.17: Graph of forward rates in a two-factor model.

Next, in Figure 18.18 we present a graph of the evolution of forward curves in a two-factor model.

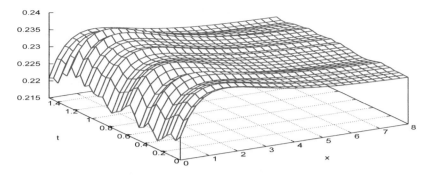

Figure 18.18: Random evolution of instantaneous forward rates in a two-factor model.

18.6 The BGM Model

The models (HJM, affine, etc.) considered in the previous chapter suffer from various drawbacks such as nonpositivity of interest rates in Vasicek model, and lack of closed-form solutions in more complex models. The Brace et al. (1997) (BGM) model has the advantage of yielding positive interest rates, and to permit to derive explicit formulas for the computation of prices for interest rate derivatives such as interest rate caps and swaptions on the LIBOR market.

In the BGM model we consider two bond prices $P(t,T_1)$, $P(t,T_2)$ with maturities T_1, T_2, and the forward probability measure $\mathbb{P}_2$ defined as

$$\frac{d\mathbb{P}_2}{d\mathbb{P}^*} = \frac{e^{-\int_0^{T_2} r_s ds}}{P(0,T_2)},$$

with numéraire $P(t,T_2)$, cf. (16.10). The forward LIBOR rate $L(t,T_1,T_2)$ is modeled as a driftless geometric Brownian motion under $\mathbb{P}_2$, *i.e.*

$$\frac{dL(t,T_1,T_2)}{L(t,T_1,T_2)} = \gamma_1(t)dB_t, \tag{18.41}$$

$0 \leqslant t \leqslant T_1$, for some deterministic volatility function of time $\gamma_1(t)$, with solution

$$L(u,T_1,T_2) = L(t,T_1,T_2) \exp\left(\int_t^u \gamma_1(s)dB_s - \frac{1}{2}\int_t^u |\gamma_1|^2(s)ds\right),$$

i.e. for $u = T_1$,

$$L(T_1,T_1,T_2) = L(t,T_1,T_2) \exp\left(\int_t^{T_1} \gamma_1(s)dB_s - \frac{1}{2}\int_t^{T_1} |\gamma_1|^2(s)ds\right).$$

Since $L(t,T_1,T_2)$ is a geometric Brownian motion under $\mathbb{P}_2$, standard caplets can be priced at time $t \in [0,T_1]$ from the Black–Scholes formula.

In the next Table 18.1 we summarize some stochastic models used for interest rates.

	Model
Short rate r_t	Mean reverting SDEs
Instantaneous forward rate $f(t,s)$	HJM model
Forward rate $f(t,T,S)$	BGM model

Table 18.1: Stochastic interest rate models.

The following Graph 18.19 summarizes the notions introduced in this chapter.

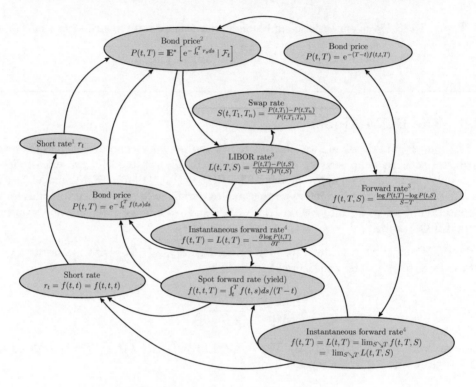

[1] Can be modeled by Vasiçek and other short rate models
[2] Can be modeled from $dP(t,T)/P(t,T)$.
[3] Can be modeled in the BGM model
[4] Can be modeled in the HJM model

Figure 18.19: Roadmap of stochastic interest rate modeling.

Exercises

Exercise 18.1 (Mamon (2004)). We consider a bond with maturity T, priced $P(t,T) = \mathbb{E}^* \left[e^{-\int_t^T r_s ds} \mid \mathcal{F}_t \right]$ at time $t \in [0,T]$.

a) Using the forward measure $\widehat{\mathbb{P}}$ with numéraire $N_t = P(t,T)$, apply the change of numéraire formula (16.9) to compute the derivative $\dfrac{\partial P}{\partial T}(t,T)$.

b) Using Relation (18.5), find an expression of the instantaneous forward rate $f(t, T)$ using the short rate r_T and the forward expectation $\widehat{\mathbb{E}}$.

c) Show that the instantaneous forward rate $(f(t, T))_{t \in [0,T]}$ is a martingale under the forward measure $\widehat{\mathbb{P}}$.

Exercise 18.2 Consider a tenor structure $\{T_1, T_2\}$ and a bond with maturity T_2 and price given at time $t \in [0, T_2]$ by

$$P(t, T_2) = \exp\left(-\int_t^{T_2} f(t, s)ds\right), \qquad t \in [0, T_2],$$

where the instantaneous yield curve $f(t, s)$ is parametrized as

$$f(t, s) = r_1 \mathbb{1}_{[0, T_1]}(s) + r_2 \mathbb{1}_{[T_1, T_2]}(s), \qquad t \leqslant s \leqslant T_2.$$

Find a formula to estimate the values of r_1 and r_2 from the data of $P(0, T_2)$ and $P(T_1, T_2)$.

Same question when $f(t, s)$ is parametrized as

$$f(t, s) = r_1 s \mathbb{1}_{[0, T_1]}(s) + (r_1 T_1 + (s - T_1) r_2) \mathbb{1}_{[T_1, T_2]}(s), \qquad t \leqslant s \leqslant T_2.$$

Exercise 18.3 (Exercise 4.15 continued). Bridge model. Assume that the price $P(t, T)$ of a zero-coupon bond with maturity $T > 0$ is modeled as

$$P(t, T) = e^{-\mu(T - t) + X_t^T}, \qquad t \in [0, T],$$

where $(X_t^T)_{t \in [0, T)}$ is the solution of the stochastic differential equation

$$dX_t^T = \sigma dB_t - \frac{X_t^T}{T - t} dt, \qquad t \in [0, T),$$

under the initial condition $X_0^T = 0$, i.e.

$$X_t^T = (T - t) \int_0^t \frac{\sigma}{T - s} dB_s, \qquad 0 \leqslant t < T,$$

with $\mu, \sigma > 0$.

a) Show that the terminal condition $P(T, T) = 1$ is satisfied.

b) Compute the forward rate

$$f(t, T, S) = -\frac{1}{S - T}(\log P(t, S) - \log P(t, T)).$$

c) Compute the instantaneous forward rate

$$f(t, T) = -\lim_{S \searrow T} \frac{1}{S - T}(\log P(t, S) - \log P(t, T)).$$

d) Show that the limit $\lim_{T \searrow t} f(t, T)$ does not exist in $L^2(\Omega)$.

e) Show that $P(t, T)$ satisfies the stochastic differential equation

$$\frac{dP(t, T)}{P(t, T)} = \sigma dB_t + \frac{\sigma^2}{2} dt - \frac{\log P(t, T)}{T - t} dt, \qquad t \in [0, T].$$

f) Rewrite the equation of Question (e) as

$$\frac{dP(t, T)}{P(t, T)} = \sigma dB_t + r_t^T dt, \qquad t \in [0, T],$$

where $(r_t^T)_{t \in [0, T]}$ is a process to be determined.

g) Show that we have the expression

$$P(t, T) = \mathbb{E}^* \left[e^{-\int_t^T r_s^T ds} \,\middle|\, \mathcal{F}_t \right], \qquad 0 \leqslant t \leqslant T.$$

h) Compute the conditional Radon–Nikodym density

$$\mathbb{E}^* \left[\frac{d\mathbb{P}_T}{d\mathbb{P}^*} \,\middle|\, \mathcal{F}_t \right] = \frac{P(t, T)}{P(0, T)} e^{-\int_0^t r_s^T ds}$$

of the forward measure $\mathbb{P}_T$ with respect to $\mathbb{P}^*$.

i) Show that the process

$$\widehat{B}_t := B_t - \sigma t, \qquad 0 \leqslant t \leqslant T,$$

is a standard Brownian motion under $\mathbb{P}_T$.

j) Compute the dynamics of X_t^S and $P(t, S)$ under $\mathbb{P}_T$.
   Hint: Show that

$$-\mu(S - T) + \sigma(S - T) \int_0^t \frac{1}{S - s} dB_s = \frac{S - T}{S - t} \log P(t, S).$$

k) Compute the bond option price

$$\mathbb{E}^* \left[e^{-\int_t^T r_s^T ds} (P(T, S) - K)^+ \,\middle|\, \mathcal{F}_t \right] = P(t, T) \, \mathbb{E}_T \left[(P(T, S) - K)^+ \,\middle|\, \mathcal{F}_t \right],$$

$0 \leqslant t < T < S.$

Hint: Given X a Gaussian random variable with mean m and variance v^2 given $\mathcal{F}_t$, we have:

$$\mathbb{E} \left[(e^X - \kappa)^+ \,\middle|\, \mathcal{F}_t \right] = e^{m + v^2/2} \Phi \left(\frac{1}{v}(m + v^2 - \log \kappa) \right)$$
$$- \kappa \Phi \left(\frac{1}{v}(m - \log \kappa) \right).$$

Exercise 18.4   Consider a short rate process $(r_t)_{t \in \mathbb{R}_+}$ of the form $r_t = h(t) + X_t$, where $h(t)$ is a deterministic function of time and $(X_t)_{\mathbb{R}_+}$ is a Vasicek process started at $X_0 = 0$.

a) Compute the price $P(0, T)$ at time $t = 0$ of a bond with maturity T, using $h(t)$ and the function $A(T)$ defined in (17.34) for the pricing of Vasicek bonds.

b) Show how the function $h(t)$ can be estimated from the market data of the initial instantaneous forward rate curve $f(0, t)$.

Exercise 18.5   (Exercise 4.12 continued). Consider two assets whose prices $S_t^{(1)}$, $S_t^{(2)}$ at time $t \in [0, T]$ follow the Bachelier dynamics

$$dS_t^{(1)} = rS_t^{(1)} dt + \sigma_1 dW_t^{(1)} \quad dS_t^{(2)} = rS_t^{(2)} dt + \sigma_2 dW_t^{(2)} \quad t \in [0, T],$$

where $\big(W_t^{(1)}\big)_{t \in [0,T]}$, $\big(W_t^{(2)}\big)_{t \in [0,T]}$ are two standard Brownian motions with correlation $\rho \in [-1, 1]$ under a risk-neutral probability measure $\mathbb{P}^*$.

Compute the price $e^{-rT} \mathbb{E}^*[(S_T - K)^+]$ of the spread option on $S_T := S_T^{(2)} - S_T^{(1)}$ with maturity $T > 0$ and strike price $K > 0$.

Exercise 18.6

a) Given two LIBOR spot rates $L(t, t, T)$ and $L(t, t, S)$, compute the corresponding LIBOR forward rate $L(t, T, S)$.

b) Assuming that $L(t, t, T) = 2\%$, $L(t, t, S) = 2.5\%$ and $t = 0$, $T = 1$, $S = 2T = 2$, would you buy a LIBOR forward contract over $[T, 2T]$ with rate $L(0, T, 2T)$ if $L(T, T, 2T)$ remained at the level $L(T, T, 2T) = L(0, 0, T) = 2\%$?

Exercise 18.7   (Exercise 17.4 continued).

a) Compute the forward rate $f(t, T, S)$ in the Ho–Lee model (17.48) with constant deterministic volatility.

In the next questions we take $a = 0$.

b) Compute the instantaneous forward rate $f(t, T)$ in this model.

c) Derive the stochastic equation satisfied by the instantaneous forward rate $f(t, T)$.

d) Check that the HJM absence of arbitrage condition is satisfied in this equation.

Exercise 18.8   Consider the two-factor Vasicek model

$$\begin{cases} dX_t = -bX_t dt + \sigma dB_t^{(1)}, \\[2mm] dY_t = -bY_t dt + \sigma dB_t^{(2)}, \end{cases}$$

where $\big(B_t^{(1)}\big)_{t \in \mathbb{R}_+}$, $\big(B_t^{(2)}\big)_{t \in \mathbb{R}_+}$ are correlated Brownian motion such that $dB_t^{(1)} \cdot dB_t^{(2)} = \rho dt$, for $\rho \in [-1, 1]$.

a) Write down the expressions of the short rates X_t and Y_t.

Hint: They can be found in Section 17.1.

b) Compute the variances $\mathrm{Var}[X_t]$, $\mathrm{Var}[Y_t]$, and the covariance $\mathrm{Cov}(X_t, Y_t)$.

Hint: The expressions of $\mathrm{Var}[X_t]$ and $\mathrm{Var}[Y_t]$ can be found in Section 17.1.

c) Compute the covariance $\mathrm{Cov}(\log P(t, T_1), \log P(t, T_2))$ for the two-factor bond prices

$$P(t, T_1) = F_1(t, X_t, T_1) F_2(t, Y_t, T_1) e^{\rho U(t, T_1)}$$

and

$$P(t, T_2) = F_1(t, X_t, T_2) F_2(t, Y_t, T_2) e^{\rho U(t, T_2)},$$

where

$$\log F_1(t, x, T) = C_1^T + x A_1^T \quad \text{and} \quad \log F_2(t, x) = C_2^T + x A_2^T.$$

Hint: We have $\mathrm{Cov}(X + Y, Z) = \mathrm{Cov}(X, Z) + \mathrm{Cov}(Y, Z)$ and $\mathrm{Cov}(c, X) = 0$ when c is a constant.

Exercise 18.9 Stochastic string model (Santa-Clara and Sornette (2001)). Consider an instantaneous forward rate $f(t, x)$ solution of

$$d_t f(t, x) = \alpha x^2 dt + \sigma d_t B(t, x), \tag{18.42}$$

with a flat initial curve $f(0, x) = r$, where x represents the time to maturity, and $(B(t, x))_{(t,x) \in \mathbb{R}_+^2}$ is a standard *Brownian sheet* with covariance

$$\mathbb{E}[B(s, x) B(t, y)] = (\min(s, t))(\min(x, y)), \qquad s, t, x, y \geqslant 0, \tag{18.43}$$

and initial conditions $B(t, 0) = B(0, x) = 0$ for all $t, x \geqslant 0$.

a) Solve the equation (18.42) for $f(t, x)$.

b) Compute the short-term interest rate $r_t = f(t, 0)$.

c) Compute the value at time $t \in [0, T]$ of the bond price

$$P(t, T) = \exp\left(-\int_0^{T-t} f(t, x) dx\right)$$

with maturity T.

d) Compute the variance $\mathbb{E}\left[\left(\int_0^{T-t} B(t, x) dx\right)^2\right]$ of the centered Gaussian random variable $\int_0^{T-t} B(t, x) dx$.

e) Compute the expected value $\mathbb{E}^*[P(t, T)]$.

f) Find the value of α such that the discounted bond price

$$e^{-rt} P(t, T) = \exp\left(-rT - \frac{\alpha}{3} t (T - t)^3 - \sigma \int_0^{T-t} B(t, x) dx\right), \quad t \in [0, T].$$

satisfies $\mathbb{E}^*[P(t, T)] = e^{-(T-t)r}$.

g) Compute the bond option price $\mathbb{E}^*\left[\exp\left(-\int_0^T r_s ds\right)(P(T, S) - K)^+\right]$ by the Black–Scholes formula, knowing that for any centered Gaussian random variable $X \simeq \mathcal{N}(0, v^2)$ with variance v^2 we have

$$\mathbb{E}[(x e^{m+X} - K)^+]$$
$$= x e^{m+v^2/2} \Phi(v + (m + \log(x/K))/v) - K\Phi((m + \log(x/K))/v).$$

Chapter 19

Pricing of Interest Rate Derivatives

Interest rate derivatives are option contracts whose payoffs can be based on fixed-income securities such as bonds, or on cash flows exchanged in *e.g.* interest rate swaps. In this chapter, we consider the pricing and hedging of interest rate and fixed income derivatives such as bond options, caplets, caps and swaptions, using the change of numéraire technique and forward measures.

19.1   Forward Measures and Tenor Structure

The maturity dates are arranged according to a discrete *tenor structure*

$$\{0 = T_0 < T_1 < T_2 < \cdots < T_n\}.$$

A sample of forward interest rate curve data is given in Table 19.1, which contains the values of $(T_1, T_2, \ldots, T_{23})$ and of $\{f(t, t + T_i, t + T_i + \delta)\}_{i=1,2,\ldots,23}$, with $t = 07/05/2003$ and $\delta = $ six months.

Maturity	2D	1W	1M	2M	3M	1Y	2Y	3Y	4Y	5Y	6Y	7Y
Rate (%)	2.55	2.53	2.56	2.52	2.48	2.34	2.49	2.79	3.07	3.31	3.52	3.71
Maturity	8Y	9Y	10Y	11Y	12Y	13Y	14Y	15Y	20Y	25Y	30Y	
Rate (%)	3.88	4.02	4.14	4.23	4.33	4.40	4.47	4.54	4.74	4.83	4.86	

Table 19.1: Forward rates arranged according to a tenor structure.

Recall that by definition of $P(t, T_i)$ and absence of arbitrage the discounted bond price process

$$t \mapsto e^{-\int_0^t r_s ds} P(t, T_i), \qquad 0 \leqslant t \leqslant T_i,$$

is an $\mathcal{F}_t$-martingale under the probability measure $\mathbb{P}^* = \mathbb{P}$, hence it satisfies the Assumption (A) on page 451 for $i = 1, 2, \ldots, n$. As a consequence the bond price process can be taken as a numéraire

$$N_t^{(i)} := P(t, T_i), \qquad 0 \leqslant t \leqslant T_i,$$

in the definition

$$\frac{d\widehat{\mathbb{P}}_i}{d\mathbb{P}^*} = \frac{1}{P(0, T_i)} e^{-\int_0^{T_i} r_s ds} \tag{19.1}$$

of the *forward measure* $\widehat{\mathbb{P}}_i$, see Definition 16.1. The following proposition will allow us to price contingent claims using the forward measure $\widehat{\mathbb{P}}_i$, it is a direct consequence of Proposition 16.5, noting that here we have $P(T_i, T_i) = 1$.

DOI: 10.1201/9781003298670-19

Proposition 19.1. *For all sufficiently integrable random variables C we have*

$$\mathbb{E}^*\left[C e^{-\int_t^{T_i} r_s ds}\ \bigg|\ \mathcal{F}_t\right] = P(t, T_i)\widehat{\mathbb{E}}_i[C \mid \mathcal{F}_t], \quad 0 \leqslant t \leqslant T_i, \quad i = 1, 2, \ldots, n. \tag{19.2}$$

Recall that by Proposition 16.4, the deflated process

$$t \mapsto \frac{P(t, T_j)}{P(t, T_i)}, \qquad 0 \leqslant t \leqslant \min(T_i, T_j),$$

is an $\mathcal{F}_t$-martingale under $\widehat{\mathbb{P}}_i$ for all $T_i, T_j \geqslant 0$.

In the sequel we assume as in (17.25) that the dynamics of the bond price $P(t, T_i)$ is given by

$$\frac{dP(t, T_i)}{P(t, T_i)} = r_t dt + \zeta_i(t)dW_t, \tag{19.3}$$

for $i = 1, 2, \ldots, n$, where $(W_t)_{t \in \mathbb{R}_+}$ is a standard Brownian motion under $\mathbb{P}^*$ and $(r_t)_{t \in \mathbb{R}_+}$ and $(\zeta_i(t))_{t \in \mathbb{R}_+}$ are adapted processes with respect to the filtration $(\mathcal{F}_t)_{t \in \mathbb{R}_+}$ generated by $(W_t)_{t \in \mathbb{R}_+}$, *i.e.*

$$P(t, T_i) = P(0, T_i)\exp\left(\int_0^t r_s ds + \int_0^t \zeta_i(s)dW_s - \frac{1}{2}\int_0^t |\zeta_i(s)|^2 ds\right),$$

$0 \leqslant t \leqslant T_i$, $i = 1, 2, \ldots, n$.

Forward Brownian motions

Proposition 19.2. *For all $i = 1, 2, \ldots, n$, the process*

$$\widehat{W}_t^i := W_t - \int_0^t \zeta_i(s)ds, \qquad 0 \leqslant t \leqslant T_i, \tag{19.4}$$

is a standard Brownian motion under the forward measure $\widehat{\mathbb{P}}_i$.

Proof. The Girsanov Proposition 16.7 applied to the numéraire

$$N_t^{(i)} := P(t, T_i), \qquad 0 \leqslant t \leqslant T_i,$$

as in (16.13), shows that

$$\begin{aligned}
d\widehat{W}_t^i &:= dW_t - \frac{1}{N_t^{(i)}}dN_t^{(i)} \cdot dW_t \\
&= dW_t - \frac{1}{P(t, T_i)}dP(t, T_i) \cdot dW_t \\
&= dW_t - \frac{1}{P(t, T_i)}(P(t, T_i)r_t dt + \zeta_i(t)P(t, T_i)dW_t) \cdot dW_t \\
&= dW_t - \zeta_i(t)dt,
\end{aligned}$$

is a standard Brownian motion under the forward measure $\widehat{\mathbb{P}}_i$ for all $i = 1, 2, \ldots, n$. $\square$

We have

$$d\widehat{W}_t^i = dW_t - \zeta_i(t)dt, \qquad i = 1, 2, \ldots, n, \tag{19.5}$$

and

$$d\widehat{W}_t^j = dW_t - \zeta_j(t)dt = d\widehat{W}_t^i + (\zeta_i(t) - \zeta_j(t))dt, \quad i, j = 1, 2, \ldots, n,$$

which shows that $(\widehat{W}_t^j)_{t \in \mathbb{R}_+}$ has drift $(\zeta_i(t) - \zeta_j(t))_{t \in \mathbb{R}_+}$ under $\widehat{\mathbb{P}}_i$.

Bond price dynamics under the forward measure

In order to apply Proposition 19.1 and to compute the price

$$\mathbb{E}^* \left[e^{-\int_t^{T_i} r_s ds} C \,\Big|\, \mathcal{F}_t \right] = P(t, T_i) \widehat{\mathbb{E}}_i [C \mid \mathcal{F}_t],$$

of a random claim payoff C, it can be useful to determine the dynamics of the underlying variables r_t, $f(t, T, S)$, and $P(t, T)$ via their stochastic differential equations written under the forward measure $\widehat{\mathbb{P}}_i$.

As a consequence of Proposition 19.2 and (19.3), the dynamics of $t \mapsto P(t, T_j)$ under $\widehat{\mathbb{P}}_i$ is given by

$$\frac{dP(t, T_j)}{P(t, T_j)} = r_t dt + \zeta_i(t) \zeta_j(t) dt + \zeta_j(t) d\widehat{W}_t^i, \quad i, j = 1, 2, \ldots, n, \tag{19.6}$$

where $(\widehat{W}_t^i)_{t \in \mathbb{R}_+}$ is a standard Brownian motion under $\widehat{\mathbb{P}}_i$, and we have

$P(t, T_j)$

$$= P(0, T_j) \exp \left(\int_0^t r_s ds + \int_0^t \zeta_j(s) dW_s - \frac{1}{2} \int_0^t |\zeta_j(s)|^2 ds \right) \qquad \text{[under } \mathbb{P}^*\text{]}$$

$$= P(0, T_j) \exp \left(\int_0^t r_s ds + \int_0^t \zeta_j(s) d\widehat{W}_s^j + \frac{1}{2} \int_0^t |\zeta_j(s)|^2 ds \right) \qquad \text{[under } \widehat{\mathbb{P}}_j\text{]}$$

$$= P(0, T_j) \exp \left(\int_0^t r_s ds + \int_0^t \zeta_j(s) d\widehat{W}_s^i + \int_0^t \zeta_j(s) \zeta_i(s) ds - \frac{1}{2} \int_0^t |\zeta_j(s)|^2 ds \right) \text{ [under } \widehat{\mathbb{P}}_i\text{]}$$

$$= P(0, T_j) \exp \left(\int_0^t r_s ds + \int_0^t \zeta_j(s) d\widehat{W}_s^i - \frac{1}{2} \int_0^t |\zeta_j(s) - \zeta_i(s)|^2 ds + \frac{1}{2} \int_0^t |\zeta_i(s)|^2 ds \right),$$

$t \in [0, T_j]$, $i, j = 1, 2, \ldots, n$. Consequently, the forward price $P(t, T_j)/P(t, T_i)$ can be written as

$$\frac{P(t, T_j)}{P(t, T_i)}$$

$$= \frac{P(0, T_j)}{P(0, T_i)} \exp \left(\int_0^t (\zeta_j(s) - \zeta_i(s)) d\widehat{W}_s^j + \frac{1}{2} \int_0^t |\zeta_j(s) - \zeta_i(s)|^2 ds \right) \qquad \text{[under } \widehat{\mathbb{P}}_j\text{]}$$

$$= \frac{P(0, T_j)}{P(0, T_i)} \exp \left(\int_0^t (\zeta_j(s) - \zeta_i(s)) d\widehat{W}_s^i - \frac{1}{2} \int_0^t |\zeta_i(s) - \zeta_j(s)|^2 ds \right), \qquad \text{[under } \widehat{\mathbb{P}}_i\text{]}$$

$$\tag{19.7}$$

$t \in [0, \min(T_i, T_j)]$, $i, j = 1, 2, \ldots, n$, which also follows from Proposition 16.8.

Short rate dynamics under the forward measure

In case the short rate process $(r_t)_{t \in \mathbb{R}_+}$ is given as the (Markovian) solution to the stochastic differential equation

$$dr_t = \mu(t, r_t) dt + \sigma(t, r_t) dW_t,$$

by (19.5) its dynamics will be given under $\widehat{\mathbb{P}}_i$ by

$$dr_t = \mu(t, r_t) dt + \sigma(t, r_t) \big(\zeta_i(t) dt + d\widehat{W}_t^i \big)$$

$$= \mu(t, r_t) dt + \sigma(t, r_t) \zeta_i(t) dt + \sigma(t, r_t) d\widehat{W}_t^i. \tag{19.8}$$

In the case of the Vašíček (1977) model, by (17.28) we have

$$dr_t = (a - br_t)dt + \sigma dW_t,$$

and

$$\zeta_i(t) = -\frac{\sigma}{b}\left(1 - e^{-b(T_i - t)}\right), \qquad 0 \leqslant t \leqslant T_i,$$

hence from (19.8) we have

$$d\widehat{W}_t^i = dW_t - \zeta_i(t)dt = dW_t + \frac{\sigma}{b}\left(1 - e^{-b(T_i - t)}\right)dt, \tag{19.9}$$

and

$$dr_t = (a - br_t)dt - \frac{\sigma^2}{b}\left(1 - e^{-b(T_i - t)}\right)dt + \sigma d\widehat{W}_t^i \tag{19.10}$$

and we obtain

$$\frac{dP(t, T_i)}{P(t, T_i)} = r_t dt + \frac{\sigma^2}{b^2}\left(1 - e^{-b(T_i - t)}\right)^2 dt - \frac{\sigma}{b}\left(1 - e^{-b(T_i - t)}\right)d\widehat{W}_t^i,$$

from (17.28).

19.2 Bond Options

The next proposition can be obtained as an application of the Margrabe formula (16.30) of Proposition 16.15 by taking $X_t = P(t, T_j)$, $N_t^{(i)} = P(t, T_i)$, and $\widehat{X}_t = X_t / N_t^{(i)} = P(t, T_j)/P(t, T_i)$. In the Vasicek model, this formula has been first obtained in Jamshidian (1989).

We work with a standard Brownian motion $(W_t)_{t \in \mathbb{R}_+}$ under $\mathbb{P}^*$, generating the filtration $(\mathcal{F}_t)_{t \in \mathbb{R}_+}$, and an $(\mathcal{F}_t)_{t \in \mathbb{R}_+}$-adapted short rate process $(r_t)_{t \in \mathbb{R}_+}$.

Proposition 19.3. *Let $0 \leqslant T_i \leqslant T_j$ and assume as in (17.25) that the dynamics of the bond prices $P(t, T_i)$, $P(t, T_j)$ under $\mathbb{P}^*$ are given by*

$$\frac{dP(t, T_i)}{P(t, T_i)} = r_t dt + \zeta_i(t)dW_t, \qquad \frac{dP(t, T_j)}{P(t, T_j)} = r_t dt + \zeta_j(t)dW_t,$$

where $(\zeta_i(t))_{t \in \mathbb{R}_+}$ and $(\zeta_j(t))_{t \in \mathbb{R}_+}$ are deterministic *volatility functions. Then, the price of a bond call option on $P(T_i, T_j)$ with payoff*

$$C := (P(T_i, T_j) - \kappa)^+$$

can be written as

$$\mathbb{E}^*\left[e^{-\int_t^{T_i} r_s ds}(P(T_i, T_j) - \kappa)^+ \,\Big|\, \mathcal{F}_t\right] \tag{19.11}$$

$$= P(t, T_j)\Phi\left(\frac{v(t, T_i)}{2} + \frac{1}{v(t, T_i)}\log\frac{P(t, T_j)}{\kappa P(t, T_i)}\right)$$

$$- \kappa P(t, T_i)\Phi\left(-\frac{v(t, T_i)}{2} + \frac{1}{v(t, T_i)}\log\frac{P(t, T_j)}{\kappa P(t, T_i)}\right),$$

where $v^2(t, T_i) := \int_t^{T_i} |\zeta_i(s) - \zeta_j(s)|^2 ds$ *and*

$$\Phi(x) := \frac{1}{\sqrt{2\pi}} \int_{-\infty}^x e^{-y^2/2} dy, \qquad x \in \mathbb{R},$$

is the Gaussian cumulative distribution function.

Proof. First, we note that using $N_t^{(i)} := P(t, T_i)$ as a numéraire the price of a bond call option on $P(T_i, T_j)$ with payoff $F = (P(T_i, T_j) - \kappa)^+$ can be written from Proposition 16.5 using the forward measure $\widehat{\mathbb{P}}_i$, or directly by (16.9), as

$$\mathbb{E}^* \left[e^{-\int_t^{T_i} r_s ds} (P(T_i, T_j) - \kappa)^+ \, \Big| \, \mathcal{F}_t \right] = P(t, T_i) \widehat{\mathbb{E}}_i \left[(P(T_i, T_j) - \kappa)^+ \, \big| \, \mathcal{F}_t \right]. \tag{19.12}$$

Next, by (19.7) or by solving (16.15) in Proposition 16.8 we can write $P(T_i, T_j)$ as the geometric Brownian motion

$$
\begin{aligned}
P(T_i, T_j) &= \frac{P(T_i, T_j)}{P(T_i, T_i)} \\
&= \frac{P(t, T_j)}{P(t, T_i)} \exp\left(\int_t^{T_i} (\zeta_j(s) - \zeta_i(s)) d\widehat{W}_s^i - \frac{1}{2} \int_t^{T_i} |\zeta_i(s) - \zeta_j(s)|^2 ds \right),
\end{aligned}
$$

under the forward measure $\widehat{\mathbb{P}}_i$, and rewrite (19.12) as

$$
\begin{aligned}
&\mathbb{E}^* \left[e^{-\int_t^{T_i} r_s ds} (P(T_i, T_j) - \kappa)^+ \, \Big| \, \mathcal{F}_t \right] \\
&= P(t, T_i) \widehat{\mathbb{E}}_i \left[\left(\frac{P(t, T_j)}{P(t, T_i)} e^{\int_t^{T_i} (\zeta_j(s) - \zeta_i(s)) d\widehat{W}_s^i - \frac{1}{2} \int_t^{T_i} |\zeta_i(s) - \zeta_j(s)|^2 ds} - \kappa \right)^+ \, \Big| \, \mathcal{F}_t \right] \\
&= \widehat{\mathbb{E}}_i \left[\left(P(t, T_j) e^{\int_t^{T_i} (\zeta_j(s) - \zeta_i(s)) d\widehat{W}_s^i - \frac{1}{2} \int_t^{T_i} |\zeta_i(s) - \zeta_j(s)|^2 ds} - \kappa P(t, T_i) \right)^+ \, \Big| \, \mathcal{F}_t \right].
\end{aligned}
$$

Since $(\zeta_i(s))_{s \in [0, T_i]}$ and $(\zeta_j(s))_{s \in [0, T_j]}$ in (19.3) are deterministic volatility functions, $P(T_i, T_j)$ is a lognormal random variable given $\mathcal{F}_t$ under $\widehat{\mathbb{P}}_i$ and we can use Lemma 7.7 to price the bond option by the zero-rate Black–Scholes formula

$$\mathrm{Bl}\big(P(t, T_j), \kappa P(t, T_i), v(t, T_i)/\sqrt{T_i - t}, 0, T_i - t \big)$$

with underlying asset price $P(t, T_j)$, strike level $\kappa P(t, T_i)$, volatility parameter

$$\frac{v(t, T_i)}{\sqrt{T_i - t}} = \sqrt{\frac{\int_t^{T_i} |\zeta_i(s) - \zeta_j(s)|^2 ds}{T_i - t}},$$

time to maturity $T_i - t$, and zero interest rate, which yields (19.11). $\qquad \square$

Note that from Corollary 16.17 the decomposition (19.11) gives the self-financing portfolio in the assets $P(t, T_i)$ and $P(t, T_j)$ for the claim with payoff $(P(T_i, T_j) - \kappa)^+$.

In the Vasicek case the above bond option price could also be computed from the joint distribution of $\left(r_T, \int_t^T r_s ds \right)$, which is Gaussian, or from the dynamics (19.6)–(19.10) of $P(t, T)$ and r_t under $\widehat{\mathbb{P}}_i$, see Kim (2002) and § 8.3 of Privault (2021).

19.3 Caplet Pricing

An interest rate caplet is an option contract that offers protection against the fluctuations of a variable (or floating) rate with respect to a fixed rate κ. The payoff of a LIBOR caplet on the yield (or spot forward rate) $L(T_i, T_i, T_{i+1})$ with strike level κ can be written as

$$(L(T_i, T_i, T_{i+1}) - \kappa)^+,$$

and priced at time $t \in [0, T_i]$ from Proposition 16.5 using the forward measure $\widehat{\mathbb{P}}_{i+1}$ as

$$\mathbb{E}^* \left[e^{-\int_t^{T_{i+1}} r_s ds} (L(T_i, T_i, T_{i+1}) - \kappa)^+ \,\Big|\, \mathcal{F}_t \right] \tag{19.13}$$

$$= P(t, T_{i+1}) \widehat{\mathbb{E}}_{i+1} \left[(L(T_i, T_i, T_{i+1}) - \kappa)^+ \mid \mathcal{F}_t \right],$$

by taking $N_t^{(i+1)} = P(t, T_{i+1})$ as a numéraire.

Proposition 19.4. *The LIBOR rate*

$$L(t, T_i, T_{i+1}) := \frac{1}{T_{i+1} - T_i} \left(\frac{P(t, T_i)}{P(t, T_{i+1})} - 1 \right), \quad 0 \leqslant t \leqslant T_i < T_{i+1},$$

is a martingale under the forward measure $\widehat{\mathbb{P}}_{i+1}$ defined in (19.1).

Proof. The LIBOR rate $L(t, T_i, T_{i+1})$ is a deflated process according to the forward numéraire process $(P(t, T_{i+1}))_{t \in [0, T_{i+1}]}$. Therefore, by Proposition 16.4 it is a martingale under $\widehat{\mathbb{P}}_{i+1}$. $\qquad\square$

The caplet on $L(T_i, T_i, T_{i+1})$ can be priced at time $t \in [0, T_i]$ as

$$\mathbb{E}^* \left[e^{-\int_t^{T_{i+1}} r_s ds} (L(T_i, T_i, T_{i+1}) - \kappa)^+ \,\Big|\, \mathcal{F}_t \right] \tag{19.14}$$

$$= \mathbb{E}^* \left[e^{-\int_t^{T_{i+1}} r_s ds} \left(\frac{1}{T_{i+1} - T_i} \left(\frac{P(t, T_i)}{P(t, T_{i+1})} - 1 \right) - \kappa \right)^+ \,\Big|\, \mathcal{F}_t \right],$$

where the discount factor is counted from the settlement date T_{i+1}. The next pricing formula (19.16) allows us to price and hedge a caplet using a portfolio based on the bonds $P(t, T_i)$ and $P(t, T_{i+1})$, cf. (19.20) below, when $L(T_i, T_i, T_{i+1})$ is modeled in the BGM model of Section 18.6.

Proposition 19.5. *(Black LIBOR caplet formula).* *Assume that $L(t, T_i, T_{i+1})$ is modeled in the BGM model as*

$$\frac{dL(t, T_i, T_{i+1})}{L(t, T_i, T_{i+1})} = \gamma_i(t) d\widehat{W}_t^{i+1}, \tag{19.15}$$

$0 \leqslant t \leqslant T_i$, $i = 1, 2, \ldots, n-1$, *where $\gamma_i(t)$ is a deterministic volatility function of time $t \in [0, T_i]$, $i = 1, 2, \ldots, n-1$. The caplet on $L(T_i, T_i, T_{i+1})$ with strike level κ is priced at time $t \in [0, T_i]$ as*

$$(T_{i+1} - T_i) \, \mathbb{E}^* \left[e^{-\int_t^{T_{i+1}} r_s ds} (L(T_i, T_i, T_{i+1}) - \kappa)^+ \,\Big|\, \mathcal{F}_t \right] \tag{19.16}$$

$$= (P(t, T_i) - P(t, T_{i+1})) \Phi(d_+(t, T_i)) - \kappa (T_{i+1} - T_i) P(t, T_{i+1}) \Phi(d_-(t, T_i)),$$

$0 \leqslant t \leqslant T_i$, where

$$d_+(t, T_i) = \frac{\log(L(t, T_i, T_{i+1})/\kappa) + (T_i - t)\sigma_i^2(t, T_i)/2}{\sigma_i(t, T_i)\sqrt{T_i - t}}, \qquad (19.17)$$

and

$$d_-(t, T_i) = \frac{\log(L(t, T_i, T_{i+1})/\kappa) - (T_i - t)\sigma_i^2(t, T_i)/2}{\sigma_i(t, T_i)\sqrt{T_i - t}}, \qquad (19.18)$$

and

$$|\sigma_i(t, T_i)|^2 = \frac{1}{T_i - t} \int_t^{T_i} |\gamma_i|^2(s)ds. \qquad (19.19)$$

Proof. Taking $P(t, T_{i+1})$ as a numéraire, the forward price

$$\widehat{X}_t := \frac{P(t, T_i)}{P(t, T_{i+1})} = 1 + (T_{i+1} - T_i)L(T_i, T_i, T_{i+1})$$

and the forward LIBOR rate process $(L(t, T_i, T_{i+1})_{t \in [0, T_i]}$ are martingales under $\widehat{\mathbb{P}}_{i+1}$ by Proposition 19.4, $i = 1, 2, \ldots, n - 1$. More precisely, by (19.15) we have

$$L(T_i, T_i, T_{i+1}) = L(t, T_i, T_{i+1}) \exp\left(\int_t^{T_i} \gamma_i(s)d\widehat{W}_s^{i+1} - \frac{1}{2} \int_t^{T_i} |\gamma_i(s)|^2 ds \right),$$

$0 \leqslant t \leqslant T_i$, *i.e.* $t \mapsto L(t, T_i, T_{i+1})$ is a geometric Brownian motion with time-dependent volatility $\gamma_i(t)$ under $\widehat{\mathbb{P}}_{i+1}$. Hence by (19.13), since $N_{T_{i+1}}^{(i+1)} = 1$, we have

$$\mathbb{E}^*\left[e^{-\int_t^{T_{i+1}} r_s ds}(L(T_i, T_i, T_{i+1}) - \kappa)^+ \Big| \mathcal{F}_t \right]$$

$$= P(t, T_{i+1})\widehat{\mathbb{E}}_{i+1}\left[(L(T_i, T_i, T_{i+1}) - \kappa)^+ \Big| \mathcal{F}_t \right]$$

$$= P(t, T_{i+1}) \left(L(t, T_i, T_{i+1})\Phi(d_+(t, T_i)) - \kappa\Phi(d_-(t, T_i)) \right)$$

$$= P(t, T_{i+1})\mathrm{Bl}(L(t, T_i, T_{i+1}), \kappa, \sigma_i(t, T_i), 0, T_i - t),$$

$t \in [0, T_i]$, where

$$\mathrm{Bl}(x, \kappa, \sigma, 0, \tau) = x\Phi(d_+(t, T_i)) - \kappa\Phi(d_-(t, T_i))$$

is the zero-interest rate Black–Scholes function, with

$$|\sigma_i(t, T_i)|^2 = \frac{1}{T_i - t} \int_t^{T_i} |\gamma_i|^2(s)ds.$$

Therefore, we obtain

$$(T_{i+1} - T_i)\,\mathbb{E}^*\left[e^{-\int_t^{T_{i+1}} r_s ds}(L(T_i, T_i, T_{i+1}) - \kappa)^+ \Big| \mathcal{F}_t \right]$$

$$= P(t, T_{i+1})L(t, T_i, T_{i+1})\Phi(d_+(t, T_i)) - \kappa P(t, T_{i+1})\Phi(d_-(t, T_i))$$

$$= P(t, T_{i+1}) \left(\frac{P(t, T_i)}{P(t, T_{i+1})} - 1 \right) \Phi(d_+(t, T_i))$$

$$\quad - \kappa(T_{i+1} - T_i)P(t, T_{i+1})\Phi(d_-(t, T_i)),$$

which yields (19.16). $\qquad \square$

In addition, from Corollary 16.17 we obtain the self-financing portfolio strategy

$$(\Phi(d_+(t,T_i)), -\Phi(d_+(t,T_i)) - \kappa(T_{i+1} - T_i)\Phi(d_-(t,T_i))) \qquad (19.20)$$

in the bonds priced $(P(t,T_i), P(t,T_{i+1}))$ with maturities T_i and T_{i+1}, cf. Corollary 16.18 and Privault and Teng (2012).

The formula (19.16) can be applied to options on underlying futures or forward contracts on commodities whose prices are modeled according to (19.15), as in the next corollary.

Corollary 19.6. *(Black (1976) formula). Let $L(t,T_i,T_{i+1})$ be modeled as in (19.15) and let the bond price $P(t,T_{i+1})$ be given as $P(t,T_{i+1}) = \mathrm{e}^{-(T_{i+1}-t)r}$. Then, (19.16) becomes*

$$\mathrm{e}^{-(T_{i+1}-t)r} L(t,T_i,T_{i+1})\Phi(d_+(t,T_i)) - \kappa\,\mathrm{e}^{-(T_{i+1}-t)r}\Phi(d_-(t,T_i)),$$

$0 \leqslant t \leqslant T_i$.

Floorlet pricing

The floorlet on $L(T_i,T_i,T_{i+1})$ with strike level κ is a contract with payoff $(\kappa - L(T_i,T_i,T_{i+1}))^+$. Floorlets are analog to put options and can be similarly priced by the call/put parity in the Black–Scholes formula.

Proposition 19.7. *Assume that $L(t,T_i,T_{i+1})$ is modeled in the BGM model as in (19.15). The floorlet on $L(T_i,T_i,T_{i+1})$ with strike level κ is priced at time $t \in [0,T_i]$ as*

$$
\begin{aligned}
&(T_{i+1} - T_i)\,\mathbb{E}^*\left[\mathrm{e}^{-\int_t^{T_{i+1}} r_s ds}(\kappa - L(T_i,T_i,T_{i+1}))^+ \,\Big|\, \mathcal{F}_t\right] \qquad (19.21)\\
&= \kappa(T_{i+1} - T_i)P(t,T_{i+1})\Phi\big(-d_-(t,T_i)\big) - (P(t,T_i) - P(t,T_{i+1}))\Phi\big(-d_+(t,T_i)\big),
\end{aligned}
$$

$0 \leqslant t \leqslant T_i$, *where $d_+(t,T_i)$, $d_-(t,T_i)$ and $|\sigma_i(t,T_i)|^2$ are defined in (19.17)–(19.19).*

Proof. We have

$$
\begin{aligned}
&(T_{i+1} - T_i)\,\mathbb{E}^*\left[\mathrm{e}^{-\int_t^{T_{i+1}} r_s ds}(\kappa - L(T_i,T_i,T_{i+1}))^+ \,\Big|\, \mathcal{F}_t\right]\\
&= (T_{i+1} - T_i)P(t,T_{i+1})\widehat{\mathbb{E}}_{i+1}\left[(\kappa - L(T_i,T_i,T_{i+1}))^+ \,|\, \mathcal{F}_t\right]\\
&= (T_{i+1} - T_i)P(t,T_{i+1})\big(\kappa\Phi\big(-d_-(t,T_i)\big) - (T_{i+1} - T_i)L(t,T_i,T_{i+1})\Phi\big(-d_+(t,T_i)\big)\big)\\
&= (T_{i+1} - T_i)P(t,T_{i+1})\kappa\Phi\big(-d_-(t,T_i)\big) - (P(t,T_i) - P(t,T_{i+1}))\Phi\big(-d_+(t,T_i)\big),
\end{aligned}
$$

$0 \leqslant t \leqslant T_i$. $\qquad\square$

Cap pricing

More generally, one can consider interest rate caps that are relative to a given tenor structure $\{T_1, T_2, \ldots, T_n\}$, with discounted payoff

$$\sum_{k=i}^{j-1}(T_{k+1} - T_k)\,\mathrm{e}^{-\int_t^{T_{k+1}} r_s ds}(L(T_k,T_k,T_{k+1}) - \kappa)^+.$$

Pricing formulas for interest rate caps are easily deduced from analog formulas for caplets, since the payoff of a cap can be decomposed into a sum of caplet payoffs. Thus, the cap price at time $t \in [0, T_i]$ is given by

$$\mathbb{E}^* \left[\sum_{k=i}^{j-1} (T_{k+1} - T_k) \, e^{-\int_t^{T_{k+1}} r_s ds} (L(T_k, T_k, T_{k+1}) - \kappa)^+ \,\middle|\, \mathcal{F}_t \right]$$

$$= \sum_{k=i}^{j-1} (T_{k+1} - T_k) \, \mathbb{E}^* \left[e^{-\int_t^{T_{k+1}} r_s ds} (L(T_k, T_k, T_{k+1}) - \kappa)^+ \,\middle|\, \mathcal{F}_t \right]$$

$$= \sum_{k=i}^{j-1} (T_{k+1} - T_k) P(t, T_{k+1}) \widehat{\mathbb{E}}_{k+1} \left[(L(T_k, T_k, T_{k+1}) - \kappa)^+ \,\middle|\, \mathcal{F}_t \right].$$

$$(19.22)$$

In the BGM model (19.15) the interest rate cap with payoff

$$\sum_{k=i}^{j-1} (T_{k+1} - T_k)(L(T_k, T_k, T_{k+1}) - \kappa)^+$$

can be priced at time $t \in [0, T_1]$ by the Black formula

$$\sum_{k=i}^{j-1} (T_{k+1} - T_k) P(t, T_{k+1}) \mathrm{Bl}(L(t, T_k, T_{k+1}), \kappa, \sigma_k(t, T_k), 0, T_k - t),$$

where

$$|\sigma_k(t, T_k)|^2 = \frac{1}{T_k - t} \int_t^{T_k} |\gamma_k|^2(s) ds.$$

SOFR Caplets

The backward-looking SOFR caplet has payoff $(R(S, T, S) - K)^+$, which is known only at time S. By Jensen's inequality we note the relation

$$\mathbb{E}_S[(R(S, T, S) - K)^+ \mid \mathcal{F}_t] = \mathbb{E}_S[\mathbb{E}_S[(R(S, T, S) - K)^+ \mid \mathcal{F}_T] \mid \mathcal{F}_t]$$

$$\geqslant \mathbb{E}_S[(\mathbb{E}_S[R(S, T, S) \mid \mathcal{F}_T] - K)^+ \mid \mathcal{F}_t]$$

$$= \mathbb{E}_S[(R(T, T, S) - K)^+ \mid \mathcal{F}_t]$$

$$= \mathbb{E}_S[(L(T, T, S) - K)^+ \mid \mathcal{F}_t],$$

hence the backward-looking SOFR caplet is more expensive than the forward-looking LIBOR caplet. The caplet on the SOFR rate $R(T_{i+1}, T_i, T_{i+1})$ with payoff $(R(T_{i+1}, T_i, T_{i+1}) - \kappa)^+$ and strike level κ can be priced at time $t \in [0, T_i]$ with a discount factor counted from the settlement date T_{i+1} from Proposition 16.5 as

$$\mathbb{E}^* \left[e^{-\int_t^{T_{i+1}} r_s ds} (R(T_{i+1}, T_i, T_{i+1}) - \kappa)^+ \,\middle|\, \mathcal{F}_t \right] \qquad (19.23)$$

$$= \mathbb{E}^* \left[e^{-\int_t^{T_{i+1}} r_s ds} \left(\frac{1}{T_{i+1} - T_i} \left(\frac{P(t, T_i)}{P(t, T_{i+1})} - 1 \right) - \kappa \right)^+ \,\middle|\, \mathcal{F}_t \right]$$

$$= P(t, T_{i+1}) \widehat{\mathbb{E}}_{i+1} \left[(R(T_{i+1}, T_i, T_{i+1}) - \kappa)^+ \mid \mathcal{F}_t \right],$$

by taking $N_t^{(i+1)} := P(t, T_{i+1})$ as a numéraire and using the forward measure $\widehat{\mathbb{P}}_{i+1}$.

Proposition 19.8. *The SOFR rate*

$$R(t, T_i, T_{i+1}) := \frac{1}{T_{i+1} - T_i} \left(\frac{P(t, T_i)}{P(t, T_{i+1})} - 1 \right), \quad 0 \leqslant T_i \leqslant t \leqslant T_{i+1},$$

is a martingale under the forward measure $\widehat{\mathbb{P}}_{i+1}$.

Proof. The SOFR rate $R(t, T_i, T_{i+1})$ is a deflated process according to the forward numéraire process $(P(t, T_{i+1}))_{t \in [0, T_{i+1}]}$. Therefore, it is a martingale under $\widehat{\mathbb{P}}_{i+1}$ by Proposition 16.4. □

The next pricing formula (19.25) allows us to price and hedge a caplet using a portfolio based on the bonds $P(t, T_i)$ and $P(t, T_{i+1})$, cf. (19.26) below, when $R(t, T_i, T_{i+1})$ is modeled in the BGM model.

Proposition 19.9. *(Black SOFR caplet formula). Assume that* $R(t, T_i, T_{i+1})$ *is modeled in the BGM model as*

$$\frac{dR(t, T_i, T_{i+1})}{R(t, T_i, T_{i+1})} = \gamma_i(t) d\widehat{W}_t^{i+1}, \tag{19.24}$$

$0 \leqslant t \leqslant T_{i+1}$, $i = 1, 2, \ldots, n-1$, *where* $\gamma_i(t)$ *is a deterministic volatility function of time* $t \in [0, T_i]$, $i = 1, 2, \ldots, n-1$. *The caplet on* $R(T_{i+1}, T_i, T_{i+1})$ *with strike level* $\kappa > 0$ *is priced at time* $t \in [0, T_{i+1}]$ *as*

$$
\begin{aligned}
&(T_{i+1} - T_i) \, \mathbb{E}^* \left[e^{- \int_t^{T_{i+1}} r_s ds} (R(T_{i+1}, T_i, T_{i+1}) - \kappa)^+ \,\Big|\, \mathcal{F}_t \right] \\
&= (P(t, T_i) - P(t, T_{i+1})) \Phi(d_+(t, T_{i+1})) - \kappa (T_{i+1} - T_i) P(t, T_{i+1}) \Phi(d_-(t, T_{i+1})),
\end{aligned}
\tag{19.25}
$$

$0 \leqslant t \leqslant T_{i+1}$, *where*

$$d_+(t, T_{i+1}) = \frac{\log(R(t, T_i, T_{i+1})/\kappa) + (T_{i+1} - t)\sigma_i^2(t, T_{i+1})/2}{\sigma_i(t, T_{i+1})\sqrt{T_{i+1} - t}},$$

and

$$d_-(t, T_{i+1}) = \frac{\log(R(t, T_i, T_{i+1})/\kappa) - (T_{i+1} - t)\sigma_i^2(t, T_{i+1})/2}{\sigma_i(t, T_{i+1})\sqrt{T_{i+1} - t}},$$

and

$$|\sigma_i(t, T_{i+1})|^2 = \frac{1}{T_{i+1} - t} \int_t^{T_{i+1}} |\gamma_i|^2(s) ds.$$

Proof. The forward price

$$\widehat{X}_t := \frac{P(t, T_i)}{P(t, T_{i+1})} = 1 + (T_{i+1} - T_i) R(T_{i+1}, T_i, T_{i+1})$$

and the SOFR rate process $(R(t, T_i, T_{i+1})_{t \in [0, T_{i+1}]}$ are martingales under $\widehat{\mathbb{P}}_{i+1}$ by Proposition 19.8, $i = 1, 2, \ldots, n-1$, and

$$R(T_{i+1}, T_i, T_{i+1}) = R(t, T_i, T_{i+1}) \exp \left(\int_t^{T_{i+1}} \gamma_i(s) d\widehat{W}_s^{i+1} - \frac{1}{2} \int_t^{T_{i+1}} |\gamma_i(s)|^2 ds \right),$$

$0 \leqslant t \leqslant T_{i+1}$, where $t \mapsto R(t, T_i, T_{i+1})$ is a geometric Brownian motion under $\widehat{\mathbb{P}}_{i+1}$ (19.24). Hence by (19.23) we have

$$
\mathbb{E}^* \left[\mathrm{e}^{- \int_t^{T_{i+1}} r_s ds} (R(T_{i+1}, T_i, T_{i+1}) - \kappa)^+ \,\middle|\, \mathcal{F}_t \right]
$$

$$
\begin{aligned}
&= P(t, T_{i+1}) \widehat{\mathbb{E}}_{i+1} \big[(R(T_{i+1}, T_i, T_{i+1}) - \kappa)^+ \,\big|\, \mathcal{F}_t \big] \\
&= P(t, T_{i+1}) \left(R(t, T_i, T_{i+1}) \Phi(d_+(t, T_{i+1})) - \kappa \Phi(d_-(t, T_{i+1})) \right) \\
&= P(t, T_{i+1}) \mathrm{Bl}(R(t, T_i, T_{i+1}), \kappa, \sigma_i(t, T_{i+1}), 0, T_{i+1} - t),
\end{aligned}
$$

$t \in [0, T_{i+1}]$, with

$$
|\sigma_i(t, T_{i+1})|^2 = \frac{1}{T_{i+1} - t} \int_t^{T_{i+1}} |\gamma_i|^2(s) ds.
$$

$\square$

In addition, we obtain the self-financing portfolio strategy

$$
(\Phi(d_+(t, T_{i+1})), -\Phi(d_+(t, T_{i+1})) - \kappa(T_{i+1} - T_i)\Phi(d_-(t, T_{i+1}))) \tag{19.26}
$$

in the bonds priced $(P(t, T_i), P(t, T_{i+1}))$, $t \in [0, T_{i+1}]$, with maturities T_i and T_{i+1}.

19.4   Forward Swap Measures

In this section we introduce the forward swap (or annuity) measures, or annuity measures, to be used for the pricing of swaptions, and we study their properties. We start with the definition of the *annuity numéraire*

$$
N_t^{(i,j)} := P(t, T_i, T_j) = \sum_{k=i}^{j-1} (T_{k+1} - T_k) P(t, T_{k+1}), \qquad 0 \leqslant t \leqslant T_i, \tag{19.27}
$$

with in particular, when $j = i + 1$,

$$
P(t, T_i, T_{i+1}) = (T_{i+1} - T_i) P(t, T_{i+1}), \qquad 0 \leqslant t \leqslant T_i.
$$

$1 \leqslant i < n$. The annuity numéraire can be also used to price a *bond ladder*. It satisfies the following martingale property, which can be proved by linearity and the fact that $t \mapsto \mathrm{e}^{- \int_0^t r_s ds} P(t, T_k)$ is a martingale for all $k = 1, 2, \ldots, n$, under Assumption (A).

Remark 19.10. *The discounted annuity numéraire*

$$
t \mapsto \mathrm{e}^{- \int_0^t r_s ds} P(t, T_i, T_j) = \mathrm{e}^{- \int_0^t r_s ds} \sum_{k=i}^{j-1} (T_{k+1} - T_k) P(t, T_{k+1}), \quad 0 \leqslant t \leqslant T_i,
$$

is a martingale under $\mathbb{P}^*$.

The forward swap measure $\widehat{\mathbb{P}}_{i,j}$ is defined, according to Definition 16.1, by

$$
\frac{\mathrm{d}\widehat{\mathbb{P}}_{i,j}}{\mathrm{d}\mathbb{P}^*} := \mathrm{e}^{- \int_0^{T_i} r_s ds} \frac{N_{T_i}^{(i,j)}}{N_0^{(i,j)}} = \mathrm{e}^{- \int_0^{T_i} r_s ds} \frac{P(T_i, T_i, T_j)}{P(0, T_i, T_j)}, \tag{19.28}
$$

$1 \leqslant i < j \leqslant n$.

Remark 19.11. *We have*

$$
\mathbb{E}^* \left[\frac{d\widehat{\mathbb{P}}_{i,j}}{d\mathbb{P}^*} \,\middle|\, \mathcal{F}_t \right] = \frac{1}{P(0, T_i, T_j)} \mathbb{E}^* \left[e^{-\int_0^{T_i} r_s ds} P(T_i, T_i, T_j) \,\middle|\, \mathcal{F}_t \right]
$$

$$
= \frac{1}{P(0, T_i, T_j)} \mathbb{E}^* \left[e^{-\int_0^{T_i} r_s ds} \sum_{k=i}^{j-1} (T_{k+1} - T_k) P(T_i, T_{k+1}) \,\middle|\, \mathcal{F}_t \right]
$$

$$
= \frac{1}{P(0, T_i, T_j)} \sum_{k=i}^{j-1} (T_{k+1} - T_k) \mathbb{E}^* \left[e^{-\int_0^{T_i} r_s ds} P(T_i, T_{k+1}) \,\middle|\, \mathcal{F}_t \right]
$$

$$
= \frac{1}{P(0, T_i, T_j)} e^{-\int_0^t r_s ds} \sum_{k=i}^{j-1} (T_{k+1} - T_k) P(t, T_{k+1})
$$

$$
= e^{-\int_0^t r_s ds} \frac{P(t, T_i, T_j)}{P(0, T_i, T_j)},
$$

$0 \leqslant t \leqslant T_i$, *by Remark 19.10, and*

$$
\frac{d\widehat{\mathbb{P}}_{i,j|\mathcal{F}_t}}{d\mathbb{P}^*_{|\mathcal{F}_t}} = e^{-\int_t^{T_i} r_s ds} \frac{P(T_i, T_i, T_j)}{P(t, T_i, T_j)}, \qquad 0 \leqslant t \leqslant T_{i+1}, \tag{19.29}
$$

by Relation (16.3) in Lemma 16.2.

Proposition 19.12. *The LIBOR swap rate*

$$
S(t, T_i, T_j) = \frac{P(t, T_i) - P(t, T_j)}{P(t, T_i, T_j)}, \qquad 0 \leqslant t \leqslant T_i,
$$

see Corollary 18.11, is a martingale under the forward swap measure $\widehat{\mathbb{P}}_{i,j}$.

Proof. We use the fact that the deflated process

$$
t \mapsto \frac{P(t, T_k)}{P(t, T_i, T_j)}, \qquad i, j, k = 1, 2, \ldots, n,
$$

is an $\mathcal{F}_t$-martingale under $\widehat{\mathbb{P}}_{i,j}$ by Proposition 16.4. $\qquad \square$

The following pricing formula is then stated for a given integrable claim with payoff of the form $P(T_i, T_i, T_j)F$, using the forward swap measure $\widehat{\mathbb{P}}_{i,j}$:

$$
\mathbb{E}^* \left[e^{-\int_t^{T_i} r_s ds} P(T_i, T_i, T_j) F \,\middle|\, \mathcal{F}_t \right] = P(t, T_i, T_j) \mathbb{E}^* \left[F \frac{d\widehat{\mathbb{P}}_{i,j|\mathcal{F}_t}}{d\mathbb{P}^*_{|\mathcal{F}_t}} \,\middle|\, \mathcal{F}_t \right]
$$

$$
= P(t, T_i, T_j) \widehat{\mathbb{E}}_{i,j}[F \mid \mathcal{F}_t], \tag{19.30}
$$

after applying (19.28) and (19.29) on the last line, or Proposition 16.5.

19.5 Swaption Pricing

Definition 19.13. *A payer (or call) swaption gives the option, but not the obligation, to enter an interest rate swap as payer of a fixed rate κ and as receiver of floating LIBOR rates $L(T_i, T_k, T_{k+1})$ at time T_{k+1}, $k = i, \ldots, j-1$, and has the payoff*

$$\left(\sum_{k=i}^{j-1} (T_{k+1} - T_k) \, \mathbb{E}^* \left[\mathrm{e}^{-\int_{T_i}^{T_{k+1}} r_s ds} \,\middle|\, \mathcal{F}_{T_i} \right] (L(T_i, T_k, T_{k+1}) - \kappa) \right)^+$$

$$= \left(\sum_{k=i}^{j-1} (T_{k+1} - T_k) P(T_i, T_{k+1})(L(T_i, T_k, T_{k+1}) - \kappa) \right)^+ \qquad (19.31)$$

at time T_i.

This swaption can be priced at time $t \in [0, T_i]$ under the risk-neutral probability measure $\mathbb{P}^*$ as

$$\mathbb{E}^* \left[\mathrm{e}^{-\int_t^{T_i} r_s ds} \left(\sum_{k=i}^{j-1} (T_{k+1} - T_k) P(T_i, T_{k+1})(L(T_i, T_k, T_{k+1}) - \kappa) \right)^+ \,\middle|\, \mathcal{F}_t \right], \qquad (19.32)$$

$t \in [0, T_i]$. When $j = i+1$, the swaption price (19.32) coincides with the price at time t of a caplet on $[T_i, T_{i+1}]$ up to a factor $\delta_i := T_{i+1} - T_i$, since

$$\mathbb{E}^* \left[\mathrm{e}^{-\int_t^{T_i} r_s ds} \left((T_{i+1} - T_i) P(T_i, T_{i+1})(L(T_i, T_i, T_{i+1}) - \kappa) \right)^+ \,\middle|\, \mathcal{F}_t \right]$$

$$= (T_{i+1} - T_i) \, \mathbb{E}^* \left[\mathrm{e}^{-\int_t^{T_i} r_s ds} P(T_i, T_{i+1}) \left(L(T_i, T_i, T_{i+1}) - \kappa \right)^+ \,\middle|\, \mathcal{F}_t \right]$$

$$= (T_{i+1} - T_i) \, \mathbb{E}^* \left[\mathrm{e}^{-\int_t^{T_i} r_s ds} \mathbb{E}^* \left[\mathrm{e}^{-\int_{T_i}^{T_{i+1}} r_s ds} \,\middle|\, \mathcal{F}_{T_i} \right] \left(L(T_i, T_i, T_{i+1}) - \kappa \right)^+ \,\middle|\, \mathcal{F}_t \right]$$

$$= (T_{i+1} - T_i) \, \mathbb{E}^* \left[\mathbb{E}^* \left[\mathrm{e}^{-\int_t^{T_i} r_s ds} \mathrm{e}^{-\int_{T_i}^{T_{i+1}} r_s ds} \left(L(T_i, T_i, T_{i+1}) - \kappa \right)^+ \,\middle|\, \mathcal{F}_{T_i} \right] \,\middle|\, \mathcal{F}_t \right]$$

$$= (T_{i+1} - T_i) \, \mathbb{E}^* \left[\mathrm{e}^{-\int_t^{T_{i+1}} r_s ds} \left(L(T_i, T_i, T_{i+1}) - \kappa \right)^+ \,\middle|\, \mathcal{F}_t \right], \qquad (19.33)$$

$0 \leqslant t \leqslant T_i$, which coincides with the caplet price (19.13) up to the factor $T_{i+1} - T_i$. Unlike in the case of interest rate caps, the sum in (19.32) cannot be taken out of the positive part. Nevertheless, the price of the swaption can be bounded as in the next proposition.

Proposition 19.14. *The payer swaption price (19.32) can be upper bounded by the interest rate cap price (19.22) as*

$$\mathbb{E}^* \left[\mathrm{e}^{-\int_t^{T_i} r_s ds} \left(\sum_{k=i}^{j-1} (T_{k+1} - T_k) P(T_i, T_{k+1})(L(T_i, T_k, T_{k+1}) - \kappa) \right)^+ \,\middle|\, \mathcal{F}_t \right]$$

$$\leqslant \sum_{k=i}^{j-1} (T_{k+1} - T_k) \, \mathbb{E}^* \left[\mathrm{e}^{-\int_t^{T_{k+1}} r_s ds} \left(L(T_i, T_k, T_{k+1}) - \kappa \right)^+ \,\middle|\, \mathcal{F}_t \right],$$

$0 \leqslant t \leqslant T_i$.

Proof. Due to the inequality

$$(x_1 + x_2 + \cdots + x_m)^+ \leqslant x_1^+ + x_2^+ + \cdots + x_m^+, \quad x_1, x_2, \ldots, x_m \in \mathbb{R},$$

we have

$$\mathbb{E}^* \left[e^{-\int_t^{T_i} r_s ds} \left(\sum_{k=i}^{j-1} (T_{k+1} - T_k) P(T_i, T_{k+1}) (L(T_i, T_k, T_{k+1}) - \kappa) \right)^+ \bigg| \mathcal{F}_t \right]$$

$$\leqslant \mathbb{E}^* \left[e^{-\int_t^{T_i} r_s ds} \sum_{k=i}^{j-1} (T_{k+1} - T_k) P(T_i, T_{k+1}) (L(T_i, T_k, T_{k+1}) - \kappa)^+ \bigg| \mathcal{F}_t \right]$$

$$= \sum_{k=i}^{j-1} (T_{k+1} - T_k) \mathbb{E}^* \left[e^{-\int_t^{T_i} r_s ds} P(T_i, T_{k+1}) (L(T_i, T_k, T_{k+1}) - \kappa)^+ \bigg| \mathcal{F}_t \right]$$

$$= \sum_{k=i}^{j-1} (T_{k+1} - T_k) \mathbb{E}^* \left[e^{-\int_t^{T_i} r_s ds} \mathbb{E}^* \left[e^{-\int_{T_i}^{T_{k+1}} r_s ds} \bigg| \mathcal{F}_{T_i} \right] (L(T_i, T_k, T_{k+1}) - \kappa)^+ \bigg| \mathcal{F}_t \right]$$

$$= \sum_{k=i}^{j-1} (T_{k+1} - T_k) \mathbb{E}^* \left[\mathbb{E}^* \left[e^{-\int_t^{T_{k+1}} r_s ds} (L(T_i, T_k, T_{k+1}) - \kappa)^+ \bigg| \mathcal{F}_{T_i} \right] \bigg| \mathcal{F}_t \right]$$

$$= \sum_{k=i}^{j-1} (T_{k+1} - T_k) \mathbb{E}^* \left[e^{-\int_t^{T_{k+1}} r_s ds} (L(T_i, T_k, T_{k+1}) - \kappa)^+ \bigg| \mathcal{F}_t \right]$$

$$= \mathbb{E}^* \left[\sum_{k=i}^{j-1} (T_{k+1} - T_k) e^{-\int_t^{T_{k+1}} r_s ds} (L(T_i, T_k, T_{k+1}) - \kappa)^+ \bigg| \mathcal{F}_t \right],$$

$0 \leqslant t \leqslant T_i$. $\square$

The payoff of the payer swaption can be rewritten as in the following lemma which is a direct consequence of the definition of the swap rate $S(T_i, T_i, T_j)$, see Proposition 18.10 and Corollary 18.11.

Lemma 19.15. *The payer swaption payoff* (19.31) *at time* T_i *with swap rate* $\kappa = S(t, T_j, T_j)$ *can be rewritten as*

$$\left(\sum_{k=i}^{j-1} (T_{k+1} - T_k) P(T_i, T_{k+1}) (L(T_i, T_k, T_{k+1}) - \kappa) \right)^+$$

$$= (P(T_i, T_i) - P(T_i, T_j) - \kappa P(T_i, T_i, T_j))^+ \qquad (19.34)$$

$$= P(T_i, T_i, T_j) (S(T_i, T_i, T_j) - \kappa)^+. \qquad (19.35)$$

Proof. The relation

$$\sum_{k=i}^{j-1} (T_{k+1} - T_k) P(t, T_{k+1}) (L(t, T_k, T_{k+1}) - S(t, T_i, T_j)) = 0$$

that defines the forward swap rate $S(t, T_i, T_j)$ shows that

$$\sum_{k=i}^{j-1}(T_{k+1} - T_k)P(t, T_{k+1})L(t, T_k, T_{k+1})$$

$$= S(t, T_i, T_j)\sum_{k=i}^{j-1}(T_{k+1} - T_k)P(t, T_{k+1})$$

$$= P(t, T_i, T_j)S(t, T_i, T_j)$$

$$= P(t, T_i) - P(t, T_j)$$

as in the proof of Corollary 18.11, hence by the definition (19.27) of $P(t, T_i, T_j)$ we have

$$\sum_{k=i}^{j-1}(T_{k+1} - T_k)P(t, T_{k+1})(L(t, T_k, T_{k+1}) - \kappa)$$

$$= P(t, T_i) - P(t, T_j) - \kappa P(t, T_i, T_j)$$

$$= P(t, T_i, T_j)\left(S(t, T_i, T_j) - \kappa\right),$$

and for $t = T_i$ we get

$$\left(\sum_{k=i}^{j-1}(T_{k+1} - T_k)P(T_i, T_{k+1})(L(T_i, T_k, T_{k+1}) - \kappa)\right)^+$$

$$= P(T_i, T_i, T_j)\left(S(T_i, T_i, T_j) - \kappa\right)^+.$$

$\square$

The next proposition simply states that a payer swaption on the LIBOR rate can be priced as a European call option on the swap rate $S(T_i, T_i, T_j)$ under the forward swap measure $\widehat{\mathbb{P}}_{i,j}$.

Proposition 19.16. *The price (19.32) of the payer swaption with payoff*

$$\left(\sum_{k=i}^{j-1}(T_{k+1} - T_k)P(T_i, T_{k+1})(L(T_i, T_k, T_{k+1}) - \kappa)\right)^+ \qquad (19.36)$$

on the LIBOR market can be written under the forward swap measure $\widehat{\mathbb{P}}_{i,j}$ as the European call price

$$P(t, T_i, T_j)\widehat{\mathbb{E}}_{i,j}\left[(S(T_i, T_i, T_j) - \kappa)^+ \big| \mathcal{F}_t\right], \qquad 0 \leqslant t \leqslant T_i,$$

on the swap rate $S(T_i, T_i, T_j)$.

Proof. As a consequence of (19.30) and Lemma 19.15, we find

$$\mathbb{E}^*\left[e^{-\int_t^{T_i} r_s ds}\left(\sum_{k=i}^{j-1}(T_{k+1} - T_k)P(T_i, T_{k+1})(L(T_i, T_k, T_{k+1}) - \kappa)\right)^+ \bigg| \mathcal{F}_t\right]$$

$$= \mathbb{E}^*\left[e^{-\int_t^{T_i} r_s ds}(P(T_i, T_i) - P(T_i, T_j) - \kappa P(T_i, T_i, T_j))^+ \big| \mathcal{F}_t\right] \qquad (19.37)$$

$$= \mathbb{E}^*\left[e^{-\int_t^{T_i} r_s ds}P(T_i, T_i, T_j)\left(S(T_i, T_i, T_j) - \kappa\right)^+ \big| \mathcal{F}_t\right]$$

$$= P(t, T_i, T_j) \, \mathbb{E}^* \left[\frac{d\widehat{\mathbb{P}}_{i,j|\mathcal{F}_t}}{d\mathbb{P}^*_{|\mathcal{F}_t}} \left(S(T_i, T_i, T_j) - \kappa \right)^+ \Big| \mathcal{F}_t \right]$$

$$= P(t, T_i, T_j) \widehat{\mathbb{E}}_{i,j} \left[\left(S(T_i, T_i, T_j) - \kappa \right)^+ \big| \mathcal{F}_t \right]. \tag{19.38}$$

$\square$

In the next Proposition 19.17 we price the payer swaption with payoff (19.36) or equivalently (19.35), by modeling the swap rate $(S(t, T_i, T_j))_{0 \leqslant t \leqslant T_i}$ using standard Brownian motion $(\widehat{W}^{i,j}_t)_{0 \leqslant t \leqslant T_i}$ under the swap forward measure $\widehat{\mathbb{P}}_{i,j}$. See Exercise 19 for swaption pricing without the Black–Scholes formula.

Proposition 19.17. *(Black swaption formula for payer swaptions). Assume that the LIBOR swap rate (18.19) is modeled as a geometric Brownian motion under $\widehat{\mathbb{P}}_{i,j}$, i.e.*

$$dS(t, T_i, T_j) = S(t, T_i, T_j) \widehat{\sigma}_{i,j}(t) d\widehat{W}^{i,j}_t, \tag{19.39}$$

where $\left(\widehat{\sigma}_{i,j}(t) \right)_{t \in \mathbb{R}_+}$ is a deterministic volatility function of time. Then, the payer swaption with payoff

$$\left(P(T, T_i) - P(T, T_j) - \kappa P(T_i, T_i, T_j) \right)^+ = P(T_i, T_i, T_j) \left(S(T_i, T_i, T_j) - \kappa \right)^+$$

can be priced using the Black–Scholes call formula as

$$\mathbb{E}^* \left[e^{- \int_t^{T_i} r_s ds} P(T_i, T_i, T_j) \left(S(T_i, T_i, T_j) - \kappa \right)^+ \Big| \mathcal{F}_t \right]$$

$$= \left(P(t, T_i) - P(t, T_j) \right) \Phi(d_+(t, T_i))$$

$$- \kappa \Phi(d_-(t, T_i)) \sum_{k=i}^{j-1} (T_{k+1} - T_k) P(t, T_{k+1}),$$

$t \in [0, T_i]$, *where*

$$d_+(t, T_i) = \frac{\log(S(t, T_i, T_j)/\kappa) + \sigma^2_{i,j}(t, T_i)(T_i - t)/2}{\sigma_{i,j}(t, T_i)\sqrt{T_i - t}}, \tag{19.40}$$

and

$$d_-(t, T_i) = \frac{\log(S(t, T_i, T_j)/\kappa) - \sigma^2_{i,j}(t, T_i)(T_i - t)/2}{\sigma_{i,j}(t, T_i)\sqrt{T_i - t}}, \tag{19.41}$$

and

$$|\sigma_{i,j}(t, T_i)|^2 = \frac{1}{T_i - t} \int_t^{T_i} |\widehat{\sigma}_{i,j}(s)|^2 ds, \qquad 0 \leqslant t \leqslant T_i. \tag{19.42}$$

Proof. Since $S(t, T_i, T_j)$ is a geometric Brownian motion with volatility function $(\widehat{\sigma}(t))_{t \in \mathbb{R}_+}$ under $\widehat{\mathbb{P}}_{i,j}$, by (19.34)–(19.35) in Lemma 19.15 or (19.37)–(19.38) we have

$$\mathbb{E}^* \left[e^{- \int_t^{T_i} r_s ds} P(T_i, T_i, T_j) \left(S(T_i, T_i, T_j) - \kappa \right)^+ \Big| \mathcal{F}_t \right]$$

$$= \mathbb{E}^* \left[e^{- \int_t^{T} r_s ds} \left(P(T, T_i) - P(T, T_j) - \kappa P(T_i, T_i, T_j) \right)^+ \Big| \mathcal{F}_t \right]$$

$$= P(t, T_i, T_j) \widehat{\mathbb{E}}_{i,j} \left[\left(S(T_i, T_i, T_j) - \kappa \right)^+ \big| \mathcal{F}_t \right]$$

$$= P(t, T_i, T_j) \mathrm{Bl}(S(t, T_i, T_j), \kappa, \sigma_{i,j}(t, T_i), 0, T_i - t)$$

$$
\begin{aligned}
&= \; P(t,T_i,T_j)\left(S(t,T_i,T_j)\Phi_+(t,S(t,T_i,T_j)) - \kappa\Phi_-(t,S(t,T_i,T_j))\right) \\
&= \; \left(P(t,T_i) - P(t,T_j)\right)\Phi_+(t,S(t,T_i,T_j)) - \kappa P(t,T_i,T_j)\Phi_-(t,S(t,T_i,T_j)) \\
&= \; \left(P(t,T_i) - P(t,T_j)\right)\Phi_+(t,S(t,T_i,T_j)) \\
&\quad -\kappa\Phi_-(t,S(t,T_i,T_j))\sum_{k=i}^{j-1}(T_{k+1}-T_k)P(t,T_{k+1}).
\end{aligned}
$$

$\square$

In addition, the hedging strategy

$$
\begin{aligned}
&\left(\Phi_+(t,S(t,T_i,T_j)), -\kappa\Phi_-(t,S(t,T_i,T_j))(T_{i+1}-T_i), \ldots\right. \\
&\left. \ldots, -\kappa\Phi_-(t,S(t,T_i,T_j))(T_{j-1}-T_{j-2}), -\Phi_+(t,S(t,T_i,T_j))\right)
\end{aligned}
$$

based on the assets $(P(t,T_i),\ldots,P(t,T_j))$ is self-financing by Corollary 16.18, see also Privault and Teng (2012). Similarly to the above, a receiver (or put) swaption gives the option, but not the obligation, to enter an interest rate swap as receiver of a fixed rate κ and as payer of floating LIBOR rates $L(T_i,T_k,T_{k+1})$ at times $T_{i+1},\ldots,T_j$, and can be priced as in the next proposition.

Proposition 19.18. *(Black swaption formula for receiver swaptions). Assume that the LIBOR swap rate (18.19) is modeled as the geometric Brownian motion (19.39) under the forward swap measure $\widehat{\mathbb{P}}_{i,j}$. Then, the receiver swaption with payoff*

$$
\left(\kappa P(T_i,T_i,T_j) - \left(P(T,T_i) - P(T,T_j)\right)\right)^+ = P(T_i,T_i,T_j)\left(\kappa - S(T_i,T_i,T_j)\right)^+
$$

can be priced using the Black–Scholes put formula as

$$
\begin{aligned}
\mathbb{E}^*&\left[e^{-\int_t^{T_i} r_s ds} P(T_i,T_i,T_j)\left(\kappa - S(T_i,T_i,T_j)\right)^+ \Big| \mathcal{F}_t\right] \\
&= \; \kappa\Phi(-d_-(t,T_i))\sum_{k=i}^{j-1}(T_{k+1}-T_k)P(t,T_{k+1}) \\
&\quad -(P(t,T_i) - P(t,T_j))\Phi(-d_+(t,T_i)),
\end{aligned}
$$

where $d_+(t,T_i)$, and $d_-(t,T_i)$ and $|\sigma_{i,j}(t,T_i)|^2$ are defined in (19.40)–(19.42).

When the SOFR swap rate (18.23) is modeled as a geometric Brownian motion under $\widehat{\mathbb{P}}_{i,j}$ as in (19.39), SOFR swaptions are priced in the same way as LIBOR swaptions.

Swaption prices can also be computed by an approximation formula, from the exact dynamics of the swap rate $S(t,T_i,T_j)$ under the forward swap measure $\widehat{\mathbb{P}}_{i,j}$, based on the bond price dynamics of the form (19.3), cf. Schoenmakers (2005), page 17.

Swaption volatilities can be estimated from swaption prices as implied volatilities from the Black pricing formula:

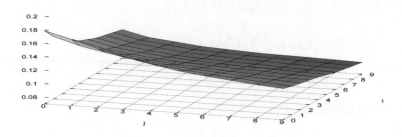

Figure 19.1: Implied swaption volatilities.

Implied swaption volatilities can then be used to calibrate the BGM model, cf. Schoenmakers (2005), Privault and Wei (2009), or § 9.5 of Privault (2021).

LIBOR-SOFR Swaps

We consider the swap contract with payoff

$$\sum_{k=i}^{j-1}(T_{k+1} - T_k)(R(T_{k+1}, T_k, T_{k+1}) - L(T_k, T_k, T_{k+1})),$$

for the exchange of a backward-looking SOFR rate $R(T_{k+1}, T_k, T_{k+1})$ with the forward-looking LIBOR rate $L(T_k, T_k, T_{k+1})$ over the time period $[T_k, T_{k+1}]$. The price of this interest rate swap vanishes at any time $t \in [0, T_1]$, as

$$(T_{k+1} - T_k)\, \mathbb{E}\left[e^{-\int_t^{T_{k+1}} r_s ds}(R(T_{k+1}, T_k, T_{k+1}) - L(T_k, T_k, T_{k+1})) \,\Big|\, \mathcal{F}_t \right]$$
$$= (T_{k+1} - T_k)P(t, T_{k+1})\, \mathbb{E}_{k+1}[R(T_{k+1}, T_k, T_{k+1}) - L(T_k, T_k, T_{k+1}) \mid \mathcal{F}_t]$$
$$= (T_{k+1} - T_k)P(t, T_{k+1})(R(t, T_k, T_{k+1}) - L(t, T_k, T_{k+1})$$
$$= 0, \qquad 0 \leqslant t \leqslant T_k.$$

see Mercurio (2018). On the other hand, for any $i = 1, \ldots, n$, we also have

$$(T_{k+1} - T_k)\, \mathbb{E}\left[e^{-\int_t^{T_{k+1}} r_s ds}(R(T_{k+1}, T_k, T_{k+1}) - L(T_k, T_k, T_{k+1})) \,\Big|\, \mathcal{F}_{T_i} \right]$$
$$= (T_{k+1} - T_k)P(T_i, T_{k+1})\, \mathbb{E}_{k+1}[R(T_{k+1}, T_k, T_{k+1}) - L(T_k, T_k, T_{k+1}) \mid \mathcal{F}_{T_k}]$$
$$= (T_{k+1} - T_k)P(T_i, T_{k+1})(R(T_i, T_k, T_{k+1}) - L(T_i, T_k, T_{k+1}))$$
$$= 0.$$

Exercises

Exercise 19.1 Consider a floorlet on a three-month LIBOR rate in nine month's time, with a notional principal amount of $10,000 per interest rate percentage point. The term structure is flat at 3.95% per year with discrete compounding, the volatility of the forward LIBOR rate in nine months is 10%, and the floor rate is 4.5%.

a) What are the key assumptions on the LIBOR rate in nine month in order to apply Black's formula to price this floorlet?

b) Compute the price of this floorlet using Black's formula as an application of Proposition 19.7 and (19.21), using the functions $\Phi(d_+)$ and $\Phi(d_-)$.

Exercise 19.2 Consider a payer swaption giving its holder the right, but not the obligation, to enter into a 3-year annual pay swap in four years, where a fixed rate of 5% will be paid and the LIBOR rate will be received. Assume that the yield curve is flat at 5% with continuous annual compounding and the volatility of the swap rate is 20%. The notional principal is $100,000 per interest rate percentage point.

a) What are the key assumptions in order to apply Black's formula to value this swaption?

b) Compute the price of this swaption using Black's formula as an application of Proposition 19.17.

Exercise 19.3 Consider a *receiver* swaption which is giving its holder the right, but not the obligation, to enter into a 2-year annual pay swap in three years, where a fixed rate of 5% will be received and the LIBOR rate will be paid. Assume that the yield curve is flat at 2% with continuous annual compounding and the volatility of the swap rate is 10%. The notional principal is $10,000 per percentage point, and the swaption price is quoted in basis points. Write down the expression of the price of this swaption using Black's formula.

Exercise 19.4 Consider two bonds with maturities T_1 and T_2, $T_1 < T_2$, which follow the stochastic differential equations

$$dP(t, T_1) = r_t P(t, T_1)dt + \zeta_1(t)P(t, T_1)dW_t$$

and

$$dP(t, T_2) = r_t P(t, T_2)dt + \zeta_2(t)P(t, T_2)dW_t.$$

a) Using Itô calculus, show that the forward process $P(t, T_2)/P(t, T_1)$ is a driftless geometric Brownian motion driven by $d\widehat{W}_t := dW_t - \zeta_1(t)dt$ under the T_1-forward measure $\widehat{\mathbb{P}}$.

b) Compute the price $\mathbb{E}^* \left[e^{-\int_t^{T_1} r_s ds} (K - P(T_1, T_2))^+ \mid \mathcal{F}_t \right]$ of a bond put option at time $t \in [0, T_1]$ using change of numéraire and the Black–Scholes formula.

Hint: Given X a Gaussian random variable with mean m and variance v^2 given $\mathcal{F}_t$, we have:

$$\mathbb{E}\left[(\kappa - e^X)^+ \mid \mathcal{F}_t \right] = \kappa \Phi\left(-\frac{1}{v}(m - \log \kappa) \right) \tag{19.43}$$
$$- e^{m + v^2/2} \Phi\left(-\frac{1}{v}(m + v^2 - \log \kappa) \right).$$

Exercise 19.5   Given two bonds with maturities T, S and prices $P(t,T)$, $P(t,S)$, consider the LIBOR rate

$$L(t,T,S) := \frac{P(t,T) - P(t,S)}{(S-T)P(t,S)}$$

at time $t \in [0,T]$, modeled as

$$dL(t,T,S) = \mu_t L(t,T,S)dt + \sigma L(t,T,S)dW_t, \quad 0 \leqslant t \leqslant T, \tag{19.44}$$

where $(W_t)_{t\in[0,T]}$ is a standard Brownian motion under the risk-neutral probability measure $\mathbb{P}^*$, $\sigma > 0$ is a constant, and $(\mu_t)_{t\in[0,T]}$ is an adapted process. Let

$$F(t) := \mathbb{E}^* \left[e^{-\int_t^S r_s ds} (\kappa - L(T,T,S))^+ \mid \mathcal{F}_t \right]$$

denote the price at time t of a floorlet option with strike level κ, maturity T, and payment date S.

a) Rewrite the value of $F(t)$ using the forward measure $\widehat{\mathbb{P}}_S$ with maturity S.

b) What is the dynamics of $L(t,T,S)$ under the forward measure $\widehat{\mathbb{P}}_S$?

c) Write down the value of $F(t)$ using the Black–Scholes formula.

    Hint: Given X a centered Gaussian random variable with variance v^2, we have

$$\mathbb{E}^*[(\kappa - e^{m+X})^+] = \kappa\Phi(-(m - \log \kappa)/v) - e^{m+v^2/2}\Phi(-v - (m - \log \kappa)/v),$$

where Φ denotes the Gaussian cumulative distribution function.

Exercise 19.6   Jamshidian's trick (Jamshidian (1989)). Consider a family $(P(t,T_l))_{l=i,...,j}$ of bond prices defined from a short rate process $(r_t)_{t\in\mathbb{R}_+}$. We assume that the bond prices are functions $P(T_i, T_{l+1}) = F_{l+1}(T_i, r_{T_i})$ of r_{T_i} that are *increasing* in the variable r_{T_i}, for all $l = i, i+1, \ldots, j-1$.

a) Compute the price $P(t, T_i, T_j)$ of the annuity numéraire paying coupons $c_{i+1}, \ldots, c_j$ at times $T_{i+1}, \ldots, T_j$ in terms of the bond prices

$$P(t, T_{i+1}), \ldots, P(t, T_j).$$

b) Show that the payoff

$$\left(P(T_i, T_i) - P(T_i, T_j) - \kappa P(T_i, T_i, T_j) \right)^+$$

of a European swaption can be rewrittten as

$$\left(1 - \kappa \sum_{l=i}^{j-1} \tilde{c}_{l+1} P(T_i, T_{l+1}) \right)^+,$$

by writing $\tilde{c}_l$ in terms of c_l, $l = i+1, \ldots, j$.

c) Assuming that the bond prices are functions $P(T_i, T_{l+1}) = F_l(T_i, r_{T_i})$ of r_{T_i} that are *increasing* in the variable r_{T_i}, for all $l = i, \ldots, j-1$, show, choosing γ_κ such that

$$\kappa \sum_{l=i}^{j-1} c_{l+1} F_{l+1}(T_i, \gamma_\kappa) = 1,$$

that the European swaption with payoff

$$\left(P(T_i, T_i) - P(T_i, T_j) - \kappa P(T_i, T_i, T_j) \right)^+ = \left(1 - \kappa \sum_{l=i}^{j-1} c_{l+1} P(T_i, T_{l+1}) \right)^+,$$

where c_j contains the final coupon payment, can be priced as a weighted sum of bond put options under the forward measure $\widehat{\mathbb{P}}_i$ with numéraire $N_t^{(i)} := P(t, T_i)$.

Exercise 19.7 (Exercise 17.4 continued). We work in the short rate model

$$dr_t = \sigma dB_t,$$

where $(B_t)_{t \in \mathbb{R}_+}$ is a standard Brownian motion under $\mathbb{P}^*$, and $\widehat{\mathbb{P}}_2$ is the forward measure defined by

$$\frac{d\widehat{\mathbb{P}}_2}{d\mathbb{P}^*} = \frac{1}{P(0, T_2)} e^{-\int_0^{T_2} r_s ds}.$$

a) State the expressions of $\zeta_1(t)$ and $\zeta_2(t)$ in

$$\frac{dP(t, T_i)}{P(t, T_i)} = r_t dt + \zeta_i(t) dB_t, \qquad i = 1, 2,$$

and the dynamics of the $P(t, T_1)/P(t, T_2)$ under $\widehat{\mathbb{P}}_2$, where $P(t, T_1)$ and $P(t, T_2)$ are bond prices with maturities T_1 and T_2.
Hint: Use Exercise 17.4 and the relation (17.25).

b) State the expression of the forward rate $f(t, T_1, T_2)$.

c) Compute the dynamics of $f(t, T_1, T_2)$ under the forward measure $\widehat{\mathbb{P}}_2$ with

$$\frac{d\widehat{\mathbb{P}}_2}{d\mathbb{P}^*} = \frac{1}{P(0, T_2)} e^{-\int_0^{T_2} r_s ds}.$$

d) Compute the price

$$(T_2 - T_1) \, \mathbb{E}^* \left[e^{-\int_t^{T_2} r_s ds} (f(T_1, T_1, T_2) - \kappa)^+ \,\Big|\, \mathcal{F}_t \right]$$

of an interest rate cap at time $t \in [0, T_1]$, using the expectation under the forward measure $\widehat{\mathbb{P}}_2$.

e) Compute the dynamics of the swap rate process

$$S(t, T_1, T_2) = \frac{P(t, T_1) - P(t, T_2)}{(T_2 - T_1) P(t, T_2)}, \qquad t \in [0, T_1],$$

under $\widehat{\mathbb{P}}_2$.

f) Using (19.33), compute the swaption price

$$(T_2 - T_1)\, \mathbb{E}^* \left[e^{-\int_t^{T_1} r_s ds} P(T_1, T_2)(S(T_1, T_1, T_2) - \kappa)^+ \,\Big|\, \mathcal{F}_t \right]$$

on the swap rate $S(T_1, T_1, T_2)$ using the expectation under the forward swap measure $\widehat{\mathbb{P}}_{1,2}$.

Exercise 19.8   Consider a LIBOR rate $L(t, T, S)$, $t \in [0, T]$, modeled as $dL(t, T, S) = \mu_t L(t, T, S) dt + \sigma(t) L(t, T, S) dW_t$, $0 \leqslant t \leqslant T$, where $(W_t)_{t \in [0, T]}$ is a standard Brownian motion under the risk-neutral probability measure $\mathbb{P}^*$, $(\mu_t)_{t \in [0, T]}$ is an adapted process, and $\sigma(t) > 0$ is a deterministic volatility function of time t.

a) What is the dynamics of $L(t, T, S)$ under the forward measure $\widehat{\mathbb{P}}$ with numéraire $N_t := P(t, S)$?

b) Rewrite the price

$$\mathbb{E}^* \left[e^{-\int_t^{S} r_s ds} \phi(L(T, T, S)) \big| \mathcal{F}_t \right] \tag{19.45}$$

at time $t \in [0, T]$ of an option with payoff function ϕ using the forward measure $\widehat{\mathbb{P}}$.

c) Write down the above option price (19.45) using an integral.

Chapter 20

Stochastic Calculus for Jump Processes

Jump processes are stochastic processes whose trajectories have discontinuities called jumps, that can occur at random times. This chapter presents the construction of jump processes with independent increments, such as the Poisson and compound Poisson processes, followed by an introduction to stochastic integrals and stochastic calculus with jumps. We also present the Girsanov Theorem for jump processes, which will be used for the construction of risk-neutral probability measures in Chapter 21 for option pricing and hedging in markets with jumps, in relation with market incompleteness.

20.1   The Poisson Process

The most elementary and useful jump process is the *standard Poisson process* $(N_t)_{t \in \mathbb{R}_+}$ which is a *counting process*, *i.e.* $(N_t)_{t \in \mathbb{R}_+}$ has jumps of size $+1$ only, and its paths are constant in between two jumps. In addition, the standard Poisson process starts at $\underline{N_0 = 0}$.

The Poisson process can be used to model discrete arrival times such as claim dates in insurance, or connection logs.

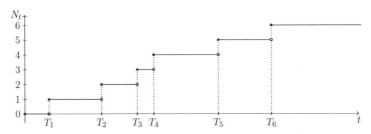

Figure 20.1: Sample path of a Poisson process $(N_t)_{t \in \mathbb{R}_+}$.

In other words, the value N_t at time t is given by[†]

$$N_t = \sum_{k \geqslant 1} \mathbb{1}_{[T_k, \infty)}(t), \qquad t \geqslant 0, \tag{20.1}$$

where

$$\mathbb{1}_{[T_k, \infty)}(t) = \begin{cases} 1 & \text{if } t \geqslant T_k, \\ 0 & \text{if } 0 \leqslant t < T_k, \end{cases}$$

[†]The notation N_t is not to be confused with the same notation used for numéraire processes in Chapter 16.

DOI: 10.1201/9781003298670-20

$k \geqslant 1$, and $(T_k)_{k \geqslant 1}$ is the increasing family of jump times of $(N_t)_{t \in \mathbb{R}_+}$ such that

$$\lim_{k \to \infty} T_k = +\infty.$$

In addition, the Poisson process $(N_t)_{t \in \mathbb{R}_+}$ is assumed to satisfy the following conditions:

1. Independence of increments: for all $0 \leqslant t_0 < t_1 < \cdots < t_n$ and $n \geqslant 1$ the increments

$$N_{t_1} - N_{t_0}, \ldots, N_{t_n} - N_{t_{n-1}},$$

   are mutually independent random variables.

2. Stationarity of increments: $N_{t+h} - N_{s+h}$ has the same distribution as $N_t - N_s$ for all $h > 0$ and $0 \leqslant s \leqslant t$.

The meaning of the above stationarity condition is that for all fixed $k \geqslant 0$ we have

$$\mathbb{P}(N_{t+h} - N_{s+h} = k) = \mathbb{P}(N_t - N_s = k),$$

for all $h > 0$, *i.e.* the value of the probability

$$\mathbb{P}(N_{t+h} - N_{s+h} = k)$$

does not depend on $h > 0$, for all fixed $0 \leqslant s \leqslant t$ and $k \geqslant 0$.

Based on the above assumption, given $T > 0$ a time value, a natural question arises:

what is the probability distribution of the random variable N_T?

We already know that N_t takes values in $\mathbb{N}$ and therefore it has a discrete distribution for all $t \in \mathbb{R}_+$.

It is a remarkable fact that the distribution of the increments of $(N_t)_{t \in \mathbb{R}_+}$, can be completely determined from the above conditions, as shown in the following theorem.

As seen in the next result, cf. Theorem 4.1 in Bosq and Nguyen (1996), the Poisson increment $N_t - N_s$ has the *Poisson distribution* with parameter $(t - s)\lambda$.

Theorem 20.1. *Assume that the counting process $(N_t)_{t \in \mathbb{R}_+}$ satisfies the above independence and stationarity Conditions 1 and 2 on page 566. Then, for all fixed $0 \leqslant s \leqslant t$ the increment $N_t - N_s$ follows the Poisson distribution with parameter $(t - s)\lambda$, i.e. we have*

$$\mathbb{P}(N_t - N_s = k) = e^{-(t-s)\lambda} \frac{((t-s)\lambda)^k}{k!}, \qquad k \geqslant 0, \qquad (20.2)$$

for some constant $\lambda > 0$.

The parameter $\lambda > 0$ is called the <u>intensity</u> of the Poisson process $(N_t)_{t \in \mathbb{R}_+}$ and it is given by

$$\lambda := \lim_{h \to 0} \frac{1}{h} \mathbb{P}(N_h = 1). \qquad (20.3)$$

The proof of the above Theorem 20.1 is technical and not included here, cf. *e.g.* Bosq and Nguyen (1996) for details, and we could in fact take this distribution property (20.2) as one of the hypotheses that define the Poisson process.

Precisely, we could restate the definition of the standard Poisson process $(N_t)_{t \in \mathbb{R}_+}$ with intensity $\lambda > 0$ as being a stochastic process defined by (20.1), which is assumed to have independent increments distributed according to the Poisson distribution, in the sense that for all $0 \leqslant t_0 \leqslant t_1 < \cdots < t_n$,

$$(N_{t_1} - N_{t_0}, \ldots, N_{t_n} - N_{t_{n-1}})$$

is a vector of independent Poisson random variables with respective parameters

$$((t_1 - t_0)\lambda, \ldots, (t_n - t_{n-1})\lambda).$$

In particular, N_t has the Poisson distribution with parameter λt, *i.e.*

$$\mathbb{P}(N_t = k) = \frac{(\lambda t)^k}{k!} e^{-\lambda t}, \qquad t > 0.$$

The *expected value* $\mathbb{E}[N_t]$ and the variance of N_t can be computed as

$$\mathbb{E}[N_t] = \operatorname{Var}[N_t] = \lambda t. \tag{20.4}$$

As a consequence, the *dispersion index* of the Poisson process is

$$\frac{\operatorname{Var}[N_t]}{\mathbb{E}[N_t]} = 1, \qquad t \geqslant 0. \tag{20.5}$$

Short time behavior

From (20.3) above we deduce the *short time asymptotics**

$$\begin{cases} \mathbb{P}(N_h = 0) = e^{-\lambda h} = 1 - \lambda h + o(h), & h \to 0, \\[2mm] \mathbb{P}(N_h = 1) = \lambda h \, e^{-\lambda h} \simeq \lambda h, & h \to 0. \end{cases}$$

By stationarity of the Poisson process we also find more generally that

$$\begin{cases} \mathbb{P}(N_{t+h} - N_t = 0) = e^{-\lambda h} = 1 - \lambda h + o(h), & h \to 0, \\[2mm] \mathbb{P}(N_{t+h} - N_t = 1) = \lambda h \, e^{-\lambda h} \simeq \lambda h, & h \to 0, \\[2mm] \mathbb{P}(N_{t+h} - N_t = 2) \simeq h^2 \frac{\lambda^2}{2} = o(h), & h \to 0, \quad t > 0, \end{cases} \tag{20.6}$$

for all $t > 0$. This means that within a "short" interval $[t, t+h]$ of length h, the increment $N_{t+h} - N_t$ behaves like a Bernoulli random variable with parameter λh. This fact can be used for the random simulation of Poisson process paths.

---

*The notation $f(h) = o(h^k)$ means $\lim_{h \to 0} f(h)/h^k = 0$, and $f(h) \simeq h^k$ means $\lim_{h \to 0} f(h)/h^k = 1$.

More generally, for $k \geqslant 1$ we have

$$\mathbb{P}(N_{t+h} - N_t = k) \simeq h^k \frac{\lambda^k}{k!}, \qquad h \to 0, \qquad t > 0.$$

The intensity of the Poisson process can in fact be made time-dependent (*e.g.* by a time change), in which case we have

$$\mathbb{P}(N_t - N_s = k) = \exp\left(-\int_s^t \lambda(u)du\right) \frac{\left(\int_s^t \lambda(u)du\right)^k}{k!}, \qquad k = 0, 1, 2, \ldots.$$

Assuming that $\lambda(t)$ is a continuous function of time t we have in particular, as h tends to zero,

$$\mathbb{P}(N_{t+h} - N_t = k)$$

$$= \begin{cases} \exp\left(-\int_t^{t+h} \lambda(u)du\right) = 1 - \lambda(t)h + o(h), & k = 0, \\[2ex] \exp\left(-\int_t^{t+h} \lambda(u)du\right) \int_t^{t+h} \lambda(u)du = \lambda(t)h + o(h), & k = 1, \\[2ex] o(h), & k \geqslant 2. \end{cases}$$

The next R code and Figure 20.2 present a simulation of the standard Poisson process $(N_t)_{t\in\mathbb{R}_+}$ according to its short time behavior (20.6).

```
1   lambda = 0.6;T=10;N=1000*lambda;dt=T*1.0/N
    t=0;s=c();for (k in 1:N) {if (runif(1)<lambda*dt) {s=c(s,t)};t=t+dt}
3   dev.new(width=T, height=5)
    plot(stepfun(s,cumsum(c(0,rep(1,length(s))))),xlim =c(0,T),xlab="t",ylab=expression('N'[t]),pch=1, cex=0.8,
        col='blue', lwd=2, main="", las = 1, cex.axis=1.2, cex.lab=1.4)
```

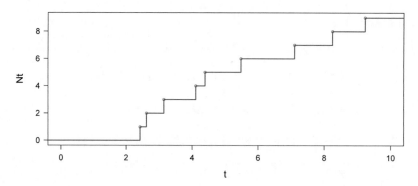

Figure 20.2: Sample path of the Poisson process $(N_t)_{t\in\mathbb{R}_+}$.

The intensity process $(\lambda(t))_{t\in\mathbb{R}_+}$ can also be made random, as in the case of Cox processes.

Poisson process jump times

In order to determine the distribution of the first jump time T_1 we note that we have the equivalence

$$\{T_1 > t\} \Longleftrightarrow \{N_t = 0\},$$

which implies

$$\mathbb{P}(T_1 > t) = \mathbb{P}(N_t = 0) = e^{-\lambda t}, \qquad t \geqslant 0,$$

i.e. T_1 has an exponential distribution with parameter $\lambda > 0$.

In order to prove the next proposition we note that more generally, we have the equivalence

$$\{T_n > t\} \Longleftrightarrow \{N_t \leqslant n - 1\},$$

for all $n \geqslant 1$. This allows us to compute the distribution of the random jump time T_n with its probability density function. It coincides with the *gamma* distribution with integer parameter $n \geqslant 1$, also known as the Erlang distribution in queueing theory.

Proposition 20.2. *For all $n \geqslant 1$ the probability distribution of T_n has the gamma probability density function*

$$t \longmapsto \lambda^n e^{-\lambda t} \frac{t^{n-1}}{(n-1)!}$$

on $\mathbb{R}_+$, i.e. for all $t > 0$ the probability $\mathbb{P}(T_n \geqslant t)$ is given by

$$\mathbb{P}(T_n \geqslant t) = \lambda^n \int_t^\infty e^{-\lambda s} \frac{s^{n-1}}{(n-1)!} ds.$$

Proof. We have

$$\mathbb{P}(T_1 > t) = \mathbb{P}(N_t = 0) = e^{-\lambda t}, \qquad t \geqslant 0,$$

and by induction, assuming that

$$\mathbb{P}(T_{n-1} > t) = \lambda \int_t^\infty e^{-\lambda s} \frac{(\lambda s)^{n-2}}{(n-2)!} ds, \qquad n \geqslant 2,$$

we obtain

$$
\begin{aligned}
\mathbb{P}(T_n > t) &= \mathbb{P}(T_n > t \geqslant T_{n-1}) + \mathbb{P}(T_{n-1} > t) \\
&= \mathbb{P}(N_t = n - 1) + \mathbb{P}(T_{n-1} > t) \\
&= e^{-\lambda t} \frac{(\lambda t)^{n-1}}{(n-1)!} + \lambda \int_t^\infty e^{-\lambda s} \frac{(\lambda s)^{n-2}}{(n-2)!} ds \\
&= \lambda \int_t^\infty e^{-\lambda s} \frac{(\lambda s)^{n-1}}{(n-1)!} ds, \qquad t \geqslant 0,
\end{aligned}
$$

where we applied an integration by parts to derive the last line. $\square$

In particular, for all $n \in \mathbb{Z}$ and $t \in \mathbb{R}_+$, we have

$$\mathbb{P}(N_t = n) = p_n(t) = e^{-\lambda t} \frac{(\lambda t)^n}{n!},$$

i.e. $p_{n-1} : \mathbb{R}_+ \to \mathbb{R}_+, n \geqslant 1$, is the probability density function of the random jump time T_n.

In addition to Proposition 20.2 we could show the following proposition which relies on the *strong Markov property*, see *e.g.* Theorem 6.5.4 of Norris (1998).

Proposition 20.3. *The (random) interjump times*

$$\tau_k := T_{k+1} - T_k$$

spent at state $k \geqslant 0$, with $T_0 = 0$, form a sequence of independent identically distributed random variables having the exponential distribution with parameter $\lambda > 0$, i.e.

$$\mathbb{P}(\tau_0 > t_0, \ldots, \tau_n > t_n) = e^{-(t_0 + t_1 + \cdots + t_n)\lambda}, \qquad t_0, t_1, \ldots, t_n \geqslant 0.$$

As the expectation of the exponentially distributed random variable τ_k with parameter $\lambda > 0$ is given by

$$\mathbb{E}[\tau_k] = \lambda \int_0^\infty x \, e^{-\lambda x} dx = \frac{1}{\lambda},$$

we can check that the *nth* jump time $T_n = \tau_0 + \cdots + \tau_{n-1}$ has the mean

$$\mathbb{E}[T_n] = \frac{n}{\lambda}, \qquad n \geqslant 1.$$

Consequently, the higher the intensity $\lambda > 0$ is (*i.e.* the higher the probability of having a jump within a small interval), the smaller the time spent in each state $k \geqslant 0$ is on average.

As a consequence of Proposition 20.2, random samples of Poisson process jump times can be generated from Poisson jump times using the following R code according to Proposition 20.3.

```
lambda = 0.6;n = 200*lambda;T=10;Z<-cumsum(c(0,rep(1,n))); tau_n <- rexp(n,rate=lambda); Tn <-
    cumsum(tau_n)
dev.new(width=T, height=5)
plot(stepfun(Tn,Z),xlim =c(0,T),ylim=c(0,8),xlab="t",ylab=expression('N'[t]),pch=1, cex=1, col="blue",
    lwd=2, main="", las = 1, cex.axis=1.2, cex.lab=1.4)
```

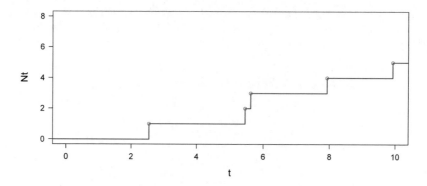

Figure 20.3: Sample path of the Poisson process $(N_t)_{t\in\mathbb{R}_+}$.

In addition, conditionally to $\{N_T = n\}$, the n jump times on $[0, T]$ of the Poisson process $(N_t)_{t\in\mathbb{R}_+}$ are independent uniformly distributed random variables on $[0, T]^n$, cf. *e.g.* § 12.1 of Privault (2018). This fact can also be useful for the random simulation of the Poisson process.

```
lambda = 0.6;T=10;n = rpois(1,lambda*T);Tn <- sort(runif(n,0,T)); Z<-cumsum(c(0,rep(1,n)));
    dev.new(width=T, height=5)
plot(stepfun(Tn,Z),xlim =c(0,T),ylim=c(0,8),xlab="t",ylab=expression('N'[t]),pch=1, cex=1, col="blue",
    lwd=2, main="", las = 1, cex.axis=1.2, cex.lab=1.4)
```

Compensated Poisson martingale

From (20.4) above we deduce that

$$\mathbb{E}[N_t - \lambda t] = 0, \tag{20.7}$$

i.e. the compensated Poisson process $(N_t - \lambda t)_{t\in\mathbb{R}_+}$ has *centered increments*.

```
lambda = 0.6;n = 20;Z<-cumsum(c(0,rep(1,n)));
tau_n <- rexp(n,rate=lambda); Tn <- cumsum(tau_n)
N <- function(t) {return(stepfun(Tn,Z)(t))};t <- seq(0,10,0.01)
dev.new(width=T, height=5)
plot(t,N(t)-lambda*t,xlim = c(0,10),ylim =
    c(-2,2),xlab="t",ylab=expression(paste('N'[t],'-t')),type="l",lwd=2,col="blue",main="", xaxs = "i", yaxs
    = "i", xaxs = "i", yaxs = "i", las = 1, cex.axis=1.2, cex.lab=1.4)
abline(h = 0, col="black", lwd =2)
points(Tn,N(Tn)-lambda*Tn,pch=1,cex=0.8,col="blue",lwd=2)
```

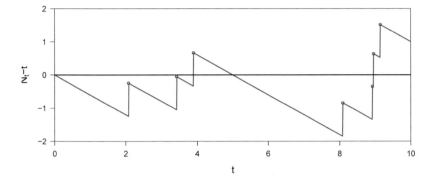

Figure 20.4: Sample path of the compensated Poisson process $(N_t - \lambda t)_{t \in \mathbb{R}_+}$.

Since in addition $(N_t - \lambda t)_{t \in \mathbb{R}_+}$ also has independent increments, we get the following proposition, see *e.g.* Example 2 page 207. We let

$$\mathcal{F}_t := \sigma\big(N_s \ : \ s \in [0,t]\big), \qquad t \geqslant 0,$$

denote the *filtration* generated by the Poisson process $(N_t)_{t \in \mathbb{R}_+}$.

Proposition 20.4. *The compensated Poisson process*

$$(N_t - \lambda t)_{t \in \mathbb{R}_+}$$

is a martingale *with respect* $(\mathcal{F}_t)_{t \in \mathbb{R}_+}$.

Extensions of the Poisson process include Poisson processes with time-dependent intensity, and with random time-dependent intensity (Cox processes). Poisson processes belong to the family of *renewal processes*, which are counting processes of the form

$$N_t = \sum_{n \geqslant 1} \mathbb{1}_{[T_n, \infty)}(t), \qquad t \geqslant 0,$$

for which $\tau_k := T_{k+1} - T_k$, $k \geqslant 0$, is a sequence of independent identically distributed random variables.

20.2 Compound Poisson Process

The Poisson process itself appears to be too limited to develop realistic price models as its jumps are of constant size. Therefore there is some interest in considering jump processes that can have random jump sizes.

Let $(Z_k)_{k \geqslant 1}$ denote a sequence of independent, identically distributed (*i.i.d.*) square-integrable random variables, distributed as a common random variable Z with probability distribution $\nu(dy)$ on $\mathbb{R}$, independent of the Poisson process $(N_t)_{t \in \mathbb{R}_+}$. We have

$$\mathbb{P}(Z \in [a, b]) = \nu([a, b]) = \int_a^b \nu(dy), \quad -\infty < a \leqslant b < \infty, \quad k \geqslant 1,$$

and when the distribution $\nu(dy)$ admits a probability density $\varphi(y)$ on $\mathbb{R}$, we write $\nu(dy) = \varphi(y)dy$ and

$$\mathbb{P}(Z \in [a, b]) = \nu([a, b]) = \int_a^b \nu(dy) = \int_a^b \varphi(y)dy, \quad -\infty < a \leqslant b < \infty, \quad k \geqslant 1.$$

Figure 20.5 shows an example of Gaussian jump size distribution.

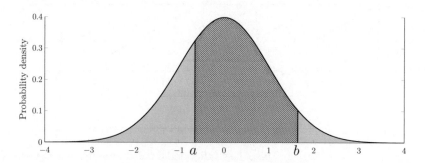

Figure 20.5: Probability density function φ.

Definition 20.5. *The process $(Y_t)_{t \in \mathbb{R}_+}$ given by the random sum*

$$Y_t := Z_1 + Z_2 + \cdots + Z_{N_t} = \sum_{k=1}^{N_t} Z_k, \quad t \geqslant 0, \tag{20.8}$$

is called a compound Poisson process.[*]

Letting Y_{t^-} denote the left limit

$$Y_{t^-} := \lim_{s \nearrow t} Y_s, \quad t > 0,$$

we note that the jump size

$$\Delta Y_t := Y_t - Y_{t^-}, \quad t \geqslant 0,$$

of $(Y_t)_{t \in \mathbb{R}_+}$ at time t is given by the relation

$$\Delta Y_t = Z_{N_t} \Delta N_t, \quad t \geqslant 0, \tag{20.9}$$

where

$$\Delta N_t := N_t - N_{t^-} \in \{0, 1\}, \quad t \geqslant 0,$$

denotes the jump size of the standard Poisson process $(N_t)_{t \in \mathbb{R}_+}$, and N_{t^-} is the left limit

$$N_{t^-} := \lim_{s \nearrow t} N_s, \quad t > 0,$$

---

[*]We use the convention $\displaystyle\sum_{k=1}^{n} Z_k = 0$ if $n = 0$ so that $Y_0 = 0$.

Example. Assume that jump sizes are Gaussian distributed with mean δ and variance η^2, with

$$\nu(dy) = \frac{1}{\sqrt{2\pi\eta^2}}\, e^{-(y-\delta)^2/(2\eta^2)} dy.$$

The next Figure 20.6 represents a sample path of a compound Poisson process, with here $Z_1 = 0.9$, $Z_2 = -0.7$, $Z_3 = 1.4$, $Z_4 = 0.6$, $Z_5 = -2.5$, $Z_6 = 1.5$, $Z_7 = -0.5$, with the relation

$$Y_{T_k} = Y_{T_k^-} + Z_k, \qquad k \geqslant 1.$$

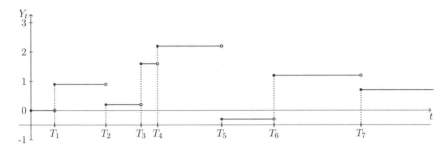

Figure 20.6: Sample path of a compound Poisson process $(Y_t)_{t \in \mathbb{R}_+}$.

```
1   N<-50;Tk<-cumsum(rexp(N,rate=0.5)); Zk<-cumsum(c(0,rexp(N,rate=0.5)))
    plot(stepfun(Tk,Zk),xlim = c(0,10),do.points = F,main="L=0.5",col="blue")
3   Zk<-cumsum(c(0,rnorm(N,mean=0,sd=1)))
    plot(stepfun(Tk,Zk),xlim = c(0,10),do.points = F,main="L=0.5",col="blue")
```

Given that $\{N_T = n\}$, the n jump sizes of $(Y_t)_{t \in \mathbb{R}_+}$ on $[0, T]$ are independent random variables which are distributed on $\mathbb{R}$ according to $\nu(dx)$. Based on this fact, the next proposition allows us to compute the *Moment Generating Function* (MGF) of the increment $Y_T - Y_t$.

Proposition 20.6. *For any $t \in [0, T]$ and $\alpha \in \mathbb{R}$ we have*

$$\mathbb{E}\left[e^{\alpha(Y_T - Y_t)}\right] = \exp\left((T-t)\lambda\left(\mathbb{E}\left[e^{\alpha Z}\right] - 1\right)\right). \tag{20.10}$$

Proof. Since N_t has a Poisson distribution with parameter $t > 0$ and is independent of $(Z_k)_{k \geqslant 1}$, for all $\alpha \in \mathbb{R}$ we have, by conditioning on the value of $N_T - N_t = n$,

$$\mathbb{E}\left[e^{\alpha(Y_T - Y_t)}\right] = \mathbb{E}\left[\exp\left(\alpha \sum_{k=N_t+1}^{N_T} Z_k\right)\right] = \mathbb{E}\left[\exp\left(\alpha \sum_{k=+1}^{N_T - N_t} Z_{k+N_t}\right)\right]$$

$$= \mathbb{E}\left[\exp\left(\alpha \sum_{k=1}^{N_T - N_t} Z_k\right)\right]$$

$$= \sum_{n \geqslant 0} \mathbb{E}\left[\exp\left(\alpha \sum_{k=1}^{N_T - N_t} Z_k\right) \bigg| N_T - N_t = n\right] \mathbb{P}(N_T - N_t = n)$$

$$= e^{-(T-t)\lambda} \sum_{n \geqslant 0} \frac{\lambda^n}{n!}(T-t)^n \mathbb{E}\left[\exp\left(\alpha \sum_{k=1}^{n} Z_k\right)\right]$$

$$= e^{-(T-t)\lambda} \sum_{n \geqslant 0} \frac{\lambda^n}{n!}(T-t)^n \prod_{k=1}^{n} \mathbb{E}\left[e^{\alpha Z_k}\right]$$

$$= e^{-(T-t)\lambda} \sum_{n\geqslant 0} \frac{\lambda^n}{n!} (T-t)^n \left(\mathbb{E}\left[e^{\alpha Z}\right]\right)^n$$

$$= \exp\left((T-t)\lambda\left(\mathbb{E}\left[e^{\alpha Z}\right] - 1\right)\right).$$

$\square$

We note that we can also write

$$\mathbb{E}\left[e^{\alpha(Y_T - Y_t)}\right] = \exp\left((T-t)\lambda \int_{-\infty}^{\infty} (e^{\alpha y} - 1)\nu(dy)\right)$$

$$= \exp\left((T-t)\lambda \int_{-\infty}^{\infty} e^{\alpha y}\nu(dy) - (T-t)\lambda \int_{-\infty}^{\infty} \nu(dy)\right)$$

$$= \exp\left((T-t)\lambda \int_{-\infty}^{\infty} (e^{\alpha y} - 1)\nu(dy)\right),$$

since the probability distribution $\nu(dy)$ of Z satisfies

$$\mathbb{E}\left[e^{\alpha Z}\right] = \int_{-\infty}^{\infty} e^{\alpha y}\nu(dy) \quad \text{and} \quad \int_{-\infty}^{\infty} \nu(dy) = 1.$$

From the moment generating function (20.10) we can compute the expectation of Y_t for fixed t as the product of the mean number of jump times $\mathbb{E}[N_t] = \lambda t$ and the mean jump size $\mathbb{E}[Z]$, *i.e.*

$$\mathbb{E}[Y_t] = \frac{\partial}{\partial \alpha} \mathbb{E}[e^{\alpha Y_t}]_{|\alpha=0} = \lambda t \int_{-\infty}^{\infty} y\nu(dy) = \mathbb{E}[N_t]\,\mathbb{E}[Z] = \lambda t\,\mathbb{E}[Z]. \tag{20.11}$$

Note that the above identity requires to exchange the differentiation and expectation operators, which is possible when the moment generating function (20.10) takes finite values for all α in a certain neighborhood $(-\varepsilon, \varepsilon)$ of 0.

Relation (20.11) states that the mean value of Y_t is the mean jump size $\mathbb{E}[Z]$ times the mean number of jumps $\mathbb{E}[N_t]$. It can be directly recovered using series summations, as

$$\mathbb{E}[Y_t] = \mathbb{E}\left[\sum_{k=1}^{N_t} Z_k\right]$$

$$= \sum_{n\geqslant 1} \mathbb{E}\left[\sum_{k=1}^{n} Z_k \,\Big|\, N_t = n\right] \mathbb{P}(N_t = n)$$

$$= e^{-\lambda t} \sum_{n\geqslant 1} \frac{\lambda^n t^n}{n!} \mathbb{E}\left[\sum_{k=1}^{n} Z_k \,\Big|\, N_t = n\right]$$

$$= e^{-\lambda t} \sum_{n\geqslant 1} \frac{\lambda^n t^n}{n!} \mathbb{E}\left[\sum_{k=1}^{n} Z_k\right]$$

$$= \lambda t\, e^{-\lambda t}\, \mathbb{E}[Z] \sum_{n\geqslant 1} \frac{(\lambda t)^{n-1}}{(n-1)!}$$

$$= \lambda t\, \mathbb{E}[Z]$$

$$= \mathbb{E}[N_t]\,\mathbb{E}[Z].$$

Regarding the variance, by (20.10) we have

$$
\begin{aligned}
\mathbb{E}\left[Y_t^2\right] &= \frac{\partial^2}{\partial \alpha^2}\,\mathbb{E}\!\left[e^{\alpha Y_t}\right]_{|\alpha=0} \\
&= \frac{\partial^2}{\partial \alpha^2}\exp\left(\lambda t\big(\mathbb{E}\left[e^{\alpha Z}\right]-1\big)\right)_{|\alpha=0} \\
&= \frac{\partial}{\partial \alpha}\left(\lambda t\,\mathbb{E}\left[Z\,e^{\alpha Z}\right]\exp\left(\lambda t\big(\mathbb{E}\left[e^{\alpha Z}\right]-1\big)\right)\right)_{|\alpha=0} \\
&= \lambda t\,\mathbb{E}\left[Z^2\right]+\left(\lambda t\,\mathbb{E}[Z]\right)^2 \\
&= \lambda t\int_{-\infty}^{\infty} y^2\nu(dy)+(\lambda t)^2\left(\int_{-\infty}^{\infty} y\nu(dy)\right)^2,
\end{aligned}
$$

which yields

$$
\operatorname{Var}\left[Y_t\right]=\lambda t\int_{-\infty}^{\infty} y^2\nu(dy)=\lambda t\,\mathbb{E}\left[|Z|^2\right]=\mathbb{E}[N_t]\,\mathbb{E}\left[|Z|^2\right]. \tag{20.12}
$$

As a consequence, the *dispersion index* of the compound Poisson process

$$
\frac{\operatorname{Var}\left[Y_t\right]}{\mathbb{E}[Y_t]}=\frac{\mathbb{E}\left[|Z|^2\right]}{\mathbb{E}[Z]},\qquad t\geqslant 0.
$$

coincides with the dispersion index of the random jump size Z. Proposition 20.6 can be used to show the next result.

Proposition 20.7. *The compound Poisson process*

$$
Y_t=\sum_{k=1}^{N_t} Z_k,\qquad t\geqslant 0,
$$

has independent increments, i.e. for any finite sequence of times $t_0 < t_1 < \cdots < t_n$, the increments

$$
Y_{t_1}-Y_{t_0},\ Y_{t_2}-Y_{t_1},\ldots,\ Y_{t_n}-Y_{t_{n-1}}
$$

are mutually independent random variables. In addition, the increment $Y_t - Y_s$ is stationary, $0\leqslant s\leqslant t$, i.e. the distribution of $Y_{t+h}-Y_{s+h}$ does not depend of $h\geqslant 0$.

Proof. This result relies on the fact that the result of Proposition 20.6 can be extended to sequences $0\leqslant t_0\leqslant t_1\leqslant\cdots\leqslant t_n$ and $\alpha_1,\alpha_2,\ldots,\alpha_n\in\mathbb{R}$, as

$$
\begin{aligned}
\mathbb{E}\left[\prod_{k=1}^{n} e^{i\alpha_k(Y_{t_k}-Y_{t_{k-1}})}\right] &= \mathbb{E}\left[\exp\left(i\sum_{k=1}^{n}\alpha_k(Y_{t_k}-Y_{t_{k-1}})\right)\right] \\
&= \exp\left(\lambda\sum_{k=1}^{n}(t_k-t_{k-1})\int_{-\infty}^{\infty}(e^{i\alpha_k y}-1)\nu(dy)\right) \tag{20.13} \\
&= \prod_{k=1}^{n}\exp\left((t_k-t_{k-1})\lambda\int_{-\infty}^{\infty}(e^{i\alpha_k y}-1)\nu(dy)\right) \\
&= \prod_{k=1}^{n}\mathbb{E}\left[e^{i\alpha_k(Y_{t_k}-Y_{t_{k-1}})}\right],
\end{aligned}
$$

which also shows the stationarity of $Y_{t+h}-Y_{s+h}$ in $h\geqslant 0$, $0\leqslant t>$ $\qquad\square$

Since the compensated compound Poisson process also has independent and centered increments by (20.7) we have the following counterpart of Proposition 20.4, cf. also Example 2 page 207.

Proposition 20.8. *The compensated compound Poisson process*

$$M_t := Y_t - \lambda t\, \mathbb{E}[Z], \qquad t \geqslant 0,$$

is a martingale.

```
  lambda = 0.6;n = 20;Zn<-cumsum(c(0,rexp(n,rate=2)));
2 tau_n <- rexp(n,rate=lambda); Tn <- cumsum(tau_n)
  Y <- function(t) {return(stepfun(Tn,Zn)(t))};t <- seq(0,10,0.01)
4 dev.new(width=T, height=5);
  par(oma=c(0,0.1,0,0))
6 plot(t,Y(t)-0.5*lambda*t,xlim = c(0,10),ylim =
  c(-2,2),xlab="t",ylab=expression(paste('Y'[t],'-t')),type="l",lwd=2,col="blue",main="", xaxs = "i", yaxs = "i",
       xaxs = "i", yaxs = "i", las = 1, cex.axis=1.2, cex.lab=1.4)
8 abline(h = 0, col="black", lwd =2)
  points(Tn,Y(Tn)-0.5*lambda*Tn,pch=1,cex=0.8,col="blue",lwd=2);grid()
```

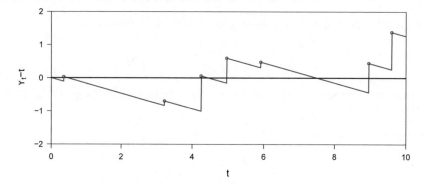

Figure 20.7: Sample path of a compensated compound Poisson process $(Y_t - \lambda t\, \mathbb{E}[Z])_{t \in \mathbb{R}_+}$.

20.3   Stochastic Integrals and Itô Formula with Jumps

Definition 20.9. *Based on the relation*

$$\Delta Y_t = Z_{N_t} \Delta N_t,$$

we define the stochastic integral of a stochastic process $(\phi_t)_{t \in [0,T]}$ *with respect to* $(Y_t)_{t \in [0,T]}$ *by*

$$\int_0^T \phi_t dY_t = \int_0^T \phi_t Z_{N_t} dN_t := \sum_{k=1}^{N_T} \phi_{T_k} Z_k. \qquad (20.14)$$

As a consequence of Proposition 20.6 we can derive the following version of the Lévy–Khintchine formula:

$$\mathbb{E}\left[\exp\left(\int_0^T f(t)dY_t\right)\right] = \exp\left(\lambda \int_0^T \int_{-\infty}^{\infty} \left(e^{yf(t)} - 1\right)\nu(dy)dt\right)$$

for $f : [0,T] \longrightarrow \mathbb{R}$ a bounded deterministic function of time.

Note that the expression (20.14) of $\int_0^T \phi_t dY_t$ has a natural financial interpretation as the value at time T of a portfolio containing a (possibly fractional) quantity ϕ_t of a risky asset at time t, whose price evolves according to random returns Z_k, generating profits/losses $\phi_{T_k} Z_k$ at random times T_k.

In particular, the compound Poisson process $(Y_t)_{t \in \mathbb{R}_+}$ in (20.5) admits the stochastic integral representation

$$Y_t = Y_0 + \sum_{k=1}^{N_t} Z_k = Y_0 + \int_0^t Z_{N_s} dN_s.$$

The next result is also called the smoothing lemma, cf. Theorem 9.2.1 in Brémaud (1999).

Proposition 20.10. *Let* $(\phi_t)_{t \in \mathbb{R}_+}$ *be a stochastic process* adapted *to the filtration generated by* $(Y_t)_{t \in \mathbb{R}_+}$, *admitting left limits and such that*

$$\mathbb{E}\left[\int_0^T |\phi_t| dt\right] < \infty, \qquad T > 0.$$

The expected value of the compound Poisson stochastic integral can be expressed as

$$\mathbb{E}\left[\int_0^T \phi_{t^-} dY_t\right] = \mathbb{E}\left[\int_0^T \phi_{t^-} Z_{N_t} dN_t\right] = \lambda\, \mathbb{E}[Z]\, \mathbb{E}\left[\int_0^T \phi_{t^-} dt\right], \qquad (20.15)$$

where ϕ_{t^-} *denotes the left limit*

$$\phi_{t^-} := \lim_{s \nearrow t} \phi_s, \qquad t > 0.$$

Proof. By Proposition 20.8 the compensated compound Poisson process $(Y_t - \lambda t\, \mathbb{E}[Z])_{t \in \mathbb{R}_+}$ is a *martingale*, and as a consequence the stochastic integral process

$$t \longmapsto \int_0^t \phi_{s^-} d(Y_s - \lambda\, \mathbb{E}[Z] ds) = \int_0^t \phi_{s^-} (Z_{N_s} dN_s - \lambda\, \mathbb{E}[Z] ds)$$

is also a martingale, by an argument similar to that in the proof of Proposition 7.1 because the adaptedness of $(\phi_t)_{t \in \mathbb{R}_+}$ to the filtration generated by $(Y_t)_{t \in \mathbb{R}_+}$, makes $(\phi_{t^-})_{t>0}$ *predictable, i.e.* adapted with respect to the filtration

$$\mathcal{F}_{t^-} := \sigma(Y_s \ : \ s \in [0, t)), \qquad t > 0.$$

It remains to use the fact that the expectation of a martingale remains constant over time, which shows that

$$
\begin{aligned}
0 &= \mathbb{E}\left[\int_0^T \phi_{t^-} (dY_t - \lambda\, \mathbb{E}[Z] dt)\right] \\
&= \mathbb{E}\left[\int_0^T \phi_{t^-} dY_t\right] - \lambda\, \mathbb{E}[Z]\, \mathbb{E}\left[\int_0^T \phi_{t^-} dt\right].
\end{aligned}
$$

$\square$

For example, taking $\phi_t = Y_t := N_t$ we have

$$\int_0^T N_{t^-} dN_t = \sum_{k=1}^{N_T} (k-1) = \frac{1}{2} N_T (N_T - 1),$$

hence

$$\mathbb{E}\left[\int_0^T N_{t^-} dN_t\right] = \frac{1}{2}\left(\mathbb{E}\left[N_T^2\right] - \mathbb{E}[N_T]\right)$$

$$= \frac{(\lambda T)^2}{2}$$

$$= \lambda \int_0^T \lambda t\, dt$$

$$= \lambda \int_0^T \mathbb{E}[N_t]\, dt,$$

as in (20.15). Note however that while the identity in expectations (20.15) holds for the left limit ϕ_{t^-}, it need not hold for ϕ_t itself. Indeed, taking $\phi_t = Y_t := N_t$ we have

$$\int_0^T N_t dN_t = \sum_{k=1}^{N_T} k = \frac{1}{2} N_T(N_T + 1),$$

hence

$$\mathbb{E}\left[\int_0^T N_t dN_t\right] = \frac{1}{2}\left(\mathbb{E}\left[N_T^2\right] + \mathbb{E}[N_T]\right)$$

$$= \frac{1}{2}\left((\lambda T)^2 + 2\lambda T\right)$$

$$= \frac{(\lambda T)^2}{2} + \lambda T$$

$$\neq \lambda \mathbb{E}\left[\int_0^T N_t dt\right].$$

Under similar conditions, the compound Poisson compensated stochastic integral can be shown to satisfy the Itô isometry (20.16) in the next proposition.

Proposition 20.11. *Let* $(\phi_t)_{t \in \mathbb{R}_+}$ *be a stochastic process* adapted *to the filtration generated by* $(Y_t)_{t \in \mathbb{R}_+}$, *admitting left limits and such that*

$$\mathbb{E}\left[\int_0^T |\phi_t|^2 dt\right] < \infty, \qquad T > 0.$$

The expected value of the squared compound Poisson compensated stochastic integral can be computed as

$$\mathbb{E}\left[\left(\int_0^T \phi_{t^-}(dY_t - \lambda\,\mathbb{E}[Z]dt)\right)^2\right] = \lambda\,\mathbb{E}\left[|Z|^2\right]\mathbb{E}\left[\int_0^T |\phi_{t^-}|^2 dt\right], \qquad (20.16)$$

Note that in (20.16), the generic jump size Z is squared but λ is not.

Proof. From the stochastic Fubini-type theorem, we have

$$\left(\int_0^T \phi_{t^-}(dY_t - \lambda\,\mathbb{E}[Z]dt)\right)^2 \qquad (20.17)$$

$$= 2\int_0^T \phi_{t^-}\int_0^{t^-} \phi_{s^-}(dY_s - \lambda\,\mathbb{E}[Z]ds)(dY_t - \lambda\,\mathbb{E}[Z]dt) \qquad (20.18)$$

$$+ \int_0^T |\phi_{t^-}|^2 |Z_{N_t}|^2 dN_t, \qquad (20.19)$$

where integration over the diagonal $\{s = t\}$ has been excluded in (20.18) as the inner integral has an upper limit t^- rather than t. Next, taking expectation on both sides of (20.17)–(20.19), we find

$$\mathbb{E}\left[\left(\int_0^T \phi_{t^-}(dY_t - \lambda \mathbb{E}[Z]dt)\right)^2\right] = \mathbb{E}\left[\int_0^T |\phi_{t^-}|^2 |Z_{N_t}|^2 dN_t\right]$$

$$= \lambda \mathbb{E}\left[|Z|^2\right] \mathbb{E}\left[\int_0^T |\phi_{t^-}|^2 dt\right],$$

where we used the vanishing of the expectation of the double stochastic integral:

$$\mathbb{E}\left[\int_0^T \phi_{t^-} \int_0^{t^-} \phi_{s^-}(dY_s - \lambda \mathbb{E}[Z]ds)(dY_t - \lambda \mathbb{E}[Z]dt)\right] = 0,$$

and the martingale property of the compensated compound Poisson process

$$t \longmapsto \left(\sum_{k=1}^{N_t} |Z_k|^2\right) - \lambda t \mathbb{E}\left[Z^2\right], \qquad t \geqslant 0,$$

as in the proof of Proposition 20.10. The isometry relation (20.16) can also be proved using simple predictable processes, similarly to the proof of Proposition 4.21. □

Next, take $(B_t)_{t\in\mathbb{R}_+}$ a standard Brownian motion independent of $(Y_t)_{t\in\mathbb{R}_+}$ and $(X_t)_{t\in\mathbb{R}_+}$ a jump-diffusion process of the form

$$X_t := \int_0^t u_s dB_s + \int_0^t v_s ds + Y_t, \qquad t \geqslant 0,$$

where $(u_t)_{t\in\mathbb{R}_+}$ is a stochastic process which is adapted to the filtration $(\mathcal{F}_t)_{t\in\mathbb{R}_+}$ generated by $(B_t)_{t\in\mathbb{R}_+}$ and $(Y_t)_{t\in\mathbb{R}_+}$, and such that

$$\mathbb{E}\left[\int_0^T |\phi_t|^2 |u_t|^2 dt\right] < \infty \quad \text{and} \quad \mathbb{E}\left[\int_0^T |\phi_t v_t| dt\right] < \infty, \quad T > 0.$$

We define the stochastic integral of $(\phi_t)_{t\in\mathbb{R}_+}$ with respect to $(X_t)_{t\in\mathbb{R}_+}$ by

$$\int_0^T \phi_t dX_t := \int_0^T \phi_t u_t dB_t + \int_0^T \phi_t v_t dt + \int_0^T \phi_t dY_t$$

$$= \int_0^T \phi_t u_t dB_t + \int_0^T \phi_t v_t dt + \sum_{k=1}^{N_T} \phi_{T_k} Z_k, \qquad T > 0.$$

For the mixed continuous-jump martingale

$$X_t := \int_0^t u_s dB_s + Y_t - \lambda t \mathbb{E}[Z], \qquad t \geqslant 0,$$

we then have the isometry:

$$\mathbb{E}\left[\left(\int_0^T \phi_{t^-} dX_t\right)^2\right] = \mathbb{E}\left[\int_0^T |\phi_{t^-}|^2 |u_t|^2 dt\right] + \lambda \mathbb{E}\left[|Z|^2\right] \mathbb{E}\left[\int_0^T |\phi_{t^-}|^2 dt\right]. \tag{20.20}$$

provided that $(\phi_t)_{t\in\mathbb{R}_+}$ is adapted to the filtration $(\mathcal{F}_t)_{t\in\mathbb{R}_+}$ generated by $(B_t)_{t\in\mathbb{R}_+}$ and $(Y_t)_{t\in\mathbb{R}_+}$. The isometry formula (20.20) will be used in Section 21.6 for mean-variance hedging in jump-diffusion models.

When $(X_t)_{t\in\mathbb{R}_+}$ takes the form

$$X_t = X_0 + \int_0^t u_s dB_s + \int_0^t v_s ds + \int_0^t \eta_s dY_s, \qquad t \geq 0,$$

the stochastic integral of $(\phi_t)_{t\in\mathbb{R}_+}$ with respect to $(X_t)_{t\in\mathbb{R}_+}$ is given by

$$\int_0^T \phi_s dX_s := \int_0^T \phi_s u_s dB_s + \int_0^T \phi_s v_s ds + \int_0^T \eta_s \phi_s dY_s$$

$$= \int_0^T \phi_s u_s dB_s + \int_0^T \phi_s v_s ds + \sum_{k=1}^{N_T} \phi_{T_k} \eta_{T_k} Z_k, \qquad T > 0.$$

Itô Formula with Jumps

The next proposition gives the simplest instance of the Itô formula with jumps, in the case of a standard Poisson process $(N_t)_{t\in\mathbb{R}_+}$ with intensity λ.

Proposition 20.12. *Itô formula for the standard Poisson process. We have*

$$f(N_t) = f(0) + \int_0^t (f(N_s) - f(N_{s^-})) dN_s, \qquad t \geq 0,$$

where N_{s^-} denotes the left limit $N_{s^-} = \lim_{h\searrow 0} N_{s-h}$.

Proof. We note that

$$N_s = N_{s^-} + 1 \quad \text{if} \quad dN_s = 1 \quad \text{and} \quad k = N_{T_k} = 1 + N_{T_k^-}, \qquad k \geq 1.$$

Hence we have the *telescoping sum*

$$f(N_t) = f(0) + \sum_{k=1}^{N_t} (f(k) - f(k-1))$$

$$= f(0) + \sum_{k=1}^{N_t} (f(N_{T_k}) - f(N_{T_k^-}))$$

$$= f(0) + \sum_{k=1}^{N_t} (f(1 + N_{T_k^-}) - f(N_{T_k^-}))$$

$$= f(0) + \int_0^t (f(1 + N_{s^-}) - f(N_{s^-})) dN_s$$

$$= f(0) + \int_0^t (f(N_s) - f(N_s - 1)) dN_s$$

$$= f(0) + \int_0^t (f(N_s) - f(N_{s^-})) dN_s,$$

where N_{s^-} denotes the left limit $N_{s^-} = \lim_{h\searrow 0} N_{s-h}$. $\square$

The next result deals with the compound Poisson process $(Y_t)_{t\in\mathbb{R}_+}$ in (20.5) via a similar argument.

Proposition 20.13. *Itô formula for the compound Poisson process $(Y_t)_{t\in\mathbb{R}_+}$. We have the pathwise Itô formula*

$$f(Y_t) = f(0) + \int_0^t (f(Y_s) - f(Y_{s^-})) dN_s, \qquad t \geq 0. \tag{20.21}$$

Proof. We have

$$
\begin{aligned}
f(Y_t) &= f(0) + \sum_{k=1}^{N_t} \left(f\left(Y_{T_k}\right) - f\left(Y_{T_k^-}\right) \right) \\
&= f(0) + \sum_{k=1}^{N_t} \left(f\left(Y_{T_k^-} + Z_k\right) - f\left(Y_{T_k^-}\right) \right) \\
&= f(0) + \int_0^t (f(Y_{s^-} + Z_{N_s}) - f(Y_{s^-}))dN_s \\
&= f(0) + \int_0^t (f(Y_s) - f(Y_{s^-}))dN_s, \qquad t \geqslant 0.
\end{aligned}
$$

$\square$

From the expression

$$
Y_t = Y_0 + \sum_{k=1}^{N_t} Z_k = Y_0 + \int_0^t Z_{N_s} dN_s,
$$

the Itô formula (20.21) can be decomposed using a compensated Poisson stochastic integral as

$$
\begin{aligned}
df(Y_t) &= (f(Y_t) - f(Y_{t^-}))dN_t - \mathbb{E}[(f(y+Z) - f(y)]_{y=Y_{t^-}} dt \qquad (20.22) \\
&\quad + \mathbb{E}[(f(y+Z) - f(y)]_{y=Y_{t^-}} dt,
\end{aligned}
$$

where

$$
(f(Y_t) - f(Y_{t^-}))dN_t - \mathbb{E}[(f(y+Z_{N_t}) - f(y)]_{y=Y_{t^-}} dt
$$

is the differential of a martingale by the smoothing lemma Proposition 20.10.

More generally, we have the following result.

Proposition 20.14. *For an Itô process of the form*

$$
X_t = X_0 + \int_0^t v_s ds + \int_0^t u_s dB_s + \int_0^t \eta_s dY_s, \qquad t \geqslant 0,
$$

we have the Itô formula

$$
\begin{aligned}
f(X_t) &= f(X_0) + \int_0^t v_s f'(X_s)ds + \int_0^t u_s f'(X_s)dB_s + \frac{1}{2}\int_0^t f''(X_s)|u_s|^2 ds \\
&\quad + \int_0^t (f(X_s) - f(X_{s^-}))dN_s, \qquad t \geqslant 0.
\end{aligned} \qquad (20.23)
$$

Proof. By combining the Itô formula for Brownian motion with the Itô formula for the compound Poisson process of Proposition 20.13, we find

$$
\begin{aligned}
f(X_t) &= f(X_0) + \int_0^t u_s f'(X_s)dB_s + \frac{1}{2}\int_0^t f''(X_s)|u_s|^2 ds + \int_0^t v_s f'(X_s)ds \\
&\quad + \sum_{k=1}^{N_T} \left(f\left(X_{T_k^-} + \eta_{T_k} Z_k\right) - f\left(X_{T_k^-}\right) \right) \\
&= f(X_0) + \int_0^t u_s f'(X_s)dB_s + \frac{1}{2}\int_0^t f''(X_s)|u_s|^2 ds + \int_0^t v_s f'(X_s)ds \\
&\quad + \int_0^t (f(X_{s^-} + \eta_s Z_{N_s}) - f(X_{s^-}))dN_s, \qquad t \geqslant 0,
\end{aligned}
$$

which yields (20.23).

$\square$

The integral Itô formula (20.23) can be rewritten in differential notation as

$$df(X_t) = v_t f'(X_t)dt + u_t f'(X_t)dB_t + \frac{|u_t|^2}{2} f''(X_t)dt + (f(X_t) - f(X_{t^-}))dN_t,$$

(20.24)

$t \geqslant 0$.

Itô multiplication table with jumps

For a stochastic process $(X_t)_{t \in \mathbb{R}_+}$ given by

$$X_t = \int_0^t u_s dB_s + \int_0^t v_s ds + \int_0^t \eta_s dN_s, \qquad t \geqslant 0,$$

the Itô formula with jumps reads

$$
\begin{aligned}
f(X_t) &= f(0) + \int_0^t u_s f'(X_s)dB_s + \frac{1}{2}\int_0^t |u_s|^2 f''(X_s)dB_s \\
&\quad + \int_0^t v_s f'(X_s)ds + \int_0^t (f(X_{s^-} + \eta_s) - f(X_{s^-}))dN_s \\
&= f(0) + \int_0^t u_s f'(X_s)dB_s + \frac{1}{2}\int_0^t |u_s|^2 f''(X_s)dB_s \\
&\quad + \int_0^t v_s f'(X_s)ds + \int_0^t (f(X_s) - f(X_{s^-}))dN_s.
\end{aligned}
$$

Given two Itô processes $(X_t)_{t \in \mathbb{R}_+}$ and $(Y_t)_{t \in \mathbb{R}_+}$ written in differential notation as

$$dX_t = u_t dB_t + v_t dt + \eta_t dN_t, \qquad t \geqslant 0,$$

and

$$dY_t = a_t dB_t + b_t dt + c_t dN_t, \qquad t \geqslant 0,$$

the Itô formula for jump processes can also be written as

$$d(X_t Y_t) = X_t dY_t + Y_t dX_t + dX_t \cdot dY_t$$

where the product $dX_t \cdot dY_t$ is computed according to the following extension of the Itô multiplication Table 4.1. The relation $dB_t \cdot dN_t = 0$ is due to the fact that $(N_t)_{t \in \mathbb{R}_+}$ has finite variation on any finite interval.

$\cdot$	dt	dB_t	dN_t
dt	0	0	0
dB_t	0	dt	0
dN_t	0	0	dN_t

Table 20.1: Itô multiplication table with jumps.

In other words, we have

$$
\begin{aligned}
dX_t \cdot dY_t &= (v_t dt + u_t dB_t + \eta_t dN_t)(b_t dt + a_t dB_t + c_t dN_t)\\
&= v_t b_t dt \cdot dt + u_t b_t dB_t \cdot dt + \eta_t b_t dN_t \cdot dt\\
&\quad + v_t a_t dt \cdot dB_t + u_t a_t dB_t \cdot dB_t + \eta_t a_t dN_t \cdot dB_t\\
&\quad + v_t c_t dt \cdot dN_t + u_t c_t dB_t \cdot dN_t + \eta_t c_t dN_t \cdot dN_t\\
&= + u_t a_t dB_t \cdot dB_t + \eta_t c_t dN_t \cdot dN_t\\
&= u_t a_t dt + \eta_t c_t dN_t,
\end{aligned}
$$

since

$$
dN_t \cdot dN_t = (dN_t)^2 = dN_t,
$$

as $\Delta N_t \in \{0,1\}$. In particular, we have

$$
(dX_t)^2 = (v_t dt + u_t dB_t + \eta_t dN_t)^2 = u_t^2 dt + \eta_t^2 dN_t.
$$

Jump processes with infinite activity

Given $\eta(s)$, $s \in \mathbb{R}_+$, a deterministic function of time and $(X_t)_{t\in\mathbb{R}_+}$ an Itô process of the form

$$
X_t := X_0 + \int_0^t v_s ds + \int_0^t u_s dB_s + \int_0^t \eta(s) dY_s, \qquad t \geqslant 0,
$$

the Itô formula with jumps (20.23) can be rewritten as

$$
\begin{aligned}
f(X_t) &= f(X_0) + \int_0^t v_s f'(X_s) ds + \int_0^t u_s f'(X_s) dB_s + \frac{1}{2}\int_0^t f''(X_s)|u_s|^2 ds\\
&\quad + \int_0^t \left(f(X_{s^-} + \eta(s)\Delta Y_s) - f(X_{s^-})\right) dN_s - \lambda \int_0^t \mathbb{E}\left[f(x + \eta(s)Z) - f(x)\right]_{|x=X_{s^-}} ds\\
&\quad + \lambda \int_0^t \int_{-\infty}^\infty \left(f(X_{s^-} + \eta(s)y) - f(X_{s^-})\right)\nu(dy)ds, \qquad t \geqslant 0,
\end{aligned}
$$

using the compensated martingale

$$
\begin{aligned}
&\int_0^t \left(f(X_s) - f(X_{s^-})\right) dN_s - \lambda \int_0^t \mathbb{E}\left[f(x + \eta(s)Z) - f(x)\right]_{|x=X_{s^-}} ds\\
&= \int_0^t \left(f(X_{s^-} + \eta(s)\Delta Y_s) - f(X_{s^-})\right) dN_s\\
&\quad - \lambda \int_0^t \int_{-\infty}^\infty \left(f(X_{s^-} + \eta(s)y) - f(X_s)\right)\nu(dy)ds,
\end{aligned}
$$

with the relation $dX_s = \eta_s \Delta Y_s$. We note that from the relation

$$
\mathbb{E}[Z] = \int_{-\infty}^\infty y\nu(dy),
$$

the above compensator can be written as

$$
\begin{aligned}
&\lambda \int_0^t \int_{-\infty}^\infty \left(f(X_{s^-} + \eta(s)y) - f(X_{s^-})\right)\nu(dy)ds\\
&= \lambda \int_0^t \int_{-\infty}^\infty \left(f(X_{s^-} + \eta(s)y) - f(X_{s^-}) - \eta(s)y f'(X_{s^-})\right)\nu(dy)ds \qquad (20.25)\\
&\quad + \lambda \mathbb{E}[Z] \int_0^t \eta(s) f'(X_{s^-})ds.
\end{aligned}
$$

The expression (20.25) above is at the basis of the extension of Itô's formula to Lévy processes with an infinite number of jumps on any interval under the conditions

$$
\int_{|y|\leqslant 1} y^2 \nu(dy) < \infty \quad \text{and} \quad \nu([-1,1]^c) < \infty,
$$

using the bound

$$|f(x+y) - f(x) - yf'(x)| \leqslant Cy^2, \qquad y \in [-1, 1],$$

that follows from Taylor's theorem for f a $\mathcal{C}^2(\mathbb{R})$ function. This yields

$$f(X_t) = f(X_0) + \int_0^t v_s f'(X_s) ds + \int_0^t u_s f'(X_s) dB_s + \frac{1}{2} \int_0^t f''(X_s) |u_s|^2 ds$$

$$+ \int_0^t \left(f(X_{s^-} + \eta(s)\Delta Y_s) - f(X_{s^-}) \right) dN_s - \lambda \int_0^t \mathbb{E}\left[f(x + \eta(s)Z) - f(x) \right]_{|x = X_{s^-}} ds$$

$$+ \lambda \int_0^t \int_{-\infty}^\infty \left(f(X_{s^-} + \eta(s)y) - f(X_{s^-}) - \eta(s)yf'(X_{s^-}) \right) \nu(dy) ds$$

$$+ \lambda \mathbb{E}[Z] \int_0^t \eta(s) f'(X_{s^-}) ds, \qquad t \geqslant 0,$$

see *e.g.* Theorem 1.16 in Øksendal and Sulem (2005) and Theorem 4.4.7 in Applebaum (2009) in the setting of Poisson random measures.

By construction, compound Poisson processes only have a *finite* number of jumps on any interval. They belong to the family of *Lévy processes* which may have an infinite number of jumps on any finite time interval, see *e.g.* § 4.4.1 of Cont and Tankov (2004). Such processes, also called "infinite activity Lévy processes" are also useful in financial modeling, cf. Cont and Tankov (2004), and include the gamma process, stable processes, variance gamma processes, inverse Gaussian processes, etc.

The sample paths of a stable process can be compared to the USD/CNY exchange rate over the year 2015, according to the date retrieved using the following code.

```
1  library(quantmod);myPars <- chart_pars();myPars$cex<-1.5
   getSymbols("USDCNY=X",from="2015-01-01",to="2015-12-06",src="yahoo")
3  rate=Ad(`USDCNY=X`);myTheme <- chart_theme();myTheme$col$line.col <- "blue"
   myTheme$rylab <- FALSE;chart_Series(rate, pars=myPars, theme = myTheme, name="USDCNY=X")
5  getSymbols("EURCHF=X",from="2013-12-30",to="2016-01-01",src="yahoo")
   rate=Ad(`EURCHF=X`);chart_Series(rate, pars=myPars, theme = myTheme)
```

The *adjusted close price* Ad() is the closing price after adjustments for applicable splits and dividend distributions.

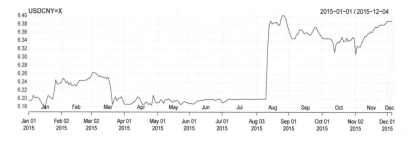

Figure 20.8: USD/CNY Exchange rate data.

Using the stochastic integral of a deterministic function $f(t)$ with respect to $(Y_t)_{t \in \mathbb{R}_+}$ defined as

$$\int_0^T f(t) dY_t = \sum_{k=1}^{N_T} Z_k f(T_k),$$

Relation (20.13) can be used to show that, more generally, the moment generating function of $\int_0^T f(t)dY_t$ is given by

$$
\begin{aligned}
\mathbb{E}\left[\exp\left(\int_0^T f(t)dY_t\right)\right] &= \exp\left(\lambda \int_0^T \int_{\mathbb{R}} \left(e^{yf(t)} - 1\right)\nu(dy)dt\right)\\
&= \exp\left(\lambda \int_0^T \left(\mathbb{E}\left[e^{f(t)Z}\right] - 1\right)dt\right).
\end{aligned}
$$

We also have

$$
\begin{aligned}
\log \mathbb{E}\left[\exp\left(\int_0^T f(t)dY_t\right)\right] &= \lambda \int_0^T \int_{\mathbb{R}} \left(e^{yf(t)} - 1\right)\nu(dy)dt\\
&= \lambda \sum_{n=1}^{\infty} \frac{1}{n!} \int_0^T \int_{\mathbb{R}} y^n f^n(t)\nu(dy)dt\\
&= \lambda \sum_{n=1}^{\infty} \frac{1}{n!} \mathbb{E}[Z^n] \int_0^T f^n(t)dt,
\end{aligned}
$$

hence the *cumulant* of order $n \geqslant 1$ of $\int_0^T f(t)dY_t$, see Definition 21.1, is given by

$$
\kappa_n = \lambda \mathbb{E}[Z^n] \int_0^T f^n(t)dt,
$$

which recovers (20.11) and (20.12) by taking $f(t) := \mathbb{1}_{[0,T]}(t)$ when $n = 1, 2$.

20.4 Stochastic Differential Equations with Jumps

In the continuous asset price model, the returns of the riskless asset price process $(A_t)_{t \in \mathbb{R}_+}$ and of the risky asset price process $(S_t)_{t \in \mathbb{R}_+}$ are modeled as

$$
\frac{dA_t}{A_t} = rdt \quad \text{and} \quad \frac{dS_t}{S_t} = \mu dt + \sigma dB_t.
$$

In this section we are interested in using jump processes in order to model an asset price process $(S_t)_{t \in \mathbb{R}_+}$.

i) Constant market return $\eta > -1$.

In the case of discontinuous asset prices, let us start with the simplest example of a constant market return η written as

$$
\eta := \frac{S_t - S_{t^-}}{S_{t^-}}, \tag{20.26}
$$

assuming the presence of a jump at time $t > 0$, *i.e.* $dN_t = 1$. Using the relation $dS_t := S_t - S_{t^-}$, (20.26) rewrites as

$$
\eta dN_t = \frac{S_t - S_{t^-}}{S_{t^-}} = \frac{dS_t}{S_{t^-}}, \tag{20.27}
$$

or

$$dS_t = \eta S_{t^-} dN_t, \tag{20.28}$$

which is a stochastic differential equation with respect to the standard Poisson process, with constant volatility $\eta \in \mathbb{R}$. Note that the left limit S_{t^-} in (20.28) occurs naturally from the definition (20.27) of market returns when dividing by the previous index value S_{t^-}.

In the presence of a jump at time t, the equation (20.26) also reads

$$S_t = (1 + \eta)S_{t^-}, \qquad dN_t = 1,$$

which can be applied by induction at the successive jump times $T_1, T_2, \ldots, T_{N_t}$ until time t, to derive the solution

$$S_t = S_0(1 + \eta)^{N_t}, \qquad t \geqslant 0,$$

of (20.28).

The use of the left limit S_{t^-} turns out to be necessary when computing pathwise solutions by solving for S_t from S_{t^-}.

ii) Time-dependent market returns η_t, $t \geqslant 0$.

Next, consider the case where η_t is time-dependent, *i.e.*

$$dS_t = \eta_t S_{t^-} dN_t. \tag{20.29}$$

At each jump time T_k, Relation (20.29) reads

$$dS_{T_k} = S_{T_k} - S_{T_k^-} = \eta_{T_k} S_{T_k^-},$$

i.e.

$$S_{T_k} = (1 + \eta_{T_k})S_{T_k^-},$$

and repeating this argument for all $k = 1, 2, \ldots, N_t$ yields the product solution

$$
\begin{aligned}
S_t &= S_0 \prod_{k=1}^{N_t} (1 + \eta_{T_k}) \\
&= S_0 \prod_{\substack{\Delta N_s = 1 \\ 0 \leqslant s \leqslant t}} (1 + \eta_s) \\
&= S_0 \prod_{0 \leqslant s \leqslant t} (1 + \eta_s \Delta N_s), \qquad t \geqslant 0.
\end{aligned}
$$

By a similar argument, we obtain the following proposition.

Proposition 20.15. *The stochastic differential equation with jumps*

$$dS_t = \mu_t S_t dt + \eta_t S_{t^-}(dN_t - \lambda dt), \tag{20.30}$$

admits the solution

$$S_t = S_0 \exp\left(\int_0^t \mu_s ds - \lambda \int_0^t \eta_s ds\right) \prod_{k=1}^{N_t} (1 + \eta_{T_k}), \qquad t \geqslant 0.$$

Note that the equations

$$dS_t = \mu_t S_{t^-} dt + \eta_t S_{t^-} (dN_t - \lambda dt)$$

and

$$dS_t = \mu_t S_t dt + \eta_t S_{t^-} (dN_t - \lambda dt)$$

are equivalent because $S_{t^-} dt = S_t dt$ as the set $\{T_k\}_{k \geqslant 1}$ of jump times has zero measure of length.

A random simulation of the numerical solution of the above equation (20.30) is given in Figure 20.9 for $\eta = 1.29$ and constant $\mu = \mu_t$, $t \geqslant 0$.

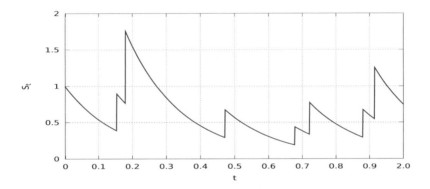

Figure 20.9: Geometric Poisson process.

Next, consider the equation

$$dS_t = \mu_t S_t dt + \eta_t S_{t^-} (dY_t - \lambda \mathbb{E}[Z] dt)$$

driven by the compensated compound Poisson process $(Y_t - \lambda \mathbb{E}[Z] t)_{t \in \mathbb{R}_+}$, also written as

$$dS_t = \mu_t S_t dt + \eta_t S_{t^-} (Z_{N_t} dN_t - \lambda \mathbb{E}[Z] dt),$$

with solution

$$S_t = S_0 \exp\left(\int_0^t \mu_s ds - \lambda \mathbb{E}[Z] \int_0^t \eta_s ds\right) \prod_{k=1}^{N_t} (1 + \eta_{T_k} Z_k) \qquad t \geqslant 0 \qquad (20.31)$$

A random simulation of the geometric compound Poisson process (20.31) is given in Figure 20.10.

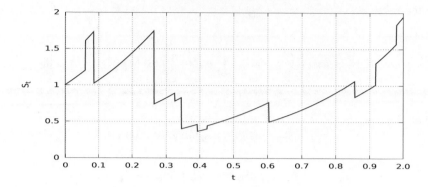

Figure 20.10: Geometric compound Poisson process.

In the case of a jump-diffusion stochastic differential equation of the form

$$dS_t = \mu_t S_t dt + \eta_t S_{t^-} (dY_t - \lambda \, \mathbb{E}[Z] dt) + \sigma_t S_t dB_t,$$

we get

$$
\begin{aligned}
S_t &= S_0 \exp\left(\int_0^t \mu_s ds - \lambda \, \mathbb{E}[Z] \int_0^t \eta_s ds + \int_0^t \sigma_s dB_s - \frac{1}{2} \int_0^t |\sigma_s|^2 ds \right) \\
&\quad \times \prod_{k=1}^{N_t} (1 + \eta_{T_k} Z_k), \qquad t \geqslant 0.
\end{aligned}
$$

A random simulation of the geometric Brownian motion with compound Poisson jumps is given in Figure 20.11.

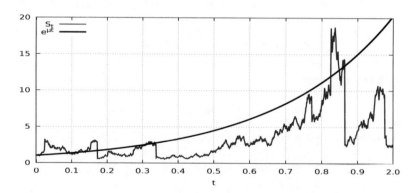

Figure 20.11: Geometric Brownian motion with compound Poisson jumps.

By rewriting S_t as

$$
\begin{aligned}
S_t &= S_0 \exp\left(\int_0^t \mu_s ds + \int_0^t \eta_s (dY_s - \lambda \, \mathbb{E}[Z] ds) + \int_0^t \sigma_s dB_s - \frac{1}{2} \int_0^t |\sigma_s|^2 ds \right) \\
&\quad \times \prod_{k=1}^{N_t} \left((1 + \eta_{T_k} Z_k) \, e^{-\eta_{T_k} Z_k} \right),
\end{aligned}
$$

$t \geqslant 0$, one can extend this jump model to processes with an infinite number of jumps on any finite time interval, cf. Cont and Tankov (2004).

20.5   Girsanov Theorem for Jump Processes

Recall that in its simplest form, cf. Section 7.2, the Girsanov Theorem 7.3 for Brownian motion states the following.

> Let $\mu \in \mathbb{R}$. Under the probability measure $\widetilde{\mathbb{P}}_{-\mu}$ defined by the Radon–Nikodym density
> $$\frac{\mathrm{d}\widetilde{\mathbb{P}}_{-\mu}}{\mathrm{d}\mathbb{P}} := \mathrm{e}^{-\mu B_T - \mu^2 T/2},$$
> the random variable $B_T + \mu T$ has the centered Gaussian distribution $\mathcal{N}(0, T)$.

This fact follows from the calculation

$$
\begin{aligned}
\widetilde{\mathbb{E}}_{-\mu}[f(B_T + \mu T)] &= \mathbb{E}[f(B_T + \mu T)\,\mathrm{e}^{-\mu B_T - \mu^2 T/2}] \\
&= \frac{1}{\sqrt{2\pi T}} \int_{-\infty}^{\infty} f(x + \mu T)\,\mathrm{e}^{-\mu x - \mu^2 T/2}\,\mathrm{e}^{-x^2/(2T)}\,dx \\
&= \frac{1}{\sqrt{2\pi T}} \int_{-\infty}^{\infty} f(x + \mu T)\,\mathrm{e}^{-(x + \mu T)^2/(2T)}\,dx \\
&= \frac{1}{\sqrt{2\pi T}} \int_{-\infty}^{\infty} f(y)\,\mathrm{e}^{-y^2/(2T)}\,dy \\
&= \mathbb{E}[f(B_T)], \tag{20.32}
\end{aligned}
$$

for any bounded measurable function f on $\mathbb{R}$, which shows that $B_T + \mu T$ is a centered Gaussian random variable under $\widetilde{\mathbb{P}}_{-\mu}$.

More generally, the Girsanov Theorem states that $(B_t + \mu t)_{t \in [0,T]}$ is a standard Brownian motion under $\widetilde{\mathbb{P}}_{-\mu}$.

When Brownian motion is replaced with a standard Poisson process $(N_t)_{t \in [0,T]}$, a spatial shift of the type

$$B_t \longmapsto B_t + \mu t$$

can no longer be used because $N_t + \mu t$ cannot be a Poisson process, whatever the change of probability applied, since by construction, the paths of the standard Poisson process has jumps of unit size and remain constant between jump times.

The correct way to extend the Girsanov Theorem to the Poisson case is to replace the space shift with a shift of the intensity of the Poisson process as in the following statement.

Proposition 20.16. *Consider a random variable N_T having the Poisson distribution $\mathcal{P}(\lambda T)$ with parameter λT under $\mathbb{P}_\lambda$. Under the probability measure $\widetilde{\mathbb{P}}_{\tilde{\lambda}}$ defined by the Radon–Nikodym density*

$$\frac{\mathrm{d}\widetilde{\mathbb{P}}_{\tilde{\lambda}}}{\mathrm{d}\mathbb{P}_\lambda} := \mathrm{e}^{-(\tilde{\lambda} - \lambda)T} \left(\frac{\tilde{\lambda}}{\lambda}\right)^{N_T},$$

the random variable N_T has a Poisson distribution with intensity $\tilde{\lambda}T$. As a consequence, the compensated process $\left(N_t - \tilde{\lambda}t\right)_{t \in [0,T]}$ is a martingale under $\widetilde{\mathbb{P}}_{\tilde{\lambda}}$.

Proof. This follows from the relation

$$
\begin{aligned}
\widetilde{\mathbb{P}}_{\tilde\lambda}(N_T = k) &= \mathrm{e}^{-(\tilde\lambda-\lambda)T}\left(\frac{\tilde\lambda}{\lambda}\right)^k \mathbb{P}_\lambda(N_T = k)\\[2mm]
&= \mathrm{e}^{-(\tilde\lambda-\lambda)T}\left(\frac{\tilde\lambda}{\lambda}\right)^k \mathrm{e}^{-\lambda T}\frac{(\lambda T)^k}{k!}\\[2mm]
&= \mathrm{e}^{-\tilde\lambda T}\frac{(\tilde\lambda T)^k}{k!}, \qquad k \geqslant 0.
\end{aligned}
$$

$\square$

Assume now that $(N_t)_{t\in[0,T]}$ is a standard Poisson process with intensity λ under a probability measure $\mathbb{P}_\lambda$. In order to extend (20.32) to the Poisson case we can replace the space shift with a *time contraction* (or dilation)

$$
N_t \longmapsto N_{(1+c)t}
$$

by a factor $1+c$, where

$$
c := -1 + \frac{\tilde\lambda}{\lambda} > -1,
$$

or $\tilde\lambda = (1+c)\lambda$. We note that

$$
\begin{aligned}
\mathbb{P}_\lambda\big(N_{(1+c)T} = k\big) &= \frac{(\lambda(1+c)T)^k}{k!}\,\mathrm{e}^{-\lambda(1+c)T}\\[2mm]
&= (1+c)^k\,\mathrm{e}^{-\lambda cT}\mathbb{P}_\lambda(N_T = k)\\[2mm]
&= \widetilde{\mathbb{P}}_{\tilde\lambda}(N_T = k), \qquad k \geqslant 0,
\end{aligned}
$$

hence

$$
\frac{\mathrm{d}\widetilde{\mathbb{P}}_{\tilde\lambda}}{\mathrm{d}\mathbb{P}_\lambda} := (1+c)^{N_T}\,\mathrm{e}^{-\lambda cT},
$$

and by analogy with (20.32) we have

$$
\begin{aligned}
\mathbb{E}_\lambda\big[f(N_{(1+c)T})\big] &= \sum_{k\geqslant 0} f(k)\mathbb{P}_\lambda\big(N_{(1+c)T} = k\big) && (20.33)\\[2mm]
&= \mathrm{e}^{-\lambda cT}\sum_{k\geqslant 0} f(k)(1+c)^k \mathbb{P}_\lambda(N_T = k)\\[2mm]
&= \mathrm{e}^{-\lambda cT}\,\mathbb{E}_\lambda\big[f(N_T)(1+c)^{N_T}\big]\\[2mm]
&= \mathbb{E}_\lambda\left[f(N_T)\frac{\mathrm{d}\widetilde{\mathbb{P}}_{\tilde\lambda}}{\mathrm{d}\mathbb{P}_\lambda}\right]\\[2mm]
&= \widetilde{\mathbb{E}}_{\tilde\lambda}[f(N_T)],
\end{aligned}
$$

for any bounded function f on $\mathbb{N}$. In other words, taking $f(x) := \mathbb{1}_{\{x\leqslant n\}}$, we have

$$
\mathbb{P}_\lambda\big(N_{(1+c)T} \leqslant n\big) = \widetilde{\mathbb{P}}_{\tilde\lambda}(N_T \leqslant n), \qquad n \geqslant 0,
$$

or

$$
\widetilde{\mathbb{P}}_{\tilde\lambda}(N_{T/(1+c)} \leqslant n) = \mathbb{P}_\lambda\big(N_T \leqslant n\big), \qquad n \geqslant 0.
$$

As a consequence, we have the following proposition.

Proposition 20.17. *Let $\lambda, \widetilde{\lambda} > 0$, and set*

$$c := -1 + \frac{\widetilde{\lambda}}{\lambda} > -1.$$

The process $\left(N_{t/(1+c)}\right)_{t \in [0,T]}$ is a standard Poisson process with intensity λ under the probability measure $\widetilde{\mathbb{P}}_{\widetilde{\lambda}}$ defined by the Radon–Nikodym density

$$\frac{\mathrm{d}\widetilde{\mathbb{P}}_{\widetilde{\lambda}}}{\mathrm{d}\mathbb{P}_\lambda} := \mathrm{e}^{-(\widetilde{\lambda}-\lambda)T} \left(\frac{\widetilde{\lambda}}{\lambda}\right)^{N_T} = \mathrm{e}^{-c\lambda T}(1+c)^{N_T}.$$

In particular, the compensated Poisson processes

$$N_{t/(1+c)} - \lambda t \quad and \quad N_t - \widetilde{\lambda}t, \qquad 0 \leqslant t \leqslant T,$$

are martingales under $\widetilde{\mathbb{P}}_{\widetilde{\lambda}}$.

Proof. As in (20.33), we have

$$\mathbb{E}_\lambda[f(N_T)] = \widetilde{\mathbb{E}}_{\widetilde{\lambda}}\left[f\left(N_{T/(1+c)}\right)\right],$$

i.e. under $\widetilde{\mathbb{P}}_{\widetilde{\lambda}}$ the distribution of $N_{T/(1+c)}$ is that of a standard Poisson random variable with parameter λT. Since $\left(N_{t/(1+c)}\right)_{t \in [0,T]}$ has independent increments, $\left(N_{t/(1+c)}\right)_{t \in [0,T]}$ is a standard Poisson process with intensity λ under $\widetilde{\mathbb{P}}_{\widetilde{\lambda}}$, and the compensated process $\left(N_{t/(1+c)} - \lambda t\right)_{t \in [0,T]}$ is a martingale under $\widetilde{\mathbb{P}}_{\widetilde{\lambda}}$ by (7.2). Similarly, the compensated process

$$\left(N_t - (1+c)\lambda t\right)_{t \in [0,T]} = \left(N_t - \widetilde{\lambda}t\right)_{t \in [0,T]}$$

has independent increments and is a martingale under $\widetilde{\mathbb{P}}_{\widetilde{\lambda}}$. $\square$

We also have

$$N_{t/(1+c)} = \sum_{n \geqslant 1} \mathbb{1}_{[T_n,\infty)}\left(\frac{t}{1+c}\right) = \sum_{n \geqslant 1} \mathbb{1}_{[(1+c)T_n,\infty)}(t), \quad t \geqslant 0,$$

which shows that the jump times $((1+c)T_n)_{n \geqslant 1}$ of $\left(N_{t/(1+c)}\right)_{t \in [0,T]}$ are distributed under $\widetilde{\mathbb{P}}_{\widetilde{\lambda}}$ as the jump times of a Poisson process with intensity λ.

The next R code shows that the compensated Poisson process $(N_{t/(1+c)} - \lambda t)_{t \in [0,T]}$, remains a martingale after the Poisson process interjump times $(\tau_k)_{k \geqslant 1}$ have been generated using exponential random variables with parameter $\widetilde{\lambda} > 0$.

```
lambda = 0.5;lambdat=2;c=-1+lambdat/lambda;n = 20;Z<-cumsum(c(0,rep(1,n)))
for (k in 1:n){tau_k <- rexp(n,rate=lambdat); Tn <- cumsum(tau_k)}
N <- function(t) {return(stepfun(Tn,Z)(t))};t <- seq(0,10,0.01)
plot(t,N(t/(1+c))-lambda*t,xlim = c(0,10),ylim =
    c(-2,2),xlab="t",ylab="Nt-t",type="l",lwd=2,col="blue",main="", xaxs = "i", yaxs = "i", xaxs = "i",
    yaxs = "i");abline(h = 0, col="black", lwd =2)
points(Tn*(1+c),N(Tn)-lambda*Tn*(1+c),pch=1,cex=0.8,col="blue",lwd=2)
```

When $\mu \neq r$, the discounted price process $(\widetilde{S}_t)_{t\in\mathbb{R}_+} = (e^{-rt}S_t)_{t\in\mathbb{R}_+}$ written as

$$\frac{d\widetilde{S}_t}{\widetilde{S}_{t^-}} = (\mu - r)dt + \sigma(dN_t - \lambda dt) \tag{20.34}$$

is not a martingale under $\mathbb{P}_\lambda$. However, we can rewrite (20.34) as

$$\frac{d\widetilde{S}_t}{\widetilde{S}_{t^-}} = \sigma\left(dN_t - \left(\lambda - \frac{\mu - r}{\sigma}\right)dt\right)$$

and letting

$$\widetilde{\lambda} := \lambda - \frac{\mu - r}{\sigma} = (1 + c)\lambda$$

with

$$c := -\frac{\mu - r}{\sigma\lambda},$$

we have

$$\frac{d\widetilde{S}_t}{\widetilde{S}_{t^-}} = \sigma\left(dN_t - \widetilde{\lambda}dt\right)$$

hence the discounted price process $(\widetilde{S}_t)_{t\in\mathbb{R}_+}$ is martingale under the probability measure $\mathbb{P}_{\widetilde{\lambda}}$ defined by the Radon–Nikodym density

$$\frac{d\mathbb{P}_{\widetilde{\lambda}}}{d\mathbb{P}_\lambda} := e^{-\lambda cT}(1 + c)^{N_T} = e^{(\mu - r)/\sigma}\left(1 - \frac{\mu - r}{\sigma\lambda}\right)^{N_T}.$$

We note that if

$$\mu - r \leqslant \sigma\lambda$$

then the risk-neutral probability measure $\mathbb{P}_{\widetilde{\lambda}}$ exists and is unique, therefore by Theorems 5.7 and 5.11 the market is without arbitrage and complete. If $\mu - r > \sigma\lambda$, then the discounted asset price process $(\widetilde{S}_t)_{t\in\mathbb{R}_+}$ is always increasing, and arbitrage becomes possible by borrowing from the savings account and investing on the risky underlying asset.

Girsanov Theorem for compound Poisson processes

In the case of compound Poisson processes, the Girsanov Theorem can be extended to variations in jump sizes in addition to time variations, and we have the following more general result.

Theorem 20.18. *Let $(Y_t)_{t\geqslant 0}$ be a compound Poisson process with intensity $\lambda > 0$ and jump size distribution $\nu(dx)$. Consider another intensity parameter $\widetilde{\lambda} > 0$ and jump size distribution $\widetilde{\nu}(dx)$, and let*

$$\psi(x) := \frac{\widetilde{\lambda}\,\widetilde{\nu}(dx)}{\lambda\,\nu(dx)} - 1, \qquad x \in \mathbb{R}. \tag{20.35}$$

Then,

under the probability measure $\widetilde{\mathbb{P}}_{\tilde{\lambda},\tilde{\nu}}$ *defined by the Radon–Nikodym density*

$$\frac{d\widetilde{\mathbb{P}}_{\tilde{\lambda},\tilde{\nu}}}{d\widetilde{\mathbb{P}}_{\lambda,\nu}} := e^{-(\tilde{\lambda}-\lambda)T} \prod_{k=1}^{N_T} (1 + \psi(Z_k)),$$

the process

$$Y_t := \sum_{k=1}^{N_t} Z_k, \qquad t \geqslant 0,$$

is a compound Poisson process with

- modified intensity $\tilde{\lambda} > 0$*, and*

- modified jump size distribution $\tilde{\nu}(dx)$*.*

Proof. For any bounded measurable function f on $\mathbb{R}$, we extend (20.33) to the following change of variable

$$\mathbb{E}_{\tilde{\lambda},\tilde{\nu}}[f(Y_T)] = e^{-(\tilde{\lambda}-\lambda)T} \mathbb{E}_{\lambda,\nu}\left[f(Y_T) \prod_{i=1}^{N_T}(1+\psi(Z_i))\right]$$

$$= e^{-(\tilde{\lambda}-\lambda)T} \sum_{k\geqslant 0} \mathbb{E}_{\lambda,\nu}\left[f\left(\sum_{i=1}^{k} Z_i\right)\prod_{i=1}^{k}(1+\psi(Z_i)) \mid N_T = k\right] \mathbb{P}_\lambda(N_T = k)$$

$$= e^{-\tilde{\lambda}T} \sum_{k\geqslant 0} \frac{(\lambda T)^k}{k!} \mathbb{E}_{\lambda,\nu}\left[f\left(\sum_{i=1}^{k} Z_i\right)\prod_{i=1}^{k}(1+\psi(Z_i))\right]$$

$$= e^{-\tilde{\lambda}T} \sum_{k\geqslant 0} \frac{(\lambda T)^k}{k!} \int_{-\infty}^{\infty}\cdots\int_{-\infty}^{\infty} f(z_1+\cdots+z_k)\prod_{i=1}^{k}(1+\psi(z_i))\nu(dz_1)\cdots\nu(dz_k)$$

$$= e^{-\tilde{\lambda}T} \sum_{k\geqslant 0} \frac{(\tilde{\lambda} T)^k}{k!} \int_{-\infty}^{\infty}\cdots\int_{-\infty}^{\infty} f(z_1+\cdots+z_k)\left(\prod_{i=1}^{k}\frac{\tilde{\nu}(dz_i)}{\nu(dz_i)}\right)\nu(dz_1)\cdots\nu(dz_k)$$

$$= e^{-\tilde{\lambda}T} \sum_{k\geqslant 0} \frac{(\tilde{\lambda} T)^k}{k!} \int_{-\infty}^{\infty}\cdots\int_{-\infty}^{\infty} f(z_1+\cdots+z_k)\tilde{\nu}(dz_1)\cdots\tilde{\nu}(dz_k).$$

This shows that under $\mathbb{P}_{\tilde{\lambda},\tilde{\nu}}$, Y_T has the distribution of a compound Poisson process with intensity $\tilde{\lambda}$ and jump size distribution $\tilde{\nu}$. We refer to Proposition 9.6 of Cont and Tankov (2004) for the independence of increments of $(Y_t)_{t\in\mathbb{R}_+}$ under $\widetilde{\mathbb{P}}_{\tilde{\lambda},\tilde{\nu}}$. $\qquad\square$

<u>Example.</u> In case $\nu \simeq \mathcal{N}(\alpha,\sigma^2)$ and $\tilde{\nu} \simeq \mathcal{N}(\beta,\eta^2)$, we have

$$\nu(dx) = \frac{dx}{\sqrt{2\pi\sigma^2}} \exp\left(-\frac{1}{2\sigma^2}(x-\alpha)^2\right), \quad \tilde{\nu}(dx) = \frac{dx}{\sqrt{2\pi\eta^2}} \exp\left(-\frac{1}{2\eta^2}(x-\beta)^2\right),$$

$x \in \mathbb{R}$, hence

$$\frac{\tilde{\nu}(dx)}{\nu(dx)} = \frac{\eta}{\sigma} \exp\left(\frac{1}{2\eta^2}(x-\beta)^2 - \frac{1}{2\sigma^2}(x-\alpha)^2\right),$$

and $\psi(x)$ in (20.35) is given by

$$1 + \psi(x) = \frac{\widetilde{\lambda}\,\widetilde{\nu}(dx)}{\lambda\,\nu(dx)} = \frac{\widetilde{\lambda}\eta}{\lambda\sigma} \exp\left(\frac{1}{2\eta^2}(x-\beta)^2 - \frac{1}{2\sigma^2}(x-\alpha)^2\right), \quad x \in \mathbb{R}.$$

Note that the compound Poisson process with intensity $\widetilde{\lambda} > 0$ and jump size distribution $\widetilde{\nu}$ can be built as

$$X_t := \sum_{k=1}^{N_{\widetilde{\lambda}t/\lambda}} h(Z_k),$$

provided that $\widetilde{\nu}$ is the *pushforward* measure of ν by the function $h : \mathbb{R} \to \mathbb{R}$, *i.e.*

$$\mathbb{P}(h(Z_k) \in A) = \mathbb{P}(Z_k \in h^{-1}(A)) = \nu(h^{-1}(A)) = \widetilde{\nu}(A),$$

for all (measurable) subsets A of $\mathbb{R}$. As a consequence of Theorem 20.18 we have the following proposition.

Proposition 20.19. *The compensated process*

$$Y_t - \widetilde{\lambda}t\,\mathbb{E}_{\widetilde{\nu}}[Z]$$

is a martingale under the probability measure $\widetilde{\mathbb{P}}_{\widetilde{\lambda},\widetilde{\nu}}$ *defined by the Radon–Nikodym density*

$$\frac{d\widetilde{\mathbb{P}}_{\widetilde{\lambda},\widetilde{\nu}}}{d\widetilde{\mathbb{P}}_{\lambda,\nu}} = e^{-(\widetilde{\lambda}-\lambda)T} \prod_{k=1}^{N_T} (1 + \psi(Z_k)).$$

Finally, the Girsanov Theorem can be extended to the linear combination of a standard Brownian motion $(B_t)_{t\in\mathbb{R}_+}$ and a compound Poisson process $(Y_t)_{t\in\mathbb{R}_+}$ independent of $(B_t)_{t\in\mathbb{R}_+}$, as in the following result which is a particular case of Theorem 33.2 of Sato (1999).

Theorem 20.20. *Let* $(Y_t)_{t\geqslant 0}$ *be a compound Poisson process with intensity* $\lambda > 0$ *and jump size distribution* $\nu(dx)$. *Consider another jump size distribution* $\widetilde{\nu}(dx)$ *and intensity parameter* $\widetilde{\lambda} > 0$, *and let*

$$\psi(x) := \frac{\widetilde{\lambda}}{\lambda}\frac{d\widetilde{\nu}}{d\nu}(x) - 1, \qquad x \in \mathbb{R},$$

and let $(u_t)_{t\in\mathbb{R}_+}$ *be a bounded adapted process. Then, the process*

$$\left(B_t + \int_0^t u_s ds + Y_t - \widetilde{\lambda}\,\mathbb{E}_{\widetilde{\nu}}[Z]t\right)_{t\in\mathbb{R}_+}$$

is a martingale under the probability measure $\widetilde{\mathbb{P}}_{u,\widetilde{\lambda},\widetilde{\nu}}$ *defined by the Radon–Nikodym density*

$$\frac{d\widetilde{\mathbb{P}}_{u,\widetilde{\lambda},\widetilde{\nu}}}{d\widetilde{\mathbb{P}}_{\lambda,\nu}} = \exp\left(-(\widetilde{\lambda}-\lambda)T - \int_0^T u_s dB_s - \frac{1}{2}\int_0^T |u_s|^2 ds\right) \prod_{k=1}^{N_T} (1 + \psi(Z_k)). \tag{20.36}$$

As a consequence of Theorem 20.20, if

$$B_t + \int_0^t v_s ds + Y_t \tag{20.37}$$

is not a martingale under $\widetilde{\mathbb{P}}_{\lambda,\nu}$, it will become a martingale under $\widetilde{\mathbb{P}}_{u,\tilde{\lambda},\tilde{\nu}}$ provided that $u, \tilde{\lambda}$ and $\tilde{\nu}$ are chosen in such a way that

$$v_s = u_s - \tilde{\lambda}\,\mathbb{E}_{\tilde{\nu}}[Z], \qquad s \in \mathbb{R}, \tag{20.38}$$

in which case (20.37) can be rewritten into the martingale decomposition

$$dB_t + u_t dt + dY_t - \tilde{\lambda}\,\mathbb{E}_{\tilde{\nu}}[Z]dt,$$

in which both $\left(B_t + \int_0^t u_s ds\right)_{t\in\mathbb{R}_+}$ and $\left(Y_t - \tilde{\lambda}t\,\mathbb{E}_{\tilde{\nu}}[Z]\right)_{t\in\mathbb{R}_+}$ are martingales under $\widetilde{\mathbb{P}}_{u,\tilde{\lambda},\tilde{\nu}}$

The following remarks will be of importance for arbitrage-free pricing in jump models in Chapter 21.

a) When $\tilde{\lambda} = \lambda = 0$, Theorem 20.20 coincides with the usual Girsanov Theorem for Brownian motion, in which case (20.38) admits only one solution given by $u = v$ and there is uniqueness of $\widetilde{\mathbb{P}}_{u,0,0}$.

b) Uniqueness also occurs when $u = 0$ in the absence of Brownian motion, and with Poisson jumps of fixed size a (*i.e.* $\tilde{\nu}(dx) = \nu(dx) = \delta_a(dx)$) since in this case (20.38) also admits only one solution $\tilde{\lambda} = v$ and there is uniqueness of $\widetilde{\mathbb{P}}_{0,\tilde{\lambda},\delta_a}$.

When $\mu \neq r$, the discounted price process $(\widetilde{S}_t)_{t\in\mathbb{R}_+} = (\mathrm{e}^{-rt}S_t)_{t\in\mathbb{R}_+}$ defined by

$$\frac{d\widetilde{S}_t}{\widetilde{S}_{t^-}} = (\mu - r)dt + \sigma dB_t + \eta(dY_t - \lambda t\,\mathbb{E}_\nu[Z])$$

is not martingale under $\mathbb{P}_{\lambda,\nu}$, however, we can rewrite the equation as

$$\frac{d\widetilde{S}_t}{\widetilde{S}_{t^-}} = \sigma(udt + dB_t) + \eta\left(dY_t - \left(\frac{u\sigma}{\eta} + \lambda\,\mathbb{E}_\nu[Z] - \frac{\mu - r}{\eta}\right)dt\right)$$

and choosing u, $\tilde{\nu}$, and $\tilde{\lambda}$ such that

$$\tilde{\lambda}\,\mathbb{E}_{\tilde{\nu}}[Z] = \frac{u\sigma}{\eta} + \lambda\,\mathbb{E}_\nu[Z] - \frac{\mu - r}{\eta}, \tag{20.39}$$

we have

$$\frac{d\widetilde{S}_t}{\widetilde{S}_{t^-}} = \sigma(udt + dB_t) + \eta\big(dY_t - \tilde{\lambda}\,\mathbb{E}_{\tilde{\nu}}[Z]dt\big).$$

Hence the discounted price process $(\widetilde{S}_t)_{t\in\mathbb{R}_+}$ is martingale under the probability measure $\widetilde{\mathbb{P}}_{u,\tilde{\lambda},\tilde{\nu}}$, and the market is without arbitrage by Theorem 5.7 and the existence of a risk-neutral probability measure $\widetilde{\mathbb{P}}_{u,\tilde{\lambda},\tilde{\nu}}$. However, the market is not complete due to the non uniqueness of solutions $(u, \tilde{\nu}, \tilde{\lambda})$ to (20.39), and Theorem 5.11 does not apply in this situation.

Exercises

Exercise 20.1   Analysis of user login activity to the DBX digibank app showed that the times elapsed between two logons are independent and exponentially distributed with mean

$1/\lambda$. Find the CDF of the time $T - T_{N_T}$ elapsed since the last logon before time T, given that the user has logged on at least once.

Hint: The number of logins until time $t > 0$ can be modeled by a standard Poisson process $(N_t)_{t \in [0,T]}$ with intensity λ.

Exercise 20.2 Consider a standard Poisson process $(N_t)_{t \in \mathbb{R}_+}$ with intensity $\lambda > 0$, started at $N_0 = 0$.

a) Solve the stochastic differential equation

$$dS_t = \eta S_{t^-} dN_t - \eta \lambda S_t dt = \eta S_{t^-}(dN_t - \lambda dt).$$

b) Using the first Poisson jump time T_1, solve the stochastic differential equation

$$dS_t = -\lambda \eta S_t dt + dN_t, \qquad t \in (0, T_2).$$

Exercise 20.3 Consider an asset price process $(S_t)_{t \in \mathbb{R}_+}$ given by the stochastic differential equation $dS_t = \mu S_t dt + \sigma S_t dB_t + \eta S_{t^-} dY_t$, *i.e.*

$$S_t = S_0 + \mu \int_0^t S_s ds + \sigma \int_0^t S_s dB_s + \eta \int_0^t S_{s^-} dY_s, \qquad t \geq 0, \tag{20.40}$$

where $S_0 > 0$, $\mu \in \mathbb{R}$, $\sigma \geq 0$, $\eta \geq 0$ are constants, and $(Y_t)_{t \in \mathbb{R}_+}$ is a compound Poisson process with intensity $\lambda \geq 0$ and *i.i.d.* jump sizes Z_k, $k \geq 1$.

a) Write a differential equation satisfied by $u(t) := \mathbb{E}[S_t]$, $t \geq 0$.

 Hint: Use the smoothing lemma Proposition 6.9.

b) Find the value of $\mathbb{E}[S_t]$, $t \geq 0$, in terms of S_0, μ, η, λ and $\mathbb{E}[Z]$.

Exercise 20.4 Consider a standard Poisson process $(N_t)_{t \in \mathbb{R}_+}$ with intensity $\lambda > 0$.

a) Solve the stochastic differential equation $dX_t = \alpha X_t dt + \sigma dN_t$ over the time intervals $[0, T_1)$, $[T_1, T_2)$, $[T_2, T_3)$, $[T_3, T_4)$, where $X_0 = 1$.

b) Write a differential equation for $f(t) := \mathbb{E}[X_t]$, and solve it for $t \in \mathbb{R}_+$.

Exercise 20.5 Consider a standard Poisson process $(N_t)_{t \in \mathbb{R}_+}$ with intensity $\lambda > 0$.

a) Solve the stochastic differential equation $dX_t = \sigma X_{t^-} dN_t$ for $(X_t)_{t \in \mathbb{R}_+}$, where $\sigma > 0$ and $X_0 = 1$.

b) Show that the solution $(S_t)_{t \in \mathbb{R}_+}$ of the stochastic differential equation

$$dS_t = r dt + \sigma S_{t^-} dN_t,$$

 is given by $S_t = S_0 X_t + r X_t \int_0^t X_s^{-1} ds$.

c) Compute $\mathbb{E}[X_t]$ and $\mathbb{E}[X_t / X_s]$, $0 \leq s \leq t$.

d) Compute $\mathbb{E}[S_t]$, $t \geq 0$.

Exercise 20.6 Let $(N_t)_{t \in \mathbb{R}_+}$ be a standard Poisson process with intensity $\lambda > 0$, started at $N_0 = 0$.

a) Is the process $t \mapsto N_t - 2\lambda t$ a *sub*martingale, a martingale, or a *super*martingale?

b) Let $r > 0$. Solve the stochastic differential equation

$$dS_t = rS_t dt + \sigma S_{t^-} (dN_t - \lambda dt).$$

c) Is the process $t \mapsto S_t$ of Question (b) a *sub*martingale, a martingale, or a *super*martingale?

d) Compute the price at time 0 of the European call option with strike price $K = S_0 e^{(r-\lambda\sigma)T}$, where $\sigma > 0$.

Exercise 20.7 Affine stochastic differential equation with jumps. Consider a standard Poisson process $(N_t)_{t \in \mathbb{R}_+}$ with intensity $\lambda > 0$.

a) Solve the stochastic differential equation $dX_t = adN_t + \sigma X_{t^-} dN_t$, where $\sigma > 0$, and $a \in \mathbb{R}$.

b) Compute $\mathbb{E}[X_t]$ for $t \in \mathbb{R}_+$.

Exercise 20.8 Consider the compound Poisson process $Y_t := \displaystyle\sum_{k=1}^{N_t} Z_k$, where $(N_t)_{t \in \mathbb{R}_+}$ is a standard Poisson process with intensity $\lambda > 0$, and $(Z_k)_{k \geqslant 1}$ is an *i.i.d.* sequence of $\mathcal{N}(0, 1)$ Gaussian random variables. Solve the stochastic differential equation

$$dS_t = rS_t dt + \eta S_{t^-} dY_t,$$

where $\eta, r \in \mathbb{R}$.

Exercise 20.9 Show, by direct computation or using the moment generating function (20.10), that the variance of the compound Poisson process Y_t with intensity $\lambda > 0$ satisfies

$$\mathrm{Var}\,[Y_t] = \lambda t \, \mathbb{E}\left[|Z|^2\right] = \lambda t \int_{-\infty}^{\infty} x^2 \nu(dx).$$

Exercise 20.10 Consider an exponential compound Poisson process of the form

$$S_t = S_0 e^{\mu t + \sigma B_t + Y_t}, \qquad t \geqslant 0,$$

where $(Y_t)_{t \in \mathbb{R}_+}$ is a compound Poisson process of the form (20.8).

a) Derive the stochastic differential equation with jumps satisfied by $(S_t)_{t \in \mathbb{R}_+}$.

b) Let $r > 0$. Find a family $(\widetilde{\mathbb{P}}_{u,\lambda,\widetilde{\nu}})$ of probability measures under which the discounted asset price $e^{-rt} S_t$ is a martingale.

Exercise 20.11   Consider $(N_t)_{t\in\mathbb{R}_+}$ a standard Poisson process with intensity $\lambda > 0$ under a probability measure $\mathbb{P}$. Let $(S_t)_{t\in\mathbb{R}_+}$ be defined by the stochastic differential equation

$$dS_t = \mu S_t dt + Z_{N_t} S_{t^-} dN_t, \tag{20.41}$$

where $(Z_k)_{k\geqslant 1}$ is an *i.i.d.* sequence of random variables of the form

$$Z_k = e^{X_k} - 1, \quad \text{where} \quad X_k \simeq \mathcal{N}(0, \sigma^2), \quad k \geqslant 1.$$

a) Solve the equation (20.41).

b) We assume that μ and the risk-free interest rate $r > 0$ are chosen such that the discounted process $(e^{-rt}S_t)_{t\in\mathbb{R}_+}$ is a martingale under $\mathbb{P}$. What relation does this impose on μ and r?

c) Under the relation of Question (b), compute the price at time t of the European call option on S_T with strike price κ and maturity $T > 0$, using a series expansion of Black–Scholes functions.

Exercise 20.12   Consider a standard Poisson process $(N_t)_{t\in\mathbb{R}_+}$ with intensity $\lambda > 0$ under a probability measure $\mathbb{P}$. Let $(S_t)_{t\in\mathbb{R}_+}$ be the mean-reverting process defined by the stochastic differential equation

$$dS_t = -\alpha S_t dt + \sigma(dN_t - \beta dt), \tag{20.42}$$

where $S_0 > 0$ and $\alpha, \beta > 0$.

a) Solve the equation (20.42) for S_t.

b) Compute $f(t) := \mathbb{E}[S_t]$ for all $t \in \mathbb{R}_+$.

c) Under which condition on α, β, σ and λ does the process S_t become a *sub*martingale?

d) Propose a method for the calculation of expectations of the form $\mathbb{E}[\phi(S_T)]$ where ϕ is a payoff function.

Exercise 20.13   Let $(N_t)_{t\in[0,T]}$ be a standard Poisson process started at $N_0 = 0$, with intensity $\lambda > 0$ under the probability measure $\mathbb{P}_\lambda$, and consider the compound Poisson process $(Y_t)_{t\in[0,T]}$ with *i.i.d.* jump sizes $(Z_k)_{k\geqslant 1}$ of distribution $\nu(dx)$.

a) Under the probability measure $\mathbb{P}_\lambda$, the process $t \mapsto Y_t - \lambda t(t + \mathbb{E}[Z])$ is a:

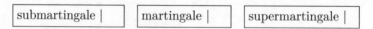

| submartingale │ | martingale │ | supermartingale │ |

b) Consider the process $(S_t)_{t\in[0,T]}$ given by

$$dS_t = \mu S_t dt + \sigma S_{t^-} dY_t.$$

Find $\widetilde{\lambda}$ such that the discounted process $(\widetilde{S}_t)_{t\in[0,T]} := (e^{-rt}S_t)_{t\in[0,T]}$ is a martingale under the probability measure $\mathbb{P}_{\widetilde{\lambda}}$ defined by the Radon–Nikodym density

$$\frac{d\mathbb{P}_{\widetilde{\lambda}}}{d\mathbb{P}_\lambda} := e^{-(\widetilde{\lambda}-\lambda)T}\left(\frac{\widetilde{\lambda}}{\lambda}\right)^{N_T}.$$

with respect to $\mathbb{P}_\lambda$.

c) Price the forward contract with payoff $S_T - \kappa$.

Exercise 20.14 Consider $(Y_t)_{t \in \mathbb{R}_+}$ a compound Poisson process written as

$$Y_t = \sum_{k=1}^{N_t} Z_k, \qquad t \in \mathbb{R}_+,$$

where $(N_t)_{t \in \mathbb{R}_+}$ a standard Poisson process with intensity $\lambda > 0$ and $(Z_k)_{k \geqslant 1}$ is an *i.i.d* family of random variables with probability distribution $\nu(dx)$ on $\mathbb{R}$, under a probability measure $\mathbb{P}$. Let $(S_t)_{t \in \mathbb{R}_+}$ be defined by the stochastic differential equation

$$dS_t = \mu S_t dt + S_{t^-} dY_t. \tag{20.43}$$

a) Solve the equation (20.43).

b) We assume that μ, $\nu(dx)$ and the risk-free interest rate $r > 0$ are chosen such that the discounted process $(e^{-rt} S_t)_{t \in \mathbb{R}_+}$ is a martingale under $\mathbb{P}$. What relation does this impose on μ, $\nu(dx)$ and r?

c) Under the relation of Question (b), compute the price at time t of the European call option on S_T with strike price κ and maturity $T > 0$, using a series expansion of integrals.

Exercise 20.15 Consider a standard Poisson process $(N_t)_{t \in [0,T]}$ with intensity $\lambda > 0$ and a standard Brownian motion $(B_t)_{t \in [0,T]}$ independent of $(N_t)_{t \in [0,T]}$ under the probability measure $\mathbb{P}_\lambda$. Let also $(Y_t)_{t \in [0,T]}$ be a compound Poisson process with *i.i.d.* jump sizes $(Z_k)_{k \geqslant 1}$ of distribution $\nu(dx)$ under $\mathbb{P}_\lambda$, and consider the jump process $(S_t)_{t \in [0,T]}$ solution of

$$dS_t = r S_t dt + \sigma S_t dB_t + \eta S_{t^-} \left(dY_t - \widetilde{\lambda} \mathbb{E}[Z_1] dt \right).$$

with $r, \sigma, \eta, \lambda, \widetilde{\lambda} > 0$.

a) Assume that $\widetilde{\lambda} = \lambda$. Under the probability measure $\mathbb{P}_\lambda$, the discounted price process $(e^{-rt} S_t)_{t \in [0,T]}$ is a:

| submartingale | | martingale | | supermartingale | |

b) Assume $\widetilde{\lambda} > \lambda$. Under the probability measure $\mathbb{P}_\lambda$, the discounted price process $(e^{-rt} S_t)_{t \in [0,T]}$ is a:

| submartingale | | martingale | | supermartingale | |

c) Assume $\widetilde{\lambda} < \lambda$. Under the probability measure $\mathbb{P}_\lambda$, the discounted price process $(e^{-rt} S_t)_{t \in [0,T]}$ is a:

| submartingale | | martingale | | supermartingale | |

d) Consider the probability measure $\widetilde{\mathbb{P}}_{\widetilde{\lambda}}$ defined by its Radon–Nikodym density

$$\frac{d\widetilde{\mathbb{P}}_{\widetilde{\lambda}}}{d\mathbb{P}_\lambda} := e^{-(\widetilde{\lambda} - \lambda)T} \left(\frac{\widetilde{\lambda}}{\lambda} \right)^{N_T}.$$

with respect to $\mathbb{P}_\lambda$. Under the probability measure $\widetilde{\mathbb{P}}_{\widetilde{\lambda}}$, the discounted price process $(e^{-rt} S_t)_{t \in [0,T]}$ is a:

| submartingale | | martingale | | supermartingale | |

Chapter 21

Pricing and Hedging in Jump Models

This chapter considers the pricing and hedging of financial derivatives using discontinuous processes that can model sharp movements in asset prices. Unlike in the case of continuous asset price modeling, the uniqueness of risk-neutral probability measures can be lost and, as a consequence, the computation of perfect replicating hedging strategies may not be possible in general.

21.1 Fitting the Distribution of Market Returns

The modeling of risky asset by stochastic processes with continuous paths, based on Brownian motions, suffers from several defects. First, the path continuity assumption does not seem reasonable in view of the possibility of sudden price variations (jumps) resulting of market crashes, gaps or opening jumps, see *e.g.* Chapter 1 of Cont and Tankov (2004). Secondly, the modeling of risky asset prices by Brownian motion relies on the use of the Gaussian distribution which tends to underestimate the probabilities of extreme events.

The following scripts allow us to fetch DJI and STI index data using Quantmod. The command diff(log(stock)) computes log-returns

$$d \log S_t \simeq \log S_{t+dt} - \log S_t = \log \frac{S_{t+dt}}{S_t}, \qquad t \geq 0,$$

with $dt = 1/365$, which are modeled by the stochastic differential equation

$$d \log S_t = \sigma dB_t + rdt - \frac{\sigma^2}{2} dt$$

satisfied by geometric Brownian motion $S_t = S_0 e^{\sigma B_t + rt - \sigma^2 t/2}$, $t \geq 0$.

```
1  install.packages("quantmod");library(quantmod)
   getSymbols("^STI",from="1990-01-03",to="2015-01-03",src="yahoo");stock=Ad(`STI`);
3  getSymbols("^DJI",from="1990-01-03",to=Sys.Date(),src="yahoo");stock=Ad(`DJI`);
   stock.rtn=diff(log(stock));returns <- as.vector(stock.rtn)
5  m=mean(returns,na.rm=TRUE);s=sd(returns,na.rm=TRUE);times=index(stock.rtn)
   n = sum(is.na(returns))+sum(!is.na(returns));x=seq(1,n);y=rnorm(n,mean=m,sd=s)
7  plot(times,returns,pch=19,xaxs="i",cex=0.03,col="blue", ylab="", xlab="", main = '')
   segments(x0 = times, x1 = times, y0 = 0, y1 = returns,col="blue")
9  points(times,y,pch=19,cex=0.3,col="red")
   abline(h = m+3*s, col="black", lwd =1);abline(h = m, col="black", lwd =1);abline(h = m-3*s, col="black",
      lwd =1)
11 length(returns[abs(returns-m)>3*s])/length(stock.rtn)
   length(y[abs(y-m)>3*s])/length(y);2*(1-pnorm(3*s,0,s))
```

The next Figures 21.1-21.6 illustrate the mismatch between the distributional properties of market log-returns *vs* standardized Gaussian returns, which tend to underestimate the probabilities of extreme events. Note that when $X \simeq \mathcal{N}(0, \sigma^2)$, 99.73% of samples of X are falling within the interval $[-3\sigma, +3\sigma]$, *i.e.* $\mathbb{P}(|X| \leqslant 3\sigma) = 0.9973002$.

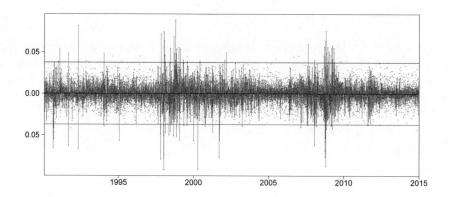

Figure 21.1: Market returns *vs* normalized Gaussian returns.

```
  stock.ecdf=ecdf(as.vector(stock.rtn));x <- seq(-0.25, 0.25, length=100);px <- pnorm((x-m)/s)
2 plot(stock.ecdf, xlab = 'Sample Quantiles', col="blue",ylab = '', main = '')
  lines(x, px, type="l", lty=2, col="red",xlab="x value",ylab="Probability", main="")
4 legend("topleft", legend=c("Empirical CDF", "Gaussian CDF"),col=c("blue", "red"), lty=1:2, cex=0.8)
```

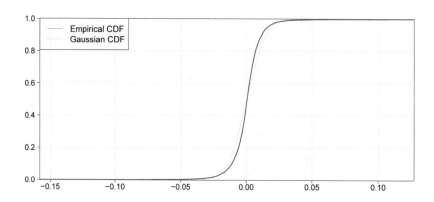

Figure 21.2: Empirical *vs* Gaussian CDF.

The following Quantile-Quantile graph is plotting the normalized empirical quantiles against the standard Gaussian quantiles and is obtained with the `qqnorm(returns)` command.

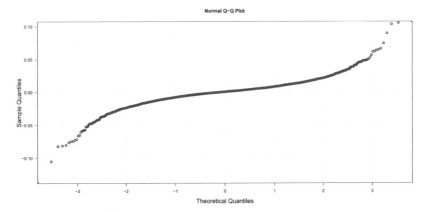

Figure 21.3: Quantile-Quantile plot.

```
  ks.test(y,"pnorm",mean=m,sd=s)
2 ks.test(returns,"pnorm",mean=m,sd=s)
```

The Kolmogorov-Smirnov test clearly rejects the null (normality) hypothesis.

One-sample Kolmogorov-Smirnov test

data: returns
D = 0.075577, p-value < 2.2e-16
alternative hypothesis: two-sided

This mismatch can be further illustrated by the empirical probability density plot in Figure 21.4, which is obtained from the following R code.

```
  x <- seq(-0.1, 0.1, length=100);qx <- dnorm(x,mean=m,sd=s)
2 returns.dens=density(stock.rtn,na.rm=TRUE)
  dev.new(width=10, height=5)
4 plot(returns.dens, xlim=c(-0.1,0.1),xlab = 'x', lwd=3, col="red",ylab = '', main = '',panel.first = abline(h = 0,
        col='grey', lwd =0.2), las=1, cex.axis=1.2, cex.lab=1.3)
  lines(x, qx, type="l", lty=2, lwd=3, col="blue",xlab="x value",ylab="Density", main="")
6 legend("topleft", legend=c("Empirical density", "Gaussian density"),col=c("red", "blue"),
  lty=1:2, cex=1.2)
```

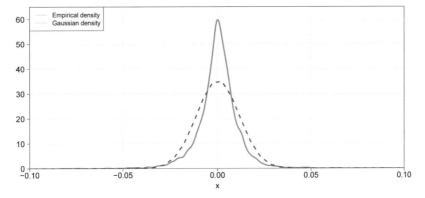

Figure 21.4: Empirical density *vs* normalized Gaussian density.

The next code and graph present a comparison to a calibrated lognormal distribution.

```
1  x <- seq(0, max(stock), length=100);qx <- dlnorm(x,mean=mean(log(stock)), sd=sd(log(stock)))
   stock.dens=density(stock,na.rm=TRUE);dev.new(width=10, height=5)
3  plot(stock.dens, xlab = 'x', lwd=3, col="red",ylab = '', main = '',panel.first = abline(h = 0, col='grey', lwd
       =0.2), las=1, cex.axis=1, cex.lab=1, xaxs='i', yaxs='i')
   lines(x, qx, type="l", lty=2, lwd=3, col="blue",xlab="x value",ylab="Density", main="")
5  legend("topright", legend=c("Empirical density", "Lognormal density"),col=c("red", "blue"), lty=1:2, cex=1.2)
```

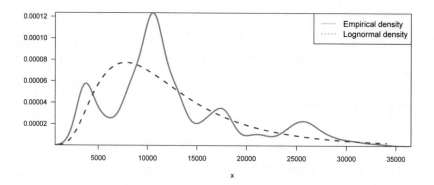

Figure 21.5: Empirical density *vs* normalized lognormal density.

Power tail distributions

We note that the empirical density has significantly higher kurtosis (leptokurtic distribution) and non zero skewness in comparison with the Gaussian probability density. On the other hand, power tail probability densities of the form $\varphi(x) \simeq C_\alpha/x^\alpha$, $x \to \infty$, can provide a better fit of empirical probability density functions, as shown in Figure 21.6.

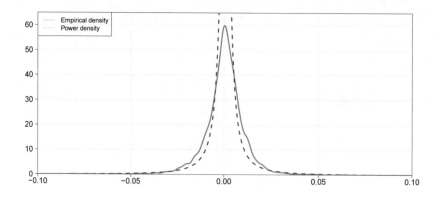

Figure 21.6: Empirical density *vs* power density.

The above fitting of empirical probability density function is using a power probability density function defined by a rational fraction obtained by the following R script.

```
1   install.packages("pracma");library(pracma);
    x <- seq(-0.25, 0.25, length=1000)
3   returns.dens=density(returns,na.rm=TRUE, from = -0.1, to = 0.1, n = 1000)
    a<-rationalfit(returns.dens$x, returns.dens$y, d1=2, d2=2)
5   dev.new(width=10, height=5)
    plot(returns.dens$x, returns.dens$y, lwd=3, type = "l",xlab = 'x', col="red",ylab = '', main = '', panel.first =
        abline(h = 0, col='grey', lwd =0.2),las=1, cex.axis=1, cex.lab=1, xaxs='i', yaxs='i')
7   lines(x,(a$p1[3]+a$p1[2]*x+a$p1[1]*x^2)/(a$p2[3]+a$p2[2]*x+a$p2[1]*x^2), type="l", lty=2, lwd=3,
        col="blue",xlab="x value",ylab="Density", main="")
    legend("topright", legend=c("Empirical density", "Power density"),col=c("red", "blue"), lty=1:2, cex=1.2)
```

The output of the **rationalfit** command is

$p1
[1] -0.184717249 -0.001591433 0.001385017

$p2
[1] 1.000000e+00 -6.460948e-04 1.314672e-05

which yields a rational fraction of the form

$$x \quad \mapsto \quad \frac{0.001385017 - 0.001591433 \times x - 0.184717249 \times x^2}{1.314672 \; 10^{-5} - 6.460948 \; 10^{-4} \times x + x^2}$$

$$\simeq \quad -0.184717249 - \frac{0.001591433}{x} + \frac{0.001385017}{x^2},$$

which approximates the empirical probability density function of DJI returns in the least squares sense.

A solution to this tail problem is to use stochastic processes with jumps, that will account for sudden variations of the asset prices. On the other hand, such jump models are generally based on the Poisson distribution which has a slower tail decay than the Gaussian distribution. This allows one to assign higher probabilities to extreme events, resulting in a more realistic modeling of asset prices. *Stable distributions* with parameter $\alpha \in (0, 2)$ provide typical examples of probability laws with power tails, as their probability density functions behave asymptotically as $x \mapsto C_\alpha / |x|^{1+\alpha}$ when $x \to \pm\infty$.

Edgeworth and Gram-Charlier expansions

Let

$$\varphi(x) := \frac{1}{\sqrt{2\pi}} \, e^{-x^2/2}, \qquad x \in \mathbb{R},$$

denote the standard normal density function, and let

$$\Phi(x) := \int_{-\infty}^{x} \varphi(y)dy, \qquad x \in \mathbb{R},$$

denote the standard normal cumulative distribution function. Let also

$$H_n(x) := \frac{(-1)^n}{\varphi(x)} \frac{\partial^n \varphi}{\partial x^n}(x), \qquad x \in \mathbb{R},$$

denote the Hermite polynomial of degree n, with $H_0(x) = 1$.

Given X a random variable, the sequence $(\kappa_n^X)_{n \geqslant 1}$ of cumulants of X has been introduced in Thiele (1899). In what follows we will use the Moment Generating Function (MGF) of the random variable X, defined as

$$\mathcal{M}_X(t) := \mathbb{E}\left[e^{tX}\right] = 1 + \sum_{n \geqslant 1} \frac{t^n}{n!} \mathbb{E}[X^n], \qquad t \in \mathbb{R}. \tag{21.1}$$

Definition 21.1. *The* cumulants *of a random variable X are defined to be the coefficients $(\kappa_n^X)_{n \geqslant 1}$ appearing in the series expansion*

$$\log \left(\mathbb{E}\left[e^{tX} \right] \right) = \log \left(1 + \sum_{n \geqslant 1} \frac{t^n}{n!} \mathbb{E}[X^n] \right) = \sum_{n \geqslant 1} \kappa_n^X \frac{t^n}{n!}, \quad t \in \mathbb{R}, \tag{21.2}$$

of the logarithmic moment generating function (log-MGF) of X.

The cumulants of X were originally called "semi-invariants" due to the property $\kappa_n^{X+Y} = \kappa_n^X + \kappa_n^Y$, $n \geqslant 1$, when X and Y are independent random variables. Indeed, in this case we have

$$
\begin{aligned}
\sum_{n \geqslant 1} \kappa_n^{X+Y} \frac{t^n}{n!} &= \log \left(\mathbb{E}\left[e^{t(X+Y)} \right] \right) \\
&= \log \left(\mathbb{E}\left[e^{tX} \right] \mathbb{E}\left[e^{tY} \right] \right) \\
&= \log \mathbb{E}\left[e^{tX} \right] + \log \mathbb{E}\left[e^{tY} \right] \\
&= \sum_{n \geqslant 1} \kappa_n^X \frac{t^n}{n!} + \sum_{n \geqslant 1} \kappa_n^Y \frac{t^n}{n!} \\
&= \sum_{n \geqslant 1} \left(\kappa_n^X + \kappa_n^Y \right) \frac{t^n}{n!}, \quad t \in \mathbb{R},
\end{aligned}
$$

showing that $\kappa_n^{X+Y} = \kappa_n^X + \kappa_n^Y$, $n \geqslant 1$.

a) First moment and cumulant. Taking $n = 1$ and $\pi = \{1\}$, we find $\kappa_1^X = \mathbb{E}[X]$.

b) Variance and second cumulant. We have

$$\kappa_2^X = \mathbb{E}\left[X^2 \right] - (\mathbb{E}[X])^2 = \mathbb{E}\left[(X - \mathbb{E}[X])^2 \right],$$

and $\sqrt{\kappa_2^X}$ is the *standard deviation* of X.

c) The third cumulant of X is given as the third central moment

$$\kappa_3^X = \mathbb{E}[(X - \mathbb{E}[X])^3],$$

and the coefficient

$$\frac{\kappa_3^X}{(\kappa_2^X)^{3/2}} = \frac{\mathbb{E}\left[(X - \mathbb{E}[X])^3 \right]}{(\mathbb{E}[(X - \mathbb{E}[X])^2])^{3/2}}$$

is the *skewness* of X.

d) Similarly, we have

$$
\begin{aligned}
\kappa_4^X &= \mathbb{E}\left[(X - \mathbb{E}[X])^4 \right] - 3(\kappa_2^X)^2 \\
&= \mathbb{E}\left[(X - \mathbb{E}[X])^4 \right] - 3\left(\mathbb{E}\left[(X - \mathbb{E}[X])^2 \right] \right)^2,
\end{aligned}
$$

and the *excess kurtosis* of X is defined as

$$\frac{\kappa_4^X}{(\kappa_2^X)^2} = \frac{\mathbb{E}[(X - \mathbb{E}[X])^4]}{(\mathbb{E}[(X - \mathbb{E}[X])^2])^2} - 3.$$

The next proposition summarizes the Gram-Charlier expansion method to obtain series expansion of a probability density function, see Gram (1883), Charlier (1914) and § 17.6 of Cramér (1946).

Proposition 21.2. *(Proposition 2.1 in Tanaka et al. (2010)) The Gram-Charlier expansion of the continuous probability density function $\phi_X(x)$ of a random variable X is given by*

$$\phi_X(x) = \frac{1}{\sqrt{\kappa_2^X}} \varphi\left(\frac{x - \kappa_1^X}{\sqrt{\kappa_2^X}}\right) + \frac{1}{\sqrt{\kappa_2^X}} \sum_{n=3}^{\infty} c_n H_n\left(\frac{x - \kappa_1^X}{\sqrt{\kappa_2^X}}\right) \varphi\left(\frac{x - \kappa_1^X}{\sqrt{\kappa_2^X}}\right),$$

where $c_0 = 1$, $c_1 = c_2 = 0$, and the sequence $(c_n)_{n \geqslant 3}$ is given from the cumulants $(\kappa_n^X)_{n \geqslant 1}$ of X as

$$c_n = \frac{1}{(\kappa_2^X)^{n/2}} \sum_{m=1}^{[n/3]} \sum_{\substack{l_1 + \cdots + l_m = n \\ l_1, \ldots, l_m \geqslant 3}} \frac{\kappa_{l_1}^X \cdots \kappa_{l_m}^X}{m! l_1! \cdots l_m!}, \qquad n \geqslant 3.$$

The coefficients c_3 and c_4 can be expressed from the skewness $\kappa_3^X / (\kappa_2^X)^{3/2}$ and the excess kurtosis $\kappa_4^X / (\kappa_2^X)^2$ as

$$c_3 = \frac{\kappa_3^X}{3!(\kappa_2^X)^{3/2}} \quad \text{and} \quad c_4 = \frac{\kappa_4^X}{4!(\kappa_2^X)^2}.$$

a) The first-order expansion

$$\phi_X^{(1)}(x) = \frac{1}{\sqrt{\kappa_2^X}} \varphi\left(\frac{x - \kappa_1^X}{\sqrt{\kappa_2^X}}\right)$$

corresponds to normal moment matching approximation.

b) The third-order expansion is given by

$$\phi_X^{(3)}(x) = \frac{1}{\sqrt{\kappa_2^X}} \varphi\left(\frac{x - \kappa_1^X}{\sqrt{\kappa_2^X}}\right)\left(1 + c_3 H_3\left(\frac{x - \kappa_1^X}{\sqrt{\kappa_2^X}}\right)\right)$$

c) The fourth-order expansion is given by

$$\phi_X^{(4)}(x) = \frac{1}{\sqrt{\kappa_2^X}} \varphi\left(\frac{x - \kappa_1^X}{\sqrt{\kappa_2^X}}\right)\left(1 + c_3 H_3\left(\frac{x - \kappa_1^X}{\sqrt{\kappa_2^X}}\right) + c_4 H_4\left(\frac{x - \kappa_1^X}{\sqrt{\kappa_2^X}}\right)\right).$$

The next R code presents a fit of first to fourth order Gram-Charlier density approximations to the empirical distribution of asset returns.

```
   install.packages("SimMultiCorrData");install.packages("PDQutils")
 2 library(SimMultiCorrData);library(PDQutils)
   x <- seq(-0.25, 0.25, length=1000);dev.new(width=10, height=5)
 4 plot(returns.dens$x, returns.dens$y, xlim=c(-0.1,0.1), xlab = 'x', type = 'l', lwd=3, col="red",ylab = '', main
        = '',panel.first = abline(h = 0, col='grey', lwd =0.2),las=1, cex.axis=1, cex.lab=1,xaxs='i', yaxs='i')
   lines(x, qx, type="l", lty=2, lwd=3, col="blue")
 6 m<-calc_moments(returns[!is.na(returns)])
   cumulants<-c(m[1],m[2]**2);d2 <- dapx_edgeworth(x, cumulants)
 8 lines(x, d2, type="l", lty=2, lwd=3, col="blue")
   cumulants<-c(m[1],m[2]**2,m[3]*m[2]**3);d3 <- dapx_edgeworth(x, cumulants)
10 lines(x, d3, type="l", lty=2, lwd=3, col="green")
   cumulants<-c(m[1],m[2]**2,0.5*m[3]*m[2]**3,0.2*m[4]*m[2]**4)
12 d4 <- dapx_edgeworth(x, cumulants);lines(x, d4, type="l", lty=2, lwd=3, col="purple")
   legend("topleft", legend=c("Empirical density", "Gaussian density", "Third order Gram-Charlier", "Fourth order
        Gram-Charlier"),col=c("red", "blue", "green", "purple"), lty=1:2,cex=1.2)
14 grid()
```

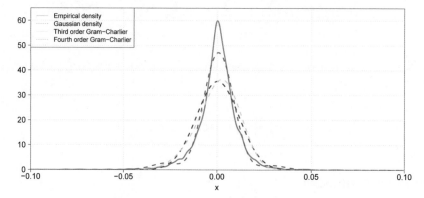

Figure 21.7: Gram-Charlier expansions

21.2   Risk-Neutral Probability Measures

Consider an asset price process modeled by the equation,

$$dS_t = \mu S_t dt + \sigma S_t dB_t + S_t \cdot dY_t, \tag{21.3}$$

where $(Y_t)_{t \in \mathbb{R}_+}$ is the compound Poisson process defined in Section 20.2, with jump size distribution $\nu(dx)$ under $\mathbb{P}_\nu$. The equation (21.3) has for solution

$$S_t = S_0 \exp\left(\mu t + \sigma B_t - \frac{\sigma^2}{2}t\right) \prod_{k=1}^{N_t}(1 + Z_k), \tag{21.4}$$

$t \geqslant 0$. An important issue for non-arbitrage pricing is to determine a risk-neutral probability measure (or martingale measure) $\mathbb{P}^*$ under which the discounted asset price process $(\widetilde{S}_t)_{t \in \mathbb{R}_+} := (e^{-rt}S_t)_{t \in \mathbb{R}_+}$ is a martingale, and this goal can be achieved using the Girsanov Theorem for jump processes, cf. Section 20.5. Similarly to Lemma 5.13, we have the following result.

Lemma 21.3. Discounting lemma. *The discounted asset price process*

$$\widetilde{S}_t := e^{-rt}S_t, \qquad t \geqslant 0,$$

satisfies the equation

$$d\widetilde{S}_t = (\mu - r)\widetilde{S}_t dt + \sigma\widetilde{S}_t dB_t + e^{-rt}\widetilde{S}_{t^-} dY_t. \tag{21.5}$$

In addition, Equation 21.5 can be rewritten as

$$d\widetilde{S}_t = (\mu - r + \tilde{\lambda}\,\mathbb{E}_{\tilde{\nu}}[Z] - \sigma u)\widetilde{S}_t dt + \sigma\widetilde{S}_t(dB_t + udt) + \widetilde{S}_{t^-}(dY_t - \tilde{\lambda}\,\mathbb{E}_{\tilde{\nu}}[Z]dt),$$

for any $u \in \mathbb{R}$. When the drift parameter u, the intensity $\tilde{\lambda} > 0$ and the jump size distribution $\tilde{\nu}$ are chosen to satisfy the condition

$$\mu - r + \tilde{\lambda}\,\mathbb{E}_{\tilde{\nu}}[Z] - \sigma u = 0 \tag{21.6}$$

with $\sigma u + r - \mu > 0$, then

$$\tilde{\lambda} = \frac{\sigma u + r - \mu}{\mathbb{E}_{\tilde{\nu}}[Z]} > 0,$$

and the Girsanov Theorem 20.20 for jump processes shows that

$$dB_t + udt + dY_t - \tilde{\lambda}\,\mathbb{E}_{\tilde{\nu}}[Z]dt$$

is a martingale under the probability measure $\widetilde{\mathbb{P}}_{u,\tilde{\lambda},\tilde{\nu}}$ defined in Theorem 20.20. As a consequence, the discounted price process $(\widetilde{S}_t)_{t\in\mathbb{R}_+} = (e^{-rt}S_t)_{t\in\mathbb{R}_+}$ becomes a martingale is a martingale under $\widetilde{\mathbb{P}}_{u,\tilde{\lambda},\tilde{\nu}}$.

In this setting, the non-uniqueness of the risk-neutral probability measure $\widetilde{\mathbb{P}}_{u,\tilde{\lambda},\tilde{\nu}}$ is apparent since additional degrees of freedom are involved in the choices of u, λ and the measure $\tilde{\nu}$, whereas in the continuous case the choice of $u = (\mu - r)/\sigma$ in (7.14) was unique.

21.3 Pricing in Jump Models

Recall that a market is without arbitrage if and only it admits at least one risk-neutral probability measure.

Consider the probability measure $\widetilde{\mathbb{P}}_{u,\tilde{\lambda},\tilde{\nu}}$ constructed in Theorem 20.20, under which the discounted asset price process

$$d\widetilde{S}_t = \sigma\widetilde{S}_t d\widehat{B}_t + \widetilde{S}_{t^-}(dY_t - \tilde{\lambda}\,\mathbb{E}_{\nu}[Z]dt),$$

is a martingale, and $\widehat{B}_t = B_t + ut$ is a standard Brownian motion under $\widetilde{\mathbb{P}}_{u,\tilde{\lambda},\tilde{\nu}}$. Then, the arbitrage-free price of a claim with payoff C is given by

$$e^{-(T-t)r}\,\mathbb{E}_{u,\tilde{\lambda},\tilde{\nu}}[C \mid \mathcal{F}_t] \tag{21.7}$$

under $\widetilde{\mathbb{P}}_{u,\tilde{\lambda},\tilde{\nu}}$.

Clearly the price (21.7) of C is no longer unique in the presence of jumps due to an infinity of possible choices of parameters $u, \tilde{\lambda}, \tilde{\nu}$ satisfying the martingale condition (21.6), and such a market is not complete, except if either $\tilde{\lambda} = \lambda = 0$, or ($\sigma = 0$ and $\tilde{\nu} = \nu = \delta_1$).

Various techniques can be used for the selection of a risk-neutral probability measure, such as the determination of a minimal entropy risk-neutral probability measure $\tilde{\mathbb{P}}_{u, \tilde{\lambda}, \tilde{\nu}}$ that minimizes the Kullback–Leibler relative entropy

$$Q \mapsto I(Q, \mathbb{P}) := \mathbb{E}\left[\frac{dQ}{d\mathbb{P}} \log \frac{dQ}{d\mathbb{P}}\right]$$

among the probability measures Q equivalent to $\mathbb{P}$.

Pricing vanilla options

The price of a vanilla option with payoff of the form $\phi(S_T)$ on the underlying asset S_T can be written from (21.7) as

$$e^{-(T-t)r} \mathbb{E}_{u, \tilde{\lambda}, \tilde{\nu}}[\phi(S_T) \mid \mathcal{F}_t], \tag{21.8}$$

where the expectation can be computed as

$$
\begin{aligned}
&\mathbb{E}_{u, \tilde{\lambda}, \tilde{\nu}}\left[\phi(S_T) \mid \mathcal{F}_t\right] \\
&= \mathbb{E}_{u, \tilde{\lambda}, \tilde{\nu}}\left[\phi\left(S_0 \exp\left(\mu T + \sigma B_T - \frac{\sigma^2}{2} T\right) \prod_{k=1}^{N_T} (1 + Z_k)\right) \Big| \mathcal{F}_t\right] \\
&= \mathbb{E}_{u, \tilde{\lambda}, \tilde{\nu}}\left[\phi\left(S_t \exp\left((T-t)\mu + (B_T - B_t)\sigma - \frac{\sigma^2}{2}(T-t)\right) \prod_{k=N_t+1}^{N_T} (1 + Z_k)\right) \Big| \mathcal{F}_t\right] \\
&= \mathbb{E}_{u, \tilde{\lambda}, \tilde{\nu}}\left[\phi\left(x \exp\left((T-t)\mu + (B_T - B_t)\sigma - \frac{\sigma^2}{2}(T-t)\right) \prod_{k=N_t+1}^{N_T} (1 + Z_k)\right)\right]_{x=S_t} \\
&= \sum_{n \geqslant 0} \mathbb{P}_{u, \tilde{\lambda}, \tilde{\nu}}(N_T - N_t = n) \\
&\qquad \mathbb{E}_{u, \tilde{\lambda}, \tilde{\nu}}\left[\phi\left(x e^{(T-t)\mu + (B_T - B_t)\sigma - (T-t)\sigma^2/2} \prod_{k=N_t+1}^{N_T} (1 + Z_k)\right) \Big| N_T - N_t = n\right]_{x=S_t} \\
&= e^{-(T-t)\tilde{\lambda}} \sum_{n \geqslant 0} \frac{((T-t)\tilde{\lambda})^n}{n!} \\
&\qquad \times \mathbb{E}_{u, \tilde{\lambda}, \tilde{\nu}}\left[\phi\left(x e^{(T-t)\mu + (B_T - B_t)\sigma - (T-t)\sigma^2/2} \prod_{k=1}^{n} (1 + Z_k)\right)\right]_{x=S_t} \\
&= e^{-\tilde{\lambda}(T-t)} \sum_{n \geqslant 0} \frac{(\tilde{\lambda}(T-t))^n}{n!} \underbrace{\int_{-\infty}^{\infty} \cdots \int_{-\infty}^{\infty}}_{n \text{ times}} \\
&\qquad \mathbb{E}_{u, \tilde{\lambda}, \tilde{\nu}}\left[\phi\left(x e^{(T-t)\mu + (B_T - B_t)\sigma - (T-t)\sigma^2/2} \prod_{k=1}^{n} (1 + z_k)\right)\right]_{x=S_t} \tilde{\nu}(dz_1) \cdots \tilde{\nu}(dz_n),
\end{aligned}
$$

hence the price of the vanilla option with payoff $\phi(S_T)$ is given by

$$e^{-(T-t)r}\, \mathbb{E}_{u,\tilde{\lambda},\tilde{\nu}}[\phi(S_T) \mid \mathcal{F}_t]$$

$$= \frac{1}{\sqrt{2(T-t)\pi}}\, e^{-(r+\tilde{\lambda})(T-t)} \sum_{n\geqslant 0} \frac{(\tilde{\lambda}(T-t))^n}{n!} \underbrace{\int_{-\infty}^{\infty} \cdots \int_{-\infty}^{\infty}}_{n+1 \text{ times}}$$

$$\phi\left(S_t\, e^{(T-t)\mu+\sigma x-(T-t)\sigma^2/2} \prod_{k=1}^{n}(1+z_k)\right)\, e^{-x^2/(2(T-t))}\tilde{\nu}(dz_1)\cdots\tilde{\nu}(dz_n)dx.$$

21.4 Exponential Lévy Models

Instead of modeling the asset price $(S_t)_{t\in\mathbb{R}_+}$ through a stochastic exponential (21.4) solution of the stochastic differential equation with jumps of the form (21.3), we may consider an exponential price process of the form

$$\begin{aligned}
S_t &:= S_0\, e^{\mu t+\sigma B_t+Y_t} \\
&= S_0 \exp\left(\mu t+\sigma B_t+\sum_{k=1}^{N_t} Z_k\right) \\
&= S_0\, e^{\mu t+\sigma B_t} \prod_{k=1}^{N_t} e^{Z_k} \\
&= S_0\, e^{\mu t+\sigma B_t} \prod_{0\leqslant s\leqslant t} e^{\Delta Y_t}, \qquad t\geqslant 0,
\end{aligned}$$

from Relation (20.9), *i.e.* $\Delta Y_t = Z_{N_t}\Delta N_t$. The process $(S_t)_{t\in\mathbb{R}_+}$ is equivalently given by the log-return dynamics

$$d\log S_t = \mu dt + \sigma dB_t + dY_t, \qquad t\geqslant 0.$$

In the exponential Lévy model we also have

$$S_t = S_0\, e^{(\mu+\sigma^2/2)t+\sigma B_t-\sigma^2 t/2+Y_t}$$

and the process S_t satisfies the stochastic differential equation

$$\begin{aligned}
dS_t &= \left(\mu+\frac{\sigma^2}{2}\right)S_t dt + \sigma S_t dB_t + S_{t^-}(e^{\Delta Y_t}-1)dN_t \\
&= \left(\mu+\frac{\sigma^2}{2}\right)S_t dt + \sigma S_t dB_t + S_{t^-}(e^{Z_{N_t}}-1)dN_t,
\end{aligned}$$

hence the process S_t has jumps of size $S_{T_k^-}(e^{Z_k}-1)$, $k\geqslant 1$, and (21.6) reads

$$\mu+\frac{\sigma^2}{2}-r = \sigma u - \tilde{\lambda}\,\mathbb{E}_{\tilde{\nu}}[e^Z-1].$$

Under this condition we can choose a risk-neutral probability measure $\widetilde{\mathbb{P}}_{u,\tilde{\lambda},\tilde{\nu}}$ under which $(e^{-rt}S_t)_{t\in\mathbb{R}_+}$ is a martingale, and the expected value

$$e^{-(T-t)r}\, \mathbb{E}_{u,\tilde{\lambda},\tilde{\nu}}[\phi(S_T) \mid \mathcal{F}_t]$$

represents a (non-unique) arbitrage-free price at time $t \in [0, T]$ for the contingent claim with payoff $\phi(S_T)$.

This arbitrage-free price can be expressed as

$$
\begin{aligned}
\mathrm{e}^{-(T-t)r}\, \mathbb{E}_{u,\tilde{\lambda},\tilde{\nu}}\left[\phi(S_T) \,|\, \mathcal{F}_t\right] &= \mathrm{e}^{-(T-t)r}\, \mathbb{E}_{u,\tilde{\lambda},\tilde{\nu}}\left[\phi(S_0\, \mathrm{e}^{\mu T + \sigma B_T + Y_T}) \,|\, \mathcal{F}_t\right] \\
&= \mathrm{e}^{-(T-t)r}\, \mathbb{E}_{u,\tilde{\lambda},\tilde{\nu}}\left[\phi(S_t\, \mathrm{e}^{(T-t)\mu + (B_T - B_t)\sigma + Y_T - Y_t}) \,|\, \mathcal{F}_t\right] \\
&= \mathrm{e}^{-(T-t)r}\, \mathbb{E}_{u,\tilde{\lambda},\tilde{\nu}}\left[\phi(x\, \mathrm{e}^{(T-t)\mu + (B_T - B_t)\sigma + Y_T - Y_t})\right]_{x=S_t} \\
&= \mathrm{e}^{-(T-t)r}\, \mathbb{E}_{u,\tilde{\lambda},\tilde{\nu}}\left[\phi\left(x\exp\left((T-t)\mu + (B_T - B_t)\sigma + \sum_{k=N_t+1}^{N_T} Z_k\right)\right)\right]_{x=S_t} \\
&= \mathrm{e}^{-(T-t)r - (T-t)\tilde{\lambda}} \\
&\quad \times \sum_{n\geqslant 0} \frac{(\tilde{\lambda}(T-t))^n}{n!}\, \mathbb{E}_{u,\tilde{\lambda},\tilde{\nu}}\left[\phi\left(x\, \mathrm{e}^{(T-t)\mu + (B_T - B_t)\sigma}\exp\left(\sum_{k=1}^{n} Z_k\right)\right)\right]_{x=S_t}.
\end{aligned}
$$

Merton (1976) model

We assume that $(Z_k)_{k\geqslant 1}$ is a family of independent identically distributed Gaussian $\mathcal{N}(\delta, \eta^2)$ random variables under $\widetilde{\mathbb{P}}_{u,\tilde{\lambda},\tilde{\nu}}$ with

$$
\mu + \frac{\sigma^2}{2} - r = \sigma u - \tilde{\lambda}\, \mathbb{E}_{\tilde{\nu}}[\mathrm{e}^Z - 1] = \sigma u - \tilde{\lambda}(\mathrm{e}^{\delta + \eta^2/2} - 1),
$$

as in (21.6), hence by the Girsanov Theorem 20.20 for jump processes, $B_t + ut + Y_t - \tilde{\lambda}\, \mathbb{E}_{\tilde{\nu}}[\mathrm{e}^Z - 1]t$ is a martingale and $B_t + ut$ is a standard Brownian motion under $\widetilde{\mathbb{P}}_{u,\tilde{\lambda},\tilde{\nu}}$. For simplicity we choose $u = 0$, which yields

$$
\mu = r - \frac{\sigma^2}{2} - \tilde{\lambda}(\mathrm{e}^{\delta + \eta^2/2} - 1).
$$

Proposition 21.4. *The price of the European call option in the Merton model is given by*

$$
\begin{aligned}
&\mathrm{e}^{-(T-t)r}\, \mathbb{E}_{\tilde{\lambda},\tilde{\nu}}\left[(S_T - K)^+ \,|\, \mathcal{F}_t\right] \\
&= \mathrm{e}^{-\tilde{\lambda}\mathrm{e}^{\delta + \eta^2/2}(T-t)} \sum_{n\geqslant 0} \frac{(\tilde{\lambda}\mathrm{e}^{\delta + n\eta^2/2}(T-t))^n}{n!} \\
&\quad \times \mathrm{Bl}\left(S_t, \kappa, \sigma^2 + n\eta^2/(T-t), r + n\frac{\delta + \eta^2/2}{T-t} - \tilde{\lambda}(\mathrm{e}^{\delta + \eta^2/2} - 1), T-t\right),
\end{aligned}
$$

$0 \leqslant t \leqslant T$.

Proof. We have

$$
\begin{aligned}
&\mathrm{e}^{-(T-t)r}\, \mathbb{E}_{\tilde{\lambda},\tilde{\nu}}\left[\phi(S_T) \,|\, \mathcal{F}_t\right] \\
&= \mathrm{e}^{-(T-t)r - (T-t)\tilde{\lambda}} \sum_{n\geqslant 0} \frac{((T-t)\tilde{\lambda})^n}{n!} \\
&\quad \times \mathbb{E}_{\tilde{\lambda},\tilde{\nu}}\left[\phi\left(x\, \mathrm{e}^{(T-t)\mu + (B_T - B_t)\sigma}\exp\left(\sum_{k=1}^{n} Z_k\right)\right)\right]_{x=S_t}
\end{aligned}
$$

$$
= \quad \mathrm{e}^{-(T-t)r-(T-t)\tilde{\lambda}} \sum_{n\geqslant 0} \frac{((T-t)\tilde{\lambda})^n}{n!} \, \mathbb{E}\left[\phi(x\,\mathrm{e}^{(T-t)\mu+n\delta+X_n})\right]_{x=S_t}
$$

$$
= \quad \mathrm{e}^{-(T-t)r-(T-t)\tilde{\lambda}} \sum_{n\geqslant 0} \frac{((T-t)\tilde{\lambda})^n}{n!} \int_{-\infty}^{\infty} \phi\big(S_t\,\mathrm{e}^{(T-t)\mu+n\delta+y}\big) \frac{\mathrm{e}^{-y^2/(2((T-t)\sigma^2+n\eta^2))}}{\sqrt{4((T-t)\sigma^2+n\eta^2)\pi}} dy,
$$

where

$$
X_n := (B_T - B_t)\sigma + \sum_{k=1}^{n}(Z_k - \delta) \simeq \mathcal{N}(0, (T-t)\sigma^2 + n\eta^2), \qquad n \geqslant 0,
$$

is a centered Gaussian random variable with variance

$$
v_n^2 := (T-t)\sigma^2 + \sum_{k=1}^{n} \mathrm{Var}\, Z_k = (T-t)\sigma^2 + n\eta^2.
$$

Hence when $\phi(x) = (x - \kappa)^+$ is the payoff function of a European call option, using the relation

$$
\mathrm{Bl}\big(x, \kappa, v_n^2/\tau, r, \tau\big) = \mathrm{e}^{-r\tau}\, \mathbb{E}\left[\big(x\,\mathrm{e}^{X_n - v_n^2/2 + r\tau} - K\big)^+\right]
$$

we get

$$
\mathrm{e}^{-(T-t)r-(T-t)\tilde{\lambda}}\, \mathbb{E}_{\tilde{\lambda},\tilde{\nu}}[(S_T - \kappa)^+ \mid \mathcal{F}_t]
$$

$$
= \quad \mathrm{e}^{-(T-t)r-(T-t)\tilde{\lambda}} \sum_{n\geqslant 0} \frac{((T-t)\tilde{\lambda})^n}{n!} \, \mathbb{E}\left[\big(x\,\mathrm{e}^{(T-t)\mu+n\delta+X_n} - \kappa\big)^+\right]_{x=S_t}
$$

$$
= \quad \mathrm{e}^{-(T-t)r-(T-t)\tilde{\lambda}} \sum_{n\geqslant 0} \frac{((T-t)\tilde{\lambda})^n}{n!}
$$
$$
\times \mathbb{E}\left[\big(x\,\mathrm{e}^{(r-\sigma^2/2-\tilde{\lambda}(\mathrm{e}^{\delta+\eta^2/2}-1))(T-t)+n\delta+X_n} - \kappa\big)^+\right]_{x=S_t}
$$

$$
= \quad \mathrm{e}^{-(T-t)r-(T-t)\tilde{\lambda}} \sum_{n\geqslant 0} \frac{((T-t)\tilde{\lambda})^n}{n!}
$$
$$
\times \mathbb{E}\left[\big(x\,\mathrm{e}^{n\delta+n\eta^2/2-\tilde{\lambda}(\mathrm{e}^{\delta+\eta^2/2}-1)(T-t)+X_n-v^2)n/2+(T-t)r} - \kappa\big)^+\right]_{x=S_t}
$$

$$
= \quad \mathrm{e}^{-(T-t)\tilde{\lambda}} \sum_{n\geqslant 0} \frac{((T-t)\tilde{\lambda})^n}{n!}
$$
$$
\times \mathrm{Bl}\big(S_t\,\mathrm{e}^{n\delta+n\eta^2/2-\tilde{\lambda}(\mathrm{e}^{\delta+\eta^2/2}-1)(T-t)}, \kappa, \sigma^2 + n\eta^2/(T-t), r, T-t\big).
$$

We may also write

$$
\mathrm{e}^{-(T-t)r-(T-t)\tilde{\lambda}}\, \mathbb{E}_{\tilde{\lambda},\tilde{\nu}}[(S_T - \kappa)^+ \mid \mathcal{F}_t]
$$

$$
= \quad \mathrm{e}^{-(T-t)\tilde{\lambda}} \sum_{n\geqslant 0} \frac{((T-t)\tilde{\lambda})^n}{n!}\, \mathrm{e}^{n\delta+n\eta^2/2-\tilde{\lambda}(\mathrm{e}^{\delta+\eta^2/2}-1)(T-t)}
$$
$$
\times \mathrm{Bl}\left(S_t, \kappa\,\mathrm{e}^{-n\delta-n\eta^2/2+\tilde{\lambda}(\mathrm{e}^{\delta+\eta^2/2}-1)(T-t)}, \sigma^2 + n\eta^2/(T-t), r, T-t\right)
$$

$$= \; e^{-\tilde{\lambda} e^{\delta + \eta^2/2}(T-t)} \sum_{n \geqslant 0} \frac{(\tilde{\lambda} e^{\delta + n\eta^2/2}(T-t))^n}{n!}$$

$$\times \mathrm{Bl}\left(S_t, \kappa, \sigma^2 + n\eta^2/(T-t), r + n\frac{\delta + \eta^2/2}{T-t} - \tilde{\lambda}(e^{\delta + \eta^2/2} - 1), T-t\right).$$

$\square$

21.5   Black–Scholes PDE with Jumps

In this section we consider the asset price process $(S_t)_{t \in \mathbb{R}_+}$ modeled by the equation (21.3), *i.e.*

$$dS_t = \mu S_t dt + \sigma S_t dB_t + S_{t^-} dY_t, \tag{21.9}$$

where $(Y_t)_{t \in \mathbb{R}_+}$ is a compound Poisson process with jump size distribution $\nu(dx)$. Recall that by the Markov property of $(S_t)_{t \in \mathbb{R}_+}$, the price (21.8) at time t of the option with payoff $\phi(S_T)$ can be written as a function $f(t, S_t)$ of t and S_t, *i.e.*

$$f(t, S_t) = e^{-(T-t)r} \, \mathbb{E}_{u, \tilde{\lambda}, \tilde{\nu}}[\phi(S_T) \mid \mathcal{F}_t] = e^{-(T-t)r} \, \mathbb{E}_{u, \tilde{\lambda}, \tilde{\nu}}[\phi(S_T) \mid S_t], \tag{21.10}$$

with the terminal condition $f(T, x) = \phi(x)$. In addition, the process

$$t \mapsto e^{(T-t)r} f(t, S_t)$$

is a martingale under $\widetilde{\mathbb{P}}_{u, \tilde{\lambda}, \tilde{\nu}}$ by the same argument as in (7.1).

In the next proposition we derive a Partial Integro-Differential Equation (PIDE) for the function $(t, x) \mapsto f(t, x)$.

Proposition 21.5. *The price $f(t, S_t)$ of the vanilla option with payoff function ϕ in the model (21.9) satisfies the Partial* Integro-Differential *Equation (PIDE)*

$$rf(t, x) \;=\; \frac{\partial f}{\partial t}(t, x) + rx\frac{\partial f}{\partial x}(t, x) + \frac{\sigma^2}{2}x^2\frac{\partial^2 f}{\partial x^2}(t, x)$$

$$+ \tilde{\lambda} \int_{-\infty}^{\infty} \left(f(t, x(1+y)) - f(t, x) - yx\frac{\partial f}{\partial x}(t, x)\right) \tilde{\nu}(dy), \tag{21.11}$$

under the terminal condition $f(T, x) = \phi(x)$.

Proof. We have

$$dS_t = rS_t dt + \sigma S_t d\widehat{B}_t + S_{t^-}(dY_t - \tilde{\lambda}\,\mathbb{E}_{\tilde{\nu}}[Z]dt), \tag{21.12}$$

where $\widehat{B}_t = B_t + ut$ is a standard Brownian motion under $\widetilde{\mathbb{P}}_{u,\tilde{\lambda},\tilde{\nu}}$. Next, by the Itô formula with jumps (20.23), we have

$$df(t, S_t)$$

$$= \frac{\partial f}{\partial t}(t, S_t)dt + rS_t\frac{\partial f}{\partial x}(t, S_t)dt + \sigma S_t\frac{\partial f}{\partial x}(t, S_t)d\widehat{B}_t + \frac{\sigma^2}{2}S_t^2\frac{\partial^2 f}{\partial x^2}(t, S_t)dt$$

$$- \tilde{\lambda}\,\mathbb{E}_{\tilde{\nu}}[Z]S_t\frac{\partial f}{\partial x}(t, S_t)dt + (f(t, S_{t^-}(1 + Z_{N_t})) - f(t, S_{t^-}))dN_t$$

$$= \sigma S_t\frac{\partial f}{\partial x}(t, S_t)d\widehat{B}_t + (f(t, S_{t^-}(1 + Z_{N_t})) - f(t, S_{t^-}))dN_t$$

$$- \tilde{\lambda}\,\mathbb{E}_{\tilde{\nu}}[(f(t, x(1 + Z)) - f(t, x))]_{x=S_t}dt$$

$$+ \left(\frac{\partial f}{\partial t}(t, S_t) + rS_t\frac{\partial f}{\partial x}(t, S_t) + \frac{\sigma^2}{2}S_t^2\frac{\partial^2 f}{\partial x^2}(t, S_t)\right)dt$$

$$+ \left(\tilde{\lambda}\,\mathbb{E}_{\tilde{\nu}}[(f(t, x(1 + Z)) - f(t, x))]_{x=S_t} - \tilde{\lambda}\,\mathbb{E}_{\tilde{\nu}}[Z]S_t\frac{\partial f}{\partial x}(t, S_t)\right)dt.$$

Based on the discounted portfolio value differential

$$d(\mathrm{e}^{-rt}f(t, S_t))$$

$$= \mathrm{e}^{-rt}\sigma S_t\frac{\partial f}{\partial x}(t, S_t)d\widehat{B}_t$$

$$+ \mathrm{e}^{-rt}\left(f(t, S_{t^-}(1 + Z_{N_t})) - f(t, S_{t^-})\right)dN_t - \tilde{\lambda}\,\mathbb{E}_{\tilde{\nu}}[(f(t, x(1 + Z)) - f(t, x))]_{x=S_t}dt)$$

$$+ \mathrm{e}^{-rt}\left(-rf(t, S_t) + \frac{\partial f}{\partial t}(t, S_t) + rS_t\frac{\partial f}{\partial x}(t, S_t) + \frac{\sigma^2}{2}S_t^2\frac{\partial^2 f}{\partial x^2}(t, S_t)\right)dt \qquad (21.13)$$

$$+ \mathrm{e}^{-rt}\left(\tilde{\lambda}\,\mathbb{E}_{\tilde{\nu}}[(f(t, x(1 + Z)) - f(t, x))]_{x=S_t} - \tilde{\lambda}\,\mathbb{E}_{\tilde{\nu}}[Z]S_t\frac{\partial f}{\partial x}(t, S_t)\right)dt, \qquad (21.14)$$

obtained from the Itô Table 20.1 with jumps, and the facts that

- the Brownian motion $(\widehat{B}_t)_{t\in\mathbb{R}_+}$ is a martingale under $\widetilde{\mathbb{P}}_{u,\tilde{\lambda},\tilde{\nu}}$,

- by the smoothing lemma Proposition 20.10, the process given by the differential

$$(f(t, S_{t^-}(1 + Z_{N_t})) - f(t, S_{t^-}))dN_t - \tilde{\lambda}\,\mathbb{E}_{\tilde{\nu}}[(f(t, x(1 + Z)) - f(t, x))]_{x=S_t}dt,$$

  is a martingale under $\widetilde{\mathbb{P}}_{u,\tilde{\lambda},\tilde{\nu}}$, see also (20.22),

- the discounted portfolio value process $t \mapsto \mathrm{e}^{-rt}f(t, S_t)$, is also a martingale under the risk-neutral probability measure $\widetilde{\mathbb{P}}_{u,\tilde{\lambda},\tilde{\nu}}$,

we conclude to the vanishing of the terms (21.13)–(21.14) above, *i.e.*

$$-rf(t, S_t) + \frac{\partial f}{\partial t}(t, S_t) + rS_t\frac{\partial f}{\partial x}(t, S_t) + \frac{\sigma^2}{2}S_t^2\frac{\partial^2 f}{\partial x^2}(t, S_t)$$

$$+ \tilde{\lambda}\,\mathbb{E}_{\tilde{\nu}}[(f(t, x(1 + Z)) - f(t, x))]_{x=S_t} - \tilde{\lambda}\,\mathbb{E}_{\tilde{\nu}}[Z]S_t\frac{\partial f}{\partial x}(t, S_t) = 0,$$

or

$$\frac{\partial f}{\partial t}(t, x) + rx\frac{\partial f}{\partial x}(t, x) + \frac{\sigma^2}{2}x^2\frac{\partial^2 f}{\partial x^2}(t, x)$$

$$+ \tilde{\lambda}\int_{-\infty}^{\infty}(f(t, x(1 + y)) - f(t, x))\tilde{\nu}(dy) - \tilde{\lambda}x\frac{\partial f}{\partial x}(t, x)\int_{-\infty}^{\infty}y\tilde{\nu}(dy) = rf(t, x),$$

which leads to the Partial *Integro-Differential* Equation (21.11). $\qquad\square$

A major technical difficulty when solving the PIDE (21.11) numerically is that the operator

$$f \mapsto \int_{-\infty}^{\infty} \left(f(t, x(1+y)) - f(t, x) - yx \frac{\partial f}{\partial x}(t, x) \right) \tilde{\nu}(dy)$$

is *nonlocal*, therefore adding significant difficulties to the application of standard discretization schemes, cf. *e.g.* Section 22.2.

In addition, we have shown that the change $df(t, S_t)$ in the portfolio value (21.10) is given by

$$df(t, S_t) = \sigma S_t \frac{\partial f}{\partial x}(t, S_t) d\widehat{B}_t + rf(t, S_t)dt \tag{21.15}$$
$$+(f(t, S_{t-}(1+Z_{N_t})) - f(t, S_{t-}))dN_t - \tilde{\lambda} \mathbb{E}_{\tilde{\nu}}[(f(t, x(1+Z)) - f(t, x))]_{x=S_t}dt.$$

Fixed jump size

In the case of Poisson jumps with fixed size a, *i.e.* when $Y_t = aN_t$ and $\nu(dx) = \delta_a(dx)$, the PIDE (21.11) reads

$$rf(t, x) \;=\; \frac{\partial f}{\partial t}(t, x) + rx\frac{\partial f}{\partial x}(t, x) + \frac{\sigma^2}{2}x^2\frac{\partial^2 f}{\partial x^2}(t, x)$$
$$+\tilde{\lambda}\left(f(t, x(1+a)) - f(t, x) - ax\frac{\partial f}{\partial x}(t, x) \right),$$

and we have

$$df(t, S_t) = \sigma S_t \frac{\partial f}{\partial x}(t, S_t) d\widehat{B}_t + rf(t, S_t)dt$$
$$+(f(t, S_{t-}(1+a)) - f(t, S_{t-}))dN_t - \tilde{\lambda}(f(t, S_t(1+a)) - f(t, S_t))dt.$$

21.6 Mean-Variance Hedging with Jumps

Consider a portfolio valued

$$V_t := \eta_t A_t + \xi_t S_t = \eta_t \mathrm{e}^{rt} + \xi_t S_t$$

at time $t \in \mathbb{R}_+$, and satisfying the self-financing condition (5.3), *i.e.*

$$dV_t = \eta_t dA_t + \xi_t dS_t = r\eta_t \mathrm{e}^{rt}dt + \xi_t dS_t.$$

Assuming that the portfolio value takes the form $V_t = f(t, S_t)$ at all times $t \in [0, T]$, by (21.12) we have

$$\begin{aligned} dV_t \;&=\; df(t, S_t) \\ &=\; r\eta_t \mathrm{e}^{rt}dt + \xi_t dS_t \\ &=\; r\eta_t \mathrm{e}^{rt}dt + \xi_t(rS_t dt + \sigma S_t d\widehat{B}_t + S_{t-}(dY_t - \tilde{\lambda}\mathbb{E}_{\tilde{\nu}}[Z]dt)) \\ &=\; rV_t dt + \sigma\xi_t S_t d\widehat{B}_t + \xi_t S_{t-}(dY_t - \tilde{\lambda}\mathbb{E}_{\tilde{\nu}}[Z]dt) \\ &=\; rf(t, S_t)dt + \sigma\xi_t S_t d\widehat{B}_t + \xi_t S_{t-}(dY_t - \tilde{\lambda}\mathbb{E}_{\tilde{\nu}}[Z]dt), \end{aligned} \tag{21.16}$$

has to match

$$df(t, S_t) = rf(t, S_t)dt + \sigma S_t \frac{\partial f}{\partial x}(t, S_t)d\widehat{B}_t \tag{21.17}$$
$$+ (f(t, S_{t^-}(1 + Z_{N_t})) - f(t, S_{t^-}))dN_t - \tilde{\lambda}\,\mathbb{E}_{\tilde{\nu}}[(f(t, x(1 + Z)) - f(t, x))]_{x = S_t}dt,$$

which is obtained from (21.15).

In such a situation we say that the claim payoff C can be exactly replicated.

Exact replication is possible in essentially only two situations:

(i) *Continuous market,* $\lambda = \tilde{\lambda} = 0$. In this case we find the usual Black–Scholes Delta:

$$\xi_t = \frac{\partial f}{\partial x}(t, S_t). \tag{21.18}$$

(ii) *Poisson jump market,* $\sigma = 0$ and $Y_t = aN_t$, $\nu(dx) = \delta_a(dx)$. In this case we find

$$\xi_t = \frac{1}{aS_{t^-}}(f(t, S_{t^-}(1 + a)) - f(t, S_{t^-})). \tag{21.19}$$

Note that in the limit $a \to 0$ this expression recovers the Black–Scholes Delta formula (21.18).

When Conditions (i) or (ii) above are not satisfied, exact replication is not possible, and this results into an hedging error given from (21.16) and (21.17) by

$$
\begin{aligned}
V_T - \phi(S_T) &= V_T - f(T, S_T) \\
&= V_0 + \int_0^T dV_t - f(0, S_0) - \int_0^T df(t, S_t) \\
&= V_0 - f(0, S_0) + \sigma \int_0^T S_t \left(\xi_t - \frac{\partial f}{\partial x}(t, S_t)\right) d\widehat{B}_t \\
&\quad + \int_0^T \xi_t S_{t^-}(Z_{N_t}dN_t - \tilde{\lambda}\,\mathbb{E}_{\tilde{\nu}}[Z]dt) \\
&\quad - \int_0^T (f(t, S_{t^-}(1 + Z_{N_t})) - f(t, S_{t^-}))dN_t \\
&\quad + \tilde{\lambda} \int_0^T \mathbb{E}_{\tilde{\nu}}[(f(t, x(1 + Z)) - f(t, x))]_{x = S_t}dt.
\end{aligned}
$$

Fixed jump size

Proposition 21.6. *Assume that* $Y_t = aN_t$, *i.e.* $\nu(dx) = \delta_a(dx)$. *The mean-square hedging error is minimized by*

$$V_0 = f(0, S_0) = e^{-rT}\,\mathbb{E}_{u,\tilde{\lambda},\tilde{\nu}}[\phi(S_T)],$$

and

$$\xi_t = \frac{\sigma^2}{\sigma^2 + a^2\tilde{\lambda}}\frac{\partial f}{\partial x}(t, S_{t^-}) + \frac{a^2\tilde{\lambda}}{\sigma^2 + a^2\tilde{\lambda}} \times \frac{f(t, S_{t^-}(1 + a)) - f(t, S_{t^-})}{aS_{t^-}}, \tag{21.20}$$

$t \in [0, T]$.

Proof. We have

$$
V_T - f(T, S_T) = V_0 - f(0, S_0) + \sigma \int_0^T S_{t^-} \left(\xi_t - \frac{\partial f}{\partial x}(t, S_{t^-}) \right) d\widehat{B}_t
$$
$$
- \int_0^T (f(t, S_{t^-}(1 + a)) - f(t, S_{t^-}) - a\xi_t S_{t^-})(dN_t - \tilde{\lambda}dt),
$$

hence the mean-square hedging error is given by

$$
\mathbb{E}_{u,\tilde{\lambda}} \left[(V_T - f(T, S_T))^2 \right]
$$
$$
= (V_0 - f(0, S_0))^2 + \sigma^2 \, \mathbb{E}_{u,\tilde{\lambda}} \left[\left(\int_0^T S_{t^-} \left(\xi_t - \frac{\partial f}{\partial x}(t, S_{t^-}) \right) d\widehat{B}_t \right)^2 \right]
$$
$$
+ \mathbb{E}_{u,\tilde{\lambda}} \left[\left(\int_0^T (f(t, S_{t^-}(1 + a)) - f(t, S_{t^-}) - a\xi_t S_{t^-})(dN_t - \tilde{\lambda}dt) \right)^2 \right]
$$
$$
= (V_0 - f(0, S_0))^2 + \sigma^2 \, \mathbb{E}_{u,\tilde{\lambda}} \left[\int_0^T S_{t^-}^2 \left(\xi_t - \frac{\partial f}{\partial x}(t, S_{t^-}) \right)^2 dt \right]
$$
$$
+ \tilde{\lambda} \, \mathbb{E}_{u,\tilde{\lambda}} \left[\int_0^T \left((f(t, S_{t^-}(1 + a)) - f(t, S_{t^-}) - a\xi_t S_{t^-}) \right)^2 dt \right],
$$

where we applied the Itô isometry (20.20). Clearly, the initial portfolio value V_0 minimizing the above quantity is

$$
V_0 = f(0, S_0) = e^{-rT} \, \mathbb{E}_{u,\tilde{\lambda},\tilde{\nu}}[\phi(S_T)].
$$

Next, let us find the optimal portfolio strategy $(\xi_t)_{t \in [0,T]}$ minimizing the remaining hedging error

$$
\mathbb{E}_{u,\tilde{\lambda}} \left[\int_0^T \left(\sigma^2 S_t^2 \left(\xi_t - \frac{\partial f}{\partial x}(t, S_{t^-}) \right)^2 + \tilde{\lambda}((f(t, S_{t^-}(1 + a)) - f(t, S_{t^-}) - a\xi_t S_{t^-})^2) \right) dt \right].
$$

For all $t \in (0, T]$, the almost-sure minimum of

$$
\xi_t \mapsto \sigma^2 S_t^2 \left(\xi_t - \frac{\partial f}{\partial x}(t, S_{t^-}) \right)^2 + \tilde{\lambda}((f(t, S_{t^-}(1 + a)) - f(t, S_{t^-}) - a\xi_t S_{t^-}))^2
$$

is given by differentiation with respect to ξ_t, as the solution of

$$
2\sigma^2 S_t^2 \left(\xi_t - \frac{\partial f}{\partial x}(t, S_{t^-}) \right) - 2a\tilde{\lambda}S_{t^-} \left((f(t, S_{t^-}(1 + a)) - f(t, S_{t^-}) - a\xi_t S_{t^-}) \right) = 0,
$$

i.e.

$$
\xi_t = \frac{\sigma^2}{\sigma^2 + a^2\tilde{\lambda}} \frac{\partial f}{\partial x}(t, S_{t^-}) + \frac{a^2\tilde{\lambda}}{\sigma^2 + a^2\tilde{\lambda}} \times \frac{f(t, S_{t^-}(1 + a)) - f(t, S_{t^-})}{aS_{t^-}},
$$

$t \in (0, T]$. $\qquad\qquad\square$

When hedging only the risk generated by the Brownian part, we let

$$
\xi_t = \frac{\partial f}{\partial x}(t, S_{t^-})
$$

as in the Black–Scholes model, and in this case the hedging error due to the presence of jumps becomes

$$\mathbb{E}_{u,\tilde{\lambda}}\left[\left(V_T - f(T, S_T)\right)^2\right] = \tilde{\lambda}\,\mathbb{E}_{u,\tilde{\lambda}}\left[\int_0^T \left((f(t, S_{t^-}(1+a)) - f(t, S_{t^-}) - a\xi_t S_{t^-})\right)^2 dt\right],$$

$t \in (0, T]$. We note that the optimal strategy (21.20) is a weighted average of the Brownian and jump hedging strategies (21.18) and (21.19) according to the respective variance parameters σ^2 and $a^2\tilde{\lambda}$ of the continuous and jump components.

Clearly, if $a\tilde{\lambda} = 0$ we get

$$\xi_t = \frac{\partial f}{\partial x}(t, S_{t^-}), \qquad t \in (0, T],$$

which is the Black–Scholes perfect replication strategy, and when $\sigma = 0$ we recover

$$\xi_t = \frac{f(t, (1+a)S_{t^-}) - f(t, S_{t^-})}{aS_{t^-}}, \qquad t \in (0, T].$$

which is (21.19). See § 10.4.2 of Cont and Tankov (2004) for mean-variance hedging in exponential Lévy model, and § 12.6 of Di Nunno et al. (2009) for mean-variance hedging by the Malliavin calculus.

Note that the fact that perfect replication is not possible in a jump-diffusion model can be interpreted as a more realistic feature of the model, as perfect replication is not possible in the real world.

See Jeanblanc and Privault (2002) for an example of a complete market model with jumps, in which continuous and jump noise are mutually excluding each other over time.

In Table 21.1 we summarize the properties of geometric Brownian motion *vs* jump-diffusion models in terms of asset price and market behaviors.

Model / Properties	Geometric Brownian motion	Jump-diffusion model	Real world
Discontinuous asset prices	✗	✓	✓
Fat tailed market returns	✗	✓	✓
Complete market	✓	✗	✗
Unique prices and risk-neutral measure	✓	✗	✗

Table 21.1: Market models and their properties.

Exercises

Exercise 21.1 Consider a standard Poisson process $(N_t)_{t \in \mathbb{R}_+}$ with intensity $\lambda > 0$ under a probability measure $\mathbb{P}$. Let $(S_t)_{t \in \mathbb{R}_+}$ be defined by the stochastic differential equation

$$dS_t = rS_t dt + \eta S_{t^-}(dN_t - \alpha dt),$$

where $\eta > 0$.

a) Find the value of $\alpha \in \mathbb{R}$ such that the discounted process $(e^{-rt}S_t)_{t \in \mathbb{R}_+}$ is a martingale under $\mathbb{P}$.

b) Compute the price at time $t \in [0, T]$ of a power option with payoff $|S_T|^2$ at maturity T.

Exercise 21.2 Consider a long forward contract with payoff $S_T - K$ on a jump diffusion risky asset $(S_t)_{t \in \mathbb{R}_+}$ given by

$$dS_t = \mu S_t dt + \sigma S_t dB_t + S_{t^-} dY_t.$$

a) Show that the forward claim admits a unique arbitrage-free price to be computed in a market with risk-free rate $r > 0$.

b) Show that the forward claim admits an exact replicating portfolio strategy based on the two assets S_t and e^{rt}.

c) Recover portfolio strategy of Question (b) using the optimal portfolio strategy formula (21.20).

Exercise 21.3 Consider $(B_t)_{t \in \mathbb{R}_+}$ a standard Brownian motion and $(N_t)_{t \in \mathbb{R}_+}$ a standard Poisson process with intensity $\lambda > 0$, independent of $(B_t)_{t \in \mathbb{R}_+}$, under a probability measure $\mathbb{P}^*$. Let $(S_t)_{t \in \mathbb{R}_+}$ be defined by the stochastic differential equation

$$dS_t = \mu S_t dt + \eta S_{t^-} dN_t + \sigma S_t dB_t. \tag{21.21}$$

a) Solve the equation (21.21).

b) We assume that μ, η and the risk-free rate $r > 0$ are chosen such that the discounted process $(e^{-rt}S_t)_{t \in \mathbb{R}_+}$ is a martingale under $\mathbb{P}^*$. What relation does this impose on μ, η, λ and r?

c) Under the relation of Question (b), compute the price at time $t \in [0, T]$ of a European call option on S_T with strike price κ and maturity T, using a series expansion of Black–Scholes functions.

Exercise 21.4 Consider $(N_t)_{t \in \mathbb{R}_+}$ a standard Poisson process with intensity $\lambda > 0$ under a probability measure $\mathbb{P}$. Let $(S_t)_{t \in \mathbb{R}_+}$ be defined by the stochastic differential equation

$$dS_t = r S_t dt + Y_{N_t} S_{t^-} dN_t,$$

where $(Y_k)_{k \geqslant 1}$ is an *i.i.d.* sequence of uniformly distributed random variables on $[-1, 1]$.

a) Show that the discounted process $(e^{-rt}S_t)_{t \in \mathbb{R}_+}$ is a martingale under $\mathbb{P}$.

b) Compute the price at time 0 of a European call option on S_T with strike price κ and maturity T, using a series of multiple integrals.

Exercise 21.5 Consider a standard Poisson process $(N_t)_{t \in \mathbb{R}_+}$ with intensity $\lambda > 0$ under a probability measure $\mathbb{P}$. Let $(S_t)_{t \in \mathbb{R}_+}$ be defined by the stochastic differential equation

$$dS_t = r S_t dt + Y_{N_t} S_{t^-} (dN_t - \alpha dt),$$

where $(Y_k)_{k \geqslant 1}$ is an *i.i.d.* sequence of uniformly distributed random variables on $[0, 1]$.

a) Find the value of $\alpha \in \mathbb{R}$ such that the discounted process $(e^{-rt} S_t)_{t \in \mathbb{R}_+}$ is a martingale under $\mathbb{P}$.

b) Compute the price at time $t \in [0, T]$ of the long forward contract with maturity T and payoff $S_T - \kappa$.

Exercise 21.6 Consider $(N_t)_{t \in \mathbb{R}_+}$ a standard Poisson process with intensity $\lambda > 0$ under a risk-neutral probability measure $\mathbb{P}^*$. Let $(S_t)_{t \in \mathbb{R}_+}$ be defined by the stochastic differential equation

$$dS_t = rS_t dt + \alpha S_{t^-} (dN_t - \lambda dt), \tag{21.22}$$

where $\alpha > 0$. Consider a portfolio with value

$$V_t = \eta_t e^{rt} + \xi_t S_t$$

at time $t \in [0, T]$, and satisfying the self-financing condition

$$dV_t = r\eta_t e^{rt} dt + \xi_t dS_t.$$

We assume that the portfolio hedges a claim payoff $C = \phi(S_T)$, and that the portfolio value can be written as a function $V_t = f(t, S_t)$ of t and S_t for all times $t \in [0, T]$.

a) Solve the stochastic differential equation (21.22).

b) Price the claim $C = \phi(S_T)$ at time $t \in [0, T]$ using a series expansion.

c) Show that under self-financing, the variation dV_t of the portfolio value V_t satisfies

$$dV_t = rf(t, S_t)dt + \alpha \xi_t S_{t^-} (dN_t - \lambda dt). \tag{21.23}$$

d) Show that the claim payoff $C = \phi(S_T)$ can be exactly replicated by the hedging strategy

$$\xi_t = \frac{1}{\alpha S_{t^-}} (f(t, S_{t^-} (1 + \alpha)) - f(t, S_{t^-})).$$

Exercise 21.7 Pricing by the Esscher transform (Gerber and Shiu (1994)). Consider a compound Poisson process $(Y_t)_{t \in [0,T]}$ with $\mathbb{E}\left[e^{\theta(Y_t - Y_s)}\right] = e^{(t-s)m(\theta)}$, $0 \leqslant s \leqslant t$, with $m(\theta)$ a function of $\theta \in \mathbb{R}$, and the asset price process $S_t := e^{rt+Y_t}$, $t \in [0, T]$. Given $\theta \in \mathbb{R}$, let

$$N_t := \frac{e^{\theta Y_t}}{\mathbb{E}\left[e^{\theta Y_t}\right]} = e^{\theta Y_t - tm(\theta)} = S_t^\theta e^{-r\theta t - tm(\theta)},$$

and consider the probability measure $\mathbb{P}^\theta$ defined as

$$\frac{d\mathbb{P}^\theta_{|\mathcal{F}_t}}{d\mathbb{P}_{|\mathcal{F}_t}} := \frac{N_T}{N_t} = e^{(Y_T - Y_t)\theta - (T-t)m(\theta)}, \qquad 0 \leqslant t \leqslant T.$$

a) Check that $(N_t)_{t \in \mathbb{R}_+}$ is a martingale under $\mathbb{P}$.

b) Find a condition on θ such that the discounted price process $(e^{-rt} S_t)_{t \in [0,T]} = (e^{Y_t})_{t \in [0,T]}$ is a martingale under $\mathbb{P}^\theta$.

c) Price the European call option with payoff $(S_T - K)^+$ by taking $\mathbb{P}^\theta$ as risk-neutral probability measure.

Chapter 22

Basic Numerical Methods

Numerical methods in finance include finite difference methods, and statistical and Monte Carlo methods for computation of option prices and hedging strategies. This chapter is a basic introduction to finite difference methods for the resolution of PDEs and stochastic differential equations. We cover the explicit and implicit finite difference schemes for the heat equations and the Black–Scholes PDE, as well as the Euler and Milshtein schemes for stochastic differential equations.

22.1 Discretized Heat Equation

Consider the heat equation

$$\frac{\partial \phi}{\partial t}(t, x) = \frac{\partial^2 \phi}{\partial x^2}(t, x) \tag{22.1}$$

with initial condition

$$\phi(0, x) = f(x)$$

on a compact time-space interval $[0, T] \times [0, X]$.

The intervals $[0, T]$ and $[0, X]$ are respectively discretized according to $\{t_0 = 0, t_1, \ldots, t_N = T\}$ and $\{x_0 = 0, x_1, \ldots, x_M = X\}$ with $\Delta t = T/N$ and $\Delta x = X/M$, from which we construct a grid

$$(t_i, x_j) = (i\Delta t, j\Delta x), \qquad i = 0, \ldots, N, \quad j = 0, \ldots, M,$$

on $[0, T] \times [0, X]$.

Our goal is to solve the heat equation (22.1) with *initial* condition $\phi(0, x)$, $x \in [0, X]$, and lateral boundary conditions $\phi(t, 0)$, $\phi(t, X)$, $t \in [0, T]$, via a discrete approximation

$$(\phi(t_i, x_j))_{0 \leqslant i \leqslant N, \, 0 \leqslant j \leqslant M}$$

of the solution to (22.1), by evaluating derivatives using finite differences.

Explicit scheme

Using the *forward* time difference approximation

$$\frac{\partial \phi}{\partial t}(t_i, x) \simeq \frac{\phi(t_{i+1}, x_j) - \phi(t_i, x_j)}{\Delta t}$$

of the time derivative, and the related space difference approximations

$$\frac{\partial \phi}{\partial x}(t, x_j) \simeq \frac{\phi(t, x_j) - \phi(t_i, x_{j-1})}{\Delta x}, \quad \frac{\partial \phi}{\partial x}(t, x_{j+1}) \simeq \frac{\phi(t, x_{j+1}) - \phi(t_i, x_j))}{\Delta x}$$

DOI: 10.1201/9781003298670-22

and

$$\frac{\partial^2 \phi}{\partial x^2}(t, x_j) \simeq \frac{1}{\Delta x}\left(\frac{\partial \phi}{\partial x}(t, x_{j+1}) - \frac{\partial \phi}{\partial x}(t, x_j)\right) = \frac{\phi(t_i, x_{j+1}) + \phi(t_i, x_{j-1}) - 2\phi(t_i, x_j)}{(\Delta x)^2}$$

of the time and space derivatives, we discretize (22.1) as

$$\frac{\phi(t_{i+1}, x_j) - \phi(t_i, x_j)}{\Delta t} = \frac{\phi(t_i, x_{j+1}) + \phi(t_i, x_{j-1}) - 2\phi(t_i, x_j)}{(\Delta x)^2}. \tag{22.2}$$

Letting $\rho = (\Delta t)/(\Delta x)^2$, this yields

$$\phi(t_{i+1}, x_j) = \rho\phi(t_i, x_{j+1}) + (1 - 2\rho)\phi(t_i, x_j) + \rho\phi(t_i, x_{j-1}),$$

$1 \leqslant j \leqslant M - 1$, $1 \leqslant i \leqslant N$, i.e.

$$\Phi_{i+1} = A\Phi_i + \rho \begin{bmatrix} \phi(t_i, x_0) \\ 0 \\ \vdots \\ 0 \\ \phi(t_i, x_M) \end{bmatrix}, \qquad i = 0, 1, \ldots, N - 1, \tag{22.3}$$

with

$$\Phi_i = \begin{bmatrix} \phi(t_i, x_1) \\ \vdots \\ \phi(t_i, x_{M-1}) \end{bmatrix}, \qquad i = 0, 1, \ldots, N,$$

and

$$A = \begin{bmatrix} 1 - 2\rho & \rho & 0 & \cdots & 0 & 0 & 0 \\ \rho & 1 - 2\rho & \rho & \cdots & 0 & 0 & 0 \\ 0 & \rho & 1 - 2\rho & \cdots & 0 & 0 & 0 \\ \vdots & \vdots & \vdots & \ddots & \vdots & \vdots & \vdots \\ 0 & 0 & 0 & \cdots & 1 - 2\rho & \rho & 0 \\ 0 & 0 & 0 & \cdots & \rho & 1 - 2\rho & \rho \\ 0 & 0 & 0 & \cdots & 0 & \rho & 1 - 2\rho \end{bmatrix}.$$

The vector

$$\begin{bmatrix} \phi(t_i, x_0) \\ 0 \\ \vdots \\ 0 \\ \phi(t_i, x_M) \end{bmatrix} = \begin{bmatrix} \phi(t_i, 0) \\ 0 \\ \vdots \\ 0 \\ \phi(t_i, X) \end{bmatrix}, \qquad i = 0, 1, \ldots, N,$$

in (22.3) can be given by the lateral boundary conditions $\phi(t, 0)$ and $\phi(t, X)$. From those boundary conditions and the initial data of

$$\Phi_0 = \begin{bmatrix} \phi(0, x_0) \\ \phi(0, x_1) \\ \vdots \\ \phi(0, x_{M-1}) \\ \phi(0, x_M) \end{bmatrix}$$

we can apply (22.3) in order to solve (22.2) recursively for $\Phi_1, \Phi_2, \Phi_3, \ldots$, see also Figure 22.1.

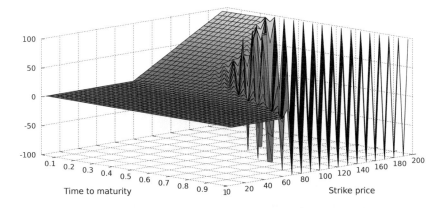

Figure 22.1: Divergence of the explicit finite difference method.

Implicit scheme

Using the *backward* time difference approximation

$$\frac{\partial \phi}{\partial t}(t_i, x) \simeq \frac{\phi(t_i, x_j) - \phi(t_{i-1}, x_j)}{\Delta t}$$

of the time derivative, we discretize (22.1) as

$$\frac{\phi(t_i, x_j) - \phi(t_{i-1}, x_j)}{\Delta t} = \frac{\phi(t_i, x_{j+1}) + \phi(t_i, x_{j-1}) - 2\phi(t_i, x_j)}{(\Delta x)^2} \tag{22.4}$$

and letting $\rho = (\Delta t)/(\Delta x)^2$ we get

$$\phi(t_{i-1}, x_j) = -\rho \phi(t_i, x_{j+1}) + (1 + 2\rho)\phi(t_i, x_j) - \rho \phi(t_i, x_{j-1}),$$

$1 \leqslant j \leqslant M - 1$, $1 \leqslant i \leqslant N$, *i.e.*

$$\Phi_{i-1} = B\Phi_i + \rho \begin{bmatrix} \phi(t_i, x_0) \\ 0 \\ \vdots \\ 0 \\ \phi(t_i, x_M) \end{bmatrix}, \qquad i = 1, 2, \ldots, N,$$

with

$$B = \begin{bmatrix} 1+2\rho & -\rho & 0 & \cdots & 0 & 0 & 0 \\ -\rho & 1+2\rho & -\rho & \cdots & 0 & 0 & 0 \\ 0 & -\rho & 1+2\rho & \cdots & 0 & 0 & 0 \\ \vdots & \vdots & \vdots & \ddots & \vdots & \vdots & \vdots \\ 0 & 0 & 0 & \cdots & 1+2\rho & -\rho & 0 \\ 0 & 0 & 0 & \cdots & -\rho & 1+2\rho & -\rho \\ 0 & 0 & 0 & \cdots & 0 & -\rho & 1+2\rho \end{bmatrix}.$$

By inversion of the matrix B, Φ_i is given in terms of Φ_{i-1} as

$$\Phi_i = B^{-1}\Phi_{i-1} - \rho B^{-1} \begin{bmatrix} \phi(t_i, x_0) \\ 0 \\ \vdots \\ 0 \\ \phi(t_i, x_M) \end{bmatrix}, \qquad i = 1, \ldots, N,$$

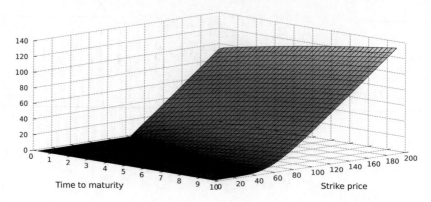

Figure 22.2: Stability of the implicit finite difference method.

which also allows for a recursive solution of (22.4), see also Figure 22.2.

22.2   Discretized Black–Scholes PDE

Consider the Black–Scholes PDE

$$r\phi(t,x) = \frac{\partial \phi}{\partial t}(t,x) + rx\frac{\partial \phi}{\partial x}(t,x) + \frac{1}{2}x^2\sigma^2\frac{\partial^2 \phi}{\partial x^2}(t,x), \tag{22.5}$$

under the terminal condition $\phi(T,x) = (x-K)^+$, *resp.* $\phi(T,x) = (K-x)^+$, for a European call, *resp.* put, option. The constant volatility coefficient σ may also be replaced with a function $\sigma(t,x)$ of the underlying asset price, in the case local volatility models.

Note that in the solution of the Black–Scholes PDE, time is run *backwards* as we start from a terminal condition $\phi(T,x)$ at time T. Thus here the explicit scheme uses *backward* differences while the implicit scheme uses *forward* differences.

Explicit scheme

Using here the *backward* time difference approximation

$$\frac{\partial \phi}{\partial t}(t_i,x) \simeq \frac{\phi(t_i,x_j) - \phi(t_{i-1},x_j)}{\Delta t}$$

of the time derivative, we discretize (22.5) as

$$\begin{aligned}
r\phi(t_i,x_j) &= \frac{\phi(t_i,x_j) - \phi(t_{i-1},x_j)}{\Delta t} + rx_j\frac{\phi(t_i,x_{j+1}) - \phi(t_i,x_{j-1})}{2\Delta x} \\
&\quad + \frac{1}{2}x_j^2\sigma^2\frac{\phi(t_i,x_{j+1}) + \phi(t_i,x_{j-1}) - 2\phi(t_i,x_j)}{(\Delta x)^2},
\end{aligned} \tag{22.6}$$

$1 \leqslant j \leqslant M-1,\, 0 \leqslant i \leqslant N-1$, *i.e.*

$$\begin{aligned}
\phi(t_{i-1},x_j) &= \frac{1}{2}(\sigma^2 j^2 - rj)\phi(t_i,x_{j-1})\Delta t + \phi(t_i,x_j)(1 - (\sigma^2 j^2 + r)\Delta t) \\
&\quad + \frac{1}{2}(\sigma^2 j^2 + rj)\phi(t_i,x_{j+1})\Delta t,
\end{aligned}$$

$1 \leqslant j \leqslant M - 1$, where the lateral boundary conditions $\phi(t_i, 0)$ and $\phi(t_i, x_M)$ are (approximately) given as follows.

European call options. We take the lateral boundary conditions

$$\phi(t_i, x_0) = 0, \quad \text{and} \quad \phi(t_i, x_M) \simeq \left(x_M - K\,\mathrm{e}^{-r(T-t_i)}\right)^+ = x_M - K\,\mathrm{e}^{-r(T-t_i)},$$

$i = 0, 1, \ldots, N$, provided that x_M is sufficiently large.

European put options. We take the lateral boundary conditions

$$\phi(t_i, x_0) \simeq \left(K\,\mathrm{e}^{-(T-t_i)r} - x_0\right)^+ = K\,\mathrm{e}^{-(T-t_i)r}, \quad \text{and} \quad \phi(t_i, x_M) = 0,$$

$i = 0, 1, \ldots, N$, with here $x_0 = 0$.

Given a terminal condition of the form

$$\phi(T, x_j) = (x_j - K)^+, \text{ resp. } \phi(T, x_j) = (K - x_j)^+, \quad j = 1, \ldots, M - 1,$$

this allows us to solve (22.6) successively for

$$\phi(t_{N-1}, x_j),\ \phi(t_{N-2}, x_j),\ \phi(t_{N-3}, x_j), \ldots, \phi(t_1, x_j),\ \phi(t_0, x_j).$$

The explicit finite difference method is nevertheless known to have a divergent behavior as time is run backwards, as illustrated in Figure 22.1.

Implicit scheme

Using the *forward* time difference approximation

$$\frac{\partial \phi}{\partial t}(t_i, x) \simeq \frac{\phi(t_{i+1}, x_j) - \phi(t_i, x_j)}{\Delta t}$$

of the time derivative, we discretize (22.5) as

$$r\phi(t_i, x_j) = \frac{\phi(t_{i+1}, x_j) - \phi(t_i, x_j)}{\Delta t} + rx_j \frac{\phi(t_i, x_{j+1}) - \phi(t_i, x_{j-1})}{\Delta x} \tag{22.7}$$
$$+ \frac{1}{2} x_j^2 \sigma^2 \frac{\phi(t_i, x_{j+1}) + \phi(t_i, x_{j-1}) - 2\phi(t_i, x_j)}{(\Delta x)^2},$$

$1 \leqslant j \leqslant M - 1,\ 0 \leqslant i \leqslant N - 1$, *i.e.*

$$\phi(t_{i+1}, x_j) = -\frac{1}{2}(\sigma^2 j^2 - rj)\phi(t_i, x_{j-1})\Delta t + \phi(t_i, x_j)(1 + (\sigma^2 j^2 + r)\Delta t)$$
$$- \frac{1}{2}(\sigma^2 j^2 + rj)\phi(t_i, x_{j+1})\Delta t,$$

$1 \leqslant j \leqslant M - 1$, *i.e.*

$$\Phi_{i+1} = B\Phi_i + \begin{bmatrix} \frac{1}{2}\left(r - \sigma^2\right)\phi(t_i, x_0)\Delta t \\ 0 \\ \vdots \\ 0 \\ -\frac{1}{2}\left(r(M-1) + (M-1)^2\sigma^2\right)\phi(t_i, x_M)\Delta t \end{bmatrix}, \tag{22.8}$$

$i = 0, 1, \ldots, N-1$, with

$$B_{j,j-1} = \frac{1}{2}\left(rj - \sigma^2 j^2\right)\Delta t, \quad B_{j,j} = 1 + \sigma^2 j^2 \Delta t + r\Delta t,$$

and

$$B_{j,j+1} = -\frac{1}{2}\left(rj + \sigma^2 j^2\right)\Delta t,$$

for $j = 1, 2, \ldots, M-1$, and $B(i, j) = 0$ otherwise.

By inversion of the matrix B, Φ_i is given in terms of Φ_{i+1} as

$$\Phi_i = B^{-1}\Phi_{i+1} - B^{-1}\begin{bmatrix} \frac{1}{2}\left(r - \sigma^2\right)\phi(t_i, x_0)\Delta t \\ 0 \\ \vdots \\ 0 \\ -\frac{1}{2}\left(r(M-1) + (M-1)^2\sigma^2\right)\phi(t_i, x_M)\Delta t \end{bmatrix},$$

$i = 0, 1, \ldots, N-1$, where the lateral boundary conditions $\phi(t_i, x_0)$ and $\phi(t_i, x_M)$ can be provided as in the case of the explicit scheme, allowing us to solve (22.7) recursively for $\phi(t_{N-1}, x_j), \phi(t_{N-2}, x_j), \phi(t_{N-3}, x_j), \ldots$

The implicit finite difference method is known to be more stable than the explicit scheme, as illustrated in Figure 22.2, in which the discretization parameters have been taken to be the same as in Figure 22.1.

22.3   Euler Discretization

In order to apply the Monte Carlo method in option pricing, we need to generate a sequence $(\widehat{X}_1, \ldots, \widehat{X}_N)$ of sample values of a random variable X, such that the empirical mean

$$\mathbb{E}[\phi(X)] \simeq \frac{\phi(\widehat{X}_1) + \cdots + \phi(\widehat{X}_N)}{N}$$

can be used according to the strong law of large number for the evaluation of the expected value $\mathbb{E}[\phi(X)]$. Despite its apparent simplicity, the Monte Carlo method can converge slowly. The optimization of Monte Carlo algorithms and of random number generators have been the object of numerous studies which are outside the scope of this text, see, *e.g.* Glasserman (2004), Korn et al. (2010).

Random samples for the solution of a stochastic differential equation of the form

$$dX_t = b(X_t)dt + a(X_t)dW_t \tag{22.9}$$

where $(W_t)_{t\in\mathbb{R}_+}$ is a standard Brownian motion, can be generated by time discretization on $\{t_0, t_1, \ldots, t_N\}$. This can be applied in particular to option pricing with local volatility, see § 9.3.

More precisely, the Euler discretization scheme for the stochastic differential equation (22.9) is given by

$$
\begin{aligned}
\widehat{X}_{t_{k+1}}^N &= \widehat{X}_{t_k}^N + \int_{t_k}^{t_{k+1}} b(X_s)ds + \int_{t_k}^{t_{k+1}} a(X_s)dW_s \\
&\simeq \widehat{X}_{t_k}^N + b(\widehat{X}_{t_k}^N)(t_{k+1} - t_k) + a(\widehat{X}_{t_k}^N)(W_{t_{k+1}} - W_{t_k}),
\end{aligned}
$$

where $W_{t_{k+1}} - W_{t_k} \simeq \mathcal{N}(0, t_{k+1} - W_{t_k})$, $k = 0, 1, \ldots, N-1$.

22.4 Milshtein Discretization

In the Milshtein scheme we use (22.9) to expand $a(X_s)$ as

$$
\begin{aligned}
a(X_s) &\simeq a(X_{t_k}) + a'(X_{t_k})(X_s - X_{t_k}) \\
&\simeq a(X_{t_k}) + a'(X_{t_k})\big(b(X_{t_k})(s - t_k) + a(X_{t_k})(W_s - W_{t_k})\big),
\end{aligned}
$$

$0 \leqslant t_k < s$. As a consequence, we get

$$
\begin{aligned}
\widehat{X}_{t_{k+1}}^N &= \widehat{X}_{t_k}^N + \int_{t_k}^{t_{k+1}} b(X_s)ds + \int_{t_k}^{t_{k+1}} a(X_s)dW_s \\
&\simeq \widehat{X}_{t_k}^N + \int_{t_k}^{t_{k+1}} b(X_s)ds + a(X_{t_k})(W_{t_{k+1}} - W_{t_k}) \\
&\quad + a'(X_{t_k})b(X_{t_k}) \int_{t_k}^{t_{k+1}} (s - t_k)dW_s \\
&\quad + a'(X_{t_k})a(X_{t_k}) \int_{t_k}^{t_{k+1}} (W_s - W_{t_k})dW_s \\
&\simeq \widehat{X}_{t_k}^N + \int_{t_k}^{t_{k+1}} b(X_s)ds + a(X_{t_k})(W_{t_{k+1}} - W_{t_k}) \\
&\quad + a'(X_{t_k})a(X_{t_k}) \int_{t_k}^{t_{k+1}} (W_s - W_{t_k})dW_s.
\end{aligned}
$$

Next, using Itô's formula we note that

$$
(W_{t_{k+1}} - W_{t_k})^2 = 2 \int_{t_k}^{t_{k+1}} (W_s - W_{t_k})dW_s + \int_{t_k}^{t_{k+1}} ds,
$$

hence

$$
\int_{t_k}^{t_{k+1}} (W_s - W_{t_k})dW_s = \frac{1}{2}\big((W_{t_{k+1}} - W_{t_k})^2 - (t_{k+1} - t_k)\big),
$$

and

$$
\begin{aligned}
\widehat{X}_{t_{k+1}}^N &\simeq \widehat{X}_{t_k}^N + \int_{t_k}^{t_{k+1}} b(X_s)ds + a(X_{t_k})(W_{t_{k+1}} - W_{t_k}) \\
&\quad + \frac{1}{2}a'(X_{t_k})a(X_{t_k})\big((W_{t_{k+1}} - W_{t_k})^2 - (t_{k+1} - t_k)\big) \\
&\simeq \widehat{X}_{t_k}^N + b(X_{t_k})(t_{k+1} - t_k) + a(X_{t_k})(W_{t_{k+1}} - W_{t_k}) \\
&\quad + \frac{1}{2}a'(X_{t_k})a(X_{t_k})\big((W_{t_{k+1}} - W_{t_k})^2 - (t_{k+1} - t_k)\big).
\end{aligned}
$$

As a consequence the Milshtein scheme is written as

$$\widehat{X}^N_{t_{k+1}} \quad \simeq \quad \widehat{X}^N_{t_k} + b(\widehat{X}^N_{t_k})(t_{k+1} - t_k) + a(\widehat{X}^N_{t_k})(W_{t_{k+1}} - W_{t_k})$$
$$+ \frac{1}{2} a'(\widehat{X}^N_{t_k}) a(\widehat{X}^N_{t_k})((W_{t_{k+1}} - W_{t_k})^2 - (t_{k+1} - t_k)),$$

i.e. in the Milshtein scheme we take into account the "small" difference

$$(W_{t_{k+1}} - W_{t_k})^2 - (t_{k+1} - t_k)$$

existing between $(\Delta W_t)^2$ and Δt. Taking $(\Delta W_t)^2$ equal to Δt brings us back to the Euler scheme.

Exercises

Exercise 22.1 Show that when the terminal condition is a constant $\phi(T, x) = c > 0$ the implicit scheme (22.8) recovers the known solution $\phi(s, x) = c e^{-r(T-s)}$, $s \in [0, T]$.

Exercise 22.2 Let X_t be the geometric Brownian motion given by the stochastic differential equation

$$dX_t = rX_t dt + \sigma X_t dW_t.$$

a) Compute the Euler discretization $\left(\widehat{X}^N_{t_k}\right)_{k=0,1,\dots,N}$ of $(X_t)_{t \in \mathbb{R}_+}$.

b) Compute the Milshtein discretization $\left(\widehat{X}^N_{t_k}\right)_{k=0,1,\dots,N}$ of $(X_t)_{t \in \mathbb{R}_+}$.

Bibliography

[1] Achdou, Y. and Pironneau, O. (2005). *Computational methods for option pricing*, volume 30 of *Frontiers in Applied Mathematics*. Society for Industrial and Applied Mathematics (SIAM), Philadelphia, PA. (Cited on page 289).

[2] Albanese, C. and Lawi, S. (2005). Laplace transforms for integrals of Markov processes. *Markov Process. Related Fields*, 11(4):677–724. (Cited on pages 251 and 486).

[3] Albrecher, H., Mayer, P., Schoutens, W., and Tistaert, J. (2007). The little Heston trap. *Wilmott Magazine*, pages 83–92. (Cited on page 266).

[4] Allegretto, W., Barone-Adesi, G., and Elliott, R. (1995). Numerical evaluation of the critical price and American options. *European Journal of Finance*, 1:69–78. (Cited on page 437).

[5] Applebaum, D. (2009). *Lévy processes and stochastic calculus*, volume 116 of *Cambridge Studies in Advanced Mathematics*. Cambridge University Press, Cambridge, second edition. (Cited on page 584).

[6] Aristotle (350 BCE). *Politics, Book one, Part XI*. The Internet Classics Archive. http://classics.mit.edu/Aristotle/politics.1.one.html. (Cited on page 4).

[7] Attari, M. (2004). Option pricing using Fourier transforms: a numerically efficient simplification. Preprint, 7 pages. (Cited on page 266).

[8] Bachelier, L. (1900). Théorie de la spéculation. *Annales Scientifiques de l'Ecole Normale Supérieure, Série 3*, 17:21–86. (Cited on pages 2, 118, 163, 197, 202, 233, and 234).

[9] Barone-Adesi, G. and Whaley, R. (1987). Efficient analytic approximation of American option values. *The Journal of Finance*, 42(2):301–320. (Cited on pages 437 and 439).

[10] Barrieu, P., Rouault, A., and Yor, M. (2004). A study of the Hartman-Watson distribution motivated by numerical problems related to the pricing of Asian options. *J. Appl. Probab.*, 41(4):1049–1058. (Cited on page 378).

[11] Bermin, H. (1998). Essays on lookback options: a Malliavin calculus approach. PhD thesis, Lund University. (Cited on page 363).

[12] Björk, T. (2004a). *Arbitrage theory in continuous time*, volume 121 of *Oxford Finance*. Oxford University Press. (Cited on page 33).

[13] Björk, T. (2004b). On the geometry of interest rate models. In *Paris-Princeton Lectures on Mathematical Finance 2003*, volume 1847 of *Lecture Notes in Mathematics*, pages 133–215. Springer, Berlin. (Cited on page 532).

[14] Black, F. (1976). The pricing of commodity contracts. *J. of Financial Economics*, 3:167–179. (Cited on page 550).

[15] Black, F., Derman, E., and Toy, W. (1990). A one-factor model of interest rates and its application to treasury bond options. *Financial Analysts Journal*, 46(1):24–32. (Cited on page 509).

[16] Black, F. and Scholes, M. (1973). The pricing of options and corporate liabilities. *J. of Political Economy*, 81. (Cited on pages 2, 3, 159, 173, and 174).

[17] Bosq, D. and Nguyen, H. (1996). *A Course in Stochastic Processes: Stochastic Models and Statistical Inference*. Mathematical and Statistical Methods. Kluwer. (Cited on pages 566 and 567).

[18] Boulding, K. (1973). *In "Energy Reorganization Act of 1973. Hearings, Ninety-third Congress, first session, on H.R. 11510"*. U.S. Government Printing Office, Washington. (Cited on pages 161 and 449).

[19] Boyle, P. and Vorst, T. (1992). Option replication in discrete time with transaction costs. *The Journal of Finance*, XLVII(1):271–293. (Cited on page 102).

[20] Brace, A., Gatarek, D., and Musiela, M. (1997). The market model of interest rate dynamics. *Math. Finance*, 7(2):127–155. (Cited on pages 3 and 537).

[21] Breeden, D. and Litzenberger, R. (1978). Prices of state-contingent claims implicit in option prices. *Journal of Business*, 51:621–651. (Cited on page 286).

[22] Brémaud, P. (1999). *Markov chains*, volume 31 of *Texts in Applied Mathematics*. Springer-Verlag, New York. (Cited on page 577).

[23] Brigo, D. and Mercurio, F. (2006). *Interest rate models—theory and practice*. Springer Finance. Springer-Verlag, Berlin, second edition. (Cited on pages 260, 493, and 536).

[24] Broadie, M. and Jain, A. (2008). The effect of jumps and discrete sampling on volatility and variance swaps. *Int. J. Theor. Appl. Finance*, 11(8):761–797. (Cited on page 274).

[25] Brody, D., Hughston, L., and Meier, D. (2018). Lévy-Vasicek models and the long-bond return process. *Int. J. Theor. Appl. Finance*, 21(3):1850026. (Cited on page 503).

[26] Brown, C., Handley, J., Ling, C.-T., and Palmer, K. (2016). Partial differential equations for Asian option prices. *Quant. Finance*, 16(3):447–460. (Cited on page 397).

[27] Brown, R. (1828). A brief account of microscopical observations made in the months of June, July and August, 1827, on the particles contained in the pollen of plants; and on the general existence of active molecules in organic and inorganic bodies. *Philosophical Magazine*, 4:161–173. (Cited on page 1).

[28] Burdzy, K. (1990). On nonincrease of Brownian motion. *Ann. Probab.*, 18(3):978–980. (Cited on page 299).

[29] Carmona, R. and Durrleman, V. (2003). Pricing and hedging spread options. *SIAM Rev.*, 45(4):627–685. (Cited on page 234).

[30] Carr, P. and Lee, R. (2008). Robust replication of volatility derivatives. Mathematics in Finance Working Paper Series, Working Paper #2008-3. (Cited on pages 254 and 274).

[31] Carr, P. and Schröder, M. (2004). Bessel processes, the integral of geometric Brownian motion, and Asian options. *Theory Probab. Appl.*, 48(3):400–425. (Cited on pages 379 and 380).

[32] Chan, K., Karolyi, G., Longstaff, F., and Sanders, A. (1992). An empirical comparison of alternative models of the short-term interest rate. *The Journal of Finance*, 47(3):1209–1227. Papers and Proceedings of the Fifty-Second Annual Meeting of the American Finance Association, New Orleans, Louisiana. (Cited on pages 504 and 505).

[33] Charlier, C. (1914). Frequency curves of type A in heterograde statistics. *Ark. Mat. Astr. Fysik*, 9(25):1–17. (Cited on page 607).

[34] Charpentier, A., editor (2014). *Computational Actuarial Science with R*. The R Series. Chapman & Hall/CRC, USA. (Cited on pages 518 and 533).

[35] Cont, R. and Tankov, P. (2004). *Financial modelling with jump processes*. Chapman & Hall/CRC Financial Mathematics Series. Chapman & Hall/CRC, Boca Raton, FL. (Cited on pages 584, 588, 593, 601, and 619).

[36] Courtadon, G. (1982). The pricing of options on default-free bonds. *The Journal of Financial and Quantitative Analysis*, 17(1):75–100. (Cited on pages 487 and 505).

[37] Cox, A. and Hobson, D. (2005). Local martingales, bubbles and option prices. *Finance Stoch.*, 9(4):477–492. (Cited on page 241).

[38] Cox, J., Ingersoll, J., and Ross, S. (1985). A theory of the term structure of interest rates. *Econometrica*, 53:385–407. (Cited on pages 197, 234, 251, 260, 486, 487, 493, 501, and 505).

[39] Cox, J., Ross, S., and Rubinstein, M. (1979). Option pricing: A simplified approach. *Journal of Financial Economics*, 7:87–106. (Cited on pages 56 and 69).

[40] Cramér, H. (1946). *Mathematical methods of statistics*. Princeton University Press, Princeton, NJ. (Cited on page 607).

[41] Crépey, S. (2013). *Financial modeling*. Springer Finance. Springer, Heidelberg. A backward stochastic differential equations perspective, Springer Finance Textbooks. (Cited on page 371).

[42] Curran, M. (1994). Valuing Asian and portfolio options by conditioning on the geometric mean price. *Management Science*, 40(12):1705–1711. (Cited on page 384).

[43] Dahl, L. and Benth, F. (2002). Fast evaluation of the Asian basket option by singular value decomposition. In *Monte Carlo and quasi-Monte Carlo methods, 2000 (Hong Kong)*, pages 201–214. Springer, Berlin. (Cited on page 385).

[44] Dana, R.-A. and Jeanblanc, M. (2007). *Financial markets in continuous time*. Springer Finance. Springer-Verlag, Berlin. Corrected Second Printing. (Cited on page 356).

[45] Dash, J. (2004). *Quantitative finance and risk management*. World Scientific Publishing Co. Inc., River Edge, NJ. (Cited on page 454).

[46] Dassios, A. and Lim, J. (2019). A variation of the Azéma martingale and drawdown options. Mathematical Finance, to appear. (Cited on page 369).

[47] Deelstra, G., Diallo, I., and Vanmaele, M. (2010). Moment matching approximation of Asian basket option prices. *J. Comput. Appl. Math.*, 234:1006–1016. (Cited on page 385).

[48] Deelstra, G., Liinev, J., and Vanmaele, M. (2004). Pricing of arithmetic basket options by conditioning. *Insurance Math. Econom.*, 34:55–57. (Cited on page 385).

[49] Demeterfi, K., Derman, E., Kamal, M., and Zou, J. (1999). More than you ever wanted to know about volatility swaps. Quantitative Strategies Research Notes. (Cited on page 275).

[50] Derman, E. and Kani, I. (1994). Riding on a smile. *Risk Magazine*, 7(2):139–145. (Cited on page 287).

[51] Di Nunno, G., Øksendal, B., and Proske, F. (2009). *Malliavin Calculus for Lévy Processes with Applications to Finance.* Universitext. Springer-Verlag, Berlin. (Cited on pages 83, 223, and 619).

[52] Doob, J. (1953). *Stochastic processes.* John Wiley & Sons Inc., New York. (Cited on page 401).

[53] Doob, J. (1984). *Classical potential theory and its probabilistic counterpart.* Springer-Verlag, Berlin. (Cited on page 401).

[54] Dothan, L. (1978). On the term structure of interest rates. *Jour. of Fin. Ec.*, 6:59–69. (Cited on pages 487 and 499).

[55] Downes, A., Joshi, M., and Denson, N. (2008). *Quant Job Interview Questions and Answers.* CreateSpace Independent Publishing Platform, first edition. (Cited on page 474).

[56] Dudley, R. (2002). *Real analysis and probability*, volume 74 of *Cambridge Studies in Advanced Mathematics.* Cambridge University Press, Cambridge. Revised reprint of the 1989 original. (Cited on page 124).

[57] Dufresne, D. (2000). Laguerre series for Asian and other options. *Math. Finance*, 10(4):407–428. (Cited on page 380).

[58] Dufresne, D. (2001). The integral of geometric Brownian motion. *Adv. in Appl. Probab.*, 33(1):223–241. (Cited on page 377).

[59] Dupire, B. (1994). Pricing with a smile. *Risk Magazine*, 7(1):18–20. (Cited on pages 287, 288, and 295).

[60] Dvoretzky, A., Erdős, P., and Kakutani, S. (1961). Nonincrease everywhere of the Brownian motion process. In *Proc. 4th Berkeley Sympos. Math. Statist. and Prob., Vol. II*, pages 103–116. University of California Press, Berkeley, California. (Cited on page 299).

[61] Einstein, A. (1905). Über die von der molekularkinetischen Theorie der Wärme geforderte Bewegung von in ruhenden Flüssigkeiten suspendierten Teilchen. *Annalen der Physik*, 17:549–560. (Cited on page 2).

[62] El Khatib, Y. (2003). Contributions to the study of discontinuous markets via the Malliavin calculus. PhD thesis, Université de La Rochelle. (Cited on page 365).

[63] El Khatib, Y. and Privault, N. (2003). Computations of replicating portfolios in complete markets driven by normal martingales. *Applicationes Mathematicae*, 30:147–172. (Cited on page 363).

[64] Elliott, R. and Kopp, P. (2005). *Mathematics of Financial Markets*. Springer Finance. Springer-Verlag, Berlin, second edition. (Cited on pages 425 and 435).

[65] Eriksson, J. and Persson, J. (2006). Pricing turbo warrants. Preprint. (Cited on pages 49 and 326).

[66] Feller, W. (1951). Two singular diffusion problems. *Ann. of Math. (2)*, 54:173–182. (Cited on pages 251 and 486).

[67] Folland, G. B. (1999). *Real analysis*. Pure and Applied Mathematics (New York). John Wiley & Sons Inc., New York, second edition. (Cited on page 115).

[68] Föllmer, H. and Leukert, P. (1999). Quantile hedging. *Finance and Stochastics*, 3:251–273. (Cited on page 243).

[69] Föllmer, H. and Schied, A. (2004). *Stochastic finance*, volume 27 of *de Gruyter Studies in Mathematics*. Walter de Gruyter & Co., Berlin. (Cited on pages 22, 27, 55, 56, 83, and 92).

[70] Fonseca, J. D. and Martini, C. (2016). The α-hypergeometric stochastic volatility model. *Stochastic Process. Appl.*, 126(5):1472–1502. (Cited on page 272).

[71] Fouque, J., Papanicolaou, G., and Sircar, K. (2000). *Derivatives in financial markets with stochastic volatility*. Cambridge University Press, Cambridge. (Cited on page 269).

[72] Fouque, J., Papanicolaou, G., Sircar, K., and Sølna, K. (2011). *Multiscale Stochastic Volatility for Equity, Interest Rate Derivatives, and Credit Derivatives*. Cambridge University Press, Cambridge. (Cited on pages 251, 269, 270, and 271).

[73] Friz, P. and Gatheral, J. (2005). Valuation of volatility derivatives as an inverse problem. *Quant. Finance*, 5(6):531–542. (Cited on pages 257, 260, and 291).

[74] Garman, M. and Kohlhagen, S. (1983). Foreign currency option values. *J. International Money and Finance*, 2:231–237. (Cited on pages 463 and 464).

[75] Gatheral, J. (2006). *The Volatility Surface: A Practitioner's Guide*. Wiley. (Cited on pages 257, 269, 273, and 293).

[76] Geman, H., El Karoui, N., and Rochet, J.-C. (1995). Changes of numéraire, changes of probability measure and option pricing. *J. Appl. Probab.*, 32(2):443–458. (Cited on pages 451 and 469).

[77] Geman, H. and Yor, M. (1993). Bessel processes, Asian options and perpetuities. *Math. Finance*, 3:349–375. (Cited on pages 376 and 380).

[78] Gerber, H. and Shiu, E. (1994). Option pricing by Esscher transforms. *Transactions of Society of Actuaries*, 46:99–191. (Cited on page 621).

[79] Gerber, H. and Shiu, E. (1996). Martingale approach to pricing perpetual American options on two stocks. *Math. Finance*, 6(3):303–322. (Cited on page 442).

[80] Glasserman, P. (2004). *Monte Carlo methods in financial engineering*, volume 53 of *Applications of Mathematics (New York)*. Springer-Verlag, New York. Stochastic Modelling and Applied Probability. (Cited on page 628).

[81] Gradshteyn, I. S. and Ryzhik, I. M. (2007). *Table of integrals, series, and products*. Elsevier/Academic Press, Amsterdam, seventh edition. (Cited on pages 260 and 297).

[82] Gram, J. (1883). Über die Entwicklung reeller Funktionen in Reihen mittelst der Methode der kleinsten Quadraten. *J. Reine Angew. Math*, 94:41–73. (Cited on page 607).

[83] Guirreri, S. (2015). *YieldCurve: Modelling and Estimation of the Yield Curve*. R package version 4.1. (Cited on page 518).

[84] Hagan, P., Kumar, D., Lesniewski, A., and Woodward, D. (2002). Managing smile risk. *Wilmott Magazine*, pages 84–108. (Cited on pages 251 and 296).

[85] Han, J., Gao, M., Zhang, Q., and Li, Y. (2013). Option prices under stochastic volatility. *Appl. Math. Lett.*, 26(1):1–4. (Cited on page 272).

[86] Hardy, G. H., Littlewood, J. E., and Pólya, G. (1988). *Inequalities*. Cambridge Mathematical Library. Cambridge University Press, Cambridge. Reprint of the 1952 edition. (Cited on page 403).

[87] Harrison, J. and Kreps, D. (1979). Martingales and arbitrage in multiperiod securities markets. *Journal of Economic Theory*, 20:341–408. (Cited on pages 55 and 56).

[88] Harrison, J. and Pliska, S. (1981). Martingales and stochastic integrals in the theory of continuous trading. *Stochastic Process. Appl.*, 11:215–260. (Cited on pages 156 and 158).

[89] Heath, D., Jarrow, R., and Morton, A. (1992). Bond pricing and the term structure of interest rates: a new methodology. *Econometrica*, 60:77–105. (Cited on pages 3 and 527).

[90] Henry-Labordère, P. (2009). *Analysis, Geometry, and Modeling in Finance*. Chapman & Hall/CRC Financial Mathematics Series. CRC Press, Boca Raton, FL. (Cited on page 296).

[91] Heston, S. (1993). A closed-form solution for options with stochastic volatility with applications to bond and currency options. *The Review of Financial Studies*, 6(2):327–343. (Cited on pages 251, 253, 265, 266, and 273).

[92] Heston, S., Loewenstein, M., and Willard, G. (2007). Options and bubbles. *The Review of Financial Studies*, 20(2):359–390. (Cited on page 241).

[93] Hiriart-Urruty, J.-B. and Lemaréchal, C. (2001). *Fundamentals of convex analysis*. Grundlehren Text Editions. Springer-Verlag, Berlin. (Cited on page 24).

[94] Hirsch, F. and Lacombe, G. (1999). *Elements of functional analysis*, volume 192 of *Graduate Texts in Mathematics*. Springer-Verlag, New York. (Cited on page 122).

[95] Ho, S. and Lee, S. (1986). Term structure movements and pricing interest rate contingent claims. *Journal of Finance*, 41:1011–1029. (Cited on page 485).

[96] Hull, J. and White, A. (1990). Pricing interest rate derivative securities. *The Review of Financial Studies*, 3:537–592. (Cited on pages 485 and 527).

[97] Ikeda, N. and Watanabe, S. (1989). *Stochastic Differential Equations and Diffusion Processes*. North-Holland. (Cited on pages 128 and 209).

[98] Itô, K. (1951). On stochastic differential equations. *Mem. Amer. Math. Soc.*, No. 4:51. (Cited on page 2).

[99] Jacka, S. (1991). Optimal stopping and the American put. *Mathematical Finance*, 1:1–14. (Cited on page 435).

[100] Jacquier, A. (2017). Advanced methods in derivatives pricing with application to volatility modelling. `https://www.ma.imperial.ac.uk/~ajacquie/IC_AMDP/IC_AMDP_Docs/AMDP.pdf`. Accessed: 2022-04-08. (Cited on page 243).

[101] Jaillet, P., Lamberton, D., and Lapeyre, B. (1990). Variational inequalities and the pricing of American options. *Acta Appl. Math.*, 21:263–289. (Cited on page 435).

[102] Jamshidian, F. (1989). An exact bond option formula. *The Journal of Finance*, XLIV(1):205–209. (Cited on pages 546 and 562).

[103] Jamshidian, F. (1996). Sorting out swaptions. *Risk Magazine*, 9(3):59–60. (Cited on page 469).

[104] Jarrow, R., Protter, P., and Shimbo, K. (2007). Asset price bubbles in complete markets. In *Advances in mathematical finance*, Appl. Numer. Harmon. Anal., pages 97–121. Birkhäuser Boston, Boston, MA. (Cited on page 241).

[105] Jeanblanc, M. and Privault, N. (2002). A complete market model with Poisson and Brownian components. In Dalang, R., Dozzi, M., and Russo, F., editors, *Seminar on stochastic analysis, random fields and applications (Ascona, 1999)*, volume 52 of *Progress in Probability*, pages 189–204. Birkhäuser, Basel. (Cited on page 619).

[106] Kakushadze, Z. (2015). Path integral and asset pricing. *Quant. Finance*, 15(11):1759–1771. (Cited on page 503).

[107] Kemna, A. and Vorst, A. (1990). A pricing method for options based on average asset values. *Journal of Banking and Finance*, 14:113–129. (Cited on page 374).

[108] Keynes, J. (1924). *A Tract on Monetary Reform*. MacMillan & Co., London. (Cited on page 480).

[109] Kim, Y.-J. (2002). Option pricing under stochastic interest rates: An empirical investigation. *Asia-Pacific Financial Markets*, 9:23–44. (Cited on page 547).

[110] Klebaner, F. (2005). *Introduction to stochastic calculus with applications*. Imperial College Press, London, second edition. (Cited on page 240).

[111] Kloeden, P. and Platen, E. (1999). *Numerical solution of stochastic differential equations*, volume 23 of *Applications of Mathematics (New York)*. Springer-Verlag, New York. Stochastic Modelling and Applied Probability. (Cited on page 140).

[112] Korn, R., Korn, E., and Kroisandt, G. (2010). *Monte Carlo methods and models in finance and insurance*. Chapman & Hall/CRC Financial Mathematics Series. CRC Press, Boca Raton, FL. (Cited on page 628).

[113] Lamberton, D. and Lapeyre, B. (1996). *Introduction to stochastic calculus applied to finance.* Chapman & Hall, London. (Cited on pages 83 and 388).

[114] Leung, T. and Sircar, K. (2015). Implied volatility of leveraged ETF options. *Applied Mathematical Finance*, 22(2):162–188. (Cited on page 204).

[115] Levy, E. (1992). Pricing European average rate currency options. *Journal of International Money and Finance*, 11:474–491. (Cited on pages 380 and 381).

[116] Lipton, A. (2001). *Mathematical methods for foreign exchange. A financial engineer's approach.* World Scientific Publishing Co., Inc., River Edge, NJ. (Cited on page 170).

[117] Longstaff, F. and Schwartz, E. (2001). Valuing American options by simulation: a simple least-squares approach. *Review of Financial Studies*, 14:113–147. (Cited on pages 436 and 438).

[118] Lyashenko, A. and Mercurio, F. (2020). Looking forward to backward-looking rates: A modeling framework for term rates replacing LIBOR. Available at SSRN: https://ssrn.com/abstract=3330240. (Cited on page 530).

[119] Lyuu, Y.-D. (2021). Course on principles of financial computing, Part 6. Barrier options. Lecture notes, National Taiwan University. (Cited on page 324).

[120] Mamon, R. (2004). Three ways to solve for bond prices in the Vasicek model. *Journal of Applied Mathematics and Decision Sciences*, 8(1):1–14. (Cited on page 538).

[121] Margrabe, W. (1978). The value of an option to exchange one asset for another. *The Journal of Finance*, XXXIII(1):177–186. (Cited on pages 467 and 471).

[122] Marsh, T. and Rosenfeld, E. (1983). Stochastic processes for interest rates and equilibrium bond prices. *The Journal of Finance*, 38(2):635–646. Papers and Proceedings Forty-First Annual Meeting American Finance Association New York, NY (Cited on pages 487 and 505).

[123] Matsumoto, H. and Yor, M. (2005). Exponential functionals of Brownian motion. I. Probability laws at fixed time. *Probab. Surv.*, 2:312–347. (Cited on page 377).

[124] Mel'nikov, A. and Petrachenko, Y. (2005). On option pricing in binomial market with transaction costs. *Finance and Stochastics*, 9:141–149. (Cited on page 102).

[125] Mel'nikov, A., Volkov, S., and Nechaev, M. (2002). *Mathematics of financial obligations*, volume 212 of *Translations of Mathematical Monographs*. American Mathematical Society, Providence, RI. Translated from the 2001 Russian original by H. H. McFaden. (Cited on page 243).

[126] Mercurio, F. (2018). A simple multi curve model for pricing SOFR futures and other derivatives. Working paper, Bloomberg LP. (Cited on page 560).

[127] Merton, R. (1973). Theory of rational option pricing. *Bell Journal of Economics*, 4(1):141–183. (Cited on page 468).

[128] Merton, R. (1976). Option pricing when underlying stock returns are discontinuous. *J. of Financial Economics*, 3:125–144. (Cited on page 612).

[129] Milevsky, M. (1998). A closed-form approximation for valuing basket options. *Journal of Derivatives*, 55:54–61. (Cited on page 385).

[130] Mörters, P. and Peres, Y. (2010). *Brownian Motion*. Cambridge Series in Statistical and Probabilistic Mathematics. Cambridge University Press, Cambridge. (Cited on page 300).

[131] Nelson, C. and Siegel, A. (1987). Parsimonious modeling of yield curves. *Journal of Business*, 60:473–489. (Cited on pages 513 and 530).

[132] Neuberger, A. (1994). The log contract. *Journal of Portfolio Management*, 20(2):74–80. (Cited on page 275).

[133] Norris, J. (1998). *Markov chains*, volume 2 of *Cambridge Series in Statistical and Probabilistic Mathematics*. Cambridge University Press, Cambridge. Reprint of 1997 original. (Cited on page 569).

[134] Øksendal, B. and Sulem, A. (2005). *Applied stochastic control of jump diffusions*. Springer-Verlag, Berlin. (Cited on page 584).

[135] Papanicolaou, A. and Sircar, K. (2014). A regime-switching Heston model for VIX and S&P 500 implied volatilities. *Quant. Finance*, 14(10):1811–1827. (Cited on pages 251 and 291).

[136] Peng, S. (2010). Backward stochastic differential equation, nonlinear expectation and their applications. In *Proceedings of the International Congress of Mathematicians. Volume I*, pages 393–432. Hindustan Book Agency, New Delhi. (Cited on page 238).

[137] Pintoux, C. and Privault, N. (2010). A direct solution to the Fokker-Planck equation for exponential Brownian functionals. *Analysis and Applications*, 8(3):287–304. (Cited on page 500).

[138] Pintoux, C. and Privault, N. (2011). The Dothan pricing model revisited. *Math. Finance*, 21:355–363. (Cited on page 499).

[139] Prayoga, A. and Privault, N. (2017). Pricing CIR yield options by conditional moment matching. *Asia-Pacific Financial Markets*, 24:19–38. (Cited on pages 253 and 501).

[140] Privault, N. (2008). Stochastic analysis of Bernoulli processes. *Probab. Surv.*, 5:435–483. arXiv:0809.3168v3. (Cited on page 83).

[141] Privault, N. (2009). *Stochastic analysis in discrete and continuous settings: with normal martingales*, volume 1982 of *Lecture Notes in Mathematics*. Springer-Verlag, Berlin. (Cited on pages 83, 84, 85, 125, 128, 208, and 223).

[142] Privault, N. (2018). *Understanding Markov Chains (Second Edition)*. Springer Undergraduate Mathematics Series. Springer. (Cited on page 570).

[143] Privault, N. (2021). *Stochastic Interest Rate Modeling With Fixed Income Derivative Pricing (3rd edition)*. Advanced Series on Statistical Science & Applied Probability. World Scientific Publishing Co., Singapore. 372 pp. (Cited on pages 527, 532, 534, 536, 547, and 560).

[144] Privault, N. and She, Q. (2016). Option pricing and implied volatilities in a 2-hypergeometric stochastic volatility model. *Appl. Math. Lett.*, 53:77–84. (Cited on page 272).

[145] Privault, N. and Teng, T.-R. (2012). Risk-neutral hedging in bond markets. *Risk and Decision Analysis*, 3:201–209. (Cited on pages 469, 550, and 559).

[146] Privault, N. and Uy, W. (2013). Monte Carlo computation of the Laplace transform of exponential Brownian functionals. *Methodol. Comput. Appl. Probab.*, 15(3):511–524. (Cited on page 500).

[147] Privault, N. and Wei, X. (2009). Calibration of the LIBOR market model - implementation in PREMIA. Bankers, Markets & Investors, 99:20–28. (Cited on page 560).

[148] Privault, N. and Yu, J. (2016). Stratified approximations for the pricing of options on average. *Journal of Computational Finance*, 19(4):95–113. (Cited on pages 383 and 501).

[149] Profeta, C., Roynette, B., and Yor, M. (2010). *Option prices as probabilities.* Springer Finance. Springer-Verlag, Berlin. A new look at generalized Black-Scholes formulae. (Cited on page 309).

[150] Protter, P. (2001). A partial introduction to financial asset pricing theory. *Stochastic Process. Appl.*, 91(2):169–203. (Cited on pages 225 and 470).

[151] Protter, P. (2004). *Stochastic integration and differential equations*, volume 21 of *Stochastic Modelling and Applied Probability.* Springer-Verlag, Berlin, second edition. (Cited on pages 135, 140, 215, 218, 219, 225, 456, 467, 491, and 492).

[152] Rebonato, R. (2009). *The SABR/LIBOR Market Model Pricing, Calibration and Hedging for Complex Interest-Rate Derivatives.* John Wiley & Sons. (Cited on page 252).

[153] Revuz, D. and Yor, M. (1994). *Continuous Martingales and Brownian Motion.* Springer-Verlag. (Cited on page 115).

[154] Rogers, L. and Shi, Z. (1995). The value of an Asian option. *J. Appl. Probab.*, 32(4):1077–1088. (Cited on page 390).

[155] Rouah, F. (2013). *The Heston Model and its Extensions in Matlab and C#.* Wiley Finance. John Wiley & Sons, Inc. (Cited on page 266).

[156] Rubinstein, M. (1991). Pay now, choose later. *Risk Magazine*, 4:13–13. (Cited on page 232).

[157] Rudin, W. (1974). *Real and Complex Analysis.* McGraw-Hill. (Cited on pages 122 and 124).

[158] Ruiz de Chávez, J. (2001). Predictable representation of the binomial process and application to options in finance. In *XXXIII National Congress of the Mexican Mathematical Society (Spanish) (Saltillo, 2000)*, volume 29 of *Aportaciones Mat. Comun.*, pages 223–230. Soc. Mat. Mexicana, México. (Cited on page 83).

[159] Rutkowski, M. and Bickersteth, M. (2021). Pricing and hedging of SOFR derivatives under differential funding costs and collateralization. Preprint arXiv:2112.14033. (Cited on page 521).

[160] Samuelson, P. (1965). Rational theory of warrant pricing. *Industrial Management Review*, 6(2):13–39. (Cited on page 2).

[161] Santa-Clara, P. and Sornette, D. (2001). The dynamics of the forward interest rate curve with stochastic string shocks. *The Review of Financial Studies*, 14(1):149–185. (Cited on page 542).

[162] Sato, K. (1999). *Lévy processes and infinitely divisible distributions*, volume 68 of *Cambridge Studies in Advanced Mathematics*. Cambridge University Press, Cambridge. (Cited on page 594).

[163] Schoenmakers, J. (2005). *Robust LIBOR modelling and pricing of derivative products*. Chapman & Hall/CRC Financial Mathematics Series. Chapman & Hall/CRC, Boca Raton, FL. (Cited on pages 559 and 560).

[164] Schroeder, T. and Coffey, B. (2018). Assessment of physical delivery mechanisms on the live cattle futures market. ResearchăReport. (Cited on page 7).

[165] Sharpe, W. (1978). *Investments*. Prentice Hall, Englewood Cliffs, NJ (Cited on page 56).

[166] Shiryaev, A. (1999). *Essentials of stochastic finance*. World Scientific Publishing Co. Inc., River Edge, NJ. (Cited on pages 156 and 158).

[167] Shreve, S. (2004). *Stochastic calculus for finance. II.* Springer Finance. Springer-Verlag, New York. Continuous-time models. (Cited on pages 309, 317, 332, 393, 423, 440, and 477).

[168] Steele, J. (2001). *Stochastic calculus and financial applications*, volume 45 of *Applications of Mathematics*. Springer-Verlag, New York. (Cited on page 433).

[169] Svensson, L. (1994). Estimating and interpreting forward interest rates: Sweden 1992-1994. National Bureau of Economic Research Working Paper 4871. (Cited on pages 513 and 531).

[170] Tanaka, K., Yamada, T., and Watanabe, T. (2010). Applications of Gram-Charlier expansion and bond moments for pricing of interest rates and credit risk. *Quant. Finance*, 10(6):645–662. (Cited on page 607).

[171] Thiele, T. (1899). On semi invariants in the theory of observations (Om Iagttagelseslærens Halvinvarianter). *Kjöbenhavn Overs.*, pages 135–141. (Cited on page 605).

[172] Turnbull, S. and Wakeman, L. (1992). A quick algorithm for pricing European average options. *Journal of Financial and Quantitative Analysis*, 26:377–389. (Cited on page 380).

[173] Üstünel, A. (2009). Probabilistic solution of the American options. *J. Funct. Anal.*, 256:3091–3105. (Cited on page 435).

[174] Vašíček, O. (1977). An equilibrium characterisation of the term structure. *Journal of Financial Economics*, 5:177–188. (Cited on pages 3, 145, 479, 493, 517, and 546).

[175] Večeř, J. (2001). A new PDE approach for pricing arithmetic average Asian options. *Journal of Computational Finance*, 4:105–113. (Cited on page 393).

[176] Watson, G. N. (1995). *A treatise on the theory of Bessel functions*. Cambridge University Press, Cambridge. Reprint of the second (1944) edition. (Cited on page 500).

[177] Widder, D. (1975). *The heat equation*. Academic Press, New York. Pure and Applied Mathematics, Vol. 67. (Cited on page 191).

[178] Wiener, N. (1923). Differential space. *Journal of Mathematics and Physics of the Massachusetts Institute of Technology*, 2:131–174. (Cited on page 2).

[179] Williams, D. (1991). *Probability with martingales*. Cambridge Mathematical Text-books. Cambridge University Press, Cambridge. (Cited on page 83).

[180] Wilmott, P. (2006). *Paul Wilmott on quantitative finance*. John Wiley & Sons. (Cited on page 442).

[181] Wong, H. and Chan, C. (2008). Turbo warrants under stochastic volatility. *Quant. Finance*, 8(7):739–751. (Cited on pages 49 and 326).

[182] Wu, X. (2000). A new stochastic duration based on the Vasicek and CIR term struc-ture theories. *Journal of Business Finance and Accounting*, 27. (Cited on page 511).

[183] Yang, Z., Ewald, C.-O., and Menkens, O. (2011). Pricing and hedging of Asian options: quasi-explicit solutions via Malliavin calculus. *Math. Methods Oper. Res.*, 74:93–120. (Cited on page 398).

[184] Yor, M. (1992). On some exponential functionals of Brownian motion. *Adv. in Appl. Probab.*, 24(3):509–531. (Cited on pages 251, 377, and 499).

Index

For Product Safety Concerns and Information please contact our
EU representative GPSR@taylorandfrancis.com Taylor & Francis
Verlag GmbH, Kaufingerstraße 24, 80331 München, Germany

Law 21 of 1896. Article.			Law 19 of 1895. Article.			Law 14 of 1894. Article.
...	...	...	90	...	...	... 54
			(Deleted from Law 21 of 1896).			
87	...	...	... 91	...	...	... 55
88	...	...	... 92	...	...	... 56
89	...	...	... 93	...	...	... 57
90	...	...	... 94	...	...	... 63
91	...	...	... 95	...	...	... 73
92	...	...	... 96	...	...	... 65
93	...	...	... 97	...	...	... 67
94	...	...	... 98	...	...	... 15
95	...	...	... 99	...	...	... 67a
96	...	...	... 100	...	...	... 30a
97	...	...	... 101	...	...	... 25
98	...	...	... 102	...	...	... 76
99	...	...	... 103	...	...	... 52a
100	...	...	... 104	...	...	... 52b
101	...	...	... 105	...	...	... 52c
102	...	...	... 106	...	...	... 52d
103	...	...	... 107	...	...	... 52e
104	...	...	... 108	...	...	... 52f
105	...	...	... 109	...	...	... 52g
106	...	...	... 110	...	...	... 52h
107	...	...	... 111	...	...	... 52i
108	...	...	... 112	...	...	... 37a
109	...	...	... 113	...	...	... 6d
110	...	...	... 114	...	...	... 6e
111	...	...	... 115	...	...	... 6f
112	...	...	... 116	...	...	... 6g
113	...	...	... 117	...	...	... 6h
114	...	...	... 118	...	...	... 6i
115	...	...	... 119	...	...	... 6k
116	...	...	... 120	...	...	... 30b
117	...	...	... 121	...	...	... 21
118	...	...	... 122	...	...	... 21a
119	...	...	... 123	...	...	... 21b
120	...	...	... 124	...	...	21c, 21d, and 21e.
121	...	...	... 125	...	...	... 21g
122	...	...	... 126	...	...	... 21l
123	...	...	... 127	...	...	... 21m
124	...	...	... 128	...	...	... 21n
125	...	...	... 129	...	...	... 40
126	...	...	... 130	...	...	... 41
127	...	...	... 131	...	...	... 42
128	...	...	... 132	...	...	... 43
129	...	...	... 133	...	...	... 43
130	...	...	... 134	...	...	... 44
131	...	...	... 135	...	...	... 45
132	...	...	... 136	...	...	... 46
133	...	...	... 137	...	...	... 47

Law 21 of 1896. Article.				Law 19 of 1895. Article.				Law 14 of 1894. Article.
134	...	...	...	138	...	...	...	48
135	...	...	...	139	...	...	...	49
136	...	...	...	140	...	...	...	86
137	...	...	...	141	...	...	...	86a
138	...	...	...	142	...	...	...	80
139	...	...	...	143	...	...	...	66a
140	...	...	...	144	...	...	...	74
141	...	...	...	145	...	...	...	81
142	...	...	...	146	...	...	...	87
143	...	...	...	147	...	...	...	68
144	...	...	...	148	...	...	...	69
145	...	...	...	149	...	...	...	71
146	...	...	...	150	...	...	...	71a
147	...	...	...	151	...	...	...	72
148	...	...	...	152	...	...	...	—
149	...	...	...	153	...	...	...	70
150	...	...	...	154	...	...	...	77
151	...	...	...	155	...	...	...	78
152	...	...	...	156	...	...	...	79
153	...	...	...	157	...	...	...	84
154	...	...	...	158	...	...	...	83
155	...	...	...	159	...	...	...	91

NOTE.—Article 61c of Law 14 of 1894, dealing with provisional prospecting licences, and Articles 82 and 82a of the same Law, dealing with transfer duty, are not included in Law 19 of 1895.

Article 78 of Law of 1895 is partly deleted and partly dealt with in Article 77 of present Law.

Articles 84 and 85 are deleted, but a portion of the subject dealt with comes under Article 77 of present Law.

Article 90 of Law of 1895 does not appear in the present Law, but is dealt with under Article 88.

ALPHABETICAL INDEX TO LAW 21, 1896.

Q 2

Extracts from the Netherlands Railway Report for 1896.

(*Report published at Amsterdam*).

EXPLOITATION.

On the 1st January, 1896, the following lines were in exploitation:

	Length. Kilometres.	Miles.
Krugersdorp-Johannesburg	32	20
Johannesburg-Elandsfontein	16	10
Elandsfontein-Springs	34	21
Mid Vaal River, Elandsfontein	66	41
Elandsfontein-Pretoria	59	37
Portuguese border-Pretoria	472	295
Kaapmuiden-Avoca	28	18
Natal Border Junction (South line)	256	160
Total	963	602

In the course of 1896 were brought in exploitation:

Avoca-Barberton	27	17
Krugersdorp-Frederickstad	85	53
So that on the 31st of December, 1896, were in exploitation ...	1075	672

On the 11th of January, 1897, the section Frederickstad-Potchefstroom was also opened for service, length, 25 kilometres or 16 miles, so that now 1,100 kilometres or 688 miles are being worked.

Again, our service of exploitation has had to cope with an extraordinary expansion of traffic, and the time has not yet come when it is possible to concentrate attention on the improvement and perfection of the service. The bringing into working of the new lines and the organisation of the service on the lines newly opened, constantly occupied a great deal of the working power of our staff.

On some parts of our system the train service was extended in such a way that it was considered necessary for safety's sake to take special precautionary measures.

On the Eastern line as well as on the Southern line the number of crossing stations was augmented considerably.

Besides the third railway track between Johannesburg and Elandsfontein, of which mention was made in the preceding report and which was almost completed during this year, it was resolved, principally in connection with the coal traffic, to double the rail section, Elandsfontein-Brakpan, 20 kilometres. The extended train service on the section, South-Eastern line to Elandsfontein, over which the Natal traffic, as well as the Cape traffic, goes, necessitated the doubling of that rail. section, of which the completion may be looked forward to in 1897.

The fact, that daily, 120 trains enter the station Elandsfontein and as many trains leave that station, that several of those trains are split or coupled on at that station, that passenger trains have to wait there for junction, because the trains from the directions Delagoa Bay, Natal, Cape Colony, Springs and Klerksdorp, join there, makes that station, as regards external service, the most important in the whole of South Africa. Thanks to a well-studied system of signals, this station is safe, but delay is oftentimes unavoidable there. In order to remedy this, the station will be freed from a portion of the traffic, by the building of a connection-curve between the south and the west, by which it will be possible to bring trains with goods exclusively destined for Johannesburg and the stations situated more westerly and coming from Natal or the Orange Free State to their destination without entering the station.

This so-called "fork" is ready now.

Besides these works of greater extent, the chapter "extension works," appearing elsewhere in this Report, will give an idea of the continual activity in this direction and also on other points of our system.

Our wagon yard also underwent, in connection with the rapid increase of the traffic, a considerable enlargement. In the course of the year we were obliged to increase the regular despatch of freight wagons from 100 to 150 per month, which was continued till far in 1897; 59 new locomotives were shipped, while the current order comprises the sending of 41 others for October, 1897.

The drastic measures for the strengthening of the traffic power of our lines made it possible for us to pretty well fulfil the requirements of the traffic, and our service might—taking into consideration the extraordinary circumstances—be called regular, were it not that a period of mishaps and calamities had marked the year 1896 as particularly unfavourable in this respect. We will come back to this subject in a following chapter.

The working of our goods service at Johannesburg, where the arrivals of foreign goods from the three chief directions principally concentrate, was a continual source of much trouble, although this year no mention is to made of blocks; and though our powers threatened to fail, the extension of our works and appliances, and also of our staff, proved to be in accord with the increase of the traffic.

A new difficulty presented itself when the principal of our two delivery contractors at Johannesburg wished to be discharged from his obligations, and when we were forced to take this portion of the working of our service under our own direction. This alteration however, only came into operation on the 1st January, 1897.

If we thereby undertook an extensive business with which technical difficulties are connected, on the other hand the gain is, that we are not dependent on a contractor independent of our service, and have it in our hands to act in the promptest manner in case of the often abnormal and rapidly changing conditions in Johannesburg. That Mr. Van Stipriaan Luiscius, head of traffic and business affairs at Johannesburg, completely knowing the requirements of the delivery service, declared himself ready to take on himself the conduct of it, made this undertaking very easy for us. As far as can be judged of the results, we have every reason for satisfaction.

The passenger traffic, although standing much behind the goods traffic as to importance, constantly develops at Johannesburg and surroundings, and assumes great dimensions.

In inland traffic the number of passengers went up from 912,198 in 1895 to 1,271,509 in this year.

Of this amount 328,766 departed from the stations of the Rand tram and from the stations between Pretoria and Elandsfontein.

From Johannesburg about 1,000 passengers per day left by local trains, besides the passengers on the direct service with the Cape Colony, Lourenço Marques, and Natal.

In the whole year there were carried in direct service :—

From Cape Colony and Orange Free State	93,850
To „ „ „	84,533
From Lourenço Marques	9,482
To „ „	12,703
From Natal	49,593
To „	52,280
Coming into the Republic	152,925 passengers.
Leaving „ „	149,516 „

These figures, however, do not give a very exact idea of the immigration, because the traffic of the coloured people (for the greatest part kaffirs) is of an altogether different character from that of the whites.

In the traffic with Lourenço Marques and Natal, the whites travel exclusively in in the first and second class, and, from the figures of the incoming and outgoing passengers, it appears that along both these routes 1346 whites less have come into the Transvaal than have left it.

In the traffic with the Cape Colony and Orange Free State to whites direct third class tickets are given; whereas, on our line, the tariff of the coloured people class has been adopted. While in that traffic 36,023 passengers, first and second class, have come in, and 34,344 have left, 43,067 whites arrived with above-mentioned third class tickets in the South African Republic, and only 26,525 passengers left it.

The increase of the white population, therefore, consists almost wholly of persons who are carried in the lowest class and, on our line, at the tariff of coloured persons. As was to be expected, the opening of the connection with the Natal South Eastern line has brought an alteration in the division of the harbour traffic.

The traffic *via* Durban was constantly increasing during the whole year, and likewise the traffic *via* Lourenço Marques, but less quickly. The traffic of the Cape Harbours, however, remained almost stationary. It was, in the middle of the year, higher than the year before, but in the latter months it began to fall off.

This natural division is very satisfactory, and confirms the expectation that the increase of the number of lines would not have a crushing effect on the existing ones, and that all would get a traffic, often so great that an increase of it has to be looked forward to with anxiety.

The following small table gives an idea of the development of the direct traffic with the connecting railways :—

GOODS TAKEN OVER (IN TONS).

MONTHS.	1895.				1896.			
	Port Border.	Natal Border.	O.F.S. Border.	Total.	Port Border.	Natal Border.	O.F.S. Border.	Total.
January ...	†4000	...	12500	16500	8500	8000	12500	29000
February ...	1500	...	11500	13000	11000	8500	21500	41000
March	3500	...	13500	·17000	11500	12500	19000	43000
April	5500	...	15000	20500	11500	11500	19500	42500
May	6000	...	19000	25000	12500	15500	28000	56000
June	5000	...	18500	23500	9500	18500	25500	53500
July	5500	...	22500	28000	12500	17500	29000	59000
August ...	9000	...	24500	33500	14500	19500	23500	57500
September ...	8000	...	19500	27500	13500	21000	21500	56000
October ...	7500	...	25000	32500	12500	20500	21000	55000
November ...	8500	2500	29000	40000	15000	18500	20500	54000
December ...	8000	2500	24500	35000	12500	17500	16500	46500

† Block in traffic through collapse of Cape Bridge.

Taking into consideration that among the goods imported *via* the Natal and Orange Free State border, is much produce of the African soil, while this is not the case, *via* the Portuguese border, it will be clearly seen what a considerable portion of the foreign traffic the harbour of Lourenço Marques has already attracted.

By some increase of hauling power, the Portuguese portion of the line was able to cope with the growing traffic in a fairly satisfactory way, but still nothing was done for the improvement of the harbour works at Lourenço Marques.

It is known to us, that big works at Lourenço Marques, constantly form the subject of enquiry, but nothing is yet to be perceived of any attempt to construct them.

The exploitation of the successively opened portions of the Klerksdorp line (South Western line) gave in the beginning no unsatisfactory results. Sight must not however be lost of the fact, that through the rinderpest, the transport per ox wagon, which in these parts, through the situation of the principal places, is the most suitable, was totally stopped, and it is not impossible that this has influenced the results of the exploitation.

The service can be done with one mixed train per day in each direction.

TRAFFIC.

This branch of our service, as has already appeared from the preceding, has caused considerable trouble in connection with maintaining adequate arrangements for dealing with the increasing demands of the service.

The usual service for the maintenance of the lines, on the older lines, more and more approached a normal condition, as the finishing and ballasting of the portions more recently brought into use was completed.

The condition of the rails, buildings, and works cannot be otherwise spoken of than with satisfaction.

The constantly increasing demands on the arrangements for the safety of trains and stations, made it necessary to establish a separate section for signalling and telegraphy, of which the organisation came into existence in the past year.

The scarcity of water, by which the whole year was marked, necessitated considerable extensions of our works for the supply of water.

TRAFFIC STATEMENTS.

The following table gives a comparative statement of the results of our exploitation during the last three years :—

	1896.	1895.	1894.
Average length in exploitation	1,004	754	445
Number of day kilometers ...	367,464	275,210	162,333
„ train „ ...	5,467,453	2,701,868	1,608,557
„ passengers, 1st class	471,301	296,614	137,462
„ „ 2nd „	490,455	371,979	327,002
„ coloured people ...	603,643	399,732	232,991
„ Government passengers	8,551	2,273	901
Baggage (English pounds) ...	5,699,186	3,056,258	1,562,885
Packages „ „ ...	7,480,814	4,691,351	2,915,333
Parcels „ „ ...	28,462,953	22,204,004	6,228,825
Normal goods „ „ ...	777,476,948 ⎱	542,468,639	403,003,351
Intermediate goods „ ...	295,334,159 ⎰		
Rough goods „ ...	2,373,531,522	1,677,778,727	1,145,144,513

The proceeds amounted to:—

	£	s.	d.	£	s.	d.	£	s.	d.
Passengers and Baggage ...	610,141	2	7	329,562	13	5	152,415	3	3
Goods and Cattle	1,945,229	17	5	1,031,626	0	4	523,966	6	5
Telegraph	5,186	18	3	3,813	19	3	2,263	15	11
Import duties	242,198	3	8	137,337	2	3	56,536	9	5
Sundries	100,759	18	6	47,731	18	0	62,200	7	0
Total	2,903,516	0	5	1,550,071	13	3	797,382	2	0

Under sundries are to be understood the extraordinary receipts from the traffic, the profits accruing from leases of bars, bookstalls, etc., rent of houses, depositing places, rolling stock in use by contractors, etc., also the payment for the use of our pier at Lourenço Marques.

For the first time the returns of the Klerksdorp line are included in the returns, and this to the amount of £13,951 10s. 1d.

The costs of working were in 1896	...	...	£1,197,841	18	8
These were in 1895 ...	...	...	868,297	15	2
And in 1894 ...	...	...	388,239	15	10

Finally we give here a comparative statement of the principal traffic figures:—

	1896.	1895.	1894.
Returns per kilometer length ...	£2,891 18 11	£2,055 15 11	£1,791 17 5
Returns per day kilometer ...	7 18 0	5 12 8	4 18 3
Returns per train kilometer ...	0 10 7⅖	0 11 5⅗	0 9 11
Cost per train kilometer ...	0 4 4⅘	0 4 11¾	0 4 10
Traffic cost in % to receipts ...	41·25%	48·49%	48·68%

FINANCIAL STATEMENT.

The unexpectedly rapid increase of the traffic on our lines compelled us, in case we wanted to satisfy the just requirements of the public, to extend in the most solid and quickest way our engine and waggon-yard, to enlarge many stations and to lay double lines on the busiest sections.

As the money necessary for those disbursements had to be obtained from the reserve fund and the Volksraad decided that doubling of rails, as an extension, had to be charged to that fund, the disbursements exceeded the receipts of the fund and the credit balance included therein.

By resolution of the Volksraad of 8th December, 1896, we were authorised to issue a loan of not more than 13,200,000f. (£1,100,000), and to charge the reserve fund with the interest and amortisation thereof.

The extraordinary meeting of shareholders held on the 9th of January, 1897, approved of the proposal of the Direction to raise a loan of 4%, amounting to 13,000,000f., or 21,970,000 reichsmark, and to redeem the 8,815,000f. still standing out in 5% obligations of the loan of 1891, unless the holders were satisfied with a reduction of interest from 5% to 4%, commencing on April 1st.

Almost all the holders availed themselves of the opportunity of having their obligations converted.

Political struggles which set in in the meantime made us resolve to postpone the issue of a portion of the new loan for a while.

Under the heading "Floating Goods," all goods are included which are sent from Europe and have not yet arrived in Africa on December 31st, or had not yet been put together and rendered fit for use. Under that heading an amount of 938,636f. (£78,219 13s. 4d.) appears for locomotives and carriages, which are to be charged to the reserve fund, as also the whole amount of 3,547,352·37f. (£297,862 13s. 11d.) for works and construction, being the extension works which were uncompleted on December 31st.

The obligatory redemptions of loans, which are deducted from the balance of the exploitation account, amounted to 208,000f. (£17,333 6s. 8d.) in 1896.

The fixed amount of 214,839·63f. (£17,903 6s. 1d.) has been paid into the reserve fund of the tramway this year, but out of that fund 622,737·25f. (£51,894 15s. 5d.) 'for extensions and 26,741·05f. (£2,228 8s. 5d.) for extraordinary repairs had to be paid. The said reserve fund remained in debt to the Company, 418,704·89f. (£34,892 1s. 6d.)

3,285,473·46f. (£273,789 9s. 1d. were paid into the reserve fund of the railway. but out of it 722,509·70f. (£60,209 2s. 10d.) were paid for extensions; 147,542·80f, (£12,295 4s. 8d.) for extraordinary repairs; and 1,795,871·05f. (£149,655 18s. 5d.) for locomotives and rolling stock.

There was on December 31st still 1,871,563·90f. (£155,963 13s. 2d.) in the fund, therefore much less than required to make the extensions appearing under "Floating goods" and "Works in construction."

An amount of 259,310f. (£21,609 3s. 4d.) will be paid this year into the amortisation fund. This amount, increased by a balance of that fund not invested, appears in the balance sheet. The South African Republic appears as creditor this year to an amount of 6,576,000f. (£548,000), being the amount given for the building of the Klerksdorp line.

This year two items appear under the charges, which we hope will never occur again. The one, amounting to 89,529·60f. (£7,460 16s.), is a donation to the victims of the dynamite explosion in Johannesburg on February 19th, 1896 ; the other, amounting to 1,824,000f. (£152,000), was given by us to the Government's Commission as a contribution for compensation for the damage caused by this explosion.

According to Article XXXIII. of the Concession, after the obligatory interest and amortisation of the loans, the contribution towards the amortisation fund and the guaranteed dividend have been deducted from the balance of the account an amount of 10,409,873·04⁵f. (£867,489 8s. 5d.) remains. According to Article XXXIV. of the

Concession, 90 per cent. thereof has to be paid out, so that as extra profit an amount of 1,040,987·30f. (£86,748 18s. 10d.) remains, to which has to be added another amount of 35,050·82f. (£2,920 18s.) brought forward from the year 1895 as undivided.

We submit to you as a recommendation the desirability of setting apart 1,050,000f (£87,500) of this amount as a payment of $7\frac{1}{2}$ per cent. extra dividend on all shares, and to carry forward 26,038·12⁵f. (£2,169 16s. 10d.) to the new account.

If you approve of this, it will be possible to pay a further dividend on July 1st of 97·50f. (£8 2s. 6d.) on the shares of the second series and of 105f. (£8 15s.) on all other shares.

The following may be given in explanation of some of the headings in the balance sheet.

As the Natal line and the branch-line to Barberton were completed in 1896, it was possible to close the construction account of our main line and of the Natal line and include it under the heading: "the Railways," which now appears in the balance sheet for an amount of 67,405,451·75f. (£5,617,120 19s. 7d.)

In this amount is comprised 2,081,483·23f. (£173,456 18s. 9d.) for extension works, which proves that in 1896 an amount of 722,509·70f. (£60,209 2s. 10d.) has been spent on works completed on December 31st.

The completed extension works on the tramway required an expenditure of 622,737·25f. (£51,894 15s. 5d.), by which amount that heading has been increased.

On the building of the Klerksdorp line 5,329,870·99f. (£444,155 18s. 4d.) was spent in 1896.

The value of the goods in the inventory increased by 422,644·79f. (£35,220 7s. 10d.) principally through the opening of the new lines and of new stations, but also through the increase of machinery in the Central workshop at Pretoria and the furnishing of new appliances for the providing of water.

The number of locomotives was increased by 59 to the value of 1,776,769·30f. (£148,064 2s. 2d.), and that of the vehicles comprising various carriages and wagons, by 1,369, to the value of 2,935,401f. (£244.616 15s.); for the increase of our locomotive and wagon stock, 749,769·30f. (£62,480 15s. 6d.) and 1,046,101·75f. (£87,175 2s. 11d.) were respectively charged to the reserve fund.

Appendix 6 gives a specification of the locomotives and carriages, which our stock consists of. Of these, however, 8 locomotives and 471 carriages were not brought into use on the December 31st.

The stock account decreased by 762,140·50f. (£63,511 14s. 2d.) through the realization of stocks ; on the other hand the deposit and "short bill account" increased by 1,904,800f. (£158,733 6s. 8d.)

The financial results of the year 1896, the fruit of extraordinary exertion and heavy labour under often unfavourable and disheartening conditions afford an idea of the expansion of the traffic in a country, which nine years ago made its first modest trial in the construction of a tramway along the goldfields in order to be able to extend the gold industry by supplying cheap coal.

Our company has existed for ten years, and has had, in that comparatively short period, to surmount many difficulties, to endure many trying periods, but its prosperity has surpassed all that the most optimistic partisan for railway exploitation in the South African Republic has ever dared to imagine.

A word of thanks to the director, who has had such a difficult task in the work of management in Africa, and to the head and other officials who have assisted him so stoutly and zealously, is certainly not misplaced here, nor is the wish that all of them will retain the ability and the desire to continue to protect the interests of the Company in the same way as in the past.

We give hereunder a comparison of the receipts, according to telegraphic statements, for the first four months of 1897, when an average of 1098 kilometers were in exploitation, and of 1896, when that average was 963 kilometers.

In those first months of the current year the English press treated the public to a series of statements regarding the sad condition of the gold industry, but the figures of gold outputs and railway receipts appeared to be completely in conflict therewith. Those statements appeared more to point to a disappointment with respect to the profits made by goldmining companies than to a shrinking of the gold industry itself. A state commission has been appointed to ascertain the causes of this disappointment, and to indicate in what way things can be improved.

The co-operation of our company, for the attaining of the object in view, can be relied upon.

RECEIPTS FOR THE FIRST FOUR MONTHS.

1897.

		January.	February.	March.	April.
Railway revenue	...	£240,750	£233,850	£260,950	£240,060
Import duties ...	...	24,050	22,550	33,050	35,540
Coal Mine, Springs	...	4,100	4,300	4,500	4,500
Total	...	£268,900	£260,700	£298,500	£280,100

1896.

Railway revenue	...	£155,100	£195,100	£194,500	£206,500
Import duties ...	...	13,900	16,100	18,300	15,900
Coal Mine, Springs	...	3,100	4,500	4,700	4,900
Total	...	£172,100	£215,700	£217,500	£227,300

BALANCE-SHEET OF THE NETHERLANDS SOUTH AFRICAN RAILWAY COMPANY

On December 31st, 1896.

Dr.

	£	s.	d.	£	s.	d.
The Railways...	£5,443,664	0	10			
Extension Works of the Railways ...	173,456	18	9	£5,617,120	19	7
Tramway and Coal Mines, Springs and Geduld ...	£400,710	3	4			
Extension of Tramway, etc. ...	112,042	19	4	512,753	2	8
Guaranteed Interest paid during Construction ...	£242,433	14	5			
Of which redeemed ...	48,946	11	8			
Construction Account, Klerksdorp ...				193,487	2	9
Inventory Goods ...				490,608	9	6
Locomotives ...				132,011	13	5
Rolling Stock ...				416,231	6	10
Cost of Erection ...				645,171	18	6
Obligations of the 4 per cent. Loan in portfolio amount-ing to £6,000,000 ...				10,829	14	6
Obligations of the 5 per cent. Loan in portfolio amount-ing to £350,000 ...				9,666	13	4
Stock Account ...				36,200	0	0
Deposits and Short Bills Account ...				98,663	14	11
Bills to Collect ...				194,566	13	4
Rate Difference of the Loans ...				516	17	10
Floating Goods (Railway Material) ...				167,202	12	8
Store Goods (Exploitation) ...				152,309	5	4
Works in Construction (with Exploitation) ...				289,778	13	8
The "Associatie Cassa," Balance ...				297,862	14	0
Cash in Netherlands and South Africa ...				1,818	6	3
The National Bank of the S.A.R., Ltd., at Pretoria ...				17,187	6	3
The Natal Government Railways ...				47,720	19	1½
The Portuguese State Railway ... London				15,149	14	7
Reserve Fund, Tramway ...				33,180	6	3¾
Sundry Debtors ...				25,386	6	3
Interest Account ...				34,892	1	6
				126,366	4	1
				1,409	6	2
				£9,568,091	18	11

Audited and approved,
Amsterdam, May 31st, 1897.
The Board of Commissioners of the Netherlands South African Railway Company.

(Signed) A. v. NAAMEN v. EEMNES, *Chairman.*
      " J. P. MOLTZER, *Secretary.*

Cr.

	£	s.	d.
Capital ...	£1,166,666	13	4
The 4 p.c. Loan amg. to 6,000,000f. at par (per resto)...	473,000	0	0
" 4 p.c. " " 15,000,000f. ...	1,237,250	0	0
" 5 p.c. " " 12,000,000f. ...	739,916	13	4
" 5 p.c. " " £350,000 ...	350,000	0	0
" 5·8 p.c. " " £2,000,000 ...	2,000,000	0	0
" 4 p.c. " " £1,250,000 ...	1,250,000	0	0
The S.A.R. gives for building Klerksdorp line ...	548,000	0	1
The "Associatie Cassa" for Outstandings ...	27,022	6	6
Labouchere, Oye s, & Co. here, ...	6,682	9	4
The National Bank of the S.A.R., Ld., Pretoria, for cheques still current ...	171,910	1	3
The Cape Government Railways ...	58,261	16	1
De Vos & Son here ...	1,329	18	0
Van Es & Van Ommeren here ...	5,105	6	2
Breuker & Wambersie here ...	91	9	0
Sundry Creditors ...	62,306	12	9½
Securities ...	7,990	13	2
Bills to be paid, Netherlands currency ...	275		
Amortisation Fund of the 5·8 p.c. Loan of £2,000,000 ...	22,179	17	5
Reserve Fund, Railway ...	53,445	6	4
Savings and Support Fund ...	2,109	5	9½
Extension Works of Railway (paid by Reserve Fund) ...	173,456	18	9
Locomotives (paid by Reserve Fund) ...	112,042	19	4
Rolling Stock ...	62,480	15	6
Payments former years (left unpaid) ...	87,175	2	11
Creditors for Interest on Loans (left unpaid) ...	2,520	10	0
Rents on Loans (not yet due) ...	104	7	6
Payment according to Article XXXIV. of Concession ...	10,107	10	0
Shareholders, for Profit in 1896 ...	780,740	9	7
	155,919	16	10
	£9,568,091	18	11

Thus compiled and provisionally fixed,
Amsterdam, May 25th, 1897.
The Direction of the Netherlands South African Railway Company.

(Signed) VAN DEN WALL BAKE.

PROFIT AND LOSS ACCOUNT OF THE NETHERLANDS SOUTH AFRICAN RAILWAY COMPANY

On December 31st, 1896.

Dr.

	£	s.	d.
To Interest and Amortisation of the 4 per cent. Loan, amounting to 6,000,000f.	£24,340	16	8
„ Interest and Amortisation of the 4 per cent. Loan, amounting to 15,000,000f.	55,990	0	0
„ Interest and Amortisation of the 5 per cent. Loan, amounting to 12,000,000f.	42,079	3	4
„ Interest Account of the 5 per cent. Loan, amounting to £350,000	15,350	0	0
„ Interest Account of the 5·8 per cent. Loan, amounting to £2,000,000	116,000	0	0
„ Interest Account of the 4 per cent. Loan, amounting to £1,250,000	50,000	0	0
„ Amortisation fund of the 5·8 per cent. Loan, amounting to £2,000,000	21,609	3	4
„ Payment Account to Article XXXIV. of the Concession	780,740	9	7
	£155,919	16	10
„ Shareholders for undivided balance of preceding year	£2,920 18 0		
„ Guaranteed dividend	66,250 0 0		
„ Share of surplus profit	86,748 18 10		
	£155,919	16	10

Hereof to pay :	£	s.	d.
13½ per cent. on 11,000,000f.	£123,750 0 0		
12 per cent. on 3,000,000f.	30,000 0 0		
To carry forward undivided to the following year	2,169 16 10		
	155,919	16	10
	£1,262,029	9	9

Cr.

	£	s.	d.
By undivided balance 1895	£2,920	18	0
„ Account Article XXXIII. par. I. of the Concession	1,259,108	11	9
	£1,262,029	9	9

R 2

Audited and Approved,
Amsterdam, May 31, 1897.
The Board of Commissioners of the Netherlands
South African Railway Company,
(Signed) A. v. NAAMEN v. EEMNES, *Chairman.*
   „ J. P. MOLITZER, *Secretary.*

Thus compiled and provisionally fixed,
Amsterdam, May 25, 1897.
The Direction of the Netherlands South African Railway Company,
(Signed) VAN DEN WALL BAKE.

INDEX.

For EU product safety concerns, contact us at Calle de José Abascal, 56–1°,
28003 Madrid, Spain or eugpsr@cambridge.org.

www.ingramcontent.com/pod-product-compliance
Ingram Content Group UK Ltd.
Pitfield, Milton Keynes, MK11 3LW, UK
UKHW012201180425
457623UK00020B/349